CHILTON'S™

GENERAL MOTORS FIER

1984-88 REPAIR MANUAL

President Dean F. Morgantini, S.A.E.
Vice President–Finance Barry L. Beck
Vice President–Sales Glenn D. Potere

Executive Editor Kevin M. G. Maher, A.S.E.
Production Manager Ben Greisler, S.A.E.
Production Assistant Melinda Possinger

Project Managers George B. Heinrich III, A.S.E., S.A.E., Will Kessler, A.S.E., S.A.E., James R. Marotta, A.S.E., S.T.S., Richard Schwartz, A.S.E., Todd W. Stidham, A.S.E.

Schematics Editor Christopher G. Ritchie

Editor Thomas A. Mellon, A.S.E., S.A.E.

CHILTON™ Automotive Books

PUBLISHED BY **W. G. NICHOLS, INC.**

Manufactured in USA

1020 Andrew Drive
West Chester, PA 19380
ISBN 0-8019-9064-5
Library of Congress Catalog Card No. 97-65892
3456789012 8765432109

HOW TO USE THIS BOOK

Chilton's Total Car Care manual is intended to help you learn more about the inner workings of your vehicle while saving you money on its upkeep and operation.

The beginning of the book will likely be referred to the most, since that is where you will find information for maintenance and tune-up. The other sections deal with the more complex systems of your vehicle. Operating systems from engine through brakes are covered to the extent that the average do-it-yourselfer becomes mechanically involved. This book will not explain such things as rebuilding a differential for the simple reason that the expertise required and the investment in special tools make this task uneconomical. It will, however, give you detailed instructions to help you change your own brake pads and shoes, replace spark plugs, and perform many more jobs that can save you money, give you personal satisfaction and help you avoid expensive problems.

A secondary purpose of this book is a reference for owners who want to understand their vehicle and/or their mechanics better. In this case, no tools at all are required.

Where to Begin

Before removing any bolts, read through the entire procedure. This will give you the overall view of what tools and supplies will be required. There is nothing more frustrating than having to walk to the bus stop on Monday morning because you were short one bolt on Sunday afternoon. So read ahead and plan ahead. Each operation should be approached logically and all procedures thoroughly understood before attempting any work.

All sections contain adjustments, maintenance, removal and installation procedures, and in some cases, repair or overhaul procedures. When repair is not considered practical, we tell you how to remove the part and then how to install the new or rebuilt replacement. In this way, you at least save the labor costs. Backyard repair of some components is just not practical.

Avoiding Trouble

Many procedures in this book require you to "label and disconnect . . ." a group of lines, hoses or wires. Don't be lulled into thinking you can remember where everything goes—you won't. If you hook up vacuum or fuel lines incorrectly, the vehicle will run poorly, if at all. If you hook up electrical wiring incorrectly, you may instantly learn a very expensive lesson.

You don't need to know the official or engineering name for each hose or line. A piece of masking tape on the hose and a piece on its fitting will allow you to assign your own label such as the letter A or a short name. As long as you remember your own code, the lines can be reconnected by matching similar letters or names. Do remember that tape will dissolve in gasoline or other fluids; if a component is to be washed or cleaned, use another method of identification. A permanent felt-tipped marker can be very handy for marking metal parts. Remove any tape or paper labels after assembly.

Maintenance or Repair?

It's necessary to mention the difference between maintenance and repair. Maintenance includes routine inspections, adjustments, and replacement of parts which show signs of normal wear. Maintenance compensates for wear or deterioration. Repair implies that something has broken or is not working. A need for repair is often caused by lack of maintenance. Example: draining and refilling the automatic transmission fluid is maintenance recommended by the manufacturer at specific mileage intervals. Failure to do this can ruin the transmission/transaxle, requiring very expensive repairs. While no maintenance program can prevent items from breaking or wearing out, a general rule can be stated: MAINTENANCE IS CHEAPER THAN REPAIR.

Two basic mechanic's rules should be mentioned here. First, whenever the left side of the vehicle or engine is referred to, it is meant to specify the driver's side. Conversely, the right side of the vehicle means the passenger's side. Second, most screws and bolts are removed by turning counterclockwise, and tightened by turning clockwise.

Safety is always the most important rule. Constantly be aware of the dangers involved in working on an automobile and take the proper precautions. See the information in this section regarding SERVICING YOUR VEHICLE SAFELY and the SAFETY NOTICE on the acknowledgment page.

Avoiding the Most Common Mistakes

Pay attention to the instructions provided. There are 3 common mistakes in mechanical work:

1. **Incorrect order of assembly, disassembly or adjustment.** When taking something apart or putting it together, performing steps in the wrong order usually just costs you extra time; however, it CAN break something. Read the entire procedure before beginning disassembly. Perform everything in the order in which the instructions say you should, even if you can't immediately see a reason for it. When you're taking apart something that is very intricate, you might want to draw a picture of how it looks when assembled at one point in order to make sure you get everything back in its proper position. We will supply exploded views whenever possible. When making adjustments, perform them in the proper order; often, one adjustment affects another, and you cannot expect even satisfactory results unless each adjustment is made only when it cannot be changed by any other.

2. **Overtorquing (or undertorquing).** While it is more common for overtorquing to cause damage, undertorquing may allow a fastener to vibrate loose causing serious damage. Especially when dealing with aluminum parts, pay attention to torque specifications and utilize a torque wrench in assembly. If a torque figure is not available, remember that if you are using the right tool to perform the job, you will probably not have to strain yourself to get a fastener tight enough. The pitch of most threads is so slight that the tension you put on the wrench will be multiplied many times in actual force on what you are tightening. A good example of how critical torque is can be seen in the case of spark plug in-

stallation, especially where you are putting the plug into an aluminum cylinder head. Too little torque can fail to crush the gasket, causing leakage of combustion gases and consequent overheating of the plug and engine parts. Too much torque can damage the threads or distort the plug, changing the spark gap.

There are many commercial products available for ensuring that fasteners won't come loose, even if they are not torqued just right (a very common brand is Loctite®). If you're worried about getting something together tight enough to hold, but loose enough to avoid mechanical damage during assembly, one of these products might offer substantial insurance. Before choosing a threadlocking compound, read the label on the package and make sure the product is compatible with the materials, fluids, etc. involved.

3. **Crossthreading.** This occurs when a part such as a bolt is screwed into a nut or casting at the wrong angle and forced. Crossthreading is more likely to occur if access is difficult. It helps to clean and lubricate fasteners, then to start threading with the part to be installed positioned straight in. Then, start the bolt, spark plug, etc. with your fingers. If you encounter resistance, unscrew the part and start over again at a different angle until it can be inserted and turned several times without much effort. Keep in mind that many parts, especially spark plugs, have tapered threads, so that gentle turning will automatically bring the part you're threading to the proper angle, but only if you don't force it or resist a change in angle. Don't put a wrench on the part until it's been tightened a couple of turns by hand. If you suddenly encounter resistance, and the part has not seated fully, don't force it. Pull it back out to make sure it's clean and threading properly.

Always take your time and be patient; once you have some experience, working on your vehicle may well become an enjoyable hobby.

TOOLS AND EQUIPMENT

Naturally, without the proper tools and equipment it is impossible to properly service your vehicle. It would also be virtually impossible to catalog every tool that you would need to perform all of the operations in this book. Of course, It would be unwise for the amateur to rush out and buy an expensive set of tools on the theory that he/she may need one or more of them at some time.

The best approach is to proceed slowly, gathering a good quality set of those tools that are used most frequently. Don't be misled by the low cost of bargain tools. It is far better to spend a little more for better quality. Forged wrenches, 6 or 12-point sockets and fine tooth ratchets are by far preferable to their less expensive counterparts. As any good mechanic can tell you, there are few worse experiences than trying to work on a vehicle with bad tools. Your monetary savings will be far outweighed by frustration and mangled knuckles.

Begin accumulating those tools that are used most frequently: those associated with routine maintenance and tune-up. In addition to the normal assortment of screwdrivers and pliers, you should have the following tools:

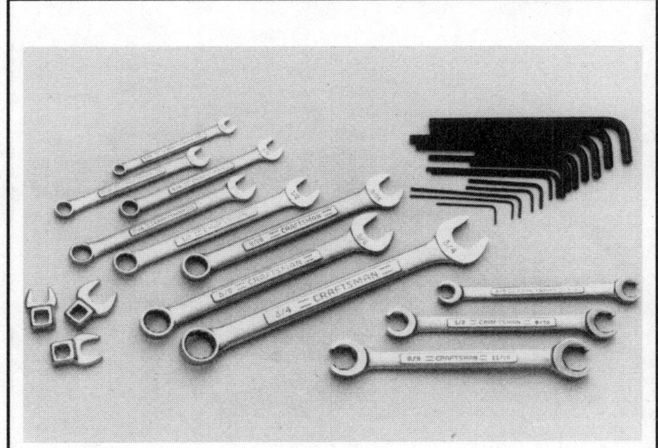

In addition to ratchets, a good set of wrenches and hex keys will be necessary

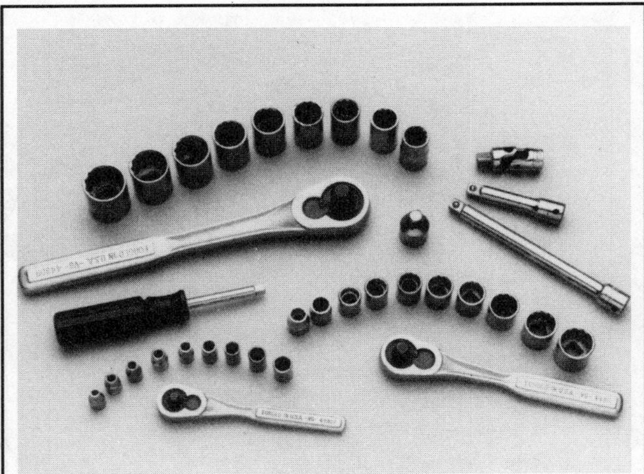

All but the most basic procedures will require an assortment of ratchets and sockets

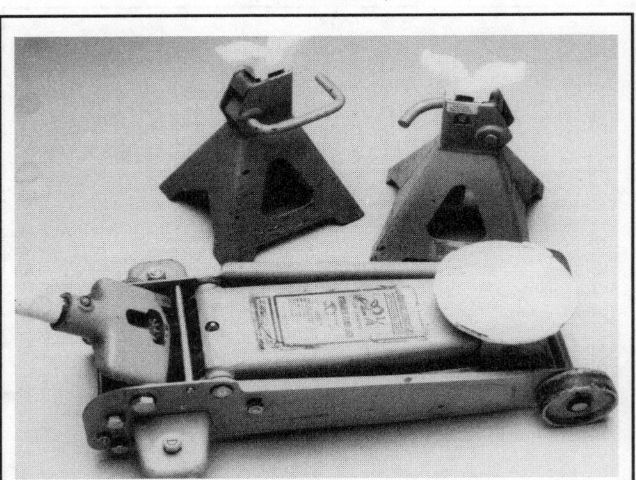

A hydraulic floor jack and a set of jackstands are essential for lifting and supporting the vehicle

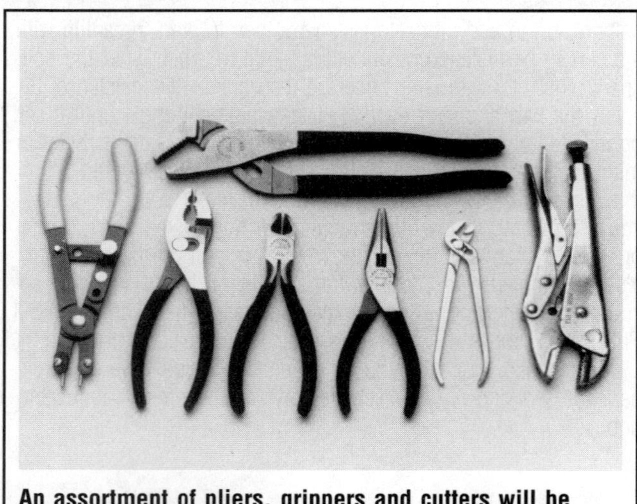

An assortment of pliers, grippers and cutters will be handy for old rusted parts and stripped bolt heads

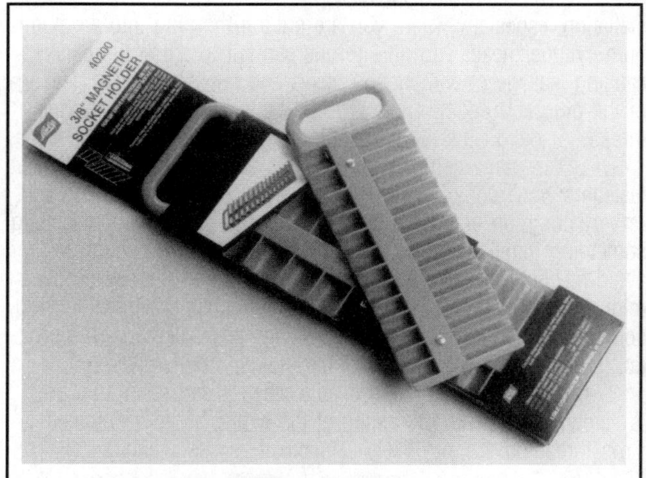

Tools from specialty manufacturers such as Lisle® are designed to make your job easier . . .

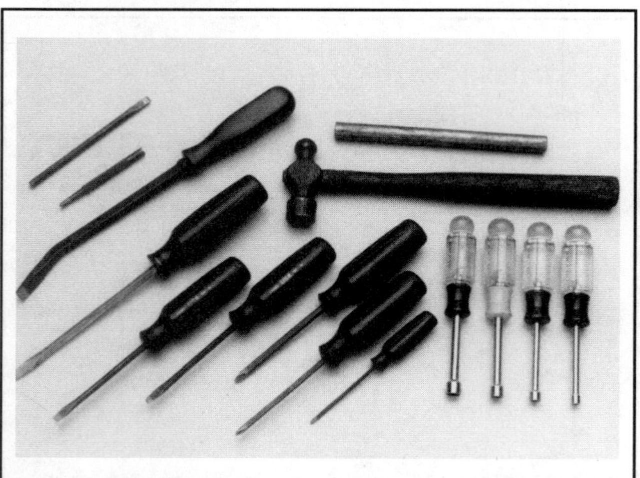

Various drivers, chisels and prybars are great tools to have in your toolbox

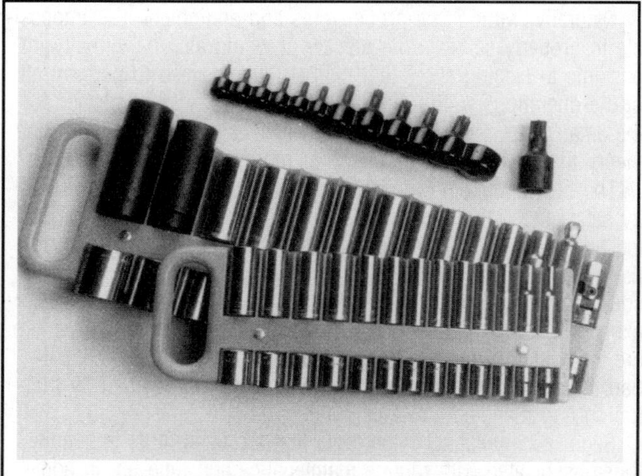

. . . these Torx® drivers and magnetic socket holders are just 2 examples of their handy products

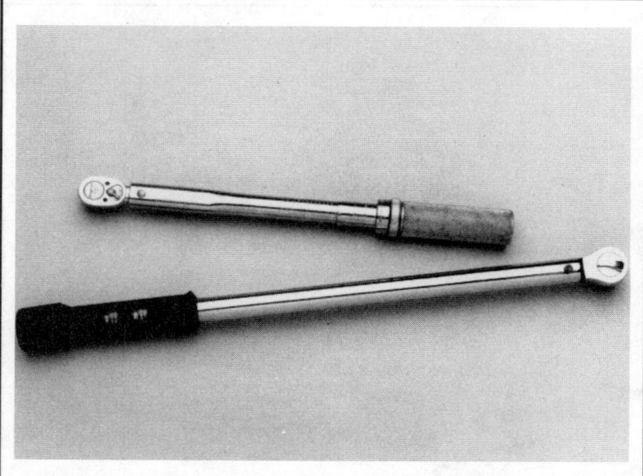

Many repairs will require the use of a torque wrench to assure the components are properly fastened

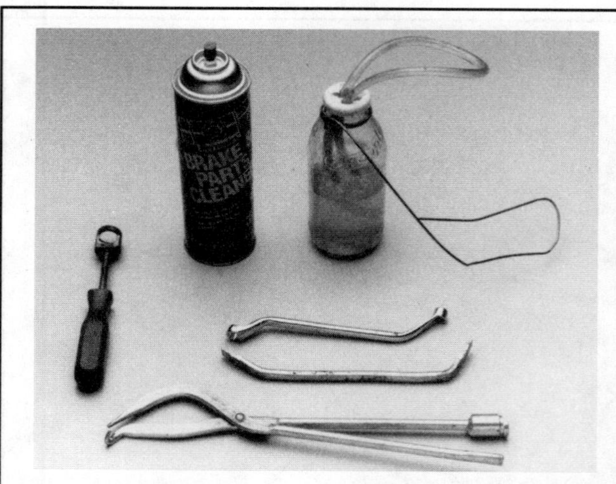

Although not always necessary, using specialized brake tools will save time

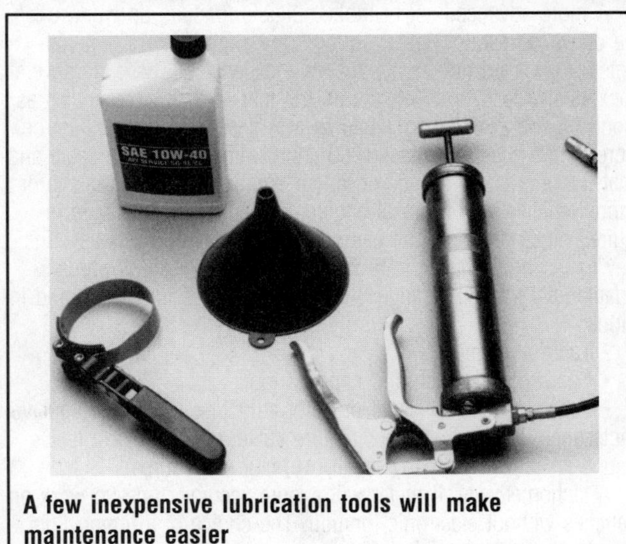

A few inexpensive lubrication tools will make maintenance easier

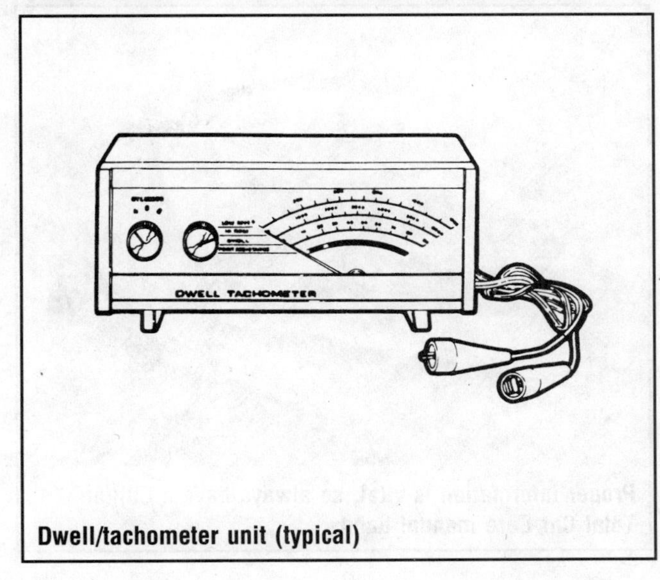

Dwell/tachometer unit (typical)

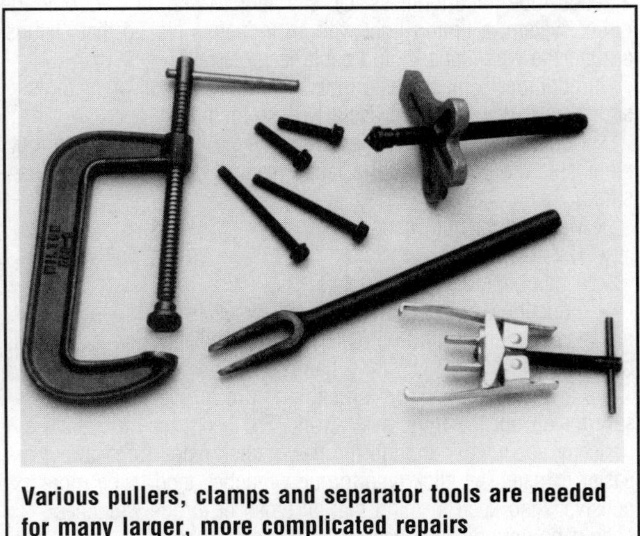

Various pullers, clamps and separator tools are needed for many larger, more complicated repairs

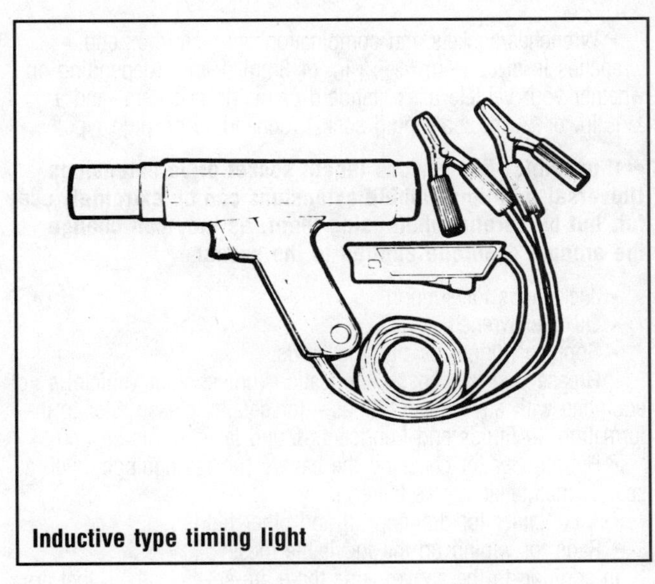

Inductive type timing light

A variety of tools and gauges should be used for spark plug gapping and installation

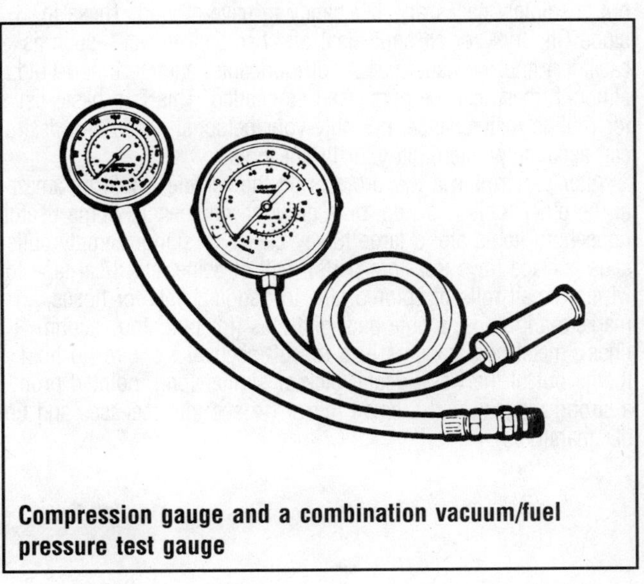

Compression gauge and a combination vacuum/fuel pressure test gauge

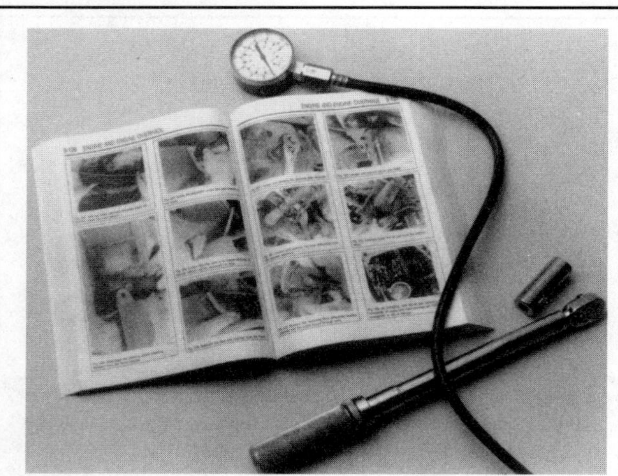

Proper information is vital, so always have a Chilton Total Car Care manual handy

• Wrenches/sockets and combination open end/box end wrenches in sizes from 1/8–3/4 in. or 3mm–19mm (depending on whether your vehicle uses standard or metric fasteners) and a 13/16 in. or 5/8 in. spark plug socket (depending on plug type).

➡If possible, buy various length socket drive extensions. Universal-joint and wobble extensions can be extremely useful, but be careful when using them, as they can change the amount of torque applied to the socket.

• Jackstands for support.
• Oil filter wrench.
• Spout or funnel for pouring fluids.
• Grease gun for chassis lubrication (unless your vehicle is not equipped with any grease fittings—for details, please refer to information on Fluids and Lubricants found later in this section).
• Hydrometer for checking the battery (unless equipped with a sealed, maintenance-free battery).
• A container for draining oil and other fluids.
• Rags for wiping up the inevitable mess.

In addition to the above items there are several others that are not absolutely necessary, but handy to have around. These include Oil Dry® (or an equivalent oil absorbent gravel—such as cat litter) and the usual supply of lubricants, antifreeze and fluids, although these can be purchased as needed. This is a basic list for routine maintenance, but only your personal needs and desire can accurately determine your list of tools.

After performing a few projects on the vehicle, you'll be amazed at the other tools and non-tools on your workbench. Some useful household items are: a large turkey baster or siphon, empty coffee cans and ice trays (to store parts), ball of twine, electrical tape for wiring, small rolls of colored tape for tagging lines or hoses, markers and pens, a note pad, golf tees (for plugging vacuum lines), metal coat hangers or a roll of mechanics's wire (to hold things out of the way), dental pick or similar long, pointed probe, a strong magnet, and a small mirror (to see into recesses and under manifolds).

A more advanced set of tools, suitable for tune-up work, can be drawn up easily. While the tools are slightly more sophisticated, they need not be outrageously expensive. There are several inexpensive tach/dwell meters on the market that are every bit as good for the average mechanic as a professional model. Just be sure that it goes to a least 1200–1500 rpm on the tach scale and that it works on 4, 6 and 8-cylinder engines. (If you own one or more vehicles with a diesel engine, a special tachometer is required since diesels don't use spark plug ignition systems). The key to these purchases is to make them with an eye towards adaptability and wide range. A basic list of tune-up tools could include:

• Tach/dwell meter.
• Spark plug wrench and gapping tool.
• Feeler gauges for valve or point adjustment. (Even if your vehicle does not use points or require valve adjustments, a feeler gauge is helpful for many repair/overhaul procedures).

A tachometer/dwell meter will ensure accurate tune-up work on vehicles without electronic ignition. The choice of a timing light should be made carefully. A light which works on the DC current supplied by the vehicle's battery is the best choice; it should have a xenon tube for brightness. On any vehicle with an electronic ignition system, a timing light with an inductive pickup that clamps around the No. 1 spark plug cable is preferred.

In addition to these basic tools, there are several other tools and gauges you may find useful. These include:

• Compression gauge. The screw-in type is slower to use, but eliminates the possibility of a faulty reading due to escaping pressure.
• Manifold vacuum gauge.
• 12V test light.
• A combination volt/ohmmeter
• Induction Ammeter. This is used for determining whether or not there is current in a wire. These are handy for use if a wire is broken somewhere in a wiring harness.

As a final note, you will probably find a torque wrench necessary for all but the most basic work. The beam type models are perfectly adequate, although the newer click types (breakaway) are easier to use. The click type torque wrenches tend to be more expensive. Also keep in mind that all types of torque wrenches should be periodically checked and/or recalibrated. You will have to decide for yourself which better fits your purpose.

Special Tools

Normally, the use of special factory tools is avoided for repair procedures, since these are not readily available for the do-it-yourself mechanic. When it is possible to perform the job with more commonly available tools, it will be pointed out, but occasionally, a special tool was designed to perform a specific function and should be used. Before substituting another tool, you should be convinced that neither your safety nor the performance of the vehicle will be compromised.

Special tools can usually be purchased from an automotive parts store or from your dealer. In some cases special tools may be available directly from the tool manufacturer.

SERVICING YOUR VEHICLE SAFELY

It is virtually impossible to anticipate all of the hazards involved with automotive maintenance and service, but care and common sense will prevent most accidents.

The rules of safety for mechanics range from "don't smoke around gasoline," to "use the proper tool(s) for the job." The trick to avoiding injuries is to develop safe work habits and to take every possible precaution.

Do's

- Do keep a fire extinguisher and first aid kit handy.
- Do wear safety glasses or goggles when cutting, drilling, grinding or prying, even if you have 20–20 vision. If you wear glasses for the sake of vision, wear safety goggles over your regular glasses.
- Do shield your eyes whenever you work around the battery. Batteries contain sulfuric acid. In case of contact with the eyes or skin, flush the area with water or a mixture of water and baking soda, then seek immediate medical attention.
- Do use safety stands (jackstands) for any undervehicle service. Jacks are for raising vehicles; jackstands are for making sure the vehicle stays raised until you want it to come down. Whenever the vehicle is raised, block the wheels remaining on the ground and set the parking brake.
- Do use adequate ventilation when working with any chemicals or hazardous materials. Like carbon monoxide, the asbestos dust resulting from some brake lining wear can be hazardous in sufficient quantities.
- Do disconnect the negative battery cable when working on the electrical system. The secondary ignition system contains EXTREMELY HIGH VOLTAGE. In some cases it can even exceed 50,000 volts.
- Do follow manufacturer's directions whenever working with potentially hazardous materials. Most chemicals and fluids are poisonous if taken internally.

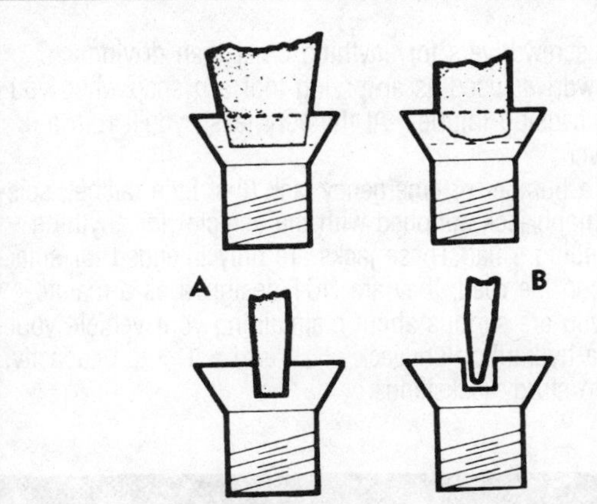

Screwdrivers should be kept in good condition to prevent injury or damage which could result if the blade slips from the screw

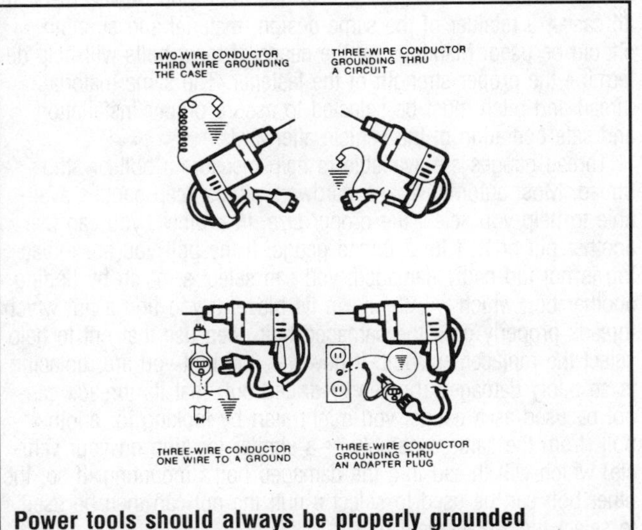

Power tools should always be properly grounded

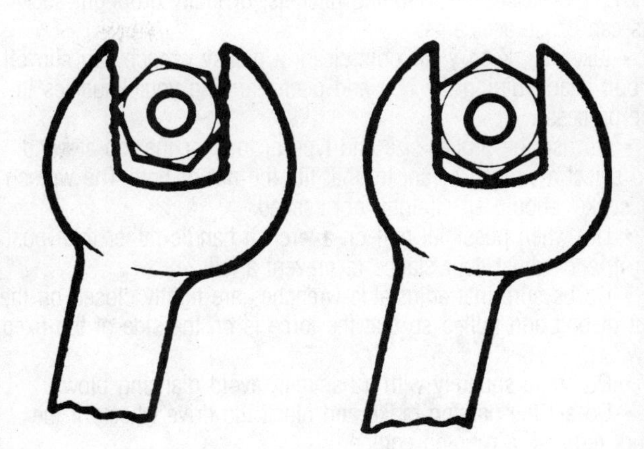

Using the correct size wrench will help prevent the possibility of rounding off a nut

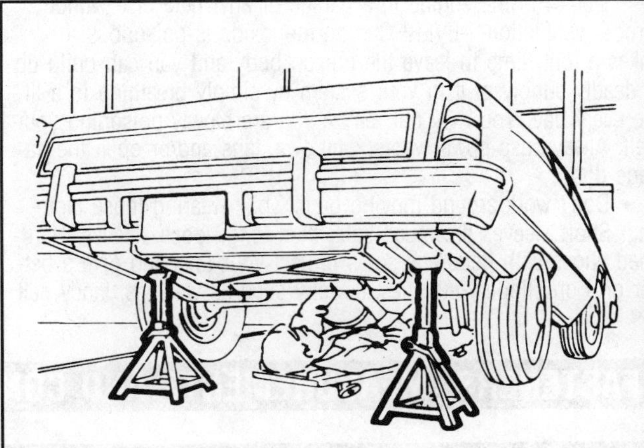

NEVER work under a vehicle unless it is supported using safety stands (jackstands)

• Do properly maintain your tools. Loose hammerheads, mushroomed punches and chisels, frayed or poorly grounded electrical cords, excessively worn screwdrivers, spread wrenches (open end), cracked sockets, slipping ratchets, or faulty droplight sockets can cause accidents.

• Likewise, keep your tools clean; a greasy wrench can slip off a bolt head, ruining the bolt and often harming your knuckles in the process.

• Do use the proper size and type of tool for the job at hand. Do select a wrench or socket that fits the nut or bolt. The wrench or socket should sit straight, not cocked.

• Do, when possible, pull on a wrench handle rather than push on it, and adjust your stance to prevent a fall.

• Do be sure that adjustable wrenches are tightly closed on the nut or bolt and pulled so that the force is on the side of the fixed jaw.

• Do strike squarely with a hammer; avoid glancing blows.

• Do set the parking brake and block the drive wheels if the work requires a running engine.

Don'ts

• Don't run the engine in a garage or anywhere else without proper ventilation—EVER! Carbon monoxide is poisonous; it takes a long time to leave the human body and you can build up a deadly supply of it in your system by simply breathing in a little every day. You may not realize you are slowly poisoning yourself. Always use power vents, windows, fans and/or open the garage door.

• Don't work around moving parts while wearing loose clothing. Short sleeves are much safer than long, loose sleeves. Hard-toed shoes with neoprene soles protect your toes and give a better grip on slippery surfaces. Jewelry such as watches, fancy belt buckles, beads or body adornment of any kind is not safe working around a vehicle. Long hair should be tied back under a hat or cap.

• Don't use pockets for toolboxes. A fall or bump can drive a screwdriver deep into your body. Even a rag hanging from your back pocket can wrap around a spinning shaft or fan.

• Don't smoke when working around gasoline, cleaning solvent or other flammable material.

• Don't smoke when working around the battery. When the battery is being charged, it gives off explosive hydrogen gas.

• Don't use gasoline to wash your hands; there are excellent soaps available. Gasoline contains dangerous additives which can enter the body through a cut or through your pores. Gasoline also removes all the natural oils from the skin so that bone dry hands will suck up oil and grease.

• Don't service the air conditioning system unless you are equipped with the necessary tools and training. When liquid or compressed gas refrigerant is released to atmospheric pressure it will absorb heat from whatever it contacts. This will chill or freeze anything it touches. Although refrigerant is normally non-toxic, R-12 becomes a deadly poisonous gas in the presence of an open flame. One good whiff of the vapors from burning refrigerant can be fatal.

• Don't use screwdrivers for anything other than driving screws! A screwdriver used as an prying tool can snap when you least expect it, causing injuries. At the very least, you'll ruin a good screwdriver.

• Don't use a bumper or emergency jack (that little ratchet, scissors, or pantograph jack supplied with the vehicle) for anything other than changing a flat! These jacks are only intended for emergency use out on the road; they are NOT designed as a maintenance tool. If you are serious about maintaining your vehicle yourself, invest in a hydraulic floor jack of at least a 1½ ton capacity, and at least two sturdy jackstands.

FASTENERS, MEASUREMENTS AND CONVERSIONS

Bolts, Nuts and Other Threaded Retainers

Although there are a great variety of fasteners found in the modern car or truck, the most commonly used retainer is the threaded fastener (nuts, bolts, screws, studs, etc). Most threaded retainers may be reused, provided that they are not damaged in use or during the repair. Some retainers (such as stretch bolts or torque prevailing nuts) are designed to deform when tightened or in use and should not be reinstalled.

Whenever possible, we will note any special retainers which should be replaced during a procedure. But you should always inspect the condition of a retainer when it is removed and replace any that show signs of damage. Check all threads for rust or corrosion which can increase the torque necessary to achieve the desired clamp load for which that fastener was originally selected. Additionally, be sure that the driver surface of the fastener has not been compromised by rounding or other damage. In some cases a driver surface may become only partially rounded, allowing the driver to catch in only one direction. In many of these occurrences, a fastener may be installed and tightened, but the driver would not be able to grip and loosen the fastener again. (This could lead to frustration down the line should that component ever need to be disassembled again).

If you must replace a fastener, whether due to design or damage, you must ALWAYS be sure to use the proper replacement. In all cases, a retainer of the same design, material and strength should be used. Markings on the heads of most bolts will help determine the proper strength of the fastener. The same material, thread and pitch must be selected to assure proper installation and safe operation of the vehicle afterwards.

Thread gauges are available to help measure a bolt or stud's thread. Most automotive and hardware stores keep gauges available to help you select the proper size. In a pinch, you can use another nut or bolt for a thread gauge. If the bolt you are replacing is not too badly damaged, you can select a match by finding another bolt which will thread in its place. If you find a nut which threads properly onto the damaged bolt, then use that nut to help select the replacement bolt. If however, the bolt you are replacing is so badly damaged (broken or drilled out) that its threads cannot be used as a gauge, you might start by looking for another bolt (from the same assembly or a similar location on your vehicle) which will thread into the damaged bolt's mounting. If so, the other bolt can be used to select a nut; the nut can then be used to select the replacement bolt.

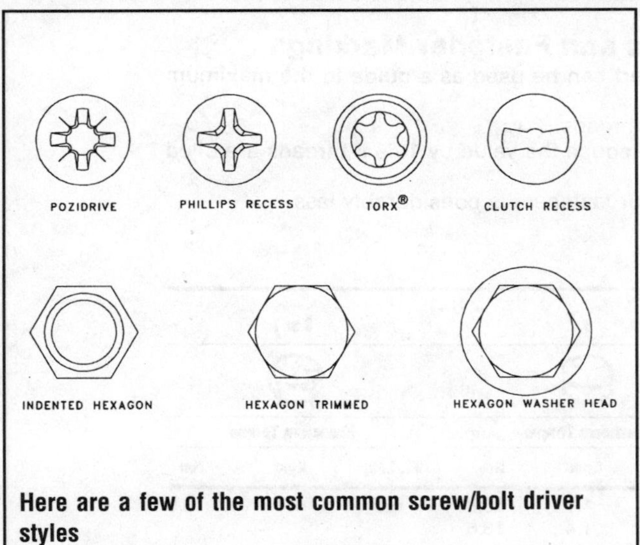

Here are a few of the most common screw/bolt driver styles

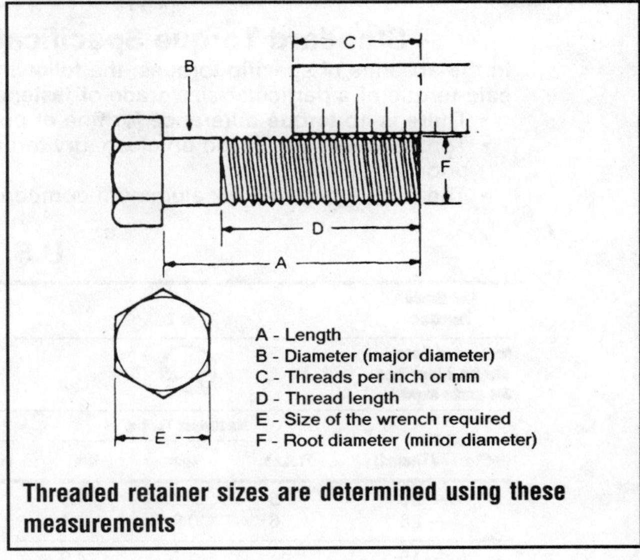

Threaded retainer sizes are determined using these measurements

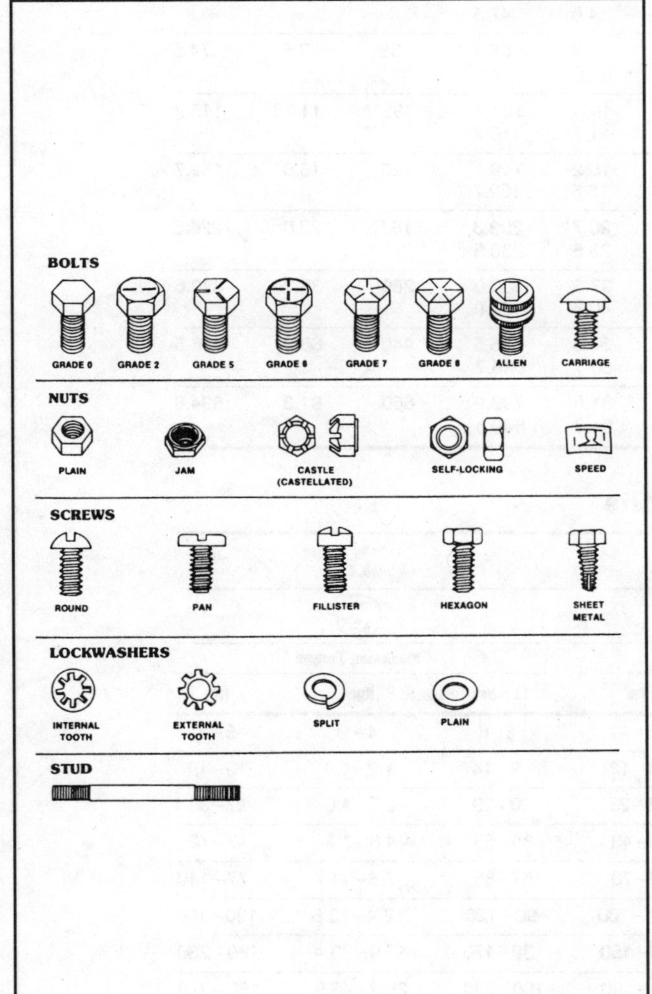

There are many different types of threaded retainers found on vehicles

T - INTERNAL DRIVE
E - EXTERNAL

Special fasteners such as these Torx® head bolts are used by manufacturers to discourage people from working on vehicles without the proper tools

In all cases, be absolutely sure you have selected the proper replacement. Don't be shy, you can always ask the store clerk for help.

✻✻ WARNING

Be aware that when you find a bolt with damaged threads, you may also find the nut or drilled hole it was threaded into has also been damaged. If this is the case, you may have to drill and tap the hole, replace the nut or otherwise repair the threads. NEVER try to force a replacement bolt to fit into the damaged threads.

Torque

Torque is defined as the measurement of resistance to turning or rotating. It tends to twist a body about an axis of rotation. A common example of this would be tightening a threaded retainer such as a nut, bolt or screw. Measuring torque is one of the most

Standard Torque Specifications and Fastener Markings

In the absence of specific torques, the following chart can be used as a guide to the maximum safe torque of a particular size/grade of fastener.

- There is no torque difference for fine or coarse threads.
- Torque values are based on clean, dry threads. Reduce the value by 10% if threads are oiled prior to assembly.
- The torque required for aluminum components or fasteners is considerably less.

U.S. Bolts

SAE Grade Number	1 or 2			5			6 or 7		
Number of lines always 2 less than the grade number.									
	Maximum Torque			Maximum Torque			Maximum Torque		
Bolt Size (Inches)—(Thread)	Ft./Lbs.	Kgm	Nm	Ft./Lbs.	Kgm	Nm	Ft./Lbs.	Kgm	Nm
¼—20	5	0.7	6.8	8	1.1	10.8	10	1.4	13.5
—28	6	0.8	8.1	10	1.4	13.6			
5/16—18	11	1.5	14.9	17	2.3	23.0	19	2.6	25.8
—24	13	1.8	17.6	19	2.6	25.7			
⅜—16	18	2.5	24.4	31	4.3	42.0	34	4.7	46.0
—24	20	2.75	27.1	35	4.8	47.5			
7/16—14	28	3.8	37.0	49	6.8	66.4	55	7.6	74.5
—20	30	4.2	40.7	55	7.6	74.5			
½—13	39	5.4	52.8	75	10.4	101.7	85	11.75	115.2
—20	41	5.7	55.6	85	11.7	115.2			
9/16—12	51	7.0	69.2	110	15.2	149.1	120	16.6	162.7
—18	55	7.6	74.5	120	16.6	162.7			
⅝—11	83	11.5	112.5	150	20.7	203.3	167	23.0	226.5
—18	95	13.1	128.8	170	23.5	230.5			
¾—10	105	14.5	142.3	270	37.3	366.0	280	38.7	379.6
—16	115	15.9	155.9	295	40.8	400.0			
⅞— 9	160	22.1	216.9	395	54.6	535.5	440	60.9	596.5
—14	175	24.2	237.2	435	60.1	589.7			
1— 8	236	32.5	318.6	590	81.6	799.9	660	91.3	894.8
—14	250	34.6	338.9	660	91.3	849.8			

Metric Bolts

Relative Strength Marking	4.6, 4.8			8.8		
Bolt Markings						
	Maximum Torque			Maximum Torque		
Bolt Size Thread Size x Pitch (mm)	Ft./Lbs.	Kgm	Nm	Ft./Lbs.	Kgm	Nm
6 x 1.0	2–3	.2–.4	3–4	3–6	4–.8	5–8
8 x 1.25	6–8	.8–1	8–12	9–14	1.2–1.9	13–19
10 x 1.25	12–17	1.5–2.3	16–23	20–29	2.7–4.0	27–39
12 x 1.25	21–32	2.9–4.4	29–43	35–53	4.8–7.3	47–72
14 x 1.5	35–52	4.8–7.1	48–70	57–85	7.8–11.7	77–110
16 x 1.5	51–77	7.0–10.6	67–100	90–120	12.4–16.5	130–160
18 x 1.5	74–110	10.2–15.1	100–150	130–170	17.9–23.4	180–230
20 x 1.5	110–140	15.1–19.3	150–190	190–240	26.2–46.9	160–320
22 x 1.5	150–190	22.0–26.2	200–260	250–320	34.5–44.1	340–430
24 x 1.5	190–240	26.2–46.9	260–320	310–410	42.7–56.5	420–550

Standard and metric bolt torque specifications based on bolt strengths—WARNING: use only as a guide

common ways to help assure that a threaded retainer has been properly fastened.

When tightening a threaded fastener, torque is applied in three distinct areas, the head, the bearing surface and the clamp load. About 50 percent of the measured torque is used in overcoming bearing friction. This is the friction between the bearing surface of the bolt head, screw head or nut face and the base material or washer (the surface on which the fastener is rotating). Approximately 40 percent of the applied torque is used in overcoming thread friction. This leaves only about 10 percent of the applied torque to develop a useful clamp load (the force which holds a joint together). This means that friction can account for as much as 90 percent of the applied torque on a fastener.

TORQUE WRENCHES

In most applications, a torque wrench can be used to assure proper installation of a fastener. Torque wrenches come in various designs and most automotive supply stores will carry a variety to suit your needs. A torque wrench should be used any time we supply a specific torque value for a fastener. A torque wrench can also be used if you are following the general guidelines in the accompanying charts. Keep in mind that because there is no worldwide standardization of fasteners, the charts are a general guideline and should be used with caution. Again, the general rule of "if you are using the right tool for the job, you should not have to strain to tighten a fastener" applies here.

Beam Type

The beam type torque wrench is one of the most popular types. It consists of a pointer attached to the head that runs the length of the flexible beam (shaft) to a scale located near the handle. As the wrench is pulled, the beam bends and the pointer indicates the torque using the scale.

Click (Breakaway) Type

Another popular design of torque wrench is the click type. To use the click type wrench you pre-adjust it to a torque setting. Once the torque is reached, the wrench has a reflex signalling feature that causes a momentary breakaway of the torque wrench body, sending an impulse to the operator's hand.

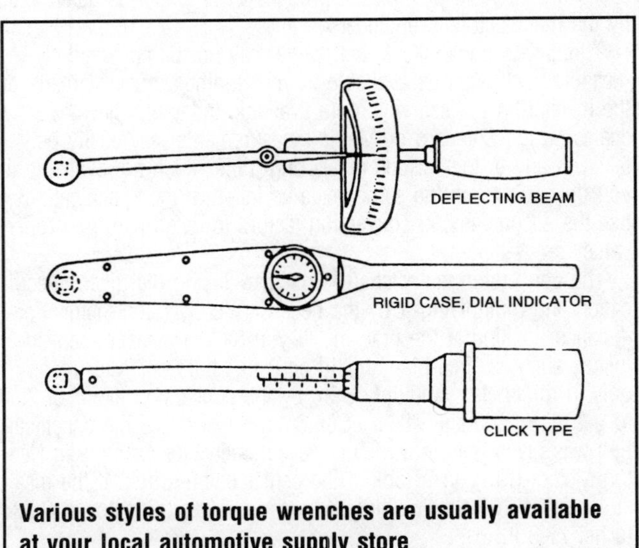

Various styles of torque wrenches are usually available at your local automotive supply store

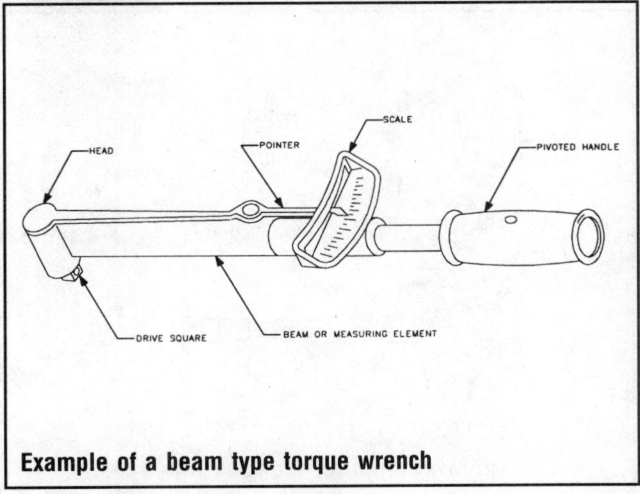

Example of a beam type torque wrench

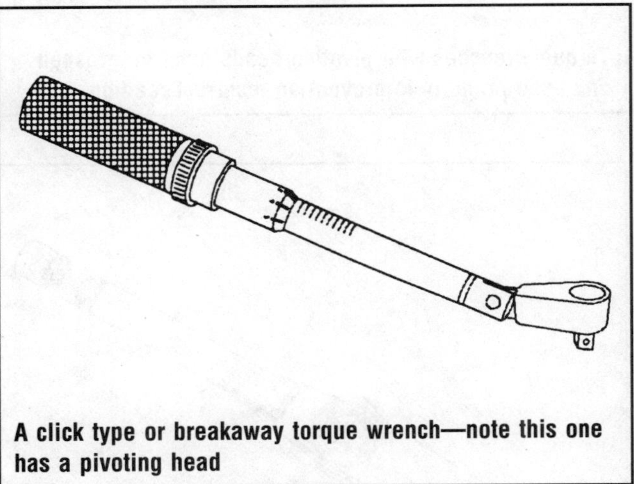
A click type or breakaway torque wrench—note this one has a pivoting head

Pivot Head Type

Some torque wrenches (usually of the click type) may be equipped with a pivot head which can allow it to be used in areas of limited access. BUT, it must be used properly. To hold a pivot head wrench, grasp the handle lightly, and as you pull on the handle, it should be floated on the pivot point. If the handle comes in contact with the yoke extension during the process of pulling, there is a very good chance the torque readings will be inaccurate because this could alter the wrench loading point. The design of the handle is usually such as to make it inconvenient to deliberately misuse the wrench.

➡It should be mentioned that the use of any U-joint, wobble or extension will have an effect on the torque readings, no matter what type of wrench you are using. For the most accurate readings, install the socket directly on the wrench driver. If necessary, straight extensions (which hold a socket directly under the wrench driver) will have the least effect on the torque reading. Avoid any extension that alters the length of the wrench from the handle to the head/driving point (such as a crow's foot). U-joint or Wobble extensions can greatly affect the readings; avoid their use at all times.

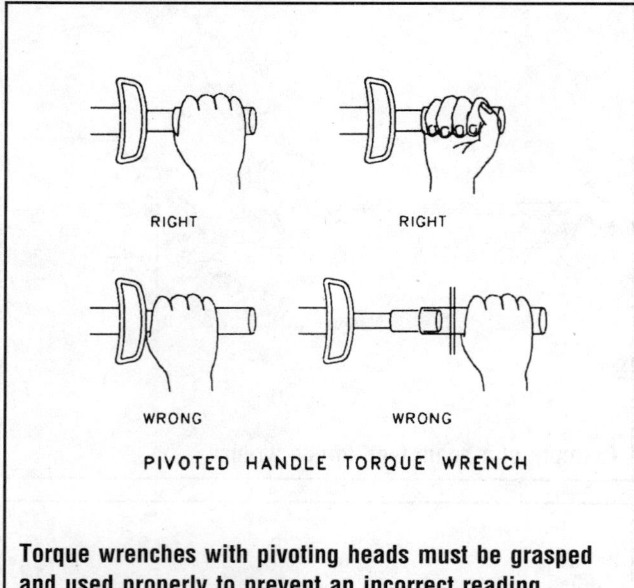

Torque wrenches with pivoting heads must be grasped and used properly to prevent an incorrect reading

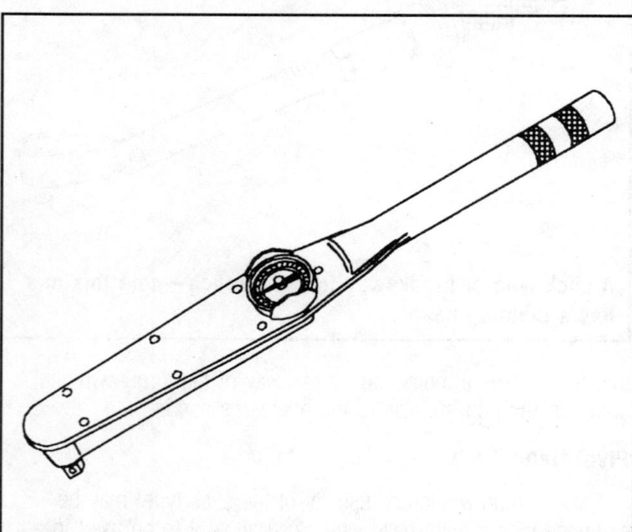

The rigid case (direct reading) torque wrench uses a dial indicator to show torque

Rigid Case (Direct Reading)

A rigid case or direct reading torque wrench is equipped with a dial indicator to show torque values. One advantage of these wrenches is that they can be held at any position on the wrench without affecting accuracy. These wrenches are often preferred because they tend to be compact, easy to read and have a great degree of accuracy.

TORQUE ANGLE METERS

Because the frictional characteristics of each fastener or threaded hole will vary, clamp loads which are based strictly on

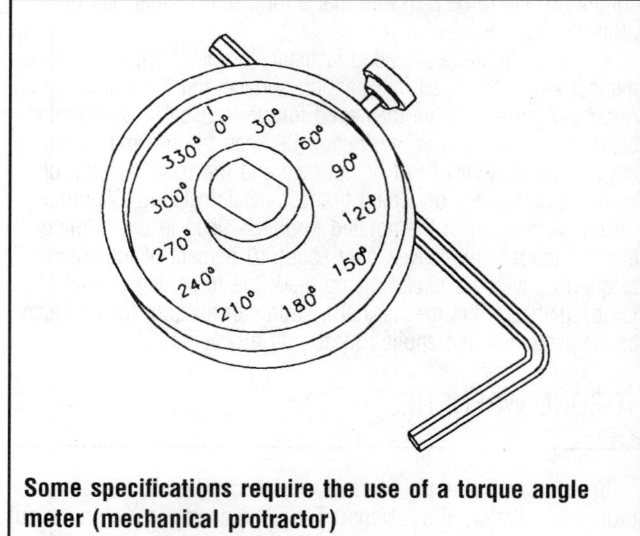

Some specifications require the use of a torque angle meter (mechanical protractor)

torque will vary as well. In most applications, this variance is not significant enough to cause worry. But, in certain applications, a manufacturer's engineers may determine that more precise clamp loads are necessary (such is the case with many aluminum cylinder heads). In these cases, a torque angle method of installation would be specified. When installing fasteners which are torque angle tightened, a predetermined seating torque and standard torque wrench are usually used first to remove any compliance from the joint. The fastener is then tightened the specified additional portion of a turn measured in degrees. A torque angle gauge (mechanical protractor) is used for these applications.

Standard and Metric Measurements

Throughout this manual, specifications are given to help you determine the condition of various components on your vehicle, or to assist you in their installation. Some of the most common measurements include length (in. or cm/mm), torque (ft. lbs., inch lbs. or Nm) and pressure (psi, in. Hg, kPa or mm Hg). In most cases, we strive to provide the proper measurement as determined by the manufacturer's engineers.

Though, in some cases, that value may not be conveniently measured with what is available in your toolbox. Luckily, many of the measuring devices which are available today will have two scales so the Standard or Metric measurements may easily be taken. If any of the various measuring tools which are available to you do not contain the same scale as listed in the specifications, use the accompanying conversion factors to determine the proper value.

The conversion factor chart is used by taking the given specification and multiplying it by the necessary conversion factor. For instance, looking at the first line, if you have a measurement in inches such as "free-play should be 2 in." but your ruler reads only in millimeters, multiply 2 in. by the conversion factor of 25.4 to get the metric equivalent of 50.8mm. Likewise, if the specification was given only in a Metric measurement, for example in Newton Meters (Nm), then look at the center column first. If the measurement is 100 Nm, multiply it by the conversion factor of 0.738 to get 73.8 ft. lbs.

CONVERSION FACTORS

LENGTH–DISTANCE

Inches (in.)	x 25.4	= Millimeters (mm)	x .0394	= Inches
Feet (ft.)	x .305	= Meters (m)	x 3.281	= Feet
Miles	x 1.609	= Kilometers (km)	x .0621	= Miles

VOLUME

Cubic Inches (in3)	x 16.387	= Cubic Centimeters	x .061	= in3
IMP Pints (IMP pt.)	x .568	= Liters (L)	x 1.76	= IMP pt.
IMP Quarts (IMP qt.)	x 1.137	= Liters (L)	x .88	= IMP qt.
IMP Gallons (IMP gal.)	x 4.546	= Liters (L)	x .22	= IMP gal.
IMP Quarts (IMP qt.)	x 1.201	= US Quarts (US qt.)	x .833	= IMP qt.
IMP Gallons (IMP gal.)	x 1.201	= US Gallons (US gal.)	x .833	= IMP gal.
Fl. Ounces	x 29.573	= Milliliters	x .034	= Ounces
US Pints (US pt.)	x .473	= Liters (L)	x 2.113	= Pints
US Quarts (US qt.)	x .946	= Liters (L)	x 1.057	= Quarts
US Gallons (US gal.)	x 3.785	= Liters (L)	x .264	= Gallons

MASS–WEIGHT

Ounces (oz.)	x 28.35	= Grams (g)	x .035	= Ounces
Pounds (lb.)	x .454	= Kilograms (kg)	x 2.205	= Pounds

PRESSURE

Pounds Per Sq. In. (psi)	x 6.895	= Kilopascals (kPa)	x .145	= psi
Inches of Mercury (Hg)	x .4912	= psi	x 2.036	= Hg
Inches of Mercury (Hg)	x 3.377	= Kilopascals (kPa)	x .2961	= Hg
Inches of Water (H_2O)	x .07355	= Inches of Mercury	x 13.783	= H_2O
Inches of Water (H_2O)	x .03613	= psi	x 27.684	= H_2O
Inches of Water (H_2O)	x .248	= Kilopascals (kPa)	x 4.026	= H_2O

TORQUE

Pounds–Force Inches (in–lb)	x .113	= Newton Meters (N·m)	x 8.85	= in–lb
Pounds–Force Feet (ft–lb)	x 1.356	= Newton Meters (N·m)	x .738	= ft–lb

VELOCITY

Miles Per Hour (MPH)	x 1.609	= Kilometers Per Hour (KPH)	x .621	= MPH

POWER

Horsepower (Hp)	x .745	= Kilowatts	x 1.34	= Horsepower

FUEL CONSUMPTION*

Miles Per Gallon IMP (MPG)	x .354	= Kilometers Per Liter (Km/L)
Kilometers Per Liter (Km/L)	x 2.352	= IMP MPG
Miles Per Gallon US (MPG)	x .425	= Kilometers Per Liter (Km/L)
Kilometers Per Liter (Km/L)	x 2.352	= US MPG

*It is common to covert from miles per gallon (mpg) to liters/100 kilometers (1/100 km), where mpg (IMP) x 1/100 km = 282 and mpg (US) x 1/100 km = 235.

TEMPERATURE

Degree Fahrenheit (°F)	= (°C x 1.8) + 32
Degree Celsius (°C)	= (°F – 32) x .56

Standard and metric conversion factors chart

SERIAL NUMBER IDENTIFICATION

Vehicle Identification Number (VIN)

See Figures 1 and 2

It is important for servicing and ordering parts to be certain of the vehicle and engine identification. The VIN (Vehicle Identification Number) is a 17 digit number visible through the windshield on the drivers side of the dash. The 10th digit indicates the model year, and the 8th digit identifies the factory installed engine.

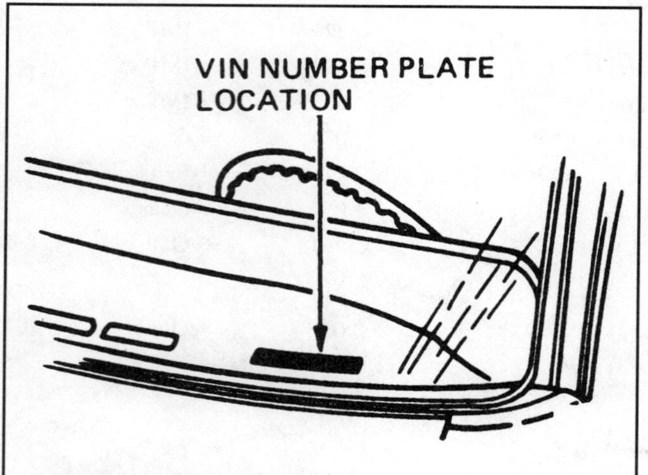

Fig. 1 Common Vehicle Identification Number (VIN) plate location on the Fiero

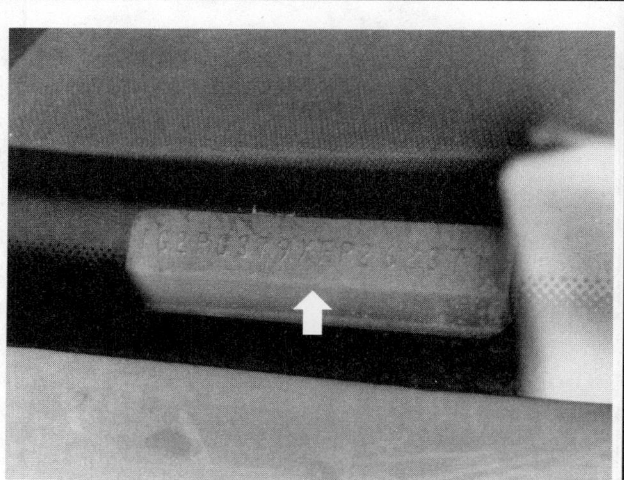

The Vehicle Identification Number (VIN) is stamped on this metal plate

Engine Code

Code	Cu. In.	Liters	Cyl.	Carb	Eng. Mfg.
R	151	2.5	4	TBI	Pontiac
9	173	2.8	6	MFI	Chev.

The seventeen digit Vehicle Identification Number can be used to determine engine application and model year. The 10th digit indicates the model year, and the 8th digit identifies the factory installed engine.
TBI (Throttle body injection)
MFI (Multi-port fuel injection)

Model Year Code

Code	Year
E	1984
F	1985
G	1986
H	1987
J	1988

Fig. 2 The Vehicle Identification Number (VIN) can be interperated as shown

Engine

➧ See Figures 3 and 4

Refer to the accompanying illustrations for the engine identification code locations.

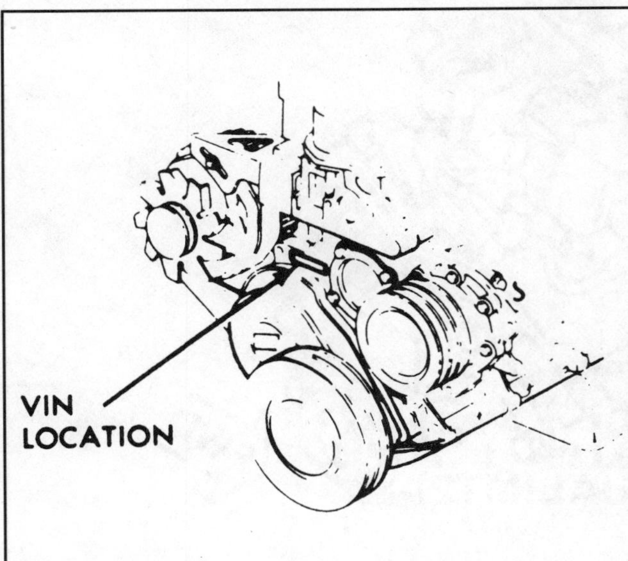

Fig. 3 Identification code location—2.5L four cylinder engine

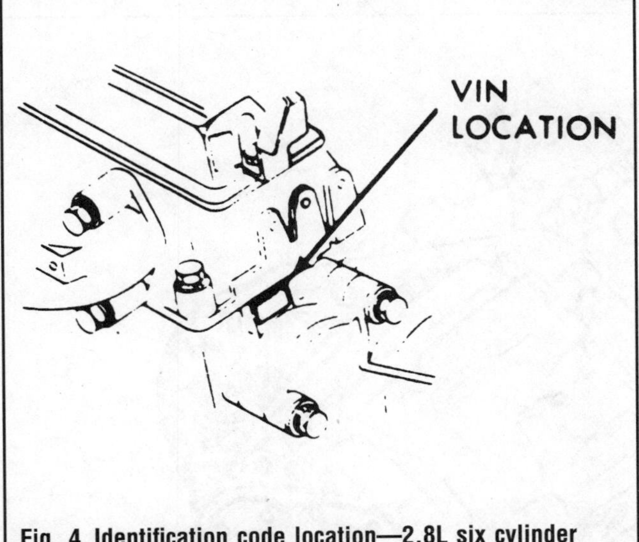

Fig. 4 Identification code location—2.8L six cylinder engine

Transmission/Transaxle

➧ See Figures 5, 6, 7 and 8

Refer to the accompanying illustrations for the transmission/transaxle identification code locations.

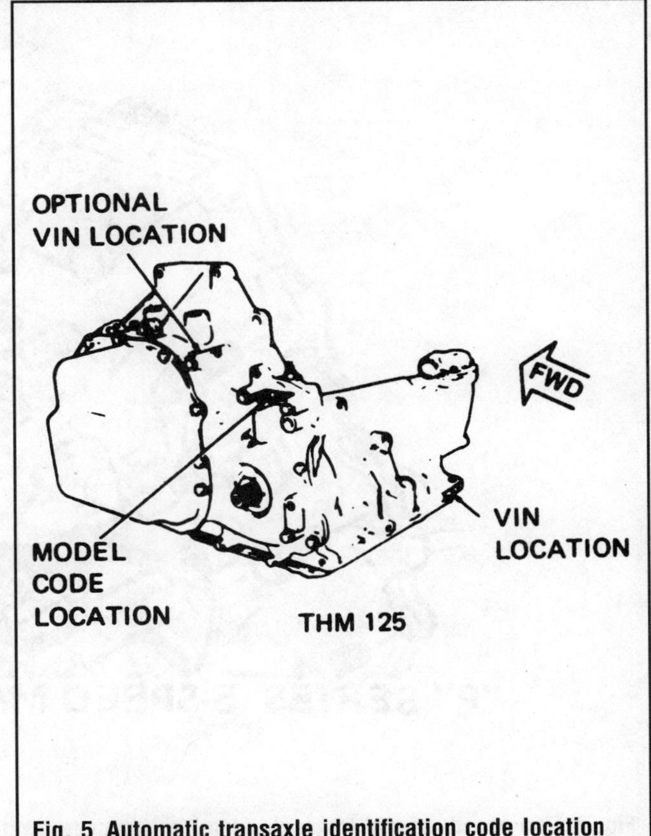

Fig. 5 Automatic transaxle identification code location

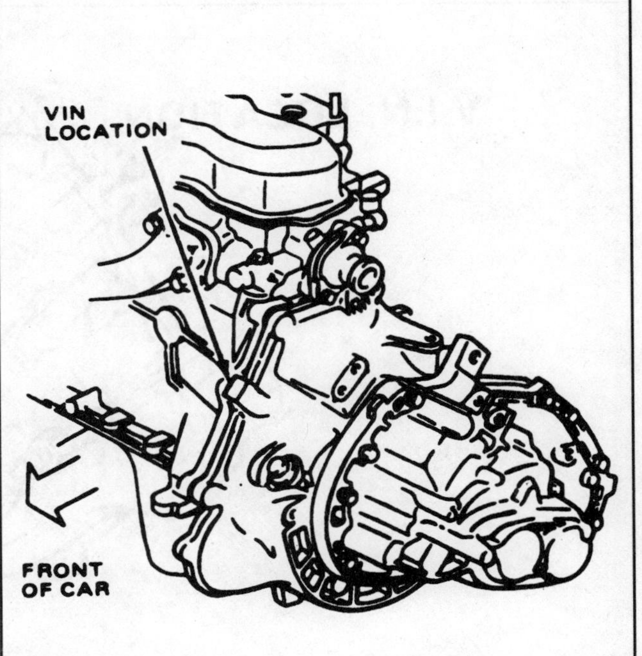

Fig. 6 Four speed manual transaxle identification code location

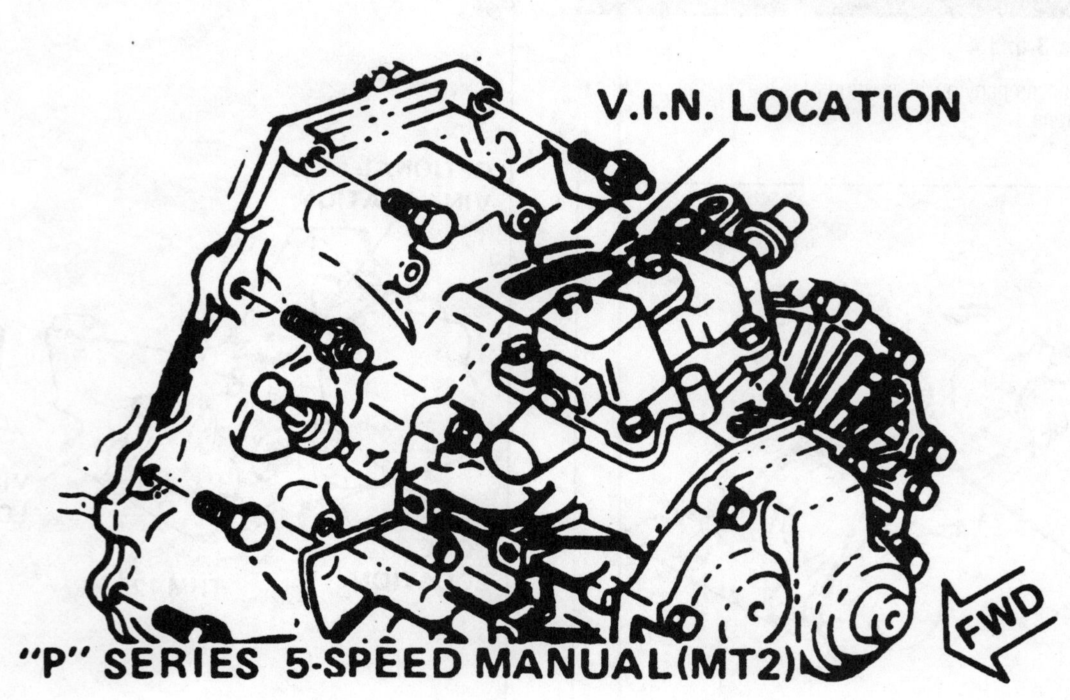

Fig. 7 Five speed manual transaxle identification code location—MT2 series

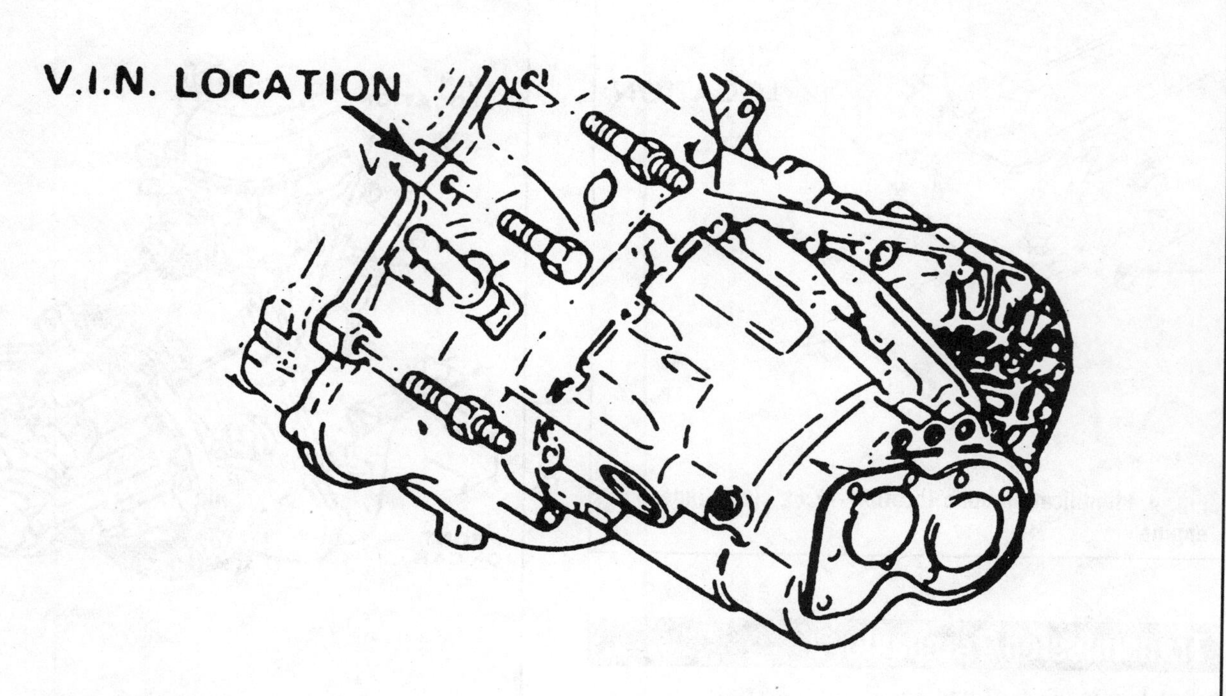

Fig. 8 Five speed transaxle identification code location—MG and MG2 series

Body Number Plate

➧ See Figure 9

The body number plate is attached to the front tie bar behind the right front or left front headlamp in the engine compartment.

The body number plate identifies numerous items such as body style, assembly plant, paint type and trim combination to name a few. This identification plate is useful when ordering body parts. Refer to the "Body Number Plate" illustration in this section.

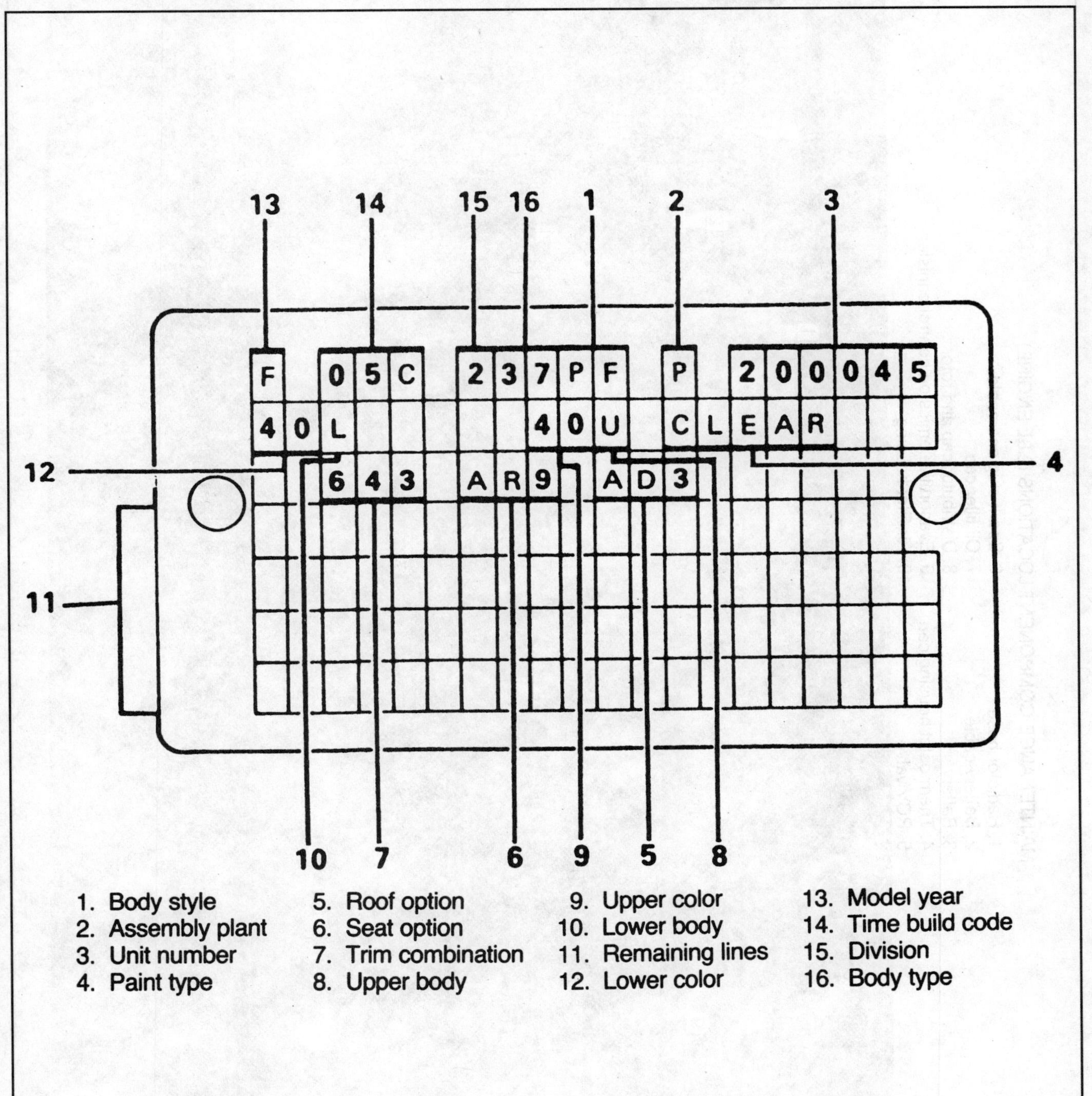

Fig. 9 The body number plate can be used to determine body style, assembly plant, original paint and trim combinations

ROUTINE MAINTENANCE

MAINTENANCE COMPONENT LOCATIONS (2.8L ENGINE)

1. Radiator hose
2. Battery cable
3. Battery
4. Thermostat housing cap
5. PCV valve
6. Spark plug and cable
7. Oil filler cap
8. Distributor cap and rotor
9. Evaporative emission control canister
10. Air filter housing

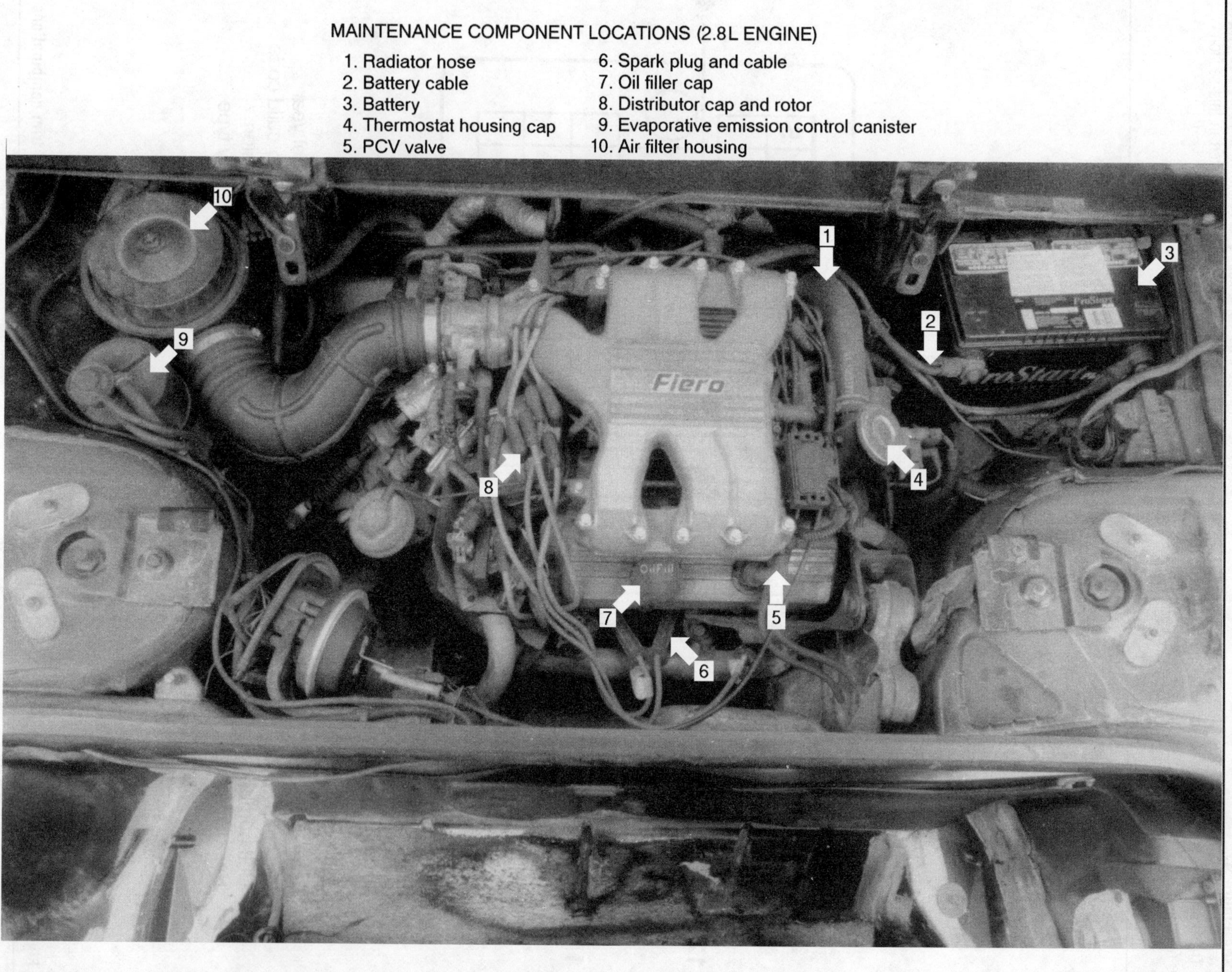

Air Cleaner and Crankcase Separator

REMOVAL & INSTALLATION

CAUTION

The air cleaner also functions as a flame arrestor in the event of an engine backfire. The air cleaner assembly should be installed at all times unless the removal is necessary for repair or maintenance. Be sure that no one is near the engine compartment before starting the engine to help reduce the risk of personal injury and property damage. If the engine backfires with the air cleaner removed, there could be a burst of flame and the possibility of a fire in the engine compartment.

4-Cylinder Engine

See Figures 10 and 11

The air filter and crankcase separator should be replaced together every 24 months or 15,000 miles (25,000 km). Replace components more often if operated under dusty conditions.

1. Remove the air cleaner cover by removing the two 10mm nuts on top of the air cleaner.
2. Remove the air cleaner element from the air cleaner.
3. To remove the separator, lift up on the air cleaner assembly and move to one side without disconnecting any rubber tubing.
4. Remove the separator from the valve cover by pulling straight up.

To install:

5. Position the separator in the valve cover, install the air cleaner element, cover and tighten the cover nuts to 4 ft. lbs. (5.4 Nm).

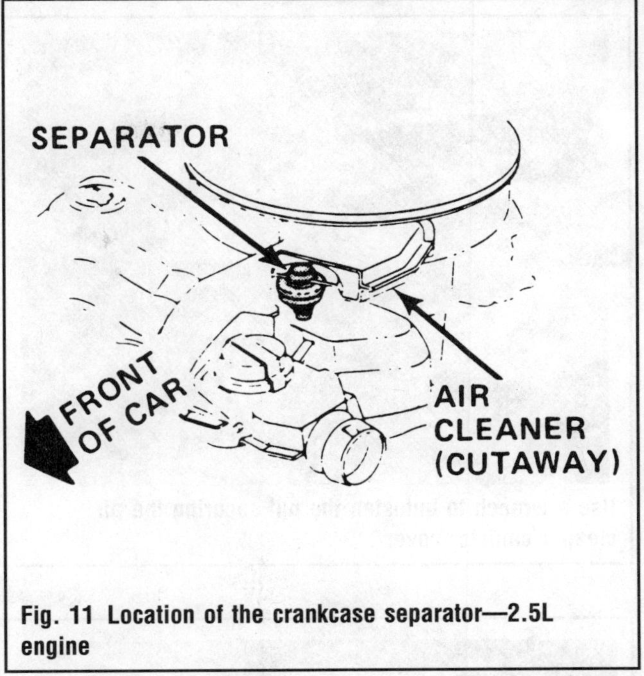

Fig. 11 Location of the crankcase separator—2.5L engine

6-Cylinder Engine

See Figure 12

The V6 uses a remotely mounted air cleaner canister, connected to the engine via a flexible duct. To replace the paper element, remove the nut securing the canister top, lift off the top and replace the element. Replace the top and tighten the nut to 4 ft. lbs. (5.4 Nm).

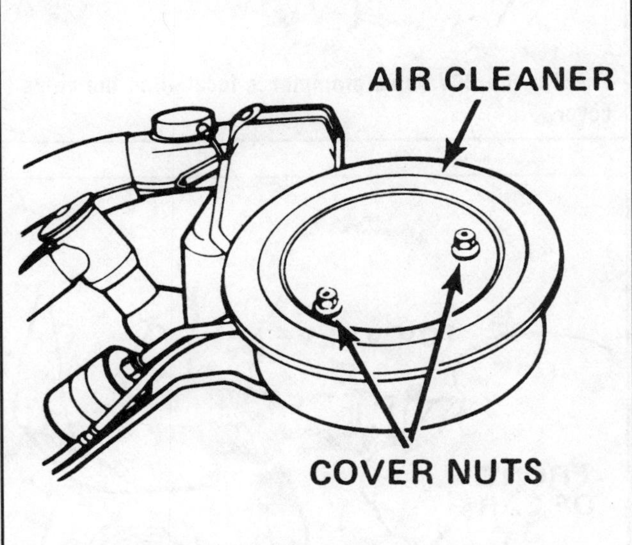

Fig. 10 The air filter cover is secured with nuts—2.5L shown

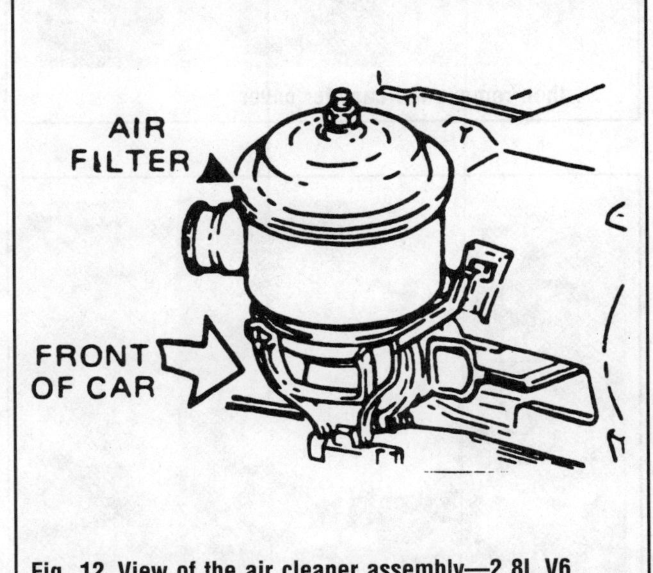

Fig. 12 View of the air cleaner assembly—2.8L V6 engine

Use a wrench to unfasten the nut securing the air cleaner canister cover . . .

. . . then remove the canister cover

Remove the filter element from the air cleaner canister

PCV Valve

REMOVAL & INSTALLATION

See Figures 13 and 14

1. With the hose attached, pull the valve out of the grommet with a twisting motion.

➡It may be necessary to roll the grommet back, in order to remove the PCV valve.

2. Push the clip tabs in the opposite direction to open the clip which holds the rubber hose in place.
3. Separate the hose and the PCV valve with a twisting motion.
4. Before installing the PCV valve, coat the end to be inserted in the rubber hose with a small amount of oil.

➡For further information and illustrations, please refer to Section 4 under PCV Systems.

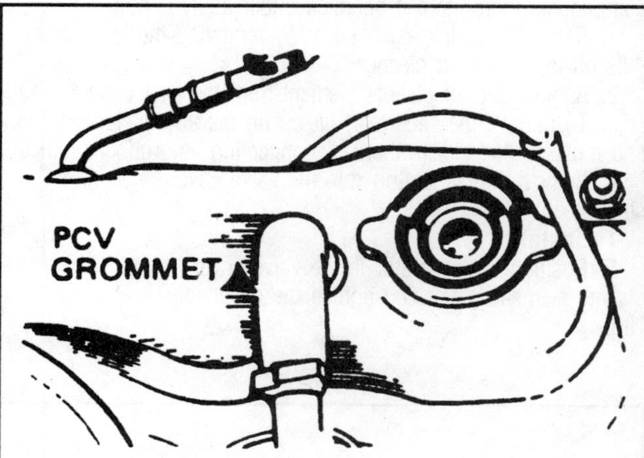

Fig. 13 The PCV valve grommet is located on the valve cover

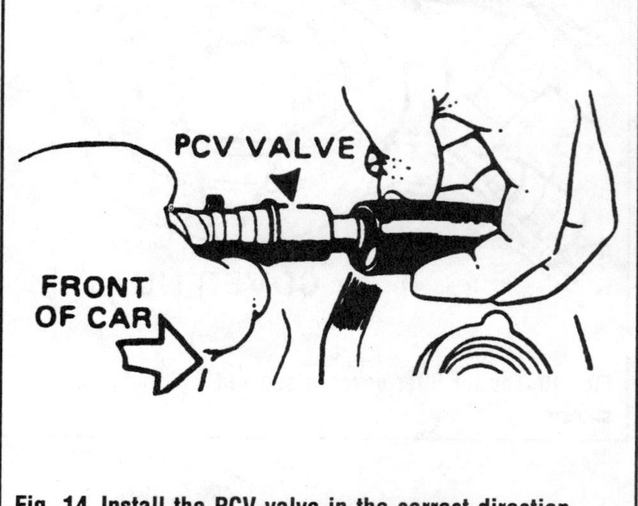

Fig. 14 Install the PCV valve in the correct direction

Pull the PCV valve from the grommet in the valve cover . . .

. . . then remove the valve from the hose using a twisting motion—2.8L shown

Evaporative Emission Control Canister

➧ See Figure 15

The evaporative control canister uses a charcoal element which stores fuel vapor from the fuel tank. The fuel vapor is removed from the canister and consumed in the normal combustion process when the engine is running.

REMOVAL & INSTALLATION

Filter

1. Loosen the screw holding the canister-to-mounting bracket.
2. Rotate the canister bracket and remove. Disconnect the canister hoses noting their position for installation.
3. Pull the filter out from the bottom of the canister with your fingers.

To install:

4. Install a new canister filter, connect the hoses in their proper location, position the canister-to-mounting bracket and tighten the retaining screw. For hose routing, refer to the "Vacuum Routing Diagrams" in Section 4.

Fuel Filter

REMOVAL & INSTALLATION

**** CAUTION**

To reduce the risk of fire and personal injury, it is necessary to relieve the fuel system pressure before servicing any fuel system component. If this procedure is not performed, fuel may be sprayed out of the connection under pressure. Always keep a dry chemical (Class B) fire extinguisher near the work area.

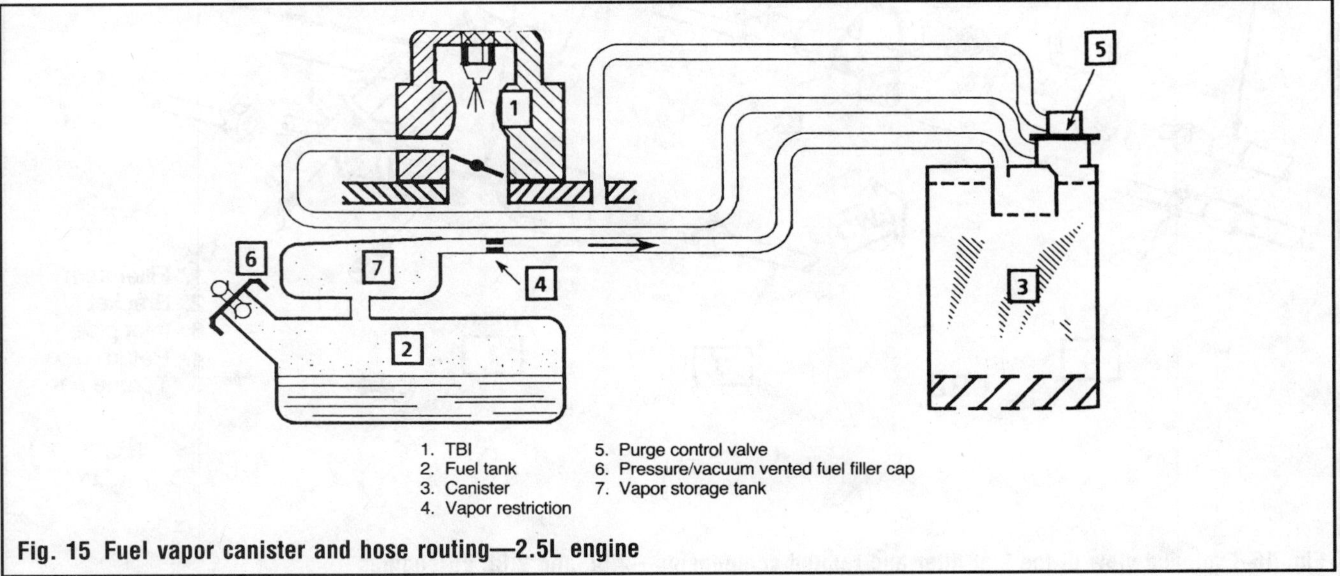

Fig. 15 Fuel vapor canister and hose routing—2.5L engine

2.5L Engine

See Figure 16

1. Remove the fuel pump fuse from the fuse block located in the passenger compartment. Start the engine and run until the engine stops due to the lack of fuel. Crank the engine for 3 seconds to ensure all pressure is relieved.
2. Disconnect the inlet and outlet steel tubes at the fuel filter using a flare nut wrench.
3. Remove the filter bracket-to-engine attaching nut and remove the filter.

To install:

4. Position the filter into the bracket and install the retaining nut. Torque the nut to 4 ft. lbs. (5.4 Nm).
5. Install the inlet and outlet steel tubes to the filter ensuring that the flow arrow is facing towards the throttle body. Refer to the following fuel filter illustration for flow direction.

2.8L Engine

1. Connect fuel gauge part No. J 34730-1 or equivalent to the fuel pressure valve on the fuel rail assembly. Wrap a towel around the fitting while connecting the gauge to prevent fuel spillage. Install the bleed hose into an approved container and open the valve to bleed the system pressure.
2. Disconnect the inlet and outlet steel tubes at the fuel filter using a flare nut wrench.
3. Remove the three filter bracket-to-torque bar attaching bolts and remove the filter.

To install:

4. Position the filter into the bracket and torque the three attaching bolts to 6 ft. lbs. (8 Nm). Install the inlet and outlet steel tubes ensuring that the flow arrow is facing in the right direction towards to the throttle body. Tighten the steel tubes with a flare nut wrench.

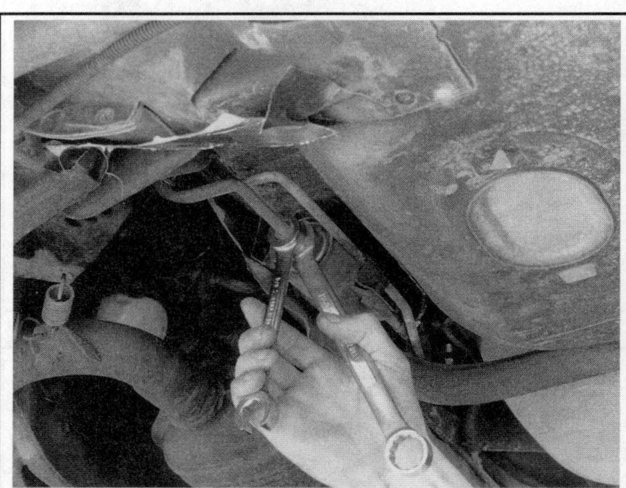

Hold the filter with an open end wrench, then loosen the fitting with a flare nut wrench

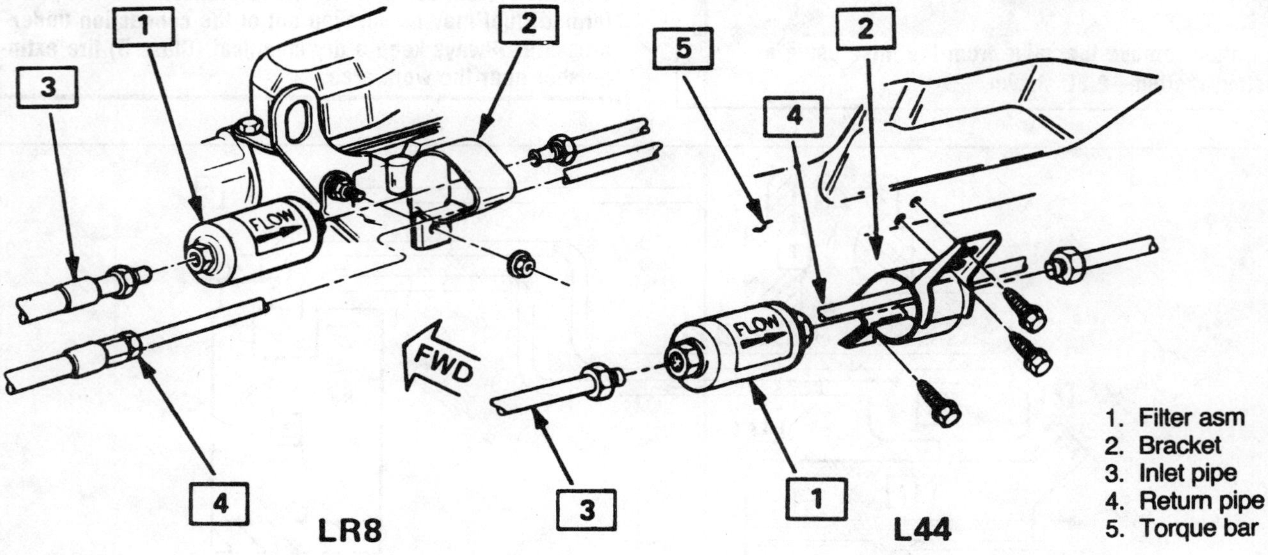

LR8 L44

1. Filter asm
2. Bracket
3. Inlet pipe
4. Return pipe
5. Torque bar

Fig. 16 Exploded view of the fuel filter and related components—2.5L and 2.8L V6 engines

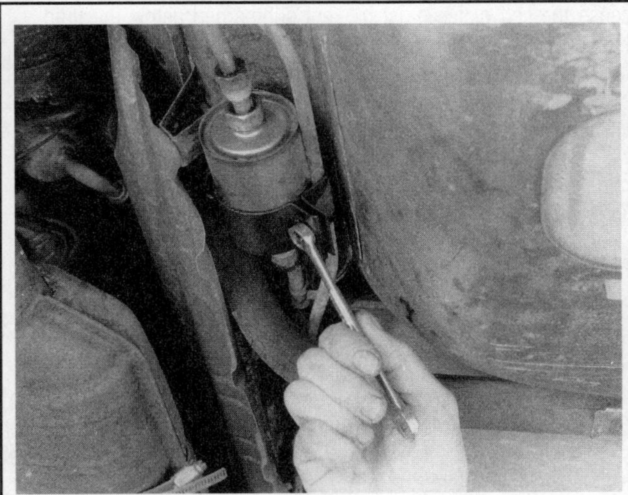

Remove the filter bracket retaining nut . . .

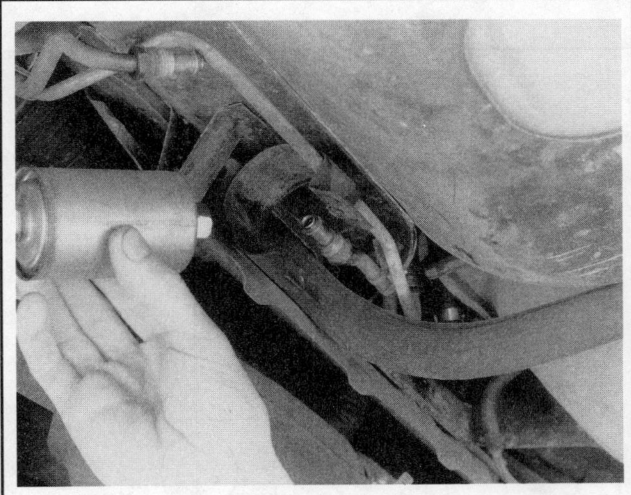

. . . then remove the fuel filter from under the vehicle

Battery

GENERAL MAINTENANCE

All batteries, regardless of type, should be carefully secured by a battery hold-down device. If this is not done, the battery terminals or casing may crack from stress applied to the battery during vehicle operation. A battery which is not secured may allow acid to leak out, making it discharge faster; such leaking corrosive acid can also eat away components under the hood. A battery that is not sealed must be checked periodically for electrolyte level. You cannot add water to a sealed maintenance-free battery (though not all maintenance-free batteries are sealed), but a sealed battery must also be checked for proper electrolyte level as indicated by the color of the built-in hydrometer "eye."

Keep the top of the battery clean, as a film of dirt can help completely discharge a battery that is not used for long periods. A solution of baking soda and water may be used for cleaning, but be careful to flush this off with clear water. DO NOT let any of the solution into the filler holes. Baking soda neutralizes battery acid and will de-activate a battery cell.

**** CAUTION**

Always use caution when working on or near the battery. Never allow a tool to bridge the gap between the negative and positive battery terminals. Also, be careful not to allow a tool to provide a ground between the positive cable/terminal and any metal component on the vehicle. Either of these conditions will cause a short circuit leading to sparks and possible personal injury.

Batteries in vehicles which are not operated on a regular basis can fall victim to parasitic loads (small current drains which are constantly drawing current from the battery). Normal parasitic loads may drain a battery on a vehicle that is in storage and not used for 6–8 weeks. Vehicles that have additional accessories such as a cellular phone, an alarm system or other devices that increase parasitic load may discharge a battery sooner. If the vehicle is to be stored for 6–8 weeks in a secure area and the alarm system, if present, is not necessary, the negative battery cable should be disconnected at the onset of storage to protect the battery charge.

Remember that constantly discharging and recharging will shorten battery life. Take care not to allow a battery to be needlessly discharged.

BATTERY FLUID

**** CAUTION**

Battery electrolyte contains sulfuric acid. If you should splash any on your skin or in your eyes, flush the affected area with plenty of clear water. If it lands in your eyes, get medical help immediately.

The fluid (sulfuric acid solution) contained in the battery cells will tell you many things about the condition of the battery. Be-

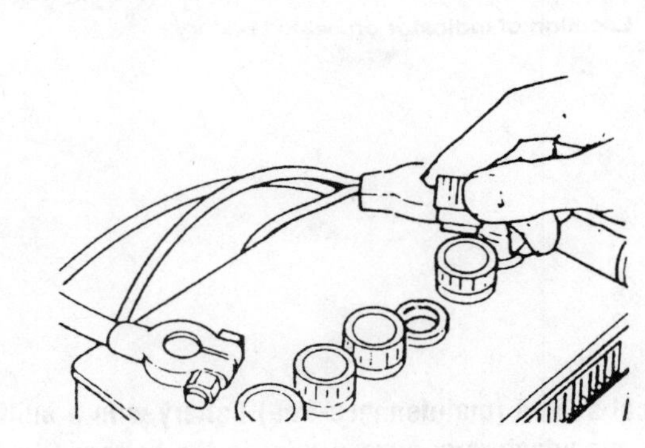

On non-maintenance free batteries, the level can be checked through the case on translucent batteries; the cell caps must be removed on other models

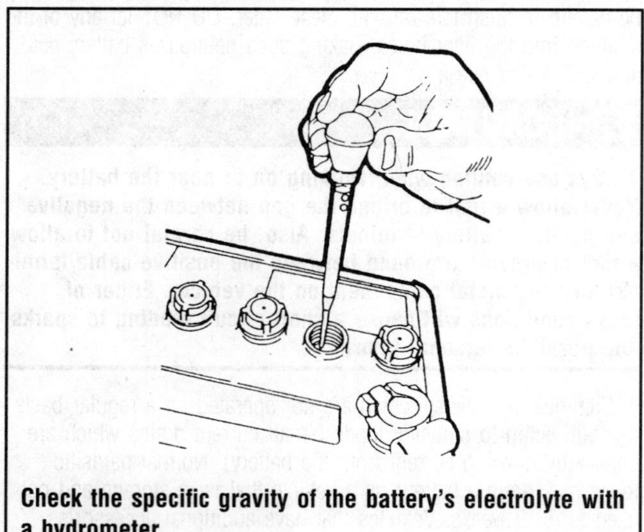

Check the specific gravity of the battery's electrolyte with a hydrometer

cause the cell plates must be kept submerged below the fluid level in order to operate, maintaining the fluid level is extremely important. And, because the specific gravity of the acid is an indication of electrical charge, testing the fluid can be an aid in determining if the battery must be replaced. A battery in a vehicle with a properly operating charging system should require little maintenance, but careful, periodic inspection should reveal problems before they leave you stranded.

Fluid Level

Check the battery electrolyte level at least once a month, or more often in hot weather or during periods of extended vehicle operation. On non-sealed batteries, the level can be checked either through the case on translucent batteries or by removing the cell caps on opaque-cased types. The electrolyte level in each cell should be kept filled to the split ring inside each cell, or the line marked on the outside of the case.

If the level is low, add only distilled water through the opening until the level is correct. Each cell is separate from the others, so

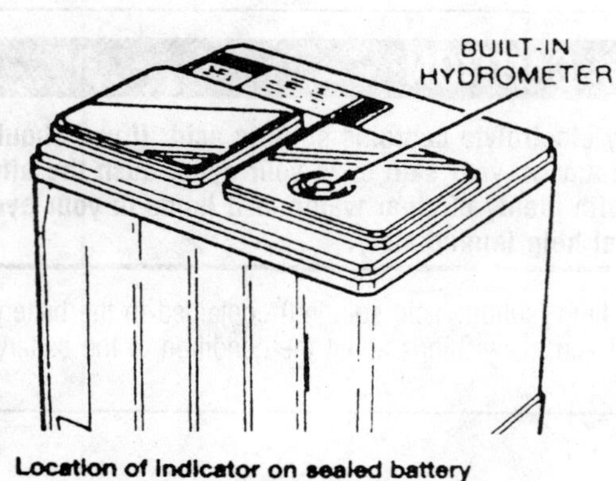

Location of indicator on sealed battery

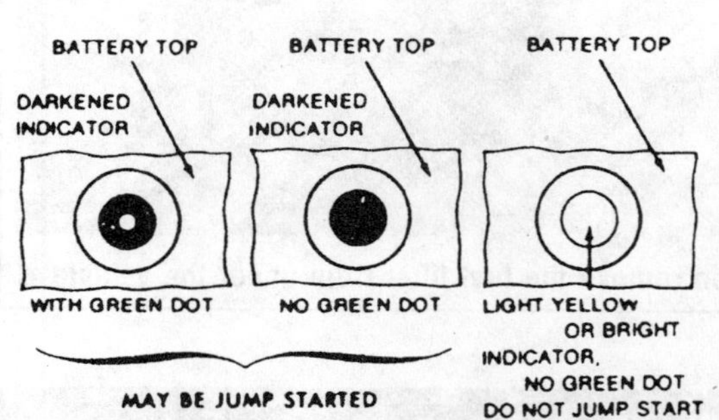

Check the appearance of the charge indicator on top of the battery before attempting a jump start; if it's not green or dark, do not jump start the car

A typical sealed (maintenance-free) battery with a built-in hydrometer—NOTE that the hydrometer eye may vary between battery manufacturers; always refer to the battery's label

each must be checked and filled individually. Distilled water should be used, because the chemicals and minerals found in most drinking water are harmful to the battery and could significantly shorten its life.

If water is added in freezing weather, the vehicle should be driven several miles to allow the water to mix with the electrolyte. Otherwise, the battery could freeze.

Although some maintenance-free batteries have removable cell caps for access to the electrolyte, the electrolyte condition and level on all sealed maintenance-free batteries must be checked using the built-in hydrometer "eye." The exact type of eye varies between battery manufacturers, but most apply a sticker to the battery itself explaining the possible readings. When in doubt, refer to the battery manufacturer's instructions to interpret battery condition using the built-in hydrometer.

➡Although the readings from built-in hydrometers found in sealed batteries may vary, a green eye usually indicates a properly charged battery with sufficient fluid level. A dark eye is normally an indicator of a battery with sufficient fluid, but one which may be low in charge. And a light or yellow eye is usually an indication that electrolyte supply has dropped below the necessary level for battery (and hydrometer) operation. In this last case, sealed batteries with an insufficient electrolyte level must usually be discarded.

Specific Gravity

As stated earlier, the specific gravity of a battery's electrolyte level can be used as an indication of battery charge. At least once a year, check the specific gravity of the battery. It should be between 1.20 and 1.26 on the gravity scale. Most auto supply stores carry a variety of inexpensive battery testing hydrometers. These can be used on any non-sealed battery to test the specific gravity in each cell.

The battery testing hydrometer has a squeeze bulb at one end and a nozzle at the other. Battery electrolyte is sucked into the hydrometer until the float is lifted from its seat. The specific gravity is then read by noting the position of the float. If gravity is low in one or more cells, the battery should be slowly charged and checked again to see if the gravity has come up. Generally, if after charging, the specific gravity between any two cells varies more than 50 points (0.50), the battery should be replaced as it can no longer produce sufficient voltage to guarantee proper operation.

On sealed batteries, the built-in hydrometer is the only way of checking specific gravity. Again, check with your battery's manufacturer for proper interpretation of its built-in hydrometer readings.

CABLES

Once a year (or as necessary), the battery terminals and the cable clamps should be cleaned. Loosen the clamps and remove the cables, negative cable first. On batteries with posts on top, the use of a puller specially made for this purpose is recommended. These are inexpensive and available in most auto parts stores. Side terminal battery cables are secured with a small bolt.

Clean the cable clamps and the battery terminal with a wire brush, until all corrosion, grease, etc., is removed and the metal is shiny. It is especially important to clean the inside of the clamp (an old knife is useful here) thoroughly, since a small deposit of foreign material or oxidation there will prevent a sound electrical connection and inhibit either starting or charging. Special tools

Maintenance is performed with household items and with special tools like this post cleaner

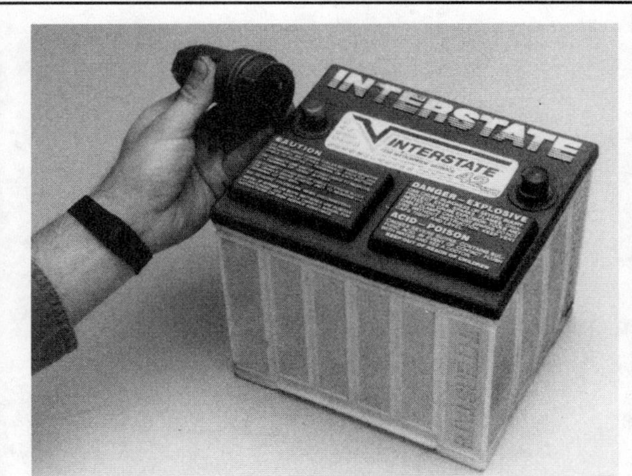

The underside of this special battery tool has a wire brush to clean post terminals

Place the tool over the terminals and twist to clean the post

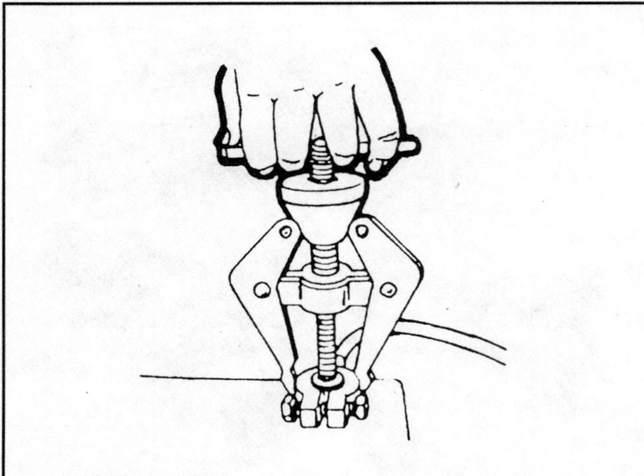

A special tool is available to pull the clamp from the post

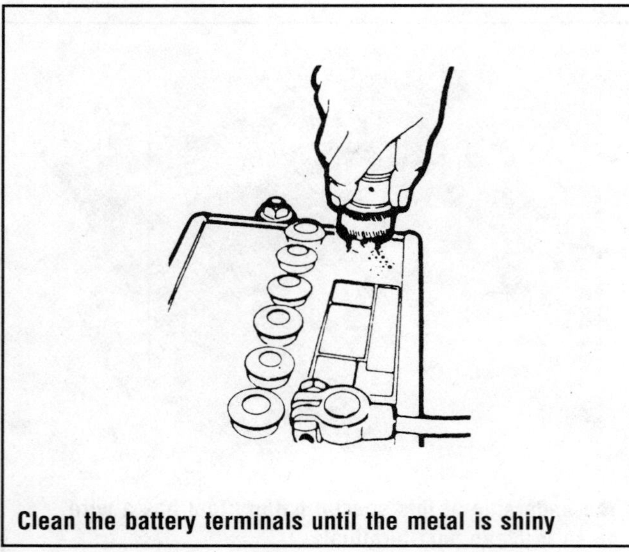

Clean the battery terminals until the metal is shiny

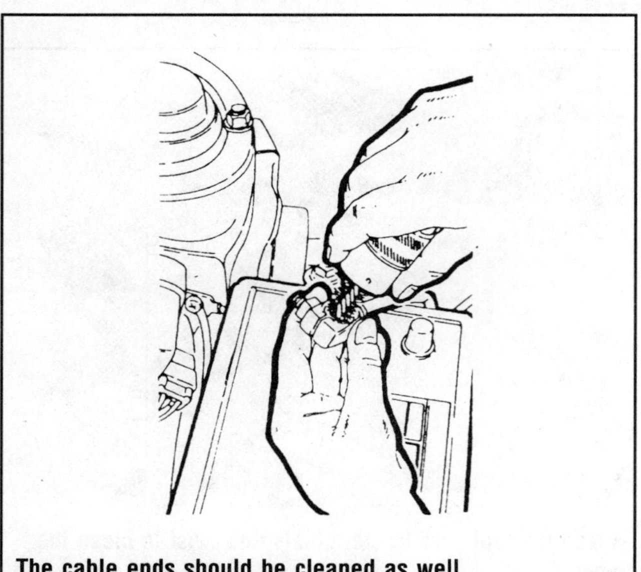

The cable ends should be cleaned as well

are available for cleaning these parts, one type for conventional top post batteries and another type for side terminal batteries.

Before installing the cables, loosen the battery hold-down clamp or strap, remove the battery and check the battery tray. Clear it of any debris, and check it for soundness (the battery tray can be cleaned with a baking soda and water solution). Rust should be wire brushed away, and the metal given a couple coats of anti-rust paint. Install the battery and tighten the hold-down clamp or strap securely. Do not overtighten, as this can crack the battery case.

After the clamps and terminals are clean, reinstall the cables, negative cable last; DO NOT hammer the clamps onto post batteries. Tighten the clamps securely, but do not distort them. Give the clamps and terminals a thin external coating of grease after installation, to retard corrosion.

Check the cables at the same time that the terminals are cleaned. If the cable insulation is cracked or broken, or if the ends are frayed, the cable should be replaced with a new cable of the same length and gauge.

CHARGING

**** CAUTION**

The chemical reaction which takes place in all batteries generates explosive hydrogen gas. A spark can cause the battery to explode and splash acid. To avoid serious personal injury, be sure there is proper ventilation and take appropriate fire safety precautions when connecting, disconnecting, or charging a battery and when using jumper cables.

A battery should be charged at a slow rate to keep the plates inside from getting too hot. However, if some maintenance-free batteries are allowed to discharge until they are almost "dead," they may have to be charged at a high rate to bring them back to "life." Always follow the charger manufacturer's instructions on charging the battery.

REPLACEMENT

When it becomes necessary to replace the battery, select one with a rating equal to or greater than the battery originally installed. Deterioration and just plain aging of the battery cables, starter motor, and associated wires makes the battery's job harder in successive years. The slow increase in electrical resistance over time makes it prudent to install a new battery with a greater capacity than the old.

ADJUSTMENT

2.5L Engine

The 4-cylinder engine is equipped with a serpentine belt that is adjusted by an automatic tensioner. This tensioner controls belt tension over a broad range of belt lengths; however, there are limits to the tensioner's ability to compensate. If the tensioner is beyond its limit, the belt should be replaced.

2.8L Engine

ALTERNATOR-A/C BELT

➧ See Figure 17

1. Disconnect the negative (−) battery cable.
2. Loosen the upper and lower alternator mounting bolts.
3. With a suitable prybar and a belt tension tool No. J 23600-B or equivalent, move the alternator outward until the belt has 145 lbs. (650 Nm) for a new belt or 70 lbs. (300 Nm) for a used belt. When specification is reached tighten the lower alternator bolt.

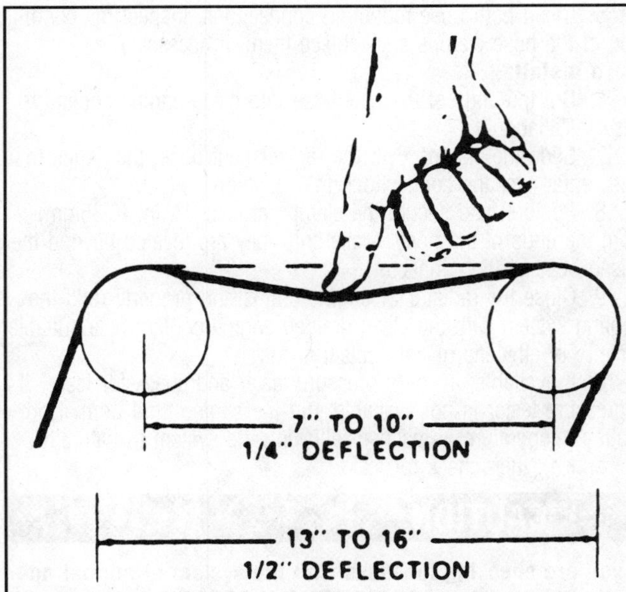

Fig. 17 A gauge is recommended, but you can check the belt tension with thumb pressure

Hoses

INSPECTION

Upper and lower radiator hoses along with the heater hoses should be checked for deterioration, leaks and loose hose clamps at least every 15,000 miles (24,000 km). It is also wise to check the hoses periodically in early spring and at the beginning of the fall or winter when you are performing other maintenance. A quick visual inspection could discover a weakened hose which might have left you stranded if it had remained unrepaired.

Whenever you are checking the hoses, make sure the engine and cooling system are cold. Visually inspect for cracking, rotting or collapsed hoses, and replace as necessary. Run your hand along the length of the hose. If a weak or swollen spot is noted when squeezing the hose wall, the hose should be replaced.

REMOVAL & INSTALLATION

1. Remove the radiator pressure cap.

✻✻ CAUTION

Never remove the pressure cap while the engine is running, or personal injury from scalding hot coolant or steam may result. If possible, wait until the engine has cooled to remove the pressure cap. If this is not possible, wrap a thick cloth around the pressure cap and turn it slowly to the stop. Step back while the pressure is released from the cooling system. When you are sure all the pressure has been released, use the cloth to turn and remove the cap.

2. Position a clean container under the radiator and/or engine draincock or plug, then open the drain and allow the cooling sys-

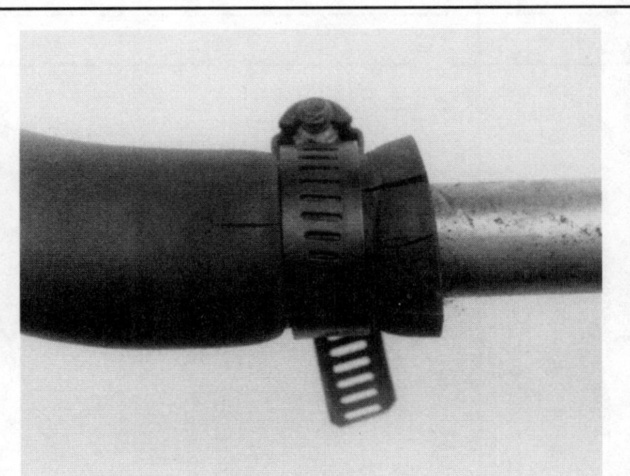

The cracks developing along this hose are a result of age-related hardening

A hose clamp that is too tight can cause older hoses to separate and tear on either side of the clamp

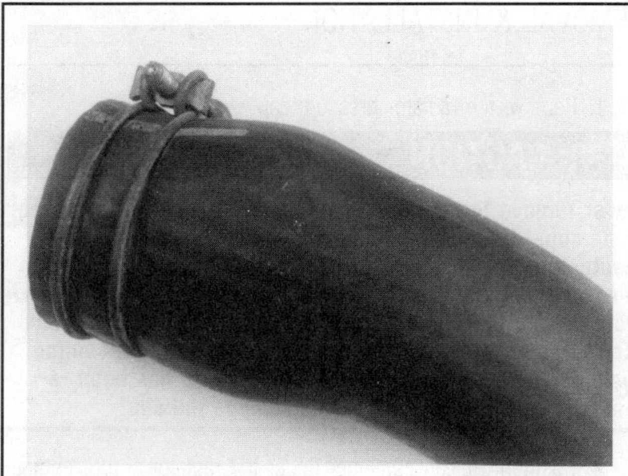

A soft spongy hose (identifiable by the swollen section) will eventually burst and should be replaced

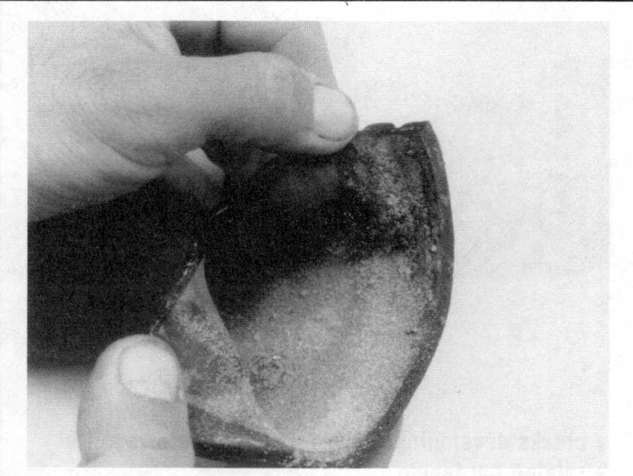

Hoses are likely to deteriorate from the inside if the cooling system is not periodically flushed

tem to drain to an appropriate level. For some upper hoses, only a little coolant must be drained. To remove hoses positioned lower on the engine, such as a lower radiator hose, the entire cooling system must be emptied.

CAUTION

When draining coolant, keep in mind that cats and dogs are attracted by ethylene glycol antifreeze, and are quite likely to drink any that is left in an uncovered container or in puddles on the ground. This will prove fatal in sufficient quantity. Always drain coolant into a sealable container. Coolant may be reused unless it is contaminated or several years old.

3. Loosen the hose clamps at each end of the hose requiring replacement. Clamps are usually either of the spring tension type (which require pliers to squeeze the tabs and loosen) or of the screw tension type (which require screw or hex drivers to loosen). Pull the clamps back on the hose away from the connection.
4. Twist, pull and slide the hose off the fitting, taking care not to damage the neck of the component from which the hose is being removed.

➡If the hose is stuck at the connection, do not try to insert a screwdriver or other sharp tool under the hose end in an effort to free it, as the connection and/or hose may become damaged. Heater connections especially may be easily damaged by such a procedure. If the hose is to be replaced, use a single-edged razor blade to make a slice along the portion of the hose which is stuck on the connection, perpendicular to the end of the hose. Do not cut deep so as to prevent damaging the connection. The hose can then be peeled from the connection and discarded.

5. Clean both hose mounting connections. Inspect the condition of the hose clamps and replace them, if necessary.

To install:

6. Dip the ends of the new hose into clean engine coolant to ease installation.
7. Slide the clamps over the replacement hose, then slide the hose ends over the connections into position.
8. Position and secure the clamps at least 1/4 in. (6.35mm) from the ends of the hose. Make sure they are located beyond the raised bead of the connector.
9. Close the radiator or engine drains and properly refill the cooling system with the clean drained engine coolant or a suitable mixture of ethylene glycol coolant and water.
10. If available, install a pressure tester and check for leaks. If a pressure tester is not available, run the engine until normal operating temperature is reached (allowing the system to naturally pressurize), then check for leaks.

CAUTION

If you are checking for leaks with the system at normal operating temperature, BE EXTREMELY CAREFUL not to touch any moving or hot engine parts. Once temperature has been reached, shut the engine OFF, and check for leaks around the hose fittings and connections which were removed earlier.

Coolant Pipes

REMOVAL & INSTALLATION

See Figures 18, 19, 20 and 21

CAUTION

When draining engine coolant, keep in mind that cats and dogs are attracted to ethylene glycol antifreeze and could drink any that is left in an uncovered container or in puddles on the ground. This will prove fatal in sufficient quantity. Always drain coolant into a sealable container. Coolant should be reused unless it is contaminated or is several years old.

1. Disconnect the negative (−) battery cable.
2. Raise the vehicle and support with jackstands.

3. Position a suitable drain pan under the radiator drain plug and drain the coolant into pan.

**** CAUTION**

Exercise extreme care when removing the cap from a hot radiator. Wait a few minutes until the engine has time to cool somewhat, then wrap a thick towel around the radiator cap and slowly turn it counterclockwise to the first stop. Step back and allow the pressure to release from the cooling system. Then, when the steam has stopped venting, press down on the cap, turn it one more stop counterclockwise and remove the cap.

4. Remove the front wheel and tire assemblies.
5. Remove the radiator and engine hoses.
6. Remove the two bolts from the pipe bracket-to-crossmember.

**** CAUTION**

Lower the pipe slowly to prevent spilling coolant into your eyes because there may be coolant still in the pipe.

7. **To install:** position the pipe into the crossmember and torque the bolts to 7 ft. lbs. (10 Nm). Install the radiator and engine coolant hoses and tighten the clamps.

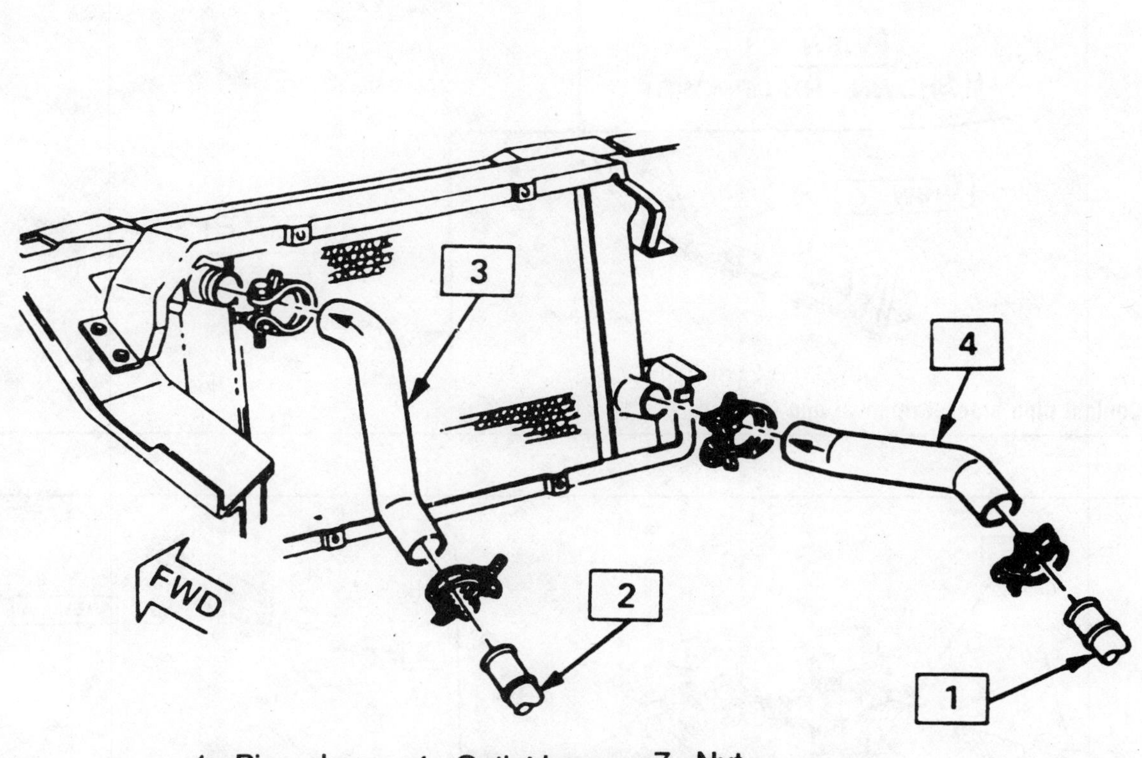

Fig. 18 Exploded view of the radiator hoses and related components

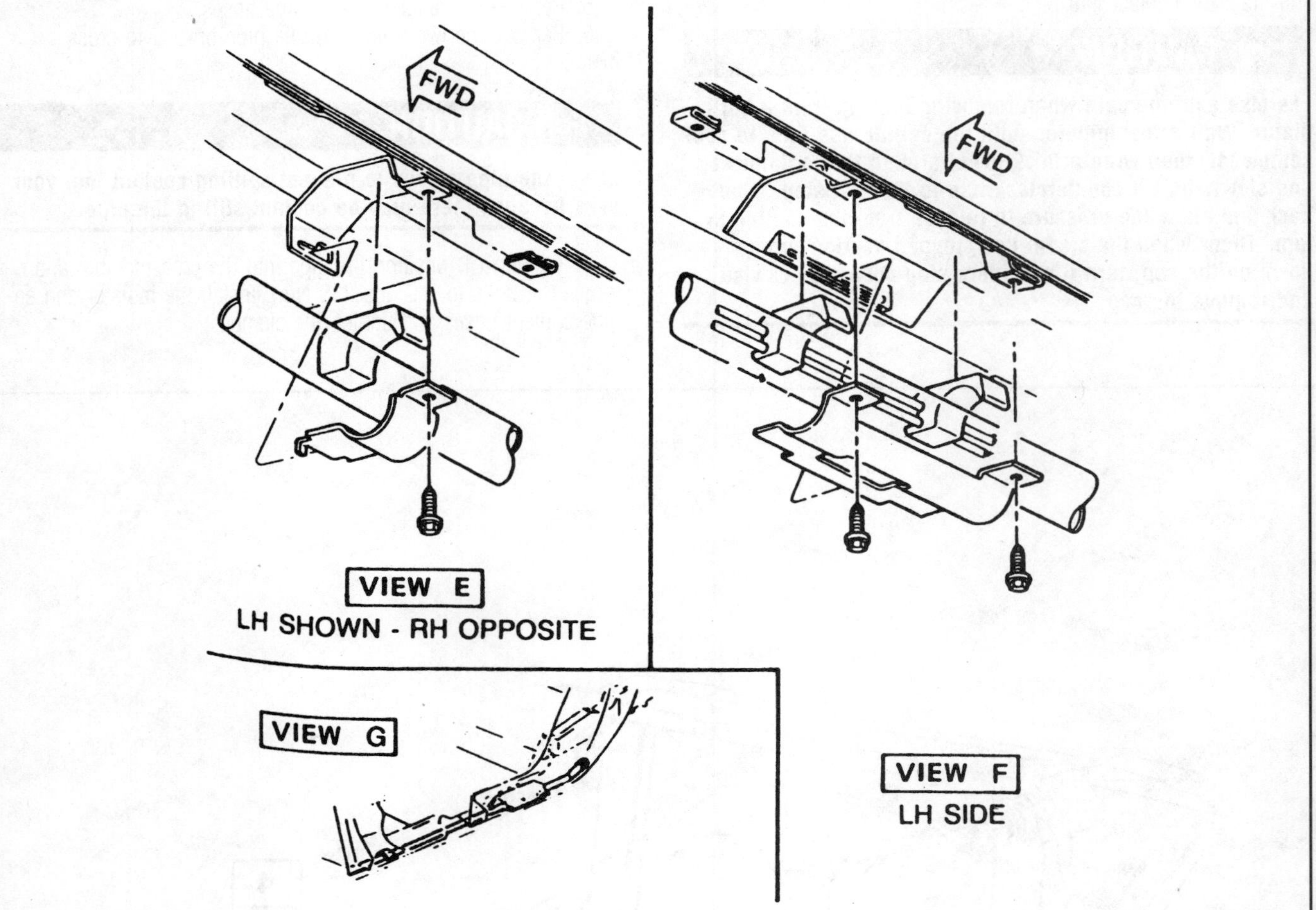

FWD
FWD
VIEW E
LH SHOWN - RH OPPOSITE
VIEW G
VIEW F
LH SIDE

Fig. 19 Coolant pipe bracket removal and location

1
A
2
5
4
FWD
3
FWD
VIEW A
2

1. Water pump outlet
2. Hose, inlet
3. Pipe, lh
4. Hose, outlet
5. Pipe, rh

Lubricate both ends of hoses.
Align arrows on hose and mating part ±15°

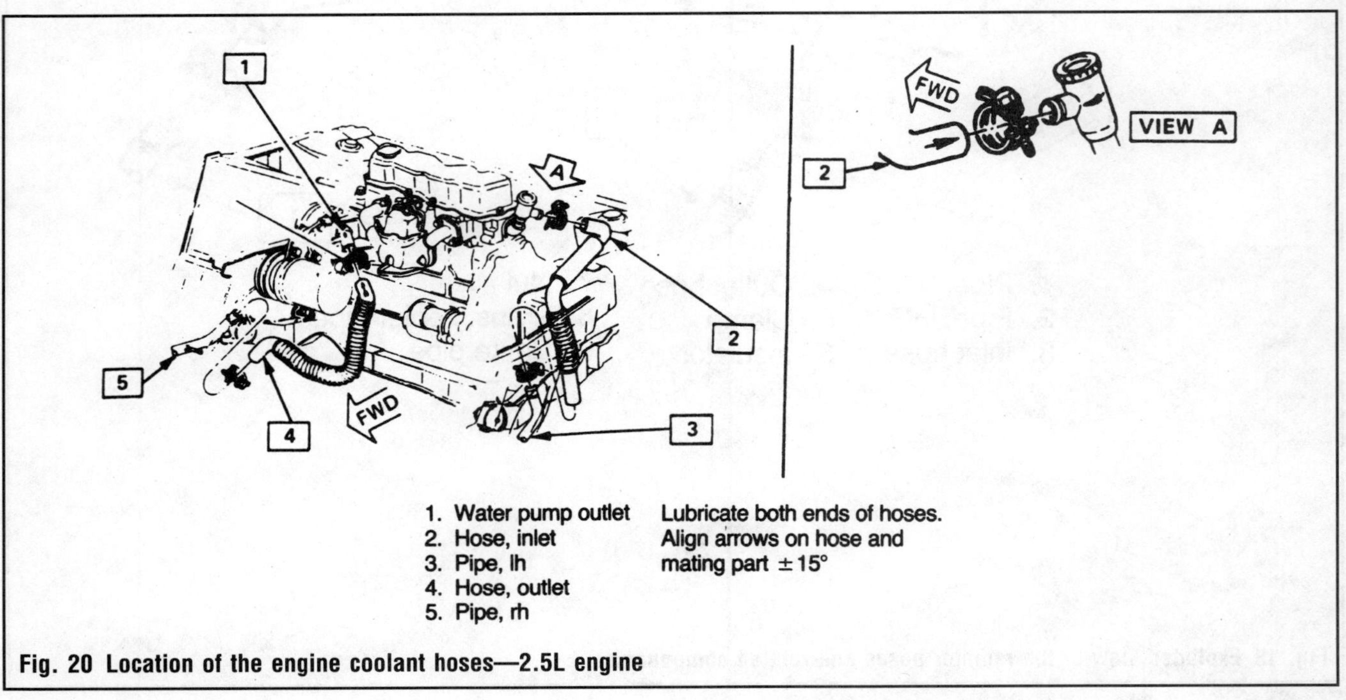

Fig. 20 Location of the engine coolant hoses—2.5L engine

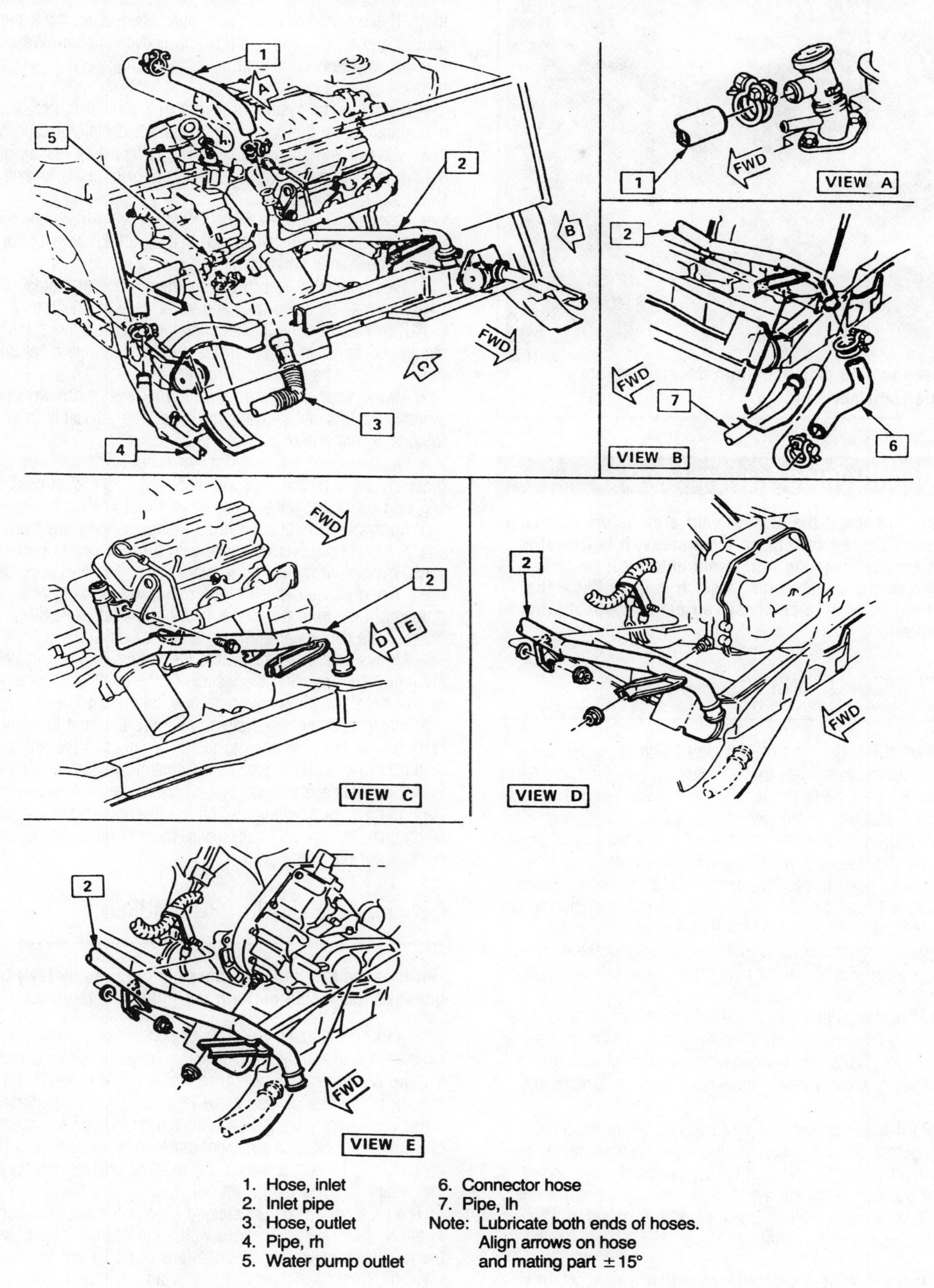

1. Hose, inlet
2. Inlet pipe
3. Hose, outlet
4. Pipe, rh
5. Water pump outlet
6. Connector hose
7. Pipe, lh

Note: Lubricate both ends of hoses. Align arrows on hose and mating part ±15°

Fig. 21 Sectional views of the engine coolant hose locations—2.8L engine

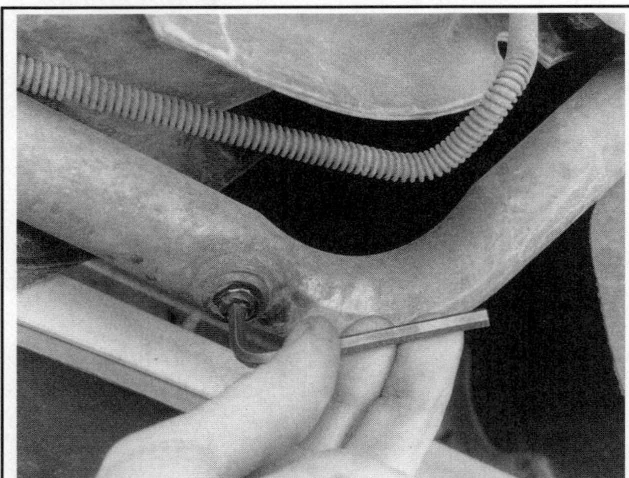
Remove the pipe plug and drain the coolant into a suitable container

Air Conditioning

➡Be sure to consult the laws in your area before servicing the air conditioning system. In most areas, it is illegal to perform repairs involving refrigerant unless the work is done by a certified technician. Also, it is quite likely that you will not be able to purchase refrigerant without proof of certification.

SAFETY PRECAUTIONS

There are two major hazards associated with air conditioning systems and they both relate to the refrigerant gas. First, the refrigerant gas (R-12) is an extremely cold substance. When exposed to air, it will instantly freeze any surface it comes in contact with, including your eyes. The other hazard relates to fire. Although normally non-toxic, the R-12 gas becomes highly poisonous in the presence of an open flame. One good whiff of the vapor formed by burning R-12 can be fatal. Keep all forms of fire (including cigarettes) well clear of the air conditioning system.

Because of the inherent dangers involved with working on air conditioning systems and R-12 refrigerant, these safety precautions must be strictly followed.

- Avoid contact with a charged refrigeration system, even when working on another part of the air conditioning system or vehicle. If a heavy tool comes into contact with a section of tubing or a heat exchanger, it can easily cause the relatively soft material to rupture.
- When it is necessary to apply force to a fitting which contains refrigerant, as when checking that all system couplings are securely tightened, use a wrench on both parts of the fitting involved, if possible. This will avoid putting torque on refrigerant tubing. (It is also advisable to use tube or line wrenches when tightening these flare nut fittings.)

➡R-12 refrigerant is a chlorofluorocarbon which, when released into the atmosphere, can contribute to the depletion of the ozone layer in the upper atmosphere. Ozone filters out harmful radiation from the sun.

- Do not attempt to discharge the system without the proper tools. Precise control is possible only when using the service gauges and a proper A/C refrigerant recovery station. Wear protective gloves when connecting or disconnecting service gauge hoses.
- Discharge the system only in a well ventilated area, as high concentrations of the gas which might accidentally escape can exclude oxygen and act as an anesthetic. When leak testing or soldering, this is particularly important, as toxic gas is formed when R-12 contacts any flame.
- Never start a system without first verifying that both service valves are properly installed, and that all fittings throughout the system are snugly connected.
- Avoid applying heat to any refrigerant line or storage vessel. Charging may be aided by using water heated to less than 125°F (50°C) to warm the refrigerant container. Never allow a refrigerant storage container to sit out in the sun, or near any other source of heat, such as a radiator or heater.
- Always wear goggles to protect your eyes when working on a system. If refrigerant contacts the eyes, it is advisable in all cases to consult a physician immediately.
- Frostbite from liquid refrigerant should be treated by first gradually warming the area with cool water, and then gently applying petroleum jelly. A physician should be consulted.
- Always keep refrigerant drum fittings capped when not in use. If the container is equipped with a safety cap to protect the valve, make sure the cap is in place when the can is not being used. Avoid sudden shock to the drum, which might occur from dropping it, or from banging a heavy tool against it. Never carry a drum in the passenger compartment of a vehicle.
- Always completely discharge the system into a suitable recovery unit before painting the vehicle (if the paint is to be baked on), or before welding anywhere near refrigerant lines.
- When servicing the system, minimize the time that any refrigerant line or fitting is open to the air in order to prevent moisture or dirt from entering the system. Contaminants such as moisture or dirt can damage internal system components. Always replace O-rings on lines or fittings which are disconnected. Prior to installation coat, but do not soak, replacement O-rings with suitable compressor oil.

GENERAL SERVICING PROCEDURES

➡It is recommended, and possibly required by law, that a qualified technician perform the following services.

The most important aspect of air conditioning service is the maintenance of a pure and adequate charge of refrigerant in the system. A refrigeration system cannot function properly if a significant percentage of the charge is lost. Leaks are common because the severe vibration encountered underhood in an automobile can easily cause a sufficient cracking or loosening of the air conditioning fittings; allowing, the extreme operating pressures of the system to force refrigerant out.

The problem can be understood by considering what happens to the system as it is operated with a continuous leak. Because the expansion valve regulates the flow of refrigerant to the evaporator, the level of refrigerant there is fairly constant. The receiver/drier stores any excess refrigerant, and so a loss will first appear there as a reduction in the level of liquid. As this level nears the bottom of the vessel, some refrigerant vapor bubbles will begin to appear in the stream of liquid supplied to the expansion valve. This vapor decreases the capacity of the expansion valve very little as the valve opens to compensate for its presence. As the quantity of liquid in the condenser decreases, the operating pressure will drop there and throughout the high side of the system. As the R-12 continues to be expelled, the pressure available to force the liquid through the expansion valve will continue to decrease, and, eventually, the valve's orifice will prove to be too much of a restriction for adequate flow even with the needle fully withdrawn.

At this point, low side pressure will start to drop, and a severe reduction in cooling capacity, marked by freeze-up of the evaporator coil, will result. Eventually, the operating pressure of the evaporator will be lower than the pressure of the atmosphere surrounding it, and air will be drawn into the system wherever there are leaks in the low side.

Because all atmospheric air contains at least some moisture, water will enter the system and mix with the R-12 and the oil. Trace amounts of moisture will cause sludging of the oil, and corrosion of the system. Saturation and clogging of the filter/drier, and freezing of the expansion valve orifice will eventually result. As air fills the system to a greater and greater extent, it will interfere more and more with the normal flows of refrigerant and heat.

From this description, it should be obvious that much of the repairman's focus in on detecting leaks, repairing them, and then restoring the purity and quantity of the refrigerant charge. A list of general rules should be followed in addition to all safety precautions:

- Keep all tools as clean and dry as possible.
- Thoroughly purge the service gauges/hoses of air and moisture before connecting them to the system. Keep them capped when not in use.
- Thoroughly clean any refrigerant fitting before disconnecting it, in order to minimize the entrance of dirt into the system.
- Plan any operation that requires opening the system beforehand, in order to minimize the length of time it will be exposed to open air. Cap or seal the open ends to minimize the entrance of foreign material.
- When adding oil, pour it through an extremely clean and dry tube or funnel. Keep the oil capped whenever possible. Do not use oil that has not been kept tightly sealed.
- Use only R-12 refrigerant. Purchase refrigerant intended for use only in automatic air conditioning systems.
- Completely evacuate any system that has been opened for service, or that has leaked sufficiently to draw in moisture and air. This requires evacuating air and moisture with a good vacuum pump for at least one hour. If a system has been open for a considerable length of time it may be advisable to evacuate the system for up to 12 hours (overnight).
- Use a wrench on both halves of a fitting that is to be disconnected, so as to avoid placing torque on any of the refrigerant lines.
- When overhauling a compressor, pour some of the oil into a clean glass and inspect it. If there is evidence of dirt, metal particles, or both, flush all refrigerant components with clean refrigerant before evacuating and recharging the system. In addition, if metal particles are present, the compressor should be replaced.
- Schrader valves may leak only when under full operating pressure. Therefore, if leakage is suspected but cannot be located, operate the system with a full charge of refrigerant and look for leaks from all Schrader valves. Replace any faulty valves.

Additional Preventive Maintenance

USING THE SYSTEM

The easiest and most important preventive maintenance for your A/C system is to be sure that it is used on a regular basis. Running the system for five minutes each month (no matter what the season) will help assure that the seals and all internal components remain lubricated.

ANTIFREEZE

In order to prevent heater core freeze-up during A/C operation, it is necessary to maintain a proper antifreeze protection. Use a hand-held antifreeze tester (hydrometer) to periodically check the condition of the antifreeze in your engine's cooling system.

➡Antifreeze should not be used longer than the manufacturer specifies.

RADIATOR CAP

For efficient operation of an air conditioned vehicle's cooling system, the radiator cap should have a holding pressure which meets manufacturer's specifications. A cap which fails to hold these pressures should be replaced.

CONDENSER

Any obstruction of or damage to the condenser configuration will restrict the air flow which is essential to its efficient operation. It is therefore a good rule to keep this unit clean and in proper physical shape.

➡Bug screens which are mounted in front of the condenser, (unless they are original equipment), are regarded as obstructions.

CONDENSATION DRAIN TUBE

This single molded drain tube expels the condensation, which accumulates on the bottom of the evaporator housing, into the engine compartment. If this tube is obstructed, the air conditioning performance can be restricted and condensation buildup can spill over onto the vehicle's floor.

SYSTEM INSPECTION

➡R-12 refrigerant is a chlorofluorocarbon which, when released into the atmosphere, can contribute to the depletion of the ozone layer in the upper atmosphere. Ozone filters out harmful radiation from the sun.

The easiest and often most important check for the air conditioning system consists of a visual inspection of the system components. Visually inspect the air conditioning system for refrigerant leaks, damaged compressor clutch, compressor drive belt tension and condition, plugged evaporator drain tube, blocked condenser fins, disconnected or broken wires, blown fuses, corroded connections and poor insulation.

A refrigerant leak will usually appear as an oily residue at the leakage point in the system. The oily residue soon picks up dust or dirt particles from the surrounding air and appears greasy. Through time, this will build up and appear to be a heavy dirt impregnated grease. Most leaks are caused by damaged or missing O-ring seals at the component connections, damaged charging valve cores or missing service gauge port caps.

An antifreeze tester can be used to determine the freezing and boiling levels of the coolant

For a thorough visual and operational inspection, check the following:

1. Check the surface of the radiator and condenser for dirt, leaves or other material which might block air flow.
2. Check for kinks in hoses and lines. Check the system for leaks.
3. Make sure the drive belt is under the proper tension. When the air conditioning is operating, make sure the drive belt is free of noise or slippage.
4. Make sure the blower motor operates at all appropriate positions, then check for distribution of the air from all outlets with the blower on **HIGH.**

➡Keep in mind that under conditions of high humidity, air discharged from the A/C vents may not feel as cold as expected, even if the system is working properly. This is because the vaporized moisture in humid air retains heat more effectively than does dry air, making the humid air more difficult to cool.

Make sure the air passage selection lever is operating correctly. Start the engine and warm it to normal operating temperature, then make sure the hot/cold selection lever is operating correctly.

DISCHARGING, EVACUATING & CHARGING

Discharging, evacuating and charging the air conditioning system must be performed by a properly trained and certified me-

RELATIVE HUMIDITY (%)	AMBIENT AIR TEMP °F	°C	LOW SIDE PSIG	ENGINE SPEED (rpm)	CENTER DUCT AIR TEMPERATURE °F	°C	HIGH SIDE PSIG
20	70	21	29	2000	40	4	150
	80	27	29		44	7	190
	90	32	30		48	9	245
	100	38	31		57	14	305
30	70	21	29	2000	42	6	150
	80	27	30		47	8	205
	90	32	31		51	11	265
	100	38	32		61	16	325
40	70	21	29	2000	45	7	165
	80	27	30		49	9	215
	90	32	32		55	13	280
	100	38	39		65	18	345
50	70	21	30	2000	47	8	180
	80	27	32		53	12	235
	90	32	34		59	15	295
	100	38	40		69	21	350
60	70	21	30	2000	48	9	180
	80	27	33		56	13	240
	90	32	36		63	17	300
	100	38	43		73	23	360
70	70	21	30	2000	50	10	185
	80	27	34		58	14	245
	90	32	38		65	18	305
	100	38	44		75	24	365
80	70	21	30	2000	50	10	190
	80	27	34		59	15	250
	90	32	39		67	19	310
90	70	21	30	2000	50	10	200
	80	27	36		62	17	265
	90	32	42		71	22	330

A/C performance chart

Troubleshooting Basic Air Conditioning Problems

Problem	Cause	Solution
There's little or no air coming from the vents (and you're sure it's on)	• The A/C fuse is blown • Broken or loose wires or connections • The on/off switch is defective	• Check and/or replace fuse • Check and/or repair connections • Replace switch
The air coming from the vents is not cool enough	• Windows and air vent wings open • The compressor belt is slipping • Heater is on • Condenser is clogged with debris • Refrigerant has escaped through a leak in the system • Receiver/drier is plugged	• Close windows and vent wings • Tighten or replace compressor belt • Shut heater off • Clean the condenser • Check system • Service system
The air has an odor	• Vacuum system is disrupted • Odor producing substances on the evaporator case • Condensation has collected in the bottom of the evaporator housing	• Have the system checked/repaired • Clean the evaporator case • Clean the evaporator housing drains
System is noisy or vibrating	• Compressor belt or mountings loose • Air in the system	• Tighten or replace belt; tighten mounting bolts • Have the system serviced
Sight glass condition		
Constant bubbles, foam or oil streaks	• Undercharged system	• Charge the system
Clear sight glass, but no cold air	• No refrigerant at all	• Check and charge the system
Clear sight glass, but air is cold	• System is OK	
Clouded with milky fluid	• Receiver drier is leaking dessicant	• Have system checked
Large difference in temperature of lines	• System undercharged	• Charge and leak test the system
Compressor noise	• Broken valves • Overcharged • Incorrect oil level • Piston slap • Broken rings • Drive belt pulley bolts are loose	• Replace the valve plate • Discharge, evacuate and install the correct charge • Isolate the compressor and check the oil level. Correct as necessary. • Replace the compressor • Replace the compressor • Tighten with the correct torque specification
Excessive vibration	• Incorrect belt tension • Clutch loose • Overcharged • Pulley is misaligned	• Adjust the belt tension • Tighten the clutch • Discharge, evacuate and install the correct charge • Align the pulley
Condensation dripping in the passenger compartment	• Drain hose plugged or improperly positioned • Insulation removed or improperly installed	• Clean the drain hose and check for proper installation • Replace the insulation on the expansion valve and hoses
Frozen evaporator coil	• Faulty thermostat • Thermostat capillary tube improperly installed • Thermostat not adjusted properly	• Replace the thermostat • Install the capillary tube correctly • Adjust the thermostat
Low side low—high side low	• System refrigerant is low • Expansion valve is restricted	• Evacuate, leak test and charge the system • Replace the expansion valve
Low side high—high side low	• Internal leak in the compressor—worn	• Remove the compressor cylinder head and inspect the compressor. Replace the valve plate assembly if necessary. If the compressor pistons, rings or

Troubleshooting Basic Air Conditioning Problems (cont.)

Problem	Cause	Solution
Low side high—high side low (cont.)		cylinders are excessively worn or scored replace the compressor
	• Cylinder head gasket is leaking	• Install a replacement cylinder head gasket
	• Expansion valve is defective	• Replace the expansion valve
	• Drive belt slipping	• Adjust the belt tension
Low side high—high side high	• Condenser fins obstructed	• Clean the condenser fins
	• Air in the system	• Evacuate, leak test and charge the system
	• Expansion valve is defective	• Replace the expansion valve
	• Loose or worn fan belts	• Adjust or replace the belts as necessary
Low side low—high side high	• Expansion valve is defective	• Replace the expansion valve
	• Restriction in the refrigerant hose	• Check the hose for kinks—replace if necessary
	• Restriction in the receiver/drier	• Replace the receiver/drier
	• Restriction in the condenser	• Replace the condenser
Low side and high side normal (inadequate cooling)	• Air in the system	• Evacuate, leak test and charge the system
	• Moisture in the system	• Evacuate, leak test and charge the system

chanic in a facility equipped with refrigerant recovery/recycling equipment that meets SAE standards for the type of system to be serviced.

If you don't have access to the necessary equipment, we recommend that you take your vehicle to a reputable service station to have the work done. If you still wish to perform repairs on the vehicle, have them discharge the system, then take your vehicle home and perform the necessary work. When you are finished, return the vehicle to the station for evacuation and charging. Just be sure to cap ALL A/C system fittings immediately after opening them and keep them protected until the system is recharged.

Windshield Wipers

ELEMENT (REFILL) CARE & REPLACEMENT

For maximum effectiveness and longest element life, the windshield and wiper blades should be kept clean. Dirt, tree sap, road tar and so on will cause streaking, smearing and blade deterioration if left on the glass. It is advisable to wash the windshield carefully with a commercial glass cleaner at least once a month. Wipe off the rubber blades with the wet rag afterwards. Do not attempt to move wipers across the windshield by hand; damage to the motor and drive mechanism will result.

To inspect and/or replace the wiper blade elements, place the wiper switch in the **LOW** speed position and the ignition switch in the **ACC** position. When the wiper blades are approximately vertical on the windshield, turn the ignition switch to **OFF.**

Examine the wiper blade elements. If they are found to be cracked, broken or torn, they should be replaced immediately. Replacement intervals will vary with usage, although ozone deterioration usually limits element life to about one year. If the wiper pattern is smeared or streaked, or if the blade chatters across the glass, the elements should be replaced. It is easiest and most sensible to replace the elements in pairs.

If your vehicle is equipped with aftermarket blades, there are several different types of refills and your vehicle might have any kind. Aftermarket blades and arms rarely use the exact same type blade or refill as the original equipment. Here are some typical aftermarket blades; not all may be available for your vehicle:

The Anco® type uses a release button that is pushed down to allow the refill to slide out of the yoke jaws. The new refill slides back into the frame and locks in place.

Some Trico® refills are removed by locating where the metal backing strip or the refill is wider. Insert a small screwdriver blade between the frame and metal backing strip. Press down to release the refill from the retaining tab.

Other types of Trico® refills have two metal tabs which are unlocked by squeezing them together. The rubber filler can then be withdrawn from the frame jaws. A new refill is installed by inserting the refill into the front frame jaws and sliding it rearward to engage the remaining frame jaws. There are usually four jaws; be certain when installing that the refill is engaged in all of them. At the end of its travel, the tabs will lock into place on the front jaws of the wiper blade frame.

Another type of refill is made from polycarbonate. The refill has a simple locking device at one end which flexes downward out of

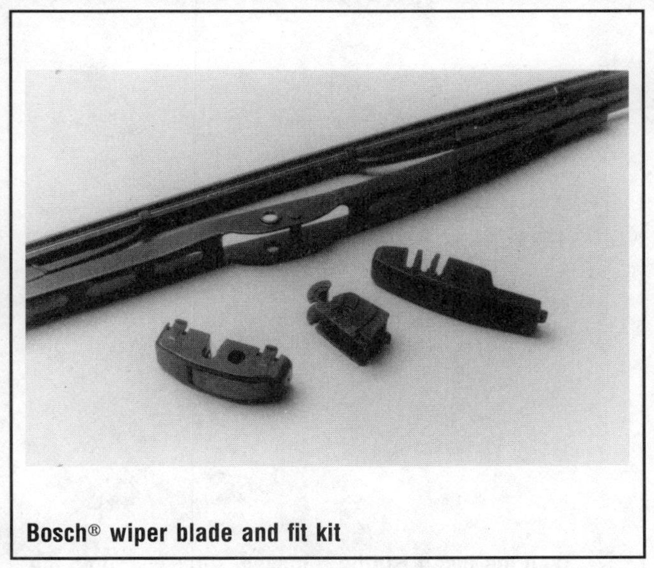

Bosch® wiper blade and fit kit

Trico® wiper blade and fit kit

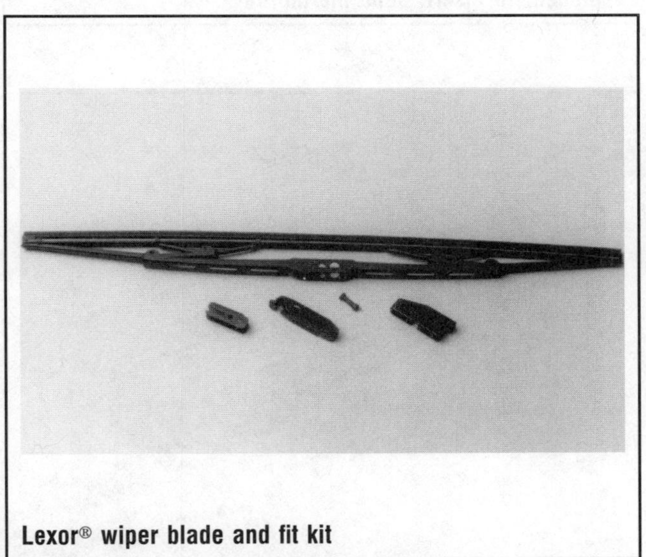

Lexor® wiper blade and fit kit

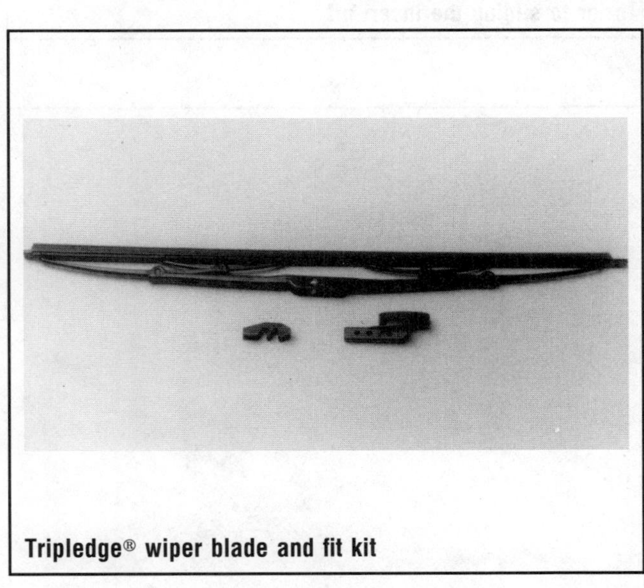

Tripledge® wiper blade and fit kit

Pylon® wiper blade and adaptor

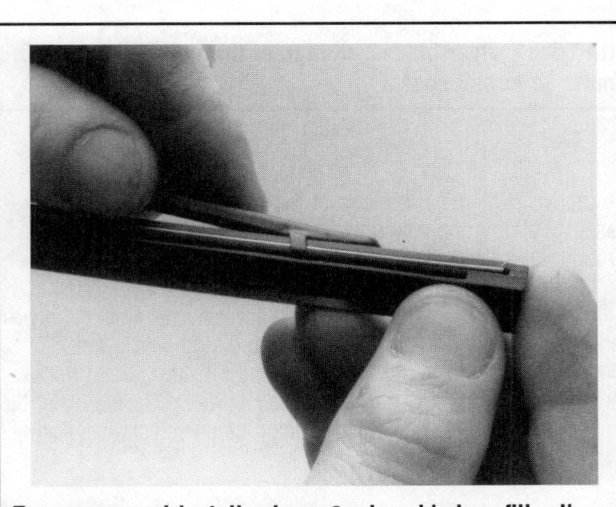

To remove and install a Lexor® wiper blade refill, slip out the old insert and slide in a new one

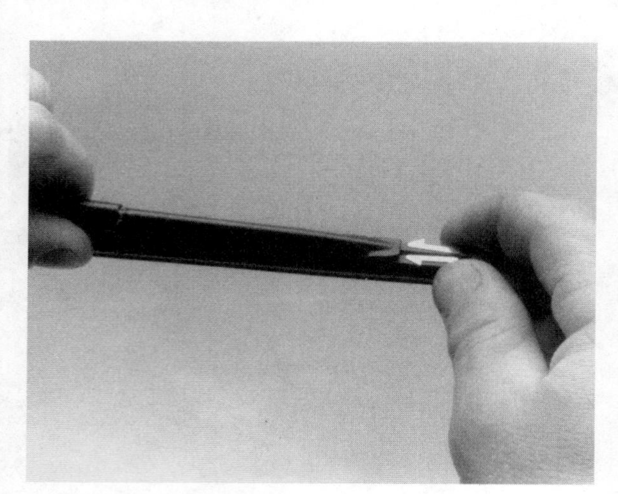

On Pylon® inserts, the clip at the end has to be removed prior to sliding the insert off

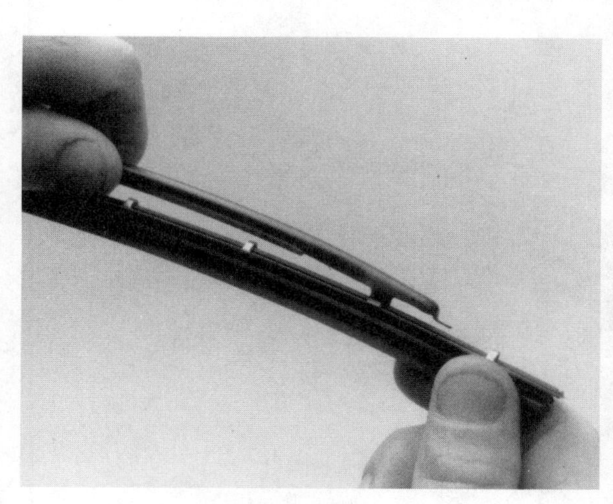

. . . then the insert can be removed. After installing the replacement insert, bend the tab back

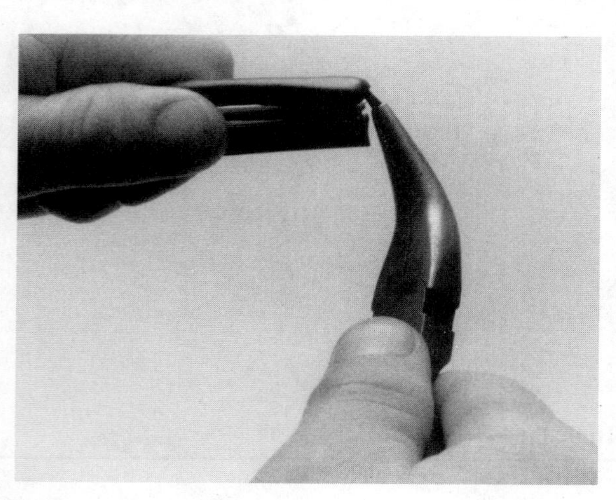

On Trico® wiper blades, the tab at the end of the blade must be turned up . . .

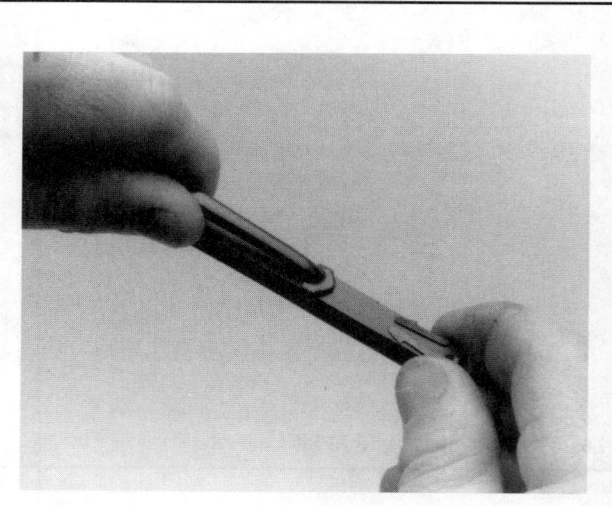

The Tripledge® wiper blade insert is removed and installed using a securing clip

the groove into which the jaws of the holder fit, allowing easy release. By sliding the new refill through all the jaws and pushing through the slight resistance when it reaches the end of its travel, the refill will lock into position.

To replace the Tridon® refill, it is necessary to remove the wiper blade. This refill has a plastic backing strip with a notch about 1 in. (25mm) from the end. Hold the blade (frame) on a hard surface so that the frame is tightly bowed. Grip the tip of the backing strip and pull up while twisting counterclockwise. The backing strip will snap out of the retaining tab. Do this for the remaining tabs until the refill is free of the blade. The length of these refills is molded into the end and they should be replaced with identical types.

Regardless of the type of refill used, be sure to follow the part manufacturer's instructions closely. Make sure that all of the frame jaws are engaged as the refill is pushed into place and locked. If the metal blade holder and frame are allowed to touch the glass during wiper operation, the glass will be scratched.

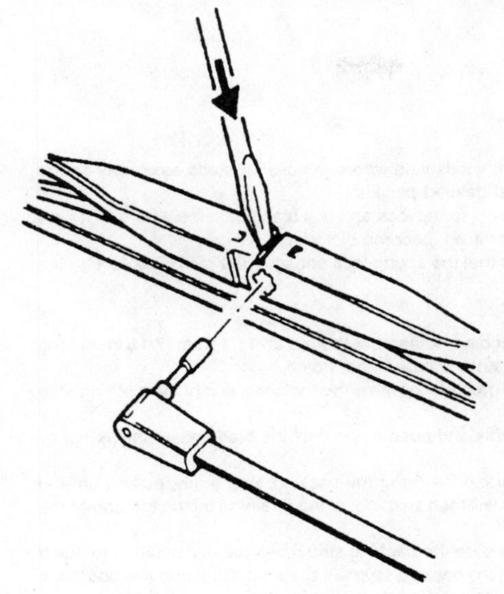

BLADE REPLACEMENT

1. CYCLE ARM AND BLADE ASSEMBLY TO UP POSITION ON THE WINDSHIELD WHERE REMOVAL OF BLADE ASSEMBLY CAN BE PERFORMED WITHOUT DIFFICULTY. TURN IGNITION KEY OFF AT DESIRED POSITION.
2. TO REMOVE BLADE ASSEMBLY, INSERT SCREWDRIVER IN SLOT, PUSH DOWN ON SPRING LOCK AND PULL BLADE ASSEMBLY FROM PIN (VIEW A)
3. TO INSTALL, PUSH THE BLADE ASSEMBLY ON THE PIN SO THAT THE SPRING LOCK ENGAGES THE PIN (VIEW A). BE SURE THE BLADE ASSEMBLY IS SECURELY ATTACHED TO PIN

VIEW A

NOTE INSERT SCREWDRIVER 3.2 mm (1/8 INCH) OR LESS PAST THIS EDGE

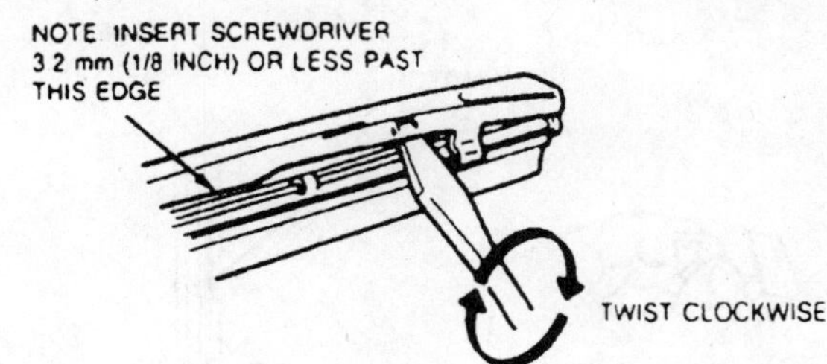

ELEMENT REPLACEMENT

1. INSERT SCREWDRIVER BETWEEN THE EDGE OF THE SUPER STRUCTURE AND THE BLADE BACKING DRIP (VIEW B) TWIST SCREWDRIVER SLOWLY UNTIL ELEMENT CLEARS ONE SIDE OF THE SUPER STRUCTURE CLAW
2. SLIDE THE ELEMENT INTO THE SUPER STRUCTURE CLAWS

VIEW B

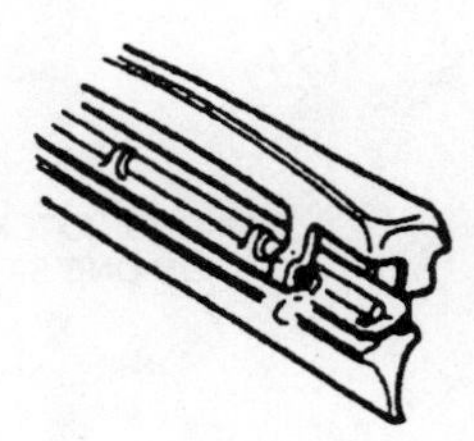

4. INSERT ELEMENT INTO ONE SIDE OF THE END CLAWS (VIEW D) AND WITH A ROCKING MOTION PUSH ELEMENT UPWARD UNTIL IT SNAPS IN (VIEW E)

VIEW D

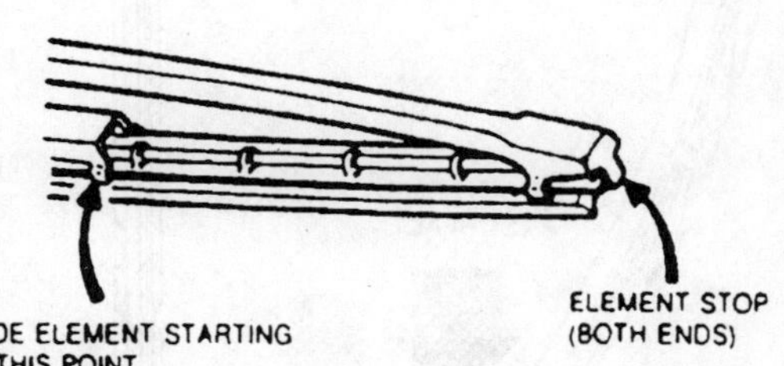

3. SLIDE THE ELEMENT INTO THE SUPER STRUCTURE CLAWS, STARTING WITH SECOND SET FROM EITHER END (VIEW C) AND CONTINUE TO SLIDE THE BLADE ELEMENT INTO ALL THE SUPER STRUCTURE CLAWS TO THE ELEMENT STOP (VIEW C)

VIEW C

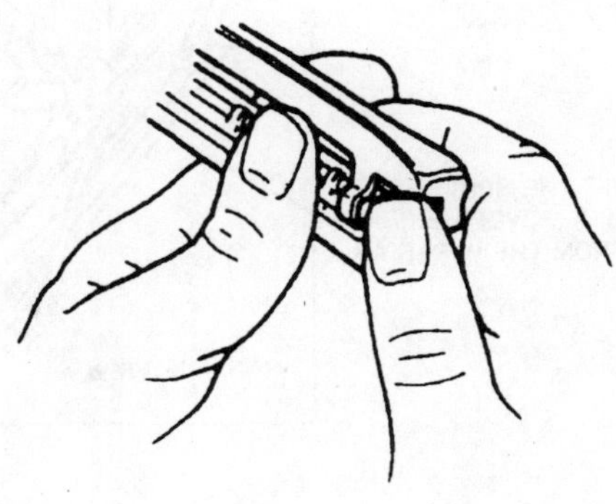

VIEW E

Trico® wiper blade insert (element) replacement

BLADE REPLACEMENT

1. Cycle arm and blade assembly to a position on the windshield where removal of blade assembly can be performed without difficulty. Turn ignition key off at desired position.
2. To remove blade assembly from wiper arm, pull up on spring lock and pull blade assembly from pin (View A). Be sure spring lock is not pulled excessively or it will become distorted.
3. To install, push the blade assembly onto the pin so that the spring lock engages the pin (View A). Be sure the blade assembly is securely attached to pin.

ELEMENT REPLACEMENT

1. In the plastic backing strip which is part of the rubber blade assembly, there is an 11.11mm (7/16 inch) long notch located approximately one inch from either end. Locate either notch.
2. Place the frame of the wiper blade assembly on a firm surface with either notched end of the backing strip visible.
3. Grasp the frame portion of the wiper blade assembly and push down until the blade assembly is tightly bowed.
4. With the blade assembly in the bowed position, grasp the tip of the backing strip firmly, pulling up and twisting C.C.W. at the same time. The backing strip will then snap out of the retaining tab on the end of the frame.
5. Lift the wiper blade assembly from the surface and slide the backing strip down the frame until the notch lines up with the next retaining tab, twist slightly, and the backing strip will snap out. Continue this operation with the remaining tabs until the blade element is completely detached from the frame.
6. To install blade element, reverse the above procedure, making sure all six (6) tabs are locked to the backing strip before installing blade to wiper arm.

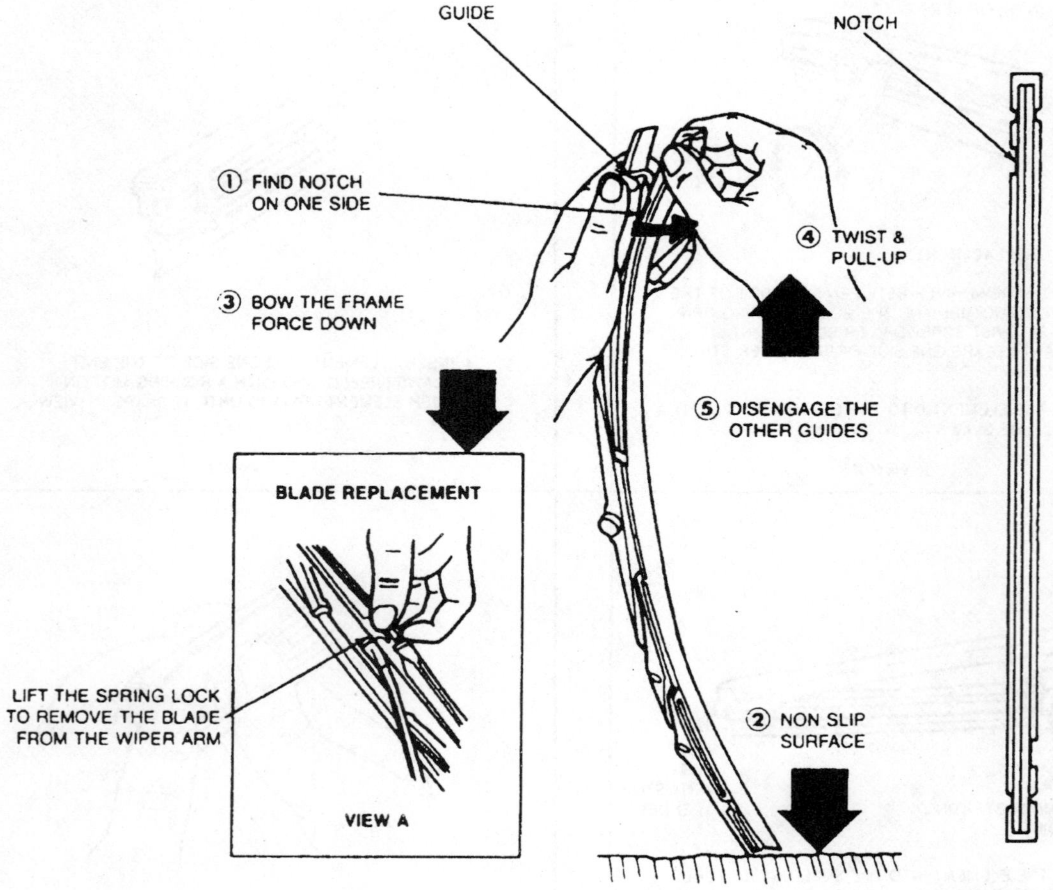

Tridon® wiper blade insert (element) replacement

Tires and Wheels

Common sense and good driving habits will afford maximum tire life. Fast starts, sudden stops and hard cornering are hard on tires and will shorten their useful life span. Make sure that you don't overload the vehicle or run with incorrect pressure in the tires. Both of these practices will increase tread wear.

➡For optimum tire life, keep the tires properly inflated, rotate them often and have the wheel alignment checked periodically.

Inspect your tires frequently. Be especially careful to watch for bubbles in the tread or sidewall, deep cuts or underinflation. Replace any tires with bubbles in the sidewall. If cuts are so deep that they penetrate to the cords, discard the tire. Any cut in the sidewall of a radial tire renders it unsafe. Also look for uneven tread wear patterns that may indicate the front end is out of alignment or that the tires are out of balance.

TIRE ROTATION

Tires must be rotated periodically to equalize wear patterns that vary with a tire's position on the vehicle. Tires will also wear in an uneven way as the front steering/suspension system wears to the point where the alignment should be reset.

Rotating the tires will ensure maximum life for the tires as a set, so you will not have to discard a tire early due to wear on only part of the tread. Regular rotation is required to equalize wear.

When rotating "unidirectional tires," make sure that they always roll in the same direction. This means that a tire used on the left side of the vehicle must not be switched to the right side and vice-versa. Such tires should only be rotated front-to-rear or rear-to-front, while always remaining on the same side of the vehicle. These tires are marked on the sidewall as to the direction of rotation; observe the marks when reinstalling the tire(s).

Some styled or "mag" wheels may have different offsets front to rear. In these cases, the rear wheels must not be used up front and vice-versa. Furthermore, if these wheels are equipped with unidirectional tires, they cannot be rotated unless the tire is remounted for the proper direction of rotation.

➡The compact or space-saver spare is strictly for emergency use. It must never be included in the tire rotation or placed on the vehicle for everyday use.

TIRE DESIGN

For maximum satisfaction, tires should be used in sets of four. Mixing of different types (radial, bias-belted, fiberglass belted) must be avoided. In most cases, the vehicle manufacturer has designated a type of tire on which the vehicle will perform best. Your first choice when replacing tires should be to use the same type of tire that the manufacturer recommends.

When radial tires are used, tire sizes and wheel diameters should be selected to maintain ground clearance and tire load ca-

Unidirectional tires are identifiable by sidewall arrows and/or the word "rotation"

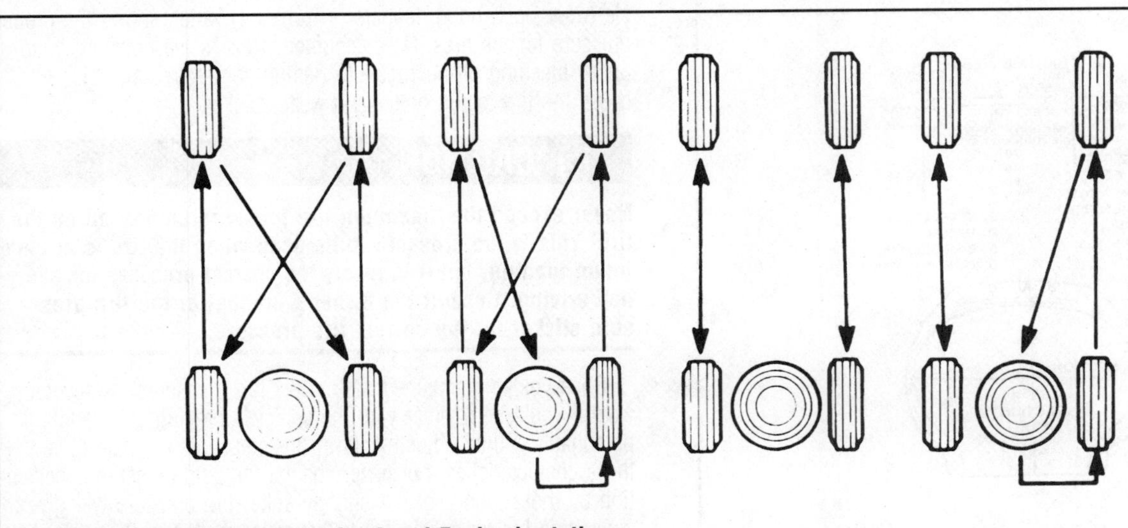

Common tire rotation patterns for 4 and 5-wheel rotations

pacity equivalent to the original specified tire. Radial tires should always be used in sets of four.

CAUTION

Radial tires should never be used on only the front axle.

When selecting tires, pay attention to the original size as marked on the tire. Most tires are described using an industry size code sometimes referred to as P-Metric. This allows the exact identification of the tire specifications, regardless of the manufacturer. If selecting a different tire size or brand, remember to check the installed tire for any sign of interference with the body or suspension while the vehicle is stopping, turning sharply or heavily loaded.

Snow Tires

Good radial tires can produce a big advantage in slippery weather, but in snow, a street radial tire does not have sufficient tread to provide traction and control. The small grooves of a street tire quickly pack with snow and the tire behaves like a billiard ball on a marble floor. The more open, chunky tread of a snow tire will self-clean as the tire turns, providing much better grip on snowy surfaces.

To satisfy municipalities requiring snow tires during weather emergencies, most snow tires carry either an M + S designation after the tire size stamped on the sidewall, or the designation "all-season." In general, no change in tire size is necessary when buying snow tires.

Most manufacturers strongly recommend the use of 4 snow tires on their vehicles for reasons of stability. If snow tires are fitted only to the drive wheels, the opposite end of the vehicle may become very unstable when braking or turning on slippery surfaces. This instability can lead to unpleasant endings if the driver can't counteract the slide in time.

Note that snow tires, whether 2 or 4, will affect vehicle handling in all non-snow situations. The stiffer, heavier snow tires will noticeably change the turning and braking characteristics of the vehicle. Once the snow tires are installed, you must re-learn the behavior of the vehicle and drive accordingly.

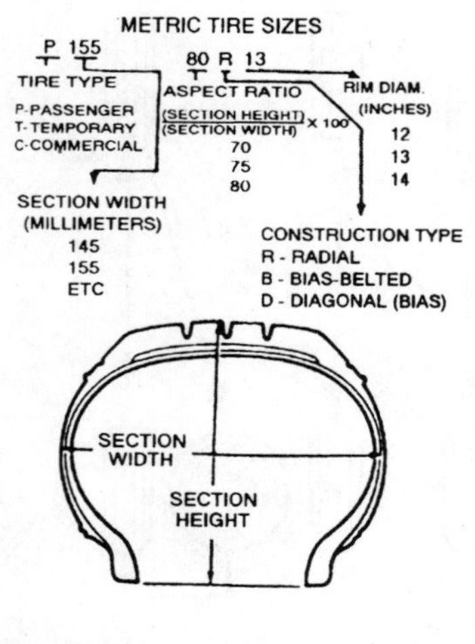

P-Metric tire coding

➡Consider buying extra wheels on which to mount the snow tires. Once done, the "snow wheels" can be installed and removed as needed. This eliminates the potential damage to tires or wheels from seasonal removal and installation. Even if your vehicle has styled wheels, see if inexpensive steel wheels are available. Although the look of the vehicle will change, the expensive wheels will be protected from salt, curb hits and pothole damage.

TIRE STORAGE

If they are mounted on wheels, store the tires at proper inflation pressure. All tires should be kept in a cool, dry place. If they are stored in the garage or basement, do not let them stand on a concrete floor; set them on strips of wood, a mat or a large stack of newspaper. Keeping them away from direct moisture is of paramount importance. Tires should not be stored upright, but in a flat position.

INFLATION & INSPECTION

The importance of proper tire inflation cannot be overemphasized. A tire employs air as part of its structure. It is designed around the supporting strength of the air at a specified pressure. For this reason, improper inflation drastically reduces the tires's ability to perform as intended. A tire will lose some air in day-to-day use; having to add a few pounds of air periodically is not necessarily a sign of a leaking tire.

Two items should be a permanent fixture in every glove compartment: an accurate tire pressure gauge and a tread depth gauge. Check the tire pressure (including the spare) regularly with a pocket type gauge. Too often, the gauge on the end of the air hose at your corner garage is not accurate because it suffers too much abuse. Always check tire pressure when the tires are cold, as pressure increases with temperature. If you must move the vehicle to check the tire inflation, do not drive more than a mile before checking. A cold tire is generally one that has not been driven for more than three hours.

A plate or sticker is normally provided somewhere in the vehicle (door post, hood, tailgate or trunk lid) which shows the proper pressure for the tires. Never counteract excessive pressure build-up by bleeding off air pressure (letting some air out). This will cause the tire to run hotter and wear quicker.

CAUTION

Never exceed the maximum tire pressure embossed on the tire! This is the pressure to be used when the tire is at maximum loading, but it is rarely the correct pressure for everyday driving. Consult the owner's manual or the tire pressure sticker for the correct tire pressure.

Once you've maintained the correct tire pressures for several weeks, you'll be familiar with the vehicle's braking and handling personality. Slight adjustments in tire pressures can fine-tune these characteristics, but never change the cold pressure specification by more than 2 psi. A slightly softer tire pressure will give a softer ride but also yield lower fuel mileage. A slightly harder tire will give crisper dry road handling but can cause skidding on wet

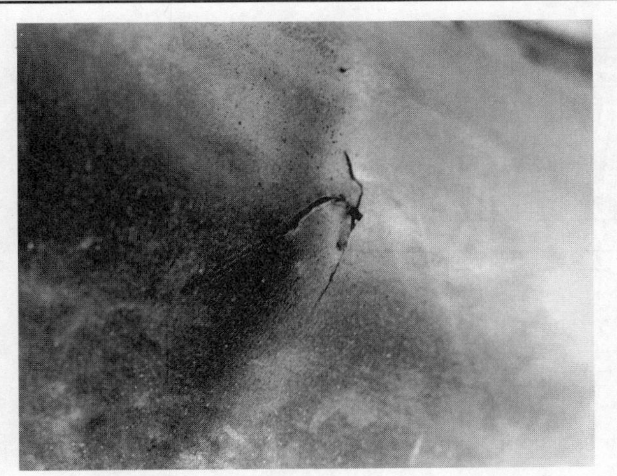
Tires should be checked frequently for any sign of puncture or damage

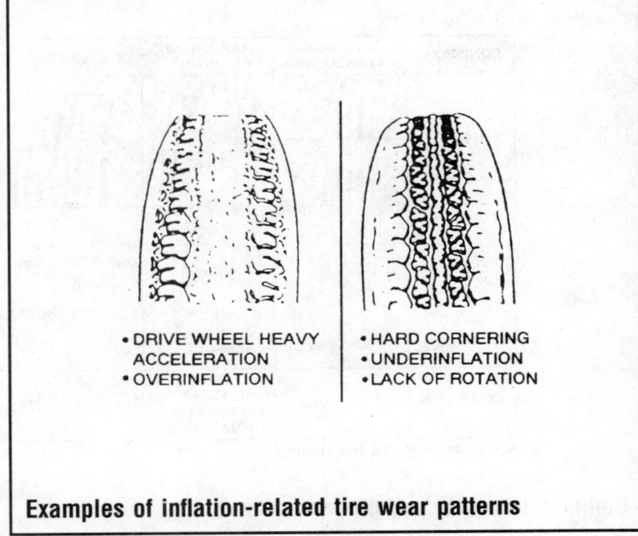

Examples of inflation-related tire wear patterns

Tires with deep cuts, or cuts which show bulging should be replaced immediately

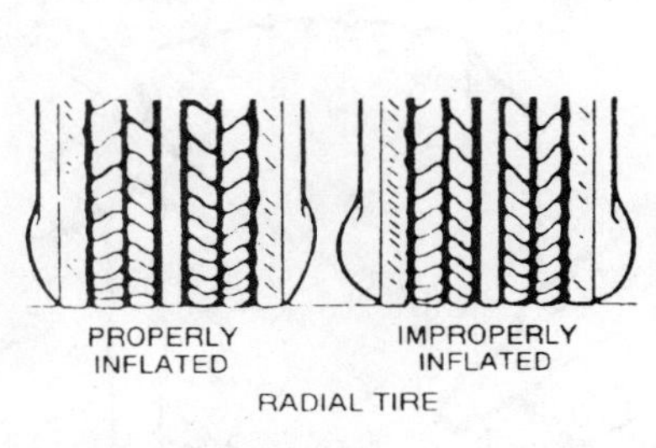

Radial tires have a characteristic sidewall bulge; don't try to measure pressure by looking at the tire. Use a quality air pressure gauge

surfaces. Unless you're fully attuned to the vehicle, stick to the recommended inflation pressures.

All tires made since 1968 have built-in tread wear indicator bars that show up as ½ in. (13mm) wide smooth bands across the tire when $\frac{1}{16}$ in. (1.5mm) of tread remains. The appearance of tread wear indicators means that the tires should be replaced. In fact, many states have laws prohibiting the use of tires with less than this amount of tread.

You can check your own tread depth with an inexpensive gauge or by using a Lincoln head penny. Slip the Lincoln penny (with Lincoln's head upside-down) into several tread grooves. If you can see the top of Lincoln's head in 2 adjacent grooves, the tire has less than $\frac{1}{16}$ in. (1.5mm) tread left and should be replaced. You can measure snow tires in the same manner by using the "tails" side of the Lincoln penny. If you can see the top of the Lincoln memorial, it's time to replace the snow tire(s).

CARE OF SPECIAL WHEELS

If you have invested money in magnesium, aluminum alloy or sport wheels, special precautions should be taken to make sure your investment is not wasted and that your special wheels look good for the life of the vehicle.

Special wheels are easily damaged and/or scratched. Occasionally check the rims for cracking, impact damage or air leaks. If any of these are found, replace the wheel. But in order to prevent this type of damage and the costly replacement of a special wheel, observe the following precautions:

• Use extra care not to damage the wheels during removal, installation, balancing, etc. After removal of the wheels from the vehicle, place them on a mat or other protective surface. If they are to be stored for any length of time, support them on strips of

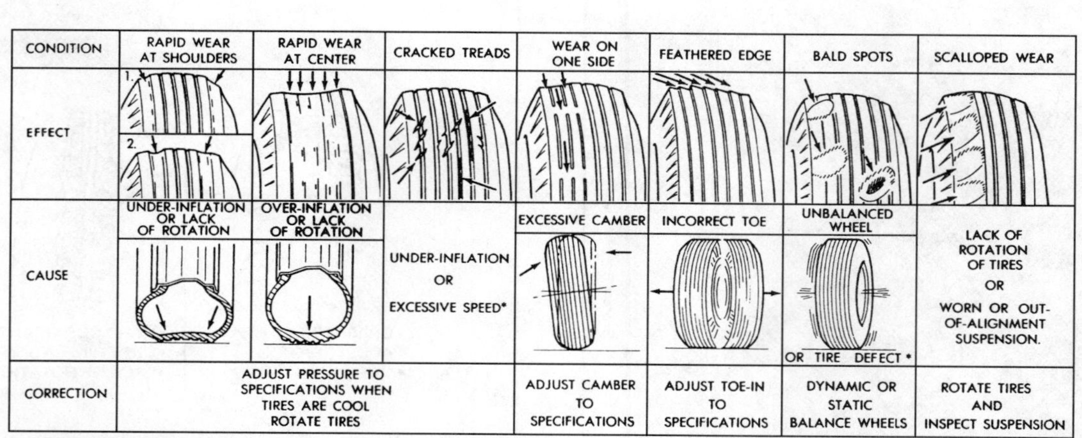

CONDITION	RAPID WEAR AT SHOULDERS	RAPID WEAR AT CENTER	CRACKED TREADS	WEAR ON ONE SIDE	FEATHERED EDGE	BALD SPOTS	SCALLOPED WEAR
EFFECT	1. 2.						
CAUSE	UNDER-INFLATION OR LACK OF ROTATION	OVER-INFLATION OR LACK OF ROTATION	UNDER-INFLATION OR EXCESSIVE SPEED*	EXCESSIVE CAMBER	INCORRECT TOE	UNBALANCED WHEEL OR TIRE DEFECT*	LACK OF ROTATION OF TIRES OR WORN OR OUT-OF-ALIGNMENT SUSPENSION.
CORRECTION	ADJUST PRESSURE TO SPECIFICATIONS WHEN TIRES ARE COOL ROTATE TIRES			ADJUST CAMBER TO SPECIFICATIONS	ADJUST TOE-IN TO SPECIFICATIONS	DYNAMIC OR STATIC BALANCE WHEELS	ROTATE TIRES AND INSPECT SUSPENSION

*HAVE TIRE INSPECTED FOR FURTHER USE.

Common tire wear patterns and causes

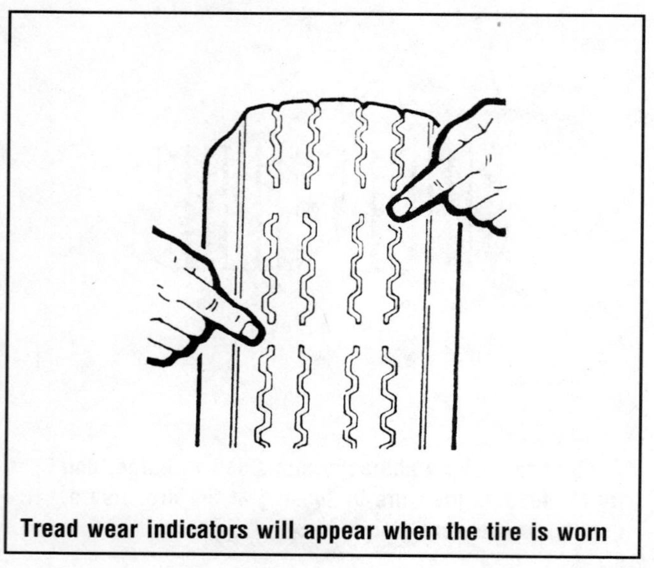

Tread wear indicators will appear when the tire is worn

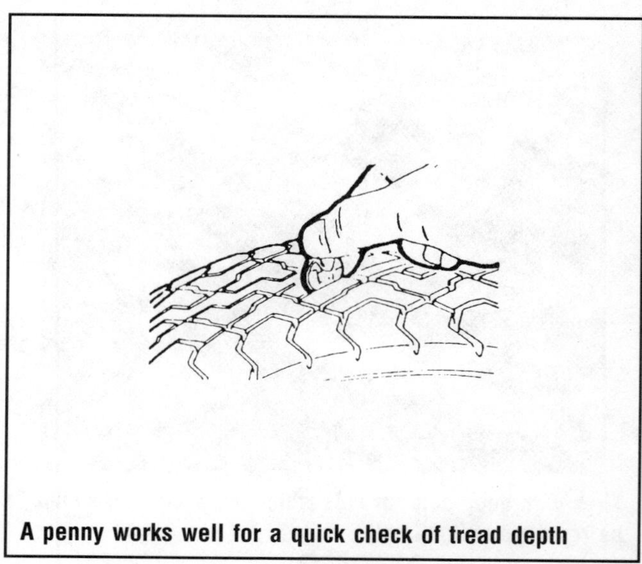

A penny works well for a quick check of tread depth

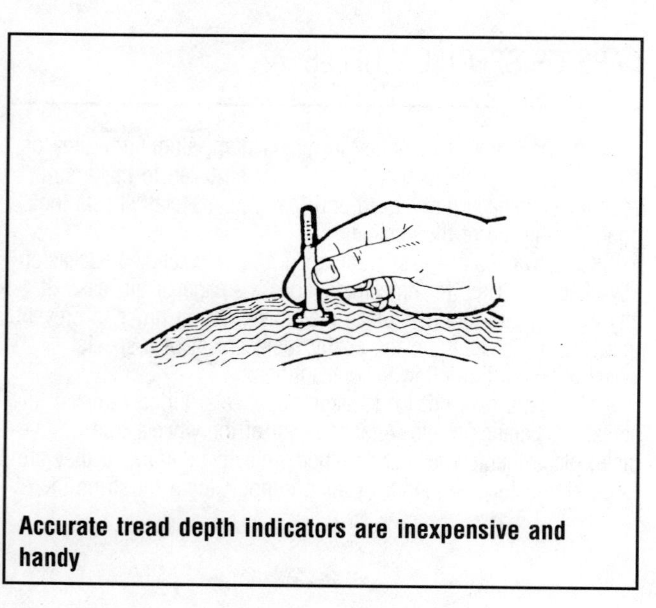

Accurate tread depth indicators are inexpensive and handy

wood. Never store tires and wheels upright; the tread may develop flat spots.

• When driving, watch for hazards; it doesn't take much to crack a wheel.

• When washing, use a mild soap or non-abrasive dish detergent (keeping in mind that detergent tends to remove wax). Avoid cleansers with abrasives or the use of hard brushes. There are many cleaners and polishes for special wheels.

• If possible, remove the wheels during the winter. Salt and sand used for snow removal can severely damage the finish of a wheel.

• Make certain the recommended lug nut torque is never exceeded or the wheel may crack. Never use snow chains on special wheels; severe scratching will occur.

Troubleshooting Basic Wheel Problems

Problem	Cause	Solution
The car's front end vibrates at high speed	• The wheels are out of balance • Wheels are out of alignment	• Have wheels balanced • Have wheel alignment checked/ adjusted
Car pulls to either side	• Wheels are out of alignment • Unequal tire pressure • Different size tires or wheels	• Have wheel alignment checked/ adjusted • Check/adjust tire pressure • Change tires or wheels to same size
The car's wheel(s) wobbles	• Loose wheel lug nuts • Wheels out of balance • Damaged wheel • Wheels are out of alignment • Worn or damaged ball joint • Excessive play in the steering linkage (usually due to worn parts) • Defective shock absorber	• Tighten wheel lug nuts • Have tires balanced • Raise car and spin the wheel. If the wheel is bent, it should be replaced • Have wheel alignment checked/ adjusted • Check ball joints • Check steering linkage • Check shock absorbers
Tires wear unevenly or prematurely	• Incorrect wheel size • Wheels are out of balance • Wheels are out of alignment	• Check if wheel and tire size are compatible • Have wheels balanced • Have wheel alignment checked/ adjusted

Troubleshooting Basic Tire Problems

Problem	Cause	Solution
The car's front end vibrates at high speeds and the steering wheel shakes	• Wheels out of balance • Front end needs aligning	• Have wheels balanced • Have front end alignment checked
The car pulls to one side while cruising	• Unequal tire pressure (car will usually pull to the low side) • Mismatched tires • Front end needs aligning	• Check/adjust tire pressure • Be sure tires are of the same type and size • Have front end alignment checked
Abnormal, excessive or uneven tire wear See "How to Read Tire Wear"	• Infrequent tire rotation • Improper tire pressure • Sudden stops/starts or high speed on curves	• Rotate tires more frequently to equalize wear • Check/adjust pressure • Correct driving habits
Tire squeals	• Improper tire pressure • Front end needs aligning	• Check/adjust tire pressure • Have front end alignment checked

Tire Size Comparison Chart

"Letter" sizes			Inch Sizes	Metric-inch Sizes		
"60 Series"	"70 Series"	"78 Series"	1965–77	"60 Series"	"70 Series"	"80 Series"
			5.50-12, 5.60-12	165/60-12	165/70-12	155-12
		Y78-12	6.00-12			
		W78-13	5.20-13	165/60-13	145/70-13	135-13
		Y78-13	5.60-13	175/60-13	155/70-13	145-13
			6.15-13	185/60-13	165/70-13	155-13, P155/80-13
A60-13	A70-13	A78-13	6.40-13	195/60-13	175/70-13	165-13
B60-13	B70-13	B78-13	6.70-13	205/60-13	185/70-13	175-13
			6.90-13			
C60-13	C70-13	C78-13	7.00-13	215/60-13	195/70-13	185-13
D60-13	D70-13	D78-13	7.25-13			
E60-13	E70-13	E78-13	7.75-13			195-13
			5.20-14	165/60-14	145/70-14	135-14
			5.60-14	175/60-14	155/70-14	145-14
			5.90-14			
A60-14	A70-14	A78-14	6.15-14	185/60-14	165/70-14	155-14
	B70-14	B78-14	6.45-14	195/60-14	175/70-14	165-14
	C70-14	C78-14	6.95-14	205/60-14	185/70-14	175-14
D60-14	D70-14	D78-14				
E60-14	E70-14	E78-14	7.35-14	215/60-14	195/70-14	185-14
F60-14	F70-14	F78-14, F83-14	7.75-14	225/60-14	200/70-14	195-14
G60-14	G70-14	G77-14, G78-14	8.25-14	235/60-14	205/70-14	205-14
H60-14	H70-14	H78-14	8.55-14	245/60-14	215/70-14	215-14
J60-14	J70-14	J78-14	8.85-14	255/60-14	225/70-14	225-14
L60-14	L70-14		9.15-14	265/60-14	235/70-14	
	A70-15	A78-15	5.60-15	185/60-15	165/70-15	155-15
B60-15	B70-15	B78-15	6.35-15	195/60-15	175/70-15	165-15
C60-15	C70-15	C78-15	6.85-15	205/60-15	185/70-15	175-15
	D70-15	D78-15				
E60-15	E70-15	E78-15	7.35-15	215/60-15	195/70-15	185-15
F60-15	F70-15	F78-15	7.75-15	225/60-15	205/70-15	195-15
G60-15	G70-15	G78-15	8.15-15/8.25-15	235/60-15	215/70-15	205-15
H60-15	H70-15	H78-15	8.45-15/8.55-15	245/60-15	225/70-15	215-15
J60-15	J70-15	J78-15	8.85-15/8.90-15	255/60-15	235/70-15	225-15
	K70-15		9.00-15	265/60-15	245/70-15	230-15
L60-15	L70-15	L78-15, L84-15	9.15-15			235-15
	M70-15	M78-15				255-15
		N78-15				

Note: Every size tire is not listed and many size comparisons are approximate, based on load ratings. Wider tires than those supplied new with the vehicle, should always be checked for clearance.

FLUIDS AND LUBRICANTS

Fluid Disposal

Used fluids such as engine oil, transmission fluid, antifreeze and brake fluid are hazardous wastes and must be disposed of properly. Before draining any fluids, consult with the local authorities; in many areas, waste oil, etc. is being accepted as a part of recycling programs. A number of service stations and auto parts stores are also accepting waste fluids for recycling.

Be sure of the recycling center's policies before draining any fluids, as many will not accept different fluids that have been mixed together, such as oil and antifreeze.

Fuel Recommendations

It is important to use fuel of the proper octane rating in your car. Octane rating is based on the quantity of anti-knock compounds added to the fuel and it determines the speed at which the gas will burn. The lower the octane rating, the faster it burns.

The higher the octane, the slower the fuel will burn and a greater percentage of compounds in the fuel prevent spark ping (knock), detonation and preignition (dieseling).

The Fiero engine is designed to use only unleaded gasoline, with an Research Octane Number (RON) rating of at least 91, or an Antiknock Index of 87.

As the temperature of the engine increases, the air/fuel mixture exhibits a tendency to ignite before the spark plug is fired. If fuel of an octane rating too low for the engine is used, this will allow combustion to occur before the piston has completed its compression stroke, thereby creating a very high pressure very rapidly.

Do not use gasolines containing more than 5 percent methanol even if they contain cosolvents and corrosion inhibitors.

Although gasolines containing 5 percent or less methanol and appropriate cosolvents and inhibitors for methanol may be suitable for use in your car, Pontiac does not endorse their use, at this time.

Look for the API oil identification label when choosing your engine oil

Oil Recommendations

➧ **See Figure 22**

Engine oils are labeled on the containers with various API (American Petroleum Institute) designations of quality. Make sure the oil you use has the API designation "SF", either alone or shown with other designations such as SF/CC or SF/CD. Oils with a label on which the designation "SF" does not appear should not be used.

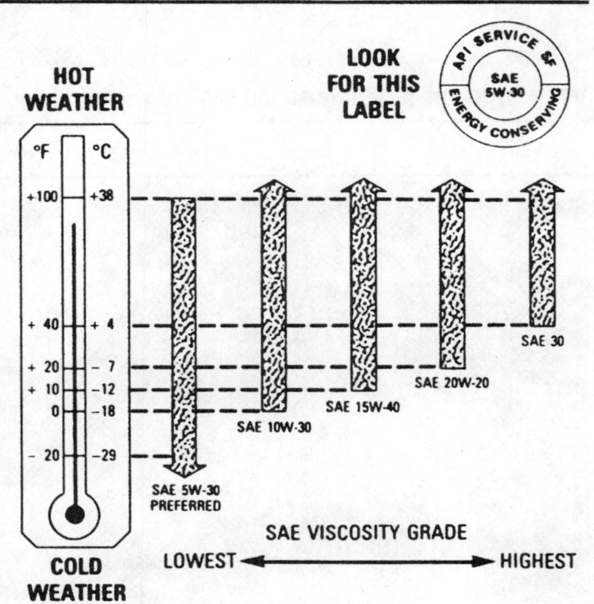

Fig. 22 Manufacturers recommended oil viscosities

Oil of the SF variety performs a multitude of functions in addition to its basic job of reducing friction of the engine's moving parts. Through a balanced formula of polymeric dispersants and metallic detergents, the oil prevents high temperature and low temperature deposits and also keeps sludge and dirt particles in suspension. Acids, particularly sulphuric acid, as well as other products of combustion of sulphur fuels, are neutralized by the oil. These acids, if permitted to concentrate, may cause corrosion and rapid wear of the internal parts of the engine.

Engine oil viscosity (thickness) should be considered according to temperature weather conditions. Lower viscosity engine oils can provide better fuel economy; however, higher temperature weather conditions require higher viscosity engine oils for satisfactory lubrication. When selecting an oil viscosity, consider the range of temperature your car will be operated in before the next oil change. Pontiac recommends that if the outside temperatures are not expected to exceed 38°C (100°F) before your next oil change, SF quality, SAE 5W-30 Energy-Conserving engine oil is the preferred viscosity grade.

Engine

OIL LEVEL CHECK

➧ **See Figure 23**

The engine oil level should be checked frequently. For instance, at each refueling stop.

1. Park the car on a level area.
2. The engine oil may be either hot or cold when checking the oil level. However, if it is hot, wait a few minutes after the engine has been shut off to allow the oil to drain back into the oil pan. If the engine is cold, do not start it before checking the oil level.
3. Open the engine compartment and locate the dipstick. Pull the dipstick from its tube, wipe it clean and reinsert it.

➡Make sure the dipstick is fully seated when checking the oil level to assure accurate readings.

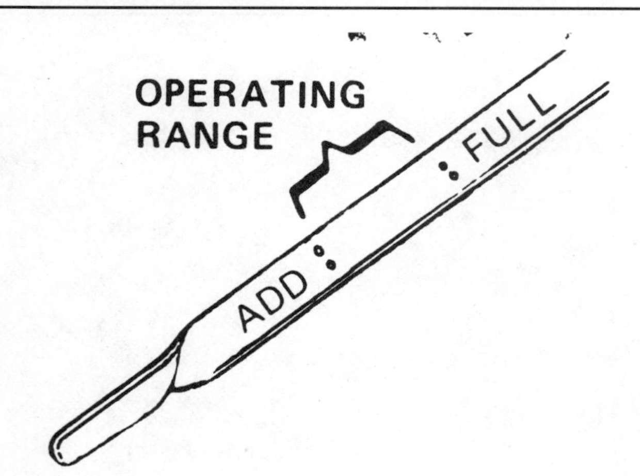

Fig. 23 The engine oil level should be in the operating range as indicated on the oil dipstick

4. Pull the dipstick out again and while holding it horizontally, read the oil level. The oil level should be above the "ADD" line but not above the "FULL" line. Do not overfill.

OIL & FILTER CHANGE

➧ See Figures 24, 25 and 26

✲✲ CAUTION

The EPA warns that prolonged contact with used engine oil may cause a number of skin disorders, including cancer! You should make every effort to minimize your exposure to used engine oil. Protective gloves should be worn when changing the oil. Wash your hands and any other exposed skin areas as soon as possible after exposure to used engine oil. Soap and water, or waterless hand cleaner should be used.

Remove the engine oil dipstick from its tube. Wipe it clean and reinsert . . .

Use a hydraulic jack to raise the vehicle . . .

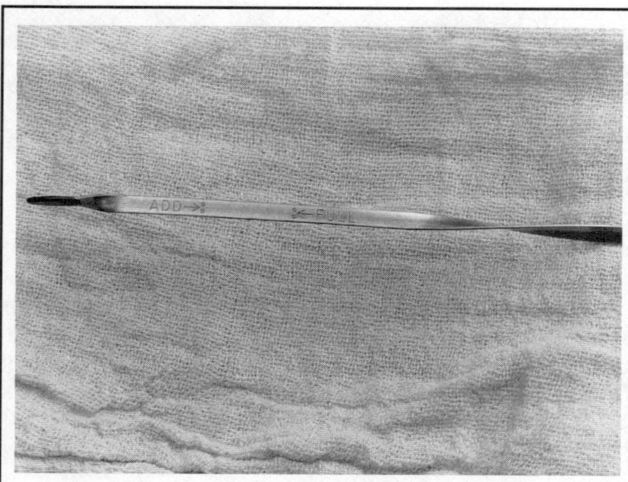
. . . then remove the dipstick again, hold it horizontally and read the oil level

. . . then support the vehicle with jackstands

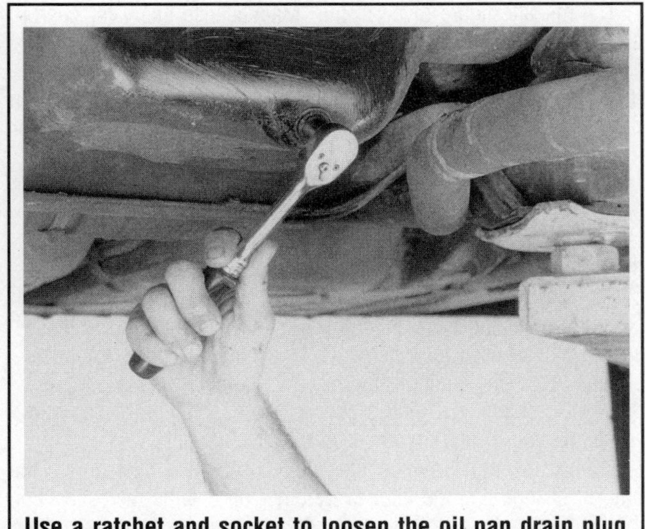

Use a ratchet and socket to loosen the oil pan drain plug

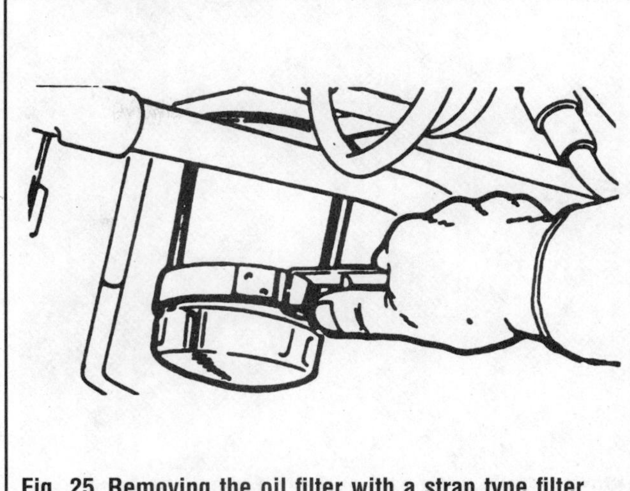

Fig. 25 Removing the oil filter with a strap type filter wrench

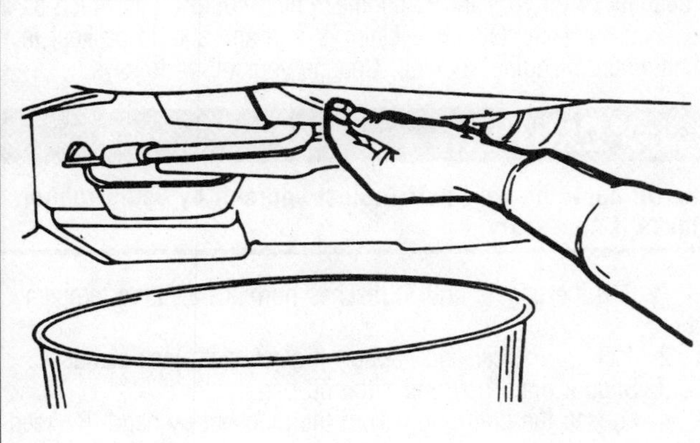

Fig. 24 Keep inward pressure on the oil drain plug as you unscrew it so oil will not escape past the threads . . .

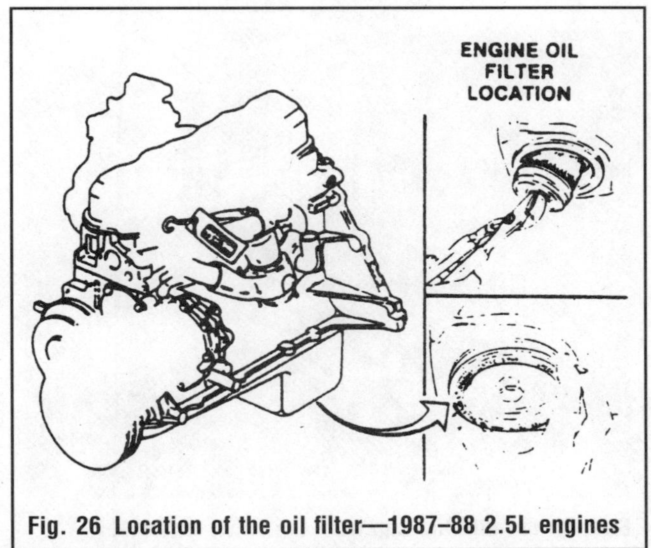

Fig. 26 Location of the oil filter—1987–88 2.5L engines

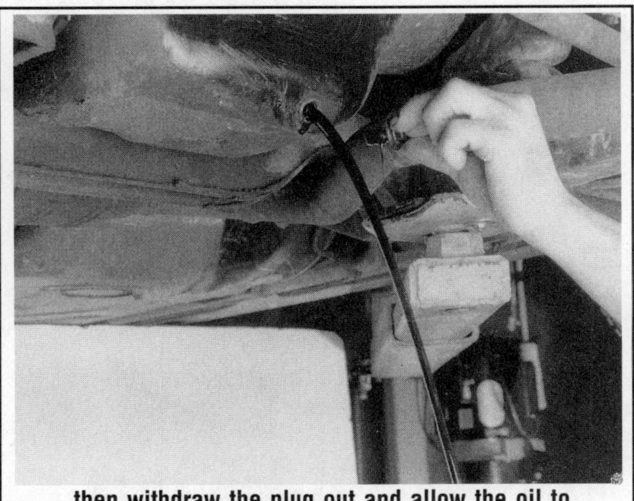

. . . then withdraw the plug out and allow the oil to drain completely into a suitable container

Before installing a new oil filter, lightly coat the rubber gasket with clean oil

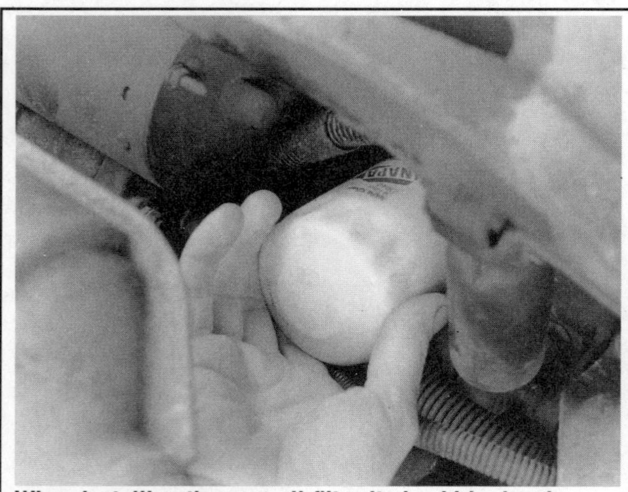
When installing the new oil filter it should be hand tightened only. Do not overtighten the filter

Remove the oil filler cap from the valve cover . . .

. . . then using a funnel, add the correct grade and amount of new engine oil

The mileage figure given in the "Maintenance Intervals" chart are the Pontiac recommended intervals for oil and filter changes assuming average driving. If your Fiero is being driven under dusty, polluted, or off road conditions, cut the mileage intervals in half. The same thing goes for cars driven in stop-and-go traffic or for only short distances.

Always drain the oil after the engine has been running long enough to bring it to operating temperature. Hot oil will flow easier and more contaminants will be removed along with the oil than if it were drained cold. You will need a large capacity drain pan (2 gls) which you can purchase at any auto store. Another necessity is containers for used oil. You will find that plastic bottles such as those used for detergents, bleaches etc., make excellent storage jugs. One ecologically desirable solution to the used oil disposal problem is to find a cooperative gas station owner who will allow you to dump your used oil into his tank.

Pontiac recommends changing both the oil and filter during the first oil change and the filter every other oil change thereafter. For the small price of an oil filter, its cheap insurance to replace the filter at every oil change. One of the larger filter manufacturers points out in its advertisements that not changing the filter leaves a quantity of dirty oil in the engine, which could be as much as a quart on some models. This claim is true and should be kept in mind when changing your oil. Change your oil as follows:

CAUTION

The oil could be very hot! Protect yourself by using rubber gloves if necessary.

1. Run the engine until it reaches normal operating temperature.
2. Jack up the car and support it safely with jack stands.
3. Slide a drain pan under the oil pan.
4. Loosen the drain plug. Turn the plug out by hand. By keeping an inward pressure on the plug as you unscrew it, oil won't escape past the threads and you can remove it without being burnt with hot oil.
5. Allow the oil to drain completely and then install the drain plug.

➡Be careful not to overtighten the plug and strip the threads in the oil pan. Torque the plug to 25 ft. lbs. (34 Nm).

6. Using a strap wrench for the 1984–86 2.5L L4 engine, remove the oil filter. Keep in mind that it's holding dirty, hot oil. Remove the oil filter through the hole in the oil pan directly above the oil drain plug on the 1987–88 2.5L L4 engines. Pull the filter through with a pliers.
7. Empty the old filter into the drain pan and dispose of the filter.
8. Using a clean rag, wipe off the filter adapter on the engine block. Be sure that the rag doesn't leave any lint which could clog an oil passage.
9. Coat the rubber gasket on the new filter with fresh oil. Spin it onto the engine by hand; when the gasket touches the adapter surface give it another ½–¾ turn. Do not overtighten or you may squash the gasket and cause it to leak.
10. Refill the engine with a correct amount of fresh oil.
    a. 2.5L L4 engine (LR8)—4 Quarts (with filter)
    b. 2.8L V6 engine (L44)—4 Quarts (with filter)

11. Check the oil level on the dipstick. It is normal for the level to be a bit above the full mark. Start the engine and allow it to idle a few minutes.

CAUTION

Do not run the engine above idle speed until it has built up oil pressure, indicated when the oil light goes out.

12. Shut off the engine, allow the oil to drain for a minute, and check the oil level. Check around the filter and drain plug for any leaks, and correct as necessary.

Automatic Transaxle

FLUID RECOMMENDATION & LEVEL CHECK

See Figure 27

The automatic transaxle fluid level should be checked at each engine oil change. When adding or changing the automatic transaxle fluid use only fluid labeled Dexron® II.

1. Set the parking brake and start the engine with the transaxle in "P" (Park).
2. With the service brakes applied, move the shift lever through all the gear ranges, ending in "P" (Park).

The fluid level must be checked with the engine running at slow idle, the car level and the fluid at least at room temperature.

The correct fluid level cannot be read if you have just driven the car for a long time at high speed, city traffic in hot weather or if the car has been pulling a trailer. In these cases, wait at least 30 minutes for the fluid to cool down.

3. Remove the dipstick located at the rear end of the engine compartment, wipe it clean, then push it back in until the cap seats.
4. Pull the dipstick out and read the fluid level. The level should be in the cross-hatched area of the dipstick.

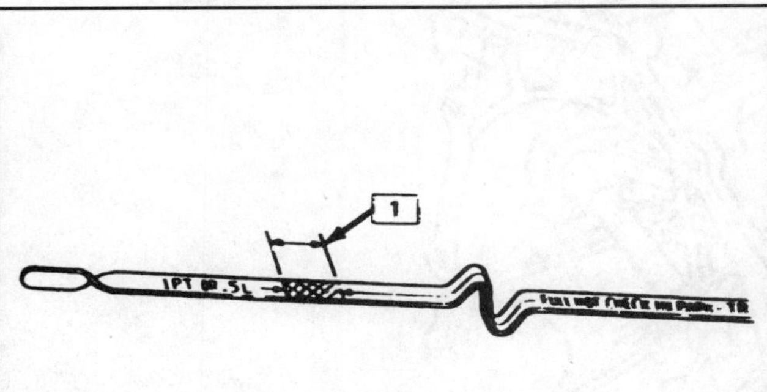

Fig. 27 THM 125C automatic transmission dipstick. The level should be in the cross hatched area when the vehicle is parked on a level surface and at normal operating temperature

5. Add fluid using a long plastic funnel in the dipstick tube. Keep in mind that it only takes one pint of fluid to raise the level from "ADD" to "FULL" with a hot transaxle.

WARNING

Damage to the automatic transaxle may result if the fluid level is above the "FULL" mark. Remove excess fluid by threading a small rubber hose into the dipstick tube and pump the fluid out with a syphon pump.

DRAIN & REFILL

See Figure 28

According to Pontiac, under normal operating conditions the automatic transmission fluid only needs to be changed every 100,000 miles unless one or more of the following driving conditions is encountered. In the following cases the fluid and filter should be changed every 15,000 miles:

a. Driving in heavy traffic when the outside temperature reaches 90°F.
b. Driving regularly in hilly or mountainous areas.
c. Towing a trailer.
d. Using a vehicle as a taxi or police car or for delivery purposes.

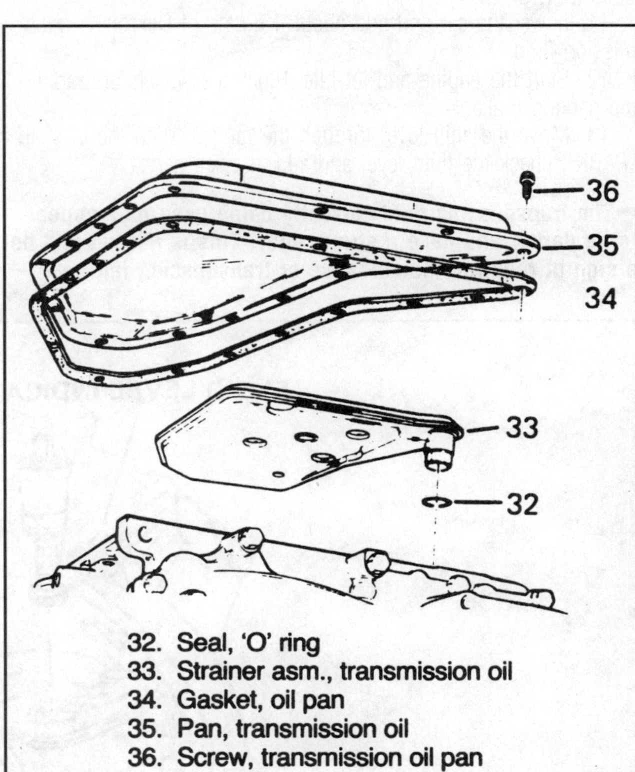

Fig. 28 Exploded view of the automatic transmission pan and gasket

Remember, these are factory recommendations, and in this case are considered to be minimum. You must determine a change interval which fits your driving habits. If your vehicle is never subjected to these conditions, a 100,000 mile change interval is adequate. If you are a normal driver, a 2-year/30,000 mile interval will be more than sufficient to maintain the long life for which your automatic transaxle was designed.

➡Use only fluid labeled Dexron® II. Use of other fluids could cause erratic shifting and transmission damage.

1. Jack up your vehicle and support it safely with jackstands.
2. Disconnect the negative (−) battery cable.
3. Remove the front and side pan bolts.
4. Loosen the rear bolts about four turns.
5. Carefully pry the oil pan loose and allow the fluid to drain.
6. Remove the remaining bolts, the pan, and the gasket or RTV sealant. Discard the old gasket.
7. Clean the pan with solvent and dry it thoroughly, with compressed air.
8. Remove the strainer and O-ring seal.
9. Install a new transaxle filter and O-ring seal, locating the strainer against the dipstick stop.

➡Always replace the filter with a new one. Do not attempt to clean the old one.

10. Install a new gasket or RTV sealant then tighten the pan bolts to 12 ft. lb. (15 Nm).
11. Lower the car and add about 4 quarts of Dexron®II transmission fluid.
12. Start the engine and let idle. Block the wheels and apply the parking brake.
13. Move the shift lever through the ranges. With the lever in "PARK", check the fluid level and add as necessary.

➡The transmission fluid currently being used may appear to be darker and have a strong odor. This is normal and not a sign of required maintenance or transmission failure.

Manual Transaxle

FLUID RECOMMENDATION

Under normal conditions, the lubricant used in the manual transaxle does require periodic changing. The fluid level in the transaxle should be checked every 12 months or 7500 miles, whichever comes first. The manual transaxle is designed to use SAE 5W-30 SF, SF/SC, or SF/CD engine oil as a lubricant.

LEVEL CHECK

➧ See Figures 29, 30, 31 and 32

1. Park the car on a level surface and turn off the engine.
2. The transaxle case must be cool to the touch. If the transaxle is hot, lubricant may flow from the filler hole when the plug is removed.
3. Remove the transaxle filler plug, dipstick or speedometer fitting which is located above the axle shaft on the driver's side of the case. When the lubricant is cool it should be level with the filler hole or at the proper level on the dipstick. Refer to the "Transaxle Fluid Level" illustrations in this section for the proper filler location.
4. Lubricant can be added by inserting the end of a funnel into one end of a rubber tube, and inserting the other end of the rubber tube into the filler hole.
5. Reinstall the filler hole plug and torque to 24 ft. lbs. (33 Nm) on the 1984 4-speed Isuzu (76mm) transaxle. Install the speedometer fitting and seat the permanent magnet generator fully on the 1985–88 4 and 5-speed Isuzu (76mm) transaxles. Install the dipstick and hand-tighten on the 1987–88 5-speed Muncie (76mm and 282) transaxles.

➡The differential assembly is part of the transaxle assembly. The transaxle fluid lubricates the differential also.

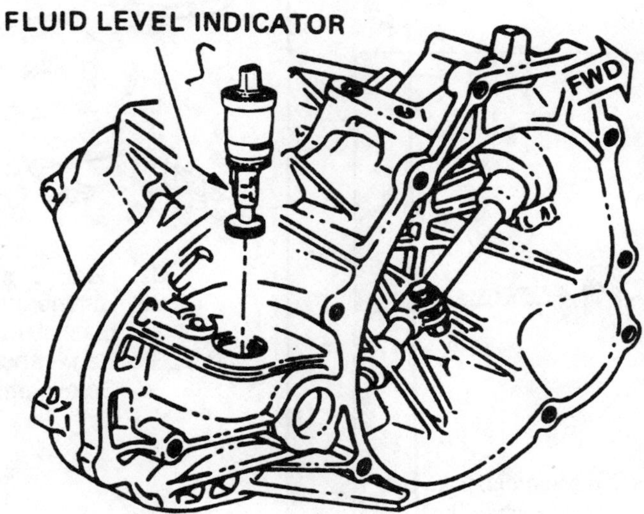

Fig. 29 Location of the manual transaxle fluid indicator—1985–88 4 and 5-speed Isuzu (76mm) models

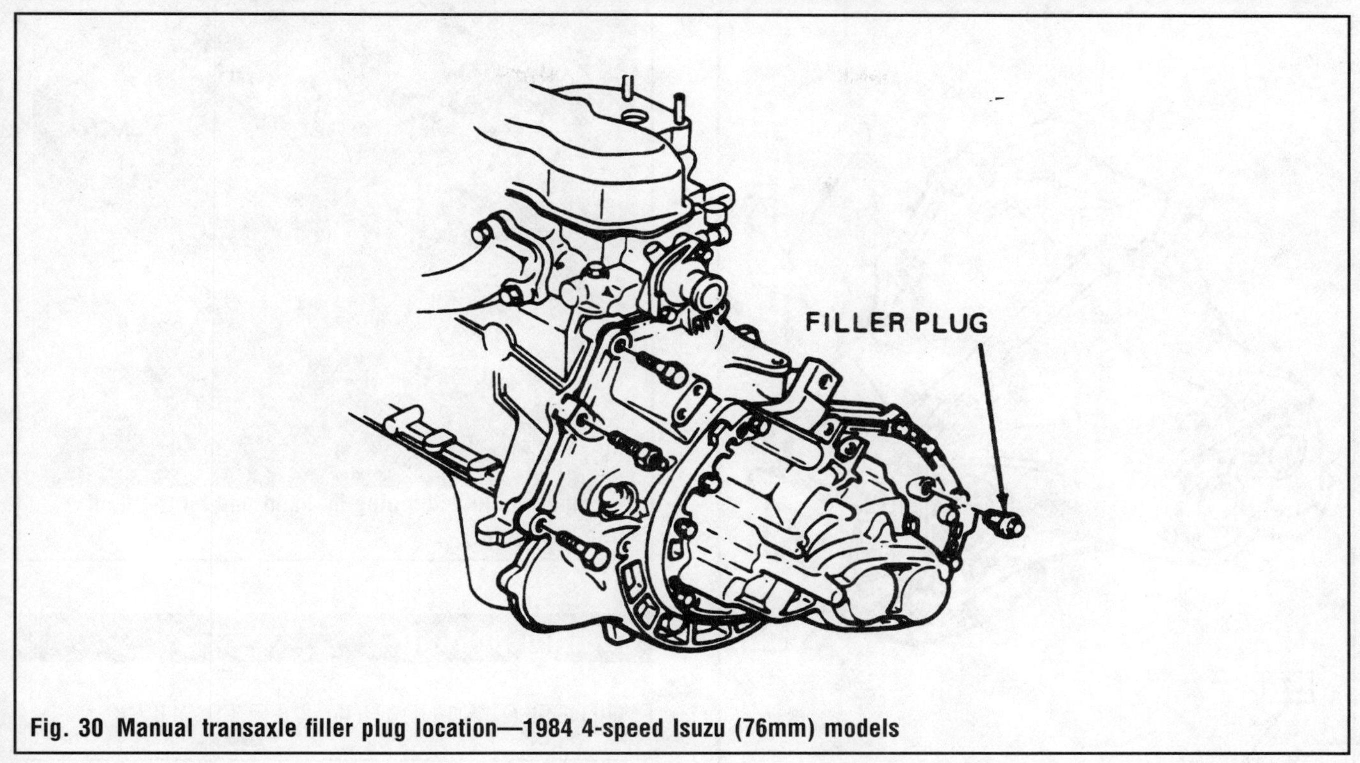

Fig. 30 Manual transaxle filler plug location—1984 4-speed Isuzu (76mm) models

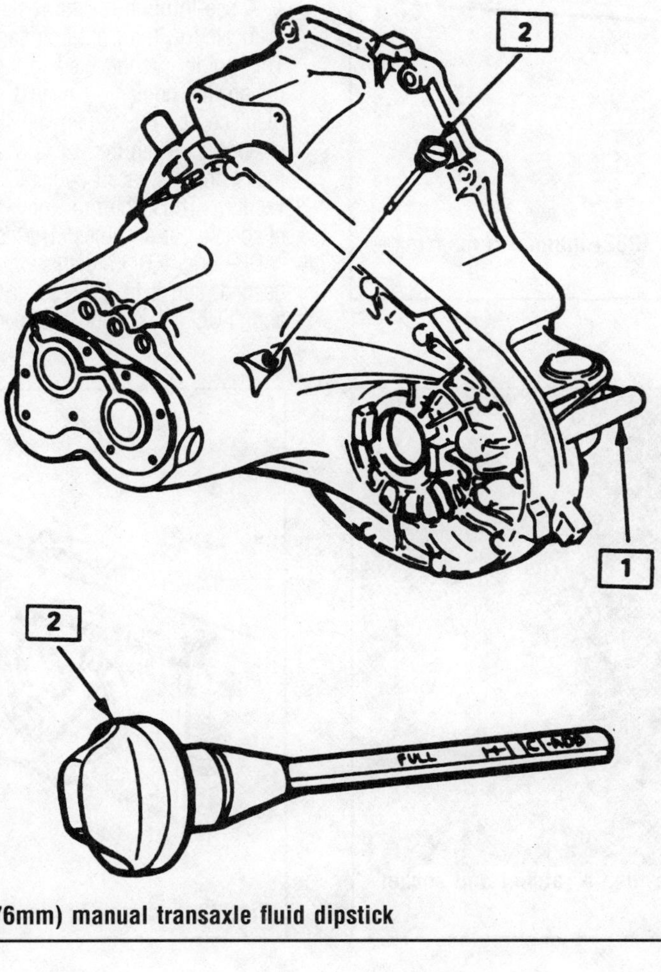

Fig. 31 1987 5-speed Muncie (76mm) manual transaxle fluid dipstick

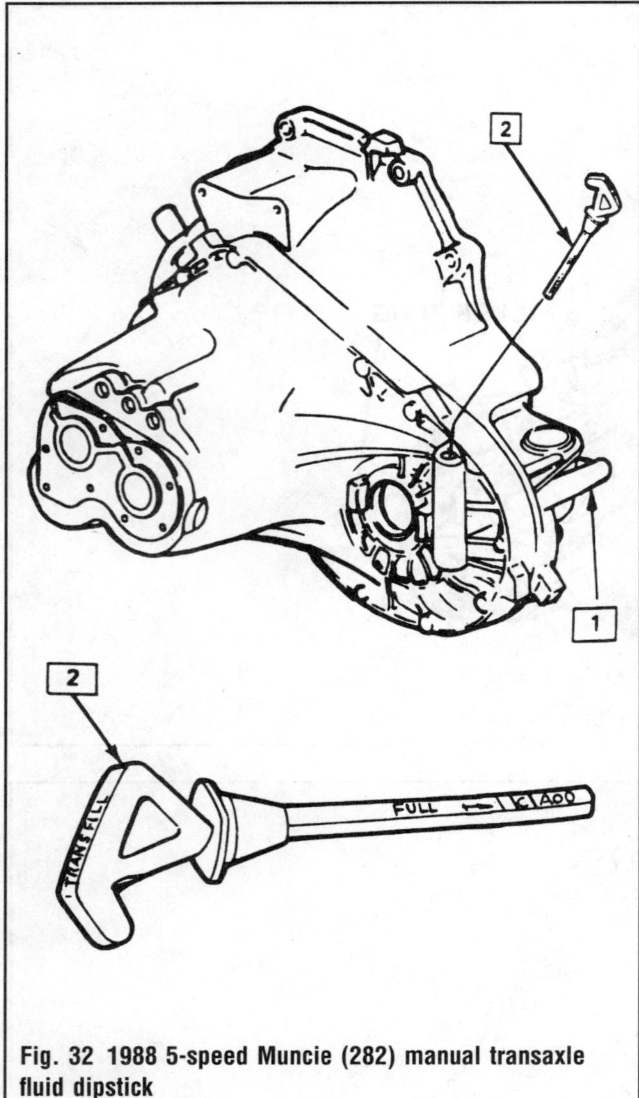

Fig. 32 1988 5-speed Muncie (282) manual transaxle fluid dipstick

. . . then remove the plug by hand and let the fluid drain completely

Cooling System

FLUID RECOMMENDATION & LEVEL CHECK

➧ See Figure 33

A see-through plastic reservoir called a coolant recovery bottle, is located in the front compartment near the radiator assembly. This bottle is connected to the radiator by a hose. As the car is driven, the coolant is heated and expands, the portion of the fluid displaced by this expansion flows from the radiator into the recovery bottle. When the car is stopped and the coolant cools and contracts, the displaced coolant is drawn back into the radiator by vacuum. Thus, the radiator is kept filled with coolant to the desired level at all times. The coolant level should be between the "ADD" and "FULL" marks on the recovery bottle. If coolant is needed, add it to the recovery bottle not the radiator. The "ADD" and "FULL" marks on the recovery bottle are approximately one

To drain the manual transaxle, use a ratchet and socket to loosen the transaxle plug . . .

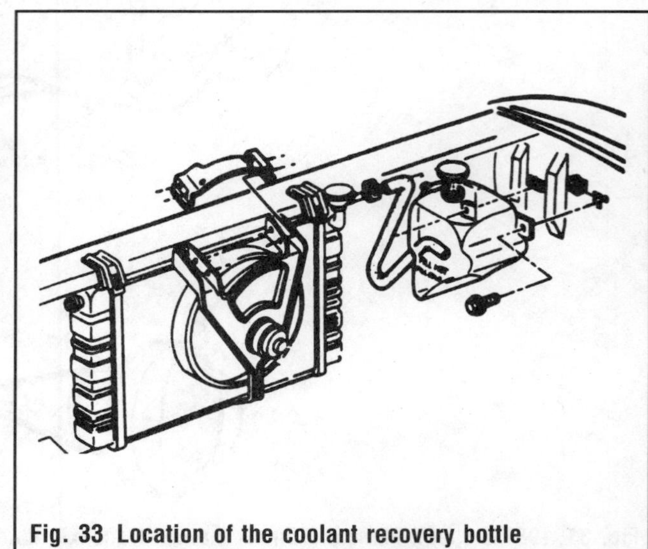
Fig. 33 Location of the coolant recovery bottle

quart apart so that a 50/50 mixture can be added (50% ethylene glycol antifreeze and 50% water).

CAUTION

Do not remove the radiator cap or the thermostat housing cap while the engine and radiator are still hot. This also includes the recovery bottle cap if coolant in the recovery bottle is boiling. Scalding fluid and steam can be blown out under pressure if any cap is taken off too soon.

The engine cooling fan is electric and can come on whether or not the engine is running. The fan can start automatically in response to a heat sensor when the ignition is in "Run." Remember to keep hands, tools and clothing away from the cooling fan when working under the compartment lid.

DRAIN & REFILL

See Figure 34

CAUTION

When draining engine coolant, keep in mind that cats and dogs are attracted to ethylene glycol antifreeze and could drink any that is left in an uncovered container or in puddles on the ground. This will prove fatal in sufficient quantity. Always drain coolant into a sealable container. Coolant should be reused unless it is contaminated or is several years old.

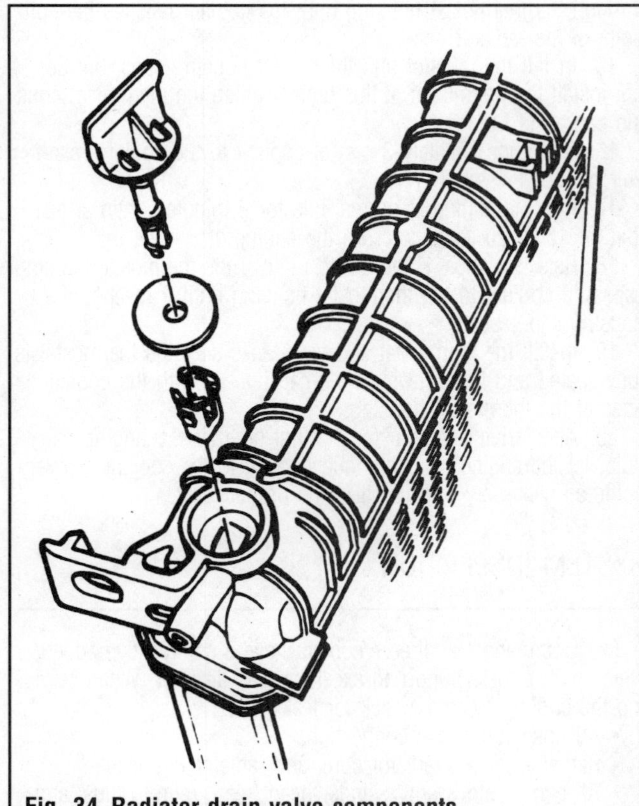

Fig. 34 Radiator drain valve components

The cooling system should be drained and refilled every 24 months or 30,000 miles. Please read the Cautions above then perform the following procedure:

➡Use a good quality antifreeze with water pump lubricants, rust inhibitors and other corrosion inhibitors along with acid neutralizers. Use a permanent type coolant that meets manufacturer's specifications.

1. When the engine is cool, open the rear engine compartment lid and turn the thermostat housing cap slowly counterclockwise until it reaches a stop.

➡Do not press down while turning the cap.

2. Wait until any remaining pressure is relieved, then press down on the cap and continue turning it counter-clockwise. Remove the cap.
3. Pull the thermostat straight out then install the cap. Run the engine at least one minute to circulate the coolant.

Check all the labels and read all the instructions before attempting to drain and refill the cooling system

After the engine has cooled remove the radiator cap

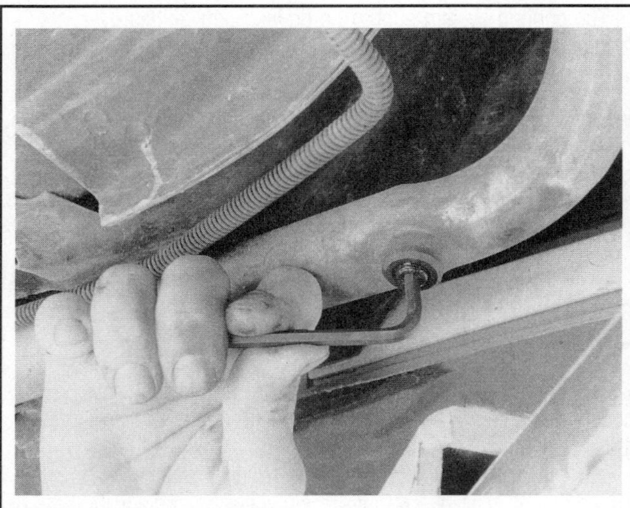
Use an allen wrench to loosen the drain plug . . .

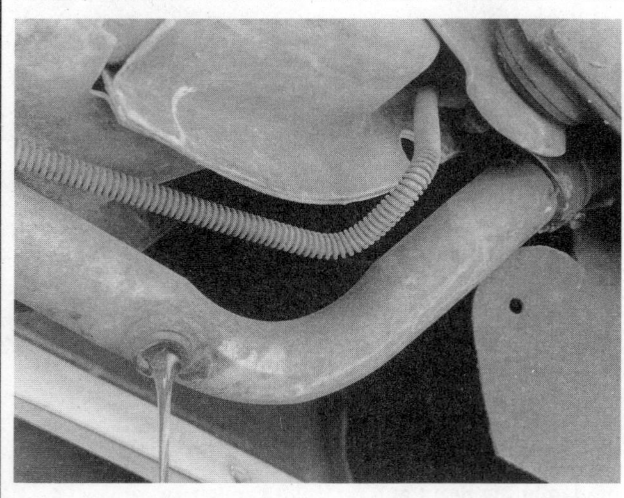
. . . then let the coolant drain into a suitable container

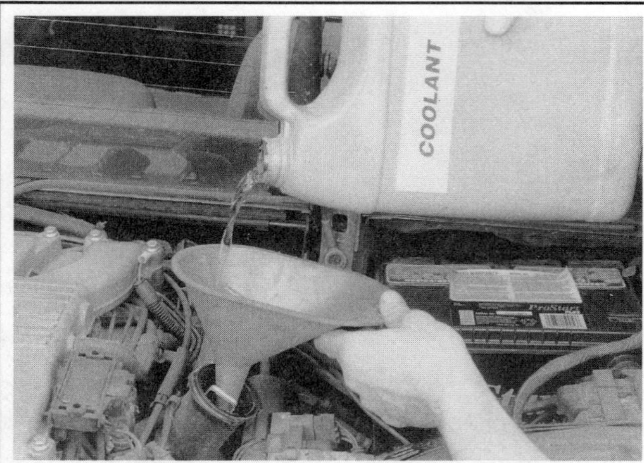

After all the old coolant has been drained and the drain plug closed, refill the system with the proper mix and amount of coolant

4. Stop the engine, then open the radiator drain valve, located on the bottom of the radiator side tank, and drain the coolant.

➡You may speed up drainage by removing the drain plugs in the engine block and in the left and right coolant pipes. The coolant pipes run underneath the car. The coolant pipe plugs are located at the rear of each pipe just ahead of the rear tires. The engine block drain plug is located on the front of the engine, on the driver's side, just above the starter.

5. Run water through the thermostat opening until the drained liquid is nearly colorless.
6. Install all drain plugs and close the radiator drain valve.
7. Remove the radiator cap and add water through the thermostat housing until the water reaches the level of the radiator neck.
8. Install the radiator and thermostat housing caps.

➡Do not install the thermostat at this time.

9. Tighten the thermostat housing cap to the first notch. At this point you should hear a clicking sound, and you will not be able to turn the cap counterclockwise without pushing it down.
10. Run the engine until the hose connected to the thermostat becomes hot. Drain the system again.
11. Install all drain plugs and close the radiator drain valve.
12. Remove, drain and clean the coolant recovery bottle, then install.
13. Add the correct amount of water and ethylene glycol antifreeze to provide the required cooling, freezing and corrosion protection. Use a solution that contains at least 50% antifreeze but not more than 70% antifreeze.
14. With the engine off, remove the radiator cap. Add coolant through the thermostat housing until the coolant reaches the spill point of the radiator neck.
15. Install the radiator and thermostat housing caps, but do not install the thermostat at this time. Tighten the thermostat housing cap as in Step 9.
16. Add approximately 3 qts. of coolant to the coolant reservoir bottle.
17. Run the engine at normal idle for 3 minutes, then at fast idle for 15 or 20 seconds. Turn the engine off.
18. Refer to Steps 1 and 2 and remove the thermostat housing cap. Add coolant to the thermostat housing until it reaches the housing cap seat.
19. Install the thermostat and cap. Make sure the thermostat is fully seated and the arrows on the cap line up with the coolant hose at the thermostat housing.
20. After driving the car for the first time after changing the fluid, let the engine cool then add coolant to the coolant recovery bottle as necessary to bring it to the proper level.

SYSTEM INSPECTION

Most permanent antifreeze/coolant have a colored dye added which makes the solution an excellent leak detector. When servicing the cooling system, check for leakage at:

- All hoses and hose connections
- Radiator seams, radiator core, and radiator draincock
- All engine block and cylinder head freeze (core) plugs, and drain plugs

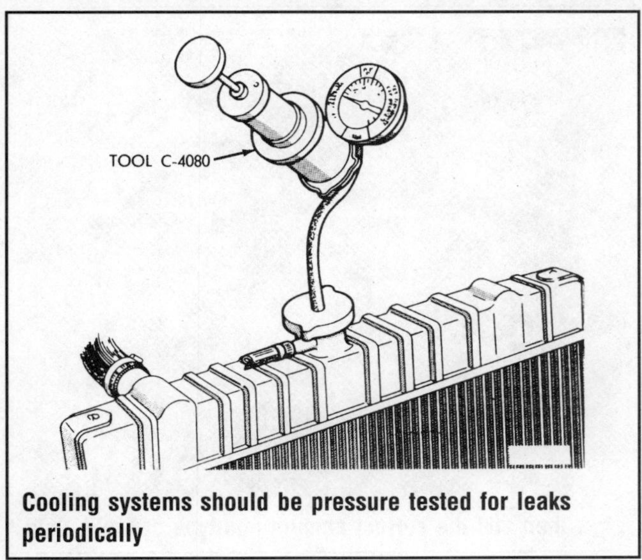

Cooling systems should be pressure tested for leaks periodically

- Edges of all cooling system gaskets (head gaskets, thermostat gasket)
- Transmission fluid cooler
- Heating system components, water pump
- Check the engine oil dipstick for signs of coolant in the engine oil. Will turn the oil a white color
- Check the coolant in the radiator for signs of oil in the coolant

Investigate and correct any indication of coolant leakage.

Check the Radiator Cap

While you are checking the coolant level, check the radiator cap for a worn or cracked gasket. If the cap doesn't seal properly, fluid will be lost and the engine will overheat.

A worn cap should be replaced with a new one.

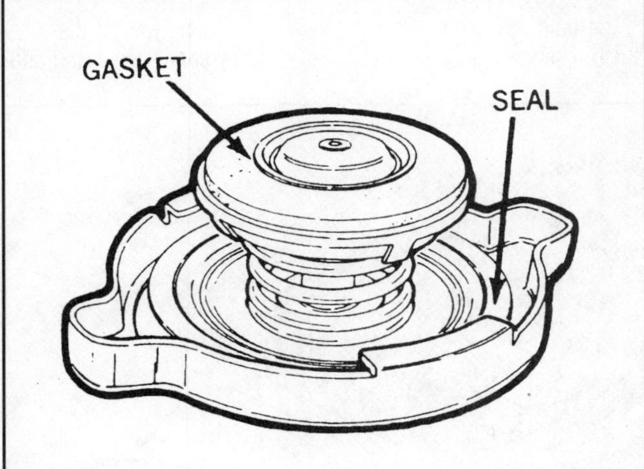

Be sure the rubber gasket on the radiator cap has a tight seal

Clean Radiator of Debris

Periodically clean any debris such as leaves, paper, insects, etc., from the radiator fins. Pick the large pieces off by hand. The smaller pieces can be washed away with water pressure from a hose.

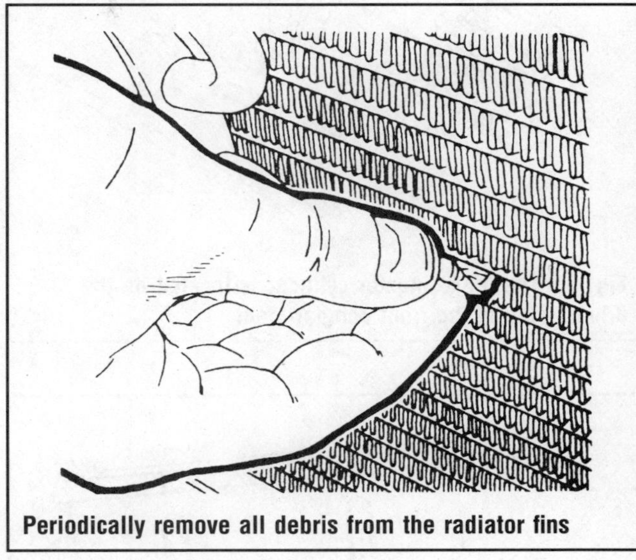
Periodically remove all debris from the radiator fins

CHECKING SYSTEM PROTECTION

A 50/50 mix of coolant concentrate and water will usually provide protection to −35°F (−37°C). Freeze protection may be checked by using a cooling system hydrometer. Inexpensive hydrometers (floating ball types) may be obtained from a local department store (automotive section) or an auto supply store. Follow the directions packaged with the coolant hydrometer when checking protection.

Brake Master Cylinder

➡The brake fluid reservoir is part of the brake master cylinder, and is located under the front engine compartment lid, on the driver's side of the car. Check the fluid level each time your engine oil is changed.

FLUID RECOMMENDATION & LEVEL CHECK

➧ See Figures 35 and 36

The fluid level can be seen through the plastic wall of the brake reservoir. The levels in both the front and rear chambers must be above the "MIN" lines. If it is necessary to add fluid, remove the cover by lifting up on the tabs on both sides of the cover. Use only Delco Supreme No. 11 or other DOT 3 specification brake fluid and add as necessary. Clean any dirt away from the cover and plastic reservoir before reinstalling.

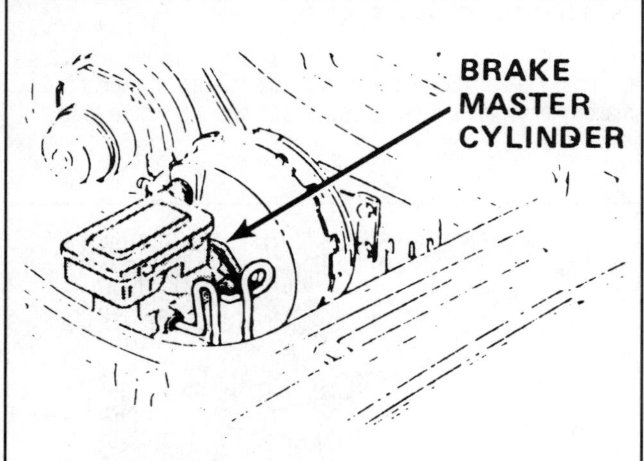

Fig. 35 The brake master cylinder is located on the drivers side of the front compartment

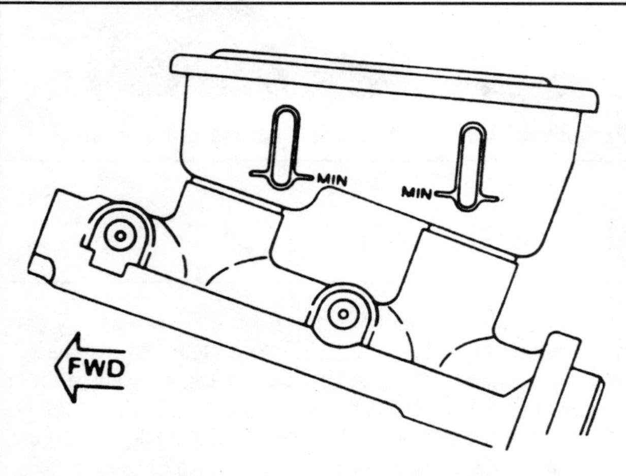

Fig. 36 Fluid level indicator marks on the side of the master cylinder reservoir

Remove the master cylinder cover by lifting up on the tabs on both sides of the cover . . .

. . . then add the correct amount and type of brake fluid

**** CAUTION**

Do not allow anyone to depress the brake pedal while the brake fluid reservoir cover is removed. Also, brake fluid will remove paint. If spilled, flush the area immediately with water.

Clutch Master Cylinder

➡The clutch master cylinder is located under the front compartment lid, on the driver's side, next to the brake master cylinder.

FLUID RECOMMENDATION & LEVEL CHECK

See Figure 37

The fluid level can be seen through the plastic wall of the clutch reservoir. Unscrew and remove the reservoir cover and add

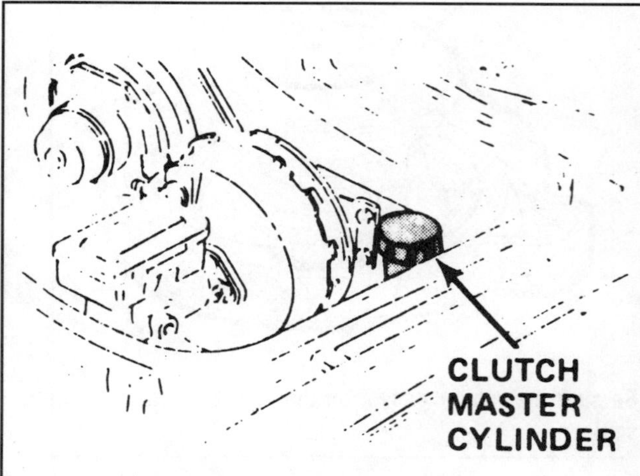

Fig. 37 The clutch master cylinder is located on the drivers side of the front compartment

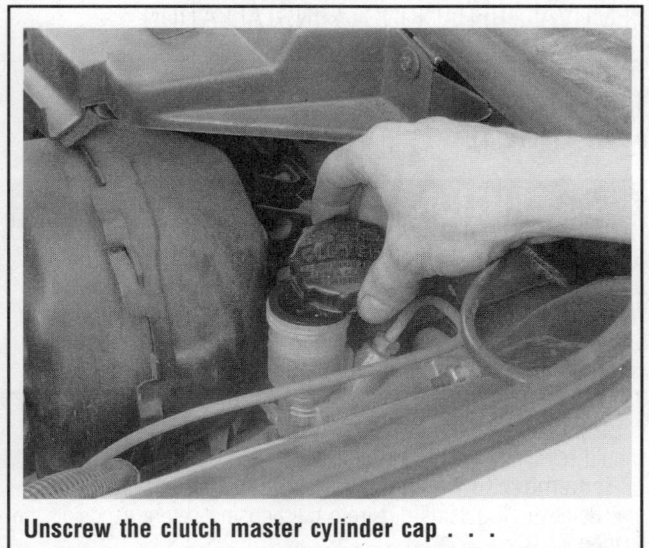
Unscrew the clutch master cylinder cap . . .

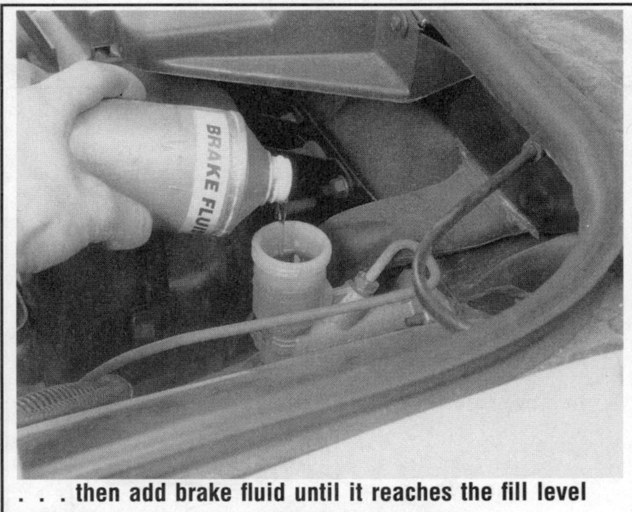

. . . then add brake fluid until it reaches the fill level indicator on the side of the master cylinder

fluid as necessary. Use only Delco Supreme No. 11 or other DOT 3 specification brake fluid. Use of other fluids may have an adverse affect on the operation of the hydraulic clutch.

***** CAUTION**

Do not allow anyone to depress the clutch pedal while the clutch fluid reservoir cover is not in place. Also, brake fluid will remove paint. If spilled, flush the area immediately with water.

Chassis Greasing

See Figures 38, 39 and 40

Every 12 months or 24,000 miles Pontiac recommends lubrication of the suspension and steering pivot points.

1. There are 6 grease fittings (3 on each side) on the front suspension and 4 grease fittings (2 on each side) on the rear suspension. Wipe each one with a clean cloth.

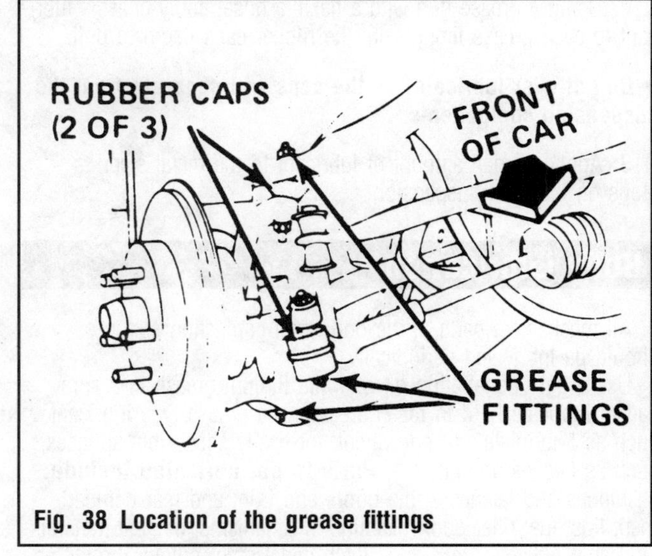

Fig. 38 Location of the grease fittings

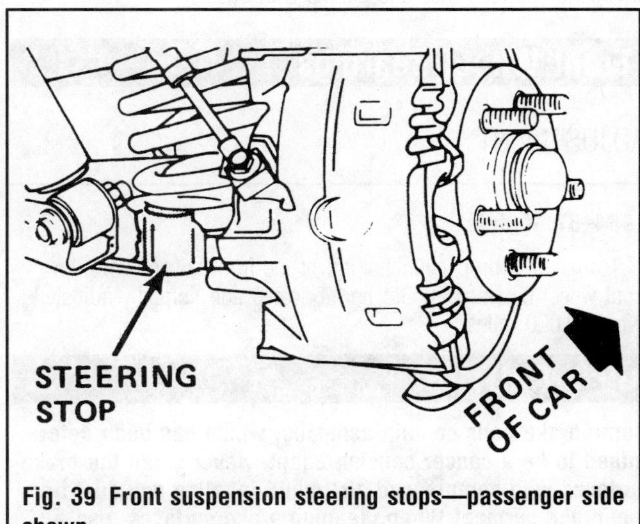

Fig. 39 Front suspension steering stops—passenger side shown

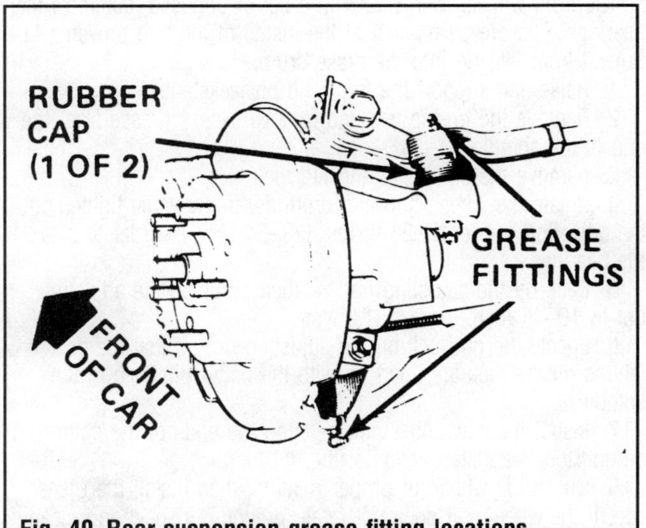

Fig. 40 Rear suspension grease fitting locations

2. Using a grease gun with a flexible hose, apply chassis lubricant to each grease fitting until the rubber caps begin to puff.

➡Do not over-lubricate, as the caps will separate from the suspension components.

3. Apply a small amount of lubricant to the metal steering stops on the front suspension.

Body Lubrication

All mechanical parts of the body with contacting surfaces should be lubricated periodically.

Use a light penetrating oil or white lithium grease in a spray can to lubricate hard to reach areas and a grease type lubricant such as Lubriplate® or equivalent, for easily accessible surfaces, such as latches and strikers. **Parts to be lubricated include:** all hinges and latches at the doors and front and rear compartment lids, fuel filler door, headlight mechanisms, manual transmission shift linkage, brake and clutch pedal pivot points, throttle and emergency brake cables and sliding seat tracks.

Front Wheel Bearings

ADJUSTMENT

1984–87 Models

To maintain proper functioning of the front suspension, the front wheel bearings should be lubricated and correctly adjusted every 30,000 miles.

CAUTION

Some brake pads contain asbestos, which has been determined to be a cancer causing agent. Never clean the brake surfaces with compressed air! Avoid inhaling any dust from any brake surface! When cleaning brake surfaces, use a commercially available brake cleaning fluid.

The front wheels each rotate on a set of opposed, tapered roller bearings. The grease retainer at the inside of the hub prevents lubricant from leaking into the brake drum.

1. Raise and support the front end on jackstands.
2. Remove the grease cap and remove excess grease from the end of the spindle.
3. Remove the cotter pin and nut lock.
4. Rotate the wheel, hub and drum assembly while tightening the adjusting nut to 17–25 ft. lbs. (23–34 Nm) in order to seat the bearings.
5. Back off the adjusting nut ½, then retighten the adjusting nut to 10–15 inch. lb. (1.2–1.8 Nm).
6. Locate the nut lock on the adjusting nut so that the castellations on the lock are lined up with the cotter pin hole in the spindle.
7. Install the new cotter pin, bending the ends of the cotter pin around the castellated flange of the nut lock.
8. Check the wheel for proper rotation, then install the grease cap. If the wheel still does not rotate properly, inspect and clean or replace the wheel bearings and cups.

REMOVAL, REPACKING & INSTALLATION

1984–87 Models

➧ See Figure 41

CAUTION

Some brake pads contain asbestos, which has been determined to be a cancer causing agent. Never clean the brake surfaces with compressed air! Avoid inhaling any dust from any brake surface! When cleaning brake surfaces, use a commercially available brake cleaning fluid.

Before handling the bearings, there are a few things that you should remember to do and not to do.

Remember to DO the following:

- Remove all outside dirt from the housing before exposing the bearing.
- Treat a used bearing as gently as you would a new one.
- Work with clean tools in clean surroundings.
- Use clean, dry canvas gloves, or at least clean, dry hands.

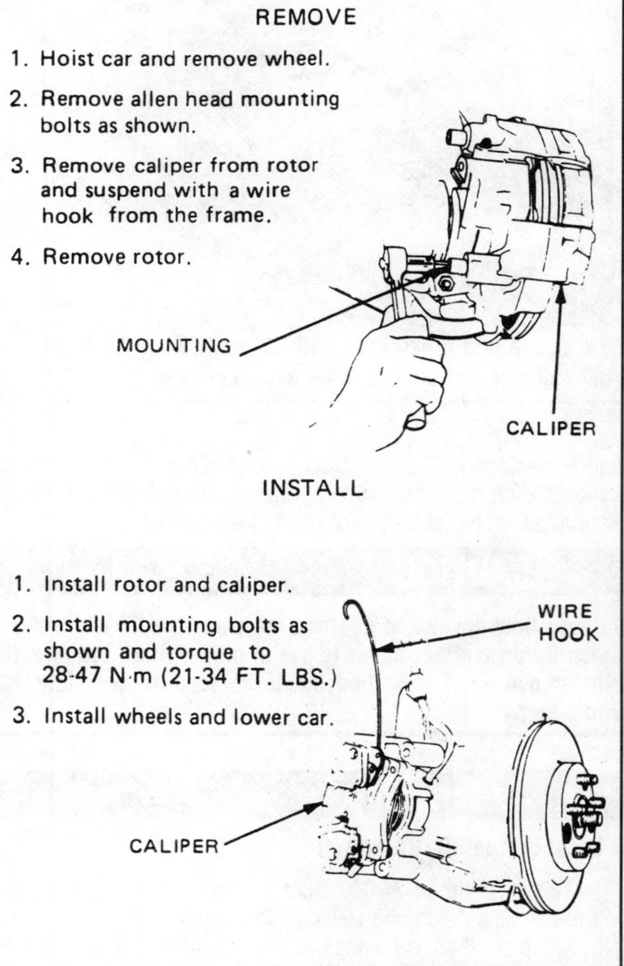

Fig. 41 Removal and installation the disc brake caliper

Pry the dust cap from the hub taking care not to distort or damage its flange

Loosen and remove the castellated nut from the spindle

Once the bent ends are cut, grasp the cotter pin and pull or pry it free of the spindle

Remove the washer from the spindle

If difficulty is encountered, gently tap on the pliers with a hammer to help free the cotter pin

With the nut and washer out of the way, the outer bearings may be removed from the hub

Pull the hub and inner bearing assembly from the spindle

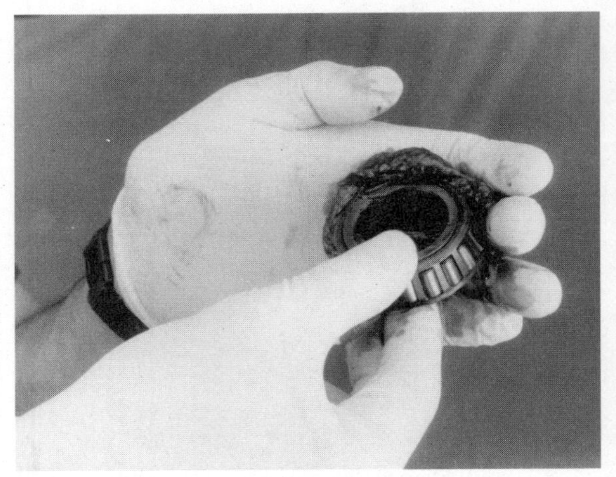
Thoroughly pack the bearing with fresh, high temperature wheel-bearing grease before installation

Use a small prytool to remove the old inner bearing seal

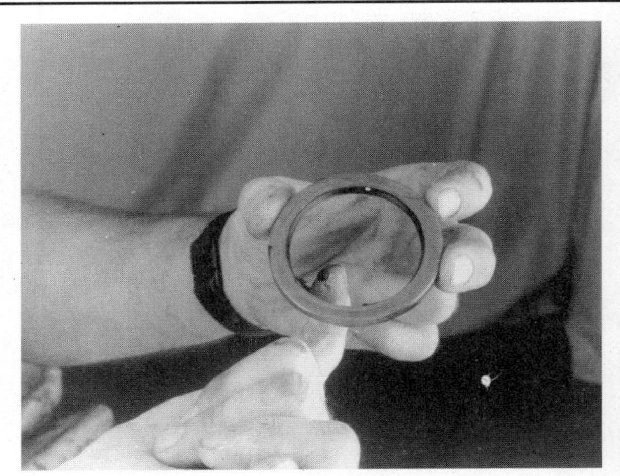
Apply a thin coat of fresh grease to the new inner bearing seal lip

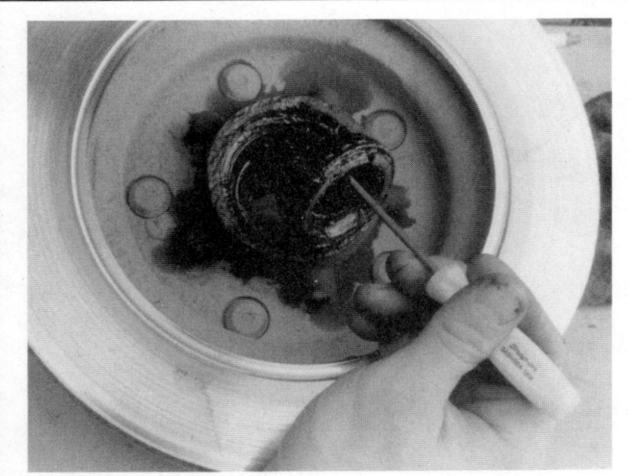
With the seal removed, the inner bearing may be withdrawn from the hub

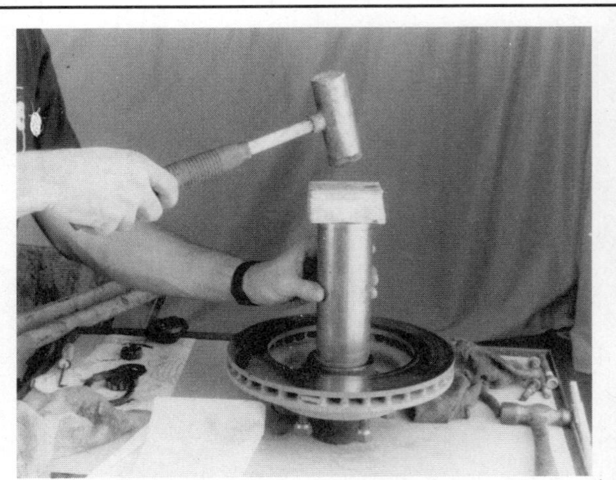
Use a suitably sized driver to install the inner bearing seal to the hub

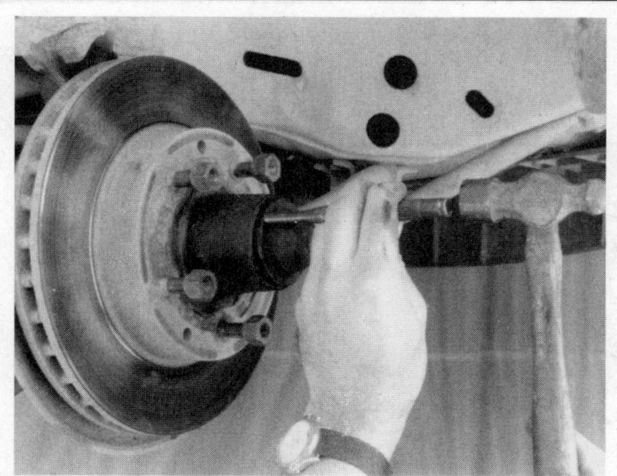

After the bearings are adjusted, install the dust cap by gently tapping on the flange—DO NOT damage the cap by hammering on the center

- Clean solvents and flushing fluids are a must.
- Use clean paper when laying out the bearings to dry.
- Protect disassembled bearings from rust and dirt. Cover them up.
- Use clean rags to wipe bearings.
- Keep the bearings in oil-proof paper when they are to be stored or are not in use.
- Clean the inside of the housing before replacing the bearing.

Do NOT do the following:

- Don't work in dirty surroundings.
- Don't use dirty, chipped or damaged tools.
- Try not to work on wooden work benches or use wooden mallets.
- Don't handle bearings with dirty or moist hands.
- Do not use gasoline for cleaning; use a safe solvent.
- Do not spin-dry bearings with compressed air. They will be damaged.
- Do not spin dirty bearings.
- Avoid using cotton waste or dirty cloths to wipe bearings.
- Try not to scratch or nick bearing surfaces.
- Do not allow the bearing to come in contact with dirt or rust at any time.

1. Raise and support the front end on jackstands.
2. Remove the wheel cover. Remove the wheel.
3. Remove the caliper from the disc and wire it to the underbody to prevent damage to the brake hose. See Chapter 9.
4. Remove the grease cap from the hub. Then, remove the cotter pin, nut lock, adjusting nut and flat washer from the spindle. Remove the outer bearing assembly from the hub.
5. Pull the hub and disc assembly off the wheel spindle.
6. Remove and discard the old grease retainer. Remove the inner bearing cone and roller assembly from the hub.
7. Clean all grease from the inner and outer bearing cups with solvent. Inspect the cups for pits, scratches, or excessive wear. If the cups are damaged, remove them with a drift.
8. Clean the inner and outer cone and roller assemblies with solvent and shake them dry. If the cone and roller assemblies show excessive wear or damage, replace them with the bearing cups as a unit.
9. Clean the spindle and the inside of the hub with solvent to thoroughly remove all old grease.

**** WARNING**

Do not submerge the rotor and hub assembly in solvent to clean the bearing areas. The porous medal will absorb the solvent and cause the new bearing grease to melt. Put a small amount of solvent on a clean rag and wipe the bearing area clean. Use a dry clean rag to wipe out the solvent still inside hub.

10. Covering the spindle with a clean cloth, brush all loose dirt and dust from the brake assembly. Remove the cloth carefully so as to not get dirt on the spindle.
11. If the inner and/or outer bearing cups were removed, install the replacement cups on the hub. Be sure that the cups seat properly in the hub.
12. It is imperative that all old grease be removed from the bearings and surrounding surfaces before repacking. Coat both bearings, bearing areas in the hub, grease seal and spindle with lithium-based grease. The new lithium-based grease is not compatible with the sodium base grease used in the past.
13. Install the hub and disc on the wheel spindle. To prevent damage to the grease seal and spindle threads, keep the hub centered on the spindle.
14. Install the outer bearing cone and roller assembly and the flat washer on the spindle. Install the adjusting nut.
15. Adjust the wheel bearings by torquing the adjusting nut to 17–25 ft. lbs. (23–34 Nm) with the wheel rotating to seat the bearing. Then back off the adjusting nut ½ turn. Retighten the adjusting nut to 10–15 inch. lb. (1.2–1.8 Nm). Install the locknut so that the castellations are aligned with the cotter pin hole. Install the cotter pin. Bend the ends of the cotter pin around the castellations of the locknut to prevent interference with the radio static collector in the grease cap. Install the grease cap.

**** WARNING**

New bolts must be used when servicing floating caliper units. The upper bolt must be tightened first. For floating caliper units, see Section 9.

16. Install the wheels.
17. Install the wheel cover, if so equipped.

1988 Models

See Figure 42

The 1988 models are equipped with sealed hub and bearing assemblies. Refer to the "Sealed Wheel Bearing Diagnosis Chart" in this section.

**** CAUTION**

Some brake pads contain asbestos, which has been determined to be a cancer causing agent. Never clean the brake surfaces with compressed air! Avoid inhaling any dust from any brake surface! When cleaning brake surfaces, use a commercially available brake cleaning fluid.

1. Raise the vehicle and support with jackstands.
2. Remove the wheel and tire assembly.
3. Remove the brake caliper and support with a wire to the surrounding body.

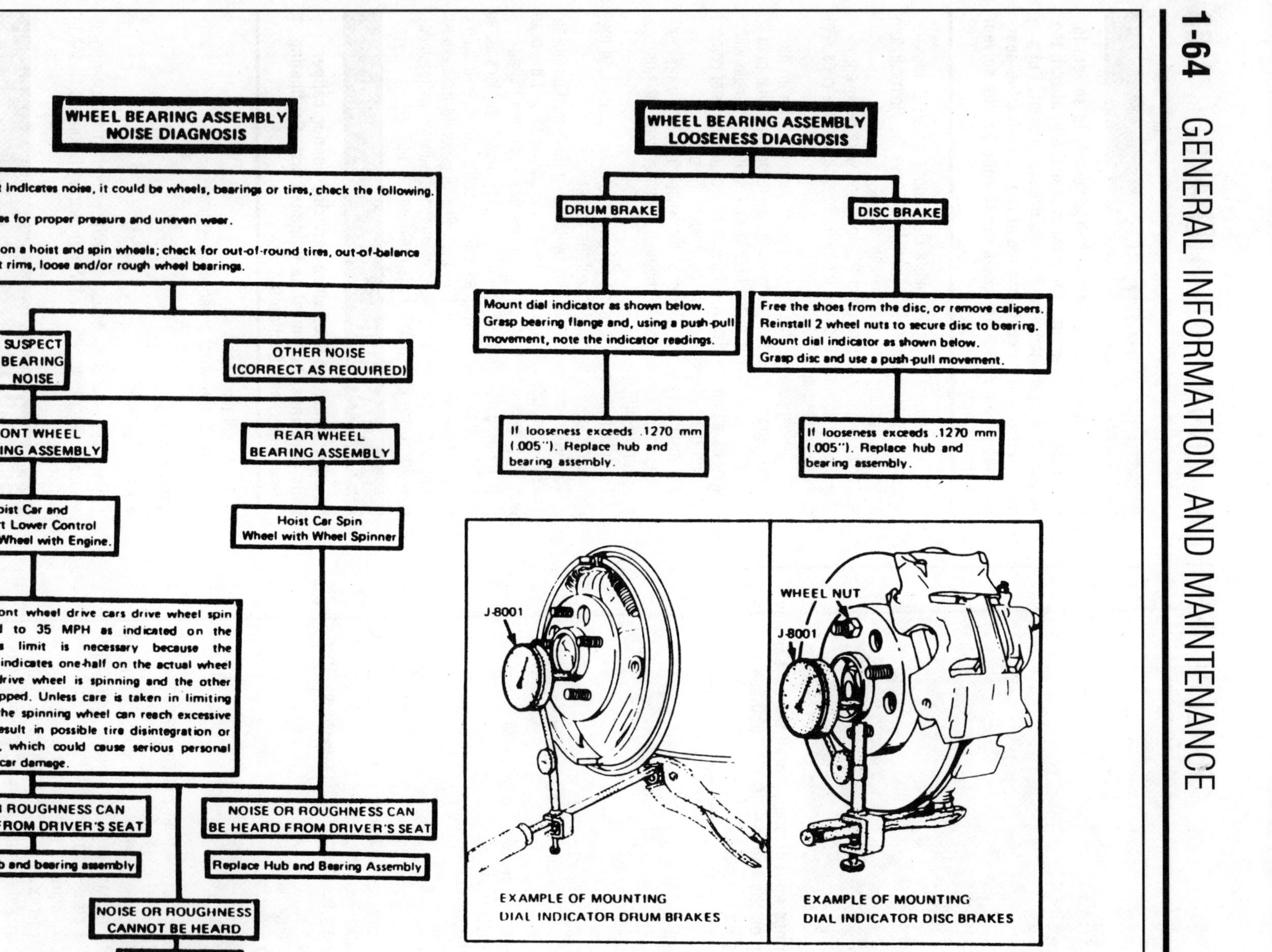

Fig. 42 Sealed bearing diagnosis chart—1988 models

4. Remove the rotor assembly.
5. Remove the three hub and bearing assembly-to-steering knuckle attaching bolts.
6. Press out the old bearing using an arbor press and press in new bearings.
7. **To install:** place the hub and bearing assembly on the spindle. Install the hub and bearing assembly-to-steering knuckle attaching bolts and torque to 220 ft. lbs. (260 Nm). Install the brake caliper and torque the mounting bolts to 74 ft. lbs. (100 Nm). Install the wheel and tire assembly. Lower the vehicle and pump the brake pedal a few times before moving the vehicle.

TOWING THE VEHICLE

Your Fiero may be towed on all four wheels only if the steering and driveline are in normal operating condition. Keep in mind the following precautions when towing your vehicle:

1. If equipped with an automatic transaxle, do not exceed a speed of 35 mph or a distance of 50 miles.
2. Make sure the steering is unlocked, the transaxle is in neutral and the parking brake is released.
3. Connect to main structural parts of the car. Do not attach to bumpers or brackets.
4. Remember, with the engine off, the power assist for the brakes will not be operating.

If your Fiero is to be towed by a wrecker, use the following precautions:

1. Follow the instructions of the wrecker manufacturer.
2. Since the Fiero is rear wheel drive, towing on the front wheels is preferred, however if necessary, it may be towed forwards on the rear drive wheels at speed up to 35 mph and for distances up to 50 miles on cars equipped with automatic transaxles. There is no restrictions on cars equipped with manual transaxles.
3. A safety chain system must be used for all towing.

TRAILER TOWING

General Recommendations

Your vehicle was primarily designed to carry passengers and cargo. It is important to remember that towing a trailer will place additional loads on your vehicles engine, drivetrain, steering, braking and other systems. However, if you decide to tow a trailer, using the prior equipment is a must.

Local laws may require specific equipment such as trailer brakes or fender mounted mirrors. Check your local laws.

Trailer Weight

The weight of the trailer is the most important factor. A good weight-to-horsepower ratio is about 35:1, 35 lbs. of Gross Combined Weight (GCW) for every horsepower your engine develops. Multiply the engine's rated horsepower by 35 and subtract the weight of the vehicle passengers and luggage. The number remaining is the approximate ideal maximum weight you should tow, although a numerically higher axle ratio can help compensate for heavier weight.

Hitch (Tongue) Weight

Calculate the hitch weight in order to select a proper hitch. The weight of the hitch is usually 9–11% of the trailer gross weight and should be measured with the trailer loaded. Hitches fall into various categories: those that mount on the frame and rear bumper, the bolt-on type, or the weld-on distribution type used for larger trailers. Axle mounted or clamp-on bumper hitches should never be used.

Check the gross weight rating of your trailer. Tongue weight is usually figured as 10% of gross trailer weight. Therefore, a trailer with a maximum gross weight of 2000 lbs. will have a maximum tongue weight of 200 lbs. Class I trailers fall into this category. Class II trailers are those with a gross weight rating of 2000–3000 lbs., while Class III trailers fall into the 3500–6000 lbs. category. Class IV trailers are those over 6000 lbs. and are for use with fifth wheel trucks, only.

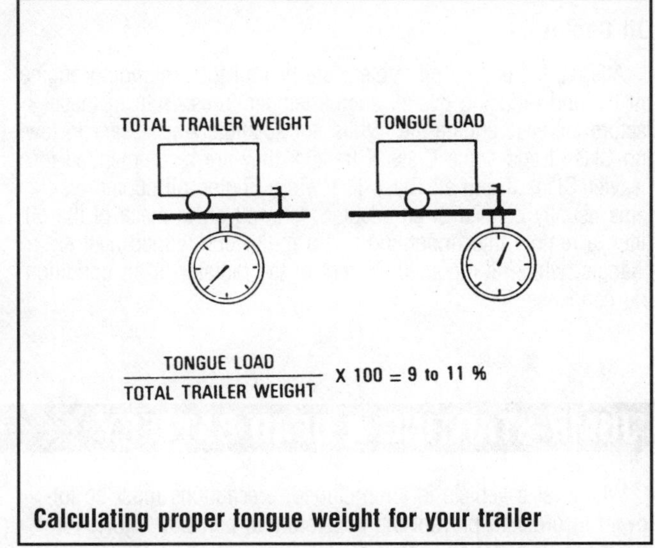

Calculating proper tongue weight for your trailer

When you've determined the hitch that you'll need, follow the manufacturer's installation instructions, exactly, especially when it comes to fastener torques. The hitch will subjected to a lot of stress and good hitches come with hardened bolts. Never substitute an inferior bolt for a hardened bolt.

Cooling

ENGINE

Overflow Tank

One of the most common, if not THE most common, problems associated with trailer towing is engine overheating. If you have a cooling system without an expansion tank, you'll definitely need to get an aftermarket expansion tank kit, preferably one with at least a 2 quart capacity. These kits are easily installed on the radiator's overflow hose, and come with a pressure cap designed for expansion tanks.

Flex Fan

Another helpful accessory for vehicles using a belt-driven radiator fan is a flex fan. These fans are large diameter units designed to provide more airflow at low speeds, by using fan blades that have deeply cupped surfaces. The blades then flex, or flatten out, at high speed, when less cooling air is needed. These fans are far lighter in weight than stock fans, requiring less horsepower to drive them. Also, they are far quieter than stock fans. If you do decide to replace your stock fan with a flex fan, note that if your vehicle has a fan clutch, a spacer will be needed between the flex fan and water pump hub.

Oil Cooler

Aftermarket engine oil coolers are helpful for prolonging engine oil life and reducing overall engine temperatures. Both of these factors increase engine life. While not absolutely necessary in towing Class I and some Class II trailers, they are recommended for heavier Class II and all Class III towing. Engine oil cooler systems usually consist of an adapter, screwed on in place of the oil filter, a remote filter mounting and a multi-tube, finned heat exchanger, which is mounted in front of the radiator or air conditioning condenser.

TRANSMISSION

An automatic transmission is usually recommended for trailer towing. Modern automatics have proven reliable and, of course, easy to operate, in trailer towing. The increased load of a trailer, however, causes an increase in the temperature of the automatic transmission fluid. Heat is the worst enemy of an automatic transmission. As the temperature of the fluid increases, the life of the fluid decreases.

It is essential, therefore, that you install an automatic transmission cooler. The cooler, which consists of a multi-tube, finned heat exchanger, is usually installed in front of the radiator or air conditioning compressor, and hooked in-line with the transmission cooler tank inlet line. Follow the cooler manufacturer's installation instructions.

Select a cooler of at least adequate capacity, based upon the combined gross weights of the vehicle and trailer.

Cooler manufacturers recommend that you use an aftermarket cooler in addition to, and not instead of, the present cooling tank in your radiator. If you do want to use it in place of the radiator cooling tank, get a cooler at least two sizes larger than normally necessary.

➡A transmission cooler can, sometimes, cause slow or harsh shifting in the transmission during cold weather, until the fluid has a chance to come up to normal operating temperature. Some coolers can be purchased with or retrofitted with a temperature bypass valve which will allow fluid flow through the cooler only when the fluid has reached above a certain operating temperature.

Handling A Trailer

Towing a trailer with ease and safety requires a certain amount of experience. It's a good idea to learn the feel of a trailer by practicing turning, stopping and backing in an open area such as an empty parking lot.

JUMP STARTING A DEAD BATTERY

Whenever a vehicle is jump started, precautions must be followed in order to prevent the possibility of personal injury. Remember that batteries contain a small amount of explosive hydrogen gas which is a by-product of battery charging. Sparks should always be avoided when working around batteries, especially when attaching jumper cables. To minimize the possibility of accidental sparks, follow the procedure carefully.

CAUTION

NEVER hook the batteries up in a series circuit or the entire electrical system will go up in smoke, including the starter!

Vehicles equipped with a diesel engine may utilize two 12 volt batteries. If so, the batteries are connected in a parallel circuit (positive terminal to positive terminal, negative terminal to negative terminal). Hooking the batteries up in parallel circuit increases battery cranking power without increasing total battery voltage output. Output remains at 12 volts. On the other hand, hooking two 12 volt batteries up in a series circuit (positive terminal to negative terminal, positive terminal to negative terminal) increases total battery output to 24 volts (12 volts plus 12 volts).

Jump Starting Precautions

- Be sure that both batteries are of the same voltage. Vehicles covered by this manual and most vehicles on the road today utilize a 12 volt charging system.
- Be sure that both batteries are of the same polarity (have the same terminal, in most cases NEGATIVE grounded).
- Be sure that the vehicles are not touching or a short could occur.
- On serviceable batteries, be sure the vent cap holes are not obstructed.
- Do not smoke or allow sparks anywhere near the batteries.

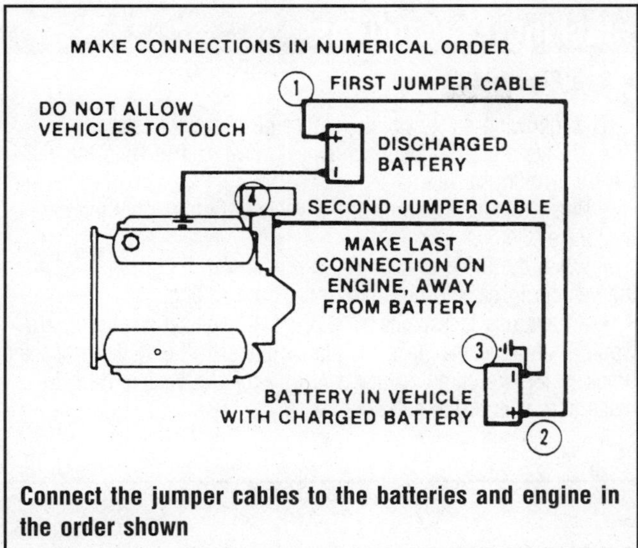

Connect the jumper cables to the batteries and engine in the order shown

- In cold weather, make sure the battery electrolyte is not frozen. This can occur more readily in a battery that has been in a state of discharge.
- Do not allow electrolyte to contact your skin or clothing.

Jump Starting Procedure

1. Make sure that the voltages of the 2 batteries are the same. Most batteries and charging systems are of the 12 volt variety.
2. Pull the jumping vehicle (with the good battery) into a position so the jumper cables can reach the dead battery and that vehicle's engine. Make sure that the vehicles do NOT touch.
3. Place the transmissions/transaxles of both vehicles in **Neutral** (MT) or **P** (AT), as applicable, then firmly set their parking brakes.

➡If necessary for safety reasons, the hazard lights on both vehicles may be operated throughout the entire procedure without significantly increasing the difficulty of jumping the dead battery.

4. Turn all lights and accessories OFF on both vehicles. Make sure the ignition switches on both vehicles are turned to the **OFF** position.
5. Cover the battery cell caps with a rag, but do not cover the terminals.
6. Make sure the terminals on both batteries are clean and free of corrosion or proper electrical connection will be impeded. If necessary, clean the battery terminals before proceeding.
7. Identify the positive (+) and negative (−) terminals on both batteries.
8. Connect the first jumper cable to the positive (+) terminal of the dead battery, then connect the other end of that cable to the positive (+) terminal of the booster (good) battery.
9. Connect one end of the other jumper cable to the negative (−) terminal on the booster battery and the final cable clamp to an engine bolt head, alternator bracket or other solid, metallic point on the engine with the dead battery. Try to pick a ground on the engine that is positioned away from the battery in order to minimize the possibility of the 2 clamps touching should one loosen during the procedure. DO NOT connect this clamp to the negative (−) terminal of the bad battery.

***** CAUTION**

Be very careful to keep the jumper cables away from moving parts (cooling fan, belts, etc.) on both engines.

10. Check to make sure that the cables are routed away from any moving parts, then start the donor vehicle's engine. Run the engine at moderate speed for several minutes to allow the dead battery a chance to receive some initial charge.
11. With the donor vehicle's engine still running slightly above idle, try to start the vehicle with the dead battery. Crank the engine for no more than 10 seconds at a time and let the starter cool for at least 20 seconds between tries. If the vehicle does not start in 3 tries, it is likely that something else is also wrong or that the battery needs additional time to charge.
12. Once the vehicle is started, allow it to run at idle for a few seconds to make sure that it is operating properly.
13. Turn ON the headlights, heater blower and, if equipped, the rear defroster of both vehicles in order to reduce the severity of voltage spikes and subsequent risk of damage to the vehicles' electrical systems when the cables are disconnected. This step is especially important to any vehicle equipped with computer control modules.
14. Carefully disconnect the cables in the reverse order of connection. Start with the negative cable that is attached to the engine ground, then the negative cable on the donor battery. Disconnect the positive cable from the donor battery and finally, disconnect the positive cable from the formerly dead battery. Be careful when disconnecting the cables from the positive terminals not to allow the alligator clips to touch any metal on either vehicle or a short and sparks will occur.

JACKING

Your vehicle was supplied with a jack for emergency road repairs. This jack is fine for changing a flat tire or other short term procedures not requiring you to go beneath the vehicle. If it is used in an emergency situation, carefully follow the instructions provided either with the jack or in your owner's manual. Do not attempt to use the jack on any portions of the vehicle other than specified by the vehicle manufacturer. Always block the diagonally opposite wheel when using a jack.

A more convenient way of jacking is the use of a garage or floor jack.

Never place the jack under the radiator, engine or transmission components. Severe and expensive damage will result when the jack is raised. Additionally, never jack under the floorpan or bodywork; the metal will deform.

Whenever you plan to work under the vehicle, you must support it on jackstands or ramps. Never use cinder blocks or stacks of wood to support the vehicle, even if you're only going to be under it for a few minutes. Never crawl under the vehicle when it is supported only by the tire-changing jack or other floor jack.

➡Always position a block of wood or small rubber pad on top of the jack or jackstand to protect the lifting point's finish when lifting or supporting the vehicle.

Small hydraulic, screw, or scissors jacks are satisfactory for raising the vehicle. Drive-on trestles or ramps are also a handy and safe way to both raise and support the vehicle. Be careful though, some ramps may be too steep to drive your vehicle onto without scraping the front bottom panels. Never support the vehicle on any suspension member (unless specifically instructed to do so by a repair manual) or by an underbody panel.

Jacking Precautions

➧ See Figure 43

The following safety points cannot be overemphasized:

- Always block the opposite wheel or wheels to keep the vehicle from rolling off the jack.
- When raising the front of the vehicle, firmly apply the parking brake.
- When the drive wheels are to remain on the ground, leave the vehicle in gear to help prevent it from rolling.
- Always use jackstands to support the vehicle when you are working underneath. Place the stands beneath the vehicle's jacking brackets. Before climbing underneath, rock the vehicle a bit to make sure it is firmly supported.

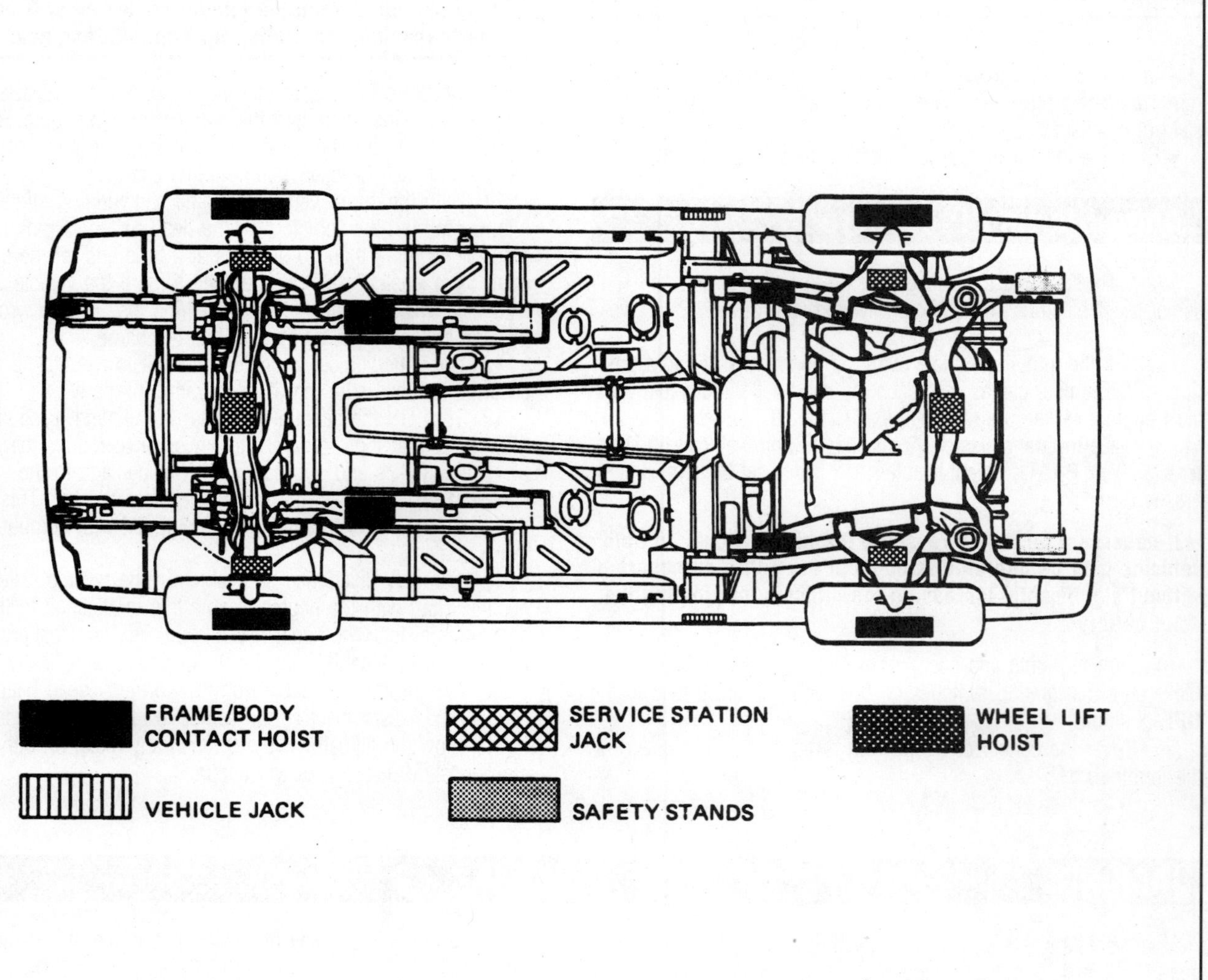

Fig. 43 Fiero lifting and jacking points

Raise the rear of the vehicle as shown. Be careful not to pinch the brake cable

Raise the front of the vehicle from the crossmember

HOW TO BUY A USED VEHICLE

Many people believe that a two or three year old used car or truck is a better buy than a new vehicle. This may be true as most new vehicles suffer the heaviest depreciation in the first two years and, at three years old, a vehicle is usually not old enough to present a lot of costly repair problems. But keep in mind, when buying a non-warranted automobile, there are no guarantees. Whatever the age of the used vehicle you might want to purchase, this section and a little patience should increase your chances of selecting one that is safe and dependable.

Tips

1. First decide what model you want, and how much you want to spend.
2. Check the used car lots and your local newspaper ads. Privately owned vehicles are usually less expensive, however, you may not get a warranty that, in many cases, comes with a used vehicle purchased from a lot. Of course, some aftermarket warranties may not be worth the extra money, so this is a point you will have to debate and consider based on your priorities.
3. Never shop at night. The glare of the lights make it easy to miss faults on the body caused by accident or rust repair.
4. Try to get the name and phone number of the previous owner. Contact him/her and ask about the vehicle. If the owner of a lot refuses this information, look for a vehicle somewhere else.

A private seller can tell you about the vehicle and maintenance. But remember, there's no law requiring honesty from private citizens selling used vehicles. There is a law that forbids tampering with or turning back the odometer mileage. This includes both the private citizen and the lot owner. The law also requires that the seller or anyone transferring ownership of the vehicle must provide the buyer with a signed statement indicating the mileage on the odometer at the time of transfer.

5. You may wish to contact the National Highway Traffic Safety Administration (NHTSA) to find out if the vehicle has ever been included in a manufacturer's recall. Write down the year, model and serial number before you buy the vehicle, then contact NHTSA (there should be a 1-800 number that your phone company's information line can supply). If the vehicle was listed for a recall, make sure the needed repairs were made.
6. Refer to the Used Vehicle Checklist in this section and check all the items on the vehicle you are considering. Some items are more important than others. Only you know how much money you can afford for repairs, and depending on the price of the vehicle, may consider performing any needed work yourself. Beware, however, of trouble in areas that will affect operation, safety or emission. Problems in the Used Vehicle Checklist break down as follows:
   - Numbers 1–8: Two or more problems in these areas indicate a lack of maintenance. You should beware.
   - Numbers 9–13: Problems here tend to indicate a lack of proper care, however, these can usually be corrected with a tune-up or relatively simple parts replacement.
   - Numbers 14–17: Problems in the engine or transmission can be very expensive. Unless you are looking for a project, walk away from any vehicle with problems in 2 or more of these areas.
7. If you are satisfied with the apparent condition of the vehicle, take it to an independent diagnostic center or mechanic for a complete check. If you have a state inspection program, have it inspected immediately before purchase, or specify on the bill of sale that the sale is conditional on passing state inspection.
8. Road test the vehicle—refer to the Road Test Checklist in this section. If your original evaluation and the road test agree—the rest is up to you.

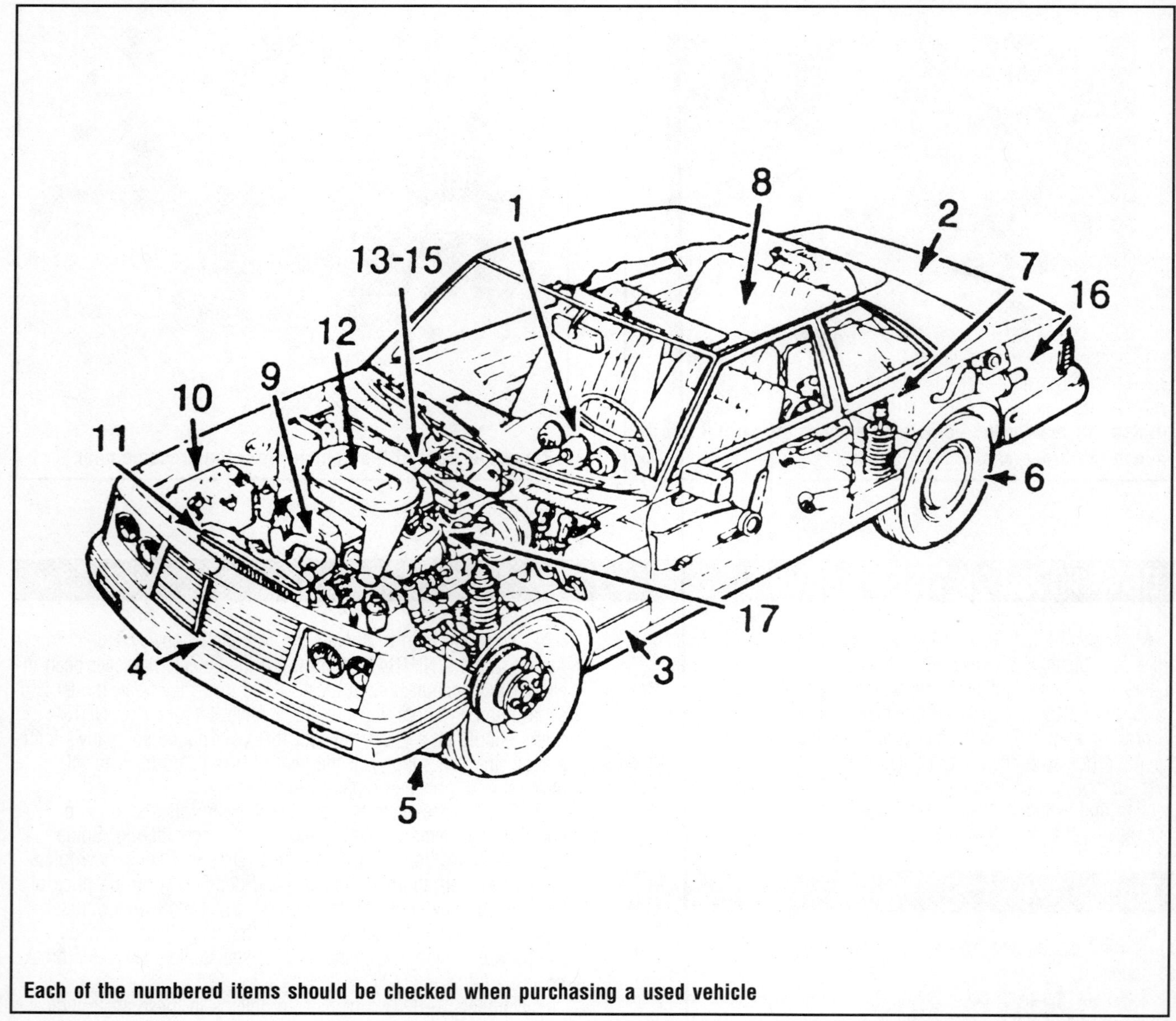

Each of the numbered items should be checked when purchasing a used vehicle

USED VEHICLE CHECKLIST

➡The numbers on the illustrations refer to the numbers on this checklist.

1. Mileage: Average mileage is about 12,000–15,000 miles per year. More than average mileage may indicate hard usage or could indicate many highway miles (which could be less detrimental than half as many tough around town miles).
2. Paint: Check around the tailpipe, molding and windows for overspray indicating that the vehicle has been repainted.
3. Rust: Check fenders, doors, rocker panels, window moldings, wheelwells, floorboards, under floormats, and in the trunk for signs of rust. Any rust at all will be a problem. There is no way to permanently stop the spread of rust, except to replace the part or panel.

➡If rust repair is suspected, try using a magnet to check for body filler. A magnet should stick to the sheet metal parts of the body, but will not adhere to areas with large amounts of filler.

4. Body appearance: Check the moldings, bumpers, grille, vinyl roof, glass, doors, trunk lid and body panels for general overall condition. Check for misalignment, loose hold-down clips, ripples, scratches in glass, welding in the trunk, severe misalignment of body panels or ripples, any of which may indicate crash work.
5. Leaks: Get down and look under the vehicle. There are no normal leaks, other than water from the air conditioner evaporator.
6. Tires: Check the tire air pressure. One old trick is to pump the tire pressure up to make the vehicle roll easier. Check the tread wear, then open the trunk and check the spare too. Uneven wear is a clue that the front end may need an alignment.
7. Shock absorbers: Check the shock absorbers by forcing

downward sharply on each corner of the vehicle. Good shocks will not allow the vehicle to bounce more than once after you let go.

8. Interior: Check the entire interior. You're looking for an interior condition that agrees with the overall condition of the vehicle. Reasonable wear is expected, but be suspicious of new seat covers on sagging seats, new pedal pads, and worn armrests. These indicate an attempt to cover up hard use. Pull back the carpets and look for evidence of water leaks or flooding. Look for missing hardware, door handles, control knobs, etc. Check lights and signal operations. Make sure all accessories (air conditioner, heater, radio, etc.) work. Check windshield wiper operation.

9. Belts and Hoses: Open the hood, then check all belts and hoses for wear, cracks or weak spots.

10. Battery: Low electrolyte level, corroded terminals and/or cracked case indicate a lack of maintenance.

11. Radiator: Look for corrosion or rust in the coolant indicating a lack of maintenance.

12. Air filter: A severely dirty air filter would indicate a lack of maintenance.

13. Ignition wires: Check the ignition wires for cracks, burned spots, or wear. Worn wires will have to be replaced.

14. Oil level: If the oil level is low, chances are the engine uses oil or leaks. Beware of water in the oil (there is probably a cracked block or bad head gasket), excessively thick oil (which is often used to quiet a noisy engine), or thin, dirty oil with a distinct gasoline smell (this may indicate internal engine problems).

15. Automatic Transmission: Pull the transmission dipstick out when the engine is running. The level should read FULL, and the fluid should be clear or bright red. Dark brown or black fluid that has distinct burnt odor, indicates a transmission in need of repair or overhaul.

16. Exhaust: Check the color of the exhaust smoke. Blue smoke indicates, among other problems, worn rings. Black smoke can indicate burnt valves or carburetor problems. Check the exhaust system for leaks; it can be expensive to replace.

17. Spark Plugs: Remove one or all of the spark plugs (the most accessible will do, though all are preferable). An engine in good condition will show plugs with a light tan or gray deposit on the firing tip.

ROAD TEST CHECKLIST

1. Engine Performance: The vehicle should be peppy whether cold or warm, with adequate power and good pickup. It should respond smoothly through the gears.

2. Brakes: They should provide quick, firm stops with no noise, pulling or brake fade.

3. Steering: Sure control with no binding harshness, or looseness and no shimmy in the wheel should be expected. Noise or vibration from the steering wheel when turning the vehicle means trouble.

4. Clutch (Manual Transmission/Transaxle): Clutch action should give quick, smooth response with easy shifting. The clutch pedal should have free-play before it disengages the clutch. Start the engine, set the parking brake, put the transmission in first gear and slowly release the clutch pedal. The engine should begin to stall when the pedal is ½–¾ of the way up.

5. Automatic Transmission/Transaxle: The transmission should shift rapidly and smoothly, with no noise, hesitation, or slipping.

6. Differential: No noise or thumps should be present. Differentials have no normal leaks.

7. Driveshaft/Universal Joints: Vibration and noise could mean driveshaft problems. Clicking at low speed or coast conditions means worn U-joints.

8. Suspension: Try hitting bumps at different speeds. A vehicle that bounces excessively has weak shock absorbers or struts. Clunks mean worn bushings or ball joints.

9. Frame/Body: Wet the tires and drive in a straight line. Tracks should show two straight lines, not four. Four tire tracks indicate a frame/body bent by collision damage. If the tires can't be wet for this purpose, have a friend drive along behind you and see if the vehicle appears to be traveling in a straight line.

Maintenance Intervals Chart

Intervals are for number of months or thousands of miles, whichever comes first.

NOTE: *Heavy-duty operation (trailer towing, prolonged idling, severe stop and start driving) should be accompanied by a 50% increase in maintenance. Cut the interval in half for these conditions.*

Item To Be Serviced	When To Perform (Months or Miles whichever comes first)
Chassis Lubrication	Every 12 mos. or 7,500 miles
Engine Oil Change Oil Filter Change	Every 7,500 miles ② Every Oil Change
Torque TBI Mounting Bolt	At first 7,500 miles
Flush and Refill Cooling System	Every 24 mos. or 30,000 miles
Repack Front Wheel Bearings	Every 30,000 miles
Change Transaxle Fluid and Filter	At 100,000 miles ①
Replace Spark Plugs	Every 30,000 miles
Inspect PCV Valve	Every 22,500
Inspect EGR System	Every 36 mos. or 30,000 miles
Air Cleaner and PCV Filter Replacement	Every 24 mos. or 22,500 miles ②
Check Engine Timing	Every 30,000 miles
Inspect Spark Plug Wires	Every 30,000 miles
Fuel Cap and Lines Inspection	Every 30,000 miles
Inspect Thermostatically Controlled Air Cleaner	Every 30,000 miles
Check Tire Inflation	Every Month

① Every 15,000 miles for Heavy Duty service

② Service more often when driven under severe or dusty conditions

Capacities

Year	VIN Code	Engine Displace Cu. In.	Eng. Mfg.	Crankcase Quarts	Transaxle Quarts Manual 4 spd	Transaxle Quarts Manual 5 spd	Transaxle Quarts Auto	Gas Tank Gal	Cooling System Qts
1984	R	151	Pont.	3.0 ①	3.0	—	6.0 ③	10.5	②
	R	151	Pont.	3.0 ①	3.0	2.7	5.0 ④	10.3	13.8 ⑤
1985	9	173	Chev.	4.0 ①	3.0	2.7	5.0 ④	10.3	13.8
	R	151	Pont.	3.0 ①	3.0	2.7	5.0 ④	10.3	13.8 ⑤
1986	9	173	Chev.	4.0 ①	3.0	2.7	5.0 ④	10.3	13.8
	R	151	Pont.	3.0 ①	—	2.7 ⑥	5.0 ④	11.9	13.8 ⑤
1987	9	173	Chev.	4.0 ①	—	2.7 ⑥	5.0 ④	11.9	13.8
	R	151	Pont.	4.0 ①	—	2.7 ⑥	5.0 ④	11.9	13.8 ⑤
1988	9	173	Chev.	4.0 ①	—	2.7 ⑥	5.0 ④	11.9	13.8

① With or without filter change.
② Non-A/C. 13.7 qts, A/C. 14.2.
③ 6.0 qts. after disassembly, 4.0 qts after pan removal.
④ 5.0 qts. after disassembly, 4.0 qts after pan removal.
⑤ 13.8 qts. auto trans, 14.1 qts manual trans.
⑥ 2.7 qts. Isuzu MT2, 2.0 qts. Muncie MG2.

ENGLISH TO METRIC CONVERSION: MASS (WEIGHT)

Current mass measurement is expressed in pounds and ounces (lbs. & ozs.). The metric unit of mass (or weight) is the kilogram (kg). Even although this table does not show conversion of masses (weights) larger than 15 lbs, it is easy to calculate larger units by following the data immediately below.

To convert ounces (oz.) to grams (g): multiply th number of ozs. by 28
To convert grams (g) to ounces (oz.): multiply the number of grams by .035

To convert pounds (lbs.) to kilograms (kg): multiply the number of lbs. by .45
To convert kilograms (kg) to pounds (lbs.): multiply the number of kilograms by 2.2

lbs	kg	lbs	kg	oz	kg	oz	kg
0.1	0.04	0.9	0.41	0.1	0.003	0.9	0.024
0.2	0.09	1	0.4	0.2	0.005	1	0.03
0.3	0.14	2	0.9	0.3	0.008	2	0.06
0.4	0.18	3	1.4	0.4	0.011	3	0.08
0.5	0.23	4	1.8	0.5	0.014	4	0.11
0.6	0.27	5	2.3	0.6	0.017	5	0.14
0.7	0.32	10	4.5	0.7	0.020	10	0.28
0.8	0.36	15	6.8	0.8	0.023	15	0.42

ENGLISH TO METRIC CONVERSION: TEMPERATURE

To convert Fahrenheit (°F) to Celsius (°C): take number of °F and subtract 32; multiply result by 5; divide result by 9

To convert Celsius (°C) to Fahrenheit (°F): take number of °C and multiply by 9; divide result by 5; add 32 to total

Fahrenheit (F)		Celsius (C)		Fahrenheit (F)		Celsius (C)		Fahrenheit (F)		Celsius (C)	
°F	°C	°C	°F	°F	°C	°C	°F	°F	°C	°C	°F
−40	−40	−38	−36.4	80	26.7	18	64.4	215	101.7	80	176
−35	−37.2	−36	−32.8	85	29.4	20	68	220	104.4	85	185
−30	−34.4	−34	−29.2	90	32.2	22	71.6	225	107.2	90	194
−25	−31.7	−32	−25.6	95	35.0	24	75.2	230	110.0	95	202
−20	−28.9	−30	−22	100	37.8	26	78.8	235	112.8	100	212
−15	−26.1	−28	−18.4	105	40.6	28	82.4	240	115.6	105	221
−10	−23.3	−26	−14.8	110	43.3	30	86	245	118.3	110	230
−5	−20.6	−24	−11.2	115	46.1	32	89.6	250	121.1	115	239
0	−17.8	−22	−7.6	120	48.9	34	93.2	255	123.9	120	248
1	−17.2	−20	−4	125	51.7	36	96.8	260	126.6	125	257
2	−16.7	−18	−0.4	130	54.4	38	100.4	265	129.4	130	266
3	−16.1	−16	3.2	135	57.2	40	104	270	132.2	135	275
4	−15.6	−14	6.8	140	60.0	42	107.6	275	135.0	140	284
5	−15.0	−12	10.4	145	62.8	44	112.2	280	137.8	145	293
10	−12.2	−10	14	150	65.6	46	114.8	285	140.6	150	302
15	−9.4	−8	17.6	155	68.3	48	118.4	290	143.3	155	311
20	−6.7	−6	21.2	160	71.1	50	122	295	146.1	160	320
25	−3.9	−4	24.8	165	73.9	52	125.6	300	148.9	165	329
30	−1.1	−2	28.4	170	76.7	54	129.2	305	151.7	170	338
35	1.7	0	32	175	79.4	56	132.8	310	154.4	175	347
40	4.4	2	35.6	180	82.2	58	136.4	315	157.2	180	356
45	7.2	4	39.2	185	85.0	60	140	320	160.0	185	365
50	10.0	6	42.8	190	87.8	62	143.6	325	162.8	190	374
55	12.8	8	46.4	195	90.6	64	147.2	330	165.6	195	383
60	15.6	10	50	200	93.3	66	150.8	335	168.3	200	392
65	18.3	12	53.6	205	96.1	68	154.4	340	171.1	205	401
70	21.1	14	57.2	210	98.9	70	158	345	173.9	210	410
75	23.9	16	60.8	212	100.0	75	167	350	176.7	215	414

ENGLISH TO METRIC CONVERSION: LENGTH

To convert inches (ins.) to millimeters (mm): multiply number of inches by 25.4

To convert millimeters (mm) to inches (ins.): multiply number of millimeters by .04

Inches	Decimals	Milli-meters	Inches to millimeters inches	mm	Inches	Decimals	Milli-meters	Inches to millimeters inches	mm
1/64	0.051625	0.3969	0.0001	0.00254	33/64	0.515625	13.0969	0.6	15.24
1/32	0.03125	0.7937	0.0002	0.00508	17/32	0.53125	13.4937	0.7	17.78
3/64	0.046875	1.1906	0.0003	0.00762	35/64	0.546875	13.8906	0.8	20.32
1/16	0.0625	1.5875	0.0004	0.01016	9/16	0.5625	14.2875	0.9	22.86
5/64	0.078125	1.9844	0.0005	0.01270	37/64	0.578125	14.6844	1	25.4
3/32	0.09375	2.3812	0.0006	0.01524	19/32	0.59375	15.0812	2	50.8
7/64	0.109375	2.7781	0.0007	0.01778	39/64	0.609375	15.4781	3	76.2
1/8	0.125	3.1750	0.0008	0.02032	5/8	0.625	15.8750	4	101.6
9/64	0.140625	3.5719	0.0009	0.02286	41/64	0.640625	16.2719	5	127.0
5/32	0.15625	3.9687	0.001	0.0254	21/32	0.65625	16.6687	6	152.4
11/64	0.171875	4.3656	0.002	0.0508	43/64	0.671875	17.0656	7	177.8
3/16	0.1875	4.7625	0.003	0.0762	11/16	0.6875	17.4625	8	203.2
13/64	0.203125	5.1594	0.004	0.1016	45/64	0.703125	17.8594	9	228.6
7/32	0.21875	5.5562	0.005	0.1270	23/32	0.71875	18.2562	10	254.0
15/64	0.234375	5.9531	0.006	0.1524	47/64	0.734375	18.6531	11	279.4
1/4	0.25	6.3500	0.007	0.1778	3/4	0.75	19.0500	12	304.8
17/64	0.265625	6.7469	0.008	0.2032	49/64	0.765625	19.4469	13	330.2
9/32	0.28125	7.1437	0.009	0.2286	25/32	0.78125	19.8437	14	355.6
19/64	0.296875	7.5406	0.01	0.254	51/64	0.796875	20.2406	15	381.0
5/16	0.3125	7.9375	0.02	0.508	13/16	0.8125	20.6375	16	406.4
21/64	0.328125	8.3344	0.03	0.762	53/64	0.828125	21.0344	17	431.8
11/32	0.34375	8.7312	0.04	1.016	27/32	0.84375	21.4312	18	457.2
23/64	0.359375	9.1281	0.05	1.270	55/64	0.859375	21.8281	19	482.6
3/8	0.375	9.5250	0.06	1.524	7/8	0.875	22.2250	20	508.0
25/64	0.390625	9.9219	0.07	1.778	57/64	0.890625	22.6219	21	533.4
13/32	0.40625	10.3187	0.08	2.032	29/32	0.90625	23.0187	22	558.8
27/64	0.421875	10.7156	0.09	2.286	59/64	0.921875	23.4156	23	584.2
7/16	0.4375	11.1125	0.1	2.54	15/16	0.9375	23.8125	24	609.6
29/64	0.453125	11.5094	0.2	5.08	61/64	0.953125	24.2094	25	635.0
15/32	0.46875	11.9062	0.3	7.62	31/32	0.96875	24.6062	26	660.4
31/64	0.484375	12.3031	0.4	10.16	63/64	0.984375	25.0031	27	690.6
1/2	0.5	12.7000	0.5	12.70					

ENGLISH TO METRIC CONVERSION: TORQUE

To convert foot-pounds (ft. lbs.) to Newton-meters: multiply the number of ft. lbs. by 1.3

To convert inch-pounds (in. lbs.) to Newton-meters: multiply the number of in. lbs. by .11

in lbs	N·m	in lbs	N·m	in lbs	N·m	in lbs	N·m	in lbs	N·m
0.1	0.01	1	0.11	10	1.13	19	2.15	28	3.16
0.2	0.02	2	0.23	11	1.24	20	2.26	29	3.28
0.3	0.03	3	0.34	12	1.36	21	2.37	30	3.39
0.4	0.04	4	0.45	13	1.47	22	2.49	31	3.50
0.5	0.06	5	0.56	14	1.58	23	2.60	32	3.62
0.6	0.07	6	0.68	15	1.70	24	2.71	33	3.73
0.7	0.08	7	0.78	16	1.81	25	2.82	34	3.84
0.8	0.09	8	0.90	17	1.92	26	2.94	35	3.95
0.9	0.10	9	1.02	18	2.03	27	3.05	36	4.0

ENGLISH TO METRIC CONVERSION: TORQUE

Torque is now expressed as either foot-pounds (ft./lbs.) or inch-pounds (in./lbs.). The metric measurement unit for torque is the Newton-meter (Nm). This unit—the Nm—will be used for all SI metric torque references, both the present ft./lbs. and in./lbs.

ft lbs	N-m	ft lbs	N-m	ft lbs	N-m	ft lbs	N-m
0.1	0.1	33	44.7	74	100.3	115	155.9
0.2	0.3	34	46.1	75	101.7	116	157.3
0.3	0.4	35	47.4	76	103.0	117	158.6
0.4	0.5	36	48.8	77	104.4	118	160.0
0.5	0.7	37	50.7	78	105.8	119	161.3
0.6	0.8	38	51.5	79	107.1	120	162.7
0.7	1.0	39	52.9	80	108.5	121	164.0
0.8	1.1	40	54.2	81	109.8	122	165.4
0.9	1.2	41	55.6	82	111.2	123	166.8
1	1.3	42	56.9	83	112.5	124	168.1
2	2.7	43	58.3	84	113.9	125	169.5
3	4.1	44	59.7	85	115.2	126	170.8
4	5.4	45	61.0	86	116.6	127	172.2
5	6.8	46	62.4	87	118.0	128	173.5
6	8.1	47	63.7	88	119.3	129	174.9
7	9.5	48	65.1	89	120.7	130	176.2
8	10.8	49	66.4	90	122.0	131	177.6
9	12.2	50	67.8	91	123.4	132	179.0
10	13.6	51	69.2	92	124.7	133	180.3
11	14.9	52	70.5	93	126.1	134	181.7
12	16.3	53	71.9	94	127.4	135	183.0
13	17.6	54	73.2	95	128.8	136	184.4
14	18.9	55	74.6	96	130.2	137	185.7
15	20.3	56	75.9	97	131.5	138	187.1
16	21.7	57	77.3	98	132.9	139	188.5
17	23.0	58	78.6	99	134.2	140	189.8
18	24.4	59	80.0	100	135.6	141	191.2
19	25.8	60	81.4	101	136.9	142	192.5
20	27.1	61	82.7	102	138.3	143	193.9
21	28.5	62	84.1	103	139.6	144	195.2
22	29.8	63	85.4	104	141.0	145	196.6
23	31.2	64	86.8	105	142.4	146	198.0
24	32.5	65	88.1	106	143.7	147	199.3
25	33.9	66	89.5	107	145.1	148	200.7
26	35.2	67	90.8	108	146.4	149	202.0
27	36.6	68	92.2	109	147.8	150	203.4
28	38.0	69	93.6	110	149.1	151	204.7
29	39.3	70	94.9	111	150.5	152	206.1
30	40.7	71	96.3	112	151.8	153	207.4
31	42.0	72	97.6	113	153.2	154	208.8
32	43.4	73	99.0	114	154.6	155	210.2

ENGLISH TO METRIC CONVERSION: FORCE

Force is presently measured in pounds (lbs.). This type of measurement is used to measure spring pressure, specifically how many pounds it takes to compress a spring. Our present force unit (the pound) will be replaced in SI metric measurements by the Newton (N). This term will eventually see use in specifications for electric motor brush spring pressures, valve spring pressures, etc.

To convert pounds (lbs.) to Newton (N): multiply the number of lbs. by 4.45

lbs	N	lbs	N	lbs	N	oz	N
0.01	0.04	21	93.4	59	262.4	1	0.3
0.02	0.09	22	97.9	60	266.9	2	0.6
0.03	0.13	23	102.3	61	271.3	3	0.8
0.04	0.18	24	106.8	62	275.8	4	1.1
0.05	0.22	25	111.2	63	280.2	5	1.4
0.06	0.27	26	115.6	64	284.6	6	1.7
0.07	0.31	27	120.1	65	289.1	7	2.0
0.08	0.36	28	124.6	66	293.6	8	2.2
0.09	0.40	29	129.0	67	298.0	9	2.5
0.1	0.4	30	133.4	68	302.5	10	2.8
0.2	0.9	31	137.9	69	306.9	11	3.1
0.3	1.3	32	142.3	70	311.4	12	3.3
0.4	1.8	33	146.8	71	315.8	13	3.6
0.5	2.2	34	151.2	72	320.3	14	3.9
0.6	2.7	35	155.7	73	324.7	15	4.2
0.7	3.1	36	160.1	74	329.2	16	4.4
0.8	3.6	37	164.6	75	333.6	17	4.7
0.9	4.0	38	169.0	76	338.1	18	5.0
1	4.4	39	173.5	77	342.5	19	5.3
2	8.9	40	177.9	78	347.0	20	5.6
3	13.4	41	182.4	79	351.4	21	5.8
4	17.8	42	186.8	80	355.9	22	6.1
5	22.2	43	191.3	81	360.3	23	6.4
6	26.7	44	195.7	82	364.8	24	6.7
7	31.1	45	200.2	83	369.2	25	7.0
8	35.6	46	204.6	84	373.6	26	7.2
9	40.0	47	209.1	85	378.1	27	7.5
10	44.5	48	213.5	86	382.6	28	7.8
11	48.9	49	218.0	87	387.0	29	8.1
12	53.4	50	224.4	88	391.4	30	8.3
13	57.8	51	226.9	89	395.9	31	8.6
14	62.3	52	231.3	90	400.3	32	8.9
15	66.7	53	235.8	91	404.8	33	9.2
16	71.2	54	240.2	92	409.2	34	9.4
17	75.6	55	244.6	93	413.7	35	9.7
18	80.1	56	249.1	94	418.1	36	10.0
19	84.5	57	253.6	95	422.6	37	10.3
20	89.0	58	258.0	96	427.0	38	10.6

ENGLISH TO METRIC CONVERSION: LIQUID CAPACITY

Liquid or fluid capacity is presently expressed as pints, quarts or gallons, or a combination of all of these. In the metric system the liter (l) will become the basic unit. Fractions of a liter would be expressed as deciliters, centiliters, or most frequently (and commonly) as milliliters.

To convert pints (pts.) to liters (l): multiply the number of pints by .47
To convert liters (l) to pints (pts.): multiply the number of liters by 2.1
To convert quarts (qts.) to liters (l): multiply the number of quarts by .95

To convert liters (l) to quarts (qts.): multiply the number of liters by 1.06
To convert gallons (gals.) to liters (l): multiply the number of gallons by 3.8
To convert liters (l) to gallons (gals.): multiply the number of liters by .26

gals	liters	qts	liters	pts	liters
0.1	0.38	0.1	0.10	0.1	0.05
0.2	0.76	0.2	0.19	0.2	0.10
0.3	1.1	0.3	0.28	0.3	0.14
0.4	1.5	0.4	0.38	0.4	0.19
0.5	1.9	0.5	0.47	0.5	0.24
0.6	2.3	0.6	0.57	0.6	0.28
0.7	2.6	0.7	0.66	0.7	0.33
0.8	3.0	0.8	0.76	0.8	0.38
0.9	3.4	0.9	0.85	0.9	0.43
1	3.8	1	1.0	1	0.5
2	7.6	2	1.9	2	1.0
3	11.4	3	2.8	3	1.4
4	15.1	4	3.8	4	1.9
5	18.9	5	4.7	5	2.4
6	22.7	6	5.7	6	2.8
7	26.5	7	6.6	7	3.3
8	30.3	8	7.6	8	3.8
9	34.1	9	8.5	9	4.3
10	37.8	10	9.5	10	4.7
11	41.6	11	10.4	11	5.2
12	45.4	12	11.4	12	5.7
13	49.2	13	12.3	13	6.2
14	53.0	14	13.2	14	6.6
15	56.8	15	14.2	15	7.1
16	60.6	16	15.1	16	7.6
17	64.3	17	16.1	17	8.0
18	68.1	18	17.0	18	8.5
19	71.9	19	18.0	19	9.0
20	75.7	20	18.9	20	9.5
21	79.5	21	19.9	21	9.9
22	83.2	22	20.8	22	10.4
23	87.0	23	21.8	23	10.9
24	90.8	24	22.7	24	11.4
25	94.6	25	23.6	25	11.8
26	98.4	26	24.6	26	12.3
27	102.2	27	25.5	27	12.8
28	106.0	28	26.5	28	13.2
29	110.0	29	27.4	29	13.7
30	113.5	30	28.4	30	14.2

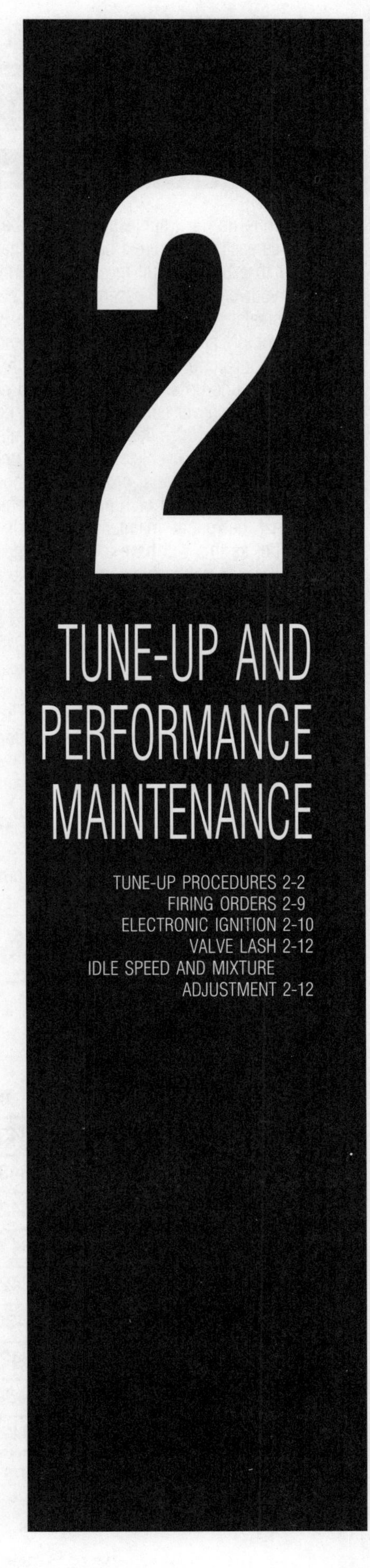

2

TUNE-UP AND PERFORMANCE MAINTENANCE

TUNE-UP PROCEDURES

General Information

Neither tune-up nor troubleshooting can be considered independently, since each has a direct bearing on the other.

In order to extract the full measure of performance and economy from your engine it is essential that it be properly tuned at regular intervals. A regular tune-up will keep your vehicle's engine running smoothly and will prevent the annoying minor breakdowns and poor performance associated with an untuned engine.

A complete tune-up should be performed every 30,000 miles or two years, whichever comes first. A tune-up check should be performed every 12,000 miles or twelve months. These intervals should be halved if the vehicle is operated under severe conditions, such as trailer towing, prolonged idling, continual stop and start driving, or if starting or running problems are noticed. It is assumed that the routine maintenance described in Section 1 has been kept up, as this will have a decided effect on the results of a tune-up. All of the applicable steps of a tune-up should be followed in order, as the result is a cumulative one.

If the specifications on the tune-up sticker in the engine compartment disagree with the Tune-Up Specifications chart in this section, the figures on the sticker must be used. The sticker often reflects changes made during the production run.

An engine tune-up is a service designed to restore the maximum capability of power, performance, economy and reliability in an engine, and, at the same time, assure the owner of a complete check and more lasting results in efficiency and trouble-free performance. Engine tune-up becomes increasingly important each year, to ensure that pollutant levels are in compliance with federal emissions standards.

It is advisable to follow a definite and thorough tune-up procedure. Tune-up consists of three separate steps: analysis, the process of determining whether normal wear is responsible for performance loss, and whether parts require replacement or service; parts replacement or service; adjustment, where engine adjustments are returned to the original factory specifications.

Troubleshooting is a logical sequence of procedures designed to lead the owner or service man to the particular cause of trouble. The troubleshooting charts in this manual is general in nature, yet specific enough to locate the problem. Service usually comprises two areas: diagnosis, and repair. While the apparent cause of trouble, in many cases, is worn or damaged parts, performance problems are less obvious. The first job is to locate the problem and cause. Once the problem has been isolated, refer to the appropriate section for repair, removal or adjustment procedures.

It is advisable to read the entire chapter before beginning a tune-up, although those who are more familiar with tune-up procedures may wish to go directly to the instructions.

Spark Plugs

A typical spark plug consists of a metal shell surrounding a ceramic insulator. A metal electrode extends downward through the center of the insulator and protrudes a small distance. Located at the end of the plug and attached to the side of the outer metal shell is the side electrode. The side electrode bends in at a 90° angle so that its tip is just past and parallel to the tip of the center electrode. The distance between these two electrodes (measured in thousandths of an inch or hundredths of a millimeter) is called the spark plug gap.

The spark plug does not produce a spark but instead provides

Gasoline Engine Tune-Up Specifications

Year	VIN	No. Cylinder Displacement cu. in. (liter)	Spark Plugs Type	Spark Plugs Gap (in.)	Ignition Timing (deg.) MT	Ignition Timing (deg.) AT	Compression Pressure (psi)	Fuel Pump (psi)	Idle Speed (rpm) MT	Idle Speed (rpm) AT	Valve Clearance In.	Valve Clearance Ex.
1984	R	151 (2.5)	R43TSX	.060	①	①	NA	9–13	①	①	Hyd.	Hyd.
1985	R	151 (2.5)	R43TSX	.060	①	①	NA	9–13	①	①	Hyd.	Hyd.
	9	173 (2.8)	R42CTS	.045	①	①	NA	41–47	①	①	Hyd.	Hyd.
1986	R	151 (2.5)	R43CTS	.060	①	①	NA	9–13	①	①	Hyd.	Hyd.
	9	173 (2.8)	R42CTS	.045	①	①	NA	34–45	①	①	Hyd.	Hyd.
1987	R	151 (2.5)	R43CTS6	.060	①	①	NA	9–13	①	①	Hyd.	Hyd.
	9	173 (2.8)	R42CTS	.045	①	①	NA	32–47	①	①	Hyd.	Hyd.
1988	R	151 (2.5)	R43CTS6	.060	①	①	NA	9–13	①	①	Hyd.	Hyd.
	9	173 (2.8)	R42CTS	.045	①	①	NA	32–47	①	①	Hyd.	Hyd.

NOTE: The underhood specifications sticker often reflects tune-up specifications changes made in production. Sticker figures must be used if they disagree with those in this chart.

① See underhood sticker.

a gap across which the current can arc. The coil produces anywhere from 20,000 to 50,000 volts (depending on the type and application) which travels through the wires to the spark plugs. The current passes along the center electrode and jumps the gap to the side electrode, and in doing so, ignites the air/fuel mixture in the combustion chamber.

SPARK PLUG HEAT RANGE

➧ **See Figure 1**

Spark plug heat range is the ability of the plug to dissipate heat. The longer the insulator (or the farther it extends into the engine), the hotter the plug will operate; the shorter the insulator (the closer the electrode is to the block's cooling passages) the cooler it will operate. A plug that absorbs little heat and remains too cool will quickly accumulate deposits of oil and carbon since it is not hot enough to burn them off. This leads to plug fouling and consequently to misfiring. A plug that absorbs too much heat will have no deposits but, due to the excessive heat, the electrodes will burn away quickly and might possibly lead to preignition or other ignition problems. Preignition takes place when plug tips get so hot that they glow sufficiently to ignite the air/fuel mixture before the actual spark occurs. This early ignition will usually cause a pinging during low speeds and heavy loads.

The general rule of thumb for choosing the correct heat range when picking a spark plug is: if most of your driving is long distance, high speed travel, use a colder plug; if most of your driving is stop and go, use a hotter plug. Original equipment plugs are generally a good compromise between the 2 styles and most people never have the need to change their plugs from the factory-recommended heat range.

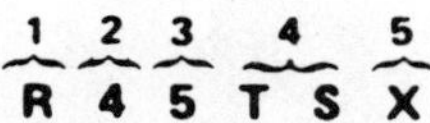

1 — R--INDICATES RESISTOR-TYPE PLUG.
2 — "4" INDICATES 14 mm THREADS.
3 — HEAT RANGE
4 — TS--TAPERED SEAT
S--EXTENDED TIP
5 — SPECIAL GAP

Fig. 1 Spark plug coding using an AC/45TSX as an example

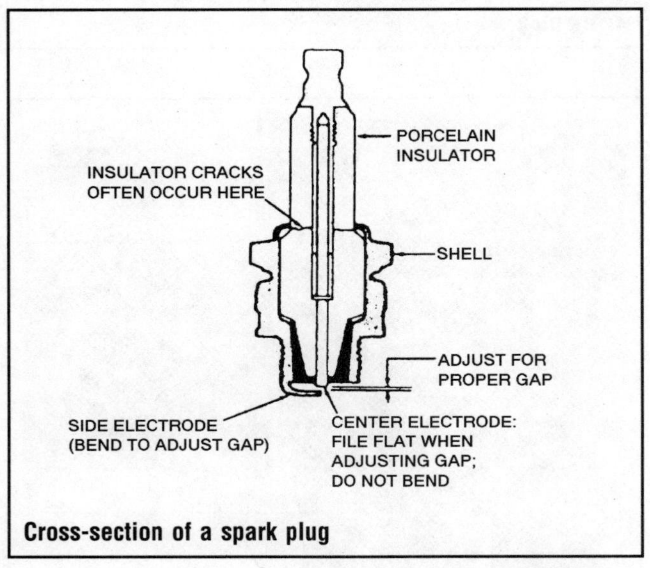

Cross-section of a spark plug

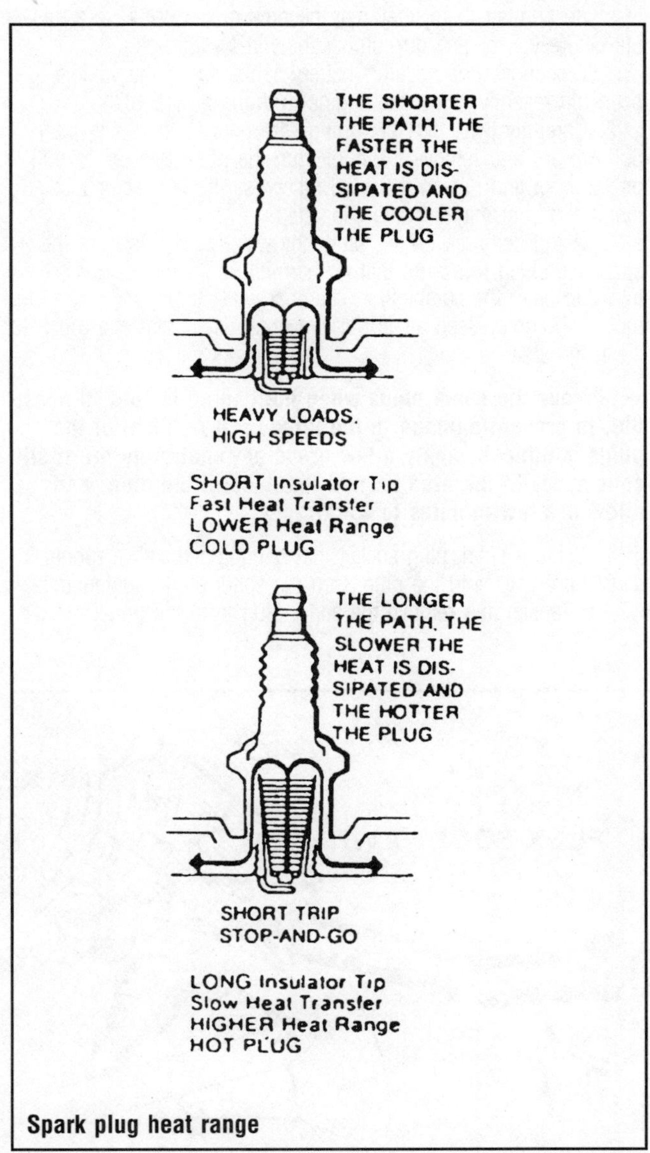

Spark plug heat range

REMOVAL & INSTALLATION

See Figure 2

A set of spark plugs usually requires replacement after about 20,000–30,000 miles (32,000–48,000 km), depending on your style of driving. In normal operation plug gap increases about 0.001 in. (0.025mm) for every 2500 miles (4000 km). As the gap increases, the plug's voltage requirement also increases. It requires a greater voltage to jump the wider gap and about two to three times as much voltage to fire the plug at high speeds than at idle. The improved air/fuel ratio control of modern fuel injection combined with the higher voltage output of modern ignition systems will often allow an engine to run significantly longer on a set of standard spark plugs, but keep in mind that efficiency will drop as the gap widdens (along with fuel economy and power).

When you're removing spark plugs, work on one at a time. Don't start by removing the plug wires all at once, because, unless you number them, they may become mixed up. Take a minute before you begin and number the wires with tape.

1. Disconnect the negative battery cable, and if the vehicle has been run recently, allow the engine to thoroughly cool.
2. Carefully twist the spark plug wire boot to loosen it, then pull upward and remove the boot from the plug. Be sure to pull on the boot and not on the wire, otherwise the connector located inside the boot may become separated.
3. Using compressed air, blow any water or debris from the spark plug well to assure that no harmful contaminants are allowed to enter the combustion chamber when the spark plug is removed. If compressed air is not available, use a rag or a brush to clean the area.

➡Remove the spark plugs when the engine is cold, if possible, to prevent damage to the threads. If removal of the plugs is difficult, apply a few drops of penetrating oil or silicone spray to the area around the base of the plug, and allow it a few minutes to work.

4. Using a spark plug socket that is equipped with a rubber insert to properly hold the plug, turn the spark plug counterclockwise to loosen and remove the spark plug from the bore.

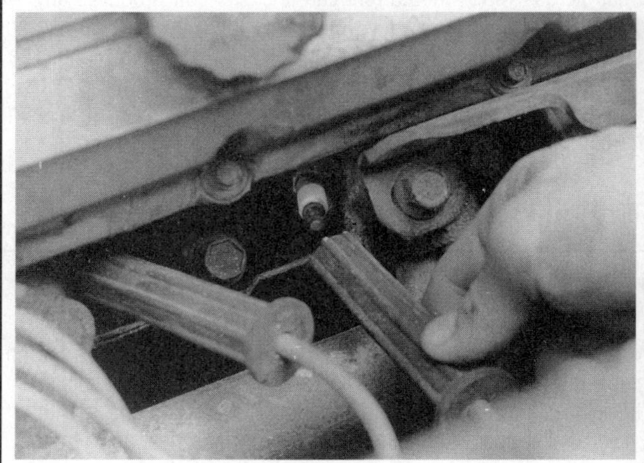

Grasp the spark plug boot and twist it to remove the wire from the plug

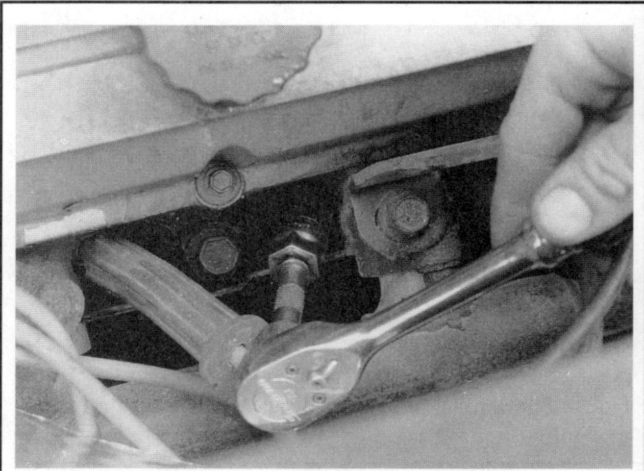

Use a spark plug socket and a ratchet to loosen the spark plug . . .

Fig. 2 A flex socket wrench may be needed to remove some of the spark plugs on the 2.8L V6 engine

. . . then remove the spark plug from the cylinder head

WARNING

Be sure not to use a flexible extension on the socket. Use of a flexible extension may allow a shear force to be applied to the plug. A shear force could break the plug off in the cylinder head, leading to costly and frustrating repairs.

To install:

5. Inspect the spark plug boot for tears or damage. If a damaged boot is found, the spark plug wire must be replaced.
6. Using a wire feeler gauge, check and adjust the spark plug gap. When using a gauge, the proper size should pass between the electrodes with a slight drag. The next larger size should not be able to pass while the next smaller size should pass freely.
7. Carefully thread the plug into the bore by hand. If resistance is felt before the plug is almost completely threaded, back the plug out and begin threading again. In small, hard to reach areas, an old spark plug wire and boot could be used as a threading tool. The boot will hold the plug while you twist the end of the wire and the wire is supple enough to twist before it would allow the plug to crossthread.

WARNING

Do not use the spark plug socket to thread the plugs. Always carefully thread the plug by hand or using an old plug wire to prevent the possibility of crossthreading and damaging the cylinder head bore.

8. Carefully tighten the spark plug. If the plug you are installing is equipped with a crush washer, seat the plug, then tighten about 1/4 turn to crush the washer. If you are installing a tapered seat plug, tighten the plug to specifications provided by the vehicle or plug manufacturer.
9. Apply a small amount of silicone dielectric compound to the end of the spark plug lead or inside the spark plug boot to prevent sticking, then install the boot to the spark plug and push until it clicks into place. The click may be felt or heard, then gently pull back on the boot to assure proper contact.

INSPECTION & GAPPING

Check the plugs for deposits and wear. If they are not going to be replaced, clean the plugs thoroughly. Remember that any kind of deposit will decrease the efficiency of the plug. Plugs can be cleaned on a spark plug cleaning machine, which can sometimes be found in service stations, or you can do an acceptable job of cleaning with a stiff brush. If the plugs are cleaned, the electrodes must be filed flat. Use an ignition points file, not an emery board or the like, which will leave deposits. The electrodes must be filed perfectly flat with sharp edges; rounded edges reduce the spark plug voltage by as much as 50%.

Check spark plug gap before installation. The ground electrode (the L-shaped one connected to the body of the plug) must be parallel to the center electrode and the specified size wire gauge (please refer to the Tune-Up Specifications chart for details) must pass between the electrodes with a slight drag.

➡NEVER adjust the gap on a used platinum type spark plug.

Always check the gap on new plugs as they are not always set correctly at the factory. Do not use a flat feeler gauge when measuring the gap on a used plug, because the reading may be inaccurate. A round-wire type gapping tool is the best way to check the gap. The correct gauge should pass through the electrode gap with a slight drag. If you're in doubt, try one size smaller and one larger. The smaller gauge should go through easily, while the larger one shouldn't go through at all. Wire gapping tools usually have a bending tool attached. Use that to adjust the side electrode until the proper distance is obtained. Absolutely never attempt to bend the center electrode. Also, be careful not to bend the side electrode too far or too often as it may weaken and break off within the engine, requiring removal of the cylinder head to retrieve it.

A normally worn spark plug should have light tan or gray deposits on the firing tip

A carbon fouled plug, identified by soft, sooty, black deposits, may indicate an improperly tuned vehicle. Check the air cleaner, ignition components and engine control system

A physically damaged spark plug may be evidence of severe detonation in that cylinder. Watch that cylinder carefully between services, as a continued detonation will not only damage the plug, but could also damage the engine

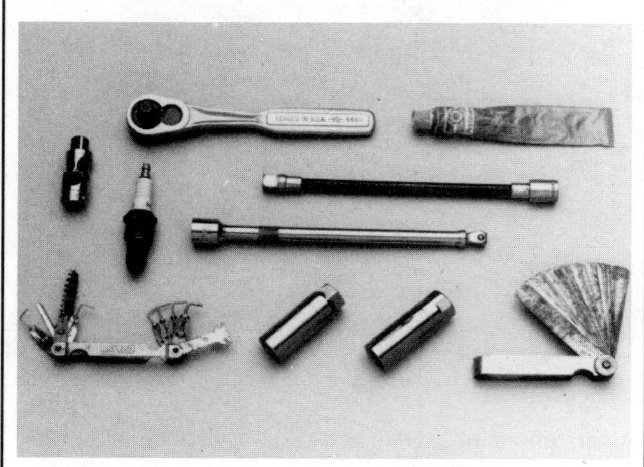

A variety of tools and gauges are needed for spark plug service

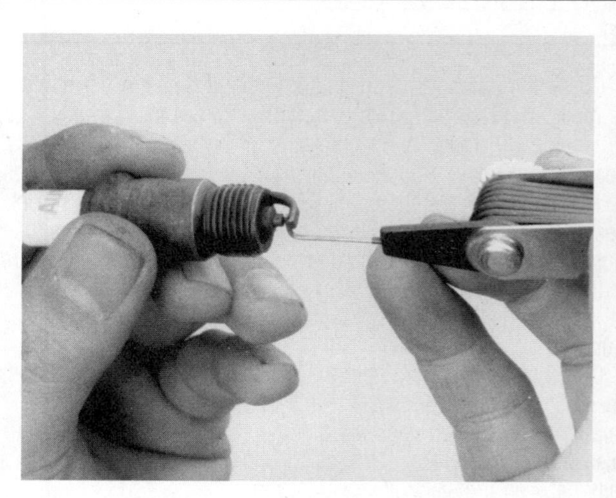

Checking the spark plug gap with a feeler gauge

An oil fouled spark plug indicates an engine with worn piston rings and/or bad valve seals allowing excessive oil to enter the chamber

This spark plug has been left in the engine too long, as evidenced by the extreme gap—Plugs with such an extreme gap can cause misfiring and stumbling accompanied by a noticeable lack of power

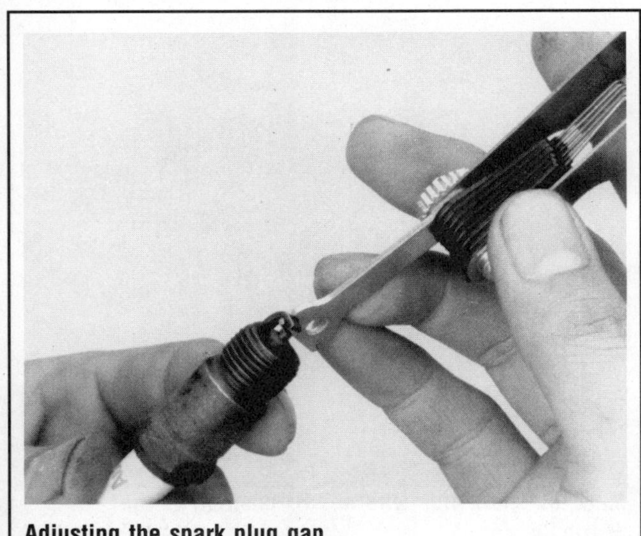
Adjusting the spark plug gap

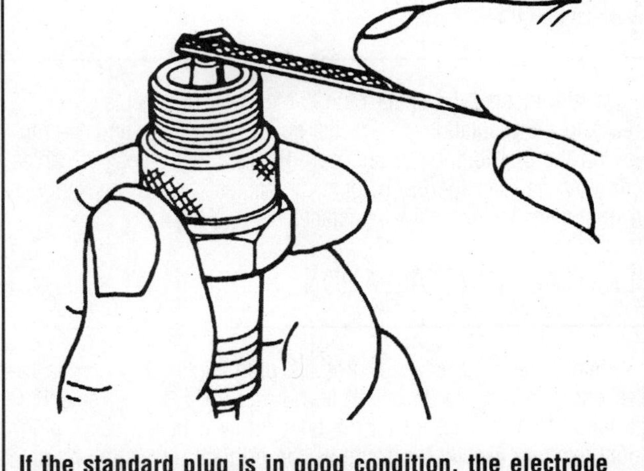
If the standard plug is in good condition, the electrode may be filed flat—CAUTION: do not file platinum plugs

A bridged or almost bridged spark plug, identified by a build-up between the electrodes caused by excessive carbon or oil build-up on the plug

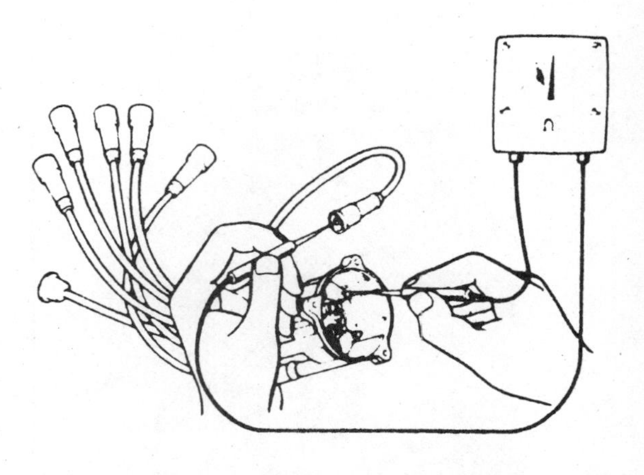

Checking plug wire resistance through the distributor cap with an ohmmeter

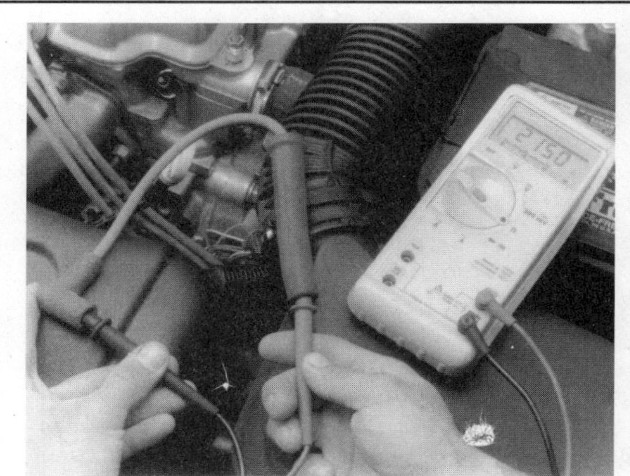

Checking individual plug wire resistance with a digital ohmmeter

Spark Plug Cables

INSPECTION

Visually inspect the spark plug cables for burns, cuts, or breaks in the insulation. Check the spark plug boots and the nipples on the distributor cap and coil. Replace any damaged cables. If no physical damage is obvious, the cables can be checked with an ohmmeter for excessive resistance.

REMOVAL & INSTALLATION

When installing a new set of spark plug cables, replace the cables one at a time so there will be no mix-up. Start by replacing the longest cable first. Install the boot firmly over the spark plug. Route the wire exactly the same as the original. Insert the nipple firmly into the tower on the distributor cap. Repeat the process for each cable.

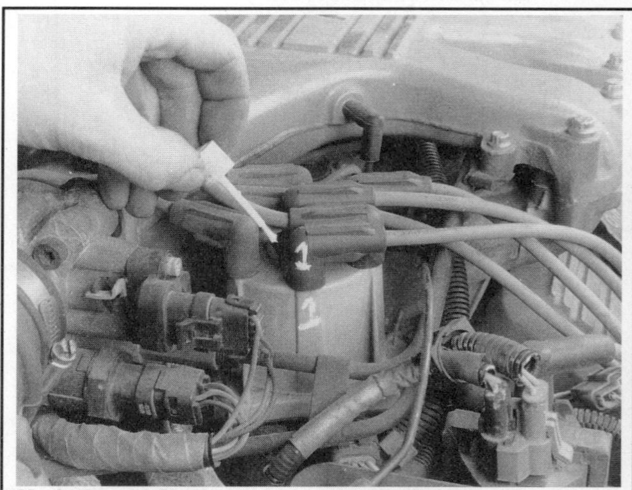

Mark the spark plug wire and its position on the distributor cap . . .

. . . then remove the wires from the distributor tower and the spark plug

FIRING ORDERS

See Figures 3, 4 and 5

To avoid confusion, replace spark plugs and wires one at a time. Or tag them with masking tape.

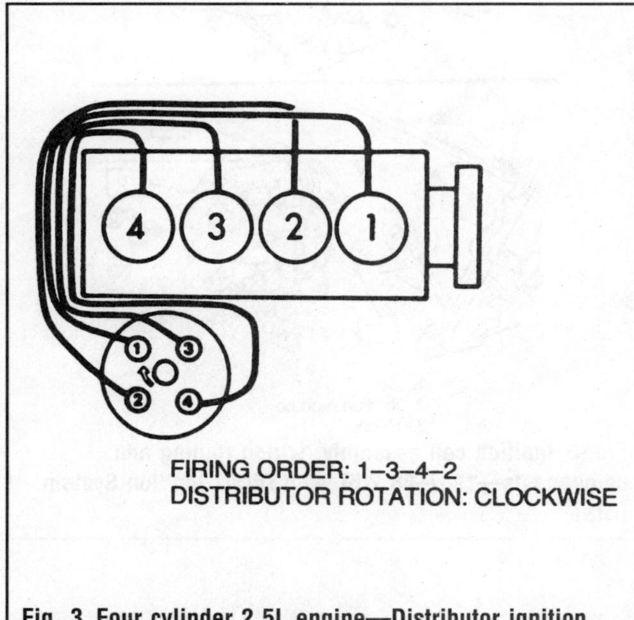

Fig. 3 Four cylinder 2.5L engine—Distributor ignition
Firing order: 1–3–4–2
Distributor rotation: Clockwise

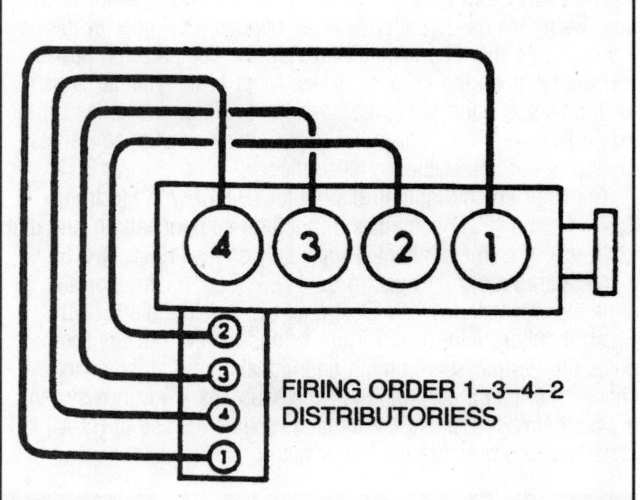

Fig. 4 Four cylinder 2.5L engine Direct Ignition System (DIS)
Firing order: 1–3–4–2
Distributor rotation: Distributorless

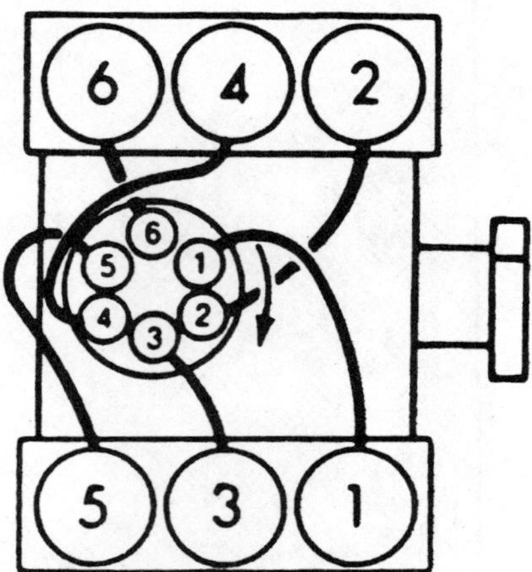

Fig. 5 Six cylinder 2.8L engine Firing order: 1–2–3–4–5–6 Distributor rotation: Clockwise

ELECTRONIC IGNITION

General Information

➧ **See Figure 6**

The Direct Ignition System (DIS) is a distributorless ignition system installed on the 1987–88 2.5L L4 engines (LR8). The DIS system uses individual coils (2), crankshaft sensor, ignition module and Electronic Control Module (ECM) to directly transfer spark to the spark plugs without the use of a distributor assembly. No vacuum or mechanical advances are used.

The DIS system uses a "Waste Spark" method of spark distribution. Each cylinder is paired with its opposing cylinder in the firing order, so that one cylinder fires on the compression stroke and the other on the exhaust stroke. Most of the voltage is used for the compression stroke because little voltage is needed on the exhaust stroke. This dual firing helps reduce exhaust emissions. Timing is not adjustable on these models.

The High Energy Ignition distributor (H.E.I.) with Electronic Spark Timing (EST) combines all ignition components in one unit (2.8L V6). The coil is mounted separately on the (1984–86 2.5L L4).

All spark timing changes in the H.E.I. (EST) distributor are done electronically by and Electronic Control Module (ECM) which monitors information from various engine sensors, computes the desired spark timing and signals the distributor to change the timing accordingly. A back-up spark advance system is incorporated to signal the ignition module in case of (ECM) failure. No vacuum or mechanical advances are used.

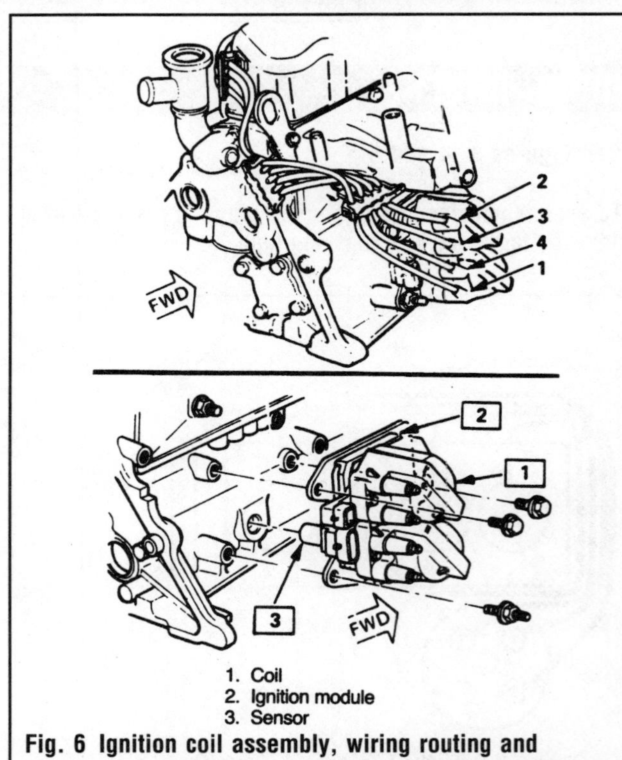

Fig. 6 Ignition coil assembly, wiring routing and components—1987–88 2.5L with Direct Ignition System (DIS)

⁂ WARNING

When using an auxiliary starter switch on HEI systems, the distributor BATT lead must be disconnected. Failure to do this may cause damage to the grounding circuit in the ignition switch.

Ignition Timing

➧ See Figures 7 and 8

TACHOMETER HOOK-UP

The tachometer (Tach) terminal is next to the ignition switch (BAT) connector on the distributor cap on the HEI systems.

⁂ CAUTION

Never ground the TACH terminal; serious module and ignition coil damage will result. If there is any doubt as to the correct tachometer hook-up, check with the tachometer manufacturer.

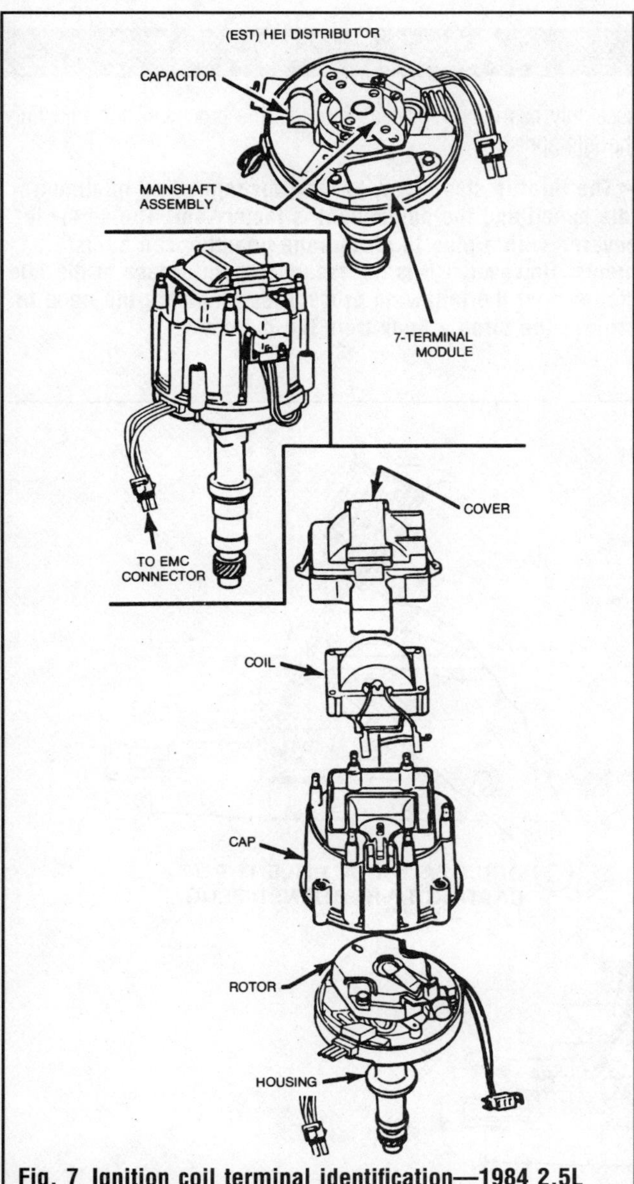

Fig. 7 Ignition coil terminal identification—1984 2.5L engine with a HEI/EST distributor

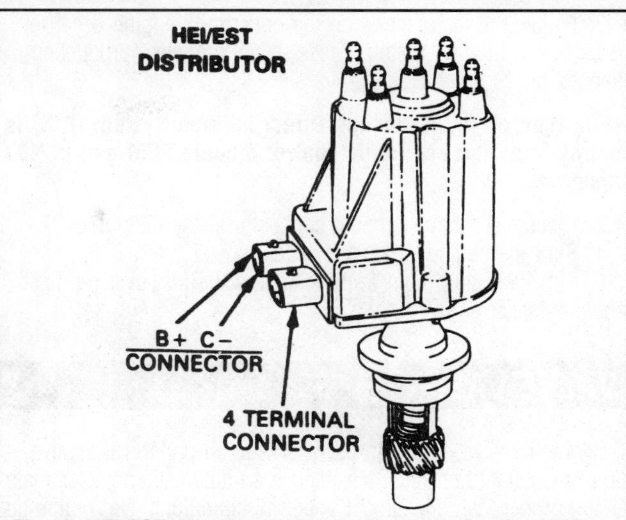

Fig. 8 HEI/EST distributor terminal connections—1986–88 models

INSPECTION & ADJUSTMENT

➧ See Figure 9

⁂ CAUTION

Do not come in contact with any spark plug wires while the engine is running. 20,000–30,000 volts are passing to the spark plugs with engine running.

1. Connect a timing light to the No. 1 spark plug wire according to the light manufacturer's instructions.

➡**Do not pierce the spark plug wire to connect the timing light.**

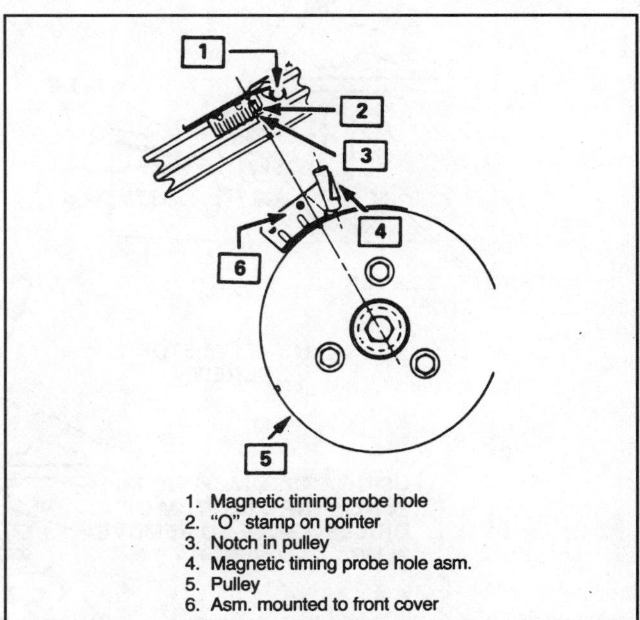

Fig. 9 Location of the ignition timing marks on vehicles equipped with HEI distributor systems

2. Follow the instructions on the underhood engine decal for checking the ignition timing. These reflect the latest production changes for your vehicle.

➡The ignition timing for the Direct Ignition System (DIS) is controlled by the electronic control module ECM and is NOT adjustable.

3. Disconnect the 4 terminal connector at the distributor.
4. Start the engine and run it at idle speed.
5. Aim the timing light at the degree scale just over the harmonic balancer.
6. Adjust the timing by loosening the securing clamp and rotating the distributor until the desired ignition advance is achieved, then tighten the clamp.
7. Loosen the distributor retaining bolt. On some engines its necessary to slide the clamp back slightly. Do not remove the retaining bolt.
8. To advance the timing, rotate the distributor opposite the normal direction of rotor rotation. Retard the timing by rotating the distributor in the normal direction of rotor rotation.

VALVE LASH

Hydraulic valve lifters are used to keep all parts of the valve train in constant contact. Each lifter is an automatic adjuster maintaining proper lash adjustment under all conditions. No routine adjustment is necessary. If further service procedures need to be performed, refer to the "Rocker Arm" procedure in section 3.

IDLE SPEED AND MIXTURE ADJUSTMENT

2.5L Engine

1984–86 MODELS

➧ See Figures 10, 11 and 12

These adjustments are controlled by the Electronic Control Module (ECM). No adjustments are necessary unless the throttle body assembly has been replaced. Below is the procedure for adjusting the idle speed.

➡The throttle stop screw is used for regulating minimum idle speed and the adjustment is factory set. The screw is covered with a plug to discourage unauthorized adjustments. However, i it is necessary to gain access to the idle stop screw, the following procedures eliminate the need to remove the throttle body from the manifold.

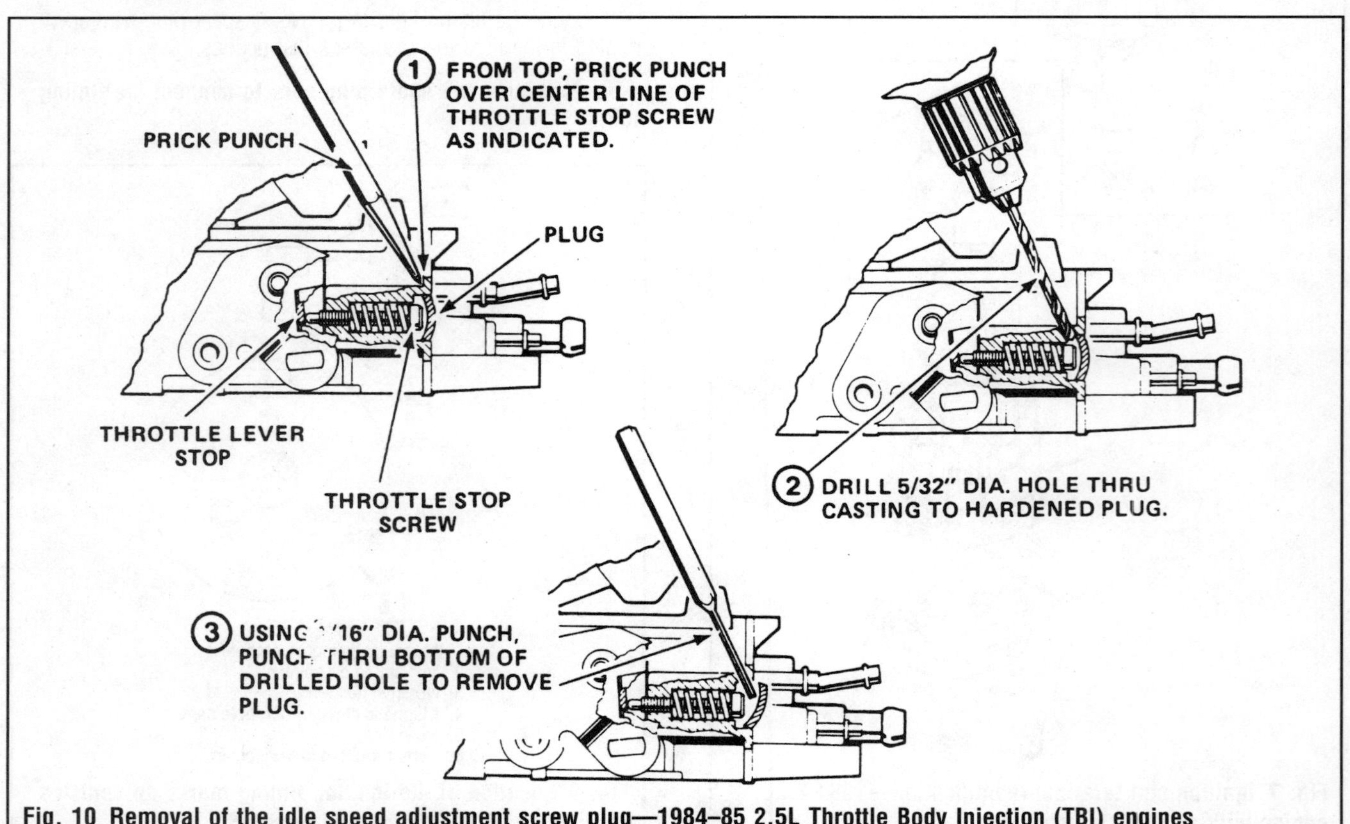

Fig. 10 Removal of the idle speed adjustment screw plug—1984–85 2.5L Throttle Body Injection (TBI) engines

CAUTION

To prevent the engine from running at high rpm, make sure the ignition is OFF and the vehicle is in NEUTRAL before connecting the Idle Air Control (IAC) valve. Failure to do so may result in the vehicle moving.

1. Disconnect the negative (−) battery cable.
2. Remove the air cleaner assembly.
3. Use a prick punch to establish a location over center line of the idle stop screw so a hole can be drilled. Refer to the idle stop screw removal illustration in this section.
4. Drill a 4mm diameter hole through the throttle body casting to the hardened plug and stop.
5. Use a 2mm diameter punch to drive through the bottom of the drilled hole and knock out the plug.

To adjust:

6. Remove the throttle valve cable from the throttle control bracket to allow access to the minimum air adjustment screw (auto trans only).
7. Set the parking brake and block drive wheels. Connect a tachometer to the engine at the distributor (TACH) terminal.
8. Disconnect the Idle Air Control (IAC) valve electrical connector. Refer to the exploded view of the throttle body assembly for IAC valve location.
9. Start the engine, put transaxle selector in PARK (NEUTRAL on manual trans) and allow the rpm to stabilize.
10. Install a J-33047 plug in the idle air passage of the throttle body. Seat the tool in the air passage until it is bottomed and no air leaks exist.
11. Using a No. 20 Torx® bit, turn the idle speed stop screw until the engine rpm is 500±25 for the 2.5L with automatic transaxle and 775±25 rpm for the 2.5L with manual transaxle.
12. Stop the engine and remove the tool from the throttle body.

To install:

13. Install the throttle valve cable into the throttle control bracket (auto trans only). Reconnect the IAC valve electrical connector.
14. Seal the drilled hole in the throttle body casting with silicone sealant or equivalent and install the air cleaner.

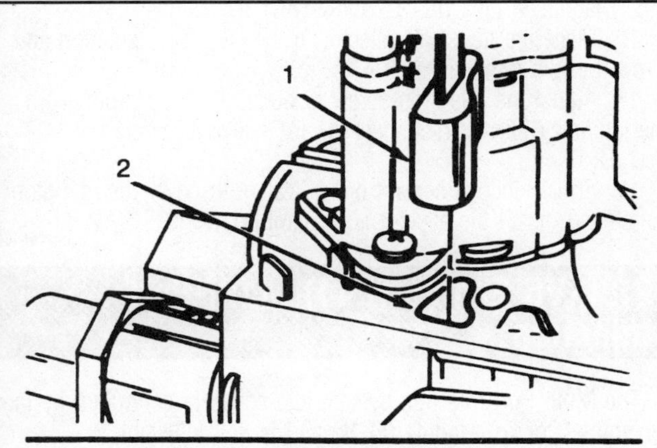

1. Idle air passage plug (J33047/BT 8207-A)
2. Idle air passage

Fig. 11 Use tool J-33047/BT 8207-A to plug the passage—1984–TBI engines

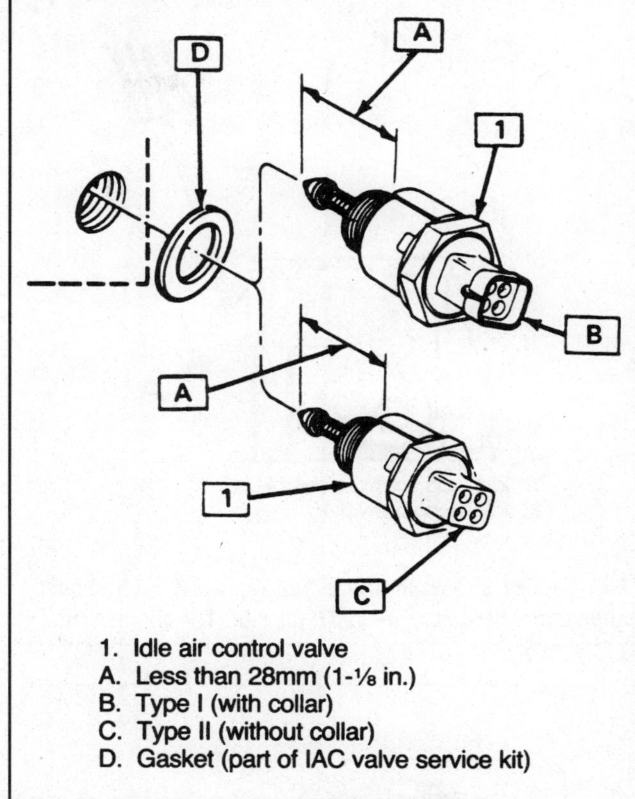

1. Idle air control valve
A. Less than 28mm (1-⅛ in.)
B. Type I (with collar)
C. Type II (without collar)
D. Gasket (part of IAC valve service kit)

Fig. 12 The Idle Air Control (IAC) identification

1987–88 MODELS

See Figures 13, 14 and 15

These adjustments are controlled by the Electronic Control Module (ECM). No adjustments are necessary unless the throttle body assembly has been replaced. Below is the procedure for adjusting the idle speed.

➡The throttle stop screw is used for regulating minimum idle speed and the adjustment is factory set. The screw is covered with a plug to discourage unauthorized adjustments. However, if it is necessary to gain access to the idle stop screw, the following procedures eliminate the need to remove the throttle body from the manifold.

CAUTION

To prevent the engine from running at high rpm, make sure the ignition is OFF and the vehicle is in NEUTRAL before connecting the IAC (Idle Air Control) valve. Failure to do so may result in the vehicle moving.

1. Start the engine and run until it reaches normal operating temperature. Then turn the ignition OFF.
2. Remove the air cleaner and gasket.
3. Pierce the idle stop screw plug with an awle and apply leverage to remove it.
4. Connect a suitable tachometer to the TACH terminal at the distributor.

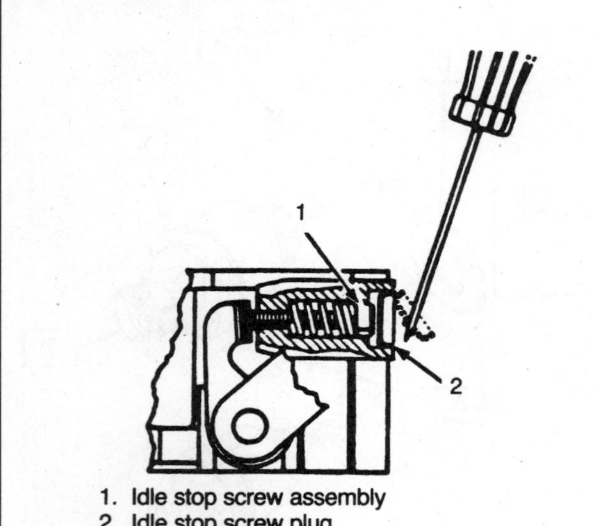

Fig. 13 Use an awl to pierce and remove the idle speed adjustment stop screw—1987–88 2.5L TBI engines

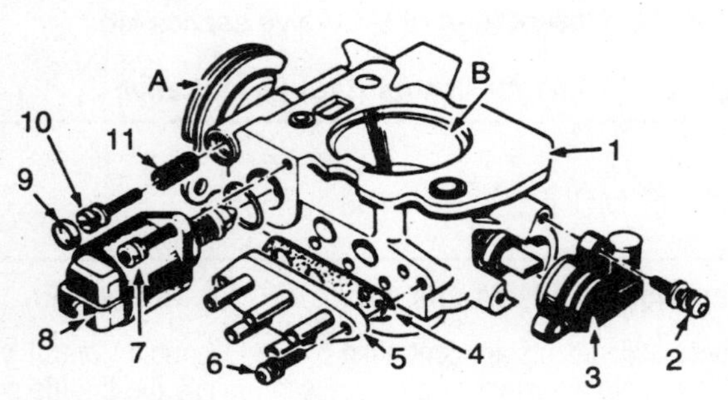

Fig. 14 The Idle Air Control (IAC) valve is located on the lower side of the throttle body assembly—1987–88 2.5L TBI engines

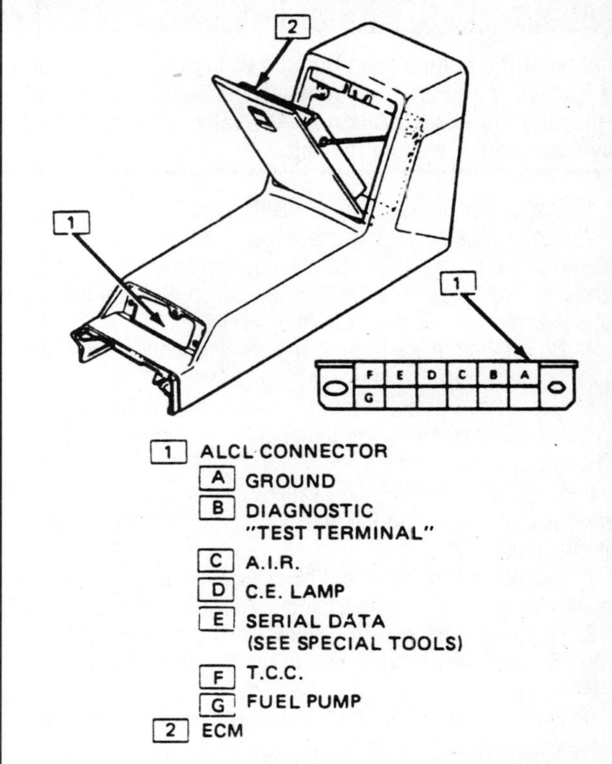

Fig. 15 The Assembly Line Diagnostic Link (ALDL) is located in the passenger compartment console

5. With the idle air control (IAC) valve connected, ground the diagnostic terminal of the Assembly Line Diagnostic Link (ALDL) connector. Refer to "ALDL Connector Location" illustration in this section.
6. Turn the ignition ON, but do *not* start the engine. Wait at least 45 seconds.
7. With the ignition ON, engine *not* running, test terminal grounded, disconnect the IAC valve electrical connector.
8. Block the drive wheels and apply the emergency brake.
9. Remove the ground from the diagnostic terminal Assembly Line Diagnostic Link (ALDL) and START the engine.
10. Place the transaxle selector in the NEUTRAL position and allow the idle to stabilize.
11. Adjust the idle stop screw to obtain 600 ± 25 rpm. Turn the ignition OFF and reconnect the IAC valve electrical connector.
12. Apply silicone sealant or equivalent to cover the idle stop screw and install the air cleaner assembly.

2.8L V6 Engine (L44) Multi-Port Injection

The Multi-Port Injection system idle speed is controlled by the Electronic Control Module (ECM) and is not adjustable.

3

ENGINE AND ENGINE OVERHAUL

ENGINE ELECTRICAL

Understanding Electricity

For any electrical system to operate, there must be a complete circuit. This simply means that the power flow from the battery must make a full circle. When an electrical component is operating, power flows from the battery to the components, passes through the component (load) causing it to function, and returns to the battery through the ground path of the circuit. This ground may be either another wire or a metal part of the vehicle (depending upon how the component is designed).

BASIC CIRCUITS

Perhaps the easiest way to visualize a circuit is to think of connecting a light bulb (with two wires attached to it) to the battery. If one of the two wires was attached to the negative post (−) of the battery and the other wire to the positive post (+), the circuit would be complete and the light bulb would illuminate. Electricity could follow a path from the battery to the bulb and back to the battery. It's not hard to see that with longer wires on our light bulb, it could be mounted anywhere on the vehicle. Further, one wire could be fitted with a switch so that the light could be turned on and off. Various other items could be added to our primitive circuit to make the light flash, become brighter or dimmer under certain conditions, or advise the user that it's burned out.

Ground

Some automotive components are grounded through their mounting points. The electrical current runs through the chassis of the vehicle and returns to the battery through the ground (−) cable; if you look, you'll see that the battery ground cable connects between the battery and the body of the vehicle.

Load

Every complete circuit must include a "load" (something to use the electricity coming from the source). If you were to connect a wire between the two terminals of the battery (DON'T do this, but take our word for it) without the light bulb, the battery would attempt to deliver its entire power supply from one pole to another almost instantly. This is a short circuit. The electricity is taking a short cut to get to ground and is not being used by any load in the circuit. This sudden and uncontrolled electrical flow can cause great damage to other components in the circuit and can develop a tremendous amount of heat. A short in an automotive wiring harness can develop sufficient heat to melt the insulation on all the surrounding wires and reduce a multiple wire cable to one sad lump of plastic and copper. Two common causes of shorts are broken insulation (thereby exposing the wire to contact with surrounding metal surfaces or other wires) or a failed switch (the pins inside the switch come out of place and touch each other).

Switches and Relays

Some electrical components which require a large amount of current to operate also have a relay in their circuit. Since these circuits carry a large amount of current (amperage or amps), the thickness of the wire in the circuit (wire gauge) is also greater. If this large wire were connected from the load to the control switch on the dash, the switch would have to carry the high amperage load and the dash would be twice as large to accommodate wiring harnesses as thick as your wrist. To prevent these problems, a relay is used. The large wires in the circuit are connected from the battery to one side of the relay and from the opposite side of the relay to the load. The relay is normally open, preventing current from passing through the circuit. An additional, smaller wire is connected from the relay to the control switch for the circuit. When the control switch is turned on, it grounds the smaller wire

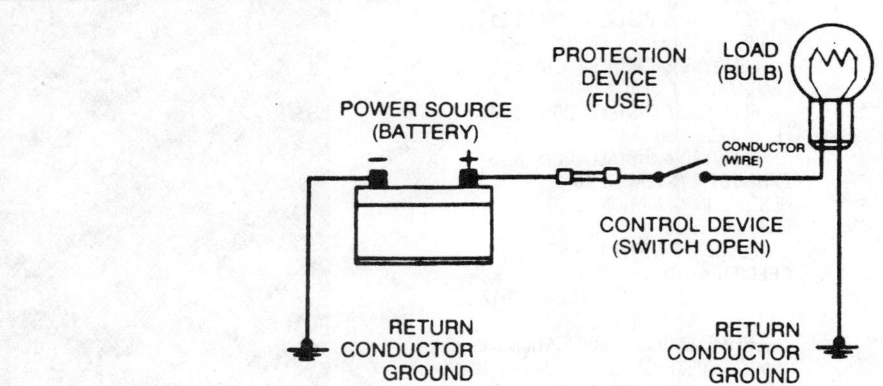

Here is an example of a simple automotive circuit. When the switch is closed, power from the positive battery terminal flows through the fuse, the switch and then the load (light bulb). The light illuminates and the circuit is completed through the return conductor and the vehicle ground. If the light did not work, the tests could be made with a voltmeter or test light at the battery, fuse, switch or bulb socket

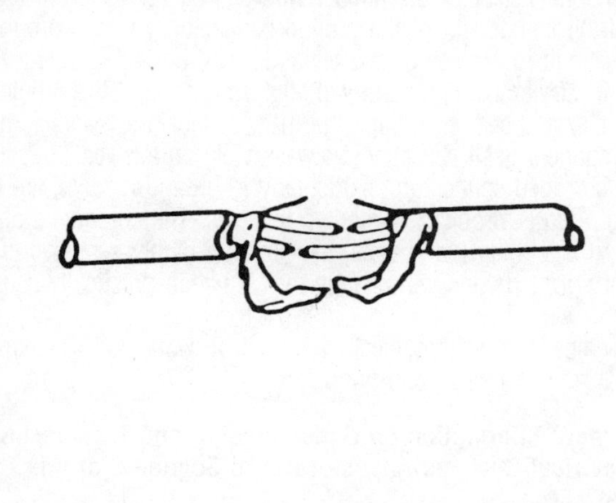

Damaged insulation can allow wires to break (causing an open circuit) or touch (causing a short circuit)

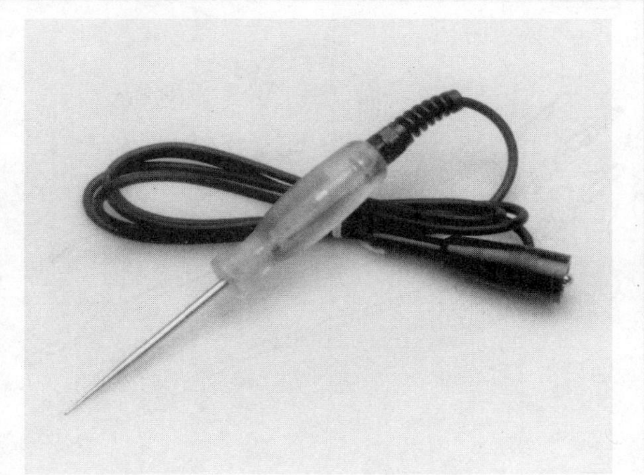

A 12 volt test light is useful when checking parts of a circuit for power

to the relay and completes its circuit. The main switch inside the relay closes, sending power to the component without routing the main power through the inside of the vehicle. Some common circuits which may use relays are the horn, headlights, starter and rear window defogger systems.

Protective Devices

It is possible for larger surges of current to pass through the electrical system of your vehicle. If this surge of current were to reach the load in the circuit, it could burn it out or severely damage it. To prevent this, fuses, circuit breakers and/or fusible links are connected into the supply wires of the electrical system. These items are nothing more than a built-in weak spot in the system. It's much easier to go to a known location (the fusebox) to see why a circuit is inoperative than to dissect 15 feet of wiring under the dashboard, looking for what happened.

When an electrical current of excessive power passes through the fuse, the fuse blows (the conductor melts) and breaks the circuit, preventing the passage of current and protecting the components.

A circuit breaker is basically a self repairing fuse. It will open the circuit in the same fashion as a fuse, but when either the short is removed or the surge subsides, the circuit breaker resets itself and does not need replacement.

A fuse link (fusible link or main link) is a wire that acts as a fuse. One of these is normally connected between the starter relay and the main wiring harness under the hood. Since the starter is usually the highest electrical draw on the vehicle, an internal short during starting could direct about 130 amps into the wrong places. Consider the damage potential of introducing this current into a system whose wiring is rated at 15 amps and you'll understand the need for protection. Since this link is very early in the electrical path, it's the first place to look if nothing on the vehicle works, but the battery seems to be charged and is properly connected.

TROUBLESHOOTING

Electrical problems generally fall into one of three areas:

- The component that is not functioning is not receiving current.

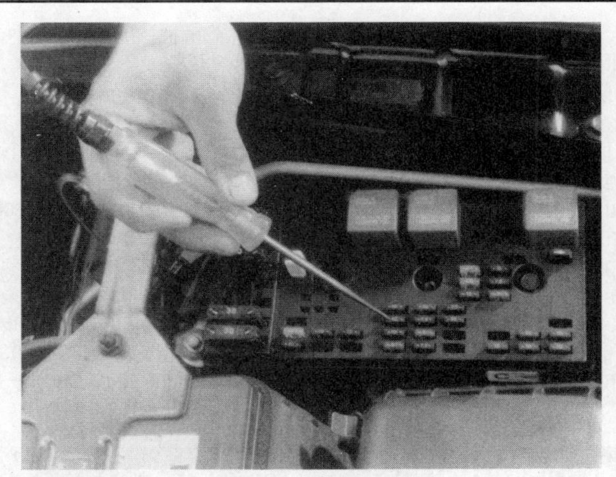

Here, someone is checking a circuit by making sure there is power to the component's fuse

- The component is receiving power but is not using it or is using it incorrectly (component failure).
- The component is improperly grounded.

The circuit can be can be checked with a test light and a jumper wire. The test light is a device that looks like a pointed screwdriver with a wire on one end and a bulb in its handle. A jumper wire is simply a piece of wire with alligator clips or special terminals on each end. If a component is not working, you must follow a systematic plan to determine which of the three causes is the villain.

1. Turn ON the switch that controls the item not working.

➡Some items only work when the ignition switch is turned ON.

2. Disconnect the power supply wire from the component.
3. Attach the ground wire of a test light or a voltmeter to a good metal ground.
4. Touch the end probe of the test light (or the positive lead of the voltmeter) to the power wire; if there is current in the wire, the light in the test light will come on (or the voltmeter will indicate

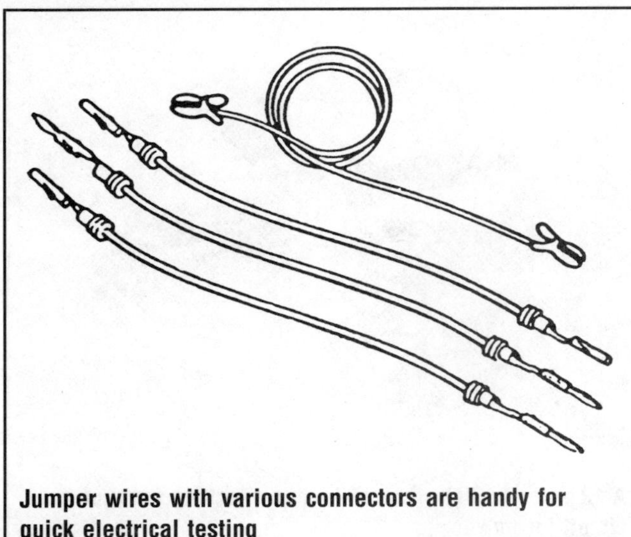

Jumper wires with various connectors are handy for quick electrical testing

the amount of voltage). You have now established that current is getting to the component.

5. Turn the ignition or dash switch **OFF** and reconnect the wire to the component.

If there was no power, then the problem is between the battery and the component. This includes all the switches, fuses, relays and the battery itself. The next place to look is the fusebox; check carefully either by eye or by using the test light across the fuse clips. The easiest way to check is to simply replace the fuse. If the fuse is blown, and upon replacement, immediately blows again, there is a short between the fuse and the component. This is generally (not always) a sign of an internal short in the component. Disconnect the power wire at the component again and replace the fuse; if the fuse holds, the component is the problem.

**** WARNING**

DO NOT test a component by running a jumper wire from the battery UNLESS you are certain that it operates on 12 volts. Many electronic components are designed to operate with less voltage and connecting them to 12 volts could destroy them. Jumper wires are best used to bypass a portion of the circuit (such as a stretch of wire or a switch) that DOES NOT contain a resistor and is suspected to be bad.

If all the fuses are good and the component is not receiving power, find the switch for the circuit. Bypass the switch with the jumper wire. This is done by connecting one end of the jumper to the power wire coming into the switch and the other end to the wire leaving the switch. If the component comes to life, the switch has failed.

**** WARNING**

Never substitute the jumper for the component. The circuit needs the electrical load of the component. If you bypass it, you will cause a short circuit.

Checking the ground for any circuit can mean tracing wires to the body, cleaning connections or tightening mounting bolts for the component itself. If the jumper wire can be connected to the case of the component or the ground connector, you can ground the other end to a piece of clean, solid metal on the vehicle. Again, if the component starts working, you've found the problem.

A systematic search through the fuse, connectors, switches and the component itself will almost always yield an answer. Loose and/or corroded connectors, particularly in ground circuits, are becoming a larger problem in modern vehicles. The computers and on-board electronic (solid state) systems are highly sensitive to improper grounds and will change their function drastically if one occurs.

Remember that for any electrical circuit to work, ALL the connections must be clean and tight.

➡For more information on Understanding and Troubleshooting Electrical Systems, please refer to Section 6 of this manual.

Battery, Starting and Charging Systems

BASIC OPERATING PRINCIPLES

Battery

The battery is the first link in the chain of mechanisms which work together to provide cranking of the automobile engine. In most modern vehicles, the battery is a lead/acid electrochemical device consisting of six 2v subsections (cells) connected in series so the unit is capable of producing approximately 12v of electrical pressure. Each subsection consists of a series of positive and negative plates held a short distance apart in a solution of sulfuric acid and water.

The two types of plates are of dissimilar metals. This sets-up a chemical reaction, and it is this reaction which produces current flow from the battery when its positive and negative terminals are connected to an electrical accessory such as a lamp or motor. The continued transfer of electrons would eventually convert the sulfuric acid to water, and make the two plates identical in chemical composition. As electrical energy is removed from the battery, its voltage output tends to drop. Thus, measuring battery voltage and battery electrolyte composition are two ways of checking the ability of the unit to supply power. During engine cranking, electrical energy is removed from the battery. However, if the charging circuit is in good condition and the operating conditions are normal, the power removed from the battery will be replaced by the alternator which will force electrons back through the battery, reversing the normal flow, and restoring the battery to its original chemical state.

Starting System

The battery and starting motor are linked by very heavy electrical cables designed to minimize resistance to the flow of current. Generally, the major power supply cable that leaves the battery goes directly to the starter, while other electrical system needs are supplied by a smaller cable. During starter operation, power flows from the battery to the starter and is grounded through the vehicle's frame/body or engine and the battery's negative ground strap.

The starter is a specially designed, direct current electric motor capable of producing a great amount of power for its size. One thing that allows the motor to produce a great deal of power is its tremendous rotating speed. It drives the engine through a tiny pinion gear (attached to the starter's armature), which drives the very large flywheel ring gear at a greatly reduced speed. Another factor allowing it to produce so much power is that only intermittent operation is required of it. Thus, little allowance for air circulation is necessary, and the windings can be built into a very small space.

The starter solenoid is a magnetic device which employs the small current supplied by the start circuit of the ignition switch. This magnetic action moves a plunger which mechanically engages the starter and closes the heavy switch connecting it to the battery. The starting switch circuit usually consists of the starting switch contained within the ignition switch, a neutral safety switch or clutch pedal switch, and the wiring necessary to connect these in series with the starter solenoid or relay.

The pinion, a small gear, is mounted to a one way drive clutch. This clutch is splined to the starter armature shaft. When the ignition switch is moved to the **START** position, the solenoid plunger slides the pinion toward the flywheel ring gear via a collar and spring. If the teeth on the pinion and flywheel match properly, the pinion will engage the flywheel immediately. If the gear teeth butt one another, the spring will be compressed and will force the gears to mesh as soon as the starter turns far enough to allow them to do so. As the solenoid plunger reaches the end of its travel, it closes the contacts that connect the battery and starter, then the engine is cranked.

As soon as the engine starts, the flywheel ring gear begins turning fast enough to drive the pinion at an extremely high rate of speed. At this point, the one-way clutch begins allowing the pinion to spin faster than the starter shaft so that the starter will not operate at excessive speed. When the ignition switch is released from the starter position, the solenoid is de-energized, and a spring pulls the gear out of mesh interrupting the current flow to the starter.

Some starters employ a separate relay, mounted away from the starter, to switch the motor and solenoid current on and off. The relay replaces the solenoid electrical switch, but does not eliminate the need for a solenoid mounted on the starter used to mechanically engage the starter drive gears. The relay is used to reduce the amount of current the starting switch must carry.

Charging System

The automobile charging system provides electrical power for operation of the vehicle's ignition system, starting system and all electrical accessories. The battery serves as an electrical surge or storage tank, storing (in chemical form) the energy originally produced by the engine driven generator. The system also provides a means of regulating output to protect the battery from being overcharged and to avoid excessive voltage to the accessories.

The storage battery is a chemical device incorporating parallel lead plates in a tank containing a sulfuric acid/water solution. Adjacent plates are slightly dissimilar, and the chemical reaction of the two dissimilar plates produces electrical energy when the battery is connected to a load such as the starter motor. The chemical reaction is reversible, so that when the generator is producing a voltage (electrical pressure) greater than that produced by the battery, electricity is forced into the battery, and the battery is returned to its fully charged state.

Newer automobiles use alternating current generators or alternators, because they are more efficient, can be rotated at higher speeds, and have fewer brush problems. In an alternator, the field usually rotates while all the current produced passes only through the stator winding. The brushes bear against continuous slip rings. This causes the current produced to periodically reverse the direction of its flow. Diodes (electrical one way valves) block the flow of current from traveling in the wrong direction. A series of diodes is wired together to permit the alternating flow of the stator to be rectified back to 12 volts DC for use by the vehicle's electrical system.

The voltage regulating function is performed by a regulator. The regulator is often built in to the alternator; this system is termed an integrated or internal regulator.

Alternator

ALTERNATOR PRECAUTIONS

To prevent damage to the alternator and regulator, the following precautions should be taken when working with the electrical system.

1. Never reverse the battery connections.
2. Booster batteries for starting must be connected properly: positive-to-positive (+) and negative-to-negative (−).
3. Disconnect the battery cables before using a fast charger; the charger has a tendency to force current through the diodes in the opposite direction for which they were designed. This burns out the diodes.
4. Never use a fast charger as a booster for starting the vehicle.
5. Never disconnect the voltage regulator while the engine is running.
6. Avoid long soldering times when replacing diodes or transistors. Prolonged heat is damaging to AC (alternating current) generators.
7. Do not use test lamps of more than 12 volts (V) for checking diode continuity.
8. Do not short across or ground any of the terminals on the AC (alternating current) generator.
9. The polarity of the battery, generator, and regulator must be matched and considered before making any electrical connections within the system.
10. Never operate the alternator on an open circuit. Make sure that all connections within the circuit are clean and tight.
11. Disconnect the battery terminals when performing any service on the electrical system. This will eliminate the possibility of accidental reversal of polarity.
12. Disconnect the battery ground cable if arc welding is to be done on any part of the car.

REMOVAL & INSTALLATION

Testing or replacing individual components in the alternator is not practical or economical for a do-it-yourself mechanic. The tools needed are expensive and would not be practical to purchase to use only a few times. Complete rebuilt units can be purchased through your local parts distributor for a fraction of the cost of a new unit.

4-2.5L Engine

1984–86 MODELS

1. Disconnect the negative (−) battery cable.

CAUTION

Failure to observe this step may cause personal injury from hot battery leads at the alternator.

2. Remove the air cleaner assembly and move out of the way.
3. Disconnect the upper strut mount.
4. Remove the alternator adjusting bolt, upper adjusting bracket and drive belt.
5. Disconnect the wiring from the back of the alternator.
6. Lower the alternator mounting bracket and remove the alternator from the bottom of the vehicle.

To install:

7. Position the alternator and bracket assembly onto engine and install the upper and lower adjusting bolts. Adjust the belt so that there is ¼ in. of play at the longest point. Torque the bolts to 25 ft. lbs. (34 Nm).

➡Do not pry on the aluminum housing of the alternator. Pry on the steel center to adjust belt tension.

8. Connect the wiring to the back of the alternator. Install the upper strut mount. Install the air cleaner assembly. Reconnect the negative (−) battery cable.

1987–88 MODELS

➧ See Figure 1

1. Disconnect the negative (−) battery cable.

CAUTION

Failure to observe this step may cause personal injury from hot battery lead at the alternator.

2. Remove the air cleaner assembly and move out of the way.
3. Remove the rear bracket from the alternator.
4. Loosen the bolt at the belt tensioner and remove the belt. Refer to the accompanying illustration.
5. Disconnect the electrical connectors from the alternator. Testing or replacing individual components in the alternator is not practical or economical for a do-it-yourself mechanic. The tools needed are expensive and would not be practical to purchase to use only a few times. Complete rebuilt units can be purchased from your local parts distributor for a fraction of the cost of new.
6. Remove the lower through bolt at the bottom of the alternator and remove the alternator.

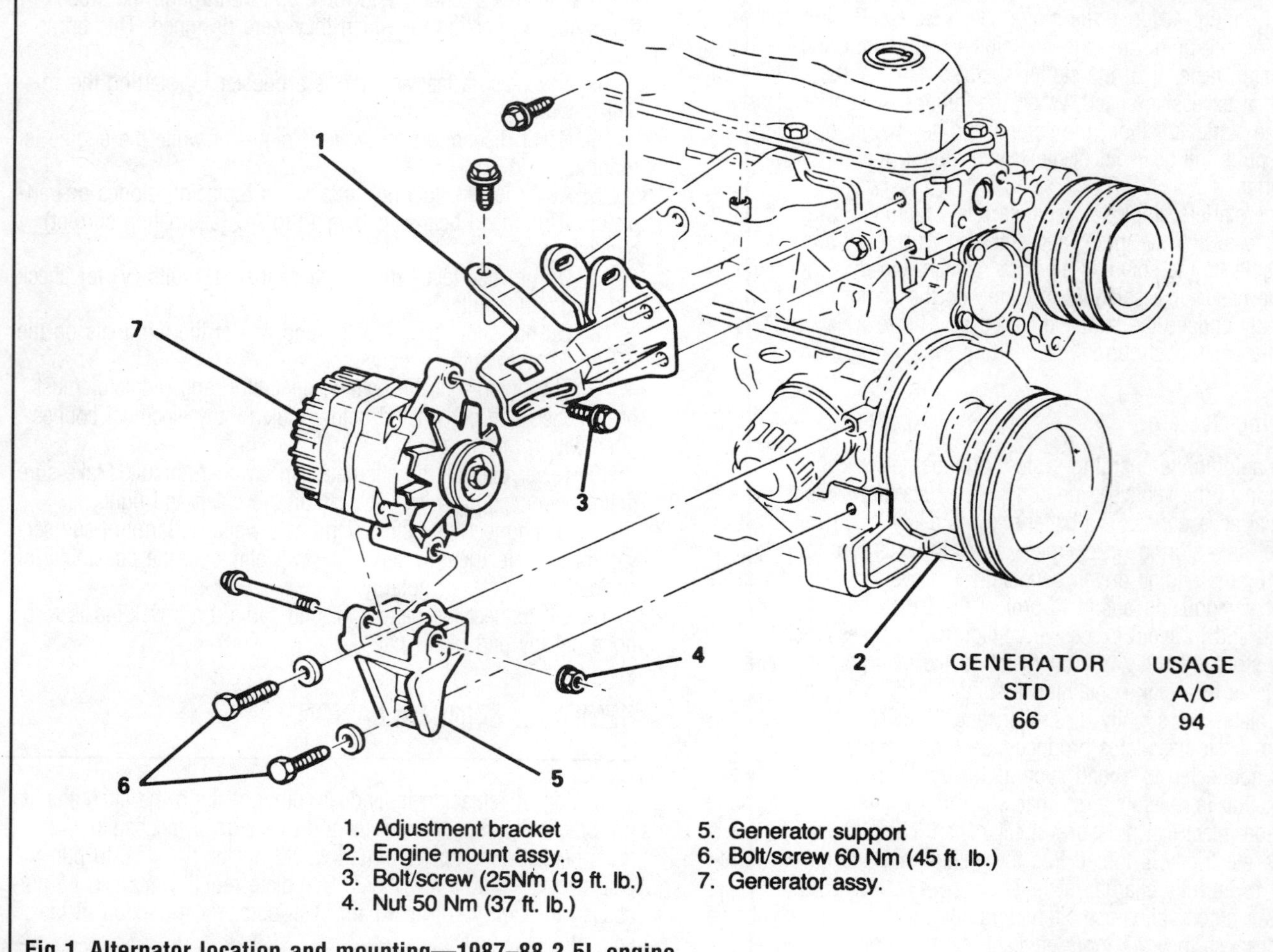

Fig.1 Alternator location and mounting—1987–88 2.5L engine

To install:

7. Position the alternator and bracket assembly onto engine and install the lower through bolt.
8. Install the belt and adjust so that there is 1/4 in. of play at the longest point.
9. Install the rear bracket bolt and torque to 20 ft. lbs. (27 Nm).

➡Do not pry on the aluminum housing of the alternator. Pry on the steel center to adjust belt tension.

10. Connect the wiring to the back of the alternator. Install the upper strut mount. Install the air cleaner assembly. Reconnect the negative (−) battery cable.

6-2.8L Engine

See Figure 2

1. Disconnect the negative (−) battery cable.

**** CAUTION**

Failure to observe this step may cause personal injury from hot battery lead at the alternator.

2. Loosen the top alternator bracket-to-engine bolt.
3. Remove the two upper alternator bracket bolts.
4. Raise the vehicle and support with jackstands.
5. Remove the rear wheel assemblies.
6. Remove the right rear splash guard.
7. Remove the outer tie rod end and swing up and to the left.
8. Lower the alternator bracket-to-engine bolt.

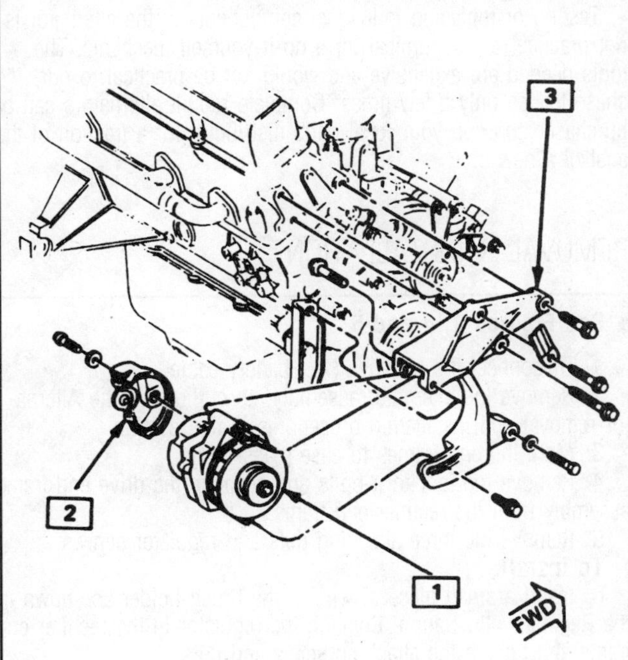

Fig. 2 View of the alternator location and mounting on a 2.8L engine—1 is the alternator, 2 is the shield and 3 is the bracket

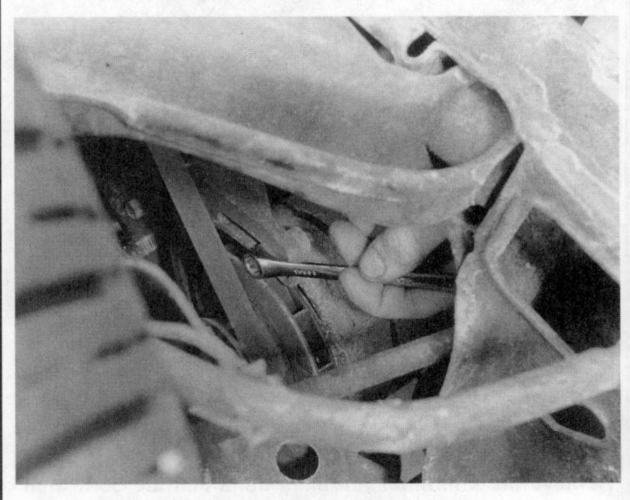
Loosen the alternator bracket adjusting bolt

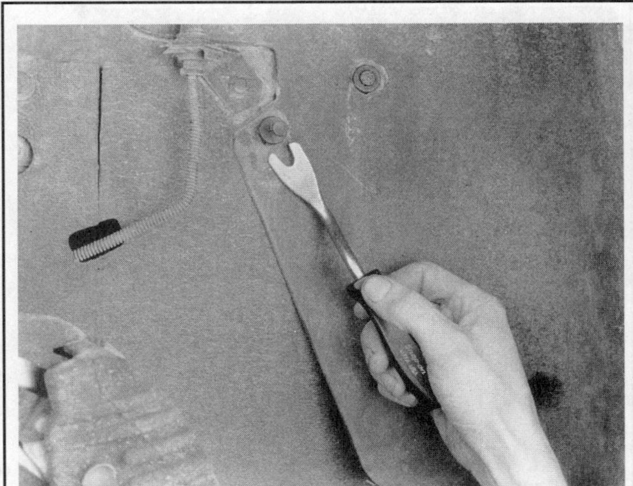
Remove the right rear splash shield retainers . . .

. . . then remove the splash shield from the vehicle

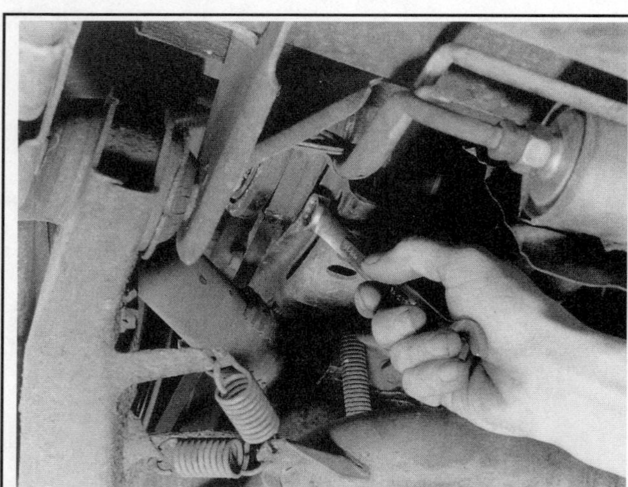
Remove the alternator retaining bolts and the belt, then . . .

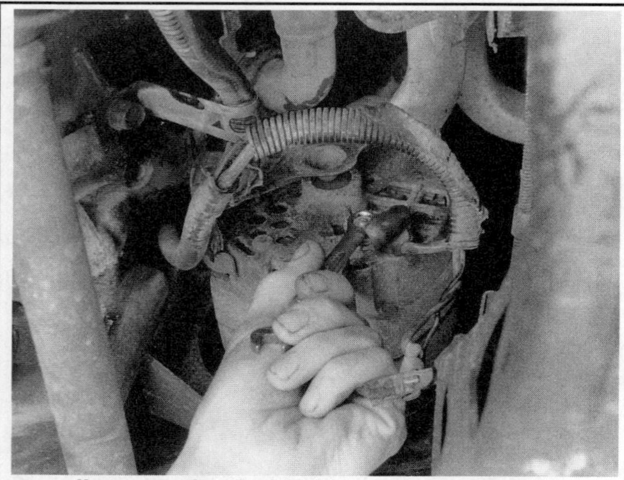
. . . disengage the electrical connectors from the rear of the alternator

Remove the alternator from the vehicle

9. Remove the alternator adjusting bolts and belt.
10. Remove the upper alternator-to-bracket bolt and electrical connectors.
11. Rotate the alternator bracket lower end toward the engine. Remove the alternator and shield.

To install:

1. Install the alternator and shield assembly.
2. Connect the electrical wires in back of alternator.
3. Install the upper alternator-to-bracket bolt and adjusting bolt.
4. Rotate the alternator and bracket up into position and install the lower alternator bracket-to-engine bolt.
5. Install the two upper alternator-to-engine bolts and torque to 37 ft. lbs. (50 Nm).
6. Install the rear alternator bracket-to-engine bolt and torque to 59 ft. lbs. (80 Nm).
7. Install the alternator belt and adjust belt. Torque the tensioner bolt to 20 ft. lbs. (27 Nm).
8. Install the tie rod end and torque the nut to 50 ft. lbs. (68 Nm). Do NOT change adjustment.
9. Install the splash guards, rear wheel assemblies and torque the lug nuts to 100 ft. lbs. (140 Nm).
10. Lower the vehicle and torque the rear alternator bracket-to-alternator bolt to 37 ft. lbs. (50 Nm). Reconnect the negative (−) battery cable.

Regulator

The voltage regulator is a solid-state, non-adjustable unit integral with the alternator. The alternator must be disassembled to remove the regulator.

Testing or replacing individual components in the alternator is not practical or economical for a do-it-yourself mechanic. The tools needed are expensive and would not be practical to purchase to use only a few times. Complete rebuilt alternators can be purchased through your local parts distributor for a fraction of the cost of a new unit.

REMOVAL & INSTALLATION

➧ See Figures 3, 4 and 5

1. Disconnect the negative (−) battery cable.
2. Remove the alternator assembly, as outlined in the Alternator removal and installation procedures in this section.
3. Mark the end frames to ease reassembly.
4. Remove the four thru-bolts and separate the drive end frame assembly from the rectifier end frame.
5. Remove the three attaching nuts and regulator screws.

To install:

6. Insert a small piece of wire in the brush holder as shown in the Regulator illustration. Position the regulator in the rectifier end frame and tighten the attaching screw and nuts.
7. Install the rectifier end frame in the same position as removed and tighten the four thru-bolts. *Make sure to remove the brush retaining wire.*
8. Install the alternator assembly on the vehicle, as outlined in the Alternator removal and installation procedures in this section.

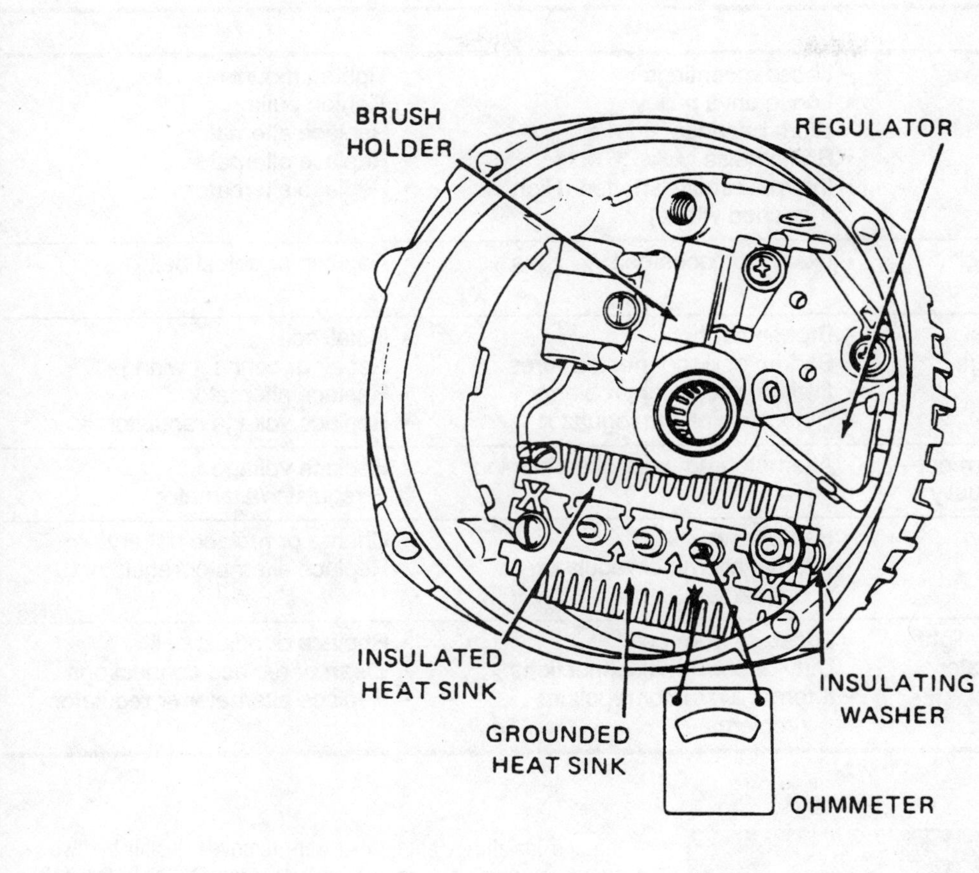

Fig. 3 Position of the voltage regulator—10SI–27SI alternators

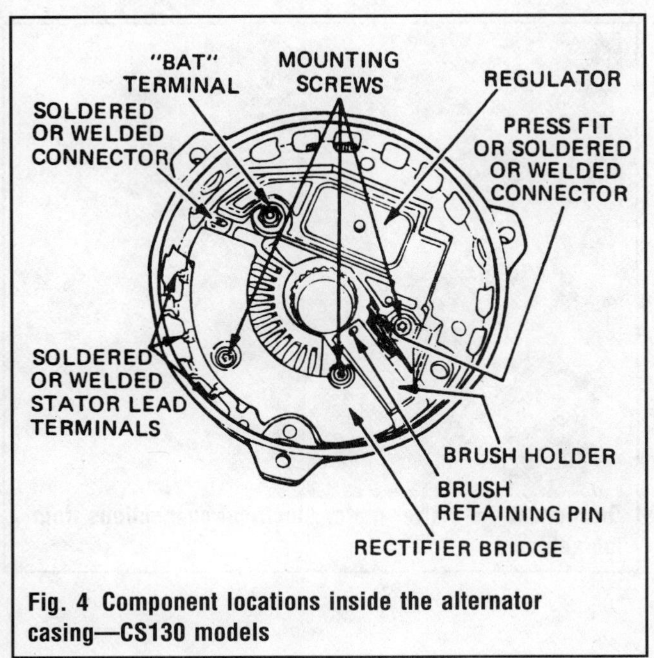

Fig. 4 Component locations inside the alternator casing—CS130 models

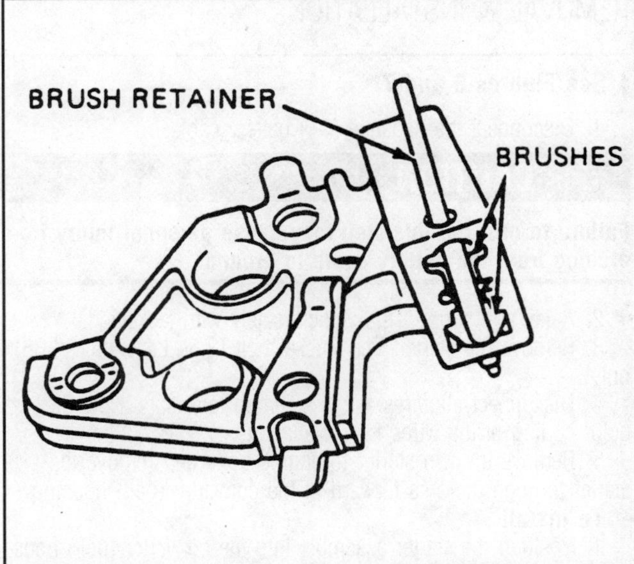

Fig. 5 Insert a small piece of wire into the brush holder to retain the brushes until the unit is properly installed

Troubleshooting Basic Charging System Problems

Problem	Cause	Solution
Noisy alternator	• Loose mountings • Loose drive pulley • Worn bearings • Brush noise • Internal circuits shorted (High pitched whine)	• Tighten mounting bolts • Tighten pulley • Replace alternator • Replace alternator • Replace alternator
Squeal when starting engine or accelerating	• Glazed or loose belt	• Replace or adjust belt
Indicator light remains on or ammeter indicates discharge (engine running)	• Broken fan belt • Broken or disconnected wires • Internal alternator problems • Defective voltage regulator	• Install belt • Repair or connect wiring • Replace alternator • Replace voltage regulator
Car light bulbs continually burn out—battery needs water continually	• Alternator/regulator overcharging	• Replace voltage regulator/alternator
Car lights flare on acceleration	• Battery low • Internal alternator/regulator problems	• Charge or replace battery • Replace alternator/regulator
Low voltage output (alternator light flickers continually or ammeter needle wanders)	• Loose or worn belt • Dirty or corroded connections • Internal alternator/regulator problems	• Replace or adjust belt • Clean or replace connections • Replace alternator or regulator

Starter

Never operate the starter motor more than 30 seconds at a time without pausing to allow it to cool for at least two minutes. Overheating, caused by excessive cranking, will seriously damage the starter motor.

REMOVAL & INSTALLATION

See Figures 6 and 7

1. Disconnect the negative (−) battery cable.

CAUTION

Failure to observe this step may cause personal injury from arching from the battery cable to ground.

2. Raise and support the vehicle safely with jackstands.
3. Remove the starter rear bracket bolt (2.5L L4 engine (LR8) only).
4. Disconnect all wires at the solenoid terminals. Note the color coding of the wires for installation.
5. Remove the two starter-to-engine bolts and remove the starter through the area forward of the converter (bell) housing.

To install:

1. Position the starter assembly into the converter (bell) housing and install any shims that were removed. Install the two starter-to-engine mounting bolts and torque to 32 ft. lbs. (43 Nm).
2. Install the rear bracket (2.5L L4 engine (LR8) only).
3. Install the heat shield, if so equipped.
4. Lower the vehicle.

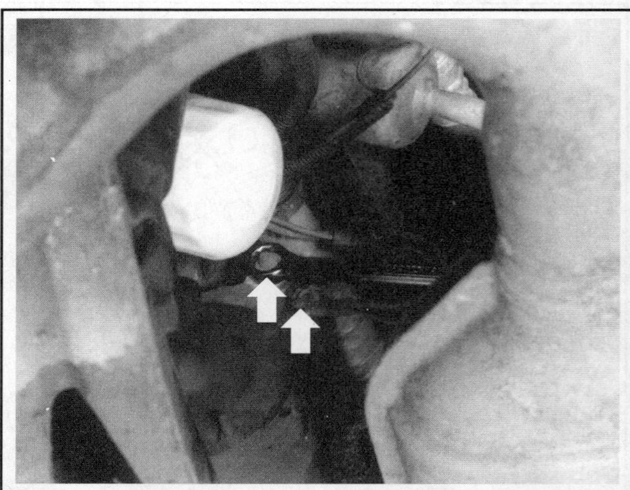

Disconnect the starter motor electrical connections from the solenoid

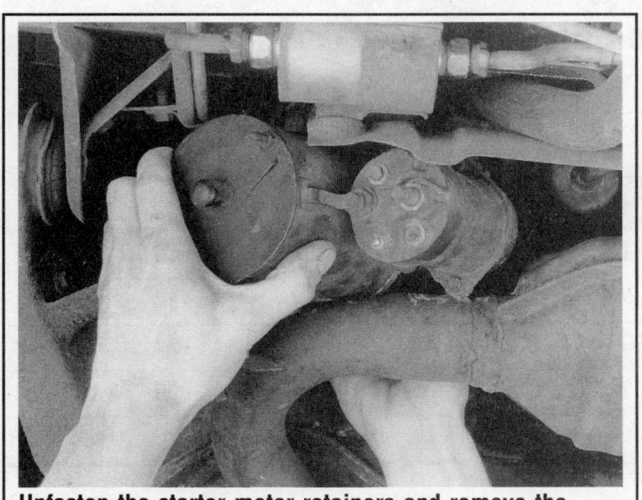

Unfasten the starter motor retainers and remove the starter from the vehicle

3
1
FWD
L44

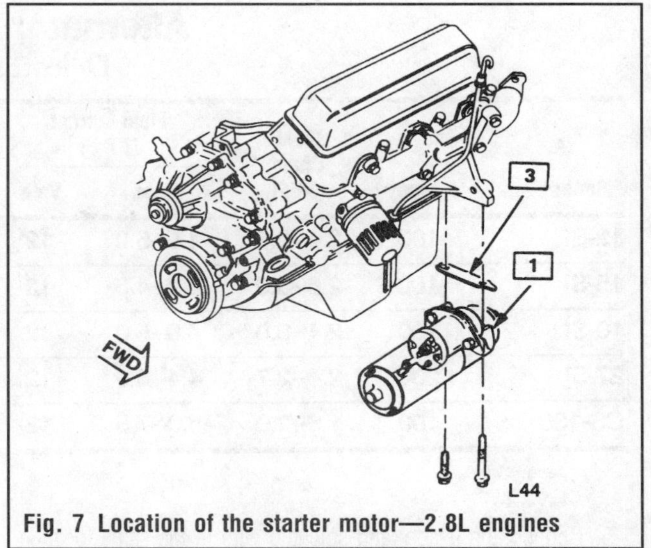

Fig. 7 Location of the starter motor—2.8L engines

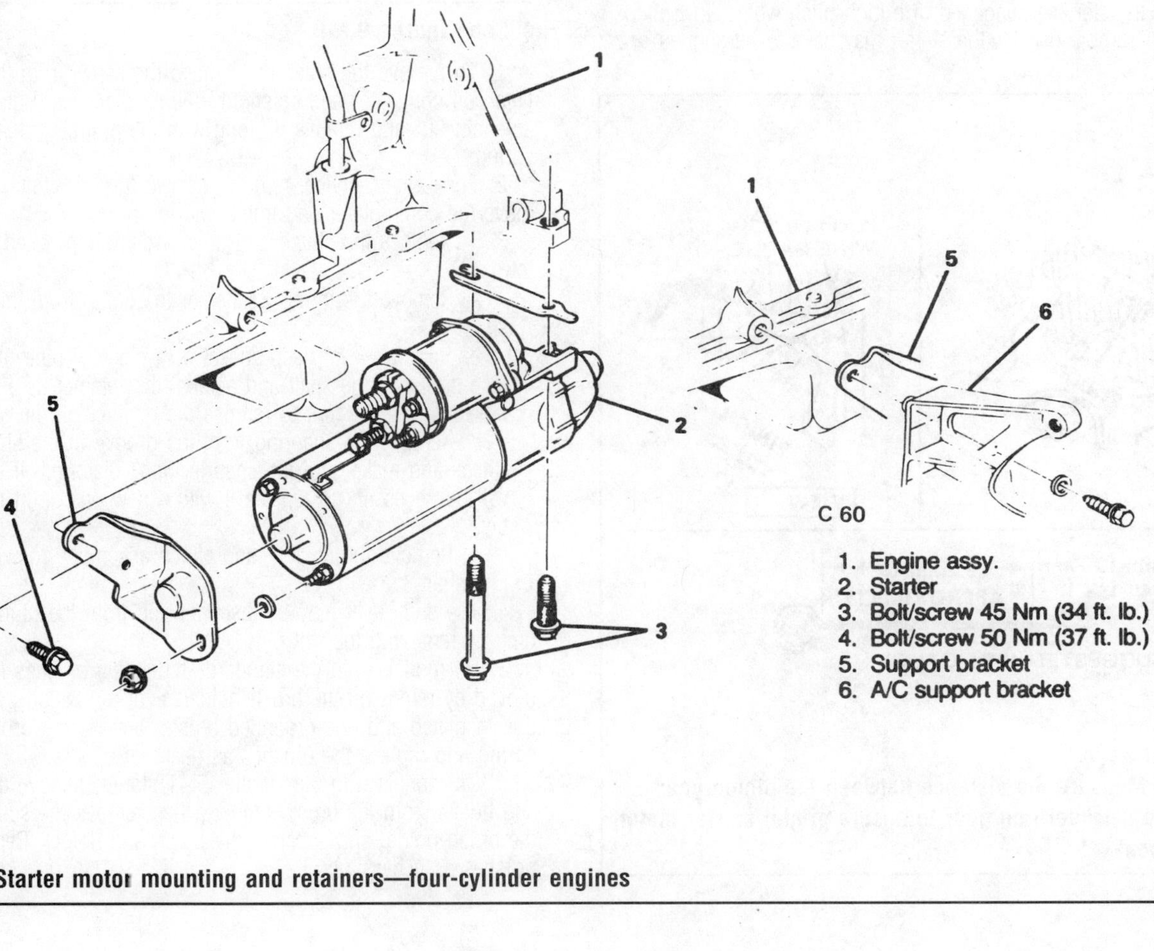

1
2
3
4
5
1
5
6
C 60
1. Engine assy.
2. Starter
3. Bolt/screw 45 Nm (34 ft. lb.)
4. Bolt/screw 50 Nm (37 ft. lb.)
5. Support bracket
6. A/C support bracket

Fig. 6 Starter motor mounting and retainers—four-cylinder engines

Alternator Specifications
Delcotran Generators

Series	Type	Field Ohms (80°F)	Field Current (80° F) Amps	Volts	Cold Output Amps	RPM	Amps	RPM	Pulley Nut Torque (Ft. lbs.)	(N.m)
12-SI	100	2.4–2.7	4.5–5.0	12	51	2000	81	7000	40–60	54–82
15-SI	100	2.6–3.0	4.0–4.6	12	57	2000	85	5000	40–60	54–82
10-SI	100	2.4–3.0	4.0–5.0	12	30	2000	51	5000	40–60	54–82
27-SI	200	2.4–2.7	4.4–4.9	12	52	2000	72	5000	40–60	54–82
CS-130	100	1.6–2.0	6.0–7.5	12	42	1600	85	6500	40–80	54–108

5. Connect the battery and solenoid wire in the same location of removal.
6. Reconnect the negative battery (−) cable.

ALIGNMENT

➧ See Figure 8

While the starter is engaged, if a high pitch whine, low pitch whoop or rumble occurs, the starter may have to be aligned or serviced with the proper shims that can be purchased at the dealer or local parts distributor. Measure the distance between the pinion gear and the flywheel ring gear as shown in the following illustration.

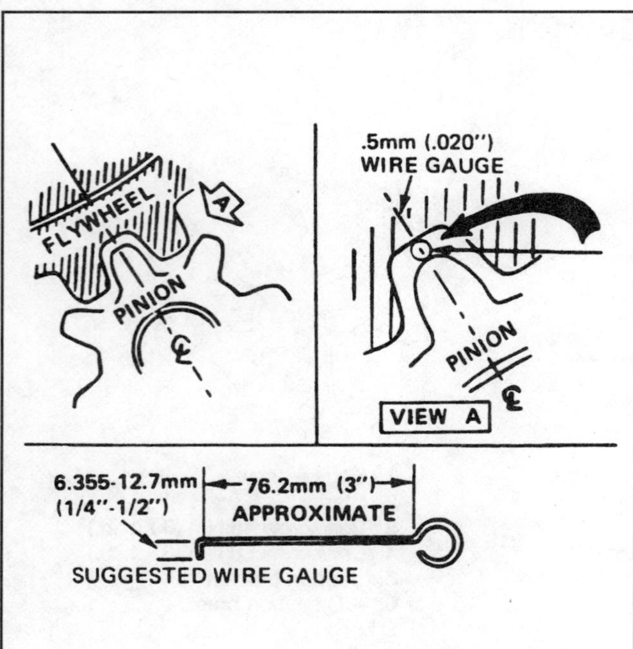

Fig. 8 Measure the distance between the pinion gear and the flywheel ring gear to ensure proper starter motor alignment

OVERHAUL

➧ See Figures 9, 10 and 11

1. To remove the solenoid, remove the screw from the field coil connector and solenoid mounting screws. Rotate the solenoid 90° and remove it along with the plunger return spring.
2. For further service, remove the two through-bolts, then remove the commutator end frame and washer.
3. To replace the clutch and drive assembly proceed as follows:
   a. Remove the thrust washer or the collar from the armature shaft.
   b. Slide a 5/8 in. deep socket or a piece of pipe of suitable size over the shaft and against the retainer as a driving tool. Tap the tool to remove the retainer off the snapring.
   c. Remove the snapring from the groove in the shaft. Check and make sure the snapring isn't distorted. If it is, it will be necessary to replace it with a new one upon reassembly.
   d. Remove the retainer and clutch assembly from the armature shaft.
4. The shift lever may be disconnected from the plunger at this time by removing the roll pin.
5. On models with the standard starter, the brushes may be removed by removing the brush holder pivot pin which positions one insulated and one grounded brush. Remove the brush and spring and replace the brushes as necessary.
6. On models with the smaller 5MT starter, remove the brush and holder from the brush support, then remove the screw from the brush holder and separate the brush and holder. Replace the brushes as necessary.

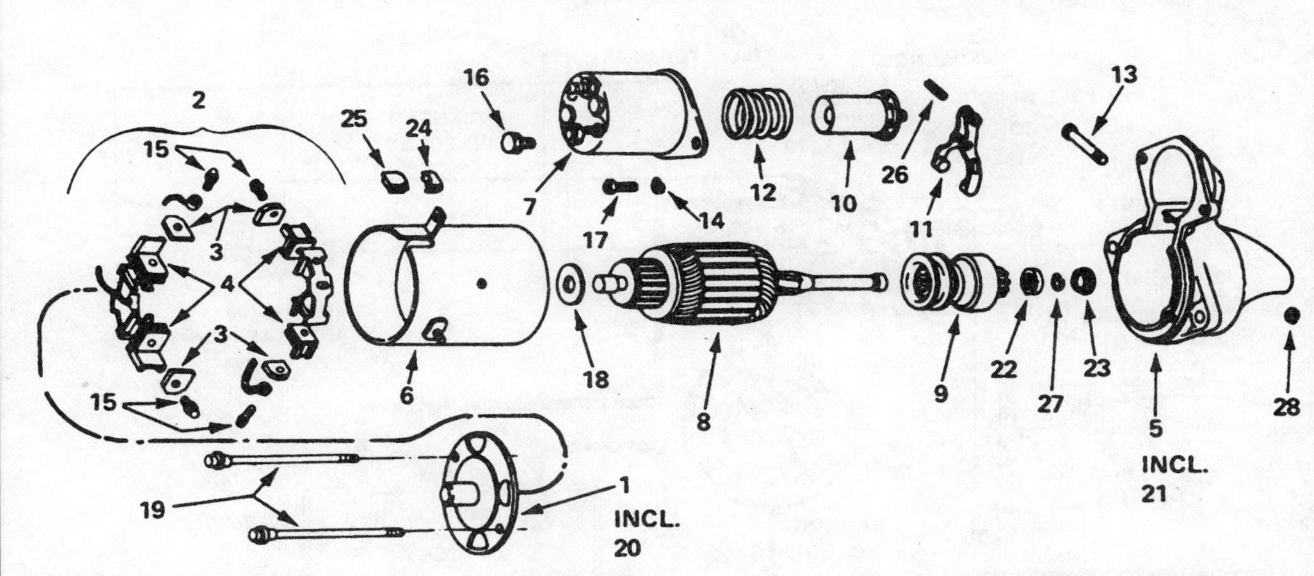

1. Frame—commutator end
2. Brush and holder pkg.
3. Brush
4. Brush holder
5. Housing—drive end
6. Frame and field asm.
7. Solenoid switch
8. Armature
9. Drive asm.
10. Plunger
11. Shift lever
12. Plunger return springer
13. Shift lever shaft
14. Lock washer
15. Screw—brush attaching
16. Screw—field lead to switch
17. Screw—switch attaching
18. Washer—brake
19. Thru bolt
20. Bushing—commutator end
21. Bushing—drive end
22. Pinion stop collar
23. Thrust collar
24. Grommet
25. Grommet
26. Plunger pin
27. Pinion stop retainer ring
28. Lever shaft retaining ring

Fig. 9 Exploded view of a common starter motor

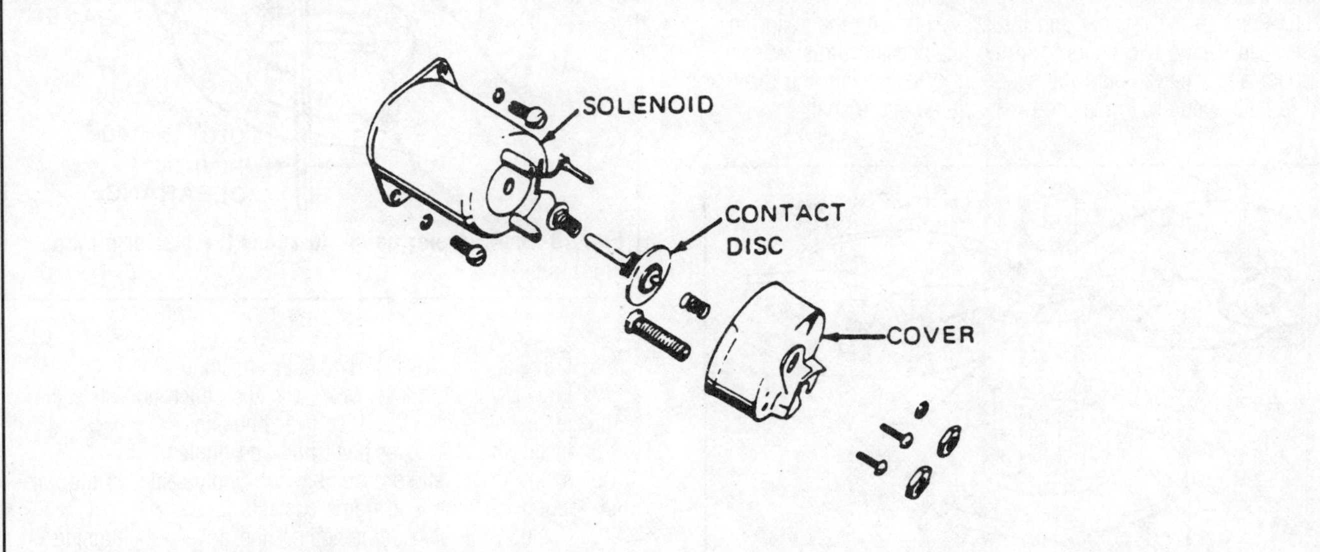

Fig. 10 Exploded view of the starter solenoid assembly

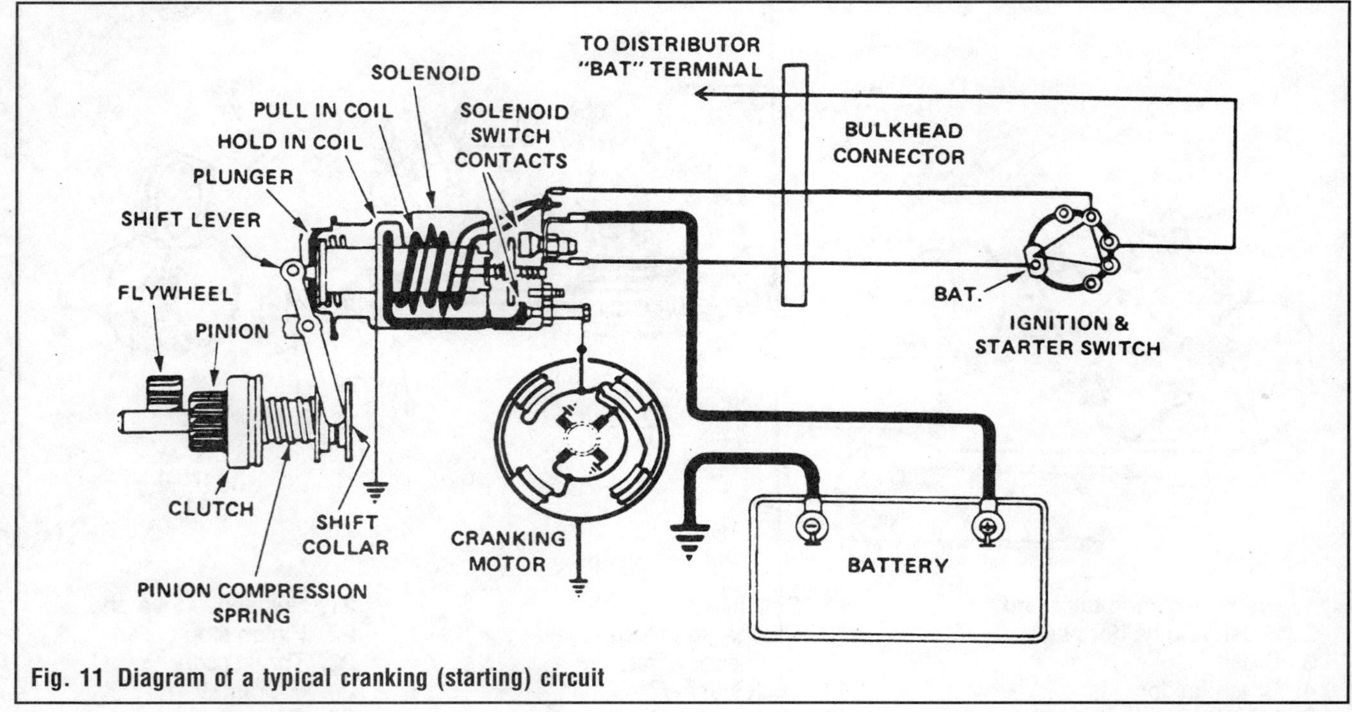

Fig. 11 Diagram of a typical cranking (starting) circuit

Reassembly

➧ See Figures 12 and 13

1. Lubricate the drive end of the armature shaft and slide the clutch assembly onto the armature shaft with the pinion away from the armature.
2. Slide the retainer onto the shaft with the cupped side facing the end of the shaft.
3. Install the snapring into the groove on the armature shaft.
4. Install the thrust washer on the shaft.
5. Position the retainer and thrust washer with the snapring in between. Using two pliers, grip the retainer and thrust washer or collar and squeeze until the snapring is forced into the retainer and is held securely in the groove in the armature shaft.

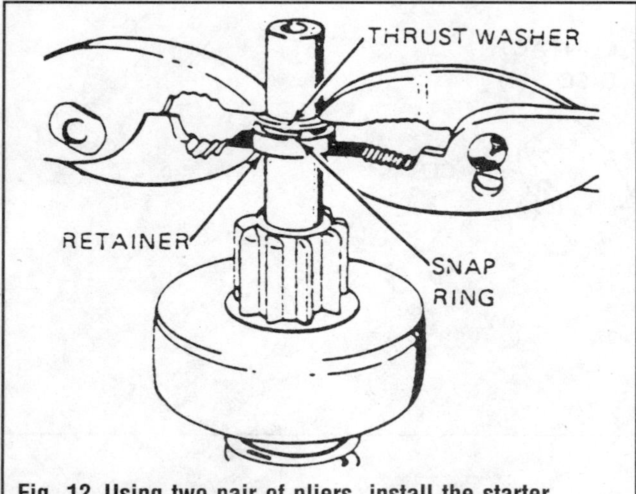

Fig. 12 Using two pair of pliers, install the starter retainer washer and ring on the armature shaft

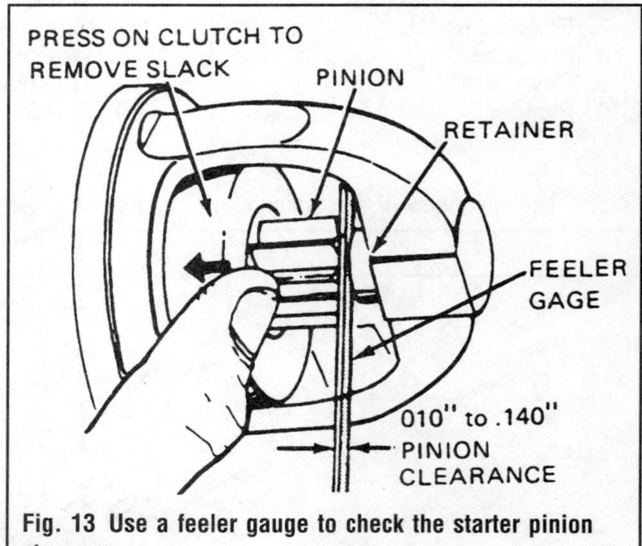

Fig. 13 Use a feeler gauge to check the starter pinion clearance

6. Lubricate the drive gear housing bushing.
7. Engage the shift lever yoke with the clutch and slide the complete assembly into the drive gear housing.
8. Install the shift lever pivot bolt and tighten.
9. Install the solenoid assembly and apply sealer to the solenoid flange where the field frame contacts it.
10. Position the field frame against the drive gear housing on the alignment pin using care to prevent damage to the brushes.
11. Lubricate the commutator end frame and install the washer on the armature shaft. Slide the end frame onto the shaft and tighten the bolts. Make sure the bolts pass through the holes in the insulator.
12. Connect the field coil connector to the solenoid terminal.

Starter Specifications

			No Load Test (includes solenoid current)			
Series	Type	Volts	Min. Amps	Max. Amps	Min. RPM	Max. RPM
5 MT	100	10	50	75	6,000	11,900
10 MT	110	10	60	90	6,500	10,500

➡When the starter motor has been disassembled or the solenoid has been replaced, it is necessary to check the pinion clearance. Pinion clearance must be correct to prevent the buttons on the shift lever yoke from rubbing on the clutch collar during cranking.

13. Check pinion clearance as follows:
   a. Disconnect the motor field coil connector from the solenoid motor terminal and insulate it carefully.
   b. Connect the (+) 12 volt battery lead to the solenoid motor terminal and the (−) lead to the motor frame.
   c. Flash a jumper lead momentarily from the solenoid motor terminal to the starter frame. This will shift the pinion into the cranking position and will remain until the battery is disconnected.
   d. Push the pinion back as far as possible to take up any movement and check the clearance with a feeler gauge. The clearance should be 0.25–0.35mm.
   e. Means for adjusting pinion clearance is not provided on the starter motor. If the clearance is not within specifications, check for improper installation or worn parts.

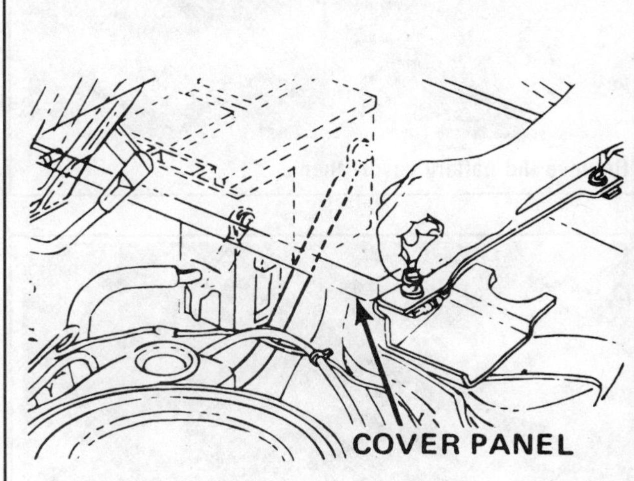

Fig. 14 Remove the retainers holding the battery cover panel to the body

Battery

The battery is located in the rear compartment on the passenger's side of the vehicle, under a cover panel.

REMOVAL & INSTALLATION

See Figures 14 and 15

1. In the rear engine compartment remove the two thumb screws holding the battery cover panel to the body, and lift the panel out.
2. Remove the black negative (−) battery cable first, then the red positive (−) cable from the battery.
3. Remove the battery retainer bolt, located on the bottom front side of the battery (terminal side).
4. Loosen the bolts which retain the heat shield and move the shield out of the way.
5. Carefully remove the battery.
6. Before installing a new battery, check the cables terminals and battery tray for corrosion and clean as necessary. Refer to the Battery Maintenance portion of Section 1.
7. Reconnect the battery terminals. Make the positive connection first. The remainder of the installation is the reverse of removal.

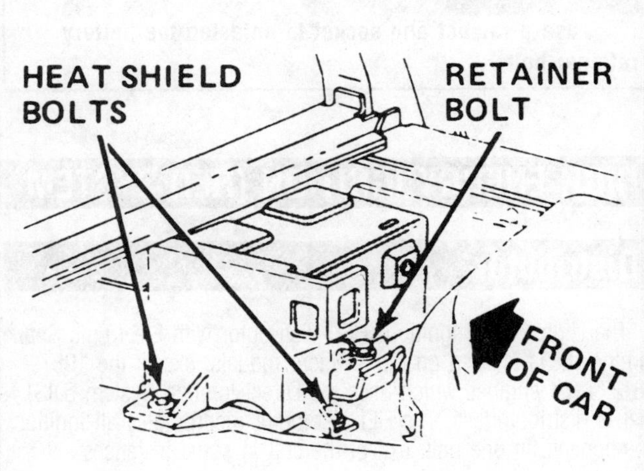

Fig. 15 After disconnecting the battery cables, unfasten the retaining bolt and heat shield bolts, then remove the battery

Remove the battery cover, then . . .

Remove the battery retainer

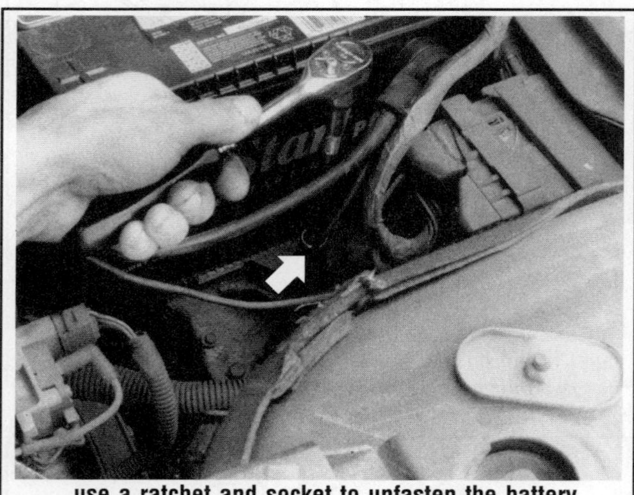

. . . use a ratchet and socket to unfasten the battery retainer bolt

Disconnect the battery cables and remove the battery from the vehicle

HIGH ENERGY IGNITION (HEI) SYSTEM

Distributor

The High Energy Ignition (HEI) distributor with Electronic Spark Timing (EST) is used on the all Fiero models, except the 1987–88 2.5L L4 engines which uses the Direct Ignition System (DIS) that is distributorless. The HEI distributor incorporates all ignition components in one unit, except the coil in some instances.

PRECAUTIONS

1. When making compression checks, disconnect the ignition switch feed wire at the distributor by releasing the locking tab and gently pulling downward.

2. No periodic lubrication is needed because the bearings are lubricated by the engine oil.

3. The tachometer (TACH) terminal is next to the ignition switch (BAT) connector on the distributor cap.

WARNING

Never ground the (TACH) terminal as damage to the ignition module may result.

4. Dwell adjustment is controlled by the ignition module, and cannot be adjusted.

5. When adjusting the ignition timing, never pierce the soft spark plug wires. The spark plug wires are routed so they will not become scuffed or burnt. The wire must be routed in their original locations to prevent this condition.

REMOVAL & INSTALLATION

1. Disconnect the negative (−) battery cable. Remove the ignition switch battery (BAT) feed wire and tachometer lead from the distributor.
2. Remove the distributor cap by turning the four latches counterclockwise. Move the cap out of the way.
3. Remove the four terminal ECM harness connector from the distributor.
4. Mark the position of the rotor on the distributor housing with a grease pen or permanent marker. Mark the position of the distributor housing at the engine block by scratching a mark with a screwdriver or equivalent.

➡To ensure correct timing of the distributor, the distributor must be installed with the rotor and housing correctly. The ignition timing will have to be checked with a timing light after the distributor is installed.

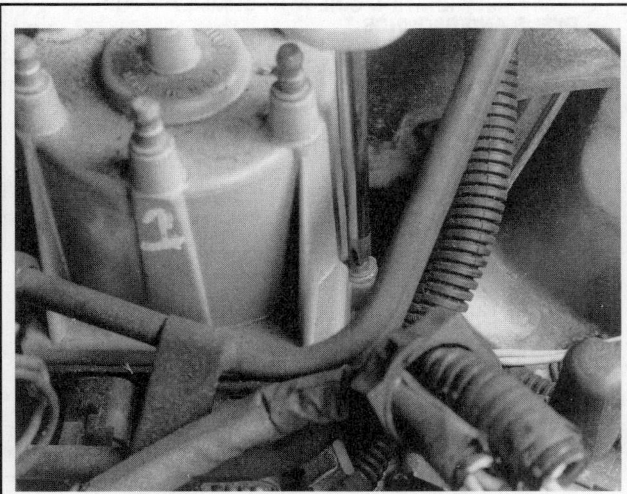

Loosen the distributor caps hold-down retainer . . .

. . . then, remove the distributor cap

If necessary, remove the rotor by pulling it up and off the shaft

5. Remove the distributor hold-down bolt and retainer. While twisting the distributor housing, pull upward and remove the distributor.

➡If the distributor will not move, spray some penetrating oil around the base where it goes into the engine and wait a few minutes for the oil to penetrate.

Engine Not Rotated

6. Rotate the distributor shaft until the rotor aligns with the second mark you made (when the shaft stopped moving). Lubricate the drive gear with clean engine oil, install the distributor in the engine.
7. Install the clamp and hold-down bolt. Tighten them until the distributor can just be moved with a little effort.
8. Connect all wires and harnesses and install the distributor cap.
9. Set the timing and tighten the hold bolt. Refer to the "Ignition Timing" procedures in Section 2.

Engine Rotated

If by chance, the engine crankshaft has moved while the distributor was removed. Refer to the following procedures to properly set initial timing so the engine will start.

1. Remove the No. 1 spark plug. Refer to the Firing Order illustrations for No. 1 spark plug location.
2. With the engine cool, place your finger over No. 1 spark plug hole and crank the engine slowly by hand until compression is felt.

**** CAUTION**

Do not crank the engine using the starter motor because it will turn too fast. Place a wrench on the crankshaft pulley bolt to turn the crankshaft or turn by hand.

3. Align the timing mark on the crankshaft pulley to the **0** mark on the engine timing indicator.

4. Turn the rotor to point at the No. 1 spark plug tower on the distributor cap.
5. Install the distributor and connect the ignition feed wire.
6. Install the cap and spark plug wires.
7. Check and adjust the engine timing with a timing light to proper specifications. Refer to the Ignition Timing procedures in Section 2.

Ignition Coil

TESTING

See Figures 16 and 17

1. Disconnect the negative (−) battery cable.
2. Disconnect the high tension coil wire and input and output connectors from the coil. Refer to the Testing Remote Ignition Coil illustration in this section.
3. Check the coil with an ohmmeter for opens and grounds as follows.
   a. Using the ohms × 1,000, connect one lead to the coil housing and the other to the input terminal. The reading should be very high (infinite), if not replace the coil.
   b. Using the ohms × 1, connect one lead to the coil input terminal and the other to the output terminal. The reading should be very low or zero, if not replace the coil.
   c. Using the ohms × 1,000, connect one lead to the coil output terminal and the other to the high tension coil wire terminal. The reading should NOT be infinite, if it is replace the coil.

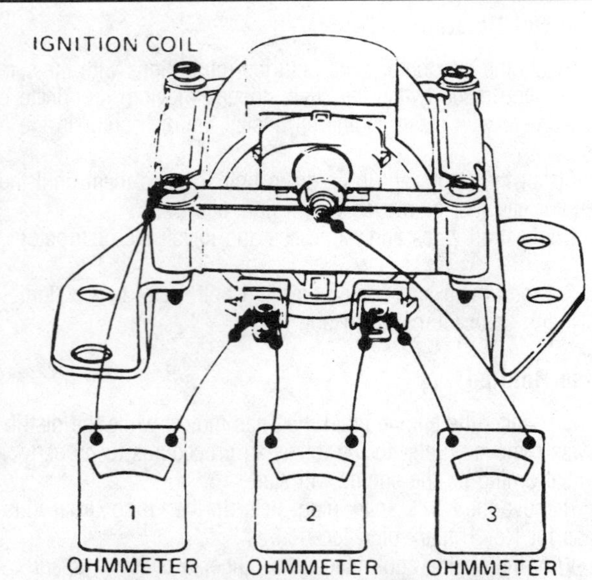

Fig. 16 Testing the remote ignition coil using an ohmmeter—older model vehicles

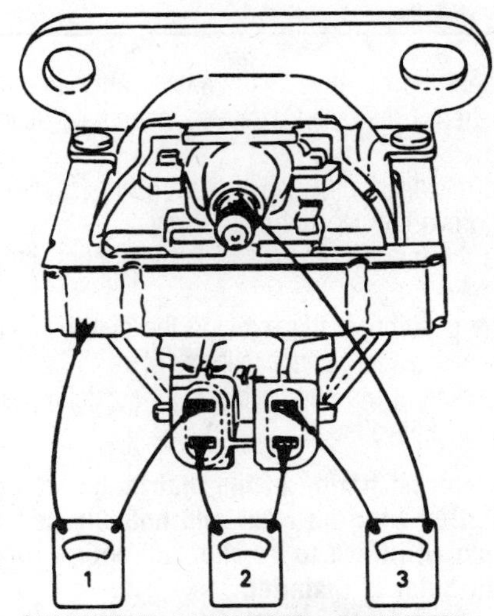

Fig. 17 Testing the remote ignition coil using an ohmmeter—newer model vehicles

REMOVAL & INSTALLATION

1. Disconnect the negative (−) battery cable.
2. Remove the high tension coil wire and input and output connectors.

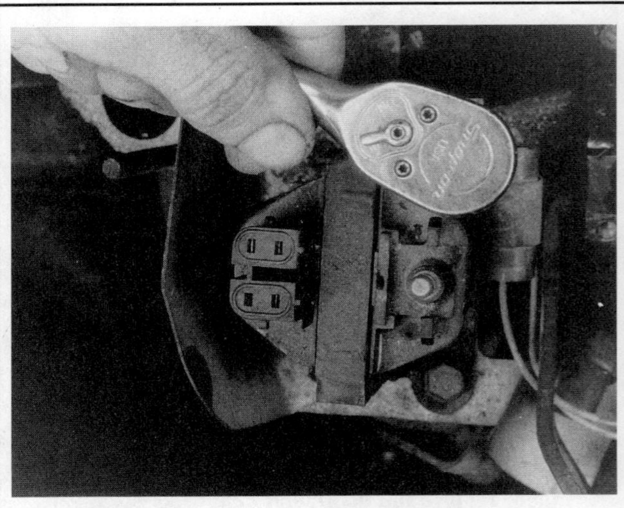

Unfasten the coil-to-bracket retaining bolts . . .

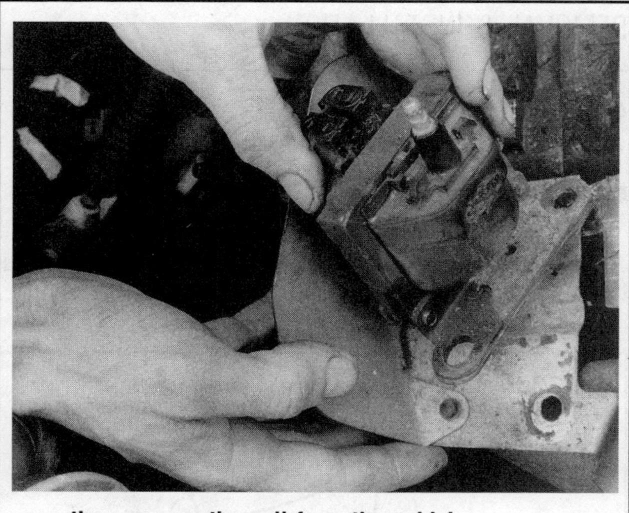

. . . then remove the coil from the vehicle

3. Remove the coil-to-body attaching bolts. Remove the coil from the vehicle.

To install:

4. Position the coil to the mounting area and install the attaching bolts. Torque the bolts to 6 ft. lbs. (8.1 Nm).
5. Apply a small amount of Dielectric Compound to the high tension coil tower and install the coil wire and input and output connectors.

Pick-up Coil

TESTING

See Figures 18 and 19

1. Disconnect the negative (−) battery cable.
2. Remove the distributor cap and lay aside.
3. Remove the two prong connector from the ignition module.

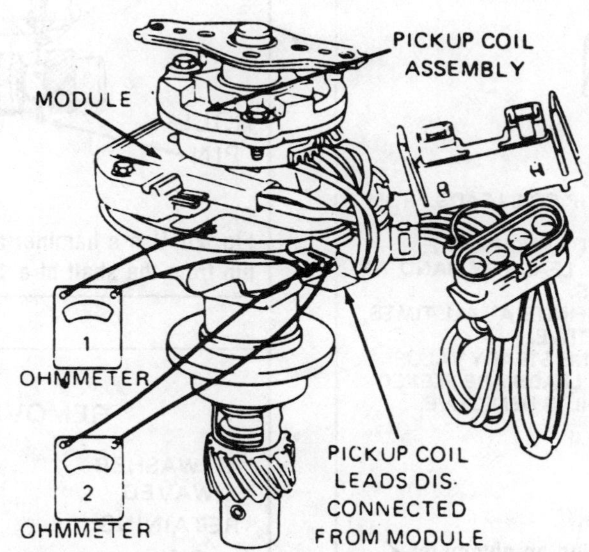

3. REMOVE ROTOR AND PICKUP COIL LEADS FROM MODULE.
4. CONNECT OHMMETER PART 1 AND PART 2.
5. IF VACUUM UNIT IS USED, CONNECT VACUUM SOURCE TO VACUUM UNIT. REPLACE VACUUM UNIT IF INOPERATIVE.
6. OBSERVE OHMMETER THROUGHOUT VACUUM RANGE: IF NO VACUUM UNIT IS USED, FLEX LEADS BY HAND TO CHECK FOR INTERMITTENT OPENS.

STEP 1 — SHOULD READ INFINITE AT ALL TIMES. IF NOT, PICKUP COIL IS DEFECTIVE.

STEP 2 — SHOULD READ ONE STEADY VALUE BETWEEN 500-1500 OHMS AS VACUUM IS OPERATED, OR AS LEADS ARE FLEXED BY HAND. IF NOT, PICKUP COIL IS DEFECTIVE.

7. OHMMETER MAY DEFLECT IF OPERATING VACUUM UNIT CAUSES TEETH TO ALIGN. THIS IS NOT A DEFECT.

Fig. 18 Using an ohmmeter to test the pick-up coil—1984 2.5L engine

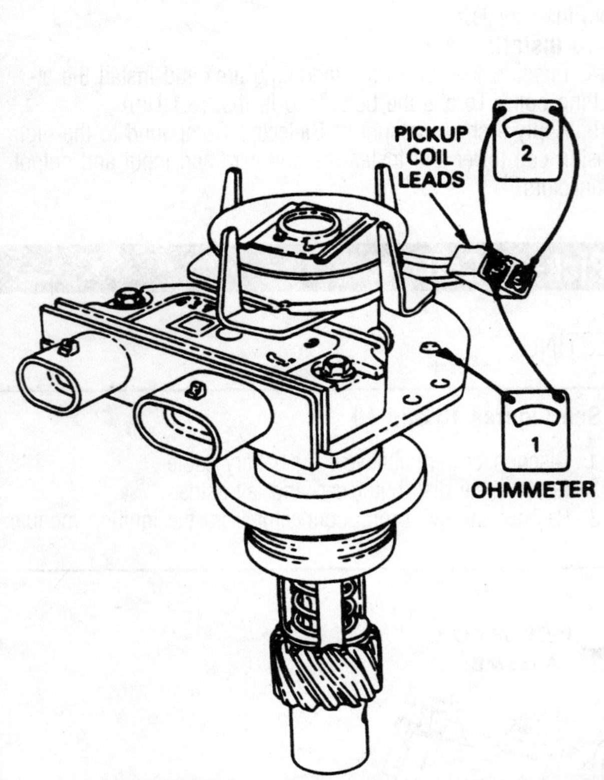

Fig. 19 Testing the pick-up coil using an ohmmeter—1985–86 2.5L engine and 1985—88 2.8L engine

Refer to the "Pick-up Coil Testing" illustrations in this section for connector locations.

4. Using an ohmmeter, follow the procedures below to test the pick-up coil.
   a. Using ohms × 1, connect the test leads as shown for test 1 of illustration. The reading should read infinite at all times. If not, replace the pick-up coil.
   b. Using ohms × 1,000, connect the test leads as shown for test 2 of illustration. The reading should be between 500–1,500Ω. If not, replace the pick-up coil.

➡If the center distributor shaft is hitting the pick-up coil as the shaft is turned. This will ground the pick-up coil and give you a false reading. Check the distributor shaft for excessive movement, replace distributor if defective. Check the pick-up coil mounting for looseness and repair if condition occurs.

REMOVAL & INSTALLATION

4-2.5L Engine

1984 MODELS

➧ See Figures 20, 21 and 22

1. Disconnect the negative (−) battery cable.
2. Remove the distributor assembly as outlined in the Distributor removal and installation procedures in this section.

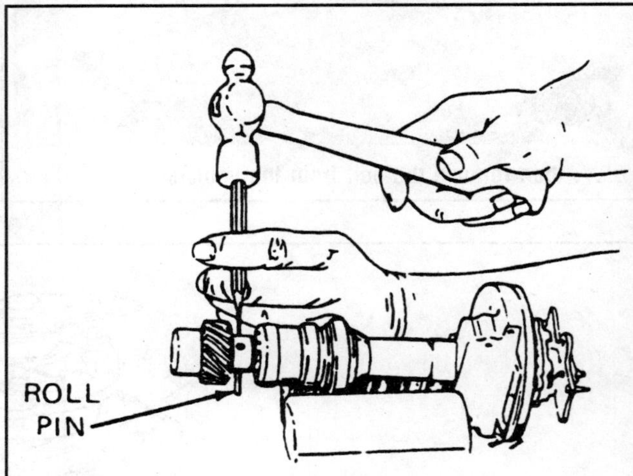

Fig. 20 Use a hammer and a punch to remove the roll pin from the shaft of a 1984 HEI distributor

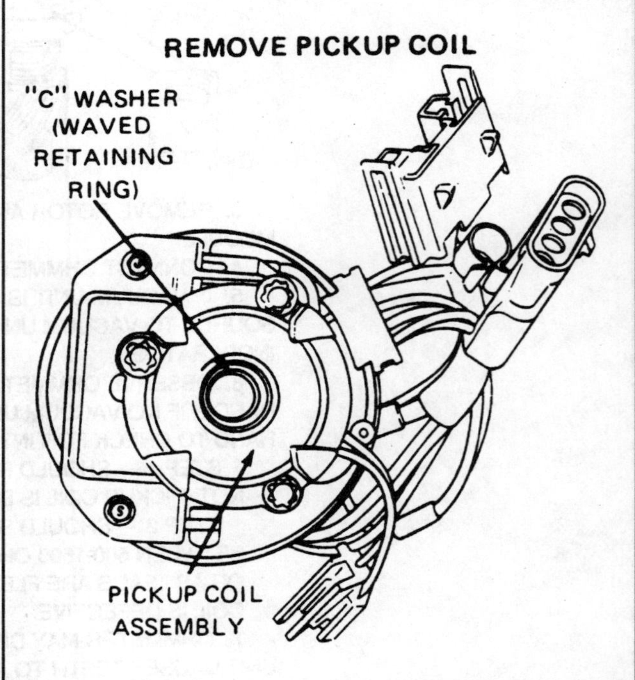

Fig. 21 Location of the pick-up coil C washer—1984 HEI distributor

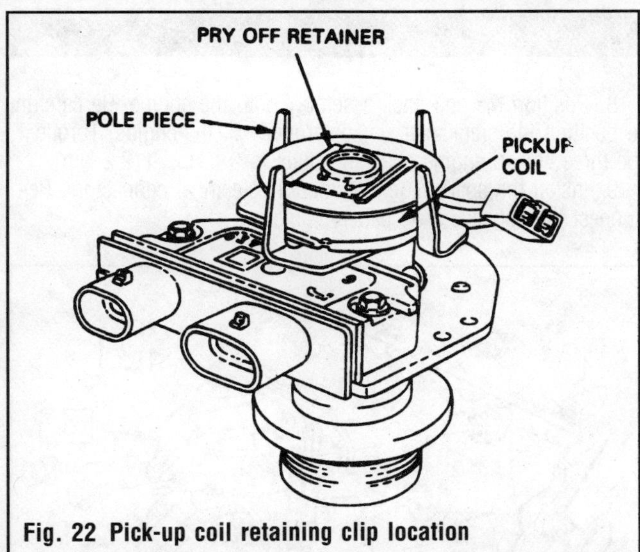

Fig. 22 Pick-up coil retaining clip location

➡Mark the position of the rotor and distributor base before pulling out the distributor. This is very important because it will save a lot of time when reinstalling. If problems occur, refer to Distributor Installation When the Engine is Disturbed procedures in this section.

3. Place the distributor assembly into a vise. Be careful not damage the aluminum distributor housing.
4. Mark the gear assembly at the end of the distributor housing for proper installation. Drive the roll pin out with a round punch and remove the gear.
5. Remove the distributor shaft by pulling and twisting the rotor mounting plate.
6. Remove the C-washer retaining ring, the three pick-up coil retaining screws, disconnect the module connector and remove the pick-up coil.

To install:

1. Install the pick-up coil and tighten the attaching screws.
2. Connect the coil connector to the module.
3. Coat the distributor shaft with clean engine oil and install the shaft into the housing.
4. Make sure the coil is mounted properly and does not hit the shaft teeth.
5. Install the shaft gear and roll pin to the same position before disassembly.
6. Install the distributor assembly in the engine as outlined in the Distributor removal and installation procedures in this section.
7. Adjust the ignition timing with an inductive timing light to the proper specifications on the emissions sticker under the engine cover. Refer to the Ignition Timing Marks illustration in Section 2.

1985–88 MODELS

➡The distributor assembly does NOT have to be removed to replace the pick-up coil for the 1985–88 HEI distributors. Early 1985 models still may have the old style distributor and will have to be removed. Refer to the illustrations to see which style you have.

1. Disconnect the negative (−) battery cable.
2. Remove the distributor cap by turning the two or four retaining latches counterclockwise. Move the distributor cap out of the way. Use a piece of string to hold it in place. Remove the rotor assembly.
3. Remove the pick-up coil retaining clip by prying off with a small punch or equivalent. Be careful not to loose the clip as it comes off.
4. Disconnect the coil electrical connector from the module and lift the pick-up coil assembly straight up to remove from the distributor.

To install:

5. Install the pick-up coil and retaining clip. Connect the electrical connector to the ignition module. Install the distributor cap as outlined in the Distributor removal and installation procedures in this section. Reconnect the negative (−) battery cable.

Ignition Module

REMOVAL & INSTALLATION

➧ See Figure 23

➡The distributor does NOT have to be removed to perform service on the ignition module.

1. Disconnect the negative (−) battery cable.
2. Remove the distributor cap by turning the two or four retaining latches counterclockwise. Move the distributor cap out of the way. Use a piece of string to hold it in place.
3. Remove the rotor assembly.
4. Disconnect the wiring connectors from the module. Remove the two module-to-distributor retaining screws and remove the module.

To install:

1. Wipe the distributor base and module clean with a rag and solvent.
2. Apply a coat of Dielectric Compound or equivalent to the module, module base and module electrical terminals.
3. Install the module to the base and tighten the two module-to-distributor retaining screws. Connect the module electrical connector.
4. Install the distributor cap and reconnect the negative (−) battery cable.

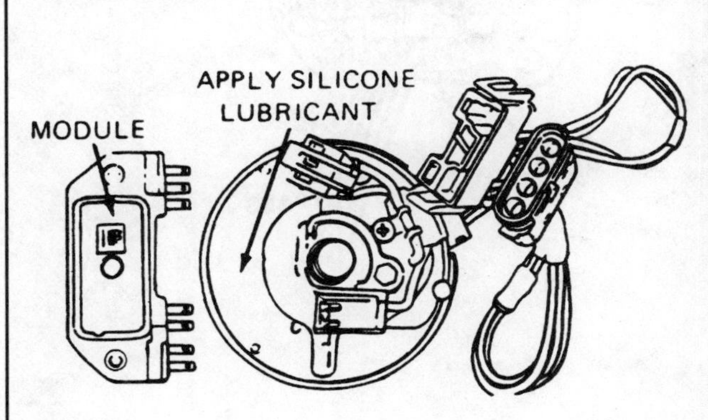

Fig. 23 Always apply silicone lubricant to the back of the ignition module before installation—1984 model shown

DIRECT IGNITION SYSTEM (DIS)

Ignition Coil

REMOVAL & INSTALLATION

➧ **See Figures 24 and 25**

1. Disconnect the negative (−) battery cable.
2. Label each spark plug wire for proper installation.
3. Remove the spark plug and module electrical connectors from the ignition coils.
4. Remove the three coil-to-engine attaching bolts.

✱✱ CAUTION

Be careful not to damage the crankshaft and module terminals when pulling the coil assemblies from the engine. Pull slowly and carefully away from the engine.

5. Gently pull the coil assemblies from the engine.
6. There are two coils that can be replaced separately. Remove the two coil retaining screws and remove the coil.

To install:

7. Position the coil on the base plate and tighten the retaining screws.
8. Position the coil pack assembly onto the engine. Be careful to position the crankshaft sensor properly in the engine. Torque the three coil-to-engine attaching bolts to 9 ft. lbs. (12.2 Nm).
9. Install the spark plug and module electrical connectors. Reconnect the negative (−) battery cable.

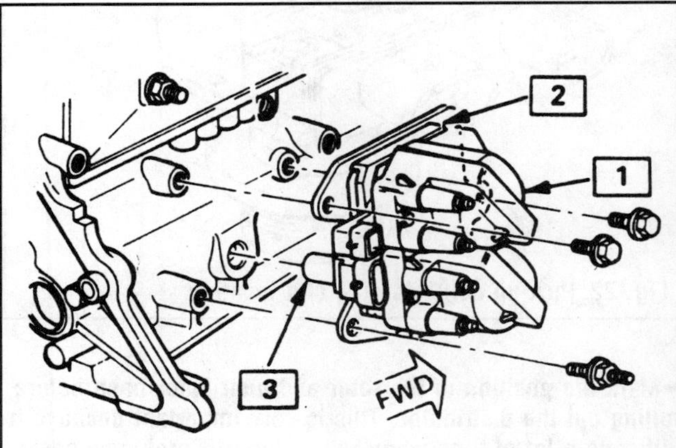

Fig. 25 Ignition coil and module location and retainers—1987–88 2.5L engine with Direct Ignition System (DIS)

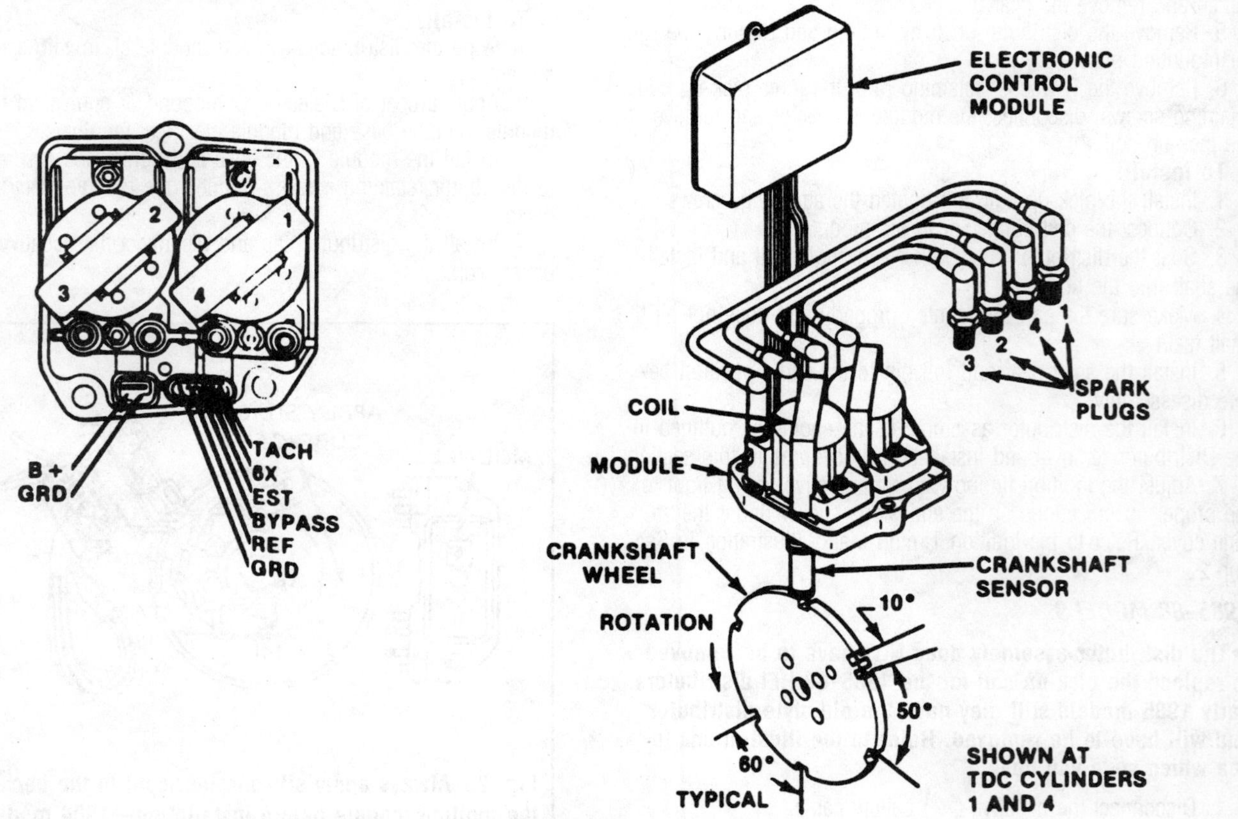

Fig. 24 Direct Ignition System (DIS) components—1987–88 2.5L engine

Ignition Module

REMOVAL & INSTALLATION

1. Disconnect the negative (−) battery cable.
2. Label each spark plug wire for proper installation.
3. Remove the spark plug and module electrical connectors from the ignition coils.
4. Remove the three coil-to-engine attaching bolts.

** CAUTION

Be careful not to damage the crankshaft and module terminals when pulling the coil assemblies from the engine. Pull slowly and carefully away from the engine.

5. Gently pull the coil assemblies from the engine.
6. Remove the four coil-to-module attaching nuts and bolts and remove the module and crankshaft sensor. Be careful not to damage the crankshaft sensor terminals. Refer to the DIS Coil illustrations in this section.

To install:

7. Position the module and crankshaft sensor onto backing plate and torque the attaching nuts and bolts to 40 inch lbs. (4.5 Nm).
8. Position the coil pack assembly onto the engine. Be careful to position the crankshaft sensor properly in the engine. Torque the three coil-to-engine attaching bolts to 9 ft. lbs. (12.2 Nm).
9. Install the spark plug and module electrical connectors. Reconnect the negative (−) battery cable.

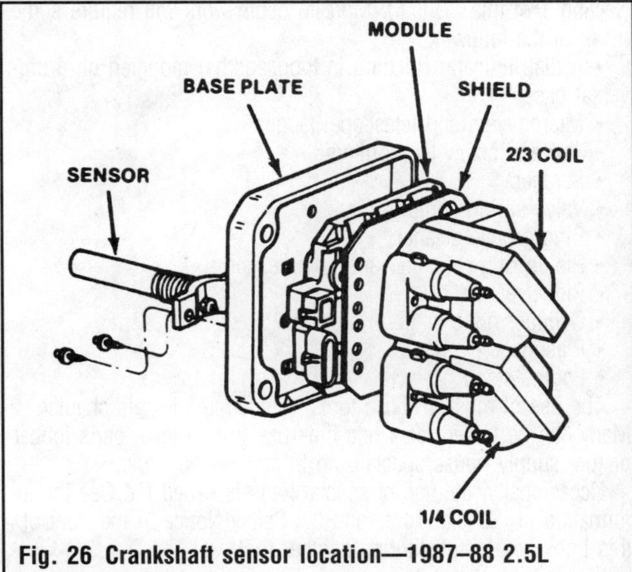

Fig. 26 Crankshaft sensor location—1987–88 2.5L engine

Crankshaft Sensor

REMOVAL & INSTALLATION

➧ **See Figure 26**

1. Disconnect the negative (−) battery cable.
2. Label each spark plug wire for proper installation.
3. Remove the spark plug and module electrical connectors from the ignition coils.
4. Remove the three coil-to-engine attaching bolts.

** CAUTION

Be careful not to damage the crankshaft and module terminals when pulling the coil assemblies from the engine. Pull slowly and carefully away from the engine.

5. Gently pull the coil assemblies from the engine.
6. Remove the two crankshaft sensor-to-coil pack and remove the sensor by carefully pulling the sensor away from the coil pack.

To install:

7. Position the coil pack assembly onto the engine. Be careful to position the crankshaft sensor properly into the engine. Torque the three coil-to-engine attaching bolts to 9 ft. lbs. (12.2 Nm).
8. Install the spark plug and module electrical connectors. Reconnect the negative (−) battery cable.

ENGINE MECHANICAL

Engine Overhaul Tips

Most engine overhaul procedures are fairly standard. In addition to specific parts replacement procedures and specifications for your individual engine, this section is also a guide to acceptable rebuilding procedures. Examples of standard rebuilding practice are given and should be used along with specific details concerning your particular engine.

Competent and accurate machine shop services will ensure maximum performance, reliability and engine life. In most instances it is more profitable for the do-it-yourself mechanic to remove, clean and inspect the component, buy the necessary parts and deliver these to a shop for actual machine work.

On the other hand, much of the rebuilding work (crankshaft, block, bearings, piston rods, and other components) is well within the scope of the do-it-yourself mechanic's tools and abilities. You will have to decide for yourself the depth of involvement you desire in an engine repair or rebuild.

This section contains the needed information to overhaul your 2.5L L4 and 2.8L V6 engine. The main components of the overhaul are cylinder block, cylinder head, crankshaft, valve train, pistons, camshaft and oiling system.

TOOLS

The tools required for an engine overhaul or parts replacement will depend on the depth of your involvement. With a few exceptions, they will be the tools found in a mechanic's tool kit (see

Section 1 of this manual). More in-depth work will require some or all of the following:

- A dial indicator (reading in thousandths) mounted on a universal base
- Micrometers and telescope gauges
- Jaw and screw-type pullers
- Scraper
- Valve spring compressor
- Ring groove cleaner
- Piston ring expander and compressor
- Ridge reamer
- Cylinder hone or glaze breaker
- Plastigage®
- Engine stand

The use of most of these tools is illustrated in this chapter. Many can be rented for a one-time use from a local parts jobber or tool supply house specializing in automotive work.

Occasionally, the use of special tools is called for. See the information on Special Tools and the Safety Notice in the front of this book before substituting another tool.

INSPECTION TECHNIQUES

Procedures and specifications are given in this chapter for inspecting, cleaning and assessing the wear limits of most major components. Other procedures such as Magnaflux® and Zyglo® can be used to locate material flaws and stress cracks. Magnaflux® is a magnetic process applicable only to ferrous materials. The Zyglo® process coats the material with a fluorescent dye penetrant and can be used on any material.

Checking for suspected surface cracks can be more readily made using spot check dye. The dye is sprayed onto the suspected area, wiped off and the area sprayed with a developer. Cracks will show up brightly.

OVERHAUL TIPS

Aluminum has become extremely popular for use in engines, due to its low weight. Observe the following precautions when handling aluminum parts:

- Never hot tank aluminum parts (the caustic hot tank solution will eat the aluminum.
- Remove all aluminum parts (identification tag, etc.) from engine parts prior to the tanking.
- Always coat threads lightly with engine oil or anti-seize compounds before installation, to prevent seizure.
- Never overtorque bolts or spark plugs especially in aluminum threads.

Stripped threads in any component can be repaired using any of several commercial repair kits (Heli-Coil®, Microdot®, Keenserts®, etc.).

When assembling the engine, any parts that will be exposed to frictional contact must be prelubed to provide lubrication at initial start-up. Any product specifically formulated for this purpose can be used, but engine oil is not recommended as a prelube in most cases.

When semi-permanent (locked, but removable) installation of bolts or nuts is desired, threads should be cleaned and coated with Loctite® or another similar, commercial non-hardening sealant.

REPAIRING DAMAGED THREADS

Several methods of repairing damaged threads are available. Heli-Coil® (shown here), Keenserts® and Microdot® are among the most widely used. All involve basically the same principle—drilling out stripped threads, tapping the hole and installing a prewound insert—making welding, plugging and oversize fasteners unnecessary.

Two types of thread repair inserts are usually supplied: a standard type for most inch coarse, inch fine, metric course and metric fine thread sizes and a spark lug type to fit most spark plug port sizes. Consult the individual tool manufacturer's catalog to determine exact applications. Typical thread repair kits will contain a selection of prewound threaded inserts, a tap (corresponding to the outside diameter threads of the insert) and an installation tool. Spark plug inserts usually differ because they require a tap equipped with pilot threads and a combined reamer/tap section. Most manufacturers also supply blister-packed thread repair in-

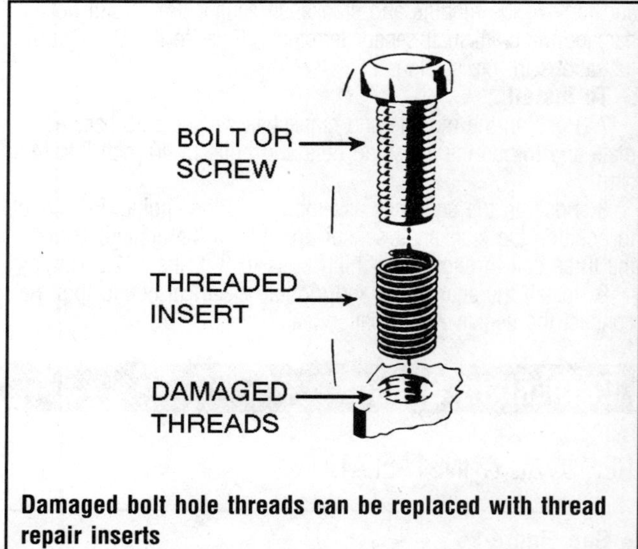

Damaged bolt hole threads can be replaced with thread repair inserts

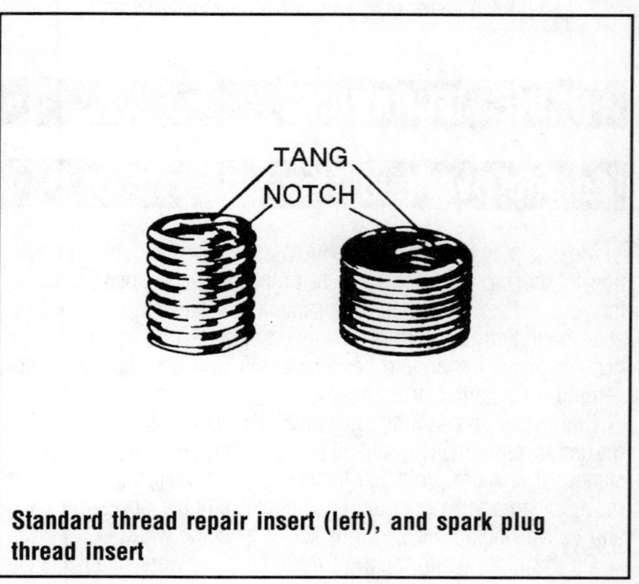

Standard thread repair insert (left), and spark plug thread insert

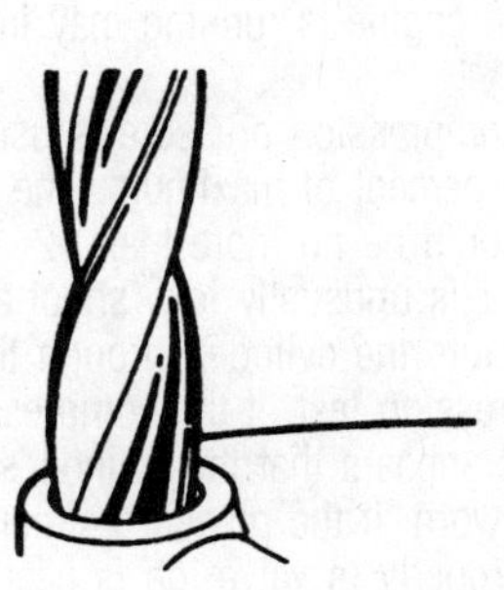

Drill out the damaged threads with the specified size bit. Be sure to drill completely through the hole or to the bottom of a blind hole

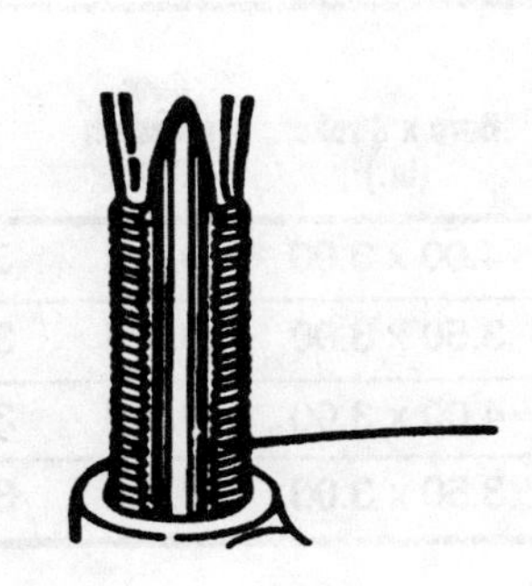

Using the kit, tap the hole in order to receive the thread insert. Keep the tap well oiled and back it out frequently to avoid clogging the threads

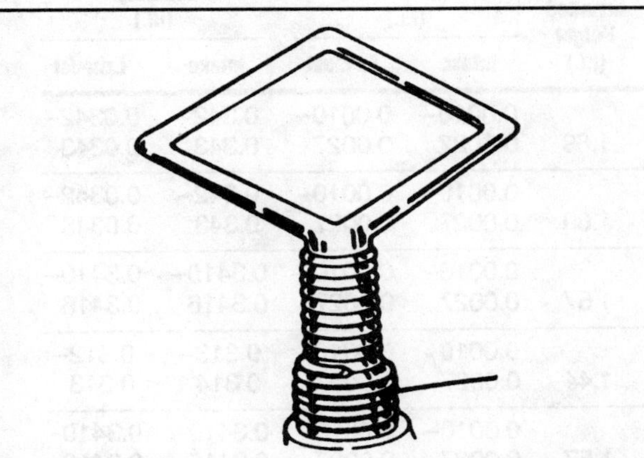

Screw the insert onto the installer tool until the tang engages the slot. Thread the insert into the hole until it is ¼–½ turn below the top surface, then remove the tool and break off the tang using a punch

serts separately in addition to a master kit containing a variety of taps and inserts plus installation tools.

Before attempting to repair a threaded hole, remove any snapped, broken or damaged bolts or studs. Penetrating oil can be used to free frozen threads. The offending item can usually be removed with locking pliers or using a screw/stud extractor. After the hole is clear, the thread can be repaired, as shown in the series of accompanying illustrations and in the kit manufacturer's instructions.

CHECKING ENGINE COMPRESSION

A noticeable lack of engine power, excessive oil consumption and/or poor fuel mileage measured over an extended period are all indicators of internal engine war. Worn piston rings, scored or worn cylinder bores, blown head gaskets, sticking or burnt valves and worn valve seats are all possible culprits here. A check of each cylinder's compression will help you locate the problems.

As mentioned in the Tools and Equipment section of Section 1, a screw-in type compression gauge is more accurate that the type you simply hold against the spark plug hole, although it takes slightly longer to use. It's worth it to obtain a more accurate reading. Follow the procedures below.

1. Warm up the engine to normal operating temperature.
2. Mark the spark plug wires and remove all the spark plugs.
3. Disconnect the BAT terminal from the HEI distributor or ignition module.
4. Remove the air cleaner assembly and fully open the throttle plates by operating the throttle linkage by hand or by having an assistant floor the accelerator pedal.
5. Coat the gauge threads with oil and screw the compression gauge into the no. 1 spark plug hole until the fitting is snug.

WARNING

Be careful not to crossthread the plug hole. On aluminum cylinder heads use extra care, as the threads in these heads are easily ruined.

6. Ask an assistant to depress the accelerator pedal fully on both carbureted and fuel injected vehicles. Then, while you read the compression gauge, ask the assistant to crank the engine two or three times in short bursts using the ignition switch. There should be four puffs per cylinder.
7. Read the compression gauge at the end of each series of cranks, and record the highest of these readings. Repeat this procedure for each of the engine's cylinders. Compare the highest reading of each cylinder to the compression pressure specification of **100 psi (689 kPa).** The lowest cylinder reading should not be less than **70 percent** of the highest reading.

NORMAL—Compression builds up quickly and evenly to the specified compression on each cylinder.

PISTON RINGS—Compression low on the first stroke, tends to build up on the following strokes, but does not reach normal. This reading should be tested with the addition of a few shots of engine oil into the cylinder. If the compression increases considerably, the rings are leaking compression.

VALVES—Low on the first stroke, does not tend to build up on following strokes. This reading will stay around the same with a few shots of engine oil.

HEAD GASKET—The compression reading is low between

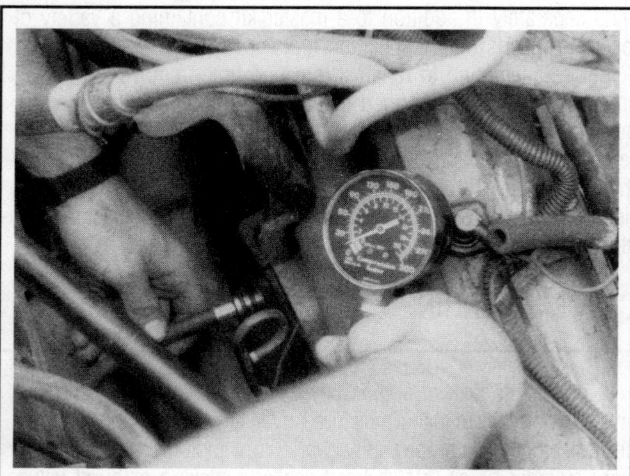
A screw-in type compression gauge is more accurate and easier to use without an assistant

two adjacent cylinders. The head gasket between the two cylinders maybe blown. If there is the sign of white smoke coming from the exhaust while the engine is running may indicate water leaking into the cylinder.

A cylinder's compression pressure is usually acceptable if it is not less than 70 percent of maximum. The difference between any two cylinders should be no more than 12–14 pounds.

8. If a cylinder is unusually low, shoot about a tablespoon of clean engine oil into the cylinder through the spark plug hole and repeat the compression test. If the compression comes up after adding the oil, it appears that the cylinder's piston rings or bore are damaged or worn. If the pressure remains low, the valves may not be seating properly (a valve job is needed), or the head gasket may be blown near that cylinder. If compression in any two adjacent cylinders is low, and if the addition of oil doesn't help the compression, there is leakage past the head gasket. Oil and coolant water in the combustion chamber can result from this problem. There may be evidence of water droplets on the engine dipstick when a head gasket has blown.

General Engine Specifications

Year	VIN	No. Cylinder Displacement cu. in. (liter)	Fuel System Type	Net Horsepower @ rpm	Net Torque @ rpm (ft. lbs.)	Bore x Stroke (in.)	Compression Ratio	Oil Pressure @ rpm
1984–86	R	151 (2.5)	TBI	90 @ 4000	132 @ 2800	4.00 x 3.00	9.0:1	36–41 @ 2000
	9	173 (2.8)	MPI	130 @ 5400	160 @ 3600	3.50 x 3.00	8.9:1	30–45 @ 2000
1987–88	R	151 (2.5)	TBI	92 @ 4400	134 @ 2800	4.00 x 3.00	8.3:1	36–41 @ 2000
	9	173 (2.8)	MPI	140 @ 5200	170 @ 3600	3.50 x 3.00	8.9:1	30–45 @ 2000

TBI—Throttle body fuel injection
MPI—Multi port fuel injection

Valve Specifications

Year	VIN	No. Cylinder Displacement cu. in. (liter)	Seat Angle (deg.)	Face Angle (deg.)	Spring Test Pressure (lbs.)	Spring Installed Height (in.)	Stem-to-Guide Clearance (in.) Intake	Stem-to-Guide Clearance (in.) Exhaust	Stem Diameter (in.) Intake	Stem Diameter (in.) Exhaust
1984	R	151 (2.5)	46	45	122–180 @ 1.254	1.69	0.0010–0.0027	0.0010–0.0027	0.342–0.343	0.0342–0.0343
1985–86	R	151 (2.5)	46	45	170–180 @ 1.26	1.69	0.0010–0.0027	0.0010–0.0027	0.342–0.343	0.0342–0.0343
	9	173 (2.8)	46	45	195 @ 1.181	1.57	0.0010–0.0027	0.0010–0.0027	0.3410–0.3416	0.3410–0.3416
1987–88	R	151 (2.5)	46	45	158–170 @ 1.040	1.44	0.0010–0.0027	0.0010–0.0027	0.313–0.314	0.312–0.313
	9	173 (2.8)	46	45	195 @ 1.181	1.57	0.0010–0.0027	0.0010–0.0027	0.3410–0.3416	0.3410–0.3416

Camshaft Specifications

All measurements given in inches.

Year	VIN	No. Cylinder Displacement cu. in. (liter)	Journal Diameter 1	2	3	4	5	Lobe Lift In.	Ex.	Bearing Clearance	Camshaft End Play
1984–88	R	151 (2.5)	1.869	1.869'	1.869	—	—	0.398	0.398	0.0007–0.0027	0.0015–0.0050
	9	173 (2.8)	1.869	1.869	1.869	1.869	—	0.231	0.263	0.0010–0.0040	—

Piston and Ring Specifications

All measurements are given in inches.

Year	VIN	No. Cylinder Displaceme... cu. in. (liter)	Piston Clearance	Ring Gap Top Compression	Ring Gap Bottom Compression	Ring Gap Oil Control	Ring Side Clearance Top Compression	Ring Side Clearance Bottom Compression	Ring Side Clearance Oil Control
1984–88	R	151 (2.5)	0.0025–0.0030	0.010–0.020	0.010–0.020	0.02–0.06	0.002–0.003	0.001–0.003	0.015–0.055
	9	173 (2.8)	0.00066–0.00169	0.010–0.020	0.010–0.020	0.02–0.06	0.0010–0.0027	0.0015–0.0037	0.00078 max

Torque Specifications

All readings in ft. lbs.

Year	VIN	No. Cylinder Displacement cu. in. (liter)	Cylinder Head Bolts	Main Bearing Bolts	Rod Bearing Bolts	Crankshaft Pulley Bolts	Flywheel Bolts	Manifold Intake	Manifold Exhaust	Spark Plugs
1984–85	R	151 (2.5)	92 ①	70	32	200	44	29	44	17–22
	9	173 (2.8)	65–75 ②	63–74	34–40	66–84	45–55	20–25	22–28	17–22
1986	R	151 (2.5)	③	70	32	162	44	④	⑤	17–22
	9	173 (2.8)	65–90 ⑥	63–74	34–40	66–84	45–55	20–25	22–28	17–22
1987–88	R	151 (2.5)	③	70	32	162	69	④	⑤	17–22
	9	173 (2.8)	65–90 ⑥	63–74	34–40	66–84	45–55	20–25	22–28	17–22

Torque in three steps in sequence using thread sealer

① a. 1st step: 31 ft. lbs.
b. 2nd step: 62 ft. lbs.
c. 3rd step: 92 ft. lbs.

② Torque in two steps in sequence
a. 1st step: 35 ft. lbs.
b. 2nd step: 65–75 ft. lbs.

③ Torque cylinder head bolts in sequence as follows
a. 1st step: 18 ft. lbs.
b. 2nd step: all bolts except #9 to 22 ft. lbs, and #9 to 29 ft. lbs.
c. Repeat sequence, turning all bolts except #9 2 flats (120 degrees), torque #9 ¼ turn (90 degrees)

④ Refer to the 1986 2.5L L4 intake manifold torquing sequence illustration in this chapter

⑤ Refer to the 1886–88 2.5L L4 exhaust manifold torquing sequence illustration in this chapter

⑥ Torque in three steps in sequence
a. 1st step: 18 ft. lbs.
b. 2nd step: 32–45 ft. lbs.
c. 3rd step: 65–90 ft. lbs.

Crankshaft and Connecting Rod Specifications

All measurements are given in inches.

Year	VIN	No. Cylinder Displacement cu. in. (liter)	Crankshaft				Connecting Rod		
			Main Brg. Journal Dia.	Main Brg. Oil Clearance	Shaft End-play	Thrust on No.	Journal Diameter	Oil Clearance	Side Clearance
1984	R	151 (2.5)	2.30	0.0005–0.0022	.0035–.0085	5	2.00	0.0005–0.0026	0.006–0.022
1985–88	R	151 (2.5)	2.30	0.0005–0.0022	.0035–.0085	5	2.00	0.0005–0.0026	0.006–0.022
	9	173 (2.8)	2.4932–2.6482	0.0016–0.0032	.002–.008	3	1.9993–1.9983	0.0014–0.0037	0.006–0.017

Engine

REMOVAL & INSTALLATION

4-2.5L Engine

➧ See Figures 27 thru 34

➡The engine assembly is removed from underneath the vehicle.

1. Disconnect the negative (−) battery cable.
2. With the cool, drain the engine coolant into a suitable drain pan.

⁂ CAUTION

When draining engine coolant, keep in mind that cats and dogs are attracted to ethylene glycol antifreeze and could drink any that is left in an uncovered container or in puddles on the ground. This will prove fatal in sufficient quantity. Always drain coolant into a sealable container. Coolant should be reused unless it is contaminated or is several years old.

3. Remove the rear engine compartment lid and also the side cover panels with an assistant.

➡Do not remove the torsion rod retaining bolts. Scribe the hinges for later assembly. Remove the trim at the sail panel below the battery side panel.

4. Remove the air cleaner assembly.
5. Disconnect the throttle and shift cables.
6. Position suitable drain pan under the engine and disconnect the heater hose at the intake manifold.
7. Disconnect the vacuum hoses from all non-engine components.
8. Disconnect the fuel lines and filter.

⁂ CAUTION

To reduce the risk of fire and personal injury, it is necessary to relieve the fuel system pressure before servicing any fuel system component. If this procedure is not performed, fuel may be sprayed out of the connection under pressure. Always keep a dry chemical (Class B) fire extinguisher near the work area.

To relieve fuel system pressure:

a. Remove the fuel pump fuse from the fuse block located in the passenger compartment.
b. Start the engine and run until the engine stops due to the lack of fuel.
c. Crank the engine for 3 seconds to ensure all pressure is relieved.

9. Disconnect the fuel pump relay and oxygen sensor.
10. On models with automatic transaxle, disconnect the transaxle cooler lines.
11. Disconnect the slave cylinder from manual transaxle equipped vehicles.
12. Disconnect the engine-to-chassis ground strap and electrical harness connector at bulkhead.
13. Disconnect the air conditioning system, if so equipped, then disconnect the air conditioning lines at the compressor and seal the ends.

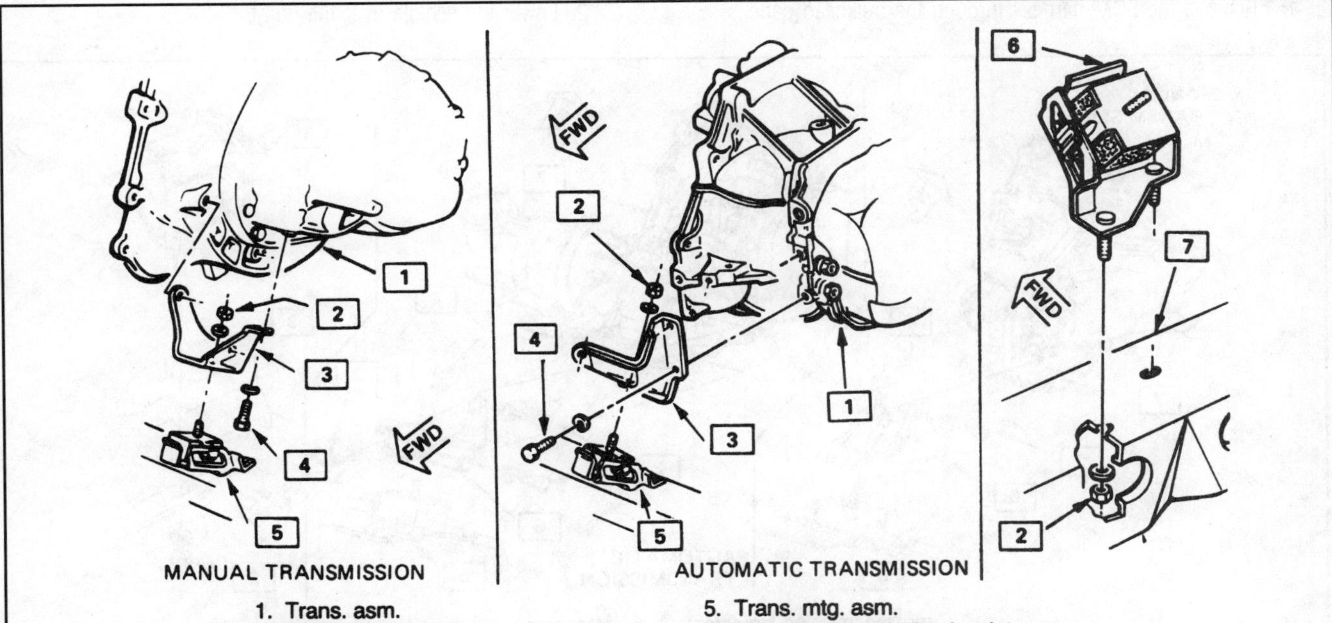

Fig. 27 Exploded views of the engine mounts used on the older model 2.5L engines with manual and automatic transaxles

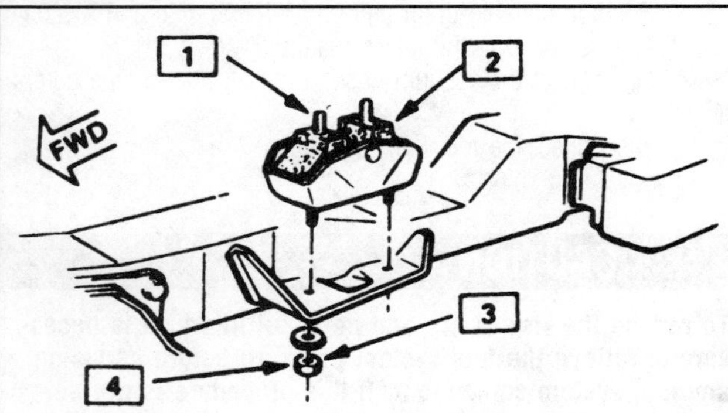

1. Insulator to support bracket studs
2. Engine insulator
3. Insulator to chassis attaching nut
4. 56 N·m (41 lb. ft.)

Fig. 28 Components of the engine mount-to-crossmember used on four-cylinder engines

** CAUTION

Please refer to Section 1 before discharging the compressor or disconnecting air conditioning lines. Damage to the air conditioning system or personal injury could result. Consult your local laws concerning refrigerant discharge and recycling. In many areas it may be illegal for anyone but a certified technician to service the A/C system. Always use an approved recovery station when discharging the air conditioning.

14. Remove the rear console.
15. Remove the ECM harness through the bulkhead panel.
16. Install an engine support fixture part No. J28467 or equivalent.
17. Remove the engine strut bracket and mark the bolt and bracket for reassembly.
18. Raise the vehicle and support with jackstands. Refer to the Engine removal illustration.
19. Remove the rear wheels.
20. On models equipped with an automatic transaxle, remove the torque converter bolts.
21. Remove the parking brake cable and calipers. Wire the calipers to the body so not to damage the brake hose.

➡Do not disconnect the brake hoses. Support the caliper out of the way with a piece of wire.

22. Remove the strut bolts and mark the struts for realignment. Refer to the MacPherson Strut removal and installation procedure in Section 8.
23. Disconnect the air conditioning wiring, if so equipped.
24. Loosen the four engine cradle bolts.
25. On the 4-cylinder engine, release the parking brake cables at the cradle. A special tool No. J-34065 is available for this procedure.

** CAUTION

Support the engine/transaxle and cradle assembly on a jack. Be sure to support the outboard ends of the lower control arms. Disconnect the engine support fixture.

26. Lower the car and attach the engine/transaxle assembly to a dolly. Remove the cradle bolts. Raise the car and roll the dolly from under the car.
27. Separate the engine and transaxle.

To install:

1. Reconnect the engine and transaxle on the cradle.
2. Lower the vehicle over the dolly.

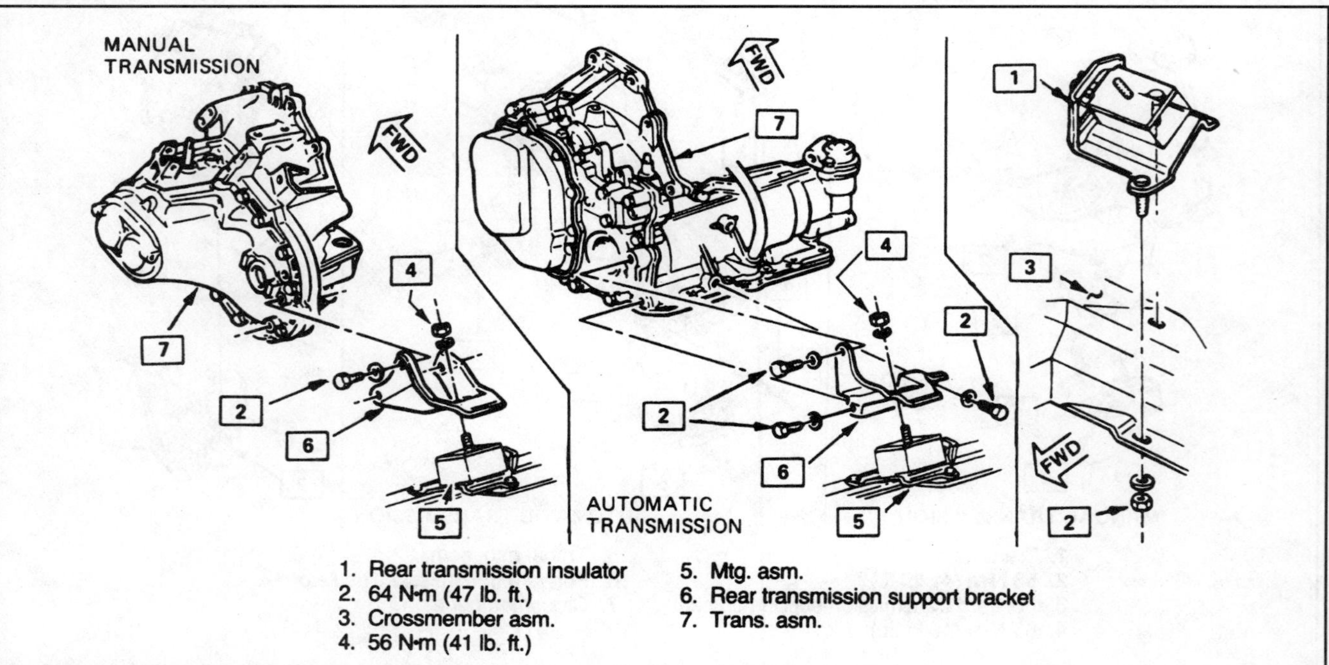

1. Rear transmission insulator
2. 64 N·m (47 lb. ft.)
3. Crossmember asm.
4. 56 N·m (41 lb. ft.)
5. Mtg. asm.
6. Rear transmission support bracket
7. Trans. asm.

Fig. 29 Exploded views of the rear transaxle mount used on older model 2.5L engines

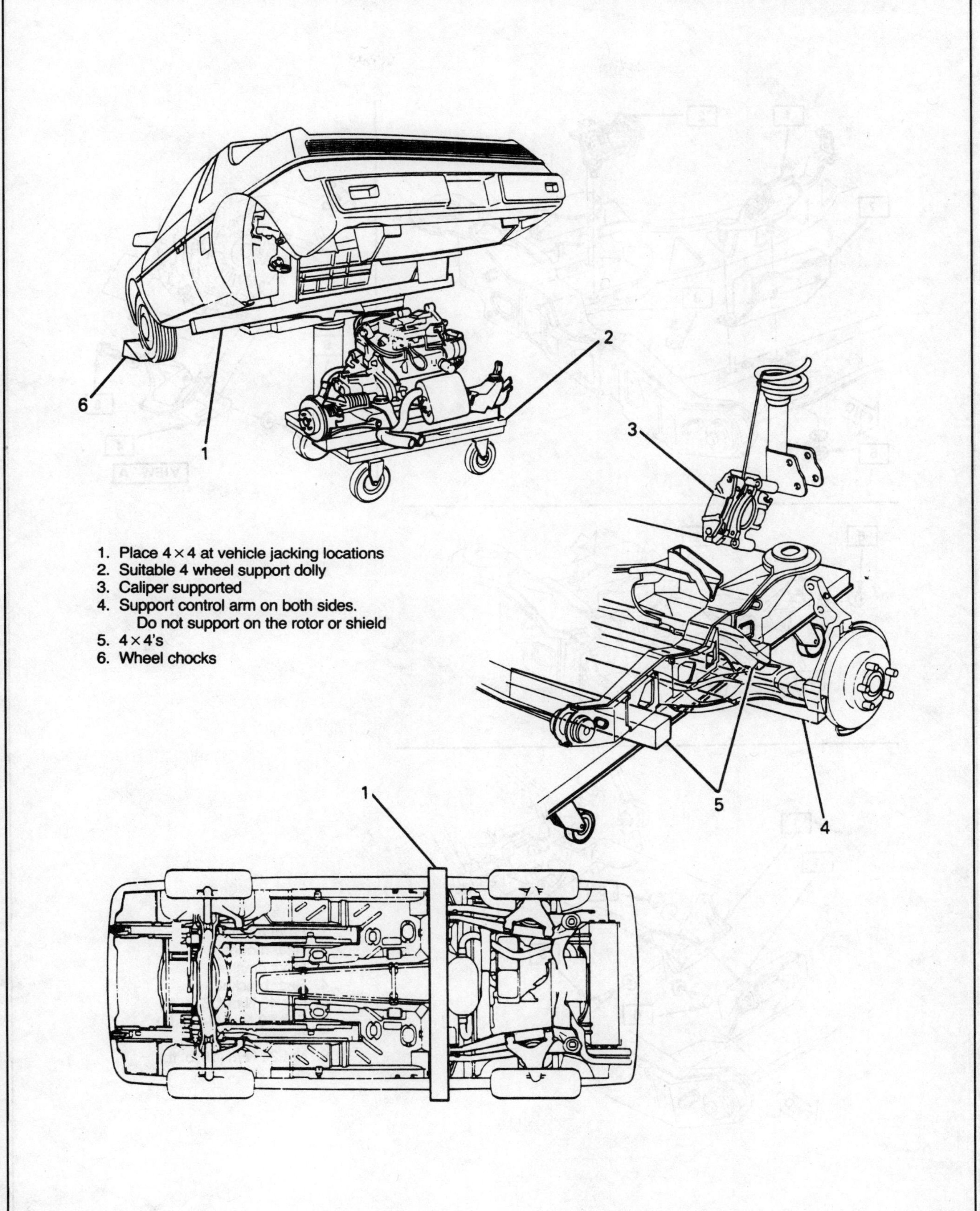

Fig. 30 Different views of some of the steps needed for engine removal and installation

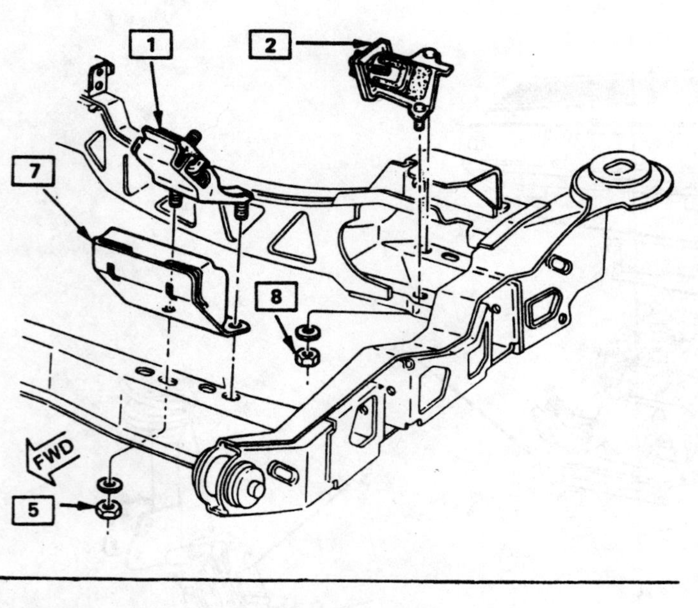

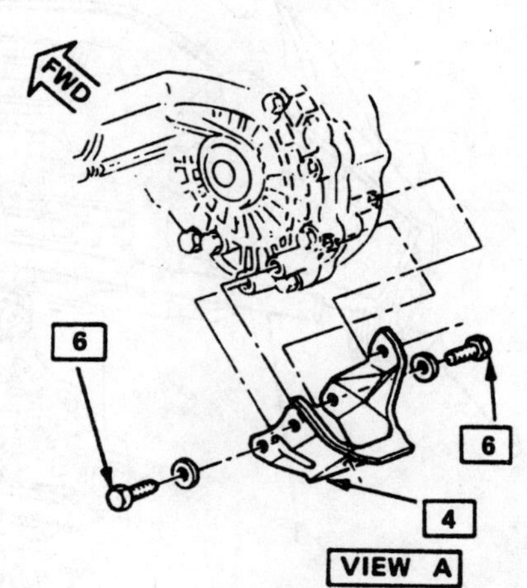

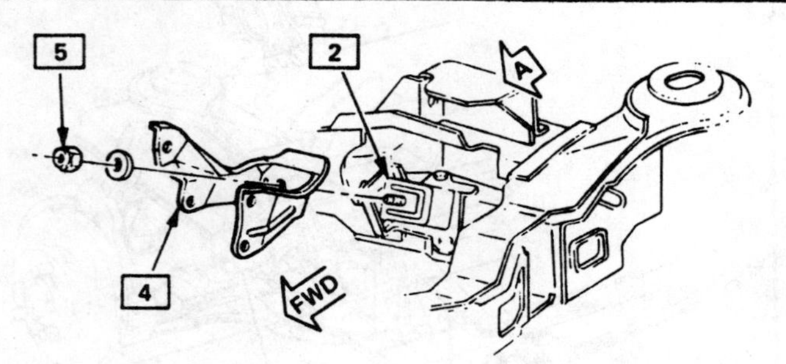

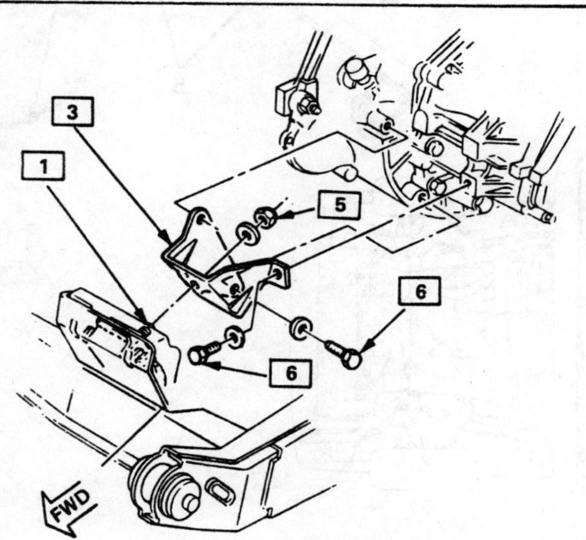

1. Front mount
2. Rear mount
3. Front bracket
4. Rear bracket
5. Nut-48 N·m (35 lb. ft.)
6. Bolt-60 N·m (44 lb. ft.)
7. Shield
8. Nut-24 N·m (18 lb. ft.)

Fig. 31 Engine mount locations—2.5L engine

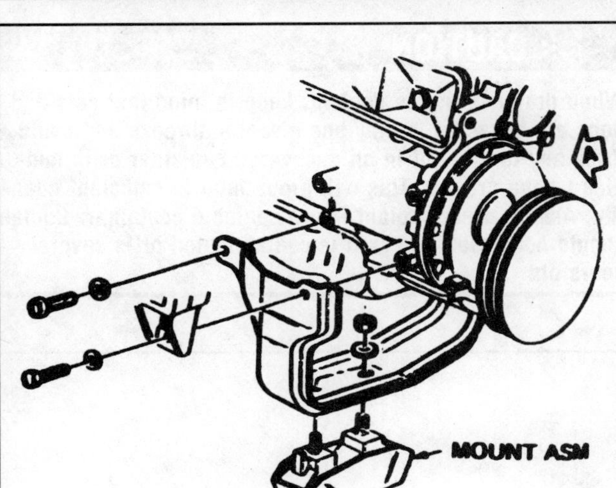

Fig. 32 Location of the engine support bracket and its retainers—2.5L engine

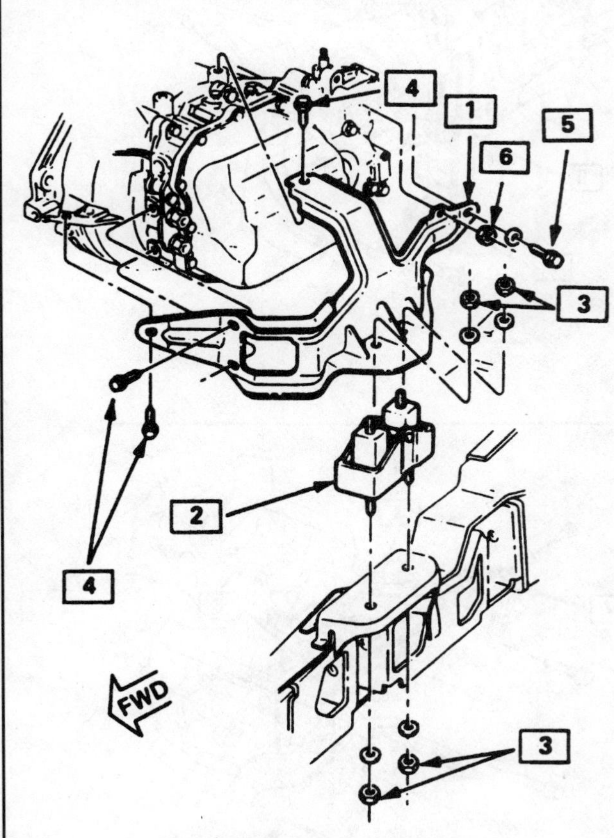

Fig. 33 Exploded view of the automatic transaxle mounting bracket and components—2.5L engine

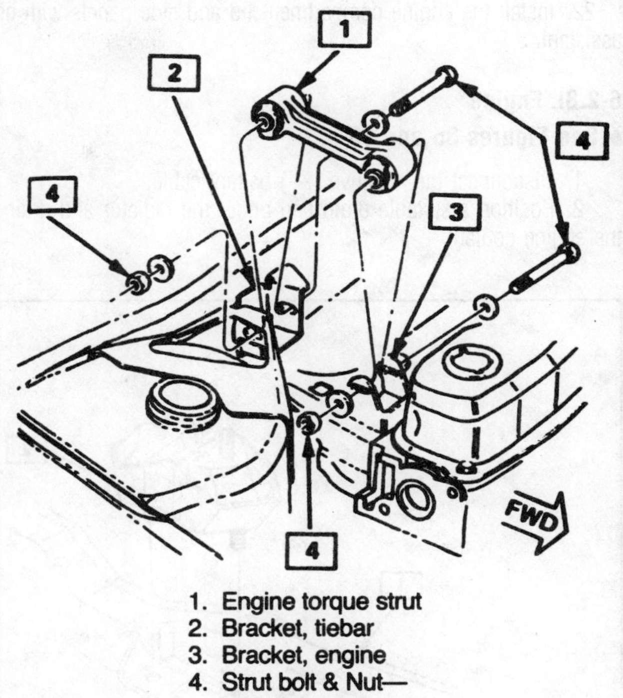

Fig. 34 Engine torque strut and related components—2.5L engine

3. Install the cradle bolts in sequence as below.
   a. Install the front bolts finger-tight.
   b. Torque the rear bolts to 76 ft. lbs. (103 Nm).
   c. Torque the front bolts to 66 ft. lbs. (90 Nm).
4. Raise the vehicle and support with jackstands. Install the MacPherson strut bolts.
5. Install the brake caliper and parking brake cable.
6. Connect the air conditioning wiring, if so equipped.
7. Install the torque converter bolts and tighten (automatic transaxle).
8. Install the rear wheels and torque the lug nuts to 100 ft. lbs. (134 Nm).
9. Lower the vehicle.
10. Install the engine strut bracket.
11. Connect the radiator and heater hoses and tighten clamps.
12. Connect the ground strap to the engine.
13. Connect the transaxle cooler lines (automatic trans. only).
14. Connect the fuel pump relay and oxygen sensor connectors, fuel lines at the throttle body and filter and all vacuum hoses.
15. Connect the throttle and shift cables and install the air cleaner assembly.
16. Connect the engine and ECM electrical harness.
17. Install the rear console.
18. Refill the engine with the specified coolant and the proper viscosity engine oil.
19. Connect the negative (−) battery cable.
20. Evacuate and recharge the air conditioning system. Refer to the Air Conditioning System recharge and evacuate procedures in section 1.

21. Install the sail panel trim below the battery side panel.
22. Install the engine compartment lid and side panels with an assistant.

6-2.8L Engine

➧ See Figures 35 and 36

1. Disconnect the negative (−) battery cable.
2. Position a suitable drain pan under the radiator and drain the engine coolant.

CAUTION

When draining engine coolant, keep in mind that cats and dogs are attracted to ethylene glycol antifreeze and could drink any that is left in an uncovered container or in puddles on the ground. This will prove fatal in sufficient quantity. Always drain coolant into a sealable container. Coolant should be reused unless it is contaminated or is several years old.

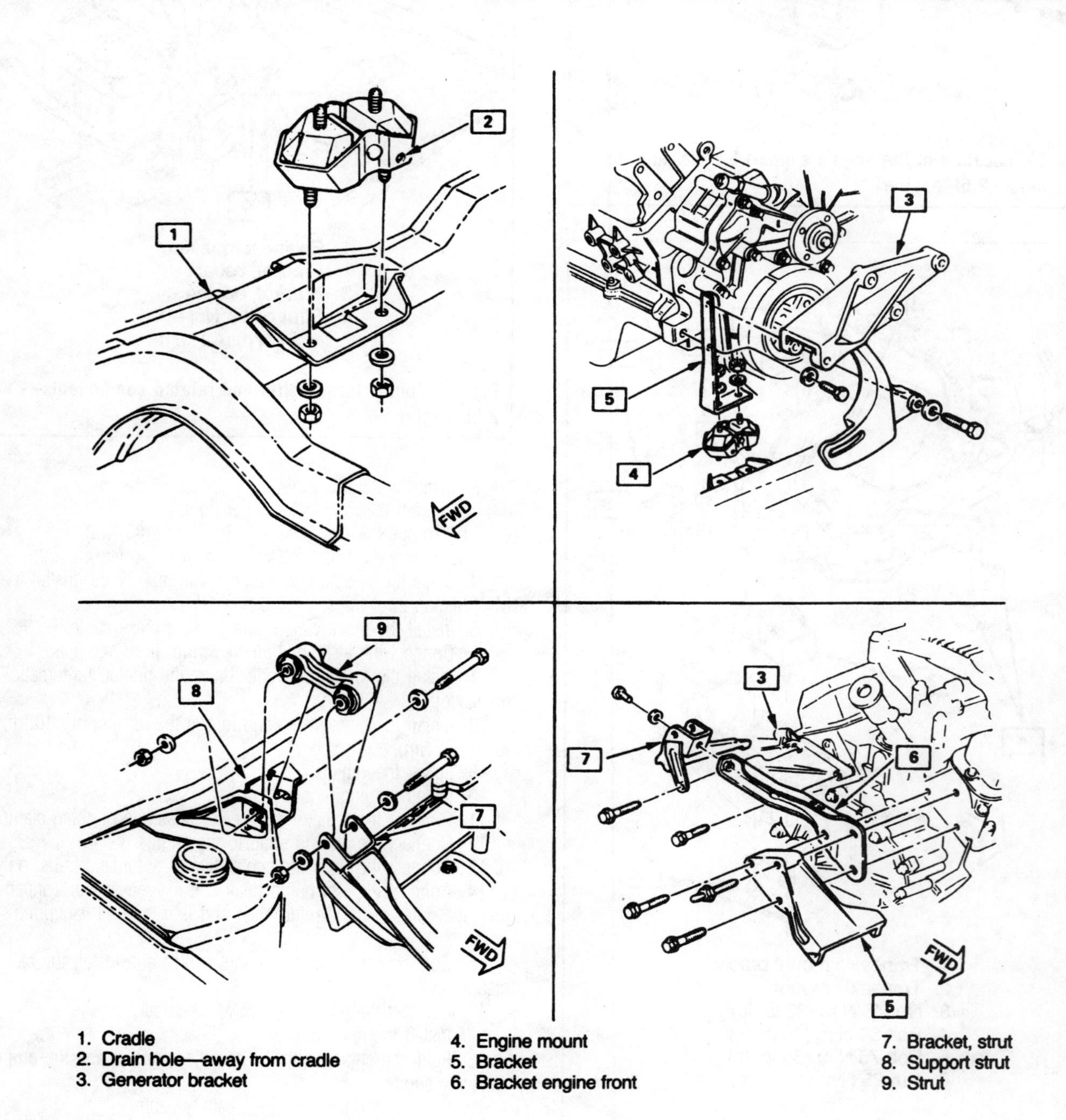

Fig. 35 Exploded view of the engine mounts and torque strut—V6 engines

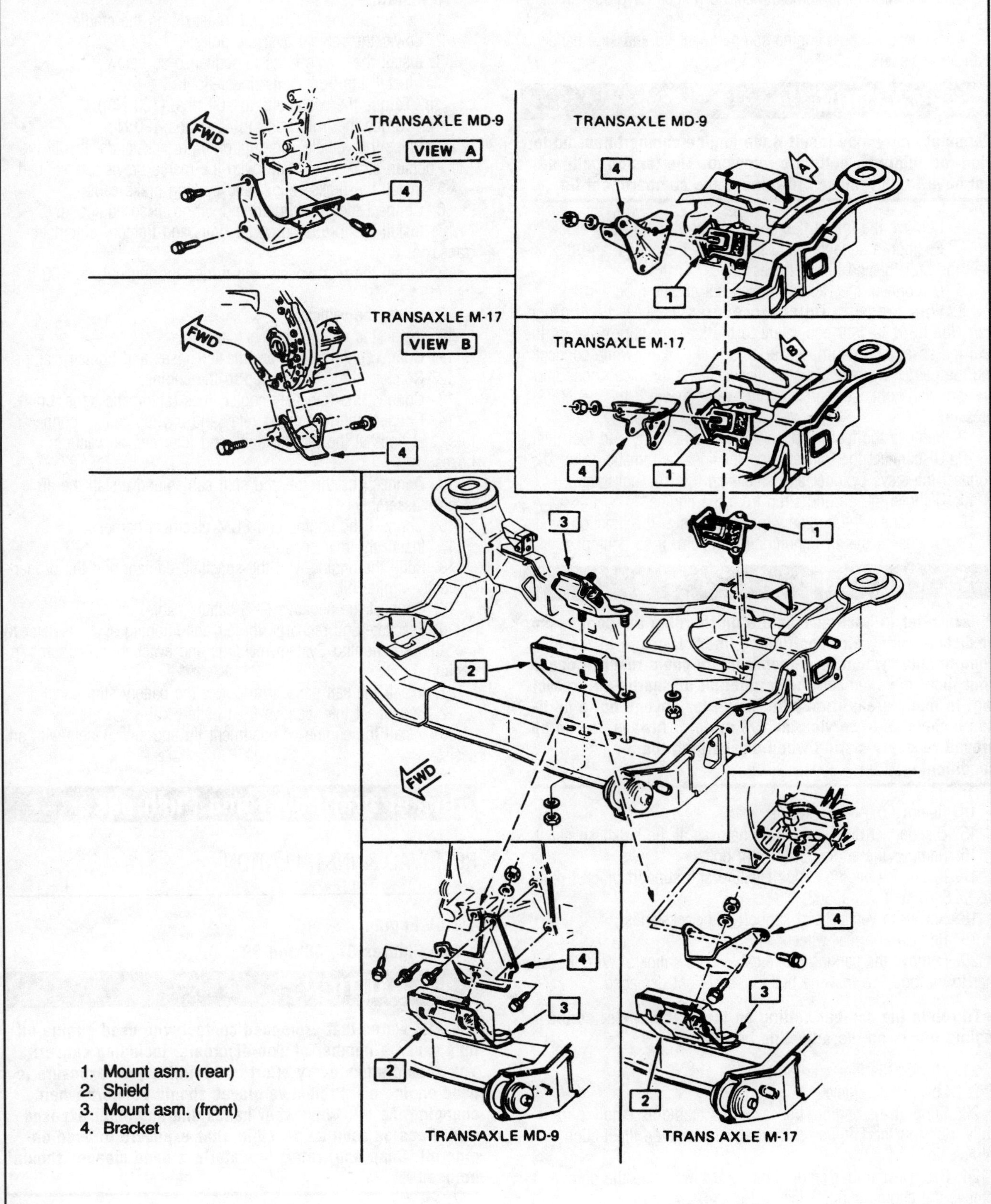

Fig. 36 Exploded view of the cradle and transaxle nuts—V6 engines

3. Mark the engine compartment lid hinges for proper installation.
4. Remove the rear engine compartment lid and side panels with an assistant.

CAUTION

Personal injury may result if the engine compartment lid torsion rod retaining bolts are removed. The torsion bolts do not have to be removed to remove the compartment lid.

5. Remove the intake flex duct and the throttle body elbow.
6. Position a suitable drain pan under the engine and disconnect the radiator and heater hoses.
7. Disconnect the vacuum hoses not engine mounted.
8. **Fuel pressure relief procedures:** connect a fuel gauge part No. J 34730-1 or equivalent to the fuel pressure valve on the fuel rail assembly. Wrap a towel around the fitting while connecting the gauge to prevent fuel spillage. Install the bleed hose into an approved container and open the valve to bleed the system pressure.
9. Remove the fuel lines from the throttle body and fuel filter.
10. Disconnect the transaxle cooler lines (automatic only). Disconnect the slave cylinder and shield on the (manual trans.).
11. Remove the ground strap from the engine.
12. Disconnect the engine wiring harness at the junction block.
13. Discharge the air conditioning system, if so equipped.

CAUTION

Please refer to Section 1 before discharging the compressor or disconnecting air conditioning lines. Damage to the air conditioning system or personal injury could result. Consult your local laws concerning refrigerant discharge and recycling. In many areas it may be illegal for anyone but a certified technician to service the A/C system. Always use an approved recovery station when discharging the air conditioning.

14. Remove the rear console.
15. Disconnect the ECM wiring harness at the bulkhead panel.
16. Remove the engine strut front bolt.
17. Install the engine support fixture and support bracket part No. J28467 and W/J35563.
18. Raise the vehicle and support with jackstands.
19. Remove the rear wheels.
20. Remove the parking brake cables and calipers. Wire the caliper to the body so that the brake hose is not damaged.

➡To retain the camber setting on the rear wheels, scribe legible marks on the adjusting bolt.

21. Loosen the four cradle bolts.
22. Lower the vehicle.
23. Support the engine, transaxle and cradle assembly on a dolly. Refer to the Engine removal and installation illustration in this section.
24. Remove the four cradle bolts and lower onto the dolly and remove the engine support fixture No. J28467.
25. Raise the vehicle leaving the engine/transaxle and cradle assembly on the dolly.
26. Separate the engine from the transaxle. Place the engine on a suitable engine stand.

To install:

1. Reconnect the engine and transaxle on the cradle.
2. Lower the vehicle over the dolly.
3. Install the cradle bolts in sequence as below.
   a. Install the front bolts finger-tight.
   b. Torque the bear bolts to 76ft. lbs. (103 Nm).
   c. Torque the front bolts to 66 ft. lbs. (90 Nm).
4. Raise the vehicle and support with jackstands. Install the MacPherson strut bolts. Align with the marks previously scribed.
5. Install the brake caliper and parking brake cable.
6. Connect the air conditioning wiring, if so equipped.
7. Install the torque converter bolts and tighten (automatic transaxle).
8. Install the rear wheels and torque the lug nuts to 100 ft. lbs. (134 Nm).
9. Lower the vehicle.
10. Install the engine strut bracket.
11. Connect the radiator and heater hoses and tighten clamps.
12. Connect the ground strap to the engine.
13. Connect the transaxle cooler lines (automatic trans. only).
14. Connect the fuel pump relay and oxygen sensor connectors, fuel lines at the throttle body and filter and all vacuum hoses.
15. Connect the throttle and shift cables and install the air cleaner assembly.
16. Connect the engine and ECM electrical harness.
17. Install the rear console.
18. Refill the engine with the specified coolant and the proper viscosity engine oil.
19. Connect the negative (−) battery cable.
20. Evacuate and recharge the air conditioning system. Refer to the Air Conditioning System recharge and evacuate procedures in section 1.
21. Install the sail panel trim below the battery side panel.
22. Reconnect the negative (−) battery cable.
23. Install the engine compartment lid and side panels with an assistant.

Rocker Arm Cover and Pushrods

REMOVAL & INSTALLATION

4-2.5L Engine

➧ See Figures 37, 38 and 39

CAUTION

The EPA warns that prolonged contact with used engine oil may cause a number of skin disorders, including cancer! You should make every effort to minimize your exposure to used engine oil. Protective gloves should be worn when changing the oil. Wash your hands and any other exposed skin areas as soon as possible after exposure to used engine oil. Soap and water, or waterless hand cleaner should be used.

1. Remove the air cleaner assembly (Refer to Section 1).
2. Remove the PCV valve and hose.
3. Remove the accelerator and throttle valve TV cables.
4. Remove the valve cover bolts.

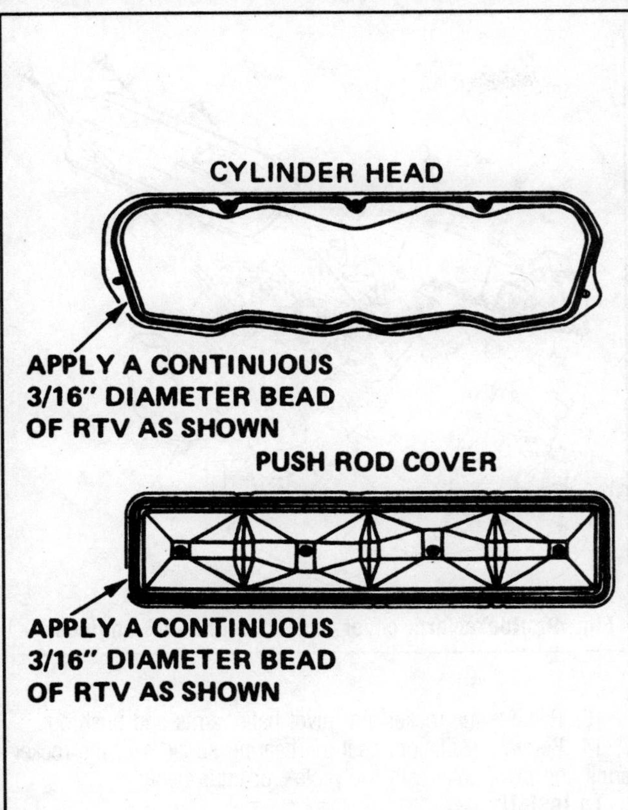

Fig. 37 Cylinder head and rocker cover RTV sealant application—four-cylinder engines

5. Disconnect and mark the wires from the spark plugs and clips.
6. Remove the valve cover by using the Rocker Arm Cover Removing tool No. J34144-A or equivalent and lightly tap with a rubber hammer.

➡Prying on the cover could cause damage to the sealing surfaces.

7. Remove the rocker arm bolt and ball.
8. If replacing the pushrod only, loosen the rocker arm bolt and swing the arm clear of the pushrod.
9. Remove the rocker arm and pushrod. If removing more than one, label each part to ensure the part is placed in its original location.

To install:

10. Clean the rocker arm cover with solvent and dry with a clean rag.
11. Install the pushrod into the same hole as removed. Place the guide, rocker arm, ball and nut over the stud and finger-tighten the nut.
12. Make sure the camshaft is on the base of the cam lob (valve in the closed position) before tightening the rocker arm nut. Torque the rocker arm nut to 24 ft. lbs. (32 Nm).
13. Apply a continuous 5mm diameter bead of RTV sealant or equivalent around the cylinder head sealing surfaces inboard at the bolt holes.

➡Keep the sealant out of the bolt holes.

14. Install the rocker arm cover and torque the attaching bolts to 4 ft. lbs. (5 Nm).
15. Install the spark plug wires and clips, PCV valve and hose, accelerator and TV cable and air cleaner assembly.

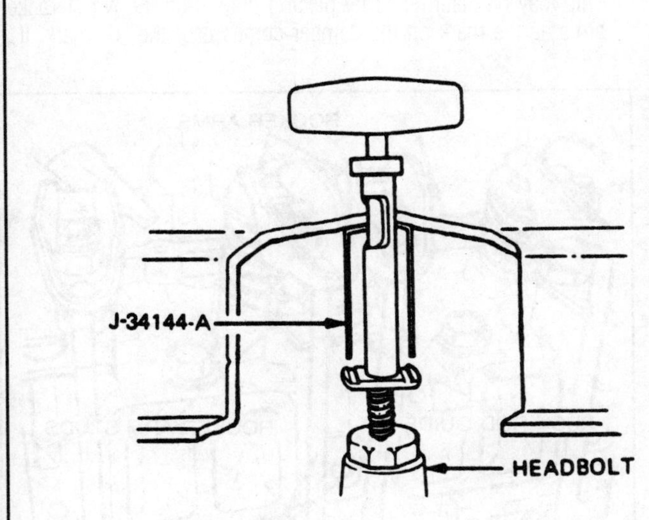

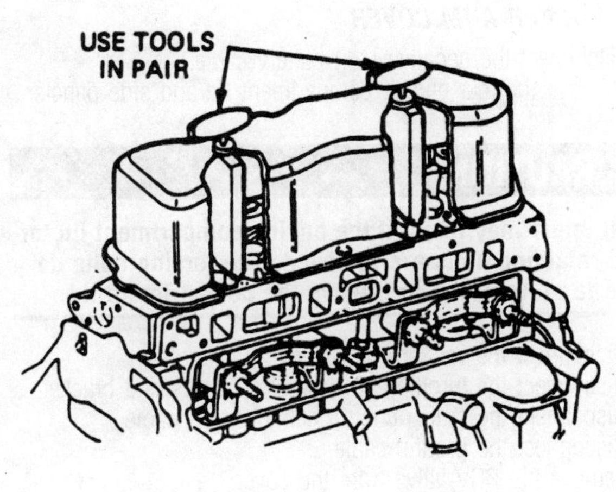

Fig. 38 Remove the valve cover by using a pair of J-34144-A tools and then gently tapping the cover with a hammer

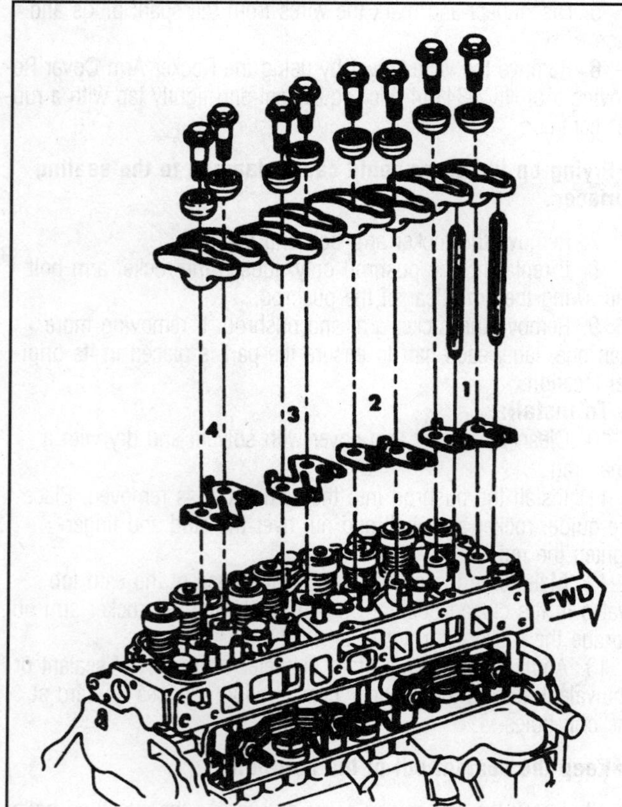

Fig. 39 Exploded view of the valve mechanisms—2.5L engine

6-2.8L Engine

➧ See Figures 40, 41 and 42

FRONT ROCKER ARM COVER

1 Disconnect the negative (−) battery cable.
2. Remove the rear engine compartment lid and side panels with an assistant.

✲✲ CAUTION

Personal injury may result if the engine compartment lid torsion rod retaining bolts are removed. The torsion bolts do not have to be removed to remove the compartment lid.

3. Disconnect the vacuum boost line and tube.
4. Disconnect the throttle and downshift cables and bracket.
5. Disconnect the cruise control cable, if applicable.
6. Disconnect the ground cable.
7. Remove the PCV valve from the cover.
8. Remove the oil dip stick tube.
9. Mark and disconnect the spark plug wires and bracket.
10. Remove the engine lift hook.
11. Remove the rocker arm cover bolts and carefully remove the cover by bumping with a rubber mallet. If prying is necessary do not distort the sealing flange.
12. Remove the rocker arm nuts.

➡Keep all components in order so that they may be installed in the same location.

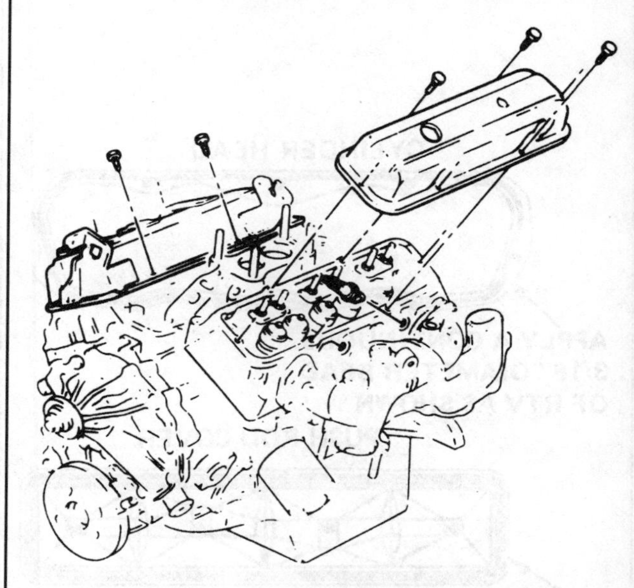
Fig. 40 Rocker arm cover and retainers—V6 engines

13. Remove the rocker arm pivot balls, arms and pushrods.
14. Before installation, coat the bearing surfaces of the rocker arms and pivot balls with Molykote® or equivalent.

To install:

15. Install the pushrods, rocker arms and pivot balls. Make sure the pushrods are seated in the valve lifters.
16. Adjust the rocker arm nuts until lash is eliminated.
 a. **Valve Lash Adjustment:** rotate the engine until the mark on the torsional damper lines up with the "0" mark on the timing tab, with the engine in the No. 1 firing position. This may be determined by placing fingers on the No. 1 rocker arms as the mark on the damper comes near the "0" mark. If

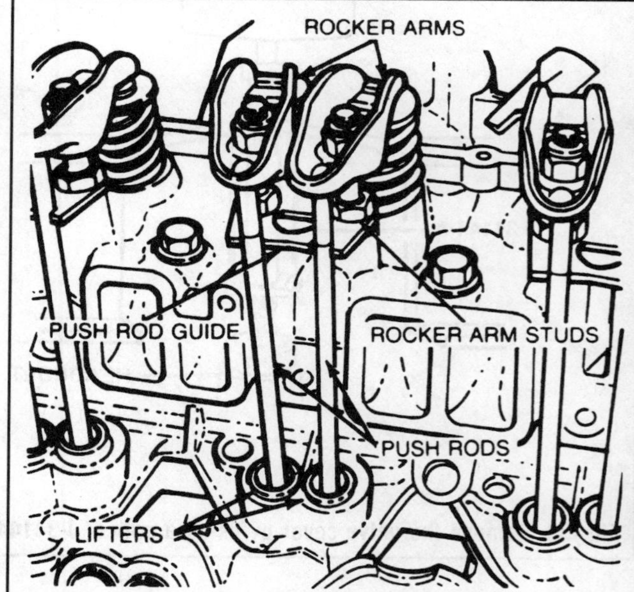

Fig. 41 Valve train components and their locations—V6 engines

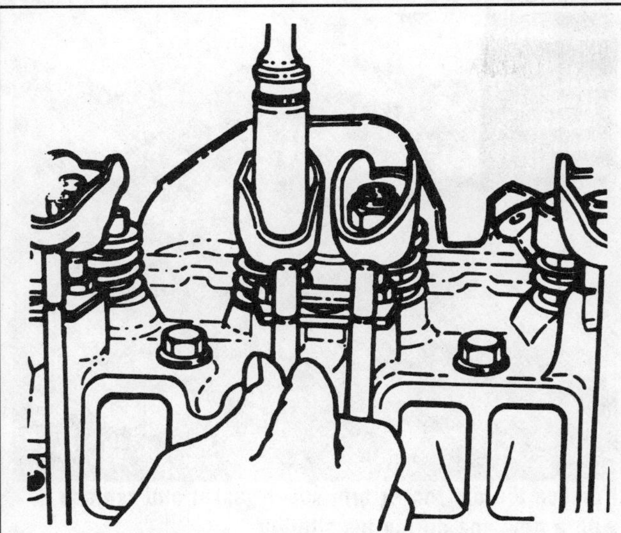

Fig. 42 Adjust the valve lash until all lash is removed—V6 engines

the valves are not moving, the engine is in the No. 1 firing position. With the engine in the No. 1 firing position, the following valves may be adjusted:

- Exhaust—1, 2, 3
- Intake—1, 5, 6

b. Back out the adjusting nut until lash is felt at the pushrod, then turn the adjusting nut until all lash is removed. This can be determined by rotating the pushrod while turning the adjusting nut. When lash has been removed, turn the adjusting nut in 1½ additional turns to center the lifter plunger.

c. Crank the engine one revolution until the timing tab "0" mark and torsional damper mark are again in alignment. This is the No. 4 firing position. With the engine in this position, the following valves may be adjusted:

- Exhaust—4, 5, 6
- Intake—2, 3, 4

17. Clean the rocker arm cover with soap and water and dry before installation.

a. Clean the surfaces on the cylinder head.

b. Place a 3mm diameter dot of RTV sealer, at the intake manifold and cylinder head split line.

c. Apply a continuous 5mm diameter bead of RTV sealer to the rocker arm cover mating surfaces. Install the rocker arm cover gasket, using care to line up the holes in the gasket with the bolt holes in the cylinder head.

d. Install the four rocker arm cover bolts and torque to 90 inch lbs. (10 Nm).

18. Install the spark plug wires and bracket in the same location as removal.

19. Install the oil dipstick tube, PCV valve and hose, ground cable, cruise control cable, and throttle control cable.

20. Install the engine compartment lid in the same location as removal with an assistant.

21. Connect the negative (−) battery cable.

REAR ROCKER ARM COVER

1. Disconnect the negative (−) battery cable.
2. Remove the torque reaction rod bolt at the cylinder head bracket.

Unfasten the torque reaction rod bolt . . .

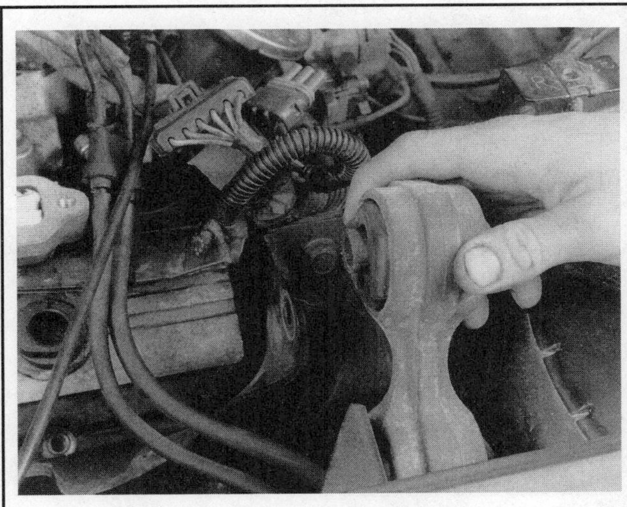

. . . then swing the torque reaction rod up

Remove the bolt connecting the cylinder head bracket to the torque reaction rod bracket

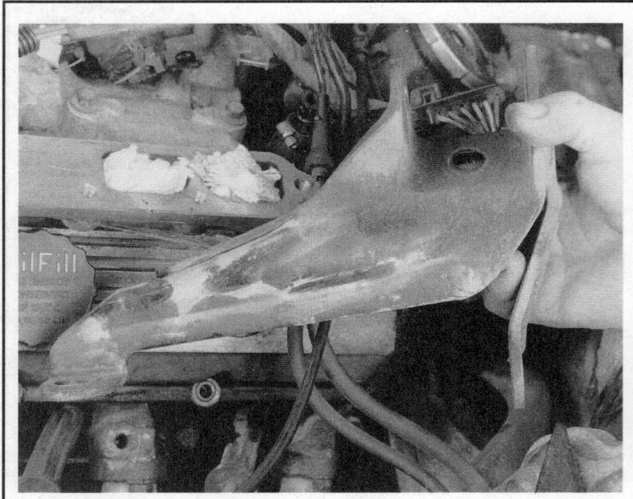
If necessary, remove the bracket from the engine

Remove the old rocker arm cover gasket and replace it with a new one during installation

Unfasten the rocker arm cover retaining bolts . . .

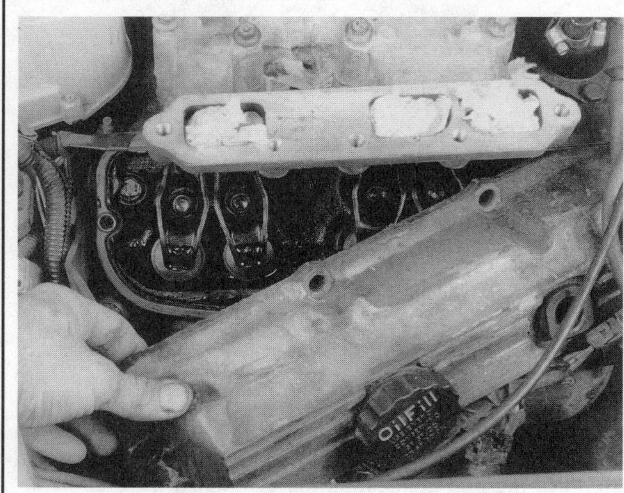
. . . then remove the rocker arm cover from the vehicle

3. Swing the torque reaction rod up and remove the bolt connecting the cylinder head bracket-to-bracket at the front of the engine.

4. Loosen the lower bolt of the torque reaction rod bracket at the front of the engine.

5. Remove the upper two bolts of the torque reaction rod bracket at the front of the engine.

6. Remove the bolt at the torque reaction rod at the exhaust manifold connector.

7. Disconnect the wiring harness between the rocker arm cover and lower intake plenum.

8. Remove the four rocker arm cover bolts and remove the cover by tapping with a rubber hammer.

To install:

9. Install the pushrods, rocker arms and pivot balls. Make sure the pushrods are seated in the valve lifters.

10. Adjust the rocker arm nuts until lash is eliminated.

a. **Valve Lash Adjustment:** rotate the engine until the mark on the torsional damper lines up with the "0" mark on the timing tab, with the engine in the No. 1 firing position. This may be determined by placing fingers on the No. 1 rocker arms as the mark on the damper comes near the "0" mark. If the valves are not moving, the engine is in the No. 1 firing position. With the engine in the No. 1 firing position, the following valves may be adjusted:

- Exhaust—1, 2, 3
- Intake—1, 5, 6

b. Back out the adjusting nut until lash is felt at the pushrod, then turn the adjusting nut until all lash is removed. This can be determined by rotating the pushrod while turning the adjusting nut. When lash has been removed, turn the adjusting nut in 1½ additional turns to center the lifter plunger.

c. Crank the engine one revolution until the timing tab "0" mark and torsional damper mark are again in alignment. This is the No. 4 firing position. With the engine in this position, the following valves may be adjusted:

- Exhaust—4, 5, 6
- Intake—2, 3, 4

11. Clean the rocker arm cover with soap and water and

dry before installation. Clean the cylinder head mating surface with a gasket scraper and clean rag to remove old gasket material.

12. Place a 1/8 in. (3mm) dot of RTV sealer or equivalent at the intake manifold and cylinder head split line.
13. Apply a continuous 5mm bead of RTV sealer to the rocker arm cover. Install the new gasket onto the cover and apply another bead of RTV sealer to the gasket.
14. Install the rocker arm cover onto the cylinder head, using care to line up the holes in the gasket with the bolt holes in the cylinder head.
15. Install the four rocker arm cover bolts and torque to 90 inch lbs. (10 Nm).
16. Install the wiring harness between the rocker arm cover and lower intake plenum.
17. Install the bolt to the torque reaction rod bracket at cylinder head and exhaust manifold.
18. Tighten the lower torque reaction rod bolt at front of the engine.
19. Install and tighten all torque reaction rod bracket bolts.
20. Connect the negative (−) battery cable.

Pushrod Cover

REMOVAL & INSTALLATION

4-2.5L Engine

1. Disconnect the negative (−) battery cable.
2. Remove the intake manifold as outlined in the "Intake Manifold" procedures in this section.

CAUTION

When draining engine coolant, keep in mind that cats and dogs are attracted to ethylene glycol antifreeze and could drink any that is left in an uncovered container or in puddles on the ground. This will prove fatal in sufficient quantity. Always drain coolant into a sealable container. Coolant should be reused unless it is contaminated or is several years old.

3. Remove the four pushrod cover attaching nuts.

➡Do not pry on the cover or damage to the sealing surface may result.

4. To remove the pushrod cover, proceed as follows:
   a. Unscrew the four nuts from the cover attaching studs, reverse the two nuts so the washers face outward and screw them back onto the inner two studs. Assemble the remaining nuts to the same two inner studs with washers facing inward.
   b. Using a small wrench on the inner nut, on each stud, jam the two nuts tightly together. Again using the small wrench, on the inner nut, unscrew the studs until the cover breaks loose.
   c. After breaking the cover loose, remove the jammed nuts from each stud. Remove the cover from the studs. Examine the stud and rubber washer assembly and replace if either stud or washer is damaged.

To install:

5. Clean the sealing surfaces on the cover and cylinder block.
6. Apply a continuous 5mm bead of RTV sealer or equivalent around the pushrod cover.
7. Install the cover and torque the bolts to 90 inch lbs. (10 Nm).
8. Install the intake manifold as outlined in the Intake Manifold installation procedures in this section.

Thermostat

REMOVAL & INSTALLATION

➧ See Figures 43 and 44

CAUTION

When draining engine coolant, keep in mind that cats and dogs are attracted to ethylene glycol antifreeze and could drink any that is left in an uncovered container or in puddles on the ground. This will prove fatal in sufficient quantity. Always drain coolant into a sealable container. Coolant should be reused unless it is contaminated or is several years old.

1. When the engine is cool, drain the coolant from the radiator until the level is below the thermostat housing cap.

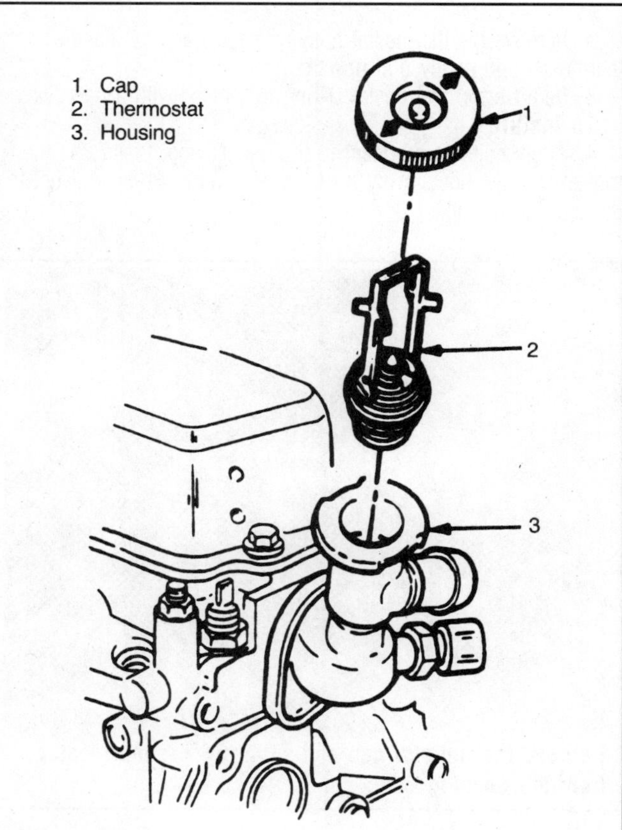

Fig. 43 Exploded view of the thermostat assembly—2.5L engines

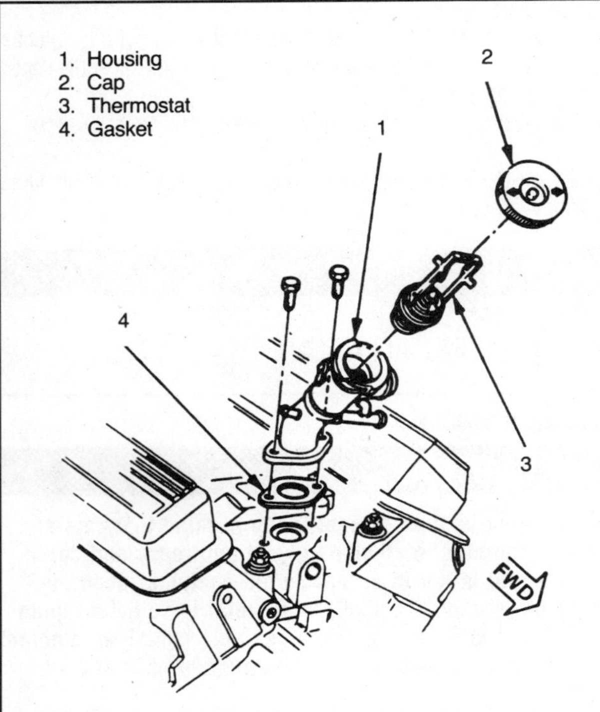

Fig. 44 Exploded view of the thermostat assembly—2.8L engines

2. Remove the thermostat housing cap, grasp the handle of the thermostat and gently pull upward.
3. Remove the thermostat O-ring to replace with a new one.

To install:

4. Apply suitable lubricant to the new O-ring. Install the thermostat into the housing by pushing downward. Be careful not to damage the O-ring.

Remove the radiator cap and withdraw the thermostat from the opening

5. Install the thermostat housing cap. Refill the radiator with the specified coolant. Install radiator cap only half way (to first stop). Start the engine and warm up to operating temperature. Remove the cap with a large towel and check coolant level and add if necessary.

Intake Manifold

REMOVAL & INSTALLATION

4-2.5L Engine

See Figures 45 and 46

CAUTION

To reduce the risk of fire and personal injury, it is necessary to relieve the fuel system pressure before servicing any fuel system component. If this procedure is not performed, fuel may be sprayed out of the connection under pressure. Always keep a dry chemical (Class B) fire extinguisher near the work area.

1. **Fuel pressure relief procedures:** remove the Fuel pump fuse from the fuse block located in the passenger compartment. Start the engine and run until the engine stops due to the lack of fuel. Crank the engine for 3 seconds to ensure all pressure is relieved.
2. Disconnect the negative (−) battery cable.
3. Remove the air cleaner assembly.
4. Remove the PCV valve and hose.
5. Drain the cooling system at the radiator.

CAUTION

When draining engine coolant, keep in mind that cats and dogs are attracted to ethylene glycol antifreeze and could drink any that is left in an uncovered container or in puddles on the ground. This will prove fatal in sufficient quantity. Always drain coolant into a sealable container. Coolant should be reused unless it is contaminated or is several years old.

6. Disconnect the fuel lines at the intake manifold.
7. Disconnect the vacuum hoses.
8. Disconnect the wiring and the throttle linkage from the throttle body assembly.
9. Disconnect the cruise control linkage, if so equipped.
10. Disconnect the throttle linkage and bell crank and place to one side.
11. Disconnect the heater hose.
12. Remove the alternator upper bracket.
13. Remove the ignition coil, on vehicles with the separately mounted coil.
14. Remove the retaining bolts and remove the manifolds by tapping with a rubber hose.

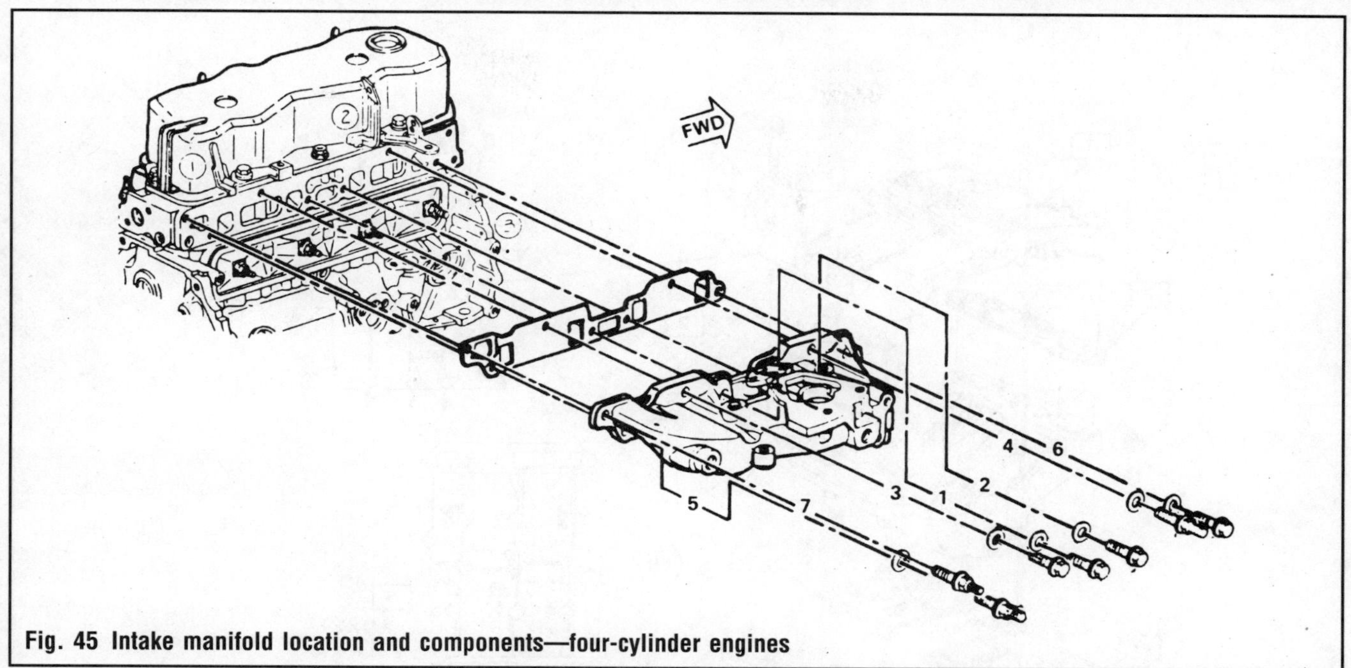

Fig. 45 Intake manifold location and components—four-cylinder engines

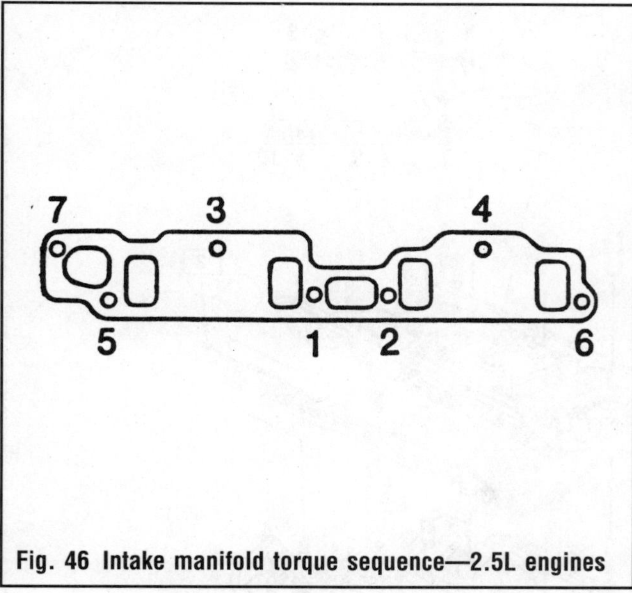

Fig. 46 Intake manifold torque sequence—2.5L engines

To install:

1. Clean the mating surfaces on the manifold and cylinder head with a gasket scraper and solvent.
2. Install the manifold with a new gasket onto the cylinder head and install the seven retaining bolts hand-tight.
3. **Important:** refer to the Torque Specifications chart in the beginning of this section for the proper torque specifications for the year of the vehicle.
4. Install the heater hose and clamps, throttle linkage and bell crank and cruise control linkage.
5. Install the wiring and throttle linkage to the throttle body.
6. Install the vacuum hoses, fuel lines, PCV valve and refill with the proper engine coolant.
7. Install the air cleaner assembly and connect the negative (−) battery cable.

2.8L V6 Engine

➧ **See Figure 47**

CAUTION

To reduce the risk of fire and personal injury, it is necessary to relieve the fuel system pressure before servicing any fuel system component. If this procedure is not performed, fuel may be sprayed out of the connection under pressure. Always keep a dry chemical (Class B) fire extinguisher near the work area.

1. Disconnect the negative battery cable.
2. **Fuel pressure relief procedures:** remove the Fuel pump fuse from the fuse block located in the passenger compartment. Start the engine and run until the engine stops due to the lack of fuel. Crank the engine for 3 seconds to ensure all pressure is relieved.
3. Remove all non engine mounting vacuum lines.
4. Remove the throttle cable bracket bolts, throttle body bolts and plenum bolts.
5. Remove the upper plenum and gaskets by gently pulling upward or tapping with a rubber hammer if will not come loose.
6. Remove both rocker arm covers. Refer to the "Rocker Arm Cover" removal and installation procedures in this section.
7. Drain the engine coolant into a suitable drain pan at the radiator.

CAUTION

When draining engine coolant, keep in mind that cats and dogs are attracted to ethylene glycol antifreeze and could drink any that is left in an uncovered container or in puddles on the ground. This will prove fatal in sufficient quantity. Always drain coolant into a sealable container. Coolant should be reused unless it is contaminated or is several years old.

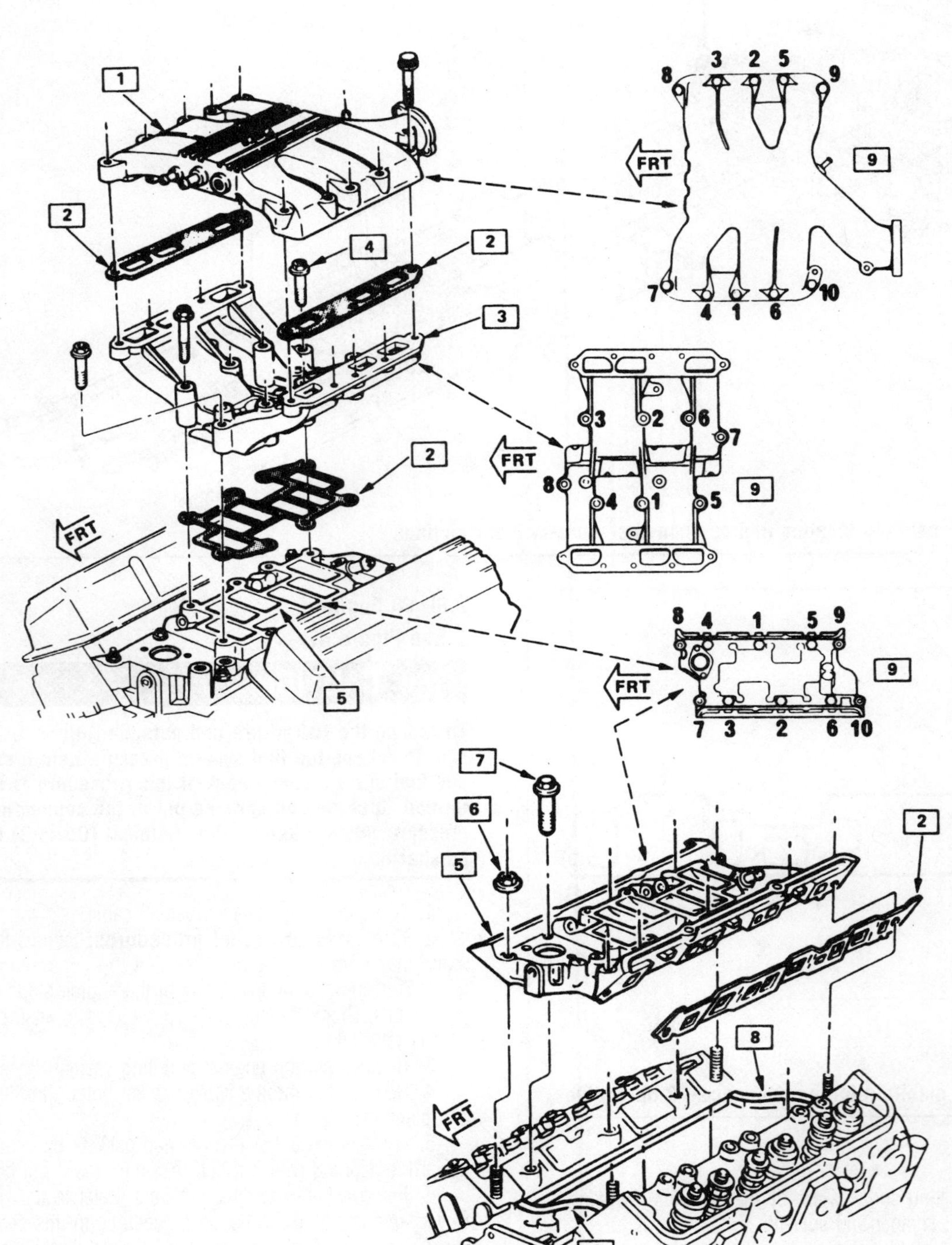

1. Manifold, upper plenum
2. Gasket
3. Intake manifold, intermediate
4. Bolt 21 N•m (15 lb. ft.)
5. Intake manifold, lower
6. Nut 26 N•m (19 lb. ft.)
7. Bolt 26 N•m (19 lb. ft.)
8. Apply a smooth—continuous bead approx. 2.0–3.0 mm wide and 3.0–3.5 mm thick on both surfaces. Bead configuration must insure complete sealing of water and oil. Surface must be free of oil and dirt to insure adequate seal.

Fig. 47 Exploded view of the intake manifold assembly and tightening sequence—2.8L engine

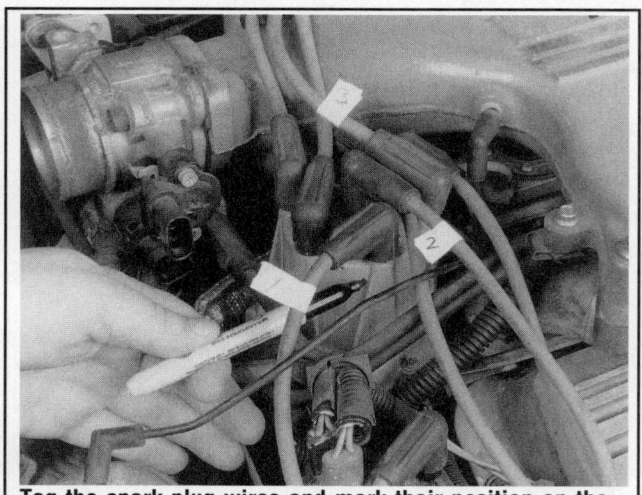
Tag the spark plug wires and mark their position on the distributor cap . . .

Disconnect the hoses and fuel lines

. . . then disengage the spark plug wires

Loosen the inlet air tube clamp and then . . .

Tag and disengage any vacuum hoses from the upper intake manifold

. . . remove the inlet air tube from the throttle body assembly

Remove the throttle linkage retaining clips . .

Use a ratchet and socket to remove the upper intake manifold retaining bolts . . .

. . . then disconnect the linkage from the throttle body assembly

. . . then remove the upper intake manifold from the vehicle

Disconnect the MAP sensor and all other electrical connections from the upper intake manifold

Unfasten its bolts and remove the intermediate intake manifold from the engine

Remove the lower intake manifold bolts . . .

. . . then remove the lower intake manifold from the vehicle

8. Remove the distributor cap and move aside. Mark the position of the distributor rotor to the distributor housing and the housing to the engine. Remove the distributor assembly.
9. Disconnect the shift, cruise control and throttle linkage.
10. Remove the throttle body-to-upper plenum connector.
11. Disconnect the heater and radiator hoses.
12. Remove the radiator fill inlet.
13. Disconnect all wiring harness and vacuum hoses while noting their locations for reassembly.
14. Disconnect the vacuum booster pipe and bracket.
15. Disconnect the EGR pipe.
16. Remove the intermediate intake manifold and gasket.
17. Remove the lower intake manifold and gaskets.

To install:

1. Clean all gasket surfaces on the intake manifolds and cylinder head.
2. Install the lower intake manifold and gasket and torque in sequence to 19 ft. lbs. (26 Nm).
3. Install both rocker arm covers as outlined in the Rocker Arm Cover removal and installation procedures in this section. Torque the bolts to 90 inch. lb. (10 Nm).
4. Install the intermediate intake manifold and gaskets and torque in sequence to 15 ft. lbs. (21 Nm).
5. Install the upper manifold plenum and gaskets and torque in sequence to 18 ft. lbs. (25 Nm).
6. Install the EGR pipe, brake booster pipe and bracket, vacuum hoses, heater hoses, and wiring harness.
7. Install the inlet and return heater hoses and pipe to throttle body. Install the radiator fill inlet and radiator hose.
8. Install the throttle body to upper plenum and torque the bolts to 12.5 ft. lbs. (17 Nm).
9. Install the throttle, downshift and cruise control (if equipped) cables.
10. Install the distributor assembly into the same position as marked upon removal. Install the distributor cap and lock the four retaining clips.
11. Refill the radiator with the specified engine coolant.
12. Connect the negative (−) battery cable.
13. Start the engine and check engine timing with a inductive timing light.
14. Check for coolant, fuel and vacuum leaks.

Exhaust Manifold

REMOVAL & INSTALLATION

4-2.5L Engine

➧ See Figures 48 and 49

1. Disconnect the negative (−) battery cable. Remove the air cleaner and the EFI bracket tube.
2. Raise the vehicle and support it with jackstands.

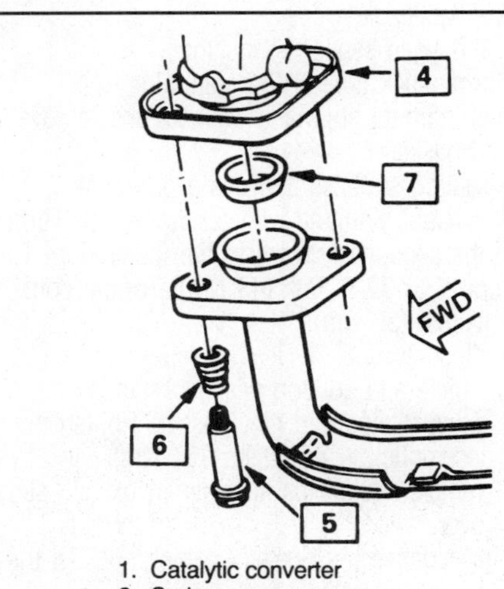

Fig. 48 Exhaust pipe-to-manifold connection and components—2.5L engine

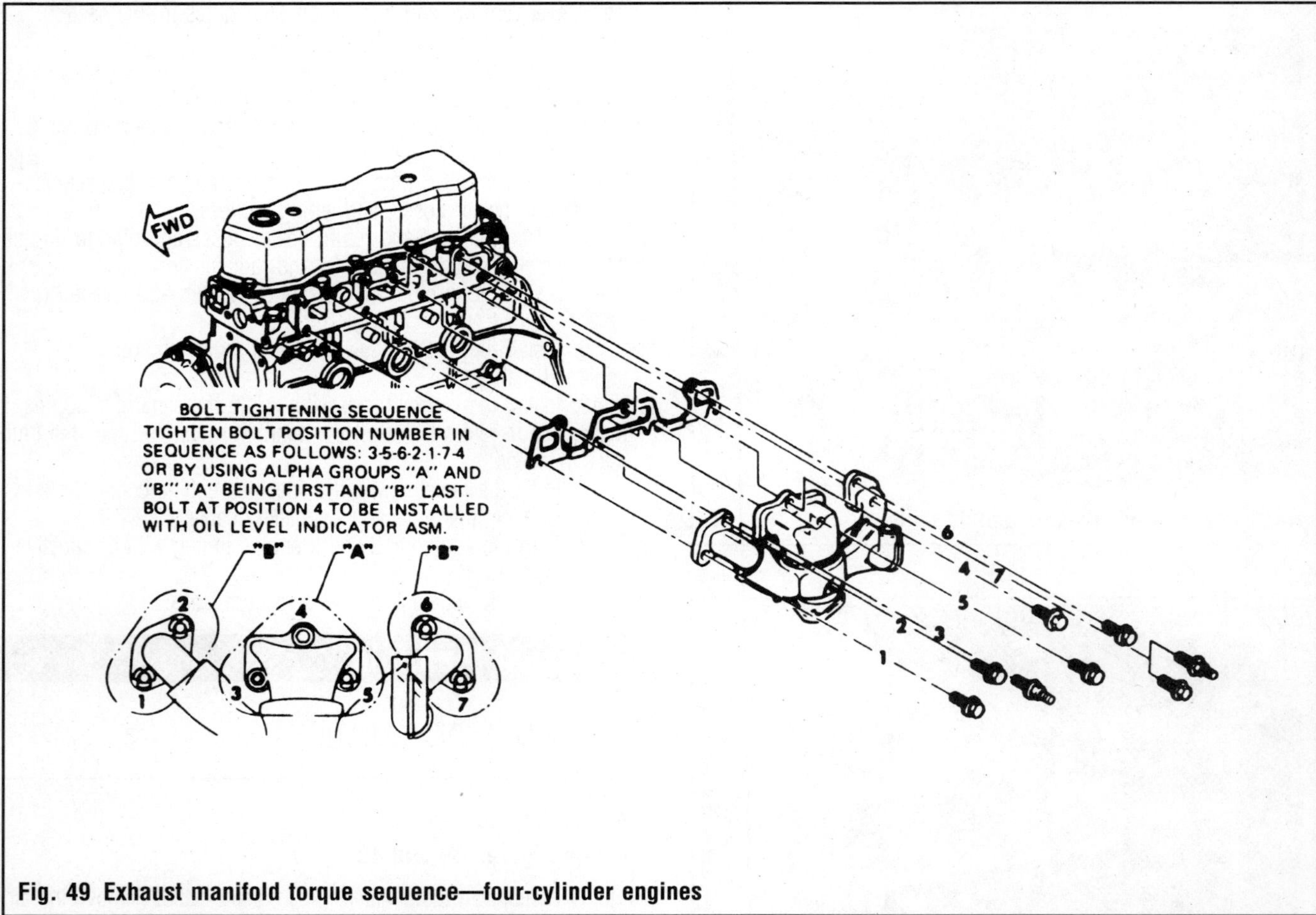

Fig. 49 Exhaust manifold torque sequence—four-cylinder engines

3. Remove the exhaust pipe and lower the vehicle.
4. Remove the battery side cover.
5. Remove the oxygen sensor connector.
6. Remove the dipstick tube at the manifold.
7. Remove the retaining bolts and washers and remove the exhaust manifold and gasket.
8. Clean the sealing surfaces and use a new gasket.
9. Install the exhaust manifold with a new gasket. Torque the retaining bolts to the sequence shown in the illustration. Torque bolts No. 1,2,6, and 7 to 32 ft. lbs. (43 Nm). Torque bolts No. 3,4, and 5 to 37 ft. lbs. (50 Nm).
10. Install the dipstick tube.
11. Raise the vehicle and support with jackstands.
12. Install the exhaust pipe and new gasket. Tighten the two bolts and spring assemblies to 40 ft. lbs. (54 Nm).
13. Lower the vehicle. Install the air cleaner, oxygen sensor and battery side cover.
14. Connect the negative (−) battery cable and start the engine and check for exhaust leaks.

6-2.8L Engine

FRONT MANIFOLD

See Figure 50

1. Disconnect the negative (−) battery cable.
2. Scribe the engine compartment lid hinges for proper reinstallation. Remove the rear compartment lid with an assistant.

CAUTION

Personal injury may result if the engine compartment lid torsion rod retaining bolts are removed. The torsion bolts do not have to be removed to remove the compartment lid.

3. Remove the brake vacuum hose.
4. Remove the manifold heat shield.
5. Remove the front crossover bolts.
6. Raise the car and support with jackstands. Remove the front converter heat shield and the lower manifold bolts.
7. Lower the car and remove the upper manifold bolts then remove the manifold.

To install:

8. With a new gasket, install manifold and torque the upper bolts to 18 ft. lbs. (24 Nm).
9. Raise the car and support with jackstands. Torque the lower bolts to 18 ft. lbs. (24 Nm).
10. Install the front converter heat shield.
11. Lower the car and torque the crossover bolts to 22 ft. lbs. (30 Nm).
12. Install the manifold heat shield and brake vacuum hose.
13. Install the engine compartment lid in the same location as removed with an assistant. Connect the negative (−) battery cable and start the engine and check for exhaust or vacuum leaks.

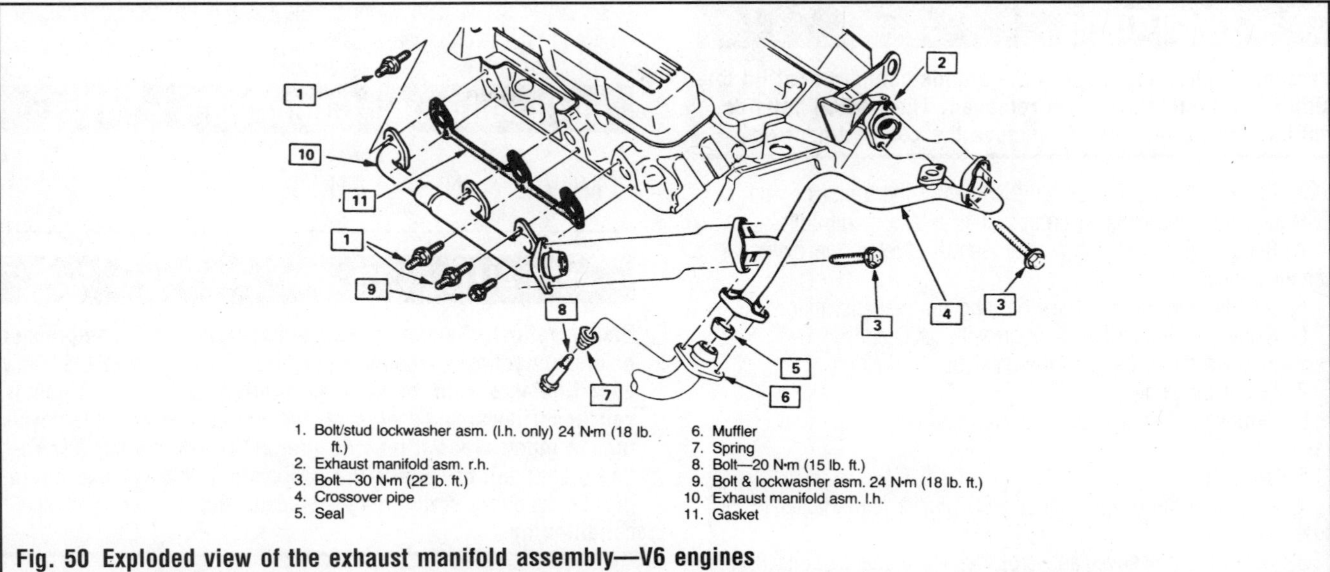

Fig. 50 Exploded view of the exhaust manifold assembly—V6 engines

Raise the vehicle and support it with jackstands

. . . then unfasten the upper bolts and remove the exhaust manifold from the vehicle

Use a box wrench or socket to remove the lower bolt from the exhaust manifold . . .

REAR MANIFOLD

1. Disconnect the negative (−) battery cable.
2. Disconnect the manifold-to-crossover bolts.
3. Remove the manifold bolts then remove the manifold.
4. Installation is the reverse of removal. Torque the manifold bolts to 18 ft. lbs. (24 Nm) and the manifold to crossover bolts to 22 ft. lbs. (30 Nm).

Crossover Pipe

REMOVAL & INSTALLATION

1. Disconnect the negative (−) battery cable.
2. Scribe the engine compartment lid hinges for proper reinstallation. Remove the rear compartment lid with an assistant.

CAUTION

Personal injury may result if the engine compartment lid torsion rod retaining bolts are removed. The torsion bolts do not have to be removed to remove the compartment lid.

3. Remove the EGR hose, shift cables at the transaxle and the EGR tube from the exhaust crossover-to-intake manifold.
4. Remove the front and rear crossover shields and oxygen sensor connector.
5. Remove the bolts at the front and rear exhaust manifolds.
6. Raise the vehicle and support with jackstands.
7. Remove the bolts from the catalytic converter.
8. Lower the vehicle.
9. Remove the crossover pipe, oxygen sensor pipe and EGR valve pipe.

To install:

1. Assemble the oxygen sensor, EGR valve and adapter to the crossover pipe.
2. Install the crossover and crossover-to-manifold bolts (front and rear). Torque the bolts to 22 ft. lbs. (30 Nm).
3. Raise the vehicle and support with jackstands.
4. Install the catalytic converter bolts and torque to 15 ft. lbs. (20 Nm).
5. Lower the vehicle. Connect the oxygen sensor. Start the engine and check for exhaust leaks.

Air Conditioning Compressor

REMOVAL & INSTALLATION

CAUTION

Please refer to Section 1 before discharging the compressor or disconnecting air conditioning lines. Damage to the air conditioning system or personal injury could result. Consult your local laws concerning refrigerant discharge and recycling. In many areas it may be illegal for anyone but a certified technician to service the A/C system. Always use an approved recovery station when discharging the air conditioning.

See Figures 51, 52 and 53

1. Disconnect the negative (−) battery cable.
2. Raise the vehicle and support with jackstands.

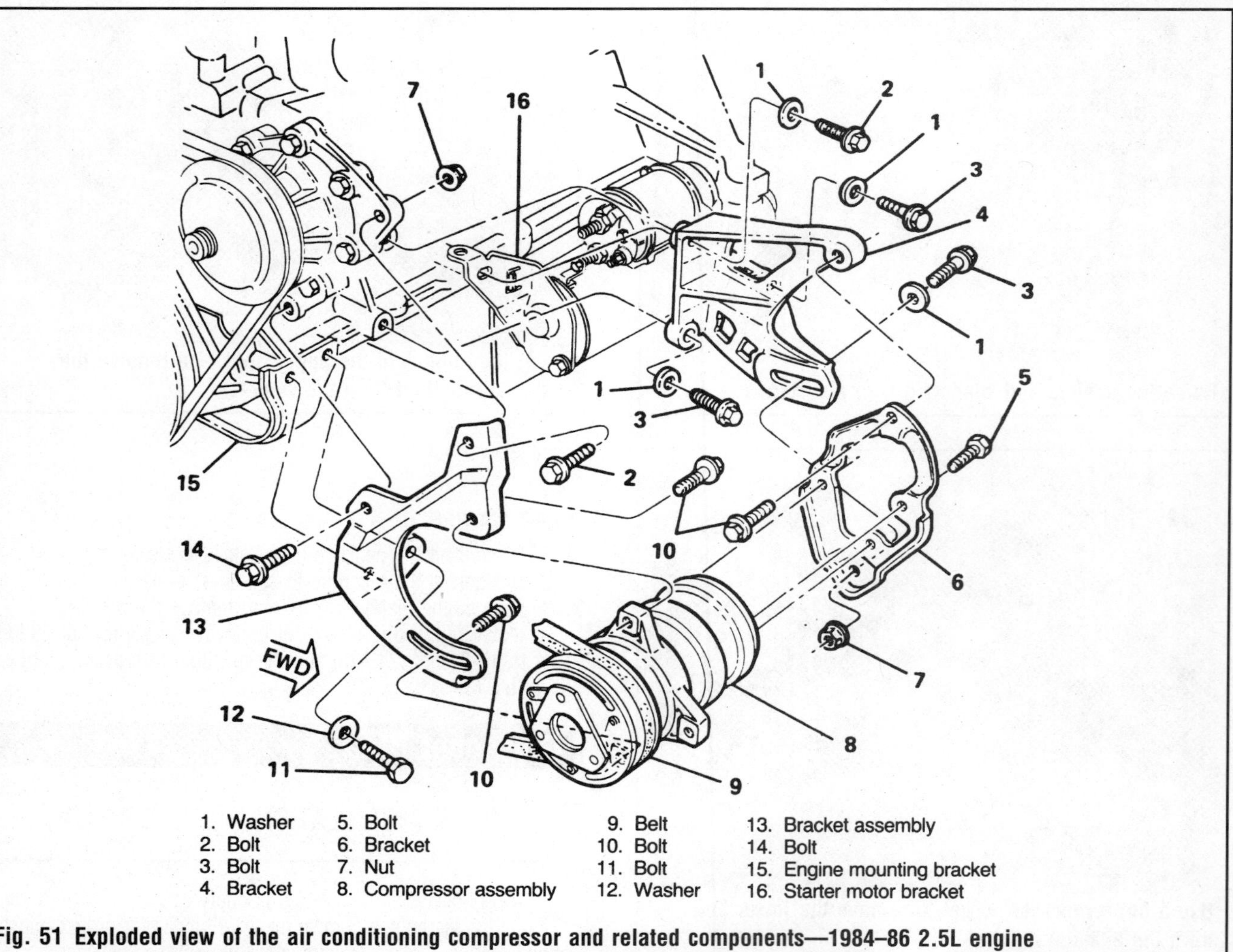

Fig. 51 Exploded view of the air conditioning compressor and related components—1984–86 2.5L engine

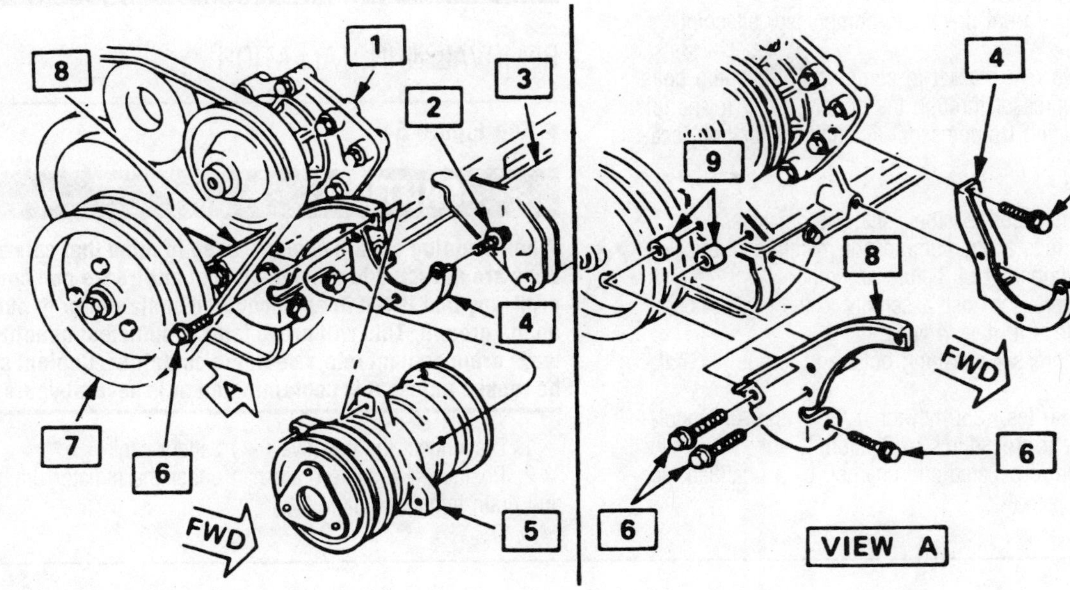

VIEW A

1. Water pump
2. 27 N·m (20 lb. ft.)
3. Starter motor
4. Bracket
5. Compressor asm.
6. 50 N·m (37 lb. ft.)
7. Crankshaft
8. Bracket
9. Spacer

Fig. 52 Exploded view of the air conditioning compressor and related components—1987–88 2.5L engine

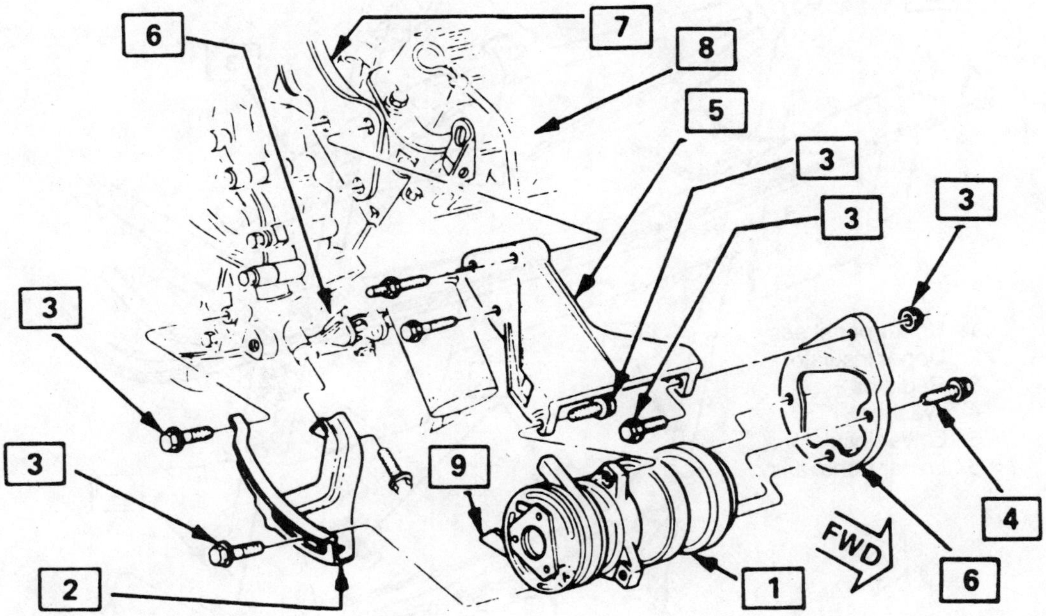

1. Compressor asm
2. Bracket
3. 40–60 N·m (30–44 lb. ft.)
4. 20–34 N·m (15–25 lb. ft.)
5. Bracket asm
6. Bracket
7. Torque strut bracket
8. Engine asm
9. Belt

Fig. 53 Exploded view of the air conditioning compressor and related components—2.8L engine

3. Disconnect and plug the compressor hose assemblies from the back of the compressor.

4. Remove the three front bracket-to-compressor attaching bolts.

5. Remove the two rear bracket-to-compressor attaching bolts and remove the compressor through the bottom. Refer to the following "Air Conditioning Compressor" illustrations for bolt locations.

To install:

1. Install the compressor assembly into the brackets.

2. Install new O-rings at the compressor manifold (lubricate with 525 viscosity refrigerant oil before assembly).

3. Install the compressor hose assembly to the back of compressor and torque to 3 ft. lbs. (4 Nm).

4. Install the compressor attaching bolts and torque to 37 ft. lbs. (50 Nm).

5. Adjust Belt to 80 lbs. (350 newtons). Refer the Air Conditioning Belt adjustment procedures in Section 1.

6. Have the system evacuated and charged by a qualified technician.

Radiator

REMOVAL & INSTALLATION

➧ See Figure 54

CAUTION

When draining engine coolant, keep in mind that cats and dogs are attracted to ethylene glycol antifreeze and could drink any that is left in an uncovered container or in puddles on the ground. This will prove fatal in sufficient quantity. Always drain coolant into a sealable container. Coolant should be reused unless it is contaminated or is several years old.

1. Disconnect the negative (−) battery cable.

2. Position a suitable drain pan under the radiator drain plug and drain engine coolant.

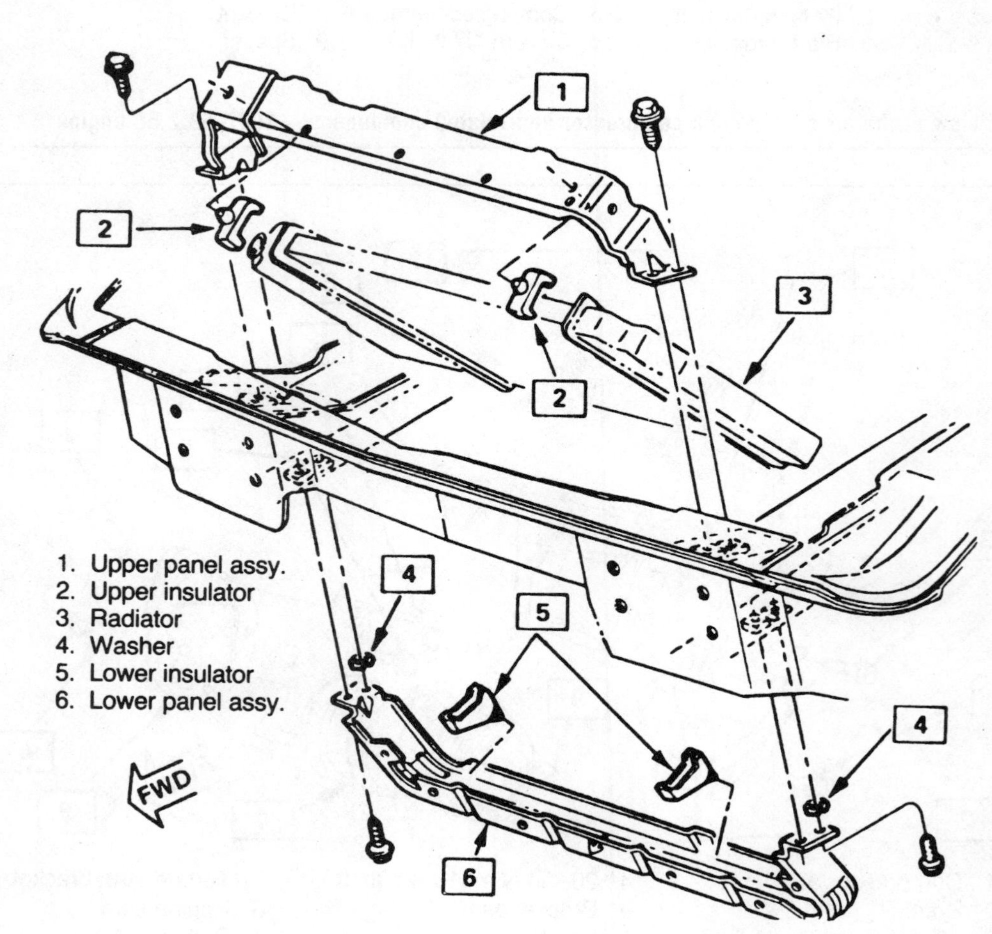

Fig. 54 Common radiator support used on Fiero models

Place a drain pan under the radiator and loosen the drain plug

. . . then lift the fan up and out of the vehicle

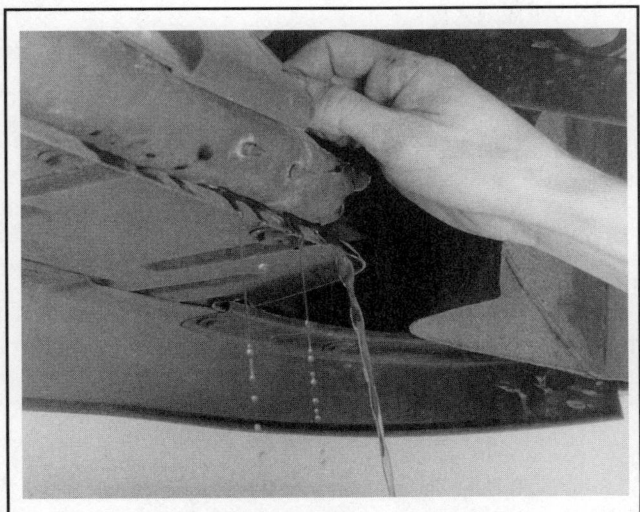
Let the coolant completely drain from the radiator

Remove the upper panel assembly bolts . . .

Loosen the fan retaining bolts . . .

. . . then remove the upper panel assembly from the vehicle

Unfasten the upper and lower radiator hose retaining clamps . . .

. . . then pull the hoses from their radiator connections

Unfasten the retaining bolts and remove the radiator from the vehicle

3. Remove the forward strut brace at the radiator and swing the strut rearward.

➡**To prevent shearing off the rubber bushing, loosen the bolt before swinging the brace.**

4. Disconnect the forward lamp harness from the fan frame and unplug the fan connector.
5. Remove the fan attaching bolts and remove the fan and frame assembly.
6. Remove the hood latch from the radiator support.

➡**Scribe the latch location before removal so to ensure reinstallation in the same position.**

7. Remove the coolant hoses from the radiator and coolant recovery tank.
8. Remove the transaxle oil cooler lines from the radiator (automatic only).
9. Remove the radiator-to-support attaching bolts and clamps. Remove the radiator from the vehicle.

To install:

1. If a new radiator is being installed, transfer all fittings from the old unit to new one.
2. Install the radiator in the vehicle. Make sure the bottom is positioned into the lower mounting pads.
3. Install the radiator-to-radiator support attaching clamps and bolts. Torque to 7 ft. lbs. (10 Nm).
4. Attach the transaxle oil cooler lines (automatic only) and torque to 20 ft. lbs. (27 Nm).
5. Install the radiator hoses and torque the clamps to 19 inch lbs. (2 Nm). Install the coolant recovery hose to radiator neck.
6. Install the hood latch in the same position as removal. Torque the bolts to 18 ft. lbs. (25 Nm).
7. Install the fan assembly making sure the bottom edge of the frame fits into the rubber grommet at the lower radiator support. Torque the fan attaching bolts to 88 inch lbs. (10 Nm).
8. Connect the fan and forward lamp harnesses to fan frame.
9. Swing the engine forward strut and brace forward until the brace contacts the radiator support. Install the bolts and torque to 37 ft. lbs. (50 Nm). Be sure to connect the engine ground strap to the strut brace.
10. Refill the radiator with the specified engine coolant. Connect the negative (−) battery cable, start the engine and check for leaks.

Air Conditioning Condenser

REMOVAL & INSTALLATION

➧ **See Figure 55**

1. Disconnect the negative (−) battery cable.

***** CAUTION**

Please refer to Section 1 before discharging the compressor or disconnecting air conditioning lines. Damage to the air conditioning system or personal injury could result. Consult your local laws concerning refrigerant discharge and recycling. In many areas it may be illegal for anyone but a certified technician to service the A/C system. Always use an approved recovery station when discharging the air conditioning.

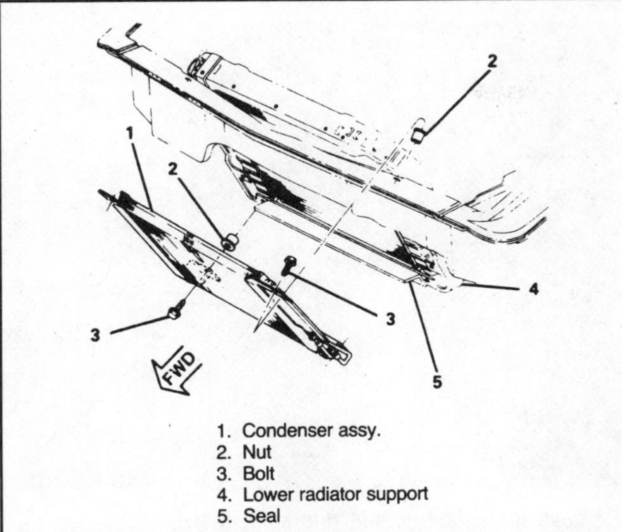

Fig. 55 Air conditioning condenser components typically found on Fiero models

2. Raise the vehicle and support with jackstands
3. Remove the front grille assembly.
4. After the system has been discharged, remove the condenser lines.

➡Use care when removing the condenser lines because they are made of soft aluminum. Use a flare nut wrench to remove the fittings.

5. Remove the lower condenser attaching bolts and remove the condenser from the vehicle.

To install:

1. Install the condenser into lower mount and torque the lower attaching bolts to 15 ft. lbs. (20 Nm).
2. Install new O-rings on both condenser lines and lubricate with 525 viscosity refrigerant oil.
3. Install both condenser lines and torque the inlet line to 13 ft. lbs. (17Nm) and the outlet line to 17 ft. lbs. (27 Nm).
4. Install the grille assembly.
5. Lower the vehicle and install the upper condenser attaching bolts and torque to 15 ft. lbs. (20 Nm).
6. Have the system evacuated and charged by a qualified technician.

Water Pump

✲✲ CAUTION

Keep hands, tools, and clothing away from the engine cooling fan to help prevent personal injury. This fan is electric and can come on whether or not the engine is running. The fan can start automatically in response to a heat sensor with the ignition in the ON position.

REMOVAL & INSTALLATION

4-2.5L Engine

➧ See Figure 56

1. Disconnect the negative (−) battery cable.
2. Position a suitable drain pan under the radiator drain plug and drain the radiator.

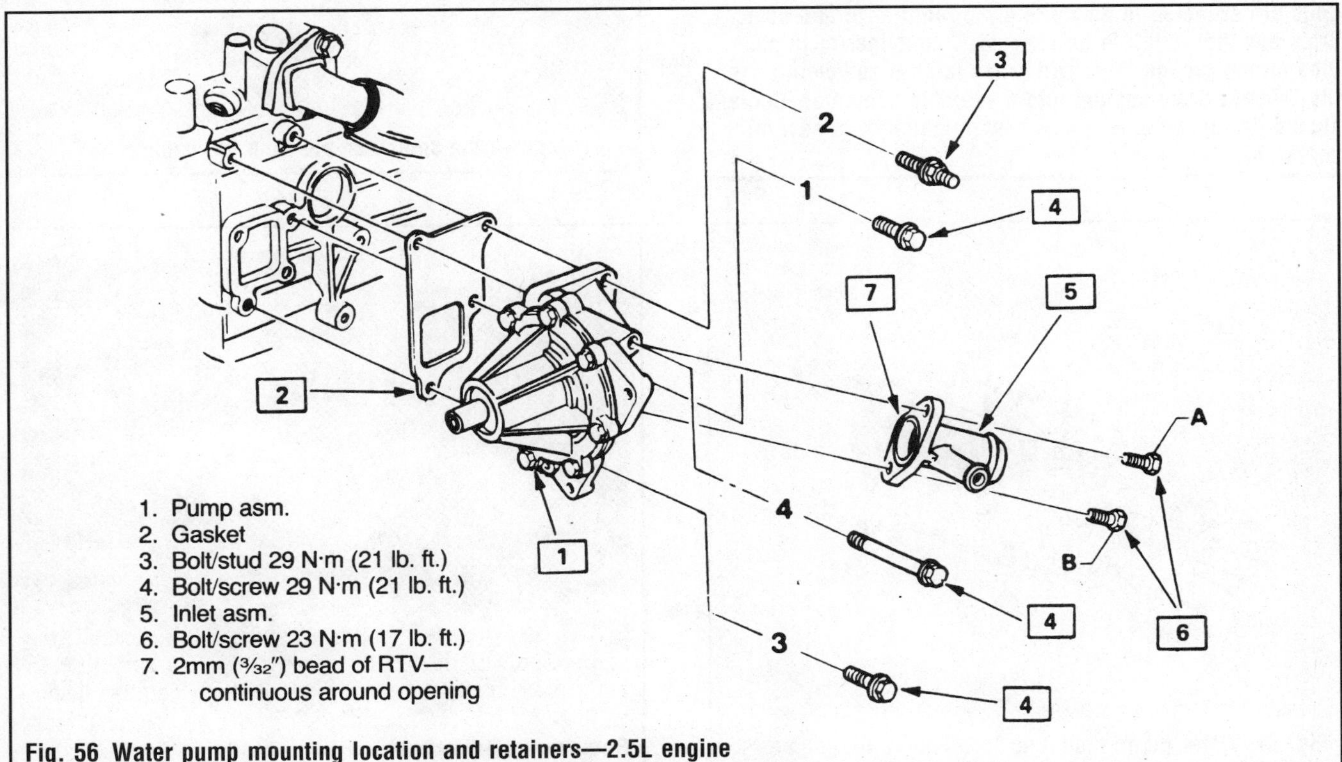

Fig. 56 Water pump mounting location and retainers—2.5L engine

✻✻ CAUTION

When draining engine coolant, keep in mind that cats and dogs are attracted to ethylene glycol antifreeze and could drink any that is left in an uncovered container or in puddles on the ground. This will prove fatal in sufficient quantity. Always drain coolant into a sealable container. Coolant should be reused unless it is contaminated or is several years old.

3. Remove the accessory drive belts.
4. Remove the water pump attaching bolts and remove the water pump.

To install:

5. If installing a new water pump, transfer the pulley from the old unit using a Pulley Remover part No. J25034-B or J29785-A.
6. With sealing surfaces cleaned, place a 3mm bead of RTV sealant, GM # 1052289 or equivalent, on the water pump sealing surface. While the sealant is still wet, install the pump and torque the bolts to 6 ft. lbs. (8 Nm).
7. Install the accessory drive belts. Refill the engine with the specified coolant.
8. Reconnect the negative (−) battery cable. Start the engine and check for coolant leaks when the engine warms up.

6-2.8L Engine

➧ See Figure 57

1. Disconnect the negative (−) battery cable.
2. Position a suitable drain pan under the radiator drain plug and drain the engine coolant.

✻✻ CAUTION

When draining engine coolant, keep in mind that cats and dogs are attracted to ethylene glycol antifreeze and could drink any that is left in an uncovered container or in puddles on the ground. This will prove fatal in sufficient quantity. Always drain coolant into a sealable container. Coolant should be reused unless it is contaminated or is several years old.

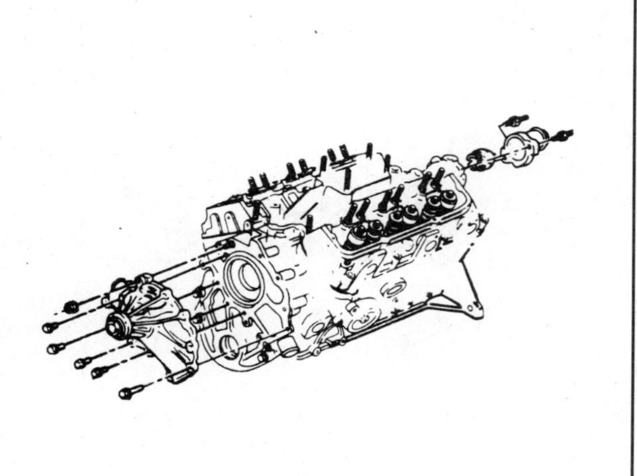

Fig. 57 Water pump mounting location—2.8L engine

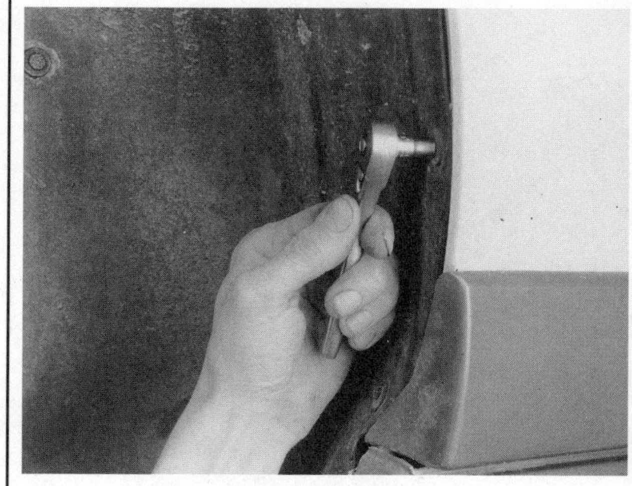

Remove the splash shield retainers, then . . .

. . . remove the splash shield from the vehicle

Remove the drive belts . . .

. . . then unfasten the lower radiator hose clamp and disengage the hose

Remove the water pump retaining bolts, then . . .

. . . remove the water pump from the vehicle

3. Remove the accessory drive belts.
4. Remove the radiator and heater hoses from the water pump.
5. Remove the water pump attaching bolts and water pump by gently tapping it with a rubber hammer.

To install:

6. Clean the water pump mating surfaces with a gasket scraper and solvent.
7. Apply a 5mm bead of RTV sealant on the water pump sealing surfaces.
8. Install the water pump and attaching bolts to the engine. Torque the bolts to 7 ft. lbs. (10 Nm).
9. Install the radiator and heater hoses and tighten the clamps.
10. Install the accessory drive belt and tighten to 135 lbs. (600 N) for a new belt, and 70 lbs. (300 N) for a used belt.
11. Refill the engine with the specified engine coolant. Reconnect the negative (−) battery cable. Start the engine and check for coolant leaks.

Cylinder Head

REMOVAL & INSTALLATION

4-2.5L Engine

See Figures 58 and 59

CAUTION

When draining engine coolant, keep in mind that cats and dogs are attracted to ethylene glycol antifreeze and could drink any that is left in an uncovered container or in puddles on the ground. This will prove fatal in sufficient quantity. Always drain coolant into a sealable container. Coolant should be reused unless it is contaminated or is several years old.

1. Disconnect the negative (−) battery cable.
2. Drain the cooling system at the radiator into a suitable drain pan.
3. Raise the vehicle and support it safely with jack stands.
4. Remove the exhaust pipe.
5. Lower the vehicle.
6. Remove the oil level indicator tube.
7. Remove the air cleaner assembly.
8. Disconnect the EFI electrical connections and vacuum hoses.
9. From the throttle body; remove the wiring connectors, throttle linkage and fuel lines.

CAUTION

To reduce the risk of fire and personal injury, it is necessary to relieve the fuel system pressure before servicing any fuel system component. If this procedure is not performed, fuel may be sprayed out of the connection under pressure. Always keep a dry chemical (Class B) fire extinguisher near the work area.

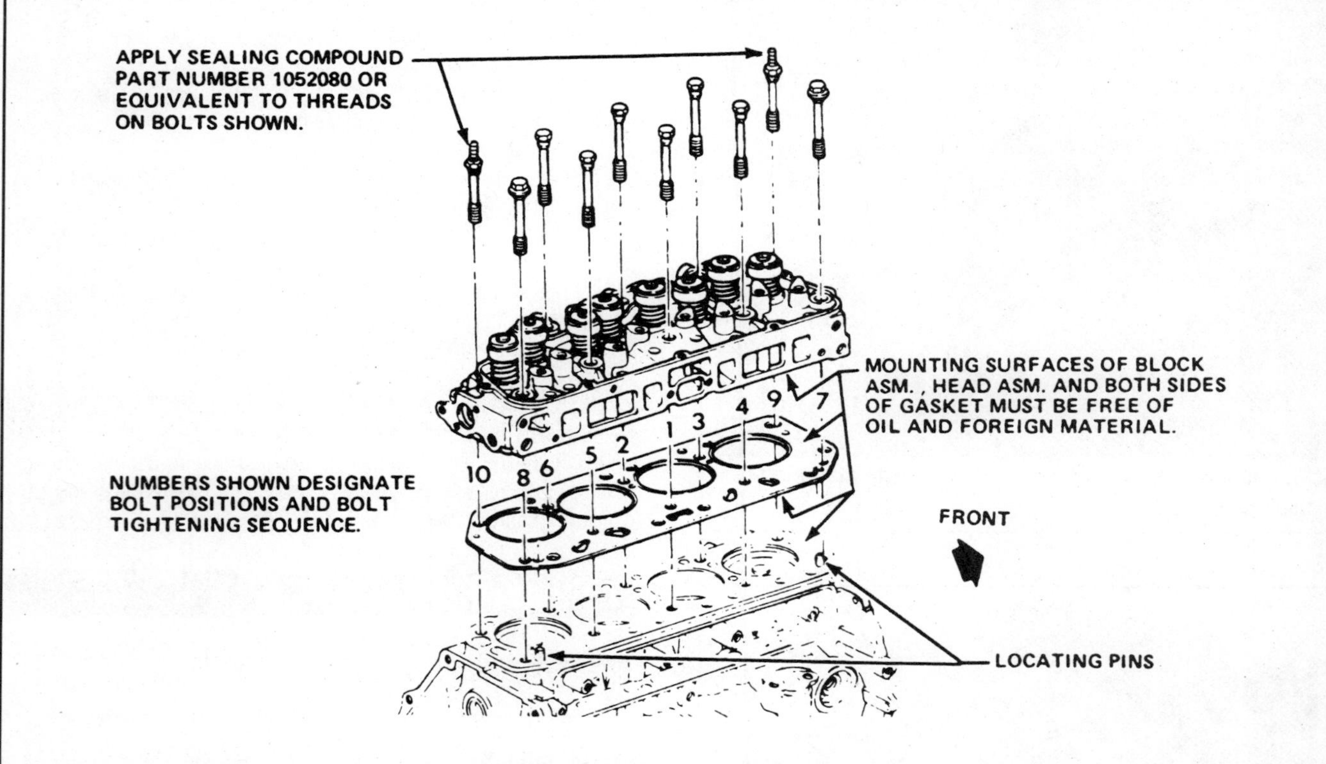

Fig. 58 Cylinder head components and bolt locations—four-cylinder engines

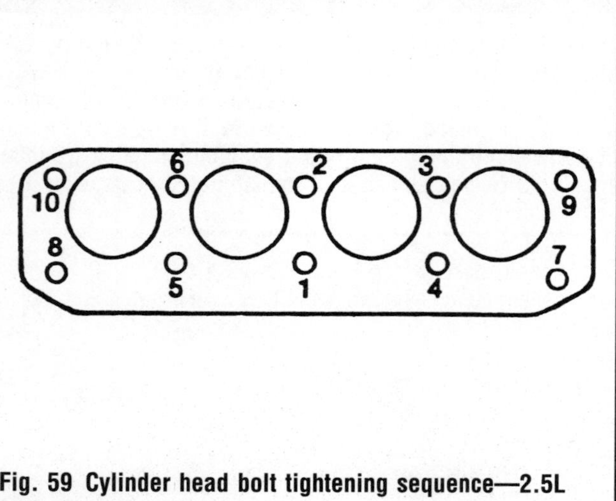

Fig. 59 Cylinder head bolt tightening sequence—2.5L engine

When removing nuts, bolts and other parts, place them in a tray or other container

Fuel pressure relief procedures:

a. Remove the fuel pump fuse from the fuse block located in the passenger compartment.

b. Start the engine and run until the engine stops due to the lack of fuel.

c. Crank the engine for 3 seconds to ensure all pressure is relieved.

10. Remove the EGR base plate.
11. Remove the heater hose from the intake manifold.
12. Remove the ignition coil from the lower mounting bolt and wiring connection.
13. Remove all wiring and vacuum connections from the intake manifold and cylinder head.
14. Remove the engine strut bolt from the upper support.
15. Remove the alternator belt and brackets to move the alternator out of the way.
16. Remove the air conditioning brackets and swing the air conditioning compressor aside if top mounted.

CAUTION

The EPA warns that prolonged contact with used engine oil may cause a number of skin disorders, including cancer! You should make every effort to minimize your exposure to used engine oil. Protective gloves should be worn when changing the oil. Wash your hands and any other exposed skin areas as soon as possible after exposure to used engine oil. Soap and water, or waterless hand cleaner should be used.

17. Remove the exhaust pipe-to-exhaust manifold attaching bolts.
18. Remove the valve cover, rocker arms and pushrods. Refer to the Rocker Arm Cover and Pushrod removal and installation procedures in this section.

➡Mark each valve component to ensure that they are replaced in the same location as removed. This is very important because each component will follow different wear patterns.

19. Remove the cylinder head bolts and remove the cylinder head and manifolds as an assembly. If the cylinder head has to be serviced, the manifolds will have to be removed from the cylinder head.

To install:

1. Before installing, clean the gasket surfaces of the head and block.
2. Check the cylinder head for warpage using a straight edge. Refer to the Cylinder Head Resurfacing procedures in this section.
3. Make sure the retaining bolt threads and the cylinder block threads are clean since dirt could affect bolt torque.
4. Match up the old head gasket with the new one to ensure the holes are EXACT. Install a new gasket over the dowel pins in the cylinder block.
5. Install the cylinder head in place over the dowel pins.
6. Coat the cylinder head bolt threads with sealing compound and install finger-tight.
7. Torque the cylinder head bolts gradually in the sequence shown in the illustration. Refer to the Torque Specifications chart in the beginning of this section for proper specs and procedures depending on the year of your Fiero.
8. Install the pushrods, rocker arms and nuts (or bolts) in the same location as removed. Torque the nuts (or bolts) to 24 ft. lbs. (32 Nm).
9. Install the rocker arm cover as outlined in the Rocker Arm Cover removal and installation procedures in this section.
10. Install the radiator hose and clamps, alternator bracket and belt and adjust the belt to 130 lbs. (600 N) for a new belt, and 70 lbs. (300 N) for a used belt.
11. Install the alternator bracket and bolt.
12. Install the air conditioning compressor and bracket (if to mounted).
13. Install the strut rod bolt.
14. Connect all wiring connectors to the intake manifold and cylinder head.
15. Install all vacuum and heater hoses to the intake manifold.
16. Install the wiring, throttle linkage and fuel lines to the throttle body assembly.
17. Install the dipstick tube, air cleaner and refill the engine with the specified engine coolant.
18. Raise the vehicle and support with jackstands.
19. Install the exhaust pipe to exhaust manifold and torque the bolts to 25 ft. lbs. (34 Nm).
20. Install the oxygen sensor connector, lower the car and connect the negative (−) battery cable. Check for completion of repair. Start the vehicle and check for fuel, vacuum, coolant and exhaust leaks.

6-2.8L Engine

LEFT CYLINDER HEAD

➧ See Figure 60

1. Disconnect the negative (−) battery cable.
2. Raise the vehicle and drain the coolant from the block.

CAUTION

When draining engine coolant, keep in mind that cats and dogs are attracted to ethylene glycol antifreeze and could drink any that is left in an uncovered container or in puddles on the ground. This will prove fatal in sufficient quantity. Always drain coolant into a sealable container. Coolant should be reused unless it is contaminated or is several years old.

3. Lower the vehicle.
4. Remove the intake manifold as outlined in the Intake Manifold removal and installation procedures in this section.

CAUTION

To reduce the risk of fire and personal injury, it is necessary to relieve the fuel system pressure before servicing any fuel system component. If this procedure is not performed, fuel may be sprayed out of the connection under pressure. Always keep a dry chemical (Class B) fire extinguisher near the work area.

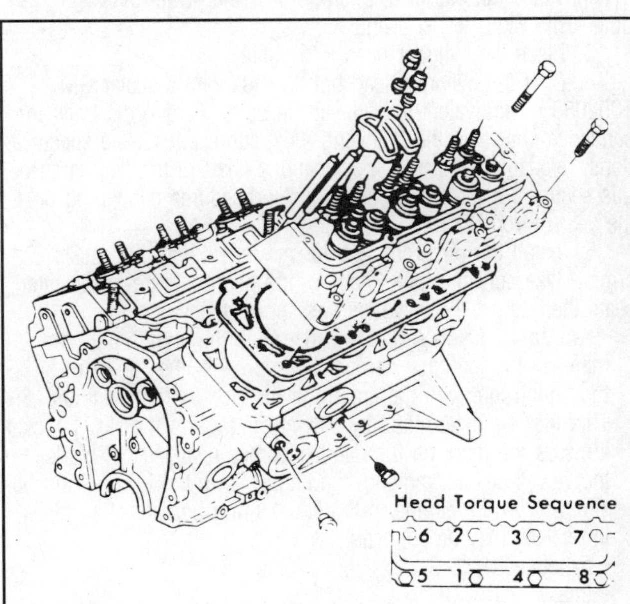

Fig. 60 Cylinder head components and bolt tightening sequence—2.8L engine

5. **Fuel pressure relief procedures:** connect a fuel gauge part No. J 34730-1 or equivalent to the fuel pressure valve on the fuel rail assembly. Wrap a towel around the fitting while connecting the gauge to prevent fuel spillage. Install the bleed hose into an approved container and open the valve to bleed the system pressure.

6. Disconnect the exhaust crossover pipe as outlined in the "Crossover Pipe" procedures in this section.

7. Disconnect the alternator bracket.

8. Remove the oil dipstick tube.

**** CAUTION**

The EPA warns that prolonged contact with used engine oil may cause a number of skin disorders, including cancer! You should make every effort to minimize your exposure to used engine oil. Protective gloves should be worn when changing the oil. Wash your hands and any other exposed skin areas as soon as possible after exposure to used engine oil. Soap and water, or waterless hand cleaner should be used.

9. Remove the rocker arm cover as outlined in the Rocker Arm Cover (Left) procedures.

10. Loosen the rocker arms until you're able to remove the pushrods. Mark each valve component so to ensure proper installation.

11. Raise the vehicle and support with jackstands.

12. Remove the bolts retaining the exhaust manifold-to-crossover pipe.

13. Remove the cylinder head bolts then remove the cylinder head.

To install:

1. Before installing, clean the gasket surfaces on the head, cylinder block and intake manifold with a gasket scraper and solvent.

2. Match the new gasket with a old one to ensure an exact match. Place the gasket in position over the dowel pins with the note "This Side UP" showing.

3. Place the cylinder head into position.

4. Coat the cylinder head bolt threads with a sealer GM 1052080 or equivalent and install the bolts. Torque the bolts in sequence shown in the following illustration. For torque specifications, refer to the Torque Specifications chart in the beginning of this section for the proper specs and procedures depending on the year of your Fiero.

5. Install the pushrods and loosely retain with the rocker arms. Make sure the lower ends of the pushrods are in the lifter seats then adjust the valve lash as shown below:

a. **Valve Lash Adjustment:** rotate the engine until the mark on the torsional damper lines up with the "0" mark on the timing tab, with the engine in the No. 1 firing position. This may be determined by placing fingers on the No. 1 rocker arms as the mark on the damper comes near the "0" mark. If the valves are not moving, the engine is in the No. 1 firing position. With the engine in the No. 1 firing position, the following valves may be adjusted:

- Exhaust—1, 2, 3
- Intake—1, 5, 6

b. Back out the adjusting nut until lash is felt at the pushrod, then turn the adjusting nut until all lash is removed. This can be determined by rotating the pushrod while turning the adjusting nut. When lash has been removed, turn the adjusting nut in 1½ additional turns to center the lifter plunger.

c. Crank the engine one revolution until the timing tab "0" mark and torsional damper mark are again in alignment. This is the No. 4 firing position. With the engine in this position, the following valves may be adjusted;

- Exhaust—4, 5, 6
- Intake—2, 3, 4

6. For further valve adjustment illustrations, refer to the Rocker Arm Cover procedures in this section.

7. Install the intake manifold assembly as outlined in the Intake Manifold procedures in this section. Also, refer to the Torque Specifications chart for proper specs and procedures for your year Fiero.

8. Install the oil dipstick tube, heat stove pipe and air supply pipe.

9. Raise the vehicle and support with jackstands.

10. Install the exhaust pipe to the exhaust manifold. Torque the attaching bolts to 25 ft. lbs. (34 Nm).

11. Install all vacuum, heater and wire connectors to the intake manifold and cylinder head.

12. Install the air conditioning compressor and alternator. Adjust the belts to specification. 135 lbs. (600 N) for a new belt, and 70 lbs. (300 N) for a used belt.

13. Install the air cleaner assembly, reconnect the negative (−) battery cable and recheck for completion of repair. Start the engine and check for vacuum, oil, fuel, exhaust and coolant leaks.

RIGHT CYLINDER HEAD

1. Disconnect the negative (−) battery cable.

2. Raise the vehicle, support it safely with jackstands.

3. With a drain pan under the radiator drain plug, drain the cooling system.

**** CAUTION**

When draining engine coolant, keep in mind that cats and dogs are attracted to ethylene glycol antifreeze and could drink any that is left in an uncovered container or in puddles on the ground. This will prove fatal in sufficient quantity. Always drain coolant into a sealable container. Coolant should be reused unless it is contaminated or is several years old.

4. Disconnect the exhaust pipe from the exhaust crossover pipe.

5. Lower the vehicle.

6. Disconnect the cruise control servo bracket.

7. Release the fuel pressure and remove the intake manifold. Refer to the Intake Manifold procedures in this section.

**** CAUTION**

To reduce the risk of fire and personal injury, it is necessary to relieve the fuel system pressure before servicing any fuel system component. If this procedure is not performed, fuel may be sprayed out of the connection under pressure. Always keep a dry chemical (Class B) fire extinguisher near the work area.

8. **Fuel pressure relief procedures:** connect a fuel gauge part No. J 34730-1 or equivalent to the fuel pressure valve on the

Loosen the rocker arm nuts, then . . .

Remove the intake manifold gaskets

. . . remove the pushrods from the engine

Use a socket and a box end wrench when disconnecting the exhaust pipe from the manifold

Tag the pushrods and keep them in the order of their removal

Remove the cylinder head bolts, then lift the cylinder head off the engine block

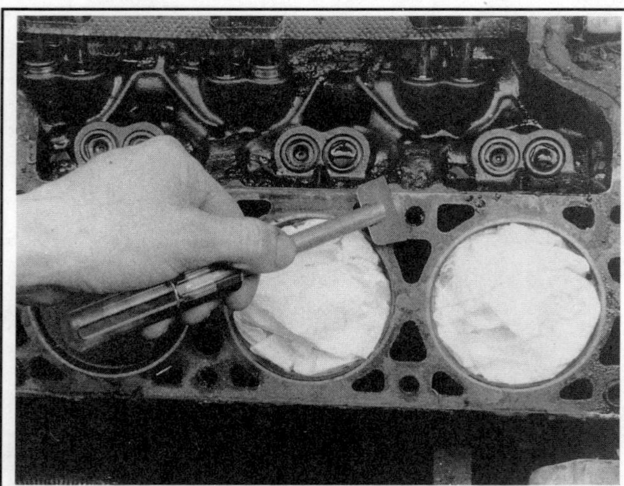
Use a gasket scraper to clean the old gasket material from the engine block

Use a torque wrench to tighten the head bolts in the proper sequence to the exact specification

fuel rail assembly. Wrap a towel around the fitting while connecting the gauge to prevent fuel spillage. Install the bleed hose into an approved container and open the valve to bleed the system pressure.

9. Disconnect the exhaust crossover pipe from the exhaust manifold.

CAUTION

The EPA warns that prolonged contact with used engine oil may cause a number of skin disorders, including cancer! You should make every effort to minimize your exposure to used engine oil. Protective gloves should be worn when changing the oil. Wash your hands and any other exposed skin areas as soon as possible after exposure to used engine oil. Soap and water, or waterless hand cleaner should be used.

10. Remove the rocker arm cover as outlined in the Rocker Arm Cover procedures in this section.

11. Loosen the rocker arm nuts far enough to remove the pushrods. Mark each valve component to ensure proper installation into the same location as removed.

12. Remove the cylinder head bolts and the cylinder head.

To install:

1. Clean the gasket surfaces on the cylinder head, intake manifold and cylinder block with a gasket scraper and solvent.
2. Check the cylinder head for flatness with a straight edge. Refer to the Cylinder Head Cleaning and Inspecting procedures in this section.
3. Match the new gasket with a old one to ensure an exact match. Place the gasket in position over the dowel pins with the note "This Side UP" showing.
4. Place the cylinder head into position.
5. Coat the cylinder head bolt threads with a sealer GM 1052080 or equivalent and install the bolts. Torque the bolts in sequence shown in the following illustration. For torque specifications, refer to the Torque Specifications chart in the beginning of this section for the proper specs and procedures depending on the year of your Fiero.
6. Install the pushrods and loosely retain with the rocker arms. Make sure the lower ends of the pushrods are in the lifter seats then adjust the valve lash as shown below:
   a. **Valve Lash Adjustment:** rotate the engine until the mark on the torsional damper lines up with the "0" mark on the timing tab, with the engine in the No. 1 firing position. This may be determined by placing fingers on the No. 1 rocker arms as the mark on the damper comes near the "0" mark. If the valves are not moving, the engine is in the No. 1 firing position. With the engine in the No. 1 firing position, the following valves may be adjusted:
   - Exhuast—1, 2, 3
   - Intake—1, 5, 6

   b. Back out the adjusting nut until lash is felt at the pushrod, then turn the adjusting nut until all lash is removed. This can be determined by rotating the pushrod while turning the adjusting nut. When lash has been removed, turn the adjusting nut in 1½ additional turns to center the lifter plunger.
   c. Crank the engine one revolution until the timing tab "0" mark and torsional damper mark are again in alignment. This is the No. 4 firing position. With the engine in this position, the following valves may be adjusted:
   - Exhuast—4, 5, 6
   - Intake—2, 3, 4
7. For further valve adjustment illustrations, refer to the "Rocker Arm Cover" procedures in this section.
8. Install the intake manifold assembly as outlined in the Intake Manifold procedures in this section. Also, refer to the Torque Specifications chart for proper specs and procedures for your year Fiero.
9. Install the cruise control servo bracket, if so equipped.
10. Raise the vehicle and support with jackstands.
11. Install the exhaust crossover pipe to the exhaust manifold. Torque the attaching bolts to 25 ft. lbs. (34 Nm).
12. Lower the vehicle.
13. Install all vacuum, heater and wire connectors to the intake manifold and cylinder head.
14. Install the air conditioning compressor and alternator. Adjust the belts to specification. 135 lbs. (600 N) for a new belt, and 70 lbs. (300 N) for a used belt.
15. Install the air cleaner assembly, reconnect the negative (−) battery cable and recheck for completion of repair. Start

the engine and check for vacuum, oil, fuel, exhaust and coolant leaks.

CLEANING & INSPECTION

➧ **See Figure 61**

✲✲✲ CAUTION

To avoid personal injury ALWAYS wear safety glasses when using a power drill and wire brush.

1. Remove all traces of carbon from the head, using a decarbon-type wire brush mounted in an electric drill. Do not use a motorized brush on any gasket mating surface.
2. Lay a straightedge across the cylinder head face and check between the straight edge and the head with feeler gauges. Make the check at six points minimum. Cylinder head flatness should be within 0.003–0.006 inch. These surfaces may be reconditioned by parallel grinding. This procedure must be done by a qualified machine shop. If more than 10% must be removed, the head should be replaced.

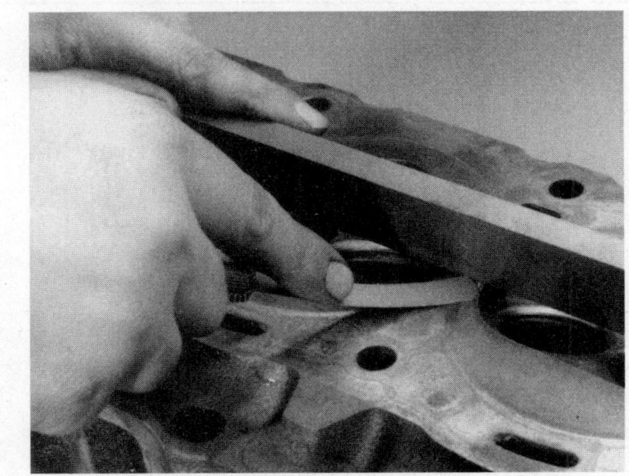

Checks should be made both straight across the cylinder head and at both diagonals

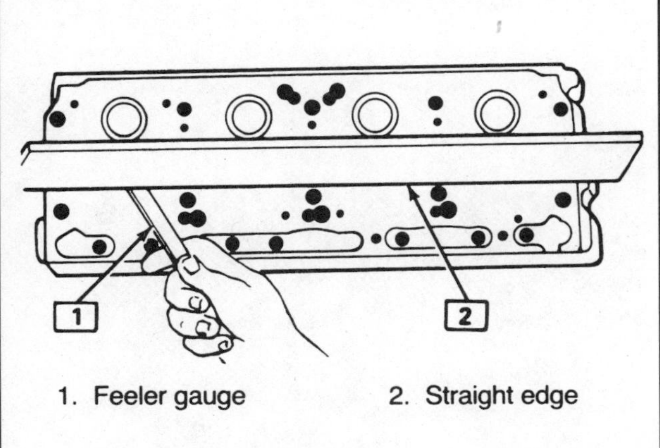

Fig. 61 Using a straightedge and a feeler gauge to check cylinder head flatness

Valves

REMOVAL & INSPECTION

➧ **See Figures 62, 63 and 64**

1. Remove the cylinder head(s) from the vehicle as previously outlined in the Cylinder Head removal and installation procedures.
2. Using a suitable valve spring compressor, compress the valve spring and remove the valve keys using a magnetic retrieval tool.
3. Slowly release the compressor and remove the valve spring caps (or rotors) and the valve springs.

A wire wheel may be used to clean the combustion chambers of carbon deposits

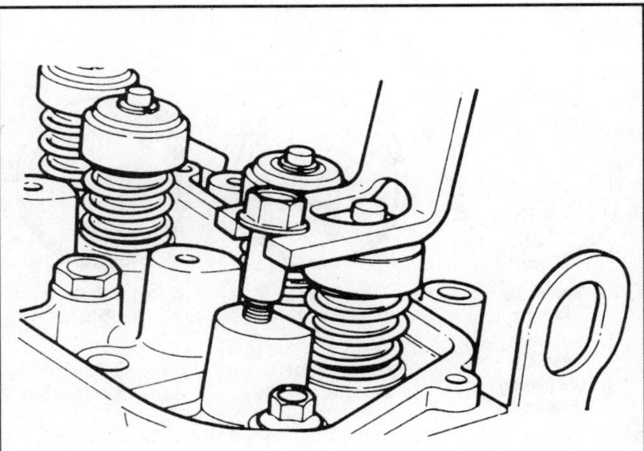

Fig. 62 Use a suitable tool to compress the valve springs

1
1
2
3
4
5
6
NEW VALVE
WORN VALVE

1. Valve tip
2. Keeper groove
3. Stem-least worn section
4. Stem-most worn section
5. Face
6. Margin

Fig. 63 Typical wear points on a common valve

CAUTION

The valve springs are under high spring load, always wear safety glasses when removing valve springs. Decompressing a valve spring quickly may cause personal injury.

4. Fabricate a valve arrangement board (piece of cardboard with holes punched through) to use when you remove the valves, which will indicate the port in which each valve was originally installed (and which cylinder head on V6 models). Also note that the valve keys, rotators, caps, etc. should be arranged in a manner which will allow you to install them on the valve on which they were originally removed.

5. Remove and discard the valve seals. On models using the umbrella type seals, note the location of the large and small seals for assembly purposes.

6. Thoroughly clean the valves on the wire wheel of a bench grinder, then clean the cylinder head mating surface with a soft wire wheel, a soft wire brush, or a wooden scraper. Avoid using a

Use a valve spring compressor to relieve spring tension and a small magnet to remove the valve keepers

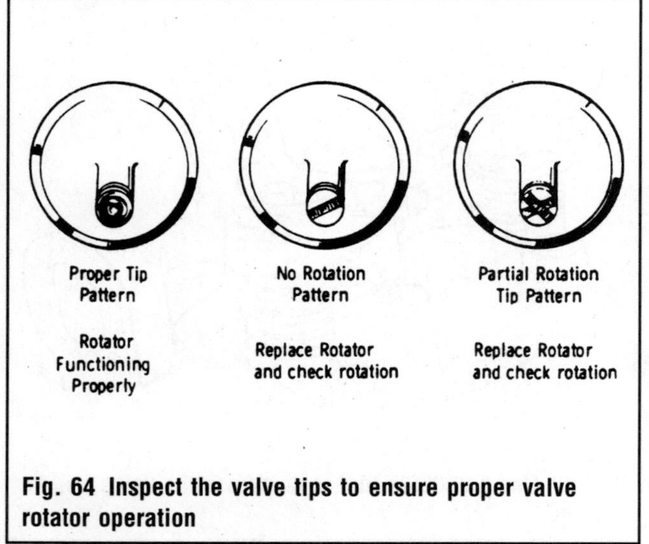

Fig. 64 Inspect the valve tips to ensure proper valve rotator operation

Remove the valve cap from the spring. . .

. . . then remove the valve shield from the spring

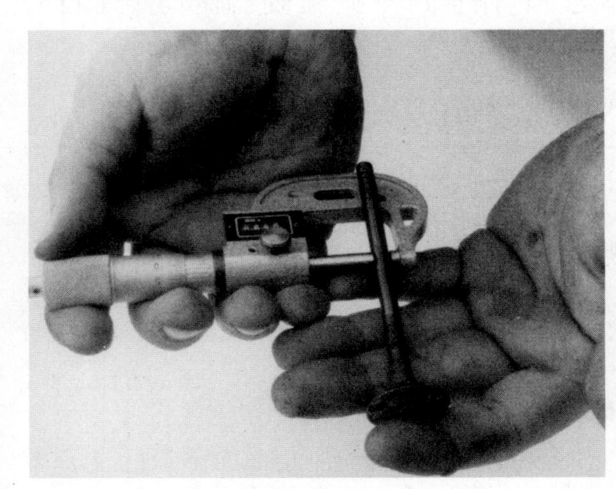
Use a micrometer to check the valve stem diameter

Invert the cylinder head and withdraw the valve from the cylinder head bore

A dial gauge may be used to check valve stem-to-guide clearance

metallic scraper, since this can cause damage to the cylinder head mating surface, especially on models with aluminum heads.

7. Using a valve guide cleaner chucked into a drill, clean all of the valve guides.
8. Install each valve into its respective port (guide) of the cylinder head.
9. Mount a dial indicator so that the stem is at 90° to the valve stem, as close to the valve guide as possible.
10. Move the valve off its seat, and measure the valve guide-to-stem clearance by rocking the stem back and forth to actuate the dial indicator.
11. Measure the valve stems using a micrometer, and compare to specifications, to determine whether stem or guide wear is responsible for excessive clearance. *Consult the machine shop for valve guide reconditioning.*

➡Consult the Specifications tables earlier in this Section.

REFACING

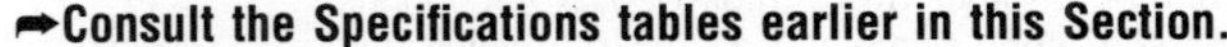

Using a valve grinder, resurface the valves according to specifications in this section.

➡All machine work should be performed by a competent, professional machine shop.

CAUTION

Valve face angle is not always identical to valve seat angle.

A minimum margin of 1/32 inch should remain after grinding the valve. The valve stem top should also be squared and resurfaced, by placing the stem in the V-block of the grinder, and turning it while pressing lightly against the grinding wheel. Be sure to chamfer the edge of the tip so that the squared edges don't dig into the rocker arm.

LAPPING

This procedure should be performed after the valves and seats have been machined, to insure that each valve mates to each seat precisely.

1. Invert the cylinder head, lightly lubricate the valve stems, and install the valves in the head as numbered.
2. Coat valve seats with fine grinding compound, and attach the lapping tool suction cup to a valve head.

➡Moisten the suction cup.

3. Rotate the tool between your palms, changing position and lifting the tool often to prevent grooving.
4. Lap the valve until a smooth and uniform wear pattern exists.
5. Remove the valve and tool, and rinse away all traces of grinding compound.

Valve Guide Service

The valve guides used in these engines are integral with the cylinder head, that is, they cannot be replaced.

➡Refer to the previous Valves—Removal and Installation to check the valve guides for wear.

Valve guides are most accurately repaired using the bronze wall rebuilding method. In this operation, "threads" are cut into the bore of the valve guide and bronze wire is turned into the threads. The bronze "wall" is then reamed to the proper diameter. This method is well received for a number of reasons: it is relatively inexpensive, it offers better valve lubrication (the wire forms channels which retain oil), it offers less valve friction, and it preserves the original valve guide-to-seat relationship.

Another popular method of repairing valve guides is to have the guides "knurled." The knurling entails cutting into the bore of the valve guide with a special tool. The cutting action "raises" metal off of the guide bore which actually narrows the inner diameter of the bore, thereby reducing the clearance between the valve guide bore and the valve stem. This method offers the same advantages as the bronze wall method, but will generally wear faster.

Either of the above services must be performed by a professional machine shop which has the specialized knowledge and tools necessary to perform the service.

Valve Seat Service

The valve seats are integral with the cylinder head on all engines. On all engines the seats are machined into the cylinder head casting itself.

Valve Springs

INSPECTION

➧ See Figures 65 and 66

Place the spring on a flat surface next to a square. Measure the height of the spring, and rotate it against the edge of the square to measure distortion. If spring height varies (by comparison) by more than 1.5mm or if distortion exceeds 1.5mm, replace the spring.

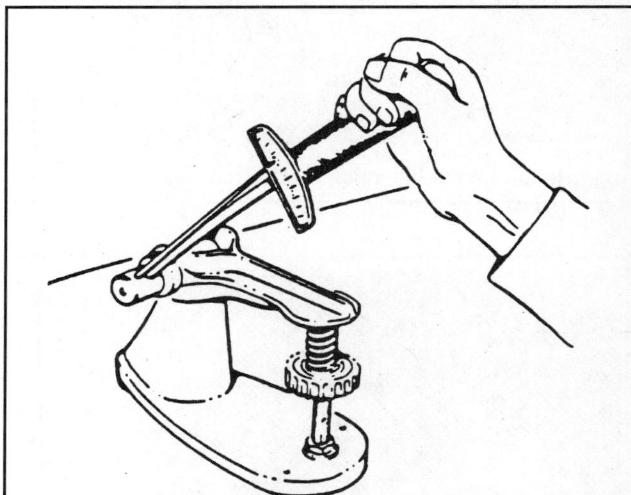

Fig. 65 Checking the valve spring load using a valve spring tester

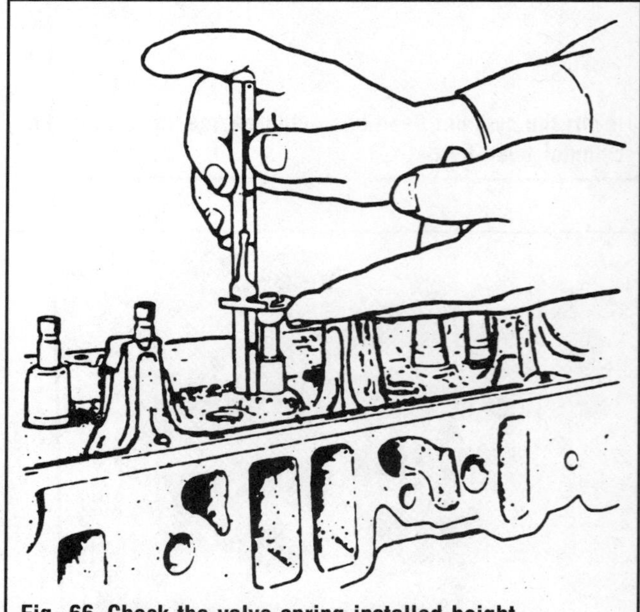

Fig. 66 Check the valve spring installed height

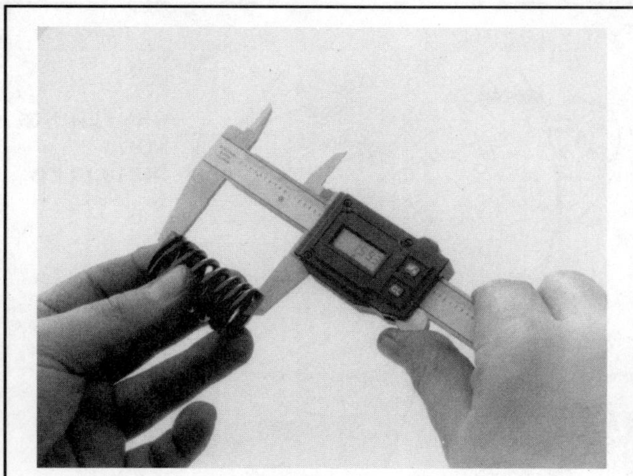

Use a caliper gauge to check the valve spring free-length

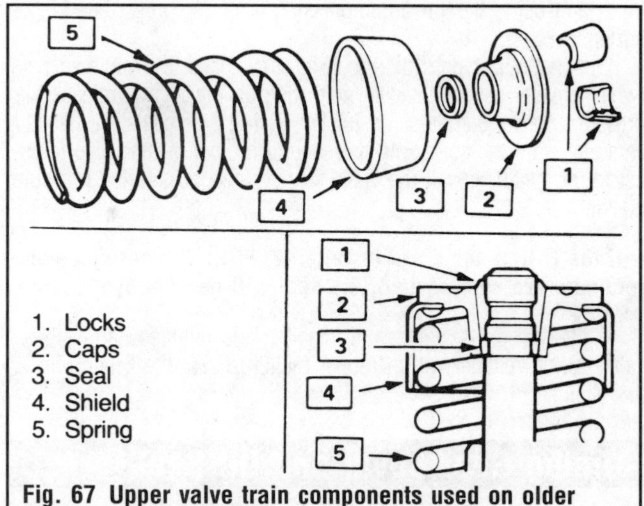

Fig. 67 Upper valve train components used on older model 2.5L engines

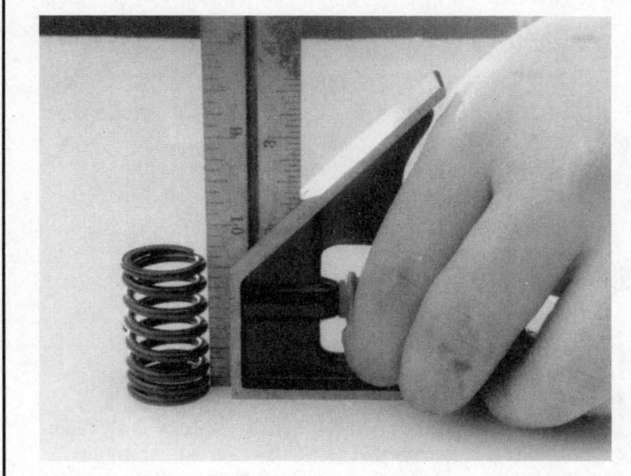

Check the valve spring for squareness on a flat service; a carpenter's square can be used

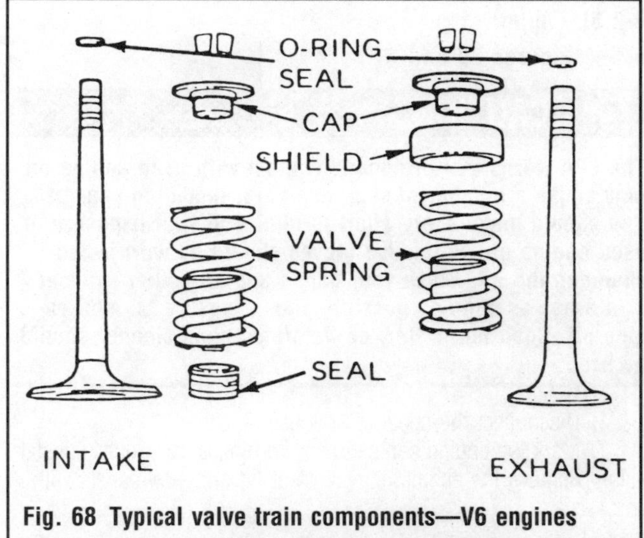

Fig. 68 Typical valve train components—V6 engines

In addition to evaluating the spring as above, test the spring pressure at the installed and compressed (installed height minus valve lift) height using a valve spring tester. Spring pressure should be ± 1 lb. of all other springs in either position.

VALVE & SPRING INSTALLATION

See Figures 67, 68 and 69

➡Be sure that all traces of lapping compound have been cleaned off before the valves are installed.

1. Lubricate all of the valve stems with a light coating of engine oil, then install the valves into the proper ports/guides.
2. If the umbrella-type valve seals are used, install them at this time. Be sure to use a seal protector to prevent damage to the seals as they are pushed over the valve keeper grooves. If O-ring seals are used, don't install them yet.
3. Install the valve springs and the spring retainers (or rota-

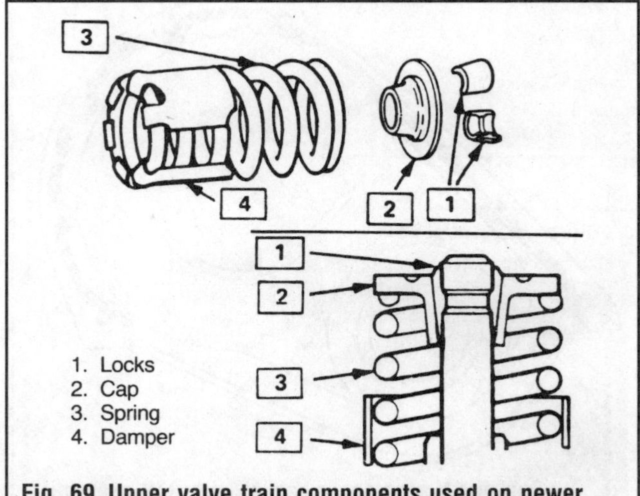

Fig. 69 Upper valve train components used on newer model 2.5L engines

tors), and using the valve compressing tool, compress the springs.

4. If umbrella-type seals are used, just install the valve keepers (white grease may be used to hold them in place) and release the pressure on the compressing tool. If O-ring type seals are used, carefully work the seals into the second groove of the valve (closest to the head), install the valve keepers and release the pressure on the tool.

➡If the O-ring seals are installed BEFORE the springs and retainers are compressed, the seal will be destroyed.

5. After all of the valves are installed and retained, tap each valve spring retainer with a rubber mallet to seat the keepers in the retainer.

Timing Gear Cover and Oil Seal

REMOVAL & INSTALLATION

4-2.5L Engine

➧ See Figures 70 and 71

✲✲ CAUTION

The EPA warns that prolonged contact with used engine oil may cause a number of skin disorders, including cancer! You should make every effort to minimize your exposure to used engine oil. Protective gloves should be worn when changing the oil. Wash your hands and any other exposed skin areas as soon as possible after exposure to used engine oil. Soap and water, or waterless hand cleaner should be used.

1. Disconnect the negative (−) battery cable.
2. Mark the engine compartment lid hinges for proper reinstallation. Remove the engine compartment lid and side panels with an assistant.

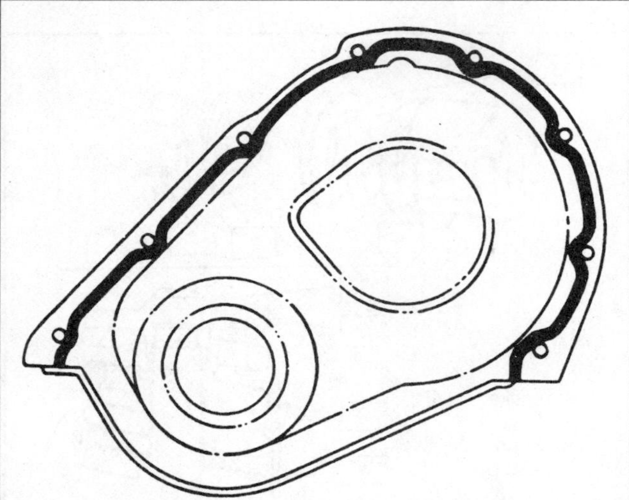

Fig. 70 Coat the timing cover gasket with RTV sealant in the areas shown—four-cylinder engines

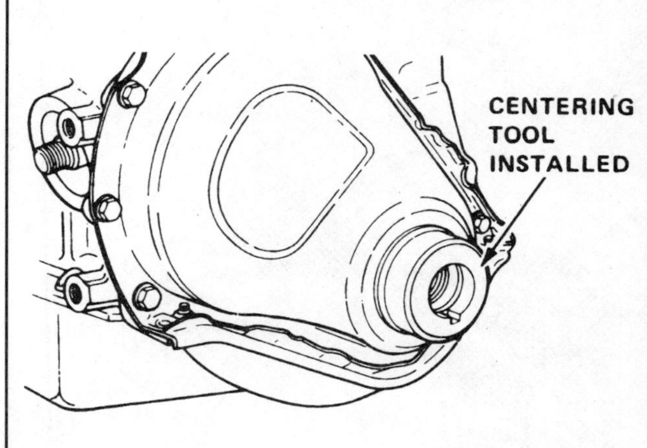

Fig. 71 Use a centering tool to align the front cover seal, then install the cover

3. Remove the trim panel at the sail panel below the battery side panel.
4. Remove the serpentine belt.
5. Raise the vehicle and support with jackstands.
6. Remove the right rear wheel assembly and inner splash shield.
7. Remove the starter motor and let hang.
8. Remove the crankshaft pulley and hub.
9. Lower vehicle and support with jackstands.
10. Install the engine support brace part No. J28467 or equivalent.
11. Raise the vehicle and support with jackstands.
12. It may be necessary to remove the alternator lower bracket.
13. Remove the front engine mounts.
14. Using a floor jack, raise the engine.
15. Remove the engine mount mounting bracket-to-cylinder blockbolts. Remove the bracket and mount as an assembly.
16. Remove the oil pan-to-front cover bolts.
17. Remove the front cover-to-block screws.
18. Pull the cover slightly forward, just enough to allow cutting of the oil pan front seal flush with the block on both sides.
19. Remove the front cover and the attached portion of the pan seal.

To install:

1. Clean the gasket surfaces on the cover, cylinder block and oil pan thoroughly.
2. Cut the tabs from the new oil pan front gasket.
3. Install the seal on the front cover, pressing the tips into the holes provided using the Front Cover Seal Installer No. J34995 or equivalent.
4. Coat the new gasket with RTV sealer and position it on the front cover.
5. Apply a 10mm wide by 5mm thick bead of silicone sealer to the joint formed at the oil pan and block.
6. Align the front cover seal with a centering tool No. J28467 and install the front cover. Torque the screws evenly to 90 inch. lb. (10 Nm).
7. Install the hub and torque the hub bolt to 160 ft. lbs. (217 Nm).
8. Install the front engine mount and remove the engine support brace J28467.

9. Install the starter, inner splash shield and right rear wheel. Torque the lug nuts to 100 ft. lbs. (136 Nm).
10. Lower the vehicle.
11. Install the serpentine belt and adjust to the specifications in the Cylinder Head installation procedures.
12. Install the trim panel at sail below the battery side panel, engine compartment lid with as assistant and the negative (−) battery cable.
13. Start the engine and check for oil leaks.

➡Coat the pulley-to-hub bolts with a locking sealant.

Timing Chain Cover

REMOVAL & INSTALLATION

6-2.8L Engine

➧ See Figures 72 and 73

1. Disconnect the negative (−) battery cable.
2. Remove the air conditioning compressor and bracket, without disconnecting the refrigerant lines, and position out of the way.
3. Drain the engine coolant at the radiator. Remove the water pump. Refer to the Water Pump removal and installation procedures in this section.

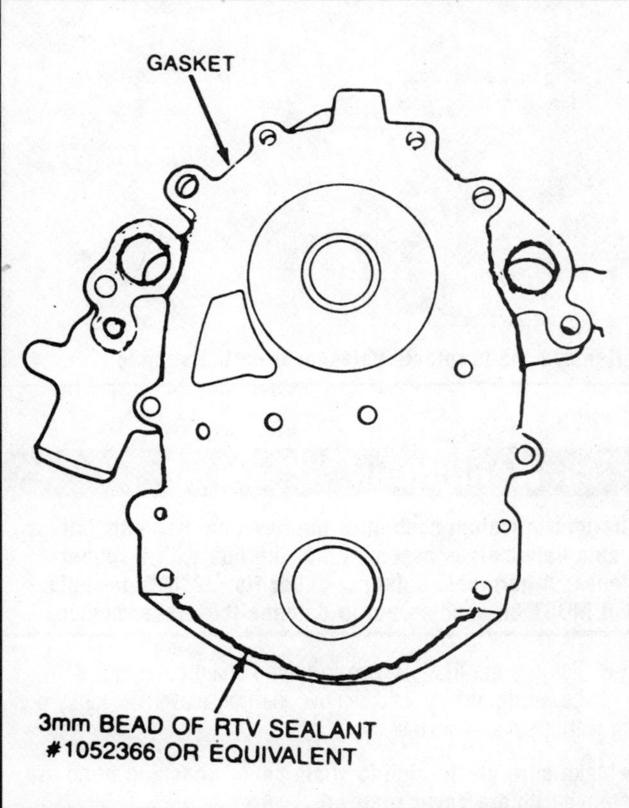

Fig. 72 Install the front cover with a new gasket and a 3mm bead of sealant to the oil pan sealing surface

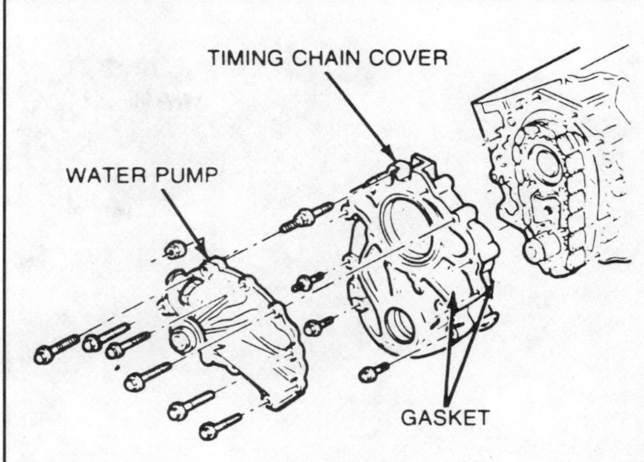

Fig. 73 To gain access to the timing chain cover, you must first remove the water pump—2.8L engine

**** CAUTION**

When draining engine coolant, keep in mind that cats and dogs are attracted to ethylene glycol antifreeze and could drink any that is left in an uncovered container or in puddles on the ground. This will prove fatal in sufficient quantity. Always drain coolant into a sealable container. Coolant should be reused unless it is contaminated or is several years old.

4. Raise the vehicle and support it safely with jackstands.
5. Remove the torsional damper (harmonic balancer) with a harmonic balancer puller No. J23523 or equivalent.

Remove the crankshaft pulley drive belt

Remove the pulley center bolt, then . . .

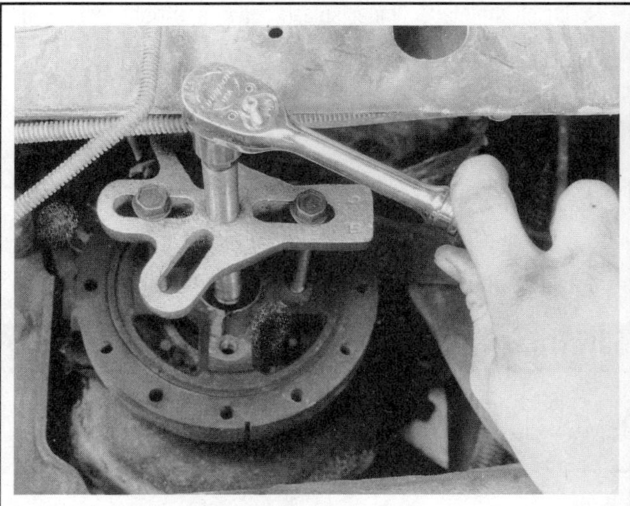
Install a puller on the harmonic balancer

. . . remove the four remaining bolts from the pulley

Remove the harmonic balancer from the vehicle

Remove the crankshaft pulley from the engine

***** WARNING**

The inertia weight section of the torsional damper (harmonic balancer) is assembled to the hub with a rubber sleeve. A harmonic balancer puller No. J23523 or equivalent MUST be used so not to damage the rubber sleeve.

6. Remove the front oil pan-to-timing chain cover bolts.
7. Lower the vehicle and remove the front cover by gently prying with a suitable prybar.

➡Make sure all the timing chain cover attaching bolts are removed before cover removal.

To install:

***** CAUTION**

The EPA warns that prolonged contact with used engine oil may cause a number of skin disorders, including cancer!

You should make every effort to minimize your exposure to used engine oil. Protective gloves should be worn when changing the oil. Wash your hands and any other exposed skin areas as soon as possible after exposure to used engine oil. Soap and water, or waterless hand cleaner should be used.

1. Before installing, clean the sealing surfaces on the front cover and cylinder block with a gasket scraper and solvent.
2. Install a new gasket and apply a continuous 3mm bead of RTV sealer to the oil pan sealing surface of the front cover.
3. Place the front cover on the engine and install the stud bolt and bolts. Torque the bolts to 20–30 ft. lbs. (27–41 Nm).
4. Install the water pump as outlined in the Water Pump installation procedures. Torque the pump bolts to 13–18 ft. lbs. (18–24 Nm).
5. Raise the vehicle and support with jackstands.
6. Install the oil pan-to-timing chain cover bolts and tighten.
7. Install the torsional damper (harmonic balancer) and torque the bolt to 66–84 ft. lbs. (90–115 Nm).
8. Lower the vehicle.
9. Install the air conditioning compressor and bracket, accessory drive belt and tighten to the specification in the Belts portion of Section 1.
10. Refill the radiator with the specified engine coolant. Connect the negative (−) battery cable and start the engine and check for coolant and oil leaks.

Front Cover Oil Seal

REMOVAL & INSTALLATION

6-2.8L Engine

CAUTION

The EPA warns that prolonged contact with used engine oil may cause a number of skin disorders, including cancer! You should make every effort to minimize your exposure to used engine oil. Protective gloves should be worn when changing the oil. Wash your hands and any other exposed skin areas as soon as possible after exposure to used engine oil. Soap and water, or waterless hand cleaner should be used.

1. Remove the torsional damper. Refer to the previous Timing Chain Cover procedures for accessory removal.

WARNING

The inertia weight section of the torsional damper (harmonic balancer) is assembled to the hub with a rubber sleeve. A harmonic balancer puller No. J23523 or equivalent MUST be used so not to damage the rubber sleeve.

2. Pry out the seal using a suitable seal removing tool.

To install:

3. Lubricate the seal with clean engine oil.
4. Insert the seal in the front cover with the lip facing the engine.
5. Using Tool No. J23042 Seal Installer, drive the seal into place.
6. Install the torsional damper and check for leaks.

Timing Chain and Sprockets

REMOVAL & INSTALLATION

6-2.8L Engine

See Figures 74 and 75

1. Disconnect the negative (−) battery cable.
2. Remove the timing chain cover as outlined in the Timing Chain Cover removal procedures in this section.

Fig. 74 The timing chain and sprockets are only accessible after the timing chain cover has been removed—V6 engines

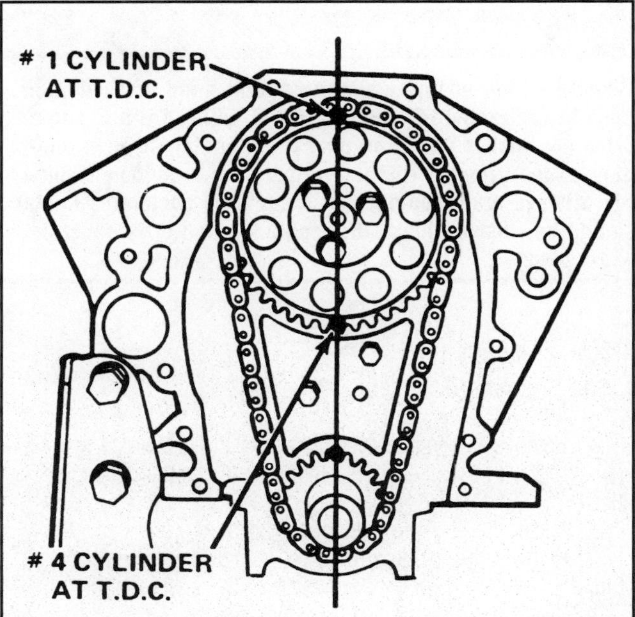

Fig. 75 Make sure the marks on the camshaft and crankshaft are aligned after the chain has been installed

3. Place the No. 1 piston at Top Dead Center, with the marks on the camshaft and crankshaft sprockets aligned.

➡If the timing chain is broken when removing, the timing marks on the camshaft and crankshaft will have to be lined up. Refer to the Camshaft Timing illustration in this section for the proper timing mark location.

4. Remove the camshaft sprocket and chain.

➡It may be necessary to use a plastic mallet on the lower edge of the sprocket to dislodge it.

5. Remove the crankshaft sprocket with Tool No. J5825.

To install:

1. Install the crankshaft sprocket with a sprocket installer tool No. J5590.
2. Apply Molykote® or equivalent to the sprocket thrust surface of the camshaft.
3. Hold the sprocket with the chain hanging down and align the marks on the camshaft and crankshaft sprockets.
4. Align the dowel in the camshaft with the dowel hole in the camshaft sprocket.
5. Draw the camshaft sprocket onto the camshaft, using the mounting bolts and torque to 15–20 ft. lbs. (20–27 Nm).
6. Lubricate the timing chain with engine oil.
7. Install the timing chain cover, water pump and torsional damper.
8. Refill the engine with coolant and start to check for oil and coolant leaks.

Camshaft and Timing Gear

REMOVAL & INSTALLATION

⁂ CAUTION

When draining engine coolant, keep in mind that cats and dogs are attracted to ethylene glycol antifreeze and could drink any that is left in an uncovered container or in puddles on the ground. This will prove fatal in sufficient quantity. Always drain coolant into a sealable container. Coolant should be reused unless it is contaminated or is several years old.

4-2.5L Engine

➧ See Figures 76, 77 and 78

1. Remove the engine assembly from the vehicle as previously described in the Engine removal procedures in this section.
2. Install the engine on a support stand.
3. Remove the rocker arm cover, loosen the valve rocker arm bolts and swing the rocker arms clear of the pushrods.
4. Remove the distributor (non DIS system).
5. Remove the pushrod cover, pushrods and valve lifters.
6. Remove the alternator, lower alternator bracket and front engine mount bracket assembly.

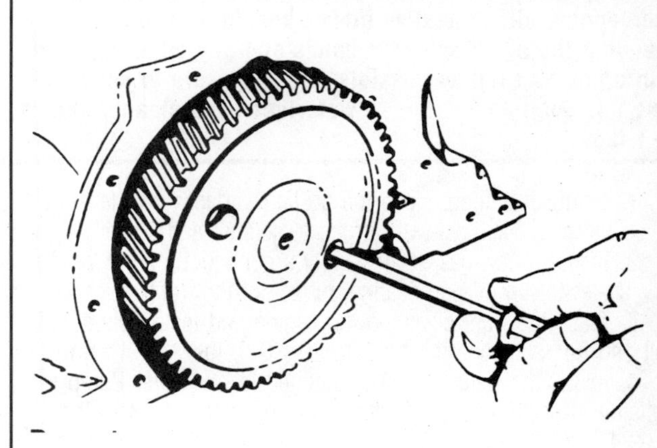

Fig. 76 Insert a screwdriver in the camshaft thrust plate screw access holes to unfasten the screws

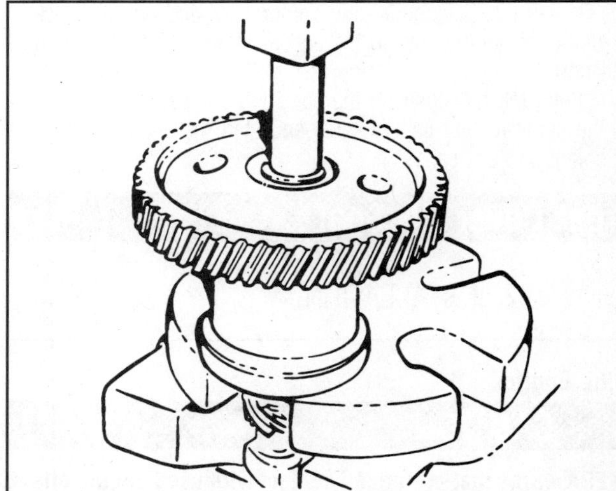

Fig. 77 If necessary, use a press to remove the camshaft timing gear—four-cylinder engines

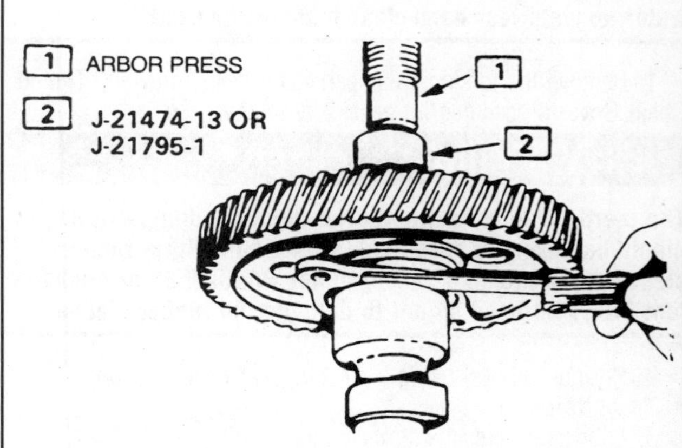

Fig. 78 Use a feeler gauge to check camshaft timing gear/thrust plate end clearance—four-cylinder engines

CAUTION

The EPA warns that prolonged contact with used engine oil may cause a number of skin disorders, including cancer! You should make every effort to minimize your exposure to used engine oil. Protective gloves should be worn when changing the oil. Wash your hands and any other exposed skin areas as soon as possible after exposure to used engine oil. Soap and water, or waterless hand cleaner should be used.

7. Remove the oil pump driveshaft and gear assembly.
8. Remove the front pulley hub and timing gear cover as outlined in the Timing Gear Cover removal procedures in this section.
9. Remove the two camshaft thrust plate screws by working through the holes in the camshaft gear. Refer to the Thrust Plate illustration in this section.
10. Remove the camshaft and gear assembly by pulling it out through the front of the block.

➡Support the shaft carefully when removing so as not to damage the camshaft bearings.

11. If the gear must be removed from the shaft, use the press plate and adapter J-971 on the press.
12. Place the tools on the table of the press. Place the camshaft through the openings in the tools, then press the shaft out of the gear using a socket or other suitable tool. Refer to the Camshaft Gear removal illustration in this section.

➡The thrust plate must be so positioned that the Woodruff key in the shaft does not damage it when the shaft is pressed out of the gear.

To install:

1. To assemble the camshaft gear, thrust plate and gear spacer ring to the camshaft, proceed as follows:
   a. Firmly support the shaft at the back of the front journal in an arbor press using press plate adapters.
   b. Place the gear spacer ring and thrust plate over the end of the shaft, and install a Woodruff key in the shaft keyway.
   c. Install the camshaft gear and press it onto the shaft until it bottoms against the gear spacer ring. The end clearance of the thrust plate should be 0.025–0.130mm. If less than 0.04mm, the thrust plate should be replaced.
2. Thoroughly coat the camshaft journals with a high quality Assembly Lube or engine oil supplement.
3. Install the camshaft assembly into the engine, being careful not to damage the bearings or cam.
4. Turn the crankshaft and camshaft so that the valve timing marks on the gear teeth will line up. The engine is now in the No. 4 firing position. Install the camshaft thrust plate-to-block screws and tighten to 90 inch lbs. (10 Nm).
5. Install the timing gear cover and gasket as outlined in the Timing Gear Cover installation procedures in this section.
6. Line up the keyway in the hub with the key on the crankshaft and slide the hub onto the shaft. Install the center bolt and torque to 162 ft. lbs. (220 Nm).
7. Coat each valve lifter with Assembly Lube® Install the valve lifters, pushrods, pushrod cover, oil pump shaft and gear assembly and fuel pump as previously described.
8. Install the distributor (non DIS system) as follows:
   a. Turn the crankshaft 360° to the firing position of the No. 1 cylinder (number 1 exhaust and intake valve lifters both on base circle of camshaft and timing mark on the harmonic balancer indexed with the TDC mark on the timing pad).
   b. Install the distributor in its original position and align the shaft so the rotor arm points toward the No. 1 cylinder spark plug contact.
9. Swing the rocker arms over the pushrods. With the lifters on the base circle of the camshaft, tighten the rocker arm bolt to 24 ft. lbs. (32 Nm). Do not over torque.
10. Install the front mount assembly, lower alternator bracket and alternator.
11. Install the engine assembly into the vehicle as outlined in the Engine installation procedures in this section.

Camshaft

REMOVAL & INSTALLATION

6-2.8L Engine

See Figure 79

CAUTION

When draining engine coolant, keep in mind that cats and dogs are attracted to ethylene glycol antifreeze and could drink any that is left in an uncovered container or in puddles on the ground. This will prove fatal in sufficient quantity. Always drain coolant into a sealable container. Coolant should be reused unless it is contaminated or is several years old.

1. Remove the engine from the vehicle and place on a suitable stand as outlined in the Engine removal procedures in this section.
2. Remove the intake manifold as outlined in the Intake Manifold removal section.

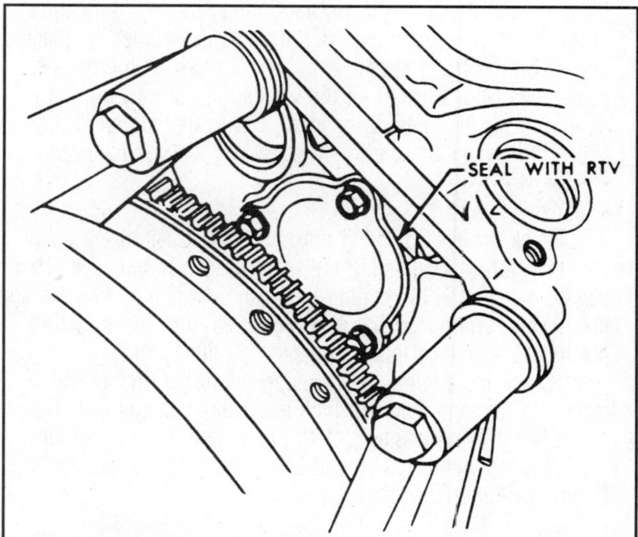

Fig. 79 Apply RTV sealant to the camshaft rear cover before installation —V6 engine

3. Remove the rocker arm covers and loosen the rocker arm bolts enough to move them aside to remove the pushrods.

➡Mark all valve components to ensure installation will be in same location as removal.

4. Remove the valve lifters. Mark each lifter to ensure installation will be in same location as removal.
5. Remove the timing chain front cover as outlined in the Timing Chain Cover removal procedures.
6. Remove the timing chain and sprocket.
7. Remove the rear cover. Refer to the Camshaft Rear Cover illustration in this section.
8. Carefully remove the camshaft to avoid damage to the bearings.

➡Install a 6 inch long M8×1.25 size bolt into the camshaft sprocket bolt hole to remove the camshaft.

To install:

1. Before installation, lubricate the camshaft journals and lobes with Assembly Lube®.

➡If a new camshaft is to be installed, coat the lobes with Assembly Lube such as GM E.O.S. or its equivalent.

2. Install the camshaft using a six inch long M8×1.25 size bolt in the camshaft sprocket bolt hole. Be careful not to damage the camshaft bearings during installation.
3. Install the camshaft sprocket and timing chain as outlined in the Timing Chain installation procedures in this section.

➡The timing marks have to be lined up at this time.

4. Apply RTV sealer to the rear camshaft cover and install the cover with the three attaching bolts. Torque the bolts to 6–9 ft. lbs. (8–12 Nm).
5. Install the timing chain front cover as outlined in the Timing Chain Cover installation procedures.
6. Apply Assembly Lube® to the valve lifters and install into their previously marked lifter bores.
7. Install the pushrods into their previously marked positions. Adjust the valve lash as follows:
   a. Rotate the engine until the mark on the torsional damper lines up with the "0" mark on the timing tab, with the engine in the No. 1 firing position. This may be determined by placing fingers on the No. 1 rocker arms as the mark on the damper comes near the "0" mark. If the valves are not moving, the engine is in the No. 1 firing position, . With the engine in the No. 1 firing position, the following valves may be adjusted:
   - Exhaust—1, 2, 3
   - Intake—1, 5, 6

   b. Back out the adjusting nut until lash is felt at the pushrod, then turn the adjusting nut until all lash is removed. This can be determined by rotating the pushrod while turning the adjusting nut. When lash has been removed, turn the adjusting nut in 1½ additional turns to center the lifter plunger.
   c. Crank the engine one revolution until the timing tab "0" mark and torsional damper mark are again in alignment. This is the No. 4 firing position. With the engine in this position, the following valves may be adjusted. Refer to the Timing Chain illustrations for timing marks:
   - Exhaust—4, 5, 6
   - Intake—2, 3, 4

8. Install the engine assembly into the vehicle as outlined in the Engine installation procedures in this section.

Camshaft Bearings

REMOVAL & INSTALLATION

4-2.5L Engine

➡Camshaft bearing removal should be done by a qualified machine shop because the tools needed are expensive and would not be economical to purchase for a one time usage.

1. Remove the engine from the vehicle as previously outlined.
2. Remove the camshaft from the engine as previously outlined.
3. Unbolt and remove the engine flywheel.
4. Drive the rear camshaft expansion plug out of the engine block from the inside using a long prybar.
5. Using a camshaft bearing service tool No. J33049 or equivalent, drive the front camshaft bearing towards the rear and the rear bearing towards the front.
6. Install the appropriate extension on the service tool and drive the center bearing out towards the rear.
7. Drive all of the new bearings into place in the opposite direction of which they were removed, making sure to align the oil holes in the engine block bores.

CAUTION

Never reuse camshaft bearings. Always use new bearings.

➡The front camshaft bearing must be driven approximately 3mm behind the front of the cylinder block to uncover the oil hole to the timing gear oiling nozzle.

To install:

8. Install the camshaft bearings so that the oil holes in the bearing is aligned with the hole in the block.
9. Install the camshaft and timing gear as outlined in the Camshaft installation procedures.
10. Install the timing gear cover, harmonic balancer, all accessories and install the engine into the vehicle as outlined in the Engine installation procedures in this section.

6-2.8L Engine

See Figures 80 and 81

➡Camshaft bearing removal should be done by a qualified machine shop because the tools needed are expensive and would not be economical to purchase for a one time usage.

Camshaft bearings can be replaced with engine completely or partially disassembled. To replace bearings without complete disassembly remove the camshaft and crankshaft leaving cylinder heads attached and pistons in place: Before removing crankshaft, install two inch pieces of rubber hose to the threads of connecting rod bolts to prevent damage to crankshaft. Fasten connecting rods against sides of engine so they will not be in the way while replacing camshaft bearings.

1. Remove the timing chain front cover and camshaft rear cover as outlined in the Timing Chain Cover and Camshaft removal procedures.
2. Using a camshaft bearing Tool J-33049 or its equivalent, with the nut and thrust washer installed to the end of the threads,

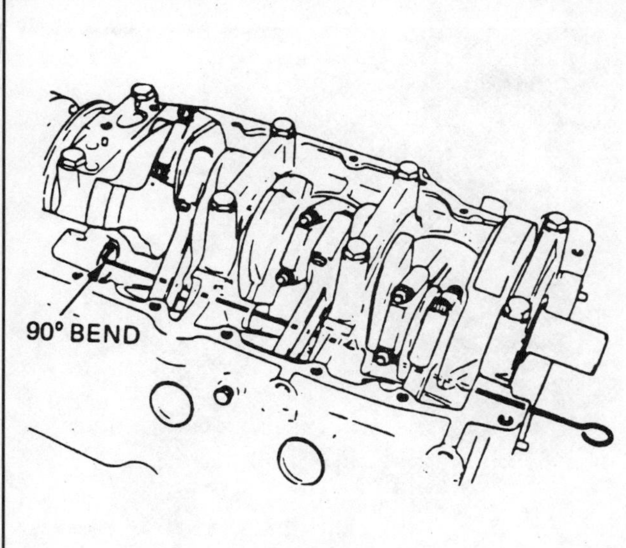

Fig. 80 Use a piece of wire bent at a ninety degree angle to align the camshaft bearing oil holes

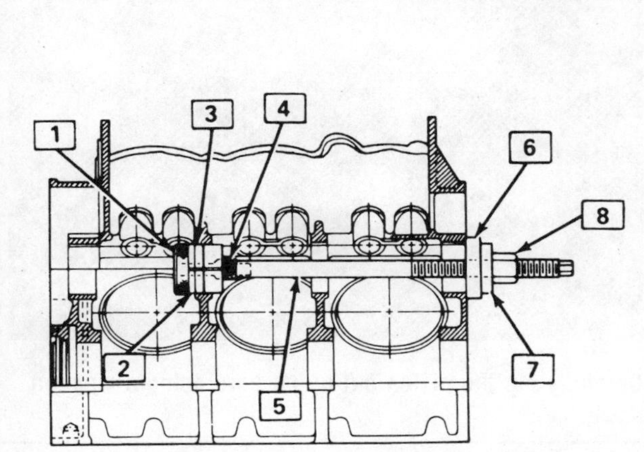

1. Back-up nut
2. Expanding collet
3. Bearing
4. Expanding mandrel
5. 2 piece puller screw
6. Pulling plate
7. Thrust bearing
8. Pulling nut

Fig. 81 Use a camshaft bearing removal/installation tool to remove the bearings. Always follow the specific tool manufacturers instructions for proper tool set-up and operation

index the pilot in the camshaft front bearing and install the puller screw through the pilot.

3. Install the remover and installer tool with the shoulder toward the bearing, making sure a sufficient number of threads are engaged.

4. Using two wrenches, hold the puller screw while turning the nut. When the bearing has been pulled from the bore, remove the remover and installer tool and bearing from the puller screw.

**** CAUTION**

The EPA warns that prolonged contact with used engine oil may cause a number of skin disorders, including cancer! You should make every effort to minimize your exposure to used engine oil. Protective gloves should be worn when changing the oil. Wash your hands and any other exposed skin areas as soon as possible after exposure to used engine oil. Soap and water, or waterless hand cleaner should be used.

5. Remove the remaining bearings (except front and rear) in the same manner. It will be necessary to index the pilot in the camshaft rear bearing to remove the rear intermediate bearing.

6. Assemble the remover and installer tool on the driver handle and remove the camshaft front and rear bearings by driving towards the center of the cylinder block.

The camshaft front and rear bearings should be installed first. These bearings will act as guides for the pilot, and center the remaining bearings being pulled into place.

7. Assemble the remover and installer tool on the driver handle and install the camshaft front and rear bearings by driving them towards the center of the cylinder block. Make sure the oil holes in the bearing line up with the holes in the block.

8. Using Tool Set J-6098, or its equivalent with the nut and thrust washer installed to end of the threads, index the pilot into the camshaft front bearing and install the puller screw through the pilot.

9. Index the camshaft bearing into the bore (with oil hole aligned as outlined below), then install the remover and installer tool on the puller screw with the shoulder toward the bearing.

- The rear and intermediate bearing oil holes must be aligned at 2:30 o'clock.
- The front bearing oil holes must be aligned at 1:00 and 2:30 o'clock (two holes).

10. Using two wrenches, hold the puller screw while turning the nut. After the bearing has been pulled into the bore, remove the remover and installer tool from the puller screw and check the alignment of the oil holes in the camshaft bearings.

11. Install the remaining bearings in the same manner. It will be necessary to index the pilot in the camshaft rear bearing to install the rear intermediate bearing.

12. Clean the rear cover mating surfaces and bolt holes then apply a 3mm bead of RTV to the cover. Install the rear cover and torque the bolts to 6–9 ft. lbs. (8–12 Nm).

13. Install the camshaft as outlined in the Camshaft installation procedures. Install the timing gear cover, all accessories and install the engine into the vehicle.

Pistons and Connecting Rod Assemblies

REMOVAL

1. Remove the engine assembly from the car, by following the Engine removal and installation procedures, earlier in this section.

2. On 6-cylinder engines, remove the intake manifold and the cylinder head over piston assembly being removed. On 4-cylinder engines, remove the cylinder head and manifolds as an assembly.

CAUTION

The EPA warns that prolonged contact with used engine oil may cause a number of skin disorders, including cancer! You should make every effort to minimize your exposure to used engine oil. Protective gloves should be worn when changing the oil. Wash your hands and any other exposed skin areas as soon as possible after exposure to used engine oil. Soap and water, or waterless hand cleaner should be used.

3. Drain the oil and remove the oil pan.
4. Remove the oil pump assembly. On 1987–88 2.5L engines, remove the force balancer assembly as outlined in the Forced Balancer removal procedures.
5. Stamp the cylinder number on the machine surfaces of the bolt bosses of the connecting rod and cap for identification when reinstalling. If the pistons are to be removed from the connecting rod, mark the cylinder number on the piston with a silver pencil or quick drying paint for proper cylinder identification and cap-to-rod location. The 2.5L L4 engine (LR8) is numbered 1-4 from front to back; the 2.8L V6 engine (L44) is numbered 1-3-5 on the right bank, 2-4-6 on the left bank.
6. Examine the cylinder bore above the ring travel. If a ridge exists, remove the ridge with a ridge reamer before attempting to remove the piston and rod assembly.
7. Remove the rod bearing cap and bearing.
8. Install guide hoses over threads of the rod bolts. This is to prevent damage to bearing journal and rod bolt threads.
9. Remove the rod and piston assembly through the top of the cylinder bore by lightly tapping the connecting rod with a wooden hammer handle.

➡If the piston rings will not clear the top of the cylinder, check to see if the ridge is completely removed.

10. Remove all other rod and piston assemblies in the same manner.

Place rubber hose over the connecting rod studs to protect the crank and bores from damage

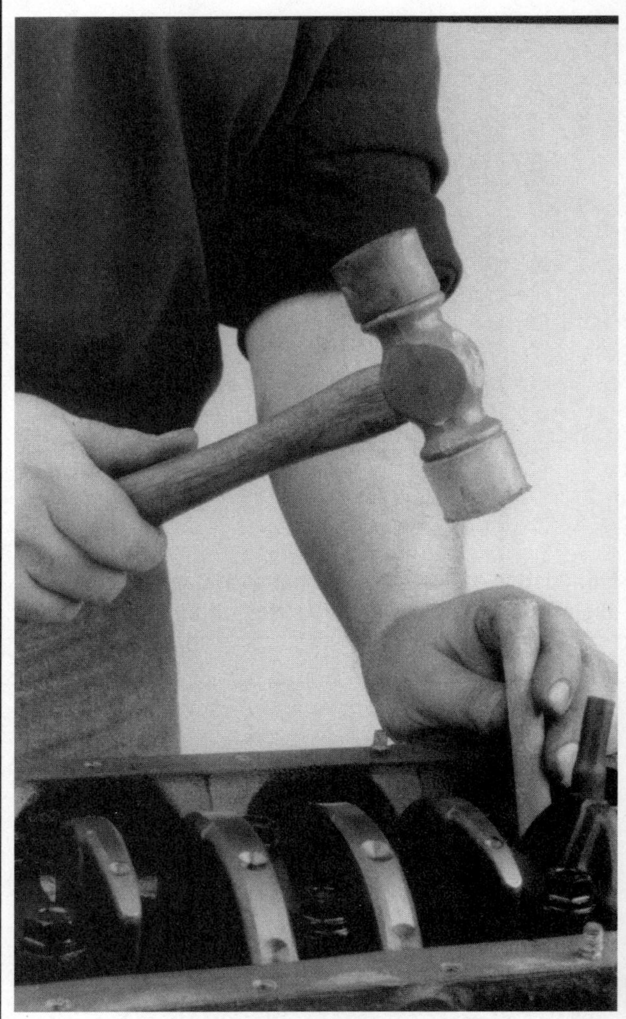

Carefully tap the piston out of the bore using a wooden dowel

CLEANING & INSPECTION

Connecting Rods

Wash connecting rods in cleaning solvent and dry with compressed air. Check for twisted or bent rods and inspect for nicks or cracks. Also check the length of the rods and replace connecting rods that are damaged.

Pistons

See Figure 82

Clean varnish from piston skirts and pins with a cleaning solvent. *Do not wire brush any part of the piston.* Clean the carbon out of the ring grooves with a ring groove cleaner or break a old ring in half. Make sure oil ring holes and slots are clean.

Inspect the piston for cracked ring lands, skirts or pin bosses,

Clean the piston grooves using a ring groove cleaner

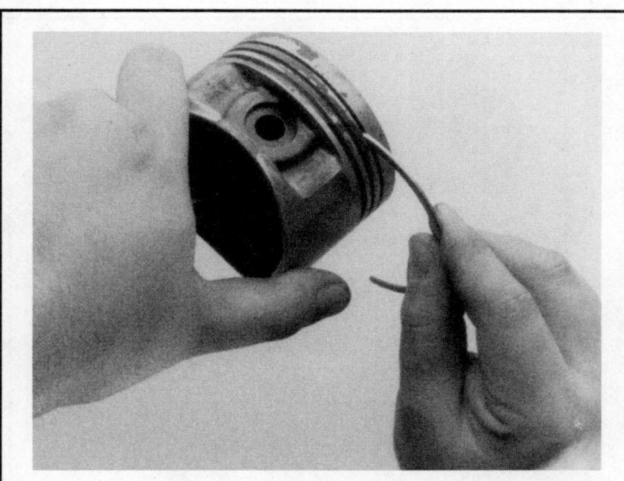

You can use a piece of an old ring to clean the piston grooves, BUT be careful, the ring is sharp

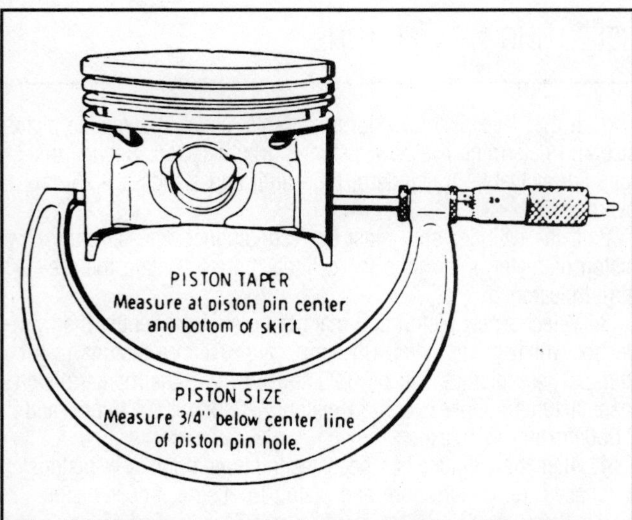

Fig. 82 Use a micrometer to measure the piston skirt

wavy or worn ring lands, scuffed or damaged skirts, eroded areas at the top of the piston. Replace pistons that are damaged or show signs of excessive wear. Inspect the grooves for nicks or burrs that might cause the rings to hang up.

Measure piston skirt (across center line of piston pin) and check piston clearance.

PISTON PIN REMOVAL & INSTALLATION

See Figures 83 and 84

Use care at all times when handling and servicing connecting rods and pistons. To prevent possible damage to these units, do not clamp the rod or piston in a vise since they may become distorted. Do not allow the pistons to strike against one another, against hard objects or bench surfaces, since distortion of the piston contour or nicks in the soft aluminum material may result.

1. Remove the piston rings using a suitable piston ring remover.

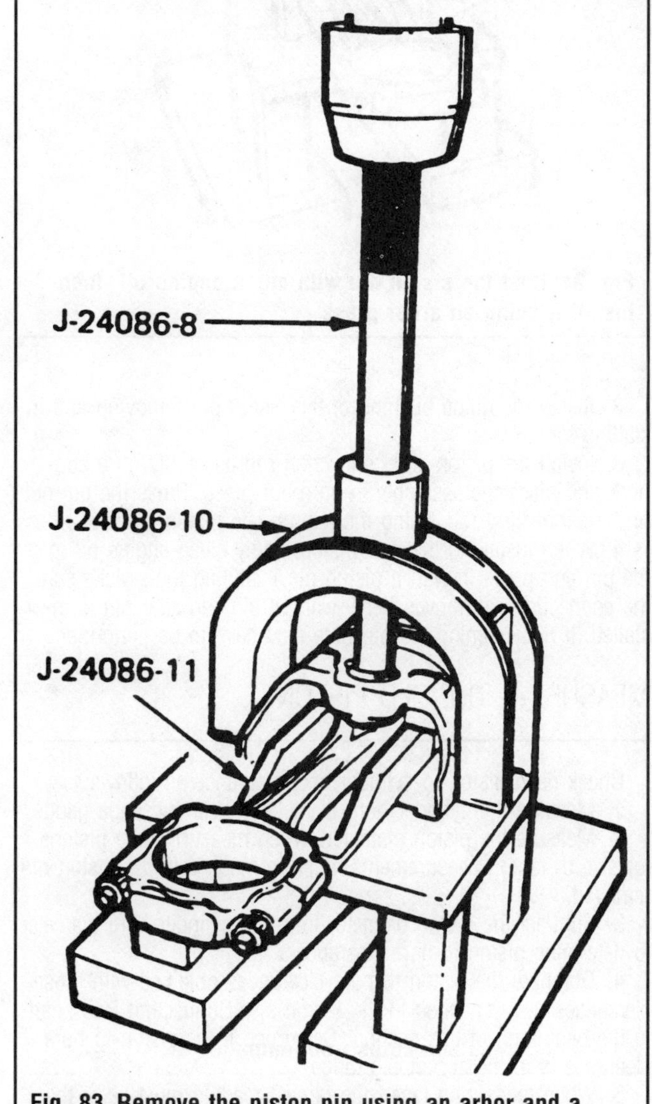

Fig. 83 Remove the piston pin using an arbor and a suitable piston pin tool

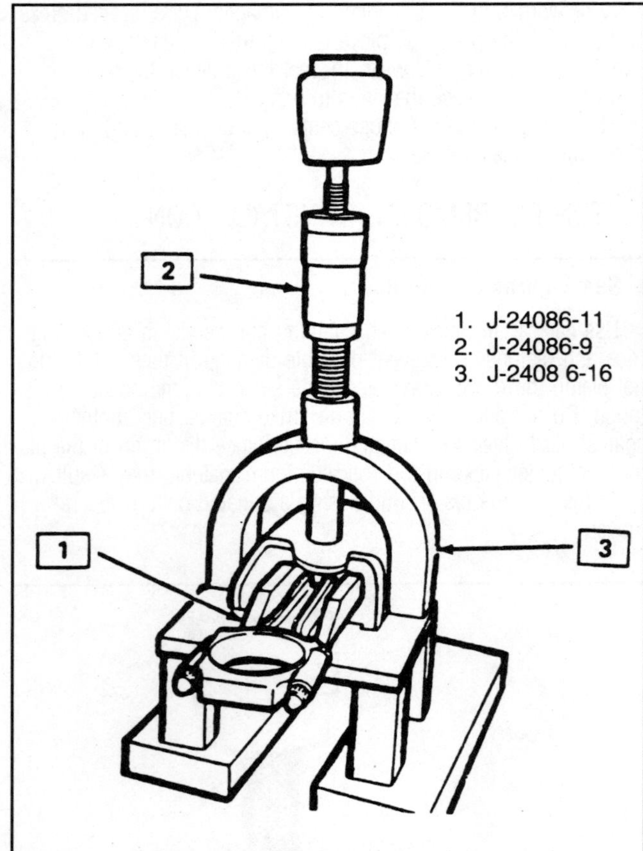

Fig. 84 Coat the piston pin with clean engine oil, then install it using an arbor press

2. Install the guide bushing of the piston pin removing and installing tool.
3. Install the piston and connecting rod assembly on a support, and place the assembly in an arbor press. Press the pin out of the connecting rod, using the appropriate piston pin tool.
4. When installing the new piston, apply clean engine oil to the pin and press in with a piston pin installing tool. Make sure the connecting rod moves freely without binding after pin is installed. If not, reaming the pin hole may have to be performed.

MEASURING THE OLD PISTONS

Check used piston-to-cylinder bore clearance as follows:

1. Measure the cylinder bore diameter with a telescope gauge.
2. Measure the piston diameter. When measuring the pistons for size or taper, measurements must be made with the piston pin removed.
3. Subtract the piston diameter from the cylinder bore diameter to determine piston-to-bore clearance.
4. Compare the piston-to-bore clearances obtained with those clearances recommended in the Piston and Connecting Rod chart in the beginning of this section. Determine if the piston-to-bore clearance is in the acceptable range.
5. When measuring taper, the largest reading must be at the bottom of the skirt.

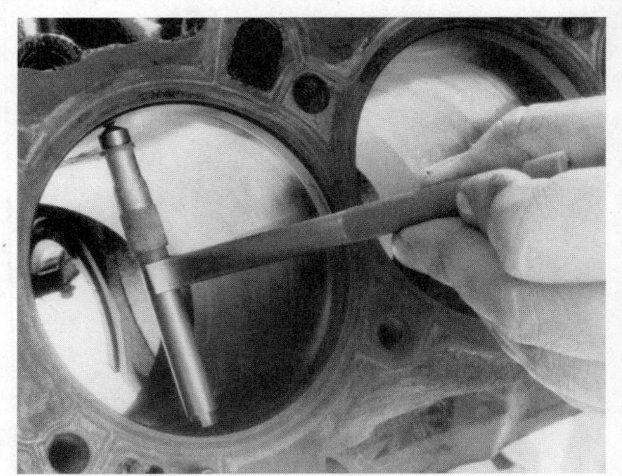

A telescoping gauge may be used to measure the cylinder bore diameter

Measure the piston's outer diameter using a micrometer

SELECTING NEW PISTONS

1. If the used piston is not acceptable, check the service piston size and determine if a new piston can be selected. Service pistons are available in standard, high limit and standard 0.25mm oversize.
2. If the cylinder bore must be reconditioned, measure the new piston diameter, then hone the cylinder bore to obtain the preferred clearance.
3. Select a new piston and mark the piston to identify the cylinder for which it was fitted. On some cars, oversize pistons may be found. These pistons will be 0.25mm oversize. Aftermarket piston manufactures supply oversized pistons 0.030mm, 0.040mm, and 0.060mm in most cases.
4. After the cylinder has been reconditioned and new pistons purchased, remeasure bore and piston to ensure proper piston fit.

CYLINDER HONING

➧ **See Figure 85**

1. When cylinders are being honed, follow the manufacturer's recommendations for the use of the hone.
2. Occasionally during the honing operation, the cylinder bore should be thoroughly cleaned and the selected piston checked for correct fit.
3. When finish-honing a cylinder bore, the hone should be moved up and down at a sufficient speed to obtain a very fine uniform surface finish in a cross-hatch pattern of approximately 45–65° included angle. The finish marks should be clean but not sharp, free from imbedded particles and torn or folded metal.
4. Permanently mark the piston for the cylinder to which it has been fitted and proceed to hone the remaining cylinders.

➡Handle pistons with care. Do not attempt to force pistons through cylinders until the cylinders have been honed to correct size. Pistons can be distorted through careless handling.

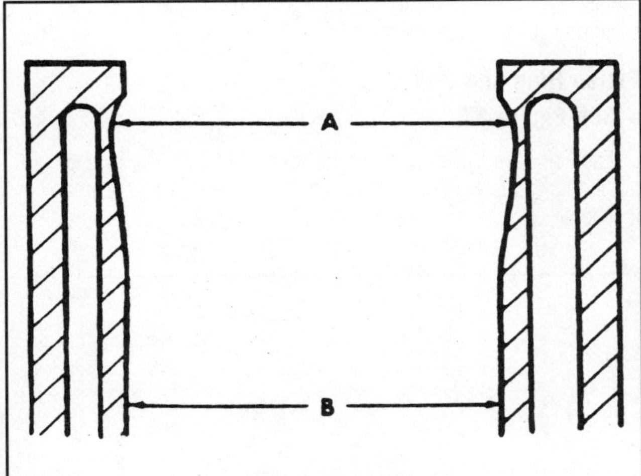

Fig. 85 Typical cylinder bore wear patterns and measuring points

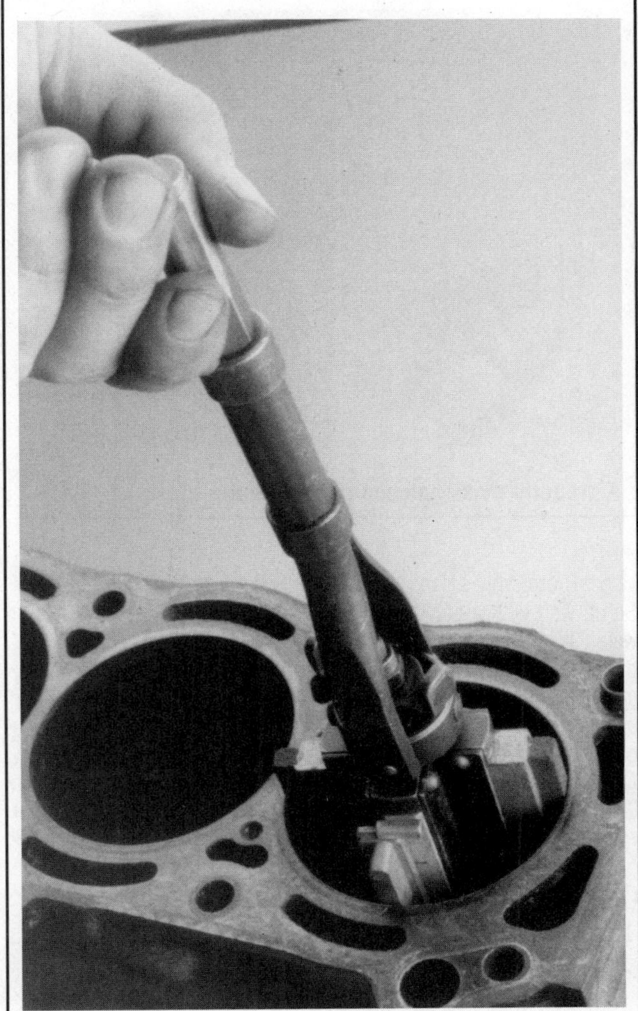

A solid hone can also be used to cross-hatch the cylinder bore

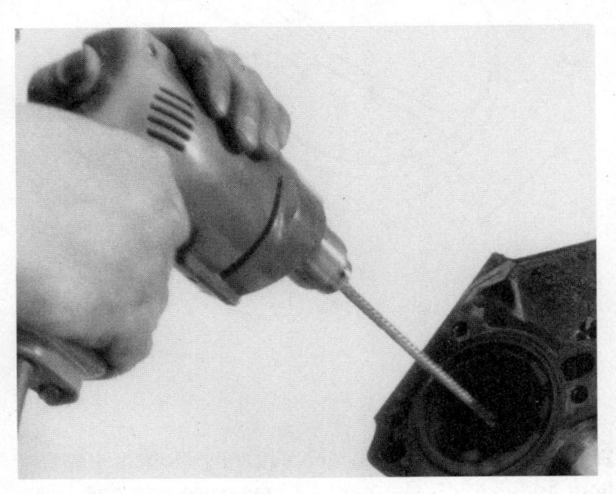

Removing cylinder glazing using a flexible hone

As with a ball hone, work the hone carefully up and down the bore to achieve the desired results

A properly cross-hatched cylinder bore

5. Thoroughly clean the bores with hot water and detergent. Scrub well with a stiff bristle brush and rinse thoroughly with hot water. It is extremely essential that a good cleaning operation be performed. If any of the abrasive material is allowed to remain in the cylinder bores, it will rapidly wear the new rings and cylinder bores. The bores should be swabbed several times with light engine oil with a clean cloth and then wiped with a clean dry cloth. *Cylinders should not be cleaned with kerosene or gasoline.* Clean the remainder of the cylinder block to remove the excess material spread during the honing operation.

CHECKING CYLINDER BORE

See Figure 86

Cylinder bore size can be measured with inside micrometers or a cylinder gauge. The most wear will occur at the top of the ring travel.

Fig. 86 Use a cylinder bore gauge to measure bore size and taper

Reconditioned cylinder bores should be held to not more than 0.025mm taper.

If the cylinder bores are smooth, the cylinder walls should not be deglazed. If the cylinder walls are scored, the walls may have to be honed before installing new rings. It is important that reconditioned cylinder bores be thoroughly washed with a soap and water solution to remove all traces of abrasive material to eliminate premature wear.

Piston Rings

The pistons have three rings (two compression rings and one oil ring). The oil ring consists of two rails and an expander. Pistons do not have oil drain holes behind the rings.

RING TOLERANCES

When installing new rings, ring gap and side clearance should be checked as in the following illustrations. Check the measurements with the specifications in the Piston and Rings chart in the beginning of the section:

Piston Ring and Rail Gap

See Figure 87

Each ring and rail gap must be measured with the ring or rail positioned squarely and at the bottom of the ring-travel area of the bore.

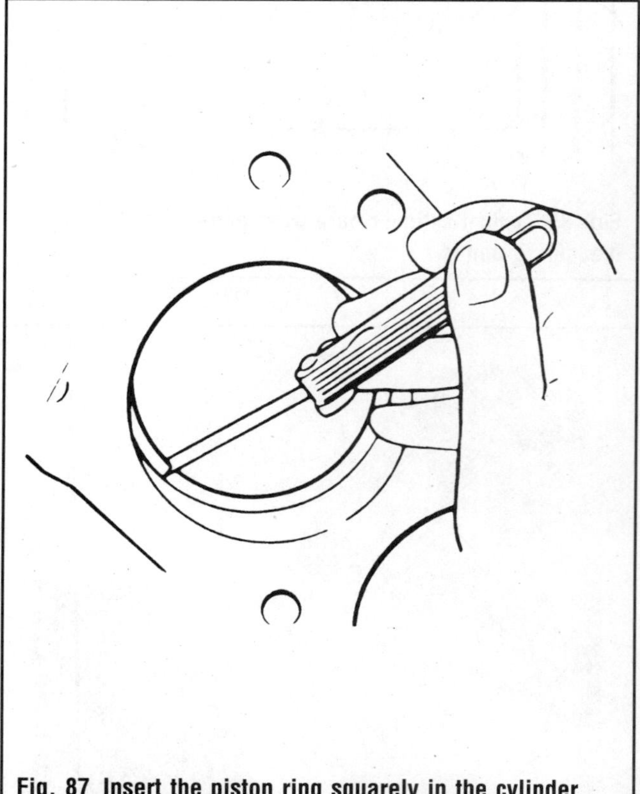

Fig. 87 Insert the piston ring squarely in the cylinder bore and use a feeler gauge to measure ring gap

Side Clearance

➧ See Figure 88

Each ring must be checked for side clearance in its respective piston groove by inserting a feeler gauge between the ring and its upper land. The piston grooves must be cleaned before checking the ring for side clearance specifications. To check oil ring side clearance, the oil rings must be installed on the piston.

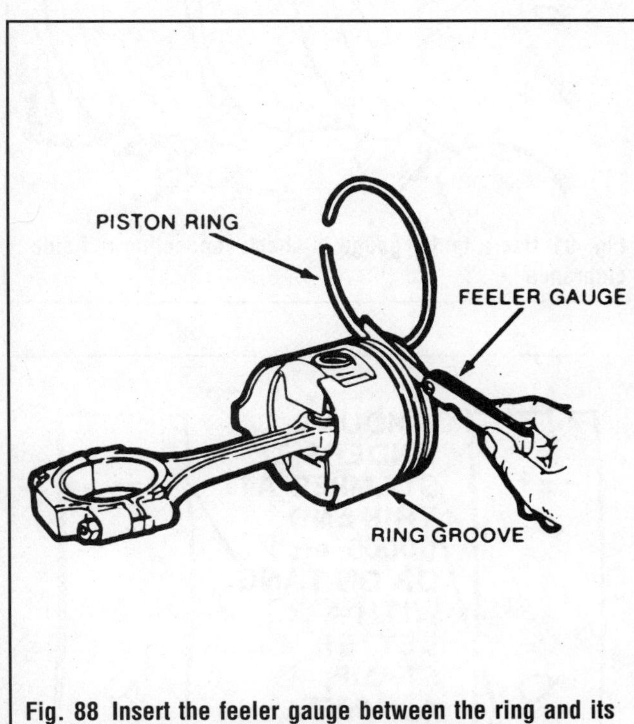

Fig. 88 Insert the feeler gauge between the ring and its upper land to measure piston ring side clearance

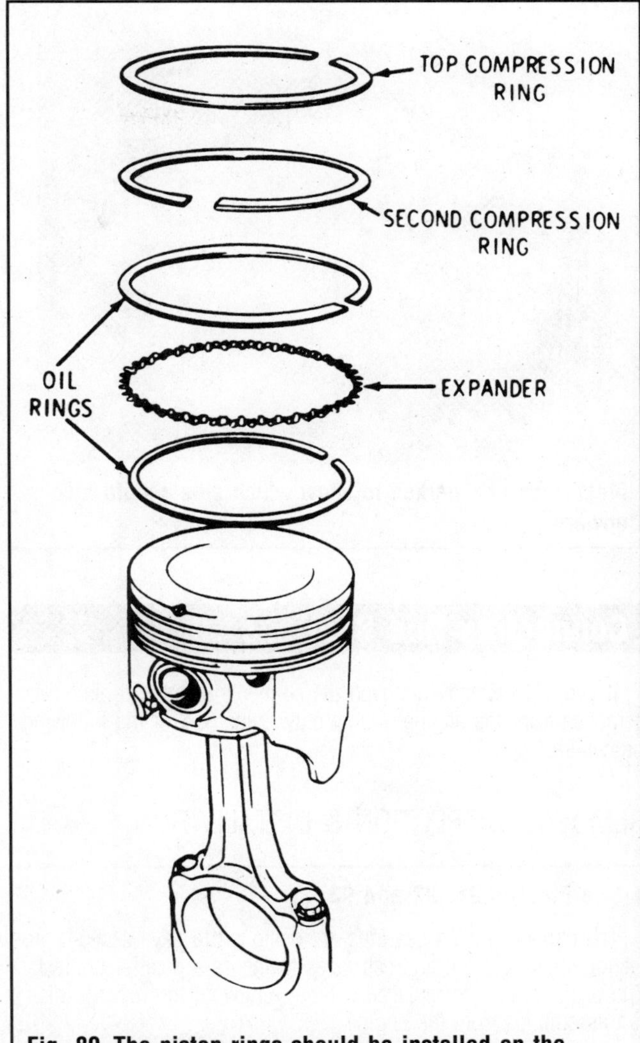

Fig. 89 The piston rings should be installed on the piston as illustrated

RING INSTALLATION

➧ See Figures 89 and 90

For service ring specifications and detailed installation productions, refer to the instructions furnished with the parts package. If oversized pistons are being used, make sure to select the proper oversize piston rings to fit the oversized pistons.

1. Using your fingers, install the oil expander.

➡Use care when installing the piston rings so not to scratch the piston skirt.

2. Install the lower oil control ring and position the gaps as shown in the Piston Ring Gap Location illustration in this section. Install the upper oil control ring.

➡Use a piston ring expander to install the compression rings. Avoid expanding the rings more than necessary, which may cause ring damage.

3. Using a piston ring installer (expander), install the second compression ring with manufacturers mark facing UP. Install the top compression ring with manufacturers mark facing UP. Position the gaps as shown in the ring gap illustration.

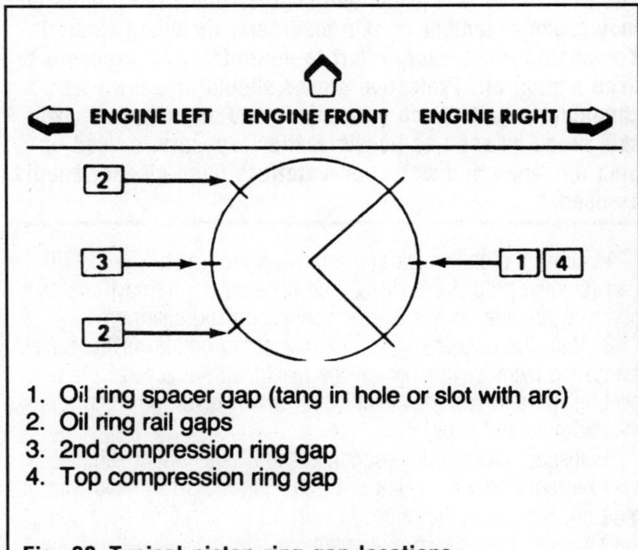

Fig. 90 Typical piston ring gap locations

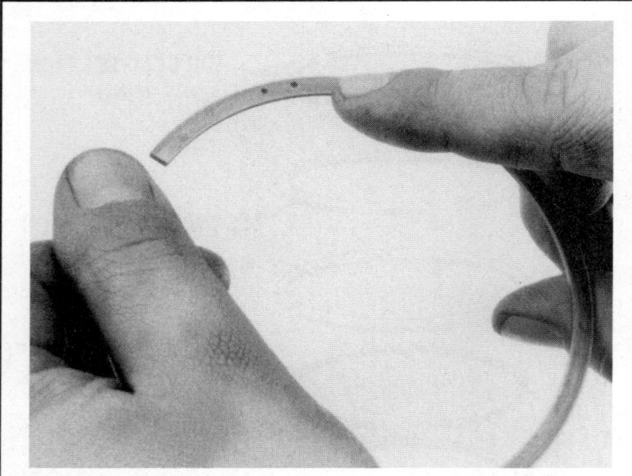

Most rings are marked to show which side should face upward

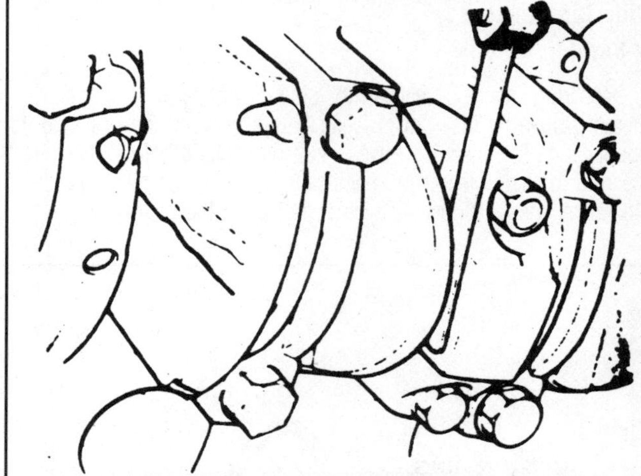

Fig. 91 Use a feeler gauge to check connecting rod side clearance

Connecting Rod Bearings

If you have already removed the connecting rod and piston assemblies from the engine, follow only Steps 3–7 of the following procedure.

REMOVAL, INSPECTION & INSTALLATION

See Figures 91, 92 and 93

The connecting rod bearings are designed to have a slight projection above the rod and cap faces to insure a positive contact. The bearings can be replaced without removing the rod and piston assemblies from the engine.

CAUTION

The EPA warns that prolonged contact with used engine oil may cause a number of skin disorders, including cancer! You should make every effort to minimize your exposure to used engine oil. Protective gloves should be worn when changing the oil. Wash your hands and any other exposed skin areas as soon as possible after exposure to used engine oil. Soap and water, or waterless hand cleaner should be used.

1. Drain the engine oil and remove the oil pan. See the Oil Pan removal procedures. It may be necessary to remove the oil pump to provide access to rear connecting rod bearings.
2. With the connecting rod journal at the bottom of the travel, stamp the cylinder number on the machined surfaces of the connecting rod and cap for identification when installing, then remove the rod nuts and caps.
3. Inspect journals for roughness and wear. Slight roughness may be removed with a fine grit polishing cloth saturated with engine oil. Burrs may be removed with a fine oil stone by moving the stone on the journal circumference. Do not move the stone back and forth across the journal. If the journals are scored or ridged, the crankshaft must be reconditioned or replaced.

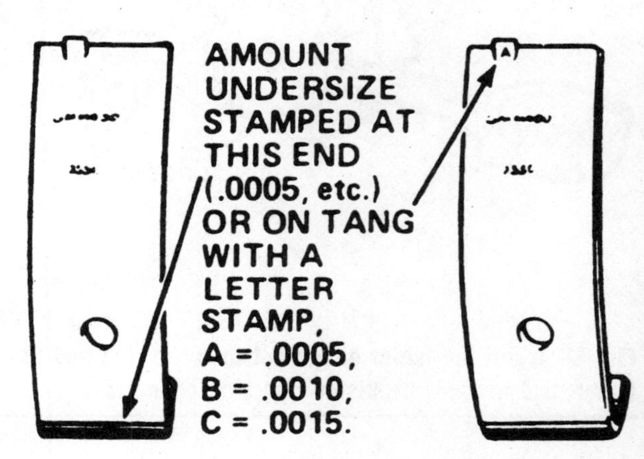

Fig. 92 Check the bearing insert size markings to ensure you are installing the proper size replacement bearings

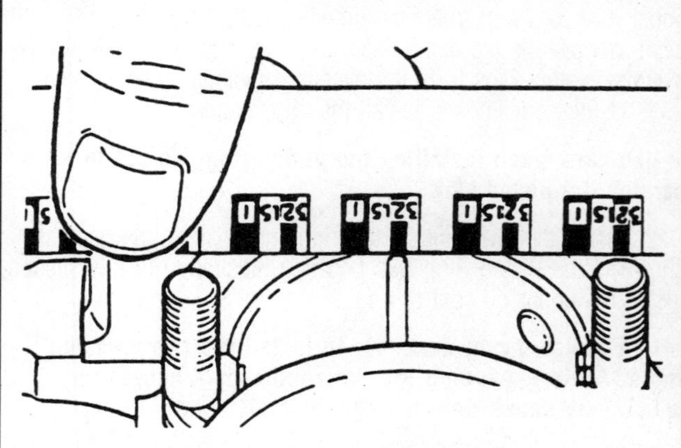

Fig. 93 Compare the reading on the plastigage® package scale to the crankshaft specifications chart to check for proper bearing clearance

4. The connecting rod journals should be checked for out-of-round and correct size with a micrometer.

➡Crankshaft rod journals will normally be standard size. If any undersized bearings are used, all will be 0.25mm undersize and 0.25mm will be stamped on the number 4 counterweight.

If Plastigage® material is to be used:

5. Clean oil from the journal bearing cap, connecting rod and outer and inner surfaces of the bearing inserts. Position the insert so that the tang is properly aligned with the notch in the rod and cap.

6. Place a piece of Plastigage® material in the center of lower bearing shell as shown in the illustration.

7. Install the bearing cap onto the connecting rod and torque to specifications. Remove the bearing cap and determine the bearing clearances by comparing the width of the flattened plastic gauging material at its widest point with the graduation on the plastigage® package. The number within the graduation on the envelope indicates the clearance in thousandths of an inch or millimeters. If this clearance is excessive, replace the bearing and recheck the clearance with the plastigage® material. Lubricate the bearing with Assembly Lube or engine oil before installation. Repeat Steps 2–7 on the remaining connecting rod bearings.

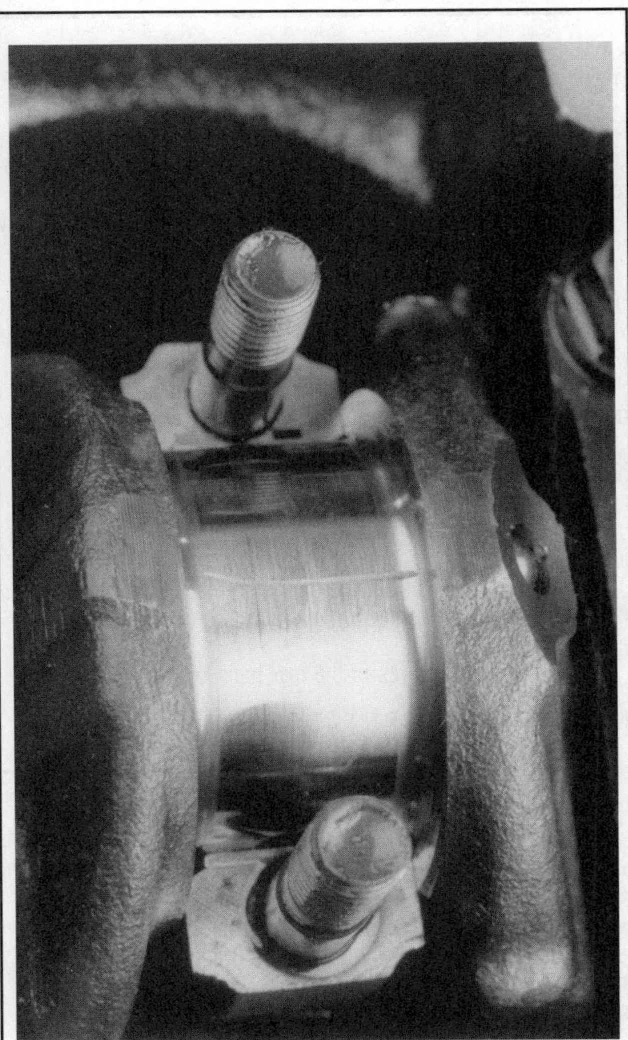
Apply a strip of gauging material to the bearing journal, then install and torque the cap

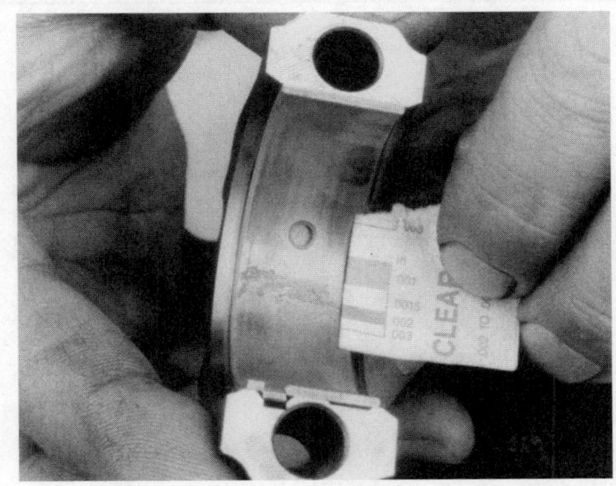
After the cap is removed again, use the scale supplied with the gauge material to check clearances

➡All rods must be connected to their journals when rotating the crankshaft, to prevent engine damage.

Piston and Connecting Rod Assembly

INSTALLATION

1. Make sure all parts are clean. Install some lengths of rubber tubing over the connecting rod bolts to prevent damage to the crankshaft journals.

✲✲ CAUTION

The EPA warns that prolonged contact with used engine oil may cause a number of skin disorders, including cancer! You should make every effort to minimize your exposure to used engine oil. Protective gloves should be worn when changing the oil. Wash your hands and any other exposed skin areas as soon as possible after exposure to used engine oil. Soap and water, or waterless hand cleaner should be used.

2. Apply engine oil to the pistons, rings and cylinder walls, then install a piston ring compressing tool on the piston.

3. Install the assembly in its respective cylinder bore with the notch in the top of the piston facing towards the FRONT of the engine.

4. Lubricate the crankshaft journal with Assembly Lube and install the connecting rod bearing and cap, with the bearing index tang in rod and cap on same side.

➡When more than one rod and piston assembly is being installed, the connecting rod cap attaching nuts should be tightened only enough to keep each rod in position until all have been installed. This will aid installation of the remaining piston assemblies.

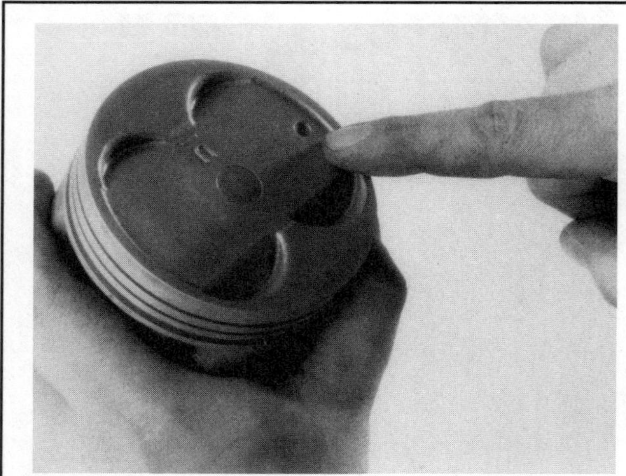

Most pistons are marked to indicate positioning in the engine (usually a mark means the side facing front)

Installing the piston into the block using a ring compressor and the handle of a hammer

The notch on the the side of the bearing cap matches the groove on the bearing insert

5. Torque the rod cap nuts to the specifications in the Torque Specifications chart in the beginning of this section.
6. Install all other parts in reverse order of removal.
7. Install the engine in the car. Refer to the Engine removal and installation procedures in this section.

Crankshaft

REMOVAL

CAUTION

The EPA warns that prolonged contact with used engine oil may cause a number of skin disorders, including cancer! You should make every effort to minimize your exposure to used engine oil. Protective gloves should be worn when changing the oil. Wash your hands and any other exposed skin areas as soon as possible after exposure to used engine oil. Soap and water, or waterless hand cleaner should be used.

1. Remove the engine assembly as previously outlined in the Engine removal procedures.
2. Remove the engine timing chain or gear front cover.
3. Remove the timing chain and sprockets (6 cylinder).
4. Remove the oil pan as outlined in the Oil Pan removal procedures.
5. Remove the oil pump, (remove the force balancer assembly on the 1987–88 2.5L L4 engine).
6. Stamp the cylinder number on the machined surfaces of the bolt boses of the connecting rods and caps for identification when installing. If the pistons are to be removed from the connecting rod, mark the cylinder number on each piston with an indelible marker, silver pencil or quick drying paint for proper cylinder identification and cap to rod location.
7. Remove the connecting rod caps and store them so that they can be installed in their original positions.
8. Mark and remove all the main bearing caps.
9. Note the position of the keyway in the crankshaft so it can be installed in the same position.
10. With an assistant, lift the crankshaft out of the block. The rods will pivot to the center of the engine when the crankshaft is removed.
11. Remove both halves of the rear main oil seal.

INSPECTION & INSTALLATION

See figure 94

1. Measure the crankshaft journals with a micrometer to determine the correct size rod and main bearings to be used. Whenever a new or reconditioned crankshaft is installed, new connecting rod bearings and main bearings must be installed. The bearing undersize are usually 0.010, 0.020 and 0.030 inch. Do not go any further undersize than 0.030 inch. See Main Bearings and Rod Bearings in the beginning of this section.
2. Clean all oil passages in the block (and crankshaft if it is being reused).

➡A new rear main seal should be installed anytime the crankshaft is removed or replaced.

A dial gauge may be used to check crankshaft end-play

Turn the crankshaft slowly by hand while checking the gauge

Carefully pry the shaft back and forth while reading the dial gauge for play

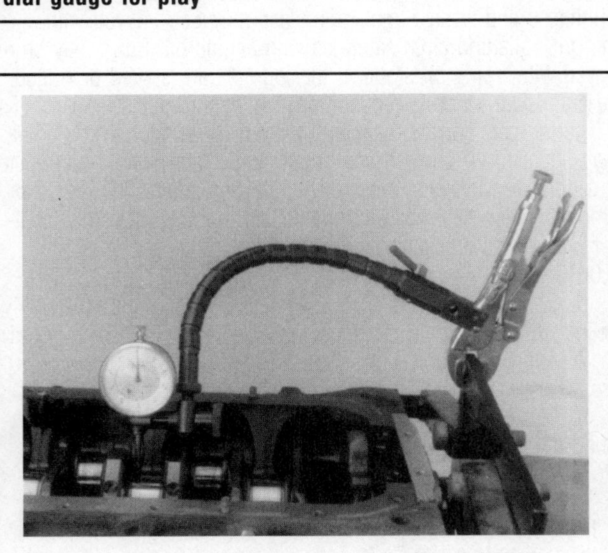

A dial gauge may also be used to check crankshaft run-out

Mounting a dial gauge to read crankshaft run-out

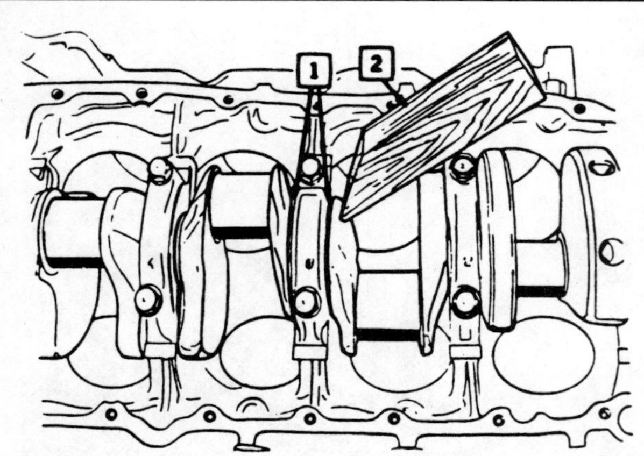

Fig. 94 Align the crankshaft thrust flanges of the main bearing (1) by bumping the crankshaft in each direction using a block of wood (2)

3. Install sufficient oil pan bolts in the block to align with the connecting rod bolts. Use rubber bands between the bolts to position the connecting rods as required. Connecting rod position can be adjusted by increasing the tension on the rubber bands with additional turns around the pan bolts or thread protectors. Install if not already done, pieces of rubber hose on the connecting rod bolts to protect the crankshaft journals during installation.

4. Position the upper half of main bearings in the block and lubricate them with Assembly Lube.

5. Position crankshaft keyway in the same position as removed, with an assistant, lower the crankshaft into the block. The connecting rods will follow the crank pins into the correct position as the crankshaft is lowered.

6. Lubricate the thrust flanges with Assembly Lube 10501609 or equivalent. Install rod caps with the lower half of the bearings lubricated with Assembly Lube. Lubricate the cap bolts with Assembly Lube and install, but do not tighten.

7. With a block of wood, bump the crankshaft in each direction to align the thrust flanges of the main bearing. After bumping the shaft in each direction, wedge the shaft to the front and hold it while torquing the thrust bearing cap bolts.

➡In order to prevent the possibility of cylinder block and/or main bearing cap damage, the main bearing caps are to be tapped into their cylinder block cavity using a wood or rubber mallet before the bolts are installed. Do not use attaching bolts to pull the main bearing caps into their seats. Failure to observe this information may damage the cylinder block or a bearing cap.

8. Torque all main bearing caps to specification in the Torque Specifications chart in this section.

9. Remove the connecting rod bolt thread protectors and lubricate the connecting rod bearings with Assembly Lube.

10. Install the connecting rod bearing caps in their original position. Torque the nuts to specifications in the Torque Specifications chart in this section.

11. Install the oil pump, oil pan, timing cover, accessories and install the engine assembly into the vehicle as outlined in the Engine installation procedures.

Main Bearings

CHECKING BEARING CLEARANCE

1. Remove the bearing cap and wipe the oil from the crankshaft journal and the outer and inner surfaces of the bearing shell.

2. Place a piece of plastic gauging material in the center of the bearing.

3. Use a floor jack or other means to hold the crankshaft against the upper bearing shell. This is necessary to obtain accurate clearance readings when using plastic gauging material.

4. Install the bearing cap and bearing. Place engine oil on the cap bolts and install. Torque the bolts to specification.

5. Remove the bearing cap and determine the bearing clearance by comparing the width of the flattened Plastigage® material at its widest point with the graduations on the Plastigage® container. The number within the graduation on the envelope indicates the clearance in millimeters or thousandths of an inch. If the clearance is greater than allowed, *replace both bearing shells as a set.* Recheck the clearance after replacing the shells. (Refer to Main Bearing Replacement).

REPLACEMENT

Main bearing clearances must be corrected by the use of selective upper and lower shells. *Under no circumstances* should the use of shims behind the shells to compensate for wear be attempted. To install the main bearing shells, proceed as follows:

1.Remove the oil pan as outlined below. On some models, the oil pump may also have to be removed.

2. Loosen all main bearing caps.

3. Remove the bearing caps and remove the lower shell.

4. Insert a flattened cotter pin or roll pin in the oil passage hole in the crankshaft, then rotate the crankshaft in the direction opposite to cranking rotation. The pin will contact the upper shell and roll it out.

5. The main bearing journals should be checked for roughness and wear. Slight roughness may be removed with a fine grit polishing cloth saturated with engine oil. Burrs may be removed with a fine oil stone. If the journals are scored or ridged, the crankshaft must be reconditioned or replaced.

The journals can be measured for out-of-round with the crankshaft installed by using a crankshaft caliper and inside micrometer or a main bearing micrometer. The upper bearing shell must be removed when measuring the crankshaft journals. Maximum out-of-round of the crankshaft journals must not exceed 0.037mm (0.0015 inch).

6. Clean the crankshaft journals and bearing caps thoroughly for installing new main bearings.

7. Apply Assembly Lube, No. 1050169 or equivalent, to the thrust flanges of bearing shells.

8. Place a new upper shell on the crankshaft journal with locating tang in the correct position and rotate the shaft to turn it into place using a cotter pin or roll pin as during removal.

9. Place a new bearing shell in the bearing cap.

10. Install a new oil seal in the rear main bearing cap and block.

11. Lubricate the main bearings with engine oil. Lubricate the thrust surface with Assembly Lube 1050169 or equivalent.

12. Lubricate the main bearing cap bolts with engine oil.

➡In order to prevent the possibility of cylinder block and/or main bearing cap damage, the main bearing caps are to be tapped into their cylinder block cavity using a wood or rubber mallet before the attaching bolts are installed. Do not use attaching bolts to pull the main bearing caps into their seats. Failure to observe this information may damage the cylinder block or a bearing cap.

13. Torque the main bearing cap bolts to the specification in the Torque Specifications chart in the beginning of this section.

Oil Pan

REMOVAL & INSTALLATION

4-2.5L Engine

➧ See Figures 95, 96 and 97

1. On some models it may be necessary to remove the engine cradle from the car as follows:

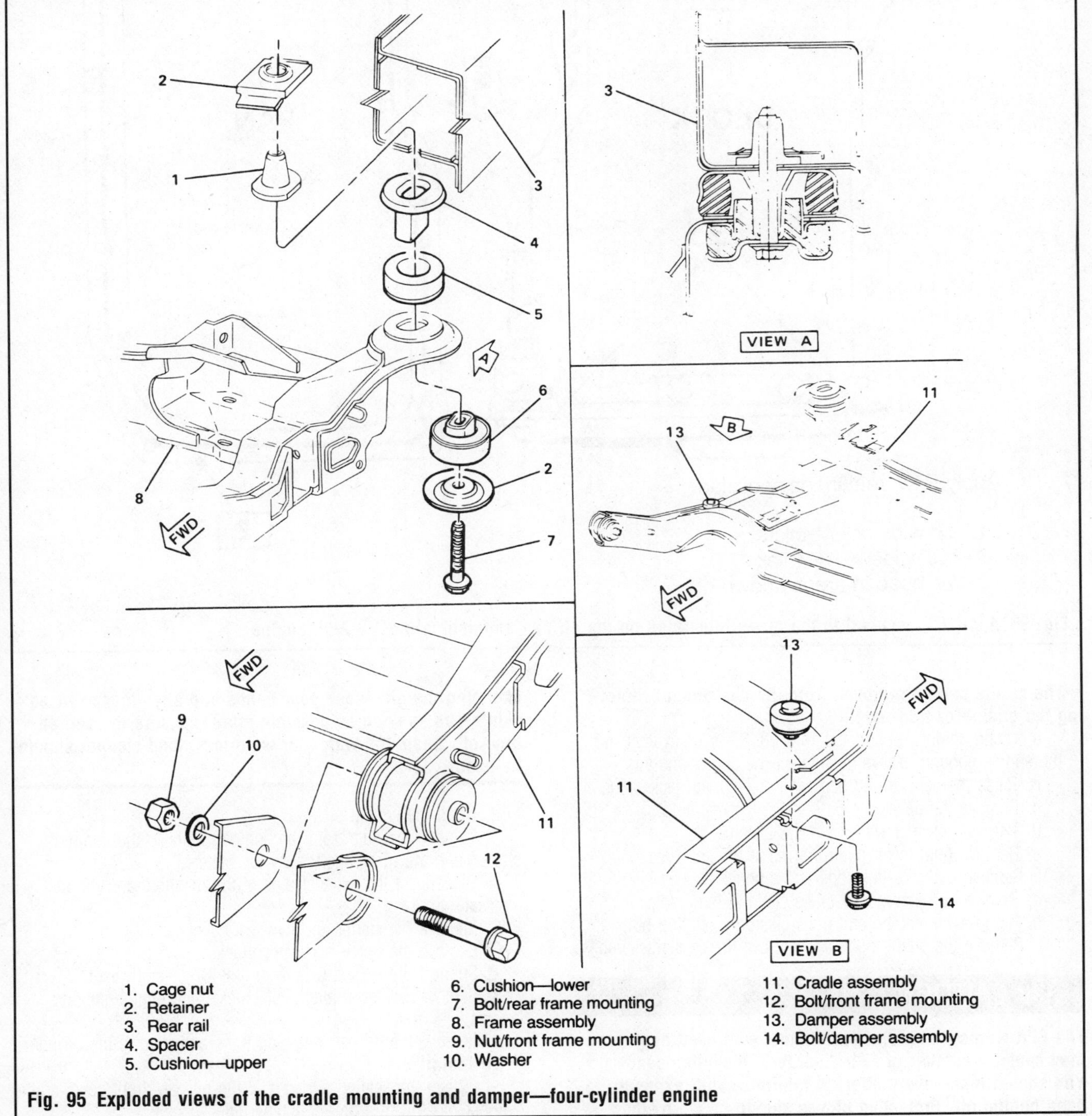

Fig. 95 Exploded views of the cradle mounting and damper—four-cylinder engine

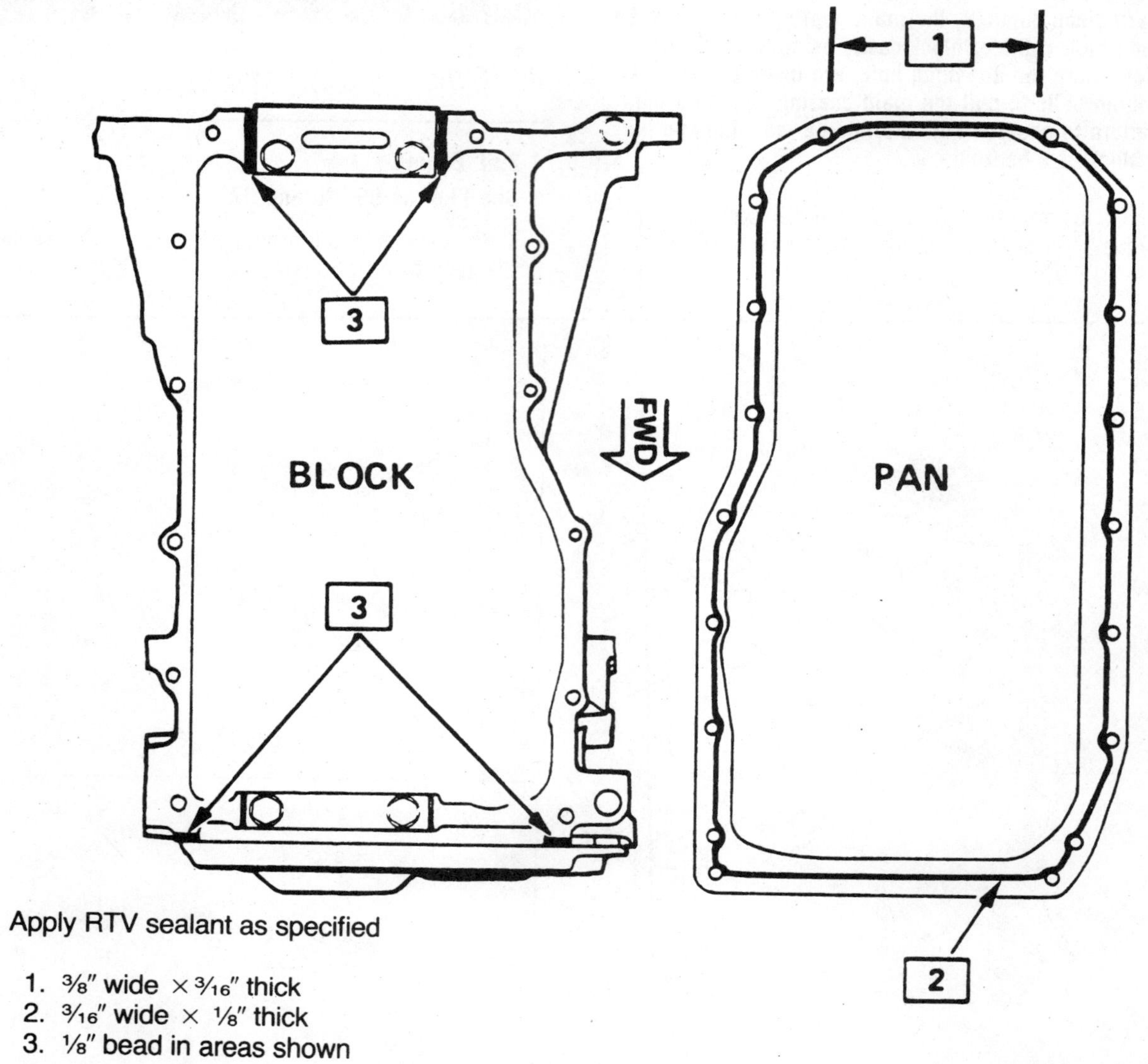

Fig. 96 Apply RTV sealant to the areas illustrated on the oil pan and engine block—2.5L engine

➡The cradle can be removed from the car without removing the engine or transaxle.

a. Using engine support fixture J-28467 or equivalent, raise the engine enough to take tension off the engine mounts.
b. Raise the vehicle and support it safely with jackstands.
c. Remove the exhaust pipe bolts at the manifold.
d. Remove the rear wheel and tire assemblies.
e. Remove both lower control arms at the knuckles.
f. Remove both toe-link rods at the knuckle.
g. Remove the emergency brake cable at the cradle.
h. Remove the engine and transmission mounting bolts.
i. Remove the cradle bolts and remove the cradle assembly.

✲✲ CAUTION

The EPA warns that prolonged contact with used engine oil may cause a number of skin disorders, including cancer! You should make every effort to minimize your exposure to used engine oil. Protective gloves should be worn when changing the oil. Wash your hands and any other exposed skin areas as soon as possible after exposure to used engine oil. Soap and water, or waterless hand cleaner should be used.

2. Drain the engine oil.
3. Remove the nuts from the engine mount to the support bracket and the trim panel below the battery.
4. Disconnect the exhaust pipe at the manifold and the rear transaxle mount.
5. Remove the starter and flywheel cover.
6. Remove the upper alternator bracket.
7. Support the engine with Tool J28467 or equivalent.
8. Remove the lower alternator bracket and engine support bracket.
9. Remove the oil pan retaining bolts and remove the oil pan.

To install:

1. Clean the sealing surfaces of the oil pan, front cover and cylinder block with a gasket scraper and solvent.

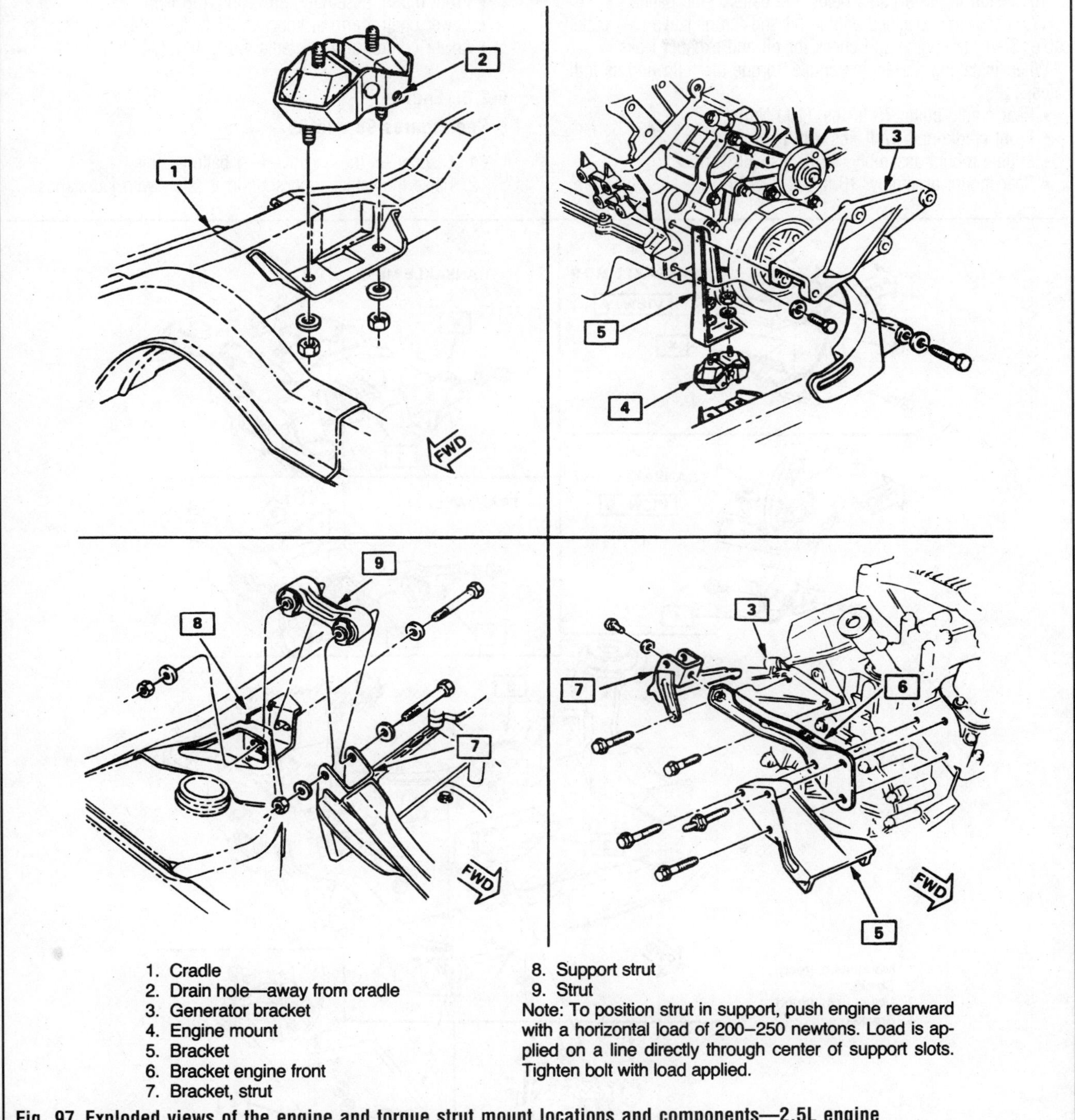

1. Cradle
2. Drain hole—away from cradle
3. Generator bracket
4. Engine mount
5. Bracket
6. Bracket engine front
7. Bracket, strut
8. Support strut
9. Strut

Note: To position strut in support, push engine rearward with a horizontal load of 200–250 newtons. Load is applied on a line directly through center of support slots. Tighten bolt with load applied.

Fig. 97 Exploded views of the engine and torque strut mount locations and components—2.5L engine

2. Apply RTV sealer to the cylinder block and oil pan as shown in the oil pan illustration.
3. Install the oil pan assembly and retaining bolts (install the oil filter on 1987–88 engines).
4. Install the engine front support bracket and mount.
5. Lower the vehicle and lower the engine into the mounts.
6. Remove the engine support tool No. J28467.
7. Install the engine torque strut.
8. Raise the vehicle and install the lower alternator bracket bolt.
9. Install the air conditioning compressor bolts, if so equipped.
10. Install the heat shield at the air conditioning compressor, if so equipped.
11. Install the front engine mount to cradle nuts.
12. Install the splash shield and starter motor.
13. Install the starter and flywheel cover.
14. Install the wheel assemblies and lower the vehicle.
15. Install the alternator and drive belts. Tighten the belt to specifications in Section 1.

16. Install the trim panel below the battery side panel.
17. Install the specified engine oil and the negative (−) battery cable. Start the engine and check for oil and exhaust leaks.

When installing the engine cradle, torque the following as indicated:

- Rear cradle bolts: 76 ft. lbs. (100 Nm).
- Front cradle nut: 67 ft. lbs. (89 Nm).
- Engine mount assembly: 42 ft. lbs. (55 Nm).
- Rear mount assembly: 18 ft. lbs. (23 Nm).
- Front mount assembly: 36 ft. lbs. (48 Nm).
- Lower control arm at knuckle: 33 ft. lbs. (44 Nm).
- Lower control arm at cradle: 69 ft. lbs. (94 Nm).

6-2.8L Engine

See Figures 98 and 99

1. Disconnect the negative (−) battery cable.
2. Raise the vehicle and support it safely with jackstands.

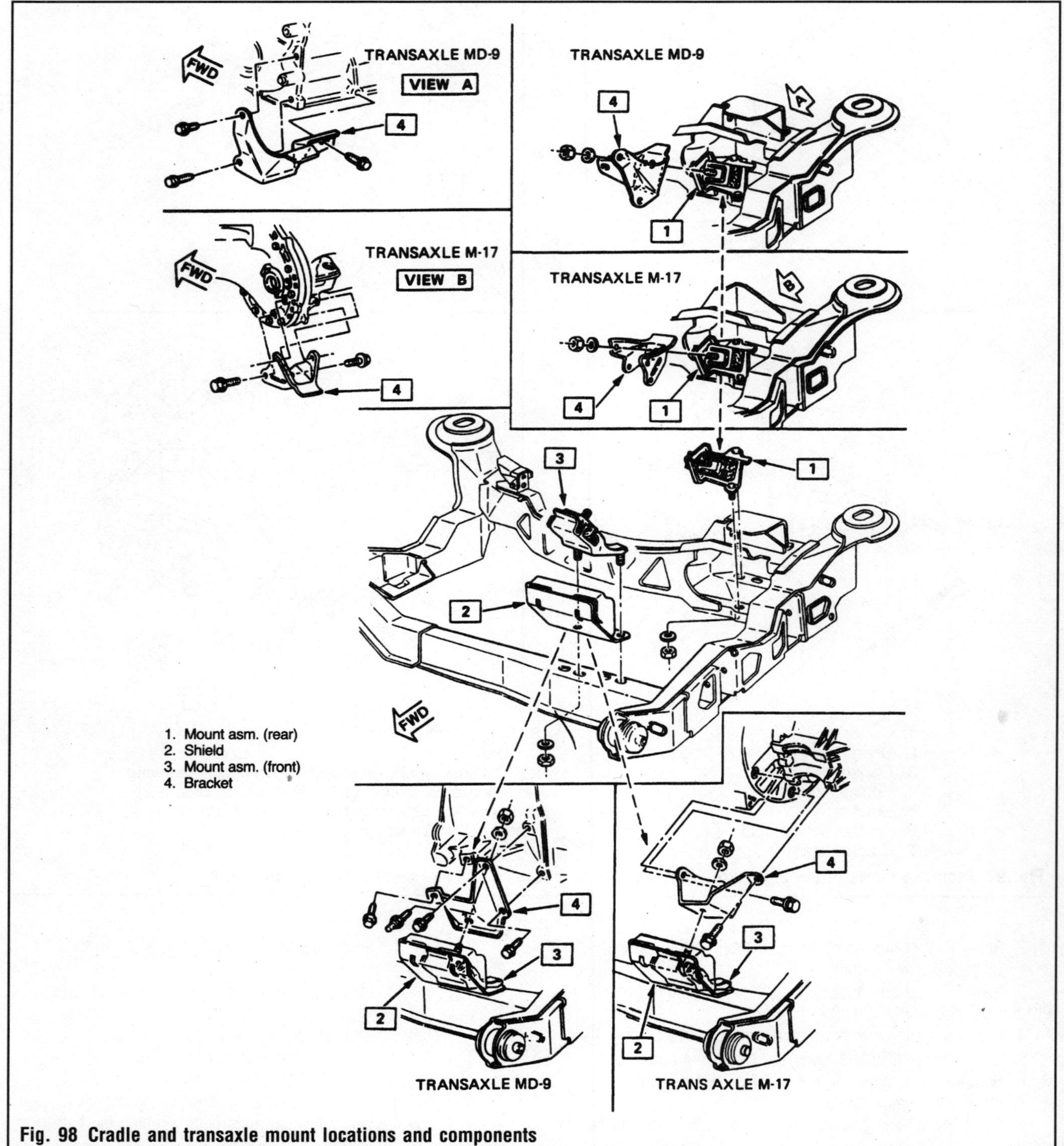

Fig. 98 Cradle and transaxle mount locations and components

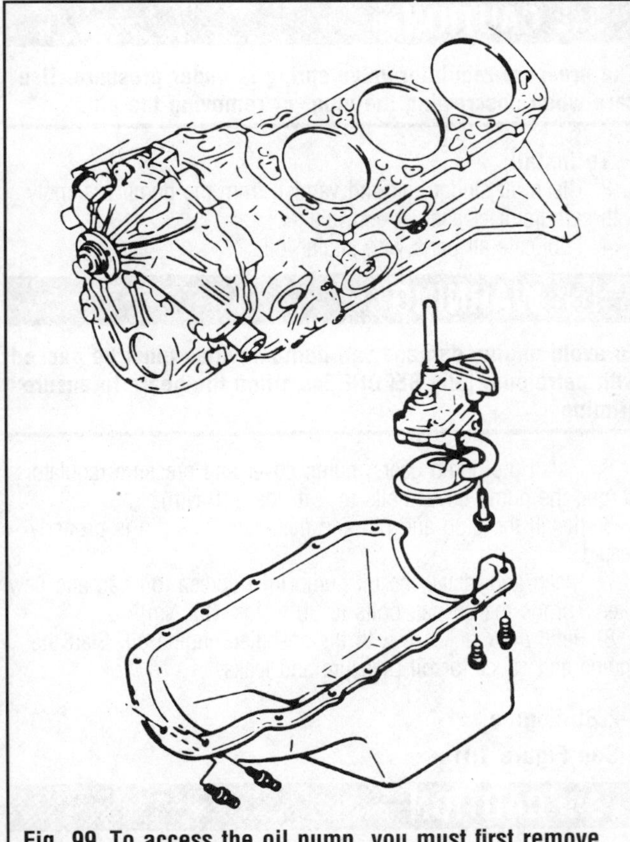

Fig. 99 To access the oil pump, you must first remove the oil pan—V6 engine

CAUTION

The EPA warns that prolonged contact with used engine oil may cause a number of skin disorders, including cancer! You should make every effort to minimize your exposure to used engine oil. Protective gloves should be worn when changing the oil. Wash your hands and any other exposed skin areas as soon as possible after exposure to used engine oil. Soap and water, or waterless hand cleaner should be used.

3. Drain the oil from the crankcase.
4. Remove the flywheel shield or clutch housing cover.
5. Remove the starter.
6. Remove the oil pan bolts and oil pan.

To install:

7. Clean all mating surfaces.
8. Place a 3mm bead of RTV sealant on the oil pan sealing flange.
9. Install the oil pan and torque the 1 inch bolts to 6–9 ft. lbs. (8–12 Nm) and the 1.5 inch bolts to 14–22 ft. lbs. (19–29 Nm).
10. Install the starter assembly.
11. Install the flywheel and clutch housing cover.
12. Lower the vehicle and refill the crankcase with the specified engine oil.
13. Install the negative (−) battery cable. Start the engine and check for oil leaks.

Drain the engine oil from the pan . . .

. . . then remove the oil pan retaining bolts

Oil Pump

REMOVAL & INSTALLATION

2.5L L4 Engine

1984–86 MODELS

➧ See Figure 100

CAUTION

The EPA warns that prolonged contact with used engine oil may cause a number of skin disorders, including cancer! You should make every effort to minimize your exposure to used engine oil. Protective gloves should be worn when changing the oil. Wash your hands and any other exposed skin areas as soon as possible after exposure to used engine oil. Soap and water, or waterless hand cleaner should be used.

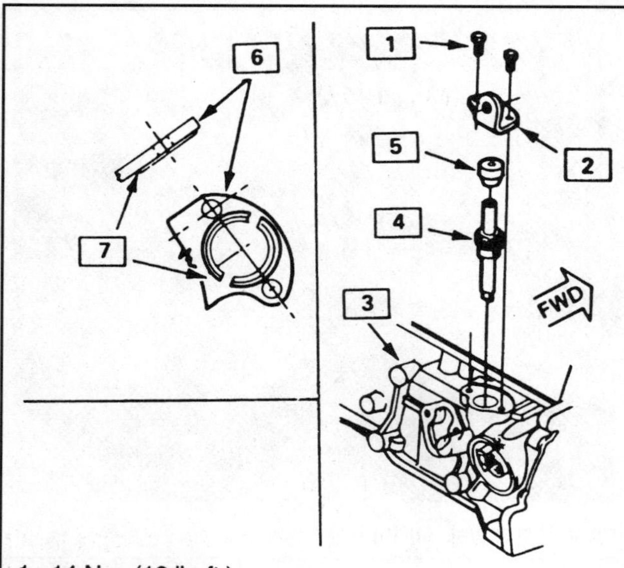

1. 14 N·m (10 lb. ft.)
2. Plate assembly
3. Cylinder block
4. Shaft and gear assembly
5. Bearing
6. Plate
7. Apply a continuous 1/16" diam. bead of RTV as shown

Fig. 100 Oil pump and driveshaft components—four-cylinder engine

1. Remove the oil pan as described in the Oil Pan removal procedures.
2. Remove the two flange mounting bolts and the nut from the main bearing cap bolt.
3. Remove the pump and screen as an assembly.

To install:

4. Align the pump shaft with the driveshaft tang. Torque the pump retaining bolts 20 ft. lbs. (27 Nm). Install the oil pan as previously shown.

1987–88 MODELS

➡1987–88 4-cylinder engines incorporate a force balance into the oil pump. The force balancer assembly does NOT have to be removed to service the oil pump or pressure regulator assemblies.

CAUTION

The EPA warns that prolonged contact with used engine oil may cause a number of skin disorders, including cancer! You should make every effort to minimize your exposure to used engine oil. Protective gloves should be worn when changing the oil. Wash your hands and any other exposed skin areas as soon as possible after exposure to used engine oil. Soap and water, or waterless hand cleaner should be used.

1. Drain the crankcase oil and remove the oil pan and filter as outlined in the Oil Pan removal procedures in this section.
2. Remove the restrictor, oil pump cover, oil pump gears and pressure regulator valve.

CAUTION

The pressure regulator valve spring is under pressure. Use care when unscrewing the plug, or removing the pin.

To install:

3. Clean all sludge, oil and varnish from the pump assembly with carburetor cleaner or equivalent.
4. Lubricate all parts with engine oil.

WARNING

To avoid engine damage, all pump cavities must be packed with petroleum jelly BEFORE installing the gears to ensure priming.

5. Install the pump gears, pump cover and pressure regulator. Torque the pump cover bolts to 7 ft. lbs. (10 Nm).
6. Install the plug and pin and make sure the pin is properly seated.
7. Clean and install the oil pump inlet screen, oil pan and new filter. Torque the oil pan bolts to 20 ft. lbs. (27 Nm).
8. Refill the crankcase with the specified engine oil. Start the engine and check for oil pressure and leaks.

6-2.8L Engine

➧ See Figure 101

CAUTION

The EPA warns that prolonged contact with used engine oil may cause a number of skin disorders, including cancer! You should make every effort to minimize your exposure to used engine oil. Protective gloves should be worn when changing the oil. Wash your hands and any other exposed skin areas as soon as possible after exposure to used engine oil. Soap and water, or waterless hand cleaner should be used.

1. Disconnect the negative (−) battery cable.
2. Drain the crankcase and remove the oil pan as outlined in the Oil Pan removal procedures in this section.

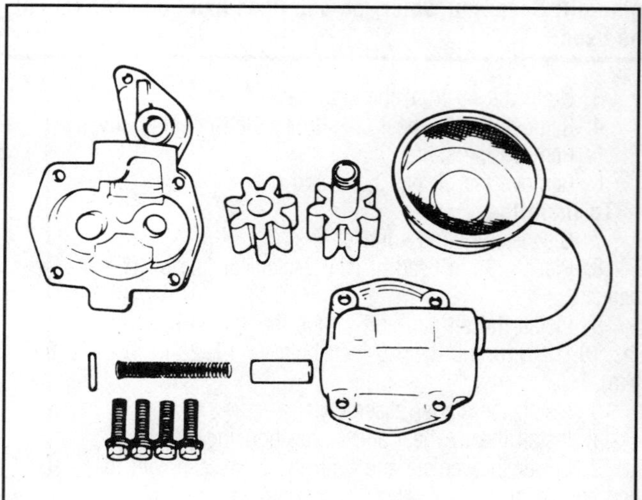

Fig. 101 Oil pump components—V6 engine

3. Remove the flywheel shield or clutch housing cover.
4. Remove the starter motor.
5. Remove the oil pan as outlined in the Oil Pan removal procedures in this section.
6. Remove the pump and driveshaft extension.

To install:

7. Engage the driveshaft extension in the cover end of the distributor drive gear.
8. Install the pump-to-rear bearing cap bolt and torque to 26–35 ft. lbs. (35–47 Nm).
9. Install the oil pan as outlined in the Oil Pan section and refill with engine oil. Start the engine and check for oil leaks.

Force Balancer Assembly

See Figure 102

The 1987–88 2.5L engine uses a force balancer assembly that is driven directly from the crankshaft. Two eccentrically weighted shafts and gears are counter rotated by a concentric gear on the crankshaft at twice the crankshaft speed. The balancer helps dampen engine vibration and includes a sump pick-up screen, a gerotor-type oil pump and an oil filter. The filter is serviced through an opening in the bottom of the oil pan.

REMOVAL & INSTALLATION

See Figures 103 and 104

1. Disconnect the negative (−) battery cable.
2. Drain the engine oil and remove the oil filter assembly.
3. Remove the oil pan assembly as outlined in the Oil Pan removal procedures in this section.
4. Remove the four force balancer attaching bolts and remove the balancer assembly. Refer to the force balancer illustrations in this section.
5. Before installation, perform the following procedures:
   a. Rotate the engine to Top Dead Center (TDC) on the No. 1 and No. 4 cylinders.
   b. Measure from the block to the first cut of the double notch on the reluctor ring as shown in the Force Balancer Adjustments illustration in this section.
   c. The dimension should be 43mm.
   d. Mount the force balancer with the counterweights parallel and pointing away from the crankshaft. Do not move the crankshaft.
6. Install the oil pan assembly as outlined in the Oil Pan installation procedures in this section.
7. Refill the crankcase with the specified engine oil. Start the engine and check for oil leaks.

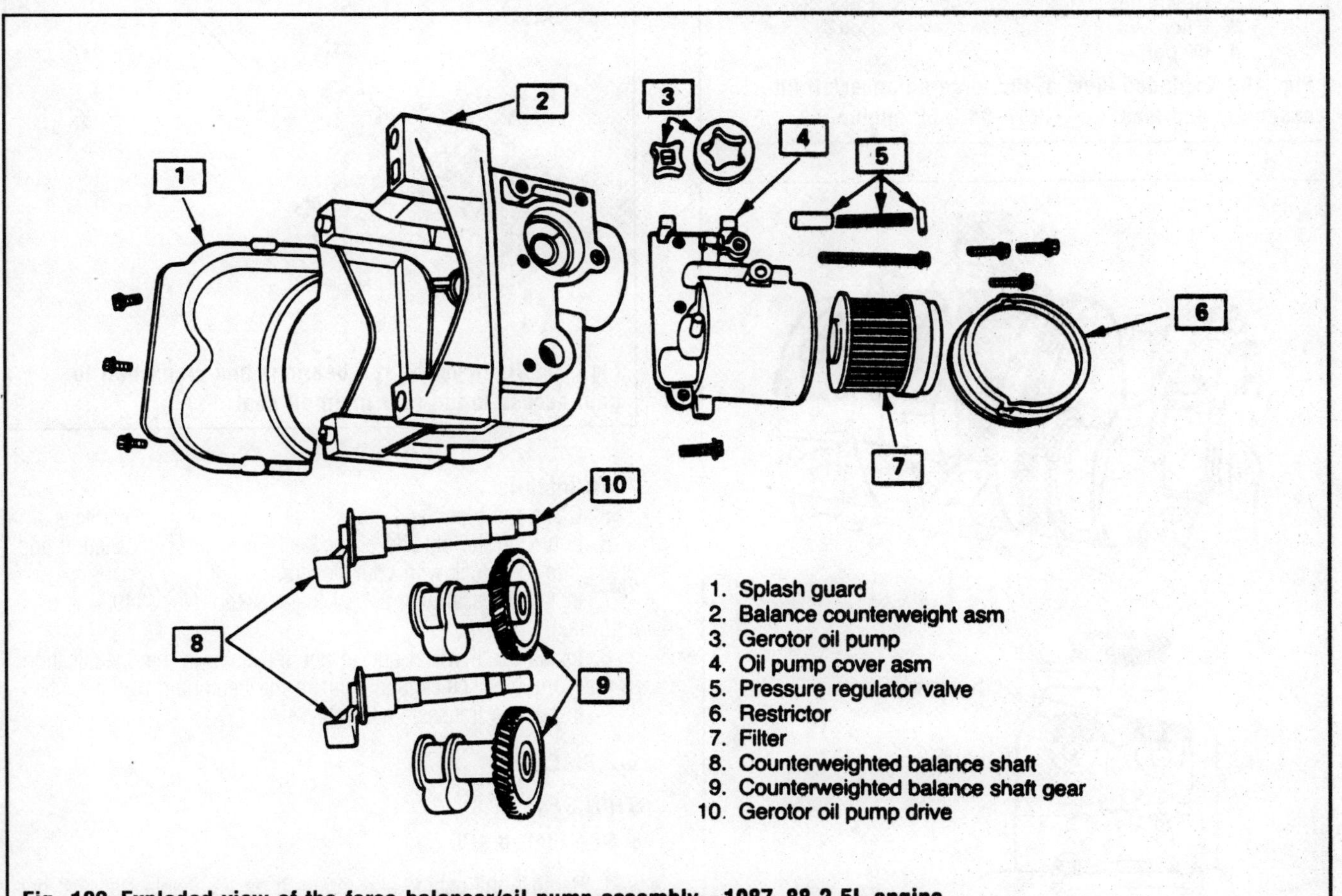

Fig. 102 Exploded view of the force balancer/oil pump assembly—1987–88 2.5L engine

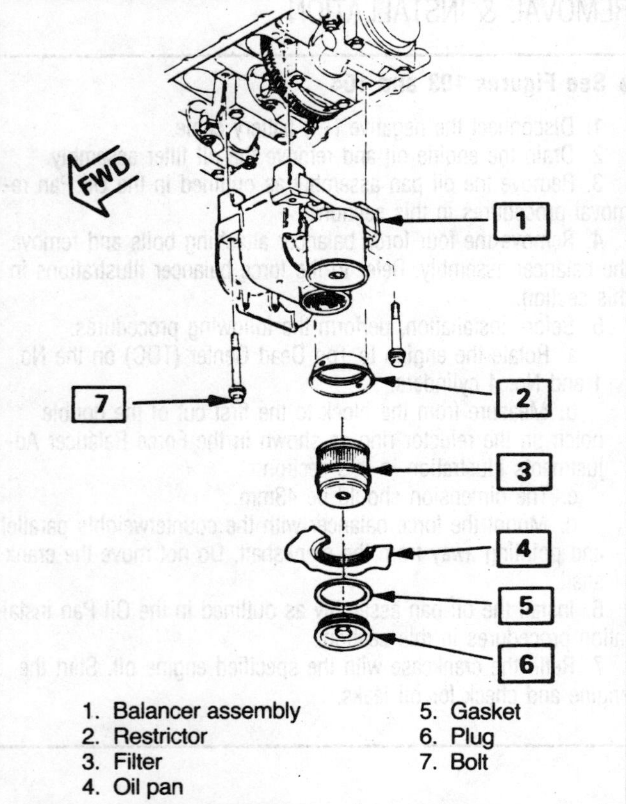

1. Balancer assembly
2. Restrictor
3. Filter
4. Oil pan
5. Gasket
6. Plug
7. Bolt

Fig. 103 Exploded view of the force balancer/oil filter assembly and location—1987–88 2.5L engine

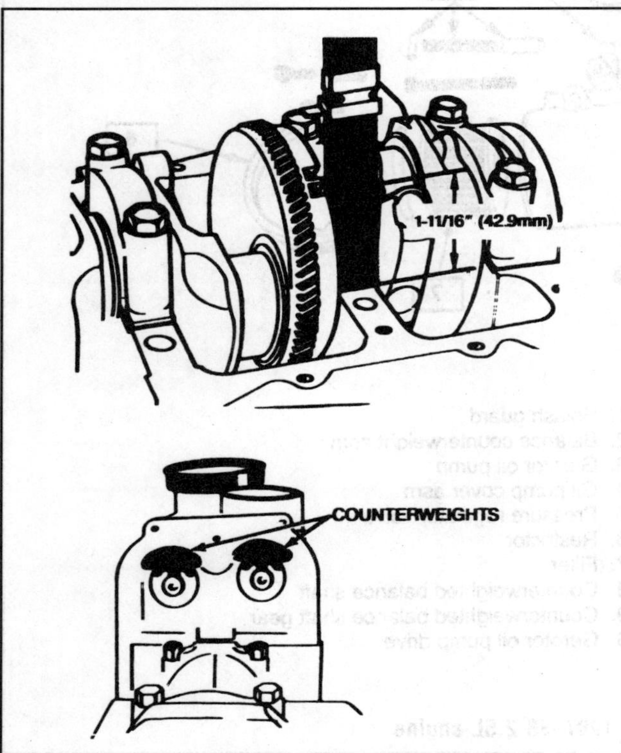

Fig. 104 Force balancer adjustments and counterweight locations—1987–88 2.5L engine

Rear Main Oil Seal

REMOVAL & INSTALLATION

4-2.5L Engine

➧ **See Figure 105**

➡This is a one piece seal and can be replaced without removal of the oil pan or crankshaft.

1. Remove the transaxle assembly as outlined in the Transaxle removal procedures in Section 7.
2. Remove the six flywheel attaching bolts and the flywheel (automatic).
3. If equipped with a (manual) transaxle, remove the pressure plate and disc.
4. Pry out the rear main seal.

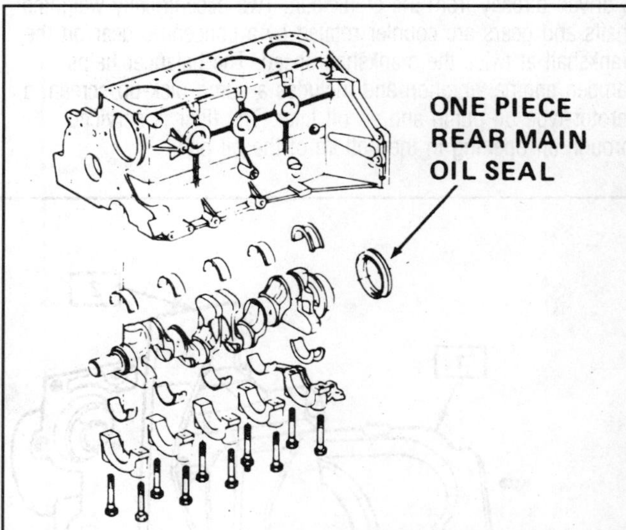

Fig. 105 Remove the rod bearings and crankshaft to gain access to the rear main oil seal

To install:

5. Clean the block and crank-shaft-to-seal mating surfaces.
6. Lubricate the outside of the seal for ease of installation and press into the block with your fingers.
7. Install the seal with a Seal Installer tool No. J34924-A or equivalent.
8. Install the flywheel and torque the bolts to the specification in the Torque Specifications chart in the beginning of the section.
9. Install the transaxle assembly.

6-2.8L Engine

THIN SEAL

➧ **See Figure 106**

1. Remove the engine and mount it on a suitable stand as outlined in the Engine removal procedures in this section.
2. Remove the oil pan and oil pump assembly.
3. Remove the front cover, then lock the chain tensioner with a pin, but do not force.

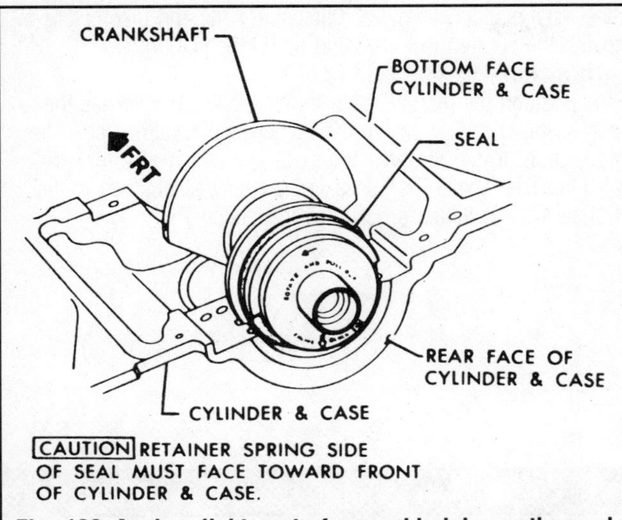

Fig. 106 Apply a light coat of assembly lube on the seal and install the seal on the end of the crankshaft

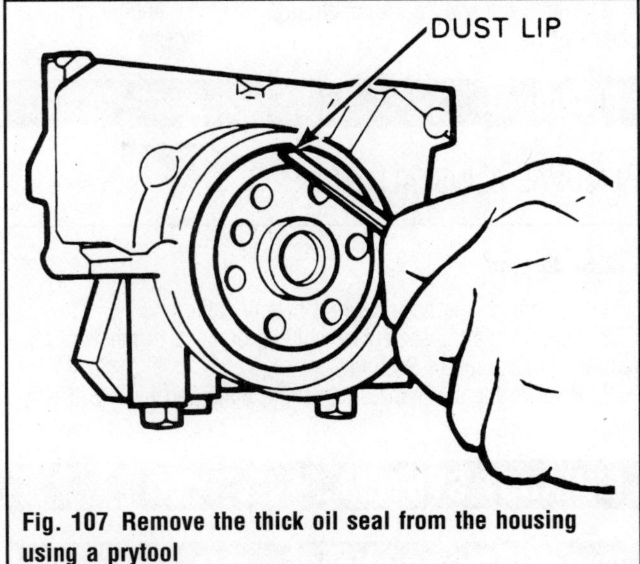

Fig. 107 Remove the thick oil seal from the housing using a prytool

4. Rotate the crankshaft until the timing marks on the cam and crank sprockets align.
5. Remove the camshaft bolt, cam sprocket and timing chain.
6. Rotate the crankshaft to the horizontal position.
7. Remove the rod bearing nuts, caps and bearings.

➡Mark each component so not to mix up bearing caps or bearing.

8. Remove the crankshaft and the old oil seal.

To install:

1. Apply a light coat of Assembly Lube® or equivalent to the outside of the seal.
2. Install the new seal and tool in the rear area of the crankshaft.
3. Install the crankshaft and tool in the engine.
4. Position the seal tool so that the arrow points toward the cylinder block and remove the tool.
5. Put a light coat of oil on the crankshaft journals.
6. Seal the rear main bearing split line surface with G.M. 1052726 or equivalent.
7. Install the connecting rod and crankshaft caps and torque to the specifications in the Torque Specifications chart in the beginning of this section.
8. Install the oil pump assembly as torque the bolts to 30 ft. lbs. (41 Nm).
9. Install the camshaft sprocket and timing chain cover, oil pan and install the engine into the vehicle as outlined in the Engine installation procedures.
10. Refill the engine with engine oil, coolant and transaxle fluid. Start the engine and check for leaks.

THICK SEAL

➧ See Figures 107 and 108

1. Refer to the Transaxle removal and installation procedures in Section 7 and remove the transaxle.

➡If equipped with an manual transaxle, remove the pressure plate and the clutch.

2. Remove the flywheel from the crankshaft.
3. Using a small prybar, pry the rear oil seal from the housing.

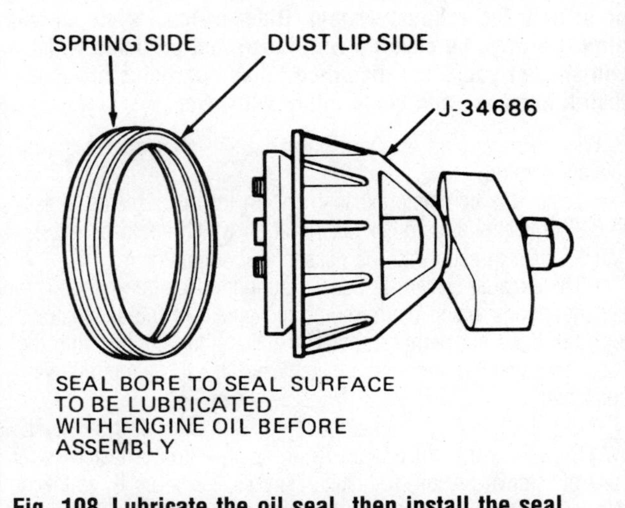

Fig. 108 Lubricate the oil seal, then install the seal using the proper installation tool—V6 engine

➡When prying the oil seal from the housing, be careful not to damage the machined surfaces.

To install:

4. Using the seal installation tool J-34686, lubricate the new oil seal lip and slide it onto the installation (dust lip side against the tool) until it seats against the tool.
5. Align the installation tool's dowel pin with the dowel pin hole in the crankshaft. Torque the mounting screws to 2–5 ft. lbs.
6. Turn the "T" handle and push the seal into the housing, until it bottoms out against the housing.
7. Loosen the "T" handle until it comes to a stop. Remove the mounting screws of the installation tool.
8. Check the seal and make sure that it is squarely seated in the bore.
9. Install the flywheel and torque to specifications in the Torque Specifications in this section.
10. Install the transaxle as outlined in the Transaxle installation procedures in Section 7.

11. Refill the engine with engine oil. Start the engine and check for oil leaks.

Flywheel

REMOVAL & INSTALLATION

4-2.5L Engine

1. Disconnect the negative (−) battery cable.
2. Remove the transaxle assembly as outlined in the Transaxle removal procedures in Section 7.
3. Remove the six flywheel attaching bolts and remove the flywheel (automatic). Remove the pressure plate and disc before removing the six flywheel attaching bolts (manual).

To install:

4. Position the flywheel onto the crankshaft and torque the bolts to the specifications in the Torque Specifications chart in this section. Install the pressure plate and clutch disc for a (manual) transaxle. Install the transaxle assembly as outlined in the "Transaxle" installation procedures in Section 7.

EXHAUST SYSTEM

General Information

➡**Safety glasses should be worn at all times when working on or near the exhaust system. Older exhaust systems will almost always be covered with loose rust particles which will shower you when disturbed. These particles are more than a nuisance and could injure your eye.**

Whenever working on the exhaust system always keep the following in mind:

- Check the complete exhaust system for open seams, holes loose connections, or other deterioration which could permit exhaust fumes to seep into the passenger compartment.
- The exhaust system is usually supported by free-hanging rubber mountings which permit some movement of the exhaust system, but does not permit transfer of noise and vibration into the passenger compartment. Do not replace the rubber mounts with solid ones.
- Before removing any component of the exhaust system, ALWAYS squirt a liquid rust dissolving agent onto the fasteners for ease of removal. A lot of knuckle skin will be saved by following this rule. It may even be wise to spray the fasteners and allow them to sit overnight.

***** CAUTION**

Allow the exhaust system to cool sufficiently before spraying a solvent exhaust fasteners. Some solvents are highly flammable and could ignite when sprayed on hot exhaust components.

- Annoying rattles and noise vibrations in the exhaust system are usually caused by misalignment of the parts. When aligning the system, leave all bolts and nuts loose until all parts are properly aligned, then tighten, working from front to rear.
- When installing exhaust system parts, make sure there is enough clearance between the hot exhaust parts and pipes and hoses that would be adversely affected by excessive heat. Also make sure there is adequate clearance from the floor pan to avoid possible overheating of the floor.

Muffler

➧ **See Figures 109, 110 and 111**

The muffler is a tri-flow design, located at the rear of the vehicle, mounted transversely. The complete exhaust system is a one

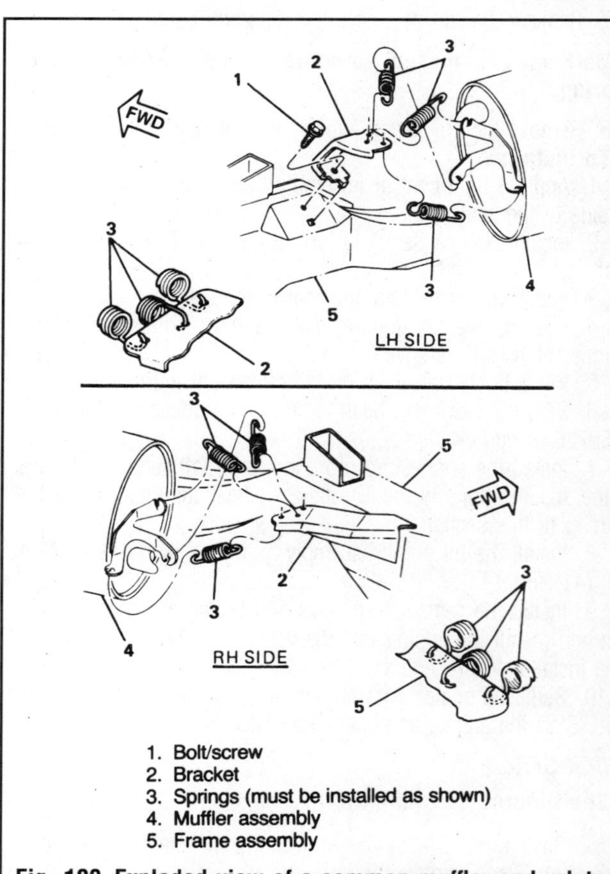

Fig. 109 Exploded view of a common muffler and related components

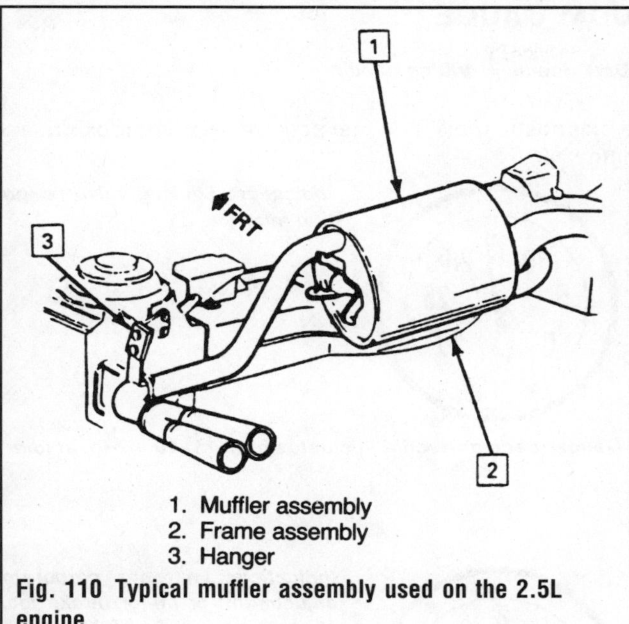

Fig. 110 Typical muffler assembly used on the 2.5L engine

piece design constructed of stainless steel. When servicing a welded connection it should be cut and the new connection clamped when installing replacement parts. Also, coat the slip joints with exhaust system sealer before assembling.

Spring type hangers are used to support the complete exhaust system. It is very important that they be installed properly to avoid annoying vibrations which are difficult to diagnose.

Catalytic Converter

The catalytic converter is an emission control device added to the exhaust system to reduce pollutants from the exhaust gas stream. The converter uses two types of catalysts to reduce three types of pollutants. The oxidation catalyst is coated with a material containing platinum and palladium which lowers the levels of hydrocarbons HC (unburned fuel) and carbon monoxide CO. The three way catalyst contains platinum and rhodium which lowers the levels of oxides of nitrogen NOx.

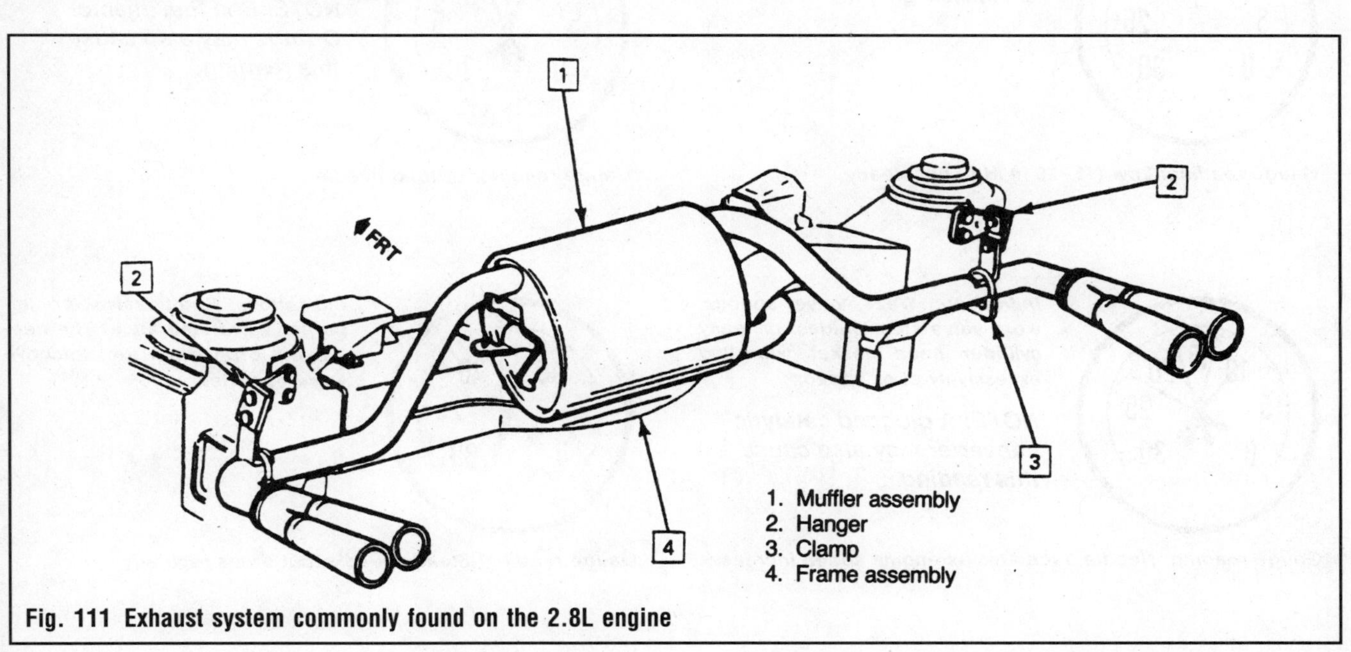

Fig. 111 Exhaust system commonly found on the 2.8L engine

USING A VACUUM GAUGE

White needle = steady needle ***Dark needle = drifting needle***

The vacuum gauge is one of the most useful and easy-to-use diagnostic tools. It is inexpensive, easy to hook up, and provides valuable information about the condition of your engine.

Indication: Normal engine in good condition

Gauge reading: Steady, from 17–22 in./Hg.

Indication: Sticking valve or ignition miss

Gauge reading: Needle fluctuates from 15–20 in./Hg. at idle

Indication: Late ignition or valve timing, low compression, stuck throttle valve, leaking carburetor or manifold gasket.

Gauge reading: Low (15–20 in./Hg.) but steady

Indication: Improper carburetor adjustment, or minor intake leak at carburetor or manifold

NOTE: Bad fuel injector O-rings may also cause this reading.

Gauge reading: Drifting needle

Indication: Weak valve springs, worn valve stem guides, or leaky cylinder head gasket (vibrating excessively at all speeds).

NOTE: A plugged catalytic converter may also cause this reading.

Gauge reading: Needle fluctuates as engine speed increases

Indication: Burnt valve or improper valve clearance. The needle will drop when the defective valve operates.

Gauge reading: Steady needle, but drops regularly

Indication: Choked muffler or obstruction in system. Speed up the engine. Choked muffler will exhibit a slow drop of vacuum to zero.

Gauge reading: Gradual drop in reading at idle

Indication: Worn valve guides

Gauge reading: Needle vibrates excessively at idle, but steadies as engine speed increases

Troubleshooting Engine Mechanical Problems

Problem	Cause	Solution
External oil leaks	• Cylinder head cover RTV sealant broken or improperly seated	• Replace sealant; inspect cylinder head cover sealant flange and cylinder head sealant surface for distortion and cracks
	• Oil filler cap leaking or missing	• Replace cap
	• Oil filter gasket broken or improperly seated	• Replace oil filter
	• Oil pan side gasket broken, improperly seated or opening in RTV sealant	• Replace gasket or repair opening in sealant; inspect oil pan gasket flange for distortion
	• Oil pan front oil seal broken or improperly seated	• Replace seal; inspect timing case cover and oil pan seal flange for distortion
	• Oil pan rear oil seal broken or improperly seated	• Replace seal; inspect oil pan rear oil seal flange; inspect rear main bearing cap for cracks, plugged oil return channels, or distortion in seal groove
	• Timing case cover oil seal broken or improperly seated	• Replace seal
	• Excess oil pressure because of restricted PCV valve	• Replace PCV valve
	• Oil pan drain plug loose or has stripped threads	• Repair as necessary and tighten
	• Rear oil gallery plug loose	• Use appropriate sealant on gallery plug and tighten
	• Rear camshaft plug loose or improperly seated	• Seat camshaft plug or replace and seal, as necessary
Excessive oil consumption	• Oil level too high	• Drain oil to specified level
	• Oil with wrong viscosity being used	• Replace with specified oil
	• PCV valve stuck closed	• Replace PCV valve
	• Valve stem oil deflectors (or seals) are damaged, missing, or incorrect type	• Replace valve stem oil deflectors
	• Valve stems or valve guides worn	• Measure stem-to-guide clearance and repair as necessary
	• Poorly fitted or missing valve cover baffles	• Replace valve cover
	• Piston rings broken or missing	• Replace broken or missing rings
	• Scuffed piston	• Replace piston
	• Incorrect piston ring gap	• Measure ring gap, repair as necessary
	• Piston rings sticking or excessively loose in grooves	• Measure ring side clearance, repair as necessary
	• Compression rings installed upside down	• Repair as necessary
	• Cylinder walls worn, scored, or glazed	• Repair as necessary

Troubleshooting Engine Mechanical Problems

Problem	Cause	Solution
Excessive oil consumption (cont.)	• Piston ring gaps not properly staggered	• Repair as necessary
	• Excessive main or connecting rod bearing clearance	• Measure bearing clearance, repair as necessary
No oil pressure	• Low oil level	• Add oil to correct level
	• Oil pressure gauge, warning lamp or sending unit inaccurate	• Replace oil pressure gauge or warning lamp
	• Oil pump malfunction	• Replace oil pump
	• Oil pressure relief valve sticking	• Remove and inspect oil pressure relief valve assembly
	• Oil passages on pressure side of pump obstructed	• Inspect oil passages for obstruction
	• Oil pickup screen or tube obstructed	• Inspect oil pickup for obstruction
	• Loose oil inlet tube	• Tighten or seal inlet tube
Low oil pressure	• Low oil level	• Add oil to correct level
	• Inaccurate gauge, warning lamp or sending unit	• Replace oil pressure gauge or warning lamp
	• Oil excessively thin because of dilution, poor quality, or improper grade	• Drain and refill crankcase with recommended oil
	• Excessive oil temperature	• Correct cause of overheating engine
	• Oil pressure relief spring weak or sticking	• Remove and inspect oil pressure relief valve assembly
	• Oil inlet tube and screen assembly has restriction or air leak	• Remove and inspect oil inlet tube and screen assembly. (Fill inlet tube with lacquer thinner to locate leaks.)
	• Excessive oil pump clearance	• Measure clearances
	• Excessive main, rod, or camshaft bearing clearance	• Measure bearing clearances, repair as necessary
High oil pressure	• Improper oil viscosity	• Drain and refill crankcase with correct viscosity oil
	• Oil pressure gauge or sending unit inaccurate	• Replace oil pressure gauge
	• Oil pressure relief valve sticking closed	• Remove and inspect oil pressure relief valve assembly
Main bearing noise	• Insufficient oil supply	• Inspect for low oil level and low oil pressure
	• Main bearing clearance excessive	• Measure main bearing clearance, repair as necessary
	• Bearing insert missing	• Replace missing insert
	• Crankshaft end-play excessive	• Measure end-play, repair as necessary
	• Improperly tightened main bearing cap bolts	• Tighten bolts with specified torque
	• Loose flywheel or drive plate	• Tighten flywheel or drive plate attaching bolts
	• Loose or damaged vibration damper	• Repair as necessary

Troubleshooting Engine Mechanical Problems

Problem	Cause	Solution
Connecting rod bearing noise	• Insufficient oil supply	• Inspect for low oil level and low oil pressure
	• Carbon build-up on piston	• Remove carbon from piston crown
	• Bearing clearance excessive or bearing missing	• Measure clearance, repair as necessary
	• Crankshaft connecting rod journal out-of-round	• Measure journal dimensions, repair or replace as necessary
	• Misaligned connecting rod or cap	• Repair as necessary
	• Connecting rod bolts tightened improperly	• Tighten bolts with specified torque
Piston noise	• Piston-to-cylinder wall clearance excessive (scuffed piston)	• Measure clearance and examine piston
	• Cylinder walls excessively tapered or out-of-round	• Measure cylinder wall dimensions, rebore cylinder
	• Piston ring broken	• Replace all rings on piston
	• Loose or seized piston pin	• Measure piston-to-pin clearance, repair as necessary
	• Connecting rods misaligned	• Measure rod alignment, straighten or replace
	• Piston ring side clearance excessively loose or tight	• Measure ring side clearance, repair as necessary
	• Carbon build-up on piston is excessive	• Remove carbon from piston
Valve actuating component noise	• Insufficient oil supply	• Check for: (a) Low oil level (b) Low oil pressure (c) Wrong hydraulic tappets (d) Restricted oil gallery (e) Excessive tappet to bore clearance
	• Rocker arms or pivots worn	• Replace worn rocker arms or pivots
	• Foreign objects or chips in hydraulic tappets	• Clean tappets
	• Excessive tappet leak-down	• Replace valve tappet
	• Tappet face worn	• Replace tappet; inspect corresponding cam lobe for wear
	• Broken or cocked valve springs	• Properly seat cocked springs; replace broken springs
	• Stem-to-guide clearance excessive	• Measure stem-to-guide clearance, repair as required
	• Valve bent	• Replace valve
	• Loose rocker arms	• Check and repair as necessary
	• Valve seat runout excessive	• Regrind valve seat/valves
	• Missing valve lock	• Install valve lock
	• Excessive engine oil	• Correct oil level

Troubleshooting Engine Performance

Problem	Cause	Solution
Hard starting (engine cranks normally)	• Faulty engine control system component	• Repair or replace as necessary
	• Faulty fuel pump	• Replace fuel pump
	• Faulty fuel system component	• Repair or replace as necessary
	• Faulty ignition coil	• Test and replace as necessary
	• Improper spark plug gap	• Adjust gap
	• Incorrect ignition timing	• Adjust timing
	• Incorrect valve timing	• Check valve timing; repair as necessary
Rough idle or stalling	• Incorrect curb or fast idle speed	• Adjust curb or fast idle speed (If possible)
	• Incorrect ignition timing	• Adjust timing to specification
	• Improper feedback system operation	• Refer to Chapter 4
	• Faulty EGR valve operation	• Test EGR system and replace as necessary
	• Faulty PCV valve air flow	• Test PCV valve and replace as necessary
	• Faulty TAC vacuum motor or valve	• Repair as necessary
	• Air leak into manifold vacuum	• Inspect manifold vacuum connections and repair as necessary
	• Faulty distributor rotor or cap	• Replace rotor or cap (Distributor systems only)
	• Improperly seated valves	• Test cylinder compression, repair as necessary
	• Incorrect ignition wiring	• Inspect wiring and correct as necessary
	• Faulty ignition coil	• Test coil and replace as necessary
	• Restricted air vent or idle passages	• Clean passages
	• Restricted air cleaner	• Clean or replace air cleaner filter element
Faulty low-speed operation	• Restricted idle air vents and passages	• Clean air vents and passages
	• Restricted air cleaner	• Clean or replace air cleaner filter element
	• Faulty spark plugs	• Clean or replace spark plugs
	• Dirty, corroded, or loose ignition secondary circuit wire connections	• Clean or tighten secondary circuit wire connections
	• Improper feedback system operation	• Refer to Chapter 4
	• Faulty ignition coil high voltage wire	• Replace ignition coil high voltage wire (Distributor systems only)
	• Faulty distributor cap	• Replace cap (Distributor systems only)
Faulty acceleration	• Incorrect ignition timing	• Adjust timing
	• Faulty fuel system component	• Repair or replace as necessary
	• Faulty spark plug(s)	• Clean or replace spark plug(s)
	• Improperly seated valves	• Test cylinder compression, repair as necessary
	• Faulty ignition coil	• Test coil and replace as necessary

Troubleshooting Engine Performance

Problem	Cause	Solution
Faulty acceleration (cont.)	• Improper feedback system operation	• Refer to Chapter 4
Faulty high speed operation	• Incorrect ignition timing	• Adjust timing (if possible)
	• Faulty advance mechanism	• Check advance mechanism and repair as necessary (Distributor systems only)
	• Low fuel pump volume	• Replace fuel pump
	• Wrong spark plug air gap or wrong plug	• Adjust air gap or install correct plug
	• Partially restricted exhaust manifold, exhaust pipe, catalytic converter, muffler, or tailpipe	• Eliminate restriction
	• Restricted vacuum passages	• Clean passages
	• Restricted air cleaner	• Cleaner or replace filter element as necessary
	• Faulty distributor rotor or cap	• Replace rotor or cap (Distributor systems only)
	• Faulty ignition coil	• Test coil and replace as necessary
	• Improperly seated valve(s)	• Test cylinder compression, repair as necessary
	• Faulty valve spring(s)	• Inspect and test valve spring tension, replace as necessary
	• Incorrect valve timing	• Check valve timing and repair as necessary
	• Intake manifold restricted	• Remove restriction or replace manifold
	• Worn distributor shaft	• Replace shaft (Distributor systems only)
	• Improper feedback system operation	• Refer to Chapter 4
Misfire at all speeds	• Faulty spark plug(s)	• Clean or relace spark plug(s)
	• Faulty spark plug wire(s)	• Replace as necessary
	• Faulty distributor cap or rotor	• Replace cap or rotor (Distributor systems only)
	• Faulty ignition coil	• Test coil and replace as necessary
	• Primary ignition circuit shorted or open intermittently	• Troubleshoot primary circuit and repair as necessary
	• Improperly seated valve(s)	• Test cylinder compression, repair as necessary
	• Faulty hydraulic tappet(s)	• Clean or replace tappet(s)
	• Improper feedback system operation	• Refer to Chapter 4
	• Faulty valve spring(s)	• Inspect and test valve spring tension, repair as necessary
	• Worn camshaft lobes	• Replace camshaft
	• Air leak into manifold	• Check manifold vacuum and repair as necessary
	• Fuel pump volume or pressure low	• Replace fuel pump
	• Blown cylinder head gasket	• Replace gasket
	• Intake or exhaust manifold passage(s) restricted	• Pass chain through passage(s) and repair as necessary
Power not up to normal	• Incorrect ignition timing	• Adjust timing
	• Faulty distributor rotor	• Replace rotor (Distributor systems only)

Troubleshooting Engine Performance

Problem	Cause	Solution
Power not up to normal (cont.)	• Incorrect spark plug gap	• Adjust gap
	• Faulty fuel pump	• Replace fuel pump
	• Faulty fuel pump	• Replace fuel pump
	• Incorrect valve timing	• Check valve timing and repair as necessary
	• Faulty ignition coil	• Test coil and replace as necessary
	• Faulty ignition wires	• Test wires and replace as necessary
	• Improperly seated valves	• Test cylinder compression and repair as necessary
	• Blown cylinder head gasket	• Replace gasket
	• Leaking piston rings	• Test compression and repair as necessary
	• Improper feedback system operation	• Refer to Chapter 4
Intake backfire	• Improper ignition timing	• Adjust timing
	• Defective EGR component	• Repair as necessary
	• Defective TAC vacuum motor or valve	• Repair as necessary
Exhaust backfire	• Air leak into manifold vacuum	• Check manifold vacuum and repair as necessary
	• Faulty air injection diverter valve	• Test diverter valve and replace as necessary
	• Exhaust leak	• Locate and eliminate leak
Ping or spark knock	• Incorrect ignition timing	• Adjust timing
	• Distributor advance malfunction	• Inspect advance mechanism and repair as necessary (Distributor systems only)
	• Excessive combustion chamber deposits	• Remove with combustion chamber cleaner
	• Air leak into manifold vacuum	• Check manifold vacuum and repair as necessary
	• Excessively high compression	• Test compression and repair as necessary
	• Fuel octane rating excessively low	• Try alternate fuel source
	• Sharp edges in combustion chamber	• Grind smooth
	• EGR valve not functioning properly	• Test EGR system and replace as necessary
Surging (at cruising to top speeds)	• Low fuel pump pressure or volume	• Replace fuel pump
	• Improper PCV valve air flow	• Test PCV valve and replace as necessary
	• Air leak into manifold vacuum	• Check manifold vacuum and repair as necessary
	• Incorrect spark advance	• Test and replace as necessary
	• Restricted fuel filter	• Replace fuel filter
	• Restricted air cleaner	• Clean or replace air cleaner filter element
	• EGR valve not functioning properly	• Test EGR system and replace as necessary
	• Improper feedback system operation	• Refer to Chapter 4

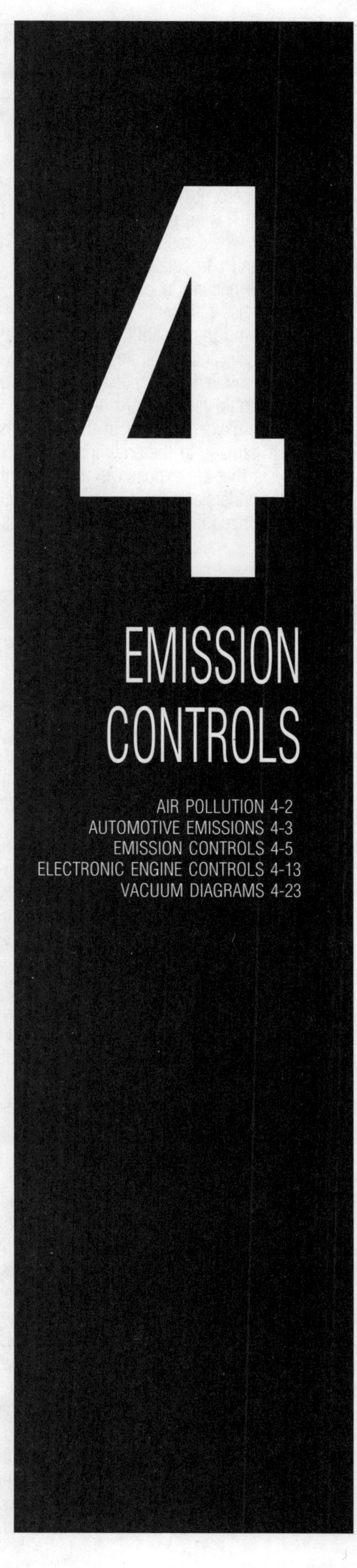

4

EMISSION CONTROLS

AIR POLLUTION

The earth's atmosphere, at or near sea level, consists approximately of 78 percent nitrogen, 21 percent oxygen and 1 percent other gases. If it were possible to remain in this state, 100 percent clean air would result. However, many varied sources allow other gases and particulates to mix with the clean air, causing our atmosphere to become unclean or polluted.

Some of these pollutants are visible while others are invisible, with each having the capability of causing distress to the eyes, ears, throat, skin and respiratory system. Should these pollutants become concentrated in a specific area and under certain conditions, death could result due to the displacement or chemical change of the oxygen content in the air. These pollutants can also cause great damage to the environment and to the many man made objects that are exposed to the elements.

To better understand the causes of air pollution, the pollutants can be categorized into 3 separate types, natural, industrial and automotive.

Natural Pollutants

Natural pollution has been present on earth since before man appeared and continues to be a factor when discussing air pollution, although it causes only a small percentage of the overall pollution problem. It is the direct result of decaying organic matter, wind born smoke and particulates from such natural events as plain and forest fires (ignited by heat or lightning), volcanic ash, sand and dust which can spread over a large area of the countryside.

Such a phenomenon of natural pollution has been seen in the form of volcanic eruptions, with the resulting plume of smoke, steam and volcanic ash blotting out the sun's rays as it spreads and rises higher into the atmosphere. As it travels into the atmosphere the upper air currents catch and carry the smoke and ash, while condensing the steam back into water vapor. As the water vapor, smoke and ash travel on their journey, the smoke dissipates into the atmosphere while the ash and moisture settle back to earth in a trail hundreds of miles long. In some cases, lives are lost and millions of dollars of property damage result.

Industrial Pollutants

Industrial pollution is caused primarily by industrial processes, the burning of coal, oil and natural gas, which in turn produce smoke and fumes. Because the burning fuels contain large amounts of sulfur, the principal ingredients of smoke and fumes are sulfur dioxide and particulate matter. This type of pollutant occurs most severely during still, damp and cool weather, such as at night. Even in its less severe form, this pollutant is not confined to just cities. Because of air movements, the pollutants move for miles over the surrounding countryside, leaving in its path a barren and unhealthy environment for all living things.

Working with Federal, State and Local mandated regulations and by carefully monitoring emissions, big business has greatly reduced the amount of pollutant introduced from its industrial sources, striving to obtain an acceptable level. Because of the mandated industrial emission clean up, many land areas and streams in and around the cities that were formerly barren of vegetation and life, have now begun to move back in the direction of nature's intended balance.

Automotive Pollutants

The third major source of air pollution is automotive emissions. The emissions from the internal combustion engines were not an appreciable problem years ago because of the small number of registered vehicles and the nation's small highway system. However, during the early 1950's, the trend of the American people was to move from the cities to the surrounding suburbs. This caused an immediate problem in transportation because the majority of suburbs were not afforded mass transit conveniences. This lack of transportation created an attractive market for the automobile manufacturers, which resulted in a dramatic increase in the number of vehicles produced and sold, along with a marked increase in highway construction between cities and the suburbs. Multi-vehicle families emerged with a growing emphasis placed on an individual vehicle per family member. As the increase in vehicle ownership and usage occurred, so did pollutant levels in and around the cities, as suburbanites drove daily to their businesses and employment, returning at the end of the day to their homes in the suburbs.

It was noted that a smoke and fog type haze was being formed and at times, remained in suspension over the cities, taking time to dissipate. At first this "smog," derived from the words "smoke" and "fog," was thought to result from industrial pollution but it was determined that automobile emissions shared the blame. It was discovered that when normal automobile emissions were exposed to sunlight for a period of time, complex chemical reactions would take place.

It is now known that smog is a photo chemical layer which develops when certain oxides of nitrogen (NOx) and unburned hydrocarbons (HC) from automobile emissions are exposed to sunlight. Pollution was more severe when smog would become stagnant over an area in which a warm layer of air settled over the top of the cooler air mass, trapping and holding the cooler mass at ground level. The trapped cooler air would keep the emissions from being dispersed and diluted through normal air flows. This type of air stagnation was given the name "Temperature Inversion."

TEMPERATURE INVERSION

In normal weather situations, surface air is warmed by heat radiating from the earth's surface and the sun's rays. This causes it to rise upward, into the atmosphere. Upon rising it will cool through a convection type heat exchange with the cooler upper air. As warm air rises, the surface pollutants are carried upward and dissipated into the atmosphere.

When a temperature inversion occurs, we find the higher air is no longer cooler, but is warmer than the surface air, causing the cooler surface air to become trapped. This warm air blanket can extend from above ground level to a few hundred or even a few thousand feet into the air. As the surface air is trapped, so are the pollutants, causing a severe smog condition. Should this stagnant air mass extend to a few thousand feet high, enough air movement with the inversion takes place to allow the smog layer to rise above ground level but the pollutants still cannot dissipate. This inversion can remain for days over an area, with the smog level only rising or lowering from ground level to a few hundred feet high. Meanwhile, the pollutant levels increase, causing eye irritation, respiratory problems, reduced visibility, plant damage and in some cases, even disease.

This inversion phenomenon was first noted in the Los Angeles, California area. The city lies in terrain resembling a basin and with certain weather conditions, a cold air mass is held in the basin while a warmer air mass covers it like a lid.

Because this type of condition was first documented as prevalent in the Los Angeles area, this type of trapped pollution was named Los Angeles Smog, although it occurs in other areas where a large concentration of automobiles are used and the air remains stagnant for any length of time.

HEAT TRANSFER

Consider the internal combustion engine as a machine in which raw materials must be placed so a finished product comes out. As in any machine operation, a certain amount of wasted material is formed. When we relate this to the internal combustion engine, we find that through the input of air and fuel, we obtain power during the combustion process to drive the vehicle. The by-product or waste of this power is, in part, heat and exhaust gases with which we must dispose.

The heat from the combustion process can rise to over 4000°F (2204°C). The dissipation of this heat is controlled by a ram air effect, the use of cooling fans to cause air flow and a liquid coolant solution surrounding the combustion area to transfer the heat of combustion through the cylinder walls and into the coolant. The coolant is then directed to a thin-finned, multi-tubed radiator, from which the excess heat is transferred to the atmosphere by 1 of the 3 heat transfer methods, conduction, convection or radiation.

The cooling of the combustion area is an important part in the control of exhaust emissions. To understand the behavior of the combustion and transfer of its heat, consider the air/fuel charge. It is ignited and the flame front burns progressively across the combustion chamber until the burning charge reaches the cylinder walls. Some of the fuel in contact with the walls is not hot enough to burn, thereby snuffing out or quenching the combustion process. This leaves unburned fuel in the combustion chamber. This unburned fuel is then forced out of the cylinder and into the exhaust system, along with the exhaust gases.

Many attempts have been made to minimize the amount of unburned fuel in the combustion chambers due to quenching, by increasing the coolant temperature and lessening the contact area of the coolant around the combustion area. However, design limitations within the combustion chambers prevent the complete burning of the air/fuel charge, so a certain amount of the unburned fuel is still expelled into the exhaust system, regardless of modifications to the engine.

AUTOMOTIVE EMISSIONS

Before emission controls were mandated on internal combustion engines, other sources of engine pollutants were discovered along with the exhaust emissions. It was determined that engine combustion exhaust produced approximately 60 percent of the total emission pollutants, fuel evaporation from the fuel tank and carburetor vents produced 20 percent, with the final 20 percent being produced through the crankcase as a by-product of the combustion process.

Exhaust Gases

The exhaust gases emitted into the atmosphere are a combination of burned and unburned fuel. To understand the exhaust emission and its composition, we must review some basic chemistry.

When the air/fuel mixture is introduced into the engine, we are mixing air, composed of nitrogen (78 percent), oxygen (21 percent) and other gases (1 percent) with the fuel, which is 100 percent hydrocarbons (HC), in a semi-controlled ratio. As the combustion process is accomplished, power is produced to move the vehicle while the heat of combustion is transferred to the cooling system. The exhaust gases are then composed of nitrogen, a diatomic gas (N_2), the same as was introduced in the engine, carbon dioxide (CO_2), the same gas that is used in beverage carbonation, and water vapor (H_2O). The nitrogen (N_2), for the most part, passes through the engine unchanged, while the oxygen (O_2) reacts (burns) with the hydrocarbons (HC) and produces the carbon dioxide (CO_2) and the water vapors (H_2O). If this chemical process would be the only process to take place, the exhaust emissions would be harmless. However, during the combustion process, other compounds are formed which are considered dangerous. These pollutants are hydrocarbons (HC), carbon monoxide (CO), oxides of nitrogen (NOx) oxides of sulfur (SOx) and engine particulates.

HYDROCARBONS

Hydrocarbons (HC) are essentially fuel which was not burned during the combustion process or which has escaped into the atmosphere through fuel evaporation. The main sources of incomplete combustion are rich air/fuel mixtures, low engine temperatures and improper spark timing. The main sources of hydrocarbon emission through fuel evaporation on most vehicles used to be the vehicle's fuel tank and carburetor float bowl.

To reduce combustion hydrocarbon emission, engine modifications were made to minimize dead space and surface area in the combustion chamber. In addition, the air/fuel mixture was made more lean through the improved control which feedback carburetion and fuel injection offers and by the addition of external controls to aid in further combustion of the hydrocarbons outside the engine. Two such methods were the addition of air injection systems, to inject fresh air into the exhaust manifolds and the installation of catalytic converters, units that are able to burn traces of hydrocarbons without affecting the internal combustion process or fuel economy.

To control hydrocarbon emissions through fuel evaporation, modifications were made to the fuel tank to allow storage of the fuel vapors during periods of engine shut-down. Modifications were also made to the air intake system so that at specific times during engine operation, these vapors may be purged and burned by blending them with the air/fuel mixture.

CARBON MONOXIDE

Carbon monoxide is formed when not enough oxygen is present during the combustion process to convert carbon (C) to carbon dioxide (CO_2). An increase in the carbon monoxide (CO) emission is normally accompanied by an increase in the hydrocarbon (HC) emission because of the lack of oxygen to completely burn all of the fuel mixture.

Carbon monoxide (CO) also increases the rate at which the photo chemical smog is formed by speeding up the conversion of nitric oxide (NO) to nitrogen dioxide (NO_2). To accomplish this, carbon monoxide (CO) combines with oxygen (O_2) and nitric oxide (NO) to produce carbon dioxide (CO_2) and nitrogen dioxide (NO_2). ($CO + O_2 + NO \quad CO_2 + NO_2$).

The dangers of carbon monoxide, which is an odorless and colorless toxic gas are many. When carbon monoxide is inhaled into the lungs and passed into the blood stream, oxygen is replaced by the carbon monoxide in the red blood cells, causing a reduction in the amount of oxygen supplied to the many parts of the body. This lack of oxygen causes headaches, lack of coordination, reduced mental alertness and, should the carbon monoxide concentration be high enough, death could result.

NITROGEN

Normally, nitrogen is an inert gas. When heated to approximately 2500°F (1371°C) through the combustion process, this gas becomes active and causes an increase in the nitric oxide (NO) emission.

Oxides of nitrogen (NOx) are composed of approximately 97–98 percent nitric oxide (NO). Nitric oxide is a colorless gas but when it is passed into the atmosphere, it combines with oxygen and forms nitrogen dioxide (NO_2). The nitrogen dioxide then combines with chemically active hydrocarbons (HC) and when in the presence of sunlight, causes the formation of photo-chemical smog.

Ozone

To further complicate matters, some of the nitrogen dioxide (NO_2) is broken apart by the sunlight to form nitric oxide and oxygen. (NO_2 + sunlight $\quad NO + O$). This single atom of oxygen then combines with diatomic (meaning 2 atoms) oxygen (O_2) to form ozone (O_3). Ozone is one of the smells associated with smog. It has a pungent and offensive odor, irritates the eyes and lung tissues, affects the growth of plant life and causes rapid deterioration of rubber products. Ozone can be formed by sunlight as well as electrical discharge into the air.

The most common discharge area on the automobile engine is the secondary ignition electrical system, especially when inferior quality spark plug cables are used. As the surge of high voltage is routed through the secondary cable, the circuit builds up an electrical field around the wire, which acts upon the oxygen in the surrounding air to form the ozone. The faint glow along the cable with the engine running that may be visible on a dark night, is called the "corona discharge." It is the result of the electrical field passing from a high along the cable, to a low in the surrounding air, which forms the ozone gas. The combination of corona and ozone has been a major cause of cable deterioration. Recently, different and better quality insulating materials have lengthened the life of the electrical cables.

Although ozone at ground level can be harmful, ozone is beneficial to the earth's inhabitants. By having a concentrated ozone layer called the "ozonosphere," between 10 and 20 miles (16–32 km) up in the atmosphere, much of the ultra violet radiation from the sun's rays are absorbed and screened. If this ozone layer were not present, much of the earth's surface would be burned, dried and unfit for human life.

OXIDES OF SULFUR

Oxides of sulfur (SOx) were initially ignored in the exhaust system emissions, since the sulfur content of gasoline as a fuel is less than 1/10 of 1 percent. Because of this small amount, it was felt that it contributed very little to the overall pollution problem. However, because of the difficulty in solving the sulfur emissions in industrial pollutions and the introduction of catalytic converter to the automobile exhaust systems, a change was mandated. The automobile exhaust system, when equipped with a catalytic converter, changes the sulfur dioxide (SO_2) into sulfur trioxide (SO_3).

When this combines with water vapors (H_2O), a sulfuric acid mist (H_2SO_4) is formed and is a very difficult pollutant to handle since it is extremely corrosive. This sulfuric acid mist that is formed, is the same mist that rises from the vents of an automobile battery when an active chemical reaction takes place within the battery cells.

When a large concentration of vehicles equipped with catalytic converters are operating in an area, this acid mist may rise and be distributed over a large ground area causing land, plant, crop, paint and building damage.

PARTICULATE MATTER

A certain amount of particulate matter is present in the burning of any fuel, with carbon constituting the largest percentage of the particulates. In gasoline, the remaining particulates are the burned remains of the various other compounds used in its manufacture. When a gasoline engine is in good internal condition, the particulate emissions are low but as the engine wears internally, the particulate emissions increase. By visually inspecting the tail pipe emissions, a determination can be made as to where an engine defect may exist. An engine with light gray or blue smoke emitting from the tail pipe normally indicates an increase in the oil consumption through burning due to internal engine wear. Black smoke would indicate a defective fuel delivery system, causing the engine to operate in a rich mode. Regardless of the color of the smoke, the internal part of the engine or the fuel delivery system should be repaired to prevent excess particulate emissions.

Diesel and turbine engines emit a darkened plume of smoke from the exhaust system because of the type of fuel used. Emission control regulations are mandated for this type of emission and more stringent measures are being used to prevent excess emission of the particulate matter. Electronic components are being introduced to control the injection of the fuel at precisely the proper time of piston travel, to achieve the optimum in fuel ignition and fuel usage. Other particulate after-burning components are being tested to achieve a cleaner emission.

Good grades of engine lubricating oils should be used, which meet the manufacturers specification. Cut-rate oils can contribute to the particulate emission problem because of their low flash or ignition temperature point. Such oils burn prematurely during the combustion process causing emission of particulate matter.

The cooling system is an important factor in the reduction of particulate matter. The optimum combustion will occur, with the cooling system operating at a temperature specified by the manufacturer. The cooling system must be maintained in the same manner as the engine oiling system, as each system is required to perform properly in order for the engine to operate efficiently for a long time.

Crankcase Emissions

Crankcase emissions are made up of water, acids, unburned fuel, oil fumes and particulates. These emissions are classified as hydrocarbons (HC) and are formed by the small amount of unburned, compressed air/fuel mixture entering the crankcase from the combustion area (between the cylinder walls and piston rings) during the compression and power strokes. The head of the compression and combustion help to form the remaining crankcase emissions.

Since the first engines, crankcase emissions were allowed into the atmosphere through a road draft tube, mounted on the lower side of the engine block. Fresh air came in through an open oil filler cap or breather. The air passed through the crankcase mixing with blow-by gases. The motion of the vehicle and the air blowing past the open end of the road draft tube caused a low pressure area (vacuum) at the end of the tube. Crankcase emissions were simply drawn out of the road draft tube into the air.

To control the crankcase emission, the road draft tube was deleted. A hose and/or tubing was routed from the crankcase to the intake manifold so the blow-by emission could be burned with the air/fuel mixture. However, it was found that intake manifold vacuum, used to draw the crankcase emissions into the manifold, would vary in strength at the wrong time and not allow the proper emission flow. A regulating valve was needed to control the flow of air through the crankcase.

Testing, showed the removal of the blow-by gases from the crankcase as quickly as possible, was most important to the longevity of the engine. Should large accumulations of blow-by gases remain and condense, dilution of the engine oil would occur to form water, soots, resins, acids and lead salts, resulting in the formation of sludge and varnishes. This condensation of the blow-by gases occurs more frequently on vehicles used in numerous starting and stopping conditions, excessive idling and when the engine is not allowed to attain normal operating temperature through short runs.

Evaporative Emissions

Gasoline fuel is a major source of pollution, before and after it is burned in the automobile engine. From the time the fuel is refined, stored, pumped and transported, again stored until it is pumped into the fuel tank of the vehicle, the gasoline gives off unburned hydrocarbons (HC) into the atmosphere. Through the redesign of storage areas and venting systems, the pollution factor was diminished, but not eliminated, from the refinery standpoint. However, the automobile still remained the primary source of vaporized, unburned hydrocarbon (HC) emissions.

Fuel pumped from an underground storage tank is cool but when exposed to a warmer ambient temperature, will expand. Before controls were mandated, an owner might fill the fuel tank with fuel from an underground storage tank and park the vehicle for some time in warm area, such as a parking lot. As the fuel would warm, it would expand and should no provisions or area be provided for the expansion, the fuel would spill out of the filler neck and onto the ground, causing hydrocarbon (HC) pollution and creating a severe fire hazard. To correct this condition, the vehicle manufacturers added overflow plumbing and/or gasoline tanks with built in expansion areas or domes.

However, this did not control the fuel vapor emission from the fuel tank. It was determined that most of the fuel evaporation occurred when the vehicle was stationary and the engine not operating. Most vehicles carry 5–25 gallons (19–95 liters) of gasoline. Should a large concentration of vehicles be parked in one area, such as a large parking lot, excessive fuel vapor emissions would take place, increasing as the temperature increases.

To prevent the vapor emission from escaping into the atmosphere, the fuel systems were designed to trap the vapors while the vehicle is stationary, by sealing the system from the atmosphere. A storage system is used to collect and hold the fuel vapors from the carburetor (if equipped) and the fuel tank when the engine is not operating. When the engine is started, the storage system is then purged of the fuel vapors, which are drawn into the engine and burned with the air/fuel mixture.

EMISSION CONTROLS

Crankcase Ventilation

OPERATION

➧ See Figures 1 and 2

A Positive Crankcase Ventilation system (PCV) is used to provide more complete burning of the crankcase vapors. Fresh air from the air cleaner or intake duct (V6), is supplied to the crankcase, mixed with blow-by gases and then passed through a Positive Crankcase Ventilation valve (PCV) into the intake manifold (four cyl.) or the Air Plenum (V6). The system is used on all models but not controlled by the Electronic Control Module (ECM).

The primary control is through the PCV valve which meters the flow at a rate depending on manifold vacuum. To maintain engine idle quality, the PCV valve restricts the flow when intake manifold vacuum is high.

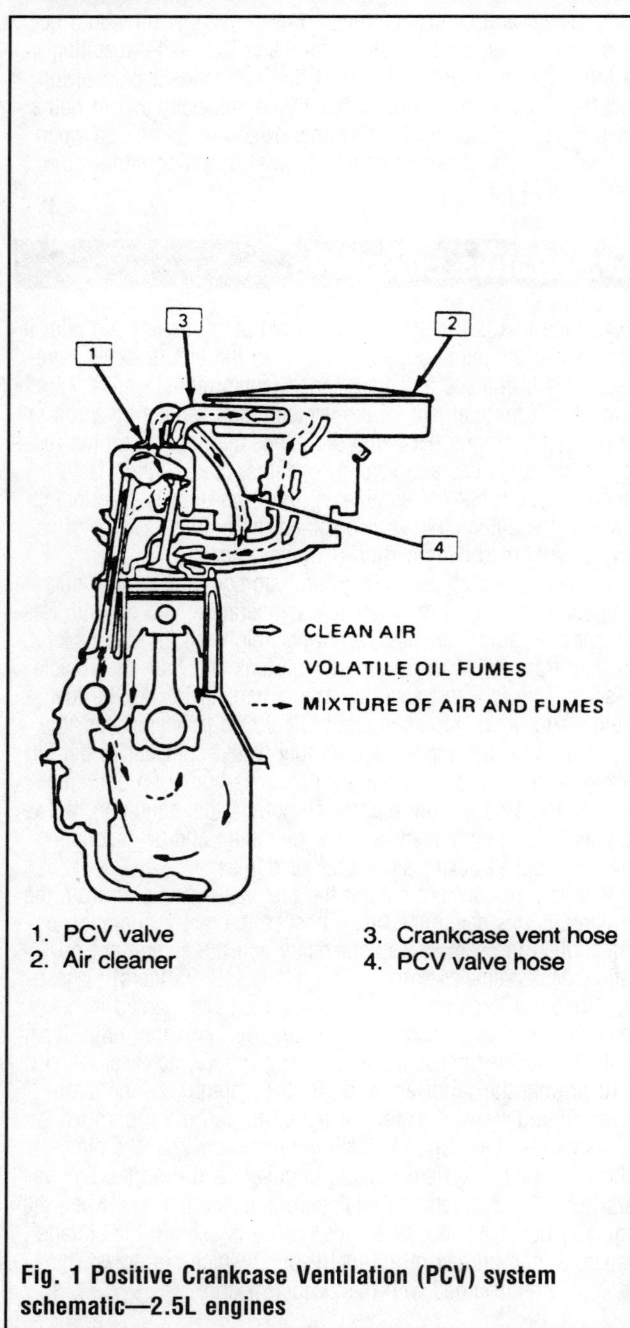

Fig. 1 Positive Crankcase Ventilation (PCV) system schematic—2.5L engines

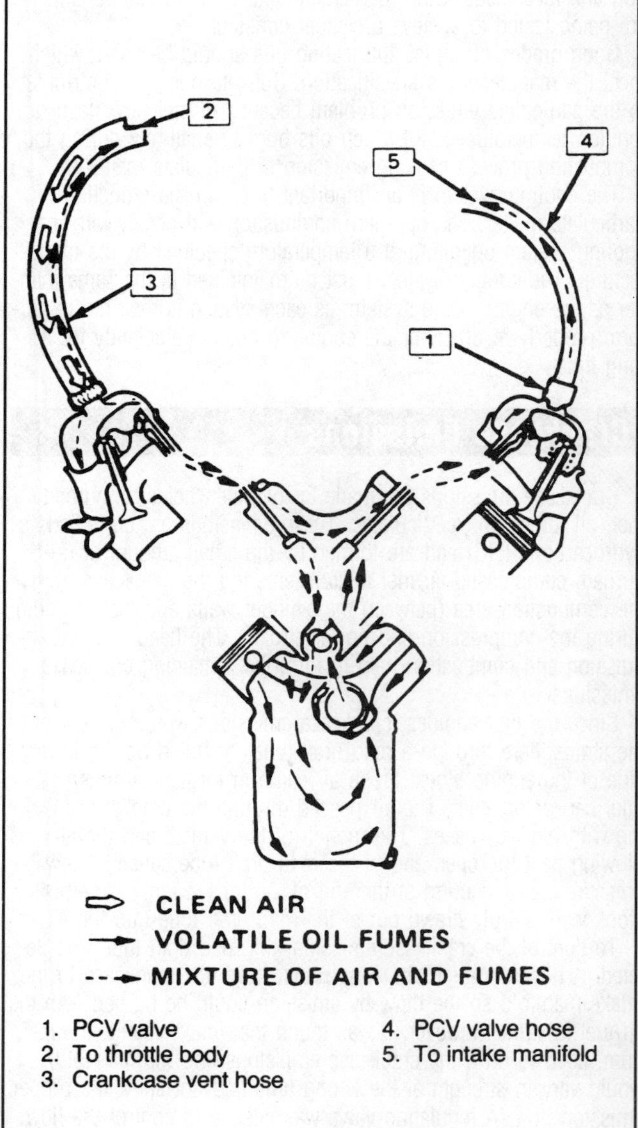

Fig. 2 Positive Crankcase Ventilation (PCV) system schematic—2.8L engines

INSPECTION & SERVICE

See Figures 3, 4 and 5

A clogged PCV valve or plugged hose could cause rough idling, stalling, oil leaks or sludge in the engine. A leaking valve or hose may cause rough idle, stalling or high idle speed. If the engine is operated without the the PCV valve installed properly, engine damage may result. Check the valve and hose as follows every 30,000 miles:

1. Remove the valve from the rocker arm cover.
2. Apply the emergency brake and place the auto transaxle in park, manual transaxle in neutral. Start the engine and run at idle.
3. Place your thumb over the end of the valve to check for vacuum. If there is no vacuum at the valve, check for plugged hoses at manifold port or PCV valve. Replace plugged or deteriorated hoses.
4. Turn off the engine and remove the PCV valve. Shake the valve and listen for the rattle of the check needle inside the valve. If the valve does not rattle, replace the valve.

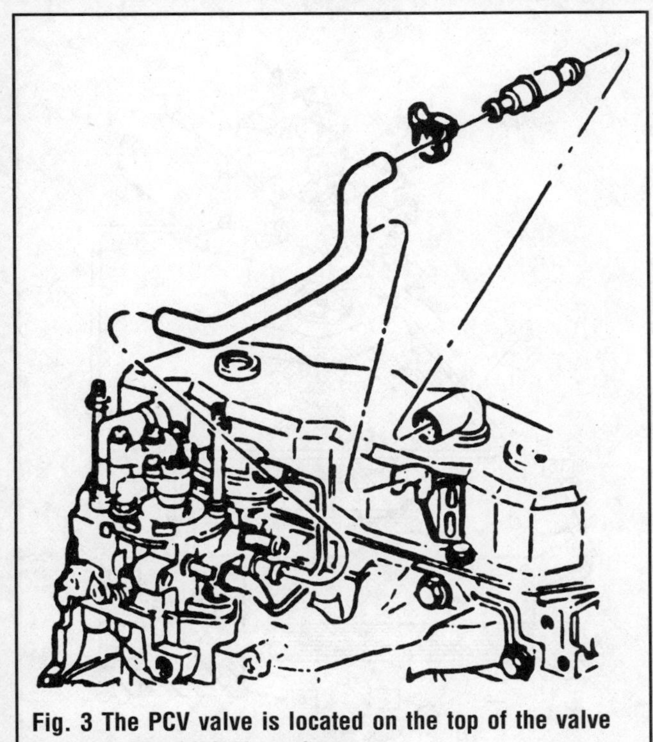

Fig. 3 The PCV valve is located on the top of the valve cover—1984–86 2.5L engines

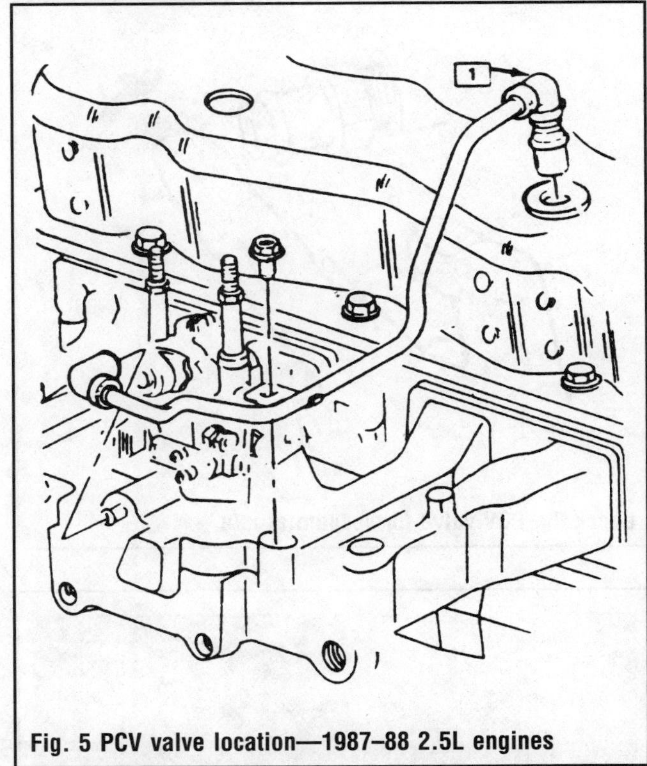

Fig. 5 PCV valve location—1987–88 2.5L engines

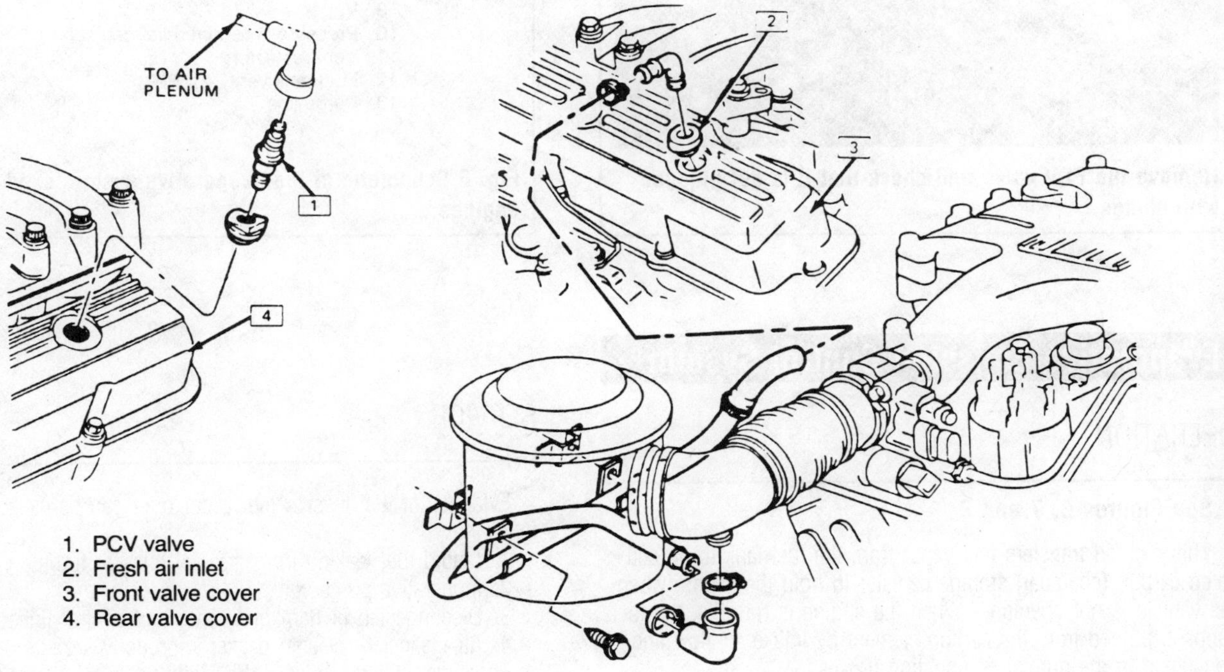

TO AIR PLENUM

1. PCV valve
2. Fresh air inlet
3. Front valve cover
4. Rear valve cover

Fig. 4 Exploded view of the PCV system used on the 2.8L engine

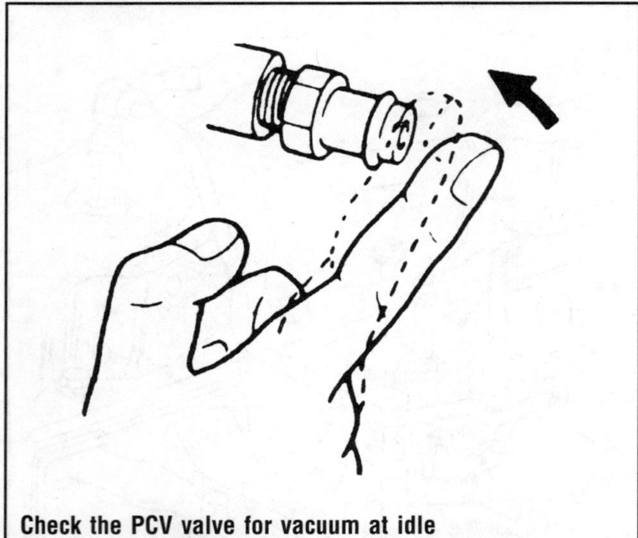

Check the PCV valve for vacuum at idle

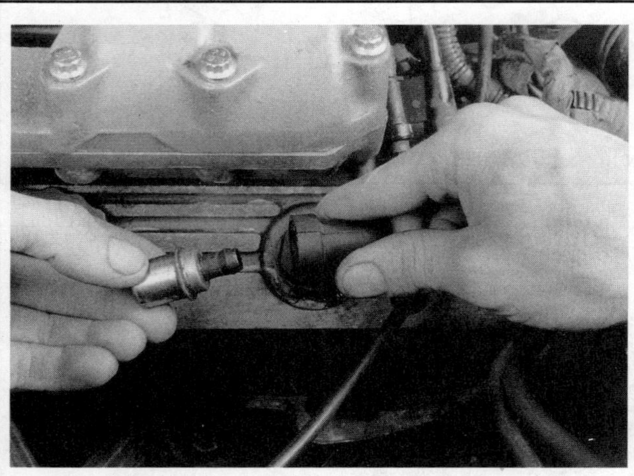

Remove the PCV valve and check that it is not plugged with sludge

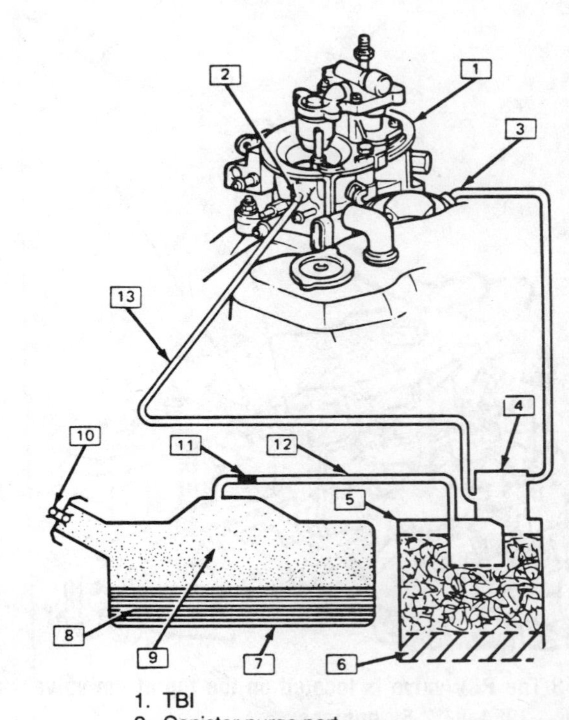

Fig. 6 Schematic of the evaporative system used on 2.5L engines

Evaporative Emission Control System

OPERATION

➧ See Figures 6, 7 and 8

This method transfers fuel vapor from the fuel tank to an activated carbon (charcoal) storage canister to hold the vapors when the vehicle is not operating. When the engine is running, the fuel vapor is purged from the carbon element by intake air flow and consumed in the normal combustion process.

The vapor canister uses a integral diaphragm operated purge valve. When the engine is running, manifold vacuum is supplied to the top tube of the purge valve, the valve opens and the vapor is pulled into the throttle body or air plenum.

SERVICE

Evidence of fuel loss or fuel vapor odor can be caused by the following:

1. Liquid fuel leaking from the fuel lines or throttle body.
2. Inoperative purge valve.
3. Disconnected or damaged vapor and control lines.
4. Air cleaner or cleaner gasket improperly seated.

Poor idle, stalling or poor driveability can be caused by the following:

1. Inoperative purge valve.
2. Damaged canister.
3. Hoses split, cracked, damaged or connected improperly.

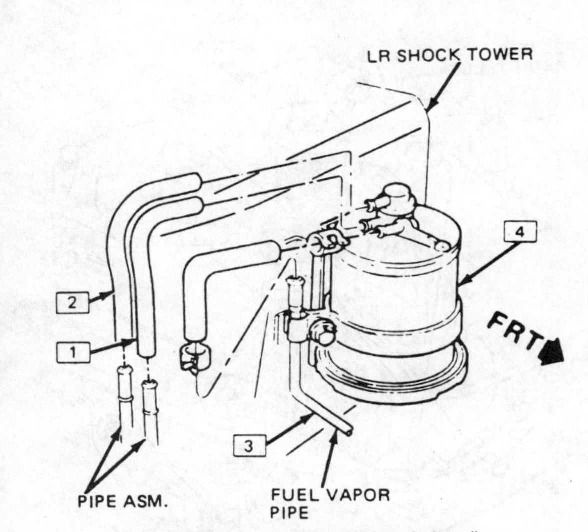

Fig. 7 Location of the evaporator canister and its related components—2.8L engines

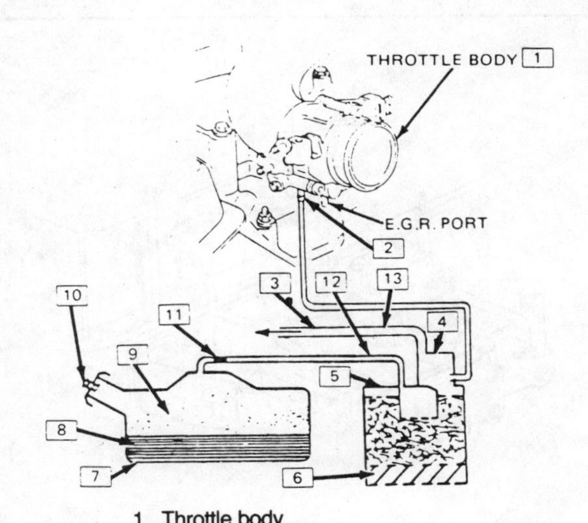

Fig. 8 Schematic of the evaporative system used on the 2.8L engine

TESTING

1. Visually check the canister for cracks or damage, replace canister.
2. If fuel is leaking from the bottom of the canister, replace canister and check for proper hose routing.
3. Check the filter at the bottom of the canister. If dirty, replace the filter.
4. Functional test the purge valve by installing a piece of hose to the lower tube of the valve and attempt to blow through it. Little or no air should pass into the canister.
5. Connect a vacuum pump and apply 15 Hg (51 kPa) of vacuum to the upper control valve tube. The diaphragm should hold vacuum for at least 20 seconds. If it does not hold vacuum, the canister must be replaced.

REMOVAL & INSTALLATION

1. Disconnect the negative (−) battery cable.
2. Remove the hoses on the canister and mark them for installation.
3. Remove the canister bracket attaching bolt.
4. Install the canister and torque the attaching bolt to 6–9 ft. lbs. (8–12 Nm). Reconnect the hoses in their original locations.
5. Start the engine and check for proper operation and fuel leaks.

Exhaust Gas Recirculation System (EGR)

OPERATION

See Figure 9

The Exhaust Gas Recirculation (EGR) System is used to lower the oxides of nitrogen (NOX) emission levels caused by high com-

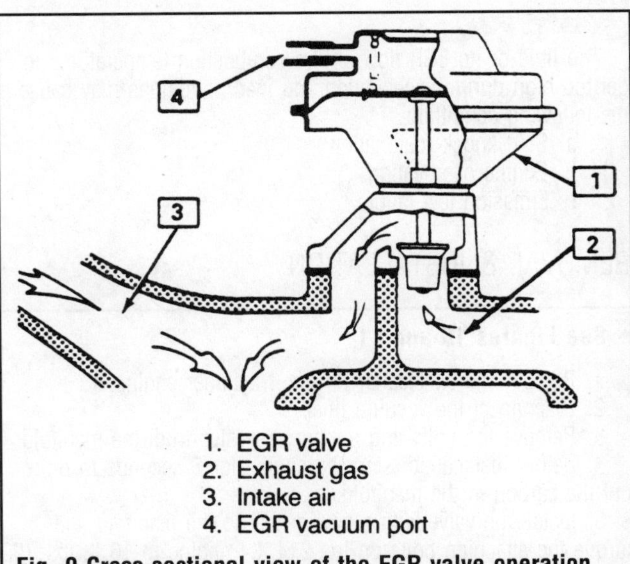

Fig. 9 Cross-sectional view of the EGR valve operation

bustion temperature. It does that by decreasing combustion temperature. The main element of the system is the EGR valve mounted on the intake manifold (4 cyl.) and on the exhaust manifold (V6). The EGR valve feeds small amounts of exhaust gas back into the combustion chamber.

The EGR valve is opened by ported manifold vacuum to let exhaust gas flow into the intake manifold. The exhaust gas mixes with the air/fuel mixture as it moves into the combustion chamber. Very little exhaust gas is allowed to enter the valve, and non at idle.

TESTING

Too much EGR flow at idle, cruise or cold operation may cause the following conditions:

a. Engine stops after cold start.
b. Engine stops at idle after deceleration.
c. Vehicle surges during cruise.
d. Rough idle.

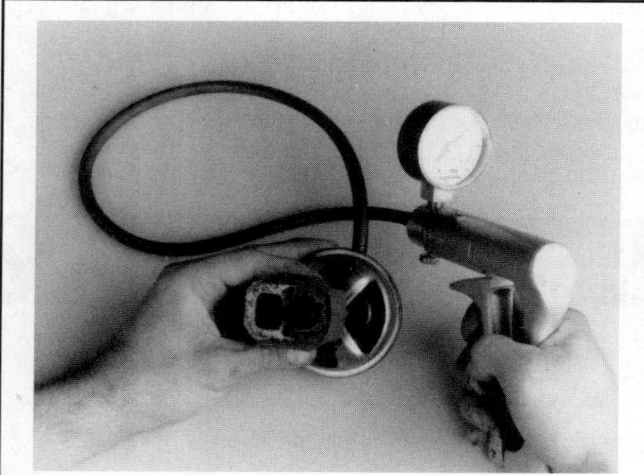

Some EGR valves may be tested using a vacuum pump by watching for diaphragm movement

Too little or no EGR flow allows combustion temperatures to get too high during acceleration and load conditions may cause the following conditions:

a. Start knock (detonation).
b. Engine overheating.
c. Emission test failure.

REMOVAL & INSTALLATION

See Figures 10 and 11

1. Remove the air cleaner on the 4 cylinder engine.
2. Disconnect the vacuum line.
3. Remove the bolts and remove the valve from the manifold.
4. Before installation, start the engine for 5 seconds to blow out the carbon in the manifold.
5. Install the valve with a new gasket to the manifold and torque the attaching bolts on the 2.5L L4 engine to 16 ft. lbs. (22 Nm). Torque the two nuts on the 2.8L V6 engine to 15 ft. lbs. (20 Nm). Install the vacuum hose. Start the engine and check for exhaust leaks.

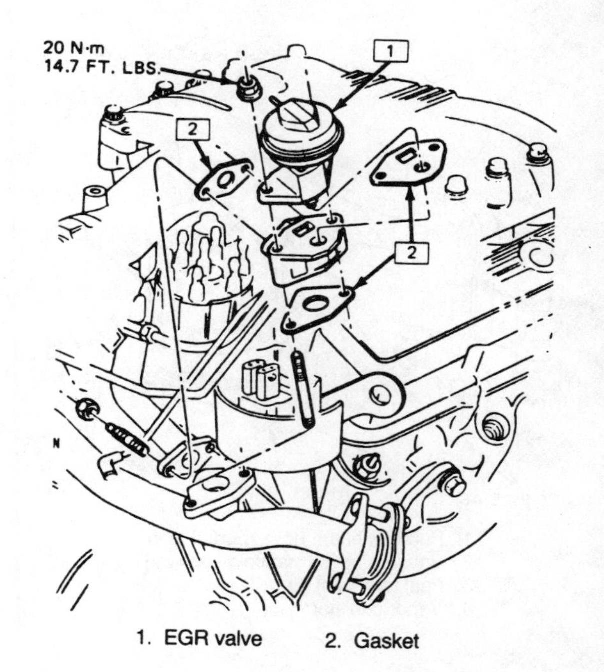

Fig. 10 Location and mounting of the EGR valve—2.8L engines

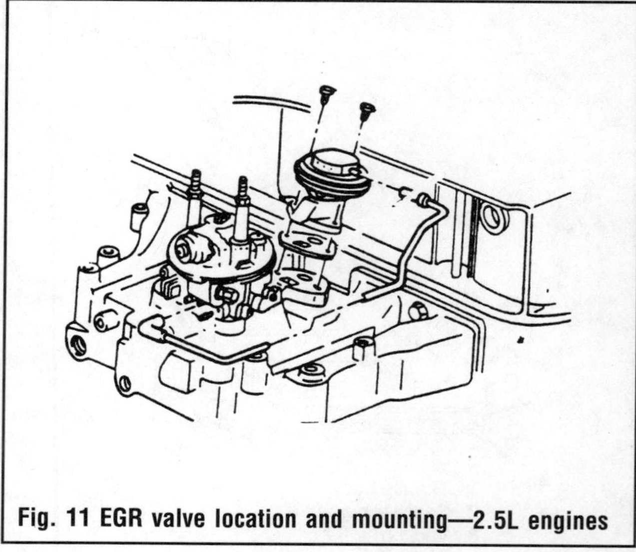

Fig. 11 EGR valve location and mounting—2.5L engines

CLEANING

1. Using a wire wheel, clean the carbon deposits from the mounting surface and around the valve.
2. Scrape any carbon deposits around the valve outlet with a suitable tool.
3. Clean all mounting surfaces.

Disengage the vacuum line from the EGR valve

Remove the EGR valve gasket . . .

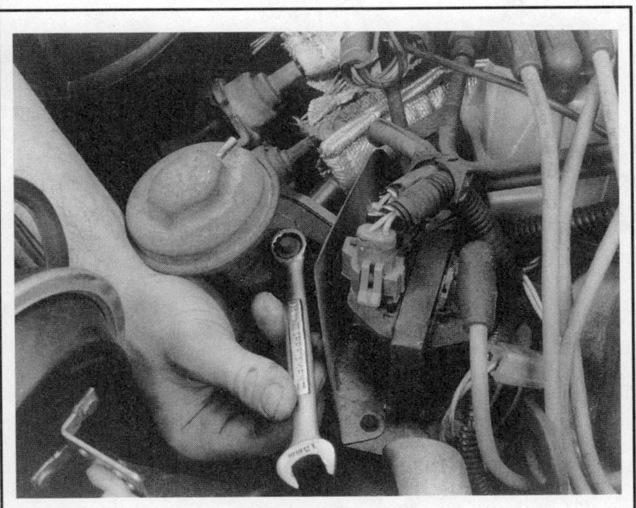

Unfasten the EGR valve retaining bolts . . .

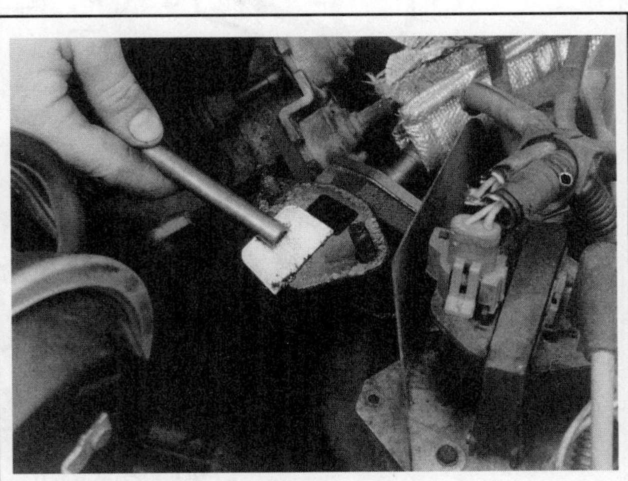

. . . then use a gasket scraper to remove any of the old gasket residue

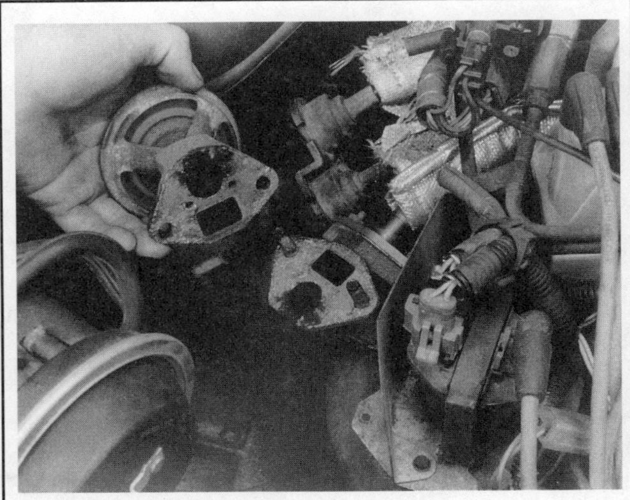

. . . then remove the EGR valve

Thermostatic Air Cleaner

OPERATION

See Figure 12

This system, used on the four cylinder engines, uses heated air and manifold vacuum to give good driveability under varying climatic conditions.

Air can enter the air cleaner from outside the engine compartment or from the heat stove built around the exhaust manifold. A vacuum diaphragm motor, built into the air cleaner snorkel, moves the damper door, to admit hot air from the exhaust manifold, outside air, or a combination of both. Inside the air cleaner is a temperature sensor that reacts to air intake temperature and controls the amount of vacuum going to the motor.

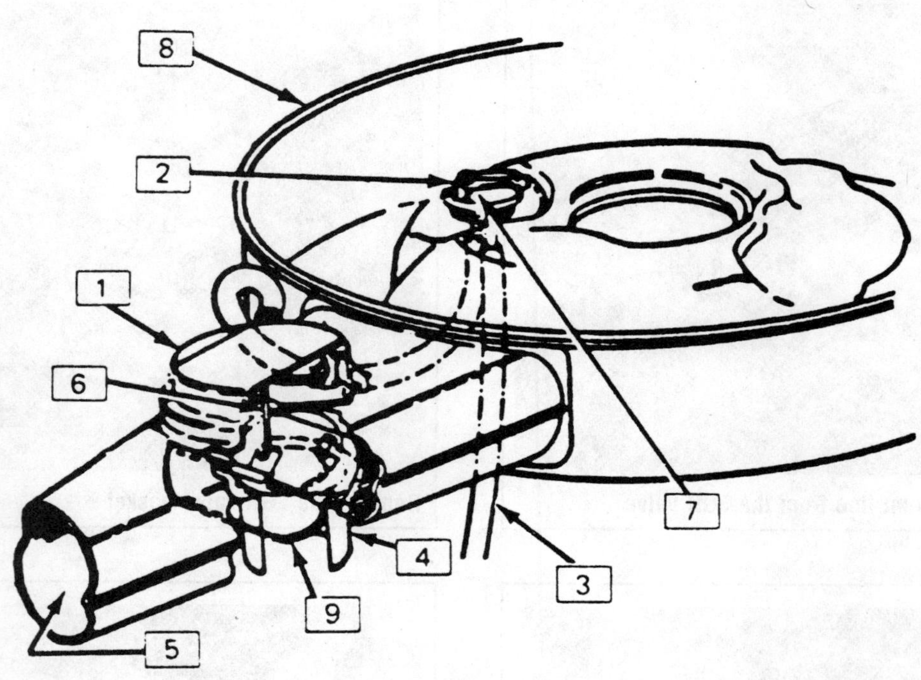

1. Vacuum diaphragm motor
2. Temperature sensor
3. Vacuum hose (to manifold vacuum)
4. Heat stove duct
5. Snorkel
6. Linkage
7. Air bleed valve
8. Air cleaner asm.
9. Damper door

Fig. 12 Components of the thermostatic air cleaner system

INSPECTION

Hesitation during warm-up may be caused by the following

a. The heat stove tube disconnected.
b. Vacuum diaphragm motor on the air cleaner inoperative.
c. No manifold vacuum.
d. Damper door does not move.
e. Missing air cleaner-to-throttle body seal.
f. Missing air cleaner cover seal or loose cover.
g. Loose air cleaner.

TESTING

1. Checked for kinked, plugged or deteriorated hoses to the vacuum motor and heat stove.
2. Check the condition of the gasket or seal between the air cleaner and TBI unit.
3. With the air cleaner assembly installed, the damper door should be open to the outside air when the engine is not running or above 86°F (30°C).
4. Start the engine. Watch the damper door in the air cleaner snorkel. When the engine is first started, the damper door should move and close off outside air.
5. As the air cleaner warms up, the damper door should open slowly to the outside air.
6. If the air cleaner fails to operate as described above, the vacuum motor or the temperature sensor may be defective.
7. Using a vacuum pump, apply at least 7 in.Hg (23 kPa) of vacuum to the vacuum diaphragm motor. If the motor will *not* hold vacuum, replace the vacuum motor. If the motor holds vacuum, check motor for binding condition. Replace the temperatures sensor if the vacuum motor is working properly.

ELECTRONIC ENGINE CONTROLS

EMISSION CONTROL COMPONENT LOCATIONS (2.8L V6)

1. Manifold Absolute Pressure (MAP) sensor
2. Positive Crankcase Ventilation (PCV) valve
3. Exhaust Gas Recirculation (EGR) valve
4. Evaporative Emission Control canister (EVAP)
5. Throttle Position Sensor (TPS)
6. Idle Air Control (IAC) valve

Automatic Transmission Converter Clutch (TCC) System

OPERATION

See Figure 13

The transmission converter clutch system is designed to eliminate power loss by the torque converter slippage. This system increases fuel efficiency because a more effective coupling to the flywheel is achieved. The converter clutch is operated by an ECM controlled solenoid within the automatic transaxle. The solenoid will not engage until the proper amount of fluid pressure is achieved.

INSPECTION

1. Install a tachometer.
2. Operate the vehicle until proper operating temperature.
3. Drive the vehicle at 50–55 mph (80–88 km/h) with light throttle.
4. Lightly touch the brake pedal and check for a slight bump when the TCC releases a slight increase in the engine RPM.
5. Release the brake and check for a re-apply of the converter clutch and a slight decrease in engine RPM.

WARNING

Do not apply 12-volts of battery current to test the TCC solenoid. Accidentally crossed wires will destroy the internal diodes of the TCC solenoid.

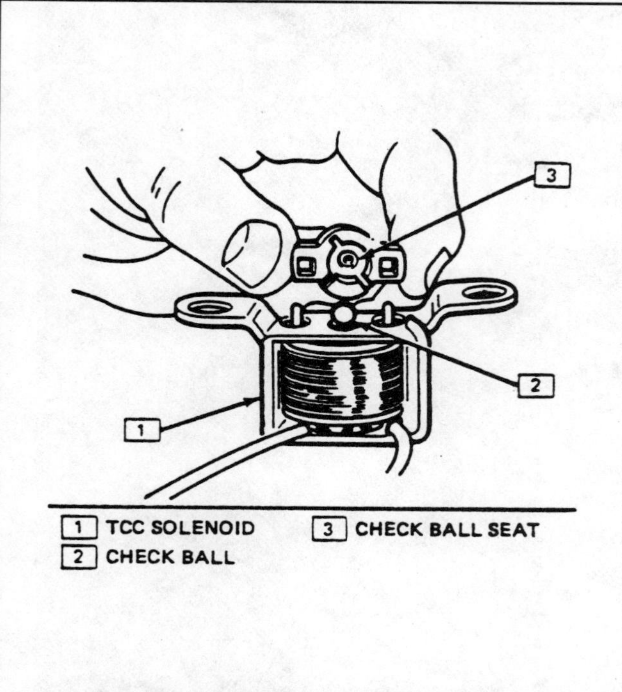

Fig. 13 Transaxle Converter Clutch (TCC) solenoid components

REMOVAL & INSTALLATION

See Figure 14

1. Raise the vehicle and support with jackstands.
2. Disconnect the negative (−) battery cable.
3. Drain the transaxle fluid into a suitable drain pan. Refer to the "Transaxle Fluid Change" procedures in Section 7.
4. Remove the valve body side cover and drain excess fluid into the drain pan.
5. Disconnect the solenoid wires from the electrical connector and the pressure switch.
6. Remove the one solenoid attaching screw and pull the TCC solenoid out of the valve body.

To install:

7. Position a new O-ring seal onto the TCC solenoid. Lubricate the O-ring with Dexron®II and install the solenoid into the valve body. Tighten the one attaching screw and reconnect the electrical wires.
8. Install the valve body side cover with a new gasket and torque the bolts to 8 ft. lbs. (11 Nm).
9. Refill the transaxle with the proper amount of Dexron®II. Refer to the "Transaxle Fluid Change" procedures in Section 7.
10. Connect the negative (−) battery cable. Start the engine and wait till operating temperature has been reached. With the emergency brake applied, move the gear selector through the gears. Put the selector in PARK, check the fluid level and fill to proper level with engine running.

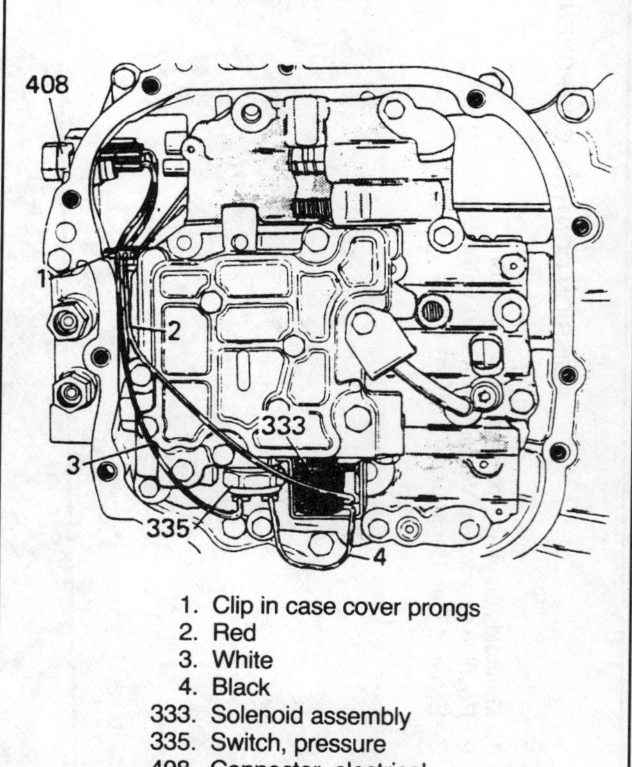

Fig. 14 The valve body side cover must be removed to gain access to the TCC solenoid

Oxygen Sensor (O_2)

The exhaust oxygen sensor is mounted in the exhaust system where it can monitor the oxygen content of the exhaust gases. The oxygen reacts to the oxygen sensor to produce a voltage output. The voltage ranges from .1 volts for lean mixtures to .9 volts for rich mixtures.

✲✲ WARNING

The oxygen sensor uses a permanently attached pigtail and connector. This pigtail should NOT be removed from the sensor. Damage to the oxygen sensor will result.

The oxygen sensor is located in the exhaust cross-over pipe on 2.8L V6 engines

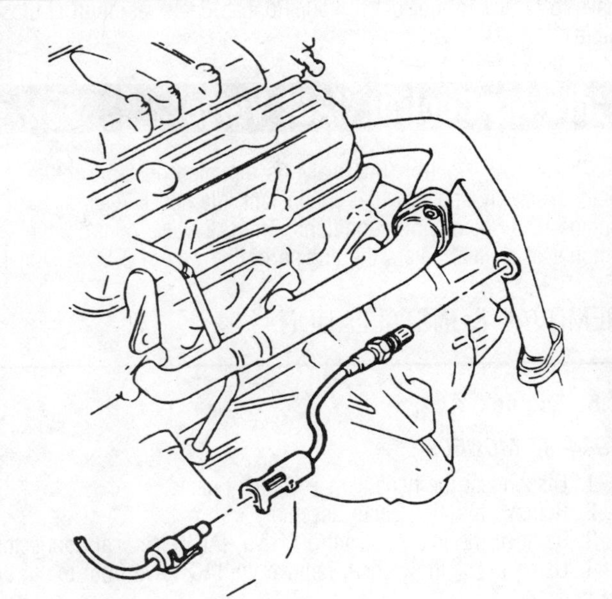

Fig. 15 Exploded view of the oxygen sensor is mounting on the 2.8L engine

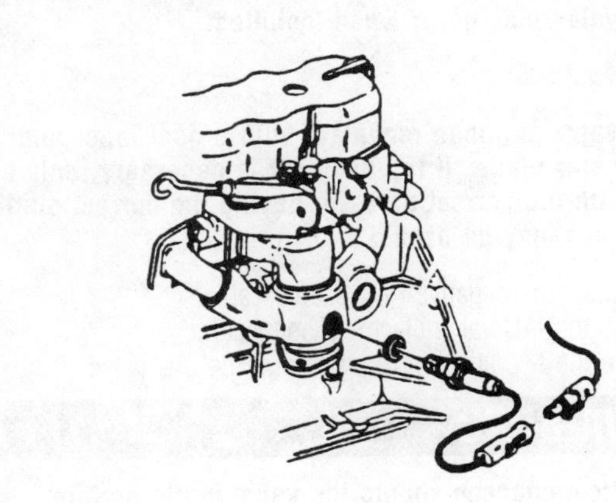

Fig. 16 The oxygen sensor is located in the exhaust manifold on the 2.5L engine

REMOVAL & INSTALLATION

See Figures 15 and 16

The oxygen sensor may be difficult to remove when the engine temperature is below 120°F (48°C). Excessive force may damage the threads in the exhaust manifold or cross-over pipe.

1. Disconnect the negative (−) battery cable.
2. Disconnect the electrical connector at the plug.
3. Remove the sensor from the exhaust manifold or crossover pipe, being careful not to damage the manifold threads.

A special anti-seize compound is used on the oxygen sensor threads to prevent thread seizure. The threads MUST be coated with anti-seize compound No. P/N 5613695 or equivalent before installation.

To install:

4. Position the sensor and seal into the exhaust manifold. Torque the sensor to 30 ft. lbs (41 Nm) and connect the electrical connector. Reconnect the negative battery cable and start the engine to check for exhaust leaks.

Emission Service Light

The Fiero models sold in the United States and some in Canada have the Computer Command Control (CCC) systems. Fieros with the Computer Command Control system include a **"Check Engine"** light on 1984–85 models and a **"Service Engine Soon"** light on 1986–88 models. This light is on the instrument panel to the right of the fuel gauge. The light will come ON during engine starting to let you know the bulb is working. Have the system serviced by your dealer if the light does not come on during starting, intermittently or continuously while driving. These conditions may indicate that the Computer Command Control (CCC) system needs servicing. In most cases, the vehicle will not have to be towed, but get to your Pontiac dealer as soon as possible.

Idle Air Control (IAC) Valve

The Idle Air Control (IAC) valve is mounted on the throttle body assembly and provides a constant idle speed regardless of engine loads or driving conditions. The IAC valve controls the amount of air that enters the engine by the way of a ECM signal.

REMOVAL & INSTALLATION

2.5L Engine

1984–86 MODELS

1. Disconnect the negative (−) battery cable.
2. Remove the air cleaner assembly.
3. Remove the Idle Air Control Valve (IAC) electrical connector.
4. Using a 1¼ in. wrench, remove the IAC valve from the throttle body.

➡Before installing a new IAC valve, measure the distance that the conical valve (pintle) extends. The measurement should be made from the valve housing to the end of the pintle cone. The distance should be no greater than 1⅛ inch (28mm). If the pintle cone is extended too far, damage to the IAC valve may occur when installed.

1987–88 MODELS

➡The IAC valve is flange mounted, with a dual taper and 10mm diameter pintle. If replacement is necessary, only an IAC valve with the correct part No. having the correct pintle shape and size may be used.

1. Disconnect the negative (−) battery cable.
2. Remove the IAC valve electrical connector.
3. Remove the two attaching screws and the IAC valve.

⁂ WARNING

Under no circumstances should the valve pintle be tampered with by hand, screwed or pushed in, or pulled out because damage may result.

To install:

4. Lubricate the new O-ring seal with automatic transmission fluid and install on the IAC valve.
5. Install the IAC valve to the throttle body.
6. Coat the two IAC valve attaching screws with thread locking compound and torque to 28 inch lb. (3.2 Nm).
7. Install the IAC electrical connector. Reconnect the negative (−) battery cable.
8. Start the engine and allow to reach operating temperature. Check the idle speed with a tachometer.

2.8L Engine

➧ See Figure 17

1. Disconnect the negative (−) battery cable.
2. Remove the air duct assembly.
3. Remove the IAC valve electrical connector.

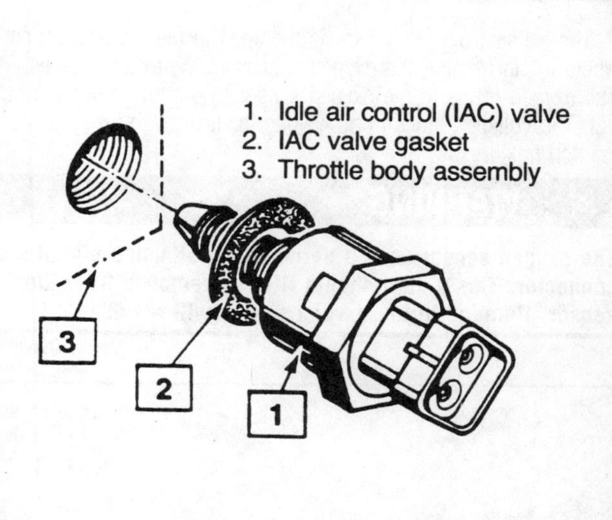

Fig. 17 The Idle Air Control (IAC) valve is threaded into the throttle body

4. Using a 1¼ inch wrench, remove the IAC valve from the throttle body.

To install:

5. With a new gasket, install the IAC valve into the throttle body and torque to 13 ft. lbs. (18 Nm).
6. Reconnect the IAC electrical connector.
7. Install the air duct and connect the negative (−) battery cable.
8. Start the engine and allow the engine to reach operating temperature and normal idle speed. Check to see if the idle speed is to specifications using a tachometer.

ADJUSTMENT

Type 1

Exert firm pressure on the conical valve (pintle cone) to retract it. A slight side to side movement may be helpful.

Type 2

➧ See Figure 18

1. Compress the retaining spring from the conical valve (pintle cone) while turning the valve IN with a clockwise motion. The return spring should be in the original position with the straight portion of the spring end aligned with the flat surface of the valve.

To install:

2. With a new gasket, install the IAC valve into the throttle body and torque to 13 ft. lbs. (18 Nm).
3. Reconnect the IAC electrical connector.
4. Install the air cleaner and connect the negative (−) battery cable.
5. Start the engine and allow the engine to reach operating temperature and normal idle speed. Check to see if the idle speed is to specifications using a tachometer.

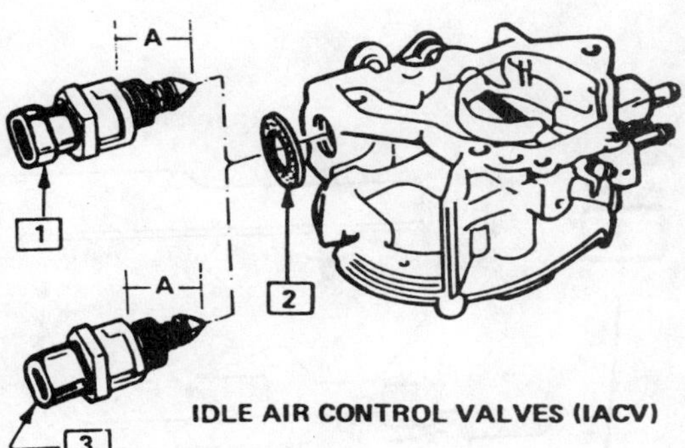

Fig. 18 Two types of Idle Air Control (IAC) valve used

Throttle Position Sensor (TPS)

The TPS is mounted on the side of the throttle body opposite the throttle lever assembly. The function of the TPS is to relay throttle valve position to the Electronic Control Module (ECM). The signal is needed to generate the proper injector controls (base pulse).

REMOVAL & INSTALLATION

Throttle Body Injection

1. Disconnect the negative (−) battery cable.
2. Remove the air cleaner assembly.
3. Remove the electrical connector from the TP sensor.
4. Remove the two attaching screws and remove the sensor.

➡The throttle position sensor TPS is an electrical component and should not be immersed in any type of liquid solvent or cleaner.

To install:

5. Position the TPS unit on the throttle body with the throttle valve normally closed. Install the sensor and rotate counter clockwise to align the mounting holes. Torque the two attaching screws to 18 inch lb. (2.0 Nm).
6. Connect the TPS electrical connector. Reconnect the negative (−) battery cable.

Multi-Port Injection

1. Disconnect the negative (−) battery cable.
2. Remove the air duct assembly.

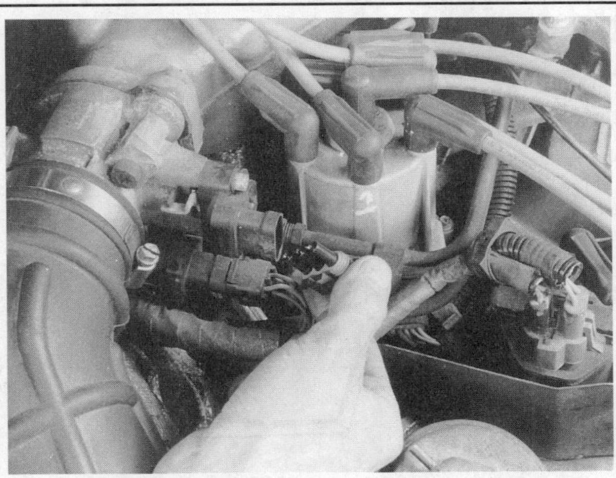

When unplugging the Throttle Position Sensor (TPS) be careful not to break the locktab

3. Remove the electrical connector from the TP sensor.
4. Remove the two attaching screws and remove the sensor.

➡The throttle position sensor TPS is an electrical component and should not be immersed in any type of liquid solvent or cleaner.

To install:

5. Position the TPS unit on the throttle body with the throttle valve normally closed. Install the sensor and rotate counter clockwise to align the mounting holes. Torque the two attaching screws to 18 inch lb. (2.0 Nm).
6. Connect the TPS electrical connector. Reconnect the negative (−) battery cable.
7. Reconnect the negative battery cable. Start the engine and check for proper operation.

ADJUSTMENT

1984–86 Model 300 Only

➧ See Figure 19

1. Connect a tachometer and check the idle speed to see if it is within specifications on the underhood sticker. If not within specifications, refer to the "Idle Speed Adjustment" procedures in section 2.
2. Remove the air cleaner and disconnect the TPS electrical connector.
3. Using three, six inch jumper wires, connect the TPS harness to the TPS as shown in the illustration.
4. Turn the ignition switch to the ON position with the engine NOT running. Measure the voltage between terminals B and C using a digital voltmeter.
5. The voltage should read 0.450–1.250 volts at closed throttle position.
6. Turn the ignition switch to the OFF position and reconnect the TPS electrical connector without the jumper wires.

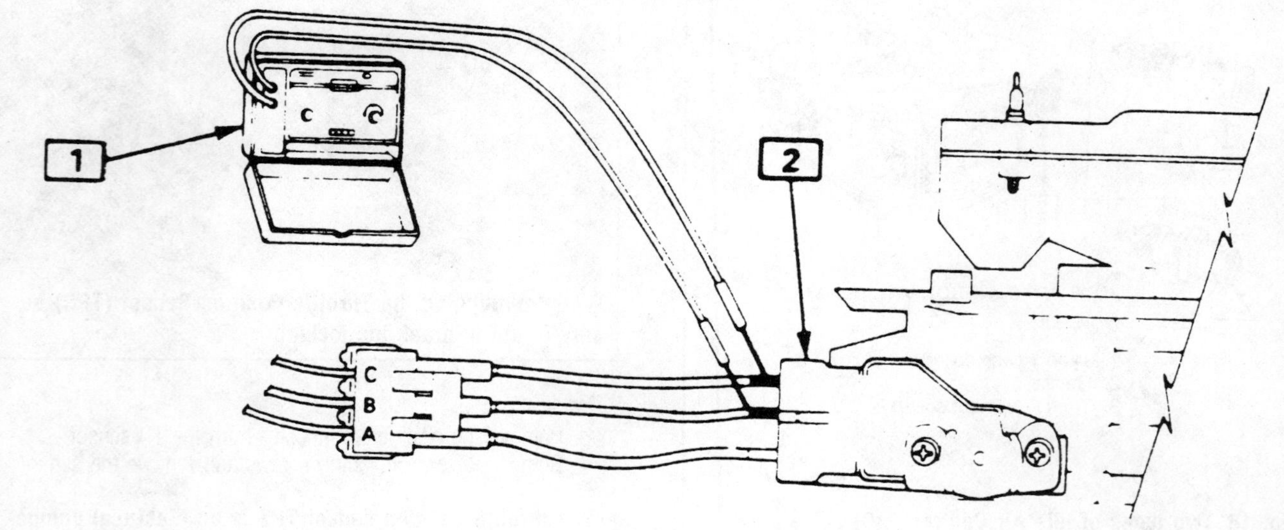

Fig. 19 Connect the multimeter to the terminals indicated

Manifold Absolute Pressure Sensor (MAP)

➧ See Figure 20

The MAP sensor measures manifold vacuum and sends the signal to the electronic control module (ECM). The sensor is mainly used for fuel calculation when the ECM is running in the throttle body backup mode. The MAP sensor also determines barometric pressure to help calculate fuel delivery. The sensor is mounted on the air plenum assembly.

REMOVAL & INSTALLATION

1. Disconnect the negative (−) battery cable.
2. Remove the vacuum and electrical connectors from the MAP sensor.
3. Remove the two MAP sensor-to-air plenum screws.

To install:

4. Position the MAP sensor onto the air plenum and torque the two attaching screws to 88 inch.lb (10.0 Nm).
5. Reconnect the vacuum and electrical connectors to the MAP sensor.
6. Reconnect the negative (−) battery cable. Start the engine and check for proper operation.

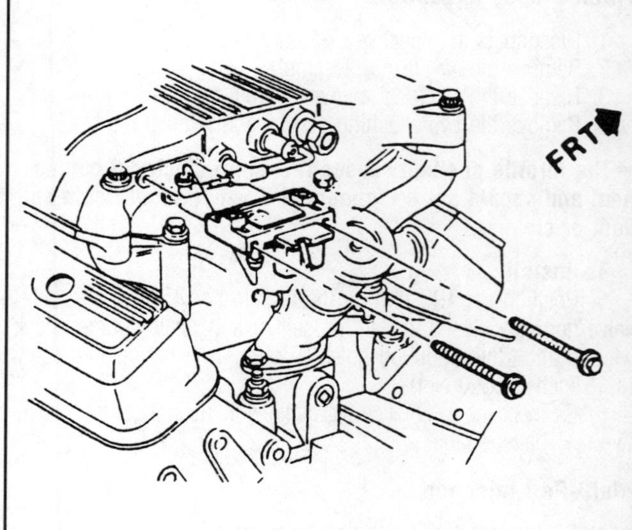

Fig. 20 Exploded view of the Manifold Absolute Pressure (MAP) sensor mounting—2.8L engine shown

Remove the bolt securing the Manifold Absolute Pressure (MAP) sensor

Disengage the MAP sensor vacuum line and electrical connection, then and remove it from the vehicle

Electronic Control Module (ECM)

The ECM is the control center for the fuel injector system. It consists of three integral systems, a separate controller (ECM without the PROM), a separate calibrator (PROM) and a calpak. To allow one model of ECM to be used for many different vehicles, a device called the calibrator or Programmable Read Only Memory (PROM) is used. The PROM is located in the ECM and is very specific to the vehicle and can not be interchanged with other models as the ECM can. The CALPAK is a device used to allow fuel delivery if certain parts of the ECM should fail. The PROM and CALPAK can be removed and replaced as individual components in the ECM.

The ECM assembly is located under the rear console assembly. The console has to removed to remove the ECM assembly. The ECM diagnostic hock-up (ALDL) is also in the console assembly. To get to the Assembly Line Diagnostic Link (ALDL), lift open the ALDL door in the console.

REMOVAL & INSTALLATION

➧ See Figure 21

⁂ CAUTION

To prevent internal ECM damage, always disconnect the negative (−) battery cable before disconnecting or reconnecting the ECM fuse, jumper cables and any other related service.

1. Disconnect the negative (−) battery cable.
2. Remove the rear console as follows:
   a. Remove the shifter trim panel and move out of the way.
   b. Open the ECM access door and remove the four rear pad attaching screws.
   c. Remove the cigar lighter and rear console assembly.

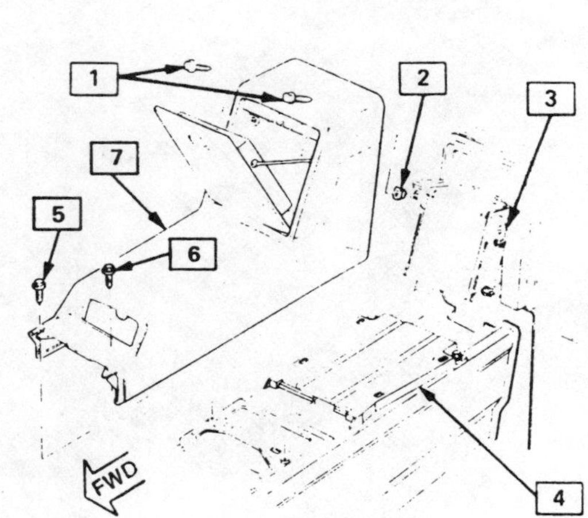

1. 1.6 N·m (14 lbs. in.); install first
2. Nut
3. ECM bracket
4. Support assembly
5. 1.6 N·m (14 lbs. in.); install second
6. 1.6 N·m (14 lbs. in.); install last
7. Rear console pad

Fig. 21 The rear console assembly must be removed to gain access to the Electronic Control Module (ECM)

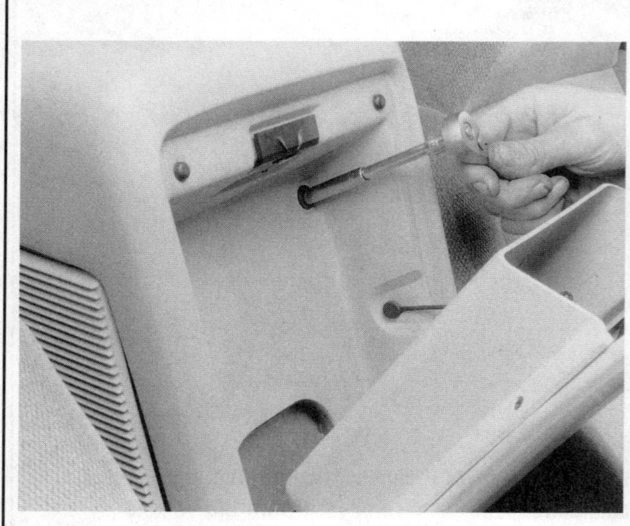

Unfasten the rear console retainers . . .

. . . then remove the panel to gain access to the Electronic Control Module (ECM)

3. Remove the ECM from the bracket.
4. Remove the ECM electrical connectors. Be careful not damage the ECM terminals.

To install:

1. Connect the ECM electrical connectors and install the ECM attaching screws. Torque the screws to 14 inch.lb. (1.6 Nm).
2. Install the rear console assembly and cigar lighter.
3. Install the shifter trim panel.
4. Reconnect the negative (−) battery cable and start the engine to check for proper operation.

PROM and CALPAK

REMOVAL & INSTALLATION

➧ See Figure 22

CAUTION

To prevent internal ECM damage, always disconnect the negative (−) battery cable before disconnecting or reconnecting the ECM fuse, jumper cables and any other related service.

1. Disconnect the negative (−) battery cable.
2. Remove the rear console as follows:
   a. Remove the shifter trim panel and move out of the way.
   b. Open the ECM access door and remove the four rear pad attaching screws.
   c. Remove the cigar lighter and rear console assembly.
3. Remove the ECM from the bracket.
4. Remove the ECM electrical connectors. Be careful not damage the ECM terminals.
5. Remove the ECM from the vehicle.
6. Remove the access cover from the ECM.
7. Remove the PROM or CALPAK by using a rocker type PROM removing tool. Engage one end of the carrier with the hooked end of the tool. Press on the vertical bar end of the tool and rock the engaged end of the PROM carrier up as far as possible. Engage the opposite end of the carrier in the same manner and rock this end up as far as possible. Repeat until the PROM is free. Remove the CALPAK in the same manner. Refer to the following illustration for help.

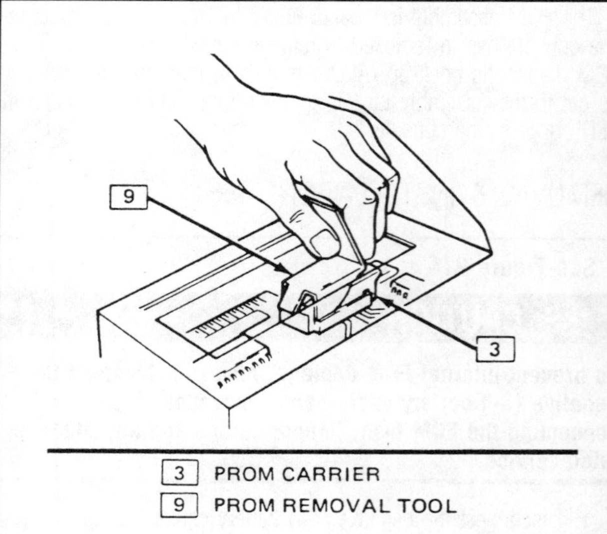

Fig. 22 Remove the PROM from the ECM using the proper removal tool

➡**Before installing a new PROM or CALPAK, check for the same part numbers as the old one. Make sure the PROM is replaced in the PROM carrier/socket and the CALPAK into the CALPAK carrier/socket.**

To install:

1. Install the PROM or CALPAK into their respective locations using the PROM removal tool. Align the small notch of the carrier to the small notch in the socket. Press on the PROM carrier until it is firmly seated in the socket. Do NOT press on the PROM, only the carrier.
2. Install the access cover.
3. Connect the ECM electrical connectors and install the unit into the console bracket. Torque the screws to 14 inch.lb. (1.6 Nm).
4. Install the rear console pad, cigar lighter and shifter trim panel.
5. Reconnect the negative (–) battery cable.
6. Start the engine and check for proper operation.

Fuel Pump/Oil Pressure Switch

REMOVAL & INSTALLATION

4-2.5L Engine

➧ **See Figures 23 and 24**

The oil pressure switch is mounted on the bulkhead side of the engine below the intake manifold. The switch is wired in parallel with the Fuel Pump Relay. If the fuel pump relay should fail, the oil pressure switch takes over after 4 psi (28 kPa) of oil pressure is reached.

The fuel pump relay is mounted in the engine compartment, in front of the air cleaner. The mounting bracket has two identical relays mounted to it. The relay on the left hand side is the air conditioning relay and the relay on the right is the fuel pump relay.

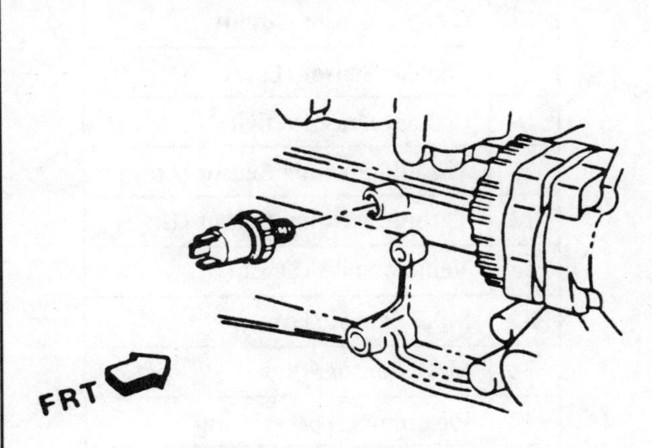

Fig. 23 The oil pressure switch is located on the bulkhead side of the engine just below the intake manifold

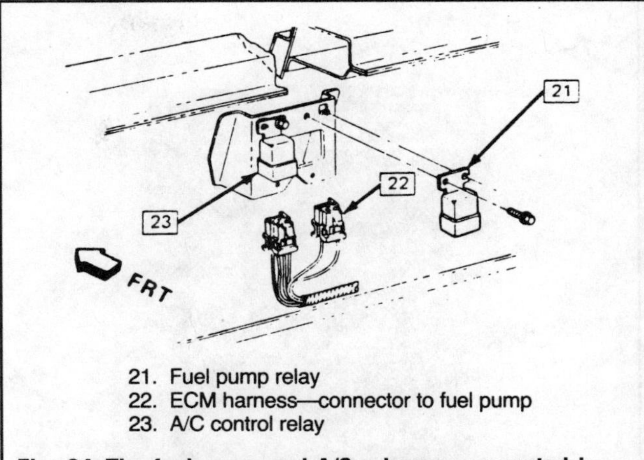

21. Fuel pump relay
22. ECM harness—connector to fuel pump
23. A/C control relay

Fig. 24 The fuel pump and A/C relays are mounted in the engine compartment, just forward of the air cleaner assembly

Check Engine Light

The "Check Engine" or "Service Engine Soon" light on the instrument panel is used as a warning lamp to tell the driver that a problem has occured in the electronic engine control system. When the self-diagnosis mode is activated by grounding the test terminal of the diagnostic connector, the check engine light will flash stored trouble codes to help isolate system problems. The Electronic Control Module (ECM) has a memory that knows what certain engine sensors should be, under certain conditions. If a sensor reading is not what the ECM thinks it should be, the control unit will illuminate the check engine light and store a trouble code in its memory. The trouble code indicates what circuit the problem is in, each circuit consisting of a sensor, the wiring harness and connectors to it and the ECM.

The Assembly Line Diagnostic Link (ALDL) is a diagnostic connector located in the passenger compartment console. It has terminals which are used in the assembly plant to check that the engine is operating properly before shipment. Terminal B is the diagnostic test terminal and Terminal A is the ground. By connecting the two terminals together with a jumper wire, the diagnostic mode is activated and the control unit will begin to flash trouble codes using the check engine light.

When the test terminal is grounded with the key **ON** and the engine stopped, the ECM will display code 12 to show that the system is working. The ECM will usually display code 12 three times, then start to display any stored trouble codes. If no trouble codes are stored, the ECM will continue to display code 12 until the test terminal is disconnected. Each trouble code will be flashed three times, then code 12 will display again. The ECM will also energize all controlled relays and solenoids when in the diagnostic mode to check function.

When the test terminal is grounded with the engine running, it will cause the ECM to enter the Field Service Mode. In this mode, the service engine soon light will indicate whether the system is in Open or Closed Loop operation. In open loop, the light will flash 2½ times per second; in closed loop, the light will stay out most of the time if the system is too lean and will stay on most of the time if the system is too rich.

A scan tool combines many standard testers into a single tool for quick and accurate diagnosis

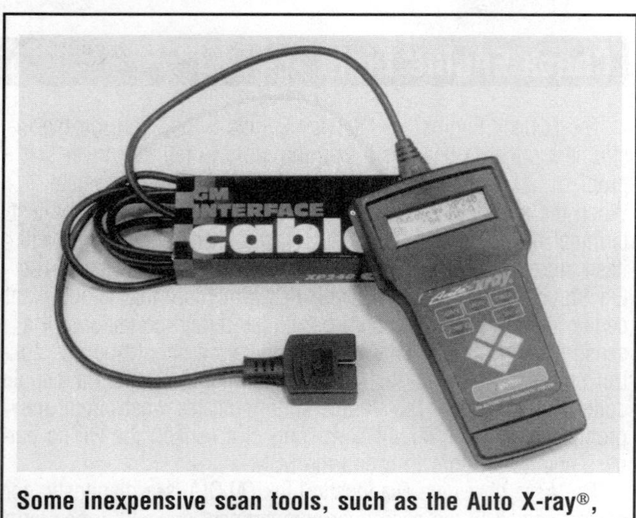

Some inexpensive scan tools, such as the Auto X-ray®, can interface with GM vehicles

➡The vehicle may be driven in the Field Service mode and system evaluated at any steady road speed. This mode is useful in diagnosing driveability problems where the system is rich or lean too long.

Trouble codes should be cleared after service is completed. To clear the trouble code memory, disconnect the battery for at least 10 seconds. This may be accomplished by disconnecting the ECM harness from the positive battery pigtail or by removing the ECM fuse.

✲✲ CAUTION

The ignition switch must be OFF when disconnecting or reconnecting power to the ECM. The vehicle should be driven after the ECM memory is cleared to allow the system to readjust itself. The vehicle should be driven at part throttle under moderate acceleration with the engine at normal operating temperature. A change in performance should be noted initially, but normal performance should return quickly.

GM Port Injection Trouble Codes

Trouble Code	Circuit
12	Normal operation
13	Oxygen sensor
14	Coolant sensor (low voltage)
15	Coolant sensor (high voltage)
21	Throttle position sensor (high voltage)
22	Throttle position sensor (low voltage)
24	Speed sensor
32	FGR vacuum control
33	Mass air flow sensor
34	Mass air flow sensor
42	Electronic spark timing
43	Electronic spark control
44	Lean exhaust
45	Rich exhaust
51	PROM failure
52	CALPAK
55	ECM failure

GM TBI TROUBLE CODES

DTC	DESCRIPTION
13	Oxygen Sensor Circuit
14	Coolant Sensor (Low)
15	Coolant Sensor (High)
21	Throttle Position Sensor (Low)
22	Throttle Position Sensor (High)
24	Vehicle Speed Sensor
33	MAP Sensor (Low)
34	MAP Sensor (High)
42	Electronic Spark Timing
44	Lean Exhaust Indication
45	Rich Exhaust Indication
51	PROM
55	ECM

VACUUM DIAGRAMS

Following are vacuum diagrams for most of the engine and emissions package combinations covered by this manual. Because vacuum circuits will vary based on various engine and vehicle options, always refer first to the vehicle emission control information label, if present. Should the label be missing, or should vehicle be equipped with a different engine from the vehicle's original equipment, refer to the diagrams below for the same or similar configuration.

If you wish to obtain a replacement emissions label, most manufacturers make the labels available for purchase. The labels can usually be ordered from a local dealer.

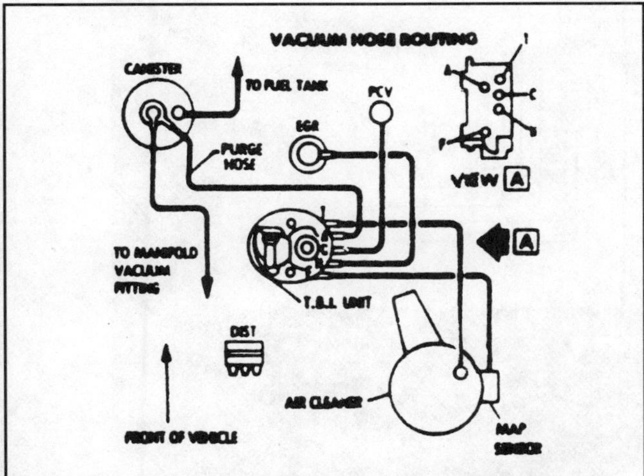

Fig. 25 Engine vacuum schematic—1984–86 2.5L engine (Federal and California)

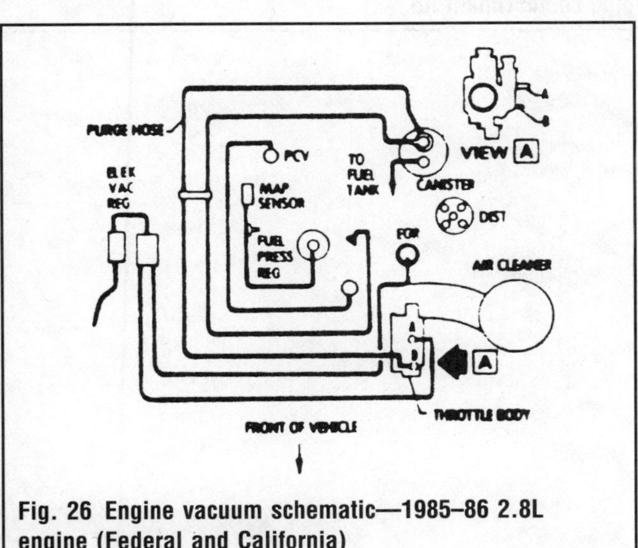

Fig. 26 Engine vacuum schematic—1985–86 2.8L engine (Federal and California)

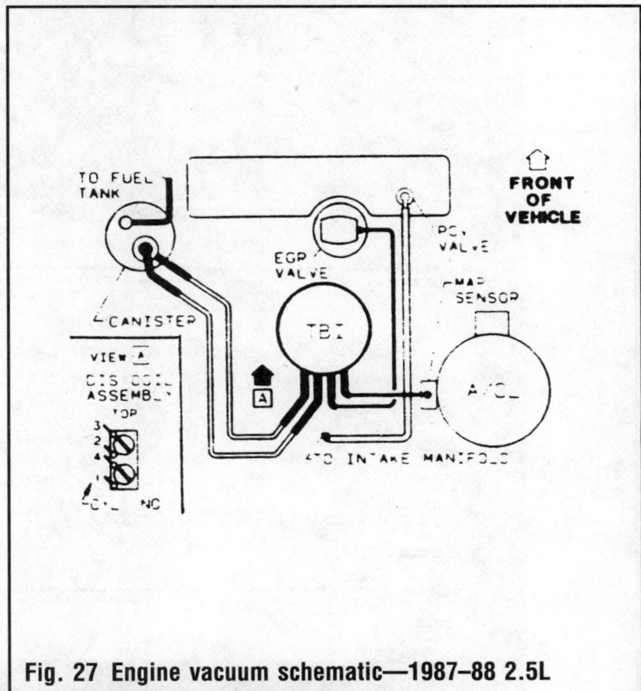

Fig. 27 Engine vacuum schematic—1987–88 2.5L engine (Federal and California)

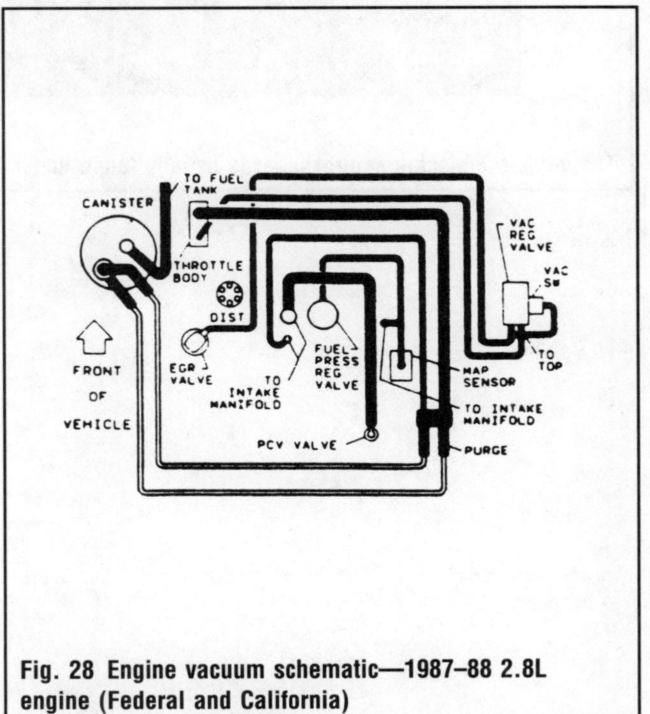

Fig. 28 Engine vacuum schematic—1987–88 2.8L engine (Federal and California)

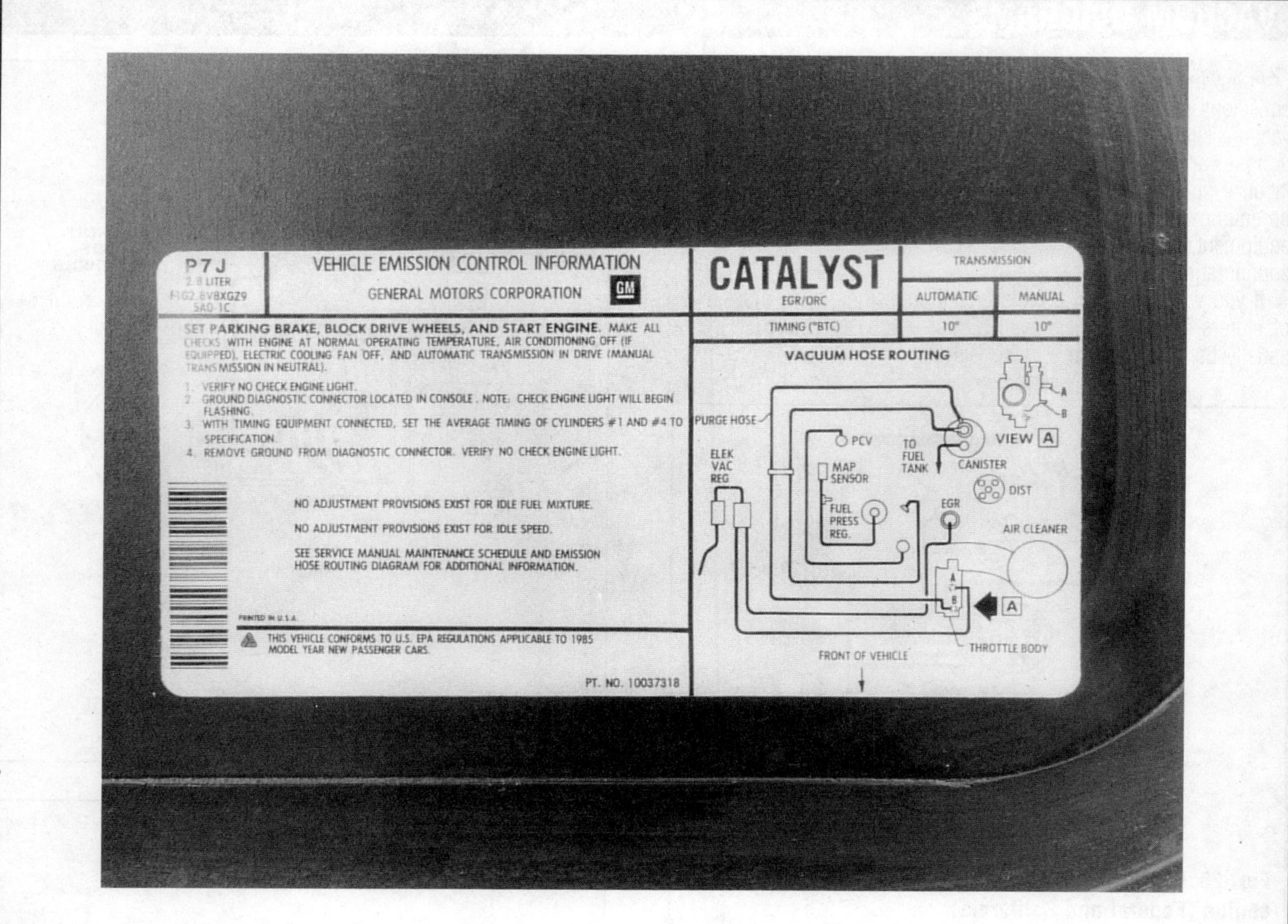

The vehicle emission control label is usually found under the engine compartment lid

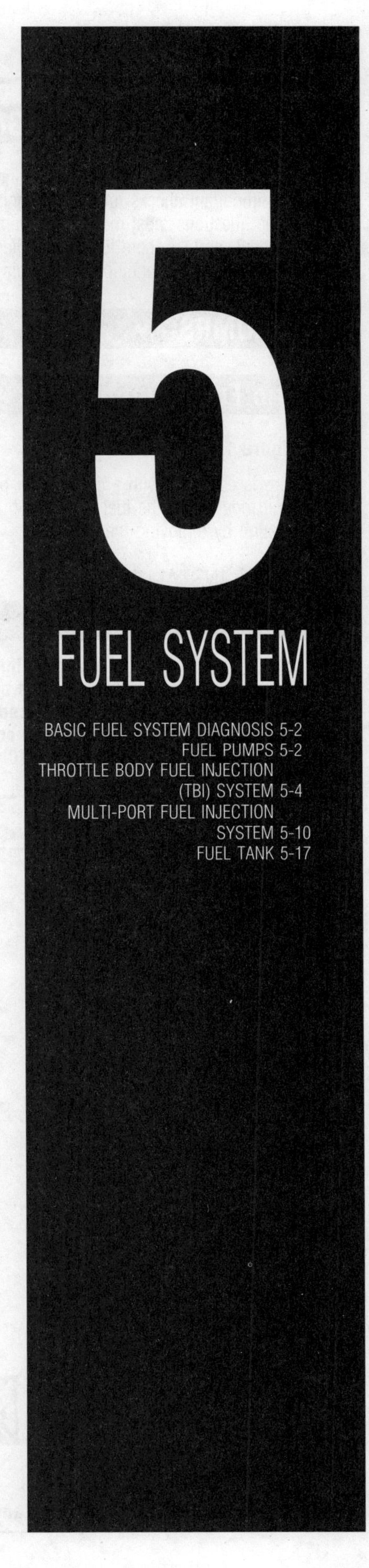

5 FUEL SYSTEM

BASIC FUEL SYSTEM DIAGNOSIS

When there is a problem starting or driving a vehicle, two of the most important checks involve the ignition and the fuel systems. The questions most mechanics attempt to answer first, "is there spark?" and "is there fuel?" will often lead to solving most basic problems. For ignition system diagnosis and testing, please refer to the information on engine electrical components and ignition systems found earlier in this manual. If the ignition system checks out (there is spark), then you must determine if the fuel system is operating properly (is there fuel?).

FUEL PUMPS

Electric Fuel Pump

See Figure 1

The Fiero is equipped with a electric fuel pump and gauge sending unit mounted in the fuel tank. The pump is serviced and a complete unit by removing the fuel tank.

REMOVAL & INSTALLATION

CAUTION

To reduce the risk of fire and personal injury, it is necessary to relieve the fuel system pressure before servicing any fuel system component. If this procedure is not performed, fuel may be sprayed out of the connection under pressure. Always keep a dry chemical (Class B) fire extinguisher near the work area.

1. Disconnect the negative (−) battery cable.
2. Relieve the fuel system pressure.

Remove the fuel pump fuse from the fuse block located in the passenger compartment. Start the engine and run until the engine stops due to the lack of fuel. Crank the engine for 3 seconds to ensure all pressure is relieved.

3. Drain all the fuel from the tank using a suction pump.
4. Raise the vehicle and support with jackstands.
5. Disconnect the wiring from the tank.
6. Remove the ground wire retaining screw from under the body.
7. Disconnect all hoses and filler neck from the tank.
8. Support the tank on a jack and remove the retaining strap nuts.
9. Lower the tank enough to disconnect the fuel sending unit wires.
10. Disconnect the fuel line, vapor line and return line.
11. Remove the tank from the vehicle.

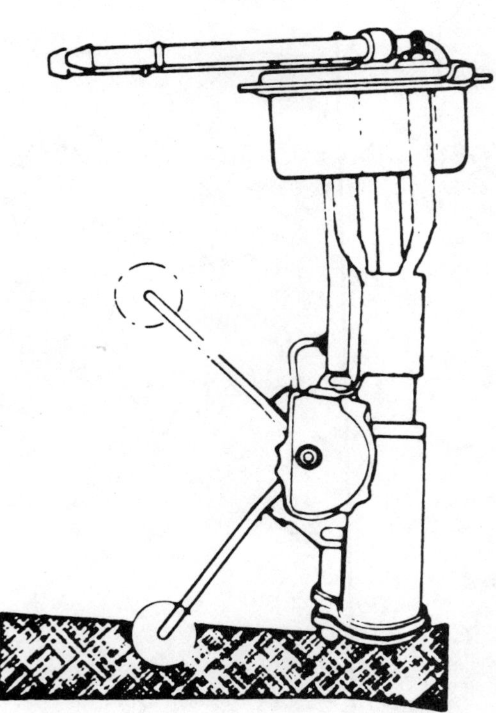

Fig. 1 View of the electric fuel pump and sending unit assembly used on Fiero models

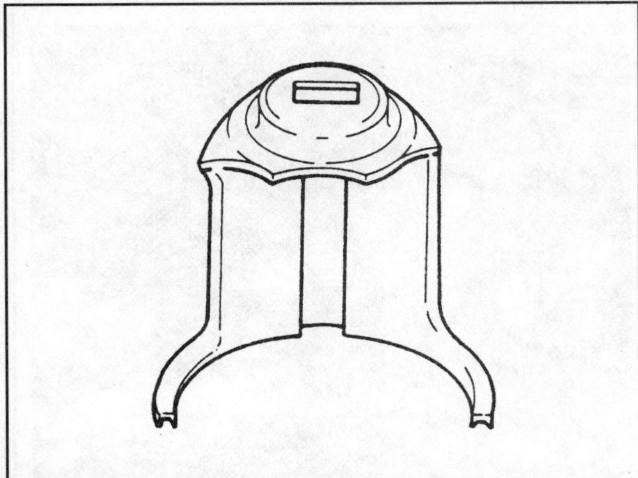
A special tool is usually available to remove or install the fuel pump locking cam

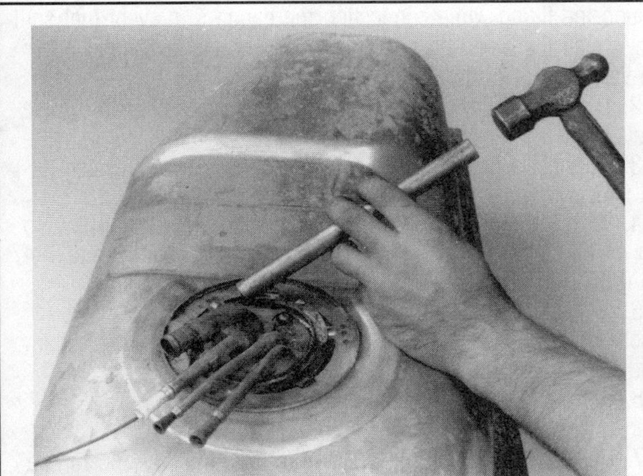
A brass drift and a hammer can be used to loosen the fuel pump locking cam

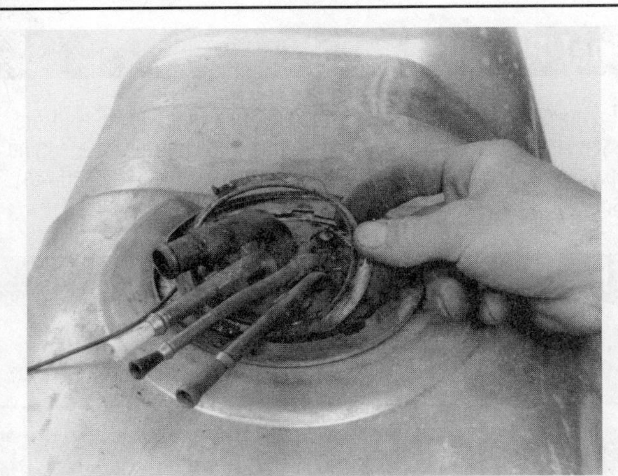
Once the locking cam is released it can be removed to free the fuel pump

12. Remove the fuel gauge/pump retaining ring by turning the cam lock ring counterclockwise using a spanner wrench such as tool J-24187.
13. Remove the gauge unit and the pump.

To install:

1. Inspect the fuel pump attaching hose for any signs of deterioration and replace if necessary. Also, check the rubber sound insulator at the bottom of the pump.
2. Push the fuel pump assembly into the attaching hose.
3. Using a new O-ring seal, install the pump assembly into the tank.
4. Install the cam lock ring over the pump and lock by turning clockwise with a spanner wrench J-24187 or equivalent.
5. Support the tank on a suitable jack.
6. Raise the tank enough to connect all fuel and filler hoses.
7. Connect all electrical wires to the pump and tank.
8. Raise the tank and install the retaining strap nuts. Use new sound reducing pad if they are damaged. Check all connections and wire to ensure proper installation before refilling the tank.
9. Refill the tank with unleaded fuel. Reconnect the negative (−) battery cable.
10. Start the engine and check for fuel leaks and gauge operation.

TESTING

2.5L Engine

PRESSURE TEST

✻✻ CAUTION

To reduce the risk of fire and personal injury, it is necessary to relieve the fuel system pressure before servicing any fuel system component. If this procedure is not performed, fuel may be sprayed out of the connection under pressure. Always keep a dry chemical (Class B) fire extinguisher near the work area.

1. Remove the fuel pump fuse from the fuse block located in the passenger compartment. Start the engine and run until the engine stops due to the lack of fuel. Crank the engine for 3 seconds to ensure all pressure is relieved.
2. Remove the air cleaner and plug the thermal vacuum port on the throttle body unit.
3. Remove the steel fuel pipe between the throttle body unit and the fuel filter using a flare nut wrench.
4. Install a fuel pressure gauge No. J-29658 or equivalent between the throttle body and fuel filter.
5. Start the vehicle and observe the reading. The pressure should be at least 9–13 psi. If not check for crimped lines or disconnected electrical connectors.
6. Relieve the fuel pressure and disconnect the pressure gauge.
7. Reinstall the steel fuel pipe to the throttle body and torque to 19–25 ft. lbs. (26–34 Nm).
8. Install the air cleaner assembly and start the engine and check for fuel leaks.

VOLUME TEST

CAUTION

To reduce the risk of fire and personal injury, it is necessary to relieve the fuel system pressure before servicing any fuel system component. If this procedure is not performed, fuel may be sprayed out of the connection under pressure. Always keep a dry chemical (Class B) fire extinguisher near the work area.

1. Remove the fuel pump fuse from the fuse block located in the passenger compartment. Start the engine and run until the engine stops due to the lack of fuel. Crank the engine for 3 seconds to ensure all pressure is relieved.
2. Disconnect the steel fuel pipe from the fuel filter to throttle body.
3. Connect a hose from the steel filter inlet pipe into a suitable fuel resistant unbreakable container.
4. Turn the ignition key to the **ON** position. The pump should supply ½ pint or more in 15 seconds. If the volume is minimum, check for fuel restrictions. If there is no restriction found, check pump pressure as outlined in the "Pressure Test" procedures.

2.8L Engine

PRESSURE TEST

CAUTION

To reduce the risk of fire and personal injury, it is necessary to relieve the fuel system pressure before servicing any fuel system component. If this procedure is not performed, fuel may be sprayed out of the connection under pressure. Always keep a dry chemical (Class B) fire extinguisher near the work area.

1. Connect a fuel gauge part No. J 34730-1 or equivalent to the fuel pressure valve on the fuel rail assembly. Wrap a towel around the fitting while connecting the gauge to prevent fuel spillage. Install the bleed hose into an approved container and open the valve to bleed the system pressure.

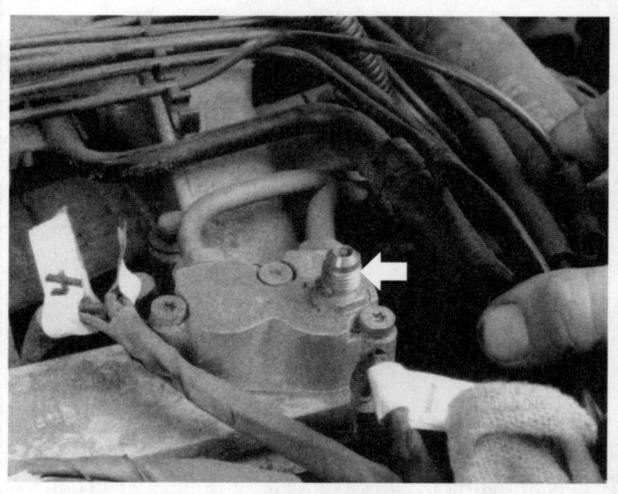

Location of the fuel system pressure test/relief valve

2. Disconnect the steel fuel pipe from the fuel filter to throttle body.
3. Connect a fuel pressure gauge J-34730-1 or equivalent to the filter inlet pipe.
4. With the ignition key in the **ON** position, the pump should run for about 2 seconds and the fuel pressure should be 40.5–47 psi (280–325 kPa).
5. If pressure is low or zero, check for a restriction or blocked fuel line. Also check for pressure regulator and the pump relay.
6. Relieve the fuel pressure and disconnect the pressure gauge.
7. Reinstall the steel fuel pipe to the throttle body and torque to 19–25 ft. lbs. (26–34 Nm).

THROTTLE BODY FUEL INJECTION (TBI) SYSTEM

General Information

The Throttle Body Injection system used by the 4-cylinder Fiero uses an electric fuel pump. The throttle body is placed on the intake manifold where the carburetor is normally mounted. The TBI unit is computer controlled and supplies the correct amount of fuel during all engine operating conditions.

The unit is made primarily of aluminum and consist of two major casting assemblies, a throttle body and fuel metering assembly.

With the TBI system, air is drawn into a single bore. The fuel is then injected into the air stream under pressure. The unit contains a pressure regulator Idle Air Control (IAC) valve, and an electrically operated solenoid that activates the fuel injector. Also attached to the TBI is a Throttle Position Sensor (TPS), a fuel inlet and a fuel return fitting.

Fuel Pressure Relief

Remove the fuel pump fuse from the fuse block located in the passenger compartment. Start the engine and run until the engine stops due to the lack of fuel. Crank the engine for 3 seconds to ensure all pressure is relieved.

Throttle Body Unit

REMOVAL & INSTALLATION

CAUTION

To reduce the risk of fire and personal injury, it is necessary to relieve the fuel system pressure before servicing any fuel system component. If this procedure is not performed, fuel may be sprayed out of the connection under

pressure. Always keep a dry chemical (Class B) fire extinguisher near the work area.

1. Relieve the fuel pressure.
2. Remove the thermac hose from the engine fitting and air cleaner.
3. Disconnect the electrical connectors to the Idle Air Control (IAC), Throttle Position Sensor (TPS) and injector.
4. Remove the throttle linkage, return spring and cruise control linkage if so equipped.
5. Disconnect the vacuum hoses from the throttle body. (Mark the hose routing for proper connection during installation.
6. Disconnect the fuel supply and return steel lines from the throttle body using a flare nut and backup wrench.
7. Remove the three bolts securing the throttle body-to-engine. Remove the throttle body assembly from the engine.

To install:

8. Clean the throttle body and intake manifold sealing surfaces with solvent and a gasket scraper.
9. Install the throttle body with a new gasket onto the manifold and torque the two or three bolts to 13 ft. lbs. (17 Nm).
10. Inspect the O-ring seals for the inlet and return lines and replace if damaged. Install the fuel lines using a flare nut and backup wrench. Torque the lines to 17 ft. lbs. (23 Nm).
11. Install the throttle return spring, throttle linkage and cruise control linkage if so equipped.
12. Reconnect the electrical connectors to the throttle position sensor, idle air control motor and injector.
13. Install the air cleaner, start the engine and check for fuel leaks.

OVERHAUL

➧ See Figures 2 and 3

➡The procedures that follow apply to complete disassembly, cleaning and reassembly of the TBI assembly removed from the engine. In many cases, service repair of individual components may be completed without removing the entire unit from the engine. Refer to the "Model 300 and 700 Throttle Body Injection" parts breakdown illustrations in this section for disassembly and reassembly.

1. Release the fuel pressure and remove the throttle body assembly. Refer to the "Throttle Body Unit" removal procedures in this section.
2. Remove the five fuel meter cover screws and lockwashers while holding the cover on the fuel meter body.
3. Lift the fuel meter cover including the fuel pressure regulator assembly off the throttle body.
4. Discard the fuel outlet passage gasket only. Leave the fuel meter cover gasket on the fuel meter body.

✱✱ CAUTION

Do not remove the four screws securing the fuel pressure regulator assembly to the fuel meter cover. The regulator cover contains a large spring under heavy tension which, if accidentally released, could cause personal injury. The assembly is serviced as a complete unit. Do not immerse the fuel meter cover in any type of industrial cleaner because damage to the pressure regulator may result.

5. Remove the sealing ring for the base of the fuel pressure regulator.
6. Clean the parts with carburetor cleaner or equivalent.

ASSEMBLY

1. Install a new dust seal for the fuel pressure regulator into the recess on the fuel meter body.
2. Install a new fuel return passage gasket on the fuel meter cover.
3. Install a new fuel meter gasket on the fuel meter body.
4. Install the fuel meter cover making sure the pressure regulator dust seal and cover gaskets are in place. Apply thread locking compound to the threads of the five fuel meter cover attaching screws. The two short screws go next to the fuel injector. Torque the five cover attaching screws to 28 inch.lb. (3.0 Nm).
5. Install the throttle body assembly as outlined in the "Throttle Body Unit" installation.

Fuel Injector

REMOVAL & INSTALLATION

Model 300 Throttle Body

1984–86 MODELS

➧ See Figures 4 and 5

✱✱ CAUTION

To reduce the risk of fire and personal injury, it is necessary to relieve the fuel system pressure before servicing any fuel system component. If this procedure is not performed, fuel may be sprayed out of the connection under pressure. Always keep a dry chemical (Class B) fire extinguisher near the work area.

1. Relieve the fuel system pressure.
2. Disconnect the negative (−) battery cable.
3. Remove the air cleaner assembly.

➡The throttle body assembly does not have to be removed from the engine to replace the fuel injector. Use care when removing the injector to prevent damage to the electrical connector pins on the top of the injector.

4. Remove the injector electrical connector by squeezing the two tabs together and pulling straight up.
5. Remove the five fuel meter cover attaching screws and remove the cover by gently pulling upward.
6. With the fuel meter cover gasket in place to prevent damage to the casting. Use a screwdriver to lift the injector carefully until it is free from the fuel meter body. Check the illustration for screwdriver placement.
7. Remove the large O-ring and steel back-up washer at the top of the injector cavity in the fuel meter body and the small O-ring at the bottom of the cavity.

To install:

8. Lubricate the new small O-ring with Automatic Transmis-

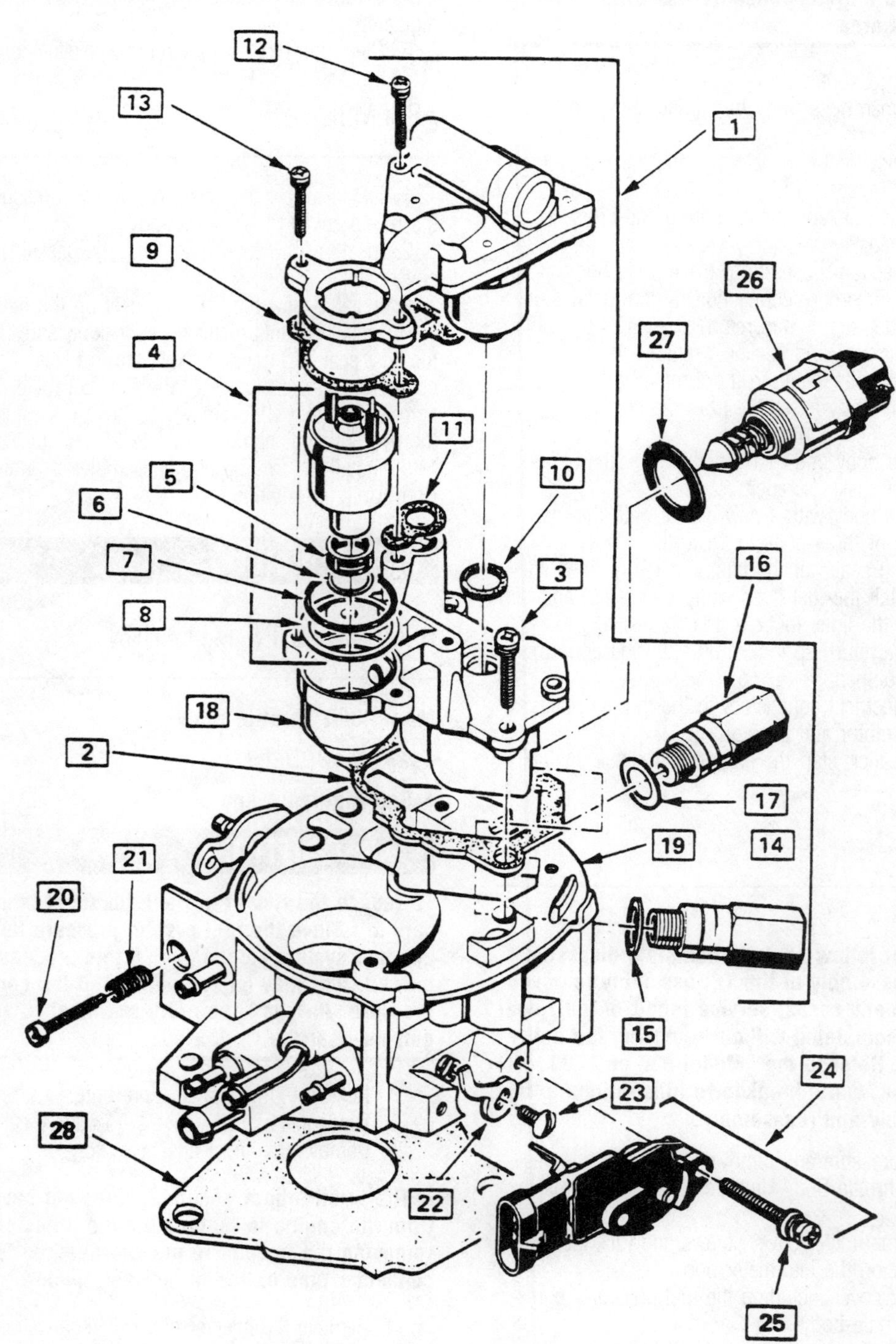

1. Fuel meter assembly
2. Gasket—fuel meter body
3. Screw & washer assy—attach. (3)
4. Fuel injector kit
5. Filter—fuel injector nozzle
6. Seal—small "O" ring
7. Seal—large "O" ring
8. Back-up washer—fuel injector
9. Gasket—fuel meter cover
10. Dust seal—press, regulator
11. Gasket—fuel meter outlet
12. Screw & washer assy—long (3)
13. Screw & washer assy—short (2)
14. Nut—fuel inlet
15. Gasket—fuel inlet nut
16. Nut—fuel outlet
17. Gasket—fuel outlet nut
18. Fuel meter body assembly
19. Throttle body assembly
20. Screw—idle stop
21. Spring—idle stop screw
22. Lever—TPS
23. Screw—TPS lever attaching
24. Sensor—throttle position kit
25. Screw—TPS attaching (2)
26. Idle air control assy.
27. Gasket—control assy. to T.B.
28. Gasket—flange mountina

Fig. 2 Exploded view of the model 300 throttle body assembly—1984–86 2.5L engine

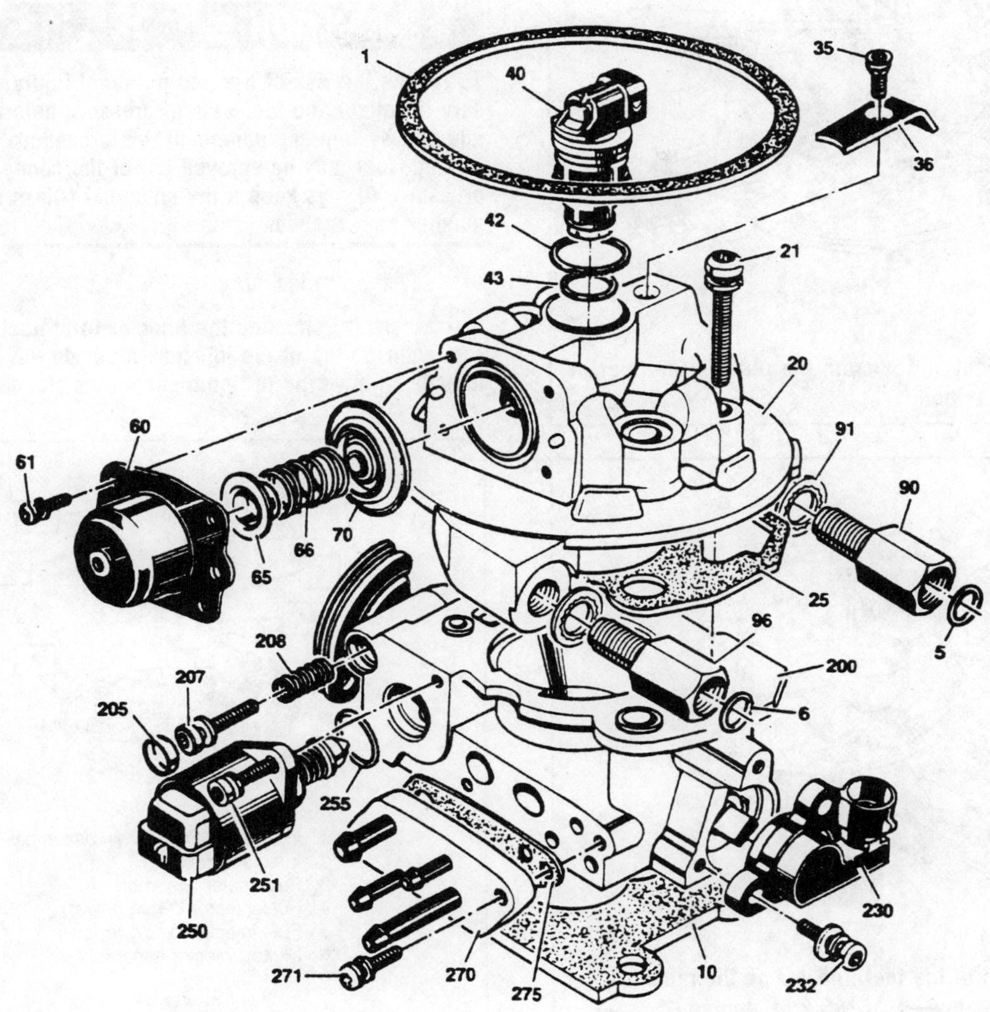

1. Gasket—air filter cleaner
5. O-ring—fuel line inlet nut
6. O-ring—fuel line outlet nut
10. Gasket—flange
20. Fuel meter assembly
21. Screw & washer assembly—fuel meter body attaching
25. Gasket—fuel meter body to throttle body
35. Screw—injector retainer
36. Retainer-injector
40. Fuel injector
42. O-ring—fuel injector—upper
43. O-ring—fuel injector—lower
60. Pressure regulator cover assembly
61. Screw—pressure regulator attaching
65. Seat—spring
66. Spring—pressure regulator
70. Pressure regulator diaphragm assembly
90. Nut—fuel inlet
91. Seal—fuel nut
96. Nut—fuel outlet
200. Throttle body assembly
205. Plug—idle stop screw
207. Screw & Washer Asembly—idle stop
208. Spring—idle stop screw
230. Sensor—throttle position (TPS)
232. Screw & washer assembly—TPS attaching
250. Idle air control (IAC) valve
251. Screw—IAC valve attaching
255. O-ring—IAC valve
270. Tube module assembly
271. Screw assembly—tube module assembly attaching
275. Gasket—tube module assembly

Fig. 3 Exploded view of the model 700 throttle body assembly—1987–88 2.5L engine

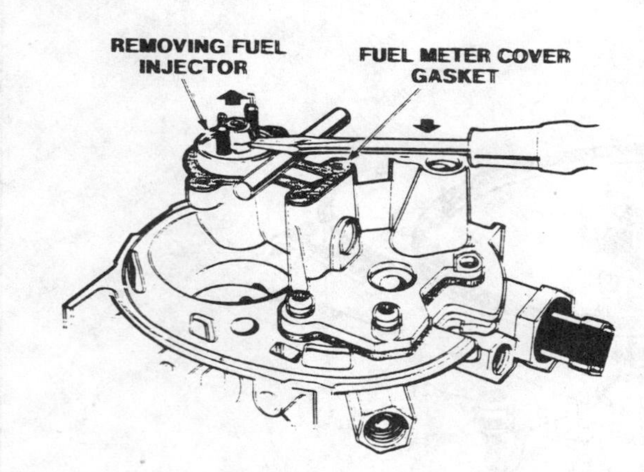

Fig. 4 Use a prytool and fulcrum the remove the injector from the fuel meter body

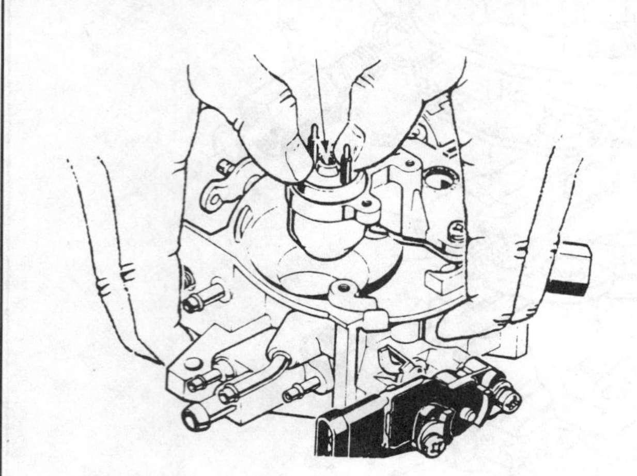

Fig. 5 Installation of the fuel injector on the model 300 throttle body assembly—1984–86 2.5L engine

sion Fluid (ATF). Push the O-ring on the nozzle end of the injector while pressing the ring up against the injector fuel filter.

9. Install the steel backup washer in the recess of the fuel meter body. Lubricate the large O-ring with ATF and install the O-ring directly above the backup washer, pressing the O-ring down into the cavity recess. The O-ring is located properly when it is flush with the fuel meter body casting surface.

➡Do not attempt to reverse this procedure and install the backup washer and O-ring after the injector is located in the cavity. This will prevent the O-ring from seating in the cavity recess.

9. Install the fuel meter cover making sure the pressure regulator dust seal and cover gaskets are in place. Apply thread locking compound to the threads of the five fuel meter cover attaching screws. The two short screws go next to the fuel injector. Torque the five cover attaching screws to 28 inch.lb. (3.0 Nm).

10. Install the injector electrical connector.

11. Reconnect the negative (−) battery cable and start the engine and check for fuel leaks. Install the air cleaner assembly.

Model 700 Throttle Body

1987–88 MODELS

➧ See Figures 6 and 7

✲✲ CAUTION

To reduce the risk of fire and personal injury, it is necessary to relieve the fuel system pressure before servicing any fuel system component. If this procedure is not performed, fuel may be sprayed out of the connection under pressure. Always keep a dry chemical (Class B) fire extinguisher near the work area.

1. Relieve the fuel pressure.

➡Use care in removing the injector to protect the electrical connector on top of the injector. Also, do not immerse the injector in any type of liquid solvent or cleaner.

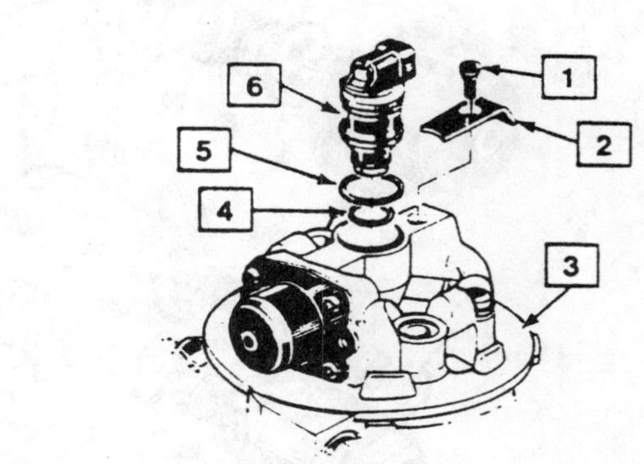

1. Injector retainer screw assembly
2. Injector retainer
3. Fuel meter assembly
4. Fuel injector O-ring (lower)
5. Fuel injector O-ring (upper)
6. Multec injector assembly

Fig. 6 Exploded view of the injector components on the model 700 throttle body assembly—1987–88 2.5L engine

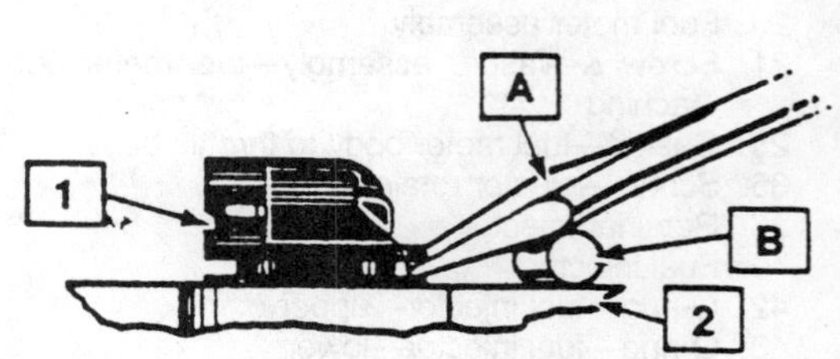

1. Fuel injector assembly
2. Fuel meter body
A. Screwdriver blade
B. Fulcrum

Fig. 7 Place the prytool and fulcrum as illustrated to remove the injector from the model 700 throttle body assembly—1987–88 2.5L engine

2. Disconnect the negative (−) battery cable.
3. Disconnect the electrical connector to the fuel injector.
4. Remove the injector screw and retainer.
5. Using a fulcrum, place a screwdriver blade under the ridge opposite the connector end and carefully pry the injector out of the cavity. Refer to the following illustrations.
6. Remove the upper and lower O-rings from the injector and cavity.
7. Inspect the injector and fuel lines for dirt and contamination. If excess contamination is present, the fuel system will have to be flushed.

➡Make sure the replacement injector is an identical part No. The injectors from other model 700 systems may fit, but are calibrated for different flow rates. Check the part No. on the side of the throttle body.

8. Lubricate the new upper and lower O-rings with Automatic Transmission Fluid (ATF) and place them on the injector. (Make sure the upper O-ring is in the groove and the lower one is flush against the filter.
9. Install the injector into the cavity by pushing straight into the fuel injector cavity.

➡Make sure the electrical connector end on the injector is facing in the general direction of the cut out in the fuel meter body for the wire grommet.

10. Install the injector retainer and coat the screw with thread locking compound. Torque the attaching screw to 27 inch.lb. (3.0 Nm).
11. Reconnect the injector electrical connector.
12. Reconnect the negative (−) battery cable.
13. With the engine NOT running, turn the ignition switch to the **ON** position and check for fuel leaks at the throttle body area.

Fuel Pressure Regulator

REMOVAL & INSTALLATION

Model 300 Throttle Body

1984–86 MODELS

➧ See Figure 8

⁂ CAUTION

To reduce the risk of fire and personal injury, it is necessary to relieve the fuel system pressure before servicing any fuel system component. If this procedure is not performed, fuel may be sprayed out of the connection under pressure. Always keep a dry chemical (Class B) fire extinguisher near the work area.

1. Relieve the fuel pressure.
2. Disconnect the negative (−) battery cable.
3. Remove the air cleaner assembly. Disconnect the electrical connector from the injector by squeezing the two tabs and pulling straight up.
4. Remove the five fuel meter cover screws and lockwashers while holding the cover on the fuel meter body.
5. Lift the fuel meter cover including the fuel pressure regulator assembly off the throttle body.

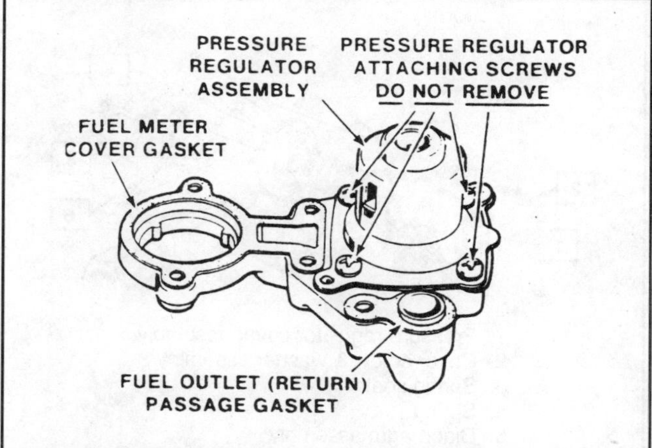

Fig. 8 Model 300 fuel pressure regulator components—1984–86 2.5L engine

6. Discard the fuel outlet passage gasket only. Leave the fuel meter cover gasket on the fuel meter body.

⁂ CAUTION

Do not remove the four screws securing the fuel pressure regulator assembly to the fuel meter cover. The regulator cover contains a large spring under heavy tension which, if accidentally released, could cause personal injury. The assembly is serviced as a complete unit. Do not immerse the fuel meter cover in any type of industrial cleaner because damage to the pressure regulator may result.

7. Remove the sealing ring for the base of the fuel pressure regulator.

To install:

8. Position the fuel meter cover to the fuel meter body with new gaskets and dust seals. Install the five fuel meter cover attaching screws and lock washers. Torque to 35 inch.lb. (4.0 Nm).
9. Install the injector electrical connector by pushing straight down until seated firmly in place.
10. Reconnect the negative (−) battery cable.
11. With the engine NOT running, turn the ignition switch to the **ON** position and check for fuel leaks at the injector area.
12. Install the air cleaner assembly.

Model 700 Throttle Body

1987–88 MODELS

➧ See Figure 9

⁂ CAUTION

To reduce the risk of fire and personal injury, it is necessary to relieve the fuel system pressure before servicing any fuel system component. If this procedure is not performed, fuel may be sprayed out of the connection under pressure. Always keep a dry chemical (Class B) fire extinguisher near the work area.

1. Relieve the fuel pressure.
2. Disconnect the negative (−) battery cable.

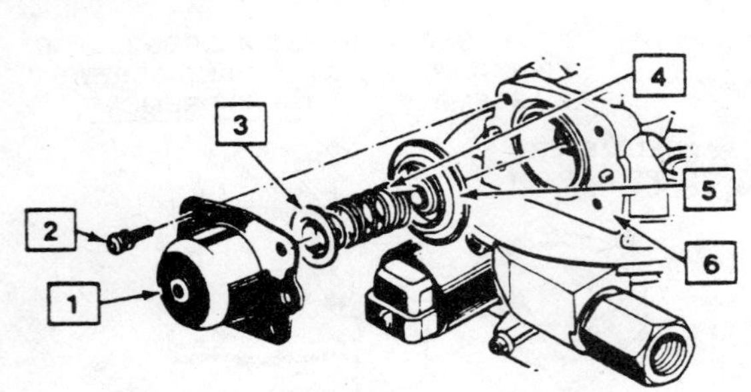

1. Pressure regulator cover assembly
2. Cover screw & washer assembly
3. Spring seat
4. Spring
5. Diaphragm assembly
6. Fuel meter assembly

Fig. 9 Exploded view of the model 700 fuel pressure regulator—1987–88 2.5L engine

CAUTION

The pressure regulator contains a large spring under heavy compression. Use care when removing the four screws to prevent personal injury.

3. Remove the pressure regulator cover assembly (4 screws).
4. Remove the regulator spring, spring seat and diaphragm assembly.

➡To prevent leaks, the pressure regulator diaphragm MUST be replaced when the cover is removed.

To install:

5. Position the new regulator diaphragm, spring, spring seat and cover on the throttle body assembly.
6. Coat the four attaching screws with thread locking compound. Install the four attaching screws and torque to 22 inch.lb. (2.5 Nm).
7. Connect the negative (−) battery cable.
8. With the engine OFF, turn the ignition switch to the **ON** position and check for fuel leaks at the injector.

MULTI-PORT FUEL INJECTION SYSTEM

General Information

On 1985 and later models, equipped with the V6 engine, a new Multi-Port Fuel Injection (MPFI) system is available. The MPFI system is controlled by an Electronic Control Module (ECM) which monitors engine operations and generates output signals to provide the correct air/fuel mixture, ignition timing and engine idle speed control. Input to the control unit is provided by an oxygen sensor, coolant temperature sensor, detonation sensor, hot film air mass sensor and throttle position sensor. The ECM also receives information concerning engine rpm, road speed, transmission gear position and air conditioning.

The main control sensor is the Oxygen (O_2) sensor, which is located in the exhaust manifold. The O_2 sensor tells the ECM how much oxygen is in the exhaust gas and the ECM changes the Air/Fuel mixture to the engine by controlling the fuel injectors. The best mixture for the engine to operate properly is a 14.7 to 1 ratio (air to fuel).

The ECM looks at the voltages from several sensors to determine how much fuel to give to each injector. The fuel is delivered under one of several conditions called "modes". All of the modes are controlled by the ECM. The modes consist of starting, clear flood, run, acceleration and deceleration.

The system uses Bosch injectors, one at each intake port, rather than the single injector found on the earlier throttle body system. The injectors are mounted on a fuel rail and are activated by a signal from the electronic control module. The injector is a solenoid-operated valve which remains open depending on the width of the electronic pulses (length of the signal) from the ECM; the longer the open time, the more fuel is injected. In this manner, the air/fuel mixture can be precisely controlled for maximum performance with minimum emissions.

Fuel is pumped from the tank by a high pressure fuel pump, located inside the fuel tank. It is a positive displacement roller vane pump. The impeller serves as a vapor separator and pre-charges the high pressure assembly. A pressure regulator maintains 28–36 psi in the fuel line to the injectors and the excess fuel is fed back to the tank. On MPFI systems, a fuel accumulator is used to dampen the hydraulic line hammer in the system created when all injectors open simultaneously.

The Mass Air Flow (MAF) Sensor is used to measure the mass of air that is drawn into the engine cylinders. It is located just ahead of the air throttle in the intake system and consists of a heated film which measures the mass of air, rather than just the volume. A resistor is used to measure the temperature of the incoming air and the air mass sensor maintains the temperature of the film at 75° above ambient temperature. As the ambient (outside) air temperature rises, more energy is required to maintain the heated film at the higher temperature and the control unit uses this difference in required energy to calculate the mass of the incoming air. The control unit uses this information to determine the duration of fuel injection pulse, timing and EGR.

The throttle body incorporates an Idle Air Control (IAC) that provides for a bypass channel through which air can flow. It consists of an orifice and pintle which is controlled by the ECM through a stopper motor. The IAC provides air flow for idle and allows additional air during cold start until the engine reaches operating temperature. As the engine temperature rises, the opening through which air passes is slowly closed.

The Throttle Position Sensor (TPS) provides the control unit with information on throttle position, in order to determine injector pulse width and hence correct mixture. The TPS is connected to the throttle shaft on the throttle body and consists of a potentiometer with one end connected to a 5 volt source from the ECM and the other to ground. A third wire is connected to the ECM to measure the voltage output from the TPS which changes as the throttle valve angle is changed (accelerator pedal moves). At the closed throttle position, the output is low (approximately .4 volts); as the throttle valve opens, the output increases to a maximum 5 volts at Wide Open Throttle (WOT). The TPS can be misadjusted open, shorted, or loose and, if it is out of adjustment, the idle quality or WOT performance may be poor. A loose TPS can cause intermittent bursts of fuel from the injectors and an unstable idle because the ECM thinks the throttle is moving. Once a trouble code is set, the ECM will use a preset value for TPS and some vehicle performance may return. A small amount of engine coolant is routed through the throttle assembly to prevent freezing inside the throttle bore during cold operation.

Fuel Pressure Relief

1. Connect fuel gauge tool #J-34730-1 or its equivalent to the fuel pressure valve on the fuel rail assembly.
2. Wrap a shop towel around the fuel fitting while connecting the gauge to prevent fuel spillage.
3. Install the bleed hose into an approved container and open the valve to bleed the system pressure.

Throttle Body Assembly

REMOVAL & INSTALLATION

➧ See Figure 10

1. Disconnect the negative (−) battery cable.
2. Remove the inlet air tube and clamp.
3. Disconnect the Throttle Position Sensor (TPS) and Idle Air Control (IAC) valve electrical connector.
4. Drain the engine coolant from the radiator.

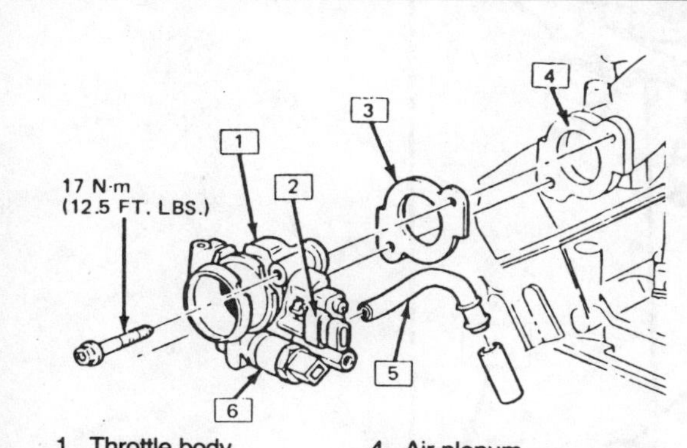

Fig. 10 Exploded view of the throttle body mounting on 2.8L engines

✲✲ CAUTION

When draining engine coolant, keep in mind that cats and dogs are attracted to ethylene glycol antifreeze and could drink any that is left in an uncovered container or in puddles on the ground. This will prove fatal in sufficient quantity. Always drain coolant into a sealable container. Coolant should be reused unless it is contaminated or is several years old.

5. Disconnect the engine coolant hoses from the throttle body assembly.
6. Remove the throttle and cruise control linkages, if so equipped.
7. Remove the two throttle body-to-air plenum bolts and remove the throttle body and gasket.

To install:

➡All throttle body parts can be cleaned in cold immersion type cleaner or equivalent, EXCEPT the Throttle Position Sensor (TPS), Idle Air Control valve (IAC). These components MUST be removed before throttle body is placed in the cleaner to prevent damage.

1. Clean all medal parts throughly and blow dry with shop air. Make sure all air passages are free of burrs and dirt.
2. Clean the throttle body and air plenum mating surfaces with a gasket scraper and solvent.
3. Install a new body-to-plenum gasket with the throttle body assembly.
4. Install the two retaining bolts and torque to 12.5 ft. lbs. (17 Nm).
5. Install the air duct and clamp, throttle linkage and coolant hoses.
6. Refill the radiator with engine coolant. Connect the negative (−) battery cable.
7. Start the engine and check for fuel and coolant leaks.

Air Plenum (Upper Intake)

REMOVAL & INSTALLATION

➧ See Figure 11

➡To remove must of the fuel injection components from the multi-port system, the air plenum must be removed first.

1. Disconnect the negative (−) battery cable.
2. Mark and remove the vacuum lines from the air plenum.
3. Remove the EGR valve and pipe.
4. Remove the throttle body linkages and throttle body bolts. Place the throttle body out of the way.
5. Remove the eight air plenum-to-intake manifold bolts. Discard the old gasket.

To install:

6. Clean the air plenum and intake manifold mating surfaces with a gasket scraper and solvent.
7. Install the air plenum assembly with a new gasket. Torque the eight air plenum-to-intake manifold attaching bolts to 18 ft. lbs. (25 Nm).
8. Install the throttle body with a new gasket. Torque the two throttle body-to-air plenum bolts to 12.5 ft. lbs. (17 Nm).
9. Install the EGR valve and pipe assembly.
10. Install the throttle linkage and vacuum lines to the throttle body. Reconnect the negative (−) battery cable. Start the engine and check for vacuum and fuel leaks.

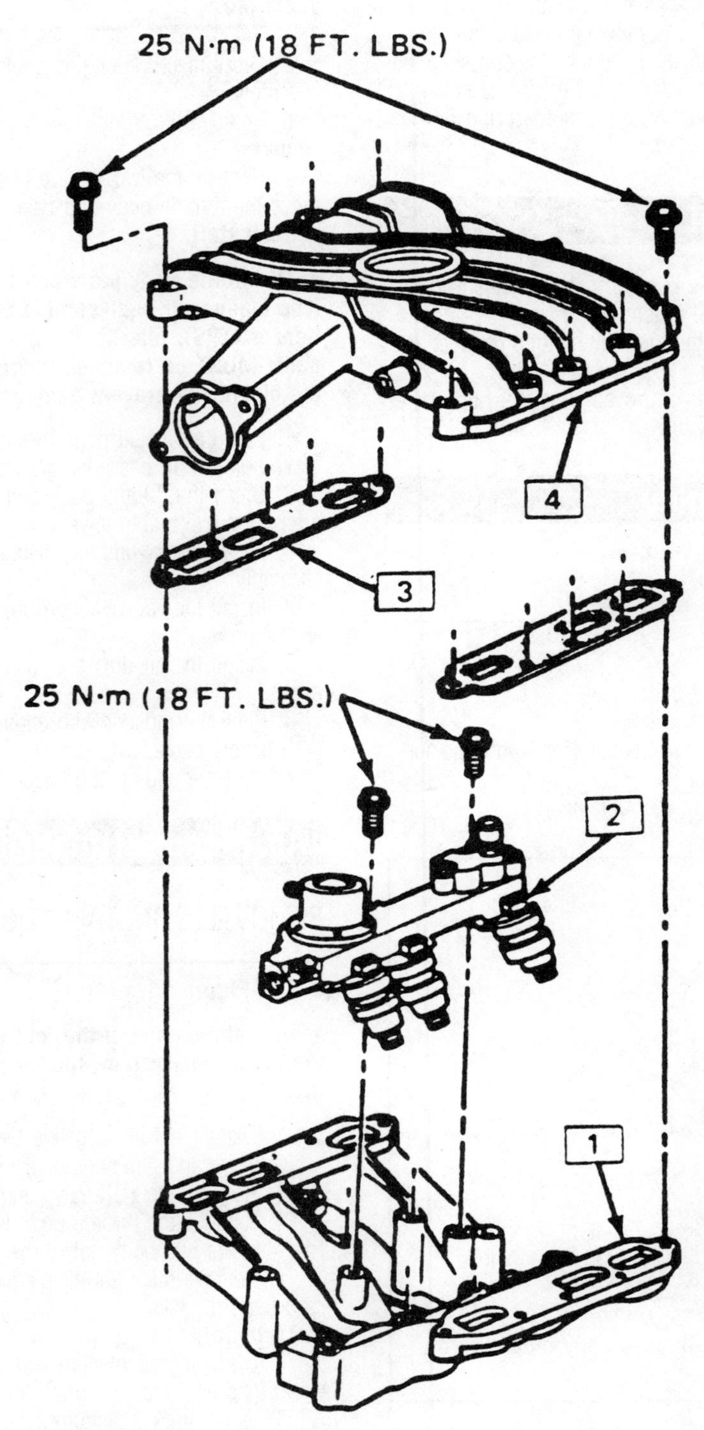

Fig. 11 View of the upper intake assembly and related components

Fuel Pressure Regulator

The pressure regulator assembly is a diaphragm operated relief valve with injector pressure on one side and manifold vacuum on the other. The regulator's function is to maintain constant pressure across the injectors at all times. The excess pressure is returned to the fuel tank through the fuel return line.

REMOVAL & INSTALLATION

1. Disconnect the negative (−) battery cable.
2. Relieve the fuel pressure as outlined below.

⁂ CAUTION

To reduce the risk of fire and personal injury, it is necessary to relieve the fuel system pressure before servicing any fuel system component. If this procedure is not performed, fuel may be sprayed out of the connection under pressure. Always keep a dry chemical (Class B) fire extinguisher near the work area.

Fuel pressure relief procedures: connect a fuel gauge part No. J 34730-1 or equivalent to the fuel pressure valve on the fuel rail assembly. Wrap a towel around the fitting while connecting the gauge to prevent fuel spillage. Install the bleed hose into an approved container and open the valve to bleed the system pressure.

3. Remove the six fuel pressure connection screws and remove the pressure regulator.
4. Discard the connection seal.

To install:

5. Clean the area around the fuel pressure connection with A/C Delco X-30A or equivalent.
6. Install a new seal on the fuel pressure connection. Install the pressure regulator and torque the six attaching screws to 88 inch.lb. (10.0 Nm).
7. Connect the negative (−) battery cable. Energize the fuel pump and check for fuel leaks.

Fuel Rail Assembly

REMOVAL & INSTALLATION

➧ See Figure 12

➡An eight digit identification number is stamped on the side of the fuel rail. Refer to this number when servicing or replacing system components. When servicing the fuel rail assembly, be careful to prevent dirt and contaminants from entering the fuel passages. Always cap or plug the fittings during servicing.

1. Relieve the fuel pressure.
2. Disconnect the negative (−) battery cable.
3. Remove the air duct and clamp.
4. Remove the air plenum assembly as outlined in the "Air Plenum" removal procedures in this section.

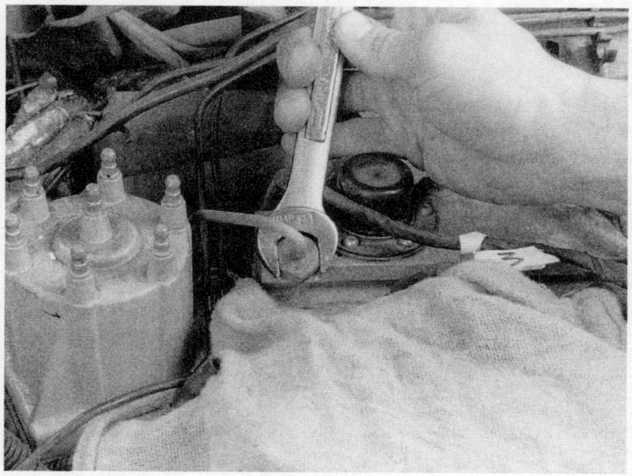

Use a wrench to loosen nut on the fuel line to the cold start injector . . .

. . . then gently pull the fuel line from the fuel rail

Disconnect the vacuum line from the fuel pressure regulator

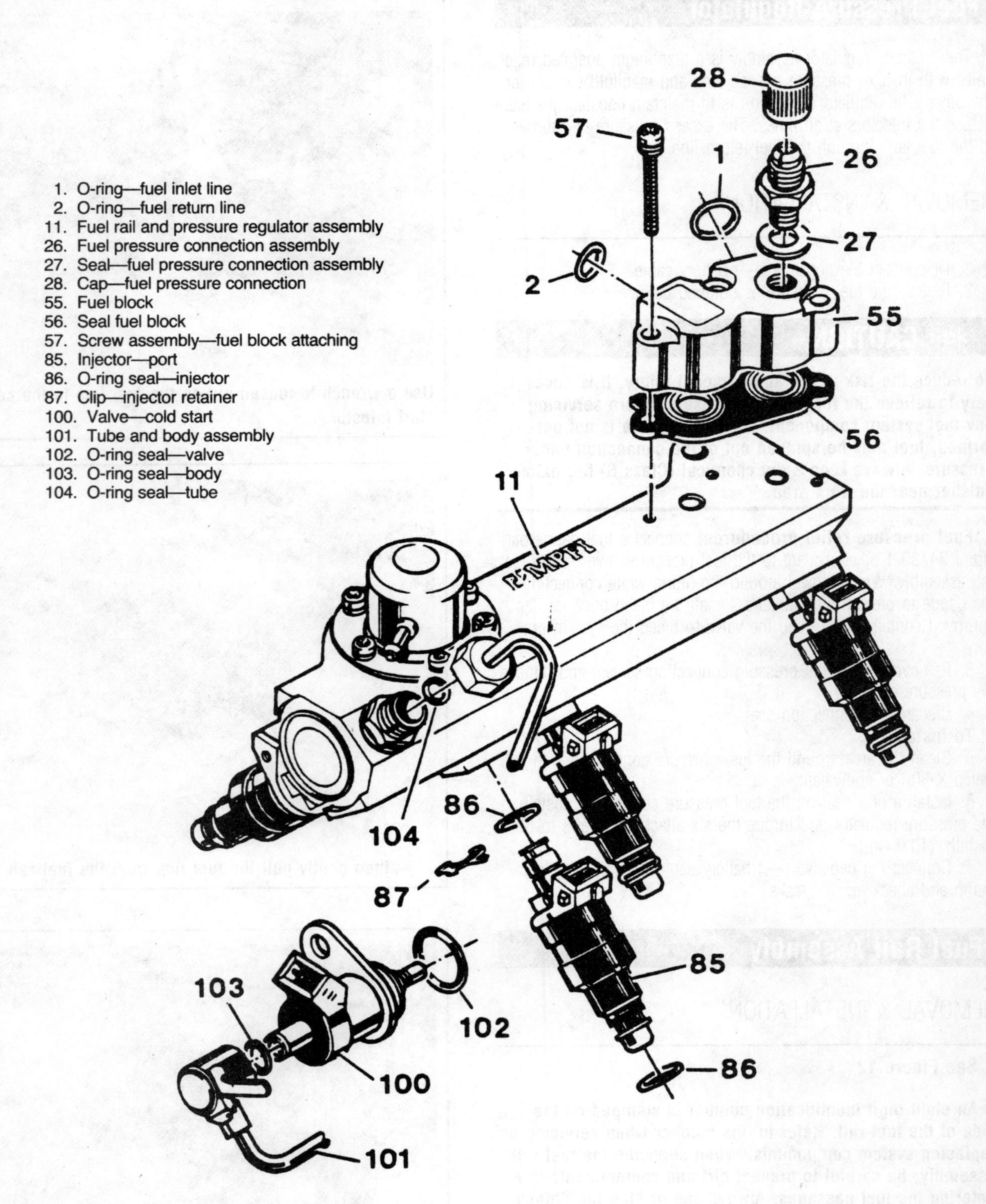

Fig. 12 Exploded view of the fuel rail assembly and its related components

5. Remove the cold start valve line at the fuel rail fitting.
6. Remove the cold start tube O-ring seal and discard.
7. Remove the fuel inlet and return lines and O-ring seals.

CAUTION

To reduce the risk of fire and personal injury, it is necessary to relieve the fuel system pressure before servicing any fuel system component. If this procedure is not performed, fuel may be sprayed out of the connection under pressure. Always keep a dry chemical (Class B) fire extinguisher near the work area.

8. Remove the vacuum line from the pressure regulator.
9. Disconnect the electrical connectors from the injectors.
10. Remove the fuel rail retaining bolts and carefully remove the fuel assembly.

➡Use care in removing the fuel rail assembly to prevent damage to the injector electrical connector terminals and injector spray tips.

To install:

11. Lubricate new injector O-rings at the each spray tip with automatic transmission fluid.
12. Install the fuel rail assembly into the intake manifold by tilting the rail so the injectors will slid into the injector holes.
13. Install the fuel rail attaching bolts and torque to 19 ft. lbs. (25 Nm).
14. Install the injector electrical connectors, vacuum connectors and fuel inlet and return with new O-rings. Torque the fittings to 88 inch.lb. (10 Nm).
15. Install the cold start valve and tube with new O-rings to the fuel rail fitting.
16. Install the air plenum as outlined in the "Air Plenum" installation procedures in this section.
17. Install the air duct and clamp. Reconnect the negative (−) battery cable.
18. Energize the fuel pump by turning the ignition switch to the **ON** position without the engine running and check for fuel, vacuum, and coolant leaks.

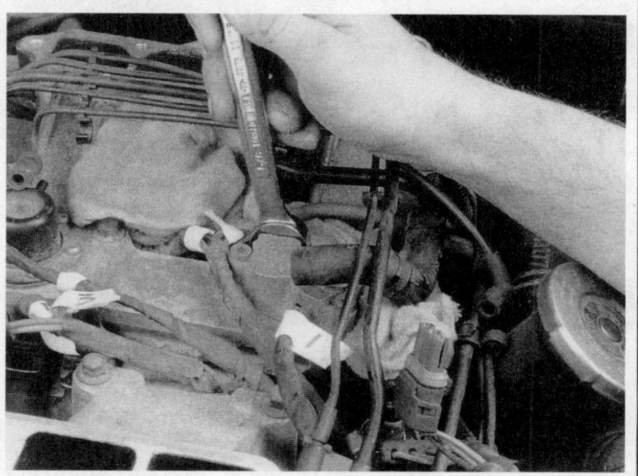

Use a flare nut wrench to loosen the fuel line nut, then disengage the line from the fuel block

Remove the fuel rail retainers . . .

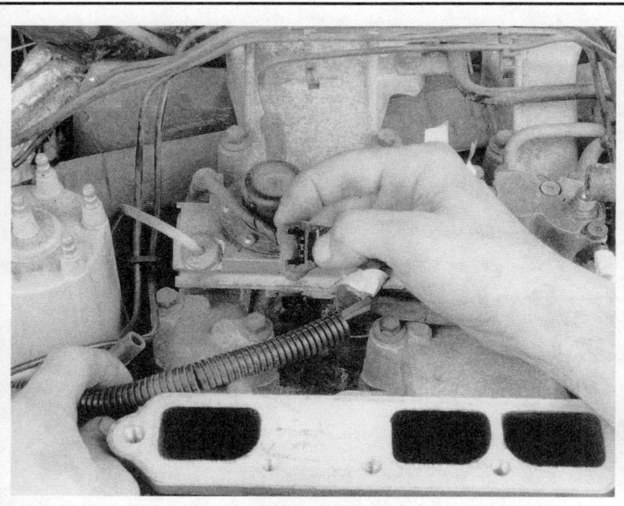

Disengage the fuel injector electrical connector

. . . then remove the fuel rail and injectors from the intake manifold assembly

Fuel Injector

REMOVAL & INSTALLATION

➧ See Figure 13

1. Disconnect the negative (−) battery cable.
2. Relieve fuel pressure.

⁂ CAUTION

To reduce the risk of fire and personal injury, it is necessary to relieve the fuel system pressure before servicing any fuel system component. If this procedure is not performed, fuel may be sprayed out of the connection under pressure. Always keep a dry chemical (Class B) fire extinguisher near the work area.

➡Use care in removing the fuel injectors to prevent damage to the electrical connector pins. The injector is serviced as a complete assembly only. Do not immerse the injector in any type of cleaner.

3. Remove the throttle body, air plenum and fuel rail assembly as outlined in this section.
4. Rotate the fuel injector retainer clip to release the injector.

➡When ordering new injectors, refer to the part No. on the side of the injector. The injectors are matched to the engine and must be identical to the original equipment.

To install:

5. Place new O-ring seals on the injector and lubricate with engine oil.
6. Install the injector into the fuel rail and turn the retaining clip counter clockwise.
7. Install the fuel rail assembly as outlined in the "Fuel Rail" installation procedures in this section.
8. Install the air plenum and throttle body assemblies as outlined in the previous procedures.
9. Install all vacuum, fuel and linkage lines to their proper positions.
10. Reconnect the negative (−) battery cable. Start the engine and check for fuel, vacuum and coolant leaks.

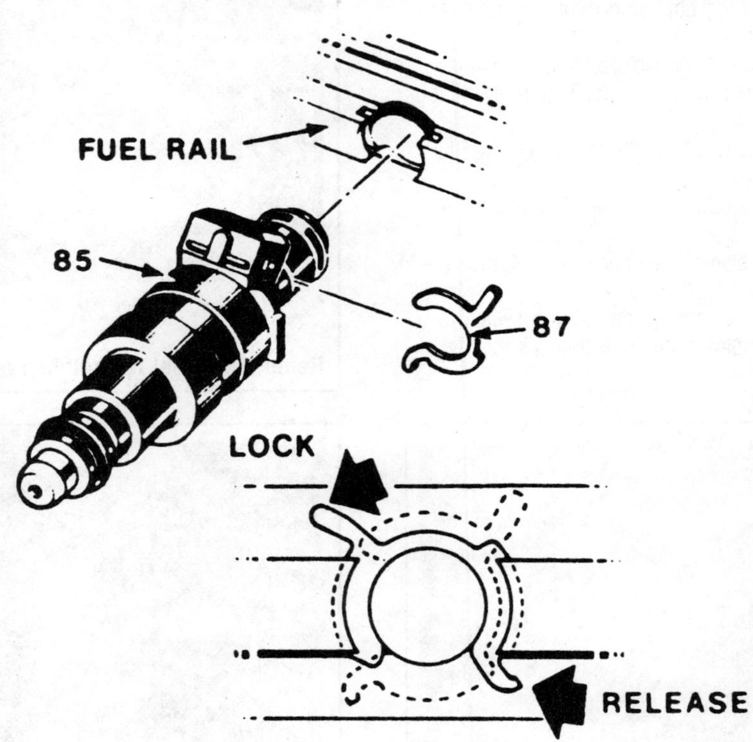

Fig. 13 To remove the fuel injector from the fuel rail the retaining clips must be rotated

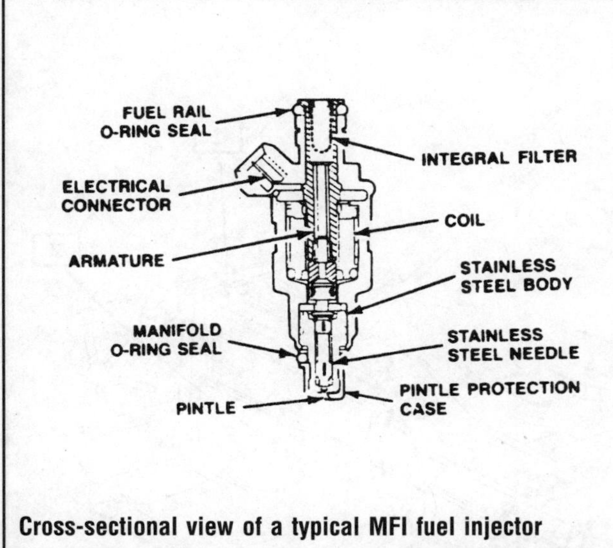

Cross-sectional view of a typical MFI fuel injector

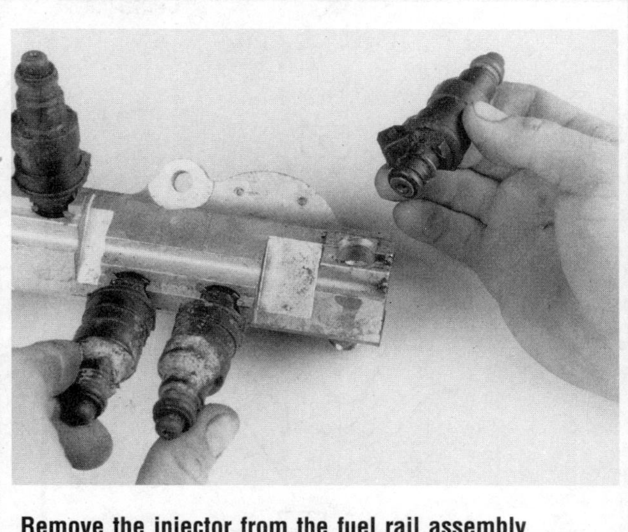

Remove the injector from the fuel rail assembly

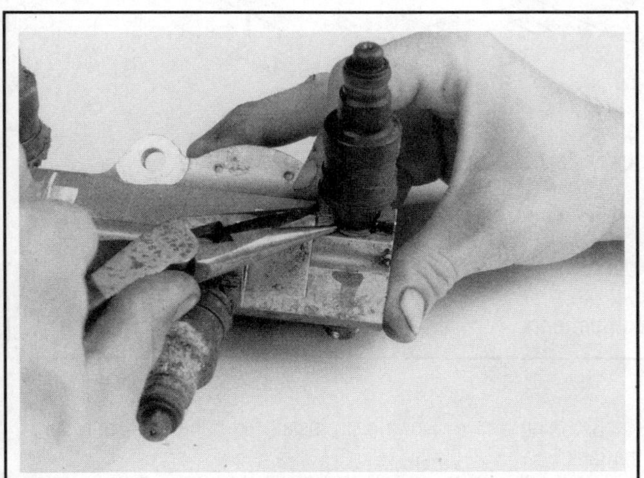

Use a pair of needle nose pliers to rotate the fuel injector retainer clip to the release position

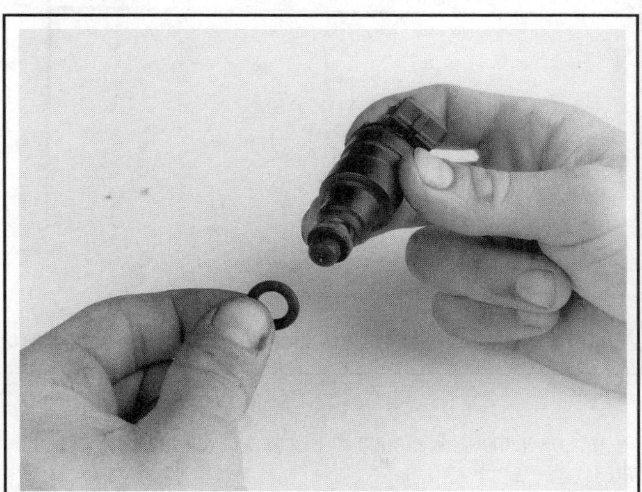

Always discard the old injector O-rings and replace them with new ones during installation

FUEL TANK

Tank Assembly

REMOVAL & INSTALLATION

See Figure 14

CAUTION

Before performing any fuel system service, it is necessary to relieve the fuel system pressure. If this procedure is not performed, there is a risk of fire and personal injury. Any time the fuel system is being worked on, always keep a dry chemical (class B) fire extinguisher near the work area.

1. Disconnect the negative (−) battery cable.
2. Relieve the fuel system pressure.

CAUTION

To reduce the risk of fire and personal injury, it is necessary to relieve the fuel system pressure before servicing any fuel system component. If this procedure is not performed, fuel may be sprayed out of the connection under pressure. Always keep a dry chemical (Class B) fire extinguisher near the work area.

3. Drain all the fuel from the tank using a suction pump.
4. Raise the vehicle and support with jackstands.
5. Disconnect the wiring from the tank.
6. Remove the ground wire retaining screw from under the body.
7. Disconnect all hoses and filler neck from the tank.
8. Support the tank on a jack and remove the retaining strap nuts.

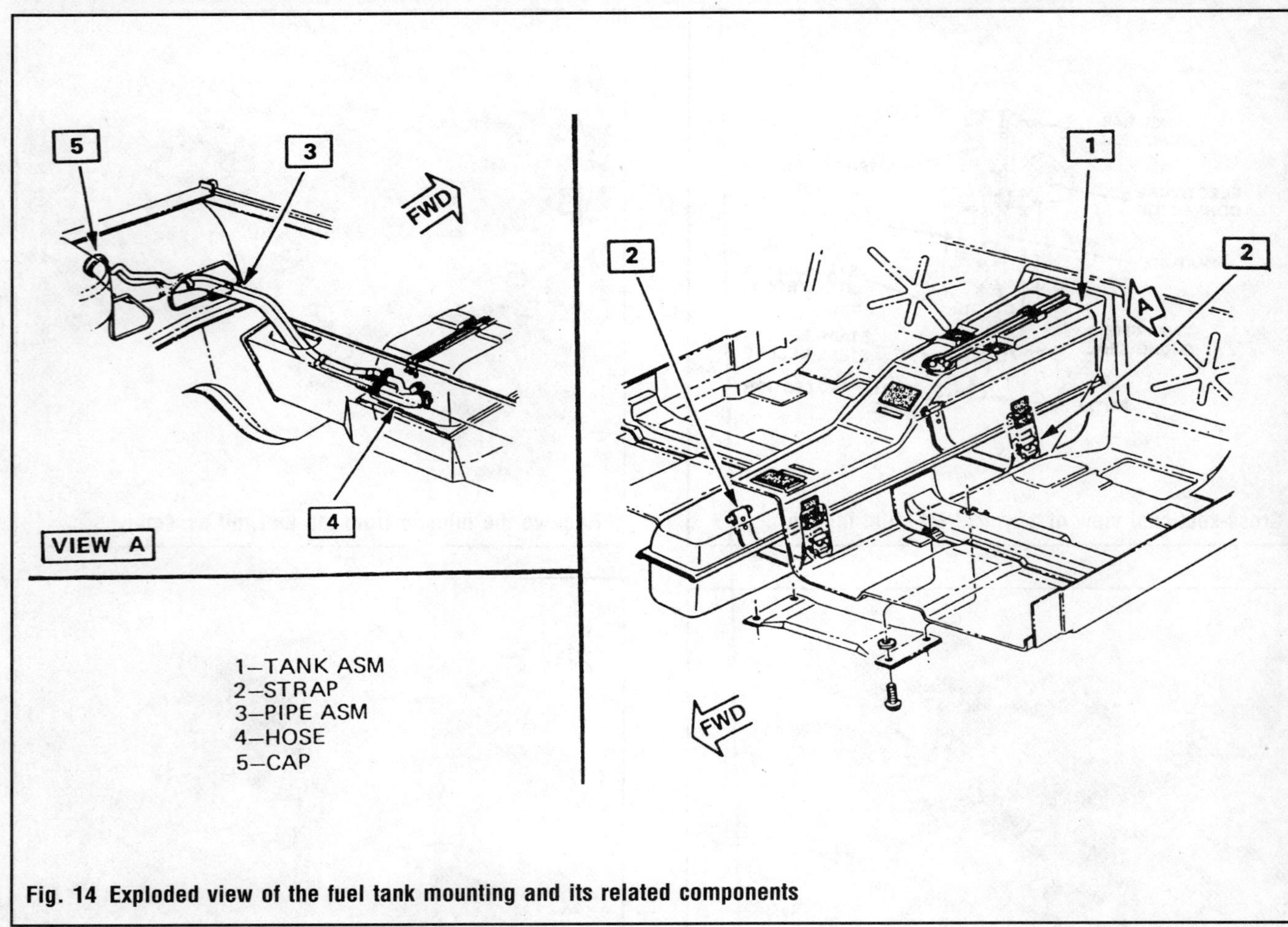

Fig. 14 Exploded view of the fuel tank mounting and its related components

9. Lower the tank enough to disconnect the fuel sending unit wires.
10. Disconnect the fuel line, vapor line and return line.
11. Remove the tank from the vehicle.
12. Remove the fuel gauge/pump retaining ring by turning the cam lock ring counterclockwise using a spanner wrench such as tool J-24187.
13. Remove the gauge unit/pump assembly.

To install:

1. Inspect the fuel pump attaching hose for any signs of deterioration and replace if necessary. Also, check the rubber sound insulator at the bottom of the pump.
2. Push the fuel pump assembly into the attaching hose.
3. Using a new O-ring seal, install the pump assembly into the tank.
4. Install the cam lock ring over the pump and lock by turning clockwise with a spanner wrench J-24187 or equivalent.
5. Support the tank on a suitable jack.
6. Raise the tank enough to connect all fuel and filler hoses.
7. Connect all electrical wires to the pump and tank.
8. Raise the tank and install the retaining strap nuts. Use new sound reducing pad if they are damaged. Check all connections and wire to ensure proper installation before refilling the tank.
9. Refill the tank with unleaded fuel. Reconnect the negative (−) battery cable.
10. Start engine and check for fuel leaks and gauge operation.

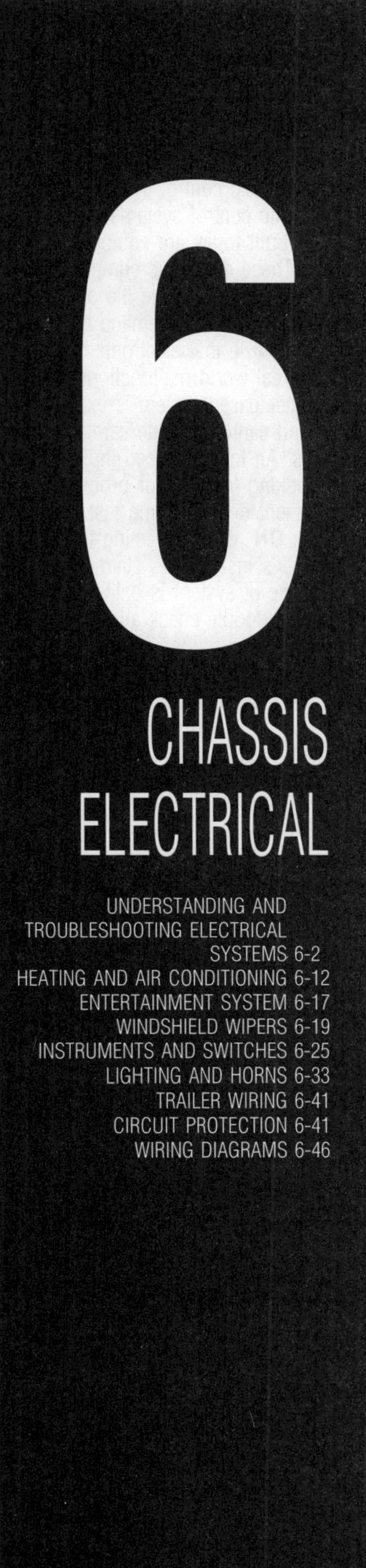
6
CHASSIS ELECTRICAL
UNDERSTANDING AND TROUBLESHOOTING ELECTRICAL SYSTEMS 6-2
HEATING AND AIR CONDITIONING 6-12
ENTERTAINMENT SYSTEM 6-17
WINDSHIELD WIPERS 6-19
INSTRUMENTS AND SWITCHES 6-25
LIGHTING AND HORNS 6-33
TRAILER WIRING 6-41
CIRCUIT PROTECTION 6-41
WIRING DIAGRAMS 6-46

UNDERSTANDING AND TROUBLESHOOTING ELECTRICAL SYSTEMS

Over the years import and domestic manufacturers have incorporated electronic control systems into their production lines. In fact, electronic control systems are so prevalent that all new cars and trucks built today are equipped with at least one on-board computer. These electronic components (with no moving parts) should theoretically last the life of the vehicle, provided that nothing external happens to damage the circuits or memory chips.

While it is true that electronic components should never wear out, in the real world malfunctions do occur. It is also true that any computer-based system is extremely sensitive to electrical voltages and cannot tolerate careless or haphazard testing/service procedures. An inexperienced individual can literally cause major damage looking for a minor problem by using the wrong kind of test equipment or connecting test leads/connectors with the ignition switch **ON**. When selecting test equipment, make sure the manufacturer's instructions state that the tester is compatible with whatever type of system is being serviced. Read all instructions carefully and double check all test points before installing probes or making any test connections.

The following section outlines basic diagnosis techniques for dealing with automotive electrical systems. Along with a general explanation of the various types of test equipment available to aid in servicing modern automotive systems, basic repair techniques for wiring harnesses and connectors are also given. Read the basic information before attempting any repairs or testing. This will provide the background of information necessary to avoid the most common and obvious mistakes that can cost both time and money. Although the replacement and testing procedures are simple in themselves, the systems are not, and unless one has a thorough understanding of all components and their function within a particular system, the logical test sequence these systems demand cannot be followed. Minor malfunctions can make a big difference, so it is important to know how each component affects the operation of the overall system in order to find the ultimate cause of a problem without replacing good components unnecessarily. It is not enough to use the correct test equipment; the test equipment must be used correctly.

Safety Precautions

✱✱ CAUTION

Whenever working on or around any electrical or electronic systems, always observe these general precautions to prevent the possibility of personal injury or damage to electronic components.

- Never install or remove battery cables with the key **ON** or the engine running. Jumper cables should be connected with the key **OFF** to avoid power surges that can damage electronic control units. Engines equipped with computer controlled systems should avoid both giving and getting jump starts due to the possibility of serious damage to components from arcing in the engine compartment if connections are made with the ignition **ON**.
- Always remove the battery cables before charging the battery. Never use a high output charger on an installed battery or attempt to use any type of "hot shot" (24 volt) starting aid.
- Exercise care when inserting test probes into connectors to insure good contact without damaging the connector or spreading the pins. Always probe connectors from the rear (wire) side, NOT the pin side, to avoid accidental shorting of terminals during test procedures.
- Never remove or attach wiring harness connectors with the ignition switch **ON**, especially to an electronic control unit.
- Do not drop any components during service procedures and never apply 12 volts directly to any component (like a solenoid or relay) unless instructed specifically to do so. Some component electrical windings are designed to safely handle only 4 or 5 volts and can be destroyed in seconds if 12 volts are applied directly to the connector.
- Remove the electronic control unit if the vehicle is to be placed in an environment where temperatures exceed approximately 176°F (80°C), such as a paint spray booth or when arc/gas welding near the control unit location.

Understanding Basic Electricity

Understanding the basic theory of electricity makes electrical troubleshooting much easier. Several gauges are used in electrical troubleshooting to see inside the circuit being tested. Without a basic understanding, it will be difficult to understand testing procedures.

THE WATER ANALOGY

Electricity is the flow of electrons—hypothetical particles thought to constitute the basic stuff of electricity. Many people have been taught electrical theory using an analogy with water. In a comparison with water flowing in a pipe, the electrons would be the water. As the flow of water can be measured, the flow of electricity can be measured. The unit of measurement is amperes, frequently abbreviated amps. An ammeter will measure the actual amount of current flowing in the circuit.

Just as the water pressure is measured in units such as pounds per square inch, electrical pressure is measured in volts. When a voltmeter's two probes are placed on two live portions of an electrical circuit with different electrical pressures, current will flow through the voltmeter and produce a reading which indicates the difference in electrical pressure between the two parts of the circuit.

While increasing the voltage in a circuit will increase the flow of current, the actual flow depends not only on voltage, but on the resistance of the circuit. The standard unit for measuring circuit resistance is an ohm, measured by an ohmmeter. The ohmmeter is somewhat similar to an ammeter, but incorporates its own source of power so that a standard voltage is always present.

CIRCUITS

An actual electric circuit consists of four basic parts. These are: the power source, such as a generator or battery; a hot wire, which conducts the electricity under a relatively high voltage to the component supplied by the circuit; the load, such as a lamp, motor, resistor or relay coil; and the ground wire, which carries the current back to the source under very low voltage. In such a circuit the bulk of the resistance exists between the point where the hot wire is connected to the load, and the point where the load is grounded. In an automobile, the vehicle's frame or body, which is made of steel, is used as a part of the ground circuit for many of the electrical devices.

Remember that, in electrical testing, the voltmeter is connected in parallel with the circuit being tested (without disconnecting any wires) and measures the difference in voltage between the locations of the two probes; that the ammeter is connected in series with the load (the circuit is separated at one point and the ammeter inserted so it becomes a part of the circuit); and the ohmmeter is self-powered, so that all the power in the circuit should be off and the portion of the circuit to be measured contacted at either end by one of the probes of the meter.

For any electrical system to operate, it must make a complete circuit. This simply means that the power flow from the battery must make a complete circle. When an electrical component is operating, power flows from the battery to the component, passes through the component causing it to perform it to function (such as lighting a light bulb) and then returns to the battery through the ground of the circuit. This ground is usually (but not always) the metal part of the vehicle on which the electrical component is mounted.

Perhaps the easiest way to visualize this is to think of connecting a light bulb with two wires attached to it to your vehicle's battery. The battery in your vehicle has two posts (negative and positive). If one of the two wires attached to the light bulb was attached to the negative post of the battery and the other wire was attached to the positive post of the battery, you would have a complete circuit. Current from the battery would flow out one post, through the wire attached to it and then to the light bulb, where it would pass through causing it to light. It would then leave the light bulb, travel through the other wire, and return to the other post of the battery.

AUTOMOTIVE CIRCUITS

The normal automotive circuit differs from this simple example in two ways. First, instead of having a return wire from the bulb to the battery, the light bulb return the current to the battery through the chassis of the vehicle. Since the negative battery cable is attached to the chassis and the chassis is made of electrically conductive metal, the chassis of the vehicle can serve as a ground wire to complete the circuit. Secondly, most automotive circuits contain switches to turn components on and off.

Some electrical components which require a large amount of current to operate also have a relay in their circuit. Since these circuits carry a large amount of current, the thickness of the wire in the circuit (gauge size) is also greater. If this large wire were connected from the component to the control switch on the instrument panel, and then back to the component, a voltage drop would occur in the circuit. To prevent this potential drop in voltage, an electromagnetic switch (relay) is used. The large wires in the circuit are connected from the vehicle battery to one side of the relay, and from the opposite side of the relay to the component. The relay is normally open, preventing current from passing through the circuit. An additional, smaller wire is connected from the relay to the control switch for the circuit. When the control switch is turned on, it grounds the smaller wire from the relay and completes the circuit.

SHORT CIRCUITS

If you were to disconnect the light bulb (from the previous example of a light-bulb being connected to the battery by two wires) from the wires and touch the two wires together (please take our word for this; don't try it), the result will be a shower of sparks. A similar thing happens (on a smaller scale) when the power supply wire to a component or the electrical component itself becomes grounded before the normal ground connection for the circuit. To prevent damage to the system, the fuse for the circuit blows to interrupt the circuit—protecting the components from damage. Because grounding a wire from a power source makes a complete circuit—less the required component to use the power—the phenomenon is called a short circuit. The most common causes of short circuits are: the rubber insulation on a wire breaking or rubbing through to expose the current carrying core of the wire to a metal part of the car, or a shorted switch.

Some electrical systems on the vehicle are protected by a circuit breaker which is, basically, a self-repairing fuse. When either of the described events takes place in a system which is protected by a circuit breaker, the circuit breaker opens the circuit the same way a fuse does. However, when either the short is removed from the circuit or the surge subsides, the circuit breaker resets itself and does not have to be replaced as a fuse does.

Troubleshooting

When diagnosing a specific problem, organized troubleshooting is a must. The complexity of a modern automobile demands that you approach any problem in a logical, organized manner. There are certain troubleshooting techniques that are standard:

1. Establish when the problem occurs. Does the problem appear only under certain conditions? Were there any noises, odors, or other unusual symptoms?
2. Isolate the problem area. To do this, make some simple tests and observations; then eliminate the systems that are working properly. Check for obvious problems such as broken wires, dirty connections or split/disconnected vacuum hoses. Always check the obvious before assuming something complicated is the cause.
3. Test for problems systematically to determine the cause once the problem area is isolated. Are all the components functioning properly? Is there power going to electrical switches and motors? Is there vacuum at vacuum switches and/or actuators? Is there a mechanical problem such as bent linkage or loose mounting screws? Performing careful, systematic checks will often turn up most causes on the first inspection without wasting time checking components that have little or no relationship to the problem.
4. Test all repairs after the work is done to make sure that the problem is fixed. Some causes can be traced to more than one component, so a careful verification of repair work is important in order to pick up additional malfunctions that may cause a problem to reappear or a different problem to arise. A blown fuse, for example, is a simple problem that may require more than another fuse to repair. If you don't look for a problem that caused a fuse to blow, a shorted wire (for example) may go undetected.

Experience has shown that most problems tend to be the result of a fairly simple and obvious cause, such as loose or corroded connectors or air leaks in the intake system. This makes careful inspection of components during testing essential to quick and accurate troubleshooting.

BASIC TROUBLESHOOTING THEORY

Electrical problems generally fall into one of three areas:

- The component that is not functioning is not receiving current.
- The component itself is not functioning.
- The component is not properly grounded.

Problems that fall into the first category are by far the most complicated. It is the current supply system to the component which contains all the switches, relay, fuses, etc.

The electrical system can be checked with a test light and a jumper wire. A test light is a device that looks like a pointed screwdriver with a wire attached to it. It has a light bulb in its handle. A jumper wire is a piece of insulated wire with an alligator clip attached to each end.

If a light bulb is not working, you must follow a systematic plan to determine which of the three causes is the villain.

1. Turn on the switch that controls the inoperable bulb.
2. Disconnect the power supply wire from the bulb.
3. Attach the ground wire to the test light to a good metal ground.
4. Touch the probe end of the test light to the end of the power supply wire that was disconnected from the bulb. If the bulb is receiving current, the test light will go on.

➡If the bulb is one which works only when the ignition key is turned on (turn signal), make sure the key is turned on.

If the test light does not go on, then the problem is in the circuit between the battery and the bulb. As mentioned before, this includes all the switches, fuses, and relays in the system. Turn to a wiring diagram and find the bulb on the diagram. Follow the wire that runs back to the battery. The problem is an open circuit between the battery and the bulb. If the fuse is blown and, when replaced, immediately blows again, there is a short circuit in the system which must be located and repaired. If there is a switch in the system, bypass it with a jumper wire. This is done by connecting one end of the jumper wire to the power supply wire into the switch and the other end of the jumper wire to the wire coming out of the switch. If the test light illuminates with the jumper wire installed, the switch or whatever was bypassed is defective.

➡Never substitute the jumper wire for the bulb, as the bulb is the component required to use the power from the power source.

5. If the bulb in the test light goes on, then the current is getting to the bulb that is not working in the car. This eliminates the first of the three possible causes. Connect the power supply wire and connect a jumper wire from the bulb to a good metal ground. Do this with the switch which controls the bulb works with jumper wire installed, then it has a bad ground. This is usually caused by the metal area on which the bulb mounts to the vehicle being coated with some type of foreign matter.
6. If neither test located the source of the trouble, then the light bulb itself is defective.

The above test procedure can be applied to any of the components of the chassis electrical system by substituting the component that is not working for the light bulb. Remember that for any electrical system to work, all connections must be clean and tight.

TEST EQUIPMENT

➡Pinpointing the exact cause of trouble in an electrical system can sometimes only be accomplished by the use of special test equipment. The following describes different types of commonly used test equipment and explains how to use them in diagnosis. In addition to the information covered below, the tool manufacturer's instructions booklet (provided with the tester) should be read and clearly understood before attempting any test procedures.

Jumper Wires

Jumper wires are simple, yet extremely valuable, pieces of test equipment. They are basically test wires which are used to bypass sections of a circuit. The simplest type of jumper wire is a length of multi-strand wire with an alligator clip at each end. Jumper wires are usually fabricated from lengths of standard automotive wire and whatever type of connector (alligator clip, spade connector or pin connector) that is required for the particular vehicle being tested. The well equipped tool box will have several different styles of jumper wires in several different lengths. Some jumper wires are made with three or more terminals coming from a common splice for special purpose testing. In cramped, hard-to-reach areas it is advisable to have insulated boots over the jumper wire terminals in order to prevent accidental grounding, sparks, and possible fire, especially when testing fuel system components.

Jumper wires are used primarily to locate open electrical circuits, on either the ground (−) side of the circuit or on the hot (+) side. If an electrical component fails to operate, connect the jumper wire between the component and a good ground. If the component operates only with the jumper installed, the ground circuit is open. If the ground circuit is good, but the component does not operate, the circuit between the power feed and component may be open. By moving the jumper wire successively back

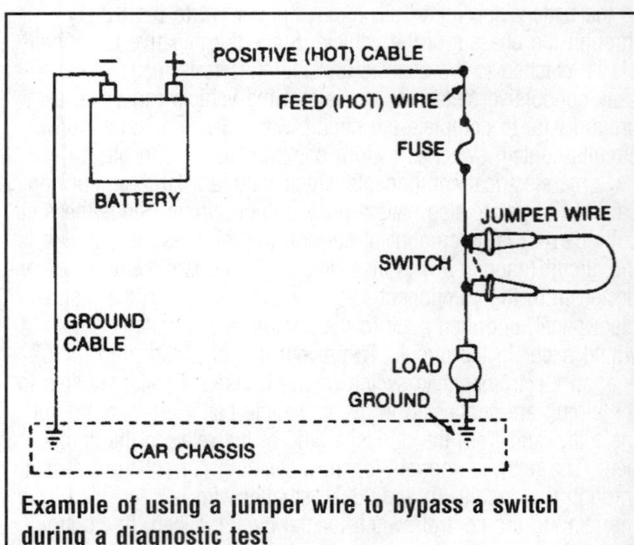

Example of using a jumper wire to bypass a switch during a diagnostic test

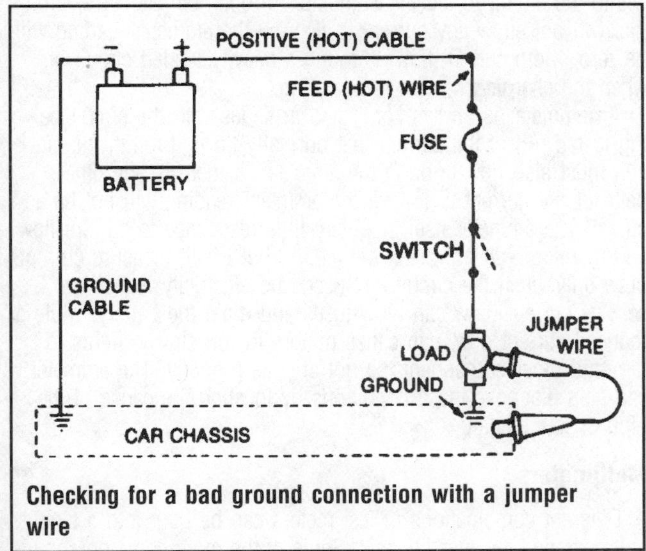

Checking for a bad ground connection with a jumper wire

from the lamp toward the power source, you can isolate the area of the circuit where the open is located. When the component stops functioning, or the power is cut off, the open is in the segment of wire between the jumper and the point previously tested.

You can sometimes connect the jumper wire directly from the battery to the hot terminal of the component, but first make sure the component uses 12 volts in operation. Some electrical components, such as fuel injectors, are designed to operate on about 4 volts and running 12 volts directly to the injector terminals can cause damage.

By inserting an in-line fuse holder between a set of test leads, a fused jumper wire can be used for bypassing open circuits. Use a 5 amp fuse to provide protection against voltage spikes. When in doubt, use a voltmeter to check the voltage input to the component and measure how much voltage is normally being applied.

✱✱ CAUTION

Never use jumpers made from wire that is of lighter gauge than that which is used in the circuit under test. If the jumper wire is of too small a gauge, it may overheat and possibly melt. Never use jumpers to bypass high resistance loads in a circuit. Bypassing resistances, in effect, creates a short circuit. This may, in turn, cause damage and fire. Jumper wires should only be used to bypass lengths of wire.

Unpowered Test Lights

The 12 volt test light is used to check circuits and components while electrical current is flowing through them. It is used for voltage and ground tests. Twelve volt test lights come in different styles but all have three main parts; a ground clip, a probe, and a light. The most commonly used 12 volt test lights have pick-type probes. To use a 12 volt test light, connect the ground clip to a good ground and probe wherever necessary with the pick. The pick should be sharp so that it can be probed into tight spaces.

✱✱ CAUTION

Do not use a test light to probe electronic ignition spark plug or coil wires. Never use a pick-type test light to probe wiring on computer controlled systems unless specifically instructed to do so. Any wire insulation that is pierced by the test light probe should be taped and sealed with silicone after testing.

Like the jumper wire, the 12 volt test light is used to isolate opens in circuits. But, whereas the jumper wire is used to bypass the open to operate the load, the 12 volt test light is used to locate the presence of voltage in a circuit. If the test light glows, you know that there is power up to that point; if the 12 volt test light does not glow when its probe is inserted into the wire or connector, you know that there is an open circuit (no power). Move the test light in successive steps back toward the power source until the light in the handle does glow. When it glows, the open is between the probe and point which was probed previously.

➡The test light does not detect that 12 volts (or any particular amount of voltage) is present; it only detects that some voltage is present. It is advisable before using the test light to touch its terminals across the battery posts to make sure the light is operating properly.

Self-Powered Test Lights

The self-powered test light usually contains a 1.5 volt penlight battery. One type of self-powered test light is similar in design to the 12 volt unit. This type has both the battery and the light in the handle, along with a pick-type probe tip. The second type has the light toward the open tip, so that the light illuminates the contact point. The self-powered test light is a dual purpose piece of test equipment. It can be used to test for either open or short circuits when power is isolated from the circuit (continuity test). A powered test light should not be used on any computer controlled system or component unless specifically instructed to do so. Many engine sensors can be destroyed by even this small amount of voltage applied directly to the terminals.

Voltmeters

A voltmeter is used to measure voltage at any point in a circuit, or to measure the voltage drop across any part of a circuit. It can also be used to check continuity in a wire or circuit by indicating current flow from one end to the other. Analog voltmeters usually have various scales on the meter dial and a selector switch to allow the selection of different voltages. The voltmeter has a positive and a negative lead. To avoid damage to the meter, always connect the negative lead to the negative (−) side of the circuit (to ground or nearest the ground side of the circuit) and connect the positive lead to the positive (+) side of the circuit (to the power source or the nearest power source). Note that the negative voltmeter lead will always be black and that the positive voltmeter will always be some color other than black (usually red).

Depending on how the voltmeter is connected into the circuit, it has several uses. A voltmeter can be connected either in parallel or in series with a circuit and it has a very high resistance to current flow. When connected in parallel, only a small amount of current will flow through the voltmeter current path; the rest will flow through the normal circuit current path and the circuit will work normally. When the voltmeter is connected in series with a circuit, only a small amount of current can flow through the circuit. The circuit will not work properly, but the voltmeter reading will show if the circuit is complete or not.

Ohmmeters

The ohmmeter is designed to read resistance (which is measured in ohms or Ω) in a circuit or component. Although there are several different styles of ohmmeters, all analog meters will usually have a selector switch which permits the measurement of different ranges of resistance (usually the selector switch allows the multiplication of the meter reading by 10, 100, 1000, and 10,000). A calibration knob allows the meter to be set at zero for accurate measurement. Since all ohmmeters are powered by an internal battery, the ohmmeter can be used as a self-powered test light. When the ohmmeter is connected, current from the ohmmeter flows through the circuit or component being tested. Since the ohmmeter's internal resistance and voltage are known values, the amount of current flow through the meter depends on the resistance of the circuit or component being tested.

The ohmmeter can be used to perform a continuity test for opens or shorts (either by observation of the meter needle or as a self-powered test light), and to read actual resistance in a circuit. It should be noted that the ohmmeter is used to check the resistance of a component or wire while there is no voltage applied to the circuit. Current flow from an outside voltage source (such as the vehicle battery) can damage the ohmmeter, so the circuit or component should be isolated from the vehicle electrical system before any testing is done. Since the ohmmeter uses its own voltage source, either lead can be connected to any test point.

➡When checking diodes or other solid state components, the ohmmeter leads can only be connected one way in order to measure current flow in a single direction. Make sure the positive (+) and negative (−) terminal connections are as described in the test procedures to verify the one-way diode operation.

In using the meter for making continuity checks, do not be concerned with the actual resistance readings. Zero resistance, or any ohm reading, indicates continuity in the circuit. Infinite resistance indicates an open in the circuit. A high resistance reading where there should be none indicates a problem in the circuit. Checks for short circuits are made in the same manner as checks for open circuits except that the circuit must be isolated from both power and normal ground. Infinite resistance indicates no continuity to ground, while zero resistance indicates a dead short to ground.

Ammeters

An ammeter measures the amount of current flowing through a circuit in units called amperes or amps. Amperes are units of electron flow which indicate how fast the electrons are flowing through the circuit. Since Ohms Law dictates that current flow in a circuit is equal to the circuit voltage divided by the total circuit resistance, increasing voltage also increases the current level (amps). Likewise, any decrease in resistance will increase the amount of amps in a circuit. At normal operating voltage, most circuits have a characteristic amount of amperes, called "current draw" which can be measured using an ammeter. By referring to a specified current draw rating, measuring the amperes, and comparing the two values, one can determine what is happening within the circuit to aid in diagnosis. An open circuit, for example, will not allow any current to flow so the ammeter reading will be zero. More current flows through a heavily loaded circuit or when the charging system is operating.

An ammeter is always connected in series with the circuit being tested. All of the current that normally flows through the circuit must also flow through the ammeter; if there is any other path for the current to follow, the ammeter reading will not be accurate. The ammeter itself has very little resistance to current flow and therefore will not affect the circuit, but it will measure current draw only when the circuit is closed and electricity is flowing. Excessive current draw can blow fuses and drain the battery, while a reduced current draw can cause motors to run slowly, lights to dim and other components to not operate properly. The ammeter can help diagnose these conditions by locating the cause of the high or low reading.

Multimeters

Different combinations of test meters can be built into a single unit designed for specific tests. Some of the more common combination test devices are known as Volt/Amp testers, Tach/Dwell meters, or Digital Multimeters. The Volt/Amp tester is used for charging system, starting system or battery tests and consists of a voltmeter, an ammeter and a variable resistance carbon pile. The voltmeter will usually have at least two ranges for use with 6, 12 and/or 24 volt systems. The ammeter also has more than one range for testing various levels of battery loads and starter current draw. The carbon pile can be adjusted to offer different amounts of resistance. The Volt/Amp tester has heavy leads to carry large amounts of current and many later models have an inductive ammeter pickup that clamps around the wire to simplify test connections. On some models, the ammeter also has a zero-center scale to allow testing of charging and starting systems without switching leads or polarity. A digital multimeter is a voltmeter, ammeter and ohmmeter combined in an instrument which gives a digital readout. These are often used when testing solid state circuits because of their high input impedance (usually 10 megohms or more).

The tach/dwell meter that combines a tachometer and a dwell (cam angle) meter is a specialized kind of voltmeter. The tachometer scale is marked to show engine speed in rpm and the dwell scale is marked to show degrees of distributor shaft rotation. In most electronic ignition systems, dwell is determined by the control unit, but the dwell meter can also be used to check the duty cycle (operation) of some electronic engine control systems. Some tach/dwell meters are powered by an internal battery, while others take their power from the vehicle battery in use. The battery powered testers usually require calibration (much like an ohmmeter) before testing.

TESTING

Open Circuits

To use the self-powered test light or a multimeter to check for open circuits, first isolate the circuit from the vehicle's 12 volt power source by disconnecting the battery or wiring harness connector. Connect the test light or ohmmeter ground clip to a good ground and probe sections of the circuit sequentially with the test light. (start from either end of the circuit). If the light is out/or there is infinite resistance, the open is between the probe and the circuit ground. If the light is on/or the meter shows continuity, the open is between the probe and end of the circuit toward the power source.

Short Circuits

By isolating the circuit both from power and from ground, and using a self-powered test light or multimeter, you can check for shorts to ground in the circuit. Isolate the circuit from power and ground. Connect the test light or ohmmeter ground clip to a good ground and probe any easy-to-reach test point in the circuit. If the light comes on or there is continuity, there is a short somewhere in the circuit. To isolate the short, probe a test point at either end of the isolated circuit (the light should be on/there should be continuity). Leave the test light probe engaged and open connectors, switches, remove parts, etc., sequentially, until the light goes out/continuity is broken. When the light goes out, the short is between the last circuit component opened and the previous circuit opened.

➡The battery in the test light and does not provide much current. A weak battery may not provide enough power to illuminate the test light even when a complete circuit is made (especially if there are high resistances in the circuit). Always make sure that the test battery is strong. To check the battery, briefly touch the ground clip to the probe; if the light glows brightly the battery is strong enough for testing. Never use a self-powered test light to perform checks for opens or shorts when power is applied to the electrical system under test. The 12 volt vehicle power will quickly burn out the light bulb in the test light.

Available Voltage Measurement

Set the voltmeter selector switch to the 20V position and connect the meter negative lead to the negative post of the battery. Connect the positive meter lead to the positive post of the battery and turn the ignition switch **ON** to provide a load. Read the voltage on the meter or digital display. A well charged battery should register over 12 volts. If the meter reads below 11.5 volts, the battery power may be insufficient to operate the electrical system properly. This test determines voltage available from the battery and should be the first step in any electrical trouble diagnosis procedure. Many electrical problems, especially on computer controlled systems, can be caused by a low state of charge in the battery. Excessive corrosion at the battery cable terminals can cause a poor contact that will prevent proper charging and full battery current flow.

Normal battery voltage is 12 volts when fully charged. When the battery is supplying current to one or more circuits it is said to be "under load." When everything is off the electrical system is under a "no-load" condition. A fully charged battery may show about 12.5 volts at no load; will drop to 12 volts under medium load; and will drop even lower under heavy load. If the battery is partially discharged the voltage decrease under heavy load may be excessive, even though the battery shows 12 volts or more at no load. When allowed to discharge further, the battery's available voltage under load will decrease more severely. For this reason, it is important that the battery be fully charged during all testing procedures to avoid errors in diagnosis and incorrect test results.

Voltage Drop

When current flows through a resistance, the voltage beyond the resistance is reduced (the larger the current, the greater the reduction in voltage). When no current is flowing, there is no voltage drop because there is no current flow. All points in the circuit which are connected to the power source are at the same voltage as the power source. The total voltage drop always equals the total source voltage. In a long circuit with many connectors, a series of small, unwanted voltage drops due to corrosion at the connectors can add up to a total loss of voltage which impairs the operation of the normal loads in the circuit. The maximum allowable voltage drop under load is critical, especially if there is more than one high resistance problem in a circuit because all voltage drops are cumulative. A small drop is normal due to the resistance of the conductors.

INDIRECT COMPUTATION OF VOLTAGE DROPS

1. Set the voltmeter selector switch to the 20 volt position.
2. Connect the meter negative lead to a good ground.
3. While operating the circuit, probe all loads in the circuit with the positive meter lead and observe the voltage readings. A drop should be noticed after the first load. But, there should be little or no voltage drop before the first load.

DIRECT MEASUREMENT OF VOLTAGE DROPS

1. Set the voltmeter switch to the 20 volt position.
2. Connect the voltmeter negative lead to the ground side of the load to be measured.
3. Connect the positive lead to the positive side of the resistance or load to be measured.
4. Read the voltage drop directly on the 20 volt scale.

Too high a voltage indicates too high a resistance. If, for example, a blower motor runs too slowly, you can determine if perhaps there is too high a resistance in the resistor pack. By taking voltage drop readings in all parts of the circuit, you can isolate the problem. Too low a voltage drop indicates too low a resistance. Take the blower motor for example again. If a blower motor runs too fast in the MED and/or LOW position, the problem might be isolated in the resistor pack by taking voltage drop readings in all parts of the circuit to locate a possibly shorted resistor.

HIGH RESISTANCE TESTING

1. Set the voltmeter selector switch to the 4 volt position.
2. Connect the voltmeter positive lead to the positive post of the battery.
3. Turn on the headlights and heater blower to provide a load.
4. Probe various points in the circuit with the negative voltmeter lead.
5. Read the voltage drop on the 4 volt scale. Some average maximum allowable voltage drops are:
   - FUSE PANEL: 0.7 volts
   - IGNITION SWITCH: 0.5 volts
   - HEADLIGHT SWITCH: 0.7 volts
   - IGNITION COIL (+): 0.5 volts
   - ANY OTHER LOAD: 1.3 volts

➡Voltage drops are all measured while a load is operating; without current flow, there will be no voltage drop.

Resistance Measurement

The batteries in an ohmmeter will weaken with age and temperature, so the ohmmeter must be calibrated or "zeroed" before taking measurements. To zero the meter, place the selector switch in its lowest range and touch the two ohmmeter leads together. Turn the calibration knob until the meter needle is exactly on zero.

➡All analog (needle) type ohmmeters must be zeroed before use, but some digital ohmmeter models are automatically calibrated when the switch is turned on. Self-calibrating digital ohmmeters do not have an adjusting knob, but its a good idea to check for a zero readout before use by touching the leads together. All computer controlled systems require the use of a digital ohmmeter with at least 10 megohms impedance for testing. Before any test procedures are attempted, make sure the ohmmeter used is compatible with the electrical system or damage to the on-board computer could result.

To measure resistance, first isolate the circuit from the vehicle power source by disconnecting the battery cables or the harness connector. Make sure the key is **OFF** when disconnecting any components or the battery. Where necessary, also isolate at least one side of the circuit to be checked in order to avoid reading parallel resistances. Parallel circuit resistances will always give a lower reading than the actual resistance of either of the branches. When measuring the resistance of parallel circuits, the total resistance will always be lower than the smallest resistance in the circuit. Connect the meter leads to both sides of the circuit (wire or component) and read the actual measured ohms on the meter scale. Make sure the selector switch is set to the proper ohm scale for the circuit being tested to avoid misreading the ohmmeter test value.

**** WARNING**

Never use an ohmmeter with power applied to the circuit. Like the self-powered test light, the ohmmeter is designed to operate on its own power supply. The normal 12 volt automotive electrical system current could damage the meter!

Wiring Harnesses

The average automobile contains about ½ mile of wiring, with hundreds of individual connections. To protect the many wires from damage and to keep them from becoming a confusing tangle, they are organized into bundles, enclosed in plastic or taped together and called wiring harnesses. Different harnesses serve different parts of the vehicle. Individual wires are color coded to help trace them through a harness where sections are hidden from view.

Automotive wiring or circuit conductors can be in any one of three forms:

1. Single strand wire
2. Multi-strand wire
3. Printed circuitry

Single strand wire has a solid metal core and is usually used inside such components as alternators, motors, relays and other devices. Multi-strand wire has a core made of many small strands of wire twisted together into a single conductor. Most of the wiring in an automotive electrical system is made up of multi-strand wire, either as a single conductor or grouped together in a harness. All wiring is color coded on the insulator, either as a solid color or as a colored wire with an identification stripe. A printed circuit is a thin film of copper or other conductor that is printed on an insulator backing. Occasionally, a printed circuit is sandwiched between two sheets of plastic for more protection and flexibility. A complete printed circuit, consisting of conductors, insulating material and connectors for lamps or other components is called a printed circuit board. Printed circuitry is used in place of individual wires or harnesses in places where space is limited, such as behind instrument panels.

Since automotive electrical systems are very sensitive to changes in resistance, the selection of properly sized wires is critical when systems are repaired. A loose or corroded connection or a replacement wire that is too small for the circuit will add extra resistance and an additional voltage drop to the circuit. A ten percent voltage drop can result in slow or erratic motor operation, for example, even though the circuit is complete. The wire gauge number is an expression of the cross-section area of the conductor. The most common system for expressing wire size is the American Wire Gauge (AWG) system.

Gauge numbers are assigned to conductors of various cross-section areas. As gauge number increases, area decreases and the conductor becomes smaller. A 5 gauge conductor is smaller than a 1 gauge conductor and a 10 gauge is smaller than a 5 gauge. As the cross-section area of a conductor decreases, resistance increases and so does the gauge number. A conductor with a higher gauge number will carry less current than a conductor with a lower gauge number.

➡Gauge wire size refers to the size of the conductor, not the size of the complete wire. It is possible to have two wires of the same gauge with different diameters because one may have thicker insulation than the other.

12 volt automotive electrical systems generally use 10, 12, 14, 16 and 18 gauge wire. Main power distribution circuits and larger accessories usually use 10 and 12 gauge wire. Battery cables are usually 4 or 6 gauge, although 1 and 2 gauge wires are occasionally used. Wire length must also be considered when making repairs to a circuit. As conductor length increases, so does resistance. An 18 gauge wire, for example, can carry a 10 amp load for 10 feet without excessive voltage drop; however if a 15 foot wire is required for the same 10 amp load, it must be a 16 gauge wire.

An electrical schematic shows the electrical current paths when a circuit is operating properly. It is essential to understand how a circuit works before trying to figure out why it doesn't. Schematics break the entire electrical system down into individual circuits and show only one particular circuit. In a schematic, no attempt is made to represent wiring and components as they physically appear on the vehicle; switches and other components are shown as simply as possible. Face views of harness connectors show the cavity or terminal locations in all multi-pin connectors to help locate test points.

If you need to backprobe a connector while it is on the component, the order of the terminals must be mentally reversed. The wire color code can help in this situation, as well as a keyway, lock tab or other reference mark.

WIRING REPAIR

Soldering is a quick, efficient method of joining metals permanently. Everyone who has the occasion to make wiring repairs should know how to solder. Electrical connections that are soldered are far less likely to come apart and will conduct electricity much better than connections that are only "pig-tailed" together. The most popular (and preferred) method of soldering is with an electrical soldering gun. Soldering irons are available in many sizes and wattage ratings. Irons with higher wattage ratings deliver higher temperatures and recover lost heat faster. A small soldering iron rated for no more than 50 watts is recommended, especially on electrical systems where excess heat can damage the components being soldered.

There are three ingredients necessary for successful soldering; proper flux, good solder and sufficient heat. A soldering flux is necessary to clean the metal of tarnish, prepare it for soldering and to enable the solder to spread into tiny crevices. When soldering, always use a rosin core solder which is non-corrosive and will not attract moisture once the job is finished. Other types of flux (acid core) will leave a residue that will attract moisture and cause the wires to corrode. Tin is a unique metal with a low melting point. In a molten state, it dissolves and alloys easily with many metals. Solder is made by mixing tin with lead. The most common proportions are 40/60, 50/50 and 60/40, with the percentage of tin listed first. Low priced solders usually contain less tin, making them very difficult for a beginner to use because more heat is required to melt the solder. A common solder is 40/60 which is well suited for all-around general use, but 60/40 melts easier and is preferred for electrical work.

Soldering Techniques

Successful soldering requires that the metals to be joined be heated to a temperature that will melt the solder, usually 360–460°F (182–238°C). Contrary to popular belief, the purpose of the soldering iron is not to melt the solder itself, but to heat the parts being soldered to a temperature high enough to melt the solder when it is touched to the work. Melting flux-cored solder on the soldering iron will usually destroy the effectiveness of the flux.

➡Soldering tips are made of copper for good heat conductivity, but must be "tinned" regularly for quick transference of heat to the project and to prevent the solder from sticking to the iron. To "tin" the iron, simply heat it and touch the flux-cored solder to the tip; the solder will flow over the hot tip. Wipe the excess off with a clean rag, but be careful as the iron will be hot.

After some use, the tip may become pitted. If so, simply dress the tip smooth with a smooth file and "tin" the tip again. Flux-cored solder will remove oxides but rust, bits of insulation and oil or grease must be removed with a wire brush or emery cloth. For maximum strength in soldered parts, the joint must start off clean and tight. Weak joints will result in gaps too wide for the solder to bridge.

If a separate soldering flux is used, it should be brushed or swabbed on only those areas that are to be soldered. Most solders contain a core of flux and separate fluxing is unnecessary. Hold the work to be soldered firmly. It is best to solder on a wooden board, because a metal vise will only rob the piece to be soldered of heat and make it difficult to melt the solder. Hold the soldering tip with the broadest face against the work to be soldered. Apply solder under the tip close to the work, using enough solder to give a heavy film between the iron and the piece being soldered, while moving slowly and making sure the solder melts properly. Keep the work level or the solder will run to the lowest part and favor the thicker parts, because these require more heat to melt the solder. If the soldering tip overheats (the solder coating on the face of the tip burns up), it should be retinned. Once the soldering is completed, let the soldered joint stand until cool. Tape and seal all soldered wire splices after the repair has cooled.

Wire Harness Connectors

Most connectors in the engine compartment or that are otherwise exposed to the elements are protected against moisture and dirt which could create oxidation and deposits on the terminals.

These special connectors are weather-proof. All repairs require the use of a special terminal and the tool required to service it. This tool is used to remove the pin and sleeve terminals. If removal is attempted with an ordinary pick, there is a good chance that the terminal will be bent or deformed. Unlike standard blade type terminals, these weather-proof terminals cannot be straightened once they are bent. Make certain that the connectors are properly seated and all of the sealing rings are in place when connecting leads. On some models, a hinge-type flap provides a backup or secondary locking feature for the terminals. Most secondary locks are used to improve connector reliability by retaining the terminals if the small terminal lock tangs are not positioned properly.

Molded-on connectors require complete replacement of the connection. This means splicing a new connector assembly into the harness. All splices should be soldered to insure proper contact. Use care when probing the connections or replacing terminals in them as it is possible to short between opposite terminals. If this happens to the wrong terminal pair, it is possible to damage certain components. Always use jumper wires between connectors for circuit checking and never probe through weatherproof seals.

Open circuits are often difficult to locate by sight because corrosion or terminal misalignment are hidden by the connectors. Merely wiggling a connector on a sensor or in the wiring harness may correct the open circuit condition. This should always be considered when an open circuit or a failed sensor is indicated. Intermittent problems may also be caused by oxidized or loose connections. When using a circuit tester for diagnosis, always probe connections from the wire side. Be careful not to damage sealed connectors with test probes.

All wiring harnesses should be replaced with identical parts, using the same gauge wire and connectors. When signal wires are spliced into a harness, use wire with high temperature insulation only. It is seldom necessary to replace a complete harness. If replacement is necessary, pay close attention to insure proper harness routing. Secure the harness with suitable plastic wire clamps to prevent vibrations from causing the harness to wear in spots or contact any hot components.

➡Weatherproof connectors cannot be replaced with standard connectors. Instructions are provided with replacement connector and terminal packages. Some wire harnesses have mounting indicators (usually pieces of colored tape) to mark where the harness is to be secured.

In making wiring repairs, its important that you always replace damaged wires with wiring of the same gauge as the wire being replaced. The heavier the wire, the smaller the gauge number. Wires are color-coded to aid in identification and whenever possible the same color coded wire should be used for replacement. A wire stripping and crimping tool is necessary to install solderless terminal connectors. Test all crimps by pulling on the wires; it should not be possible to pull the wires out of a good crimp.

Wires which are open, exposed or otherwise damaged are repaired by simple splicing. Where possible, if the wiring harness is accessible and the damaged place in the wire can be located, it is best to open the harness and check for all possible damage. In an inaccessible harness, the wire must be bypassed with a new insert, usually taped to the outside of the old harness.

When replacing fusible links, be sure to use fusible link wire, NOT ordinary automotive wire. Make sure the fusible segment is of the same gauge and construction as the one being replaced and double the stripped end when crimping the terminal connector for a good contact. The melted (open) fusible link segment of the wiring harness should be cut off as close to the harness as possible, then a new segment spliced in as described. In the case of a damaged fusible link that feeds two harness wires, the harness connections should be replaced with two fusible link wires so that each circuit will have its own separate protection.

➡Most of the problems caused in the wiring harness are due to bad ground connections. Always check all vehicle ground connections for corrosion or looseness before performing any power feed checks to eliminate the chance of a bad ground affecting the circuit.

Hard-Shell Connectors

Unlike molded connectors, the terminal contacts in hard-shell connectors can be replaced. Weatherproof hard-shell connectors with the leads molded into the shell have non-replaceable terminal ends. Replacement usually involves the use of a special terminal removal tool that depresses the locking tangs (barbs) on the connector terminal and allows the connector to be removed from the rear of the shell. The connector shell should be replaced if it shows any evidence of burning, melting, cracks, or breaks. Replace individual terminals that are burnt, corroded, distorted or loose.

➡The insulation crimp must be tight to prevent the insulation from sliding back on the wire when the wire is pulled. The insulation must be visibly compressed under the crimp tabs, and the ends of the crimp should be turned in for a firm grip on the insulation.

The wire crimp must be made with all wire strands inside the crimp. The terminal must be fully compressed on the wire strands with the ends of the crimp tabs turned in to make a firm grip on the wire. Check all connections with an ohmmeter to insure a good contact. There should be no measurable resistance between the wire and the terminal when connected.

Fusible Links

The fuse link is a short length of special, Hypalon (high temperature) insulated wire, integral with the engine compartment wiring harness and should not be confused with standard wire. It is several wire gauges smaller than the circuit which it protects. Under no circumstances should a fuse link replacement repair be made using a length of standard wire cut from bulk stock or from another wiring harness.

To repair any blown fuse link use the following procedure:

1. Determine which circuit is damaged, its location and the cause of the open fuse link. If the damaged fuse link is one of three fed by a common No. 10 or 12 gauge feed wire, determine the specific affected circuit.
2. Disconnect the negative battery cable.
3. Cut the damaged fuse link from the wiring harness and discard it. If the fuse link is one of three circuits fed by a single feed wire, cut it out of the harness at each splice end and discard it.
4. Identify and procure the proper fuse link with butt connectors for attaching the fuse link to the harness.

➡Heat shrink tubing must be slipped over the wire before crimping and soldering the connection.

5. To repair any fuse link in a 3-link group with one feed:
   a. After cutting the open link out of the harness, cut each of the remaining undamaged fuse links close to the feed wire weld.
   b. Strip approximately ½ in. (13mm) of insulation from the detached ends of the two good fuse links. Insert two wire ends into one end of a butt connector, then carefully push one stripped end of the replacement fuse link into the same end of the butt connector and crimp all three firmly together.

➡Care must be taken when fitting the three fuse links into the butt connector as the internal diameter is a snug fit for three wires. Make sure to use a proper crimping tool. Pliers, side cutters, etc. will not apply the proper crimp to retain the wires and withstand a pull test.

   c. After crimping the butt connector to the three fuse links, cut the weld portion from the feed wire and strip approximately ½ in. (13mm) of insulation from the cut end. Insert the stripped end into the open end of the butt connector and crimp very firmly.
   d. To attach the remaining end of the replacement fuse link, strip approximately ½ in. (13mm) of insulation from the wire end of the circuit from which the blown fuse link was removed, and firmly crimp a butt connector or equivalent to the stripped wire. Then, insert the end of the replacement link into the other end of the butt connector and crimp firmly.
   e. Using rosin core solder with a consistency of 60 percent tin and 40 percent lead, solder the connectors and the wires at the repairs then insulate with electrical tape or heat shrink tubing.
6. To replace any fuse link on a single circuit in a harness, cut out the damaged portion, strip approximately ½ in. (13mm) of insulation from the two wire ends and attach the appropriate replacement fuse link to the stripped wire ends with two proper size butt connectors. Solder the connectors and wires, then insulate.
7. To repair any fuse link which has an eyelet terminal on one end such as the charging circuit, cut off the open fuse link behind the weld, strip approximately ½ in. (13mm) of insulation from the cut end and attach the appropriate new eyelet fuse link to the cut stripped wire with an appropriate size butt connector. Solder the connectors and wires at the repair, then insulate.
8. Connect the negative battery cable to the battery and test the system for proper operation.

➡Do not mistake a resistor wire for a fuse link. The resistor wire is generally longer and has print stating, "Resistor-don't cut or splice."

When attaching a single No. 16, 17, 18 or 20 gauge fuse link to a heavy gauge wire, always double the stripped wire end of the fuse link before inserting and crimping it into the butt connector for positive wire retention.

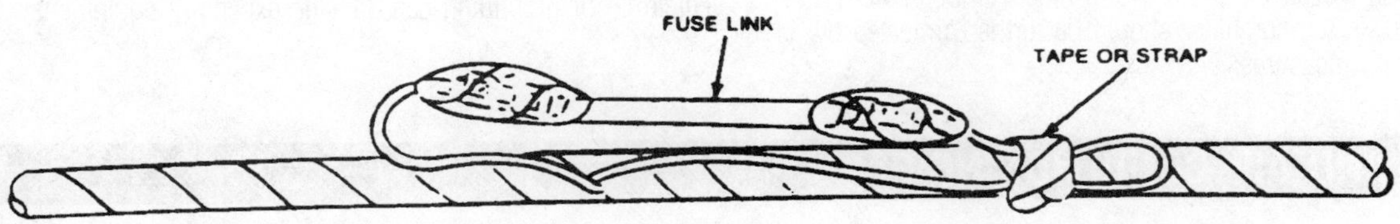

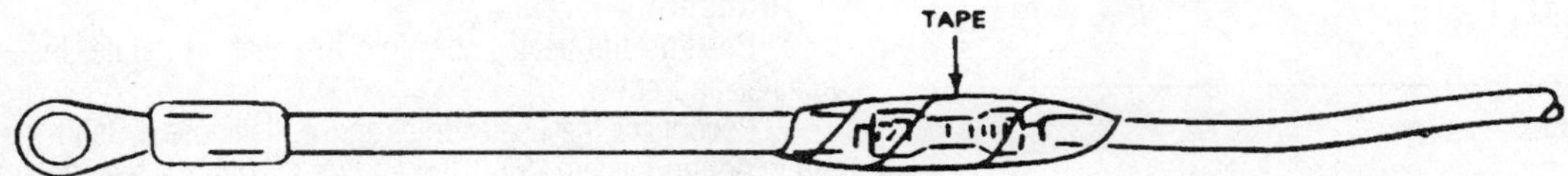

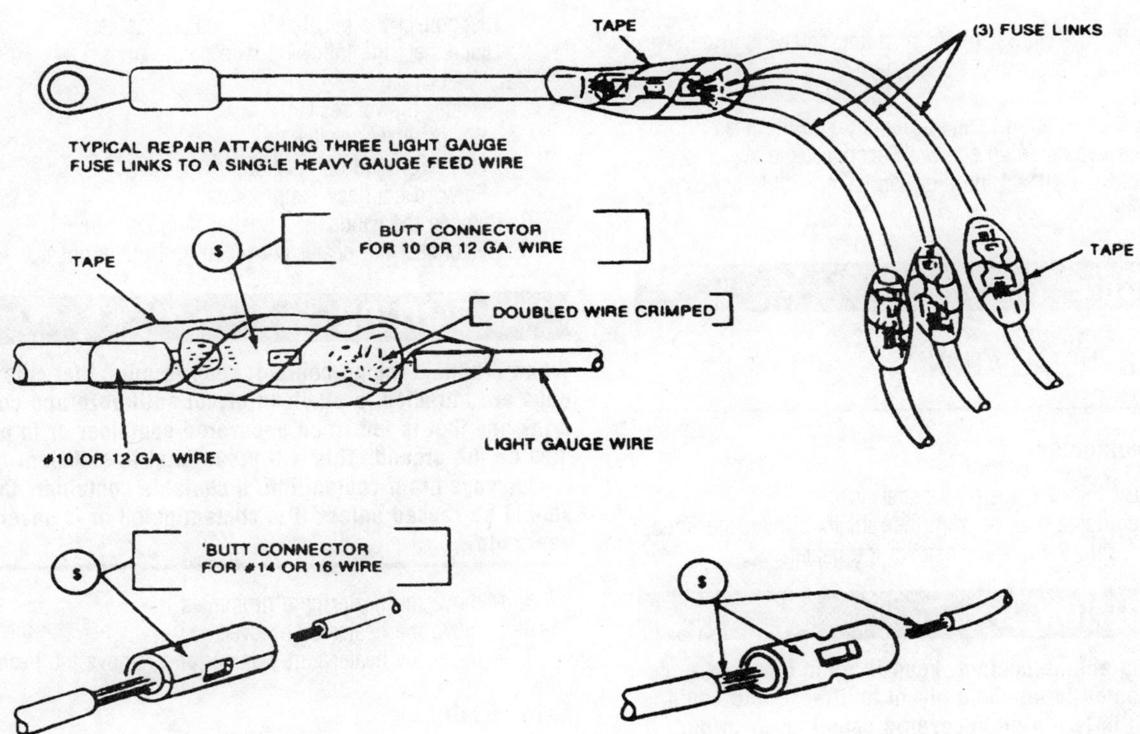

General fusible link repair—never replace a fusible link with regular wire or a fusible link rated at a higher amperage than the one being replaced

Add-On Electrical Equipment

The electrical system in your vehicle is designed to perform under reasonable operating conditions without interference between components. Before any additional electrical equipment is installed, it is recommended that you consult your dealer or a reputable repair facility that is familiar with the vehicle and its systems.

If the vehicle is equipped with mobile radio equipment and/or mobile telephone, it may have an effect upon the operation of any on-board computer control modules. Radio Frequency Interference (RFI) from the communications system can be picked up by the vehicle's wiring harnesses and conducted into the control module, giving it the wrong messages at the wrong time. Although well shielded against RFI, the computer should be further protected by taking the following measures:

- Install the antenna as far as possible from the control module. For instance, if the module is located behind the center console area, then the antenna should be mounted at the rear of the vehicle.
- Keep the antenna wiring a minimum of eight inches away from any wiring running to control modules and from the module itself. NEVER wind the antenna wire around any other wiring.
- Mount the equipment as far from the control module as possible. Be very careful during installation not to drill through any wires or short a wire harness with a mounting screw.
- Insure that the electrical feed wire(s) to the equipment are properly and tightly connected. Loose connectors can cause interference.
- Make certain that the equipment is properly grounded to the vehicle. Poor grounding can damage expensive equipment.

HEATING AND AIR CONDITIONING

Blower Motor and Cage

REMOVAL & INSTALLATION

See Figures 1 and 2

1. Disconnect the negative (−) battery cable.
2. Remove the cooling tube.
3. Disconnect electrical connections from the blower switch and ground.
4. Remove the five blower motor retaining screws and remove the blower and cage assembly.

To install:

5. Position the motor and cage assembly into the heater housing. Tighten the five retaining screws. Reconnect the switch and ground connectors. Connect the negative battery cable and check for proper operation.

Heater Core

REMOVAL & INSTALLATION

With Air Conditioning

1. Disconnect the negative (−) battery cable.
2. Drain the engine coolant from the radiator. Under the hood, disconnect and plug the heater hoses at the heater.

CAUTION

When draining engine coolant, keep in mind that cats and dogs are attracted to ethylene glycol antifreeze and could drink any that is left in an uncovered container or in puddles on the ground. This will prove fatal in sufficient quantity. Always drain coolant into a sealable container. Coolant should be reused unless it is contaminated or is several years old.

3. Remove the speaker grille and the speaker.
4. Remove the heater core cover, retainers and the heater core.

To install:

5. Position the heater core into the heater module. Install the retainer and cover.
6. Reconnect the heater inlet and outlet hoses. Refill the engine cooling system. Start the engine and check for coolant leaks.

Without Air Conditioning

1. Disconnect the negative (−) battery cable.
2. Disconnect the following wire connections:
   a. Heater relay.
   b. Heater blower resistor.
   c. Heater blower switch.
   d. Heater ground connection.
   e. Forward courtesy lamp socket.
3. Remove the windshield washer fluid container.
4. Disconnect the heater core inlet and outlet hoses.

CAUTION

When draining engine coolant, keep in mind that cats and dogs are attracted to ethylene glycol antifreeze and could drink any that is left in an uncovered container or in puddles on the ground. This will prove fatal in sufficient quantity. Always drain coolant into a sealable container. Coolant should be reused unless it is contaminated or is several years old.

5. Remove the heater core grommets.
6. Remove the heater case cover.
7. Remove the heater core retainer and remove the heater core.

To install:

8. Position the heater core and seals into the heater case. Install the retainer and cover assembly. Tighten the cover attaching screws.
9. Connect the heater wiring to the heater case cover. (heater relay, resistor, blower switch and ground)

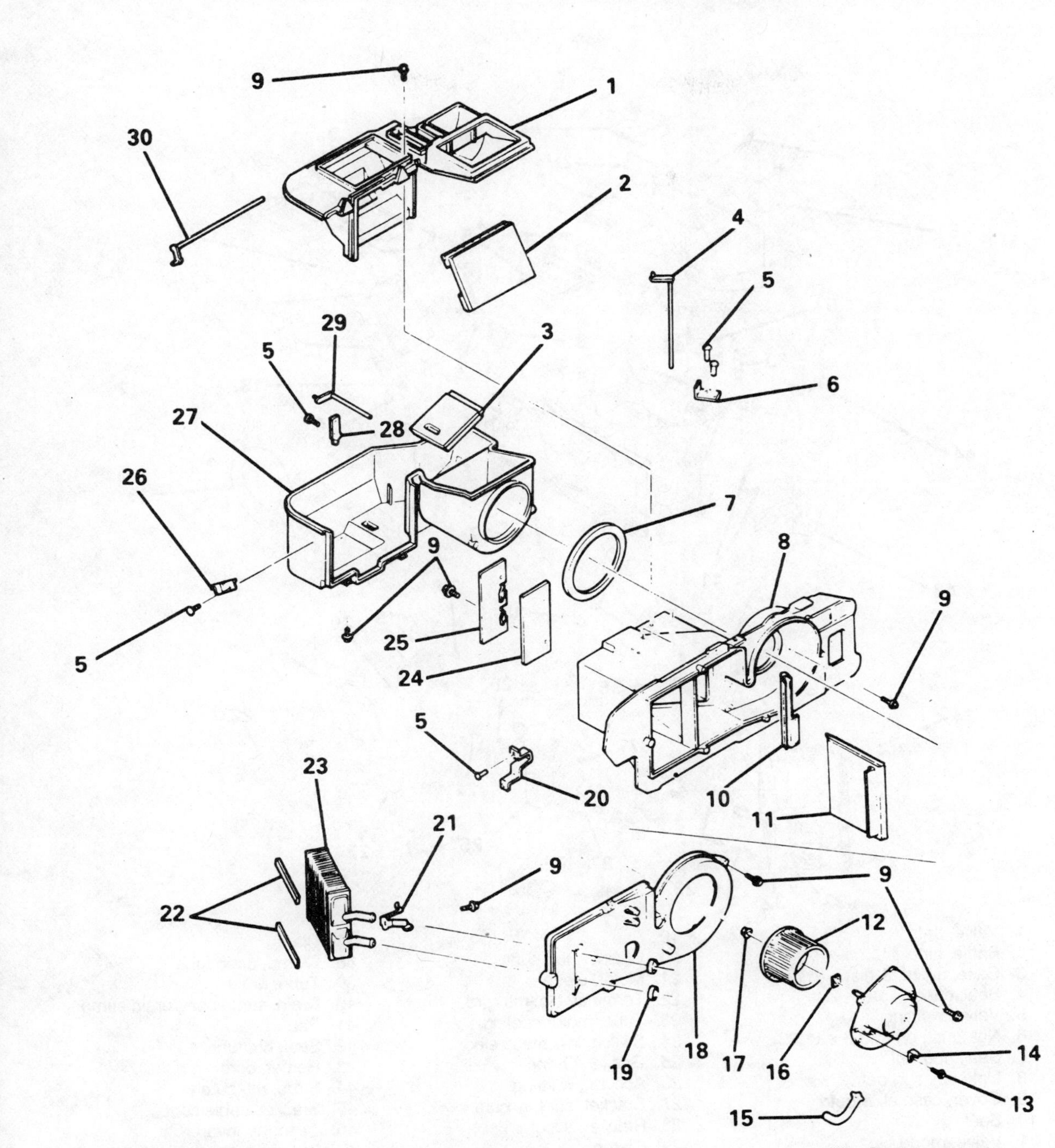

1. Cover, air inl. & dist.
2. Valve, vent
3. Valve, defr.
4. Shaft, w/lvr., temp. vlv.
5. Rivet, truss hd (9/16″ x 1/4″)
6. Bracket, cbl. mtg.
7. Seal, htr. & blo. case
8. Case, htr.
9. Screw, hwh tap (M4.2 x 1.41 x 13)
10. Baffle, air
11. Valve, temp.
12. Fan, blo.
13. Screw, hwh tap (M4.2 x 1.41 x 14)
14. Terminal, blo. mtr. grd. (2.530)
15. Tube, mtr. clg. (9.218)
16. Washer, fan supt. (9.216)
17. Nut, blo. fan
18. Cover, blo.
19. Seal, htr. core tube
20. Bracket, mt.
21. Clamp, core mt.
22. Seal, htr. core
23. Core, htr.
24. Seal, htr. core case
25. Clip, htr. core mt.
26. Bracket, cbl. mt.
27. Case, air inl. & distr.
28. Bracket, cbl. mt.
29. Shaft, w/lvr., defr. vlv.
30. Shaft, w/lvr., vent vlv.

Fig. 1 Exploded view of the heater control module used on models not equipped with A/C

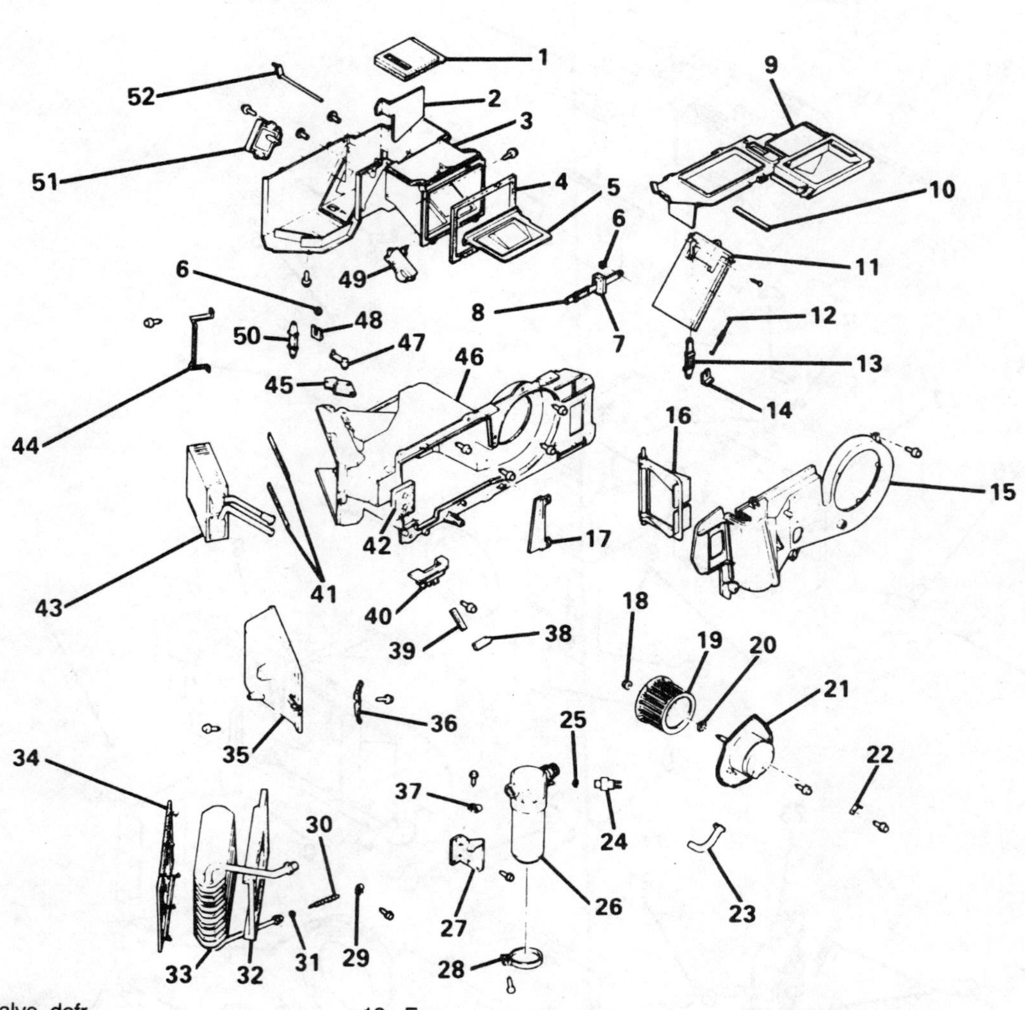

1. Valve, defr.
2. Baffle, air
3. Case, air int. & dist.
4. Seal, case
5. Valve, w/fitting
6. Nut, push on (M3.6 x 11.23)
7. Seal, opg. link
8. Link, adj. spr. defr.
9. Cover, case al. & defr.
10. Seal
11. Valve, mode
12. Spring, ext.
13. Link, adj. spr. mode
14. Retainer
15. Case, blower
16. Valve, temp.
17. Baffle, air
18. Nut
19. Fan
20. Washer, fan supt.
21. Motor, elec.
22. Terminal, blo. mtr. grd.
23. Tube, motor cooling
24. Switch, low press elec.
25. Gasket, O-ring
26. Accum., w/fitting
27. Bracket, supt. accum.
28. Bracket, accum.
29. Clamp
30. Orifice
31. Gasket, O-ring
32. Seal, core evap.
33. Core, w/tube asm. evap.
34. Filter, water core
35. Cover, heater
36. Clip, spl. mt. core
37. Clamp
38. Clamp, drain tube
39. Tube, drain
40. Drain, sump seal, drain sump
41. Seal
42. Seal, htr. tube
43. Heater, core
44. Strap, mt. core
45. Bracket, cable cont.
46. Case, htr. evap.
47. Lever, cont.
48. Clip, tet link
49. Actuator, elec. al.
50. Link, adj. spr. al.
51. Actuator, elec. mode
52. Shaft, w/lever defr.

Fig. 2 Exploded view of the heater and A/C module

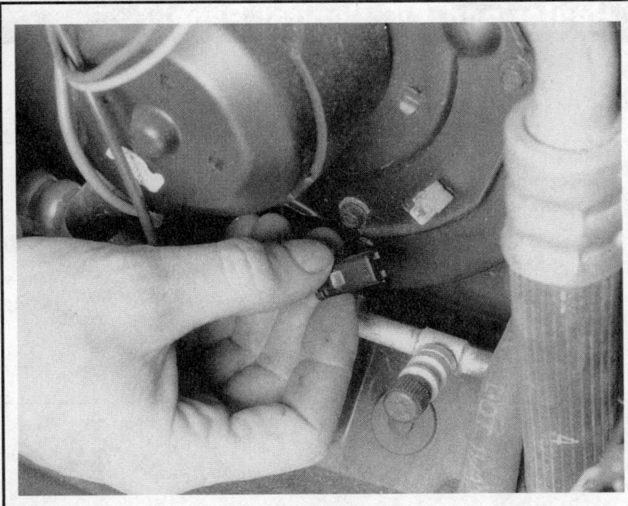
Disengage the blower motor electrical connection

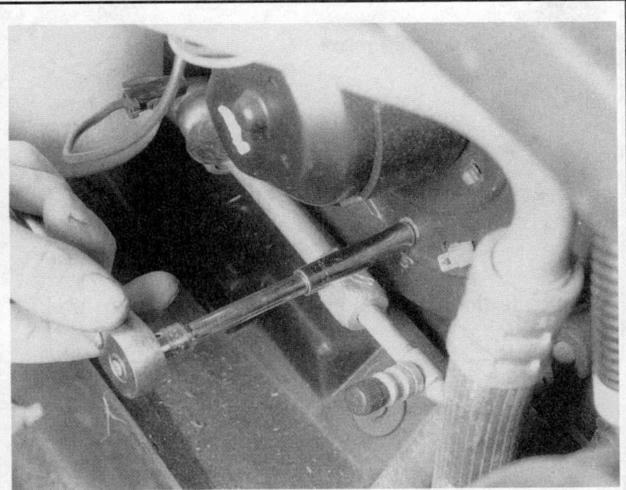
Remove the blower motor retainers . . .

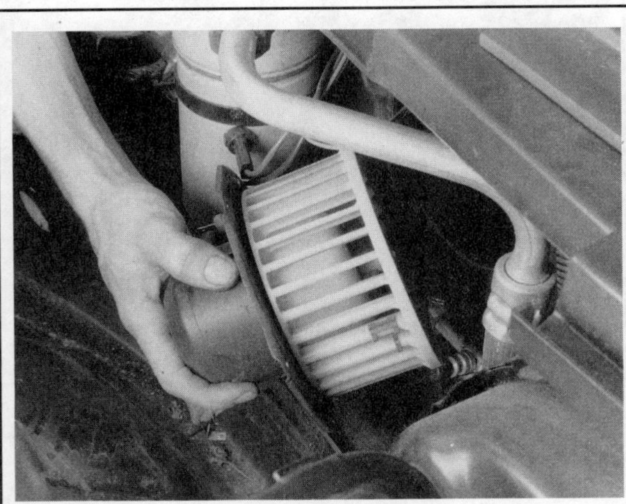
. . . then remove the blower motor and cage

10. Install the heater inlet and outlet hoses. Refill the cooling system.
11. Reconnect the negative (−) battery cable and start the engine to check for coolant leaks.

Air Conditioning Evaporator Core

REMOVAL & INSTALLATION

1. Disconnect the negative () battery cable.
2. Discharge the A/C system as outlined in the "A/C System Discharge" procedure in Section 1.
3. Remove the blower relay bracket.
4. Disconnect and mark all electrical connectors at the heater module.
5. Disconnect the evaporator core tube-to-accumulator fitting using a flare nut and backup wrench.

⁂ WARNING

Damage to the aluminum fittings may result if the proper size flare nut wrenches are not used. Always use a backup wrench on the accumulator.

6. Drain the engine coolant at the radiator.

⁂ CAUTION

When draining engine coolant, keep in mind that cats and dogs are attracted to ethylene glycol antifreeze and could drink any that is left in an uncovered container or in puddles on the ground. This will prove fatal in sufficient quantity. Always drain coolant into a sealable container. Coolant should be reused unless it is contaminated or is several years old.

7. Disconnect the heater inlet and outlet hoses.
8. Remove the washer fluid reservoir.
9. Remove the bolts from the front blower housing.
10. Remove the blower housing assembly.
11. Remove the evaporator-to-condenser tube.
12. Remove the evaporator core from the housing.

To install:

1. Install the evaporator core into the housing.
2. Install new O-ring to all A/C connections. Lubricate the seals with 525 viscosity refrigerant oil.
3. Connect the evaporator-to-condenser tube and torque to 17 ft. lbs. (24 Nm) with a flare nut and backup wrench.

⁂ WARNING

Damage to the aluminum fittings may result if the proper size flare nut wrenches are not used. Always use a backup wrench on the accumulator.

4. Install the blower housing and connect the heater hoses at the heater core.
5. Install the housing bolts and tighten.
6. Connect the evaporator core tube-to-accumulator and torque to 30 ft. lbs. (41 Nm) with a flare nut and backup wrench.
7. Install the relay bracket and all electrical connectors.
8. Evacuate and recharge the A/C system as outlined in the "A/C Evacuation and Recharge" procedure in Section 1.
9. Install the washer fluid reservoir and reconnect the negative (−) battery cable.
10. Start the engine and check for proper operation of the control assembly, fan blower switch, compressor, clutch cycling, proper cooling and coolant leaks.

Heater and A/C Control Panel

REMOVAL & INSTALLATION

1. Remove the console trim plate.
2. Remove the control panel retaining bolts.
3. Slide the control panel forward, disengage the electrical connections and control cables.
4. Remove the control panel.
5. Installation is the reverse of removal.

Remove the control panel retainers . . .

Disengage the electrical connections from the control panel . . .

. . . then slide the panel forward from its mounting

. . . then disconnect the control cable and remove the control panel

ENTERTAINMENT SYSTEM

Radio

REMOVAL & INSTALLATION

➧ **See Figure 3**

1. Remove the console trim plate assembly.
2. Disconnect the side retaining nuts and the rear retaining bolt.
3. Disconnect the electrical and antenna connections.
4. Remove the radio through the front of the console.
5. Installation is the reverse of removal.

➡It is very important when doing any radio work to avoid pinching the speaker wires. A short circuit to ground from either wire will cause damage to the output circuit of the radio.

Clock

The clock is located in the LED electronic tuning display of the radio. It can be seen when the ignition key is in the **ON** position or when the clock recall button is pushed. The time of day is displayed until a tuning change is made.

SETTING

AM Radios

To set the time of day, use a ball-point pen and push in on the hour display button to set the desired hour and then push in on the minute display button to set the minute display.

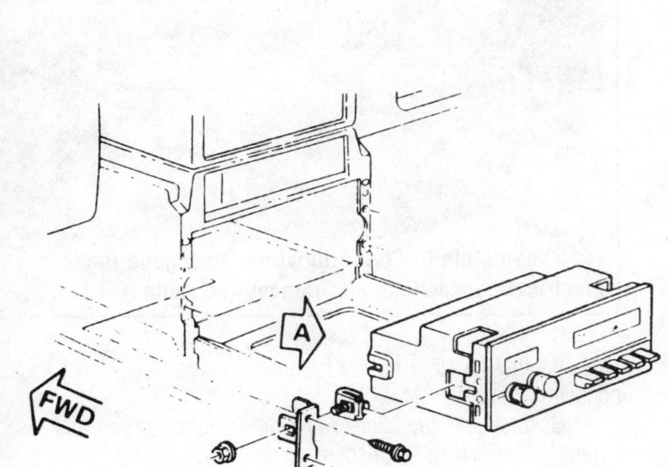

Fig. 3 The radio is retained using rear and side mounted nuts and bolts

Remove the console trim plate retaining screws . . .

Remove the radio retaining bolts . . .

. . . then remove the trim plate

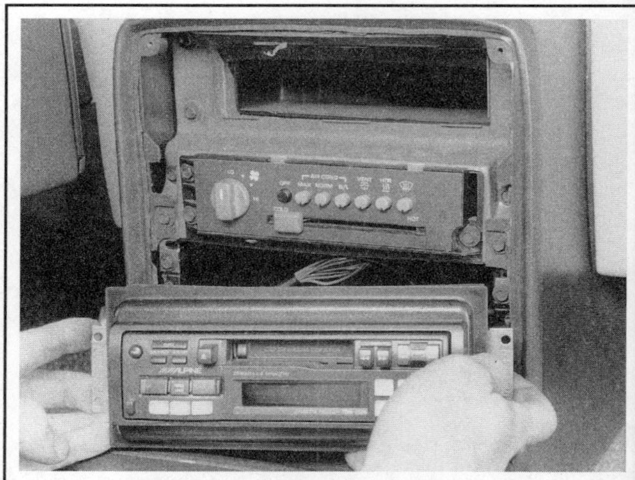

. . . then slide the radio forward. Disengage the electrical connections and remove the radio

Seek and Scan Radios

To set the hour, press the SET button. The SET indicator light on the dial will then light up and the radio frequency will be displayed. Then press the SCAN button, holding the SCAN button until the correct hour appears.

To set the minutes, press the SET button. The SET indicator light will then light up and the radio frequency will be displayed. Then press the SEEK button, holding the SEEK button in until the correct minute is displayed. The clock frequency will only be displayed when the SEEK or SCAN button is pushed.

Radio Amplifier

REMOVAL & INSTALLATION

1. Disconnect the negative (−) battery cable.
2. Remove the console shift plate, console pad and the carpet from the retainers.
3. Remove the four button fasteners. Remove the carpet and console side cover.
4. Unscrew the amplifier-to-bracket retaining screws and disconnect the electrical connectors.

To install:

5. Position the amplifier assembly into the bracket and tighten the retaining screws.
6. Install the carpet, four button fasteners and console side cover.
7. Install the console pad and shift plate.

WINDSHIELD WIPERS

Wiper Arm

REMOVAL & INSTALLATION

➧ **See Figure 4**

The wiper arms are retained on the serrated transmission spindle by an integral locking clip. Carefully lift up on the wiper arm using Tool J-8966 or equivalent. Installation is the reverse of removal.

Windshield Wipers

ELEMENT (REFILL) CARE & REPLACEMENT

For maximum effectiveness and longest element life, the windshield and wiper blades should be kept clean. Dirt, tree sap, road tar and so on will cause streaking, smearing and blade deterioration if left on the glass. It is advisable to wash the windshield carefully with a commercial glass cleaner at least once a month. Wipe off the rubber blades with the wet rag afterwards. Do not attempt to move wipers across the windshield by hand; damage to the motor and drive mechanism will result.

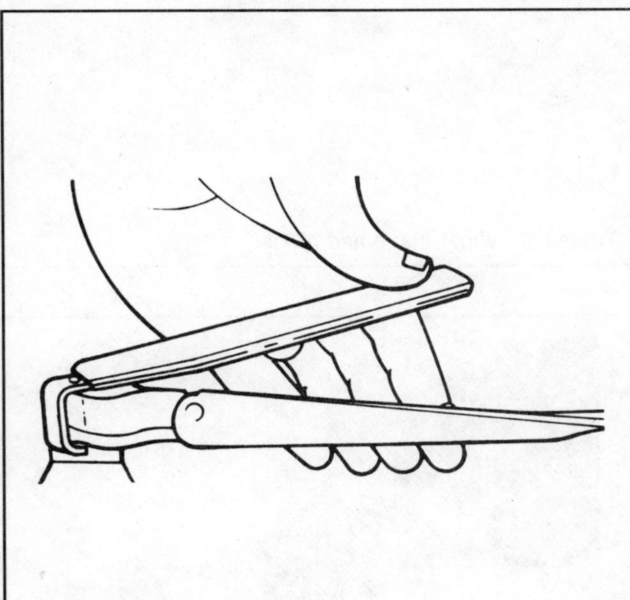

Fig. 4 Use tool J-8966 or its equivalent to disengage the wiper arm from the retaining locking clip

To inspect and/or replace the wiper blade elements, place the wiper switch in the **LOW** speed position and the ignition switch in the **ACC** position. When the wiper blades are approximately vertical on the windshield, turn the ignition switch to **OFF.**

Examine the wiper blade elements. If they are found to be cracked, broken or torn, they should be replaced immediately. Replacement intervals will vary with usage, although ozone deterioration usually limits element life to about one year. If the wiper pattern is smeared or streaked, or if the blade chatters across the glass, the elements should be replaced. It is easiest and most sensible to replace the elements in pairs.

If your vehicle is equipped with aftermarket blades, there are several different types of refills and your vehicle might have any kind. Aftermarket blades and arms rarely use the exact same type blade or refill as the original equipment. Here are some typical aftermarket blades; not all may be available for your vehicle:

The Anco® type uses a release button that is pushed down to allow the refill to slide out of the yoke jaws. The new refill slides back into the frame and locks in place.

Some Trico® refills are removed by locating where the metal backing strip or the refill is wider. Insert a small screwdriver blade between the frame and metal backing strip. Press down to release the refill from the retaining tab.

Other types of Trico® refills have two metal tabs which are unlocked by squeezing them together. The rubber filler can then be withdrawn from the frame jaws. A new refill is installed by inserting the refill into the front frame jaws and sliding it rearward to engage the remaining frame jaws. There are usually four jaws; be certain when installing that the refill is engaged in all of them. At the end of its travel, the tabs will lock into place on the front jaws of the wiper blade frame.

Another type of refill is made from polycarbonate. The refill has a simple locking device at one end which flexes downward out of the groove into which the jaws of the holder fit, allowing easy release. By sliding the new refill through all the jaws and pushing through the slight resistance when it reaches the end of its travel, the refill will lock into position.

To replace the Tridon® refill, it is necessary to remove the wiper blade. This refill has a plastic backing strip with a notch about 1 in. (25mm) from the end. Hold the blade (frame) on a hard surface so that the frame is tightly bowed. Grip the tip of the backing strip and pull up while twisting counterclockwise. The backing strip will snap out of the retaining tab. Do this for the remaining tabs until the refill is free of the blade. The length of these refills is molded into the end and they should be replaced with identical types.

Regardless of the type of refill used, be sure to follow the part manufacturer's instructions closely. Make sure that all of the frame jaws are engaged as the refill is pushed into place and locked. If the metal blade holder and frame are allowed to touch the glass during wiper operation, the glass will be scratched.

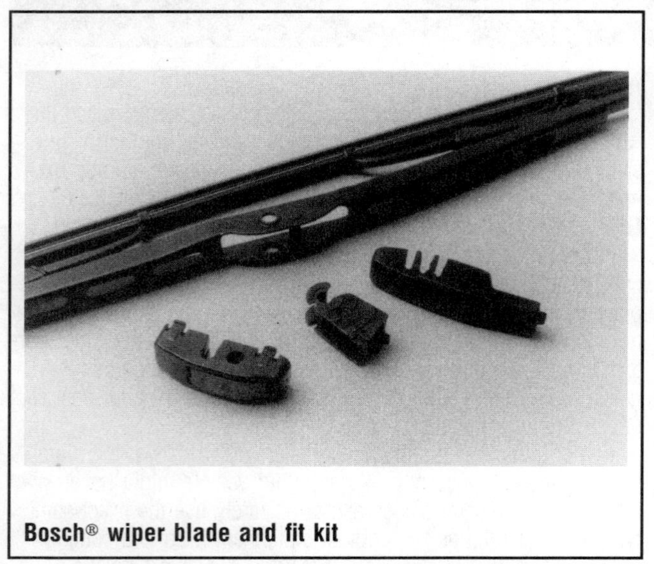
Bosch® wiper blade and fit kit

Trico® wiper blade and fit kit

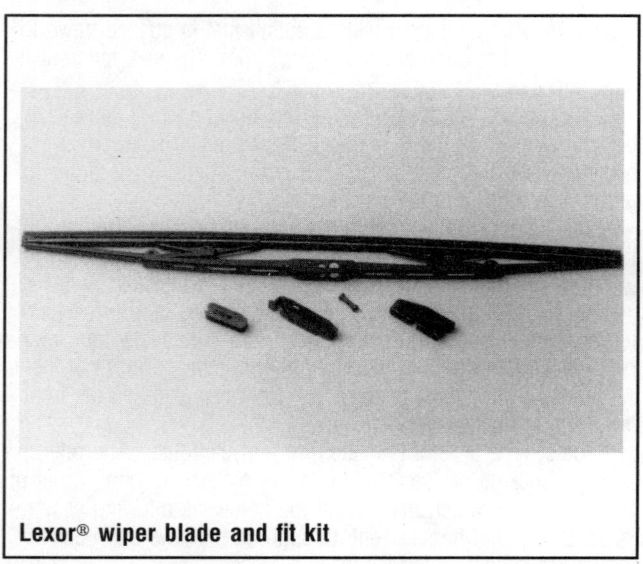
Lexor® wiper blade and fit kit

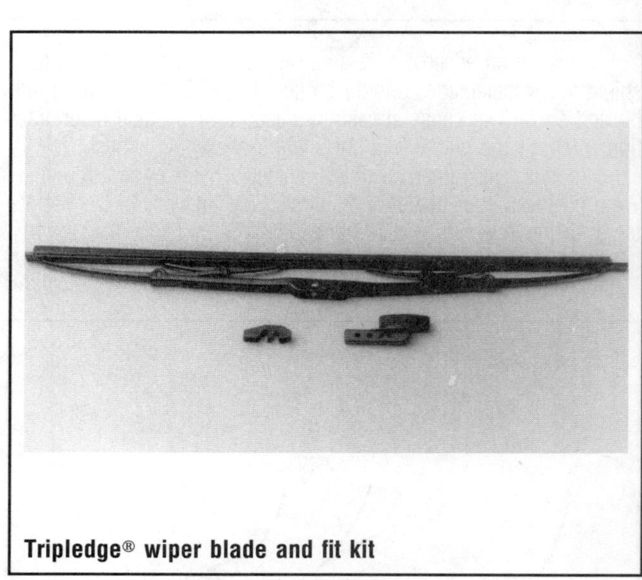
Tripledge® wiper blade and fit kit

Pylon® wiper blade and adaptor

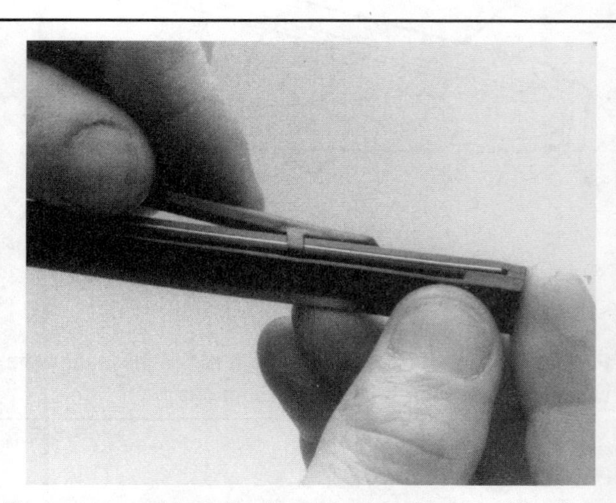
To remove and install a Lexor® wiper blade refill, slip out the old insert and slide in a new one

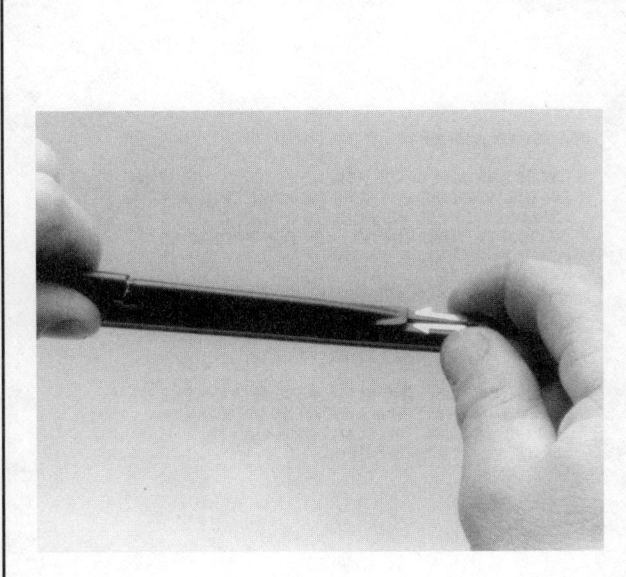

On Pylon® inserts, the clip at the end has to be removed prior to sliding the insert off

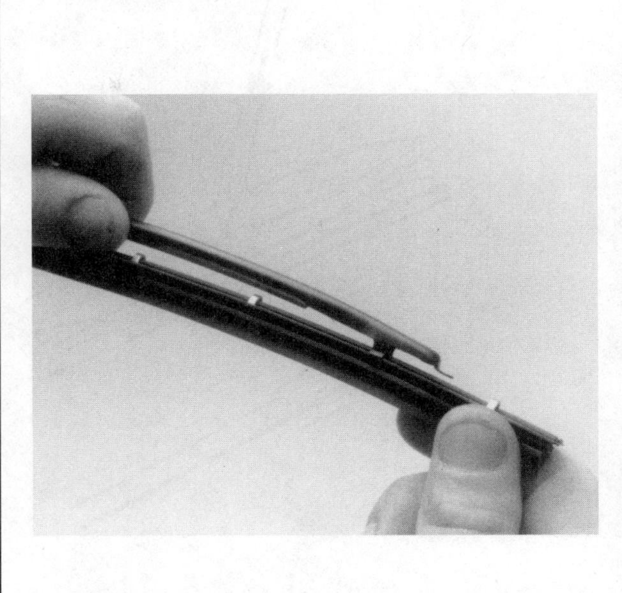

. . . then the insert can be removed. After installing the replacement insert, bend the tab back

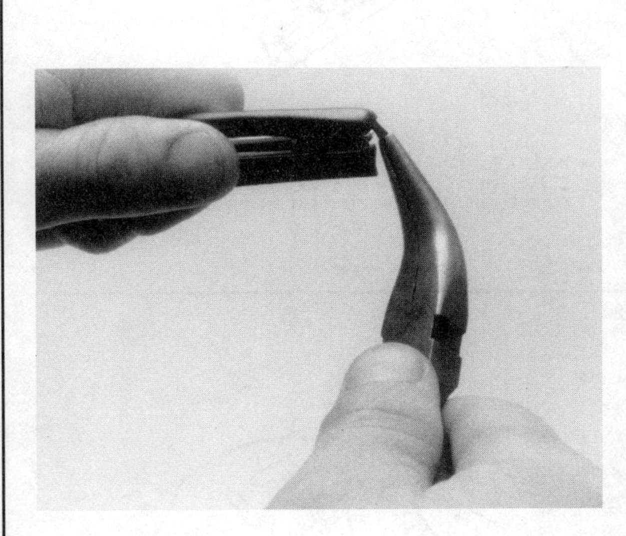

On Trico® wiper blades, the tab at the end of the blade must be turned up . . .

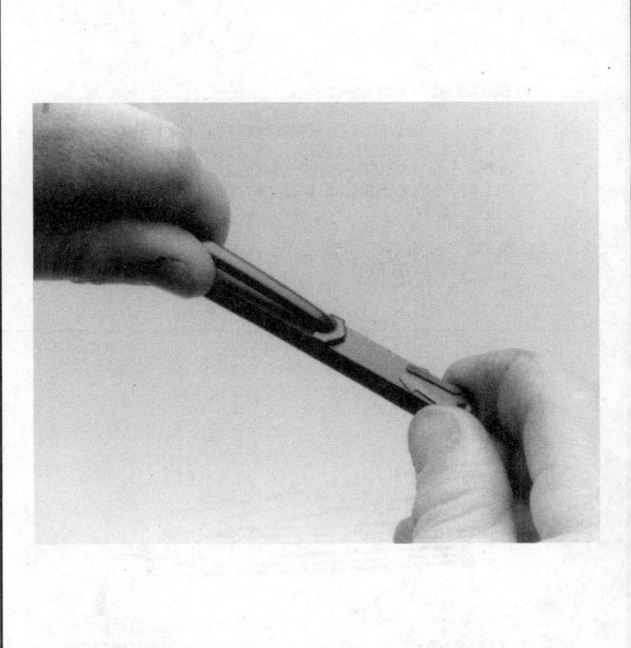

The Tripledge® wiper blade insert is removed and installed using a securing clip

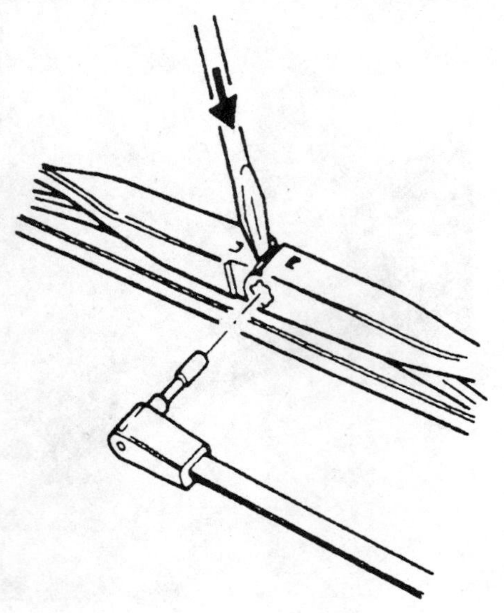

BLADE REPLACEMENT

1. CYCLE ARM AND BLADE ASSEMBLY TO UP POSITION-ON THE WINDSHIELD WHERE REMOVAL OF BLADE ASSEMBLY CAN BE PERFORMED WITHOUT DIFFICULTY. TURN IGNITION KEY OFF AT DESIRED POSITION.

2. TO REMOVE BLADE ASSEMBLY, INSERT SCREWDRIVER IN SLOT, PUSH DOWN ON SPRING LOCK AND PULL BLADE ASSEMBLY FROM PIN (VIEW A)

3. TO INSTALL, PUSH THE BLADE ASSEMBLY ON THE PIN SO THAT THE SPRING LOCK ENGAGES THE PIN (VIEW A). BE SURE THE BLADE ASSEMBLY IS SECURELY ATTACHED TO PIN

VIEW A

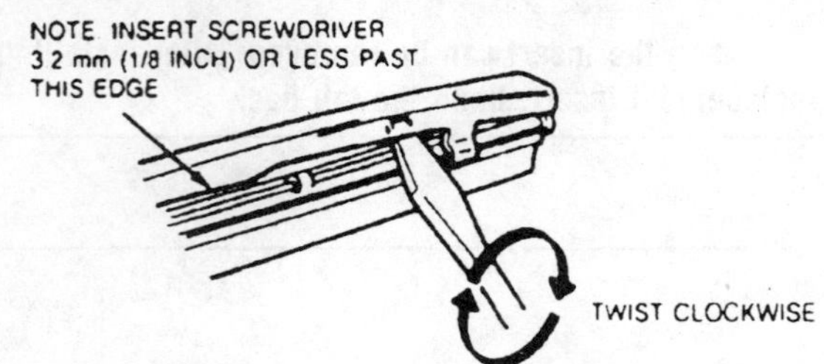

ELEMENT REPLACEMENT

1. INSERT SCREWDRIVER BETWEEN THE EDGE OF THE SUPER STRUCTURE AND THE BLADE BACKING DRIP (VIEW B) TWIST SCREWDRIVER SLOWLY UNTIL ELEMENT CLEARS ONE SIDE OF THE SUPER STRUCTURE CLAW

2. SLIDE THE ELEMENT INTO THE SUPER STRUCTURE CLAWS

VIEW B

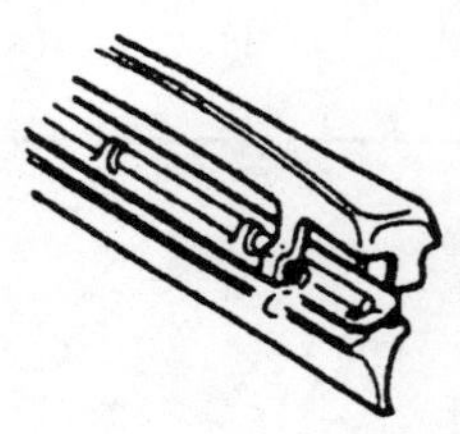

4. INSERT ELEMENT INTO ONE SIDE OF THE END CLAWS (VIEW D) AND WITH A ROCKING MOTION PUSH ELEMENT UPWARD UNTIL IT SNAPS IN (VIEW E)

VIEW D

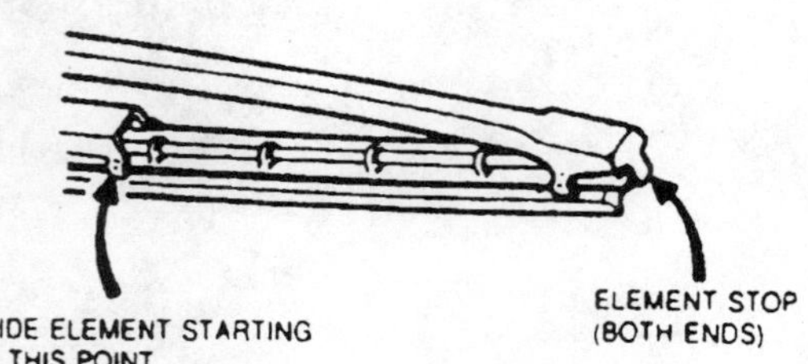

3. SLIDE THE ELEMENT INTO THE SUPER STRUCTURE CLAWS, STARTING WITH SECOND SET FROM EITHER END (VIEW C) AND CONTINUE TO SLIDE THE BLADE ELEMENT INTO ALL THE SUPER STRUCTURE CLAWS TO THE ELEMENT STOP (VIEW C)

VIEW C

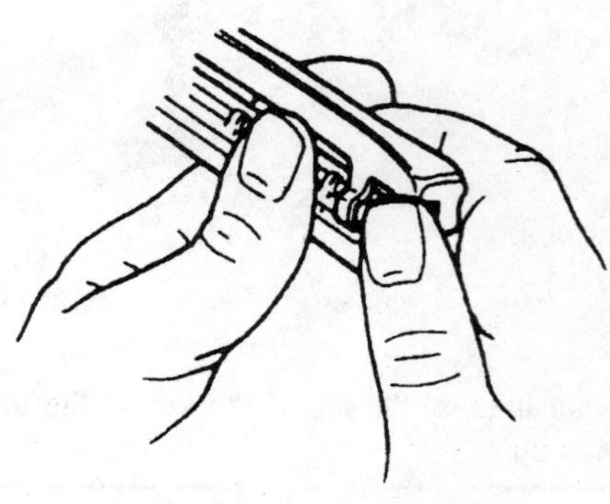

VIEW E

Trico® wiper blade insert (element) replacement

BLADE REPLACEMENT

1. Cycle arm and blade assembly to a position on the windshield where removal of blade assembly can be performed without difficulty. Turn ignition key off at desired position.
2. To remove blade assembly from wiper arm, pull up on spring lock and pull blade assembly from pin (View A). Be sure spring lock is not pulled excessively or it will become distorted.
3. To install, push the blade assembly onto the pin so that the spring lock engages the pin (View A). Be sure the blade assembly is securely attached to pin.

ELEMENT REPLACEMENT

1. In the plastic backing strip which is part of the rubber blade assembly, there is an 11.11mm (7/16 inch) long notch located approximately one inch from either end. Locate either notch.
2. Place the frame of the wiper blade assembly on a firm surface with either notched end of the backing strip visible.
3. Grasp the frame portion of the wiper blade assembly and push down until the blade assembly is tightly bowed.
4. With the blade assembly in the bowed position, grasp the tip of the backing strip firmly, pulling up and twisting C.C.W. at the same time. The backing strip will then snap out of the retaining tab on the end of the frame.
5. Lift the wiper blade assembly from the surface and slide the backing strip down the frame until the notch lines up with the next retaining tab, twist slightly, and the backing strip will snap out. Continue this operation with the remaining tabs until the blade element is completely detached from the frame.
6. To install blade element, reverse the above procedure, making sure all six (6) tabs are locked to the backing strip before installing blade to wiper arm.

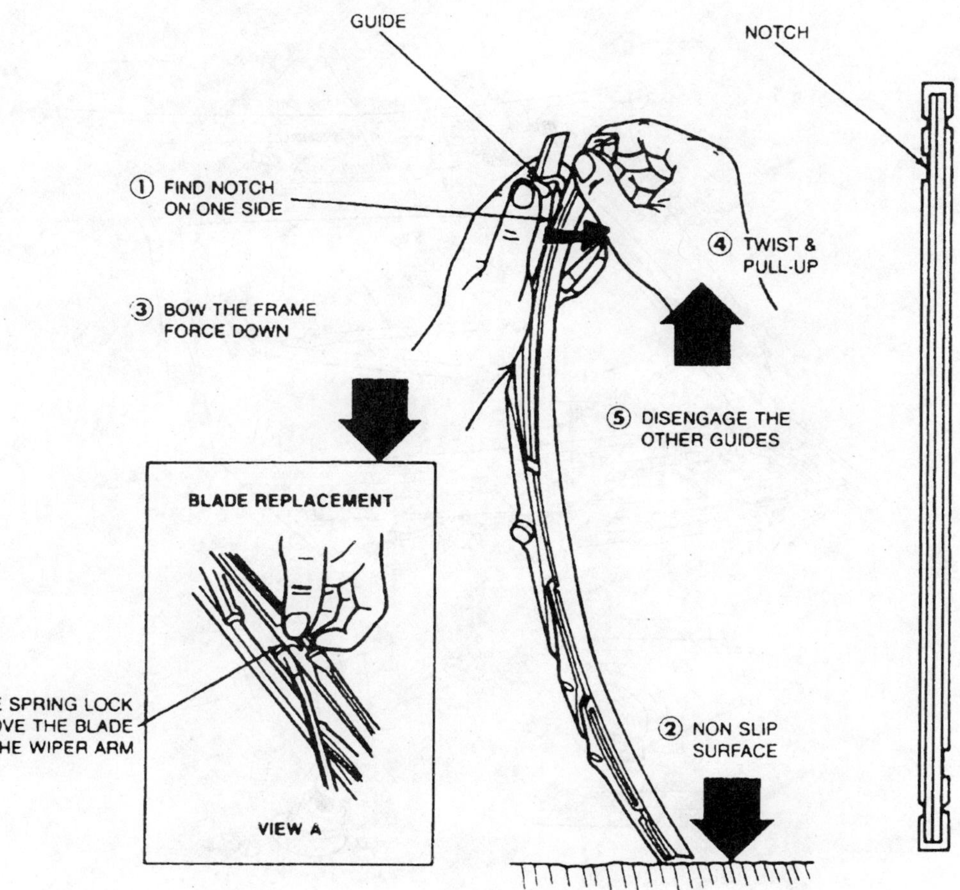

Tridon® wiper blade insert (element) replacement

Wiper Motor

The wiper motor is protected by a circuit breaker in addition to a fuse. If the motor overheats due to overloading caused by heavy snow or ice, the wiper motor will remain stopped until the motor cools. Do not continuously operate an overheating wiper motor. The automatic reset type circuit breaker is located inside the motor on the brush holder assembly.

REMOVAL & INSTALLATION

1. Disconnect the negative (−) battery cable.
2. Remove the wiper arms.
3. Remove the shroud top vent screen.
4. Remove the drive link from the crank arm.
5. Disconnect the electrical leads.
6. Remove the three attaching screws and remove the wiper arm.

To install:

7. Make sure the wiper motor is in the park position before installing the wiper arms and the shroud top screen.
8. Install the motor by placing the crank arm through the opening in the body.
9. Install the three motor-to-body attaching bolts and torque to 48 inch.lb. (5.5 Nm).
10. Install the drive link to the crank arm. Reconnect the electrical connectors.
11. Replace the shroud top vent screen and wiper arms.
12. Reconnect the negative (−) battery cable and check for proper wiper operation.

Wiper Transmission Assembly (Linkage)

REMOVAL & INSTALLATION

➧ **See Figure 5**

1. Disconnect the negative (−) battery cable.
2. Remove the wiper arms.
3. Remove the shroud top vent screen.
4. Remove the drive link from the crank arm.

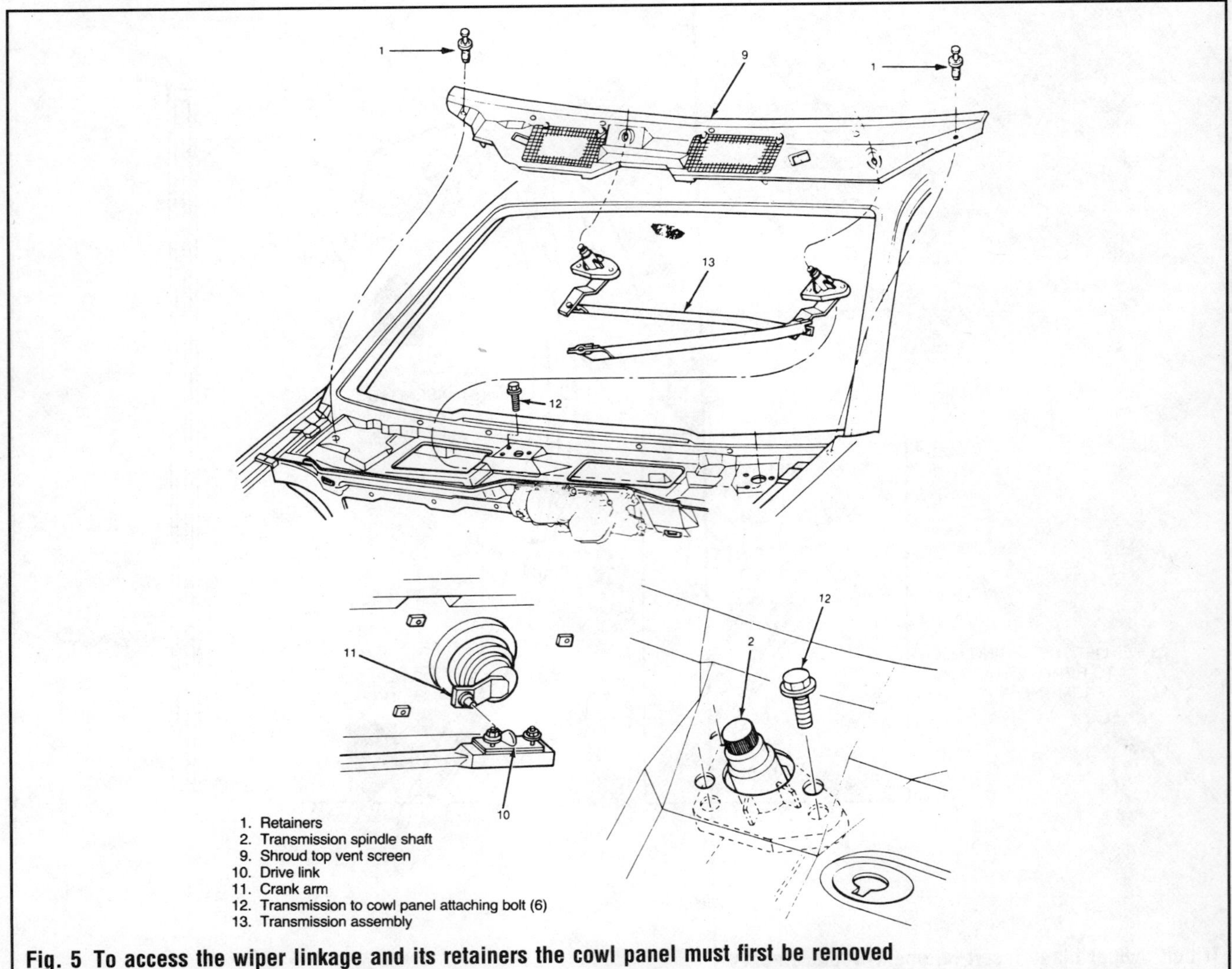

Fig. 5 To access the wiper linkage and its retainers the cowl panel must first be removed

5. Remove the six bolts attaching the transmission to the cowl panel and remove the transmission.

To install:

6. Position the transmission assembly into the cowl panel and install the six attaching bolts and torque to 64 inch.lb. (7.0 Nm).

7. Install the drive link, shroud vent screen, wiper arms and connect the negative (−) battery cable to check for proper operation.

INSTRUMENTS AND SWITCHES

Instrument Cluster

REMOVAL & INSTALLATION

See Figures 6, 7 and 8

1. Disconnect the negative (−) battery cable.
2. Remove the rear cluster cover.
3. Remove the front trim plate.
4. Remove the steering column cover.
5. Remove the cluster attaching screws, disconnect the wiring harness, and remove the cluster assembly.

The speedometer, tach and gauges may be serviced by removing the front cluster lens.

To install:

1. Reconnect the wiring harnesses.
2. Install the cluster into the housing and tighten the attaching screws.
3. Install rear cluster cover, front trim plate and steering column cover.
4. Reconnect the negative (−) battery cable. Turn the ignition to the ON position and check for proper gauge operation.

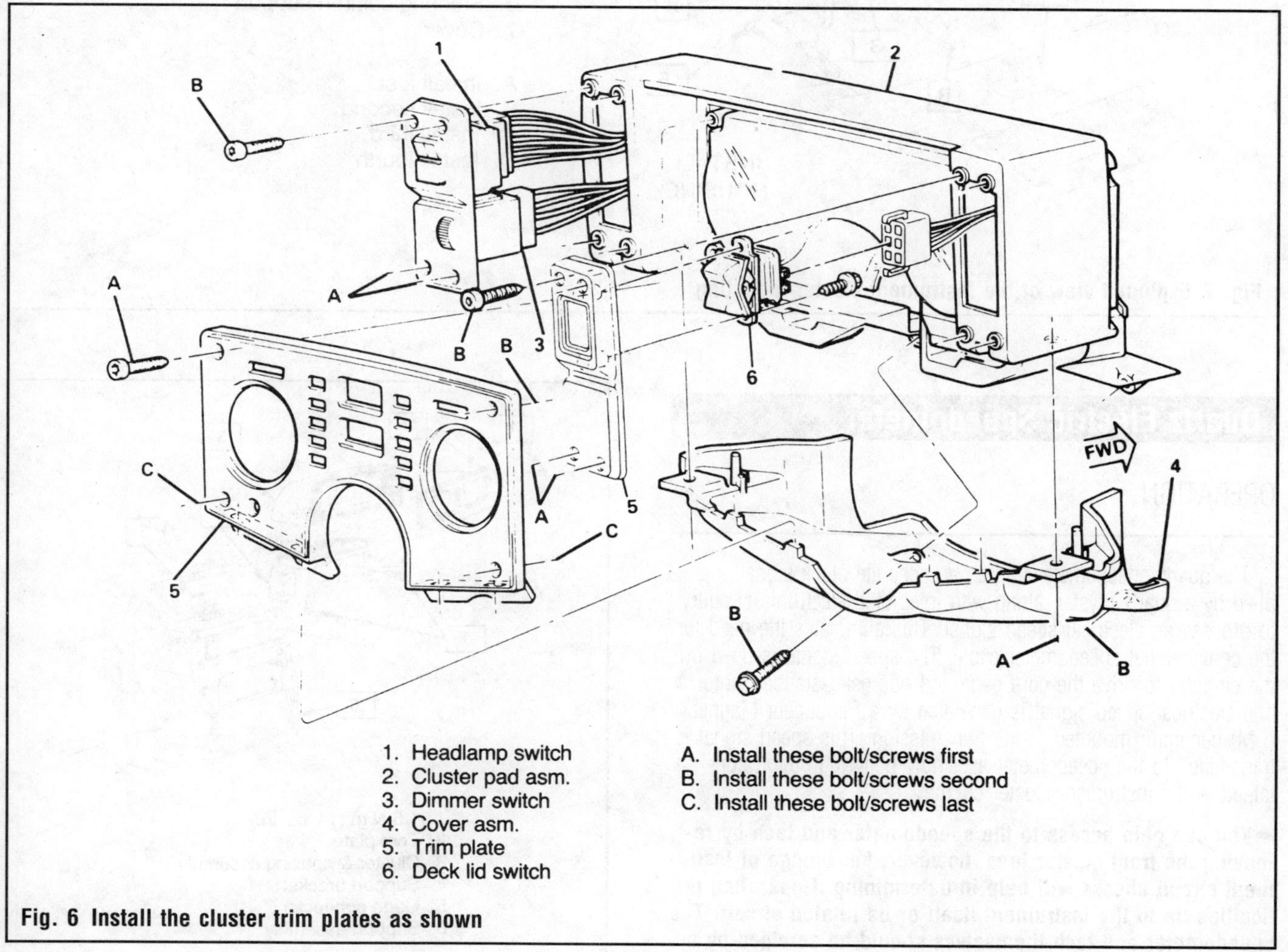

Fig. 6 Install the cluster trim plates as shown

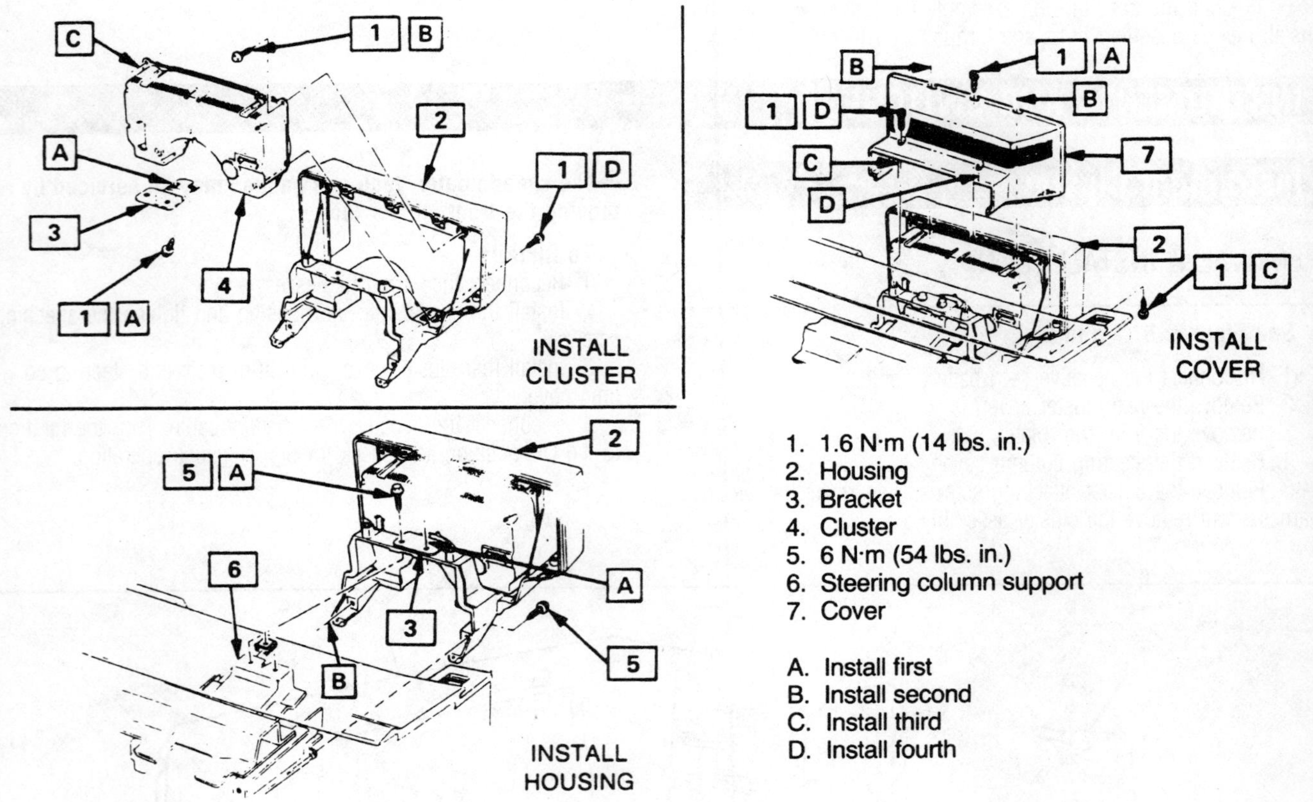

C
1 B
2
A
1 D
3
4
1 A
INSTALL
CLUSTER
B
1 A
1 D
B
C
7
D
2
1 C
INSTALL
COVER
2
5 A
6
A
3
5
B
INSTALL
HOUSING
1. 1.6 N·m (14 lbs. in.)
2. Housing
3. Bracket
4. Cluster
5. 6 N·m (54 lbs. in.)
6. Steering column support
7. Cover
A. Install first
B. Install second
C. Install third
D. Install fourth

Fig. 7 Exploded view of the instrument cluster mounting

Quartz Electric Speedometer

OPERATION

The quartz speedometer utilizes an accurate clock signal supplied by a quartz crystal, along with integrated electronic circuitry to process an electrical speed signal. This eliminates the need for the conventional speedometer cable. The speed signal is used by the circuitry to drive the core gage and odometer stepper motor. The electrical speed signal is generated by a Permanent Magnet (PM) generator mounted in the transmission. This speed signal is transmitted to the speedometer assembly buffering circuit contained in the instrument cluster circuitry.

➡You can gain access to the speedometer and tach by removing the front cluster lens, however, knowledge of instrument circuit checks will help in determining if operating difficulties lie in the instrument itself or its related circuit. The speedometer and tach themselves should be serviced by a Specified Service Center. If a speedometer problem develops, it is suggested that you contact an authorized Pontiac dealer.

1
2
3
4
5
1
6
1. 1.6 N·m (14 lbs. in.)
2. Trim plate
3. Cluster & housing assembly
4. Support bracket
5. Gage connector
6. Support assembly

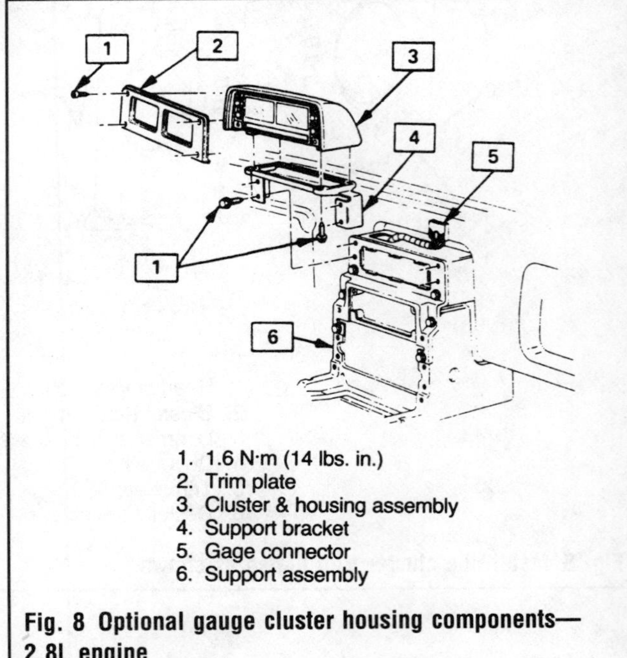

Fig. 8 Optional gauge cluster housing components—2.8L engine

Speedometer Sensor

REMOVAL & INSTALLATION

Automatic Transaxle

➧ See Figure 9

1. Disconnect the negative (−) battery cable.
2. The speed sensor is located on top of the governor assembly, horizontally mounted.
3. Disconnect the electrical connector from the speed sensor.
4. Remove the sensor retaining clip.
5. Remove the sensor by gently twisting and pulling it out of the governor housing.

To install:

6. Install a new O-ring on the sensor and lubricate with transmission fluid.
7. Install the drive gear to the sensor and position assembly into the governor housing.
8. Insert the retaining clip into the housing and reconnect the electrical connector.
9. Reconnect the negative (−) battery cable and drive the vehicle to check for proper operation.

Manual Transaxle

1. Disconnect the negative (−) battery cable.
2. The speed sensor is located on top of the differential portion of the transaxle housing, vertically mounted.
3. Remove the sensor bolt and retainer.
4. Disconnect the electrical connector from the sensor.
5. Remove the sensor by gently twisting and pulling it out of the transaxle.

To install:

6. Install a new O-ring seal on the sensor and lubricate with automatic transmission fluid.
7. Install the drive gear to the sensor and position assembly into the transaxle housing.
8. Install the sensor retainer and bolt. Torque the bolt to 45 inch.lb. (5 Nm).
9. Reconnect the electrical connector and negative (−) battery cable.
10. Drive the vehicle to check for proper operation.

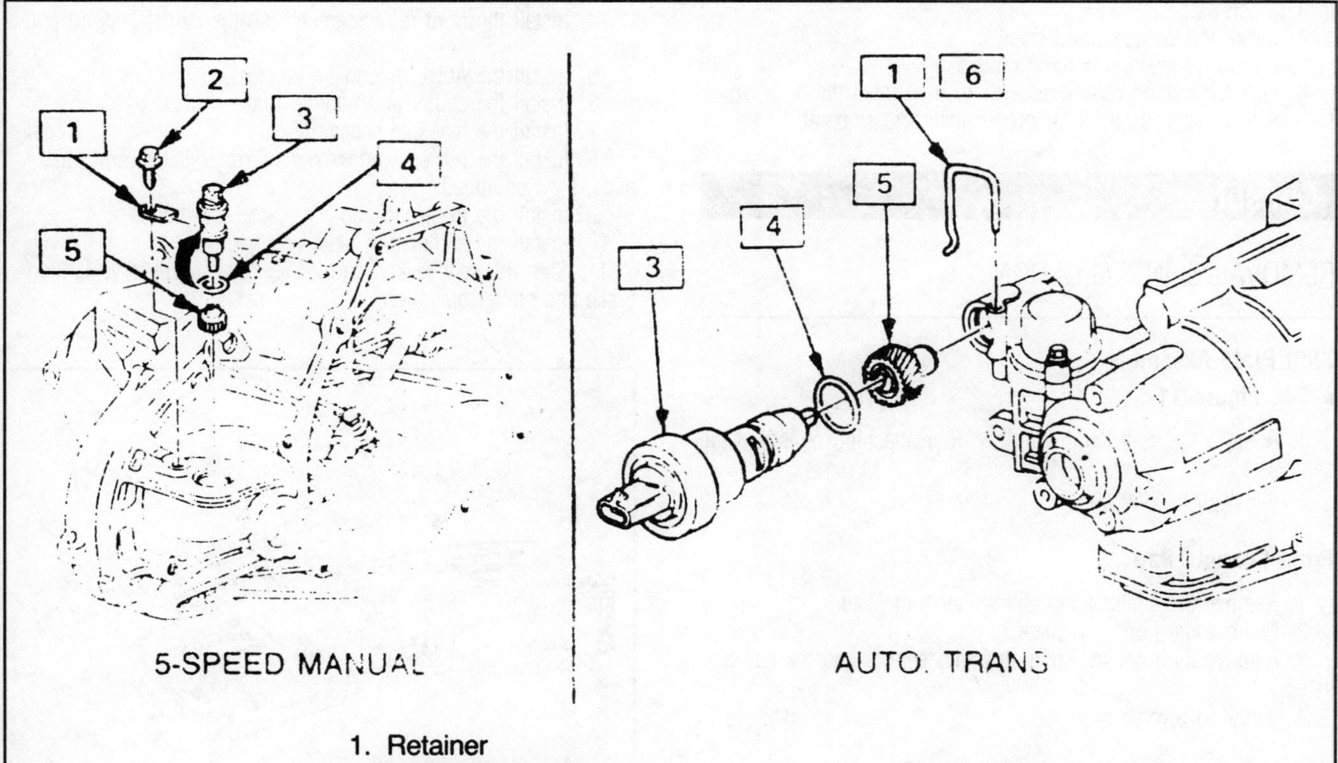

Fig. 9 Location of the speed sensors on the manual and automatic transmissions

Instrument Panel

REMOVAL & INSTALLATION

➧ See Figure 10

1. Disconnect the negative (−) battery cable.
2. Remove the hood release assembly.
3. Remove the steering column cover.
4. Remove the speaker grills and speakers.
5. Remove the instrument panel attaching screws and service cover.
6. Loosen the shift trim plate.
7. Remove the front console trim plate and pad assembly.
8. Remove the instrument panel reinforcement screws and panel assembly.

To install:

➡Coat the edge and frame contact points with silicone sealer to help prevent squeaks and rattles.

1. Install the instrument panel and reinforcement screws.
2. Install the front console pad and trim plate.
3. Install the instrument panel service cover and panel attaching screws.
4. Install the speakers and grills.
5. Install the steering column covers.
6. Install the hood release assembly. Reconnect the negative (−) battery cable to check for proper instrument operation.

Console

REMOVAL & INSTALLATION

Shift Plate Assembly

➧ See Figure 11

1. Remove the shift knob, ash tray, four attaching bolts and the shift plate.
2. Install in reverse order.

Front Console Pad

1. Remove the shifter knob and shifter trim plate.
2. Remove the front trim plate.
3. Remove the front trim pad attaching screws and the pad assembly.
4. Install in reverse order.

Rear Console Pad

1. Remove the shifter trim plate and move out of the way.
2. Remove the rear pad attaching screws.
3. Disconnect the cigar lighter wiring and remove the lighter.
4. Remove the rear console pad.

To install:

5. Position the cigar lighter into the pad assembly and connect the wire.
6. Install the rear pad attaching screws.
7. Install the shifter trim plate.

Console Support Assembly

➧ See Figure 12

1. Remove the shifter knob, shifter trim panel and power window and mirror switches, if so equipped.
2. Remove the parking brake cable.
3. Disconnect the shift cable.
4. Remove the front trim and pad assembly.
5. Remove the rear trim and pad assembly.
6. Remove the twelve carpet clips and carpet support.
7. Remove the ALDL diagnostic connection.
8. Remove the two mounting screws on the sides of the support assembly. Remove the front reinforcement.
9. Remove the heater control and radio assemblies.
10. Remove the console support assembly.

To install:

1. Install the console support assembly (loosely).
2. Install the radio and heater control.
3. Install the two console side mounting screws.
4. Install the front reinforcement and the carpet support and clips.
5. Install the ALDL diagnostic connection.
6. Install the shifter and parking brake cables.
7. Install the rear pad assembly.
8. Install the power window and mirror switches and trim plate, if so equipped.
9. Install the front pad and trim plate assemblies.
10. Install the shifter trim plate and knob.
11. Start the vehicle and check for proper accessary, parking brake and shifter operation.

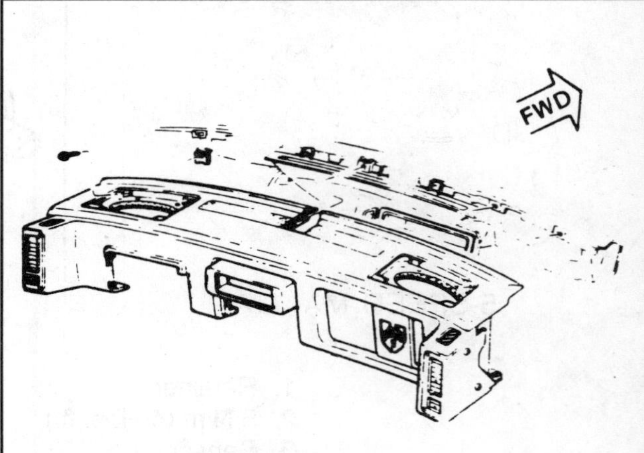

Fig. 10 Common instrument panel assembly used on Fiero models

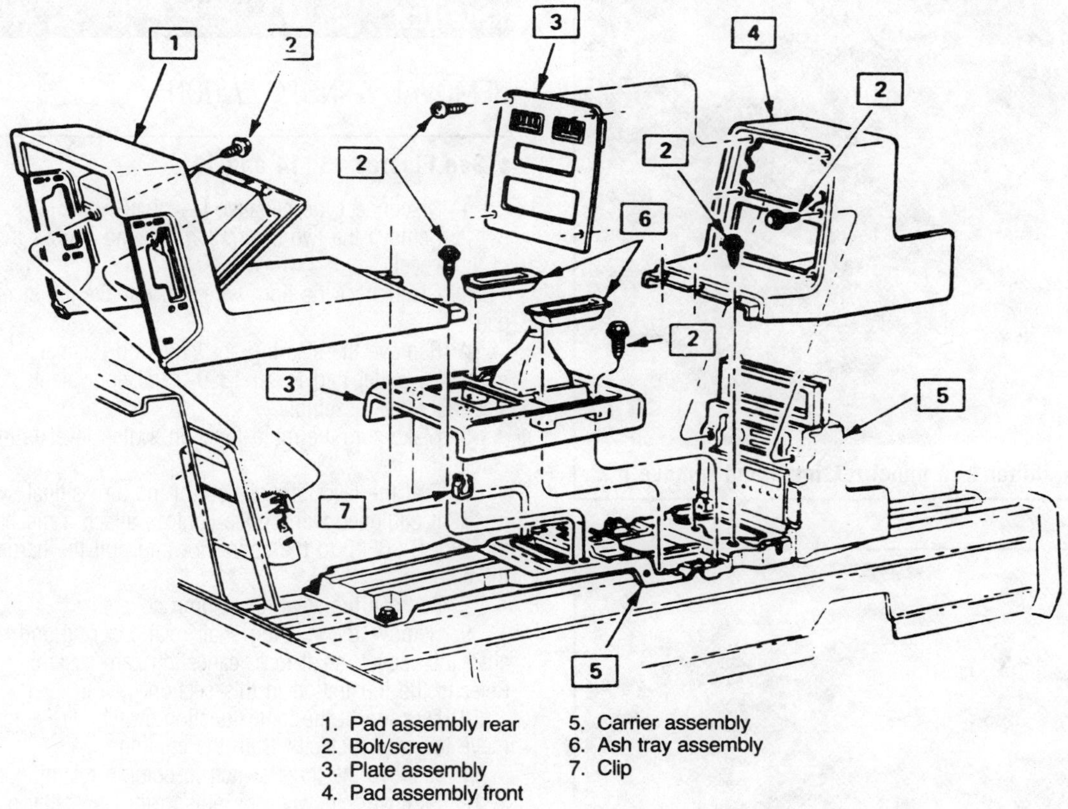

Fig. 11 Exploded view of the console assembly components

Fig. 12 Exploded view of the console support assembly

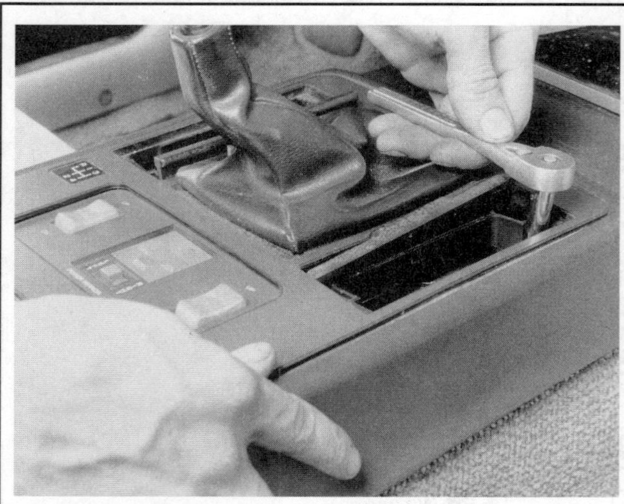
Unfasten the shifter trim panel retainers and remove it

Remove the power window and mirror switch retainers . . .

. . . then lift the switch assembly up and disengage the electrical connections

Windshield Wiper (Multi-Function) Switch

REMOVAL & INSTALLATION

➧ **See Figures 13, 14 and 15**

1. Disconnect the negative (−) battery cable.
2. Remove the two steering wheel pad screws from the back of the wheel.
3. Disconnect the horn wire and remove the steering wheel pad.
4. Remove the steering shaft nut and retainer. Using a steering wheel puller part No. J-1859-03 or equivalent, remove the steering wheel assembly.
5. Make sure the multi-function switch lever is in the OFF position.
6. Pull the lever straight out of the turn signal switch.
7. If equipped with cruise control, attach a mechanics wire or tool No. BT-6810 to the connector and pull the harness through the column.
8. Remove the steering column covers.
9. Remove the steering shaft retaining ring and remove the shaft lock cover, shaft lock, canceling cam assembly and spring. Refer to the illustration in this section.
10. Disconnect the multi-function switch wire connector and remove the wire protector from the column.
11. Remove the three switch-to-column retaining screws.
12. Remove the switch by pulling the assembly out of the column cover guiding the wiring harness through the opening in the cover.

To install:

1. Wrap the wiring harness connector with electrical tape to prevent damage.

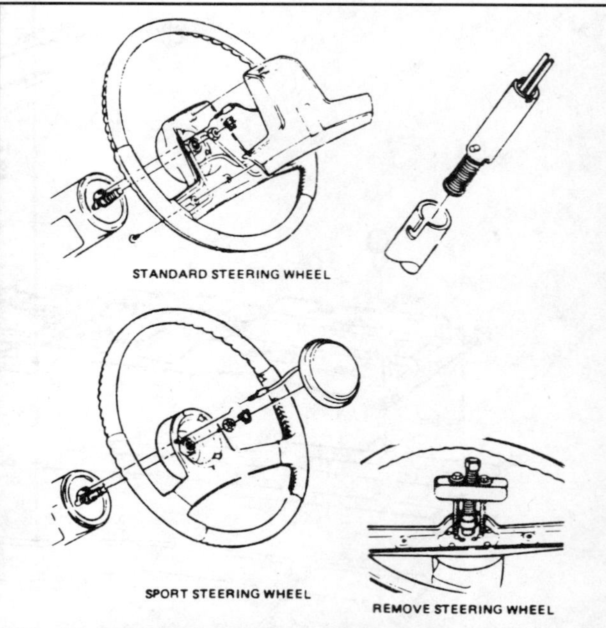

Fig. 13 The steering wheel must be removed first to gain access to the multi-function lever and switch

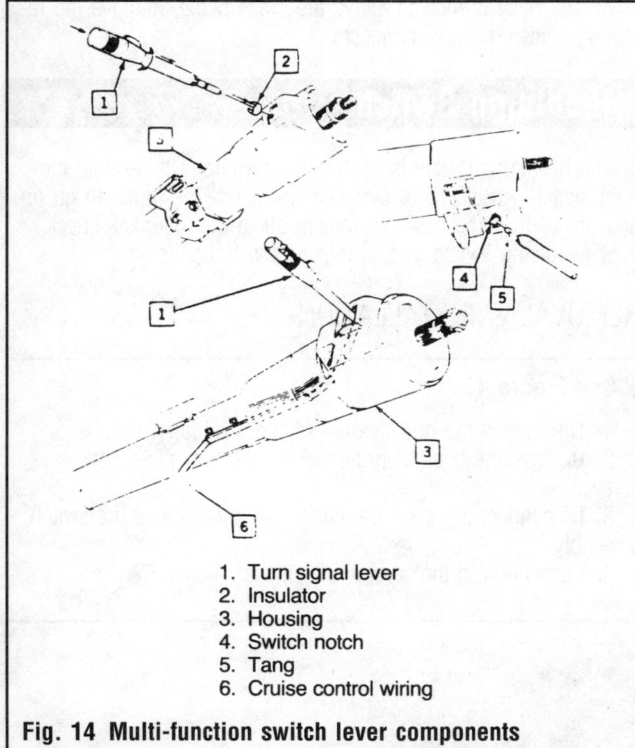

Fig. 14 Multi-function switch lever components

2. Thread the multi-switch wiring harness through the column cover using a stiff piece of coat hanger. Be careful not to damage the wiring harness.
3. Locate the switch into the cover and install the three retaining screws.
4. Remove the electrical tape, connect the wiring harness and install the wire protector.
5. Install the lower steering column covers.
6. Install the spring, canceling cam assembly, shaft lock, retaining ring and shaft lock cover in that order to the steering shaft.
7. Align the steering wheel with the mark on the shaft and install the nut. Torque the nut to 30 ft. lbs. (41 Nm). Install the shaft retainer.
8. Connect the horn wire and install the pad onto the wheel. Tighten the two horn pad retaining screws.
9. Install the multi-function switch lever by connecting the cruise control wiring harness, if so equipped. Push the lever into the switch.

Rear Defogger Switch and Relay

REMOVAL & INSTALLATION

➧ **See Figure 16**

1. Disconnect the negative (−) battery cable.
2. The defogger switch is located on the right hand side of the instrument panel below the rear compartment lid release switch.
3. To remove, unscrew the four trim plate retaining Torx® screws and pull out the trim plate far enough to get access to the switch wiring.
4. Remove the wire connector and two retaining screws and remove the switch.

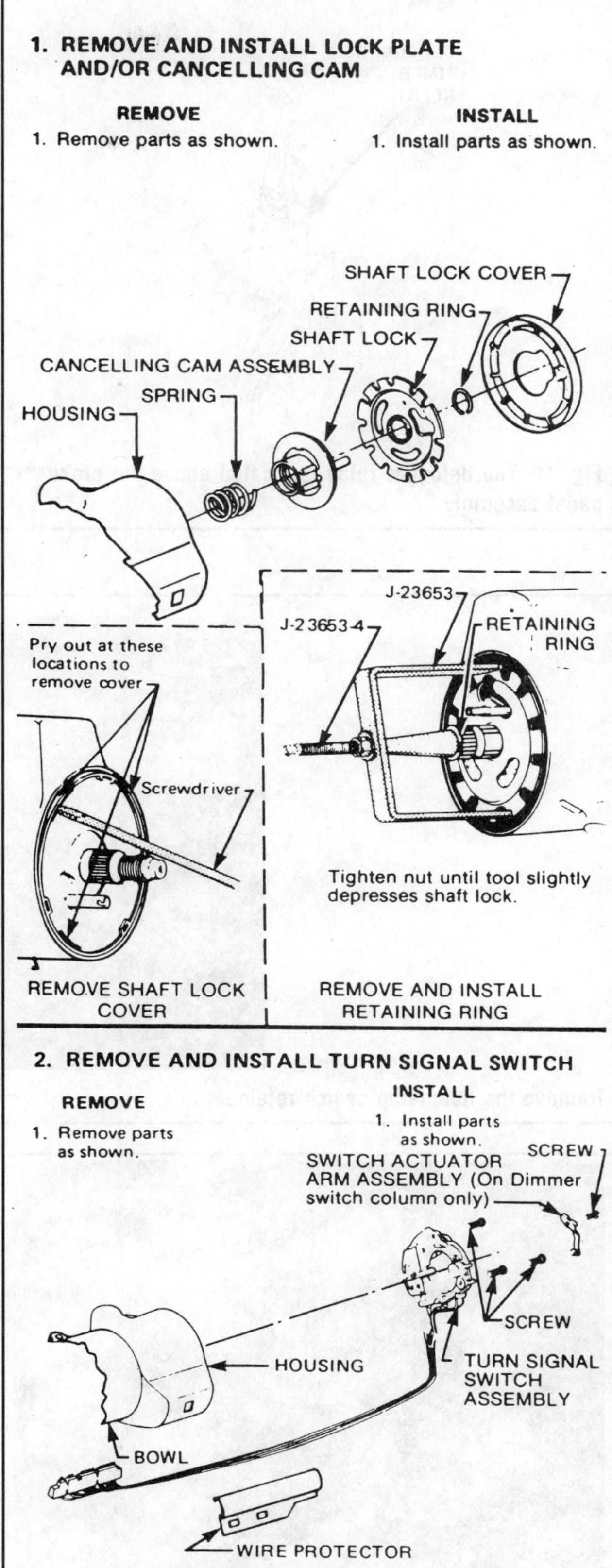

Fig. 15 Use the steps in the illustration to remove the shaft lock cover, shaft lock, canceling cam assembly and spring

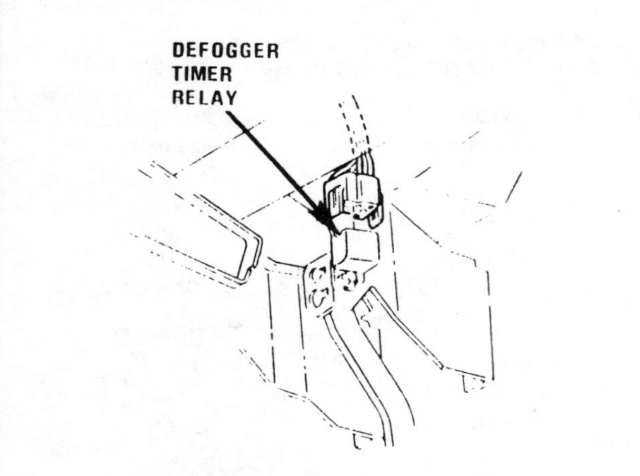

Fig. 16 The defogger relay is located above the brake pedal assembly

5. The relay is located above the brake pedal. Remove the retaining screw and wire connector.

Headlamp Switch

The headlamp circuit is protected by a circuit breaker in the light switch. An electrical overload will cause the lights to go on and off, or in some cases to remain off. If this happens check your headlamp switch and wiring for short circuits.

REMOVAL & INSTALLATION

See Figure 17

1. Disconnect the negative (−) battery cable.
2. Remove the headlamp/dimmer switch trim plate Torx® screws.
3. Disconnect the electrical connector and remove the switch assembly.
4. Installation is the reverse of removal.

Remove the headlamp switch retainers . . .

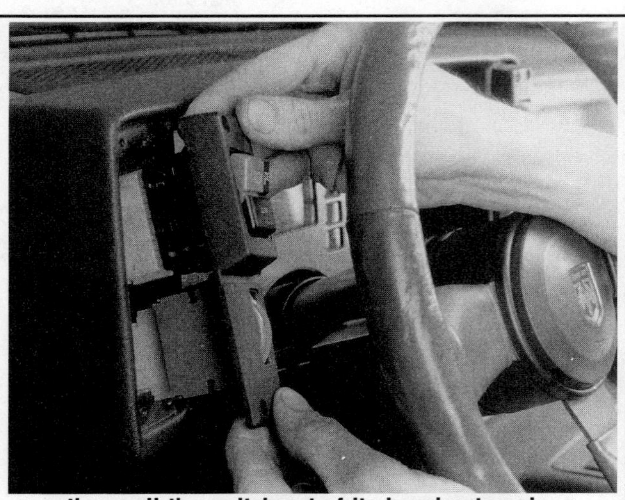

. . . then pull the switch out of its housing to gain access to the electrical connection

Disengage the electrical connections and remove the switch

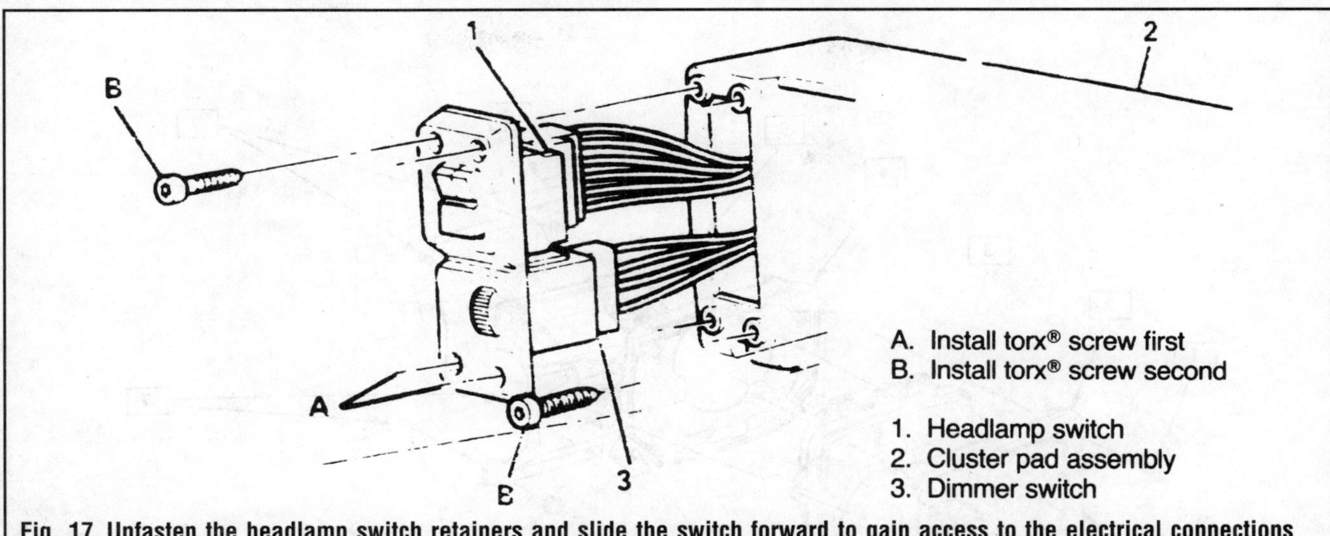

Fig. 17 Unfasten the headlamp switch retainers and slide the switch forward to gain access to the electrical connections

LIGHTING AND HORNS

Headlamp

REMOVAL & INSTALLATION

➧ **See Figure 18**

1. Disconnect the negative (−) battery cable.
2. Open the hood and disconnect the electrical connections at the lamps.
3. Raise the headlamps, then close the hood.
4. Remove the Torx® screw at the top right and left side of the bezel.
5. Remove the black plastic bezel.
6. Raise the hood.
7. Remove the four chrome retaining ring screws and remove the retaining ring. Be careful not to let the bulb fall to the ground after the retaining ring is removed.
8. Remove the bulb assembly.

To install:

9. Use replacement bulb Trade No. 2057, 32/2 candlepower. Install the bulb into the socket and position the chrome retaining ring into position. Tighten the four retaining ring screws. Install the electrical connector and bezel.

Headlamp Actuator

REMOVAL & INSTALLATION

➧ **See Figure 19**

➡Before removing the headlamp actuator bracket from the front panel compartment, mark the position by scribing around the two upper attaching bolts and onto the headlamp mounting bracket.

1. Disconnect the negative (−) battery cable.
2. Open the hood and remove the electrical connections from the bulb and actuator.
3. Remove the three retaining bolts, one at each side of the lamp assembly and one at the link assembly.
4. Remove the bulb and bezel.
5. Remove the headlamp mounting bracket.
6. Remove the clip at the actuator cam linkage.

➡Mark the position of the linkage-to-actuator before removal to aid in reassembly.

7. Remove the linkage.
8. Remove the three actuator attaching bolts and the actuator.

To install:

1. Install the actuator and three actuator attaching bolts.
2. Install the linkage and retaining clip.
3. Install the electrical connections to the mounting bracket.
4. Install the headlamp mounting bracket and align the marks previously scribed. Torque the four bolts to 80 inch.lb. (9 Nm).
5. Install the headlamp bulb into the mounting bracket.
6. Align the bulb in the bracket and install the chrome retaining ring and four screws. Install the headlamp bezel.
7. Install the three bolts, one at each side of the lamp assembly and one at the link assembly.
8. Connect the electrical connector to the bulb and reconnect the negative (−) battery cable. Turn the headlamp switch ON to check for proper operation.

EMERGENCY MANUAL HEADLAMP OPERATION

1. Turn the headlamps OFF.
2. Open the hood.
3. For each inoperative headlamp, rotate the door motor's manual control knob in the direction of the arrow on top of the knob

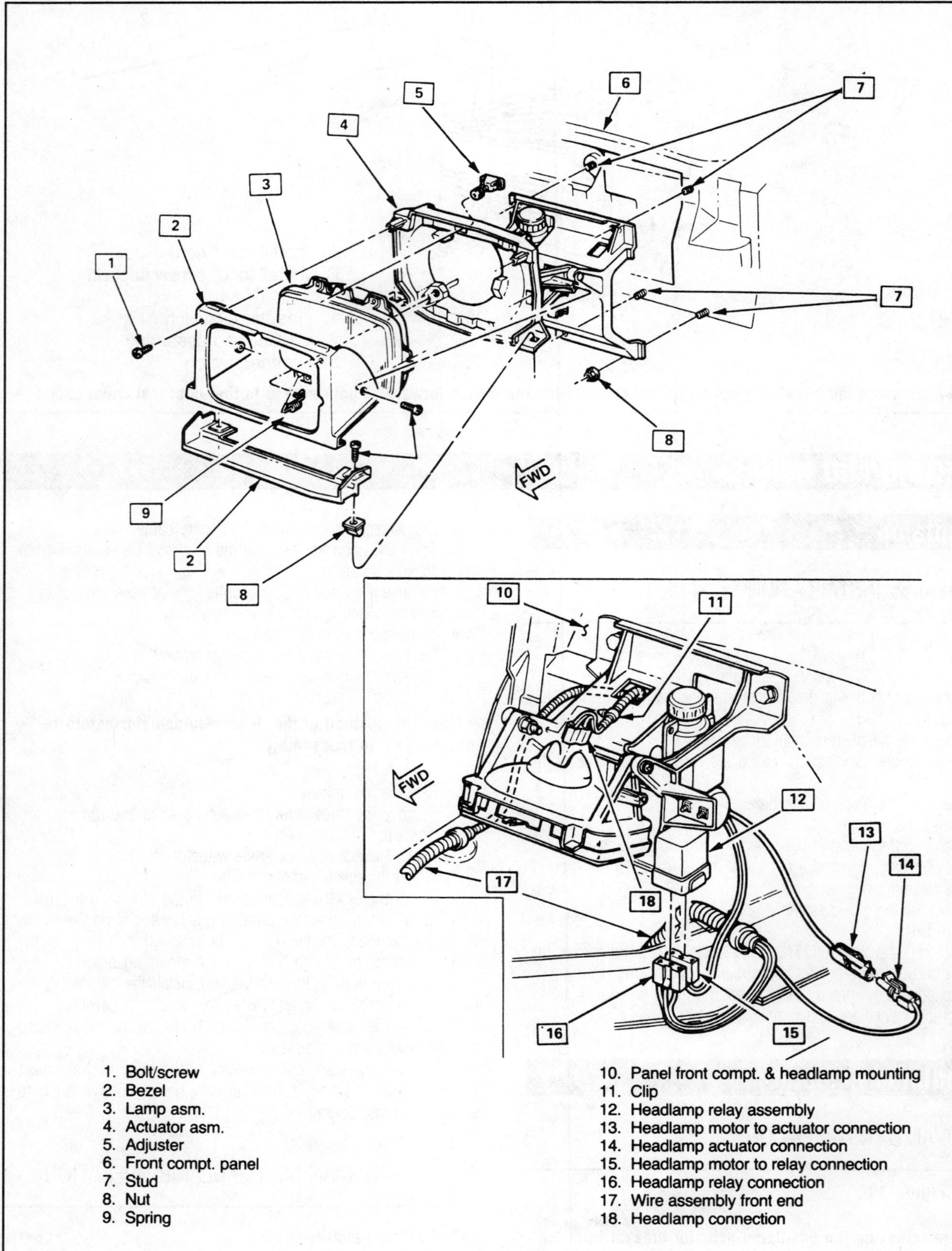

Fig. 18 Exploded view of the headlamp and actuator assembly—1984–86 models

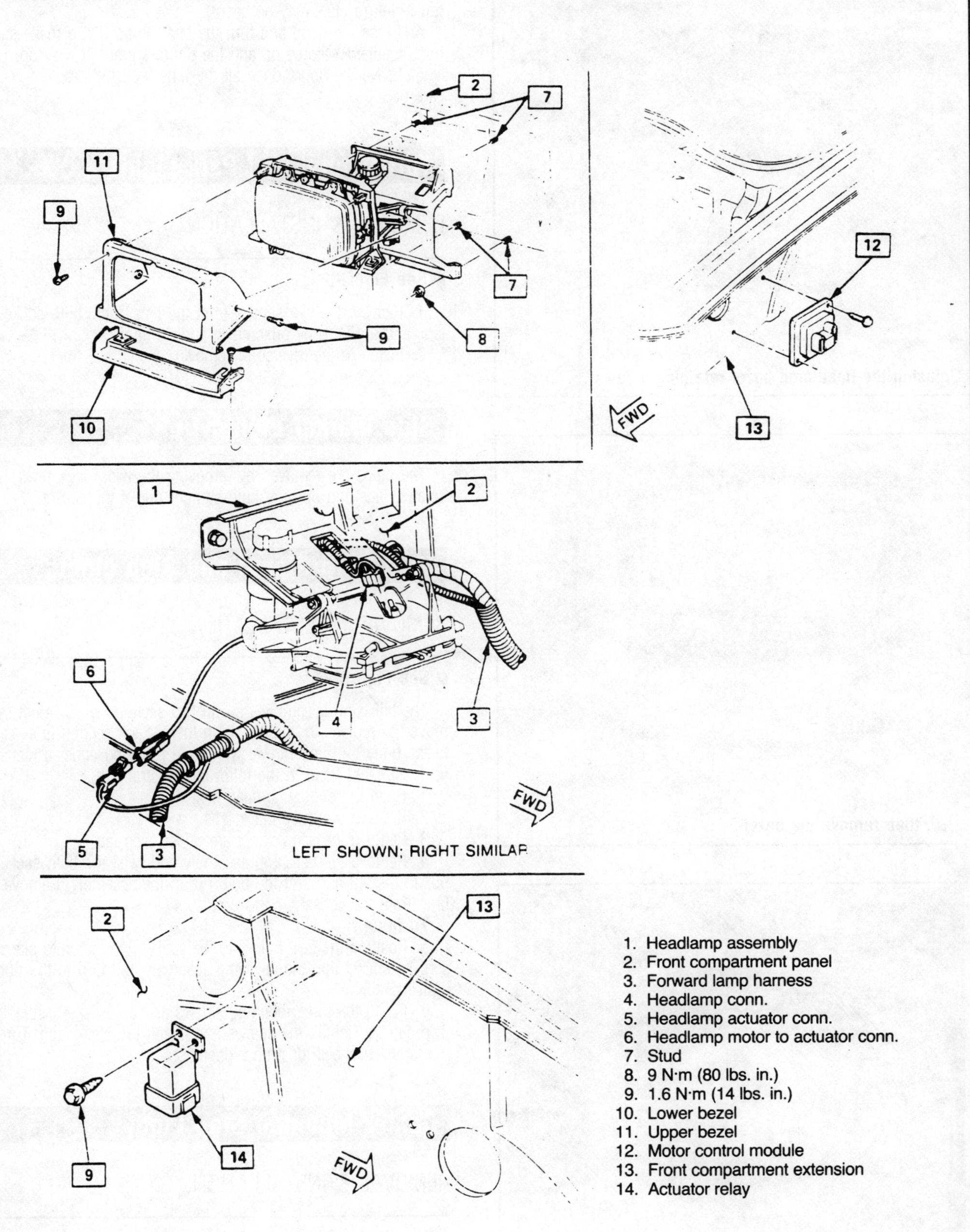

Fig. 19 Exploded view of the headlamp and actuator assembly—1987–88 models

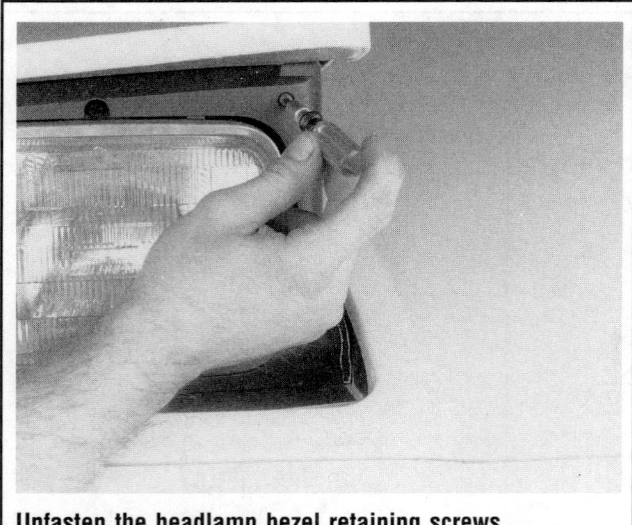
Unfasten the headlamp bezel retaining screws . . .

. . . then remove the bezel

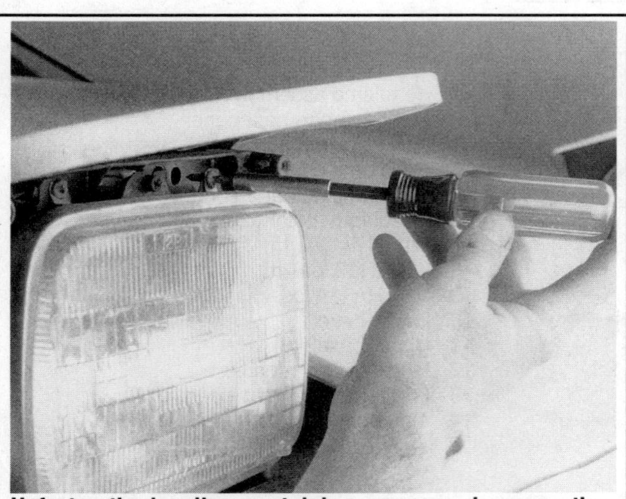
Unfasten the headlamp retaining screws and remove the headlamp

(towards open). Continue turning the knob until an increase in effort is felt (a click may be heard).

4. Close the hood and turn the headlamps ON to make sure both headlamps come on and the doors are all the way up.
5. Leave the doors open all the time until the problem is taken care of.

Turn Signal and Park Lights

REMOVAL & INSTALLATION

See Figure 20

1. Remove the two screws from the lens, lens, bulb socket at lens and the bulb by pushing in and turning.
2. Install in the reverse of removal.

Side Marker Lights

The bulbs are removed by removing the two Torx® head screws, lens and pull the bulb straight out of the socket.

Rear Turn Signal and Stop Lights

REMOVAL & INSTALLATION

See Figure 21

The tail lamp assemblies are in two sections which must be removed to replace the bulbs within them. Each section is attached to the body by three screws which are recessed under a rectangular black tabs. Refer to the following illustration.

1. Open the engine compartment lid.
2. Remove the three black tabs.
3. Remove the screws that are under each tab.
4. Remove the tail lamp assembly and twist the bulb socket 90° to the left and pull the bulb out of the assembly. Remove the bulb from the socket.

To install:

5. Position the new bulb into the socket and lock into place. Insert the socket into the tail lamp assembly and turn to the right until locked.
6. Install the three retaining screws and adjust the assembly to fit properly. Tighten the screws and install the black tabs. Turn on the lights to check for proper operation.

Center Mounted Stop Light

REMOVAL & INSTALLATION

See Figure 22

A center mounted stop light has been installed on later model vehicles to aid in stop lamp illumination. This light can be ser-

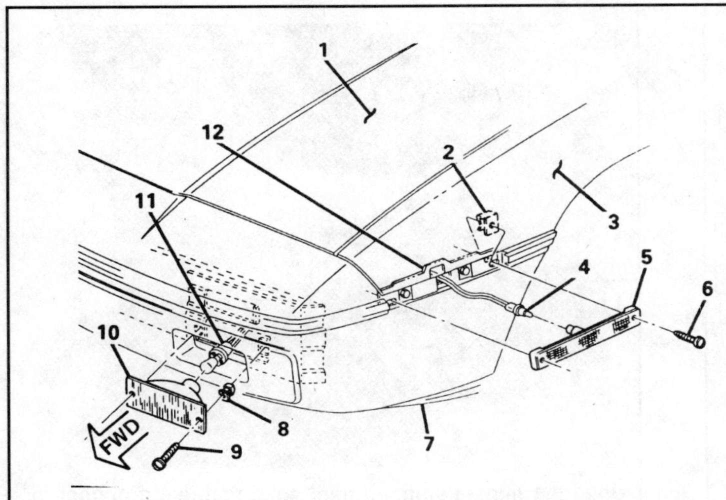

1 – HOOD PANEL
2 – U-NUT
3 – FRONT FENDER
4 – BULB & SOCKET ASSY
5 – LAMP ASSY – LEFT & RIGHT
6 – BOLT
7 – FRONT FASCIA ASSY.
8 – NUT
9 – BOLT
10 – LAMP ASSY. LEFT & RIGHT
11 – BULB & SOCKET ASSY.
12 – BACKING PLATE

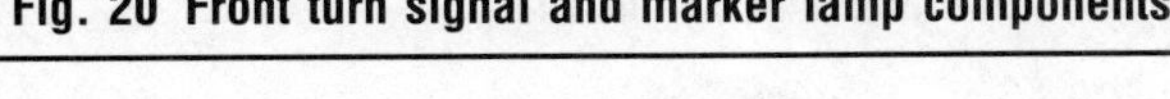

Fig. 20 Front turn signal and marker lamp components

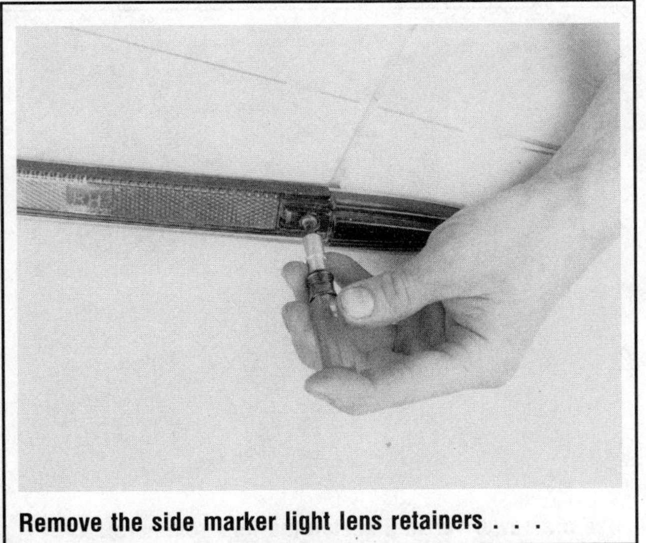

Remove the side marker light lens retainers . . .

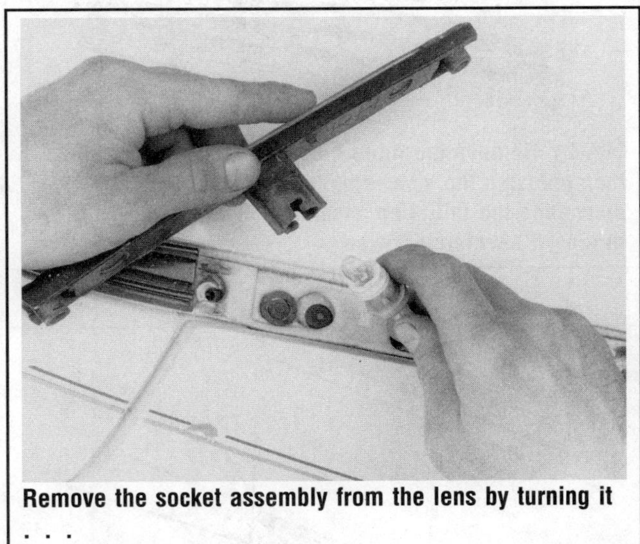

Remove the socket assembly from the lens by turning it . . .

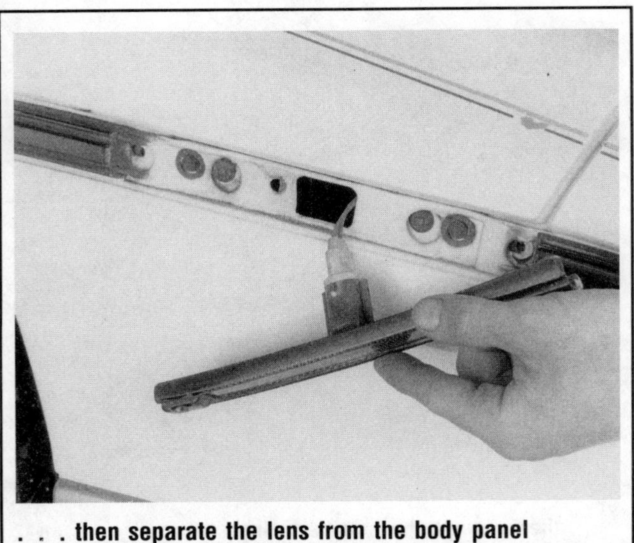

. . . then separate the lens from the body panel

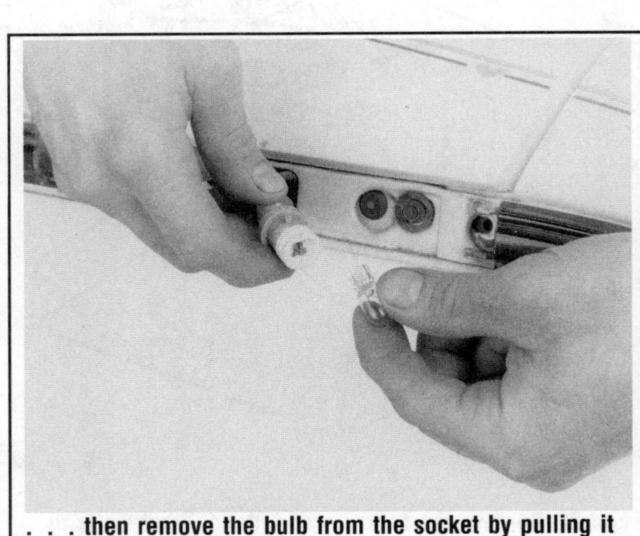

. . . then remove the bulb from the socket by pulling it out

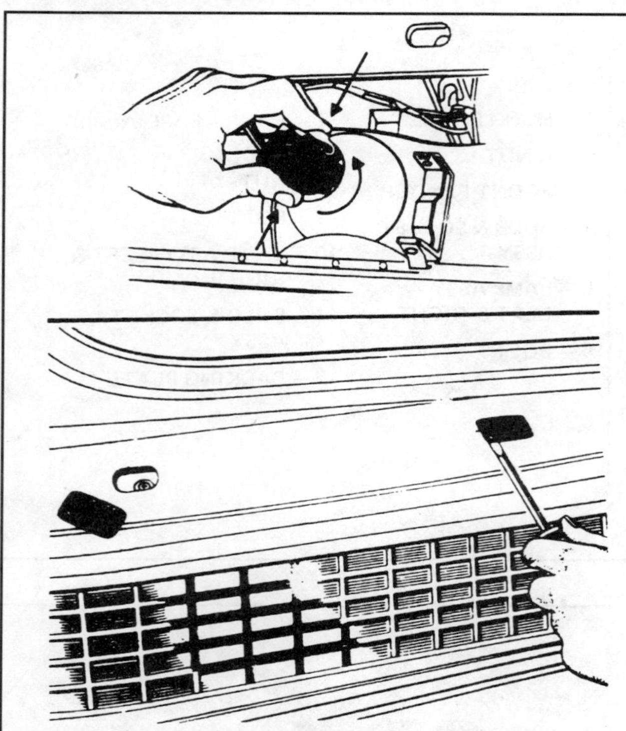
Fig. 21 Remove the three black tabs using a prytool, then unfasten the screws underneath the tabs to disengage the tail lamp assembly. Remove the bulb by turning it counterclockwise

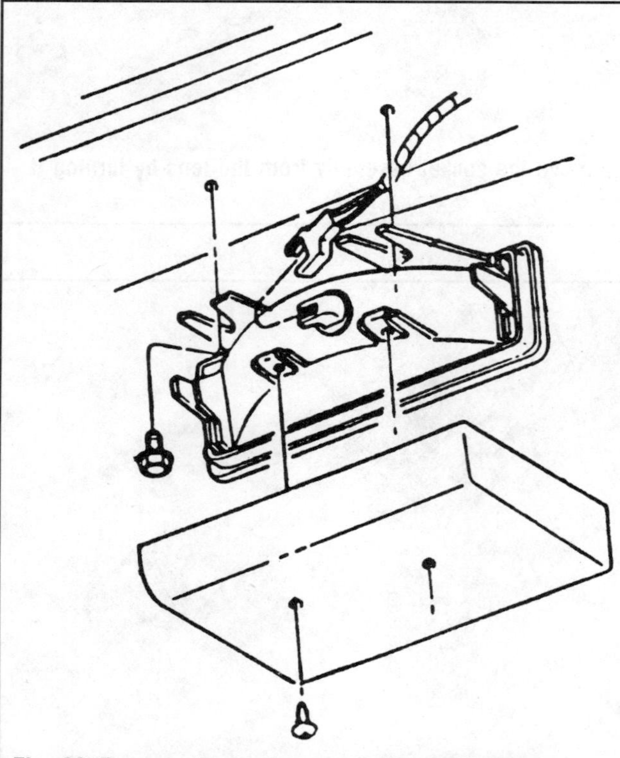
Fig. 22 Remove the center mounted stop light cover to access the bulb assemblies

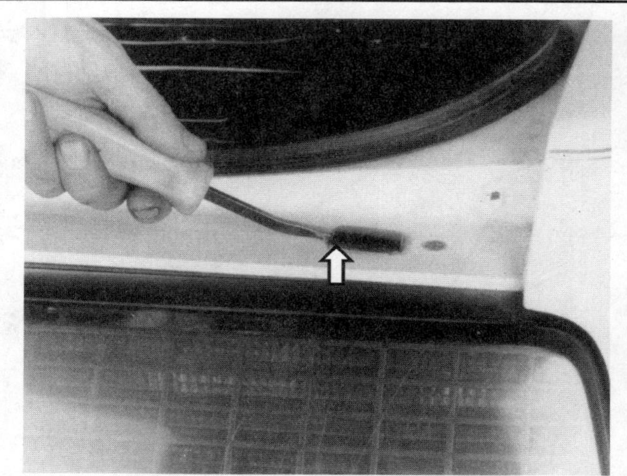
Open the engine compartment hood and use a prytool to remove the black tabs on the sill

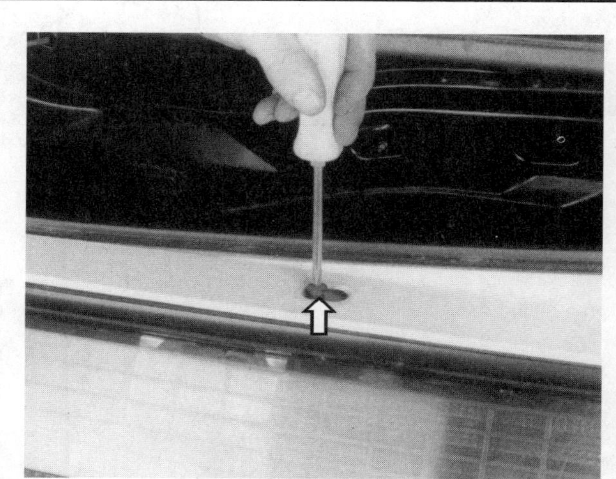
Use a screwdriver to unfasten the lens retainers . . .

. . . then remove the lens retaining screws

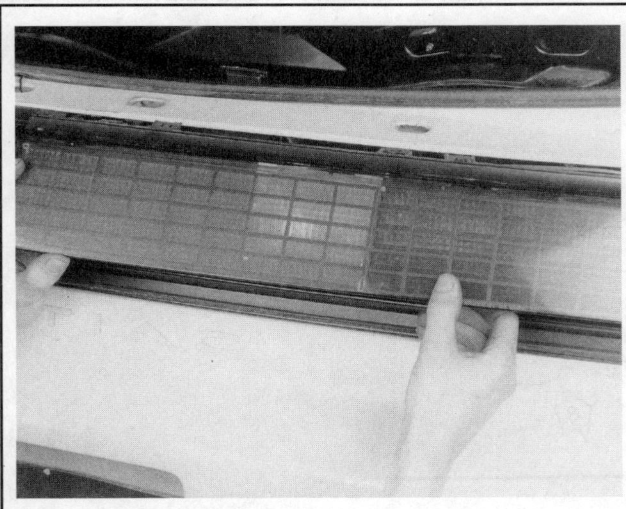
Pull the lens assembly forward

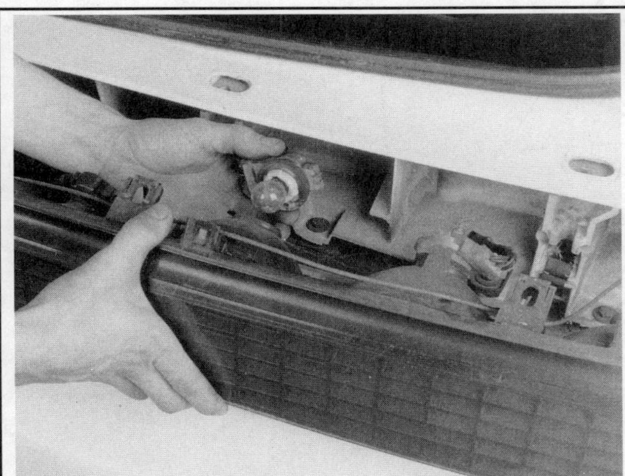
Twist the bulb socket to the left and disengage it from the lens assembly

Remove the bulb from the socket by turning it counterclockwise

viced from inside the vehicle. To remove the bulb; unscrew the two cover screws, remove the cover, light sockets and replace the two bulbs.

Horns

POOR HORN TONE

1. Poor horn tone—tighten the bolts in the mounting area.
2. Low pitched moan—Sounds like "mooing" caused by the current too high. Refer to the following **Adjustment** procedures.
3. Weak tone—current too low, correct poor connections, ground, or adjust as follows.
4. Weak stained tone—remove foreign object in the horn.
5. Harsh vibration—bend bracket so horn is not touching any sheet metal.

ADJUSTMENT

The current draw for a horn while operating should be 4.5 to 5.5 amperes at 11.5 to 12.5 volts. High current (more than 20 amperes) indicates an overheated winding or shorted horn; replace the horn if this condition exists. A current reading of 18 amperes means the contact points are not opening; adjust the horn current as follows.

1. To increase current—turn the adjusting screw clockwise.
2. To decrease current—turn the adjusting screw counterclockwise.
3. Current adjustments should be made ¼ turn (90°) at a time.

REMOVAL & INSTALLATION

➧ **See Figure 23**

There are two horn assemblies installed at the front compartment frame rails, one on the left and the other on the right frame rail. Remove the electrical connector and retaining bolt. Note that the right and left horns have different mounting brackets. Install the horn and torque the bolt to 12 ft. lbs. (15 Nm).

Horn Relay

REMOVAL & INSTALLATION

The horn relay is located in the convenience center on the right side of the A/C and heater module under the instrument panel. To remove the relay, pull it straight out of the center. Refer to the "Convenience Center" procedures in this section.

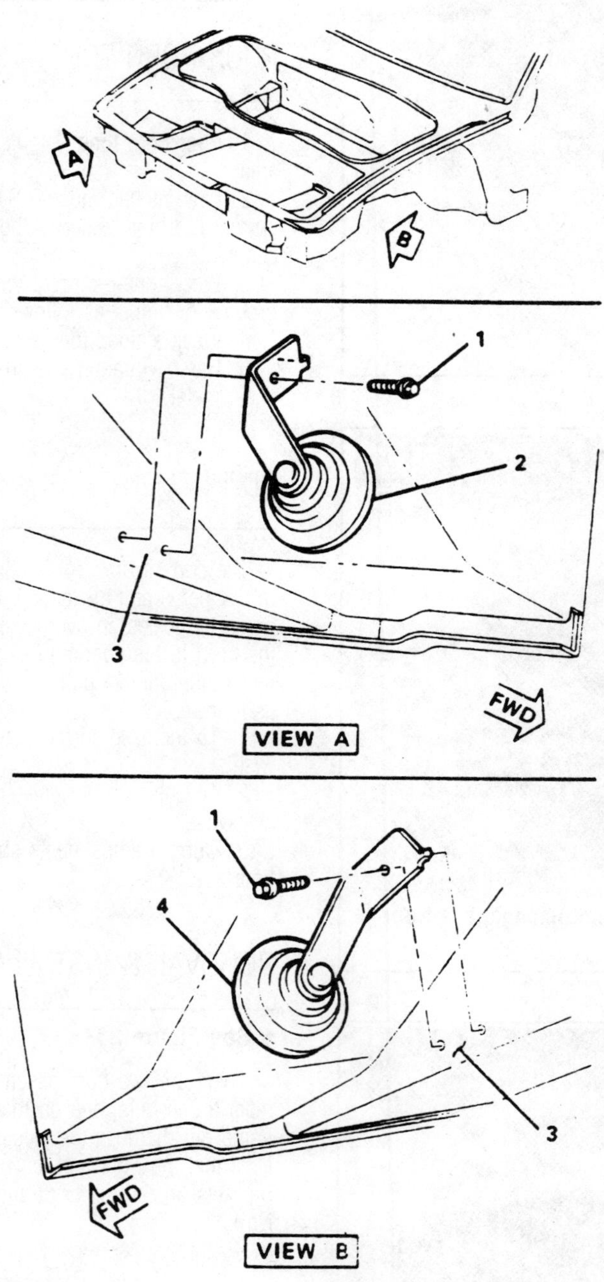

Fig. 23 Exploded view of the horn assembly location and components

TRAILER WIRING

Wiring the vehicle for towing is fairly easy. There are a number of good wiring kits available and these should be used, rather than trying to design your own.

All trailers will need brake lights and turn signals as well as tail lights and side marker lights. Most areas require extra marker lights for overwide trailers. Also, most areas have recently required back-up lights for trailers, and most trailer manufacturers have been building trailers with back-up lights for several years.

Additionally, some Class I, most Class II and just about all Class III trailers will have electric brakes. Add to this number an accessories wire, to operate trailer internal equipment or to charge the trailer's battery, and you can have as many as seven wires in the harness.

Determine the equipment on your trailer and buy the wiring kit necessary. The kit will contain all the wires needed, plus a plug adapter set which includes the female plug, mounted on the bumper or hitch, and the male plug, wired into, or plugged into the trailer harness.

When installing the kit, follow the manufacturer's instructions. The color coding of the wires is usually standard throughout the industry. One point to note: some domestic vehicles, and most imported vehicles, have separate turn signals. On most domestic vehicles, the brake lights and rear turn signals operate with the same bulb. For those vehicles with separate turn signals, you can purchase an isolation unit so that the brake lights won't blink whenever the turn signals are operated, or, you can go to your local electronics supply house and buy four diodes to wire in series with the brake and turn signal bulbs. Diodes will isolate the brake and turn signals. The choice is yours. The isolation units are simple and quick to install, but far more expensive than the diodes. The diodes, however, require more work to install properly, since they require the cutting of each bulb's wire and soldering in place of the diode.

One, final point, the best kits are those with a spring loaded cover on the vehicle mounted socket. This cover prevents dirt and moisture from corroding the terminals. Never let the vehicle socket hang loosely; always mount it securely to the bumper or hitch.

CIRCUIT PROTECTION

Fuse Block

➧ See Figures 24 and 25

The fuse block is a swing-down unit located in the underside of the instrument panel left of the steering column. The fuse block uses miniaturized fuses, designed for increased circuit protection and greater reliability. Various convenience connectors, which snap-lock into the fuse block, add to the serviceability of this unit.

The fuses can be removed by grasping the middle of the fuse with a needle nose pliers and pulling straight out of the fuse block. The fuses can be tested while they are still in the fuse block. Insert a fuse tester or a point type test light into the two medal tangs on the top of the fuse. With the ignition key ON, the test light should light.

CAUTION

When replacing fuses, only use the correct amperage replacement fuse. Each fuse has a number stamped on the top which indicates the amperage rating. Damage to the electrical system may result if the incorrect fuses are used.

Convenience Center

➧ See Figure 26

The convenience center is a stationary unit. It is located on the right side of the heater or A/C module in the vehicle, under the instrument panel. This location provides easy access to the audio alarm, 4-way flasher, the horn relay and the seat belt key and headlamp warning alarm. All units are serviced by plug-in replacements.

Fusible Link

Added protection is provided to all battery feed circuits and other selected circuits by a fusible link. This link is a short piece of copper wire approximately 4 inches long, inserted in series with the circuit and acts as a fuse. The link is two (2) or more gauges smaller in size than the circuit wire it is protecting and will burn out without damage to the circuit in case of current overload.

LOCATION

➧ See Figures 27, 28 and 29

The Fiero is equipped with up to nine fusible links. Most of them are located at the RH front of the engine compartment, at the battery junction block. There is one at the forward lamp harness, to the right of the brake master cylinder. The last one is located at the lower LH front of engine, at the starter solenoid. Refer to the "Fusible Link Location" illustrations in this section.

Power Distribution

1. Fusible link A—Feeds the ignition switch
2. Fusible link B—Feeds the vehicle lighting
3. Fusible link C—Feeds the headlamp door module
4. Fusible link D—Feeds the headlamp door module
5. Fusible link E—Feeds the charging system
6. Fusible link F—Feeds the electronic control module (ECM)
7. Fusible link G—Feeds the starter solenoid and fuel system
8. Fusible link H—Feeds the ignition system
9. Fusible link X—Feeds the electro-hydraulic power steering

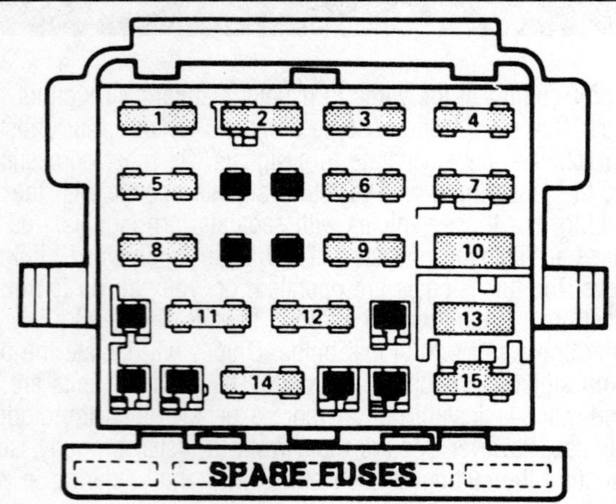

1. FUSE 10 AMP. IGN. RED (E. F. I. E. C. M. & INJ.) (C. C. C., E. C. M.)
2. FUSE 10 AMP. IGN. RED (FUEL PUMP RELAY & OIL PRESSURE SW. FEED)
3. FUSE 20 AMP. BATT. YEL. (STOP LAMP SW., HAZARD FLASHER, CHIME)
4. FUSE 20 AMP. IGN. YEL. (COOLANT FAN RELAY COIL)
5. FUSE 20 AMP. IGN. YEL. (TURN SIGNAL FLASHER, BACK-UP LAMPS)
6. FUSE 20 AMP BATT. YEL (TAIL LAMPS, PARKING, SIDE MARKER & LICENSE LAMPS)
7. FUSE 20 AMP. IGN. YEL. (HEATER, A/C)
8. FUSE 20 AMP. IGN. RED (C49 RELAY, C49 OFF-ON SW, CHIME, VOLTMETER, CRUISE, V. S. S., A/C RELAY T. C. C. BRAKE SW. & R. R. DECK LID)
9. FUSE 20 AMP BATT YEL (DOME LAMPS, HORN RELAY, CLOCK, LIGHTER, POWER LOCKS RELAY, POWER MIRROR)
10. CIRCUIT BREAKER 30 AMP. (POWER WINDOWS)
11. FUSE 5 AMP. IGN. TAN (INST. PANEL LAMPS, HEADLAMP WARNING)
12. FUSE 10 AMP. IGN. RED (RADIO FEED & CRUISE)
13. CIRCUIT BREAKER 30 AMP. (AU3/C49) (POWER LOCKS, REAR DEFOG)
14. FUSE 20 AMP. IGN. YEL. (WINDSHIELD WIPER MOTOR)
15. FUSE 3 AMP. IGN. TAN (CRANK SIGNAL TO E. C. M.)

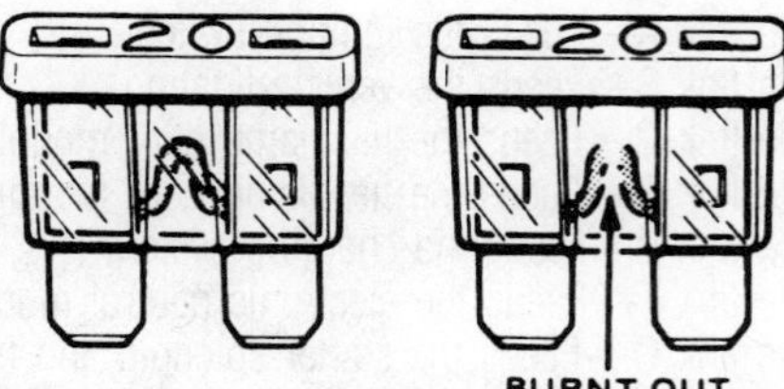

Fig. 24 Typical fuse block and fuse locations—1984–85 models

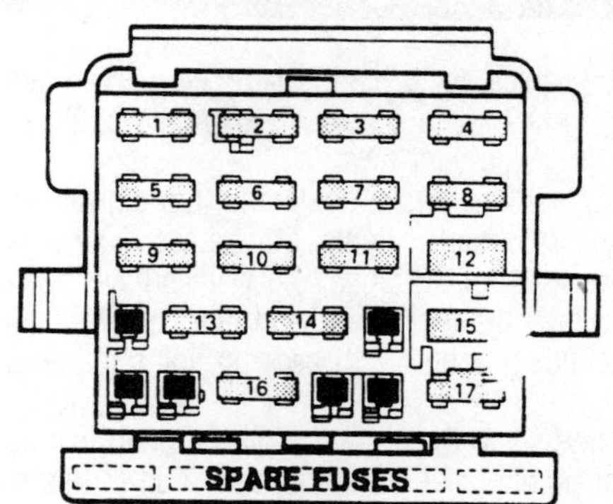

1. Fuse (10 amp. red)—computer cammand control E.C.M., L4 electronic fuel injection
2. Fuse (10 amp. red)—fuel pump relay, oil pressure switch feed
3. Fuse (20 amp. yellow)—tail lights, parking and side marker lights, license plate illumination
4. Fuse (20 amp. yellow)—coolant fan relay coil
5. Fuse (20 amp. yellow)—turn signal flasher, back-up lights
6. Fuse (5 amp. tan)—V6 fuel injection
7. Fuse (20 amp. yellow)—stop light switch, hazard flasher, warning chime
8. Fuse (25 amp. white)—heater, air conditioner
9. Fuse (10 amp. red)—rear defogger switch & relay, warning chime, generator light, V.S.S., T.C.C. brake switch, I.P. cluster
10. Fuse (5 amp. tan)—V6 fuel injection
11. Fuse (20 amp. yellow)—horn relay, dome lights, clock, cigar lighter
12. Circuit breaker (30 amp.)—power windows
13. Fuse (5 amp. tan)—I.P. lights, headlight warning
14. Fuse (10 amp. red)—radio, cruise control
15. Circuit breaker (30 amp.)—power door locks, rear defogger
16. Fuse (20 amp. yellow)—windshield wiper motor
17. Fuse (20 amp. yellow)—rear compartment lid release, rear compartment light, power door lock relay, power sport mirrors control

Fig. 25 Location of the fuses in the fuse block assembly—1986–88 models

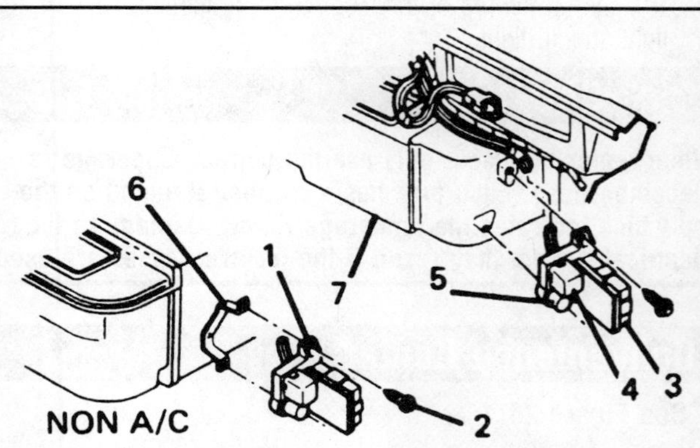

1. Convenience center
2. Screw
3. Alarm
4. Relay (horn)
5. Flasher (4-way)
6. Bracket
7. Heater and A/C module

Fig. 26 The convenience center is usually found on the right side of the heater or A/C module

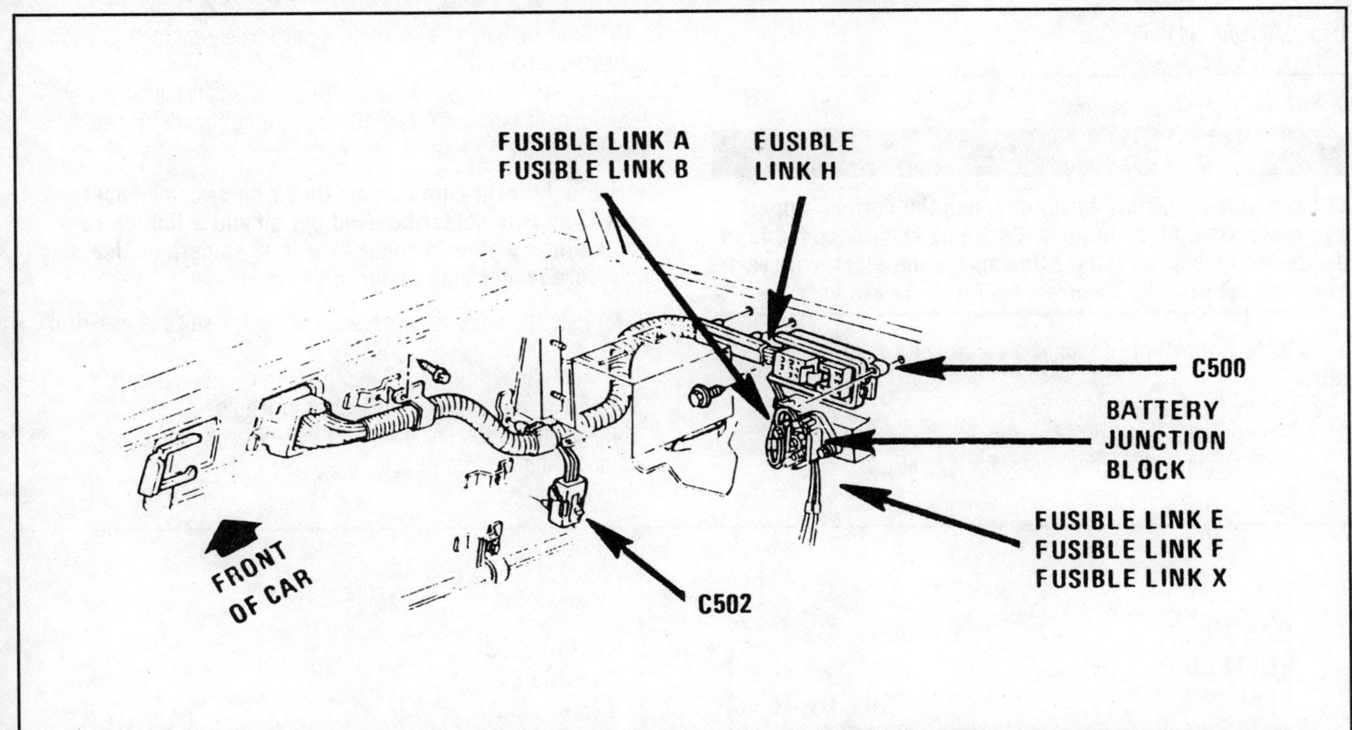

Fig. 27 Location of the fusible links in the right hand front of the engine compartment next to the battery junction block

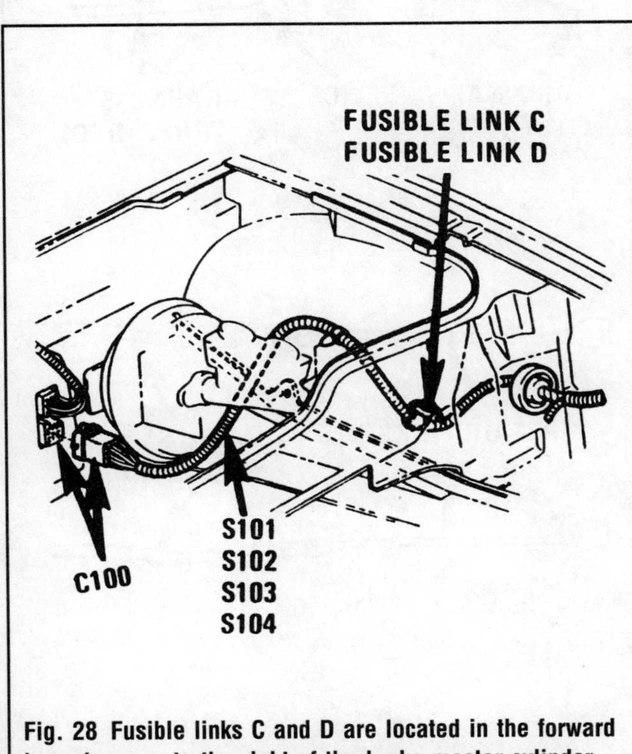

Fig. 28 Fusible links C and D are located in the forward lamp harness to the right of the brake master cylinder

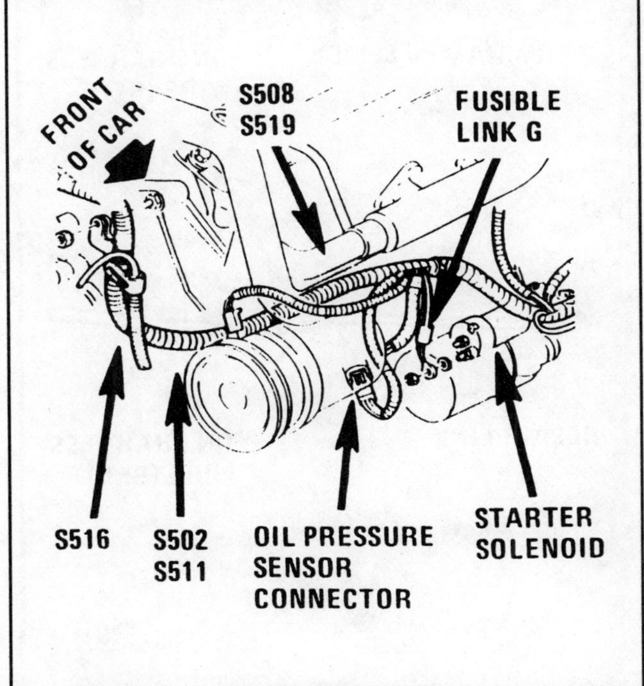

Fig. 29 Location of fusible link G at the lower left hand front of the engine at the starter solenoid

REPLACEMENT

➧ See Figure 30

⁂ CAUTION

When replacing fusible links, only use the correct amperage replacement fusible links. Each link is color coded to indicate the amperage rating. Damage to the electrical system may result if the incorrect fusible links are used.

1. **Very Important:** disconnect the negative (−) battery cable.
2. Locate the burned out link.
3. Strip away all melted harness insulation.
4. Cut the burned link ends from the circuit wire.
5. Strip the circuit wire back approximately ½ inch to allow soldering of new link.
6. Using a fusible link four (4) gauges smaller than the protected circuit (approximately 10 inches long), solder a new link into the circuit.

➡Use only resin core solder. Under no circumstances should an acid solder be used nor should a link be connected in any other manner except by soldering. Use of acid core solder may result in corrosion.

7. Tape the soldered ends securely, using suitable electrical tape.
8. After taping the wire, tape the harness leaving an exposed loop of wire approximately 5 inches in length.
9. Reconnect the negative (−) battery cable and check for operation of the affected circuit.

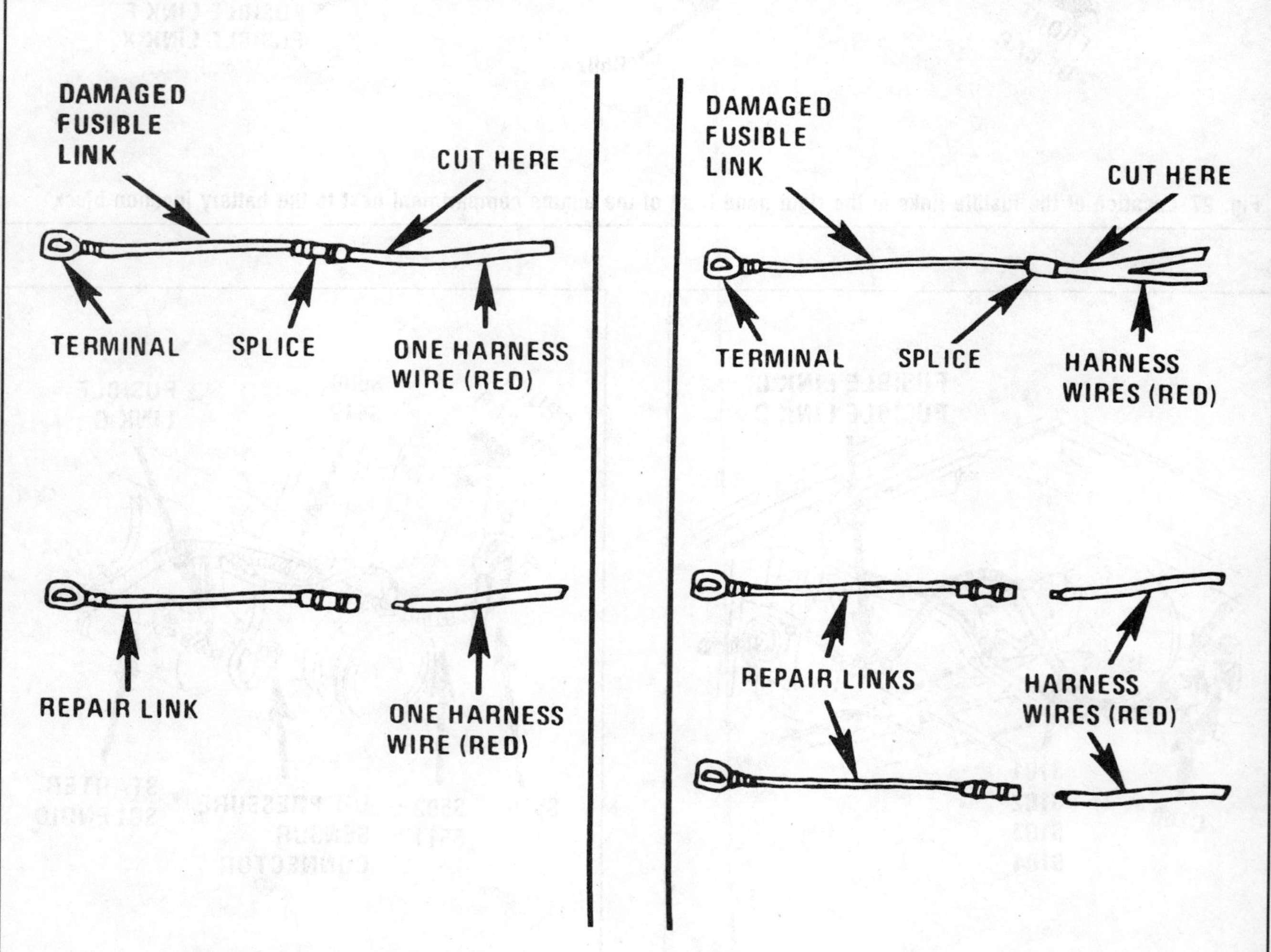

Fig. 30 Fusible links may be repaired by removing the damaged piece and soldering a new piece of wire in its place

Circuit Breakers

Circuit breakers are used in conjunction or instead of fuses to protect the circuit from an overload. If the circuit becomes overloaded, the circuit breaker heats up and at a specified temperature, the contacts in the breaker will open to stop the flow of current. When the circuit breaker cools down, the contacts will close and restore current flow. This condition usually causes the affected circuit to blink on and off until the problem is repaired.

LOCATION

1. Lighting Circuit—in the headlamp switch assembly
2. Windshield Wipers—in the wiper motor assembly
3. Power Windows—in the #12 slot of the fuse block (30 amp)
4. Power Door Locks, Rear Defogger—in the #15 slot of the fuse block (30 amp)

Flashers

REMOVAL & INSTALLATION

Turn Signals

➧ See Figure 31

1. Disconnect the negative (−) battery cable.
2. The turn signal flasher is located to the left of the steering column support bracket under the instrument panel.
3. Remove the electrical connector and slide the flasher assembly out of the bracket.

To install:

4. Reconnect the electrical connector and position the flasher into the bracket. Connect the negative (−) battery cable and turn the ignition key to the ON position. Operate the turnsignal switch in both directions to check for proper flasher operation.

Hazard (4-way)

1. Disconnect the negative (−) battery cable.
2. The hazard flasher is located in the convenience center at the RH side of the A/C and heater module under the instrument panel. Refer to the "Convenience Center" procedures in this section.
3. Disconnect the electrical connector and gently pull the flasher straight out of the convenience center.

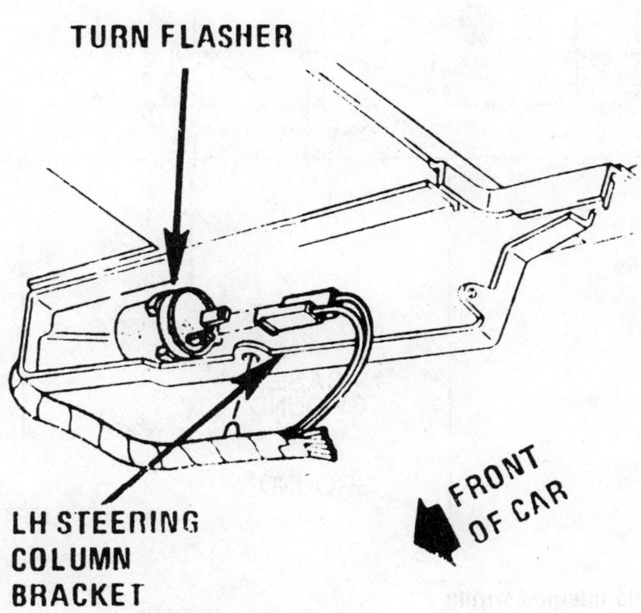

Fig. 31 The turn signal flasher is located on the left hand side of the steering column support

WIRING DIAGRAMS

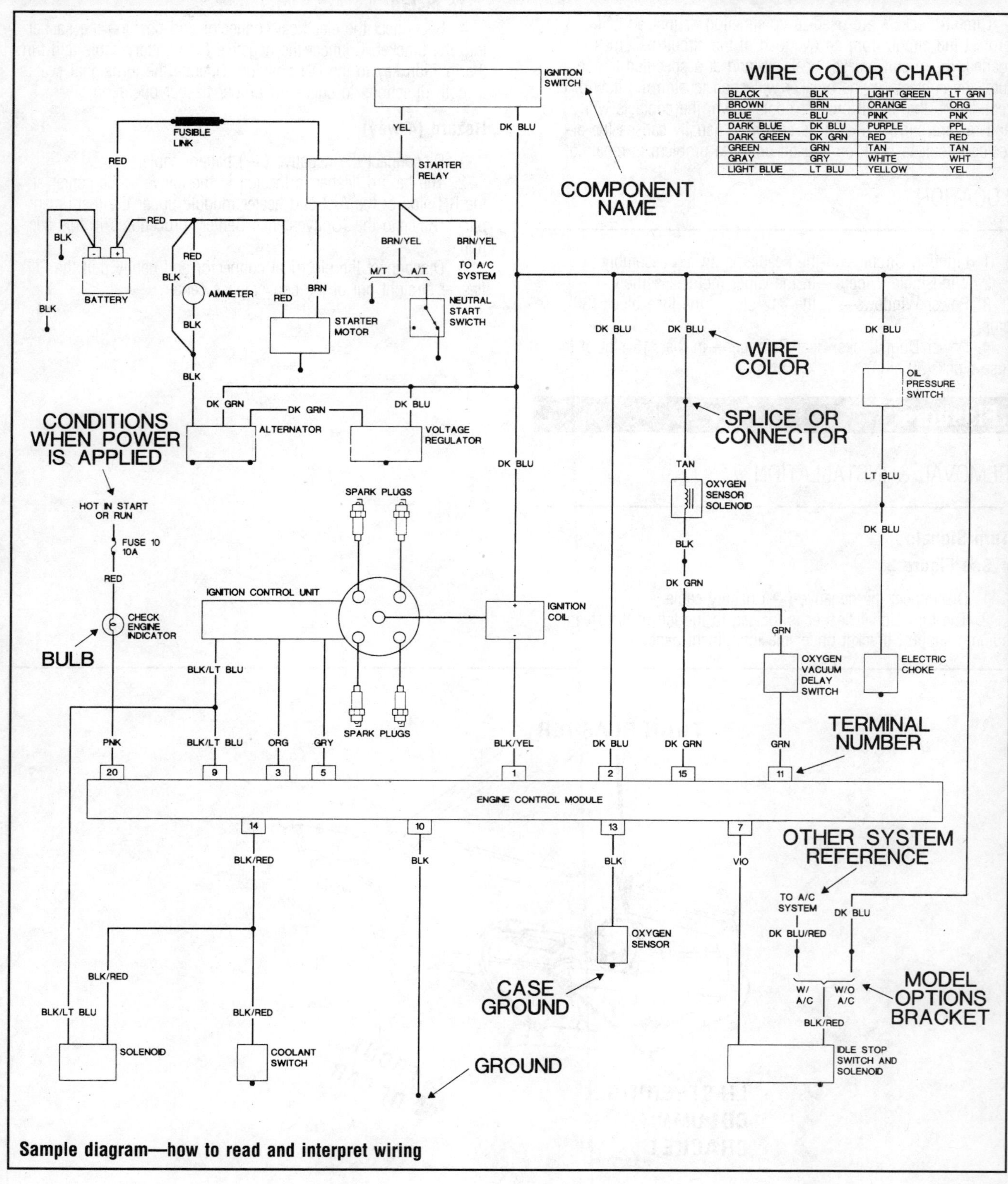

BLACK	BLK	LIGHT GREEN	LT GRN
BROWN	BRN	ORANGE	ORG
BLUE	BLU	PINK	PNK
DARK BLUE	DK BLU	PURPLE	PPL
DARK GREEN	DK GRN	RED	RED
GREEN	GRN	TAN	TAN
GRAY	GRY	WHITE	WHT
LIGHT BLUE	LT BLU	YELLOW	YEL

Sample diagram—how to read and interpret wiring

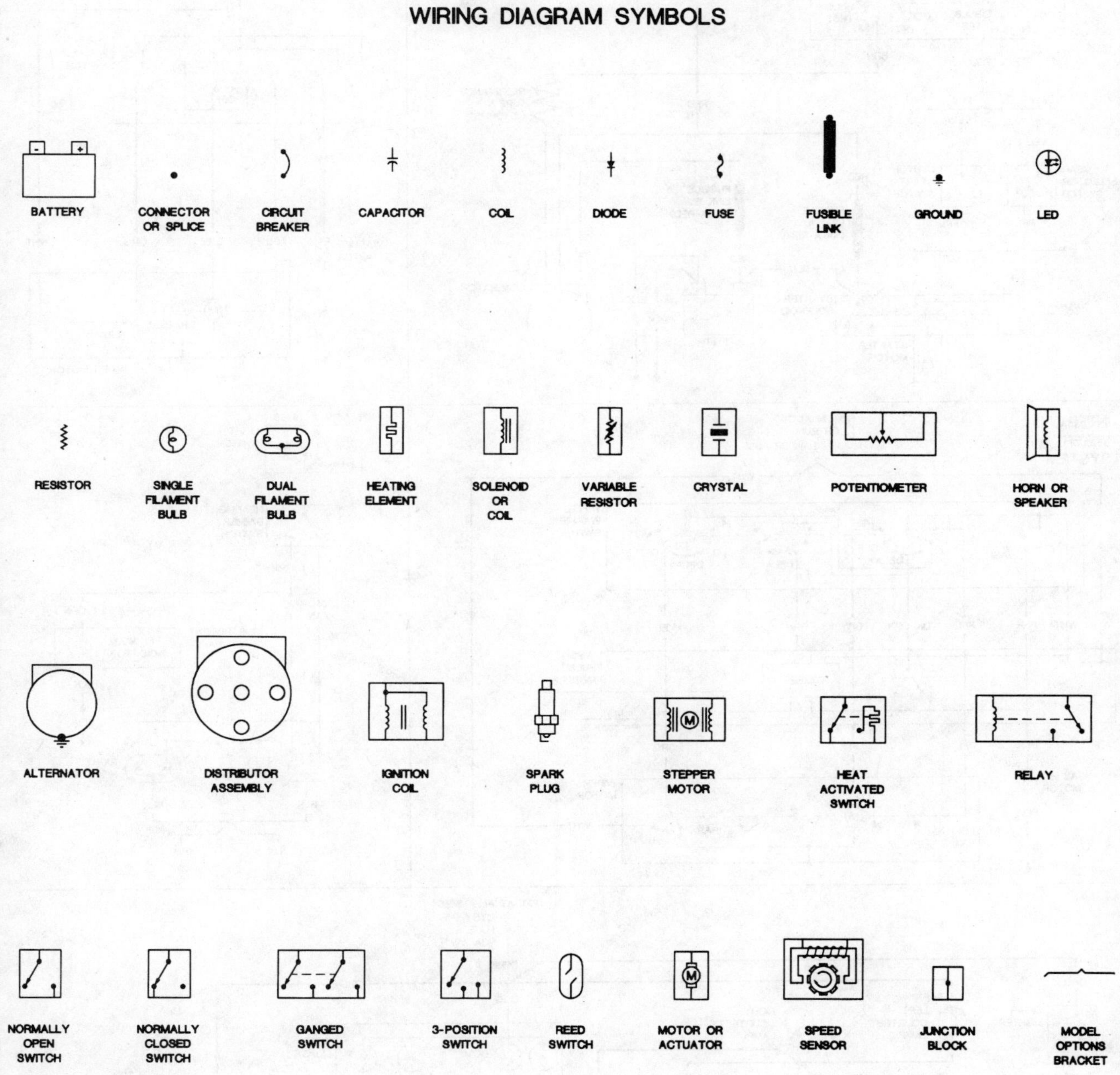

WIRING DIAGRAM SYMBOLS

BATTERY
CONNECTOR OR SPLICE
CIRCUIT BREAKER
CAPACITOR
COIL
DIODE
FUSE
FUSIBLE LINK
GROUND
LED
RESISTOR
SINGLE FILAMENT BULB
DUAL FILAMENT BULB
HEATING ELEMENT
SOLENOID OR COIL
VARIABLE RESISTOR
CRYSTAL
POTENTIOMETER
HORN OR SPEAKER
ALTERNATOR
DISTRIBUTOR ASSEMBLY
IGNITION COIL
SPARK PLUG
STEPPER MOTOR
HEAT ACTIVATED SWITCH
RELAY
NORMALLY OPEN SWITCH
NORMALLY CLOSED SWITCH
GANGED SWITCH
3-POSITION SWITCH
REED SWITCH
MOTOR OR ACTUATOR
SPEED SENSOR
JUNCTION BLOCK
MODEL OPTIONS BRACKET

Common wiring diagram symbols

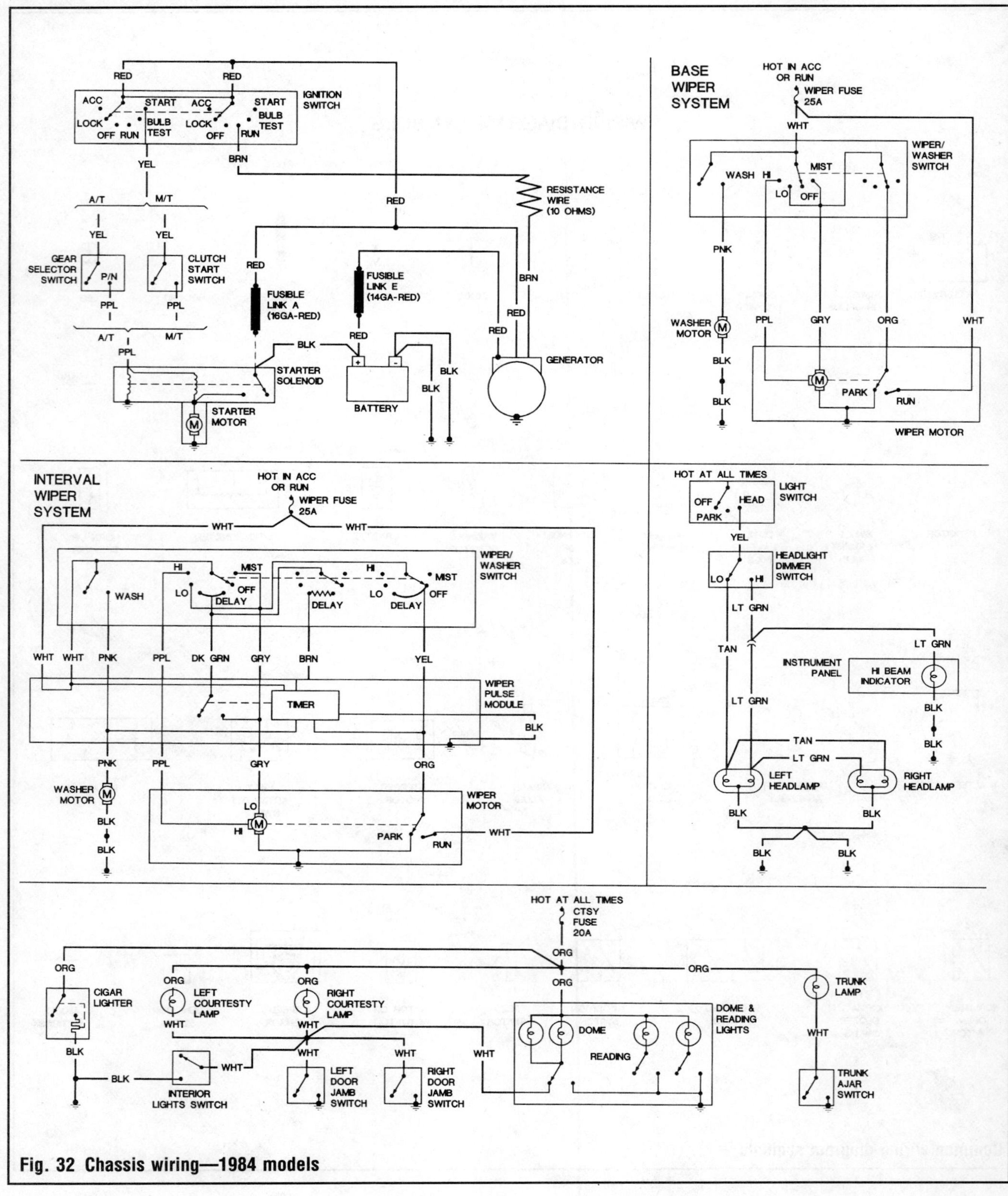

Fig. 32 Chassis wiring—1984 models

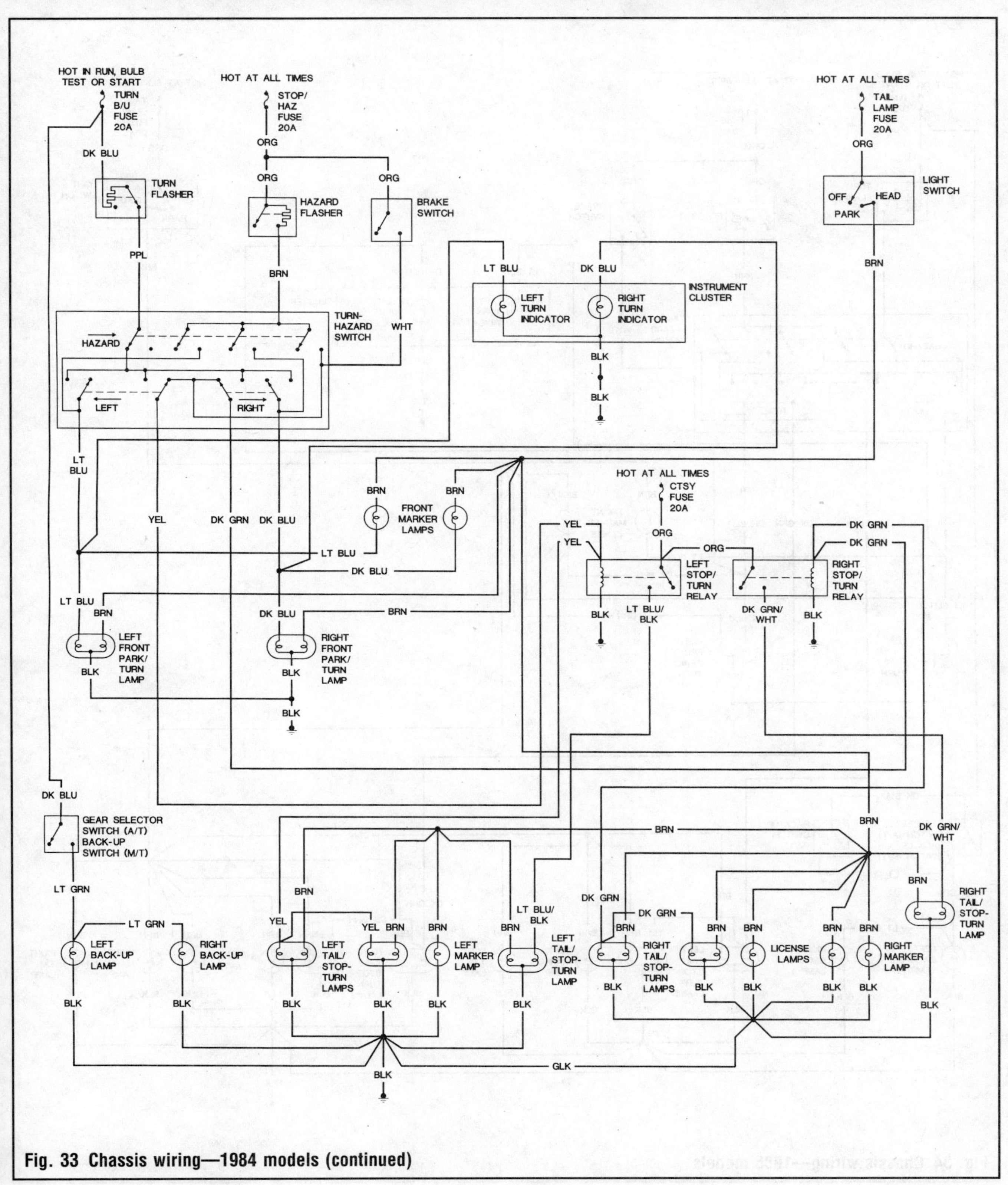

Fig. 33 Chassis wiring—1984 models (continued)

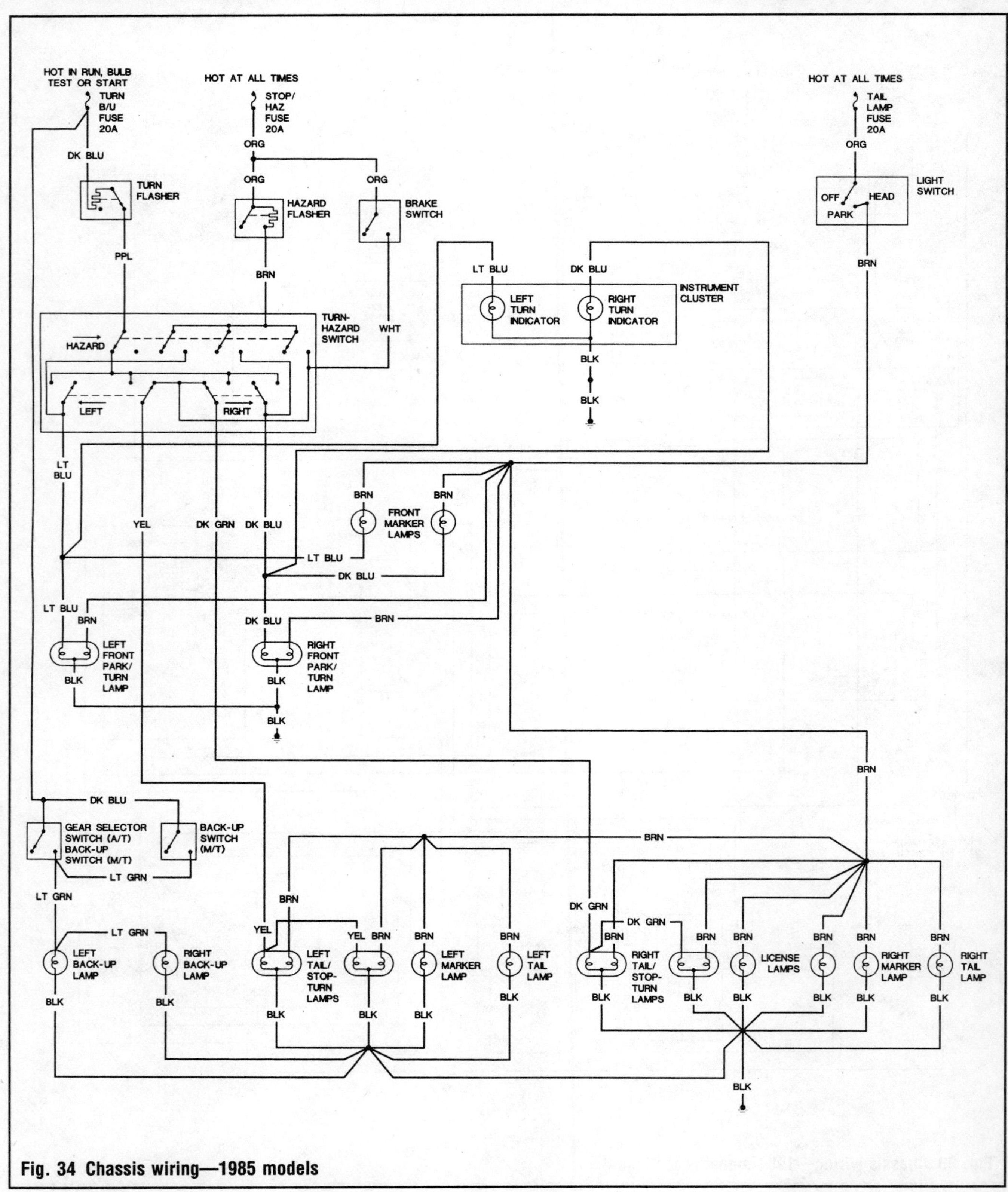

Fig. 34 Chassis wiring—1985 models

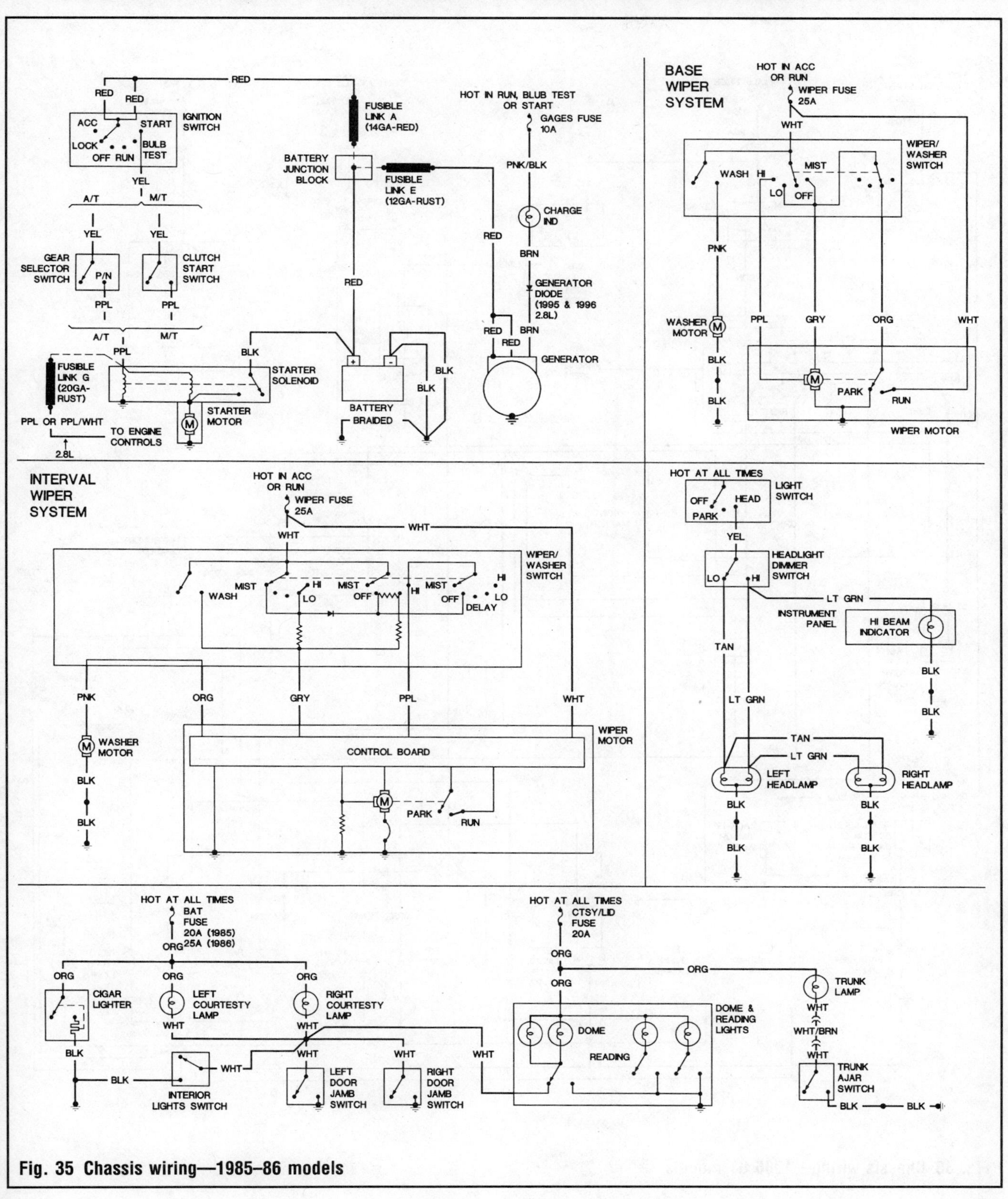

Fig. 35 Chassis wiring—1985–86 models

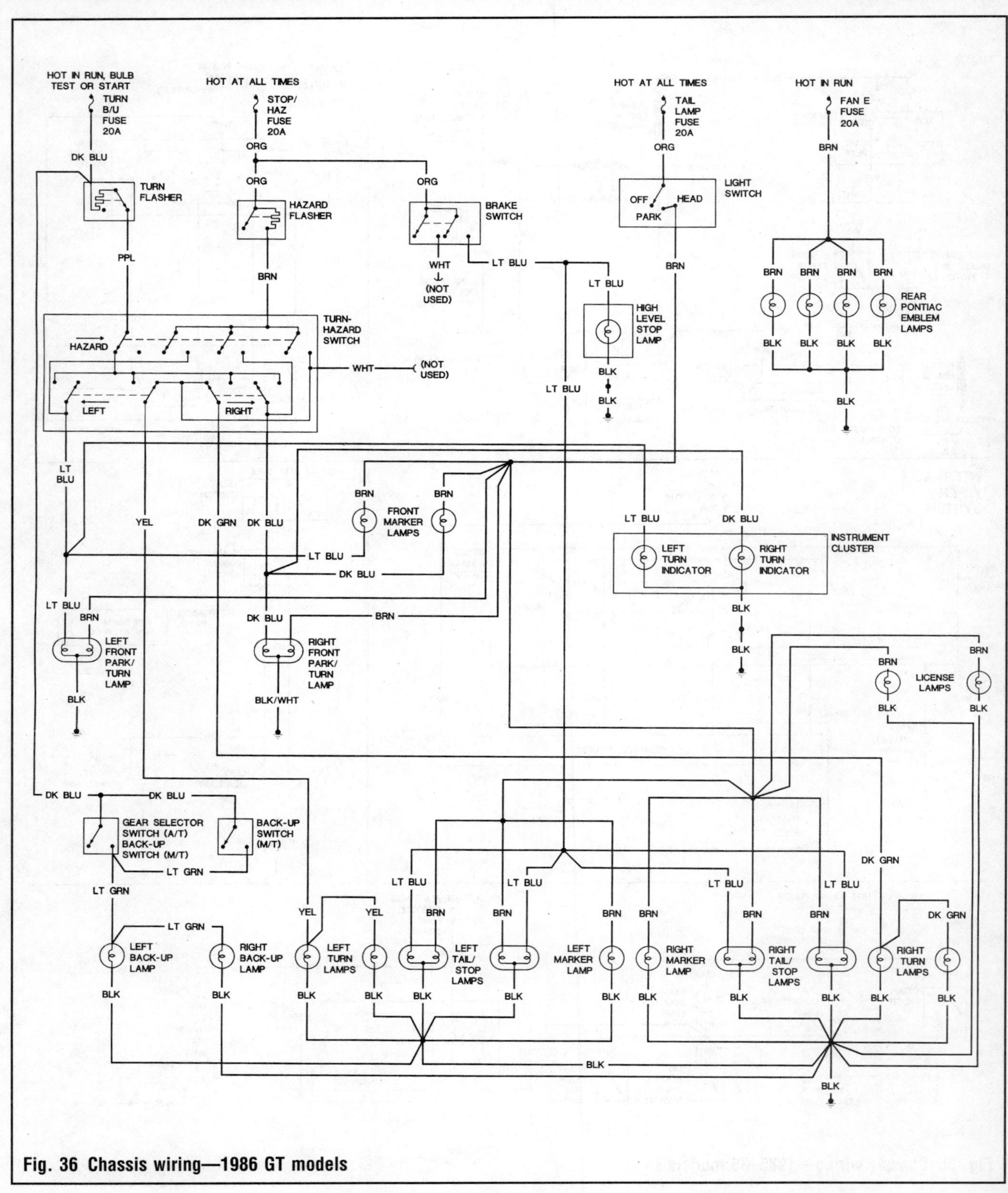

Fig. 36 Chassis wiring—1986 GT models

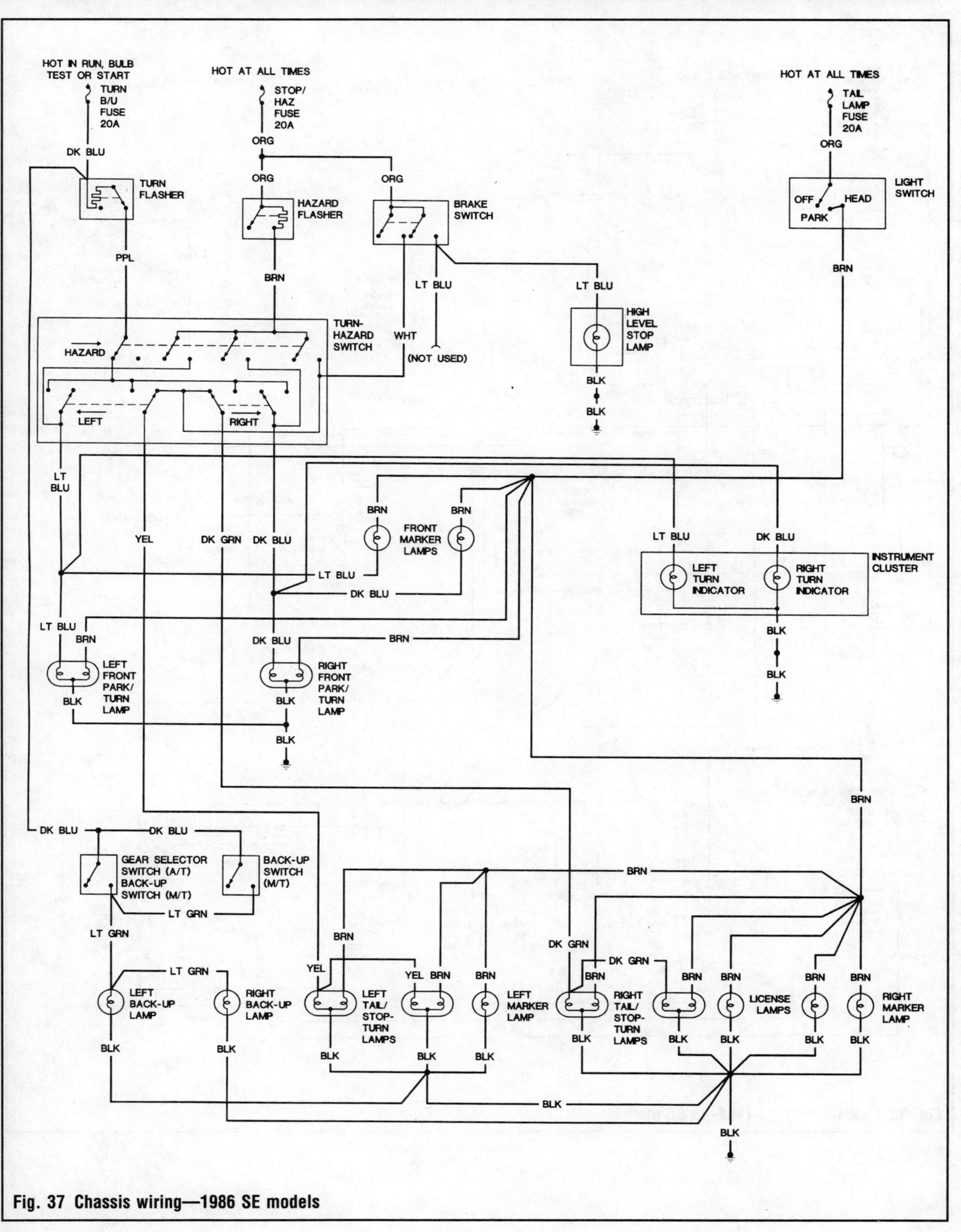

Fig. 37 Chassis wiring—1986 SE models

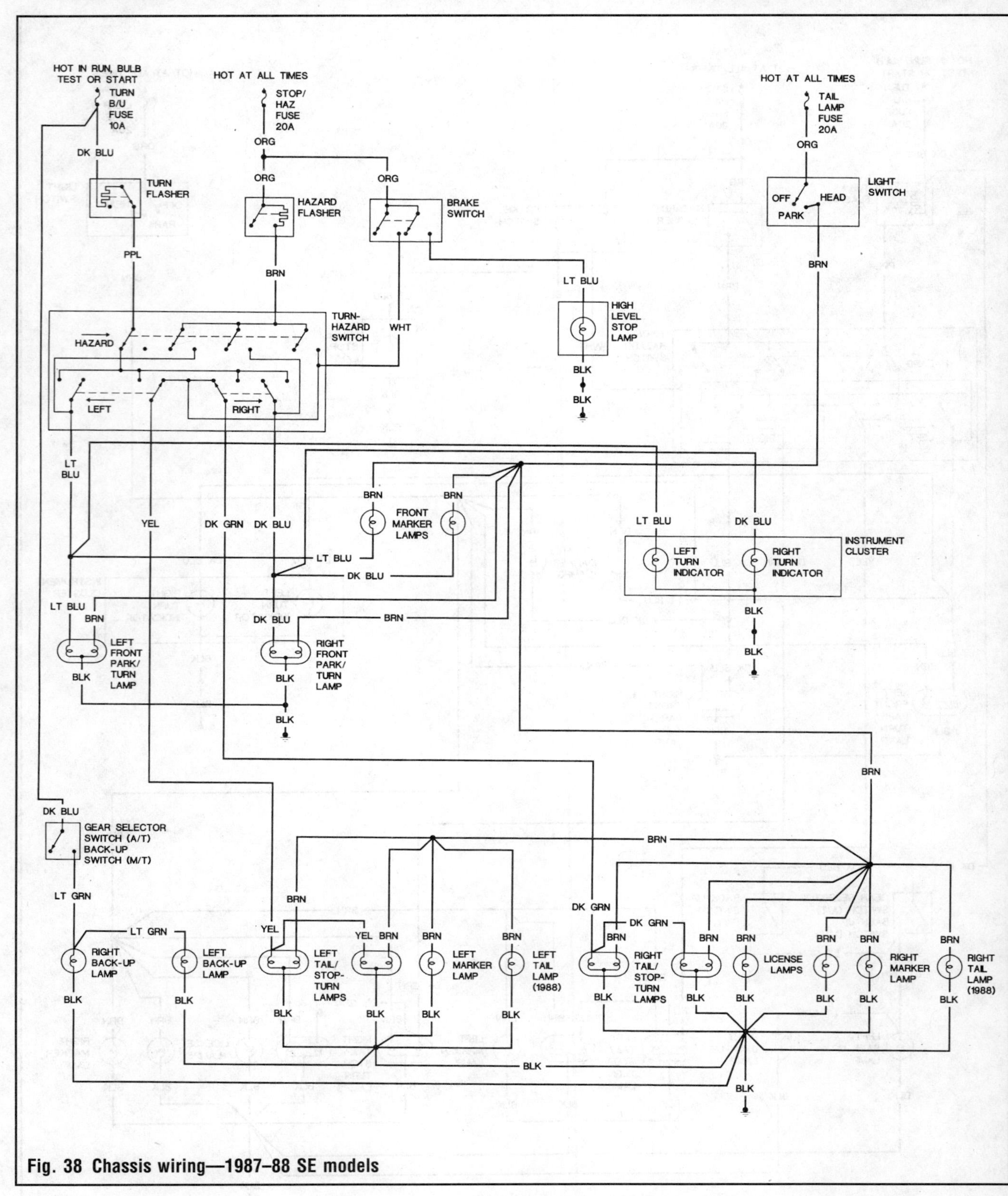

Fig. 38 Chassis wiring—1987–88 SE models

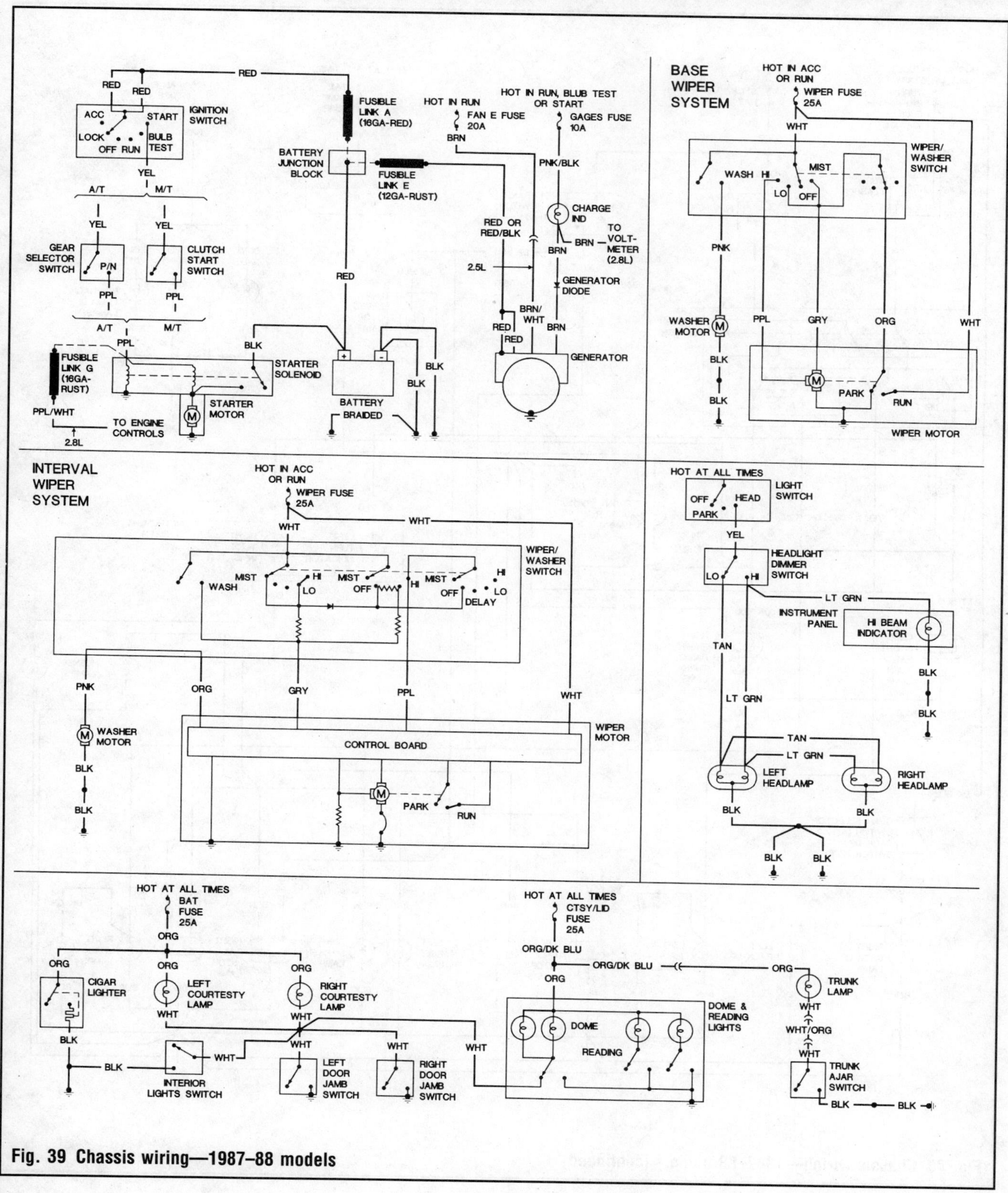

Fig. 39 Chassis wiring—1987–88 models

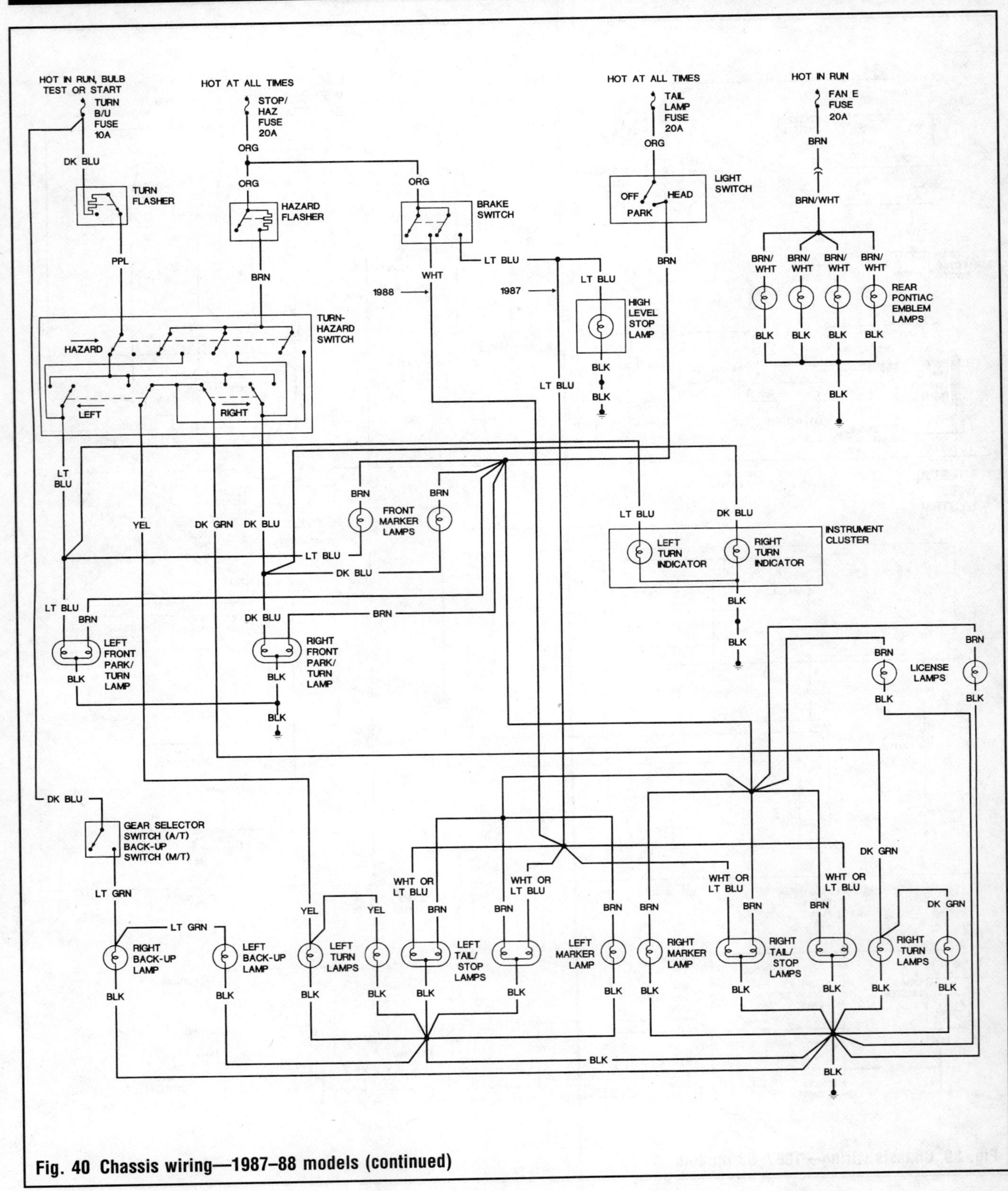

Fig. 40 Chassis wiring—1987–88 models (continued)

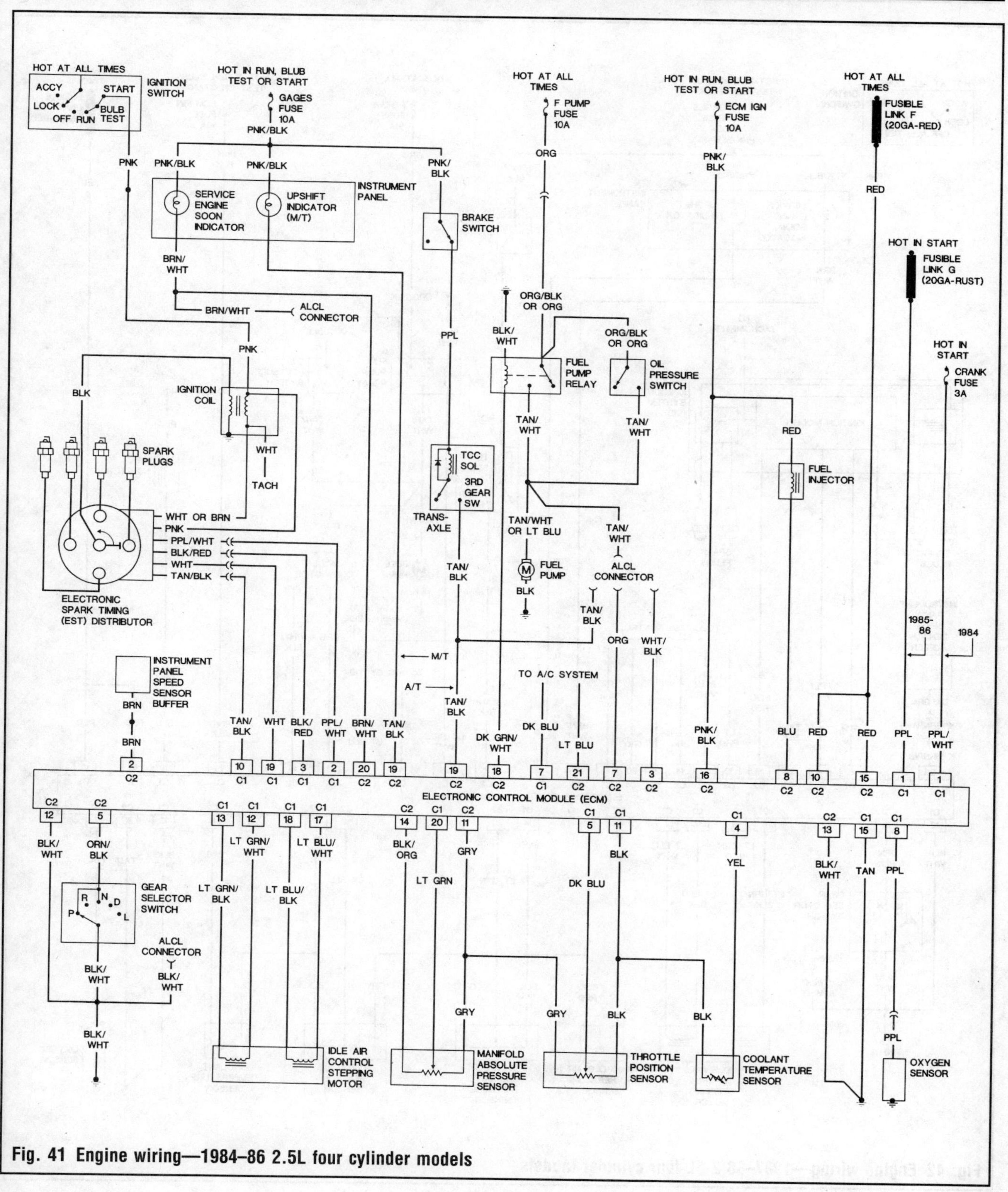

Fig. 41 Engine wiring—1984–86 2.5L four cylinder models

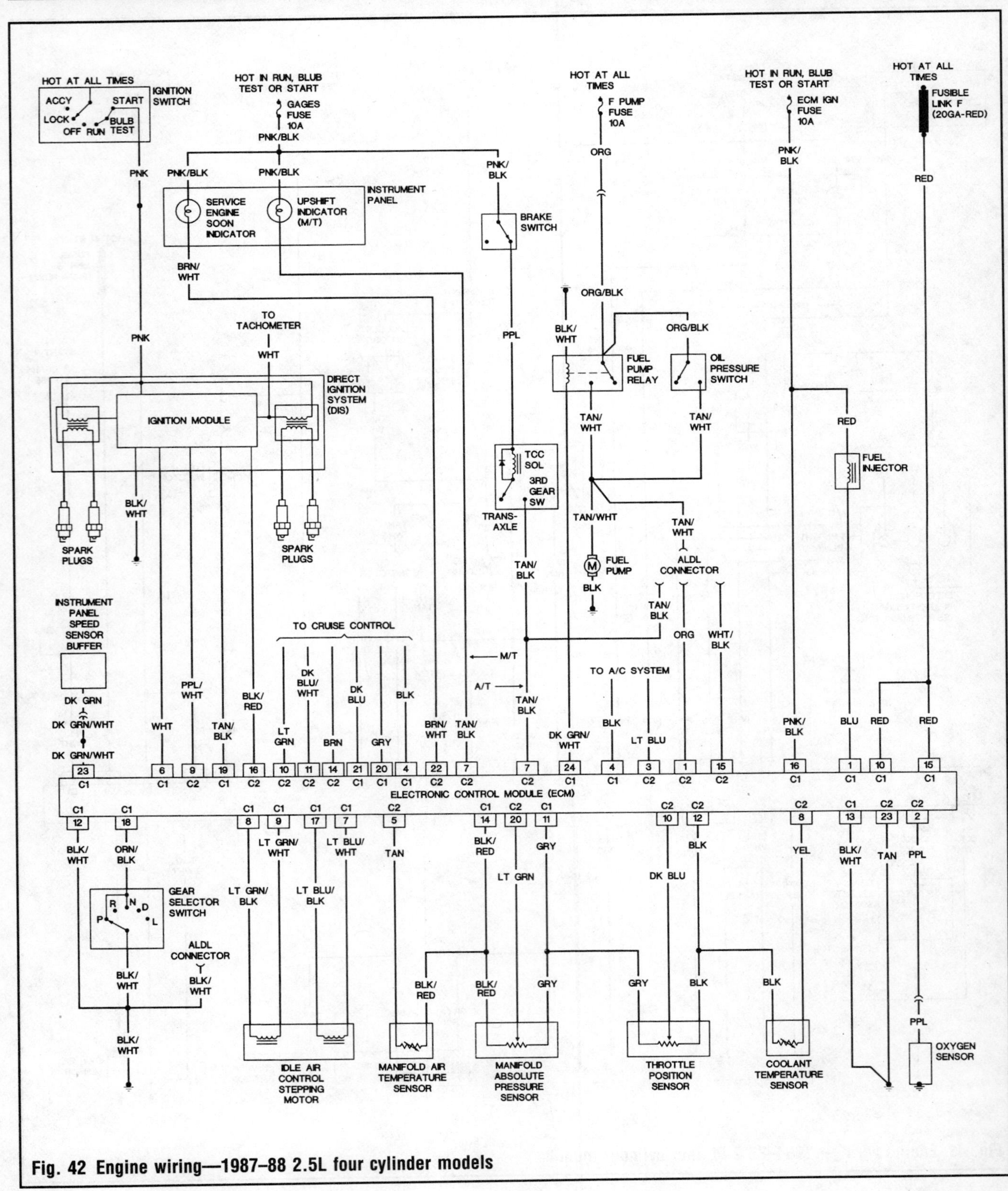

Fig. 42 Engine wiring—1987–88 2.5L four cylinder models

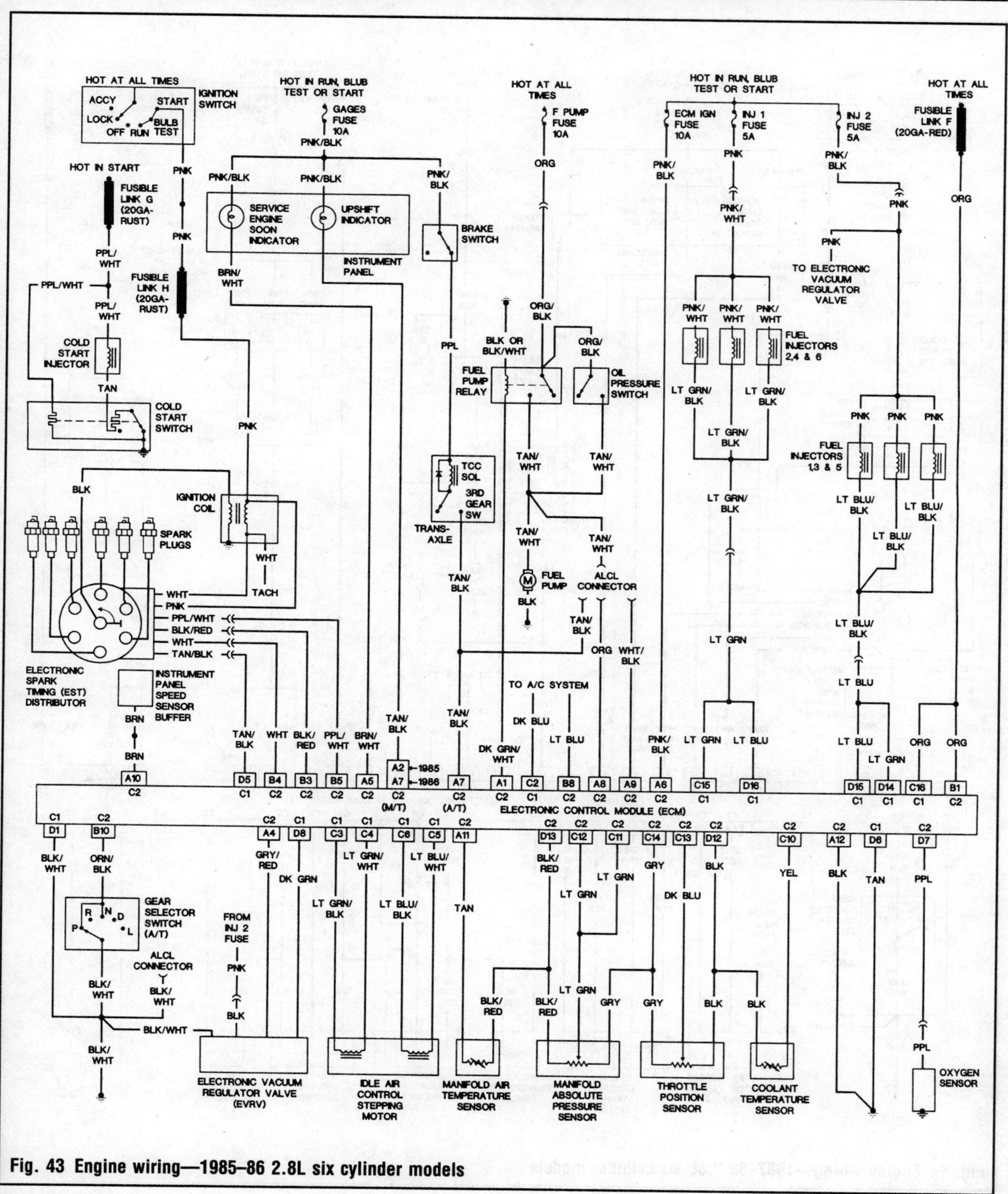

Fig. 43 Engine wiring—1985–86 2.8L six cylinder models

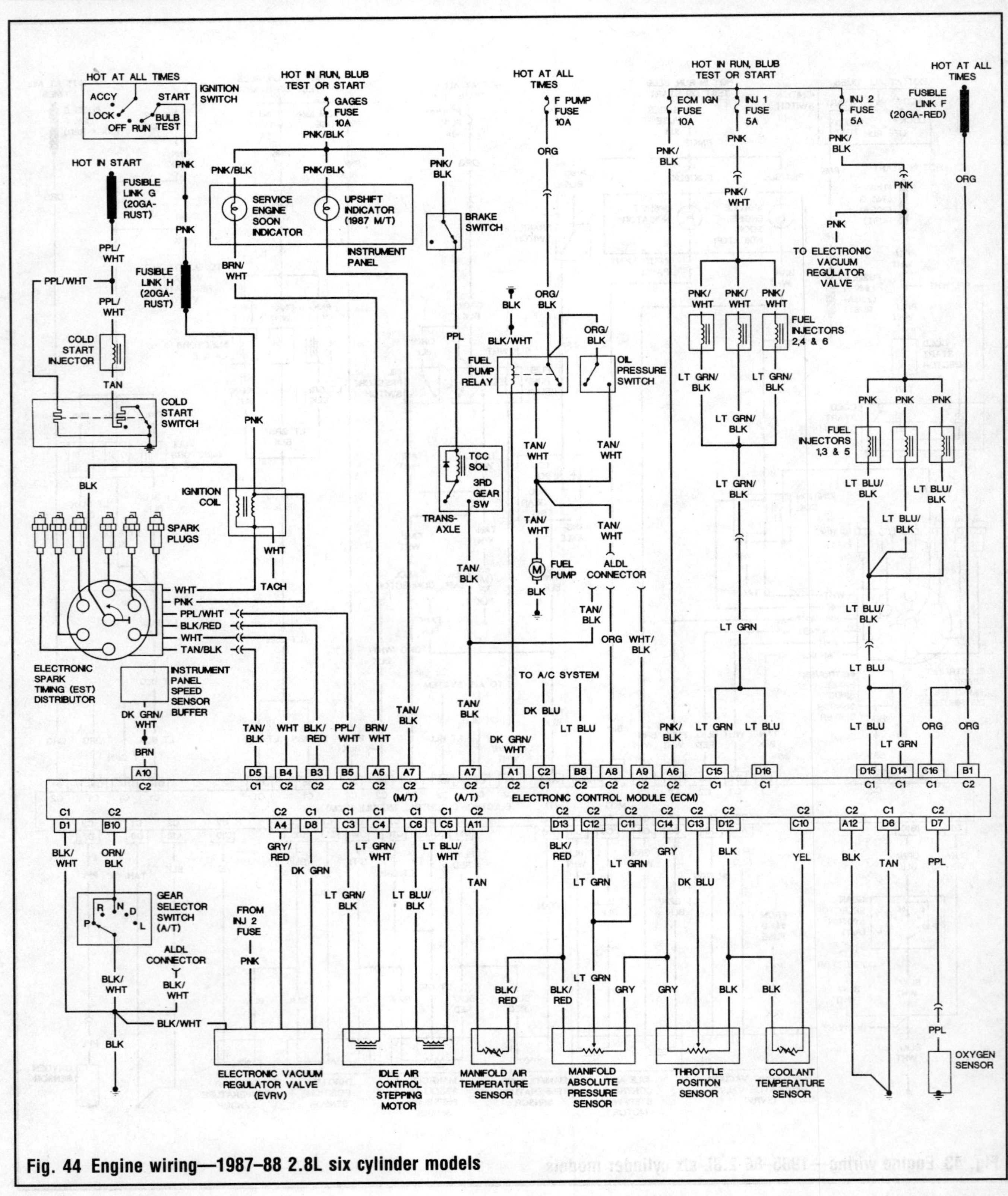

Fig. 44 Engine wiring—1987–88 2.8L six cylinder models

7 DRIVE TRAIN

MANUAL TRANSAXLE

Understanding the Manual Transaxle

Because of the way an internal combustion engine breathes, it can produce torque, or twisting force, only within a narrow speed range. Most modern, overhead valve pushrod engines must turn at about 2500 rpm to produce their peak torque. By 4500 rpm they are producing so little torque that continued increases in engine speed produce no power increases. The torque peak on overhead camshaft engines is generally much higher, but much narrower.

The manual transaxle and clutch are employed to vary the relationship between engine speed and the speed of the wheels so that adequate engine power can be produced under all circumstances. The clutch allows engine torque to be applied to the transaxle input shaft gradually, due to mechanical slippage. Consequently, the vehicle may be started smoothly from a full stop. The transaxle changes the ratio between the rotating speeds of the engine and the wheels by the use of gears. The gear ratios allow full engine power to be applied to the wheels during acceleration at low speeds and at highway/passing speeds.

In a front wheel drive transaxle, power is usually transmitted from the input shaft to a mainshaft or output shaft located slightly beneath and to the side of the input shaft. The gears of the mainshaft mesh with gears on the input shaft, allowing power to be carried from one to the other. All forward gears are in constant mesh and are free from rotating with the shaft unless the synchronizer and clutch is engaged. Shifting from one gear to the next causes one of the gears to be freed from rotating with the shaft and locks another to it. Gears are locked and unlocked by internal dog clutches which slide between the center of the gear and the shaft. The forward gears employ synchronizers; friction members which smoothly bring gear and shaft to the same speed before the toothed dog clutches are engaged.

Identification

See Figures 1 and 2

The Pontiac Fiero that is equipped with a manual transaxle uses one of three types. The early fieros were equipped with either a 4-speed 76mm Isuzu or 5-speed 76mm Isuzu transaxles. The external components are basically the same with the differences in the internal components. The later model Fieros came equipped with 5-speed 282 Muncie transaxles. This model trans has been redesigned to conform with the increased horsepower ratings of the newer engines.

The manual transaxle uses a hydraulic clutch system that supplies hydraulic pressure to the slave cylinder to actuate the clutch assembly.

Two cable assemblies are used to shift the gears, one being the transaxle selector cable and the other a transaxle shifter cable. The cables are routed rearward through the floor pan extension. They are anchored to the transaxle and floor pan through the use of clips.

The identification tag is located on the transaxle bell housing.

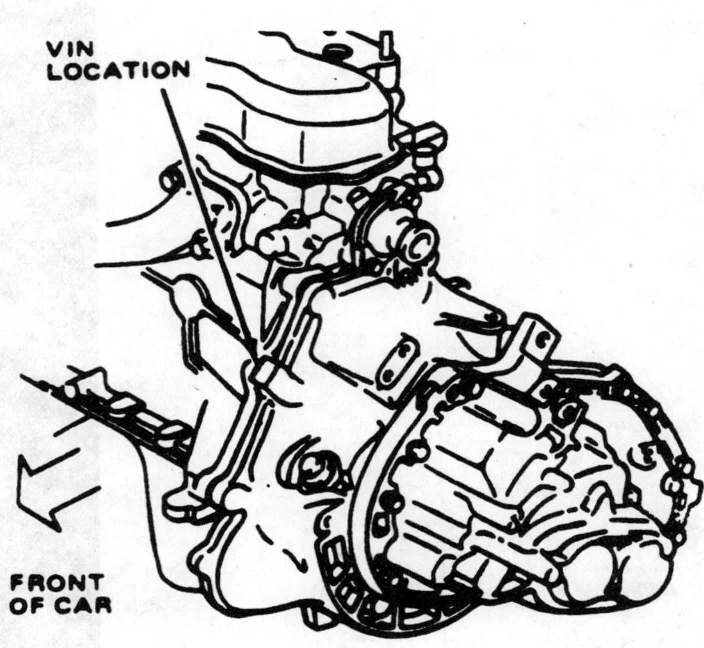

Fig. 1 Isuzu 4 and 5-speed (76mm) manual transmission identification tag location

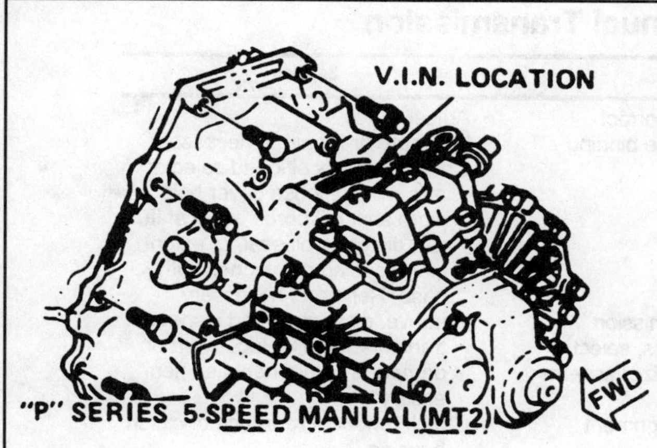

Fig. 2 Muncie 5–speed 282 manual transaxle identification tag location

The 4 and 5-speed Isuzu transaxles have the tag on the side of the bell housing. The 5-speed Muncie transaxles have the tag on the top of the bell housing.

Adjustments

SHIFT CABLES

4-speed 76mm Isuzu

➧ See Figure 3

1. Remove the reverse inhibitor fitting spring and washer from the end of housing.
2. Position the shifter shaft in the 2nd gear.
3. Measure the dimension A (end of housing to shoulder just behind the end of the shaft).
4. Apply a load of 4–6 Kg on the opposite end of the shaft.

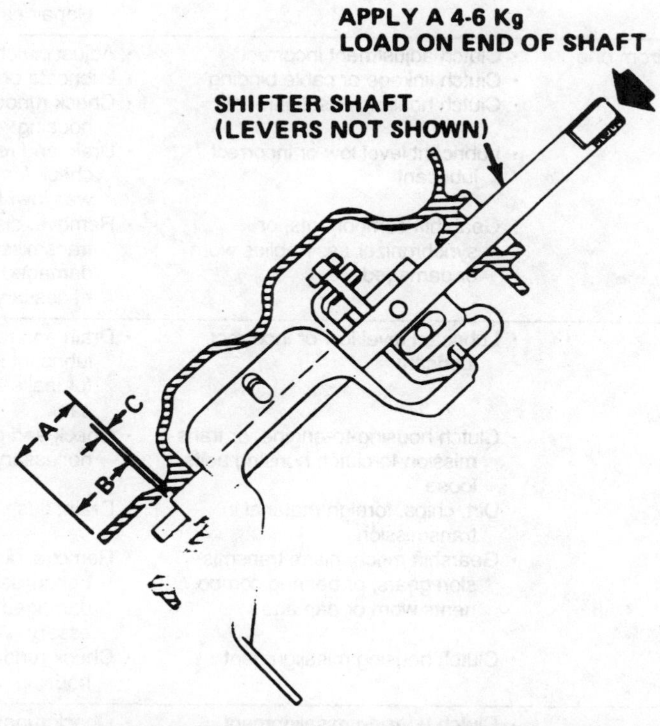

SHIM PART NO.	DIM C (MM)	COLOR & NO. OF STRIPES
14008235	1.8	3 WHITE
476709	2.1	1 ORANGE
476710	2.4	2 ORANGE
476711	2.7	3 ORANGE
476712	3.0	1 BLUE
476713	3.3	2 BLUE
476714	3.6	3 BLUE
476715	3.9	1 WHITE
476716	4.2	2 WHITE

Fig. 3 Manual shift shaft adjustment and shim chart—4-speed (76mm) Isuzu transaxle

Troubleshooting the Manual Transmission

Problem	Cause	Solution
Transmission shifts hard	• Clutch adjustment incorrect • Clutch linkage or cable binding • Shift rail binding	• Adjust clutch • Lubricate or repair as necessary • Check for mispositioned selector arm roll pin, loose cover bolts, worn shift rail bores, worn shift rail, distorted oil seal, or extension housing not aligned with case. Repair as necessary.
	• Internal bind in transmission caused by shift forks, selector plates, or synchronizer assemblies	• Remove, dissemble and inspect transmission. Replace worn or damaged components as necessary.
	• Clutch housing misalignment	• Check runout at rear face of clutch housing
	• Incorrect lubricant	• Drain and refill transmission
	• Block rings and/or cone seats worn	• Blocking ring to gear clutch tooth face clearance must be 0.030 inch or greater. If clearance is correct it may still be necessary to inspect blocking rings and cone seats for excessive wear. Repair as necessary.
Gear clash when shifting from one gear to another	• Clutch adjustment incorrect • Clutch linkage or cable binding • Clutch housing misalignment	• Adjust clutch • Lubricate or repair as necessary • Check runout at rear of clutch housing
	• Lubricant level low or incorrect lubricant	• Drain and refill transmission and check for lubricant leaks if level was low. Repair as necessary.
	• Gearshift components, or synchronizer assemblies worn or damaged	• Remove, disassemble and inspect transmission. Replace worn or damaged components as necessary.
Transmission noisy	• Lubricant level low or incorrect lubricant	• Drain and refill transmission. If lubricant level was low, check for leaks and repair as necessary.
	• Clutch housing-to-engine, or transmission-to-clutch housing bolts loose	• Check and correct bolt torque as necessary
	• Dirt, chips, foreign material in transmission	• Drain, flush, and refill transmission
	• Gearshift mechanism, transmission gears, or bearing components worn or damaged	• Remove, disassemble and inspect transmission. Replace worn or damaged components as necessary.
	• Clutch housing misalignment	• Check runout at rear face of clutch housing
Jumps out of gear	• Clutch housing misalignment	• Check runout at rear face of clutch housing
	• Gearshift lever loose	• Check lever for worn fork. Tighten loose attaching bolts.
	• Offset lever nylon insert worn or lever attaching nut loose	• Remove gearshift lever and check for loose offset lever nut or worn insert. Repair or replace as necessary.
	• Gearshift mechanism, shift forks, selector plates, interlock plate, selector arm, shift rail, detent plugs, springs or shift cover worn or damaged	• Remove, disassemble and inspect transmission cover assembly. Replace worn or damaged components as necessary.
	• Clutch shaft or roller bearings worn or damaged	• Replace clutch shaft or roller bearings as necessary

Troubleshooting the Manual Transmission (cont.)

Problem	Cause	Solution
Jumps out of gear (cont.)	· Gear teeth worn or tapered, synchronizer assemblies worn or damaged, excessive end play caused by worn thrust washers or output shaft gears	· Remove, disassemble, and inspect transmission. Replace worn or damaged components as necessary.
	· Pilot bushing worn	· Replace pilot bushing
Will not shift into one gear	· Gearshift selector plates, interlock plate, or selector arm, worn, damaged, or incorrectly assembled	· Remove, disassemble, and inspect transmission cover assembly. Repair or replace components as necessary.
	· Shift rail detent plunger worn, spring broken, or plug loose	· Tighten plug or replace worn or damaged components as necessary
	· Gearshift lever worn or damaged	· Replace gearshift lever
	· Synchronizer sleeves or hubs, damaged or worn	· Remove, disassemble and inspect transmission. Replace worn or damaged components.
Locked in one gear—cannot be shifted out	· Shift rail(s) worn or broken, shifter fork bent, setscrew loose, center detent plug missing or worn	· Inspect and replace worn or damaged parts
	· Broken gear teeth on countershaft gear, clutch shaft, or reverse idler gear	· Inspect and replace damaged part
	Gearshift lever broken or worn, shift mechanism in cover incorrectly assembled or broken, worn damaged gear train components	· Disassemble transmission. Replace damaged parts or assemble correctly.

Then measure dimension B (end of housing to end of shifter shaft major diameter).

5. Subtract: dimension A minus dimension B equals distance C.
6. Compare result of step 5 with the chart and choose the proper shim for use on reinstallation.

5-speed 76mm Isuzu

➧ See Figure 4

1. Disconnect the negative (−) battery cable.
2. Place the transaxle in first gear.
3. Loosen the shift cable attaching nuts (E) at the transaxle levers (D) and (F) shown in the "Cable Adjustment" illustration.
4. Remove the console and trim plates as required for access to shifter assembly.
5. With the shifter lever in first gear position (pulled to left and held against the stop), insert an alignment pin H and G as shown in view C.
6. Remove the lash from the transaxle by rotating lever D in the direction of the arrow while tightening the nut E in view (A). Levers D and F should be kept from moving during this process. Tighten nut E and F. Again levers D and F must remain stationary. Nut E on levers D and F tightened to 20 ft. lbs. (27 Nm).
7. Ensure reverse inhibit cam is against the roller and align if necessary.
8. Remove the alignment pins H and G at the shifter assembly.
9. Replace the console trim plate.
10. Reconnect the negative battery cable.

5-speed 282 Muncie

➧ See Figure 5

➡Only the shift cable is adjustable and is adjusted at the transaxle. Do not adjust the select cable.

1. Disconnect the negative (−) battery cable.
2. Loosen the nut on the transaxle shift lever ball stud on the shift cable only.
3. Place the transaxle in third gear.
4. Remove the front and shifter trimplate.
5. Place the pin in the floor shift mechanism is third gear.
6. Torque the nut on the shift cable ball stud to 18 ft. lbs. (25 Nm).
7. Install the trim plates and shift knob.
8. Reconnect the negative (−) battery cable and check shifter operation.

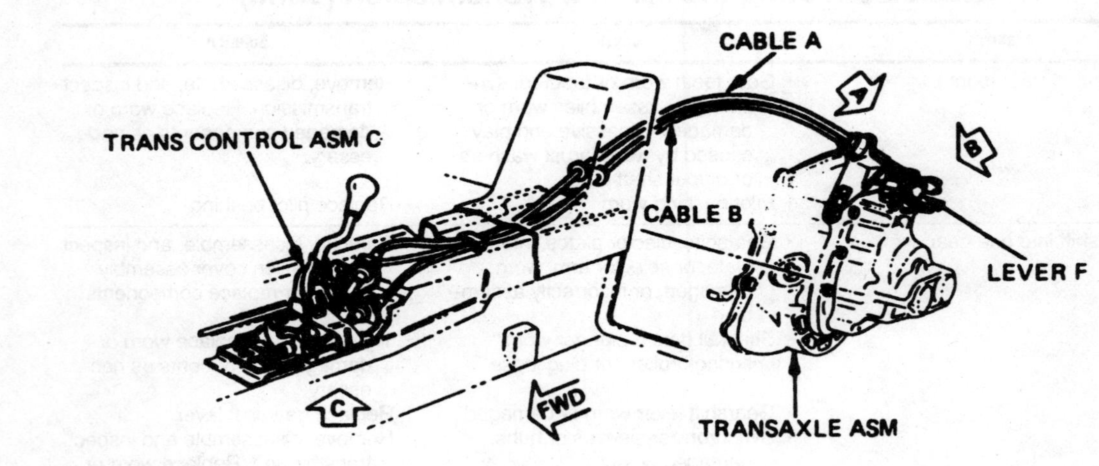

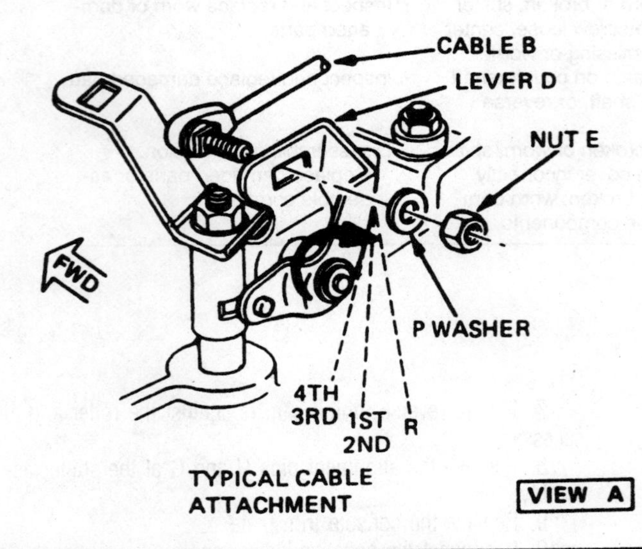

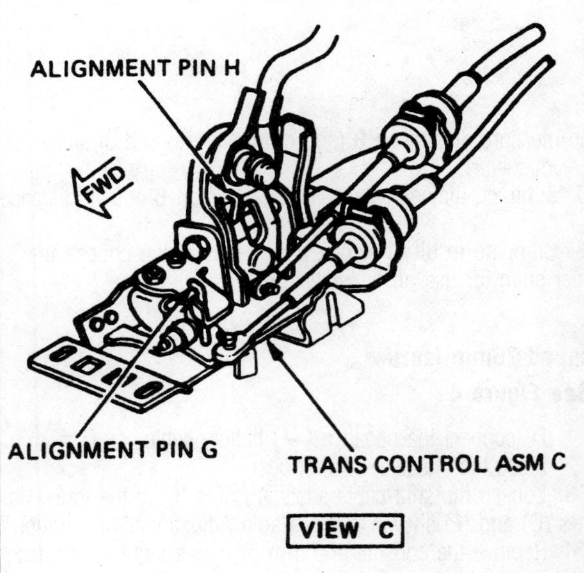

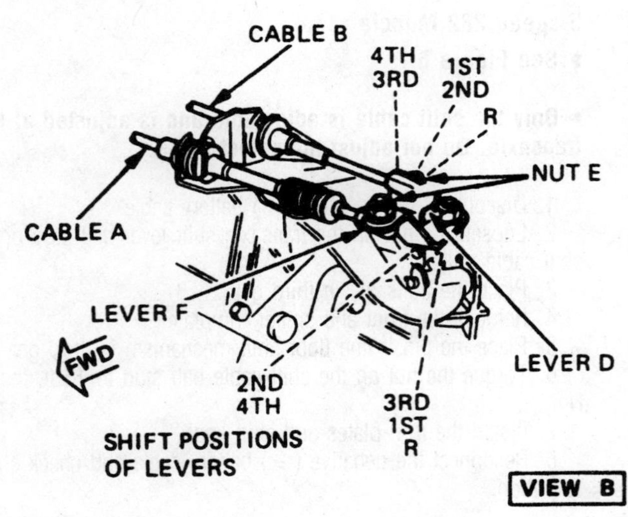

Fig. 4 Shift cable adjustment—5-speed (76mm) Isuzu transaxle

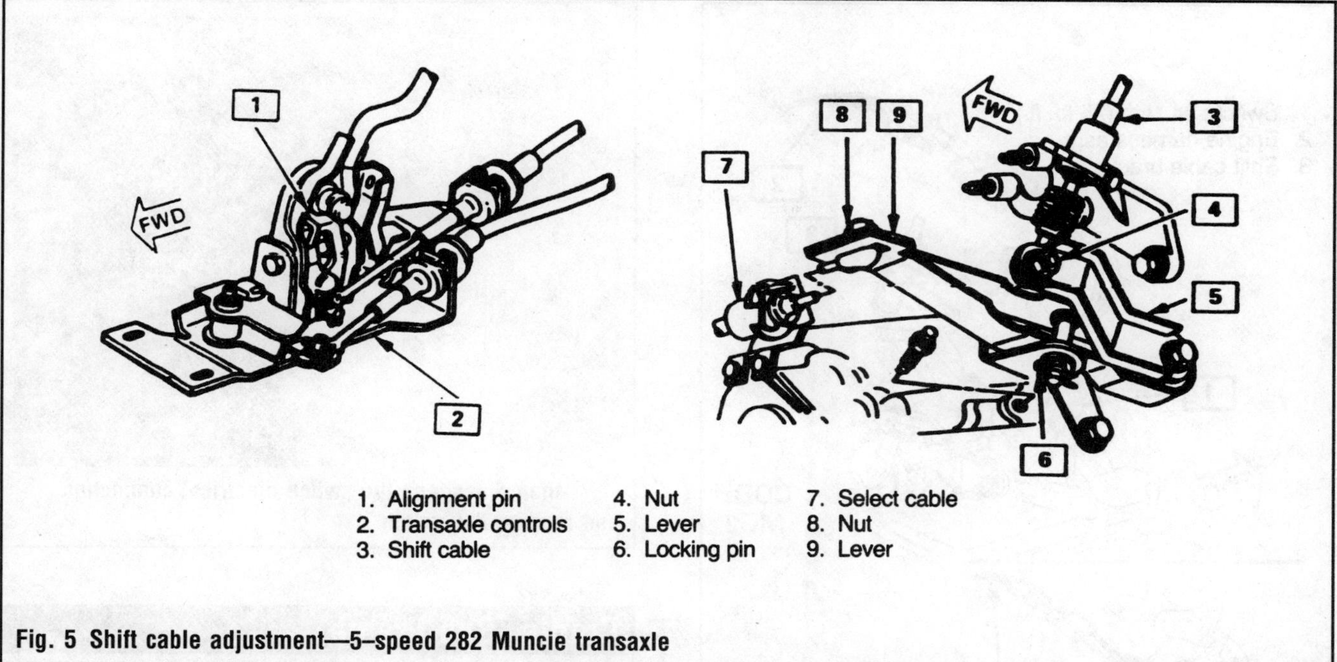

Fig. 5 Shift cable adjustment—5-speed 282 Muncie transaxle

CLUTCH ADJUSTMENT

The hydraulic clutch system locates the clutch pedal and provides automatic clutch adjustment. No adjustment of clutch linkage or pedal position is required.

Backup Lamp Switch

REMOVAL & INSTALLATION

1984–86 Models

➧ See Figures 6 and 7

1. Disconnect the negative (−) battery cable.
2. Remove the shift trim plate. Refer to the "Console" procedures in Section 6.
3. Disconnect the electrical connector at the switch.
4. Remove the switch retainer and switch.

To install:

5. Position the switch into the holder and install the retainer clip. Reconnect the electrical connector and reinstall the shift trim plate.

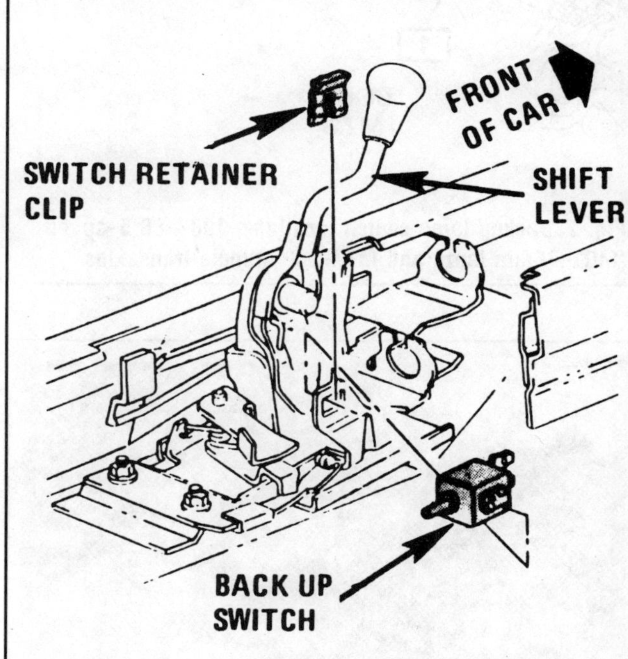

Fig. 6 Location of the backup lamp switch—1984–86 4 and 5-speed manual transaxles

1987–88 Models

1. Disconnect the negative (−) battery cable.
2. At the transaxle, disconnect the backup lamp switch electrical connector and remove the harness from the shift cable bracket.
3. Remove the switch from the transaxle assembly.

To install:

4. Lubricate the switch seal with engine oil and install into the transaxle housing. Torque the switch to 25 ft. lbs. (34 Nm).
5. Reconnect the switch electrical connector and negative (−) battery cable.

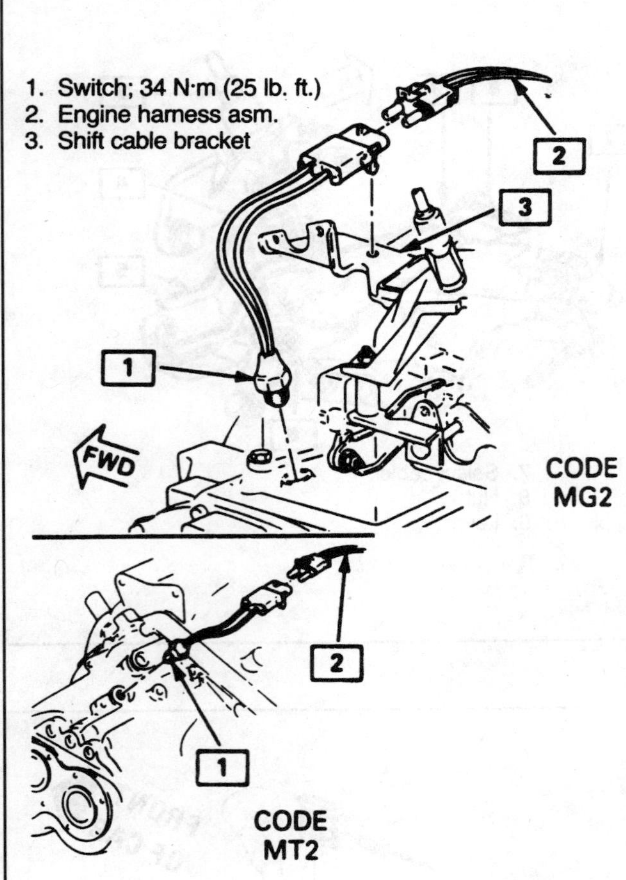

Fig. 7 Backup lamp switch location—1987–88 5-speed (MG2–76mm Isuzu and MT2–282 Muncie transaxles

Remove the backup lamp switch retaining clip . . .

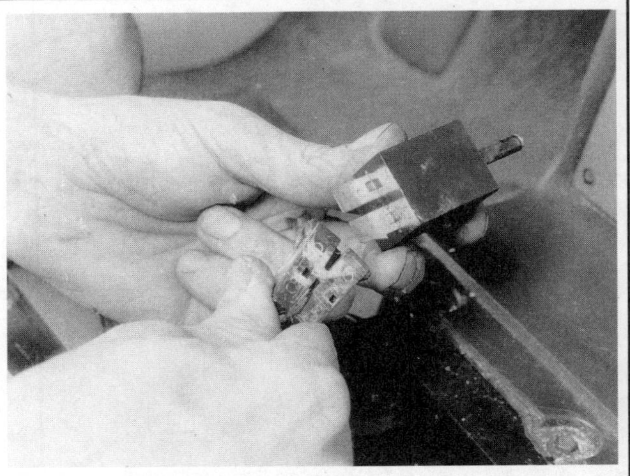
. . . then disengage the switch electrical connection and remove the switch

Cradle (Sub-Frame)

REMOVAL & INSTALLATION

See Figure 8

CAUTION

If you are using a twin post hoist, place safety stands at the rear most points as shown in the "Jacking" illustration in Section 1. If using a single post hoist, place two safety stands in the front and two in the rear at the points shown in the "Jacking" illustration.

1. Disconnect the negative (−) battery cable.
2. Remove the exhaust pipe bolts at the manifold.
3. Remove the rear wheel assemblies.
4. Remove both rear lateral control arms, fixed adjusting links and trailing arms at the knuckle.
5. Remove the stabilizer brackets at the cradle (GT only).
6. Remove the engine and transaxle mount bolts.
7. Remove the cradle bolts and cradle.

To install:

1. Install the cradle assembly and tighten the retaining bolts finger tight.
2. Install the engine and transaxle mounting bolts and torque to 36 ft. lbs. (48 Nm).
3. Install the parking brake cable at the cradle.
4. Reconnect the stabilizer brackets.
5. Install both trailing arms, fixed adjustable links and lateral control arms at the knuckle.
6. Install the exhaust pipe at the manifold.
7. Install the rear wheel assemblies.
8. Torque the front cradle retaining bolts to 67 ft. lbs. (90 Nm) and the rear bolts to 76 ft. lbs. (103 Nm).

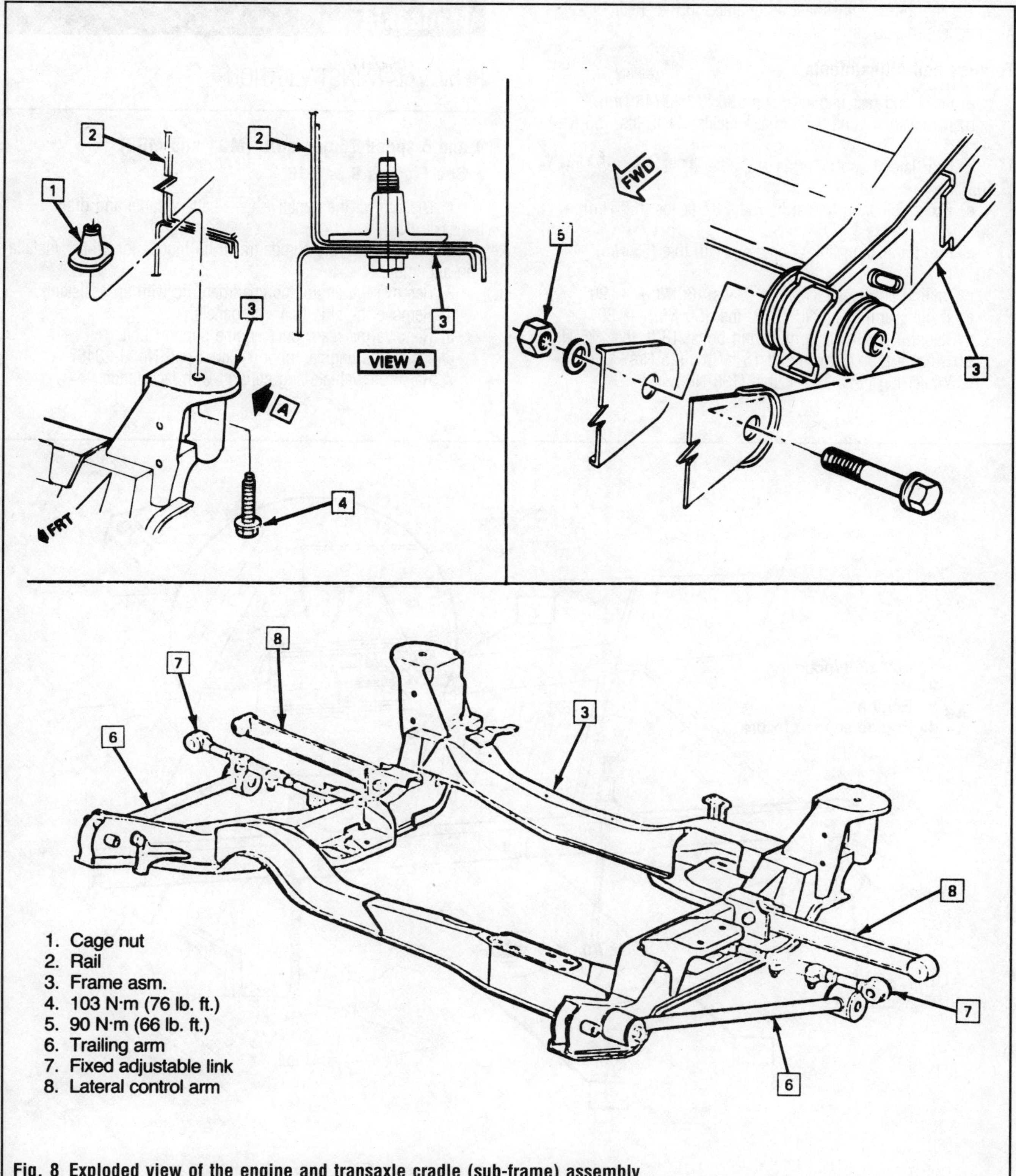

Fig. 8 Exploded view of the engine and transaxle cradle (sub-frame) assembly

9. Set the toe-in adjustment as outlined in the "Rear Wheel Alignment" procedures in Section 8.

Torques and Adjustments

a. Front and rear engine mount: 36 ft. lbs. (48 Nm).
b. Rear lateral control arms at knuckle: 41 ft. lbs. (55 Nm) + 90°.
c. Rear lateral control arms at cradle: 41 ft. lbs. (55 Nm) + 105°.
d. Fixed adjusting link at knuckle: 37 ft. lbs. (50 Nm) + 90°.
e. Fixed adjusting link at cradle: 41 ft. lbs. (55 Nm) + 105°.
f. Trailing arm to knuckle: 44 ft. lbs. (60 Nm) + 90°.
e. Trailing arm to cradle: 37 ft. lbs. (50 Nm) + 80°.
f. Stabilizer bar bracket mounting bolts: 18 ft. lbs. (25 Nm).
g. Exhaust pipe to manifold: 18 ft. lbs. (25 Nm).
h. Wheel lug nuts: 100 ft. lbs. (136 Nm).

Transaxle

REMOVAL & INSTALLATION

4 and 5-speed 76mm Isuzu (MG1 and MG2)

➧ See Figures 9 and 10

1. Disconnect the negative (−) battery cable and drain transaxle fluid.
2. Mark the engine compartment lid hinges for proper installation alignment.
3. Remove the engine compartment lid with an assistant.
4. Remove the side louvered panels.
5. Remove the rear upper engine support bolt.
6. Install the engine support fixture part No. J-28467-A.
7. Raise the vehicle and support with jackstands.

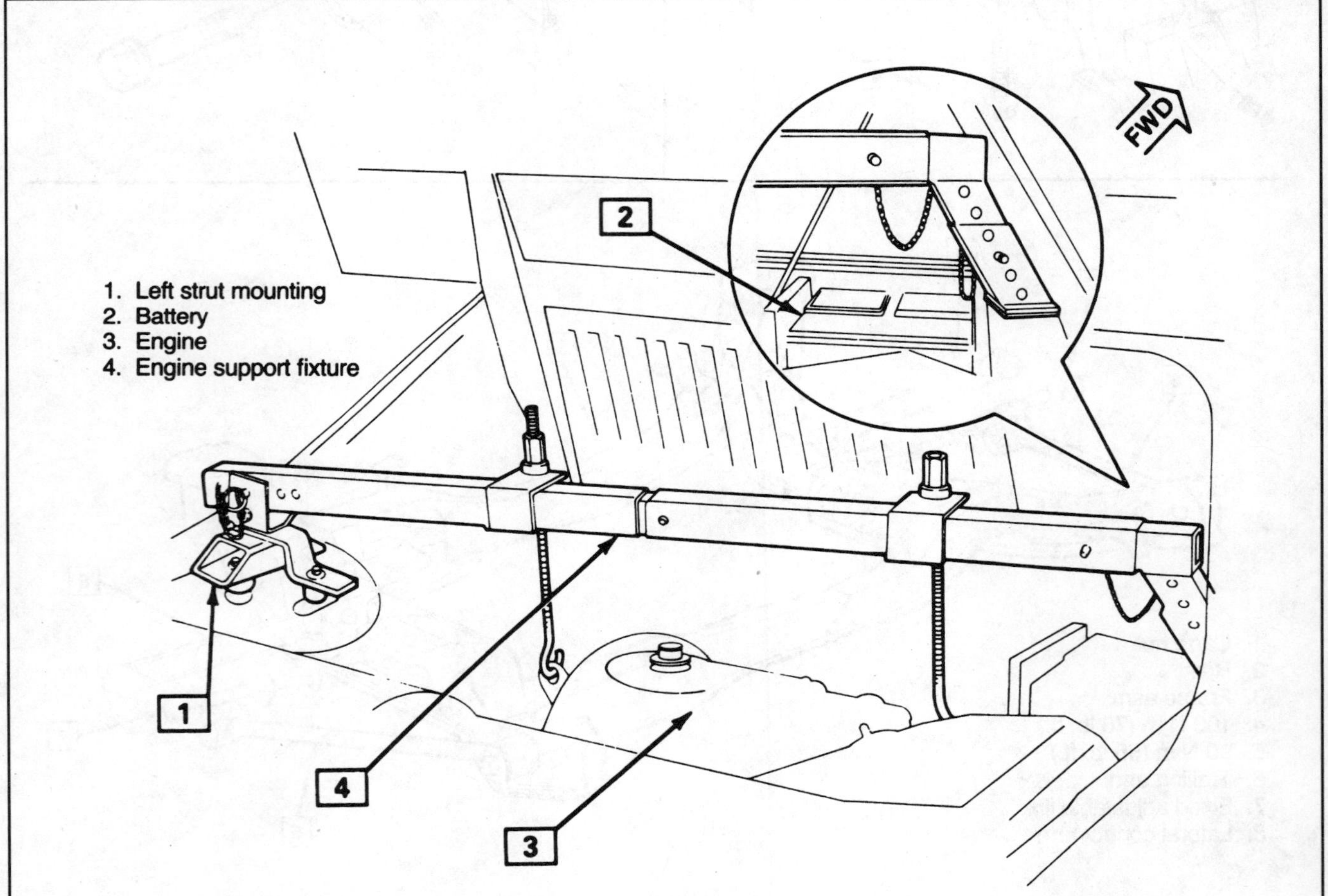

Fig. 9 When the transaxle is to being removed, the engine must be supported using engine support fixture No. J-28467-A or its equivalent

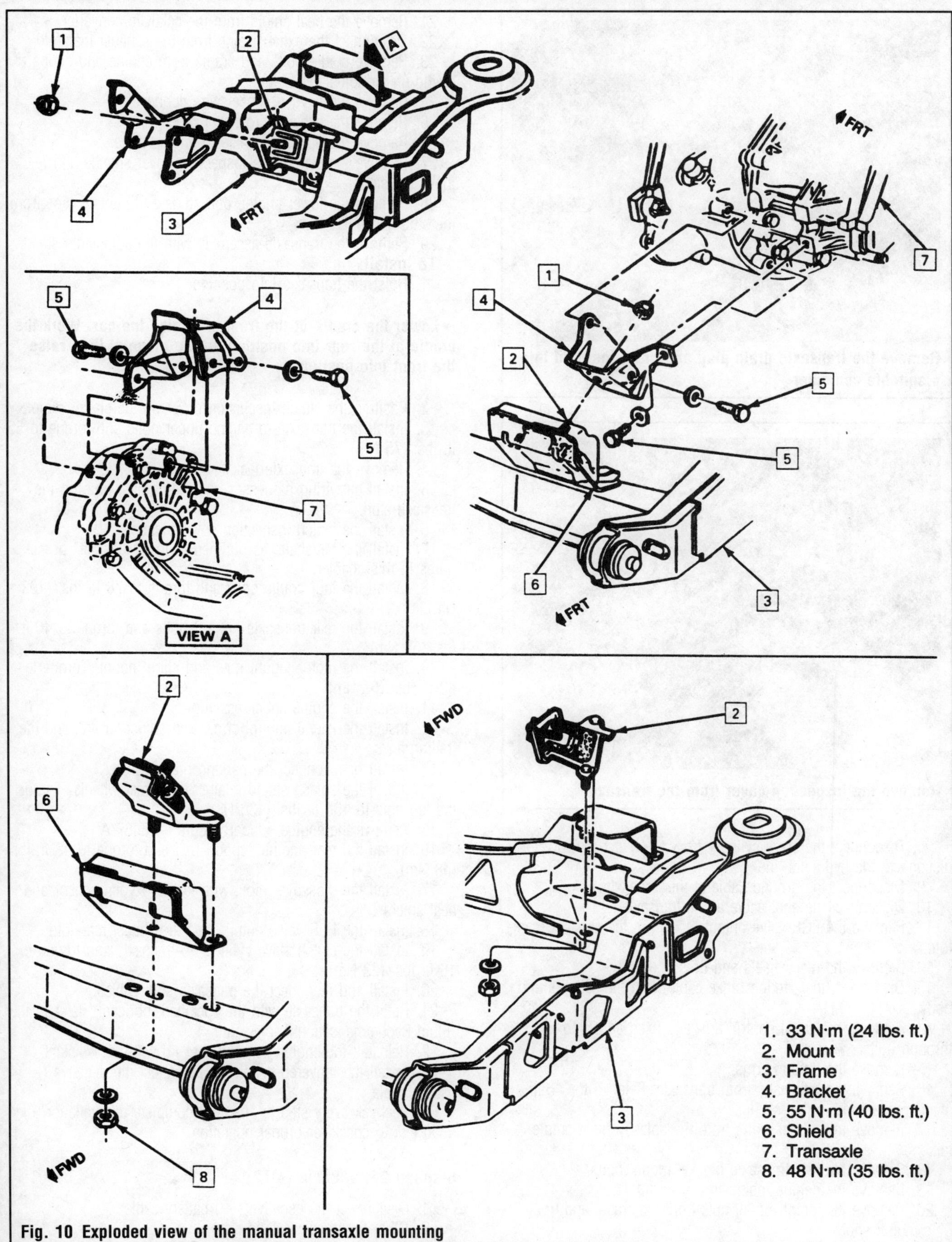

Fig. 10 Exploded view of the manual transaxle mounting

Remove the transaxle drain plug and drain the fluid into a suitable container

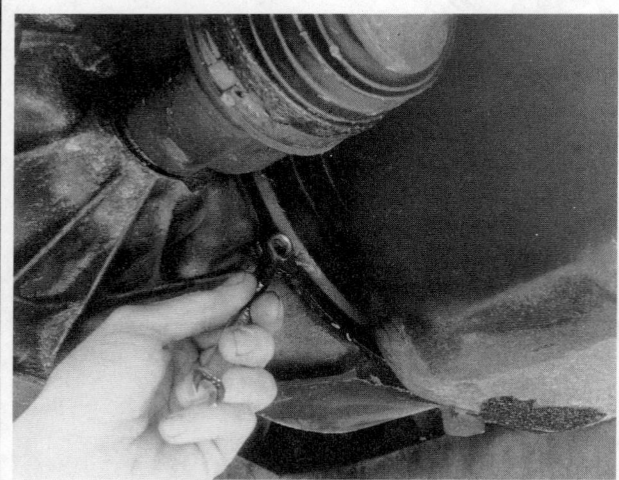

Remove the inspection cover from the transaxle

8. Disconnect the slave cylinder from the clutch but do not disconnect the hydraulic line.
9. Disconnect the ground cable at the transaxle.
10. Disconnect the shift cable at the transaxle.
11. Remove the EGR valve output pipe from the exhaust manifold.
12. Remove the rear wheels and tires.
13. Disconnect the parking brake cable from the calipers and body.
14. Remove the lateral control arm and fixed adjusting link through bolts.
15. Remove the trailing arms.
16. Remove the halfshafts from transaxle. Refer to the "Halfshaft" procedures in this section.
17. Remove the rubber skirts from the splash shield cradle retainers.
18. Remove the rear transaxle bracket mount bolts.
19. Remove the engine mount-to-cradle nuts.
20. Remove the motor mount nuts from the cradle and front engine mount shock.
21. Remove the heat shield from the catalytic converter.
22. Disconnect the exhaust pipe from the exhaust manifold.
23. Remove cradle bolts and cradle from engine and support cradle on an adjustable stand.
24. Remove the oxygen sensor wire connector.
25. Remove the exhaust crossover pipe.
26. Remove the upper transaxle-to-engine bolts.
27. Remove the starter and inspection cover shields and remove the starter.
28. Remove the lower engine bolt studs and coolant pipe from the stud and nut.
29. Remove the transaxle assembly with the adjustable stand.

To install:

1. Hoist the transaxle into position.

➡Lower the cradle at the front and raise the car. Work the cradle at the rear into position on the mounts, then raise the front into position.

2. Position the clutch inspection cover on the starter motor.
3. Install the transaxle-to-engine upper bolts and torque to 55 ft. lbs. (75 Nm).
4. Remove the transaxle jackstand.
5. Install all wiring harnesses and the coolant pipe on the transaxle stud.
6. Install the clutch inspection cover plate.
7. Install the halfshafts as outlined in the "Halfshaft" procedures in this chapter.
8. Install the four cradle bolts and torque to 76 ft. lbs. (103 Nm).
9. Install the rear transaxle bracket bolts and torque to 40 ft. lbs. (54 Nm).
10. Install the motor mount nuts and align mount. Torque to 42 ft. lbs. (57 Nm).
11. Install the engine shock assembly.
12. Install the lateral control arm, fixed adjusting link and the trailing arms.
13. Install or reconnect the parking brake cables.
14. Install the splash shield retainers and rear wheels. Torque the lug nuts to 100 ft. lbs. (136 Nm).
15. Remove the engine support fixture J-28467-A.
16. Install the rear engine support bolt and torque to 43 ft. lbs. (58 Nm).
17. Install the crossover pipe, wire to the oxygen sensor and heat shields.
18. Install the EGR valve output pipe to exhaust manifold.
19. Install the clutch slave cylinder-to-transaxle and torque to 16 ft. lbs. (22 Nm).
20. Install and reconnect the transaxle shift cables.
21. Refill the transaxle with the specified lubricant. Refer to the "Fluid Recommendations" in Section 1.
22. Reinstall the engine compartment lid with an assistant.
23. Install the louvered panel and reconnect the negative (−) battery cable.
24. Recheck every step to ensure a complete reinstallation. Road test to check for proper operation.

5-speed 282 Muncie (MT2)

1. Disconnect the negative (−) battery cable.
2. Drain the transaxle fluid.

3. Remove the select and shift cables nuts securing the cables to the transaxle bracket.
4. Disconnect the backup lamp switch.
5. Remove the shift cables and nut on the stud securing bracket to transaxle.
6. Remove the select cable mount.
7. Remove the clutch slave cylinder attaching bolts. Do not disconnect the hydraulic hose.
8. Remove the exhaust pipe from the manifold and crossover pipe (6-cyl).
9. Remove the three bolts and one stud from the upper transaxle-to-engine.
10. Install the engine support fixture No. J-28467-A or J-35563. Refer to the illustration in the previous procedures.
11. Disconnect the front and rear transaxle mounts.
12. Raise the vehicle and support with jackstands.
13. Remove the four clutch inspection plate screws and the plate.
14. Remove the lower frame (cradle) as follows in the "Cradle (sub-frame)" procedures in this section.
15. Remove the halfshafts as outlined in the "Halfshaft" procedures in this section.
16. Remove the two nuts retaining the wire harness on the two lower studs.
17. Remove the two studs and transaxle from the bottom of the vehicle. The engine may have to be tilted down for clearance.

To install:

1. Position the transaxle through the bottom and attach the engine to the transaxle with the two studs. Do not tighten studs.
2. Raise the cradle as outlined in the "Cradle" procedures in this section.
3. Install the halfshafts as outlined in the "Halfshaft" procedures in this section.
4. Install the clutch inspection plate and four screws, torque to 10 ft. lbs. (13 Nm).
5. Install the front and rear transaxle mounts.
6. Lower the vehicle and remove the engine support fixture J-28467-A or J-35563.
7. Install the three upper transaxle-to-engine bolts and one stud. Torque the upper and lower bolts and studs to 55 ft. lbs. (75 Nm).
8. Install the wiring harnesses to the two studs and torque the nuts to 13 ft. lbs. (17 Nm).
9. Install the exhaust crossover or single pipe and torque the nuts to 18 ft. lbs. (25 Nm).
10. Install the clutch slave cylinder and torque the two attaching bolts to 37 ft. lbs. (50 Nm).
11. Install the cable mount and torque to 89 inch.lb. (10 Nm).
12. Install the select and shift cable and torque the nuts to 89 inch.lb. (10 Nm).
13. Install the backup lamp switch and wire, torque to 25 ft. lbs. (34 Nm).
14. Install the fluid drain plug and torque to 18 ft. lbs. (24 Nm).
15. Refill the transaxle with syncromesh transmission fluid (12345349) or equivalent.
16. Recheck every operation to check for proper reinstallation. Road test to check for proper operation.

4-speed 76mm Isuzu (MG1) Overhaul

DISASSEMBLY

➧ **See Figures 11 thru 17**

1. Remove the transaxle assembly from the vehicle and place on a suitable work stand.
2. Remove the fifteen clutch cover-to-transaxle attaching bolts. Tap the clutch cover with a rubber hammer to work it loose.
3. Remove the ring gear/differential assembly.
4. Position the shifter shaft in the neutral position so the shifter moves freely and is not engaged in any drive gear.
5. Bend back the tab on the lock and remove the bolt from the shifter shaft. Remove the shifter shaft and fork from the synchronizer forks.
6. Remove the reverse shift fork by disengaging the guide pin and interlock bracket.
7. Remove the lock bolt securing the reverse idler gear shaft. Remove the gear/shaft and spacer as an assembly.
8. Remove the detent shift lever and interlock assembly. Leave the shift forks engaged with the synchronizers.
9. Grasp the input and output shafts and then lift them as an assembly from the case. Note the positions of the shift forks to aid in reinstallation. Remove shift forks.

Shaft Disassembly

➧ **See Figures 18, 19, 20 and 21**

➡The terms R.H. and L.H. refer to the installed position on the vehicle. RH refers to the end nearest the clutch and the LH refers to the end farthest from the clutch.

INPUT SHAFT

1. Slide the LH bearing and 4th gear from the input shaft.
2. Remove the brass blocker ring and snapring from the 3-4 synchronizer.
3. Using a support plate behind 3rd gear, press the 3rd gear off the shaft.
4. Remove the RH bearing from the shaft using tool No. J-26946.

OUTPUT SHAFT

1. Using support plates behind the 4th gear, press on the end of the output shaft to remove the 4th gear and the LH bearing.
2. Remove the 3rd gear snapring.
3. Slide the 1-2 synchronizer into the first gear position to allow the press plates to support the 2nd gear. Press the 2nd speed gear and 3rd gear from the output shaft and remove the brass blocker rings.
4. Remove the snapring retaining the 1-2 synchronizer.
5. Using press plates behind the 1st speed gear, then press the 1st gear and 1-2 synchronizer from the output shaft.
6. Install tool No. J-22227-A on the RH bearing and remove the bearing by pressing on tool No. J-26943 pilot.

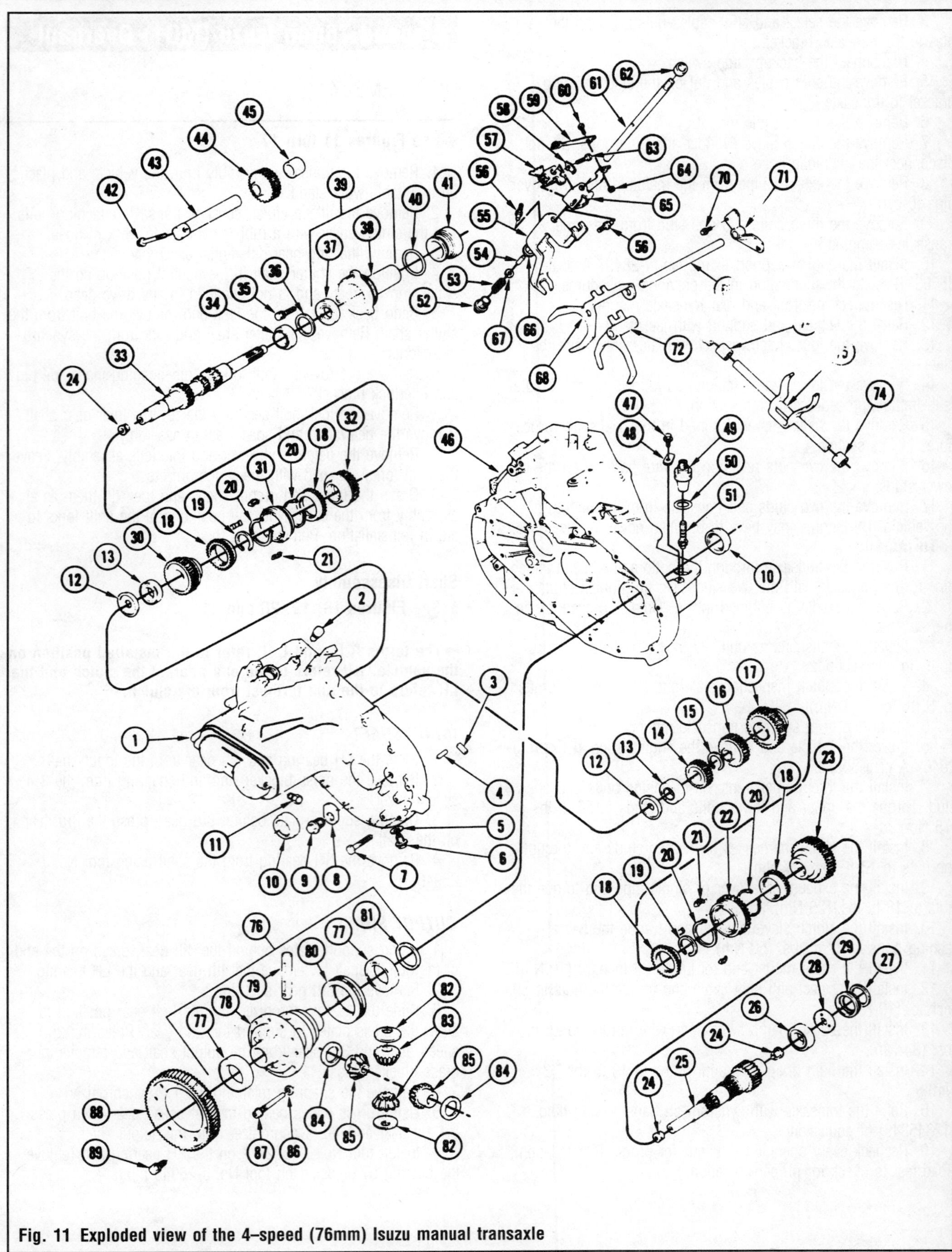

Fig. 11 Exploded view of the 4-speed (76mm) Isuzu manual transaxle

1. Case assembly
2. Vent assembly
3. Magnet
4. Pin
5. Washer, drain screw
6. Screw, drain
7. Bolt
8. Washer, fill plug
9. Plug, fill
10. Seal asembly, axle shaft
11. Plug
12. Shield, oil
13. Bearing assembly
14. Gear, 4th speed output
15. Ring, 3rd speed output gear retaining
16. Gear, 3rd speed output
17. Gear, 2nd speed output
18. Ring, synchronizer blocking
19. Ring, synchronizer retaining
20. Spring, synchronizer key retaining
21. Key, synchronizer
22. Synchronizer assembly
23. Gear, 1st speed output
24. Sleeve, oil shield
25. Gear, output
26. Bearing assembly, output
27. Shim, output gear bearing adjustment
28. Shield, output bearing oil
29. Retainer, output gear bearing oil shield
30. Gear, 4th speed input
31. Synchronizer assembly
32. Gear, 3rd speed input
33. Gear, input cluster
34. Bearing assembly, input
35. Screw
36. Shim, input gear bearing adjustment
37. Seal assembly, input gear
38. Retainer, input gear
39. Retainer assembly, input gear bearing
40. Seal, input gear bearing retainer
41. Bearing assembly, clutch release
42. Screw & washer, reverse idler
43. Shaft, reverse idler
44. Gear assembly, reverse idler
45. Spacer, reverse idler shaft
46. Housing assembly, clutch & differential
47. Screw
48. Retainer, speedo gear fitting
49. Sleeve, speedo driven gear
50. Seal, speedo gear sleeve
51. Gear, speedo driven
52. Seat, reverse inhibitor spring
53. Spring, reverse inhibitor
54. Pin
55. Lever, reverse shift
56. Stud, reverse lever locating
57. Lever assembly, detent
58. Washer, lock detent lever
59. Spring, detent
60. Bolt
61. Shaft, shift
62. Seal assembly, shift shaft
63. Bolt
64. Nut
65. Interlock, shift
66. Shim, shift shaft
67. Washer, reverse inhibitor spring
68. Fork, 3rd & 4th shift
69. Shaft, shift fork
70. Screw
71. Guide, oil
72. Fork, 1st & 2nd shift
73. Seal assembly, clutch fork shaft
74. Bearing, clutch fork shaft
75. Shaft assembly, clutch fork
76. Differential assembly
77. Bearing assembly, differential
78. Case, differential
79. Shaft, differential pinion
80. Gear, speedo drive
81. Shim, differential bearing adjustment
82. Washer, pinion thrust
83. Gear, differential pinion
84. Washer, side gear thrust
85. Gear, differential side
86. Lockwasher
87. Screw, pinion shaft
88. Gear, differential ring
89. Bolt

Fig. 12 Isuzu 4–speed (76mm) manual transaxle component list

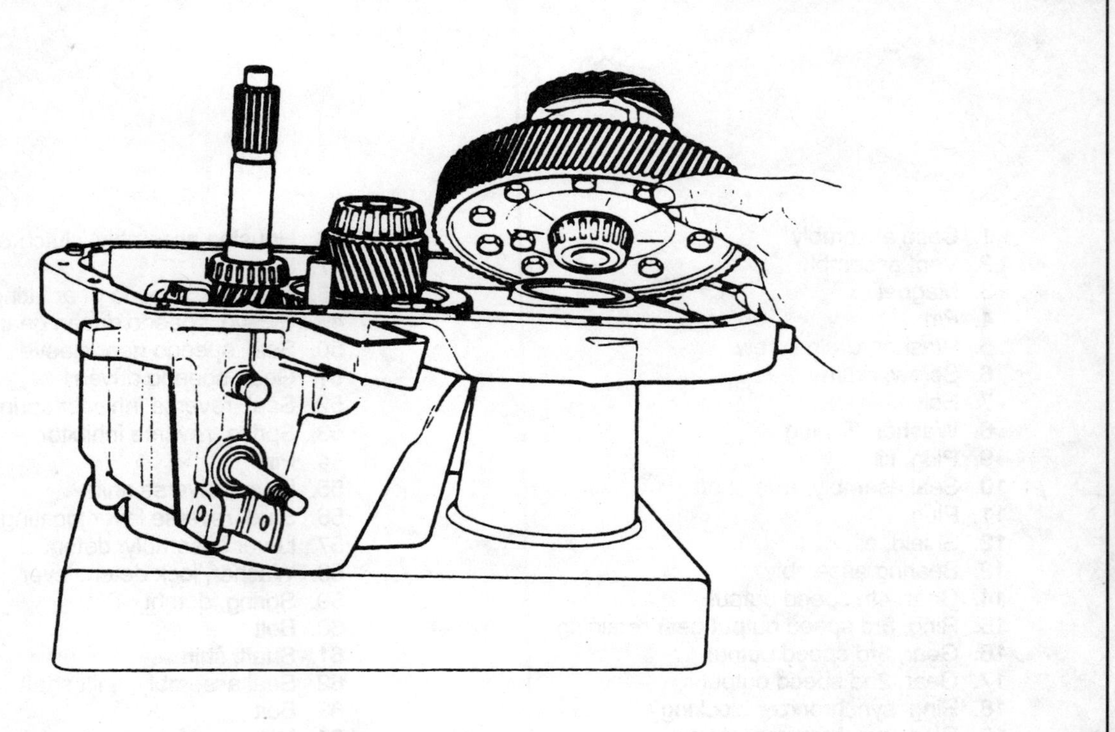

Fig. 13 Remove the ring gear and differential assembly . . .

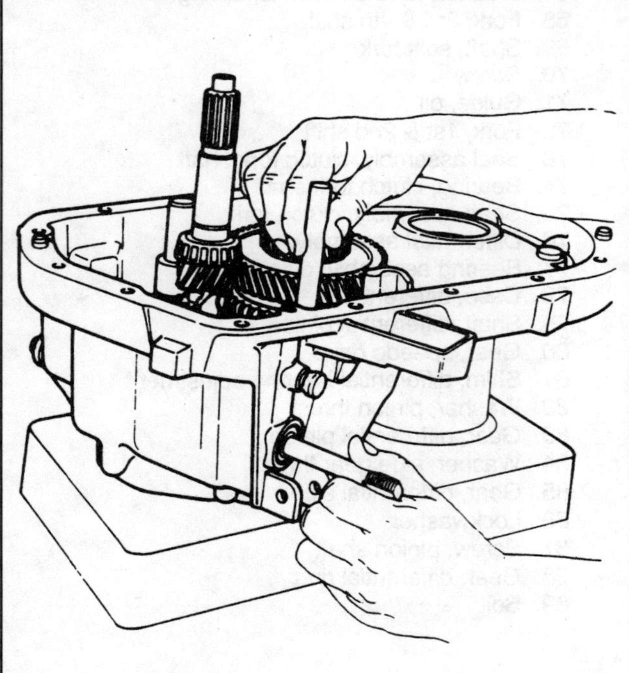

Fig. 14 . . . then place the shifter shaft in neutral. Bend back the tab on the lock and unfasten the bolt so that the shift shaft may be disengaged from the synchronizer forks

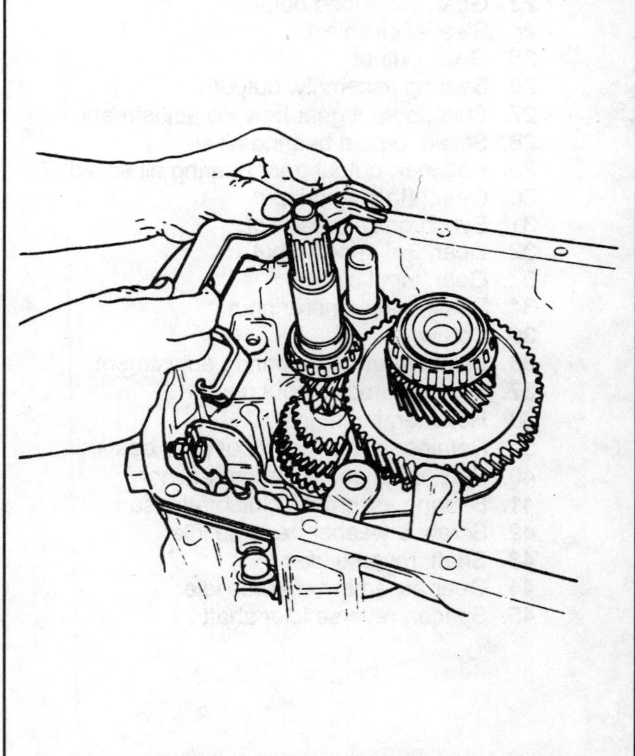

Fig. 15 Disengage the guide pin and interlock bracket to remove the reverse shift link

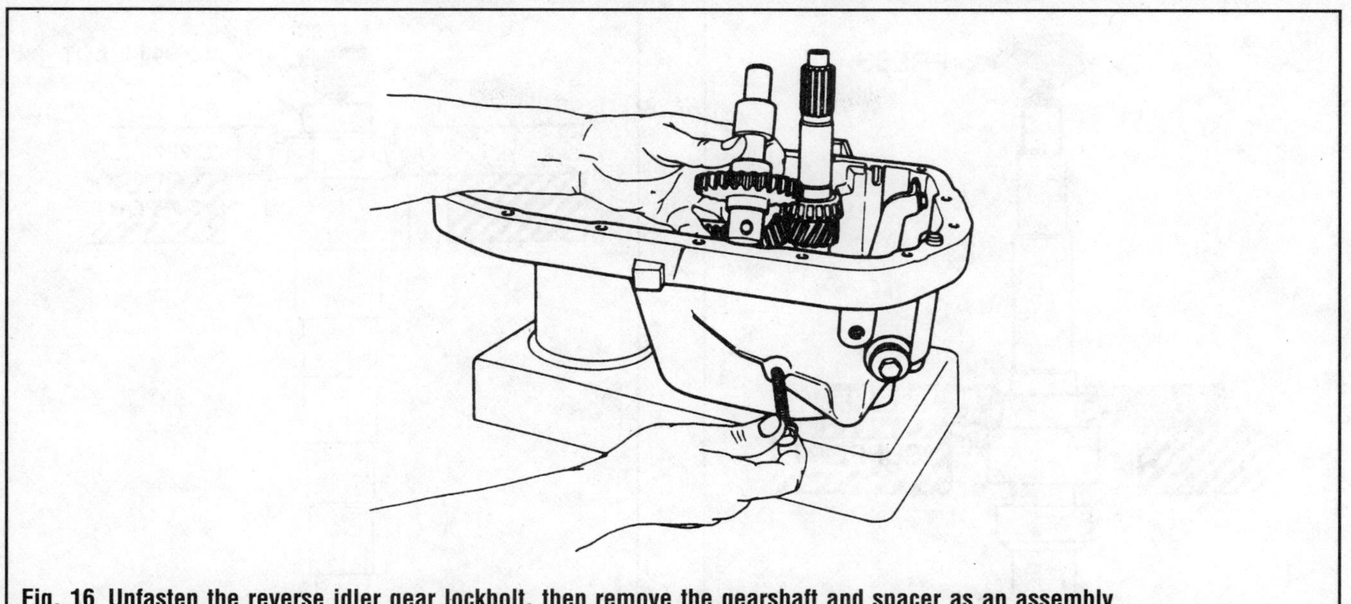

Fig. 16 Unfasten the reverse idler gear lockbolt, then remove the gearshaft and spacer as an assembly

Fig. 17 View of the shift shaft and fork assembly

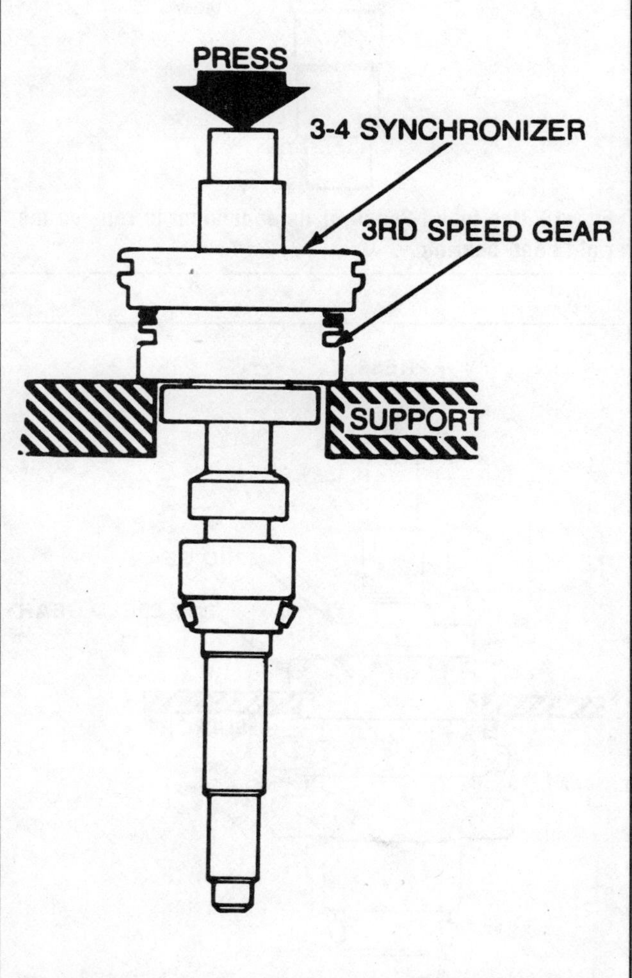

Fig. 18 Use a press to remove the 3rd gear synchronizer and gear

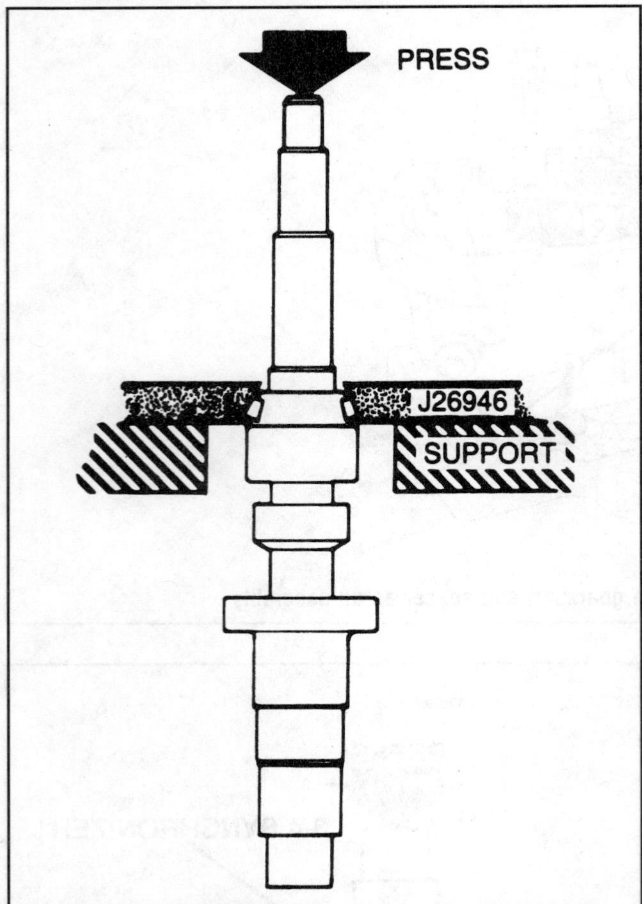

Fig. 19 Use tool J-26946 or its equivalent to remove the right hand bearing

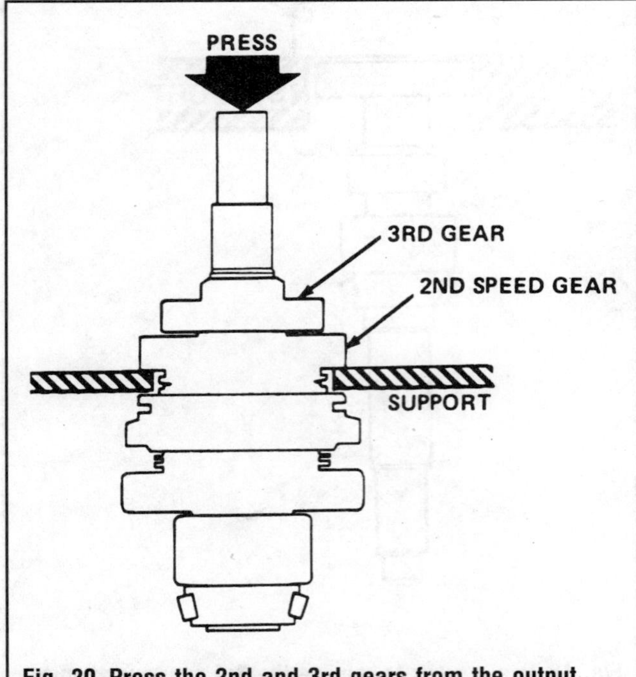

Fig. 20 Press the 2nd and 3rd gears from the output shaft and remove the brass blocker rings

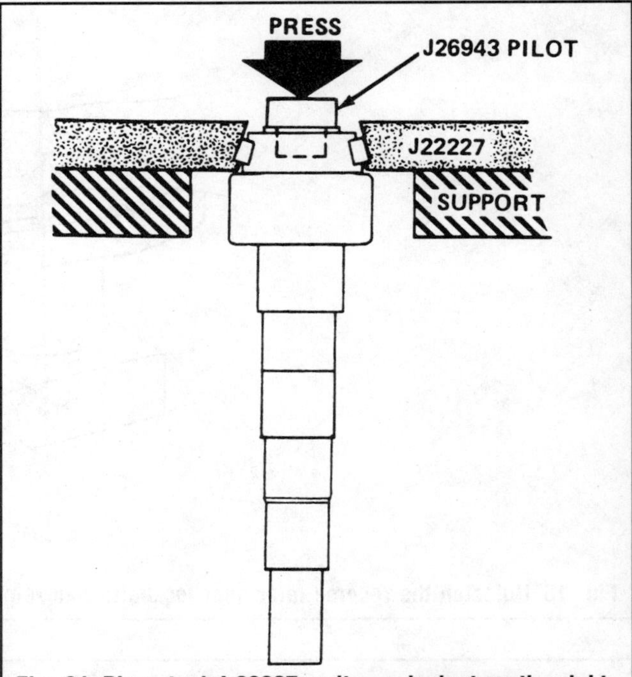

Fig. 21 Place tool J-22227 or its equivalent on the right hand bearing and press out the bearing using pilot tool J-26943

SYNCHRONIZER OVERHAUL

See Figure 22

1. Carefully pry out both synchronizer key springs from the synchronizer.
2. Separate the hub, sleeve and 3 keys after noting their positions for reinstallation.
3. Clean all parts with solvent.
4. Assemble the hub to the sleeve with the extruded lip on the hub directed away from the shift fork groove in the sleeve and align the assembly as previously marked.
5. Install the retaining ring, and carefully pry the ring back and

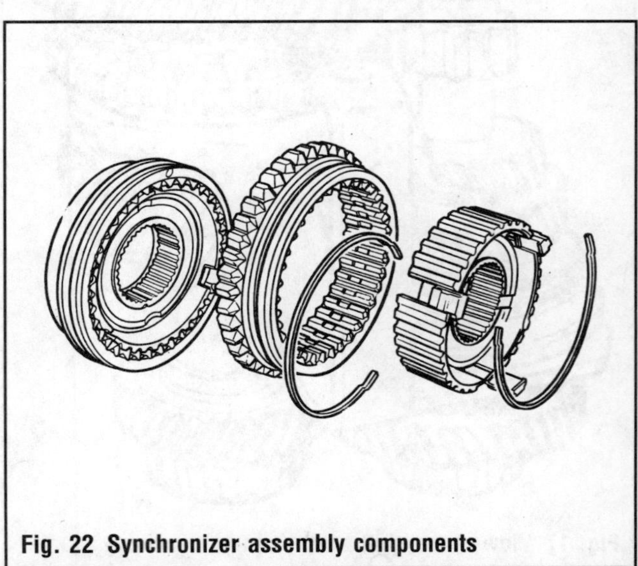
Fig. 22 Synchronizer assembly components

insert the keys, one at a time. Make sure to position the ring so it is captured by the keys.

6. Install the ring on the opposite side with the open segment of the ring with the open segment on the other side.

Shaft Reassembly

➡Before assembling the shafts, apply a coat of specified lubricant to the thrust washers, all gears and washers.

INPUT SHAFT

➧ See Figure 23

1. Install RH bearing onto shaft using tool J-28406.
2. Place the 3rd gear onto the shaft, install the brass blocker ring onto the gear cone and install the 3-4 synchronizer, using the appropriate cylinder to contact the hub near the shaft. Do not press on the sleeve portion. Both synchronizers hubs are a press fit to the shaft.
3. Install the snapring to retain 3-4 synchronizer. The beveled edges should be away from the synchronizer for later access with the snapring pliers.
4. Install the brass blocker ring.
5. Slide the 4th gear onto shaft, position it toward the 3-4 synchronizer and slide the LH bearing onto the shaft.

OUTPUT SHAFT

1. Install the RH bearing onto the shaft.
2. Place the 1st gear onto the shaft near the 1-2 synchro. Install the brass blocker ring onto the cone, install the 1-2 synchro using the appropriate cylinder to press to the hub. Do not press on the sleeve.
3. Install the snapring to retain 1-2 synchro. and install blocker ring.
4. Place the 2nd gear onto the shaft, press 3rd gear onto shaft with its hub towards the 4th gear.
5. Install the snapring to retain 3rd gear.
6. Press the 4th gear onto the shaft with its hub towards the 3rd gear. Install the LH bearing onto the shaft using tool No. J-26942.

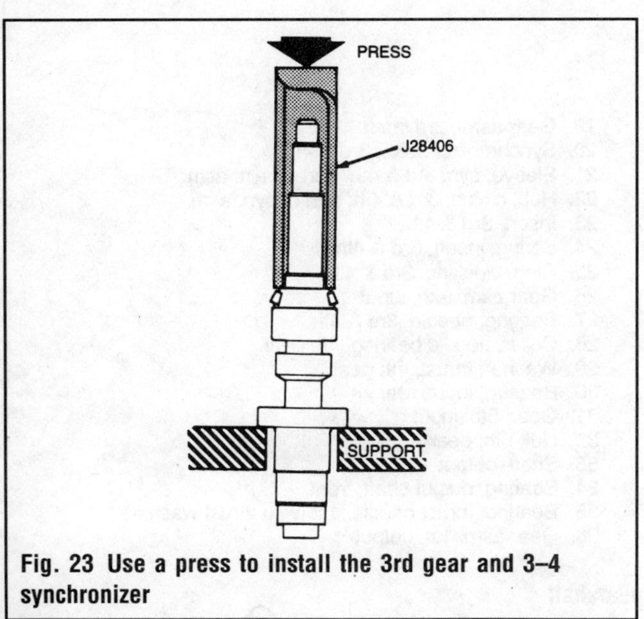

Fig. 23 Use a press to install the 3rd gear and 3–4 synchronizer

Case Reassembly

1. Place the input and output shaft together and install the two shift forks on a bench.
2. Hold the shafts as an assembly and carefully lower into the transaxle case.
3. Place the interlock bracket onto the guide pin tool J-28411. Make sure the bracket engages the fingers on the shift forks.
4. Use a straight edge on both sides of the interlock to determine if the detent is out of alignment with the interlock.

➡The straight edge should rest on both side of the interlock without interference on either side.

   a. Place the detent and interlock in a vise and with light pressure, push it into alignment.
   b. Loosen the nut securing the detent spring to the interlock. The spring is slotted for proper alignment.
   c. Tighten the nut while exerting light pressure on the spring with your thumb.
   d. Check detent alignment with a straight edge.

5. Install detent lever into interlock. Install shifter shaft through the interlock bracket and the detent lever but do not extend any further.
6. Install the reverse shift fork onto guide pin. Install the reverse idler gear and shaft into position. The long end points upward. Install the spacer onto the shaft.
7. The flat on the reverse idler shaft faces the input gear.
8. Fully install the shifter shaft through the reverse shift fork until it pivots into the inhibitor spring.
9. Remove the dummy shaft, place shaft in neutral position, install the bolt and lock through the detent shift lever and bend the tab of the lock over the bolt head.
10. Install the shift fork through the synchro forks and into the bores in the case and install the magnet.
11. Apply a thin bead of anaerobic sealant (not RTV) to the clutch cover, then carefully install the cover onto the transaxle case using the dowel pins to guide the cover into position. Gently tap the housing with a rubber hammer to ensure the parts are seated.
12. Install the fifteen attaching bolts and torque to 16 ft. lbs. (21 Nm).
13. Torque the idler shaft retaining bolts in case to 16 ft. lbs. (21 Nm).
14. Test the gear ranges by shifting the shift shaft. If freedom is not felt, remove the clutch cover to check for problem.
15. Install all other external parts needed before transaxle installation.
16. Install the transaxle assembly into the vehicle as outlined in the "Transaxle and Cradle" procedures in this section.

5-speed 76mm Isuzu (MT2) Overhaul

DISASSEMBLY

➧ See Figures 24 thru 31

1. Remove the transaxle and cradle assembly from the vehicle as outlined in the "Transaxle and Cradle" procedures in this section.
2. Remove the clutch release bearing and place the transaxle assembly in a holding fixture tool J-33366 or equivalent.

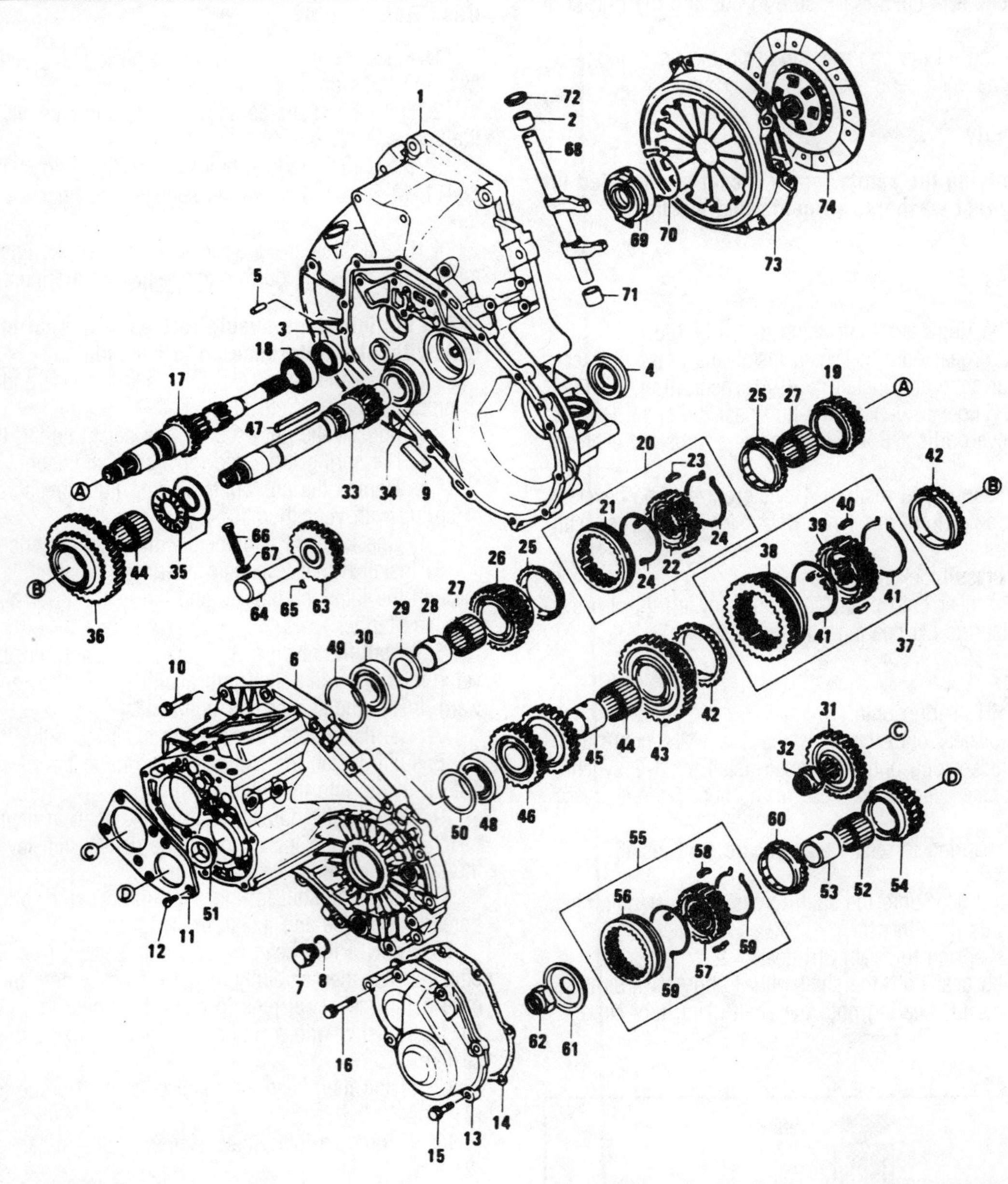

1. Housing, clutch and diff
2. Bush, clutch shaft
3. Seal, oil, input shaft
4. Seal, oil, drive shaft
5. Pin, straight knock
6. Case, transaxle
7. Plug, drain
8. Packing, O-ring, plug
9. Magnet, case
10. Bolt, housing to case
11. Retainer, bearing
12. Screw, retainer to trans. case
13. Cover, rear
14. Packing, case to rear cover
15. Bolt, rear cover to trans. case
16. Bolt, rear cover to trans. case
17. Shaft, input
18. Bearing, input shaft, front
19. Gear asm., 3rd input
20. Synchronizer asm., 3rd & 4th
21. Sleeve, syn. 3rd & 4th, part of syn. asm.
22. Hub, clutch, 3rd & 4th, part of syn. asm.
23. Insert, 3rd & 4th
24. Spring, insert, 3rd & 4th
25. Ring, blocking, 3rd & 4th
26. Gear asm., 4th, input
27. Bearing, needle, 3rd & 4th
28. Collar, needle bearing, 4th gear
29. Washer, thrust, 4th gear
30. Bearing, input, rear
31. Gear, 5th, input
32. Nut, 5th, gear
33. Shaft, output
34. Bearing, output shaft, front
35. Bearing, thrust needle, 1st (with thrust washer)
36. Gear asm. 1st, output

Fig. 24A Exploded view of the 5-speed (76mm) Isuzu transaxle gearshaft

37. Synchronizer asm., 1st & 2nd
38. Gear, rev. & sleeve, part of syn. asm.
39. Hub, clutch, rev. part of syn asm.
40. Insert, 1st & 2nd
41. Spring, insert, 1st & 2nd
42. Ring, blocking, 1st & 2nd
43. Gear asm., 2nd, output
43. Gear asm., 2nd, output
44. Bearing, 1st & 2nd
45. Collar, needle bearing, 2nd gear
46. Gear, output, 3rd & 4th
47. Key, feather, 3rd & 4th
48. Bearing, output, rear
49. Shim, bearing, input shaft
50. Shim, bearing, output shaft
51. Washer, thrust, 5th gear
52. Bearing, needle, 5th gear
53. Collar, needle brg., 5th gear
54. Gear asm., output 5th
55. Synchronizer asm., 5th gear
56. Sleeve, syn. 5th part of sn. asm.
57. Hub, clutch, 5th gear, part of syn. asm.
58. Insert, 5th
59. Spring, insert, 5th
60. Ring, blocking, 5th
61. Plate, stopper, insert
62. Nut, sleeve & hub
63. Gear asm., idler, rev.
64. Shaft, idler, rev.
65. Pin, straight
66. Bolt, idle shaft rev.
67. Gasket, idle shaft
68. Shaft asm., clutch fork
69. Bearing, clutch release
70. Spring, release bearing
71. Bush, clutch shaft
72. Seal, clutch shaft
73. Plate asm., clutch pressure
74. Disc asm., clutch w/facing

Fig. 24 Isuzu 5–speed (76mm) transaxle gearshaft component list

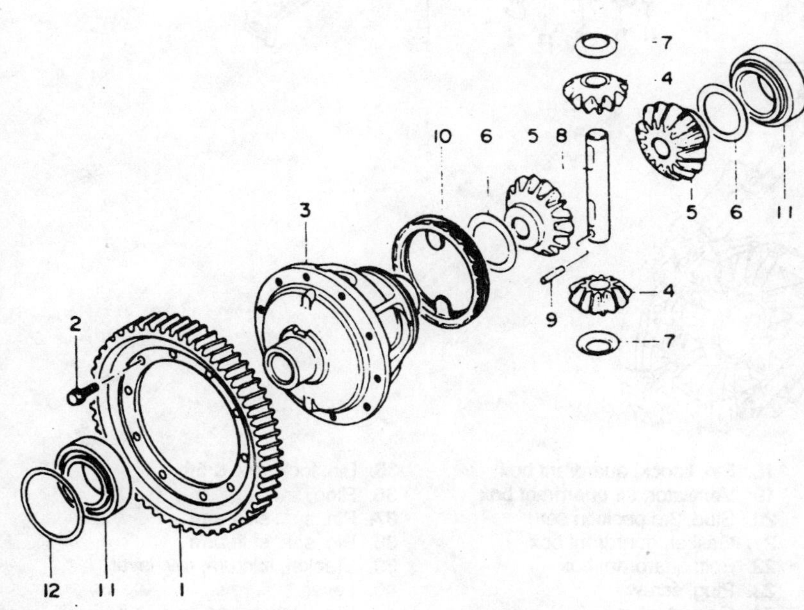

1. Ring gear
2. Ring gear bolt
3. Differential case
4. Differential pinion gear
5. Differential side gear
6. Side gear thrust washer
7. Pinion gear thrust washer
8. Cross pin
9. Lock pin
10. Speedometer drive gear
11. Side bearing
12. Side bearing shim

Fig. 25 Exploded view of the differential assembly components

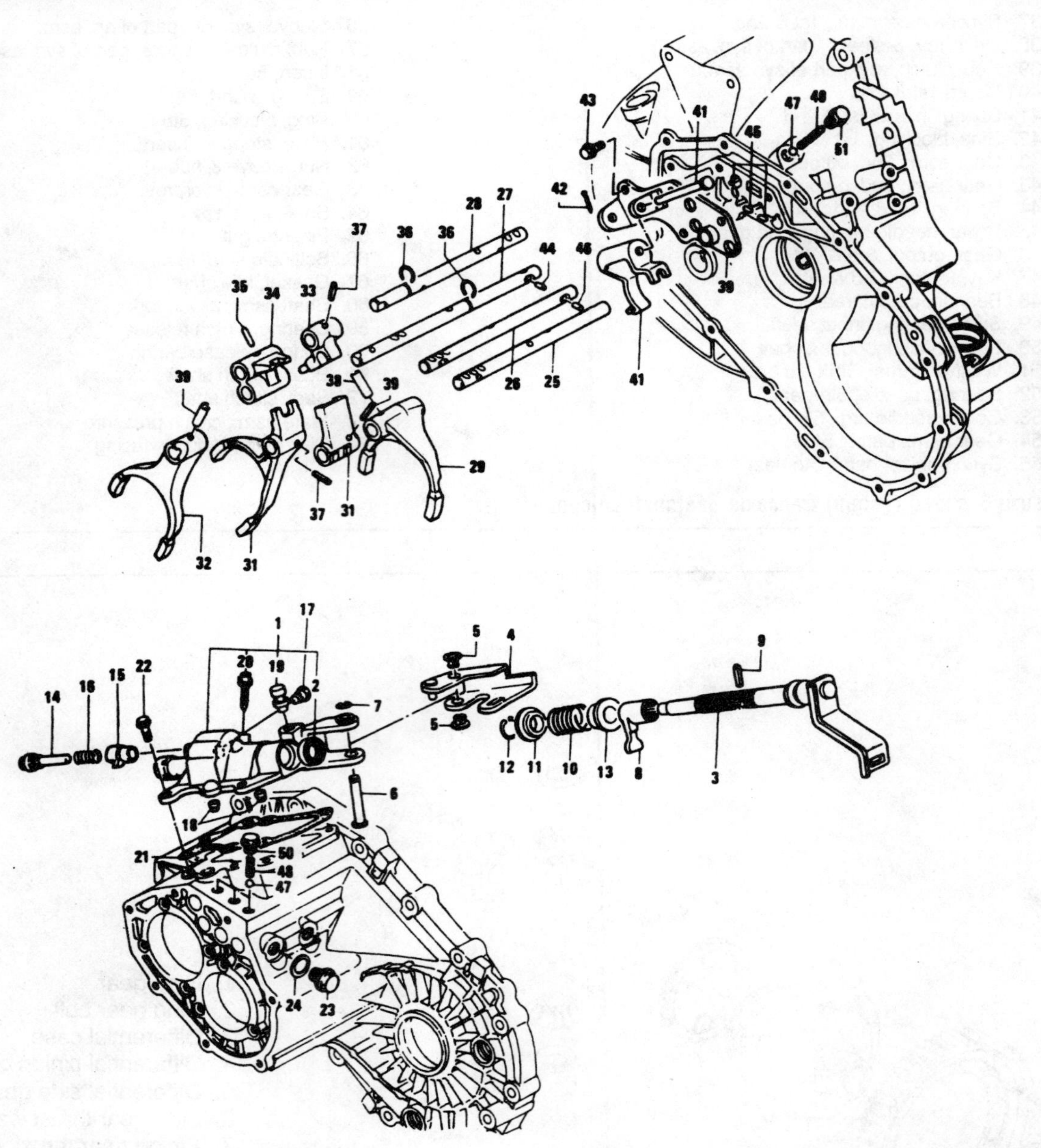

1. Box sub asm., quardrant, shift cont
2. Seal, oil quardrant box
3. Lever asm., shift, external
4. Lever asm., select external
5. Bush, select lever
6. Pin, select lever
7. Ring, snap, select lever
8. Lever, shift internal
9. Pin, spring, internal levr
10. Spring, select stop, 1st & 2nd
11. Seat, spring select stop
12. Ring, snap, spring seat
13. Stopper, rev. inhibitor
14. Bolt, rev. inhibitor
15. Cam, stopper, rev. inhibitor
16. Spring, stopper cam
17. Bolt, stopper cam
18. Pin, knock, quardrant box
19. Ventilator, air quardrant box
20. Stud, 3rd position set
21. Gasket, quardrant box
22. Bolt, quardrant box
23. Plug, screw
24. Gasket, plug
25. Shaft, arm, gear shift, 1st & 2nd
26. Shaft, arm, gear shift, 3rd & 4th
27. Shaft, arm, gear shift, 5th
28. Shaft, arm, gear shift, rev.
29. Fork, shift 1st & 2nd
30. Block, shift, 1st & 2nd
31. Fork, shift, 3rd & 4th
32. Fork, shift, 5th
33. Lever, shift rev.
34. Block, shift rev. & 5th
35. Pin, lock, rev. & 5th
36. Ring, snap
37. Pin, spr., shift arm
38. Pin, spr., shift arm
39. Bracket, fulcrum, rev. lever
40. Lever, shift rev.
41. Pin, fulcrum brkt, rev. shift
42. Cotter pin, snap, fulcrum pin
43. Bolt, fulcrum brkt
44. Pin, lock, 5th shaft
45. Pin, inter lock
46. Pin, lock, 3rd & 4th shaft
47. Ball, detent, gear shift
48. Spring, detent ball
49. Spring, detent ball, rev.
50. Plug, detent spring

Fig. 26 Components of the Isuzu 5-speed (76mm) transaxle shift mechanism

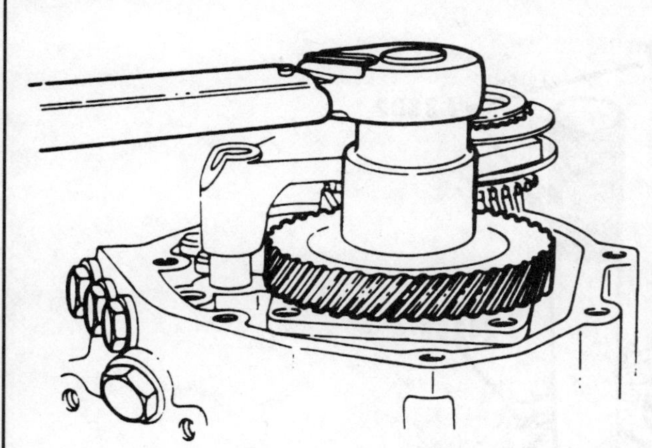
Fig. 27 Use a ratchet and socket to remove the 5th gear retaining nut . . .

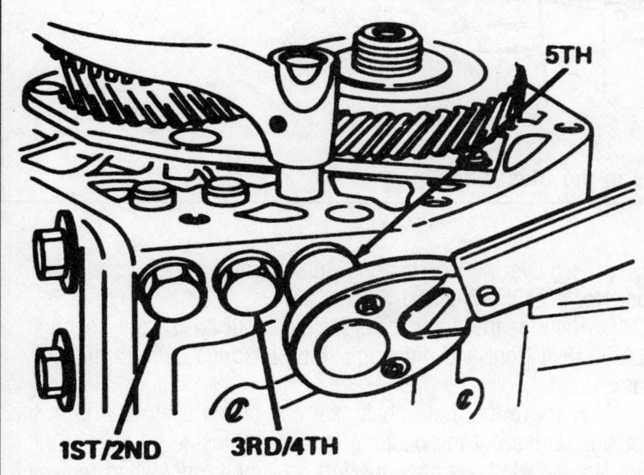

Fig. 28 . . . then remove the 1st–5th gear detent spring and balls

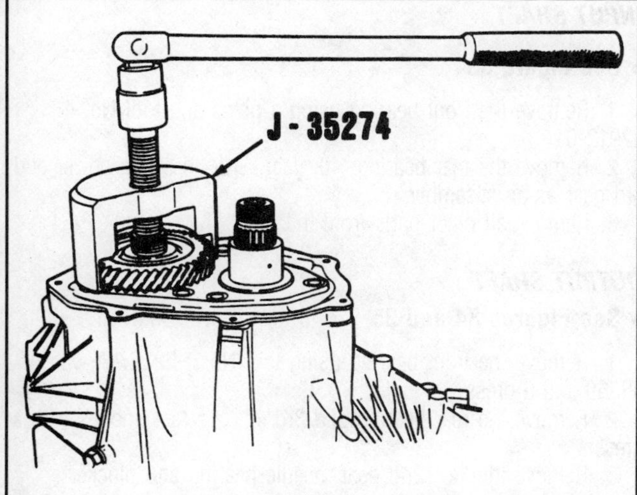

Fig. 29 Install tool J-35274 and remove the gear from the input shaft

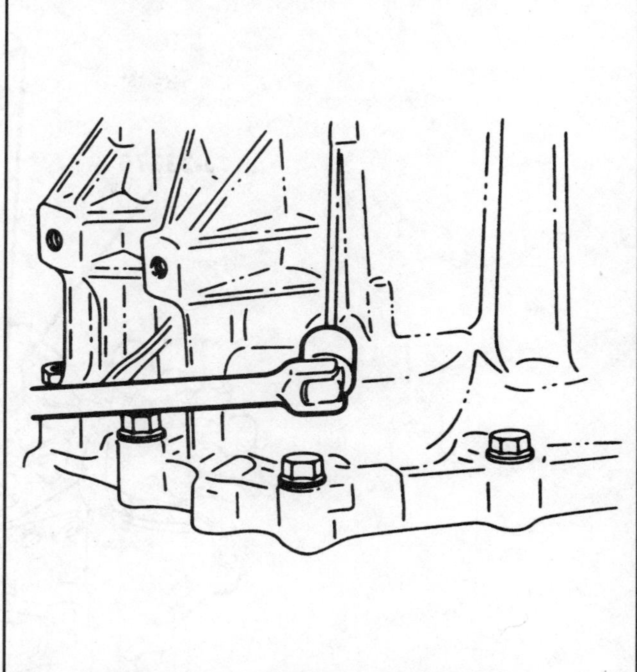
Fig. 30 Remove the reverse idle shaft bolt using a breaker bar and socket

Fig. 31 Use a punch and hammer to drive out the 1–2 shift fork roll pin

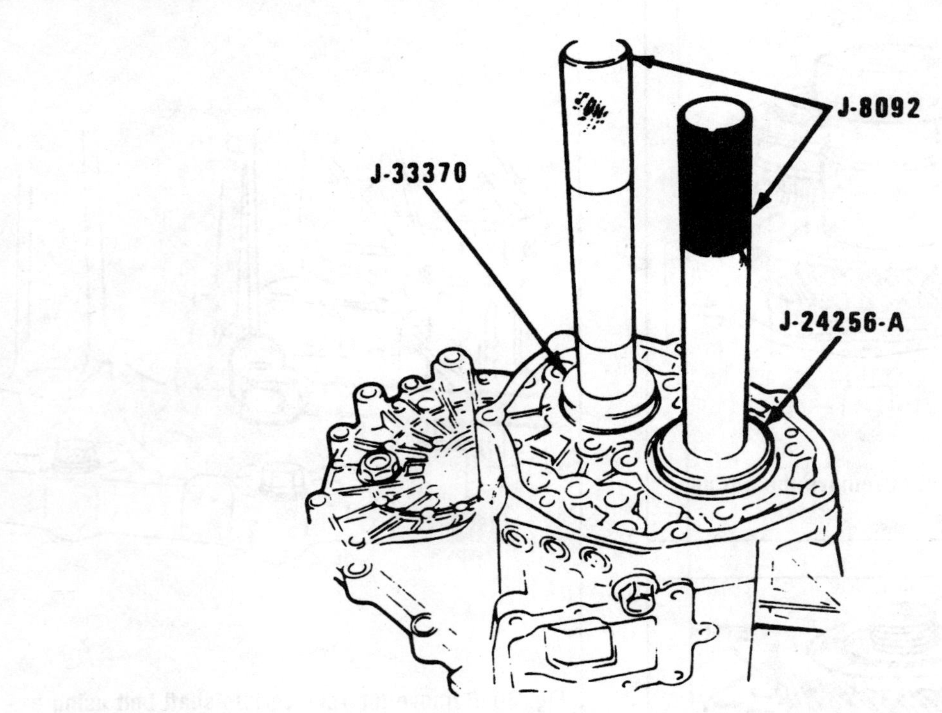

Fig. 32 Remove the input and output bearing races using the tools in the illustration

3. Remove the seven bolts from the rear cover and remove the cover.
4. Remove the shift control box and four bolts.
5. Using a screwdriver, shift the transaxle into gear. Remove the 5th gear drive and driven gear retaining nuts from the input and output shaft. Shift the transaxle into neutral, aligning the detents on the shift rails.
6. Remove the 1-2, 3-4, reverse-5 detent spring retaining bolts and balls.
7. Place the 5th gear synchronizer in neutral. Remove the roll pin at the 5th gear shift fork. Remove the 5th gear synchro hub, sleeve, roller bearing and gear with the fork as an assembly. Using tool No. J-35274, remove the 5th gear from the input shaft.
8. Remove the reverse idler shaft retaining bolt at the transaxle case.
9. Remove the collar and thrust washer from the output shaft using tool No. J-22888 and J-22888-30.
10. Remove the fourteen bolts retaining the transaxle case to the clutch housing and separate the two housings. Gently tap the clutch case with a rubber hammer.
11. Remove the reverse idle gear and idle shaft. Lift the 5th gear shaft, with the detent aligned facing the same way and remove the 5th and reverse shafts at the same time.
12. Using a punch and hammer, remove the roll pin from the 1-2 shift fork. Slide the 1-2 shaft upward to clear the housing and remove the fork and shaft.
13. Remove the input and output shafts with 3-4 shift fork and shaft as an assembly.
14. Remove the differential case assembly. Remove the reverse shift bracket with the four bolts and take the three interlock pins out.
15. Remove the rear bearing outer races from the case with tool No. J-24256-A and J-33370.
16. Remove the outer races for the input shaft front bearing, output shaft front and differential side bearings using a slide hammer.
17. Remove the input shaft seal and clutch shaft seal from the housing. Drive out the bushing toward the inside by the use of tool No. J-28412. Remove the fork assembly only when replacing the clutch fork assembly.

Shaft Disassembly

INPUT SHAFT

➧ **See Figure 33**

1. Remove the front bearing using a press and tool No. J-22912-01.
2. Remove the rear bearing, 4th gear, 3rd/4th synchronizer and 3rd gear as an assembly.
3. Remove all other parts from the input shaft.

OUTPUT SHAFT

➧ **See Figures 34 and 35**

1. Remove the front bearing using tool No. J-22227-A with J-33369 and a press.
2. Remove the rear bearing and 3rd/4th gear assemblies with a press.
3. Remove the key, 2nd gear, needle bearing and blocker rings.
4. Remove the collar, reverse gear and 1st gear as an assembly by the use of a press.

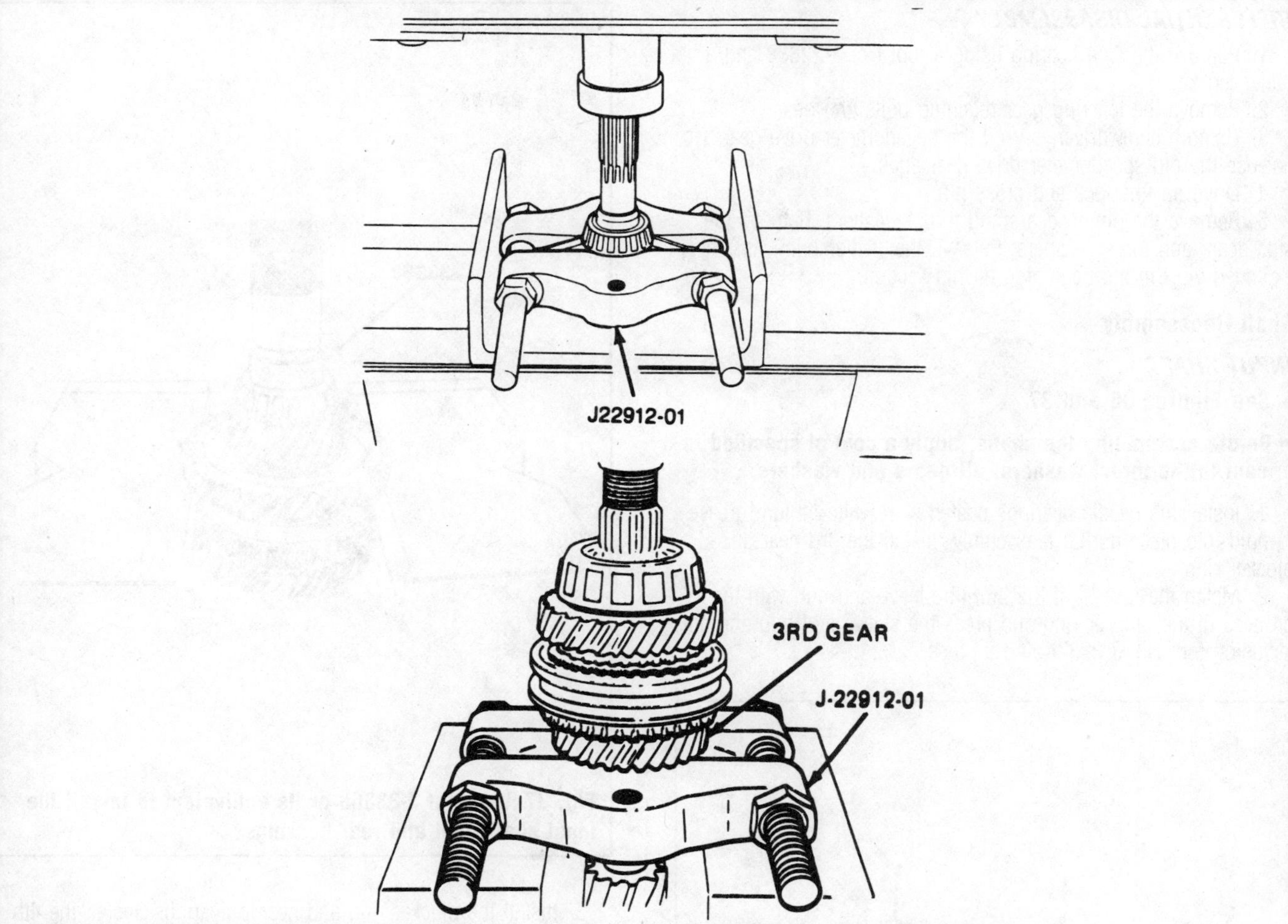

Fig. 33 Use tool J-22912-01 or its equivalent and a press to remove the input shaft front bearing

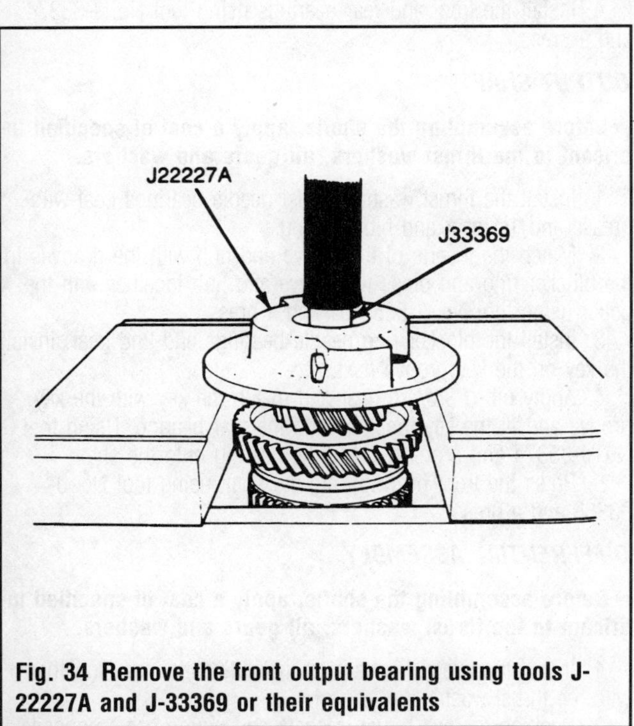

Fig. 34 Remove the front output bearing using tools J-22227A and J-33369 or their equivalents

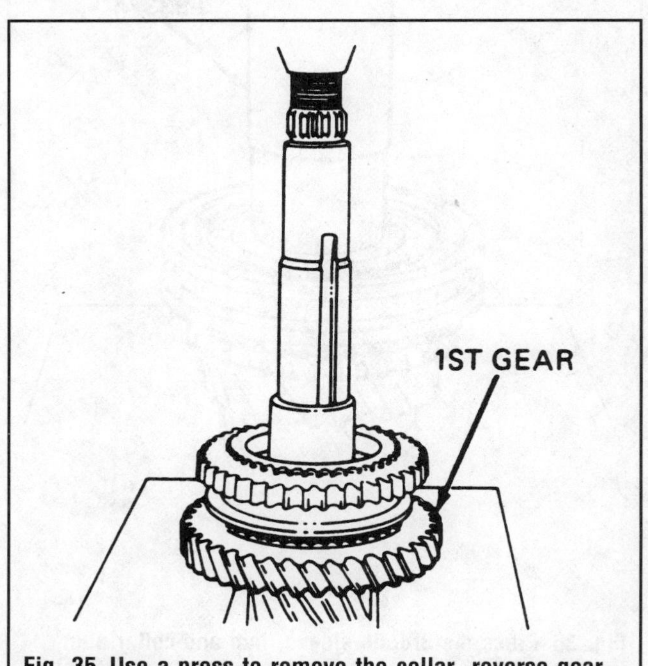

Fig. 35 Use a press to remove the collar, reverse gear and 1st gear from the output shaft

DIFFERENTIAL DISASSEMBLY

1. Remove the side bearing using a tool No. J-22888 and a puller leg kit.
2. Remove the ten ring gear retaining bolts and gear.
3. Using a screwdriver, pry off the speedometer drive gear. Do not use the old speedometer drive gear again.
4. Drive out the lock and cross pin.
5. Remove the pinion gears and thrust washers. Remove the side gears and thrust washers. Refer to the "Differential" assembly exploded view in the beginning of this section.

Shaft Reassembly

INPUT SHAFT

See Figures 36 and 37

Before assembling the shafts, apply a coat of specified lubricant to the thrust washers, all gears and washers.

1. Install the needle bearings coated with white lithium grease to hold into place during reassembly. Install the 3rd gear and blocker ring.
2. Match the inserts of the 3rd/4th sleeve and hub with the grooves of the blocker ring and press the sleeve and hub and collar using tool No. J-33374 and a press.

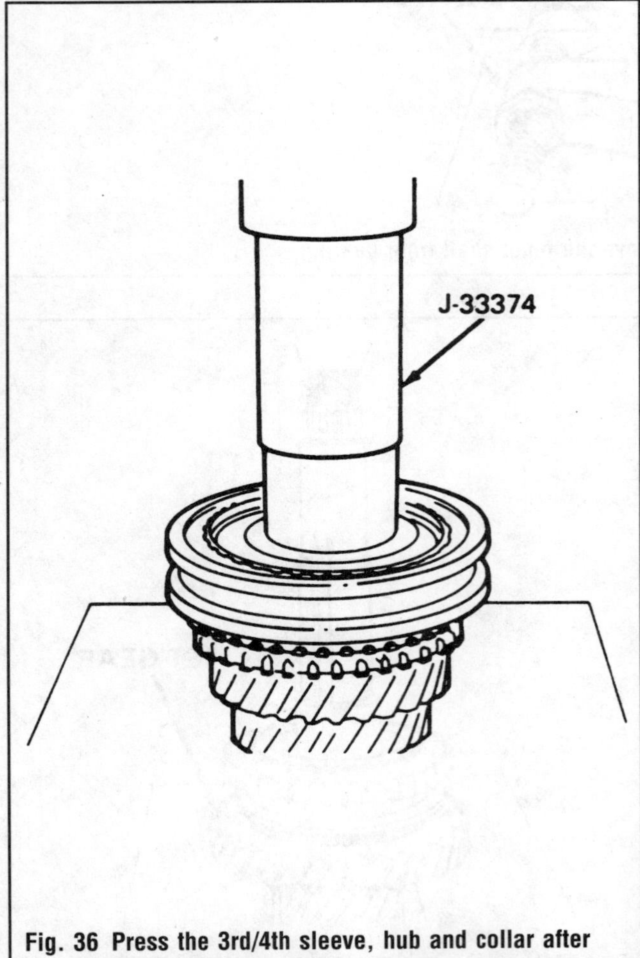

Fig. 36 Press the 3rd/4th sleeve, hub and collar after their inserts have been matched with the grooves on the blocker ring

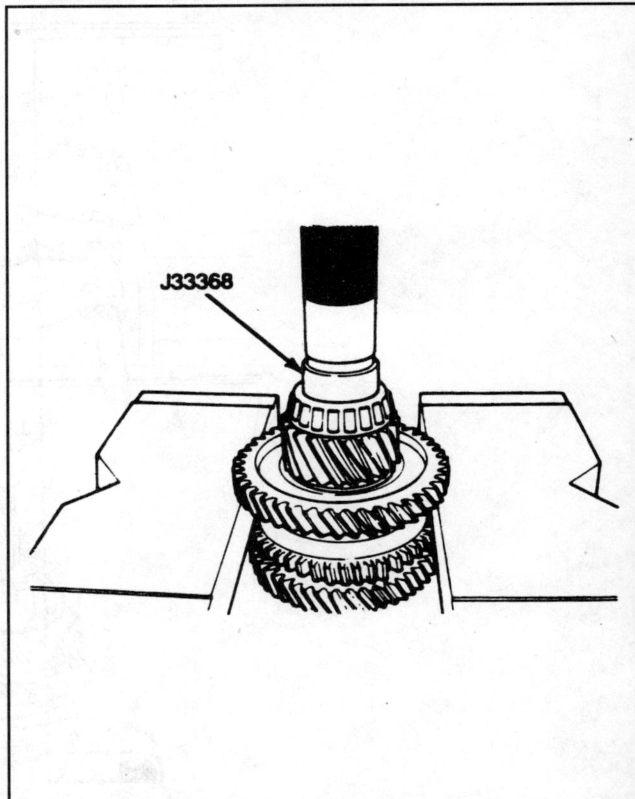

Fig. 37 Use tool J-33368 or its equivalent to install the input shaft front and rear bearings

3. Install the blocker ring and needle bearings. Install the 4th gear and thrust washer next. The thrust washer goes with the recessed area facing the 4th gear.
4. Install the front and rear bearings using tool No. J-33374 and a press.

OUTPUT SHAFT

Before assembling the shafts, apply a coat of specified lubricant to the thrust washers, all gears and washers.

1. Install the thrust washer, thrust needle bearings coat with grease and 1st gear and blocker ring.
2. Match the inserts of the sleeve and hub with the grooves in the blocker ring and press the sleeve and hub together with the collar using tool No. J-8853-01 and a press.
3. Install the blocker ring needle bearings and 2nd gear. Install the key on the key groove next.
4. Apply oil to 3rd/4th gear and match the key with the key groove and fit the key together with the rear bearing. Using tool No. J-33374 and a press, press the bearing onto the shaft.
5. Press the front bearing onto the shaft using tool No. J-33368 and a press.

DIFFERENTIAL ASSEMBLY

Before assembling the shafts, apply a coat of specified lubricant to the thrust washers, all gears and washers.

1. Install the two side gears on the differential case together with the thrust washers.
2. Position the two thrust washers and pinion gears opposite

of each other. Install them in their positions by turning the side gears.

3. Insert the cross pin and make sure the gear backlash is within the rated range of 0.03–0.08mm.

4. Install the lock pin and stake it when the correct backlash is achieved.

5. Heat the speedometer drive gear to about 203°F (95°C) with a hot oil dryer or equivalent. Install the gear on the differential.

6. Install the ring gear onto the differential case and install the ten new bolts. Torque the bolts to 73–79 ft. lbs. (98–107 Nm) in a diagonal sequence.

7. Install the side bearings on the differential case using an arbor press.

Case Reassembly

See Figures 38 thru 43

Before assembling the shafts, apply a coat of specified lubricant to the thrust washers, all gears and washers.

1. Install a new input shaft seal using tool J-26540.

2. Install the front outer bearing races for the input shaft, output shaft and differential into the clutch housing. Press the input and output races into the housing using tools J-33371, J-8092, J-7817, J-8611-01 and an arbor press.

3. Apply grease to the interlock pins and install them on the clutch housing.

4. Install the reverse shift bracket onto the clutch housing. Use the 3rd/4th shift rod to align the bracket to housing. Install the retaining bolts and torque to 11–16 ft. lbs. (15–22 Nm). Make sure the rod operates properly.

5. Install the differential assembly first, then install the input and output shaft with the 3rd/4th shift fork and shaft as an assembly into the clutch housing. Make sure the interlock pin is in the 3rd/4th shifter shaft before installing.

6. The 3rd/4th shift shaft is installed into the raised collar of the reverse shift lever bracket.

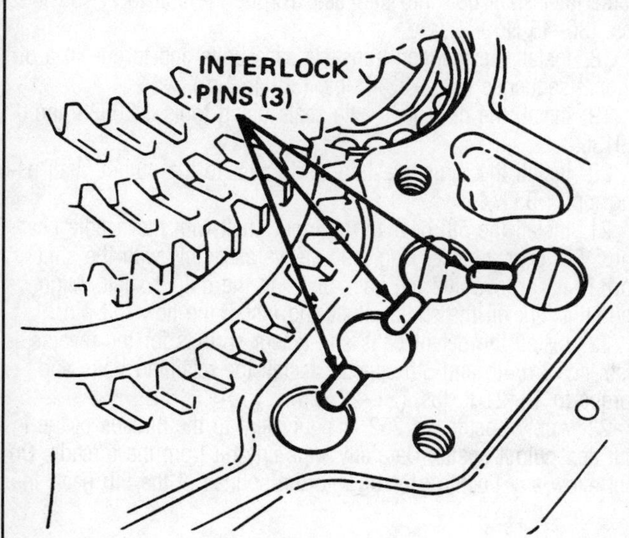

Fig. 38 Ensure that the interlock pin is in the 5th gear shifter shaft before installation

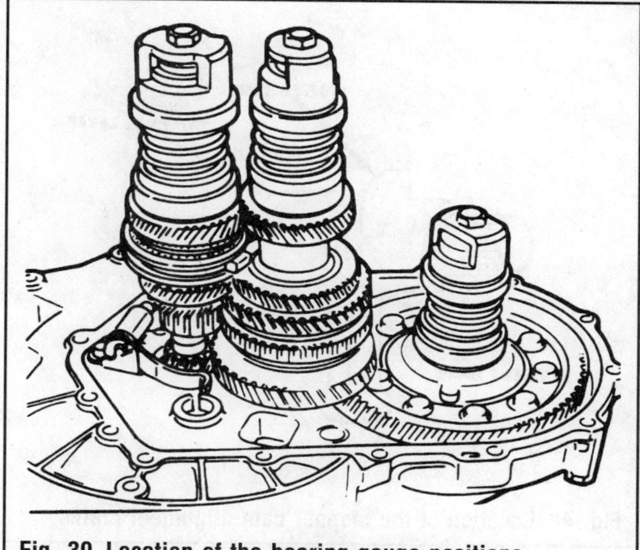

Fig. 39 Location of the bearing gauge positions

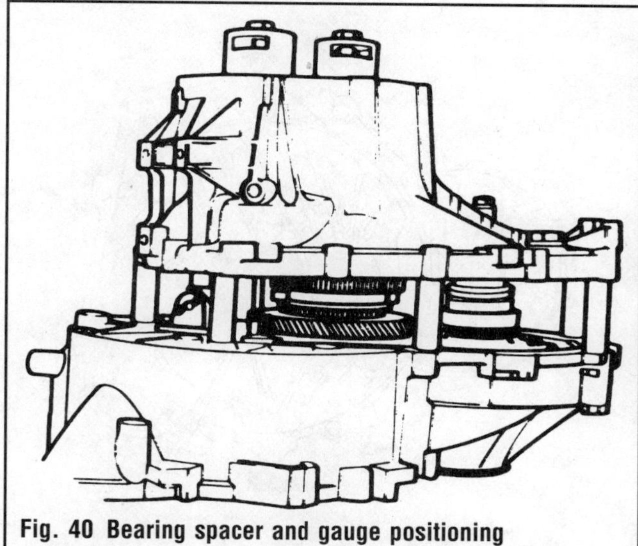

Fig. 40 Bearing spacer and gauge positioning

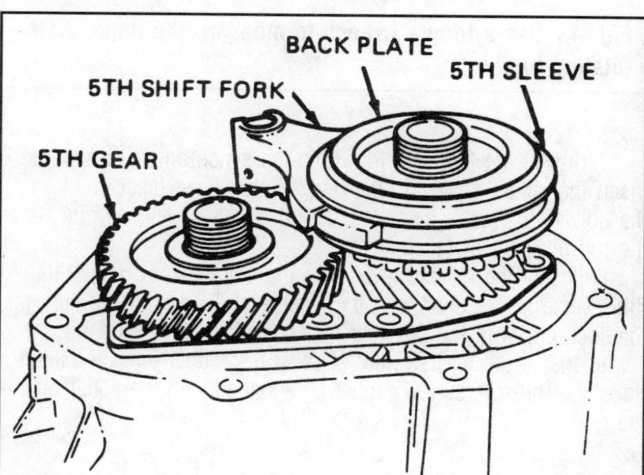

Fig. 41 The 5th gear, shift fork and other components should be in this position

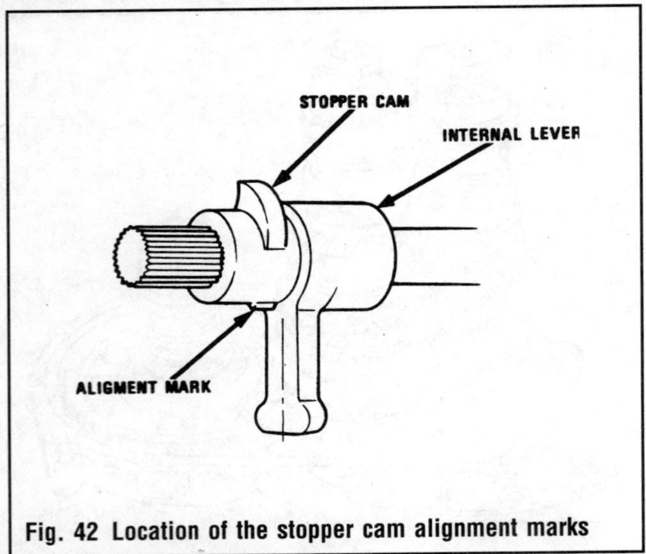

Fig. 42 Location of the stopper cam alignment marks

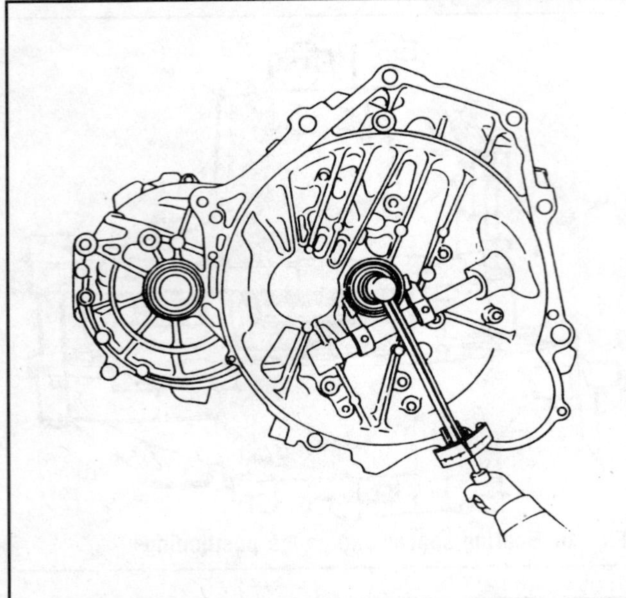

Fig. 43 Use a torque wrench to measure the input shaft rotating torque

7. Install the 1-2 shift fork onto the synchronizer sleeve and insert the shifter shaft into the reverse shift lever bracket. Align the hole in the fork with the shaft and install a new roll pin. Stake the roll pin after installation.

8. Install the reverse lever onto the shift bracket. Install the 5th/reverse shifter shaft with the reverse shift lever. Make sure the interlock pin is in the 5th gear shifter shaft before installing.

9. Install the reverse idler shaft with the gear into the clutch housing. The reverse lever must be engaged with the collar on the gear.

10. Measure and determine the shim size using tool J-33373 as follows:

a. Position the outer bearing races on the input, output and differential bearings. Position the shim selection gauges on the bearing races. The three gauges are identical.

b. Place seven spacers provided with tool J-33373 evenly around the perimeter of the clutch housing.

c. Install the bearing and shim retainer on the transaxle case. Torque the screws to 11–16 ft. lbs. (15–22 Nm). After torquing the screws, stake the screws to the retaining plate.

d. Position the transaxle case over the gauges and on the spacers. Install the seven bolts provided with the tool kit and tighten the bolts alternately until the case is seated on the spacers. Torque the bolts to 10 ft. lbs. (15 Nm).

e. Rotate the gauges to seat the bearings. Rotate the differential case through three revolutions in each direction.

f. With the three gauges compressed, measure the gap between the outer sleeve and the base pad using the available shim sizes in the following "Preload Shim Size" chart. The input shaft shim should be one size smaller than the largest shim that will fit in the gap. The differential should use a shim three sizes larger than that which will smoothly fit in the gap. The output shaft should use the largest shim that can be placed into the gap and drawn through without binding.

g. When each of the shims have been selected, remove the transaxle case, seven spacers and three gauges.

11. Position the shim selected for the input, output and differential into the bearing race bores in the transaxle case.

12. Install the rear input shaft bearing race using tool J-24256 with J-8092.

13. Install the rear output shaft bearing race using tool J-33370 with J-8092.

14. Install the differential case bearing race using tool J-8611-01 with J-8092 and a press. Press in the bearing until it is in its bore.

15. Apply a 1/8 inch bead of Loctite® #514 to the mating surfaces of the clutch housing and transaxle case.

16. Make sure the magnet is installed into the case.

17. Install the transaxle case to the clutch housing and the reverse idler shaft bolt into the case. Torque the bolt to 22–33 ft. lbs. (30–45 Nm).

18. Install the fourteen transaxle case bolts and torque in a diagonal sequence to 22–33 ft. lbs. (30–45 Nm).

19. Install the new drive axle seals using tools J-26938 and J-29130.

20. Install the thrust washers and collar to the output shaft using tool J-33374.

21. Install the 5th gear to the input shaft with the needle bearings, 5th gear, blocker ring, hub/sleeve assembly with the shift fork in its groove and the back plate on the output shaft. Align the shift fork on the shifter shaft and install the new roll pin.

22. Install the detent balls and detent springs for the reverse, 1st/2nd, 3rd/4th and 5th speeds. Install the retaining bolts and torque to 15–21 ft. lbs. (21–29 Nm).

23. Apply Loctite® # 262 or equivalent to the threads of the input and output shafts. Carefully wipe any oil from the threads. Do not allow any Loctite® to run into the splines of the 5th gear. In-

Preload Shim Sizes

THICKNESS		AVAILABLE			THICKNESS		AVAILABLE		
	mm(in.)	INPUT	OUTPUT	DIFF		mm(in.)	INPUT	OUTPUT	DIFF
1.00	0.0394	●			1.76	0.0693	●		●
1.04	0.0410	●			1.80	0.0709	●	●	●
1.08	0.0426	●		●	1.84	0.0725	●		●
1.12	0.0441	●		●	1.88	0.0741	●	●	●
1.16	0.0457	●	●	●	1.92	0.0756	●		●
1.20	0.0473	●		●	1.96	0.0772	●	●	●
1.24	0.0489	●	●	●	2.00	0.0788	●		●
1.28	0.0504	●		●	2.04	0.0804	●	●	
1.32	0.0520	●	●	●	2.08	0.0820	●		
1.36	0.0536	●		●	2.12	0.0835	●	●	
1.40	0.0552	●	●	●	2.16	0.0851	●		
1.44	0.0567	●		●	2.20	0.0867	●	●	
1.48	0.0583	●	●	●	2.24	0.0883	●		
1.52	0.0599	●		●	2.28	0.0899	●	●	
1.56	0.0615	●	●	●	2.32	0.0914	●		
1.60	0.0630	●		●	2.36	0.0930	●	●	
1.64	0.0646	●	●	●	2.40	0.0946	●		
1.68	0.0662	●		●	2.44	0.0961	●	●	
1.72	0.0678	●	●	●	2.48	0.0977	●		

stall the new retaining nuts and torque to 87–101 ft. lbs. (118–137 Nm). Stake the nuts after reaching final torque.

24. Assemble the control box as follows:
   a. Assemble the stopper cam and internal lever. Make sure the serrations on the stopper cam and internal lever are aligned.
   b. Install the stopper cam and internal lever to the shift lever.
   c. Align the stopper cam alignment mark with the center on the internal lever.
   d. Check to see that the reverse inhibitor mechanism operates properly.
   e. Use a new roll pin to attach the internal lever during assembly.
25. Install the gasket and control box on the transaxle case and torque the four bolts to 11–16 ft. lbs. (15–22 Nm).
26. Make sure the transaxle shifts properly before installing rear cover.
27. Install the gasket and rear cover with the seven bolts. Torque the bolts to 11–16 ft. lbs. (15–22 Nm).
28. Install the clutch fork assembly if it has been removed. Install the bushing into the upper hole using tool J-28412 and install the oil seal next using tool J-28406.
29. Install the clutch release bearing as outlined in the "Clutch" procedures in this section. Measure the rotating torque on the input shaft. The rotating torque should be less than 7 inch.lb.

5-speed 282 Muncie (MG2) Overhaul

DISASSEMBLY

External Mounts and Linkage

➧ See Figures 44, 44A, 45 and 45A

1. Remove the transaxle from the vehicle and place in a suitable holding fixture. Refer to the "Manual Transaxle" removal and installation procedures in this Section 1.
2. Remove the shift lever nut, do not allow the lever to move during removal of nut. Use a ⅜ inch drive wrench to hold the external shift lever.
3. Remove the washer, lever, retainer, pivot pin and pivot, bolts and bracket, fluid level indicator and the electronic speedometer retainer and assembly.

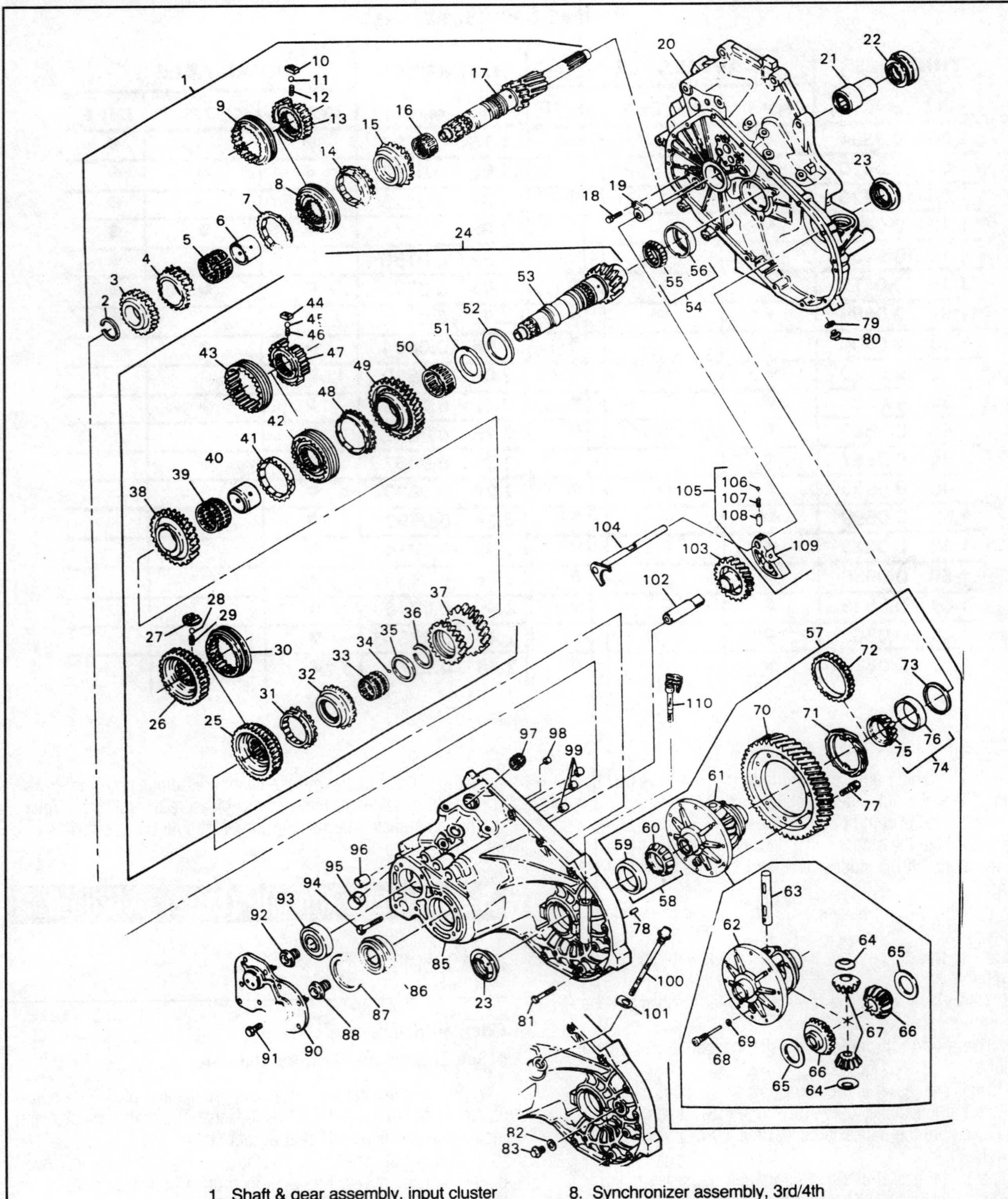

1. Shaft & gear assembly, input cluster
2. Snap ring
3. Gear, fifth input
4. Gear, fourth input
5. Bearing, cage
6. Race, needle
7. Ring, blocker 4th
8. Synchronizer assembly, 3rd/4th
9. Sleeve, 3rd/4th synchronizer
10. Key, 3rd/4th synchronizer (three)
11. Ball, 3rd/4th synchronizer (three)
12. Spring, 3rd/4th synchronizer (three)
13. Hub, clutch, 3rd/4th synchronizer
14. Ring, blocker 3rd

Fig. 44 Exploded view of the 282 Muncie 5-speed (MG2) manual transaxle gear shaft

15. Gear, third input
16. Bearing, cage (two)
17. Shaft, input
18. Bolt/screw, M6 × 1 × 12
19. Guide, reverse shift rail
20. Housing, clutch and differential
21. Bearing/sleeve assembly, input shaft
22. Bearing assembly, clutch release
23. Seal, oil drive axle
24. Shaft & gear assembly, output cluster
25. Gear, reverse output/5th synchronizer assembly
26. Gear, reverse
27. Key, 5th synchronizer (three)
28. Ball, 5th synchronizer (three)
29. Spring, 5th synchronizer (three)
30. Sleeve, 5th synchronizer
31. Ring, blocker 5th gear
32. Gear, 5th speed output
33. Bearing, 5th speed output
34. Ball, thrust washer positioner
35. Washer, thrust
36. Snap ring
37. Gear, 3rd/4th cluster
38. Gear, 2nd output
39. Bearing, 2nd output
40. Race, bearing 2nd output
41. Ring, blocker 2nd gear
42. Synchronizer assembly, 1st/2nd gear
43. Sleeve, 1st/2nd synchronizer
44. Key, 1st/2nd synchronizer (three)
45. Ball, 1st/2nd synchronizer (three)
46. Spring, 1st/2nd synchronizer (three)
47. Hub, 1st/2nd synchronizer
48. Ring, blocker 1st gear
49. Gear, 1st output
50. Bearing, 1st output
51. Bearing, thrust
52. Washer, thrust
53. Shaft, output
54. Bearing, output shaft support
55. Bearing, output
56. Race, bearing output
57. Gear and differential assembly
58. Bearing assembly, differential
59. Race, bearing differential
60. Bearing, differential
61. Case, differential assembly
62. Case, differential
63. Pin, cross differential
64. Washer, thrust pinion gear
65. Washer, thrust side gear
66. Gear, side differential
67. Gear, pinion differential
68. Bolt/screw, pinion gear shaft
69. Washer, lock
70. Gear, ring differential
71. Gear, speedo output (mechanical)
72. Gear, speedo output (electronic)
73. Shim, differential (selective)
74. Bearing assembly, differential
75. Bearing, differential
76. Race, bearing differential
77. Bolt/screw, differential ring (10)
78. Pin (two)
79. Plug, oil drain
80. Washer
81. Bolt/screw, transmission case, M8 × 1.25.50 (15)
82. Washer
83. Plug
85. Case, transmission
86. Bearing, output gear
87. Shim, output gear (selective)
88. Retainer, output gear bearing
90. End plate, transmission case
91. Bolt/screw, M8 × 1 × 18 (9)
92. Retainer, input gear bearing
93. Bearing, input gear
94. Bolt/screw, reverse idler, M8 × 1.25.50
95. Bushing, detent lever
96. Bushing, sliding sleeve
97. Bearing, needle shift shaft
98. Bushing, reverse rail
99. Bushing, shift rail (three)
100. Washer, fluid level indicator
101. Fluid level indicator
102. Shaft, reverse idler
103. Gear, reverse idler
104. Rail, reverse shift idler gear
105. Bracket assembly, reverse idler gear
106. Ball, bracket reverse idler gear
107. Spring, bracket reverse idler gear
108. Sleeve, detent bracket reverse idler gear
109. Bracket, reverse idler gear
110. Indicator assembly, transmission fluid level

Fig. 44A Muncie 282 5-speed (MG2) manual transaxle gear shaft component list

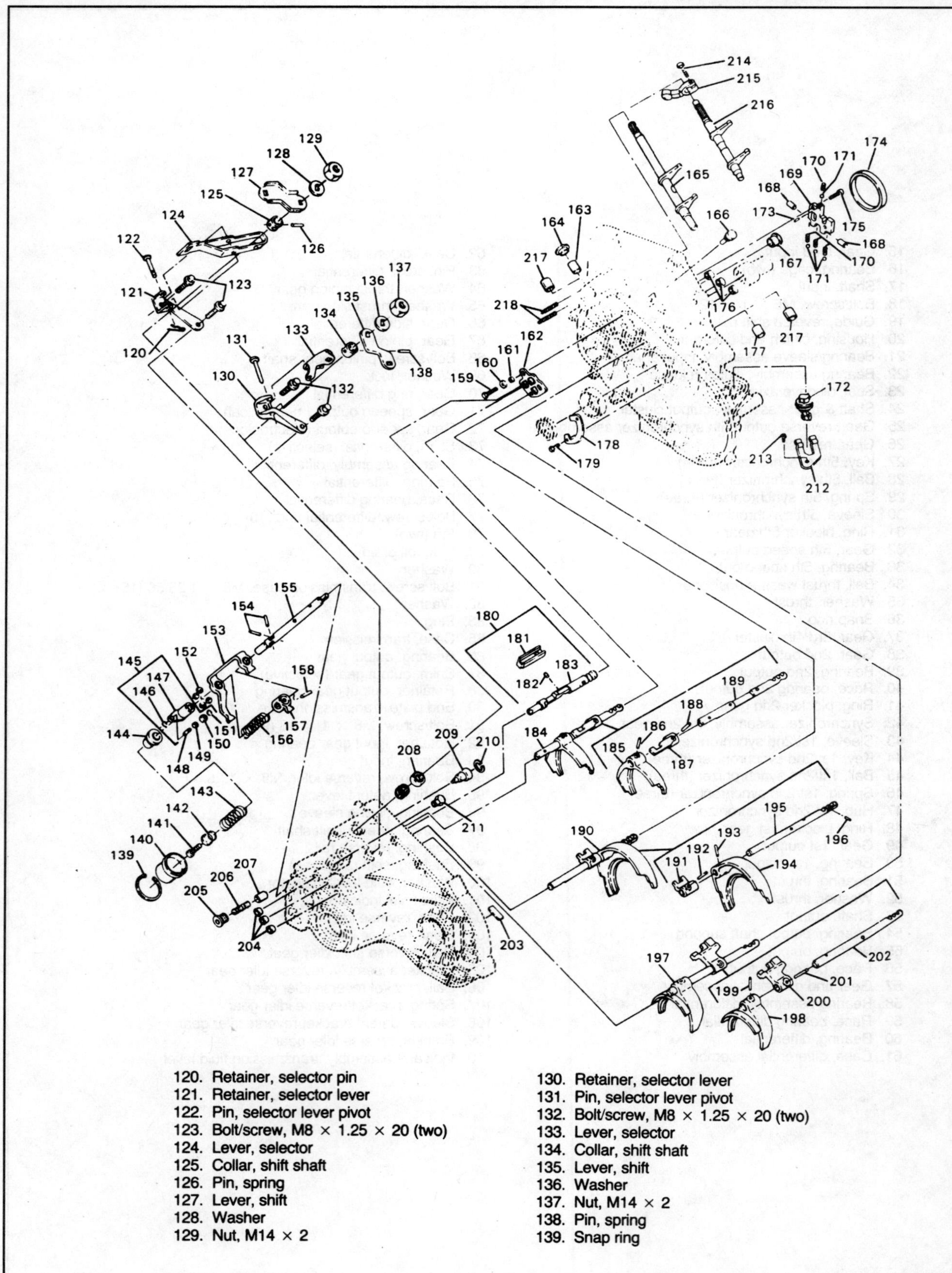

Fig. 45 Exploded view of the 282 Muncie 5-speed (MG2) manual transaxle shift mechanism

140. Cover, shift shaft
141. Bolt/screw, M20 × 1.5
142. Seat, spring 5th detent outer
143. Spring
144. Seat, spring 5th detent inner
145. Lever, detent assembly
146. Retainer, pin detent
147. Lever, detent
148. Pin, detent lever
149. Spacer, detent lever
150. Roller, detent lever
151. Retainer, pin detent
152. Roller, detent (four)
153. Lever, reverse
154. Pin, detent lever rollers (two)
155. Shaft, shift
156. Spring, 3rd/4th bias
157. Lever, shift
158. Pin, roll
159. Bolt/screw, M6 × 1 × 12 (three)
160. Washer, flat (three)
161. Spacer (three)
162. Plate, shift interlock
163. Bushing, outer clutch fork
164. Seal, clutch fork
165. Shaft, clutch fork
166. Breather assembly
167. Bushing, reverse shift rail
168. Pin, interlock (two)
169. Holder, detent
170. Spring, detent (four)
171. Ball, detent (four)
172. Speedo signal assembly
173. Pin, spring
174. Cover, detent holder
175. Bolt/screw, M6 × 1 × 30 (two)
176. Bushings, shift rail (three)
177. Bushing, inner clutch fork
178. Retainer, output bearing race
179. Bolt/screw, M6 × 1 × 12 (two)
180. Rail, reverse shift assembly
181. Shift gate, 5th/reverse
182. Roller, gear disengage
183. Shaft, reverse shift
184. Rail, 3rd/4th shift assembly
185. Fork, 3rd/4th shift shaft
186. Pin, fork retainer
187. Lever, 3rd/4th select
188. Pin, lever retainer
189. Shaft, 3rd/4th shift
190. Rail, 1st/2nd shift assembly
191. Lever, 1st/2nd select
192. Pin, lever retainer
193. Pin, fork retainer
194. Fork, 1st/2nd shift
195. Shaft, 1st/2nd shift
196. Pin, lock
197. Rail, 5th shift assembly
198. Fork, 5th shift
199. Pin, fork retainer
200. Lever, 5th shift
201. Pin, lever retainer
202. Shaft, 5th shift
203. Magnet, chip collector
204. Plug, shift rail (three)
205. Bolt/screw, M2 × 1.5
206. Spring, sliding sleeve
207. Sleeve, sliding
208. Seal, shift shaft
209. Plug
210. Snap ring
211. Stud
212. Speedo signal assembly, retainer
213. Bolt
214. Bolt
215. Lever, clutch release
216. Shaft, clutch fork
217. Bearing, clutch shaft (two)
218. Stud, clutch cylinder (two)

Fig. 45A Muncie 282 5–speed (MG2) manual transaxle shift mechanism component list

Shift Rail Detent and Clutch Housing

➧ See Figures 46 and 47

1. Remove the clutch disengage bearing.
2. Remove the detent holder cover by puncturing the cover in the middle and prying off.
3. Remove the detent holder bolts, holder, detent, springs and interlock pins.
4. Remove the detent balls and bushing.

Shift Shaft Detent in Transaxle Housing

➧ See Figure 48

1. Remove the detent cover snapring, cover, screw and outer spring seat and the 5th/reverse bias spring/inner spring seat.

Transaxle Case and Clutch Housing Separation

➧ See Figure 49

1. Remove the fifteen clutch housing retaining bolts.
2. Transaxle must be in neutral. Remove the clutch housing by gently tapping the housing with a rubber hammer.
3. Remove the differential gear assembly, magnet and bearing.

Shift Shaft Components

➧ See Figure 50

1. Remove the shift shaft pin using a punch.
2. Remove the shift shaft assembly consisting of the shaft, rollers, 1st/2nd bias spring and shift and reverse lever.

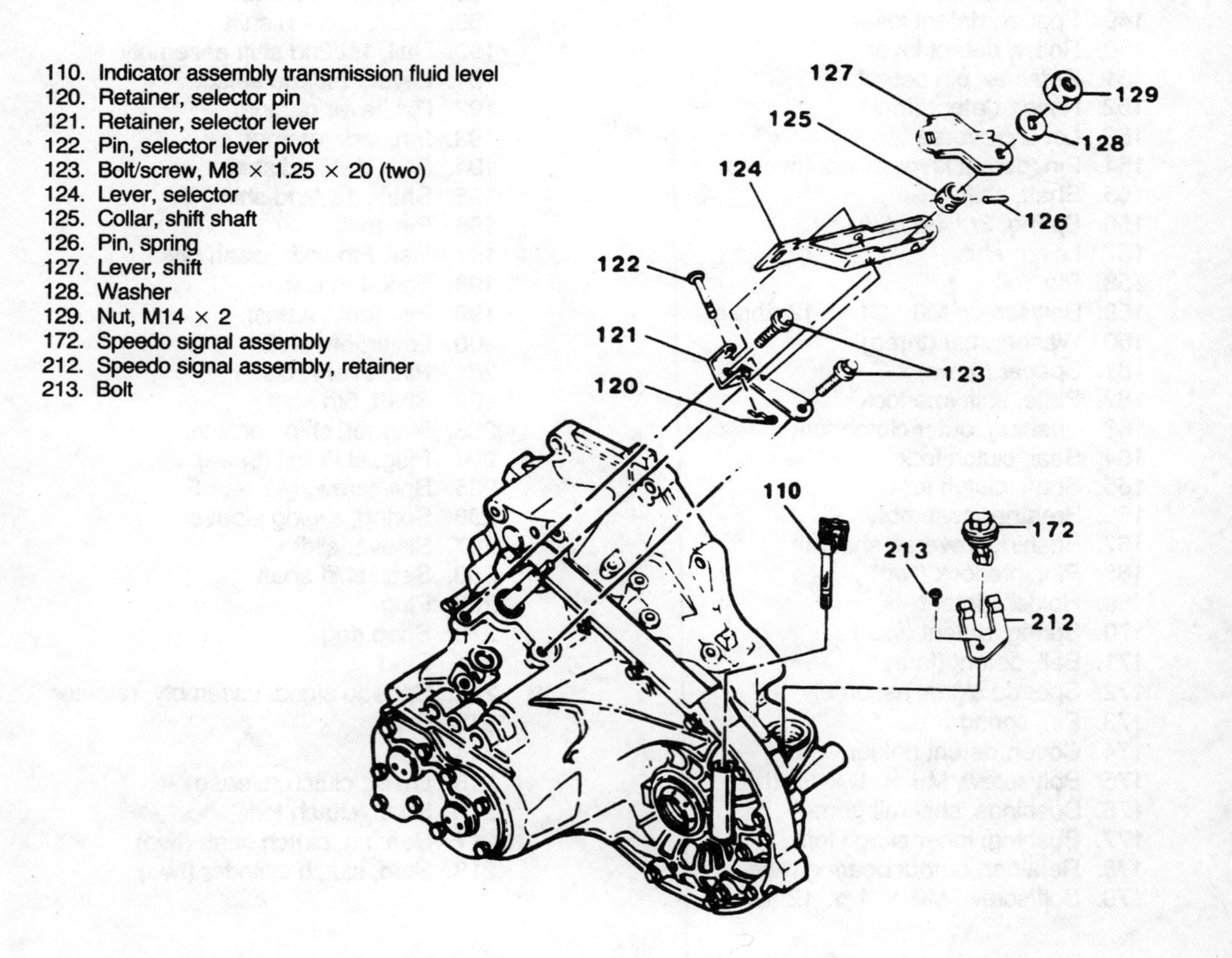

Fig. 46 Exploded view of the 5-speed Muncie transaxle external mounts

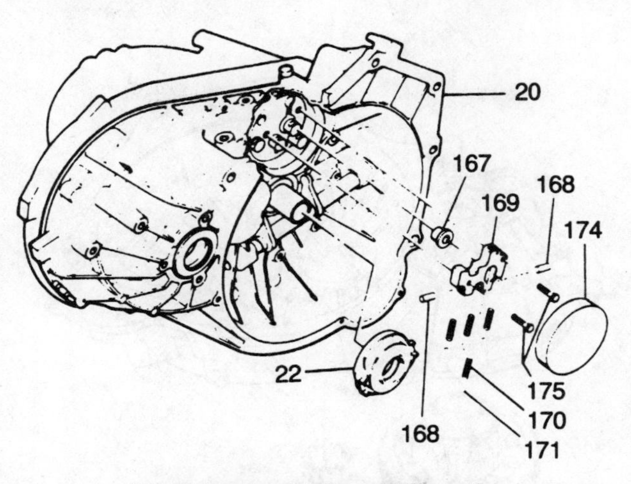

20. Housing, clutch and differential
22. Bearing, clutch disengage
167. Bushing, reverse shift rail
168. Pin, interlock (two)
169. Holder, detent
170. Spring, detent (four)
171. Ball, detent (four)
174. Cover, detent holder
175. Bolt (two), 9 N·m (84 lb. in.)

Fig. 47 The shift rail components are located inside the clutch housing

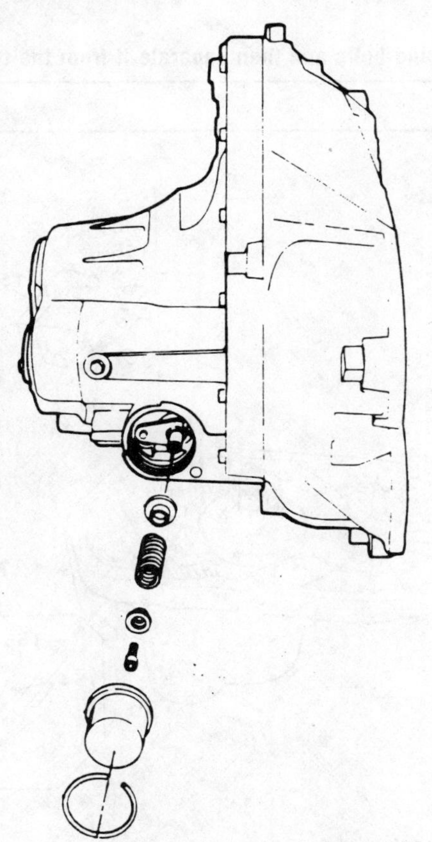

Fig. 48 Remove the shift shaft cover snapring to gain access to the shift shaft assembly

Fig. 49 Remove the clutch housing retaining bolts and then separate it from the transaxle case

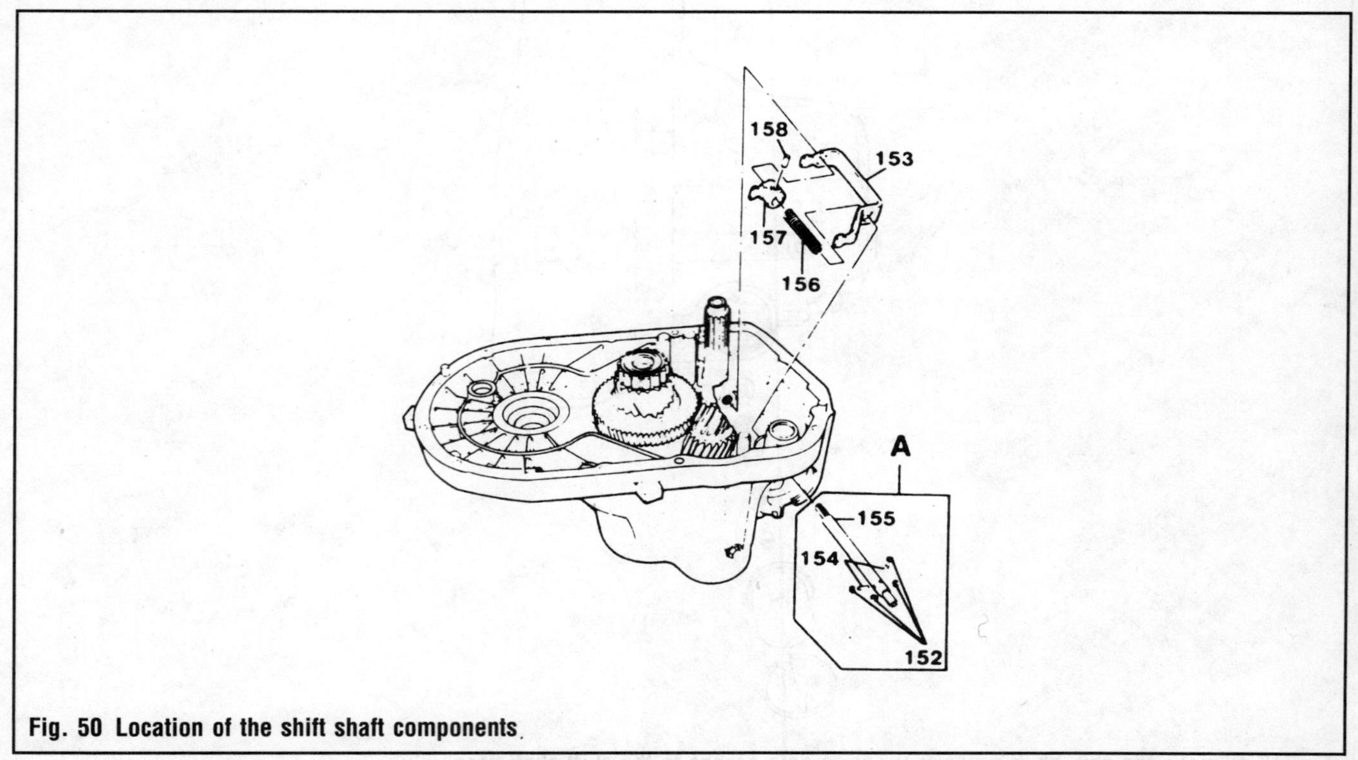

Fig. 50 Location of the shift shaft components

Gear Cluster Support Components

➧ See Figure 51

1. Engage the gear cluster in 4th (A) and reverse (B) by pushing down on the gear rails.
2. Remove the nine bearing retainer cover bolts and cover. Using tool J-36031, remove the bearing retainer Hex bolts and selective shim.

Gear Clusters

➧ See Figure 52

1. Using tool J-36182-1 and J-36182I-2, position in a hydraulic press.
2. Position the transaxle case and gear cluster assembly in the press. Align the shift rail and shaft pilots to the fixture.
3. Position tool J-36185 on the shaft support bearings and pilots. Using the press, separate the shaft and gear clusters from the transaxle case.

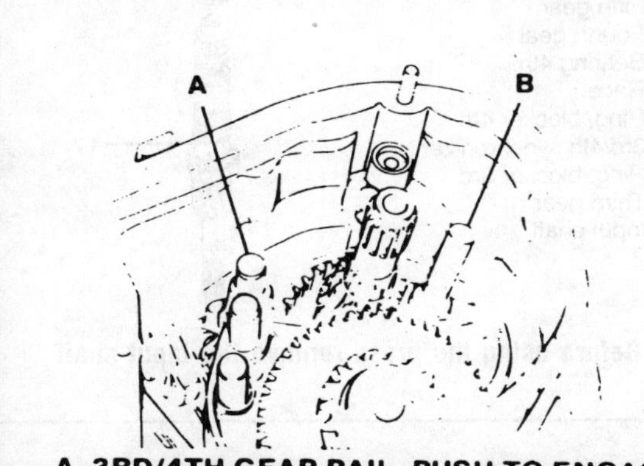

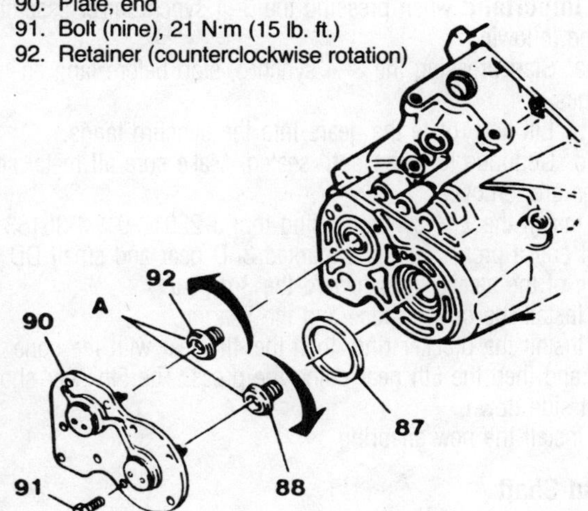

Fig. 51 The gear cluster support components at the rear of the transaxle components

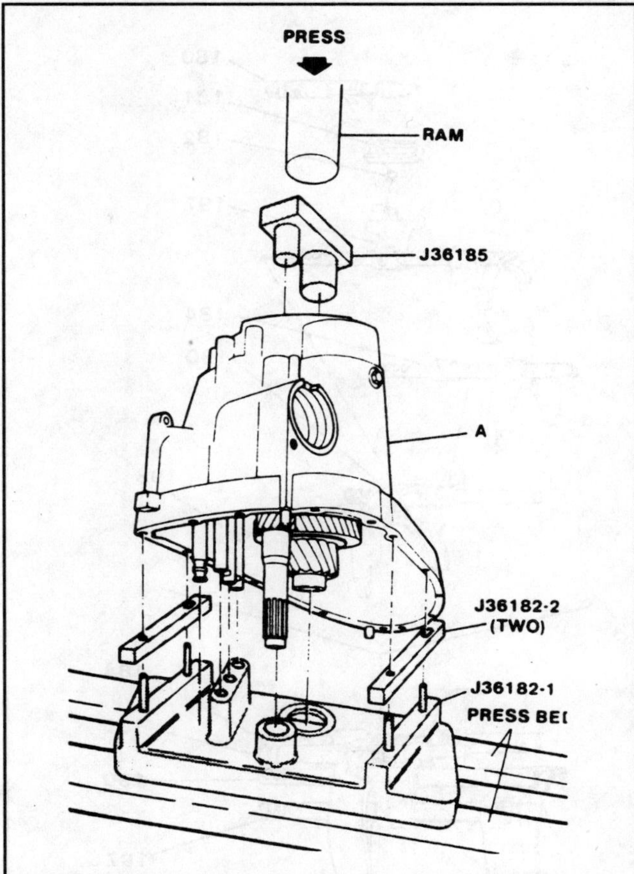

Fig. 52 Use a press to separate the gear cluster from the transaxle case

Gear Clusters and Shift Rails

➧ See Figure 53

1. Remove the 1-2 shift rail assembly and lock pin.
2. Remove the 3-4 shift rail assembly.
3. Remove the 5th shift rail assembly and reverse assembly.
4. Remove the shift gate and disengage roller.

UNIT DISASSEMBLY & REPAIR

Input Shaft

DISASSEMBLY

➧ See Figure 54

1. **Important** identify the blocker ring for the 3rd gear and 4th gear blocker ring. Do not mix the blocker rings.
2. Remove the input shaft snapring before using the press.
3. Remove 4th and 5th gears, bearings, race, blocker ring, synchronizer and gear using an arbor press.
4. Remove the 3rd gear bearing.

INSPECTION

1. Clean all parts with solvent and blow dry with compressed air.

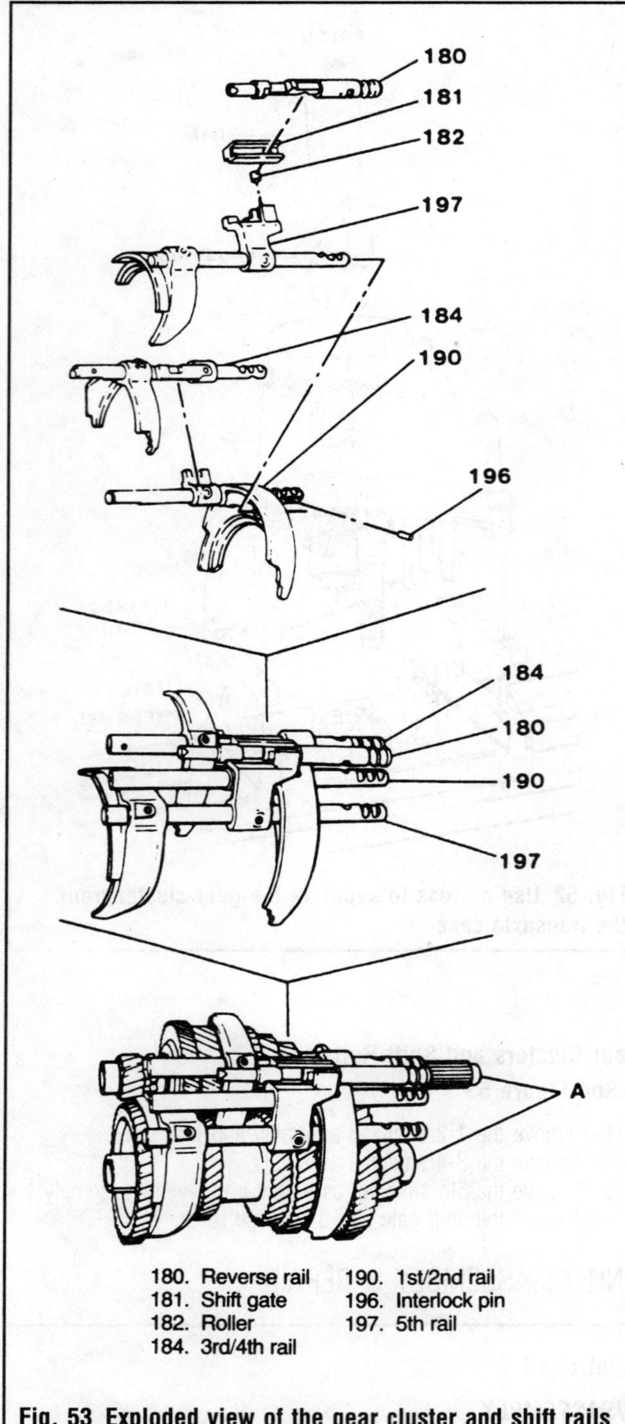

Fig. 53 Exploded view of the gear cluster and shift rails

2. Inspect; input shaft splines for cracks or wear, gear teeth for scuffed, nicked, burred or broken teeth, bearings for roughness of rotation, burred or pitted conditions and bearing races for scoring, wear or overheating. Inspect the synchronizers for scuffs, nicks, burrs or scoring. If any condition exists for any component, restore or replace the component. It is much easier to replace worn components while the transaxle is disassembled than when it is in the vehicle.

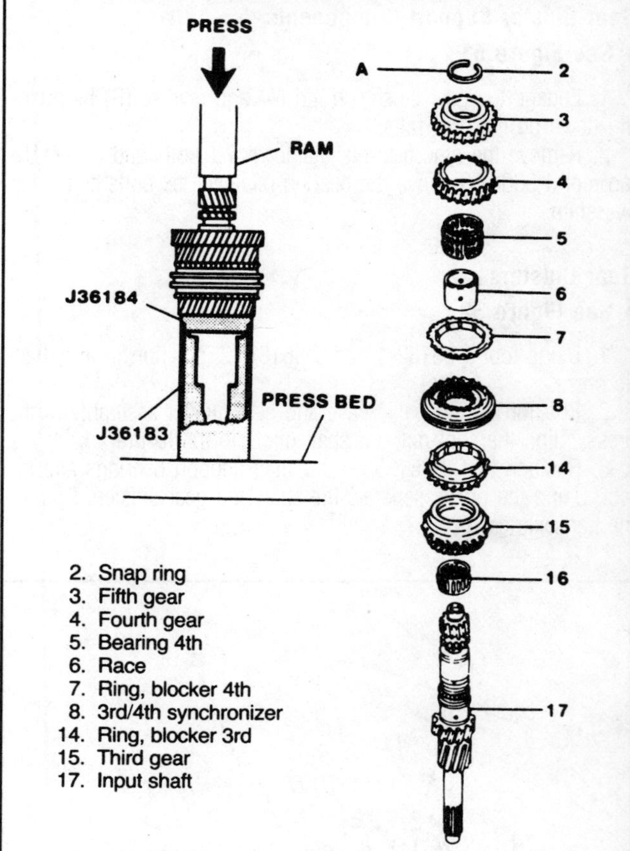

Fig. 54 Before using the press remove the input shaft snapring

ASSEMBLY

➧ **See Figure 55**

1. Install the input bearing, 3rd gear with the cone up and blocker ring.
2. **Important:** when pressing the 3–4 synchronizer assembly use the following:
   a. Start pressing the 3–4 synchro, stop before tang engages.
   b. Lift and rotate the gears into the synchro tangs.
   c. Continue to press until seated. Make sure all metal shavings are removed.
3. Install the 3–4 synchro using tool J-22912-01, J-36183, J-36184 and a press. The side marked 3RD gear and small OD groove of the sleeve goes toward the 3rd gear.
4. Install the bearing race and the bearing.
5. Install the blocker ring, then the 4th gear with the cone down and then the 5th gear using the press. The 5th gear should be flat side down.
6. Install the new snapring.

Output Shaft

DISASSEMBLY

➧ **See Figure 56**

1. **Important:** identify the blocker ring for 5th gear, ring for 2nd gear and ring for 1st gear. Do not mix the blocker rings.

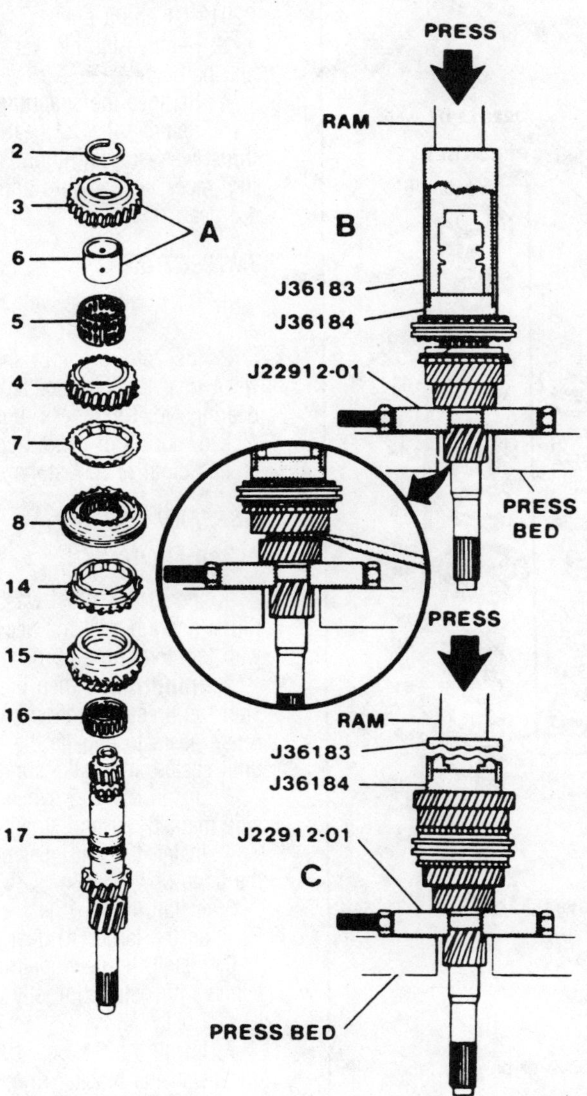

A. Fifth gear (3), bearing race (6) require heating prior to installation
B. Start press operation of 3rd/4th gear synchronizer (8). Do not contact blocker ring (14)
Lift gears (15) and (14) with probe to engage blocker ring (14) into synchronizer (8). Continue press operation
C. Press fifth gear (3)

2. Snap ring
3. 5th gear
4. 4th gear
5. Bearing, 4th gear
6. Race, bearing 4th gear
7. Blocker ring, 4th gear
8. Synchronizer assembly, 3rd/4th gear
14. Blocker ring, 3rd gear
15. 3rd gear
16. Bearing, 3rd gear
17. Shaft, input

Fig. 55 Exploded view of input shaft assembly

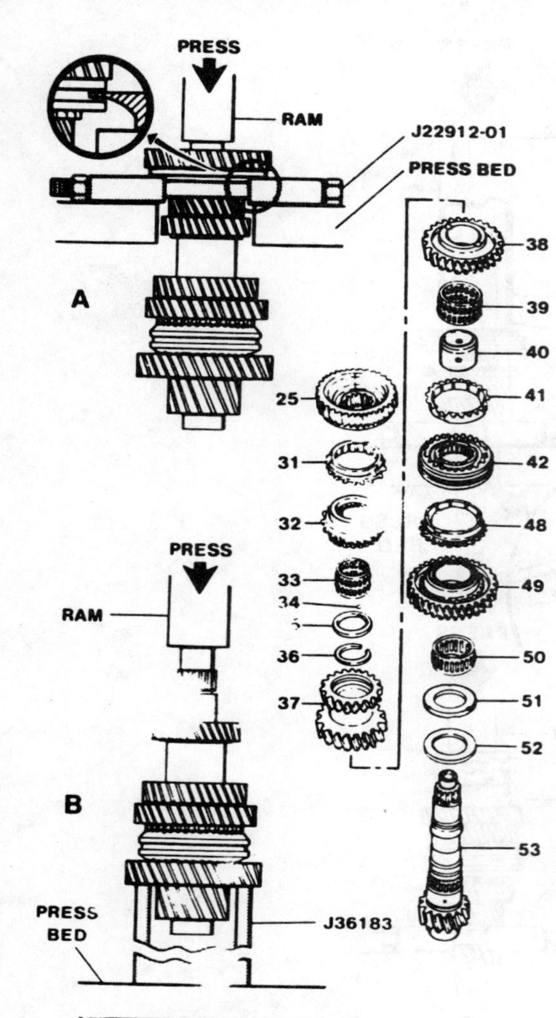

A. Install J22912-01 in sleeve groove or on gear face only
B. Snap ring (36) must be removed prior to press operation. First gear (49) on J36183

25. Reverse gear/5th gear synchronizer
31. Blocker ring, 5th gear
32. Gear, 5th speed
33. Bearing, 5th gear
34. Ball, thrust washer positioner
35. Thrust washer
36. Snap ring
37. Gear, 3rd/4th cluster
38. Gear, 2nd speed
39. Bearing, 2nd gear
40. Race, 2nd gear bearing
41. Blocker ring, 2nd gear
42. Synchronizer assembly, 1st/2nd gear
48. Blocker ring, 1st gear
49. Gear, 1st speed
50. Bearing, 1st gear
51. Bearing, thrust
52. Washer, thrust
53. Shaft, output

Fig. 56 Use an arbor press to disassemble the output shaft assembly

2. Remove the 5th/reverse synchronizer assembly using tool J-22912-01 and a press.
3. Remove the blocker ring, 5th gear, bearing, thrust washer and ball.
4. Remove the snapring.
5. Remove the 1st gear, bearing, caged thrust bearing and thrust washer using tool J-36183 and a press. The 2nd gear, bearing, race, 1–2 synchro and blocker rings will press off with the 1st gear.

INSPECTION

1. Clean all parts with solvent and blow dry with compressed air.
2. Inspect the output shaft for spline wear, cracks or excessive wear, gear teeth for scuffed, nicked, burred or broken teeth and bearings for roughness, burred or pitted conditions. If scuffed, nicked, burred or scored conditions can not be removed with fine crocus cloth or soft stone, replace the component.

ASSEMBLY

➧ See Figure 57

1. Install the thrust washer with the chamfer down, caged thrust bearing with the needles down, 1st gear bearing, 1st gear with the cone up and the blocker ring.
2. **Important:** when pressing the 1–2 synchronizer assembly, start the press operation and stop before tangs engages. Lift and rotate gears to engage the blocker ring tangs. Continue to press until seated and make sure all metal shavings are removed.
3. Install the 1–2 synchro using tool J-36183 and a press. The side marked 1st and small OD groove goes toward the 1st gear.
4. Install the 2nd gear bearing race, bearing and 2nd gear with the cone down.
5. Install the 3–4 gear cluster using tool J-36183 and a press. Position the large OD gear down.
6. Install the new snapring, thrust washer positioning ball retained with petroleum jelly and the slotted thrust washer. Align the ID slot with ball.
7. Install the 5th gear bearing and the 5th gear with the cone up. Install the blocker ring.
8. **Important:** when pressing on the reverse gear and 5th synchro, start the press operation and stop before tangs engage. Lift and rotate the 5th gear and blocker ring (thrust washer must stay down) until the tangs engage.
9. Install the 5th/reverse gear synchro assembly using tool J-36183 and a press.

Transaxle Case

DISASSEMBLY

➧ See Figure 58

➡Remove bearings and bushings only when there is evidence of damage and the component can not be reused.

1. Remove snapring, plug, screw, spring and sliding sleeve.
2. Remove bushing using tool J-36034 and J-36190.
3. Remove detent lever, bushing and seal using a small prybar.
4. Remove the shift shaft seal using tool J-36027.
5. Remove the axle seal, outer race, plugs, input shaft support bearing and the output shaft support bearing.
6. Remove the three shift rail bushing using tool J-36029, the

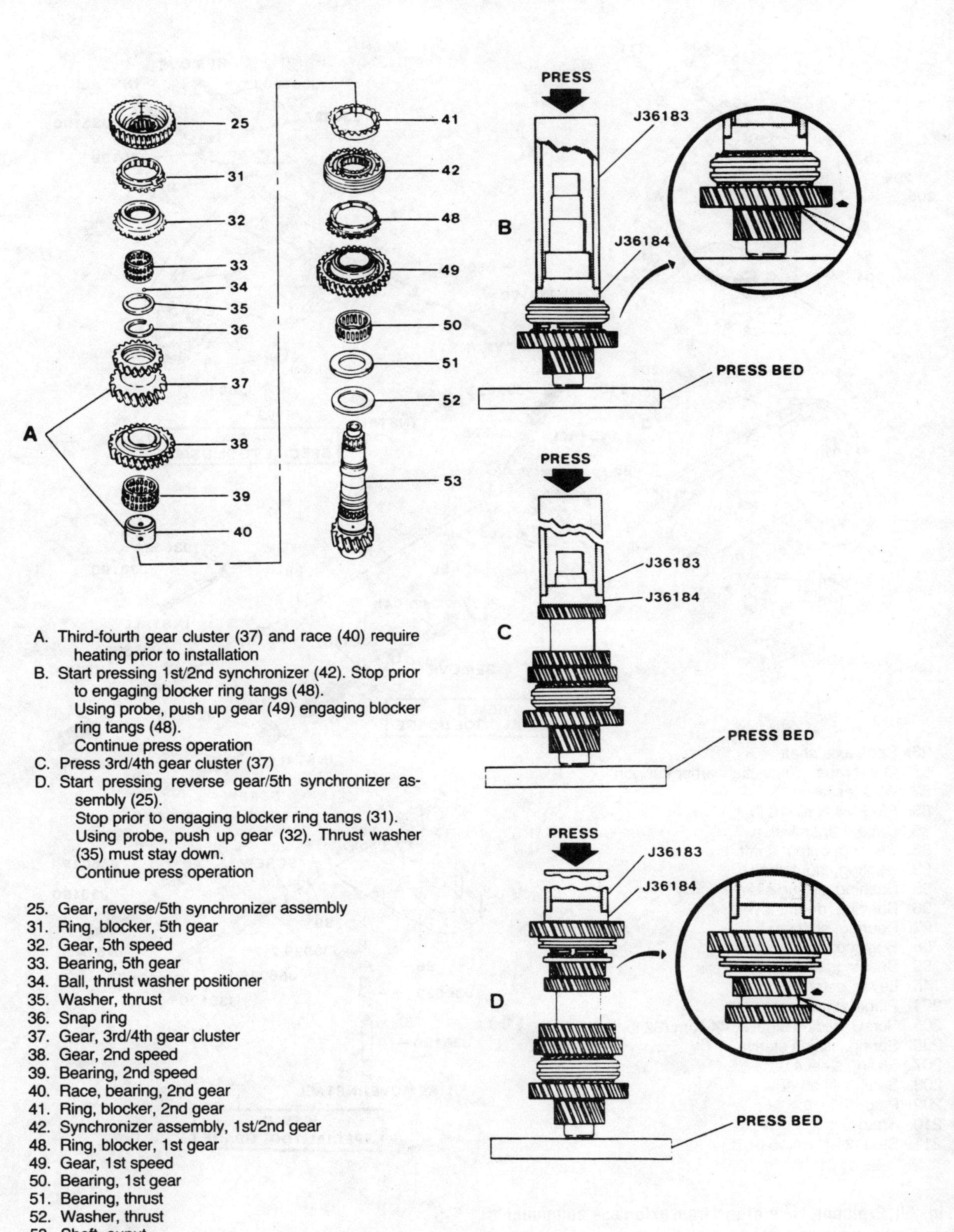

A. Third-fourth gear cluster (37) and race (40) require heating prior to installation
B. Start pressing 1st/2nd synchronizer (42). Stop prior to engaging blocker ring tangs (48).
Using probe, push up gear (49) engaging blocker ring tangs (48).
Continue press operation
C. Press 3rd/4th gear cluster (37)
D. Start pressing reverse gear/5th synchronizer assembly (25).
Stop prior to engaging blocker ring tangs (31).
Using probe, push up gear (32). Thrust washer (35) must stay down.
Continue press operation

25. Gear, reverse/5th synchronizer assembly
31. Ring, blocker, 5th gear
32. Gear, 5th speed
33. Bearing, 5th gear
34. Ball, thrust washer positioner
35. Washer, thrust
36. Snap ring
37. Gear, 3rd/4th gear cluster
38. Gear, 2nd speed
39. Bearing, 2nd speed
40. Race, bearing, 2nd gear
41. Ring, blocker, 2nd gear
42. Synchronizer assembly, 1st/2nd gear
48. Ring, blocker, 1st gear
49. Gear, 1st speed
50. Bearing, 1st gear
51. Bearing, thrust
52. Washer, thrust
53. Shaft, ouput

Fig. 57 Exploded view of the output shaft assembly

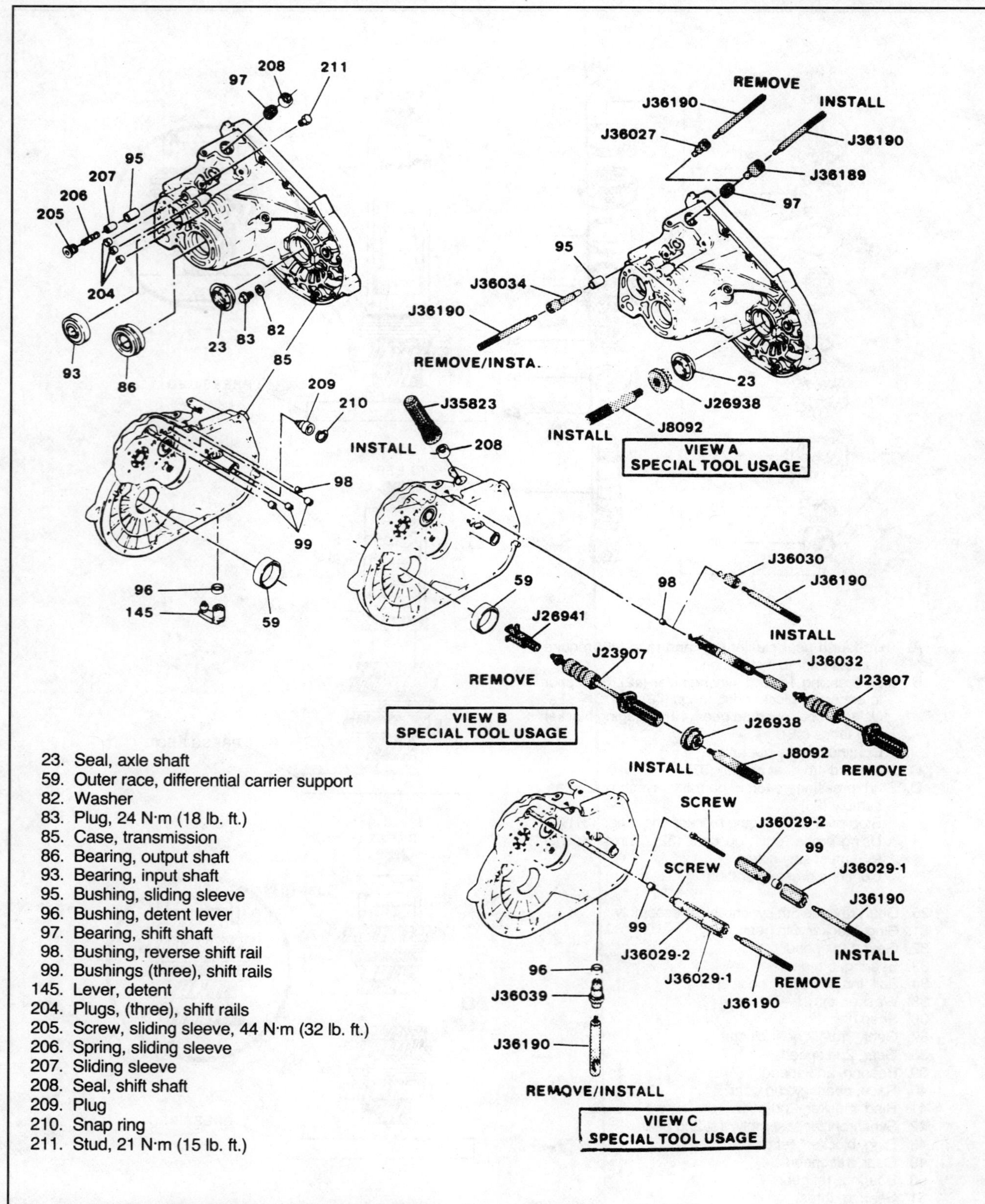

Fig. 58 Exploded view of the transaxle case components

reverse shift rail bushing by driving down and removing through the back-up light switch hole.

ASSEMBLY

1. Install the shift shaft bearing and seal using tool J-36189 and J-36190.
2. Install the three shift rail bushing using tool J-36029.
3. Install the reverse rail bushing using tool J-36030 and J-36190.
4. Install the differential carrier outer race, axle seal and plugs.
5. Install detent lever bushings, sliding sleeve bushing using tools J-36039 and J-36034.
6. Install detent lever, sleeve, spring and screw tightened to 32 ft. lbs. (44 Nm).
7. Install plug, snapring and stud with the chamfer end out torqued to 15 ft. lbs. (21 Nm).

Synchronizers

DISASSEMBLY

See Figures 59, 60 and 61

1. Place 1–2, 3–4, and 5th-reverse synchronizers in a separate shop towel. Wrap the assemblies and press against the inner hub.
2. Clean with solvent and blow dry with compressed air.

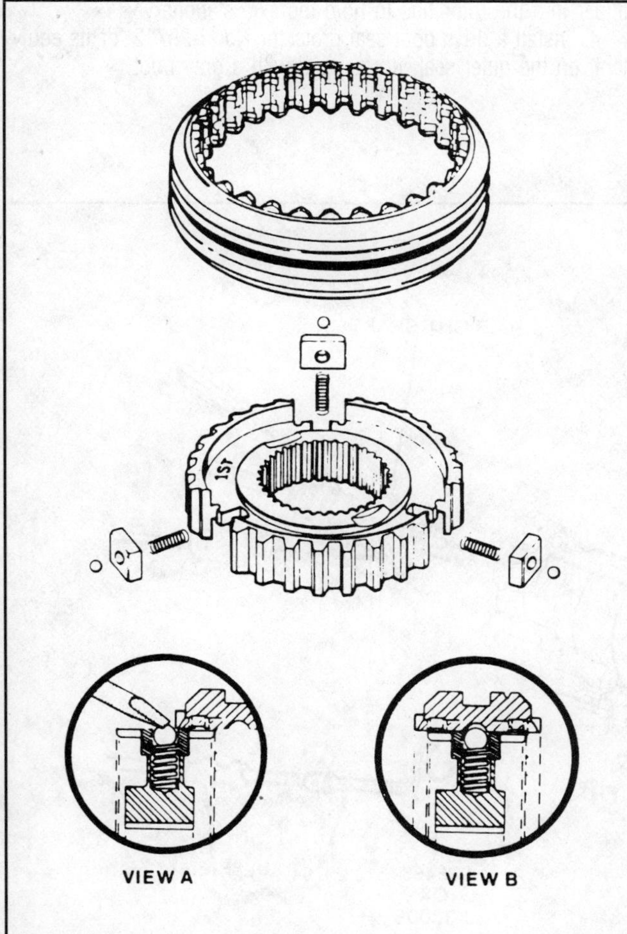

Fig. 59 Check the 1st-2nd gear synchronizer for broken teeth

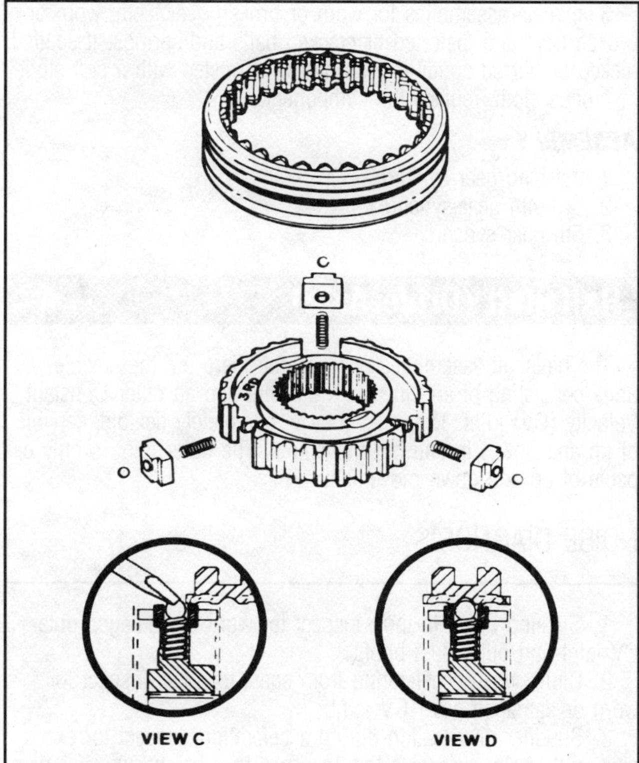

Fig. 60 Inspect the 3rd-4th gear synchronizer for worn or broken keys

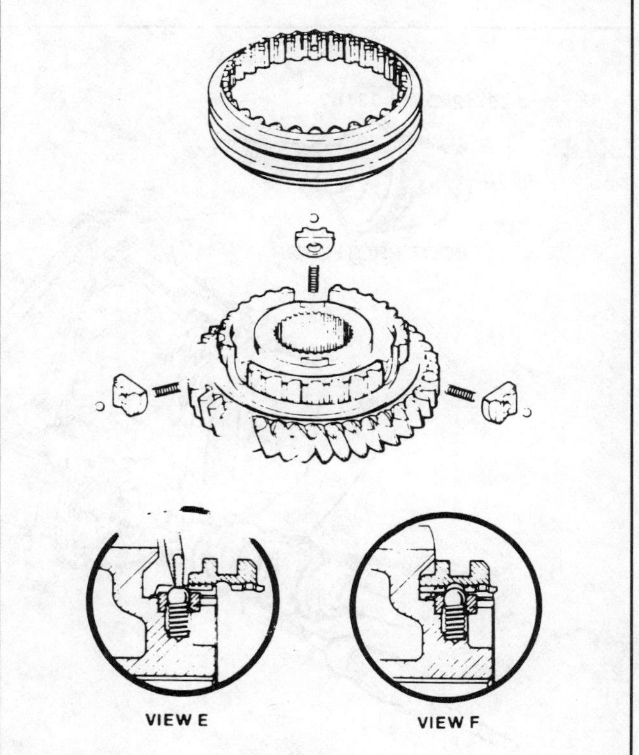

Fig. 61 Check the 5th gear synchronizer for distorted or cracked balls or springs

3. Inspect assemblies for worn or broken gear teeth, worn or broken keys and distorted or cracked balls and springs. If scuffed, nicked or burred condition can not be corrected with a soft stone or crocus cloth, replace the component.

ASSEMBLY

1. 1st–2nd gear synchro.
2. 3rd–4th gear synchro.
3. 5th gear synchro.

Halfshaft (Drive Axle)

The halfshaft assemblies used on the Fiero are the flexible units consisting of an inner Tri-Pod joint and an outer Constant Velocity (CV) joint. The inner joint is completely flexible, capable of up and down, in and out movement. The outer joint is only capable of up and down movement.

NOISE DIAGNOSIS

1. Clicking noise in turn: inspect for worn or damaged outer CV joint and outer dust boots.
2. Clunk when accelerating from coast to drive: inspect for worn or damaged outer CV joint.
3. Shudder or vibration during acceleration: inspect for excessive joint angle, excessive toe, incorrect trim height, worn or damaged outer CV joint and sticking spider assembly.
4. Vibration at highway speeds: inspect for out of balance rear tires or wheels, out of round tires or wheels, worn outer CV joint and binding or tight joint.

➡Some vehicles use a gray boot on the halfshaft axle joints. Use boot protector J-33162 on these boots. All other boots are made of thermoplastic material black and do not require use of a boot protector.

REMOVAL & INSTALLATION

See Figure 62

CAUTION

Use care when removing the halfshaft. Tri-pot joints can be damaged if the drive axle is over-extended. It is important to handle the halfshaft in a manner to prevent overextending.

1. Disconnect the negative (−) battery cable.
2. Raise the car and support with jackstands. Remove the wheel and tire.
3. Remove the hub nut by inserting a drift punch through the caliper into the rotor fins to hold the axle stationary.
4. Install a drive boot seal protector No. J-28712, or its equivalent, on the outer seal, if equipped with a gray boot.

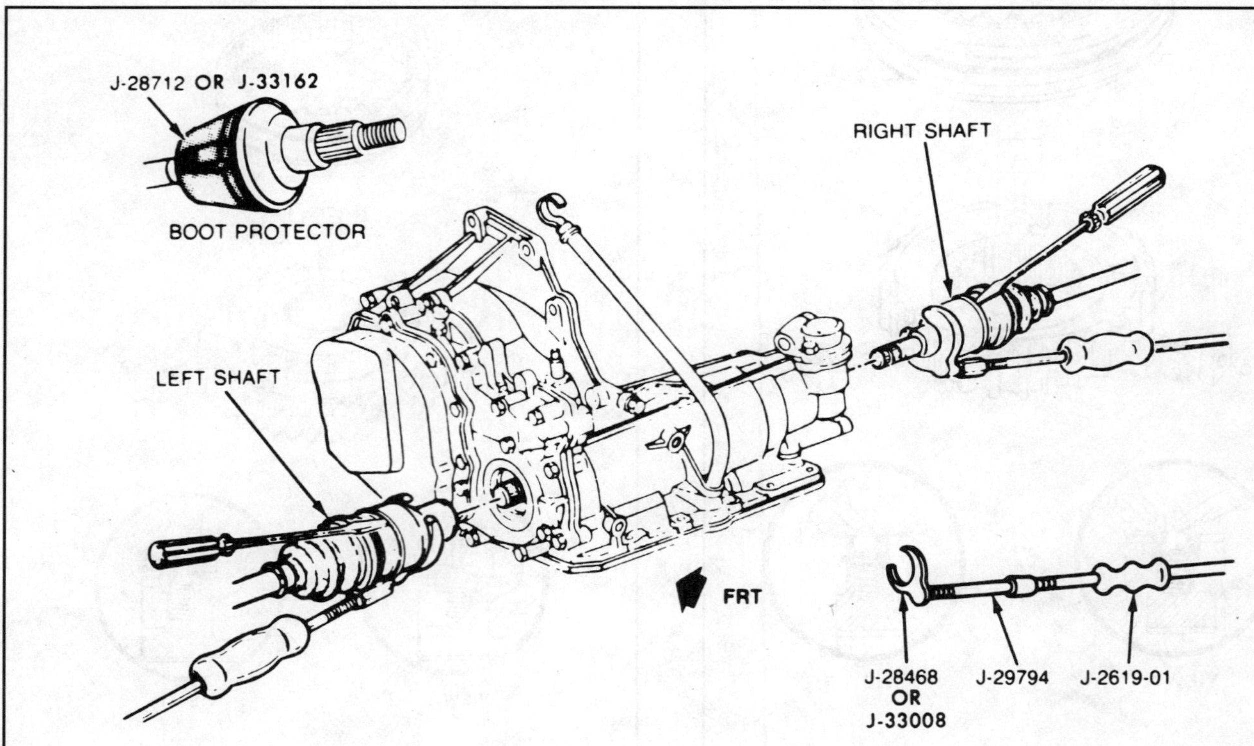

Fig. 62 Disengage the snaprings holding the halfshaft, then remove the drive axle from the transaxle

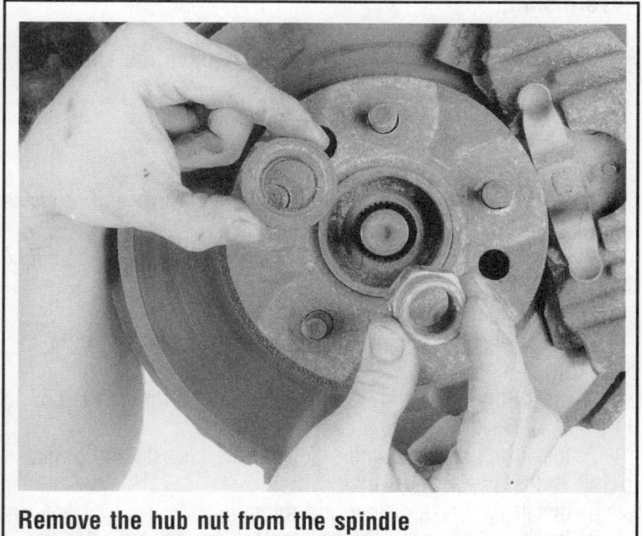

Remove the hub nut from the spindle

Remove the brake caliper assembly and support it with mechanics wire or a bungee cord

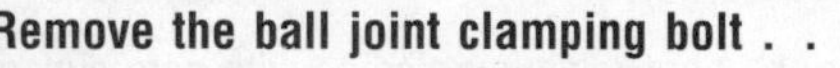

Remove the ball joint clamping bolt . . .

Install a puller on the hub assembly . . .

. . . then separate the control arm from the hub assembly

. . . then separate the hub assembly from the CV joint

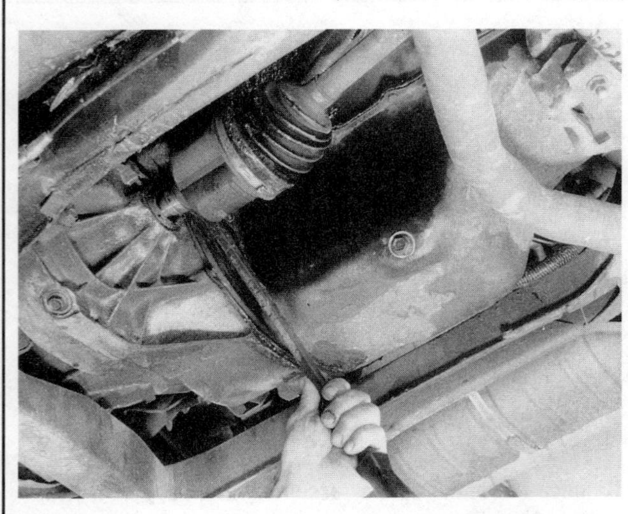
Gently pry the drive axle from the transaxle assembly

Remove the drive axle from the vehicle

5. Disconnect the toe link rod, trailing arm and lateral control arm at the knuckle assembly.
6. Remove the brake caliper and rotor.
7. Using tool No. J-28468 or its equivalent hub spindle remover, remove the halfshaft from the hub and bearing assembly.
8. Support the halfshaft with a piece of wire to the body.
9. Remove the clamp bolt from the lower control arm ball stud.
10. Separate the knuckle from the lower control arm.
11. Pull the strut, knuckle and caliper assembly away from the body and secure it in this position.
12. Using tool no. J-33008 and No. J-2619-01 or their equivalents, disengage the snaprings which are retaining the halfshaft at the transaxle, then remove the drive axle.

To install:

➡If the drive axle is being replaced, replace the knuckled seal.

1. Install the halfshaft seal protectors J-33162 for gray silicone boots.
2. Start the halfshaft into the transaxle and push until it snaps into place.
3. Coat the outer splines with anti-seize compound and align the hub with the halfshaft. Slide the splines into the hub.
4. Loosely install the strut mounting bolts.
5. Install the fixed adjusting link, lateral control arm through bolt. Torque the bolt to 37 ft. lbs. (50 Nm) +90°.
6. Install the trailing arm at the knuckle and torque the bolt to 44 ft. lbs. (60 Nm) +90°.
7. Install the strut mounting bolts at the knuckle and torque to 140 ft. lbs. (190 Nm).
8. Install the brake caliper and rotor.
9. Insert a drift punch through the caliper into the rotor fins to hold the rotor stationary. Torque the new hub nut and washer to 183–208 ft. lbs. (250–285 Nm).
10. Remove the halfshaft seal boot protector if used.
11. Install the wheel and tire assembly. Torque the lug nuts to 100 ft. lbs. (136 Nm).
12. Recheck all procedures to ensure proper installation and tightening. Road test vehicle to check for proper operation.

CV-JOINT OVERHAUL

Deflector Ring

See Figures 63, 64, 65 and 66

1. Use a brass drift to tap off deflector ring.
2. To install, use a 2½ in. pipe coupling and a piece of sheet metal to turn the deflector ring onto the joint as in Step 1.

Outer Joint Boot

1. Cut and remove the boot retaining clamps with wire cutters.
2. Remove the race retaining ring with snapring pliers. Remove the joint and boot assembly from the axle shaft. Refer to Step 2 of the CV joint procedures.
3. Flush the grease from the joint and repack the boot with half of the grease provided with the new boot.
4. Install the new boot and clamps first. Second, install the joint and snap the race retaining ring into place. Put the remainder of the grease into the joint.
5. Using an axle seal clamp tool J-35910 and a torque wrench, torque the small clamp to 100 ft. lbs. (136 Nm). Torque the large clamps to 130 ft. lbs. (176 Nm).

Outer Joint Assembly

1. Remove the large boot clamp and joint assembly from the axle as previously mentioned. Clean out the grease from the joint to aid in disassembly.
2. Use a brass drift to gently tap on the cage until tilted

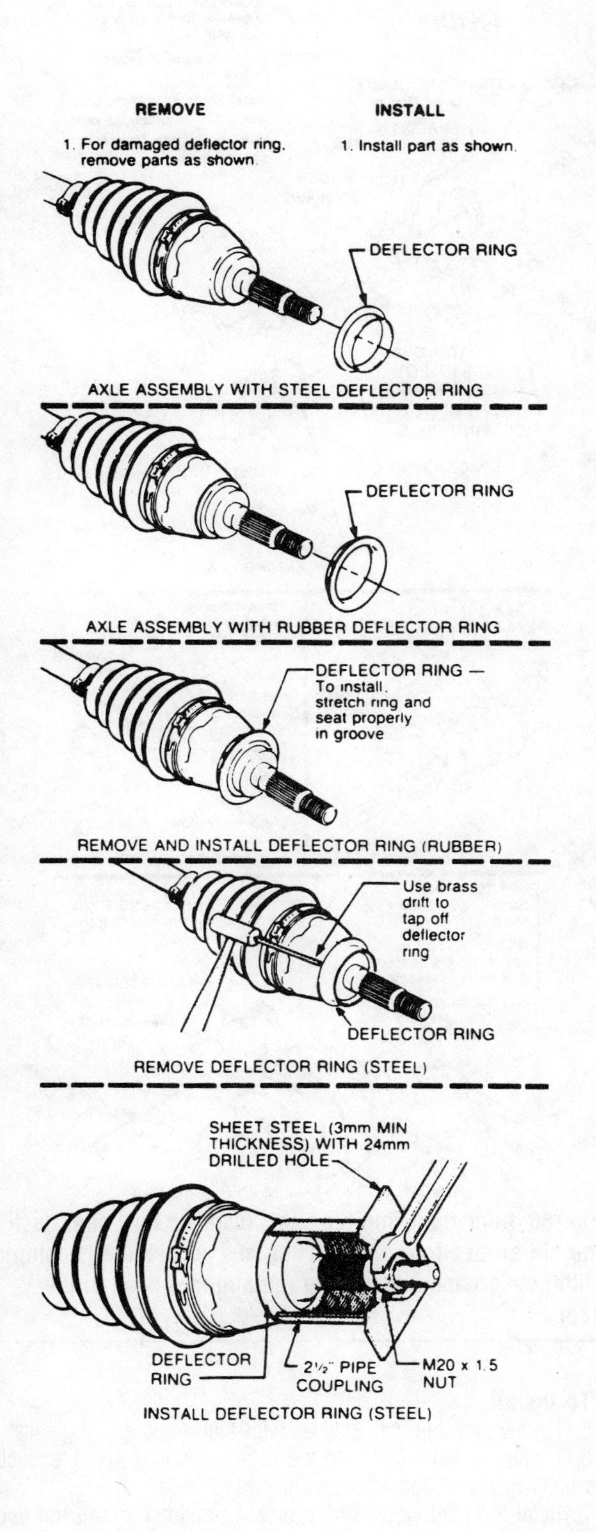

Fig. 63 Follow the illustration for removal and installation the deflector ring

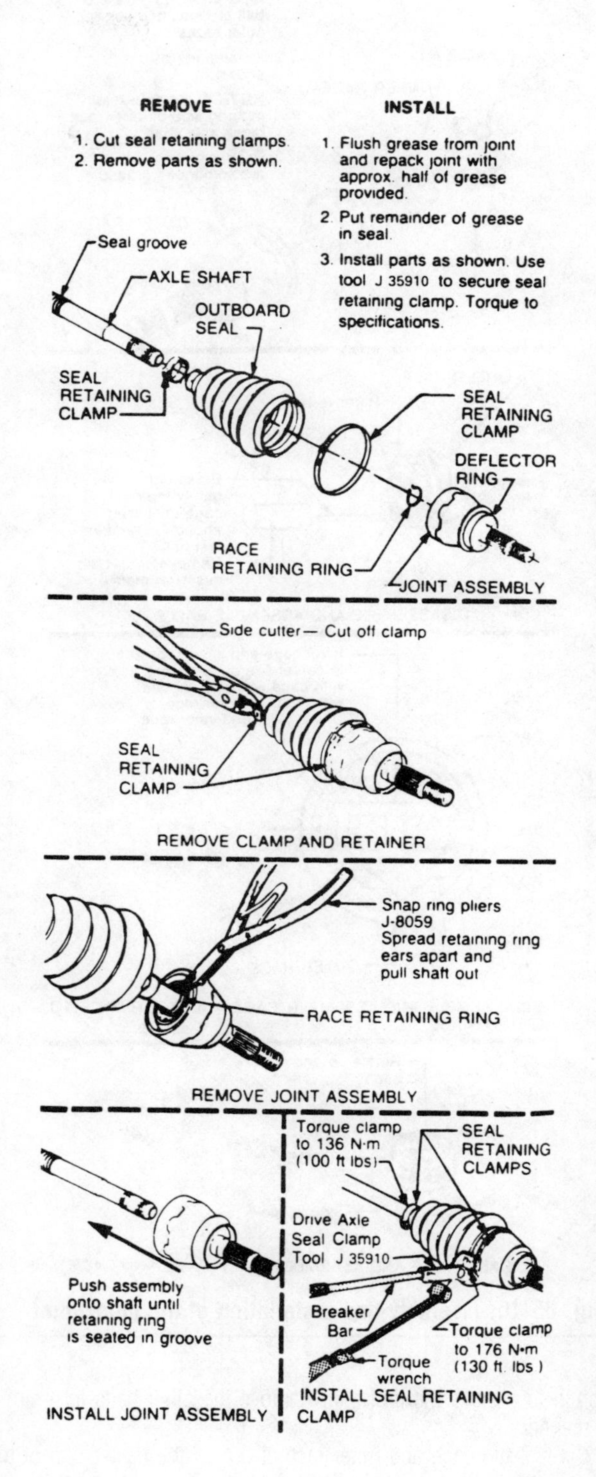

Fig. 64 Use a pair of side cutters to remove the clamp and retainers when disassembling the seal

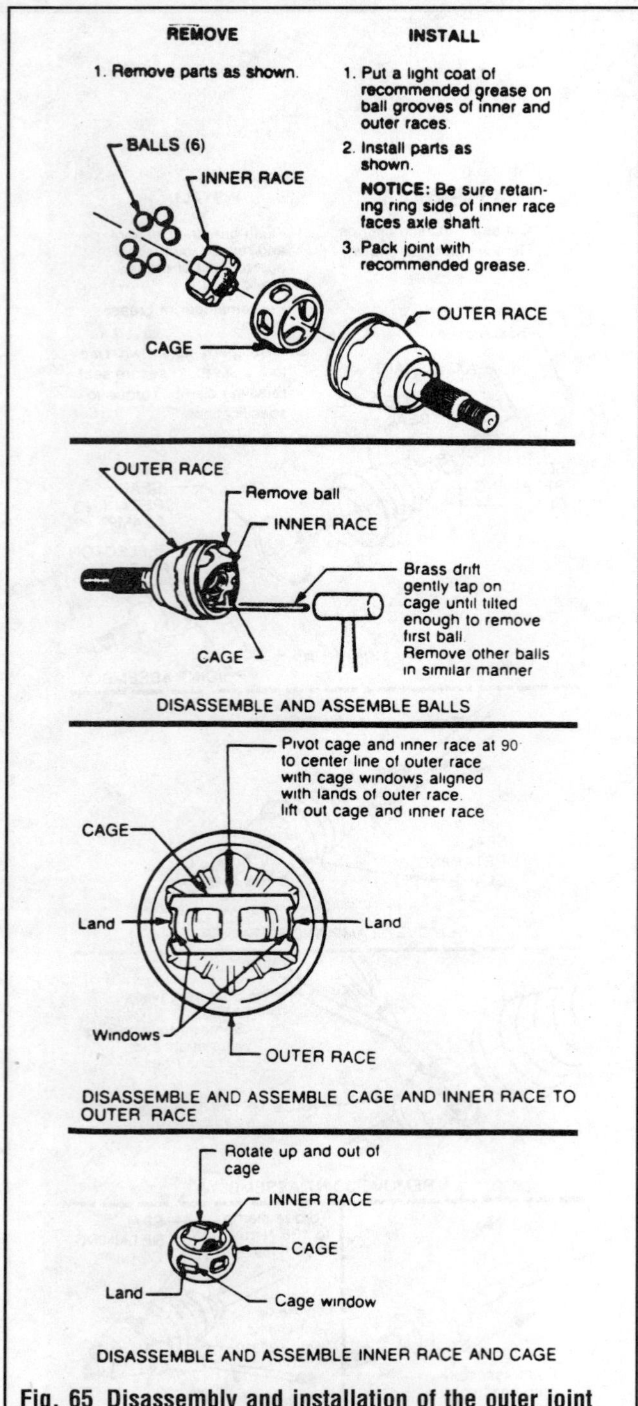

Fig. 65 Disassembly and installation of the outer joint

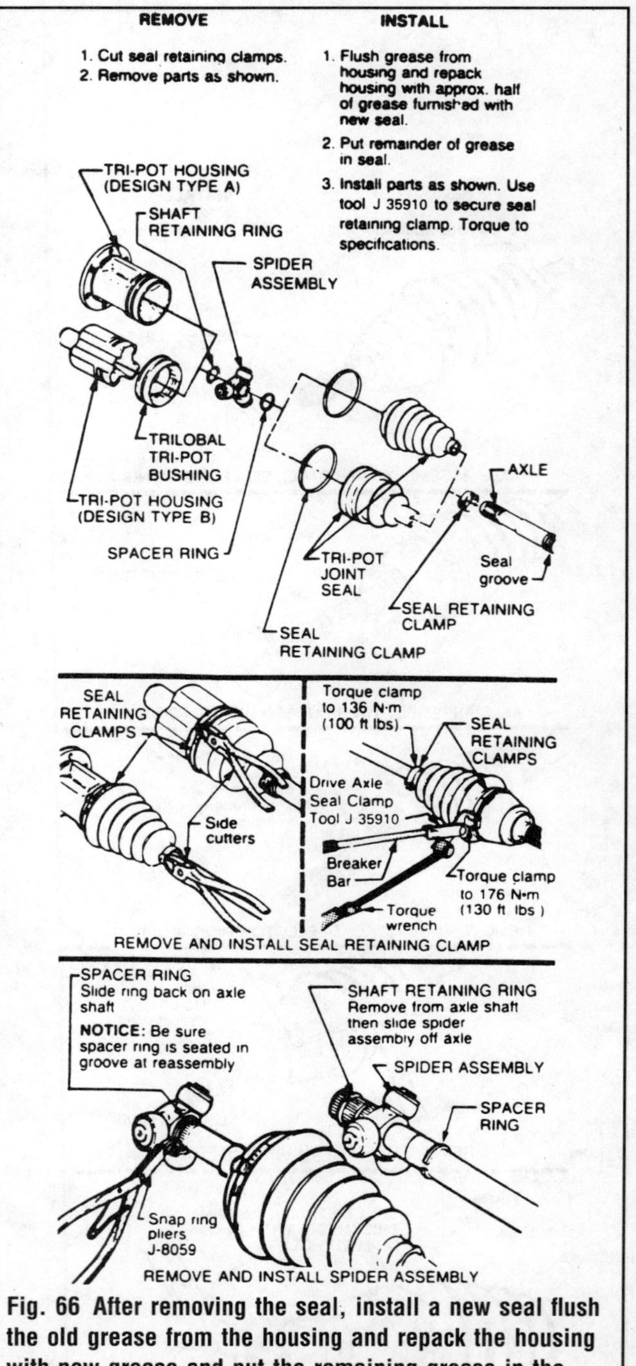

Fig. 66 After removing the seal, install a new seal flush the old grease from the housing and repack the housing with new grease and put the remaining grease in the seal

enough to remove the first ball. Remove the other balls in a simular manner.

3. Pivot the cage and inner race at 90° to the center line of the outer race with the cage windows aligned with the lands of the outer race. Lift the cage out with the inner race. Refer to Step 3 of the CV joint procedures.

4. Rotate the inner race up and out of the cage as in Step 2. Clean all parts with solvent and blow dry with compressed air.

To install:

5. Lightly coat the ball grooves with the provided CV grease.

6. Install the inner race into the cage, cage into the outer race and balls into the cage as removed.

7. Refill the joint with half the grease provided. Install the boot and clamps. Install the joint onto the axle. Fill the joint with the remaining grease and torque the clamps as in the previous procedure.

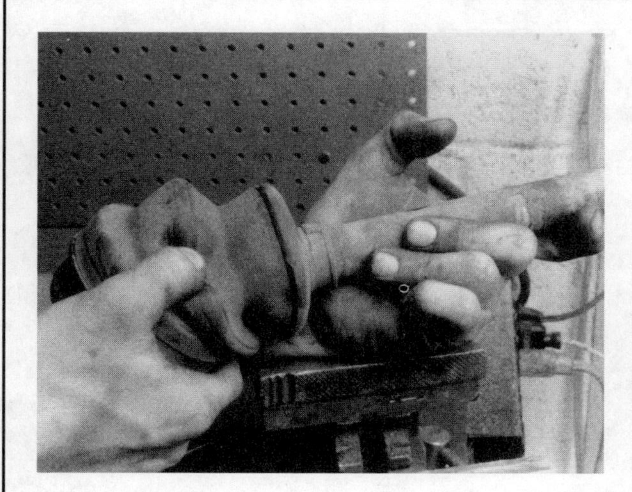
Check the CV-boot for wear

Removing the CV-boot from the joint housing

Removing the outer band from the CV-boot

Clean the CV-joint housing prior to removing boot

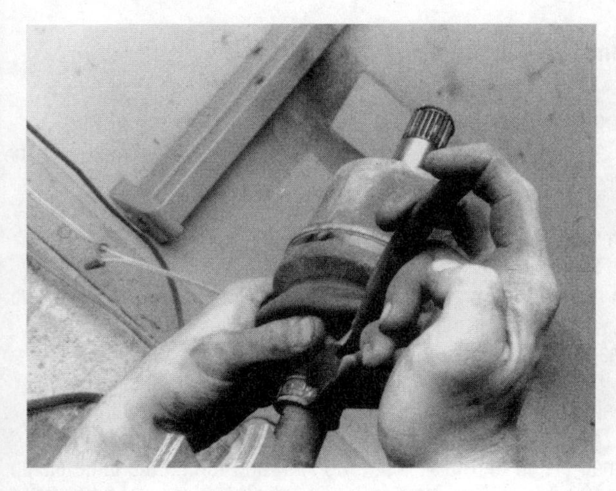
Removing the inner band from the CV-boot

Removing the CV-joint housing assembly

Removing the CV-joint

Checking the CV-joint snapring for wear

Inspecting the CV-joint housing

CV-joint snapring (typical)

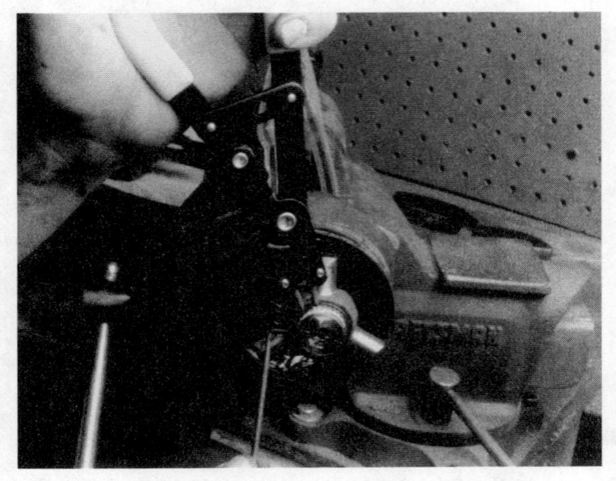
Removing the CV-joint outer snapring

Inner Tri-Pod Boot

1. Cut the clamps from the boot.
2. Remove the axle from the Tri-Pod housing as in Step 4.
3. Remove the spider assembly from the axle by removing the shaft retaining snaprings.
4. Clean all metal parts with solvent and blow dry with compressed air.

To install:

5. Refill the housing with half of the grease provided with the new boot. Install the boot and clamps first, then the spider and snapring assembly onto the axle.
6. Position the axle into the Tri-Pod housing. Install the remaining grease into the joint.
7. Using a seal clamp tool J-35910 or equivalent, torque the small clamp to 100 ft. lbs. (136 Nm) and torque the large clamp to 130 ft. lbs. (176 Nm) as in Step 4. Side cutters can be used to tighten the boot clamps, but care must be used so not to cut the new clamps.

CLUTCH

Understanding the Clutch

⁂ CAUTION

The clutch driven disc may contain asbestos, which has been determined to be a cancer causing agent. Never clean clutch surfaces with compressed air! Avoid inhaling any dust from any clutch surface! When cleaning clutch surfaces, use a commercially available brake cleaning fluid.

The purpose of the clutch is to disconnect and connect engine power at the transaxle. A vehicle at rest requires a lot of engine torque to get all that weight moving. An internal combustion engine does not develop a high starting torque (unlike steam engines) so it must be allowed to operate without any load until it builds up enough torque to move the vehicle. Torque increases with engine rpm. The clutch allows the engine to build up torque by physically disconnecting the engine from the transaxle, relieving the engine of any load or resistance.

The transfer of engine power to the transaxle (the load) must be smooth and gradual; if it weren't, drive line components would wear out or break quickly. This gradual power transfer is made possible by gradually releasing the clutch pedal. The clutch disc and pressure plate are the connecting link between the engine and transaxle. When the clutch pedal is released, the disc and plate contact each other (the clutch is engaged) physically joining the engine and transaxle. When the pedal is pushed inward, the disc and plate separate (the clutch is disengaged) disconnecting the engine from the transaxle.

Most clutches utilize a single plate, dry friction disc with a diaphragm-style spring pressure plate. The clutch disc has a splined hub which attaches the disc to the input shaft. The disc has friction material where it contacts the flywheel and pressure plate. Torsion springs on the disc help absorb engine torque pulses. The pressure plate applies pressure to the clutch disc, holding it tight against the surface of the flywheel. The clutch operating mechanism consists of a release bearing, fork and cylinder assembly.

The release fork and actuating linkage transfer pedal motion to the release bearing. In the engaged position (pedal released) the diaphragm spring holds the pressure plate against the clutch disc, so engine torque is transmitted to the input shaft. When the

Troubleshooting Basic Clutch Problems

Problem	Cause
Excessive clutch noise	Throwout bearing noises are more audible at the lower end of pedal travel. The usual causes are: • Riding the clutch • Too little pedal free-play • Lack of bearing lubrication A bad clutch shaft pilot bearing will make a high pitched squeal, when the clutch is disengaged and the transmission is in gear or within the first 2" of pedal travel. The bearing must be replaced. Noise from the clutch linkage is a clicking or snapping that can be heard or felt as the pedal is moved completely up or down. This usually requires lubrication. Transmitted engine noises are amplified by the clutch housing and heard in the passenger compartment. They are usually the result of insufficient pedal free-play and can be changed by manipulating the clutch pedal.
Clutch slips (the car does not move as it should when the clutch is engaged)	This is usually most noticeable when pulling away from a standing start. A severe test is to start the engine, apply the brakes, shift into high gear and SLOWLY release the clutch pedal. A healthy clutch will stall the engine. If it slips it may be due to: • A worn pressure plate or clutch plate • Oil soaked clutch plate • Insufficient pedal free-play
Clutch drags or fails to release	The clutch disc and some transmission gears spin briefly after clutch disengagement. Under normal conditions in average temperatures, 3 seconds is maximum spin-time. Failure to release properly can be caused by: • Too light transmission lubricant or low lubricant level • Improperly adjusted clutch linkage
Low clutch life	Low clutch life is usually a result of poor driving habits or heavy duty use. Riding the clutch, pulling heavy loads, holding the car on a grade with the clutch instead of the brakes and rapid clutch engagement all contribute to low clutch life.

clutch pedal is depressed, the release bearing pushes the diaphragm spring center toward the flywheel. The diaphragm spring pivots the fulcrum, relieving the load on the pressure plate. Steel spring straps riveted to the clutch cover lift the pressure plate from the clutch disc, disengaging the engine drive from transaxle and enabling the gears to be changed.

The clutch is operating properly if:

1. It will stall the engine when released with the vehicle held stationary.
2. The shift lever can be moved freely between 1st and reverse gears when the vehicle is stationary and the clutch disengaged.

CLUTCH ADJUSTMENT

The clutch release system is operated by hydraulic pressure and consists of a clutch pedal, master cylinder, slave cylinder and hose assemblies. The hydraulic clutch system locates the clutch pedal and provides automatic clutch adjustment. No adjustment of the clutch linkage or pedal position is required.

Driven Disc and Pressure Plate

REMOVAL & INSTALLATION

➧ See Figure 67

⁂ CAUTION

The clutch driven disc contains asbestos, which has been determined to be a cancer causing agent. Never clean the clutch surfaces with compressed air! Avoid inhaling any dust from any clutch surface! When cleaning the clutch surfaces, use a commercially available brake cleaning fluid.

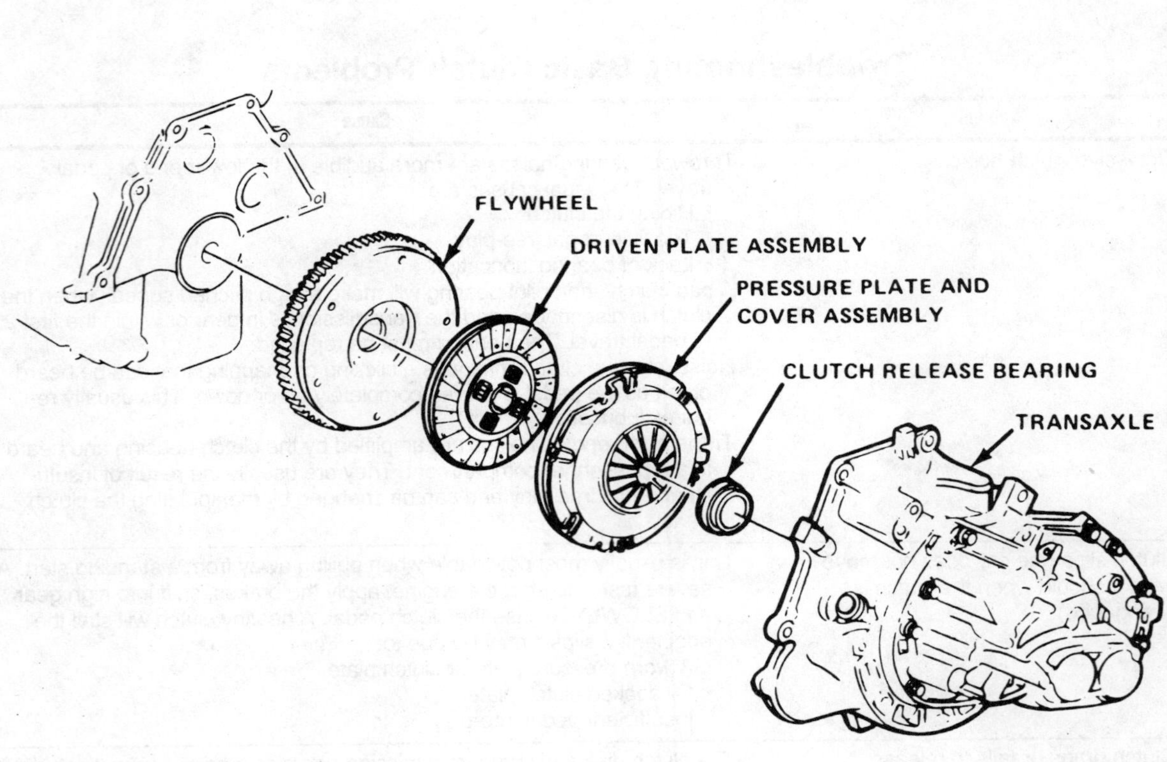

Fig. 67 Exploded view of the clutch assembly

1. Disconnect the negative (−) battery cable.
2. Remove the transaxle as outlined in the "Transaxle" removal procedures in this section.
3. Mark the pressure plate assembly and flywheel so that they can be assembled in the same position. They were balanced as an assembly at the factory.
4. Loosen the pressure plate attaching bolts one turn at a time until spring tension is relieved.
5. Support the pressure plate and remove the bolts. Remove the pressure plate and clutch disc. Do not disassemble the pressure plate assembly; replace it if it is defective.

To install:

6. Inspect the flywheel, clutch disc, pressure plate, release bearing and the clutch fork and pivot shaft assembly for wear. Replace the parts as required. If the flywheel shows any signs of overheating, or if it badly grooved or scored, it should be resurfaced or replaced.

Clutch plate and pressure plate installed with the alignment arbor in place

Install a clutch alignment arbor, to align the clutch assembly during installation

Pressure plate-to-flywheel bolt holes should align

Clutch plate installed with the arbor in place

You may want to use a thread locking compound on the clutch assembly bolts

➡After spending all this time to remove the transaxle and clutch assembly, you do not want to reinstall used parts that will fail after a short time. It is recommended that when servicing the clutch, replace the pressure plate, clutch disc and release bearing as an assembly. Also check the flywheel for burning or scoring, if these conditions exist have the flywheel resurfaced or replaced. Remanufactured clutch components can be purchased at your local parts distributor at a fraction of the cost of new.

7. Clean the pressure plate and flywheel mating surfaces thoroughly. Place the clutch disc and pressure plate into the installed position, and support with a dummy (pilot) shaft or clutch aligning tool. The clutch plate is aligned with the damper springs offset towards the transaxle. One side of the factory supplied clutch disc is stamped "Flywheel Slide".
8. Install the pressure plate-to-flywheel bolts and tighten them gradually in a criss-cross pattern. The final torque specification for the pressure plate-to-flywheel attaching bolts is 15 ft. lbs. (20 Nm).
9. Lubricate the outside groove and the inside recess of the release bearing with high temperature grease. Wipe off any excess. Install the release bearing.
10. Install the transaxle input shaft into the clutch disc by aligning the splines of the input shaft to the splines of the clutch disc. If the splines will not align, the input shaft may have to be turned or the clutch disc may have to be realigned with the pilot shaft.

WARNING

Do NOT try to draw the transaxle to the engine by the use of the transaxle to engine mounting bolts. If there is a gap between the two housings, damage to the transaxle and clutch disc may result if the housings are forced together. Realign the clutch disc with the pilot shaft and repeat the procedures until the two housings come together.

11. Finish installing the transaxle as outlined in the "Transaxle" installation procedures in this section.

Clutch Master Cylinder

REMOVAL & INSTALLATION

See Figure 68

1. Disconnect the negative (−) battery cable.
2. Disconnect the cylinder pushrod at the clutch pedal.
3. Disconnect and plug the hydraulic line at the master cylinder.
4. Remove the nuts attaching the cylinder to the cowl, then remove the cylinder.

To install:

1. Position the cylinder pushrod through the cowl and loosely install the cylinder-to-cowl nuts.
2. Connect the cylinder pushrod to the clutch pedal with the spring clip.
3. Tighten the cylinder-to-cowl nuts to 13 ft. lbs. (17 Nm).
4. Connect the hydraulic line to the master cylinder and torque it to 13 ft. lbs. (17 Nm).
5. Fill the clutch master cylinder with the recommended fluid.

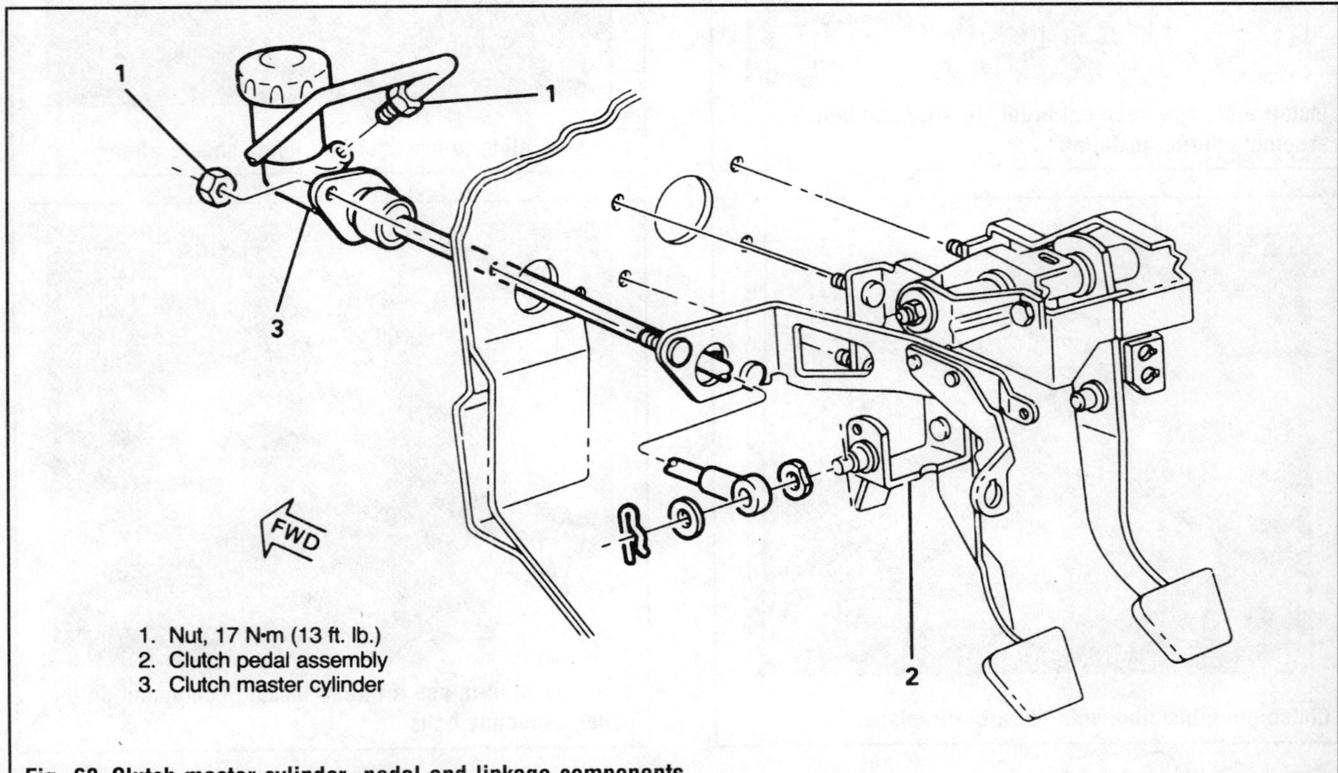

Fig. 68 Clutch master cylinder, pedal and linkage components

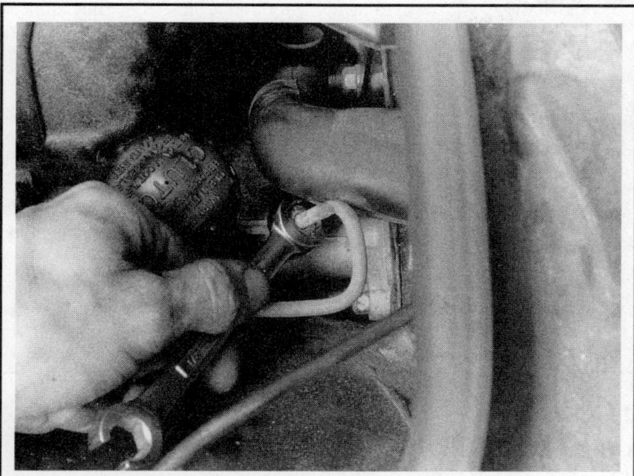
Use a flare nut wrench to loosen the clutch master cylinder hydraulic line . . .

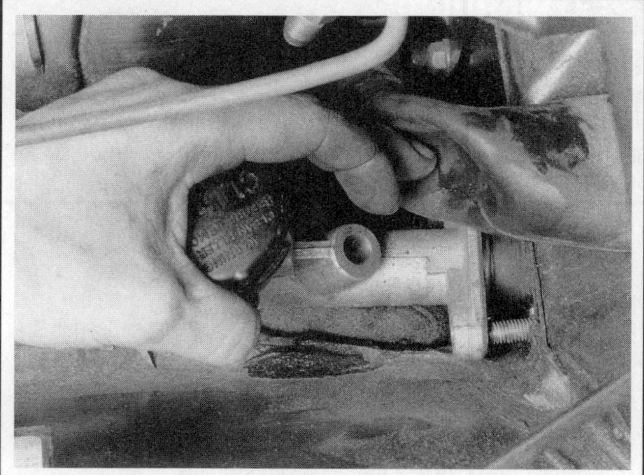
. . . then remove the clutch master cylinder from the vehicle

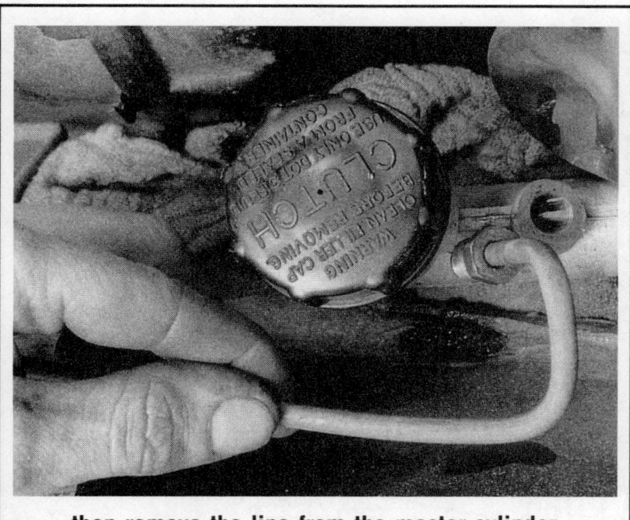

. . . then remove the line from the master cylinder

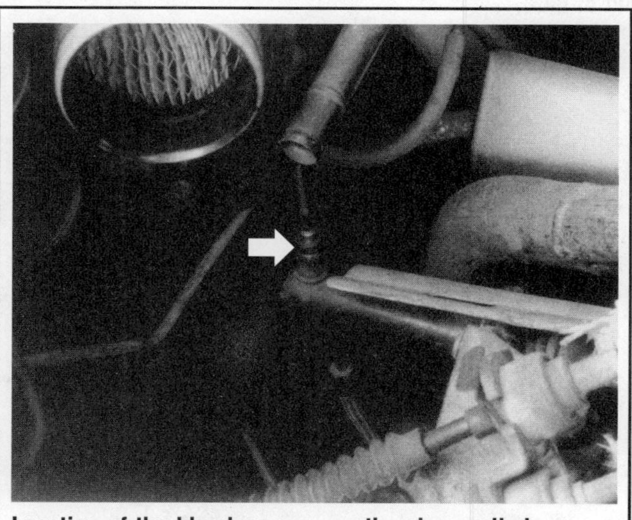
Location of the bleeder screw on the slave cylinder

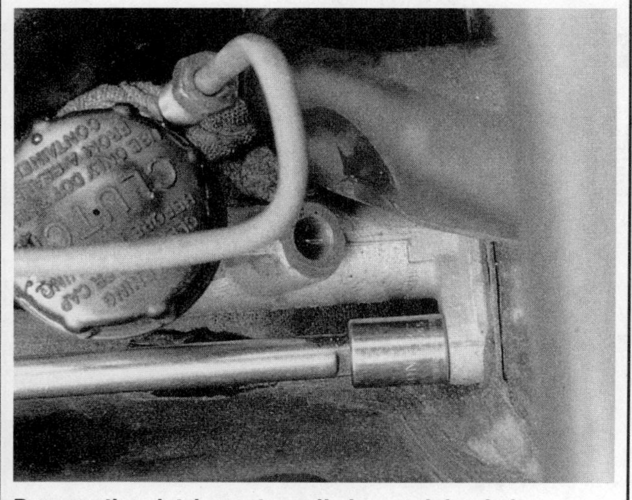
Remove the clutch master cylinder retaining bolts . . .

Attach a clear piece of plastic hose to the slave cylinder bleeder screw and submerge the other end in a container of brake fluid

✱✱ WARNING

Do not use mineral or parafin base oils in the clutch hydraulic system. These fluids may cause damage to the internal rubber parts. When adding fluid to the system after service operations use GM Delco Supreme No. 11 brake fluid or an equivalent fluid that meets DOT 3 specifications.

Clutch System Bleeding:

6. When the hydraulic portion of the clutch system has been opened, air enters the system and has to be removed before proper operation can be restored. Use the following procedures to bleed the clutch hydraulic system.

a. Fill the fluid reservoir directly from a can of unused Delco Supreme No. 11 brake fluid or equivalent. Do not use the old fluid because old fluid is contaminated with moisture and dirt which may damage the hydraulic system.

➡Make sure the fluid reservoir is kept full of fluid. If not, air will be pulled into the system when the reservoir runs out of fluid.

b. Remove the floor mat or any other object that may obstruct the full stroke of the clutch pedal.

c. Unscrew the bleeder screw at the slave cylinder enough to allow fluid to be pumped out (½–1 full turn).

d. Push the clutch pedal down through the full stroke.

e. Have an assistant close the bleeder while the pedal is still fully extended. Allow the pedal to return quickly to its stop (with the bleeder Closed).

f. Repeat this procedure until no air bubbles can be seen in the fluid.

OVERHAUL

Disassembly

➧ See Figure 69

1. Unscrew the filler cap and drain the excess fluid.
2. Pull back the dust cover.
3. Remove the circlip together with the retaining washer and pushrod.

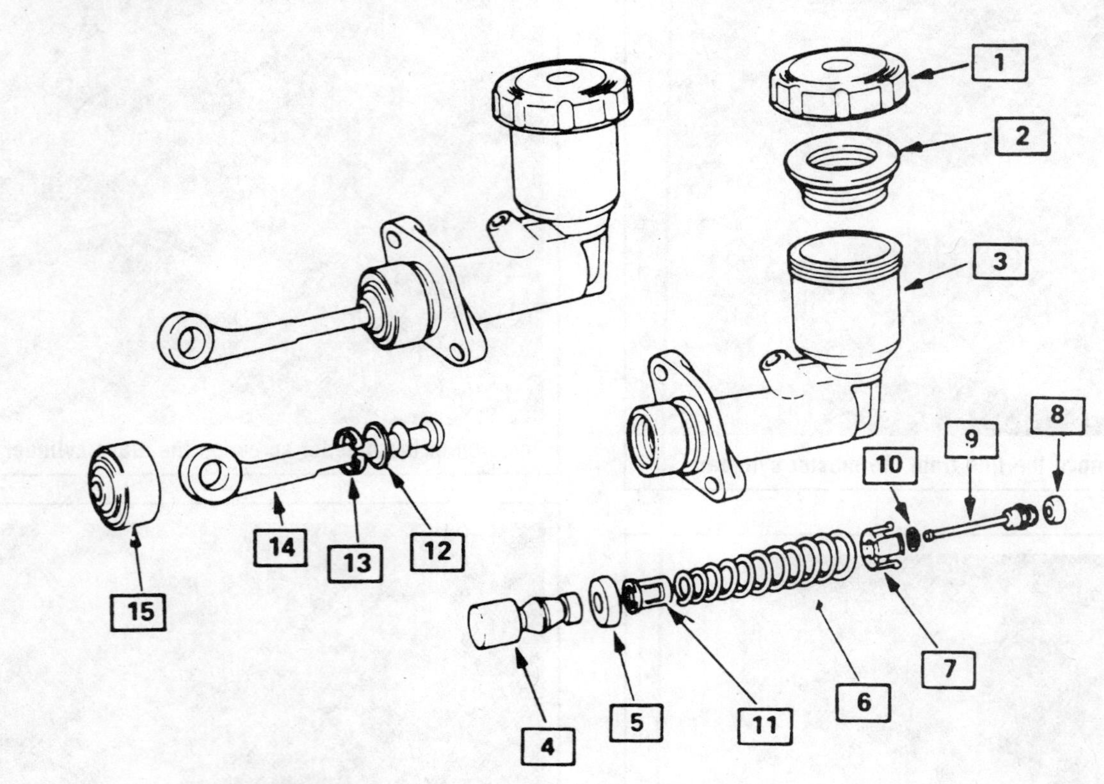

1. Reserve cap
2. Baffle*
3. Cyllinder body and reservoir assembly
4. Plunger
5. Seal*
6. Spring
7. Valve spacer
8. Center valve seal*
9. Valve stem
10. Spring
11. Spring retainer
12. Retaining washer
13. Circlip*
14. Push rod
15. Dust cover*

*Parts included in service kit

Fig. 69 Exploded view of the clutch master cylinder components

4. Shake the cylinder to eject the plunger assembly.
5. Remove the spring and retainer from the plunger. Compress the spring to free the valve stem from the key hole of the spring retainer.

➡Remove the seal carefully from the plunger not to damage the plunger surfaces.

Assembly

1. Replace all serviceable seals and parts. Clean the remaining parts thoroughly with denatured alcohol and place them on a clean piece of paper. Examine the bore of the cylinder for visible signs of scores and ridges. If these conditions are excessive, the cylinder will have to be replaced.
2. Install the plunger seal to plunger.
3. Fit the valve seal with the smallest diameter leading to the valve head.
4. Position the spring washer on the valve stem so that it flares away from the valve stem shoulder. Then install the valve spacer and springs.
5. Fit the spring retainer to the spring and compress the spring until the valve stem passes through the key hole slot and engages in the center.
6. Lubricate the seal with DOT 3 brake fluid and insert the plunger into the cylinder with the valve end leading.
7. Position the pushrod and retaining washer into the cylinder and secure the circlip.
8. Lubricate the inside of the dust seal with Silicone Lubricant No. 5459912 or equivalent and install the dust seal.
9. Install the filler cap and remount the cylinder assembly to vehicle as outlined in the previous section. Bleed the system as outlined in the "Clutch System Bleeding" procedures in this section.

Clutch Slave Cylinder

➡Prior to any vehicle service that requires removal of the slave cylinder, the master cylinder pushrod must be disconnected from the clutch pedal. If it is not disconnected, permanent damage to the slave cylinder will occur if the clutch pedal is depressed while the slave cylinder is disconnected.

REMOVAL & INSTALLATION

➧ See Figure 70

1. Disconnect the negative (−) battery cable.
2. Disconnect and plug the hydraulic line at the slave cylinder.
3. Remove the slave cylinder-to-bracket bolts, and remove the slave cylinder.

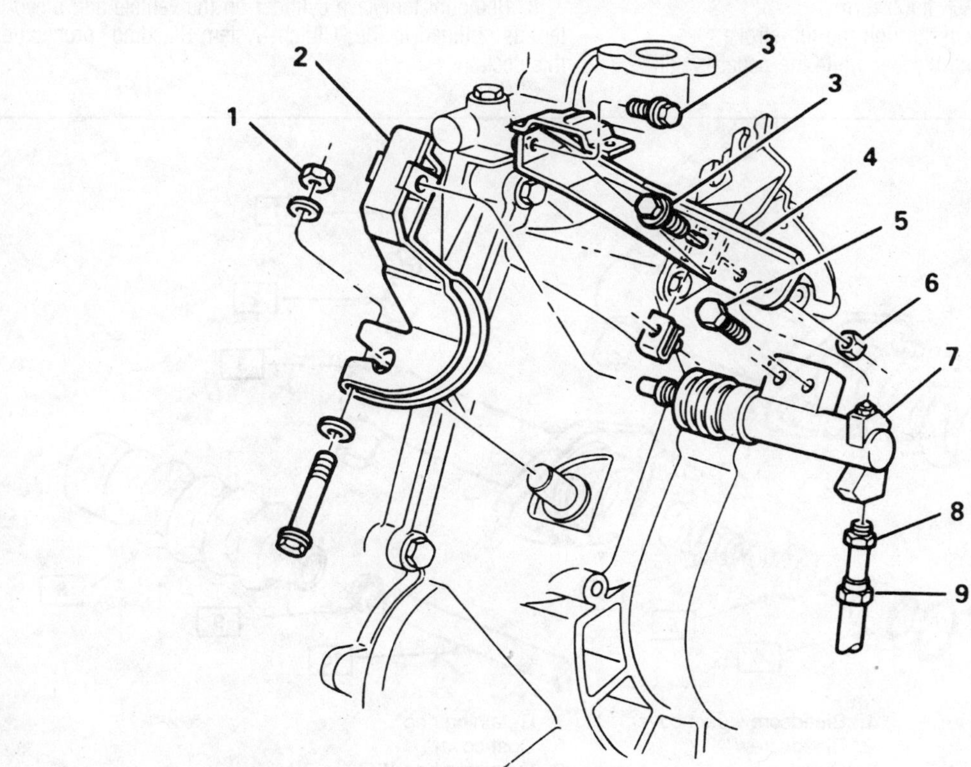

1. Nut, 38 N•m (28 ft. lb.)
2. Clutch lever
3. Bolt—50 N•m (32 ft. lb.)
4. Bracket
5. Bolt—27 N•m (20 ft. lb.)
6. Nut—22 N•m (16 ft. lb.)
7. Slave cylinder
8. Nut—17 N•m (13 ft. lb.)
9. Pipe & hose assembly

Fig. 70 Tighten the clutch slave cylinder retainers to the specifications in the illustration

To install:

1. Place the slave cylinder at the mounting bracket and position the cylinder pushrod into the clutch release lever.
2. Install the slave cylinder-to-bracket nuts and tighten them to 16 ft. lbs. (22 Nm).
3. Install the hydraulic line to the slave cylinder and tighten it to 13 ft. lbs. (17 Nm).
4. Fill the clutch master cylinder with the recommended brake fluid and bleed the system as follows.

CLUTCH SYSTEM BLEEDING

When the hydraulic portion of the clutch system has been opened, air enters the system and has to be removed before proper operation can be restored. Use the following procedures to bleed the clutch hydraulic system.

1. Fill the fluid reservoir directly from a can of unused Delco Supreme No. 11 brake fluid or equivalent. Do not use the old fluid because old fluid is contaminated with moisture and dirt which may damage the hydraulic system.

➡Make sure the fluid reservoir is kept full of fluid. If not, air will be pulled into the system when the reservoir runs out of fluid.

2. Remove the floor mat or any other object that may obstruct the full stroke of the clutch pedal.
3. Unscrew the bleeder screw at the slave cylinder enough to allow fluid to be pumped out (½–1 full turn).
4. Push the clutch pedal down through the full stroke.
5. Have an assistant close the bleeder while the pedal is still fully extended. Allow the pedal to return quickly to its stop (with the bleeder Closed).
6. Repeat this procedure until no air bubbles can be seen in the fluid.

➡It is extremely important that cleanliness be maintained throughout the bleeding operation.

OVERHAUL

See Figure 71

1. Remove the slave cylinder from the vehicle as outlined in the previous section.
2. Pull the dust cover back and remove the circlip together with the retaining ring and pushrod.
3. Shake the cylinder to remove the piston and seal.

To install:

4. Replace all serviceable seals and parts. Clean the remaining parts thoroughly with denatured alcohol and place them on a clean piece of paper. Examine the bore of the cylinder for visible signs of scores and ridges. If these conditions are excessive, the cylinder will have to be replaced.
5. Lubricate the seal and piston bore with unused DOT 3 brake fluid and insert the seal and piston assembly into the cylinder.
6. Install the pushrod and secure with the circlip.
7. Coat the inside of the dust cover with Silicone Lubricant No. 5459912 or equivalent. Install the dust cover onto the cylinder housing end.
8. Remount the slave cylinder on the vehicle and bleed the system as outlined in the "Clutch System Bleeding" procedures in this section.

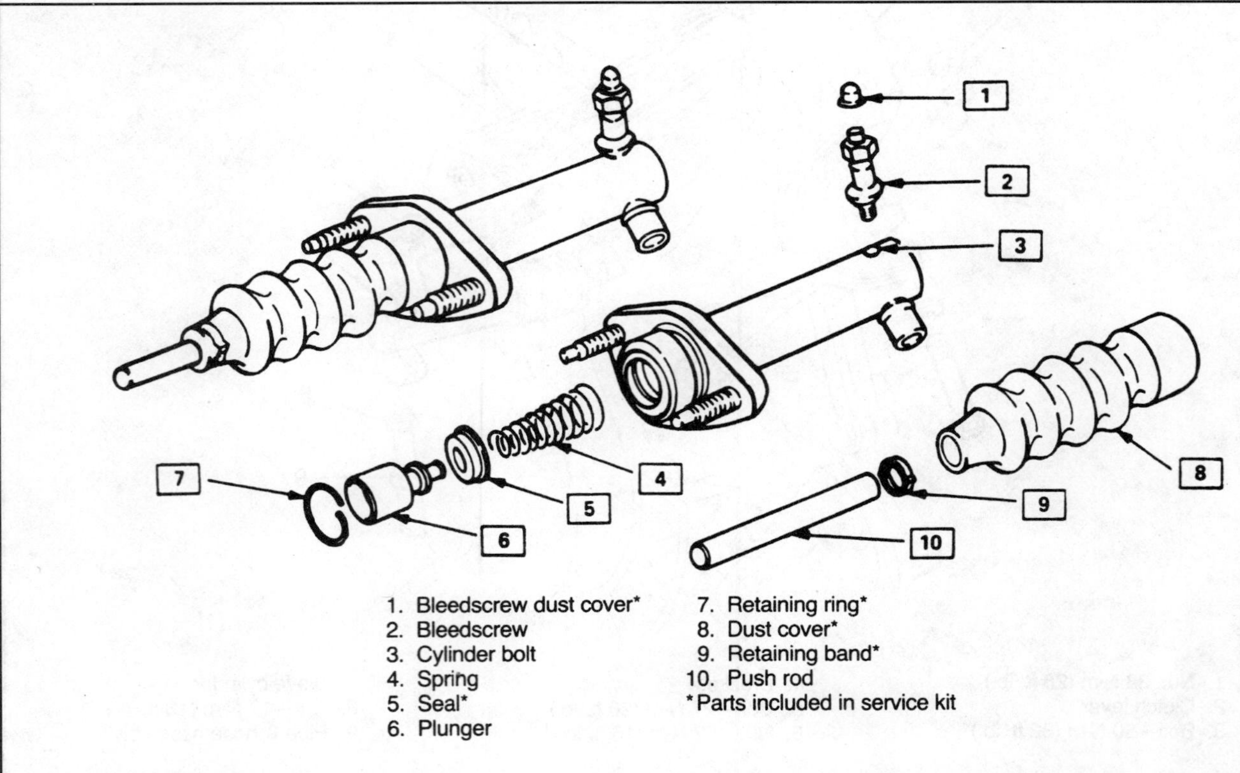

Fig. 71 Exploded view of the clutch slave cylinder components

AUTOMATIC TRANSAXLE

Understanding Automatic Transmissions

The automatic transmission allows engine torque and power to be transmitted to the rear wheels within a narrow range of engine operating speeds. It will allow the engine to turn fast enough to produce plenty of power and torque at very low speeds, while keeping it at a sensible rpm at high vehicle speeds (and it does this job without driver assistance). The transmission uses a light fluid as the medium for the transmission of power. This fluid also works in the operation of various hydraulic control circuits and as a lubricant. Because the transmission fluid performs all of these functions, trouble within the unit can easily travel from one part to another. For this reason, and because of the complexity and unusual operating principles of the transmission, a very sound understanding of the basic principles of operation will simplify troubleshooting.

TORQUE CONVERTER

The torque converter replaces the conventional clutch. It has three functions:

1. It allows the engine to idle with the vehicle at a standstill, even with the transmission in gear.
2. It allows the transmission to shift from range-to-range smoothly, without requiring that the driver close the throttle during the shift.
3. It multiplies engine torque to an increasing extent as vehicle speed drops and throttle opening is increased. This has the effect of making the transmission more responsive and reduces the amount of shifting required.

The torque converter is a metal case which is shaped like a sphere that has been flattened on opposite sides. It is bolted to the rear end of the engine's crankshaft. Generally, the entire metal case rotates at engine speed and serves as the engine's flywheel.

The case contains three sets of blades. One set is attached directly to the case. This set forms the torus or pump. Another set is directly connected to the output shaft, and forms the turbine. The third set is mounted on a hub which, in turn, is mounted on a stationary shaft through a one-way clutch. This third set is known as the stator.

A pump, which is driven by the converter hub at engine speed, keeps the torque converter full of transmission fluid at all times. Fluid flows continuously through the unit to provide cooling.

Under low speed acceleration, the torque converter functions as follows:

The torus is turning faster than the turbine. It picks up fluid at the center of the converter and, through centrifugal force, slings it outward. Since the outer edge of the converter moves faster than the portions at the center, the fluid picks up speed.

The fluid then enters the outer edge of the turbine blades. It then travels back toward the center of the converter case along the turbine blades. In impinging upon the turbine blades, the fluid loses the energy picked up in the torus.

If the fluid was now returned directly into the torus, both halves of the converter would have to turn at approximately the same speed at all times, and torque input and output would both be the same.

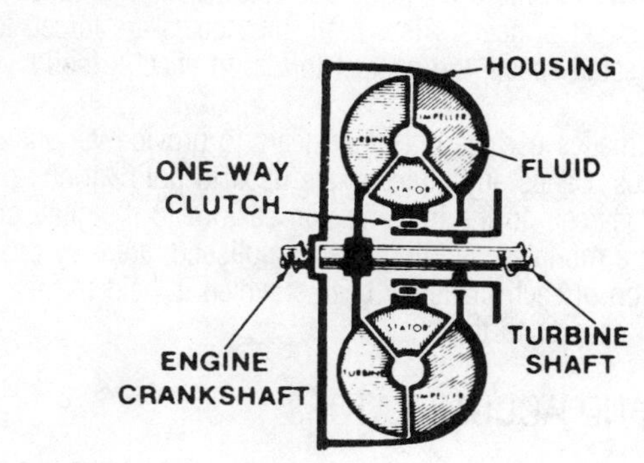

The torque converter housing is rotated by the engine's crankshaft, and turns the impeller—The impeller then spins the turbine, which gives motion to the turbine shaft, driving the gears

In flowing through the torus and turbine, the fluid picks up two types of flow, or flow in two separate directions. It flows through the turbine blades, and it spins with the engine. The stator, whose blades are stationary when the vehicle is being accelerated at low speeds, converts one type of flow into another. Instead of allowing the fluid to flow straight back into the torus, the stator's curved blades turn the fluid almost 90° toward the direction of rotation of the engine. Thus the fluid does not flow as fast toward the torus, but is already spinning when the torus picks it up. This has the effect of allowing the torus to turn much faster than the turbine. This difference in speed may be compared to the difference in speed between the smaller and larger gears in any gear train. The result is that engine power output is higher, and engine torque is multiplied.

As the speed of the turbine increases, the fluid spins faster and faster in the direction of engine rotation. As a result, the ability of the stator to redirect the fluid flow is reduced. Under cruising conditions, the stator is eventually forced to rotate on its one-way clutch in the direction of engine rotation. Under these conditions, the torque converter begins to behave almost like a solid shaft, with the torus and turbine speeds being almost equal.

PLANETARY GEARBOX

The ability of the torque converter to multiply engine torque is limited. Also, the unit tends to be more efficient when the turbine is rotating at relatively high speeds. Therefore, a planetary gearbox is used to carry the power output of the turbine to the driveshaft.

Planetary gears function very similarly to conventional transmission gears. However, their construction is different in that three elements make up one gear system, and, in that all three elements are different from one another. The three elements are: an outer gear that is shaped like a hoop, with teeth cut into the inner surface; a sun gear, mounted on a shaft and located at the very center of the outer gear; and a set of three planet gears, held by pins in a ring-like planet carrier, meshing with both the sun gear and the outer gear. Either the outer gear or the sun gear may be held stationary, providing more than one possible torque multiplication factor for each set of gears. Also, if all three gears are forced to rotate at the same speed, the gearset forms, in effect, a solid shaft.

Most automatics use the planetary gears to provide various reductions ratios. Bands and clutches are used to hold various portions of the gearsets to the transmission case or to the shaft on which they are mounted. Shifting is accomplished, then, by changing the portion of each planetary gearset which is held to the transmission case or to the shaft.

SERVOS AND ACCUMULATORS

The servos are hydraulic pistons and cylinders. They resemble the hydraulic actuators used on many other machines, such as bulldozers. Hydraulic fluid enters the cylinder, under pressure, and forces the piston to move to engage the band or clutches.

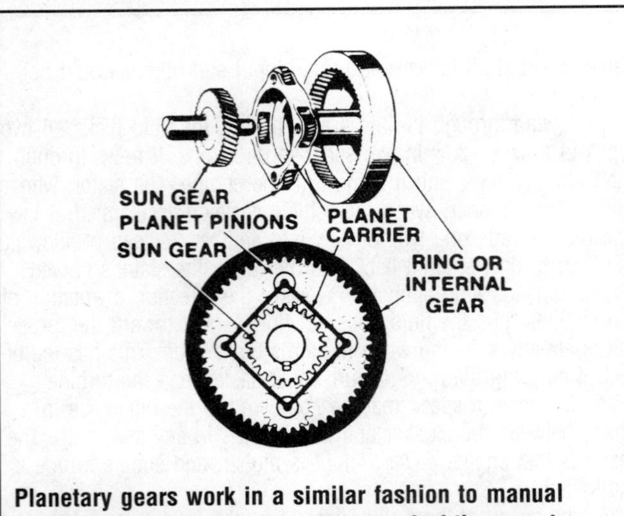

Planetary gears work in a similar fashion to manual transmission gears, but are composed of three parts

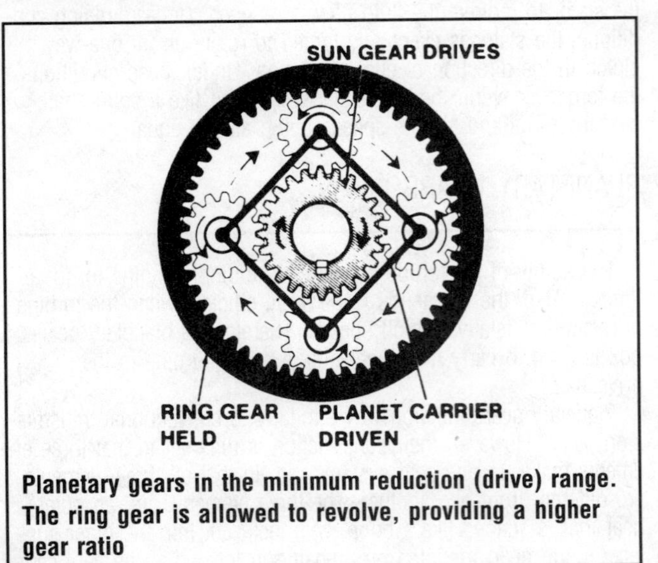

Planetary gears in the minimum reduction (drive) range. The ring gear is allowed to revolve, providing a higher gear ratio

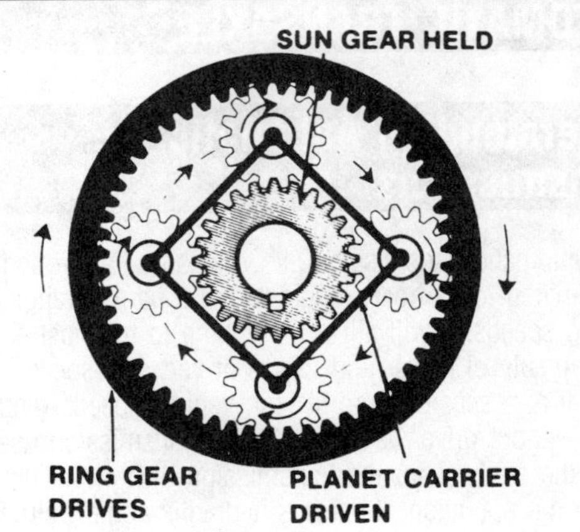

Planetary gears in the minimum reduction (drive) range. The ring gear is allowed to revolve, providing a higher gear ratio

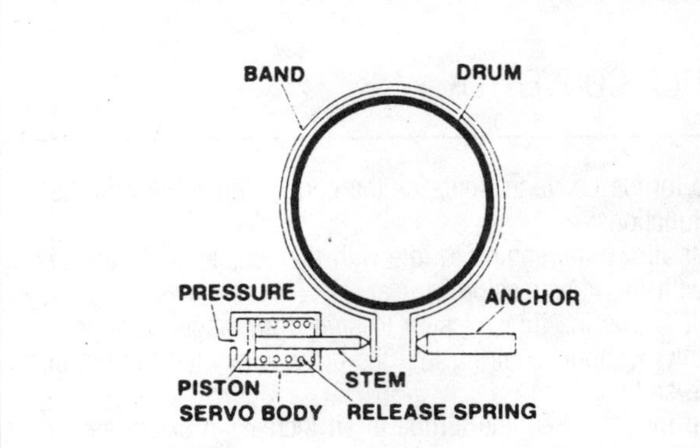

Servos, operated by pressure, are used to apply or release the bands, to either hold the ring gear or allow it to rotate

The accumulators are used to cushion the engagement of the servos. The transmission fluid must pass through the accumulator on the way to the servo. The accumulator housing contains a thin piston which is sprung away from the discharge passage of the accumulator. When fluid passes through the accumulator on the way to the servo, it must move the piston against spring pressure, and this action smooths out the action of the servo.

HYDRAULIC CONTROL SYSTEM

The hydraulic pressure used to operate the servos comes from the main transmission oil pump. This fluid is channeled to the various servos through the shift valves. There is generally a manual shift valve which is operated by the transmission selector lever and an automatic shift valve for each automatic upshift the transmission provides.

➡**Many new transmissions are electronically controlled. On these models, electrical solenoids are used to better control the hydraulic fluid. Usually, the solenoids are regulated by an electronic control module.**

There are two pressures which affect the operation of these valves. One is the governor pressure which is effected by vehicle speed. The other is the modulator pressure which is effected by intake manifold vacuum or throttle position. Governor pressure rises with an increase in vehicle speed, and modulator pressure rises as the throttle is opened wider. By responding to these two pressures, the shift valves cause the upshift points to be delayed with increased throttle opening to make the best use of the engine's power output.

Most transmissions also make use of an auxiliary circuit for downshifting. This circuit may be actuated by the throttle linkage the vacuum line which actuates the modulator, by a cable or by a solenoid. It applies pressure to a special downshift surface on the shift valve or valves.

The transmission modulator also governs the line pressure, used to actuate the servos. In this way, the clutches and bands will be actuated with a force matching the torque output of the engine.

Identification

➧ See Figure 72

All automatic transaxles have a metal identification nameplate attached to the case exterior. This nameplate will assist in the servicing and determination of replacement parts when ordering.

The Fiero equipped with a automatic transaxle uses a GM Turbo Hydra-Matic (THM 125C). This transaxle assembly is a fully automatic unit for front and mid engine GM vehicles. The THM 125C has three forward gear ranges and one reverse. The major components of the assembly consist of a 4 element hydraulic torque converter, compound planetary gear set, dual sprocket and drive link, three multiple disc clutch packs, intermediate band, valve body and vane type oil pump.

SHIFT SELECTION

1. **P** = Park position prevents the vehicle from rolling either forward or backward.
2. **R** = Reverse allows the vehicle to be operated in a rearward direction.
3. **N** = Neutral allow the engine to be started and operated without driving the vehicle. The engine can be restarted in the Neutral position.
4. **D** = Drive position is used for all normal driving conditions. It provides three gear ratios plus converter clutch operation. Downshifts are available for safe passing.
5. **2** = Manual second is used to provide acceleration and engine braking. This range may be selected at any vehicle speed.
6. **1** = Manual Low is used to provide maximum engine braking. This range may also be selected at any vehicle speed.

Fluid Pan

REMOVAL & INSTALLATION

➧ See Figure 73

➡Use only fluid labeled Dexron®II. Use of other fluids could cause erratic shifting and transmission damage.

1. Disconnect the negative (−) battery cable.
2. Raise your vehicle and support it safely with jackstands.

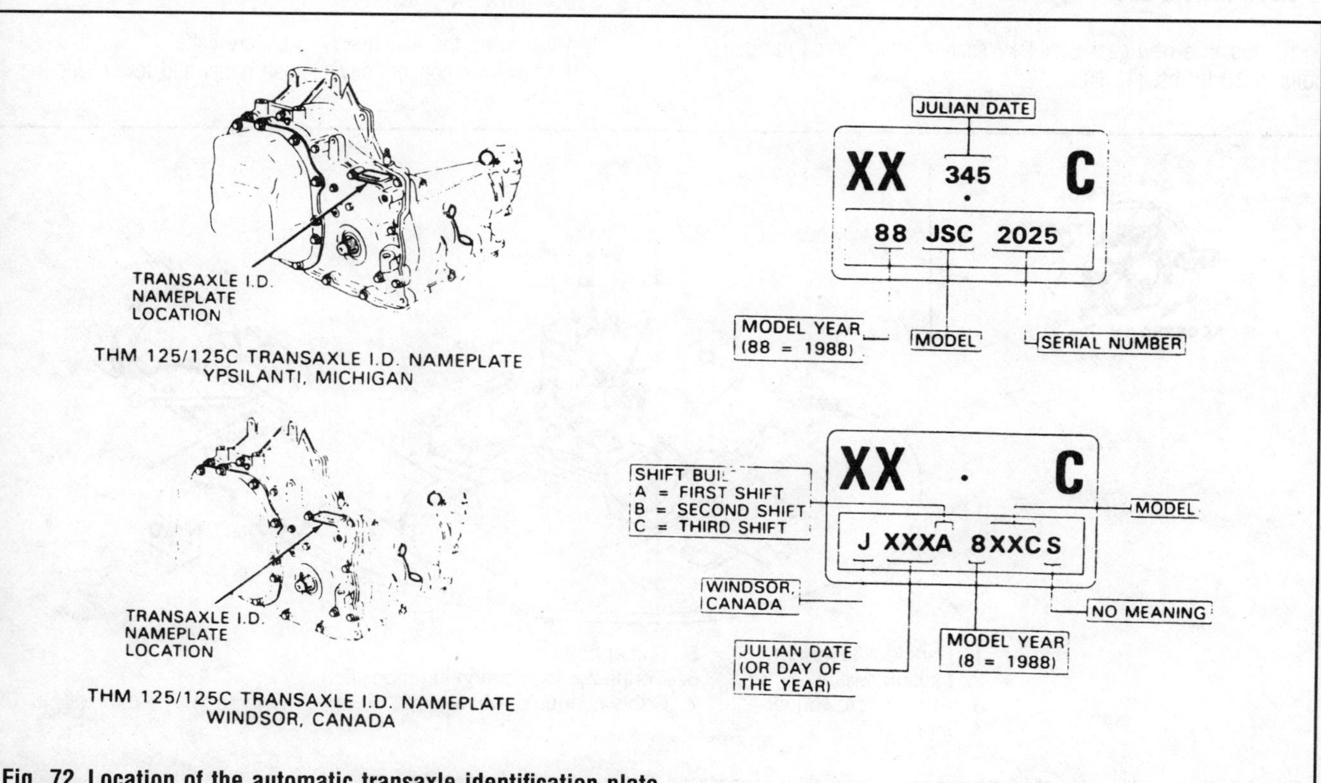

Fig. 72 Location of the automatic transaxle identification plate

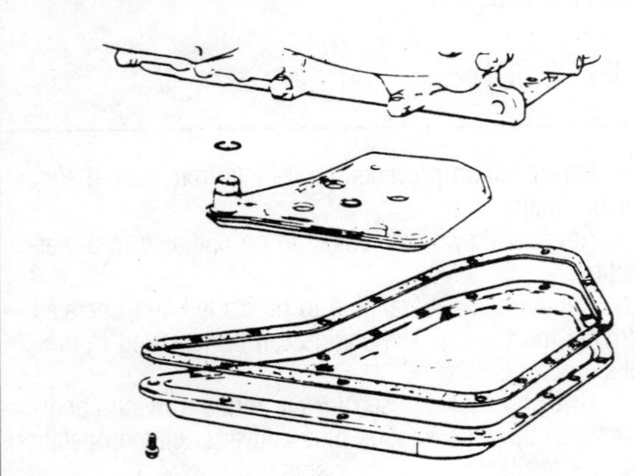

Fig. 73 The automatic transaxle pan must be removed to allow access to the transaxle filter

3. Remove the front and side pan bolts.
4. Loosen the rear bolts about four turns.
5. Carefully pry the oil pan loose and allow the fluid to drain.
6. Remove the remaining bolts, the pan, and the gasket or RTV sealant. Discard the old gasket.
7. Clean the pan with solvent and dry it thoroughly, with compressed air.
8. Remove the strainer, filter and O-ring seal.
9. Install a new transaxle filter and O-ring seal, locating the strainer against the dipstick stop.

➡Always replace the filter with a new one. Do not attempt to clean the old one.

10. Install a new gasket or RTV sealant then tighten the pan bolts to 12 ft. lbs. (15 Nm).
11. Lower the car and add about 4 quarts of Dexron®II transmission fluid. Reconnect the negative (−) battery cable.
12. Start the engine and let idle. Block the wheels and apply the parking brake.
13. Move the shift lever through the ranges. With the lever in "PARK", check the fluid level and add as necessary. Do not overfill the transaxle.

➡The transmission fluid currently being used may appear to be darker and have a strong odor. This is normal and not a sign of required maintenance or transmission failure.

Adjustments

TRANSAXLE CONTROL CABLE

1. Disconnect the negative (−) battery cable.
2. Place the shift lever in N (neutral) position.
3. Place the transaxle lever in the Neutral position by rotating the transaxle lever clockwise from Park through Reverse into Neutral.
4. Insert a threaded pin (part of shift cable assembly) upward through the slotted hole in the lever and hand start the nut. The lever must be held out of Park when torquing the nut. Torque the nut to 15–25 ft. lbs. (20–34 Nm).

Park/Lock Control Cable

REMOVAL & INSTALLATION

➧ See Figure 74

1. Disconnect the negative (−) battery cable.
2. Remove the console cover, hush panel and lower steering

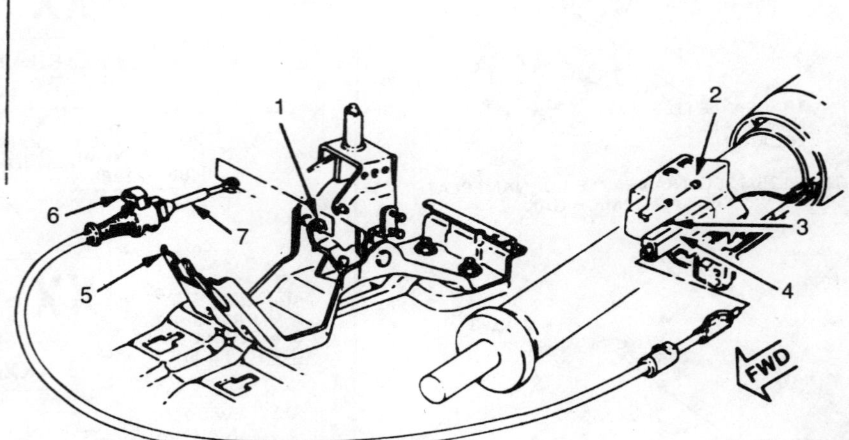

1. Park lock lever pin
2. Ignition switch
3. Slot for screwdriver
4. Inhibitor
5. Shifter base
6. Connector lock button in up position
7. Cable connector nose

Fig. 74 The park lock cable components and adjustments on the automatic transaxle

column as necessary for access to the Park lock cable. Refer to the "Console and Steering Column" procedures in Section 6.

3. Put the shifter lever in Park position.
4. Put the ignition switch in the Run position.
5. Remove the cable from the inhibitor.

➡To release the cable from the inhibitor, insert a screwdriver blade into the inhibitor slot and depress the cable latch and pull the cable from the inhibitor.

6. Remove the cable from the park lock lever pin.
7. Remove the cable from the shifter base and remove the cable.

To install:

1. Install the shift lever in the Park position and snap the cable connector lock button to the up position.
2. Snap the cable connector to the base and turn the ignition key to the OFF position.
3. Snap the cable into the inhibitor housing and turn the ignition key to the LOCK position.
4. Snap the cable to the park lock lever pin. Push the cable connector nose forward toward the connector to remove the slack.
5. With no load applied to the nose, snap the cable connector lock button down.
6. Place the shift lever in the Park position and turn the ignition key to the Lock position.
7. The shifter lever should not be able to move to another position and the ignition key should be removable from the key lock.
8. Turn the key to the Run position and put the shift lever in Neutral, ignition key should not be removable from the lock.

Neutral Safety and Backup Lamp Switch

REMOVAL & INSTALLATION

➧ **See Figure 75**

1. Disconnect the negative (−) battery cable.
2. The combination switch is located on top of the automatic transaxle housing.
3. Open the engine compartment lid and remove the electrical connector from the switch.

➡The clip on the switch must be opened before attempting to remove the electrical connector from the switch. Damage to the switch may occur if this step is ignored.

4. Pry the cable from the pivot pin at the bottom of the shift lever.
5. Remove the nut attaching the shift lever to the transaxle shift shaft.
6. Remove the two switch attaching bolts at transaxle and remove the switch.

To install:

1. Install the backup/neutral start switch to transaxle.
2. Install the two attaching bolts and torque to 20 ft. lbs. (27 Nm).
3. Install the shift lever-to-transaxle shift shaft attaching nut and torque to 20 ft. lbs. (27 Nm). Install the cable assembly to the pivot pin and reconnect the negative (−) battery cable.

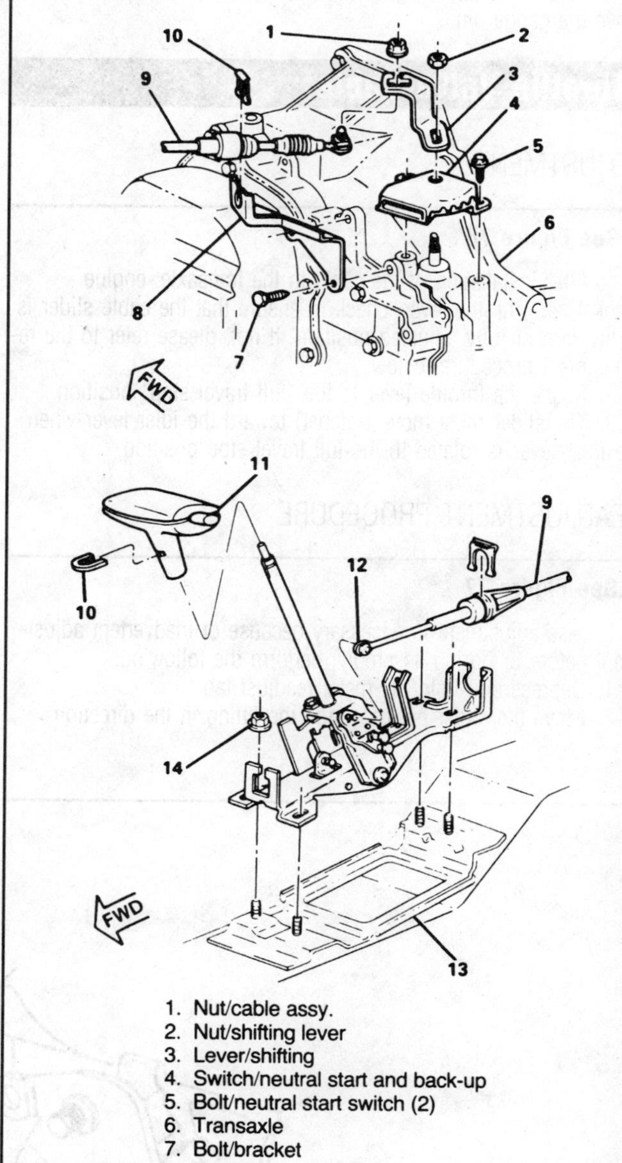

1. Nut/cable assy.
2. Nut/shifting lever
3. Lever/shifting
4. Switch/neutral start and back-up
5. Bolt/neutral start switch (2)
6. Transaxle
7. Bolt/bracket
8. Bracket
9. Cable assy.
10. Retainer assy.
11. T handle
12. Snap securely onto pin
13. Gear shift support
14. Nut 23 N·m (17 ft. lb.)

Fig. 75 Exploded view of the transaxle control components and the cable attachment and neutral switch components

ADJUSTMENT

1. Place the transaxle shifter in the Neutral position.
2. Loosen the bolts attaching the switch to the transaxle case.
3. Insert a 2.34mm dia. gauge pin (or rounded shank of a 3⁄32 in. drill bit) into the service adjustment hole. Rotate the switch until the gauge pin drops to a depth of 9mm.

4. Torque the attaching bolts to 20 ft. lbs. (27 Nm) and remove the gauge pin.

Throttle Valve Cable

ADJUSTMENT

➧ **See Figure 76**

1. After installation of the cable to the transaxle, engine bracket, and throttle lever, check to ensure that the cable slider is in the zero or fully adjusted position. If not, please refer to the readjustment procedure, below.
2. Rotate the throttle lever to the "full travel stop" position.
3. The slider must move (ratchet) toward the idler lever when the idler lever is rotated to the full travel stop position.

READJUSTMENT PROCEDURE

➧ **See Figure 77**

In case adjustment is necessary because of inadvertent adjustment before or during assembly, perform the following:

1. Depress and hold the metal readjust tab.
2. Move the slider back through the fitting in the direction away from the throttle lever until the slider stops against the fitting.
3. Release the metal readjust tab.
4. Rotate the throttle lever to the "full travel stop" position.

Automatic Transaxle

REMOVAL & INSTALLATION

1. Disconnect the negative (−) battery cable and drain transaxle fluid into a suitable drain pan.
2. Remove the air cleaner.
3. Remove the right and left engine vent covers.
4. Remove the throttle valve cable at fuel injection unit, shift cable at transaxle bracket and the neutral start/backup switch electrical connector at transaxle.
5. Remove the transaxle converter clutch, speedometer pickup and transaxle to engine electrical connectors.
6. Remove the transaxle cooler line support bracket.
7. Remove the five transaxle-to-engine retaining bolts.
8. Install the engine support fixture tool No. J-28467-A or equivalent.
9. Raise the vehicle and support with jackstands. Remove the rear wheel assemblies and install the rear halfshaft boot protectors

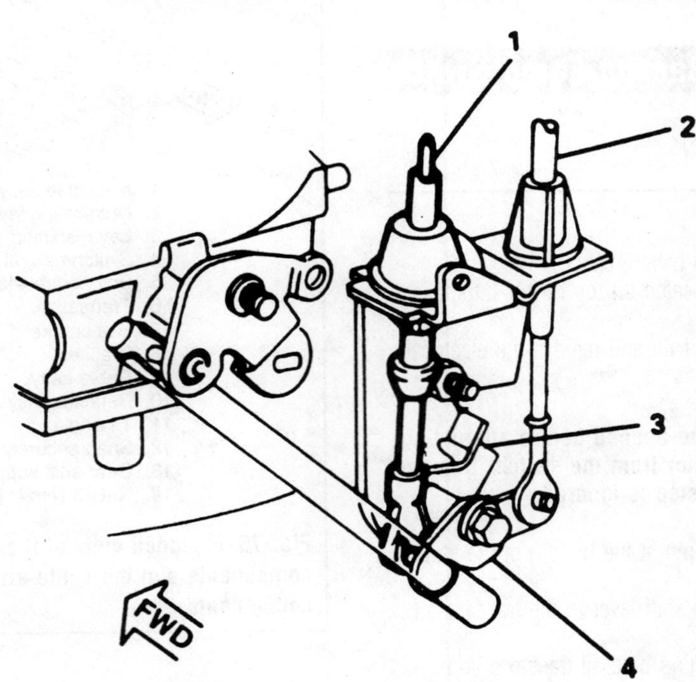

1. Cable T.V.
2. Cable accelerator
3. Lever throttle idler "at full travel stop"
4. Lever throttle idler

Fig. 76 Throttle valve cable adjustment points

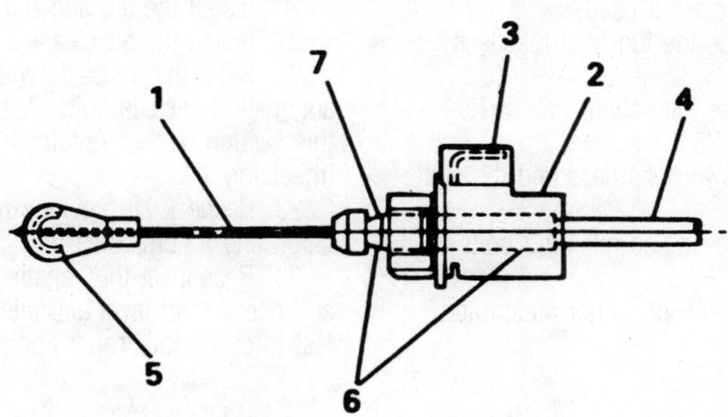

1. To throttle idler
2. Fitting
3. Tab readjustment
4. Cable
5. Terminal
6. Slider
7. Slider against fitting zero or readjust position

Fig. 77 Readjustment of the throttle valve cable

if equipped with the gray silicone boots. For further assistance, refer to the "Halfshaft" removal procedures in this section.

10. Remove the fixed adjusting link, lateral control arm through bolts and the trailing arms at the knuckle. Refer to the "Cradle" removal procedures in this section.

➡Do NOT allow the Tri-Pod halfshaft joints to overextend. Overextending the joint may result in the separation of the internal components causing failure of the joint.

11. Remove the rear halfshafts from the transaxle as outlined in the "Halfshaft" section in this section. Support the shafts to the body with wire.
12. Remove the splash shields, brake cables at calipers and brake control cable at the frame.
13. Remove the exhaust pipe-to-manifold attaching nuts.
14. Remove the two engine mount-to-cradle nuts.
15. Remove the two transaxle-to-cradle nuts.
16. Remove the two front and two rear cradle-to-body bolts and remove the cradle assembly with a jack.
17. Remove the starter/flexplate shield and flexplate bolts.
18. Remove and plug the transaxle cooler lines and drain excess fluid into a drain pan.
19. Install a transaxle support jack.
20. Remove the two transaxle support brackets at back right.
21. Remove the remaining transaxle-to-engine retaining bolts and any other component needed to free the transaxle assembly from the vehicle.
22. Remove the transaxle from the vehicle slowly while watching for undisconnected items.

To install:

1. Position the transaxle assembly in the vehicle and engage the torque converter to the flexplate.
2. Install the transaxle-to-engine retaining bolts and ground wire.
3. Install the front and rear transaxle support brackets and remove the transaxle jack.
4. Unplug and reconnect the transaxle cooler lines.
5. Install the flexplate-to-torque converter bolt and install starter/flexplate shield.
6. Install the cradle to the body and the two rear and two front cradle retaining bolts.
7. Install the two transaxle-to-cradle mount nuts and the two engine-to-cradle mount nuts.
8. Install the exhaust pipe-to-manifold nuts.
9. Install the brake control cable-to-frame and the brake cable-to-calipers.
10. Install the splash shields and disconnect the rear halfshaft from the support. Install the halfshaft into the transaxle as outlined in the "Halfshaft" installation procedures in this section.
11. Install the trailing arms at knuckle and torque the bolts to 44 ft. lbs. (60 Nm) +90° turn.

12. Install the fixed adjusting/lateral control arm through bolts and torque to 37 ft. lbs. (50 Nm) +90° turn.

13. Remove the halfshaft boot protectors if used.

14. Install the rear wheels and torque the lug nuts to 100 ft. lbs. (136 Nm).

15. Remove the jackstands and lower the vehicle safely. Remove the engine support fixture tool J-28467-A.

16. Install the neutral start/backup switch harness and the shift cable bracket.

17. Install the remaining transaxle-to-engine retaining bolts and the cooler line support bracket.

18. Reconnect the engine, speedometer, converter clutch and neutral start switch wiring connectors.

19. Install the shift cable-to-transaxle bracket and the throttle valve cable-to-fuel injection unit.

20. Install the left and right engine vent covers.

21. Install the air cleaner.

22. Refill the transaxle with the specified amount of Dexron® II automatic transaxle fluid. Refer to the "Fluid Pan" procedures in this section or the "Automatic Transaxle Fluid Change" Procedure in section 1.

23. Recheck all previous procedures to check for proper installation and a completed job.

23. Reconnect the negative (−) battery cable, start the vehicle and check fluid level and after fluid level has been obtained, road test to check for proper operation.

Troubleshooting Basic Automatic Transmission Problems

Problem	Cause	Solution
Fluid leakage	• Defective pan gasket	• Replace gasket or tighten pan bolts
	• Loose filler tube	• Tighten tube nut
	• Loose extension housing to transmission case	• Tighten bolts
	• Converter housing area leakage	• Have transmission checked professionally
Fluid flows out the oil filler tube	• High fluid level	• Check and correct fluid level
	• Breather vent clogged	• Open breather vent
	• Clogged oil filter or screen	• Replace filter or clean screen (change fluid also)
	• Internal fluid leakage	• Have transmission checked professionally
Transmission overheats (this is usually accompanied by a strong burned odor to the fluid)	• Low fluid level	• Check and correct fluid level
	• Fluid cooler lines clogged	• Drain and refill transmission. If this doesn't cure the problem, have cooler lines cleared or replaced.
	• Heavy pulling or hauling with insufficient cooling	• Install a transmission oil cooler
	• Faulty oil pump, internal slippage	• Have transmission checked professionally
Buzzing or whining noise	• Low fluid level	• Check and correct fluid level
	• Defective torque converter, scored gears	• Have transmission checked professionally
No forward or reverse gears or slippage in one or more gears	• Low fluid level	• Check and correct fluid level
	• Defective vacuum or linkage controls, internal clutch or band failure	• Have unit checked professionally
Delayed or erratic shift	• Low fluid level	• Check and correct fluid level
	• Broken vacuum lines	• Repair or replace lines
	• Internal malfunction	• Have transmission checked professionally

Lockup Torque Converter Service Diagnosis

Problem	Cause	Solution
No lockup	• Faulty oil pump • Sticking governor valve • Valve body malfunction (a) Stuck switch valve (b) Stuck lockup valve (c) Stuck fail-safe valve • Failed locking clutch • Leaking turbine hub seal • Faulty input shaft or seal ring	• Replace oil pump • Repair or replace as necessary • Repair or replace valve body or its internal components as necessary • Replace torque converter • Replace torque converter • Repair or replace as necessary
Will not unlock	• Sticking governor valve • Valve body malfunction (a) Stuck switch valve (b) Stuck lockup valve (c) Stuck fail-safe valve	• Repair or replace as necessary • Repair or replace valve body or its internal components as necessary
Stays locked up at too low a speed in direct	• Sticking governor valve • Valve body malfunction (a) Stuck switch valve (b) Stuck lockup valve (c) Stuck fail-safe valve	• Repair or replace as necessary • Repair or replace valve body or its internal components as necessary
Locks up or drags in low or second	• Faulty oil pump • Valve body malfunction (a) Stuck switch valve (b) Stuck fail-safe valve	• Replace oil pump • Repair or replace valve body or its internal components as necessary
Sluggish or stalls in reverse	• Faulty oil pump • Plugged cooler, cooler lines or fittings • Valve body malfunction (a) Stuck switch valve (b) Faulty input shaft or seal ring	• Replace oil pump as necessary • Flush or replace cooler and flush lines and fittings • Repair or replace valve body or its internal components as necessary
Loud chatter during lockup engagement (cold)	• Faulty torque converter • Failed locking clutch • Leaking turbine hub seal	• Replace torque converter • Replace torque converter • Replace torque converter
Vibration or shudder during lockup engagement	• Faulty oil pump • Valve body malfunction • Faulty torque converter • Engine needs tune-up	• Repair or replace oil pump as necessary • Repair or replace valve body or its internal components as necessary • Replace torque converter • Tune engine
Vibration after lockup engagement	• Faulty torque converter • Exhaust system strikes underbody • Engine needs tune-up • Throttle linkage misadjusted	• Replace torque converter • Align exhaust system • Tune engine • Adjust throttle linkage
Vibration when revved in neutral Overheating: oil blows out of dip stick tube or pump seal	• Torque converter out of balance • Plugged cooler, cooler lines or fittings • Stuck switch valve	• Replace torque converter • Flush or replace cooler and flush lines and fittings • Repair switch valve in valve body or replace valve body
Shudder after lockup engagement	• Faulty oil pump • Plugged cooler, cooler lines or fittings • Valve body malfunction • Faulty torque converter • Fail locking clutch • Exhaust system strikes underbody • Engine needs tune-up • Throttle linkage misadjusted	• Replace oil pump • Flush or replace cooler and flush lines and fittings • Repair or replace valve body or its internal components as necessary • Replace torque converter • Replace torque converter • Align exhaust system • Tune engine • Adjust throttle linkage

Transmission Fluid Indications

The appearance and odor of the transmission fluid can give valuable clues to the overall condition of the transmission. Always note the appearance of the fluid when you check the fluid level or change the fluid. Rub a small amount of fluid between your fingers to feel for grit and smell the fluid on the dipstick.

If the fluid appears:	It indicates:
Clear and red colored	• Normal operation
Discolored (extremely dark red or brownish) or smells burned	• Band or clutch pack failure, usually caused by an overheated transmission. Hauling very heavy loads with insufficient power or failure to change the fluid, often result in overheating. Do not confuse this appearance with newer fluids that have a darker red color and a strong odor (though not a burned odor).
Foamy or aerated (light in color and full of bubbles)	• The level is too high (gear train is churning oil) • An internal air leak (air is mixing with the fluid). Have the transmission checked professionally.
Solid residue in the fluid	• Defective bands, clutch pack or bearings. Bits of band material or metal abrasives are clinging to the dipstick. Have the transmission checked professionally.
Varnish coating on the dipstick	• The transmission fluid is overheating

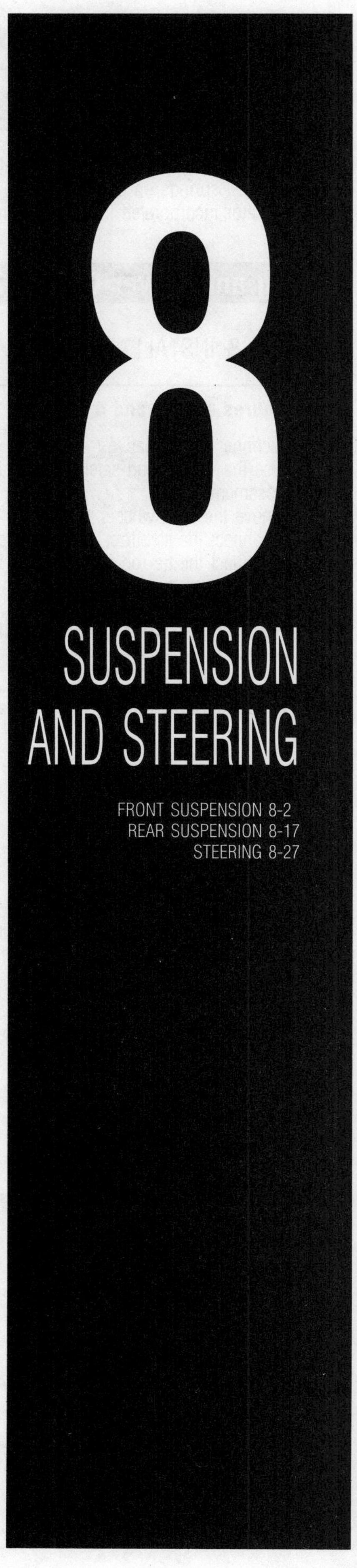
8
SUSPENSION AND STEERING
FRONT SUSPENSION 8-2
REAR SUSPENSION 8-17
STEERING 8-27

FRONT SUSPENSION

The front suspension uses a conventional long and short arm design with coil springs on both sides. The lower ball joints have a wear indicator incorporated into the assembly.

Spring and Lower Control Arm

REMOVAL & INSTALLATION

See Figures 1, 2, 3 and 4

1. Disconnect the negative (−) battery cable.
2. Raise the vehicle and safely support it with jackstands under the crossmember.
3. Remove the front wheels.
4. Disconnect the stabilizer bar from the lower control arm.
5. Disconnect the tie rod from the steering knuckle.
6. Disconnect the shock absorber at the lower control arm.
7. Support the lower control arm with a jack.

CAUTION

This procedure must be followed because it keeps the coil spring compressed. Use care to support the lower control arm adequately because the coil spring is under heavy load, if released too quickly personal injury could result.

8. Remove the nut from the lower ball joint, then use a ball joint separator tool J-26407 or its equivalent to press the ball joint out of the knuckle.
9. Swing the knuckle and hub out of the way.
10. Loosen the lower control arm pivot bolts. Make sure the jack is still under the lower control arm.
11. Install a chain through the coil spring as a safety precaution.

Troubleshooting Basic Steering and Suspension Problems

Problem	Cause	Solution
Hard steering (steering wheel is hard to turn)	• Low or uneven tire pressure • Loose power steering pump drive belt • Low or incorrect power steering fluid • Incorrect front end alignment • Defective power steering pump • Bent or poorly lubricated front end parts	• Inflate tires to correct pressure • Adjust belt • Add fluid as necessary • Have front end alignment checked/adjusted • Check pump • Lubricate and/or replace defective parts
Loose steering (too much play in the steering wheel)	• Loose wheel bearings • Loose or worn steering linkage • Faulty shocks • Worn ball joints	• Adjust wheel bearings • Replace worn parts • Replace shocks • Replace ball joints
Car veers or wanders (car pulls to one side with hands off the steering wheel)	• Incorrect tire pressure • Improper front end alignment • Loose wheel bearings • Loose or bent front end components • Faulty shocks	• Inflate tires to correct pressure • Have front end alignment checked/adjusted • Adjust wheel bearings • Replace worn components • Replace shocks
Wheel oscillation or vibration transmitted through steering wheel	• Improper tire pressures • Tires out of balance • Loose wheel bearings • Improper front end alignment • Worn or bent front end components	• Inflate tires to correct pressure • Have tires balanced • Adjust wheel bearings • Have front end alignment checked/adjusted • Replace worn parts
Uneven tire wear	• Incorrect tire pressure • Front end out of alignment • Tires out of balance	• Inflate tires to correct pressure • Have front end alignment checked/adjusted • Have tires balanced

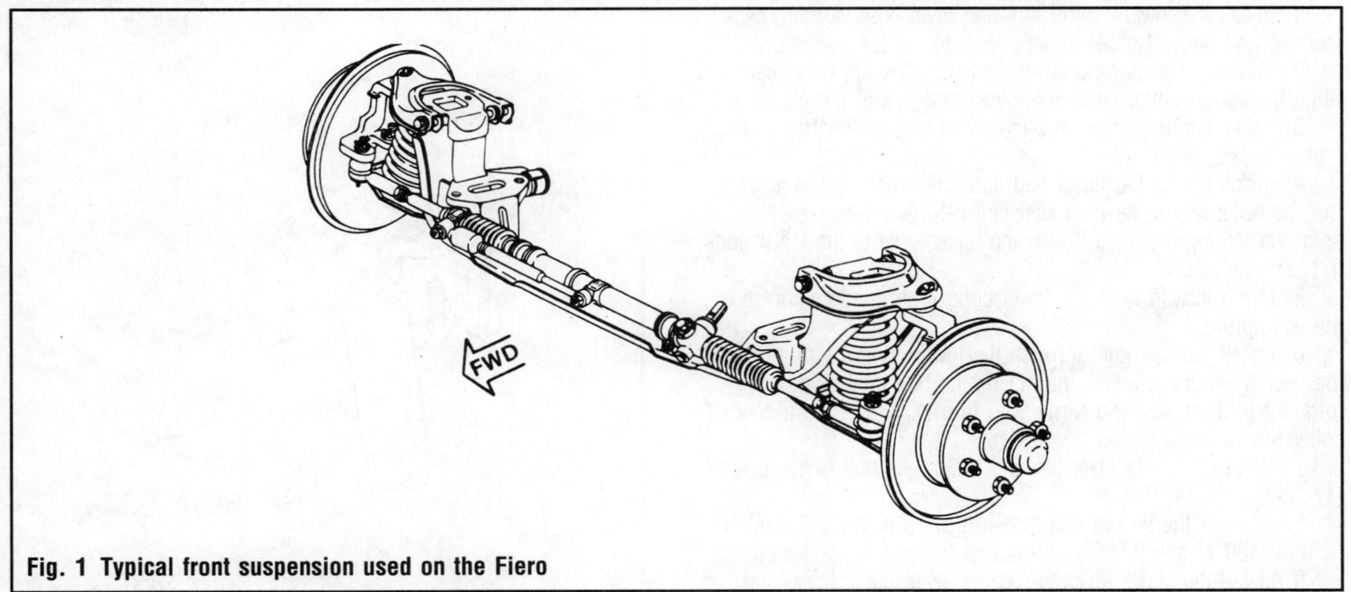

Fig. 1 Typical front suspension used on the Fiero

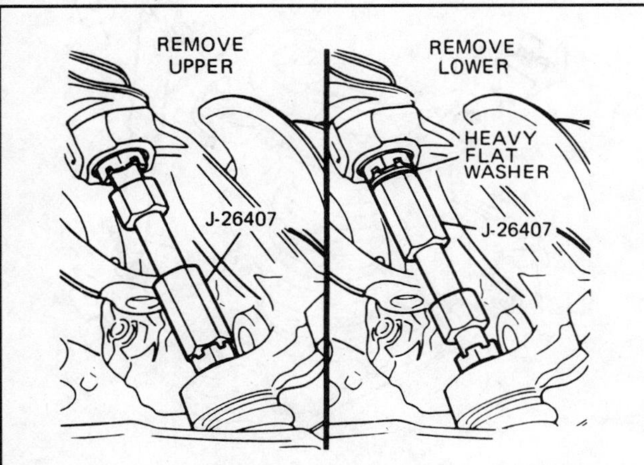

Fig. 2 Use a ball joint tool to separate the ball joint from the knuckle

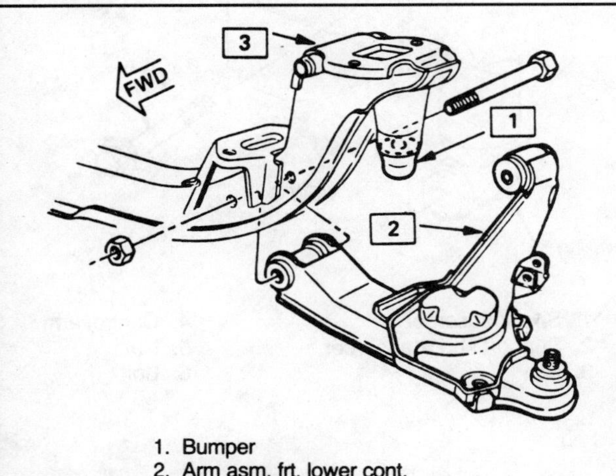

1. Bumper
2. Arm asm. frt. lower cont.
3. Frt. crossmember asm.

Fig. 3 Lower control arm location and its related components

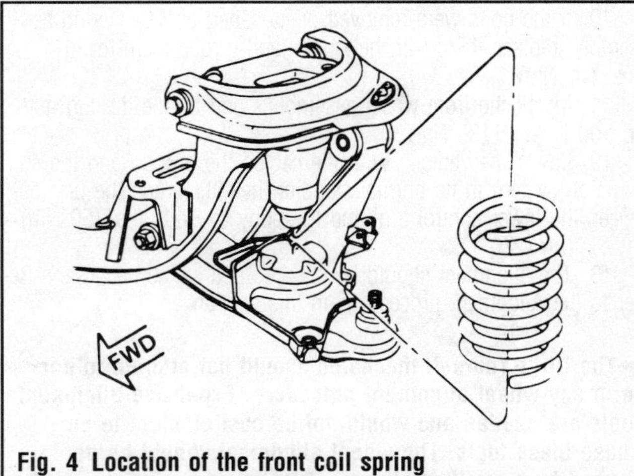

Fig. 4 Location of the front coil spring

⁂ CAUTION

The coil spring is under load and could result in personal injury if it is released too quickly. Be sure to install a chain and slowly lower the jack.

12. Slowly lower the jack and remove the spring.
13. Remove the pivot bolts at the chassis and the crossmember and remove the lower control arm.

➡Removal of the pivot bolt at the crossmember may require the loosening or removal of the steering assembly mounting bolts.

To install:

⁂ CAUTION

Any handling of the coil spring must not cause any damage to the corrosion protection coating on the springs. Hard steel contact must be avoided. Spring with damaged corrosion coating should not be used.

1. Install the lower control arm and pivot bolts at the crossmember and body. Tighten slightly, but do not torque the bolts.
2. Position the spring and insulator into the upper pocket. Align the spring bottom with the lower control arm pocket.
3. Install a safety chain through the spring as a safety precaution.
4. Install the spring lower end onto the lower control arm. It may be necessary to have an assistant help you compress the spring far enough to slide it over the raised area of the lower control arm seat.
5. Use a jack to raise the lower control arm and compress the coil spring.
6. Install the ball joint through the lower control arm and into the steering knuckle. Install the nut on the ball joint stud, and torque it to 37 ft. lbs. (50 Nm) + ¾ turn (270°). Install a new cotter pin.
7. Connect the stabilizer bar and torque the bolt to 12 ft. lbs. (17 Nm).
8. Connect the tie rod and torque it to 15 ft. lbs. (20 Nm) + ½ turn (180°), note: Maximum 1⁄16 turn to align the cotter pin.
9. Install the shock absorber on the lower control arm and torque the bolt to 20 ft. lbs. (27 Nm).
10. If the bolts were removed or loosened at the steering assembly, replace them with new bolts and torque them to 20 ft. lbs. (27 Nm).
11. Install the front wheel assemblies and torque the lug nuts to 100 ft. lbs. (136 Nm).
12. Lower the vehicle. With the car on the ground and the suspension system in its normal standing height, torque the bolt between the lower control arm and the body to 37 ft. lbs. (50 Nm) + ¾ turn (270°).
13. The alignment should be checked and set as necessary. Refer to the Alignment procedures in this section.

➡The Do-it-Yourself mechanic should not attempt to perform any wheel alignment procedure. Expensive alignment tools are needed and would not be cost efficient to purchase these tools. The wheel alignment should be performed by a certified alignment technician using the proper alignment tools.

Shock Absorber

REMOVAL & INSTALLATION

See Figure 5

1. Raise the vehicle and support it safely with jackstands.
2. Remove the wheel and tire assembly.
3. Remove the two upper retaining bolts.
4. Remove the nut and bolt from the lower end of the shock absorber and remove the shock absorber from the vehicle.

To install:

5. Place the lower portion of the shock into position and hand-tighten the nut and bolt.
6. Extend the shock absorber up into the support and torque both bolts to 8 ft. lbs. (11 Nm).
7. Torque the lower nut and bolt to 20 ft. lbs. (27 Nm).
8. Replace the wheel and tire assemblies and torque the lug nuts to 100 ft. lbs. (136 Nm).

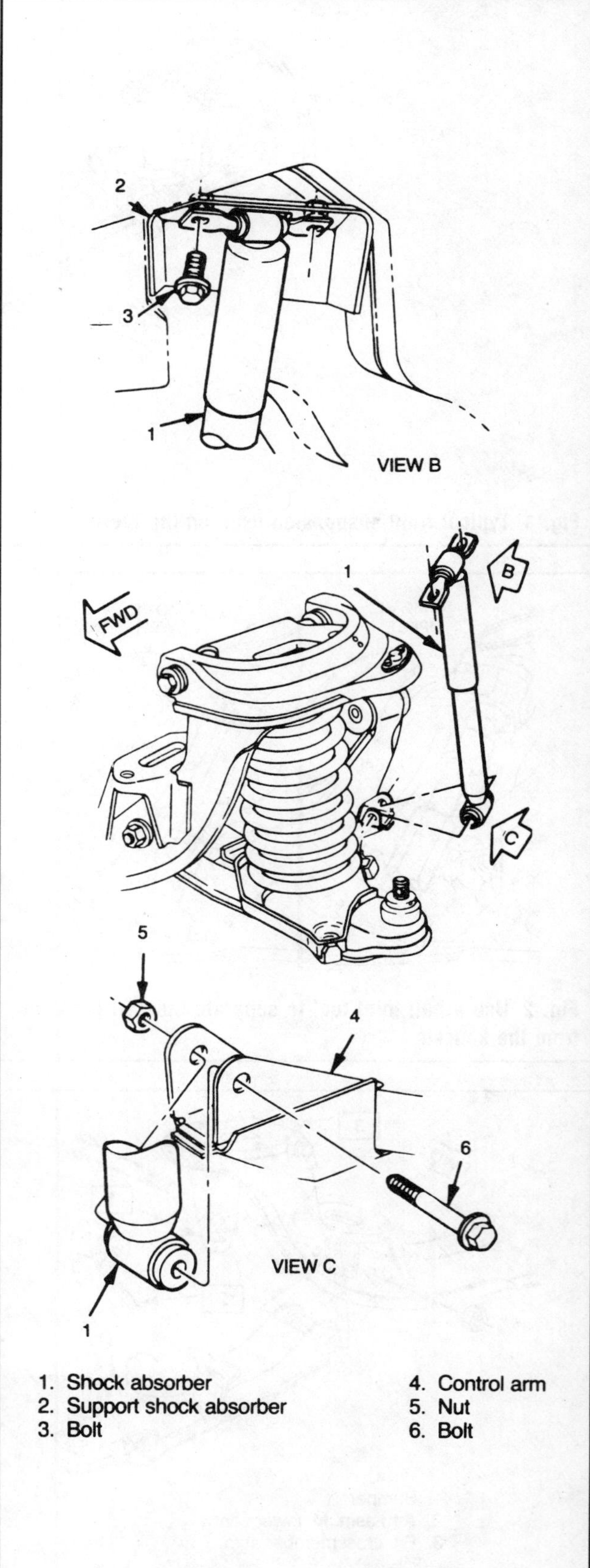

Fig. 5 Exploded view of the shock absorber mounting

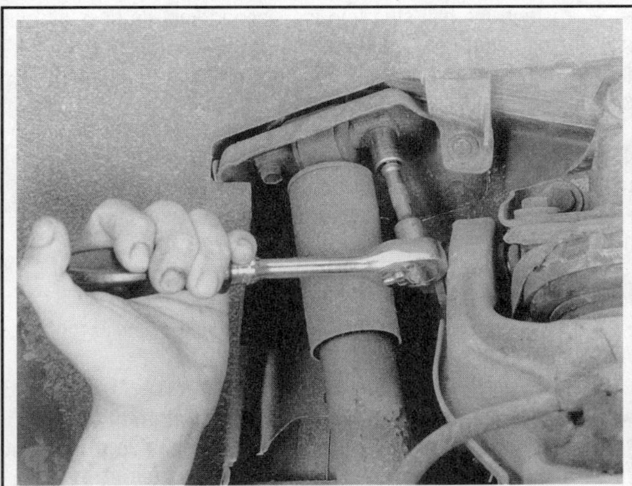

Remove the two shock absorber upper retaining bolts, then . . .

. . . unfasten the nut and bolt from the lower end and remove the shock absorber

Ball Joints

REMOVAL & INSTALLATION

Upper

➧ **See Figure 6**

1. Raise the vehicle and support it safely with jackstands.
2. Remove the tire and wheel assembly.
3. Support the lower control arm with a floor jack.
4. Remove the upper ball stud nut, then install the nut finger-tight.
5. Install a ball joint separator tool J-26407 or equivalent with the cup end over the lower ball stud nut.
6. Turn the threaded end of the tool until the upper ball stud is free of the steering knuckle.
7. Remove the tool and remove the nut from the ball stud.
8. On 1984–86 models, remove the two nuts and bolts attaching the ball joint to the upper control arm. Note which way the flat of the ball joint is pointing before removing it. The direction of the flat on the new ball joint should be in the same direction as the one removed unless a change in camber is desired.
9. On 1987–88 models, center punch the three rivets and drill a pilot hole with an 1/8 inch bit. Drill out the rivet head using an 1/4 inch drill bit and drive the rivets out with a punch.
10. Remove the ball joint.

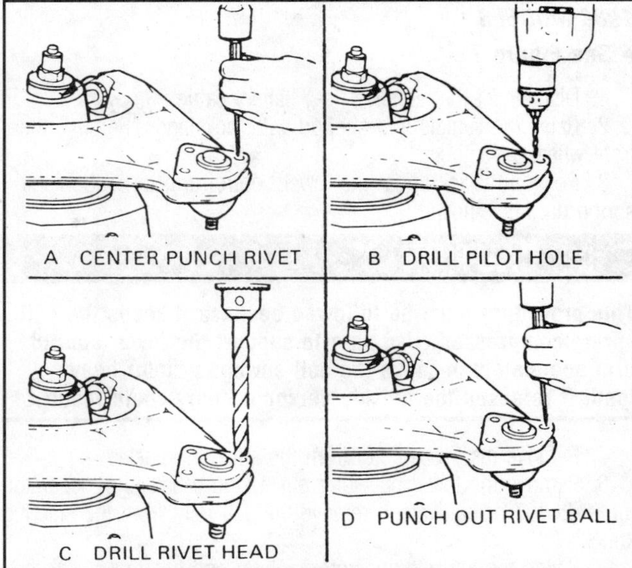

Fig. 6 Use a punch and a drill to remove the upper ball joint rivets—1987–88 models

➡Inspect the tapered hole in the steering knuckle. Remove any dirt and if any out-of-roundness, deformation, or damage is noted, the knuckle must be replaced.

To install:

1. On 1984–86 models, install the two bolts and nuts attaching the ball joint to the upper control arm and torque them to 28 ft. lbs. (38 Nm), then mate the upper control arm ball stud to the steering knuckle.
2. On 1987–88 models, install the three bolts and nuts provided with new ball joint to the upper control arm and torque to the specification given by the service repair package.
3. Install the ball joint to knuckle nut and torque it to 30–40 ft. lbs. (40–55 Nm) + 1/16 turn to align it with the cotter pin hole, and install the cotter pin.
4. Install the tire and wheel assembly and torque the lug nuts to 100 ft. lbs. (136 Nm). Lower the vehicle.

➡The toe adjustment must be checked and adjusted as necessary. Refer to the Alignment procedures in this section.

Lower

1984–87 MODELS

The lower ball joint is welded to the lower control arm and cannot be serviced separately. Replacement of the entire lower control arm will be necessary if the lower ball joint requires replacement. Refer to the Front Spring/Lower Control Arm Removal and Installation procedure.

1988 MODELS

➧ **See Figure 7**

1. Disconnect the negative (−) battery cable.
2. Raise the vehicle and support with jackstands. Remove the front wheel assemblies.
3. Position a jack under the lower control arm to support the spring during removal.

⁂ CAUTION

This procedure must be followed because it keeps the coil spring compressed. Use care to support the lower control arm adequately because the coil spring is under heavy load, if released too quickly personal injury could result.

4. Remove the tie rod end from the steering knuckle.
5. Remove the lower ball joint nut. Using a ball joint separator tool J-26407 or equivalent, remove the ball joint from the steering knuckle.
6. Swing the knuckle and rotor, caliper and bearing out of the way.

➡Inspect the tapered hole in the steering knuckle for out-of-roundness, deformation and damage. Replace the knuckle if these conditions exist. Clean all dirt and rust out the tapered hole before installation.

7. Remove the ball joint using a lower ball joint removing and installation tool No. J-9519-10 and J-9519-18. Refer to the accompanying illustration.

To install:

1. Install the lower ball joint into the lower control arm using the Lower Ball Joint installation and remove tools No. J-37161-3, J-37161-1, J-37161-4 and J-37161-2. Refer to the accompanying illustration.
2. Press the ball joint into the lower control arm.
3. Position the ball stud into the steering knuckle boss and install the ball stud nut. Torque the nut 26 ft. lbs. (35 Nm) + ½ turn (180°). Give an additional ⅙ turn maximum to align and install the cotter pin.
4. Install the tie rod end to the steering knuckle and torque to 15 ft. lbs. (20 Nm) + ½ turn (180°). Give an additional ⅙ turn maximum to align and install the cotter pin.
5. Install the front wheel assemblies and torque the lug nuts to 100 ft. lbs. (136 Nm).
6. Remove the jack from under the lower control arm and lower the vehicle to the ground.
7. Check and align the front end as outlined in the "Front Alignment" in this section.

➡The Do-it-Yourself mechanic should not attempt to perform any wheel alignment procedures. Expensive alignment tools are needed and it would not be cost efficient to purchase these tools. The wheel alignment should be performed by a certified alignment technician using the proper alignment tools.

Upper Control Arm

REMOVAL & INSTALLATION

1984–87 Models

➧ **See Figure 8**

1. Raise the vehicle and support it on jackstands.
2. Remove the tire and wheel assembly.
3. Remove the rivet holding the brake line clip to the upper control arm.
4. Support the lower control arm with a floor jack.

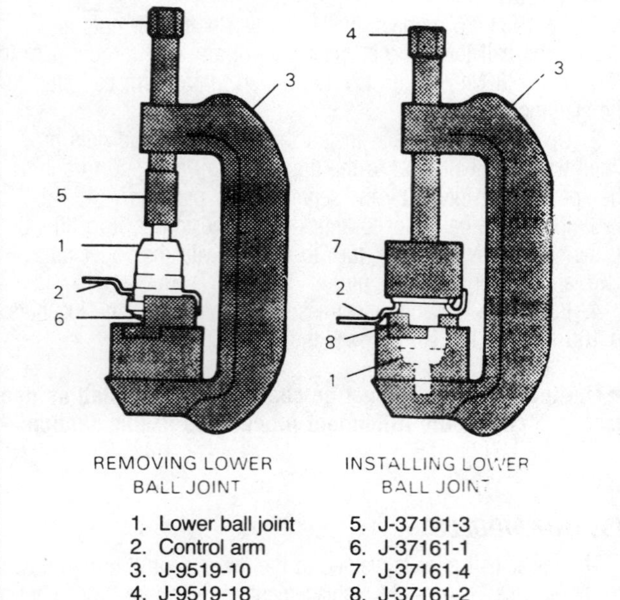

Fig. 7 Removal and installation of the lower ball joint—1988 models

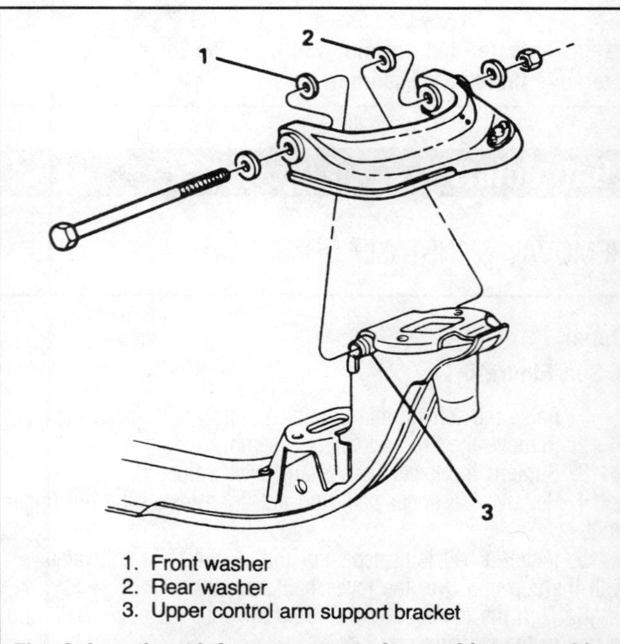

Fig. 8 Location of the upper control arm shim assembly and bushing components—1984–87 models

CAUTION

This procedure must be followed because it keeps the coil spring compressed. Use care to support the lower control arm adequately because the coil spring is under heavy load, if released too quickly personal injury could result.

5. Remove the upper ball joint from the steering knuckle using a Ball Joint Separator tool J-26407 or equivalent. This procedure has been used earlier in this section.
6. Remove the control arm pivot bolt and remove the control arm from the vehicle.
7. Transfer the ball joint if not damaged or worn.

To install:

➡Washers and shims must be installed as removed unless a change in steering geometry is desired.

1. Install the upper control arm and pivot bolt on the vehicle. The inner pivot bolt must be installed with the bolt head toward the front.
2. Install the pivot bolt nut.
3. Position the control arm in a horizontal plane and torque the nut to 66 ft. lbs. (90 Nm).

➡The bolt may turn when torqued to minimum if the nut is not backed up with a wrench. This does not mean the joint is loose.

4. Install the ball joint on the upper control arm and to the steering knuckle, as described earlier. Install the nut and torque it to 35 ft. lbs. (47 Nm). Install a new cotter pin.
5. Install the wheel and tire and torque the lug nuts to 100 ft. lbs. (136 Nm). Lower the vehicle to the floor.

1988 Models

➧ See Figure 9

1. Raise the vehicle and support safely with jackstands.
2. Remove the front wheel assemblies.
3. Support the lower control arm with a floor jack.

CAUTION

This procedure must be followed because it keeps the coil spring compressed. Use care to support the lower control arm adequately because the coil spring is under heavy load, if released too quickly personal injury could result.

4. Remove the bolt attaching the brake line clip-to-upper control arm.
5. Remove the tie rod end from the steering knuckle and swing knuckle outboard.
6. Remove the upper ball joint from the steering knuckle using a Ball Joint Separator tool J-26407 or equivalent. This procedure has been used earlier in this section.
7. Remove the two bolts and paddle nut assemblies attaching the upper control arm shaft to the crossmember and remove the control arm from the vehicle.

To install:

1. Install the upper control arm to the crossmember with a new paddle nut assembly. Do not apply the final torque until the alignment has been performed.

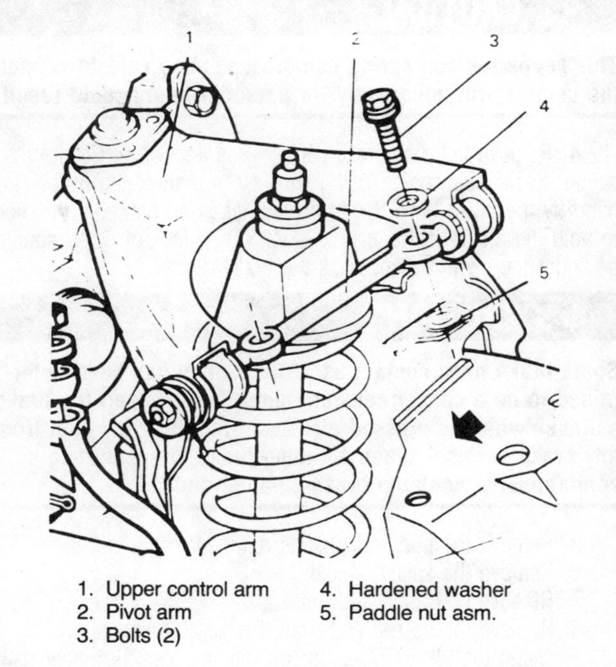

Fig. 9 Upper control arm assembly and its related components—1988 models

➡Inspect the tapered hole in the steering knuckle for out-of-roundness, deformation and damage. Replace the knuckle if these conditions exist. Clean all dirt and rust out the tapered hole before installation.

2. Install the upper control arm to the steering knuckle and torque the nut to 30–40 ft. lbs. (40–55 Nm) + 1⁄6 turn to align and install the cotter pin. Do not exceed 55 ft. lbs. (75 Nm) of torque to the nut.
3. Install the brake line clip-to-upper control arm attaching bolt.
4. Install the front wheel assemblies and torque the lug nuts to 100 ft. lbs. (136 Nm).
5. Remove the jack under the lower control arm and lower the vehicle to the ground.
6. Check and align the front end as outlined in the Front Alignment portion of this section.

➡The Do-it-Yourself mechanic should not attempt to perform any wheel alignment procedures. Expensive alignment tools are needed and it would not be cost efficient to purchase these tools. The wheel alignment should be performed by a certified alignment technician using the proper alignment tools.

Knuckle and Spindle

REMOVAL & INSTALLATION

1. Raise the vehicle on and support it on jackstands under the front crossmember.
2. Remove the front wheel assemblies.
3. Support the lower control arm with a floor jack.

✻✻ CAUTION

This keeps the coil spring compressed. Use care to support the control arm adequately, or personal injury could result.

4. Remove the disc brake caliper. See Section 9. Secure the caliper to the suspension using wire. Do not allow the caliper to hang by the brake hose. Insert a piece of wood between the shoes to hold the piston in the caliper bore. (The block of wood should be about the same thickness as the brake disc.).

✻✻ CAUTION

Some brake pads contain asbestos, which has been determined to be a cancer causing agent. Never clean the brake surfaces with compressed air! Avoid inhaling any dust from any brake surface! When cleaning brake surfaces, use a commercially available brake cleaning fluid.

5. Remove the hub and disc as outlined in this section.
6. Remove the splash shield.
7. Remove both ball stud nuts.
8. Remove the tie rod end from the steering knuckle.
9. Using tool J-26407 or its equivalent, press the upper ball stud from the steering knuckle.
10. Reverse tool J-26407 to the other ball stud nut and press the lower ball stud from the steering knuckle.
11. Remove the ball stud nuts and remove the steering knuckle.

To install:

➡Inspect the tapered hole in the steering knuckle for out-of-roundness, deformation and damage. Replace the knuckle if these conditions exist. Clean all dirt and rust out the tapered hole before installation.

1. Place the steering knuckle in position and insert the upper and lower ball studs into the knuckle bosses.
2. Install the upper control arm ball stud nut and torque to 30–40 ft. lbs. (40–55 Nm). Give an additional ⅙ turn maximum to align the cotter pin, but do NOT exceed 55 ft. lbs. (75 Nm). Torque the lower control arm stud nut to 26 ft. lbs. (35 Nm) + ½ turn (180°). Give an additional ⅙ turn maximum to align the cotter pin. Install the cotter pins.
3. Install the splash shield to the steering knuckle and torque to 7 ft. lbs. (10 Nm).
4. Install the tie rod end to the steering knuckle. Torque to 15 ft. lbs. (20 Nm) + ½ turn (180°), plus an additional ⅙ turn maximum to align the cotter pin. Install the cotter pin.
5. Repack the front wheel bearings then install the hub and disc, bearings and nut. Refer to the Front Wheel Bearings Procedure in this section.
6. Install the brake caliper.
7. Install the tire and wheel assembly and torque the lug nuts to 100 ft. lbs. (136 Nm).
8. Remove the jackstands and lower the vehicle to the ground.
9. Have the front end aligned by a qualified alignment technician.

➡The Do-it-Yourself mechanic should not attempt to perform any wheel alignment procedures. Expensive alignment tools are needed and it would not be cost efficient to purchase these tools. The wheel alignment should be performed by a certified alignment technician using the proper alignment tools.

Stabilizer Bar

REMOVAL & INSTALLATION

See Figures 10 and 11

➡Tape or mark the stabilizer bar on the right end prior to removal. This will ensure proper orientation of the part during installation.

✻✻ CAUTION

Some brake pads contain asbestos, which has been determined to be a cancer causing agent. Never clean the brake surfaces with compressed air! Avoid inhaling any dust from any brake surface! When cleaning brake surfaces, use a commercially available brake cleaning fluid.

1. Raise the vehicle and support safely with jackstands.
2. Remove both front wheel assemblies.
3. Remove both tie rods from the steering knuckle with a tie rod separator.
4. Remove both brake line clip-to-control arm attaching bolts.

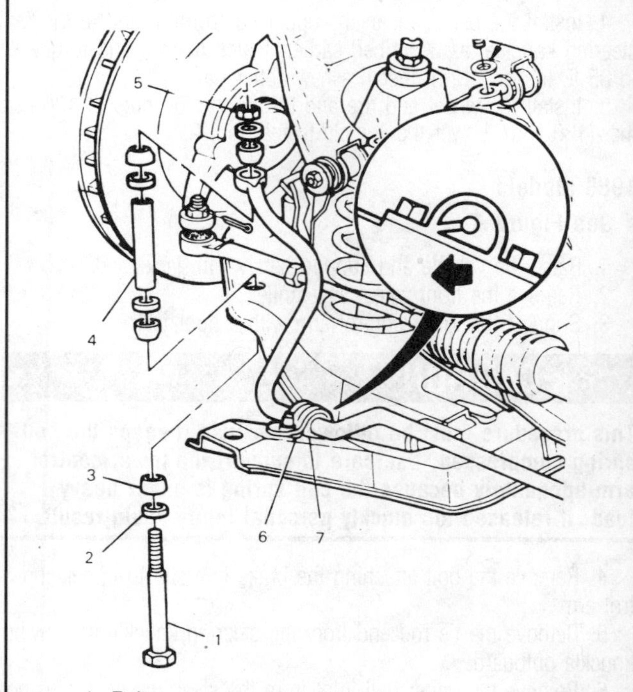

1. Bolt
2. Washer (4)
3. Insulator (4)
4. Spacer
5. Nut
6. Clamp
7. Bushing *Note slit must be toward front of vehicle

Fig. 10 Exploded view of the stabilizer bar assembly components—1988 models

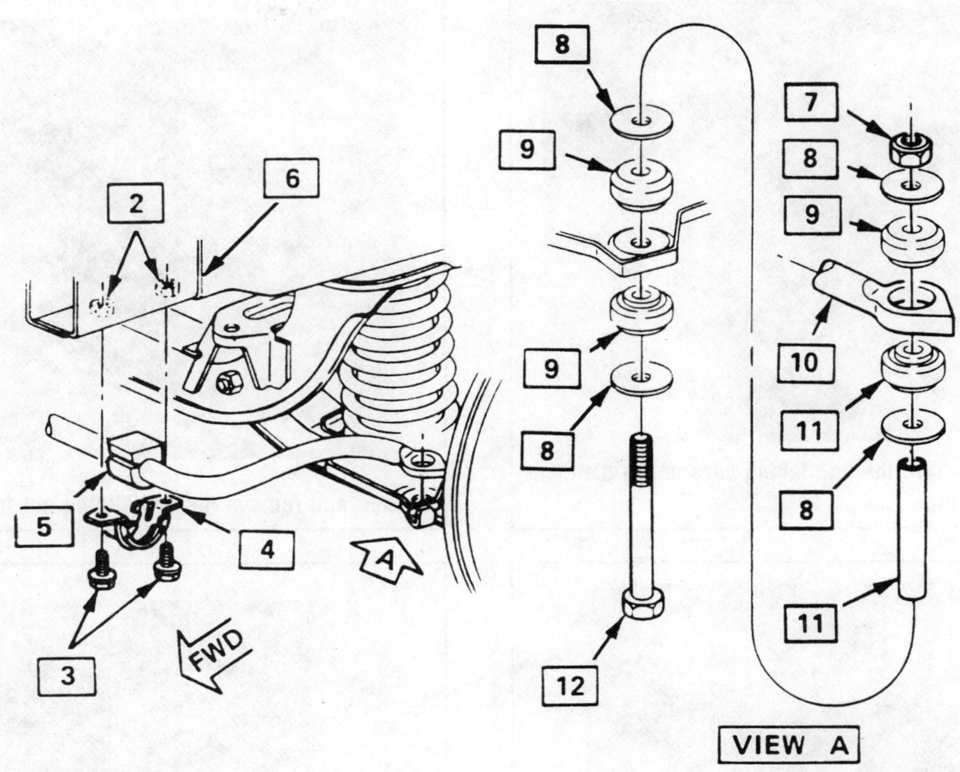

1. Spring
2. Weld nuts
3. Bolt/screw torque 18–24 N·m (13–17 ft. lb.)
4. Clamp
5. Bushing
6. Front rail
7. Note: tighten until nut bottoms on end of bolt thread
8. Washer
9. Grommet
10. Shaft front stabilizer note protruding shape on left-hand end
11. Spacer
12. Bolt note: torque from this end 17 N (13 ft.)
13. Shock absorber
14. Support shock absorber
15. Bolt
16. Control arm
17. Nut
18. Bolt

Fig. 11 Exploded view of the stabilizer bar retainers and their locations—1984–87 models

5. Remove the left side caliper, rotor, and splash shield. Suspend the caliper by a wire from the frame or body so not to damage the brake hose.
6. Remove the two bolts at each stabilizer bar clamp and bushing.
7. Remove the bar from the underside of the vehicle by moving the bar to the left side of the vehicle until the right side clears the frame rail.

To install:

1. Install the stabilizer bar to the underside of the vehicle.
2. It is important on 1988 models that the slit in the stabilizer bushing must be installed toward the front of the vehicle. Refer to the 1988 Stabilizer illustration.
3. Install the clamps and bushings. Hand-tighten the bolt to hold in place.
4. Install the link assemblies from the stabilizer bar to the lower control arm. Torque the bolts to 12 ft. lbs. (17 Nm).
5. Torque the bushing clamps to 20 ft. lbs. (27 Nm).
6. Install the tie rod ends and torque the nuts to 15 ft. lbs. (20 Nm) + ½ turn (180°), plus a maximum of ⅙ turn to align the cotter pin. Install and bend over a new cotter pin.
7. Install the left caliper, rotor and splash shield. Reconnect the brake line clip attaching bolts.
8. Install the front wheel assemblies and torque the lug nuts to 100 ft. lbs. (136 Nm). Lower the vehicle and check for proper operation.

Front Wheel Bearings

REMOVAL, REPACKING & INSTALLATION

1984–87 Models

To maintain proper functioning of the front suspension, the front wheel bearings should be lubricated and correctly adjusted every 30,000 miles.

Pry the dust cap from the hub taking care not to distort or damage its flange

Loosen and remove the castellated nut from the spindle

Once the bent ends are cut, grasp the cotter pin and pull or pry it free of the spindle

Remove the washer from the spindle

If difficulty is encountered, gently tap on the pliers with a hammer to help free the cotter pin

With the nut and washer out of the way, the outer bearings may be removed from the hub

Pull the hub and inner bearing assembly from the spindle

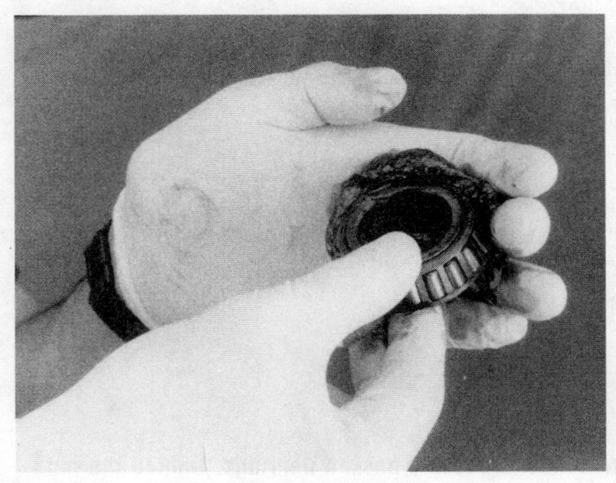
Thoroughly pack the bearing with fresh, high temperature wheel-bearing grease before installation

Use a small prytool to remove the old inner bearing seal

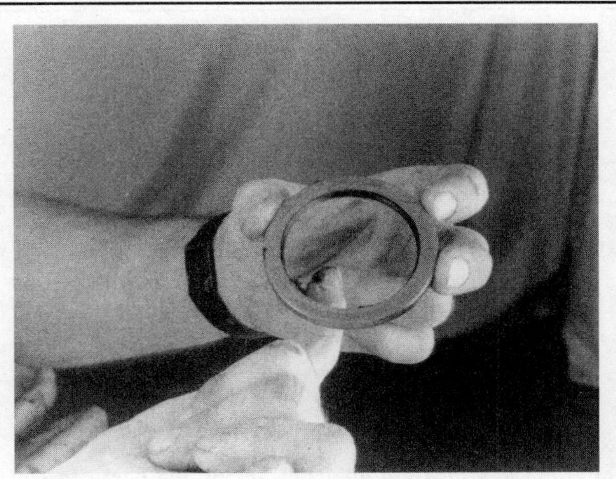
Apply a thin coat of fresh grease to the new inner bearing seal lip

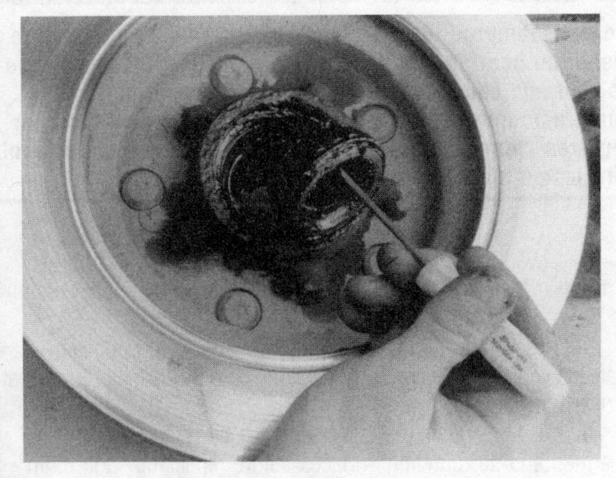
With the seal removed, the inner bearing may be withdrawn from the hub

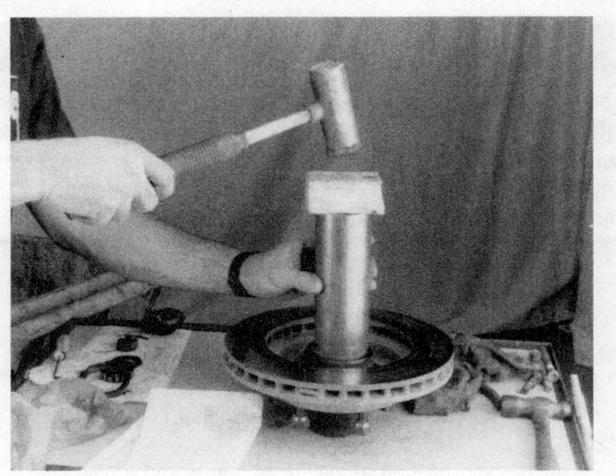
Use a suitably sized driver to install the inner bearing seal to the hub

With new or freshly packed bearings, tighten the nut while gently spinning the wheel, then adjust the bearings

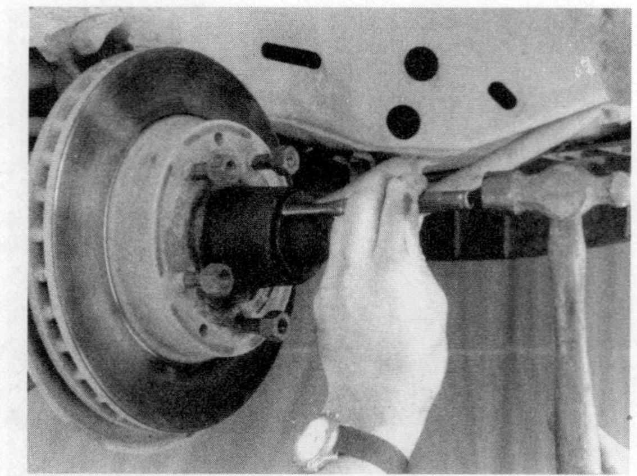
After the bearings are adjusted, install the dust cap by gently tapping on the flange—DO NOT damage the cap by hammering on the center

CAUTION

Some brake pads contain asbestos, which has been determined to be a cancer causing agent. Never clean the brake surfaces with compressed air! Avoid inhaling any dust from any brake surface! When cleaning brake surfaces, use a commercially available brake cleaning fluid.

Before handling the bearings, there are a few things that you should remember to do and not to do

Remember to DO the following:

- Remove all outside dirt from the housing before exposing the bearing.
- Treat a used bearing as gently as you would a new one.
- Work with clean tools in clean surroundings.
- Use clean, dry canvas gloves, or at least clean, dry hands.
- Clean solvents and flushing fluids are a must.
- Use clean paper when laying out the bearings to dry.
- Protect disassembled bearings from rust and dirt. Cover them up.
- Use clean rags to wipe bearings.
- Keep the bearings in oil-proof paper when they are to be stored or are not in use.
- Clean the inside of the housing before replacing the bearing.

Do NOT do the following:

- Don't work in dirty surroundings.
- Don't use dirty, chipped or damaged tools.
- Try not to work on wooden work benches or use wooden mallets.
- Don't handle bearings with dirty or moist hands.
- Do not use gasoline for cleaning; use a safe solvent.
- Do not spin-dry bearings with compressed air. They will be damaged.
- Do not spin dirty bearings.
- Avoid using cotton waste or dirty cloths to wipe bearings.
- Try not to scratch or nick bearing surfaces.
- Do not allow the bearing to come in contact with dirt or rust at any time.

1. Raise and support the front end on jackstands.
2. Remove the wheel cover. Remove the wheel.
3. Remove the caliper from the disc and wire it to the underbody to prevent damage to the brake hose. See Section 9.
4. Remove the grease cap from the hub. Then, remove the cotter pin, nut lock, adjusting nut and flat washer from the spindle. Remove the outer bearing assembly from the hub.
5. Pull the hub and disc assembly off the wheel spindle.
6. Remove and discard the old grease retainer. Remove the inner bearing cone and roller assembly from the hub.
7. Clean all grease from the inner and outer bearing cups with solvent. Inspect the cups for pits, scratches, or excessive wear. If the cups are damaged, remove them with a drift.
8. Clean the inner and outer cone and roller assemblies with solvent and shake them dry. If the cone and roller assemblies show excessive wear or damage, replace them with the bearing cups as a unit.
9. Clean the spindle and the inside of the hub with solvent to thoroughly remove all old grease.

WARNING

Do not submerge the rotor and hub assembly in solvent to clean the bearing areas. The porous medal will absorb the solvent and cause the new bearing grease to melt. Put a small amount of solvent on a clean rag and wipe the bearing area clean. Use a dry clean rag to wipe out the solvent still inside hub.

10. Covering the spindle with a clean cloth, brush all loose dirt and dust from the brake assembly. Remove the cloth carefully so as to not get dirt on the spindle.
11. If the inner and/or outer bearing cups were removed, install the replacement cups on the hub. Be sure that the cups seat properly in the hub.
12. It is imperative that all old grease be removed from the bearings and surrounding surfaces before repacking. Coat both bearings, bearing areas in the hub, grease seal and spindle with lithium-based grease. The new lithium-based grease is not compatible with the sodium base grease used in the past.
13. Install the hub and disc on the wheel spindle. To prevent

damage to the grease seal and spindle threads, keep the hub centered on the spindle.

14. Install the outer bearing cone and roller assembly and the flat washer on the spindle. Install the adjusting nut.

15. Adjust the wheel bearings by torquing the adjusting nut to 17–25 ft. lbs. (23–34 Nm) with the wheel rotating to seat the bearing. Then back off the adjusting nut to 10–15 in. lbs. (1.2–1.8 Nm). Install the locknut so that the castellations are aligned with the cotter pin hole. Install the cotter pin. Bend the ends of the cotter pin around the castellations of the locknut to prevent interference with the radio static collector in the grease cap. Install the grease cap.

WARNING

New bolts must be used when servicing floating caliper units. The upper bolt must be tightened first. For floating caliper units, see Section 9.

16. Install the wheels and torque the lug nuts to 100 ft. lbs. (136 Nm).

17. Install the wheel cover, if so equipped.

1988 Models

The 1988 models are equipped with sealed hub and bearing assemblies. Refer to the "Sealed Wheel Bearing Diagnosis Chart" in chapter 1.

CAUTION

Some brake pads contain asbestos, which has been determined to be a cancer causing agent. Never clean the brake surfaces with compressed air! Avoid inhaling any dust from any brake surface! When cleaning brake surfaces, use a commercially available brake cleaning fluid.

1. Raise the vehicle and support with jackstands.
2. Remove the wheel and tire assembly.
3. Remove the brake caliper and support with a wire to the surrounding body.
4. Remove the rotor assembly.
5. Remove the three hub and bearing assembly-to-steering knuckle attaching bolts.
6. Press out the old bearing using an arbor press and press in new bearings.

To install:

7. Place the hub and bearing assembly on the spindle.
8. Install the hub and bearing assembly-to-steering knuckle attaching bolts and torque to 220 ft. lbs. (260 Nm).
9. Install the brake caliper and torque the mounting bolts to 74 ft. lbs. (100 Nm).
10. Install the wheel and tire assembly. Lower the vehicle and pump the brake pedal a few times before moving the vehicle.

ADJUSTMENT

1984–87

The front wheels each rotate on a set of opposed, tapered roller bearings. The grease retainer at the inside of the hub prevents lubricant from leaking into the brake drum.

1. Raise and support the front end on jackstands.
2. Remove the grease cap and remove excess grease from the end of the spindle.
3. Remove the cotter pin and nut lock.
4. Rotate the wheel, hub and drum assembly while tightening the adjusting nut to 17–25 ft. lbs. (23–34 Nm) in order to seat the bearings.
5. Back off the adjusting nut ½, then retighten the adjusting nut to 10–15 inch. lbs. (1.2–1.8 Nm).
6. Locate the nut lock on the adjusting nut so that the castellations on the lock are lined up with the cotter pin hole in the spindle.
7. Install the new cotter pin, bending the ends of the cotter pin around the castellated flange of the nut lock.
8. Check the wheel for proper rotation, then install the grease cap. If the wheel still does not rotate properly, inspect and clean or replace the wheel bearings and cups.

Front End Alignment

➡The following procedures require the use of alignment equipment. The Do-it-Yourself mechanic should not attempt to perform any wheel alignment procedures. Expensive alignment tools are needed and would not be cost efficient to purchase these tools. The wheel alignment should be performed by a certified alignment technician using the proper alignment tools.

Front end alignment refers to the angular relationship between the front wheels, the front suspension attaching parts and the ground. The angle of the knuckle away from the vertical, the pointing in or "toe-in" of the front wheels, the tilt of the front wheels from vertical (when viewed from the front of the vehicle) and the tilt of the suspension members from vertical (when viewed from the side of the vehicle), all these are involved in front alignment.

The Pontiac Fiero is designed with independent front and rear suspension that is service adjustable, making four wheel alignment possible.

CAMBER

1984–87 Models

♦ See Figure 12

The Camber angle is the tilting of the wheels from the vertical when viewed from the rear of the car. When the wheels tilt outward at the top, the camber is said to be positive (+). When the wheels tilt inward at the top, the camber is said to be negative (−). Negative camber is the most common because as the springs sag down, the camber becomes negative which will wear the inside of the tires. The amount of tilt is measured in degrees from the vertical and the measurement is called camber angle.

Camber angle can be increased approximately 1° by removing the upper ball joint, rotating it one-half turn, and installing it with the flat of the upper flange on the inboard side of the control arm. For assistance, refer to the "Upper Ball Joint" procedures in this section.

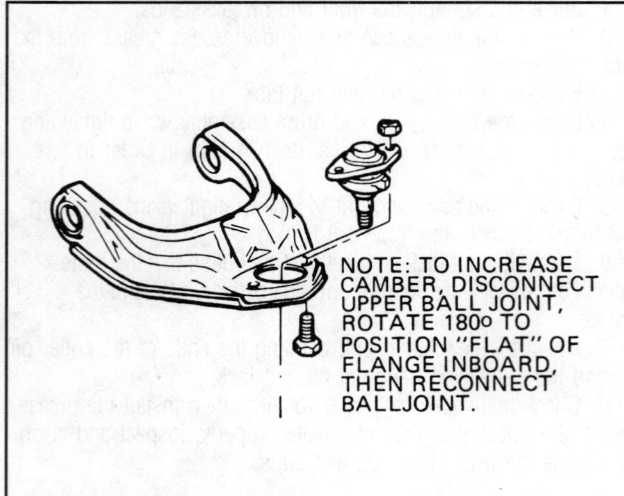

Fig. 12 The front camber angle can be adjusted by rotating the ball joint—1984–87 models

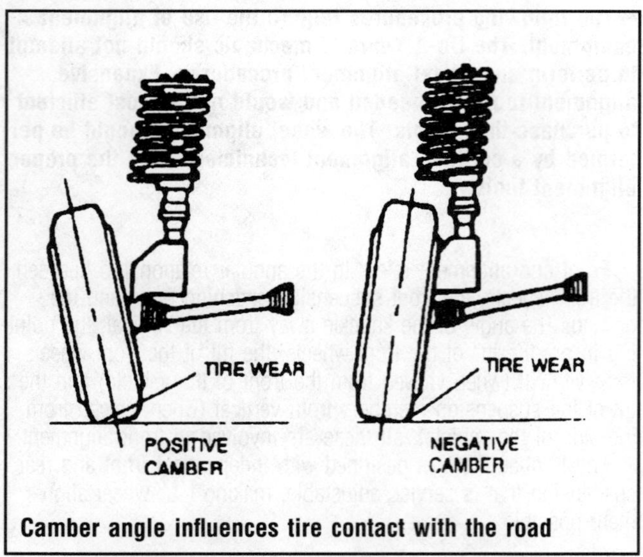

Camber angle influences tire contact with the road

CASTER

1984–87 Models

➧ **See Figure 13**

Caster angle can be changed by 1° by changing the position of the washers located between the legs of the upper control arm. Placing the thinner washer in front will increase caster, while placing it at the back will reduce caster.

➡**A kit is available containing two washers, one of 3mm thickness and one of 9mm thickness. Whenever adjusting caster, it is important to always use two washers totaling 12mm thickness, with one washer at each end of locating tube.**

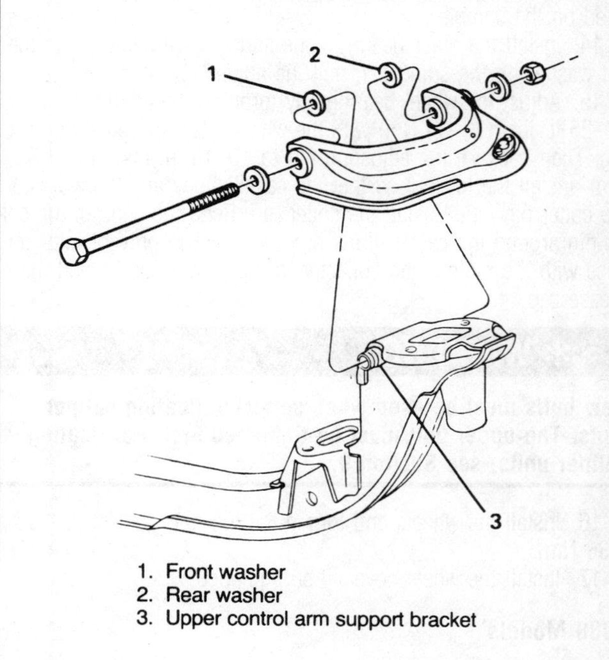

Fig. 13 The front caster angle can be adjusted by using different sized shims—1984–87 models

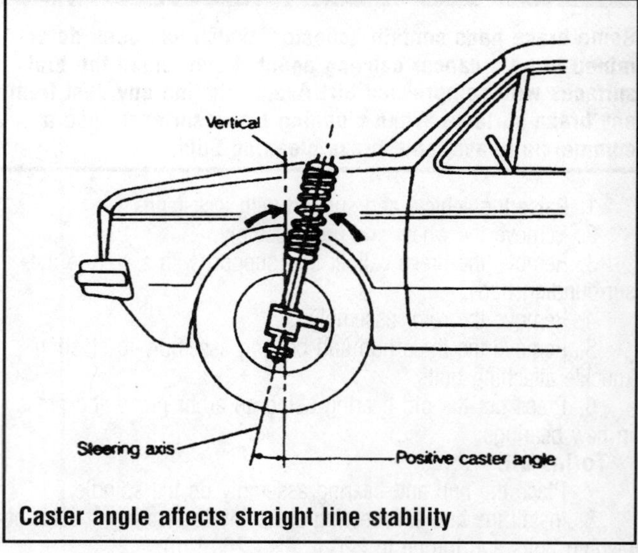

Caster angle affects straight line stability

CAMBER AND CASTER

1988 Models

➧ **See Figure 14**

The caster angle is the forward or rearward tilting of the wheel axis (at the top) from the vertical. A rearward tilt is a positive (+) angle, and a forward tilt is a negative (−) angle. Caster in-

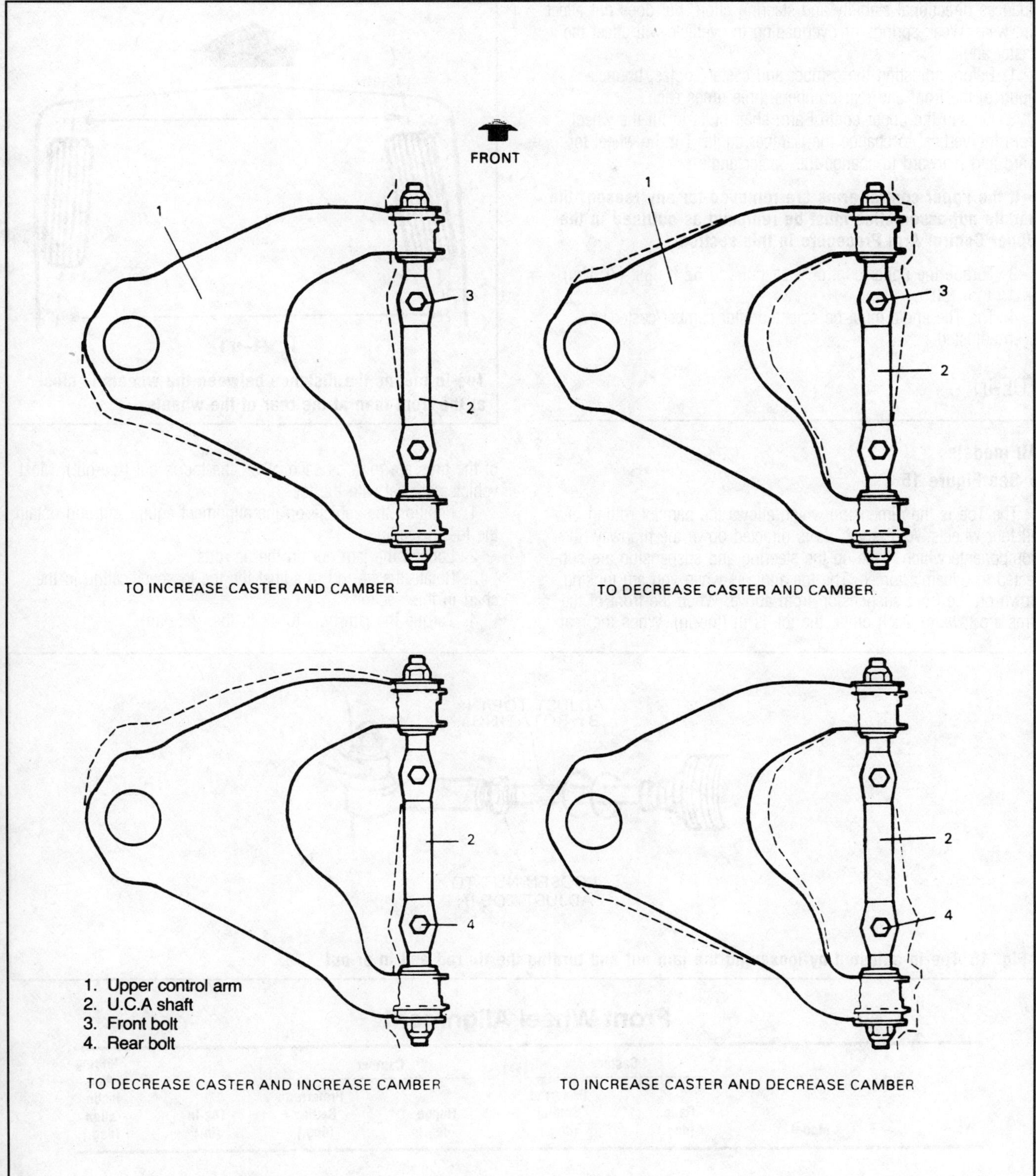

Fig. 14 Views of different camber and caster adjustments combinations—1988 models

fluences directional stability and steering effort, but does not affect tire wear. Weak springs or overloading the vehicle will affect the caster angle.

1. Before adjusting the camber and caster angles, bounce (jounce) the front and rear bumpers three times each.
2. Loosen the upper control arm shaft bolts to tilt the wheel from the vertical to change the Camber angle. Tilt the wheel forward and rearward to change the Caster angle.

➡If the upper control arms are removed for any reason, the paddle nut assemblies must be replaced as outlined in the Upper Control Arm Procedure in this section.

3. Torque the upper control shaft bolts to 52 ft. lbs. (70 Nm) + 1/4 turn (90°).
4. The Toe angle must be adjusted after camber/caster have been adjusted.

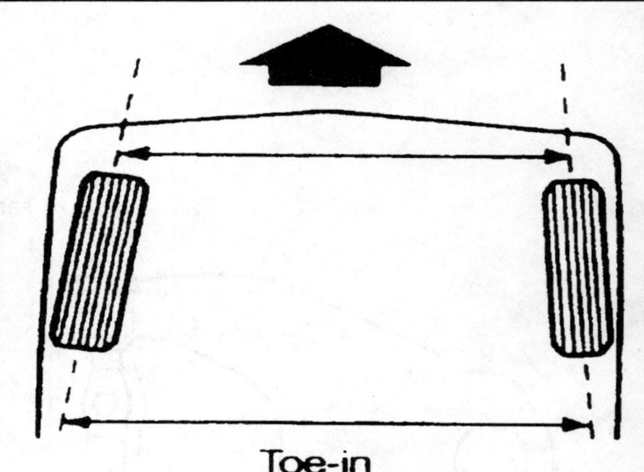

Toe-in means the distance between the wheels is closer at the front than at the rear of the wheels

TOE-IN

All models

➧ See Figure 15

The Toe is the dimension which allows the parallel rolling of all four wheels. As the vehicle is directed down the highway, the components which make up the steering and suspension are subjected to dynamic forces. The toe angle is when you are looking down on the front suspension from above. When the front of the tires are towards each other, the toe is in (toe-in). When the rear of the tires are towards each other, the toe is out (toe-out). Most vehicles are set with the toe-in.

1. Position the vehicle on the alignment equipment and obtain the toe-in reading.
2. Loosen the jam nut on the tie rods.
3. Rotate the tie rod to adjust the toe to specification in the chart in this section.
4. Torque the jam nuts to 47 ft. lbs. (64 Nm).

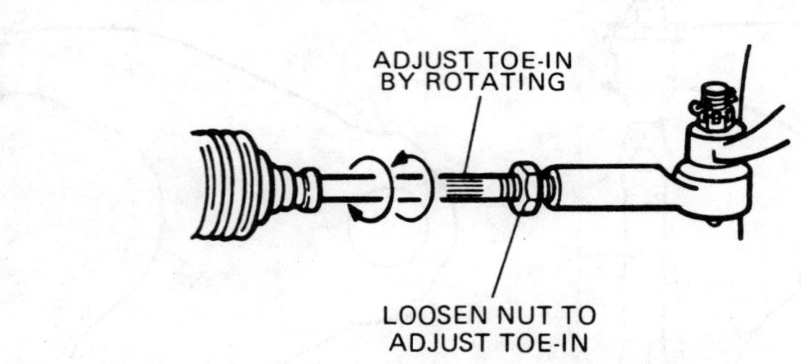

Fig. 15 Toe-in adjusted by loosening the jam nut and turning the tie rod end in or out

Front Wheel Alignment

Year	Model	Caster Range (deg.)	Caster Preferred Setting (deg.)	Camber Range (deg.)	Camber Preferred Setting (deg.)	Toe-in (in.)	Steering Axis Inclination (deg.)
84–86	All	3–7	5	−5/16–1 5/16	1/2	1/16–1/4	9 3/8
'87	All	3–7	5	−5/16–1 5/16	1/2	①	—
'88	Except GT	2 1/2–3 1/2	3	−1/2–1/2	0	1/16–1/4	—
	GT Formula	4 1/2–5 1/2	5	−1/2–1/2	0	1/16–1/4	—

① 3/32 (out), 3/32 (in)—0 preferred

REAR SUSPENSION

➧ **See Figures 16 and 17**

The rear suspension is a MacPherson Strut design. This combination strut and spring adapts to the rear wheel drive. The lower control arms pivot from the engine cradle. The cradle has isolation mounts to the body and conventional rubber bushings to the lower control arm pivots. The upper end of the struts are isolated by a rubber mount.

1. Strut asm.
2. Toe link rods
3. Spring
4. Rear control arm
5. Drive axles
1
2
3
2
5
5
4

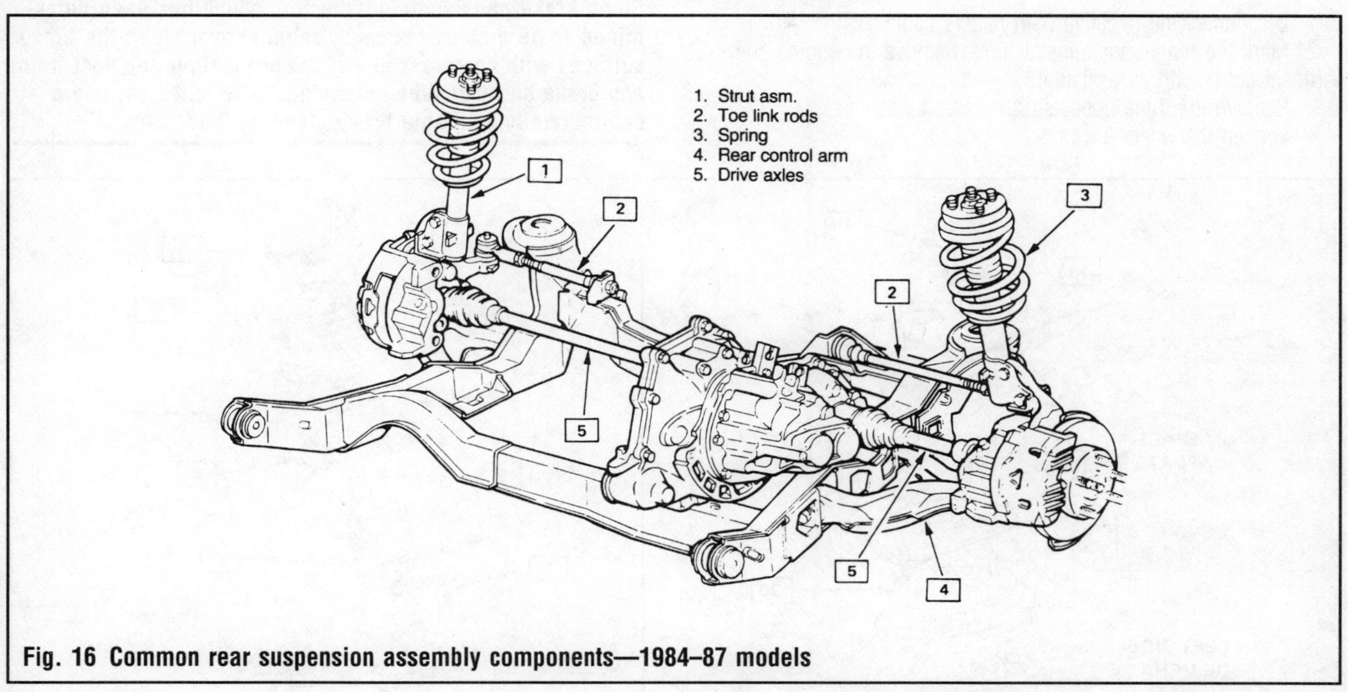

Fig. 16 Common rear suspension assembly components—1984–87 models

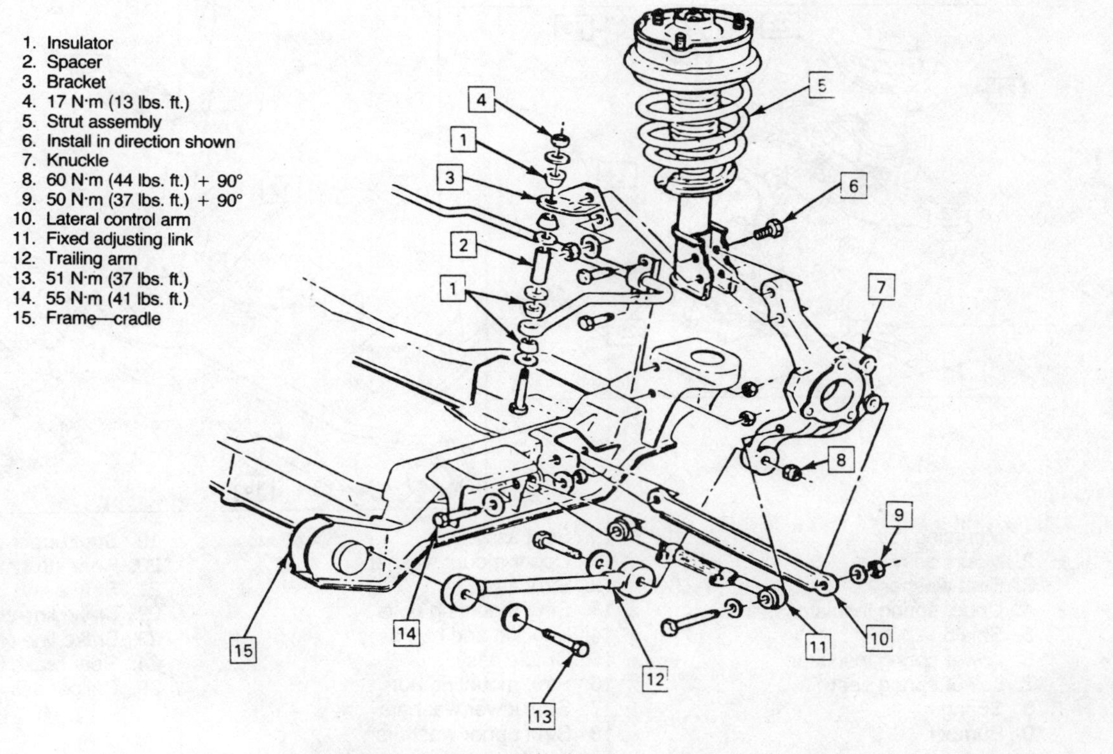

1. Insulator
2. Spacer
3. Bracket
4. 17 N·m (13 lbs. ft.)
5. Strut assembly
6. Install in direction shown
7. Knuckle
8. 60 N·m (44 lbs. ft.) + 90°
9. 50 N·m (37 lbs. ft.) + 90°
10. Lateral control arm
11. Fixed adjusting link
12. Trailing arm
13. 51 N·m (37 lbs. ft.)
14. 55 N·m (41 lbs. ft.)
15. Frame—cradle

Fig. 17 Exploded view of the rear suspension assembly—1988 models

MacPherson Strut

REMOVAL & INSTALLATION

➧ **See Figures 18 and 19**

1. Disconnect the negative (−) battery cable.
2. Mark the hinges for reinstallation. Remove the engine compartment cover with an assistant.
3. Remove the three upper strut nuts and washers.
4. Loosen the wheel lug nuts.
5. Raise the vehicle and support it on jackstands under the frame members. Support the rear control arm with a floor jack.
6. Remove the wheel and tire assemblies.

✲✲ CAUTION

Some brake pads contain asbestos, which has been determined to be a cancer causing agent. Never clean the brake surfaces with compressed air! Avoid inhaling any dust from any brake surface! When cleaning brake surfaces, use a commercially available brake cleaning fluid.

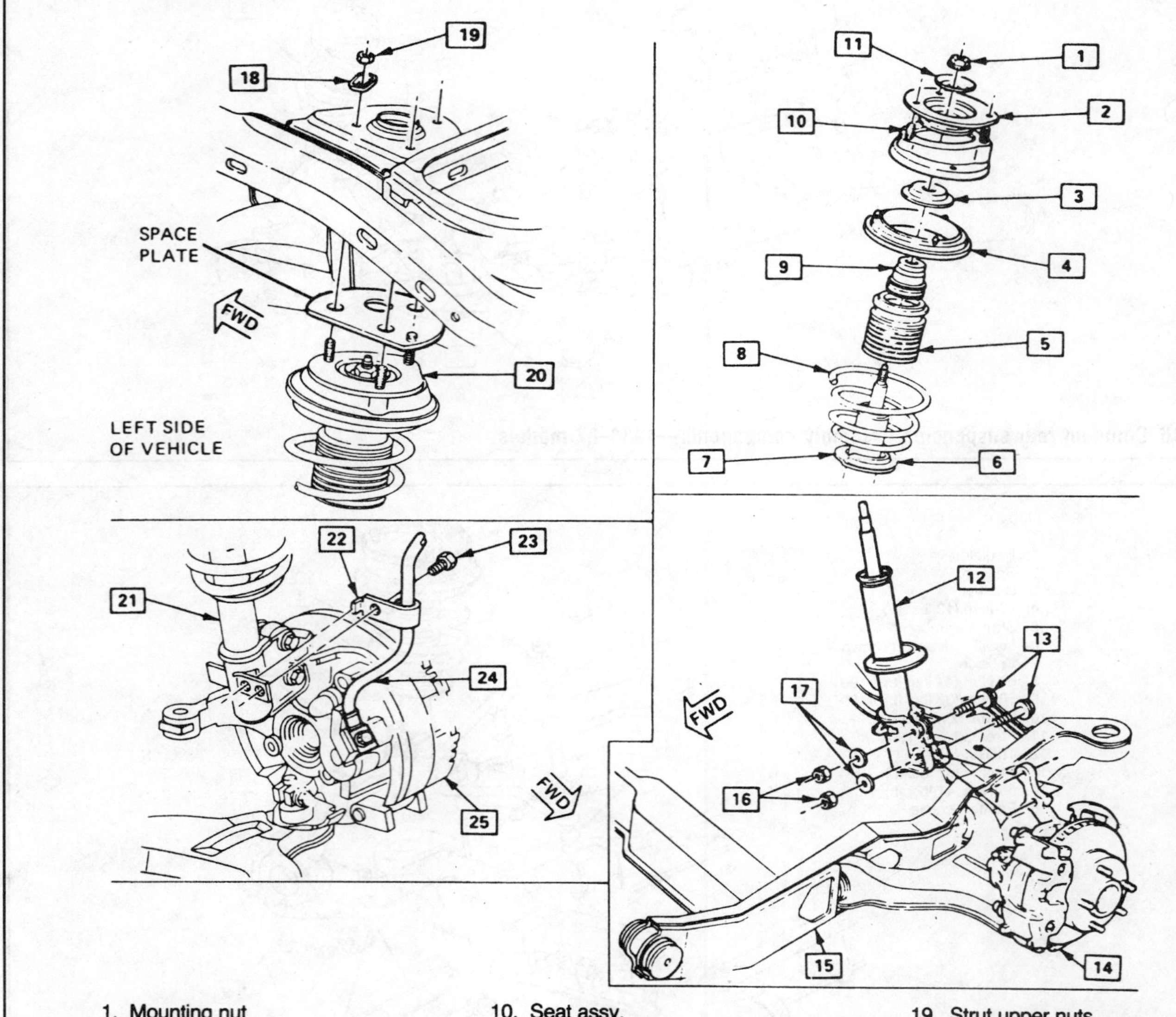

1. Mounting nut
2. Mount assy.
3. Seat washer
4. Upper spring insulator
5. Shield
6. Lower spring insulator
7. Lower spring seat
8. Spring
9. Bumper
10. Seat assy.
11. Upper mount washer
12. Strut assy.
13. Strut mounting bolts
14. Knuckle and hub assy.
15. Cradle assy.
16. Strut mounting nuts
17. Strut lower washers
18. Strut upper washers
19. Strut upper nuts
20. Rear strut mount assy.
21. Strut assy.
22. Brake line clip
23. Brake line clip bolt
24. Rear brake hose
25. Caliper assy.

Fig. 18 Exploded view of the strut assembly components and their removal/installation

7. Remove the brake line clip.
8. Scribe the strut and knuckle as shown in the accompanying illustration.
   a. Using a sharp tool, scribe the knuckle along the lower outboard strut radius, as in view A.
   b. Scribe the strut flange, on the inboard side, along the curve of the knuckle, as in view B.
   c. Make a chisel mark across the strut/knuckle interface, as shown in view C.
9. Remove the two strut mounting nuts and bolts and remove the strut assembly and spacer plate.

To install:

1. Position the strut and spacer plate assembly into the vehicle aligning the upper and lower mounts.
2. Install the two strut-to-knuckle bolts and nuts. Align the scribe marks on the strut and knuckle. Replace the bolts in the same order in which they were removed.
3. Torque the two bolts and nuts to 140 ft. lbs. (190 Nm).
4. Install the brake line clip and the wheel and tire assemblies. Torque the lug nuts to 100 ft. lbs. (136 Nm).

Matchmark the strut and knuckle, then . . .

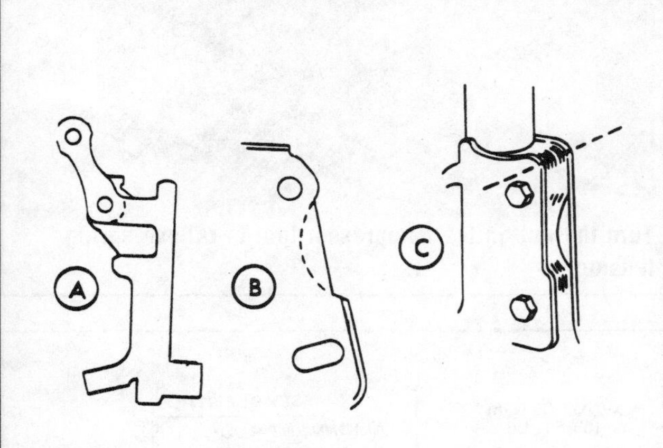

Fig. 19 Scribe the strut and knuckle positions before removing the MacPherson strut assembly

. . . remove the strut mounting nuts and bolts

Remove the nuts and washers from the top of the strut tower

Remove the strut assembly from the vehicle

5. Lower the vehicle and install the three upper strut mount-to-body nut and washers. Torque the nuts to 18 ft. lbs. (24 Nm).

6. With an assistant, install the engine compartment lid in the same position as removed.

7. Have a Rear End Alignment performed by a qualified alignment technician.

OVERHAUL

See Figure 20

➡A MacPherson Strut Compressor, special tool No. J-26584 or its equivalent MUST be used to disassemble and assemble the strut damper. Care must be used not to damage the special coating on the coil springs or damage could occur to the coils.

CAUTION

This procedure must be followed because it keeps the coil spring compressed. Use care to support the strut assembly adequately because the coil spring is under heavy load, if released too quickly personal injury could result. Never remove the center strut nuts unless the spring is compressed with a MacPherson Strut Spring Compressor tool J-26584 or equivalent.

Disassembly

1. Remove the strut assembly from the vehicle as previously outlined.

2. Clamp strut tool J-34013-A in the holding fixture J-32289-20 as outlined in the "Strut Disassembly" illustration in this section.

3. Place the strut assembly in the bottom adapter of the strut compressor and install tool J-26584-89 (make sure the strut adapter captures the strut and the locating pins are engaged).

4. Rotate the strut to align the top mounting lip with the strut compressor support notch.

5. Insert tool J-26584-450 top adapter on the top spring seal. Position the top adapters so that the long stud is at the high location to the strut flange.

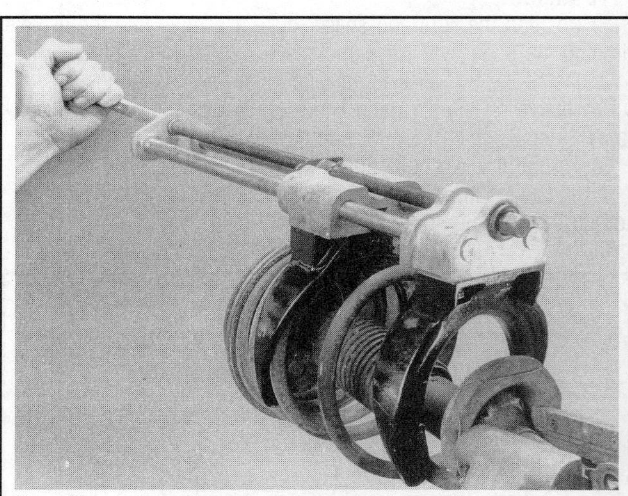

Turn the nut on the compressor tool to relieve spring tension

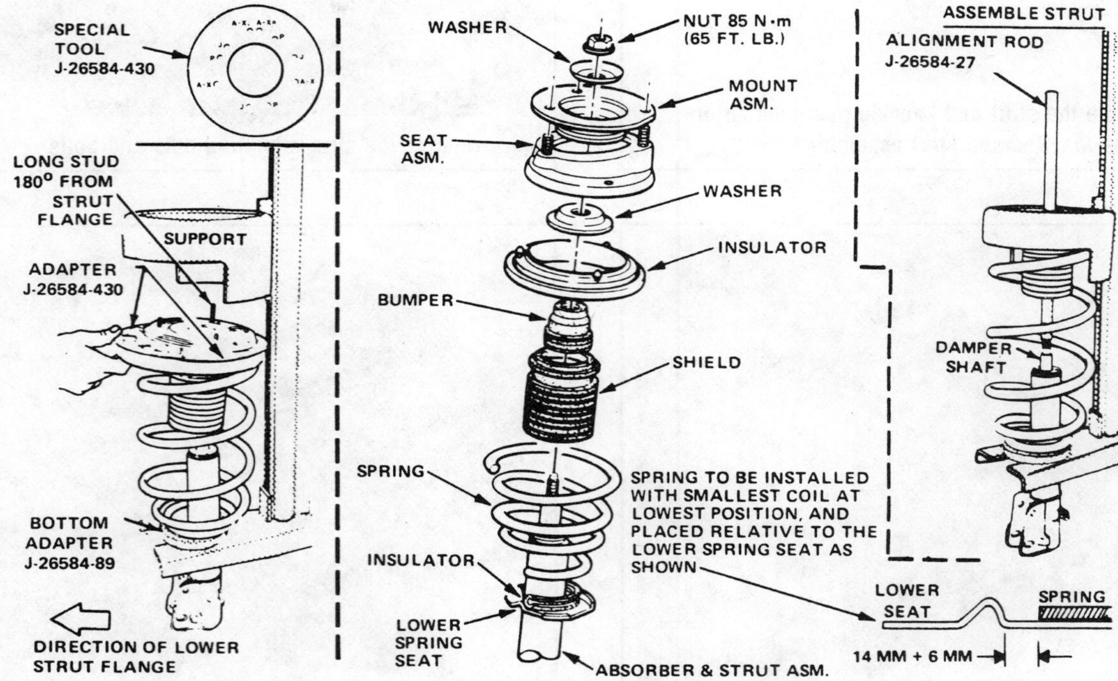

Fig. 20 A special compressor tool is needed for strut disassembly

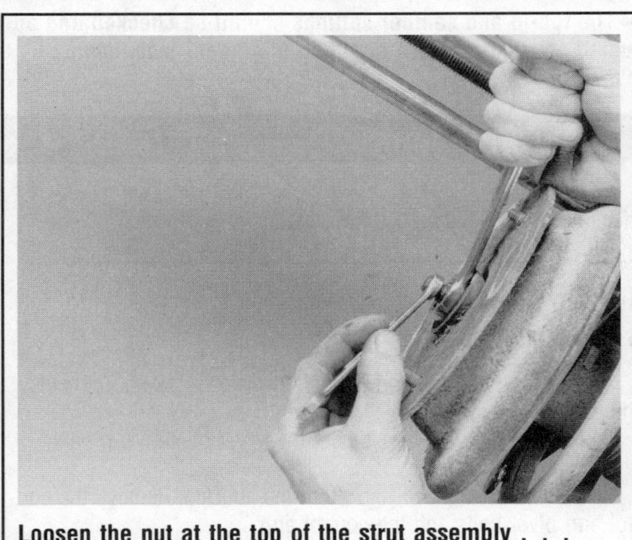
Loosen the nut at the top of the strut assembly . . .

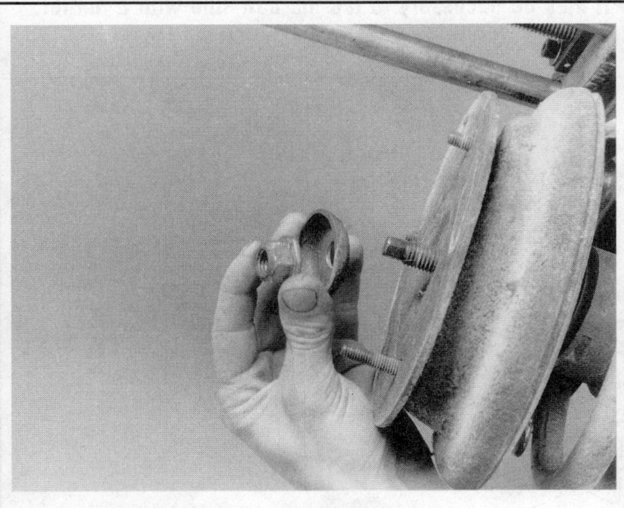
. . . then remove the nut and washer

Remove the mount assembly from the strut

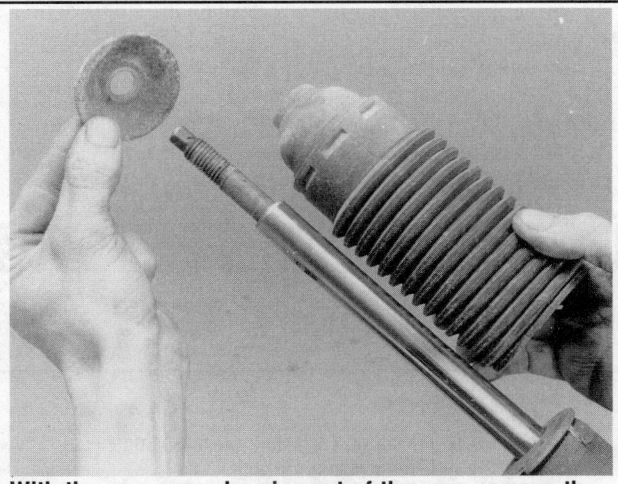
With the compressed spring out of the way, remove the washer, bumper and shield

6. Using a ratchet with a 1 inch socket, turn the compressor forcing the screw clockwise until the top support flange contacts the tool J-26584-430 top adapter. Continue turning the screw until the spring is compressed.
7. Place tool J-26584-430 top adapter over the spring seat.
8. Turn the strut compressor forcing the screw counterclockwise until the strut spring tension is relieved. Remove the top adapters, bottom adapter and the strut spring by removing the center nut.

Assembly

1. Clamp the strut compressor body tool J-26584 in a vise.
2. Place the strut assembly in the bottom adapter of the compressor and install tool J-26584-89 (make sure the adapter captures the strut and locating pins are engaged).
3. Rotate the strut assembly until the mounting flange is facing out directly opposite the compressor forcing screw.
4. Position the spring and components on the strut as shown in the accompanying illustration. Make sure the spring is properly seated on the bottom spring plate.
5. Install the strut spring seat on top of the spring. The long stud must be 180 degrees from the strut mounting flange.
6. Place tool J-26584-450 top adapter over the spring seat.
7. Turn the compressor forcing screw until the compressor support just contacts the top adapters (do not compress the spring at this time).
8. Install tool J-26584-27 Strut Alignment Rod through the spring seat and thread rod into the damper shaft and hand-tighten.
9. Compress the spring by turning the screw clockwise until enough of the damper shaft is exposed to install the washer and nut securely. Thread the nut onto the shaft far enough to properly secure.

WARNING

Do not compress the spring until it bottoms. Damage to the spring may result.

10. Remove the alignment rod and position the strut mount over the damper shaft and spring seat studs. Torque the damper nut to 65 ft. lbs. (85 Nm). Do not overtighten.
11. Turn the forcing screw counterclockwise to back off the support and remove the strut assembly from the compressor.

➡The toe-in and camber settings should be checked and adjusted as required by a qualified alignment technician.

Lower Control Arm

REMOVAL & INSTALLATION

See Figure 21

1. Raise the car and support it safely on jackstands.
2. Remove the ball joint clamping bolt.
3. Separate the knuckle from the ball joint.
4. Remove the lower control arm pivot bolts at the frame and remove the control arm.
5. Installation is the reverse of removal.

Lower Ball Joint

REMOVAL & INSTALLATION

1984–87 Models

See Figure 22

1. Raise the car, support it safely on jackstands and remove the wheel.
2. Remove the clamp bolt from the lower control arm ball stud.
3. Disconnect the ball joint from the knuckle. Remove the control arm pivot bolts and the control arm.

➡It may be necessary to tap the ball stud with a mallet.

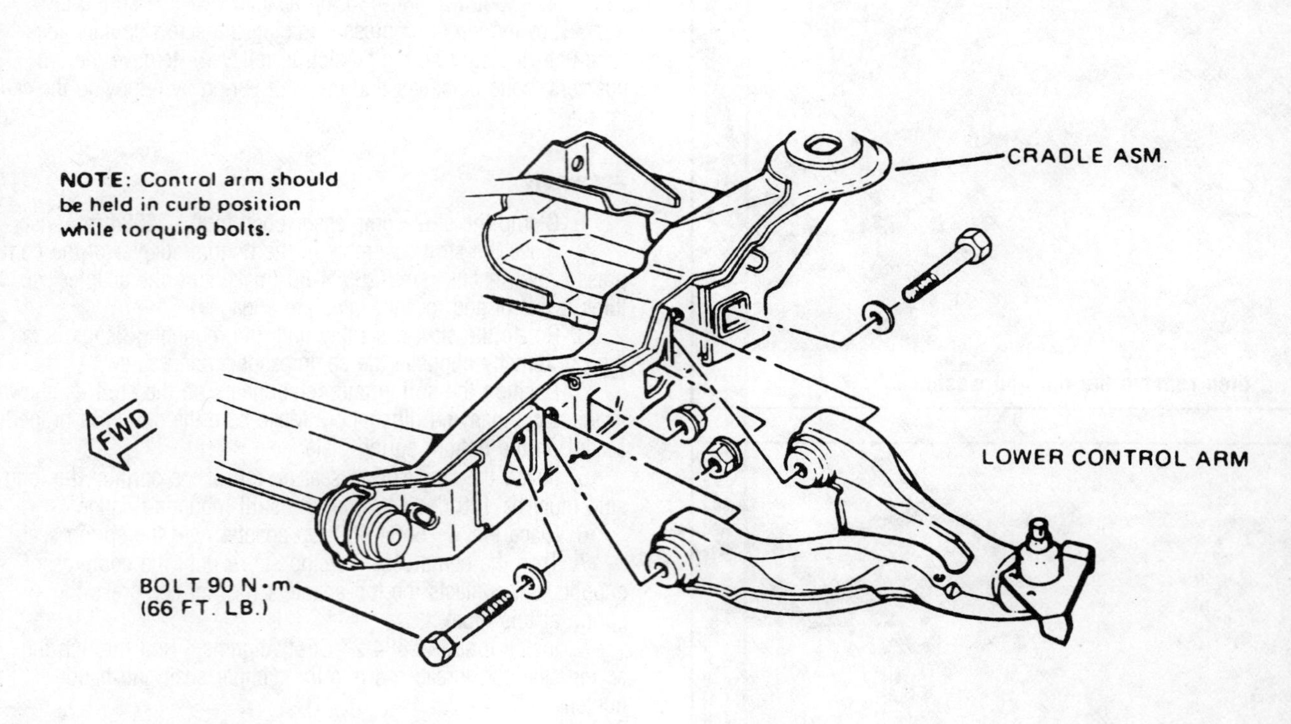

Fig. 21 Components of the lower control arm used on 1984–87 models

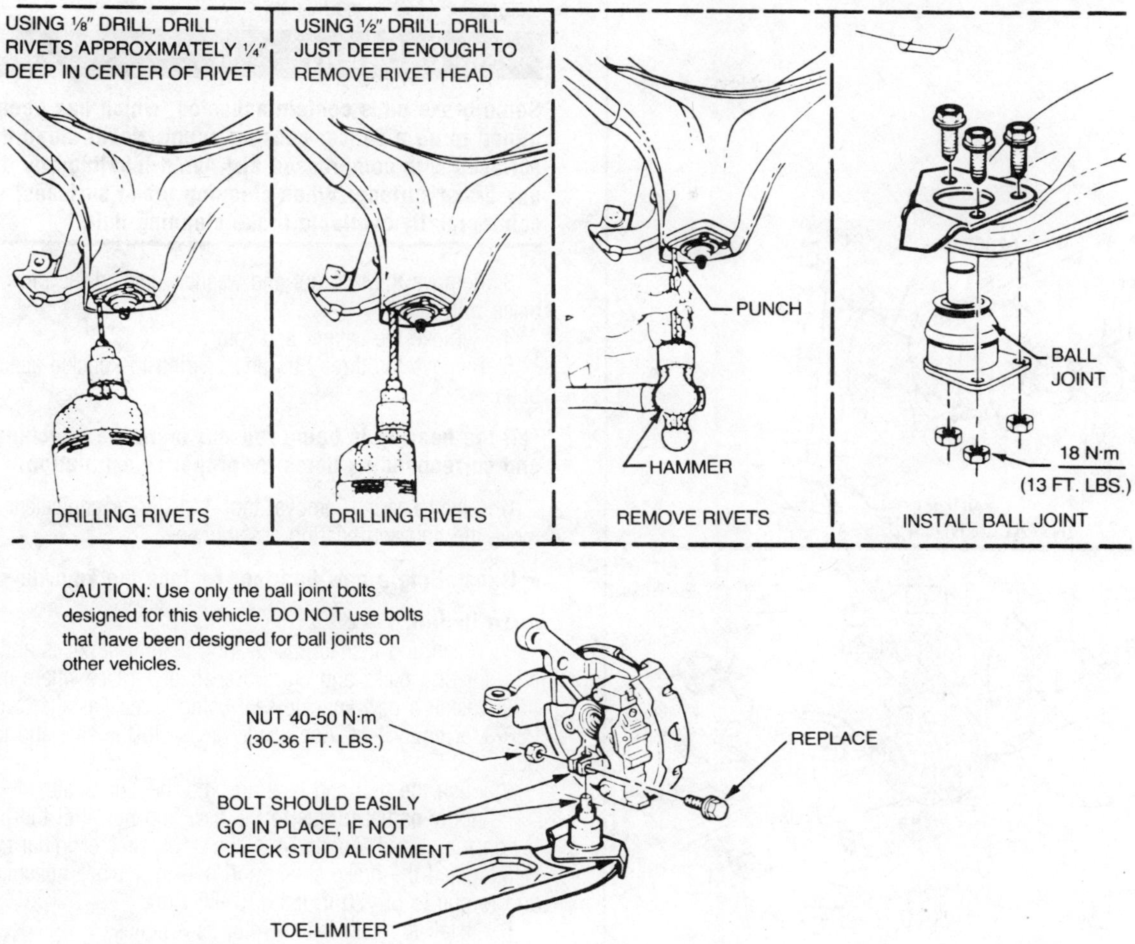

USING ⅛" DRILL, DRILL RIVETS APPROXIMATELY ¼" DEEP IN CENTER OF RIVET

DRILLING RIVETS

USING ½" DRILL, DRILL JUST DEEP ENOUGH TO REMOVE RIVET HEAD

DRILLING RIVETS

PUNCH

HAMMER

REMOVE RIVETS

BALL JOINT

18 N·m (13 FT. LBS.)

INSTALL BALL JOINT

CAUTION: Use only the ball joint bolts designed for this vehicle. DO NOT use bolts that have been designed for ball joints on other vehicles.

NUT 40-50 N·m (30-36 FT. LBS.)

REPLACE

BOLT SHOULD EASILY GO IN PLACE, IF NOT CHECK STUD ALIGNMENT

TOE-LIMITER

Fig. 22 Typical lower ball joint removal and installation—1984–87 models

After removing the ball joint clamping bolt, separate the knuckle from the ball joint

4. Using a ⅛ in. drill, drill the rivets approximately ¼ in. deep in the center of the rivet as shown in the "Ball Joint" removal illustration in this section.
5. Use a ½ in. drill and drill just deep enough to remove the rivet head.
6. Remove the rivets using a hammer and a punch.
7. The ball joint is replaced using nuts and bolts. Torque to 13 ft. lbs. (17 Nm). Check the toe-in setting and adjust as necessary.

Rear Wheel Bearings

REMOVAL & INSTALLATION

➧ **See Figure 23**

1. Remove the hub cap and loosen lug nuts. Raise the vehicle and support with jackstands.

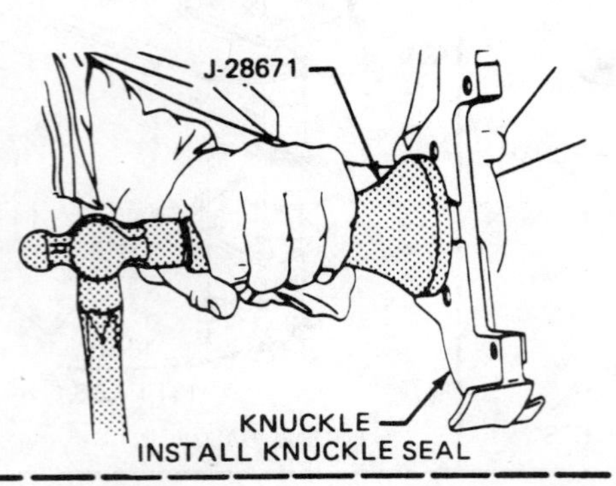

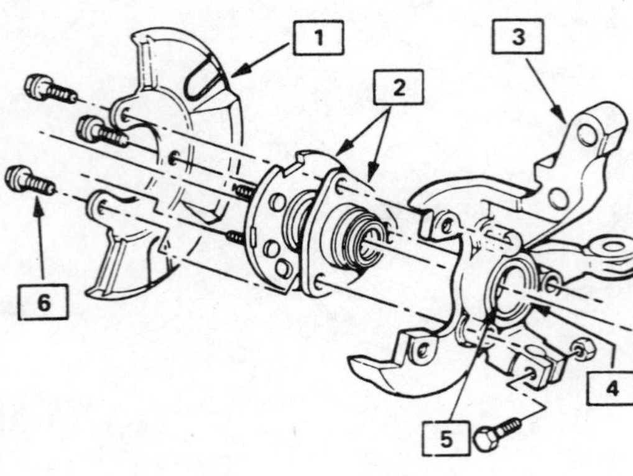

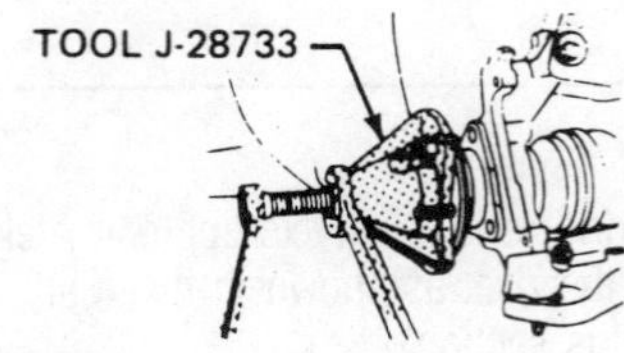

1. Shield
2. Hub and bearing asm.
3. Knuckle
4. Knuckle seal asm.
5. Fill hub bearing cavity between sealing lips with .8 grams of chassis lubricant
6. Bolt 75–95 N·m (55–70 ft. lb.)

Fig. 23 Exploded views of a common rear wheel bearing removal and installation

2. Remove the wheel assemblies and install halfshaft boot protectors J-33162 or equivalent.

CAUTION

Some brake pads contain asbestos, which has been determined to be a cancer causing agent. Never clean the brake surfaces with compressed air! Avoid inhaling any dust from any brake surface! When cleaning brake surfaces, use a commercially available brake cleaning fluid.

3. Remove the hub nut and washer, discard the old nut to replace with new.
4. Remove the caliper and rotor.
5. Remove the three hub and bearing-to-knuckle attaching bolts.

➡If the bearing is being reused, mark the attaching bolts and corresponding holes for proper reinstallation.

6. Install bearing removal tool J-28733 or equivalent and remove the hub and bearing assembly.

➡If installing a new bearing, replace the knuckle seal.

To install:

1. Clean and inspect the bearing mating surfaces and knuckle bore for dirt, nicks and burrs. Repair or replace where necessary.
2. Install a new knuckle seal using a seal installer tool J-28671 or equivalent. Apply axle grease to the seal and knuckle bore.
3. Push the hub and bearing onto the axle shaft.
4. Apply partial torque to the new hub nut until the hub and bearing is seated. About 74 ft. lbs. (100 Nm) of initial torque.
5. Install the brake shield and hub-to-knuckle attaching bolts and torque to 55–70 ft. lbs. (75–95 Nm).
6. Install the caliper and rotor assemblies.
7. Install the wheel assemblies and torque the lug nuts to 100 ft. lbs. (136 Nm). Lower the vehicle.
8. Apply final torque to the hub nut, 200 ft. lbs. (270 Nm).

➡This torque setting is very important to provide proper bearing load.

Knuckle

REMOVAL & INSTALLATION

1984–87 Models

See Figure 24

1. Remove the rear wheel bearings as outlined in the previous section.
2. Remove the toe link rod at the knuckle.
3. Remove the lower ball joint clamp nut and lower control arm from the knuckle. The knuckle may have to be tapped with a plastic hammer to remove the lower ball joint. Be careful not to damage the grease boot.
4. Remove both through bolts holding the strut-to-knuckle and remove the knuckle.

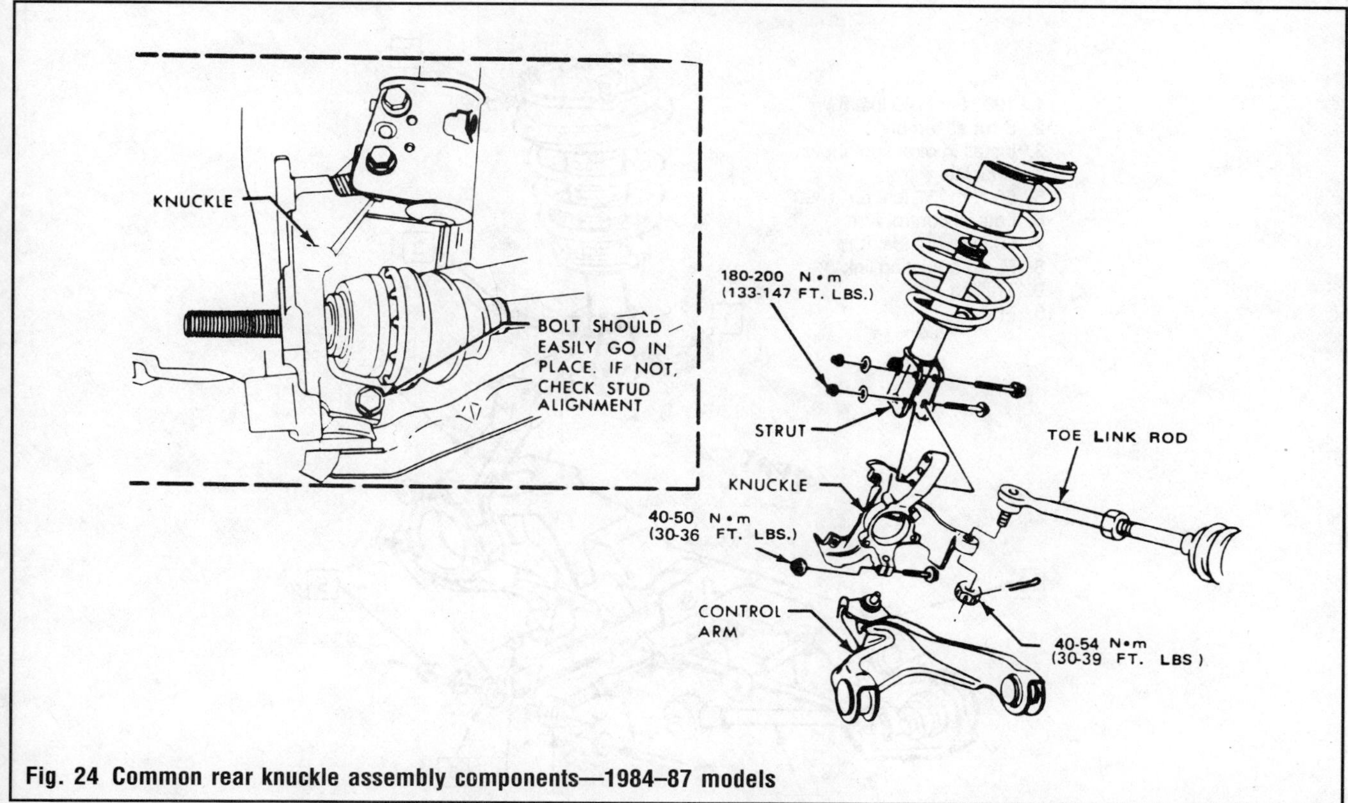

Fig. 24 Common rear knuckle assembly components—1984–87 models

To install:

5. Position the knuckle to the ball joint and loosely install the knuckle to strut.
6. Install the toe link rod-to-knuckle and torque to 30–39 ft. lbs. (40–54 Nm).
7. Torque the strut attaching bolts to 133–147 ft. lbs. (180–200 Nm).
8. Install the hub and bearing assembly as outlined in the previous procedure.
9. Install the wheel assemblies and torque the lug nuts to 100 ft. lbs. (136 Nm).
10. Have a rear wheel alignment performed by a qualified alignment technician.

1988 Models

➧ See Figure 25

1. Raise the vehicle and support with jackstands.
2. Install halfshaft boot protectors J-33162 or equivalent.
3. Remove the rear wheel assemblies.
4. Remove the hub nut.

CAUTION

Some brake pads contain asbestos, which has been determined to be a cancer causing agent. Never clean the brake surfaces with compressed air! Avoid inhaling any dust from any brake surface! When cleaning brake surfaces, use a commercially available brake cleaning fluid.

5. Remove the caliper and rotor, trailing arm at knuckle, fixed adjusting link/lateral control arm through bolts and strut mounting bolts.
6. Remove the hub/knuckle assembly from the drive axle.

To install:

1. Install the hub/knuckle to the drive axle.
2. Loosely install the strut mounting bolts with the bolt heads to the rear.
3. Install the fixed adjusting link/lateral control arm through bolts and torque to 37 ft. lbs. (50 Nm) + 90° turn.
4. Install the trailing arm and torque the nut to 44 ft. lbs. (60 Nm).
5. Torque the strut mounting bolts to 140 ft. lbs. (190 Nm).
6. Install the brake rotor and caliper as outlined in the Rear Brake Caliper procedures in Section 9.
7. Partially torque the NEW hub nut and washer to 74 ft. lbs. (100 Nm).
8. Remove the halfshaft boot protectors and install the rear wheel assemblies. Torque the lug nuts to 100 ft. lbs. (136 Nm).
9. Lower the vehicle.
10. Apply the final torque to the hub nut at 200 ft. lbs. (270 Nm).

➡This torque setting is very important to provide proper bearing load.

11. Have the rear camber and toe aligned by a qualified alignment technician.

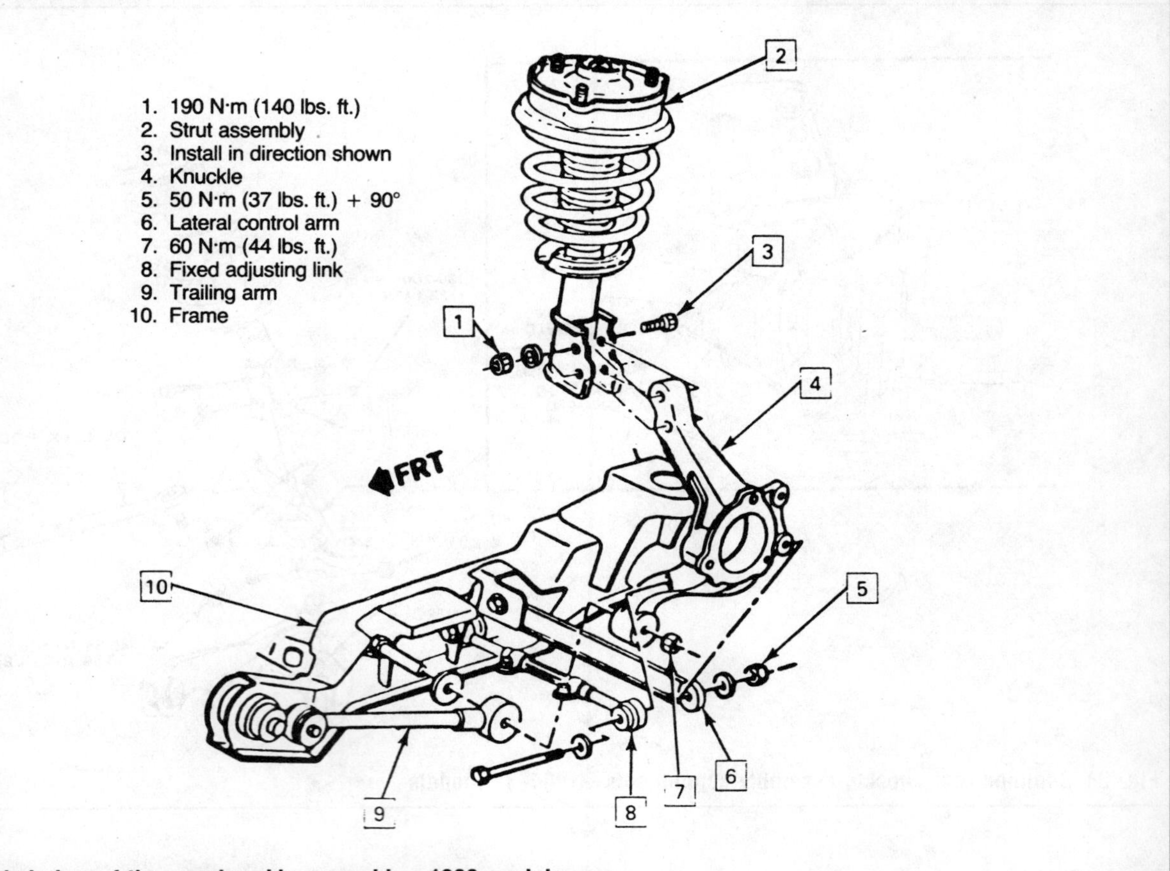

Fig. 25 Exploded view of the rear knuckle assembly—1988 models

Rear End Alignment

➡The Do-it-Yourself mechanic should not attempt to perform any wheel alignment procedures. Expensive alignment tools are needed and would not be cost efficient to purchase these tools. The wheel alignment should be performed by a certified alignment technician using the proper alignment tools.

Rear alignment refers to the angular relationship between the rear wheels, the rear suspension attaching parts and the ground. Camber and toe are the only adjustments required.

CAMBER

Camber can be adjusted by loosening both strut to knuckle bolts enough to allow movement between the strut and knuckle and grasping the top of the tire and moving it inboard or outboard until the correct camber is obtained.

TOE

Toe-in is adjusted by loosening the jam nuts on the toe link rods (fixed adjusting rods) then rotating the toe link rods to adjust the toe to specifications. Torque the clamp bolts to 47 ft. lbs. (64 Nm).

Rear Wheel Alignment

Year	Model	Caster Range (deg.)	Caster Preferred Setting (deg.)	Camber Range (deg.)	Camber Preferred Setting (deg.)	Toe-in (in.)	Steering Axis Inclination (deg.)
84–86	All	—	—	−1½–½	−1	①	—
'87	All	—	—	−1½–½	−1	①	—
'88	All	—	—	−½–1½	−1	1/16–¼	—

① 3/32 (out), 3/32 (in)—0 preferred

STEERING

Steering Wheel

REMOVAL & INSTALLATION

See Figure 26

1. Disconnect the negative (−) battery cable.
2. Pry off the center cap or remove the two pad screws. Remove the retainer clip and nut.

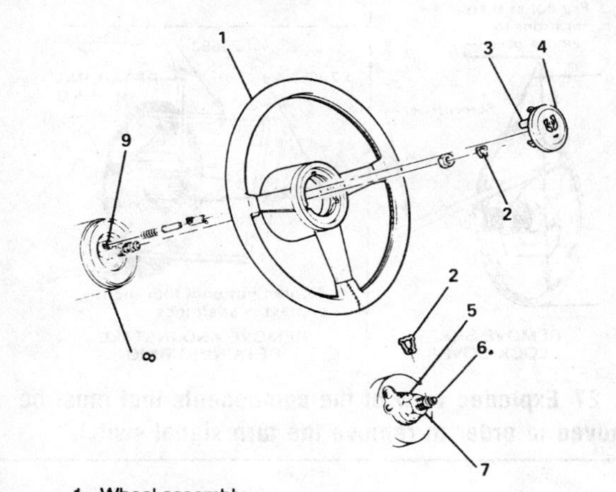

1. Wheel assembly
2. Retainer
3. Visually inspect cap to insure nylon shrink tube is secured to cap
4. Cap assembly
5. Align index mark on steering wheel with index mark on steering shaft within one female serration
6. Steering column shaft
7. 48 N·m (35 ft. lbs.)
8. Steering column
9. Caution: canceling cam tower must be centered in slot of lock plate cover before assembling wheel

Fig. 26 Exploded view of the steering wheel assembly

Remove the horn cap from the steering wheel

A pair of snapring pliers is helpful in removing the retainer clip

Remove the horn button, then . . .

. . . use a ratchet and socket to remove the steering wheel retaining nut

Use a suitable threaded puller to loosen the steering wheel from the shaft

Remove the steering wheel from the shaft

3. Remove the steering wheel using a steering wheel puller tool J-1859-03 or BT-61-9.

4. When installing, align the index mark on the steering wheel with the index mark on the steering shaft. Torque the retaining nut to 35 ft. lbs. (47 Nm).

CAUTION

The canceling cam tower must be centered in the slot of the lock plate cover before assembling the wheel.

Turn Signal (Multi-Function) Switch

REMOVAL & INSTALLATION

See Figure 27

1. Disconnect the negative (−) battery cable.
2. Remove the steering wheel and trim cover by pushing down

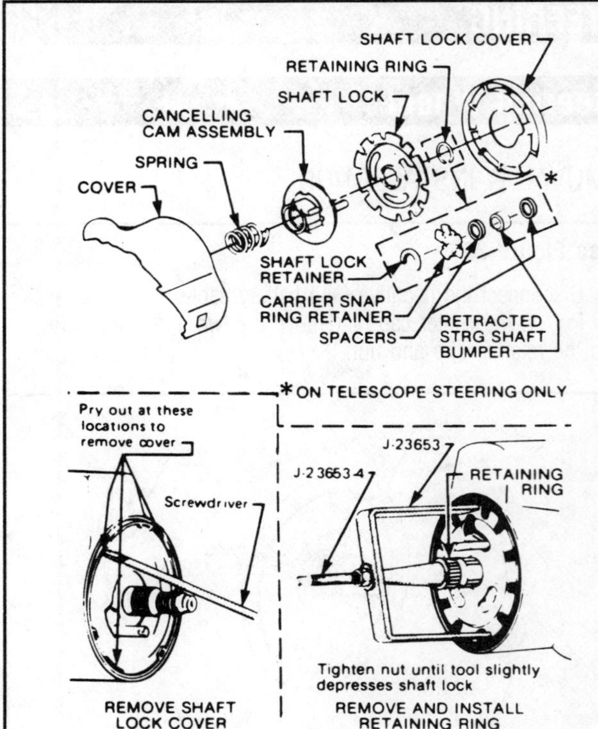

Fig. 27 Exploded view of the components that must be removed in order to remove the turn signal switch

on the trim cover and turn until unlocked (Sport Wheel). Remove the two pad retaining screws and the pad cover (Standard Wheel).

3. Remove the steering column cover attaching screws and remove the cover from the steering column.
4. Position a U-shaped lockplate compressing tool on the end of the steering shaft and compress the lockplate by turning the shaft nut clockwise. Pry the wire snapring out of the shaft groove.
5. Remove the tool and lift the lockplate off the shaft.
6. Slip the canceling cam, upper bearing preload spring, and thrust washer off the shaft.
7. Remove the turn signal lever. Remove the hazard flasher button retaining screw and remove the button spring and knob.
8. Pull the switch connector out of the mast jacket and tape the upper part to facilitate switch removal. Attach a long piece of wire to the turn signal switch connector. When installing the turn signal switch, feed this wire through the column first, and then use this wire to pull the switch connector into position. On tilt wheels, place the turn signal and shifter housing in the low position and remove the harness cover.
9. Remove the three switch mounting screws. Remove the switch by pulling it straight up while guiding the wiring harness cover through the column.

To install:

1. Install the replacement switch by working the connector and cover down through the housing and under the bracket. On tilt models, the connector is worked down through the housing, under the bracket, and then the cover is installed on the harness. Reconnect the electrical connector and cover.
2. Install the switch mounting screws and the connector on the mast jacket bracket. Install the column-to-dash trim plate.
3. Install the flasher knob and turn signal lever.

4. With the turn signal lever in neutral and the flasher knob out, slide the thrust washer, upper bearing preload spring, and canceling cam onto the shaft.

5. Position the lock plate on the shaft and press it down until a new snapring can be inserted in the shaft groove. Always use a new snapring when assembling.

6. Install the cover and the steering wheel. Torque the steering shaft nut to 30 ft. lbs. (41 Nm).

Ignition Lock Cylinder

REMOVAL & INSTALLATION

➧ See Figure 28

1. Disconnect the negative (−) battery cable.
2. Remove the steering wheel and pad as previously outlined.
3. Turn the lock to the RUN position.
4. Remove the lock plate, turn signal switch or combination switch, and the key warning buzzer switch. The warning buzzer switch can be fished out with a bent paper clip.
5. Remove the lock cylinder retaining screw and lock cylinder. Refer to the accompanying illustration.

✲✲✲ CAUTION

If the screw is dropped on removal, it could fall into the column, requiring complete disassembly to retrieve the screw.

To install:

6. Rotate the cylinder clockwise to align the cylinder key with the keyway in the housing.

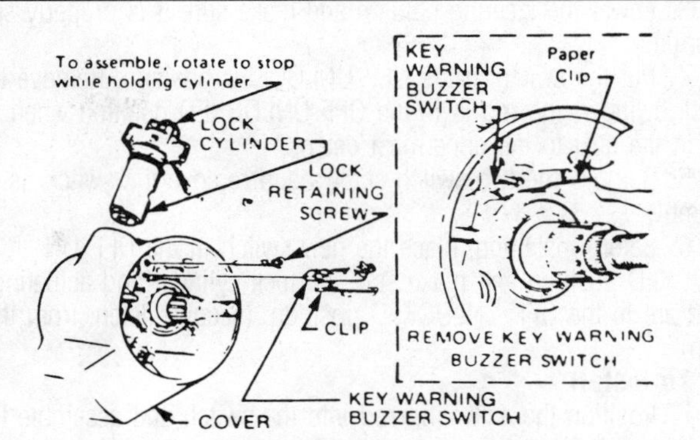

Fig. 28 After removing the lock plate, turn signal switch and key buzzer switch, remove the lock cylinder retaining screw and the lock cylinder

7. Push the lock all the way in.
8. Install the screw and torque to 15 inch lbs. (1.6 Nm).
9. Install the multi-function switch, lock plate, and steering wheel as previously outlined in this section.

Ignition Switch

REMOVAL & INSTALLATION

➧ See Figure 29

1. Disconnect the negative (−) battery cable.
2. Remove the steering wheel and lock plate as previously outlined.

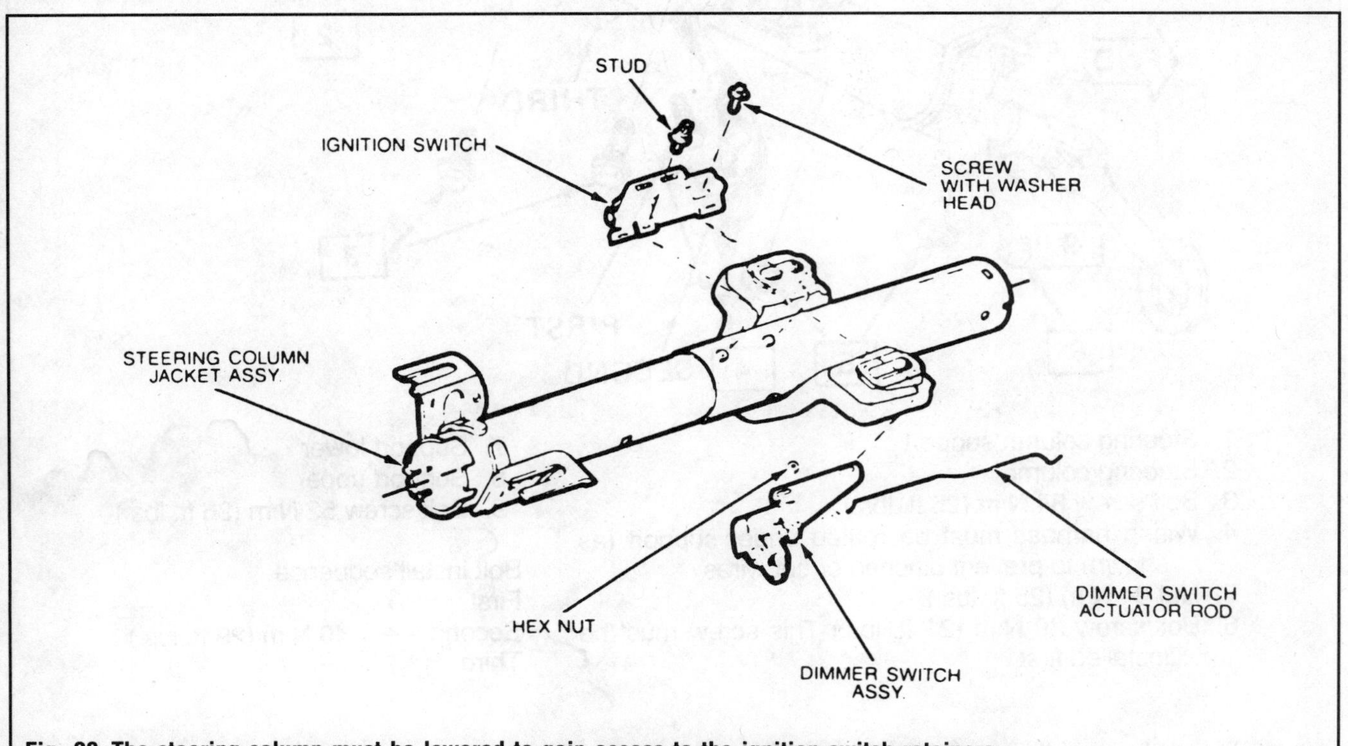

Fig. 29 The steering column must be lowered to gain access to the ignition switch retainers

3. Lower the steering column and make sure it is properly supported.

4. Put the switch in the OFF UNLOCKED position. Remove the lock cylinder, the rod is in the OFF UNLOCKED position when it is in the next to the uppermost detent.

5. Remove the two switch screws and remove the switch assembly.

6. Before installing, place the new switch in the OFF UNLOCKED position and make sure the lock cylinder and actuating rod are in the OFF UNLOCKED position. (second detent from the top).

To install:

7. Position the activating rod into the switch and assemble the switch on the column. Tighten the mounting screws. Use only the specified screws, since over length screws could impair the collapsibility of the column.

8. Reinstall the steering column, lock cylinder, lock plate and steering wheel. Torque the steering shaft nut to 30 ft. lbs. (41 Nm).

Steering Column

REMOVAL & INSTALLATION

See Figures 30 and 31

1. Disconnect the negative (−) battery cable.

2. Remove the left instrument panel sound absorber, trim pad and steering column trim collar.

3. Remove the horn pad and steering wheel as previously outlined in this section.

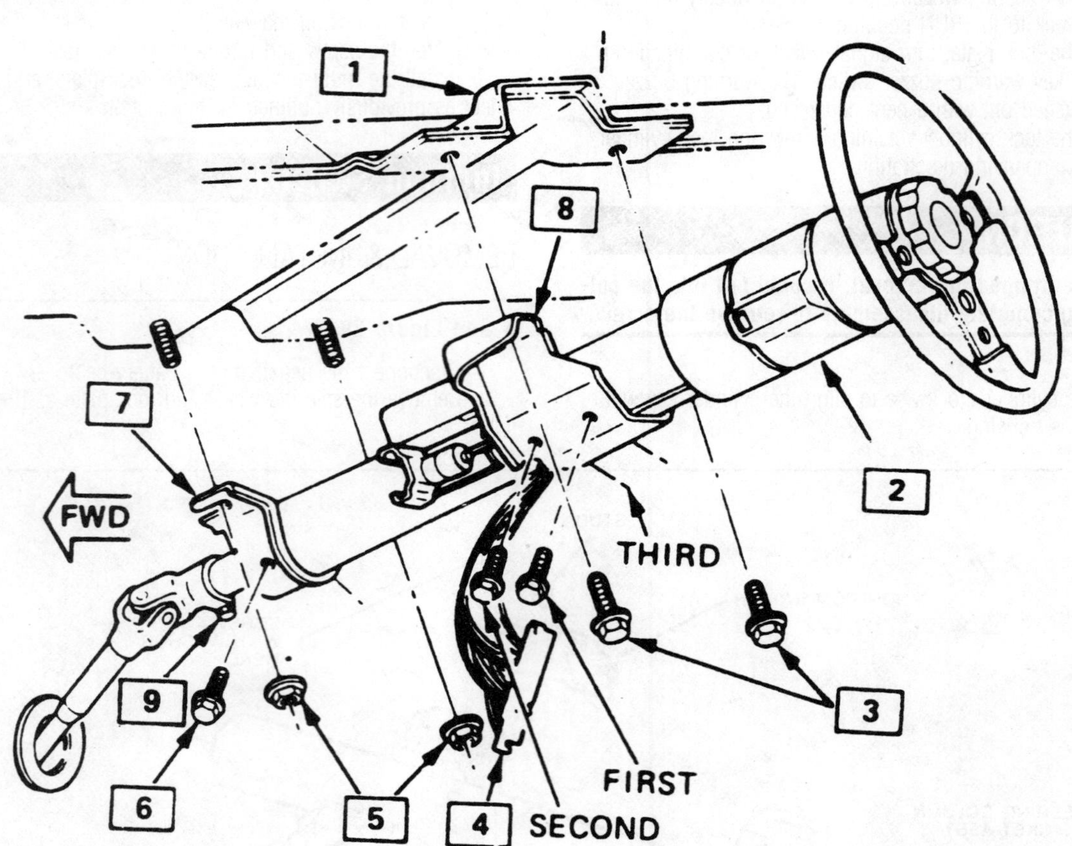

Fig. 30 Exploded view of the steering column mounting

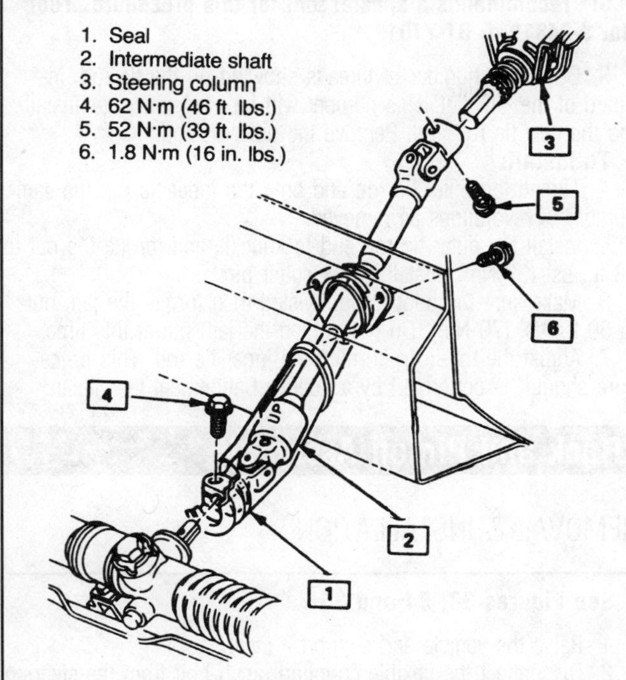

Fig. 31 Exploded view of the intermediate shaft mounting

4. Raise the front of the vehicle and support with jackstands. Remove the steering shaft-to-intermediate shaft connection.
5. Remove the column bracket support nut and bolts.
6. Remove the shift indicator cable and all electrical connectors.
7. Remove the shift cable at the actuator and housing holder and remove the column assembly.

To install:

1. Install the column assembly to the instrument panel.
2. Install the shift cable and housing, electrical connectors and shift indicator cable.
3. Install the support nut and bolts and torque in the correct sequence as shown in the illustration. Torque the bolts to 29 ft. lbs. (40 Nm).
4. Install the intermediate shaft-to-upper shaft bolt and torque the bolt to 46 ft. lbs. (62 Nm).
5. Install the steering wheel and horn pad as outlined earlier in this section.
6. Install the steering column trim covers and sound insulator. Reconnect the negative (−) battery cable and check for proper operation of serviced components.

Tie Rod End

REMOVAL & INSTALLATION

➧ **See Figure 32**

1. Loosen the jam nut.
2. Remove the tie rod-to-knuckle cotter pin and nut. Remove the tie rod from the steering knuckle.

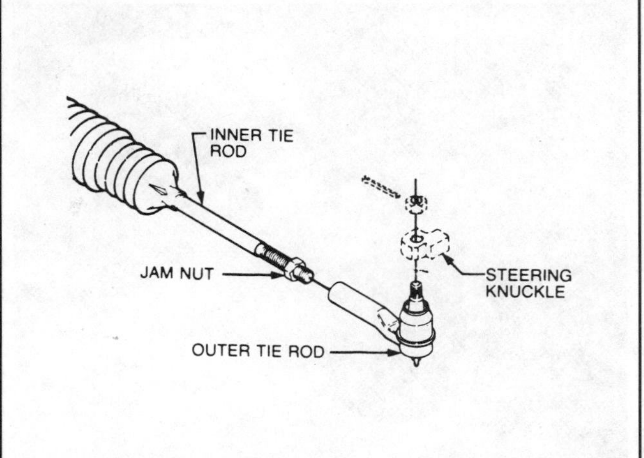

Fig. 32 Location of a common outer tie rod (tie rod end) and its related components

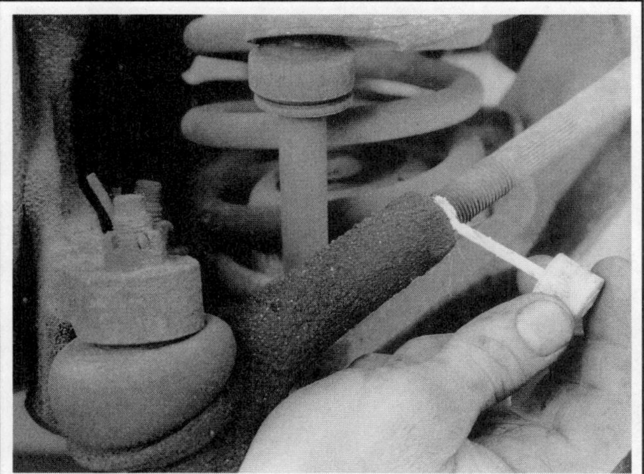

Matchmark the tie rod and tie rod end before removal, to aid in installation

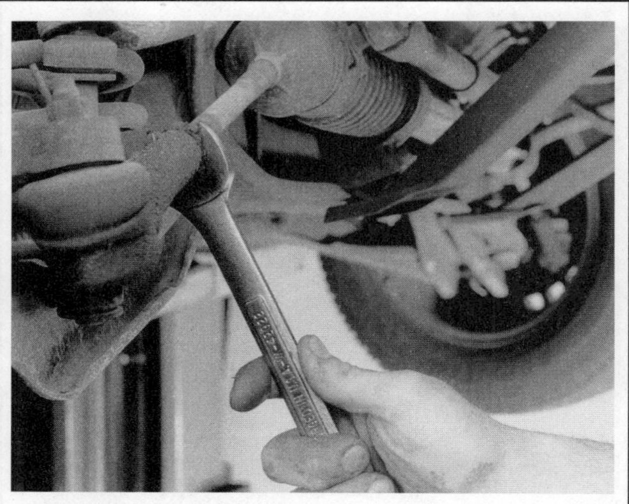

Loosen tie rod end jam nut

Remove the tie rod-to-knuckle cotter pin, then . . .

Use a ratchet and socket to remove the tie rod-to-knuckle retaining nut

Unthread and remove the tie rod end from the tie rod

➡GM recommends a special tool for this procedure. Tool No. J-24319 or BT-7101.

3. Count the number of threads showing on the tie rod, inboard of the jam nut. This number will be a reference for installing the new tie rod end. Remove the outer tie rod.

To install:

4. Thread the outer tie rod end onto the inner tie rod the same number of revolutions as removed.
5. Install the outer tie rod end-to-knuckle and torque the nut to 28 ft. lbs. (39 Nm). Install a new cotter pin.
6. Make sure the boot is not twisted then torque the jam nut to 50 ft. lbs. (70 Nm). Do not tighten the jam nut at this time.
7. Adjust the toe-in by turning the inner tie rod. This procedure should be performed by a qualified alignment technician.

Rack and Pinion Assembly

REMOVAL & INSTALLATION

See Figures 33, 34 and 35

1. Raise the vehicle and support it safely.
2. Disconnect the flexible coupling pinch bolt from the steering shaft.
3. Remove the outer tie rod cotter pins and nuts on the left and right sides.
4. Disconnect the tie rods from the steering knuckle as outlined in the previous procedure.
5. Remove the four bolts retaining the steering assembly to the crossmember and remove the steering assembly.

To install:

6. Position the steering assembly to the crossmember and torque the four retaining bolts to 20 ft. lbs. (27 Nm).
7. Install and tighten the flexible coupling bolt to 46 ft. lbs. (62 Nm).
8. Install the tie rod ends, nuts and torque to 15 ft. lbs. (20 Nm), followed by a 1⁄6 turn to align the cotter pin. Install new cotter pins.
9. Lower the vehicle and have the front end aligned by a qualified alignment technician.

OVERHAUL

The following two procedures can be performed without removing the rack and pinion assembly.

Steering Damper Assembly (1984–87 Models)

1. Hold the stud while removing the hex nut and flat washer and remove the damper assembly.

To install:

2. Position the damper assembly onto the rack assembly, install the flat washers and nuts and torque to 32 ft. lbs. (43 Nm).

Boot Seal

1. Remove the tie rod end and jam nut.
2. Cut the boot clamp and discard. The steering damper stud must be removed on the right side boot on 1984–87 models. Slide the boot off the rack assembly.

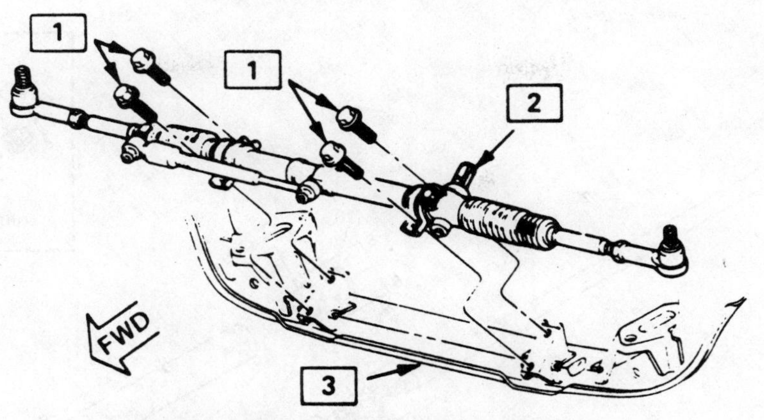

STEERING GEAR TO CROSS MEMBER

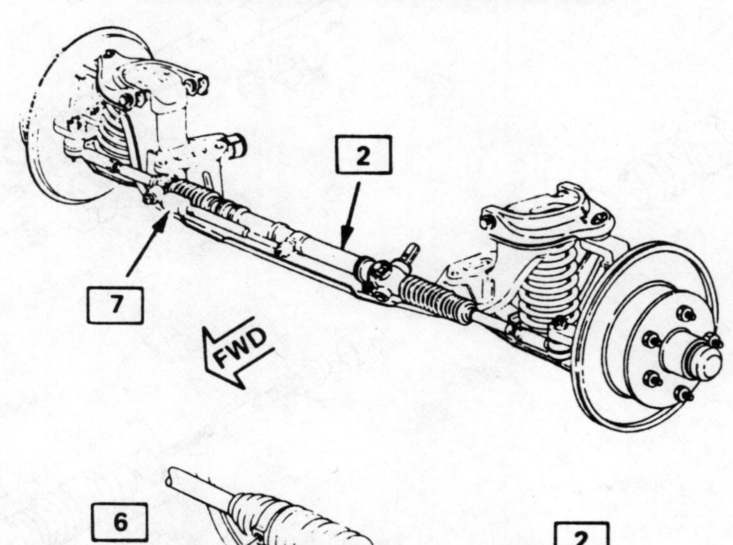

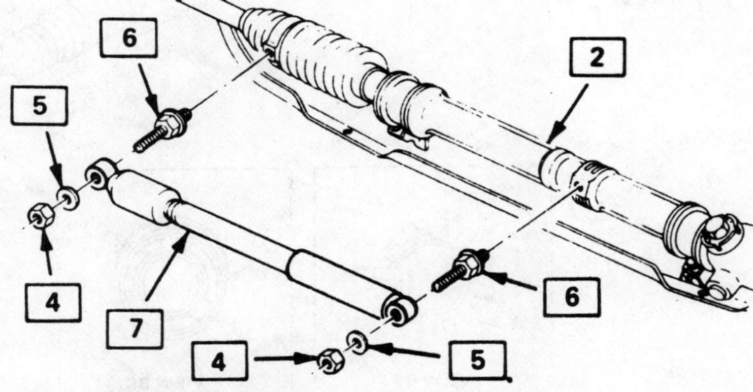

STEERING LINKAGE DAMPER ASM.

1. Bolt 29 N·m (21 ft. lbs.)
2. Steering assembly
3. Cross member
4. Nut 43 N·m (32 ft. lbs.)
5. Washer
6. Stud assembly 48 N·m (36 ft. lbs.)
7. Damper, steering link

Fig. 33 Exploded view of the rack and pinion assembly location and mounting

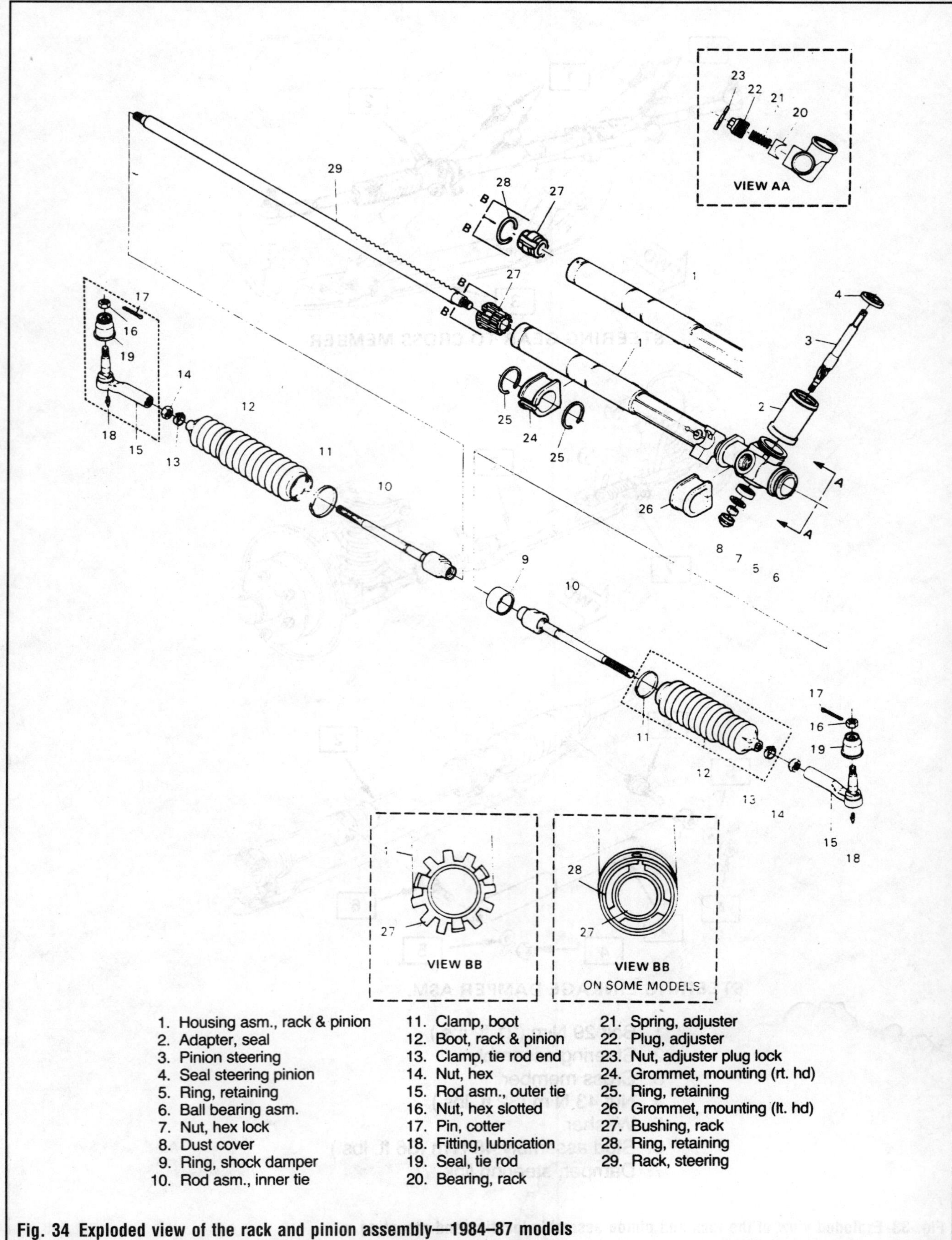

Fig. 34 Exploded view of the rack and pinion assembly—1984–87 models

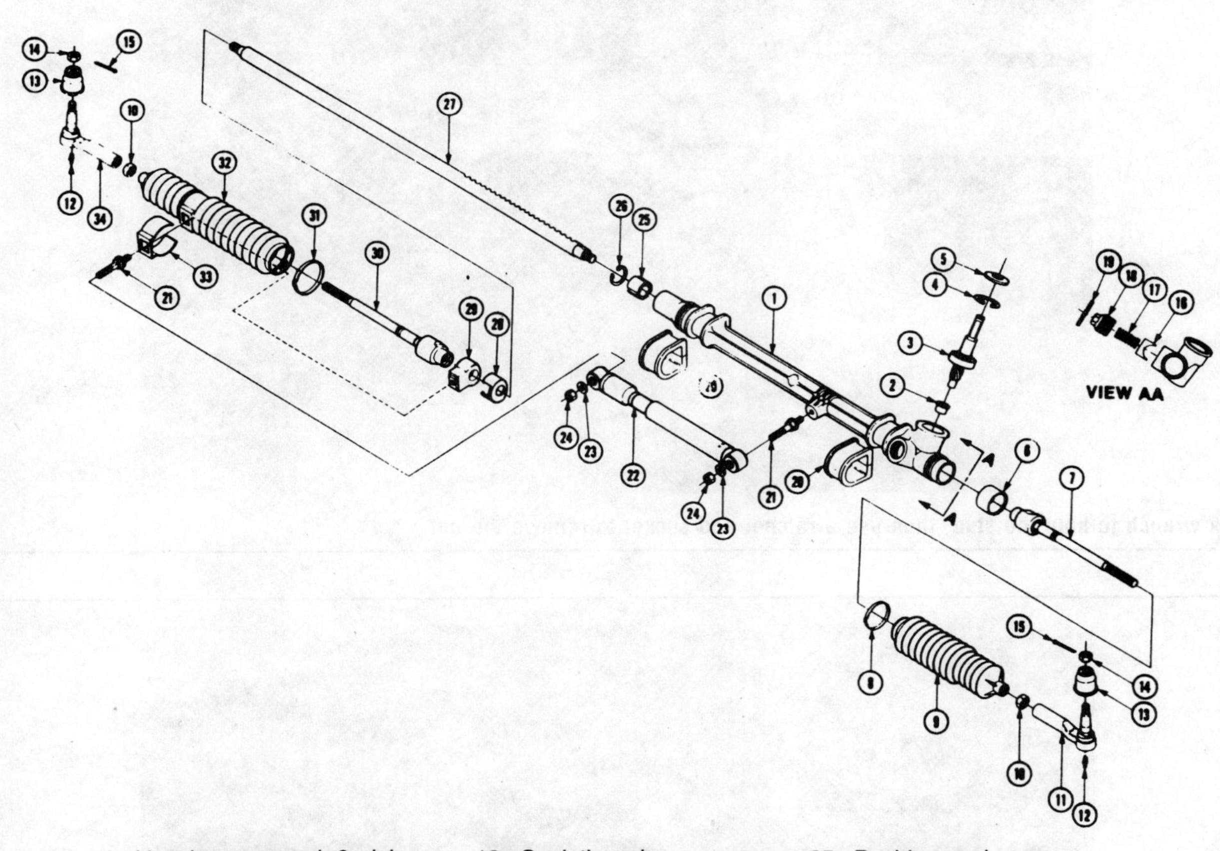

1. Housing asm, rack & pinion
2. Bearing asm, roller
3. Pinion asm, bearing &
4. Ring, retaining
5. Seal, steering pinion
6. Ring, shock damper
7. Rod asm, inner tie
8. Clamp, boot
9. Boot, rack & pinion
10. Nut, hex
11. Rod asm, outer tie
12. Fitting, lubrication
13. Seal, tie rod
14. Nut, hex
15. Pin, cotter
16. Bearing, rack
17. Spring, adjuster
18. Plug, adjuster
19. Nut, adjuster plug lock
20. Grommet, mounting
21. Stud, shock damper
22. Damper asm, steering
23. Washer, flat
24. Nut, hex
25. Bushing, rack
26. Ring, retaining
27. Rack, steering
28. Ring, shock damper
29. Adapter, steering damper
30. Rod asm, inner tie
31. Clamp, boot
32. Boot, rack & pinion
33. Support, boot
34. Rod asm, outer tie

Fig. 35 Exploded view of the rack and pinion components—1988 models

Use a wrench to hold the stud, then use a ratchet and socket to remove the nut

Separate the damper from the steering assembly

To install:

3. Slide the boot and clamps into position and torque the steering damper stud to 35 ft. lbs. (48 Nm).

4. Using a boot clamp tool J-22610, secure the boot clamps.

The following procedures can be performed by removing the rack and pinion assembly.

Inner Tie Rod End

See Figures 36 and 37

1. Remove the outer tie rod end, jam nut, boot seal and clamps.

2. Use a wrench on the rack when either the left or right-hand tie rods are removed.

Use a wrench on the rack teeth to avoid internal gear damage, as shown in the illustration in this section.

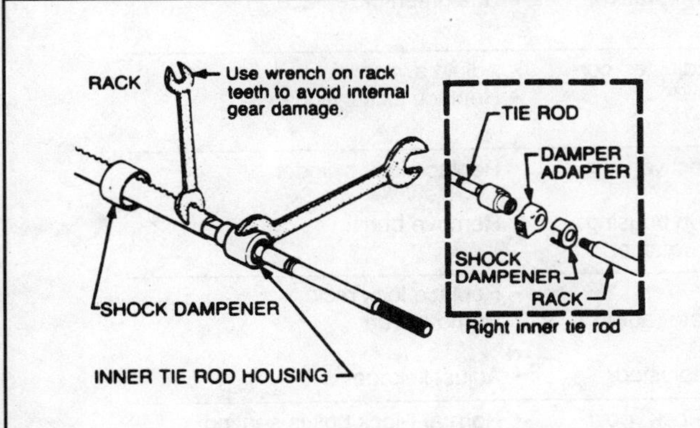

Fig. 36 Use a back-up wrench when removing the inner tie rod end

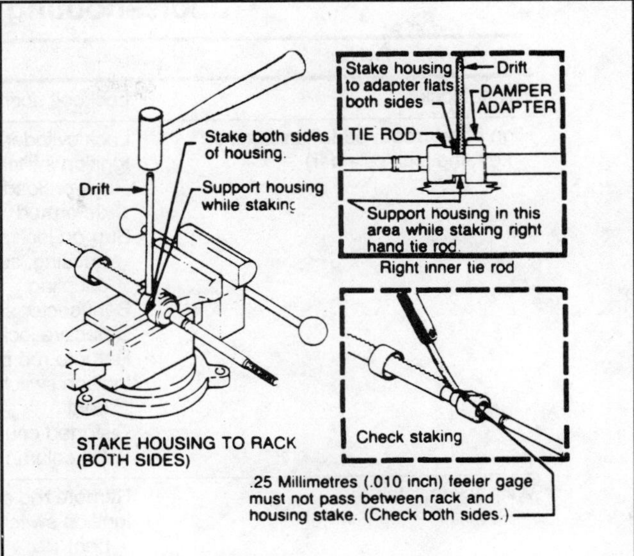

Fig. 37 Use a drift and a hammer to stake both sides of the tie rod end housing

To install:

3. Screw the tie rod end onto the steering rack and torque to 70 ft. lbs. (95 Nm).

4. Using a drift, stake the housing to the adapter flats on both sides.

5. Install the boot, clamps, jam nut and outer tie rod ends.

Further overhaul of the rack and pinion assembly is not economical or practical because a complete remanufactured unit can be purchased at your local parts distributor for a fraction of the price of new.

Troubleshooting the Steering Column

Problem	Cause	Solution
Will not lock	• Lockbolt spring broken or defective	• Replace lock bolt spring
High effort (required to turn ignition key and lock cylinder)	• Lock cylinder defective • Ignition switch defective • Rack preload spring broken or deformed • Burr on lock sector, lock rack, housing, support or remote rod coupling • Bent sector shaft • Defective lock rack • Remote rod bent, deformed • Ignition switch mounting bracket bent • Distorted coupling slot in lock rack (tilt column)	• Replace lock cylinder • Replace ignition switch • Replace preload spring • Remove burr • Replace shaft • Replace lock rack • Replace rod • Straighten or replace • Replace lock rack
Will stick in "start"	• Remote rod deformed • Ignition switch mounting bracket bent	• Straighten or replace • Straighten or replace
Key cannot be removed in "off-lock"	• Ignition switch is not adjusted correctly • Defective lock cylinder	• Adjust switch • Replace lock cylinder
Lock cylinder can be removed without depressing retainer	• Lock cylinder with defective retainer • Burr over retainer slot in housing cover or on cylinder retainer	• Replace lock cylinder • Remove burr
High effort on lock cylinder between "off" and "off-lock"	• Distorted lock rack • Burr on tang of shift gate (automatic column) • Gearshift linkage not adjusted	• Replace lock rack • Remove burr • Adjust linkage
Noise in column	• One click when in "off-lock" position and the steering wheel is moved (all except automatic column) • Coupling bolts not tightened • Lack of grease on bearings or bearing surfaces • Upper shaft bearing worn or broken • Lower shaft bearing worn or broken • Column not correctly aligned • Coupling pulled apart • Broken coupling lower joint • Steering shaft snap ring not seated • Shroud loose on shift bowl. Housing loose on jacket—will be noticed with ignition in "off-lock" and when torque is applied to steering wheel.	• Normal—lock bolt is seating • Tighten pinch bolts • Lubricate with chassis grease • Replace bearing assembly • Replace bearing. Check shaft and replace if scored. • Align column • Replace coupling • Repair or replace joint and align column • Replace ring. Check for proper seating in groove. • Position shroud over lugs on shift bowl. Tighten mounting screws.
High steering shaft effort	• Column misaligned • Defective upper or lower bearing • Tight steering shaft universal joint • Flash on I.D. of shift tube at plastic joint (tilt column only) • Upper or lower bearing seized	• Align column • Replace as required • Repair or replace • Replace shift tube • Replace bearings
Lash in mounted column assembly	• Column mounting bracket bolts loose • Broken weld nuts on column jacket • Column capsule bracket sheared	• Tighten bolts • Replace column jacket • Replace bracket assembly

Troubleshooting the Steering Column (cont.)

Problem	Cause	Solution
Lash in mounted column assembly (cont.)	• Column bracket to column jacket mounting bolts loose • Loose lock shoes in housing (tilt column only) • Loose pivot pins (tilt column only) • Loose lock shoe pin (tilt column only) • Loose support screws (tilt column only)	• Tighten to specified torque • Replace shoes • Replace pivot pins and support • Replace pin and housing • Tighten screws
Housing loose (tilt column only)	• Excessive clearance between holes in support or housing and pivot pin diameters • Housing support-screws loose	• Replace pivot pins and support • Tighten screws
Steering wheel loose—every other tilt position (tilt column only)	• Loose fit between lock shoe and lock shoe pivot pin	• Replace lock shoes and pivot pin
Steering column not locking in any tilt position (tilt column only)	• Lock shoe seized on pivot pin • Lock shoe grooves have burrs or are filled with foreign material • Lock shoe springs weak or broken	• Replace lock shoes and pin • Clean or replace lock shoes • Replace springs
Noise when tilting column (tilt column only)	• Upper tilt bumpers worn • Tilt spring rubbing in housing	• Replace tilt bumper • Lubricate with chassis grease
One click when in "off-lock" position and the steering wheel is moved	• Seating of lock bolt	• None. Click is normal characteristic sound produced by lock bolt as it seats.
High shift effort (automatic and tilt column only)	• Column not correctly aligned • Lower bearing not aligned correctly • Lack of grease on seal or lower bearing areas	• Align column • Assemble correctly • Lubricate with chassis grease
Improper transmission shifting—automatic and tilt column only	• Sheared shift tube joint • Improper transmission gearshift linkage adjustment • Loose lower shift lever	• Replace shift tube • Adjust linkage • Replace shift tube

Troubleshooting the Ignition Switch

Problem	Cause	Solution
Ignition switch electrically inoperative	• Loose or defective switch connector • Feed wire open (fusible link) • Defective ignition switch	• Tighten or replace connector • Repair or replace • Replace ignition switch
Engine will not crank	• Ignition switch not adjusted properly	• Adjust switch
Ignition switch wil not actuate mechanically	• Defective ignition switch • Defective lock sector • Defective remote rod	• Replace switch • Replace lock sector • Replace remote rod
Ignition switch cannot be adjusted correctly	• Remote rod deformed	• Repair, straighten or replace

Troubleshooting the Turn Signal Switch

Problem	Cause	Solution
Turn signal will not cancel	• Loose switch mounting screws • Switch or anchor bosses broken • Broken, missing or out of position detent, or cancelling spring	• Tighten screws • Replace switch • Reposition springs or replace switch as required
Turn signal difficult to operate	• Turn signal lever loose • Switch yoke broken or distorted • Loose or misplaced springs • Foreign parts and/or materials in switch • Switch mounted loosely	• Tighten mounting screws • Replace switch • Reposition springs or replace switch • Remove foreign parts and/or material • Tighten mounting screws
Turn signal will not indicate lane change	• Broken lane change pressure pad or spring hanger • Broken, missing or misplaced lane change spring • Jammed wires	• Replace switch • Replace or reposition as required • Loosen mounting screws, reposition wires and retighten screws
Turn signal will not stay in turn position	• Foreign material or loose parts impeding movement of switch yoke • Defective switch	• Remove material and/or parts • Replace switch
Hazard switch cannot be pulled out	• Foreign material between hazard support cancelling leg and yoke	• Remove foreign material. No foreign material impeding function of hazard switch—replace turn signal switch.
No turn signal lights	• Inoperative turn signal flasher • Defective or blown fuse • Loose chassis to column harness connector • Disconnect column to chassis connector. Connect new switch to chassis and operate switch by hand. If vehicle lights now operate normally, signal switch is inoperative • If vehicle lights do not operate, check chassis wiring for opens, grounds, etc.	• Replace turn signal flasher • Replace fuse • Connect securely • Replace signal switch • Repair chassis wiring as required
Instrument panel turn indicator lights on but not flashing	• Burned out or damaged front or rear turn signal bulb • If vehicle lights do not operate, check light sockets for high resistance connections, the chassis wiring for opens, grounds, etc. • Inoperative flasher • Loose chassis to column harness connection • Inoperative turn signal switch • To determine if turn signal switch is defective, substitute new switch into circuit and operate switch by hand. If the vehicle's lights operate normally, signal switch is inoperative.	• Replace bulb • Repair chassis wiring as required • Replace flasher • Connect securely • Replace turn signal switch • Replace turn signal switch
Stop light not on when turn indicated	• Loose column to chassis connection • Disconnect column to chassis connector. Connect new switch into system without removing old.	• Connect securely • Replace signal switch

Troubleshooting the Turn Signal Switch (cont.)

Problem	Cause	Solution
Stop light not on when turn indicated (cont.)	Operate switch by hand. If brake lights work with switch in the turn position, signal switch is defective. • If brake lights do not work, check connector to stop light sockets for grounds, opens, etc.	 • Repair connector to stop light circuits using service manual as guide
Turn indicator panel lights not flashing	• Burned out bulbs • High resistance to ground at bulb socket • Opens, ground in wiring harness from front turn signal bulb socket to indicator lights	• Replace bulbs • Replace socket • Locate and repair as required
Turn signal lights flash very slowly	• High resistance ground at light sockets • Incorrect capacity turn signal flasher or bulb • If flashing rate is still extremely slow, check chassis wiring harness from the connector to light sockets for high resistance • Loose chassis to column harness connection • Disconnect column to chassis connector. Connect new switch into system without removing old. Operate switch by hand. If flashing occurs at normal rate, the signal switch is defective.	• Repair high resistance grounds at light sockets • Replace turn signal flasher or bulb • Locate and repair as required • Connect securely • Replace turn signal switch
Hazard signal lights will not flash—turn signal functions normally	• Blow fuse • Inoperative hazard warning flasher • Loose chassis-to-column harness connection • Disconnect column to chassis connector. Connect new switch into system without removing old. Depress the hazard warning lights. If they now work normally, turn signal switch is defective. • If lights do not flash, check wiring harness "K" lead for open between hazard flasher and connector. If open, fuse block is defective	• Replace fuse • Replace hazard warning flasher in fuse panel • Conect securely • Replace turn signal switch • Repair or replace brown wire or connector as required

Troubleshooting the Manual Steering Gear

Problem	Cause	Solution
Hard or erratic steering	• Incorrect tire pressure	• Inflate tires to recommended pressures
	• Insufficient or incorrect lubrication	• Lubricate as required (refer to Maintenance Section)
	• Suspension, or steering linkage parts damaged or misaligned	• Repair or replace parts as necessary
	• Improper front wheel alignment	• Adjust incorrect wheel alignment angles
	• Incorrect steering gear adjustment	• Adjust steering gear
	• Sagging springs	• Replace springs
Play or looseness in steering	• Steering wheel loose	• Inspect shaft spines and repair as necessary. Tighten attaching nut and stake in place.
	• Steering linkage or attaching parts loose or worn	• Tighten, adjust, or replace faulty components
	• Pitman arm loose	• Inspect shaft splines and repair as necessary. Tighten attaching nut and stake in place
	• Steering gear attaching bolts loose	• Tighten bolts
	• Loose or worn wheel bearings	• Adjust or replace bearings
	• Steering gear adjustment incorrect or parts badly worn	• Adjust gear or replace defective parts
Wheel shimmy or tramp	• Improper tire pressure	• Inflate tires to recommended pressures
	• Wheels, tires, or brake rotors out-of-balance or out-of-round	• Inspect and replace or balance parts
	• Inoperative, worn, or loose shock absorbers or mounting parts	• Repair or replace shocks or mountings
	• Loose or worn steering or suspension parts	• Tighten or replace as necessary
	• Loose or worn wheel bearings	• Adjust or replace bearings
	• Incorrect steering gear adjustments	• Adjust steering gear
	• Incorrect front wheel alignment	• Correct front wheel alignment
Tire wear	• Improper tire pressure	• Inflate tires to recommended pressures
	• Failure to rotate tires	• Rotate tires
	• Brakes grabbing	• Adjust or repair brakes
	• Incorrect front wheel alignment	• Align incorrect angles
	• Broken or damaged steering and suspension parts	• Repair or replace defective parts
	• Wheel runout	• Replace faulty wheel
	• Excessive speed on turns	• Make driver aware of conditions
Vehicle leads to one side	• Improper tire pressures	• Inflate tires to recommended pressures
	• Front tires with uneven tread depth, wear pattern, or different cord design (i.e., one bias ply and one belted or radial tire on front wheels)	• Install tires of same cord construction and reasonably even tread depth, design, and wear pattern
	• Incorrect front wheel alignment	• Align incorrect angles
	• Brakes dragging	• Adjust or repair brakes
	• Pulling due to uneven tire construction	• Replace faulty tire

Troubleshooting the Power Steering Gear

Problem	Cause	Solution
Hissing noise in steering gear	• There is some noise in all power steering systems. One of the most common is a hissing sound most evident at standstill parking. There is no relationship between this noise and performance of the steering. Hiss may be expected when steering wheel is at end of travel or when slowly turning at standstill.	• Slight hiss is normal and in no way affects steering. Do not replace valve unless hiss is extremely objectionable. A replacement valve will also exhibit slight noise and is not always a cure. Investigate clearance around flexible coupling rivets. Be sure steering shaft and gear are aligned so flexible coupling rotates in a flat plane and is not distorted as shaft rotates. Any metal-to-metal contacts through flexible coupling will transmit valve hiss into passenger compartment through the steering column.
Rattle or chuckle noise in steering gear	• Gear loose on frame	• Check gear-to-frame mounting screws. Tighten screws to 88 N·m (65 foot pounds) torque.
	• Steering linkage looseness	• Check linkage pivot points for wear. Replace if necessary.
	• Pressure hose touching other parts of car	• Adjust hose position. Do not bend tubing by hand.
	• Loose pitman shaft over center adjustment **NOTE:** A slight rattle may occur on turns because of increased clearance off the "high point." This is normal and clearance must not be reduced below specified limits to eliminate this slight rattle.	• Adjust to specifications
	• Loose pitman arm	• Tighten pitman arm nut to specifications
Squawk noise in steering gear when turning or recovering from a turn	• Damper O-ring on valve spool cut	• Replace damper O-ring
Poor return of steering wheel to center	• Tires not properly inflated	• Inflate to specified pressure
	• Lack of lubrication in linkage and ball joints	• Lube linkage and ball joints
	• Lower coupling flange rubbing against steering gear adjuster plug	• Loosen pinch bolt and assemble properly
	• Steering gear to column misalignment	• Align steering column
	• Improper front wheel alignment	• Check and adjust as necessary
	• Steering linkage binding	• Replace pivots
	• Ball joints binding	• Replace ball joints
	• Steering wheel rubbing against housing	• Align housing
	• Tight or frozen steering shaft bearings	• Replace bearings
	• Sticking or plugged valve spool	• Remove and clean or replace valve
	• Steering gear adjustments over specifications	• Check adjustment with gear out of car. Adjust as required.
	• Kink in return hose	• Replace hose
Car leads to one side or the other (keep in mind road condition and wind. Test car in both directions on flat road)	• Front end misaligned	• Adjust to specifications
	• Unbalanced steering gear valve **NOTE:** If this is cause, steering effort will be very light in direction of lead and normal or heavier in opposite direction	• Replace valve

Troubleshooting the Power Steering Gear (cont.)

Problem	Cause	Solution
Momentary increase in effort when turning wheel fast to right or left	• Low oil level • Pump belt slipping • High internal leakage	• Add power steering fluid as required • Tighten or replace belt • Check pump pressure. (See pressure test)
Steering wheel surges or jerks when turning with engine running especially during parking	• Low oil level • Loose pump belt • Steering linkage hitting engine oil pan at full turn • Insufficient pump pressure • Pump flow control valve sticking	• Fill as required • Adjust tension to specification • Correct clearance • Check pump pressure. (See pressure test). Replace relief valve if defective. • Inspect for varnish or damage, replace if necessary
Excessive wheel kickback or loose steering	• Air in system • Steering gear loose on frame • Steering linkage joints worn enough to be loose • Worn poppet valve • Loose thrust bearing preload adjustment • Excessive overcenter lash	• Add oil to pump reservoir and bleed by operating steering. Check hose connectors for proper torque and adjust as required. • Tighten attaching screws to specified torque • Replace loose pivots • Replace poppet valve • Adjust to specification with gear out of vehicle • Adjust to specification with gear out of car
Hard steering or lack of assist	• Loose pump belt • Low oil level **NOTE:** Low oil level will also result in excessive pump noise • Steering gear to column misalignment • Lower coupling flange rubbing against steering gear adjuster plug • Tires not properly inflated	• Adjust belt tension to specification • Fill to proper level. If excessively low, check all lines and joints for evidence of external leakage. Tighten loose connectors. • Align steering column • Loosen pinch bolt and assemble properly • Inflate to recommended pressure
Foamy milky power steering fluid, low fluid level and possible low pressure	• Air in the fluid, and loss of fluid due to internal pump leakage causing overflow	• Check for leak and correct. Bleed system. Extremely cold temperatures will cause system aeriation should the oil level be low. If oil level is correct and pump still foams, remove pump from vehicle and separate reservoir from housing. Check welsh plug and housing for cracks. If plug is loose or housing is cracked, replace housing.
Low pressure due to steering pump	• Flow control valve stuck or inoperative • Pressure plate not flat against cam ring	• Remove burrs or dirt or replace. Flush system. • Correct
Low pressure due to steering gear	• Pressure loss in cylinder due to worn piston ring or badly worn housing bore • Leakage at valve rings, valve body-to-worm seal	• Remove gear from car for disassembly and inspection of ring and housing bore • Remove gear from car for disassembly and replace seals

Troubleshooting the Power Steering Pump

Problem	Cause	Solution
Chirp noise in steering pump	• Loose belt	• Adjust belt tension to specification
Belt squeal (particularly noticeable at full wheel travel and stand still parking)	• Loose belt	• Adjust belt tension to specification
Growl noise in steering pump	• Excessive back pressure in hoses or steering gear caused by restriction	• Locate restriction and correct. Replace part if necessary.
Growl noise in steering pump (particularly noticeable at stand still parking)	• Scored pressure plates, thrust plate or rotor • Extreme wear of cam ring	• Replace parts and flush system • Replace parts
Groan noise in steering pump	• Low oil level • Air in the oil. Poor pressure hose connection.	• Fill reservoir to proper level • Tighten connector to specified torque. Bleed system by operating steering from right to left—full turn.
Rattle noise in steering pump	• Vanes not installed properly • Vanes sticking in rotor slots	• Install properly • Free up by removing burrs, varnish, or dirt
Swish noise in steering pump	• Defective flow control valve	• Replace part
Whine noise in steering pump	• Pump shaft bearing scored	• Replace housing and shaft. Flush system.
Hard steering or lack of assist	• Loose pump belt • Low oil level in reservoir **NOTE:** Low oil level will also result in excessive pump noise • Steering gear to column misalignment • Lower coupling flange rubbing against steering gear adjuster plug • Tires not properly inflated	• Adjust belt tension to specification • Fill to proper level. If excessively low, check all lines and joints for evidence of external leakage. Tighten loose connectors. • Align steering column • Loosen pinch bolt and assemble properly • Inflate to recommended pressure
Foaming milky power steering fluid, low fluid level and possible low pressure	• Air in the fluid, and loss of fluid due to internal pump leakage causing overflow	• Check for leaks and correct. Bleed system. Extremely cold temperatures will cause system aeriation should the oil level be low. If oil level is correct and pump still foams, remove pump from vehicle and separate reservoir from body. Check welsh plug and body for cracks. If plug is loose or body is cracked, replace body.
Low pump pressure	• Flow control valve stuck or inoperative • Pressure plate not flat against cam ring	• Remove burrs or dirt or replace. Flush system. • Correct
Momentary increase in effort when turning wheel fast to right or left	• Low oil level in pump • Pump belt slipping • High internal leakage	• Add power steering fluid as required • Tighten or replace belt • Check pump pressure. (See pressure test)
Steering wheel surges or jerks when turning with engine running especially during parking	• Low oil level • Loose pump belt • Steering linkage hitting engine oil pan at full turn • Insufficient pump pressure	• Fill as required • Adjust tension to specification • Correct clearance • Check pump pressure. (See pressure test). Replace flow control valve if defective.

Troubleshooting the Power Steering Pump (cont.)

Problem	Cause	Solution
Steering wheel surges or jerks when turning with engine running especially during parking (cont.)	• Sticking flow control valve	• Inspect for varnish or damage, replace if necessary
Excessive wheel kickback or loose steering	• Air in system	• Add oil to pump reservoir and bleed by operating steering. Check hose connectors for proper torque and adjust as required.
Low pump pressure	• Extreme wear of cam ring • Scored pressure plate, thrust plate, or rotor • Vanes not installed properly • Vanes sticking in rotor slots • Cracked or broken thrust or pressure plate	• Replace parts. Flush system. • Replace parts. Flush system. • Install properly • Freeup by removing burrs, varnish, or dirt • Replace part

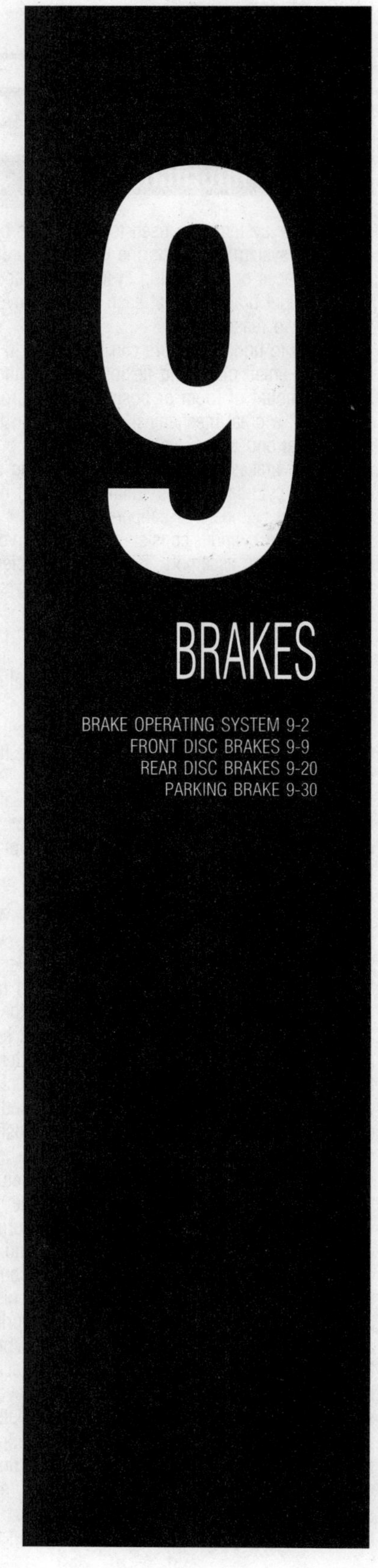

9 BRAKES

BRAKE OPERATING SYSTEM

General Information

Hydraulic systems are used to actuate the brakes of all automobiles. The system transports the power required to force the frictional surfaces of the braking system together from the pedal to the individual brake units at each wheel. A hydraulic system is used for two reasons.

First, fluid under pressure can be carried to all parts of an automobile by small pipes and flexible hoses without taking up a significant amount of room or posing routing problems.

Second, a great mechanical advantage can be given to the brake pedal end of the system, and the foot pressure required to actuate the brakes can be reduced by making the surface area of the master cylinder pistons smaller than that of any of the pistons in the wheel cylinders or calipers.

The master cylinder consists of fluid reservoir and a double cylinder and piston assembly. Double type master cylinders are designed to separate the front and rear braking systems hydraulically in case of a leak.

Steel lines carry the brake fluid to a point on the vehicle's frame near each of the vehicle's wheels. The fluid is then carried to the calipers by flexible tubes in order to allow for suspension and steering movements.

In disc brake systems, the cylinders are part of the calipers. One cylinder in each caliper is used to force the brake pads against the disc.

All pistons employ some type of seal, usually made of rubber, to minimize fluid leakage. A rubber dust boot seals the outer end of the cylinder against dust and dirt. The boot fits around the outer end of the piston on disc brake calipers, and around the brake actuating rod on wheel cylinders.

The hydraulic system operates as follows: When at rest, the entire system, from the piston(s) in the master cylinder to those in the wheel cylinders or calipers, is full of brake fluid. Upon application of the brake pedal, fluid trapped in front of the master cylinder piston(s) is forced through the lines to the wheel cylinders.

Upon release of the brake pedal, a spring located inside the master cylinder immediately returns the master cylinder pistons to the normal position. The pistons contain check valves and the master cylinder has compensating ports drilled in it. These are uncovered as the pistons reach their normal position. The piston check valves allow fluid to flow toward the wheel cylinders or calipers as the pistons withdraw. Then, as the return springs force the brake pads into the released position, the excess fluid reservoir through the compensating ports. It is during the time the pedal is in the released position that any fluid that has leaked out of the system will be replaced through the compensating ports.

Dual circuit master cylinders employ two pistons, located one behind the other, in the same cylinder. The primary piston is actuated directly by mechanical linkage from the brake pedal through the power booster. The secondary piston is actuated by fluid trapped between the two pistons. If a leak develops in front of the secondary piston, it moves forward until it bottoms against the front of the master cylinder, and the fluid trapped between the pistons will operate the rear brakes. If the rear brakes develop a leak, the primary piston will move forward until direct contact with the secondary piston takes place, and it will force the secondary piston to actuate the front brakes. In either case, the brake pedal moves further when the brakes are applied, and less braking power is available.

All dual circuit systems use a switch to warn the driver when only half of the brake system is operational. This switch is located in a valve body which is mounted on the firewall or the frame below the master cylinder. A hydraulic piston receives pressure from both circuits, each circuit's pressure being applied to one end of the piston. When the pressures are in balance, the piston remains stationary. When one circuit has a leak, however, the greater pressure in that circuit during application of the brakes will push the piston to one side, closing the switch and activating the brake warning light.

In disc brake systems, this valve body also contains a metering valve and, in some cases, a proportioning valve. The metering valve keeps pressure from traveling to the disc brakes on the front wheels until the brake shoes on the rear wheels have contacted the drums, ensuring that the front brakes will never be used alone. The proportioning valve controls the pressure to the rear brakes to lessen the chance of rear wheel lock-up during very hard braking.

Warning lights may be tested by depressing the brake pedal and holding it while opening one of the wheel cylinder bleeder screws. If this does not cause the light to go on, substitute a new lamp, make continuity checks, and, finally, replace the switch as necessary.

The hydraulic system may be checked for leaks by applying pressure to the pedal gradually and steadily. If the pedal sinks very slowly to the floor, the system has a leak. This is not to be confused with a springy or spongy feel due to the compression of air within the lines. If the system leaks, there will be a gradual change in the position of the pedal with a constant pressure.

Check for leaks along all lines and at wheel cylinders. If no external leaks are apparent, the problem is inside the master cylinder.

Adjustments

The Fiero is equipped with front and rear disc brakes. The design of the disc brake system eliminates the need for adjustment of the brake pads. As the brake pad wears, the caliper piston moves towards the rotor to ensure proper adjustment. In other words, the piston will return just far enough to release the brake pads from the rotor.

Stop Lamp Switch

ADJUSTMENT

➧ **See Figure 1**

The stop lamp switch is located above the brake pedal on the support bracket.

1. With the brake pedal in the fully released position, the stop lamp switch plunger should be fully depressed against the brake pedal shank.
2. Adjust the switch by moving in or out as necessary.

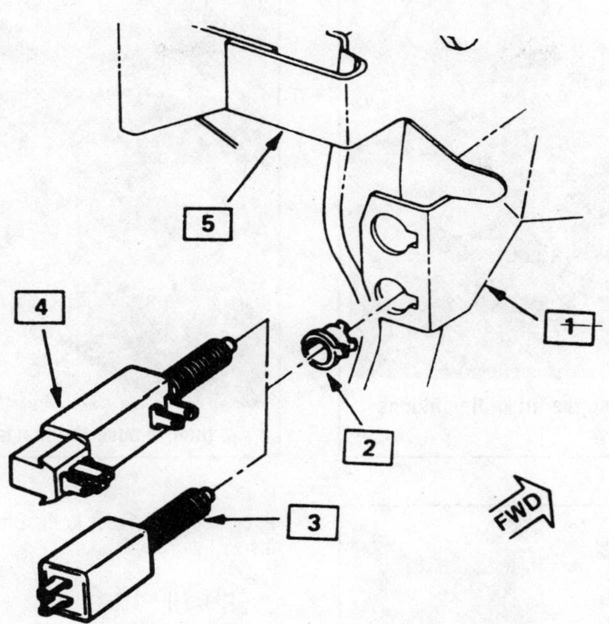

Fig. 1 Exploded view of the stop lamp switch assembly mounting

➡Make sure that the tubular clip is in the brake pedal mounting bracket.

Master Cylinder

REMOVAL & INSTALLATION

➧ See Figure 2

1. Place a number of cloths or a container under the master cylinder to catch the brake fluid. Disconnect the brake tubes from the master cylinder, using a flare nut wrench only. Cap the open ends of the tubes.

➡Brake fluid dissolves paint. Wipe up any spilled fluid immediately, then flush the area with clear water.

2. Remove the two nuts attaching the master cylinder to the booster or firewall, then remove the master cylinder.

To install:

3. Position the master cylinder and install the retaining bolts. Torque to 22–30 ft. lbs. (29–41 Nm).
4. Reconnect the fluid tubes using flare nut wrenches to 17 ft. lbs. (23 Nm).
5. Bleed the brake system at the furthest wheel from the mas-

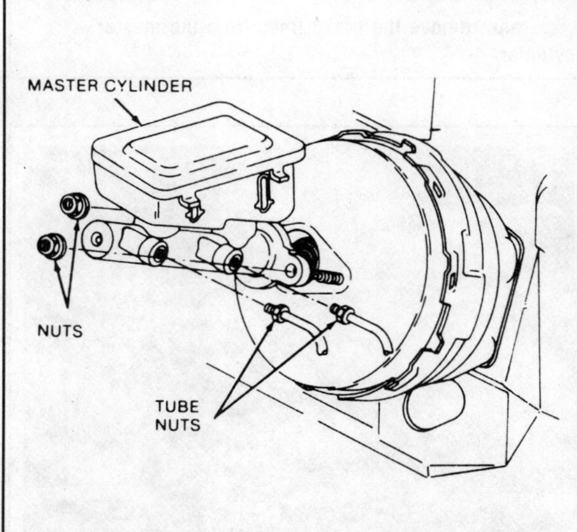

Fig. 2 The master cylinder is mounted on the power booster and retained with two nuts

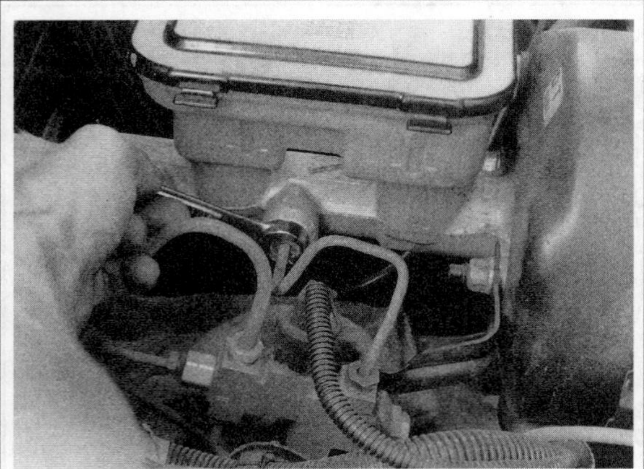
Use a flare nut wrench to loosen the brake line fittings . . .

. . . then remove the master cylinder from its mounting

. . . and remove the brake lines from the master cylinder

Remove the master cylinder retaining nuts . . .

ter cylinder first. Refer to the Brake System Bleeding procedure in this section.

OVERHAUL

➧ See Figure 3

1. Remove the reservoir cover and diaphragm and discard any fluid in the reservoir.
2. Depress the primary piston and remove the lock ring from the end of the housing.
3. Direct compressed air into the outlet at the blind end of the bore, and plug the other outlet to remove the primary and secondary pistons.
4. Remove the spring retainer and seals from the secondary piston.
5. Clamp the master cylinder in a vise and use an appropriate prybar to remove the plastic reservoir.

➡Do not clamp on the master cylinder body. Do not attempt to remove the quick take-up valve from the body. The valve is not serviceable separately.

6. Remove the reservoir grommets.
7. Inspect the master cylinder bore for corrosion. If the bore is corroded, replace the master cylinder. Do not use any abrasives on the bore.
8. Lubricate the new reservoir grommets with silicone brake lube and press them into the master cylinder body. Make sure the grommets are properly seated.
9. Lay the reservoir upside down on a flat, hard surface. Press the master cylinder body onto the reservoir using a rocking motion.
10. Lubricate new seals with clean brake fluid and install them on the secondary piston. Install the spring retainer.
11. Install the spring and secondary piston assembly into the cylinder.
12. Lubricate the primary piston seals with clean brake fluid. Install the primary piston, depress, and install the lock ring.
13. Fit the diaphragm in the reservoir cover and install on the reservoir.

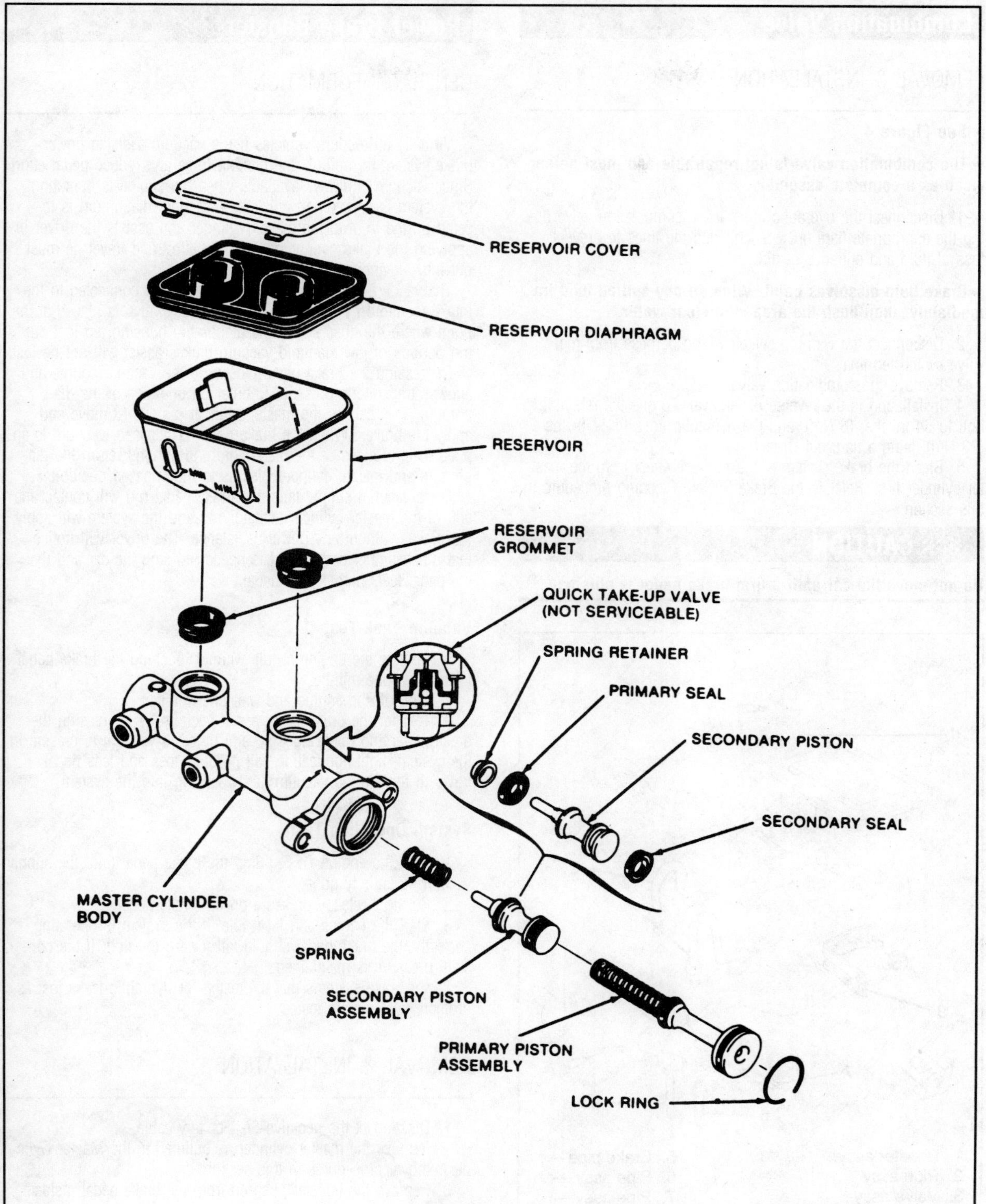

Fig. 3 Exploded view of the master cylinder components

Combination Valve

REMOVAL & INSTALLATION

➧ See Figure 4

➡The combination valve is not repairable and must be serviced as a complete assembly.

1. Disconnect the hydraulic lines at the combination valve using the appropriate flare nut wrench. Plug the lines to prevent loss of fluid and entrance of dirt.

➡Brake fluid dissolves paint. Wipe up any spilled fluid immediately, then flush the area with clear water.

2. Disconnect the warning switch wiring harness from the valve switch terminal.
3. Remove the combination valve.
4. Installation is the reverse of removal. Torque the retaining bolt to 54 in. lbs. (6 Nm), and the hydraulic lines to 17 ft. lbs. (23 Nm) using a flare nut wrench.
5. Bleed the brake system at the furthest wheel from the master cylinder first. Refer to the Brake System Bleeding procedure in this section.

CAUTION

Do not move the car until a firm brake pedal is obtained.

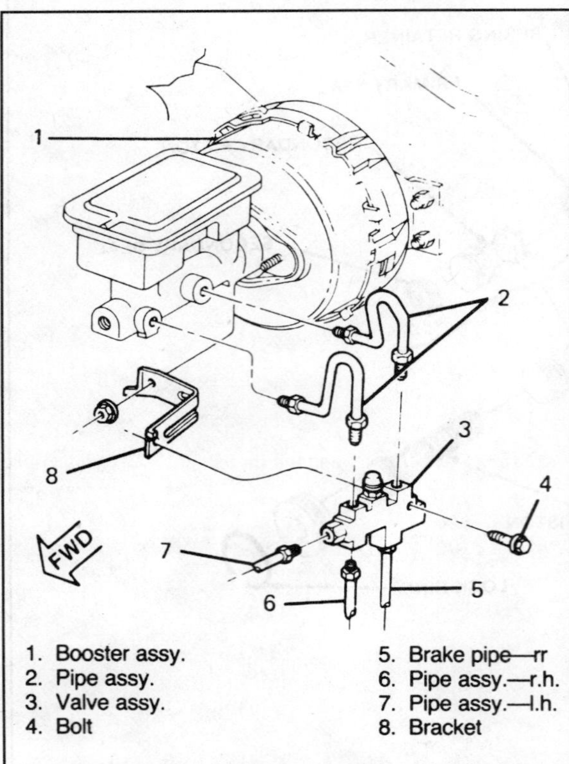

Fig. 4 Exploded view of the combination valve mounting

Power Brake Booster

GENERAL INFORMATION

Virtually all modern vehicles use a vacuum assisted power brake system to multiply the braking force and reduce pedal effort. Since vacuum is always available when the engine is operating, the system is simple and efficient. A vacuum diaphragm is located on the front of the master cylinder and assists the driver in applying the brakes, reducing both the effort and travel he must put into moving the brake pedal.

The vacuum diaphragm housing is normally connected to the intake manifold by a vacuum hose. A check valve is placed at the point where the hose enters the diaphragm housing, so that during periods of low manifold vacuum brakes assist will not be lost.

Depressing the brake pedal closes off the vacuum source and allows atmospheric pressure to enter on one side of the diaphragm. This causes the master cylinder pistons to move and apply the brakes. When the brake pedal is released, vacuum is applied to both sides of the diaphragm and springs return the diaphragm and master cylinder pistons to the released position.

If the vacuum supply fails, the brake pedal rod will contact the end of the master cylinder actuator rod and the system will apply the brakes without any power assistance. The driver will notice that much higher pedal effort is needed to stop the car and that the pedal feels harder than usual.

Vacuum Leak Test

1. Operate the engine at idle without touching the brake pedal for at least one minute.
2. Turn off the engine and wait one minute.
3. Test for the presence of assist vacuum by depressing the brake pedal and releasing it several times. If vacuum is present in the system, light application will produce less and less pedal travel. If there is no vacuum, air is leaking into the system.

System Operation Test

1. With the engine **OFF**, pump the brake pedal until the supply vacuum is entirely gone.
2. Put light, steady pressure on the brake pedal.
3. Start the engine and let it idle. If the system is operating correctly, the brake pedal should fall toward the floor if the constant pressure is maintained.

Power brake systems may be tested for hydraulic leaks just as ordinary systems are tested.

REMOVAL & INSTALLATION

1. Disconnect the negative (−) battery cable.
2. Remove the master cylinder as outlined in the Master Cylinder removal procedures in this section.
3. Remove the booster pushrod from the brake pedal inside the vehicle.
4. From inside the vehicle, remove the four booster-to-firewall attaching nuts.
5. Remove the booster from the vehicle.

To install:

6. Position the booster assembly to the vehicle firewall.
7. From inside the vehicle, install the four booster attaching nuts and torque to 15 ft. lbs. (21 Nm). Install the booster pushrod to the brake pedal.
8. Install the master cylinder as outlined in the Master Cylinder procedure in this section.
9. Bleed the brake system at the furthest wheel from the master cylinder first. Refer to the Brake System Bleeding procedure in this section.

Power Brake Booster Filter

REMOVAL & INSTALLATION

See Figures 5 and 6

1. Open the engine compartment lid. The air cleaner may have to be removed to access the booster filter.
2. Remove the two vacuum hose clamps and hoses from the filter.
3. Remove the filter from the bracket.

To install:

4. Position the filter to the bracket and tighten. Install the vacuum hoses and clamps. Close the engine compartment lid.

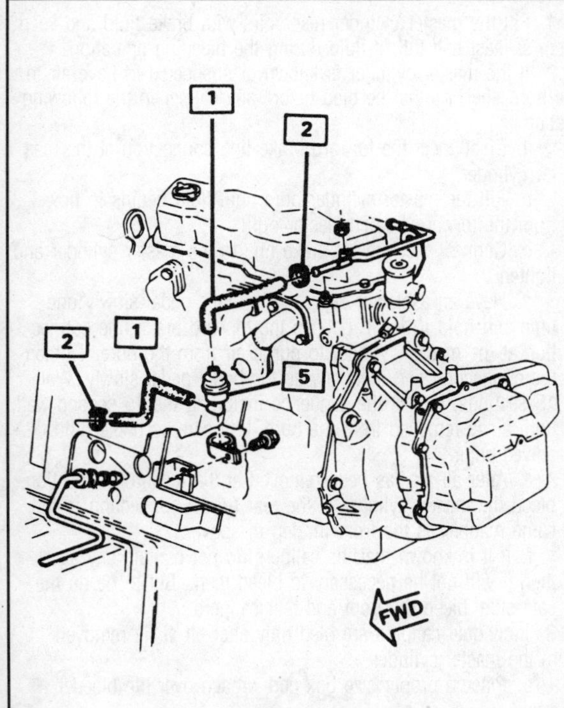

Fig. 5 Location of the power brake booster filter (5), vacuum hoses (1) and clamps (2)—2.5L engine

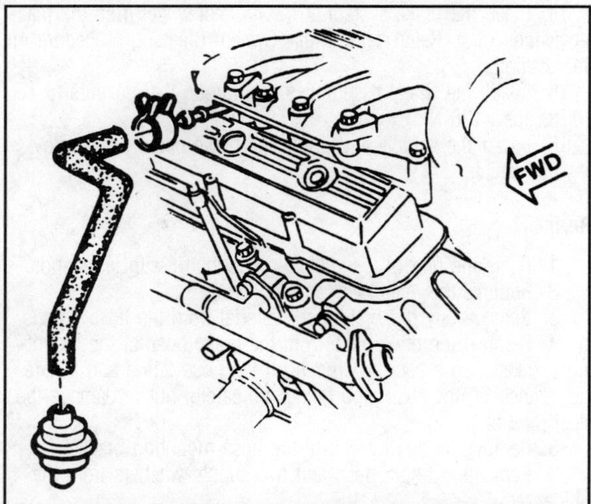

Fig. 6 Power brake booster filter location—2.8L engine

Brake Hoses

REMOVAL & INSTALLATION

Front

1. Raise the front of the vehicle and support with jackstands.
2. Remove the front wheel assemblies.
3. Remove any dirt and foreign material from the hoses and fittings.
4. Remove the bolt attaching the brake hose to the upper control arm.
5. Using a backup wrench on the hose fitting and a flare nut wrench on the steel pipe fitting, loosen and disconnect the two hoses. Be careful not damage the steel fluid pipe.
6. Remove the spring clip from the female fitting at the bracket.
7. Remove the hose from the bracket.
8. Remove the bolt, hose and two copper washers from the caliper. Replace the two copper washer with new.

To install:

9. Install the two new copper washer, brake hose and bolt to the caliper and torque the bolt to 33 ft. lbs. (45 Nm).

➡The fitting flange must engage the caliper orientation ledge.

10. Install the hose to the bracket and make sure there is no kinks in the hose.
11. Install the hose clip-to-upper control arm and torque to 54 inch. lb. (6 Nm).
12. Install the spring clip at the hose mounting bracket.
13. Reconnect the brake steel pipe to hose using a backup wrench on the hose and a flare nut wrench on the steel pipe. Torque the fittings to 11 ft. lbs. (15 Nm).

14. Bleed the brake system at the furthest wheel from the master cylinder first. Refer to the Brake System Bleeding procedure in this section.
15. Install the wheel assemblies and torque the lug nuts to 100 ft. lbs. (136 Nm).
16. Lower the vehicle and pump the brake pedal before moving the vehicle.

Rear

1. Raise the rear of the vehicle and support with jackstands.
2. Remove the rear wheel assemblies.
3. Remove any dirt or foreign material from the hose fittings.
4. Remove the brake pipe from the brake hose at the mounting bracket. Use a backup wrench on the hose fitting and a flare nut wrench on the steel pipe fitting. Be careful not to damage the steel pipe or fitting.
5. Remove the spring clip at the hose mounting bracket.
6. Remove the bolt, hose and two copper washers from the caliper.

To install:

7. Install new copper washer with the hose and bolt. Torque the bolt to 33 ft. lbs. (45 Nm).
8. Install the hose into the bracket and ensure there is no kinks in the hose.
9. Install the brake hose to the steel pipe using a backup wrench on the hose and a flare nut wrench on the steel pipe. Torque the fittings to 11 ft. lbs. (15 Nm). Be careful not to damage the steel fitting.
10. Bleed the brake system at the furthest wheel from the master cylinder first. Refer to the Brake System Bleeding procedure in this section.
11. Install the wheel assemblies and torque the lug nuts to 100 ft. lbs. (136 Nm).
12. Lower the vehicle and pump the brake pedal before moving the vehicle.

Bleeding the Brake System

** CAUTION

Some brake pads contain asbestos, which has been determined to be a cancer causing agent. Never clean the brake surfaces with compressed air! Avoid inhaling any dust from any brake surface! When cleaning brake surfaces, use a commercially available brake cleaning fluid.

MANUAL BLEEDING

It is necessary to bleed the brake system any time air is introduced into the hydraulic system.

It may be necessary to bleed the hydraulic system at all four brakes positions, and/or the master cylinder, if air has been introduced through low fluid level or by disconnecting the brake lines at the master cylinder. If a brake line is disconnected at any wheel, then that wheel caliper only need be bled. If lines are disconnected at any fitting located between the master cylinder and brakes, then the brake system served by the disconnected line must be bled.

With a hose attached to the fitting and submerged in a container of brake fluid, open and close the fitting

➡The time required to bleed the hydraulic system can be reduced if the master cylinder is filled with fluid and as much air as possible is expelled before the cylinder is installed on the vehicle. Power brakes require removing the vacuum reserve by applying the brakes several times with the engine off.

1. Fill the master cylinder reservoirs with brake fluid and keep them at least half full of fluid during the bleeding operation.
2. If the master cylinder is known or suspected to have air in the bore, then it must be bled before any caliper in the following matter.
   a. Disconnect the forward brake line connection at the master cylinder.
   b. Fill the master cylinder bore until fluid begins to flow from the forward line connector port.
   c. Connect the forward brake line to the master cylinder and tighten it.
   d. Have an assistant depress the brake pedal slowly one time and hold it down. Loosen the forward brake line connection at the master cylinder to purge air from the bore. Tighten the connection and then release the brake pedal slowly. Wait 15 seconds. Repeat the sequence including the 15 second wait, until air is removed from the bore. Use care as brake fluid dissolves paint.
   e. After all air has been removed at the forward connection, bleed the master cylinder at the rear (cowl) connection in the same manner as the front in step d, above.
   f. If it is known that the calipers do not contain any air, then it will not be necessary to bleed them. But to be on the safe side, bleed the front and rear calipers.
3. Individual calipers are bled only after all air is removed from the master cylinder.
   a. Place a proper size box end wrench over the bleeder valve.
   b. Attach a transparent tube over the valve and allow the tube to hang submerged in brake fluid in a transparent container.
   c. Depress the brake pedal slowly one time and hold.
   d. Loosen the bleeder valve to purge the air from the cylinder.
   e. Tighten the bleeder screw and slowly release the pedal.

f. Wait 15 seconds and repeat the above sequence including the 15 second wait until all air is removed.

➡It may be necessary to repeat the sequence 10 or more times until all air is removed from the system. Rapid pumping of the brake pedal pushes the master cylinder secondary piston down the bore in a manner that makes it difficult to bleed the rear side of the system.

4. If it is necessary to bleed all of the calipers, the following sequence should be followed: right rear; left rear; right front; left front (furthest from master cylinder to closest).

➡Check the brake pedal for sponginess and the brake warning light for indication of unbalanced pressure. To correct either of these two conditions repeat the entire bleeding procedure.

PRESSURE BLEEDING

⁂ CAUTION

Some brake pads contain asbestos, which has been determined to be a cancer causing agent. Never clean the brake surfaces with compressed air! Avoid inhaling any dust from any brake surface! When cleaning brake surfaces, use a commercially available brake cleaning fluid.

➡Pressure bleeding equipment must be the diaphragm type and must have a rubber diaphragm between the air supply and the brake fluid to prevent air, moisture and other contaminants from entering the hydraulic system.

1. Install the bleeder adapter J-29567 to the master cylinder reservoir.
2. Charge the bleeder tool J-29532 to 20–25 psi (140–172 kPa).
3. Connect the line to the adapter. Open the line valve and depress the bleed-off valve on top of the adapter until a few drops of fluid appears.
4. Raise the vehicle and support with jackstands. Remove the wheel assemblies at the axle being bled.
5. Bleed the brakes in the following sequence: right rear, left rear, right front and left front. Attach a clear tube over the bleeder screw. Using the proper size box wrench, open the bleeder screw and bleed until no air is seen in the fluid.
6. Close the bleeder screw and repeat step 5 for each caliper being bled.
7. Install the wheel assemblies and torque the lug nuts to 100 ft. lbs. (136 Nm). Lower the vehicle and check for a spongy brake pedal or if the brake warning light is on. If these problems occur, repeat the bleeding procedure until the brake pedal is firm at all times when the engine is not running.
8. Remove the brake bleeding equipment and fill the reservoir to the FULL level. Clean the reservoir cap and diaphragm with a clean towel and reinstall.

FRONT DISC BRAKES

⁂ CAUTION

Some brake pads contain asbestos, which has been determined to be a cancer causing agent. Never clean the brake surfaces with compressed air! Avoid inhaling any dust from any brake surface! When cleaning brake surfaces, use a commercially available brake cleaning fluid.

Brake Pads

INSPECTION

➧ See Figure 7

The pad thickness should be inspected every time that the wheels are removed. Pad thickness can be checked by looking down through the inspection hole in the top of the caliper. If the thickness of the pad is worn to within 0.030 in. (0.76mm) of the rivet at either end of the pad, all the pads should be replaced. A thermal material is sandwiched between the lining and backing. Don't include this material when determining the lining thickness. This is the factory recommended measurement. Your state's automobile inspection laws may be different.

➡Always replace all pads on both front wheels at the same time. Failure to do so will result in uneven braking action and premature wear.

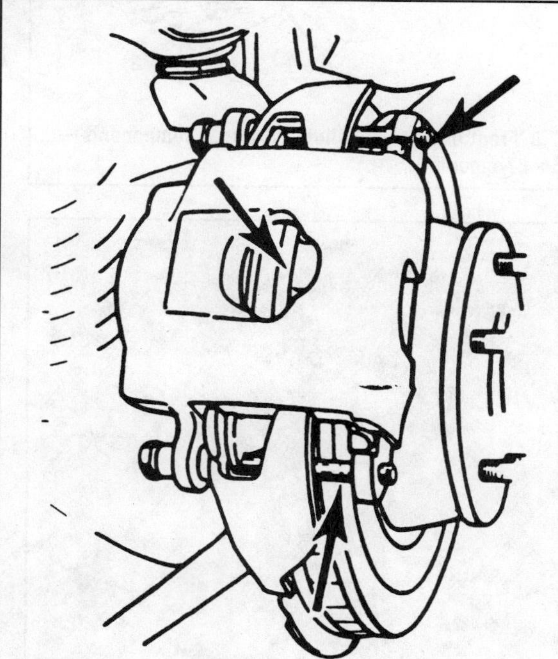

Fig. 7 Look through the inspection hole in the caliper housing to observe the brake pad lining thickness

REMOVAL & INSTALLATION

1984–87 Models

➧ See Figures 8 thru 14

1. Siphon ⅔ of the brake fluid from the master cylinder reservoir.
2. Loosen the wheel lug nuts and raise the car. Support the car safely with jackstands then remove the wheel.
3. Remove the two boots and mounting bolts using a No. 50 Torx® wrench.
4. Position 4-inch adjustable pliers over the inboard surface of the caliper housing and caliper support bracket.
5. Squeeze the pliers to compress the piston back into the caliper bore and provide clearance between the linings and rotor.
6. Remove the caliper from the rotor and suspend with a wire hook from the suspension. Do not allow the caliper to hang by the hose.
7. Remove the shoe and lining assemblies from the caliper.

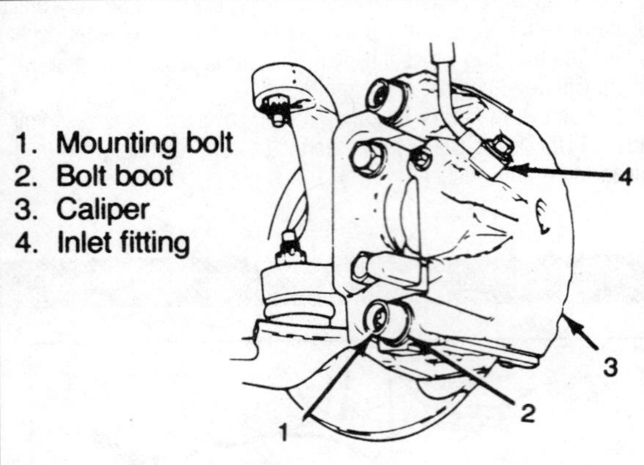

Fig. 8 Front disc brake calipers external components—1984–87 models

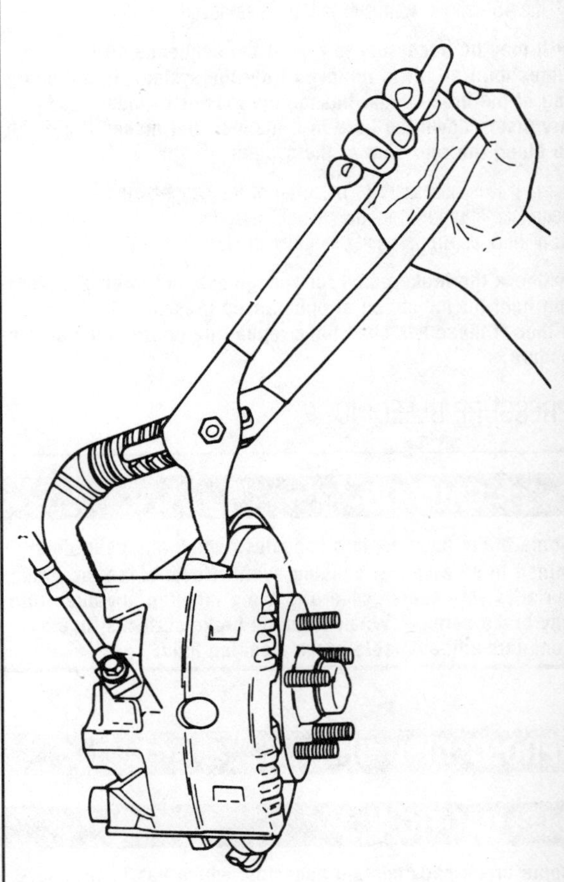

Fig. 9 Compress the piston using adjustable pliers—1984–87 models

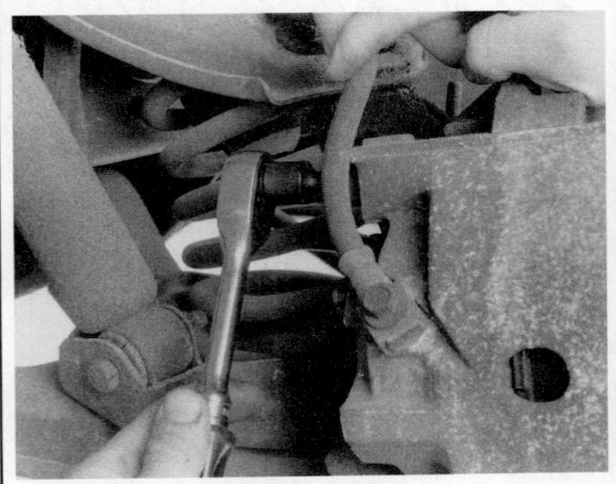

Remove the caliper mounting Torx® bolts

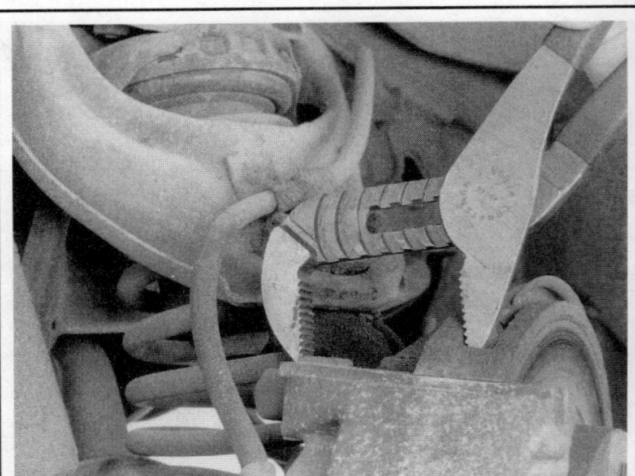

Position the pliers over the caliper support bracket and inboard caliper housing

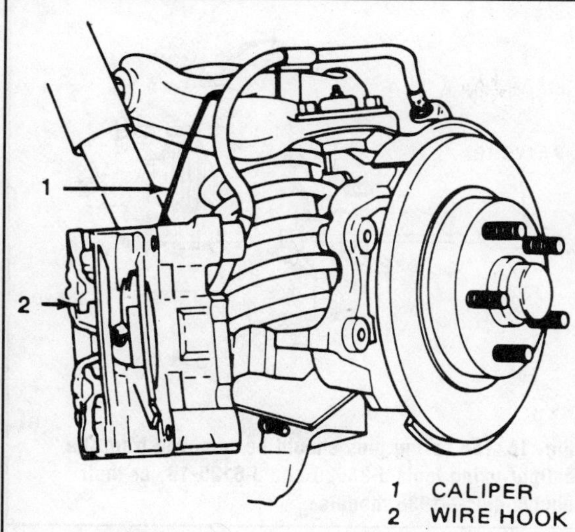

Fig. 10 The brake caliper should not hang by the hose. Use a piece of wire or bungee cord to support the caliper

The brake pads can now be removed from the caliper

To remove the outboard shoe and lining use a suitable tool to disengage the buttons on the shoe from the holes in the caliper.

8. Remove the sleeves from the mounting bolt holes.
9. Remove the bushings from the grooves in the mounting bolt holes.

To install:

10. Bottom the piston in the caliper bore before installing new linings. This can be done with a large C-clamp.
11. Use new bushings and sleeves and lubricate with a silicone lubricant.
12. Install the inboard shoe and lining as shown in the illustration.
13. Install the outboard shoe and lining with the wear sensor at the leading edge of the shoe during forward wheel rotation.

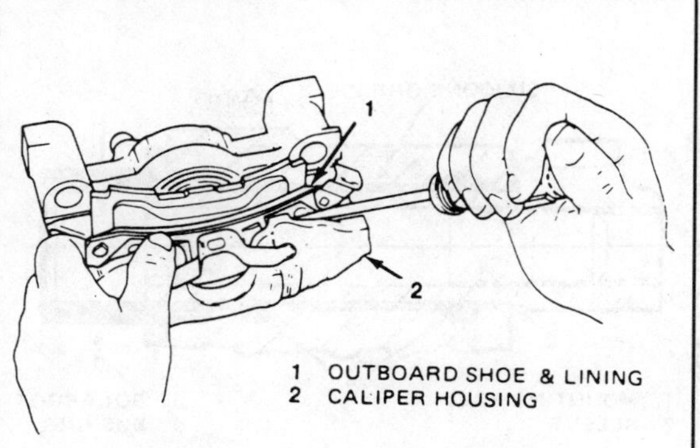

Fig. 11 Remove the outboard shoe using a suitable prytool

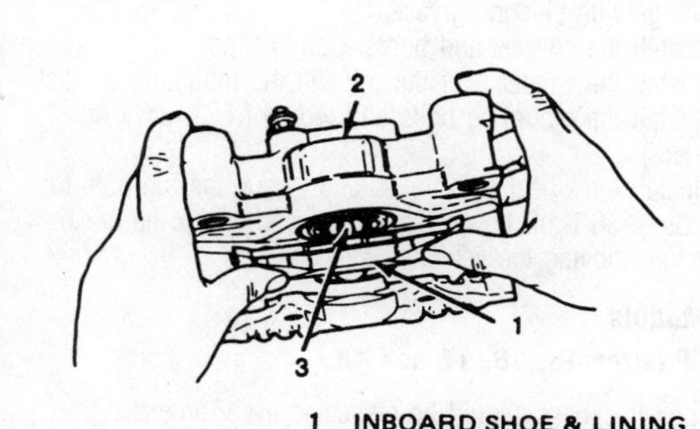

Fig. 12 Install the inboard brake pad in the caliper

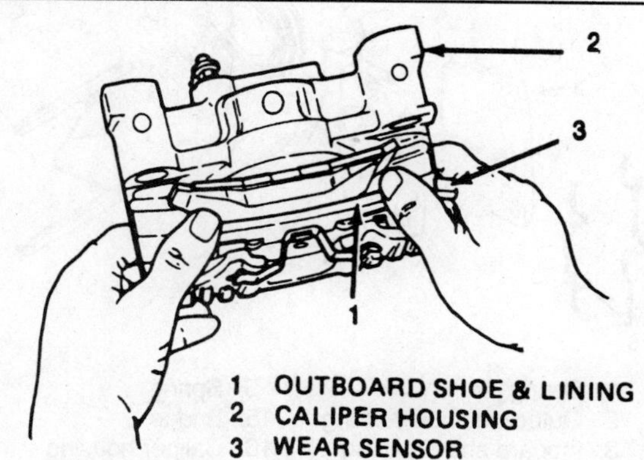

Fig. 13 When installing the outboard brake pad, make sure the wear sensor is at the leading edge of the pad during forward wheel rotation

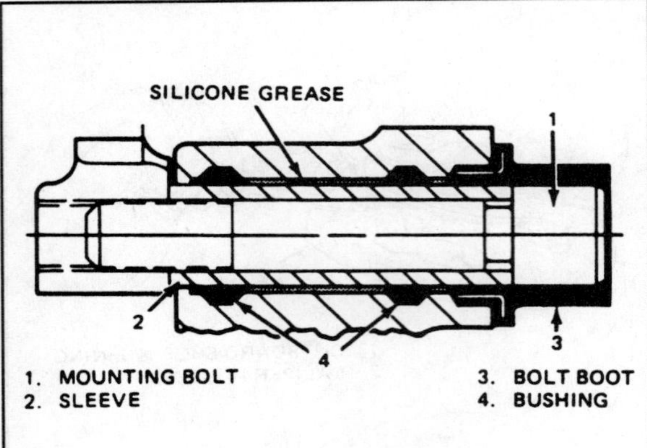

Fig. 14 The caliper housing cavities should be liberally lubricated using silicone grease

14. Liberally fill both cavities in the caliper housing between the bushings with silicone grease.
15. Install the sleeves and boots in the caliper.
16. Install the caliper over the rotor in the mounting bracket.
17. Install the mounting bolts and torque to 21–35 ft. lbs. (28–41 Nm).
18. Install the wheel assemblies and torque the lug nuts to 100 ft. lbs. (136 Nm). Lower the vehicle and pump the brake pedal before moving the vehicle.

1988 Models

See Figures 15, 16, 17 and 18

The pad thickness should be inspected every time that the wheels are removed. Pad thickness can be checked by looking

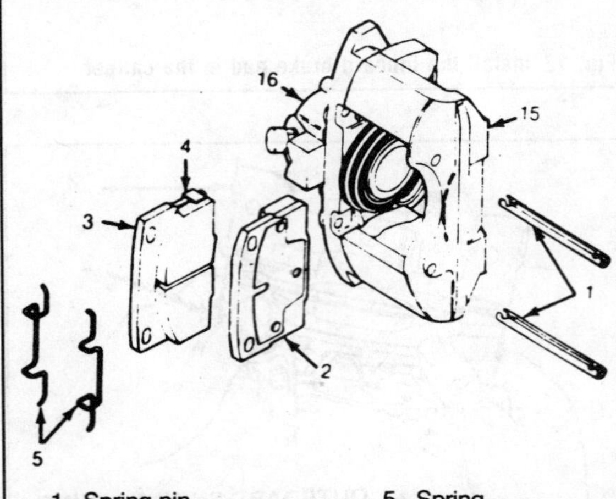

Fig. 15 Components of the front caliper and brake pad assemblies—1988 models

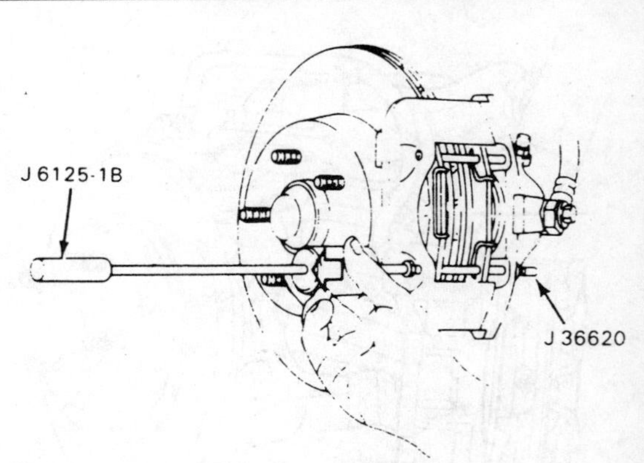

Fig. 16 The spring pins should be removed from the caliper using tools J-36620 and J-6125-1B, or their equivalents—1988 models

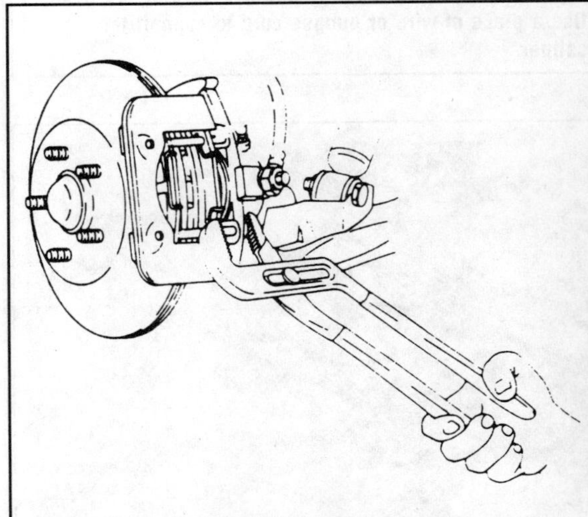

Fig. 17 A pair of adjustable pliers may be used to compress the caliper piston—1988 models

down through the inspection hole in the top of the caliper. If the thickness of the pad is worn to within 0.030 in. (0.76mm) of the rivet at either end of the pad, all the pads should be replaced. A thermal material is sandwiched between the lining and backing. Don't include this material when determining the lining thickness. This is the factory recommended measurement. Your state's automobile inspection laws may be different.

CAUTION

Some brake pads contain asbestos, which has been determined to be a cancer causing agent. Never clean the brake surfaces with compressed air! Avoid inhaling any dust from any brake surface! When cleaning brake surfaces, use a commercially available brake cleaning fluid.

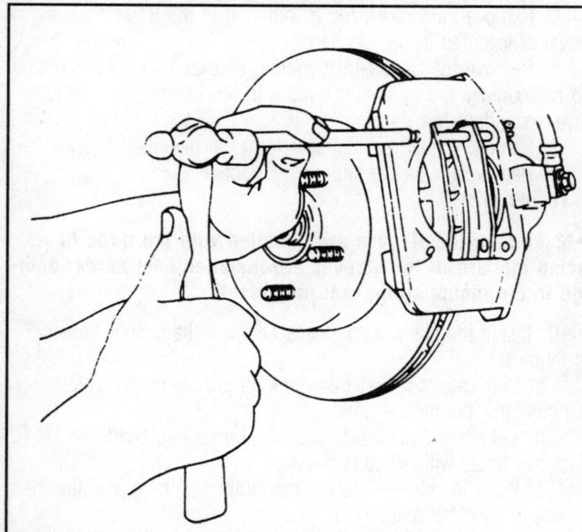

Fig. 18 Install the spring pin in the caliper assembly by tapping it into position using a soft brass drift and a hammer—1988 models

➡Always replace all pads on both front wheels at the same time. Failure to do so will result in uneven braking action and premature wear.

1. Siphon ⅔ of the brake fluid from the master cylinder reservoir.
2. Loosen the wheel lug nuts and raise the car. Support the car safely with jackstands then remove the wheels.
3. Install two adjacent lug nuts to retain the rotor.
4. Bottom the piston into the caliper bore to provide clearance between the brake pads and rotor. This can be done with a caliper compressing tool J-36621 or a pair of locking pliers.

⁂ CAUTION

Be prepared to catch the springs when removing spring pins. Springs may fly out causing personal injury.

5. Remove the spring pins with the use of spring pin removing tools J-36620 onto J-6125-1B. Insert the rod completely through the pin and install the threaded tip as far as possible. Thrust weight on J-6125-1B outward against the tool handle to drive the pin out and remove the springs.
6. Remove both brake pads by pulling straight out of the caliper with the locking pliers.

To install:

7. Before installing new brake pads, the piston must be bottomed into the caliper bore.
8. Install the inboard pad with the wear sensor at the leading edge of the shoe during forward wheel rotation. Install the outboard brake pad in the same way.

⁂ WARNING

Do not use a steel drift to install the spring pins. This will damage the ends of the pins causing later removal difficult.

9. Install one spring pin while aligning the holes in the brake pads. Tap the pin with a soft brass drift and hammer until the end of the pin just emerges from the inboard face of the caliper housing.
10. Install the springs and the remaining spring pin. The hock end of the spring has to be under the spring pin. Make sure the springs are centered on the pad flanges with each spring end projecting under the pins.
11. Install the wheel assemblies and torque the lug nuts to 100 ft. lbs. (136 Nm). Lower the vehicle and pump the brake pedal before moving the vehicle.

Brake Caliper

REMOVAL & INSTALLATION

1984–87 Models

1. Remove ⅔ of the brake fluid from the master cylinder.
2. Raise the vehicle and support it safely with jackstands.
3. Remove the wheel and tire assembly.
4. Install two lug nuts to retain the rotor.
5. Remove the bolt attaching the fluid inlet fitting to the caliper. Plug the brake hose after removal.
6. Remove the boots and mounting bolts using a No. 50 Torx® wrench.
7. Position a 4-inch adjustable pliers over the inboard surface of the caliper housing and caliper support bracket.
8. Squeeze the pliers to compress the piston back into the caliper bore and provide clearance between the linings and rotor.
9. Inspect the mounting bolts and sleeves for corrosion. If corrosion is found, use new bushings, bolts and sleeves when installing the caliper.
10. Liberally fill both cavities in the caliper housing between the bushings with silicone grease.

To install:

11. Position the sleeves and boots in the caliper.
12. Position the caliper over the rotor in the mounting bracket.
13. Install the mounting bolts and torque to 21–35 ft. lbs. (28–48 Nm).
14. Measure the clearance between the caliper and bracket stops and if necessary file the ends of the bracket stops to provide the proper clearance.
15. Install the fluid inlet fitting and torque to 18–30 ft. lbs. (25–40 Nm).
16. Install the wheel and tire assembly. Torque the lug nut to 100 ft. lbs. (136 Nm).
17. Fill the master cylinder to the proper level and bleed the brake system as outlined in the Brake System Bleeding procedures in this section.

1988 Models

➧ See Figure 19

1. Remove ⅔ of the brake fluid from the master cylinder.
2. Raise the vehicle and support it safely with jackstands.
3. Remove the wheel and tire assembly.
4. Install two lug nuts to retain the rotor.
5. Remove the bolt attaching the fluid inlet fitting to the caliper. Plug the brake hose after removal.

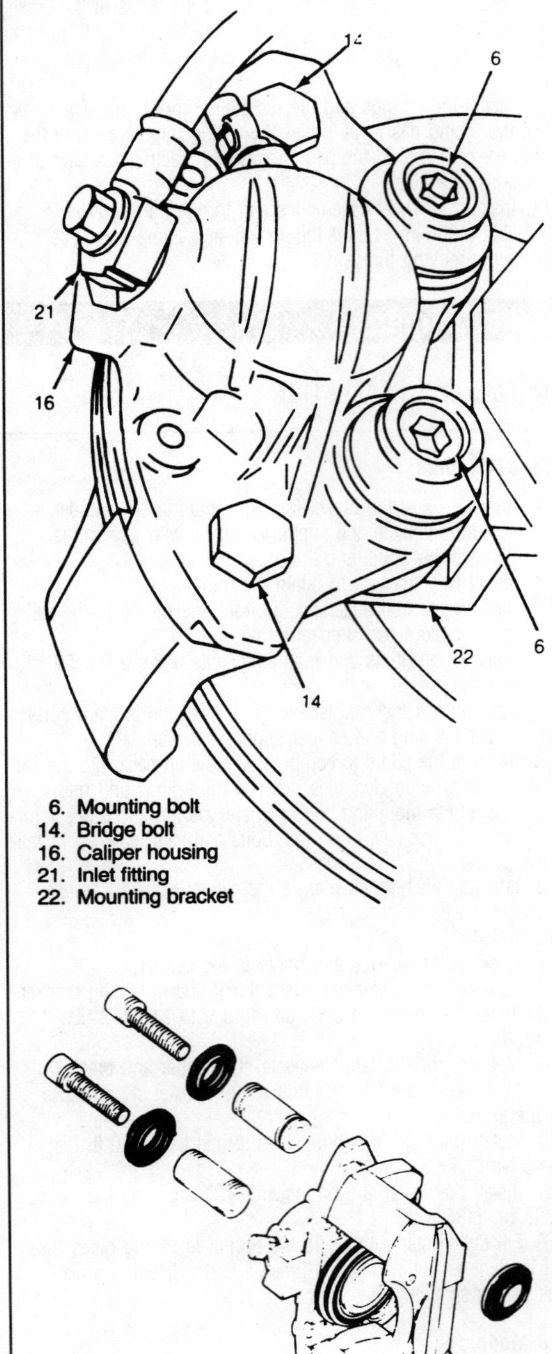

Fig. 19 View of the caliper mounting components (top); exploded view of the caliper sleeves and sleeve boots (bottom)—1988 models

6. Remove the brake pads as outlined in the Brake Pad removal procedures in this section.
7. Remove the caliper-to-mounting bracket Torx® #55 bolts. Do not confuse the mounting bolts with the bridge bolts, which have a standard hex head.
8. Remove the caliper housing from the mounting bracket.
9. Remove the sleeve and sleeve boots.

To install:

➡Make sure the sleeves are installed with the large holes facing inboard. If the sleeves are installed backwards, damage to the mounting bracket may result.

10. Install the sleeve and sleeve boots in the caliper housing as follows:
    a. Lubricate the sleeve and mounting hole in the caliper housing with silicone grease.
    b. Lubricate both inside and outside sealing beads on the sleeve boots with silicone grease.
    c. Push the sleeve into the mounting bolt hole past the inside of installed sleeve boot position.
    d. Install the remaining sleeve boot.
    e. Push the sleeve back the other way and seat the beads of both sleeve boots.
11. Install the caliper housing over the rotor to the mounting bracket with the mounting Torx® #55 bolts. Torque the bolts to 74 ft. lbs. (100 Nm). Make sure the mounting bolts are properly torqued.
12. Install the brake hose with new copper washer and torque the hose bolt to 33 ft. lbs. (45 Nm).
13. Install the brake pads as outlined in the Brake Pad installation procedures in this section.
14. Fill the master cylinder to the proper level and bleed the brake system as outlined in the Brake System Bleeding procedures in this section.
15. Install the wheel and tire assembly. Torque the lug nut to 100 ft. lbs. (136 Nm). Lower the vehicle and pump the brake pedal before moving the vehicle.

OVERHAUL

1984–87 Models

➧ See Figures 20, 21, 22 and 23

1. Remove the caliper and pads as outlined in this section.
2. Place some cloths in front of the piston. Remove the piston by applying compressed air to the fluid inlet fitting. Use just enough air pressure to ease the piston from the bore.

✲✲ CAUTION

Do not try to catch the piston with your fingers, as it could result in serious injury.

3. Remove the piston boot using a suitable prying tool, working carefully so that the piston bore is not scratched.
4. Remove the bleeder screw. If the bleeder screw can not be removed or it breaks, the caliper assembly will have to be replaced.
5. Inspect the piston for scoring, nicks, corrosion, wear, etc., and replace the piston if any defects are found.
6. Remove the piston seal from the caliper bore groove using

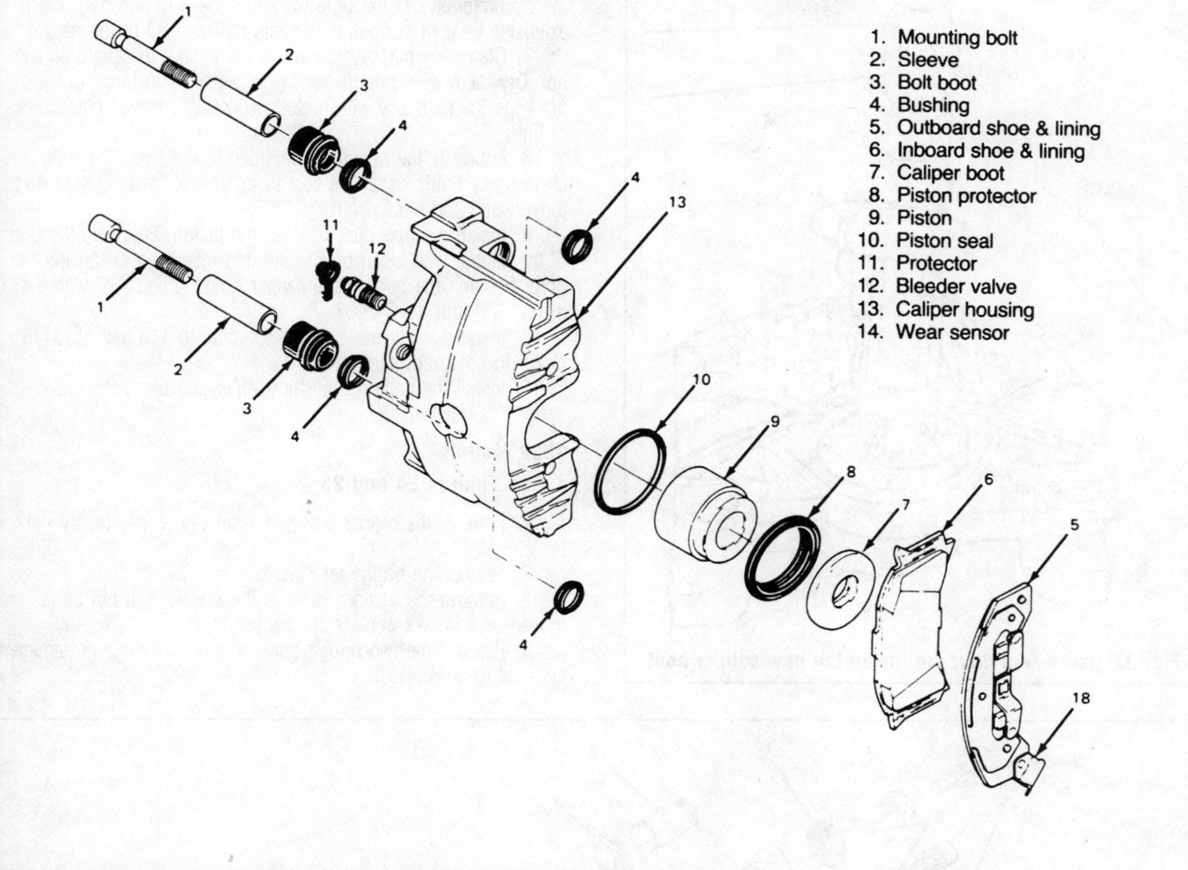

1
2
3
4
4
13
11
12
1
2
3
4
10
9
8
7
6
5
18
4
1. Mounting bolt
2. Sleeve
3. Bolt boot
4. Bushing
5. Outboard shoe & lining
6. Inboard shoe & lining
7. Caliper boot
8. Piston protector
9. Piston
10. Piston seal
11. Protector
12. Bleeder valve
13. Caliper housing
14. Wear sensor

Fig. 20 Exploded view of the front caliper assembly—1984–87 models

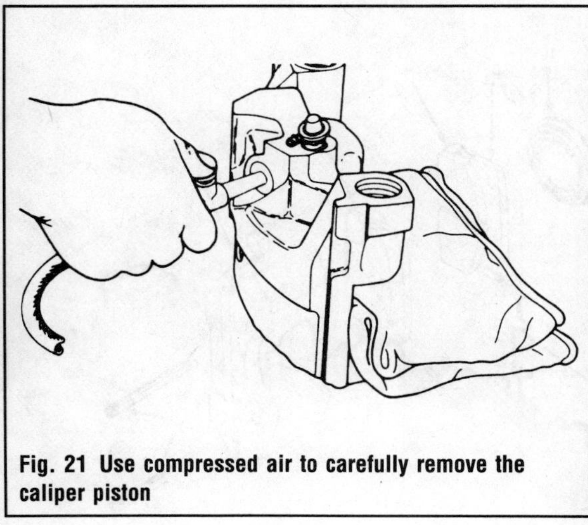

Fig. 21 Use compressed air to carefully remove the caliper piston

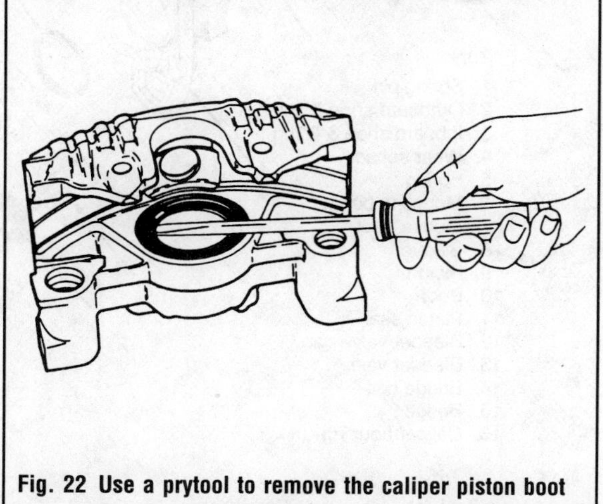

Fig. 22 Use a prytool to remove the caliper piston boot

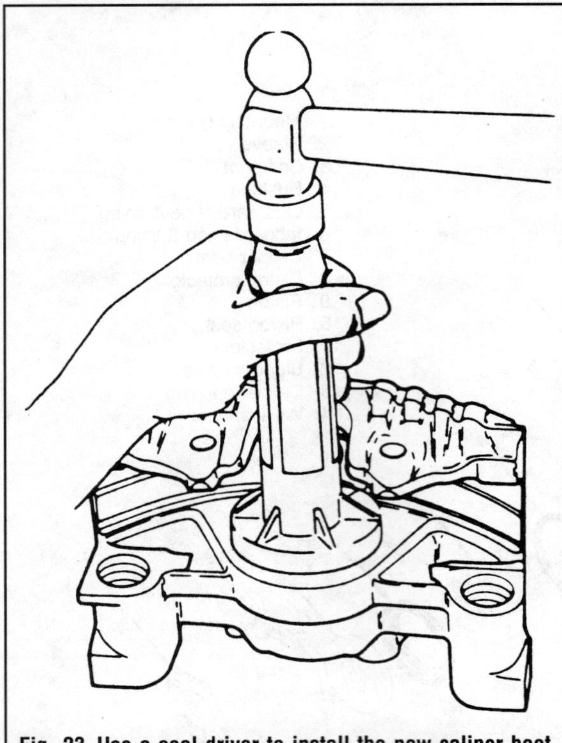

Fig. 23 Use a seal driver to install the new caliper boot

a piece of wood or plastic. Do not use a metal tool as damage to the bore could result. Very light wear can be cleaned up with a crocus cloth. Use finger pressure to rub the crocus cloth around the circumference of the bore (do not slide it in and out). More extensive wear or corrosion warrants replacement of the part.

7. Clean any parts which are to be reused, in denatured alcohol. Dry them with compressed air or allow them to air dry. Do not wipe the parts dry with a cloth, which will leave behind bits of lint.

8. Lubricate the new seal, provided in the repair kit, with clean brake fluid. Install the seal in its groove, making sure it is fully seated and not twisted.

9. Install the new dust boot on the piston. Lubricate the bore of the caliper with clean brake fluid and insert the piston into its bore. Position the boot in the caliper housing and seat with a seal driver, GM tool no. J-2907.

10. Install the bleeder screw, tightening to 116 inch lbs. (13 Nm). Do not overtighten.

11. Install the pads, install the caliper and bleed the brake system.

1988 Models

➧ See Figures 24 and 25

1. Remove the caliper and pad assembly as previously outlined.
2. Inspect the bridge for cracks.
3. Remove the bleeder valve. If the bleeder can not be removed or it breaks, replace the caliper.
4. Remove the two bridge bolts only if the bridge is damaged and has to be replaced.

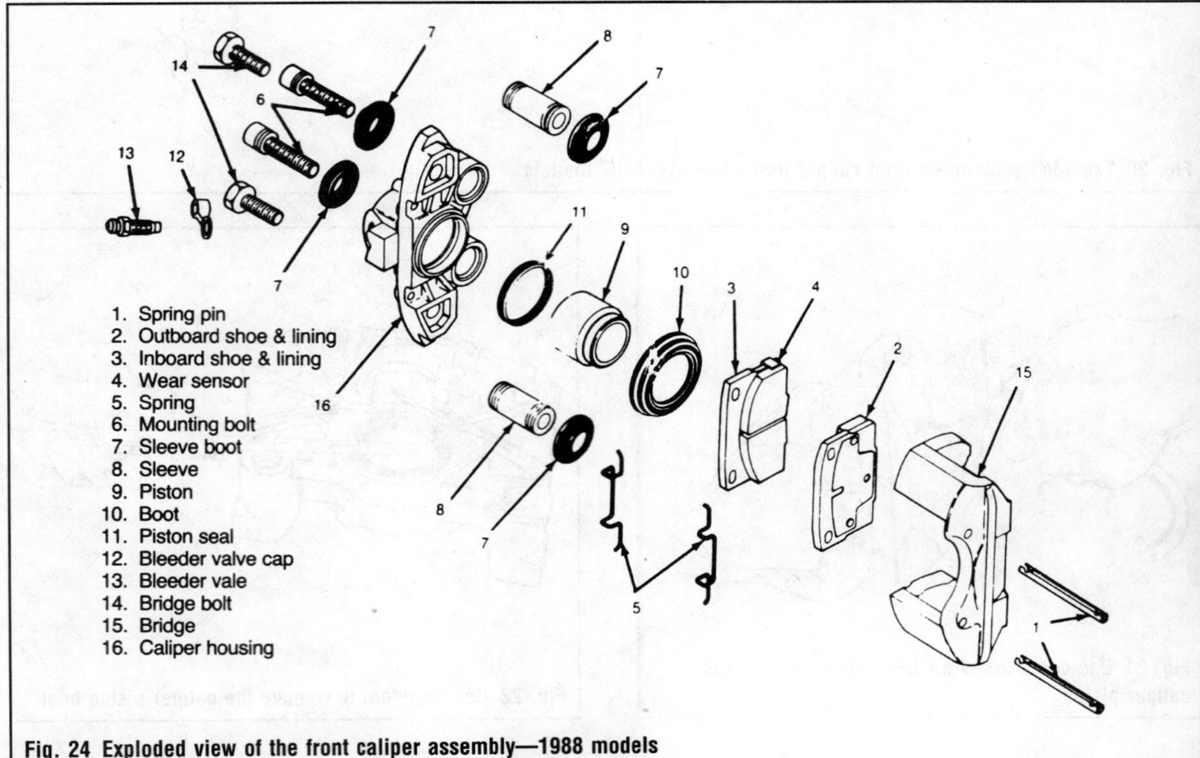

Fig. 24 Exploded view of the front caliper assembly—1988 models

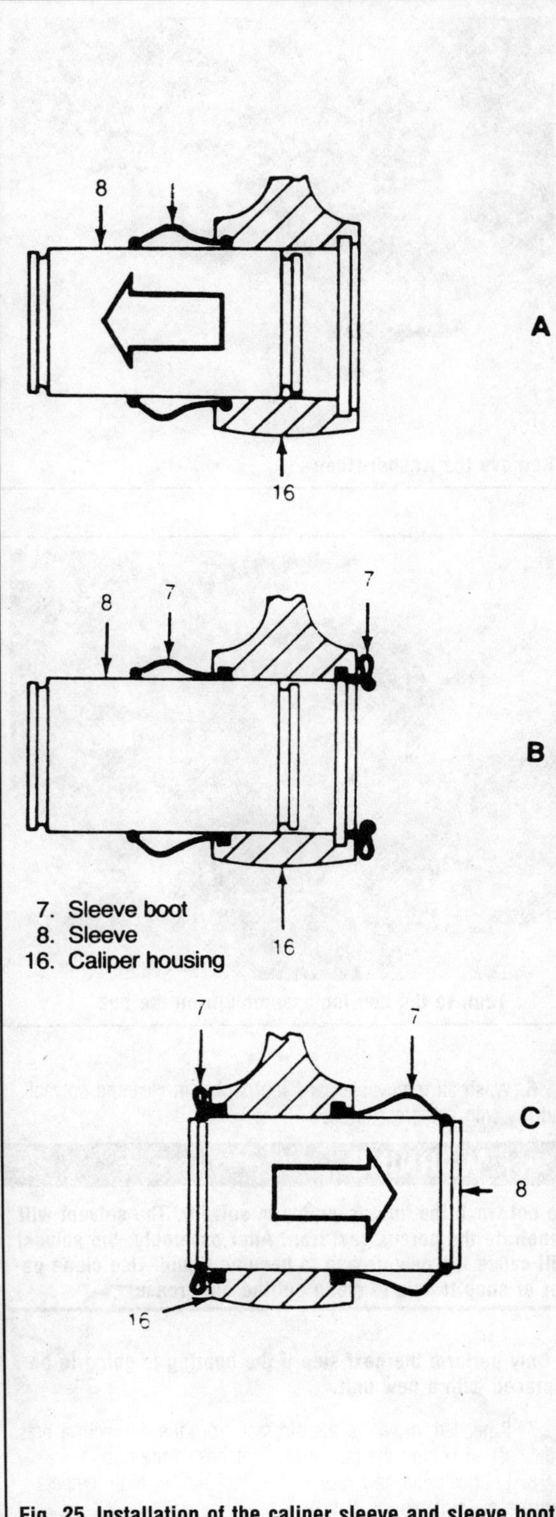

Fig. 25 Installation of the caliper sleeve and sleeve boot assembly—1988 models

➡The caliper can be overhauled without removing the bridge.

5. Use shop towels as a pad over the bridge during piston removal. Remove the piston by applying compressed air into the caliper inlet hole.

CAUTION

Do not try to catch the piston with your fingers, as it could result in serious injury!

6. Inspect the piston and bore for scoring, nicks and corrosion to the piston chrome plating. Replace the piston or bore if any of these conditions exist.
7. Remove the piston boot by prying up with a screwdriver.
8. Remove the piston seal using a plastic seal removing tool. Do not use any metal tool to remove the piston seal.
9. Use crocus cloth to polish out light corrosion. Replace parts if they will not clean up with crocus cloth.

Assembly:

10. Clean all parts in denatured alcohol and dry with compressed air.
11. Install the bridge and bolts, if removed. Torque the bolts to 74 ft. lbs. (100 Nm).
12. Install the bleeder valve and torque to 116 ft. lbs. (13 Nm).
13. Lubricate the new piston seal with new brake fluid and install the seal into the piston bore. Make sure the seal is not twisted.
14. Install the piston with the boot into the bore and push down in a rocking motion. Seat the piston boot onto the caliper housing using your fingers or a small piece of wood.
15. Install the caliper as previously described in this section.

Wheel Hub/Rotor and Bearings

REMOVAL & INSTALLATION

1984–87 Models

➡This procedure also includes repacking and adjustment of the wheel bearings.

CAUTION

Some brake pads contain asbestos, which has been determined to be a cancer causing agent. Never clean the brake surfaces with compressed air! Avoid inhaling any dust from any brake surface! When cleaning brake surfaces, use a commercially available brake cleaning fluid.

1. Raise the vehicle and support it safely with jackstands.
2. Remove the wheel and tire assembly.
3. Remove the brake caliper from the knuckle as outlined in the Brake Caliper procedure in this section.
4. Remove the dust cap, cotter pin, spindle nut and washer, and remove the hub and bearing.

➡Do not allow the bearing to fall out of the hub when removing the hub from the spindle.

5. Remove the outer bearing with your fingers, then remove the inner bearing by prying out the grease seal. Discard the seal.

Use a prytool to remove the dust cap, then . . .

Remove the washer, then . . .

. . . remove the cotter pin using a pair of pliers

. . . remove the bearing assembly from the hub

Remove the castellated nut from the spindle

6. Wash all removable parts thoroughly in cleaning solvent and dry with compressed air.

✻✻ WARNING

Do not wash the hub assembly in solvent. The solvent will penetrate the porous cast iron. After assembly, the solvent will cause the new grease to become liquid. Use clean paper or shop towels to clean out the old grease.

➡Only perform the next step if the bearing is going to be replaced with a new unit.

7. If needed, drive out the old race from the hub with a brass drift inserted behind the race in the notches in the hub.
8. Lubricate the new race with a light film of high temperature grease, suitable for disc brakes.
9. Start the race squarely into the hub and carefully seat the race using an appropriate tool.

➡Check the bearings for cracks or pitting. Check the races for scoring or pitting. If it is necessary to replace either the outer or inner bearing, it will be necessary to replace the bearing as an assembly (bearing, inner and outer race).

To install:

10. Use a high temperature front wheel bearing grease to repack the inner and outer bearings before installation. Apply grease to the inside of the hub assembly before installing the inner bearing.

➡Do not mix different kinds of greases, as mixing may change the grease properties and result in poor performance.

11. Apply a thin film of grease to the spindle at the inner and outer bearing seat, shoulder, and seal seat.
12. Put a small quantity of grease inboard of each bearing race in the hub.
13. Fill the bearing cone and roller assemblies 100% full of grease. It is extremely important to work the grease thoroughly into the bearings between the rollers, cone and the cage.
14. Place the inner bearing cone and roller assembly into the hub. Then, using your finger, put an additional quantity of grease outboard of the bearing.
15. Install a new grease seal using a flat plate until the seal is flush with the hub. Lubricate the seal lip with a thin layer of grease.
16. Carefully install the hub and rotor assembly.
17. Place the outer bearing cone and roller assembly in the outer bearing race. Install the washer and nut. Draw up the spindle nut. Do not overtighten.
18. Torque the spindle nut to 12 ft. lbs. (15 Nm), while turning the rotor assembly forward by hand to fully seat the bearings.
19. Back off the nut to the just-loose position. Tighten the spindle nut by hand, then loosen until either hole in the spindle lines up with a slot in the nut (Not more than ½ flat). Install a new cotter pin and bend the ends of the cotter pin against the nut. Cut off any extra length to ensure that the ends will not interfere with the dust cap. Install the dust cap using a rubber hammer.
20. Install the brake caliper then install the wheel and tire. Torque the lug nuts to 100 ft. lbs. (136 Nm).
21. Lower the vehicle to the floor. Pump the brake pedal before moving the vehicle to check brake operation and to fill the calipers with fluid.

1988 Models

The 1988 models are equipped with sealed hub and bearing assemblies. Refer to the Sealed Wheel Bearing Diagnosis Chart in Section 1.

⁂ CAUTION

Some brake pads contain asbestos, which has been determined to be a cancer causing agent. Never clean the brake surfaces with compressed air! Avoid inhaling any dust from any brake surface! When cleaning brake surfaces, use a commercially available brake cleaning fluid.

1. Raise the vehicle and support with jackstands.
2. Remove the wheel and tire assembly.
3. Remove the brake caliper and support with a wire to the surrounding body.
4. Remove the rotor assembly.
5. Remove the three hub and bearing assembly-to-steering knuckle attaching bolts.
6. Press out the old bearing using an arbor press and press in new bearings.

To install:

7. Place the hub and bearing assembly on the spindle. Install the hub and bearing assembly-to-steering knuckle attaching bolts and torque to 220 ft. lbs. (260 Nm). Install the brake caliper and torque the mounting Torx® bolts to 74 ft. lbs. (100 Nm). Install the wheel and tire assembly and torque the lug nuts to 100 ft. lbs. (136 Nm). Lower the vehicle and pump the brake pedal a few times before moving the vehicle.

ROTOR INSPECTION

Thickness Variation Check

The thickness variation can be checked by measuring the thickness of the rotor at four or more points. All of the measurements must be made at the same distance from the edge of the rotor. A rotor the varies by more than 0.0005 (0.013mm) can cause a pulsation in the brake pedal. If these measurement are excessive, the rotor should be refinished or replaced.

Lateral Run-out Check

1. Remove the caliper and hang from the body with a piece of wire. Install two inverted lug nuts to retain the rotor.
2. Install a dial indicator to the steering knuckle so that the indicator button contacts the rotor about 1 inch from the rotor edge.
3. Zero the dial indicator.
4. Move the rotor one complete revolution and observe the total indicated run-out.
5. If the rotor run-out exceeds 0.0015 in. (0.040mm) have the rotor refinished or replaced.

Refinishing Brake Rotors

All brake rotors have a minimum thickness dimension cast onto them. Do not use a brake rotor that will not meet minimum thickness specifications in the Brake Specifications chart at the end of this section.

Accurate control of rotor tolerances is necessary for proper brake performance and safety. Machining of the rotor should be done by a qualified machine shop with the proper machining equipment.

The optimum speed for refinishing the rotor surface is a spindle speed of 200 rpm. Crossfeed for rough cutting should range from 0.010-0.006 in. (0.254-0.152mm) per revolution. The finish cuts should be made at crossfeeds no greater than 0.002 in. (0.051mm) per revolution.

REAR DISC BRAKES

CAUTION

Some brake pads contain asbestos, which has been determined to be a cancer causing agent. Never clean the brake surfaces with compressed air! Avoid inhaling any dust from any brake surface! When cleaning brake surfaces, use a commercially available brake cleaning fluid.

Brake Pads

INSPECTION

The pad thickness should be inspected every time that the wheels are removed. Pad thickness can be checked by looking down through the inspection hole in the top of the caliper. If the thickness of the pad is worn to within 0.030 in. (0.76mm) of the rivet at either end of the pad, all the pads should be replaced. A thermal material is sandwiched between the lining and backing. Don't include this material when determining the lining thickness. This is the factory recommended measurement. Your state's automobile inspection laws may be different.

➡Always replace all pads on both front wheels at the same time. Failure to do so will result in uneven braking action and premature wear.

REMOVAL & INSTALLATION

1984–87 Models

➧ See Figures 26, 27, 28 and 29

CAUTION

Some brake pads contain asbestos, which has been determined to be a cancer causing agent. Never clean the brake surfaces with compressed air! Avoid inhaling any dust from any brake surface! When cleaning brake surfaces, use a commercially available brake cleaning fluid.

1. Remove ⅔ of the brake fluid from the master cylinder assembly.
2. Raise the vehicle and support it safely with jackstands.
3. Remove the wheel and tire assembly then install two lug nuts to retain the rotor.
4. Loosen the tension on the parking brake cable at the equalizer.
   a. Remove the cable and spring from the lever.
   b. Remove the locknut while holding the lever.
   c. Remove the lever, lever seal and anti-friction washer.
5. Remove the caliper mounting bolts with a No. 50 Torx® wrench.
6. Position 4-inch adjustable pliers over the inboard surface of the caliper housing and outboard surface of the mounting bracket.
7. Squeeze the pliers to compress the piston back into the caliper bore and provide clearance between the brake pad and the rotor.

➡Use the pliers only to move the caliper back far enough to remove the caliper and brake pad assemblies. The caliper has to be turned into the bottom of the bore using a Caliper Piston Turning Tool.

8. Remove the caliper from the rotor and mounting bracket and support it to prevent strain on the brake hose.
9. Use a suitable tool and disengage the shoe buttons from the holes in the caliper and remove the brake pad assemblies.
10. Remove the sleeves from the mounting bolt holes.
11. Remove the boots and bushings from the caliper.

To install:

12. Bottom the piston into the caliper bore using tool J-36621. Turn the left piston in a counterclockwise direction and the right

Typical rear disc brake assembly used on the Fiero

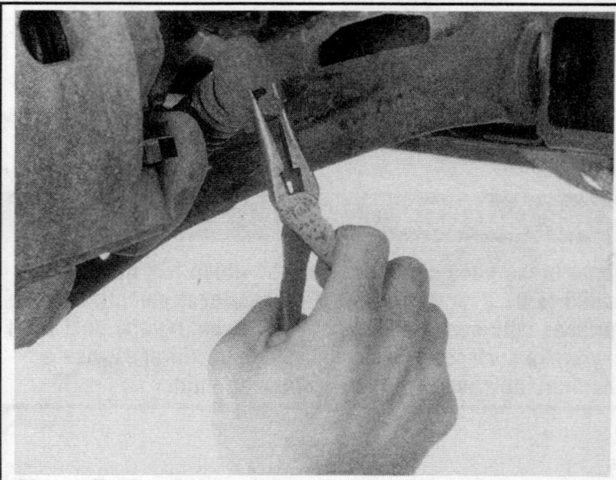

After relieving the tension at the equalizer, use a pair of pliers to disengage the cable from the lever . . .

. . . then remove the return spring assembly

Remove the parking brake lever seal, then . . .

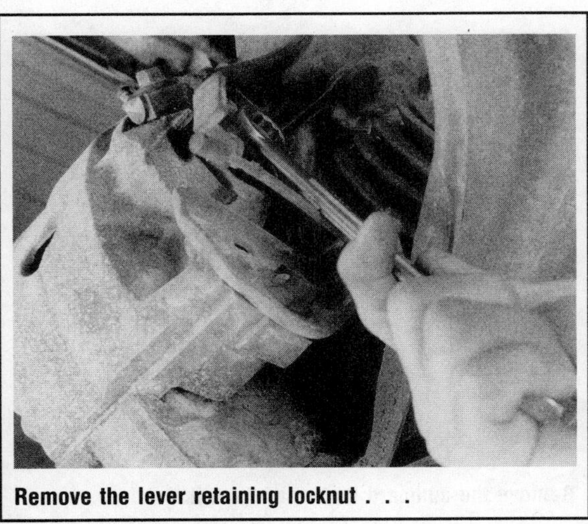
Remove the lever retaining locknut . . .

. . . remove the anti-friction washer

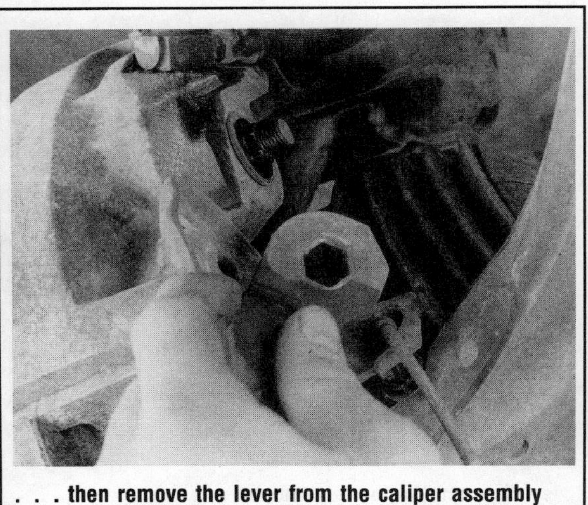
. . . then remove the lever from the caliper assembly

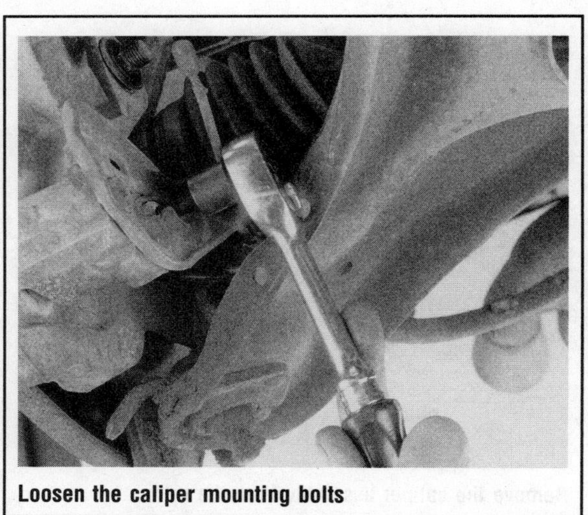
Loosen the caliper mounting bolts

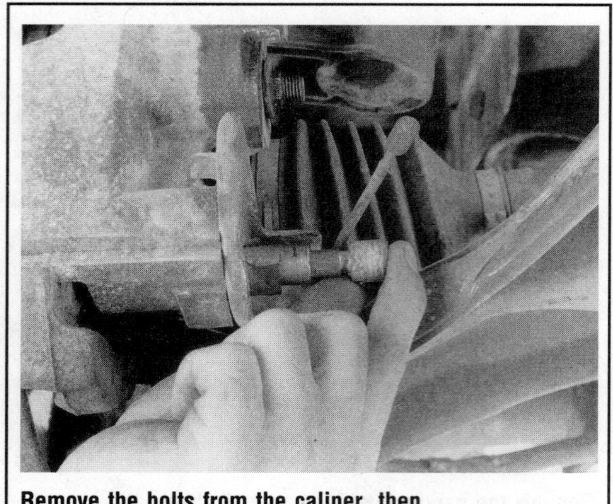
Remove the bolts from the caliper, then . . .

Support the caliper with a bungee cord or a piece of wire. Never let the caliper hang by the brake hose

. . . use a pair of pliers to compress the caliper piston

Remove the outboard brake pad from the caliper . . .

Remove the caliper assembly from the rotor

. . . then remove the inboard pad

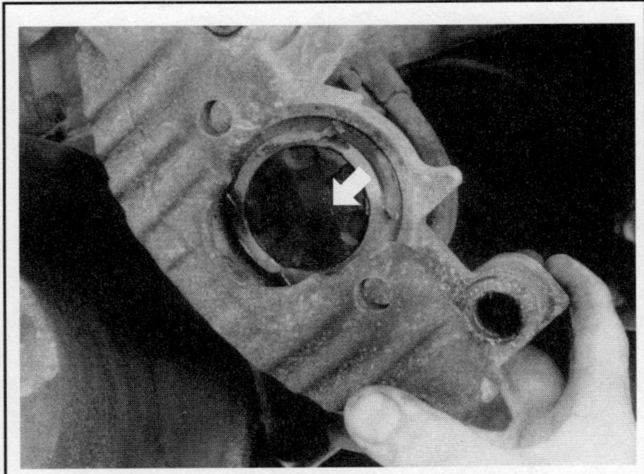

The notched piston must be turned into its bore with a special tool before installing new pads

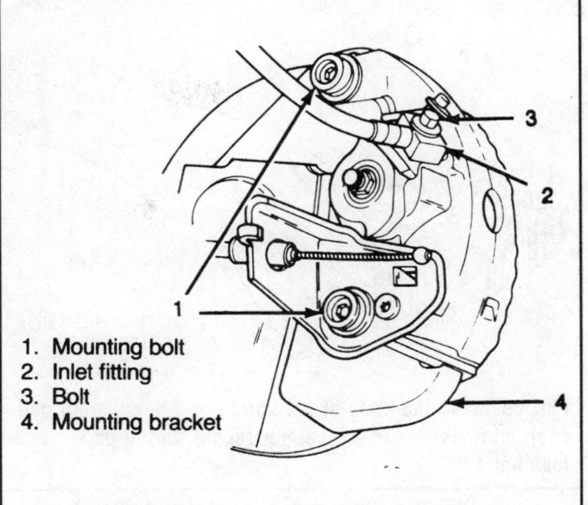

Fig. 27 Rear caliper mounting retainers and their locations—1984–87 models

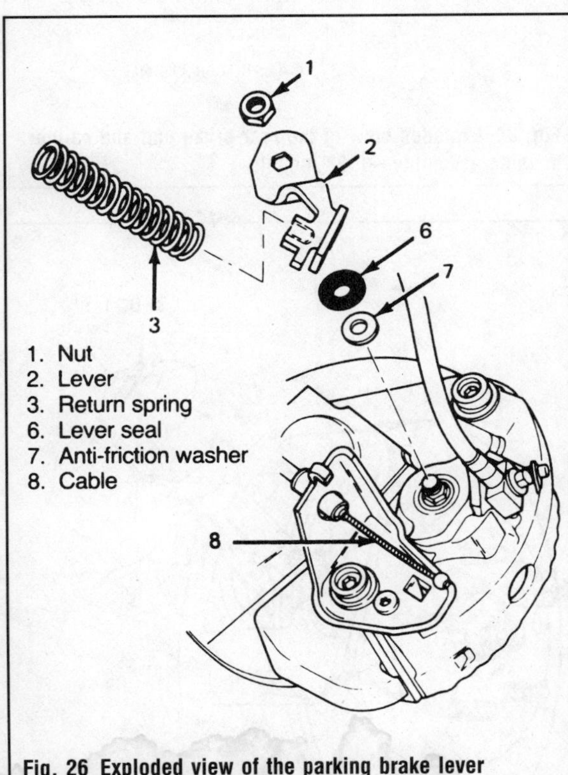

Fig. 26 Exploded view of the parking brake lever assembly—1984–87 models

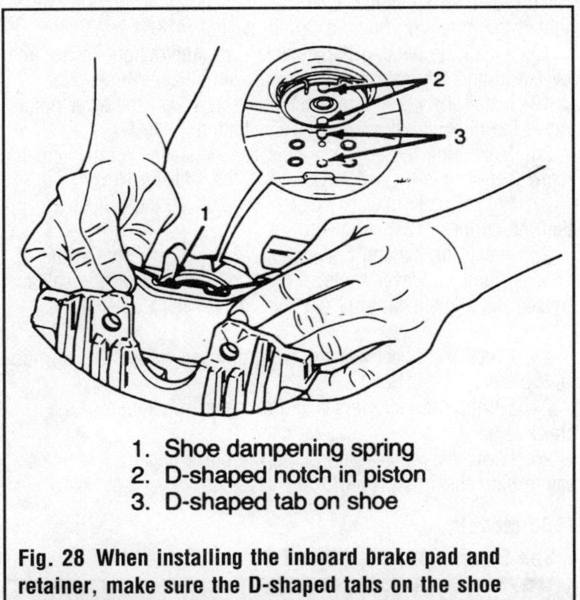

Fig. 28 When installing the inboard brake pad and retainer, make sure the D-shaped tabs on the shoe engage the D-shaped notches in the caliper piston

piston in a clockwise direction to move the piston back into the bore. The piston must be bottomed in the bore to install new brake pads.

13. Use new bushings, boots and sleeves in the mounting bolt holes and lubricate these parts with a silicone grease.

14. Use a new two-way check valve and press into the end of the piston.

15. Install the inboard shoe and lining into the caliper and make sure that the D-shaped tabs on the shoe will engage with the D-shape notches in the piston. Also make sure the wear sensor is at the leading edge of the shoe during forward wheel rotation. Slide the edge of the inboard metal shoe under the edge of the dampening spring and snap the shoe into position against the piston.

➡If the D-shaped tabs and notches do not line up, the piston will have to be turned. Pontiac recommends the use of Tool No. J-7624 or its equivalent to turn the piston.

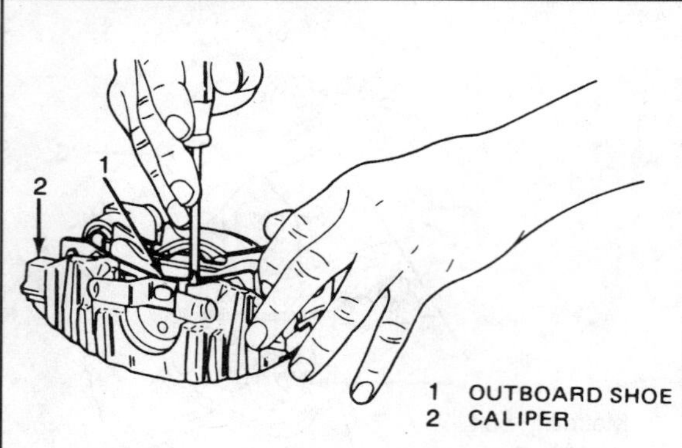

Fig. 29 Make the ends of the spring on the outboard pad snap into position in the caliper recess during pad installation

16. Install the outboard shoe and lining and make sure the ends of the spring on the outboard shoe snap into the caliper recesses.
17. Position the caliper over the rotor mounting bracket and tighten the mounting bolts to 30–45 ft. lbs. (41–61 Nm).
18. Install the parking brake cable lever antifriction washer and lever seal and lubricate the lever seal with silicone brake lube.
19. Install the lever on the actuator screw with the lever pointing in the direction shown in the illustration.
20. Make sure the lever stays properly installed on the actuator screw then torque the nut to 30–40 ft. lbs. (41–54 Nm).
21. Rotate the lever back against the stop on the caliper and install the spring.
22. Install the parking brake cable. Tighten the cable at the equalizer until the lever starts to move off the stop on the caliper. Loosen the adjustment until the lever moves back against the stop.
23. Install the wheel and tire assembly and torque the lug nuts to 100 ft. lbs. (136 Nm).
24. Fill the master cylinder and check the operation of the brake pedal.
25. Lower the vehicle and pump the brake pedal a few times before the vehicle is moved.

1988 Models

➧ See Figures 30, 31, 32 and 33

CAUTION

Some brake pads contain asbestos, which has been determined to be a cancer causing agent. Never clean the brake surfaces with compressed air! Avoid inhaling any dust from any brake surface! When cleaning brake surfaces, use a commercially available brake cleaning fluid.

1. Remove ⅔ of the brake fluid from the master cylinder assembly.
2. Raise the vehicle and support it safely with jackstands.
3. Remove the wheel and tire assembly then install two lug nuts to retain the rotor.

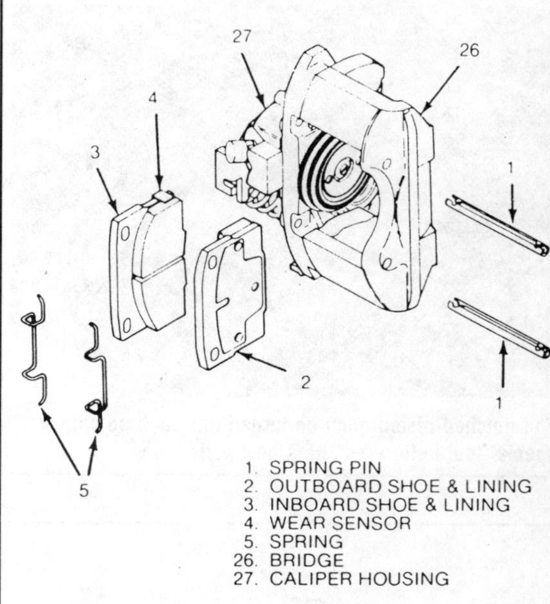

Fig. 30 Exploded view of the rear brake pad and caliper housing assembly—1988 models

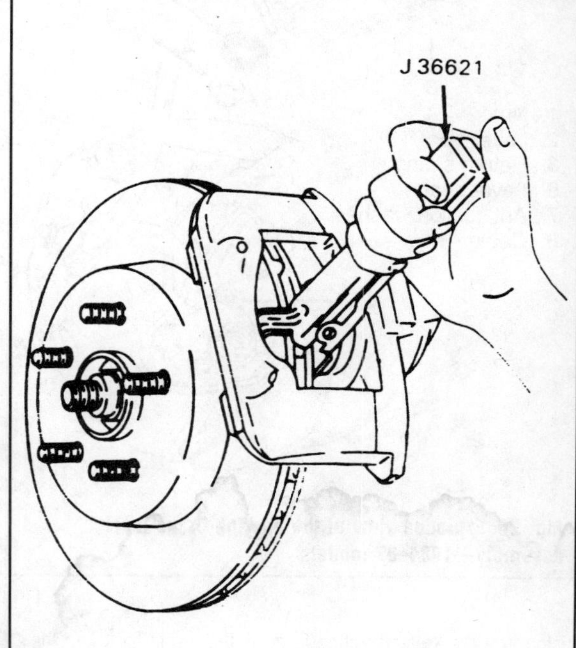

Fig. 31 Use tool J-36621 or its equivalent to compress the caliper piston

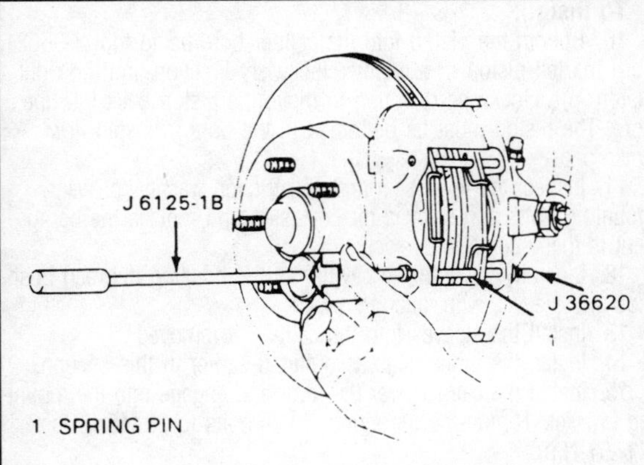

Fig. 32 Remove the spring pins from the caliper housing using the proper tools—1988 models

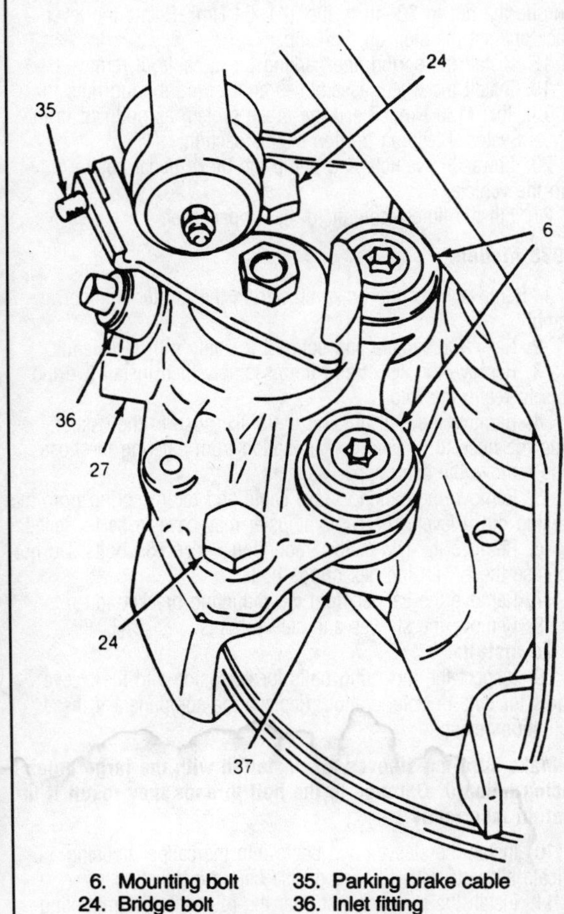

Fig. 33 Location of the rear caliper mounting components—1988 models

CAUTION

Be sure to catch the springs when removing spring pins. Springs may fly out causing personal injury.

4. Remove the spring pins by connecting a spring pin removing tool J-36620 onto J-6125-1B or equivalent. Thrust weight on J-6125-1B outward against the tool handle to drive the pin out.
5. Remove the springs from the inboard and outboard pad flanges.
6. Remove the two brake pads by twisting and pulling straight out of the caliper housing. A locking pliers may have to be used to remove the pads.
7. Remove the two way check valve from the end of the piston assembly using a small screwdriver.

➡If leakage is noted from the piston hole after the check valve is removed, the caliper will have to be overhauled or replaced.

To install:

8. Bottom the piston into the caliper bore using tool J-36621. Turn the left piston in a counterclockwise direction and the right piston in a clockwise direction to move the piston back into the bore. The piston must be bottomed in the bore to install new brake pads.
9. Lubricate a new two way check valve with silicone grease and install into the end of the piston assembly.
10. Install the inboard brake pad with the wear sensor at the leading edge of the pad during forward wheel rotation. Install the outboard brake shoe.
11. Install one spring pin while aligning the holes in the pads. Tap in the pin with a soft brass drift and hammer until the end of the pin just emerges from the inboard face of the caliper housing.

➡Do not use a steel drift to drive in the spring pins. This will damage the pin ends and make later removal of pins difficult.

12. Install the two springs and remaining spring pin. Position the pins so that the slots in the pins face each other. Make sure the springs are centered on the pad flanges with each spring end projecting and equal distance under the pins.
13. Install the parking brake cable. Tighten the cable at the equalizer until the lever starts to move off the stop on the caliper. Loosen the adjustment until the lever moves back against the stop.
14. Install the wheel and tire assembly and torque the lug nuts to 100 ft. lbs. (136 Nm).
15. Fill the master cylinder and check the operation of the brake pedal.
16. Lower the vehicle and pump the brake pedal a few times before the vehicle is moved.

Brake Caliper

REMOVAL & INSTALLATION

1984–87 Models

1. Remove ⅔ of the brake fluid from the master cylinder assembly.

2. Raise the vehicle and support it safely with jackstands.
3. Remove the wheel and tire assembly then install two lug nuts to retain the rotor.
4. Remove the bolt holding the brake hose to the caliper. Plug the hose to prevent contamination from entering the hose. Also remove the two copper washers.
5. Loosen the tension on the parking brake cable at the equalizer.
   a. Remove the cable and spring from the lever.
   b. Remove the locknut while holding the lever.
   c. Remove the lever, lever seal and anti-friction washer.
6. Remove the caliper mounting bolts with a No. 50 Torx® wrench.
7. Position 4-inch adjustable pliers over the inboard surface of the caliper housing and outboard surface of the mounting bracket.
8. Squeeze the pliers to compress the piston back into the caliper bore and provide clearance between the brake pad and the rotor.
9. Remove the caliper from the rotor and mounting bracket.

Loosen the brake hose mounting bolt, then . . .

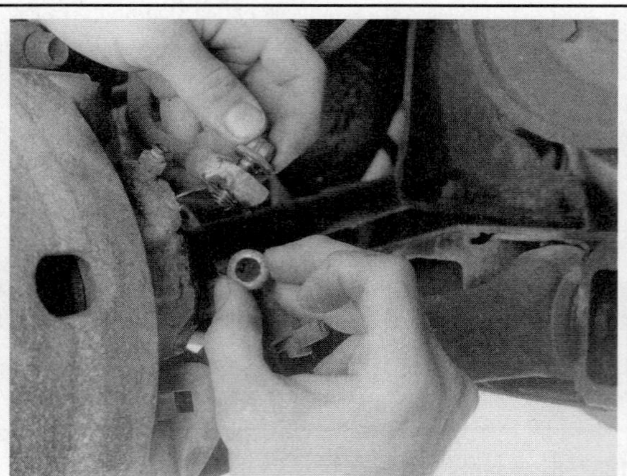

. . . disengage the hose from the caliper and remove the copper washers

To install:

10. Bottom the piston into the caliper bore using tool J-36621. Turn the left piston in a counterclockwise direction and the right piston in a clockwise direction to move the piston back into the bore. The piston must be bottomed in the bore to install new brake pads.
11. Inspect the lever seal and anti-friction washer for wear, mounting bolts and sleeves for corrosion and replace the component is these conditions exist.
12. Liberally fill both the cavities in the housing between bushings and sleeves with silicone grease.
13. Install the sleeves into the caliper, if removed.
14. Install the brake pads as outlined earlier in this section.
15. Install the caliper over the rotor and engage into the mounting bracket. Torque the mounting Torx® bolts to 30–45 ft. lbs. (41–61 Nm).
16. Install the brake hose with new copper washer. Torque the bolt to 30 ft. lbs. (40 Nm).
17. Lubricate the lever seal with silicone grease and install the lever, anti-friction washer and hex nut. Make sure the lever stays properly installed on the actuator screw hex as the nut is torqued. Torque the nut to 30–40 ft. lbs. (41–54 Nm). Rotate the lever back against the stop on the caliper.
18. Install the spring and parking brake cable, if removed.
19. Install the wheel assemblies and torque the lug nuts to 100 ft. lbs. (136 Nm). Bleed the brake system as outlined in the Brake System Bleeding portion of this section.
20. Lower the vehicle and pump the brake pedal before moving the vehicle.
21. Fill the fluid reservoir to the proper level.

1988 Models

1. Remove ⅔ of the brake fluid from the master cylinder assembly.
2. Raise the vehicle and support it safely with jackstands.
3. Remove the wheel and tire assembly then install two lug nuts to retain the rotor.
4. Remove the bolt holding the brake hose to the caliper. Plug the hose to prevent contamination from entering the hose. Also remove the two copper washers.
5. Remove the parking brake cable and return spring from the parking brake lever. The cable adjuster may have to be loosened.
6. Remove the two caliper mounting Torx® #55 bolts. Do not confuse these with the hex bridge bolts.
7. Remove the caliper from the mounting bracket and rotor.
8. Remove the sleeves and sleeve boots.

To install:

9. Inspect the mounting bolts for corrosion and the sleeve boots for cuts or deterioration. Replace the component if these conditions exist.

➡Make sure the sleeves are installed with the large holes facing inboard. Damage to the bolt threads may result if installed incorrectly.

10. Install the sleeves and boots into the caliper housing. Lubricate all parts with silicone grease before installation.
11. Install the brake caliper over the rotor into the mounting bracket and torque the two Torx® bolts to 74 ft. lbs. (100 Nm). Make sure the mounting Torx® bolts are properly torqued.
12. Install the brake hose, two copper washers and retaining bolt to the caliper. Torque the hose retaining bolt to 33 ft. lbs. (45 Nm).

13. Install the brake pads as outlined in the Brake Pad installation procedures in this section.
14. Install the spring and parking brake cable, if removed.
15. Bleed the brake system as outlined in the Brake System Bleeding procedure in this section.
16. Install the wheel assemblies and torque the lug nuts to 100 ft. lbs. (136 Nm).
17. Lower the vehicle and pump the brake pedal before moving the vehicle.
18. Fill the fluid reservoir to the proper level.

OVERHAUL

1984–87 Models

See Figures 34 and 35

1. Remove the brake pads and caliper as outlined in the Brake Pad and Caliper portions of this section.
2. Remove the bleeder valve and cap. If the bleeder will not come out or breaks off in the housing, the caliper will have to be replaced.
3. Remove the brake pad dampening spring from the end of the piston. Refer to the Rear Brake Caliper exploded view.
4. Remove the parking brake lever, nut and washers from the housing.
5. Support the caliper in a vise. Using a wrench, rotate the actuator screw in the parking brake direction (right side rotates clockwise and left side rotates counterclockwise).
6. Remove the actuator screw by pressing on the threaded end. Remove the shaft seal and thrust washer.
7. Remove the piston boot by prying it off with a small prybar. Do not damage the housing.
8. Remove the piston by applying compressed air to the caliper fluid inlet.

CAUTION

Do not try to catch the piston with your fingers, as it could result in serious injury. Use a piece of wood or rolled up towels to prevent injury.

9. Remove the piston seal with a piece of wood or plastic so not to damage the piston bore with a metal tool.

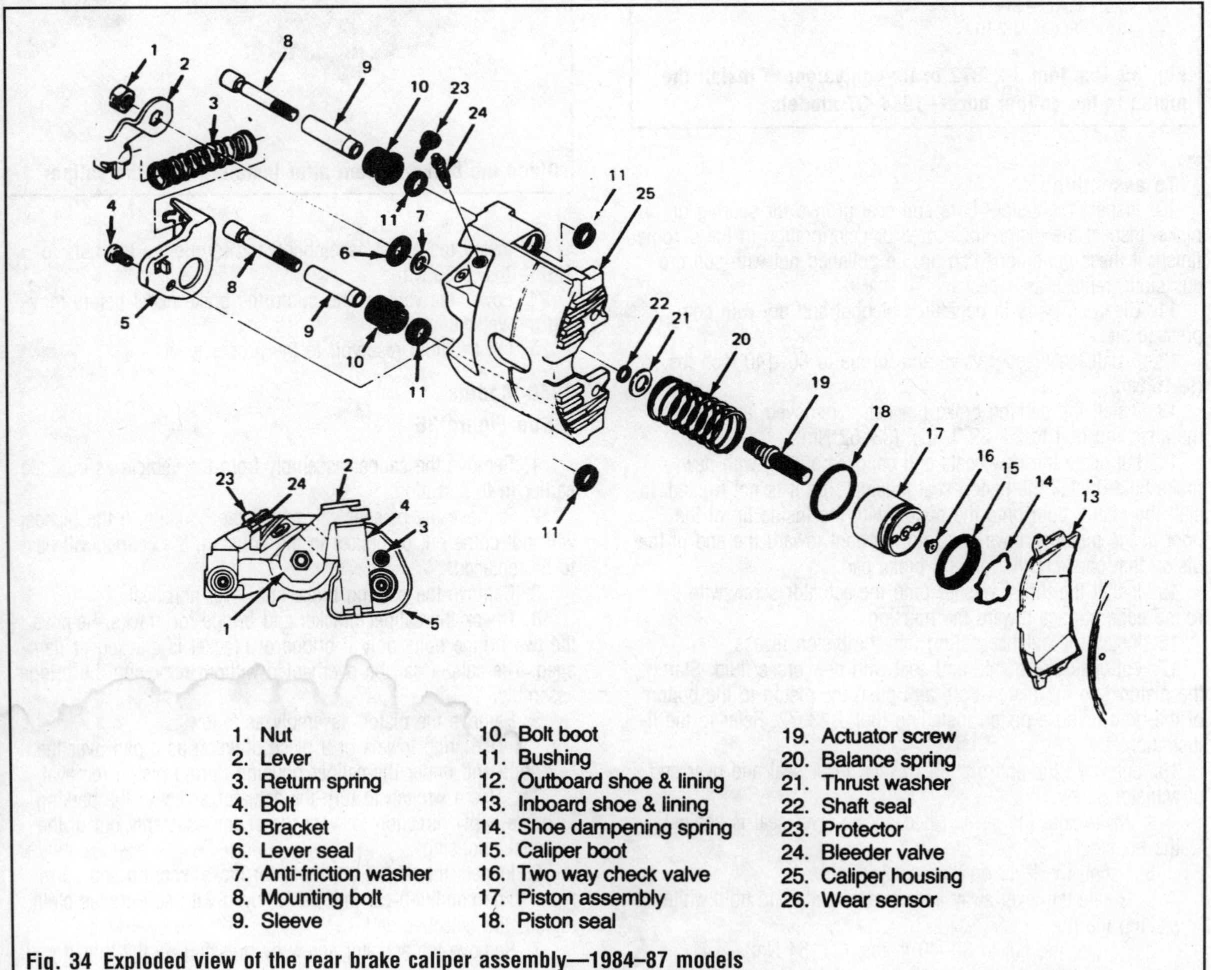

Fig. 34 Exploded view of the rear brake caliper assembly—1984–87 models

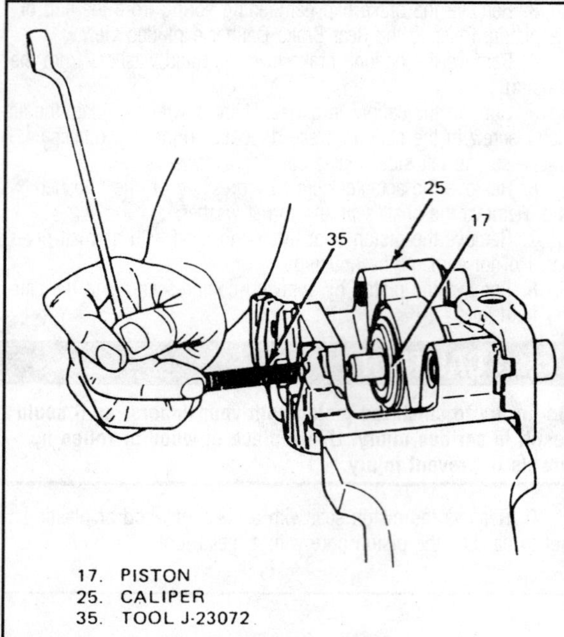

Fig. 35 Use tool J-23072 or its equivalent to install the piston in the caliper bore—1984–87 models

To assemble:

10. Inspect the caliper bore and seal groove for scoring or nicks. Inspect the piston for scores or deterioration in the chrome finish. If these conditions can not be polished out with soft crocus cloth, replace as necessary.
11. Clean all parts in denatured alcohol and dry with compressed air.
12. Install the bleeder valve and torque to 80–140 inch lbs. (9–16 Nm).
13. Install the parking brake bracket, if removed, and torque the attaching bolt to 24–39 ft. lbs. (33–52 Nm).
14. Lubricate the new seals and caliper housing with new brake fluid. Install the piston seal making sure it is not twisted. Install the piston boot onto the piston with the inside lip of the boot in the piston groove and fold the boot toward the end of the piston that contacts the inboard brake pad.
15. Install the thrust washer onto the actuator screw with the round edge surface toward the housing.
16. Install the balance spring into the piston recess.
17. Lubricate the piston and seal with new brake fluid. Start the piston into the piston bore and push the piston to the bottom of the bore using a piston installing tool J-23072. Refer to the illustration.
18. Lubricate the anti-friction washer, lever seal and over end of actuator screw.
    a. Make sure the sealing bed on the lever seal is against the housing.
    b. Install the lever on the actuator screw.
    c. Rotate the lever away from stop slightly and hold while installing the nut.
    d. Torque the nut to 30–40 ft. lbs. (41–54 Nm).
19. Install the boot in the caliper counterbore and seat using tool No. J-28678 or equivalent.
20. Install the dampening spring in the groove in the end of the piston. It may be necessary to move the parking brake lever off the stop to extend the piston and make the spring groove accessible.
21. Install the caliper and brake pads as outlined earlier in this section.
22. Bleed the brake system as outlined in the Brake System Bleeding procedure in this section.

Bleed the brake system after installation of the caliper

23. Install the wheel assemblies and torque the lug nuts to 100 ft. lbs. (136 Nm).
24. Lower the vehicle and pump the brake pedal before moving the vehicle.
25. Fill the fluid reservoir to the proper level.

1988 Models

➧ **See Figure 36**

1. Remove the caliper assembly from the vehicle as outlined earlier in this section.
2. Remove the bleeder valve from the housing. If the bleeder with not come out or breaks in the housing, the caliper will have to be replaced.
3. Remove the parking brake nut, lever and seal.
4. Check the caliper bracket and bridge for cracks. Remove the two bridge bolts only if bridge or bracket is cracked or damaged. The caliper can be overhauled without removing the bridge assembly.
5. Remove the piston assembly as follows:
    a. Use shop towels or a piece of wood as a pad over the bridge and under the caliper housing during piston removal.
    b. Use a wrench to turn the actuator screw in the parking brake apply direction to work the piston assembly out of the caliper housing.
6. Inspect the piston and bore for nicks, scoring and corrosion. If the condition can not be removed with soft crocus cloth, replace the defective part.
7. Remove the actuator screw by pressing on the thread end.

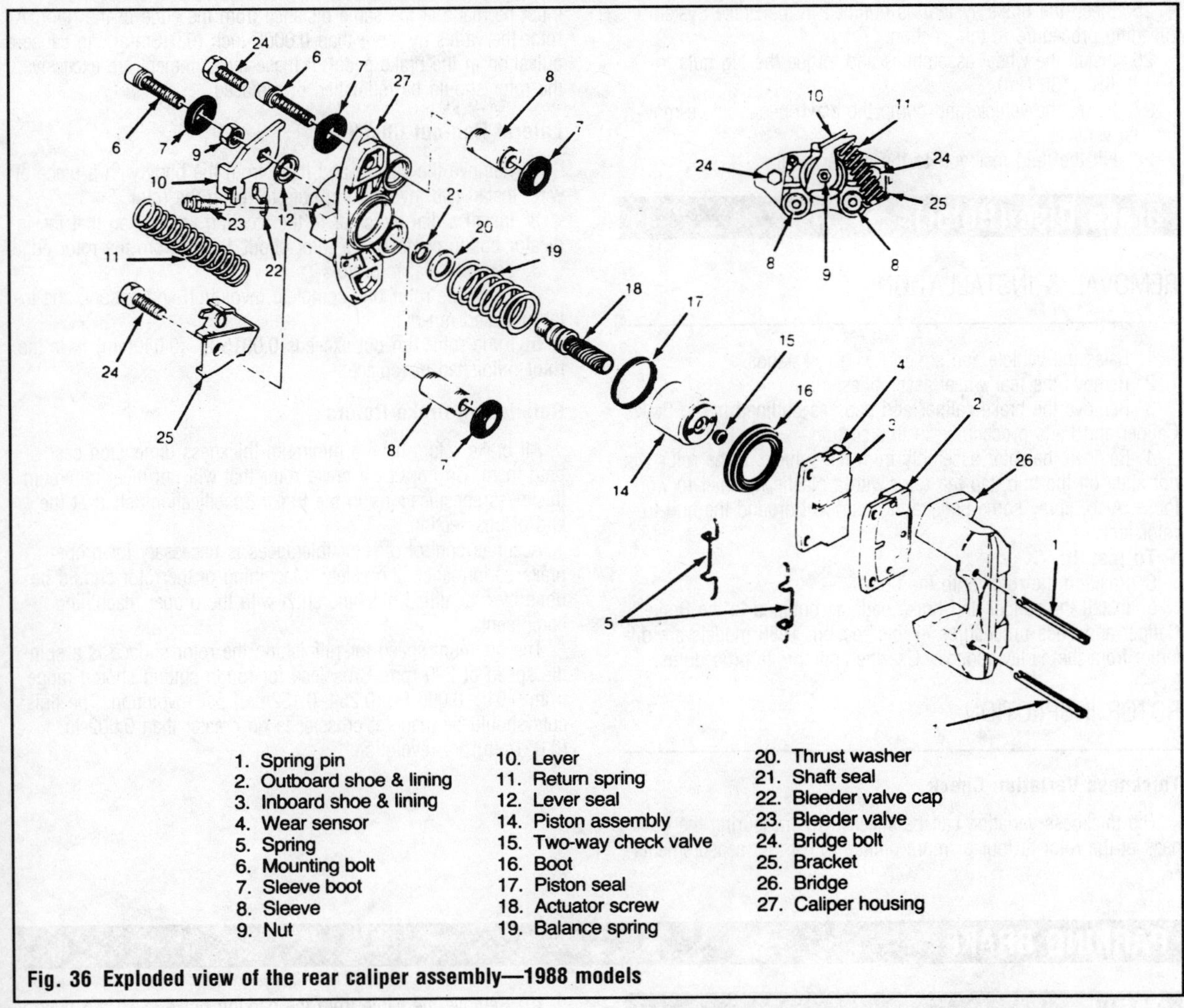

Fig. 36 Exploded view of the rear caliper assembly—1988 models

8. Remove the balance spring, shaft seal and thrust washer from the actuator screw.
9. Remove the piston boot being careful not to scratch the piston bore.
10. Remove the piston seal with a plastic or wooden seal removal tool. Do not use any metal tools.
11. Clean the piston bore and seal groove with crocus cloth.

To assemble:

12. Clean all parts with denatured alcohol and dry with compressed air.
13. If the bridge was removed, torque the bolts to 74 ft. lbs. (100 Nm).
14. Install the bleeder valve and torque to 116 inch lbs. (13 Nm).
15. Lubricate the new piston seal with new brake fluid and install into the seal groove. Make sure the seal is not twisted.
16. Install the thrust washer onto the actuator screw with the copper side of washer towards the piston.
17. Lubricate the shaft seal and piston boot. Install the boot onto the piston.
18. Lubricate the actuator screw and install with the shaft seal and thrust washer into the caliper housing.
19. Install the balance spring into the housing bore with the end of the spring in the recess at the bottom of the bore.
20. Lubricate the piston and boot. Install the assembly by pushing the piston toward the bottom of the bore using a piston installer tool J-36623 or equivalent. Turn the actuator screw as necessary to move the piston to the bottom of the bore.
21. Lubricate the parking lever seal and install so that the rubber sealing bead on the seal is against the lever and the copper side is against the housing.
22. Hold the lever back against the stop on the housing while torquing the nut. Install the lever and nut and torque to 35 ft. lbs. (47 Nm).
23. Set the piston boot to the housing by pressing down with a boot tool J-36622 and J-36623 or equivalent. A piece of wood can be used.
24. Install the caliper and brake pads as outlined earlier in this chapter.

25. Bleed the brake system as outlined in the Brake System Bleeding procedure in this section.
26. Install the wheel assemblies and torque the lug nuts to 100 ft. lbs. (136 Nm).
27. Lower the vehicle and pump the brake pedal before moving the vehicle.
28. Fill the fluid reservoir to the proper level.

Brake Disc (Rotor)

REMOVAL & INSTALLATION

1. Raise the vehicle and support with jackstands.
2. Remove the rear wheel assemblies.
3. Remove the brake caliper and pads as outlined in the Brake Caliper and Pads procedures in this section.
4. Remove the rotor assembly from the vehicle. If the rotor will not slide off the hub, tap the rotor with a plastic hammer to work loose. Also, spray some penetrating lubricant around the hub-to-rotor area.

To install:

5. Position the rotor onto the hub.
6. Install the caliper and brake pads as outlined in the Brake Caliper and Pads procedures in this section. 1988 models are different from the earlier models. Use the appropriate procedures.

ROTOR INSPECTION

Thickness Variation Check

The thickness variation can be checked by measuring the thickness of the rotor at four or more points. All of the measurements must be made at the same distance from the edge of the rotor. A rotor the varies by more than 0.0005 inch (0.013mm) can cause a pulsation in the brake pedal. If these measurement are excessive, the rotor should be refinished or replaced.

Lateral Run-out Check

1. Remove the caliper and hang from the body with a piece of wire. Install two inverted lug nuts to retain the rotor.
2. Install a dial indicator to the steering knuckle so that the indicator button contacts the rotor about 1 inch from the rotor edge.
3. Zero the dial indicator.
4. Move the rotor one complete revolution and observe the total indicated run-out.
5. If the rotor run-out exceeds 0.0015 in. (0.040mm) have the rotor refinished or replaced.

Refinishing Brake Rotors

All brake rotors have a minimum thickness dimension cast onto them. Do not use a brake rotor that will not meet minimum thickness specifications in the Brake Specifications chart at the end of this section.

Accurate control of rotor tolerances is necessary for proper brake performance and safety. Machining of the rotor should be done by a qualified machine shop with the proper machining equipment.

The optimum speed for refinishing the rotor surface is a spindle speed of 200 rpm. Crossfeed for rough cutting should range from 0.010–0.006 in. (0.254–0.152mm) per revolution. The finish cuts should be made at crossfeeds no greater than 0.002 in. (0.051mm) per revolution.

PARKING BRAKE

CABLE

REMOVAL & INSTALLATION

Front

➧ See Figure 37

1. Raise the vehicle and support it safely with jackstands.
2. Loosen the adjusting nut at the equalizer and separate the cables.
3. Remove the clip from the cable.
4. Remove the two retaining clip bolts in the left wheel well.
5. Lower the vehicle then unsnap the clip holding the parking brake boot to the lever.
6. Remove the seat belt bolt and carpeting finishing molding.
7. Remove the shoulder harness retaining bolt.
8. Remove the quarter trim finishing molding.
9. Pull the carpet back and note how the cable is routed.
10. Remove the cable from the parking brake lever and push it through the body.
11. Installation is the reverse of removal.

Rear

1. Raise the vehicle and support it safely with jackstands.
2. Loosen the adjusting nut at the equalizer and separate the cables.
3. Remove the cables at the calipers.
4. Disconnect the cables at the cradle. Pontiac recommends using tool No. J-34065 for this step.
5. Installation is the reverse of removal. Adjust the parking brake.

ADJUSTMENT

Adjustment of the parking brake is necessary anytime the rear brake cables have been disconnected or if the hydraulic system operates with good reserve, but the parking brake hand lever travel is more than 9 ratchet clicks.

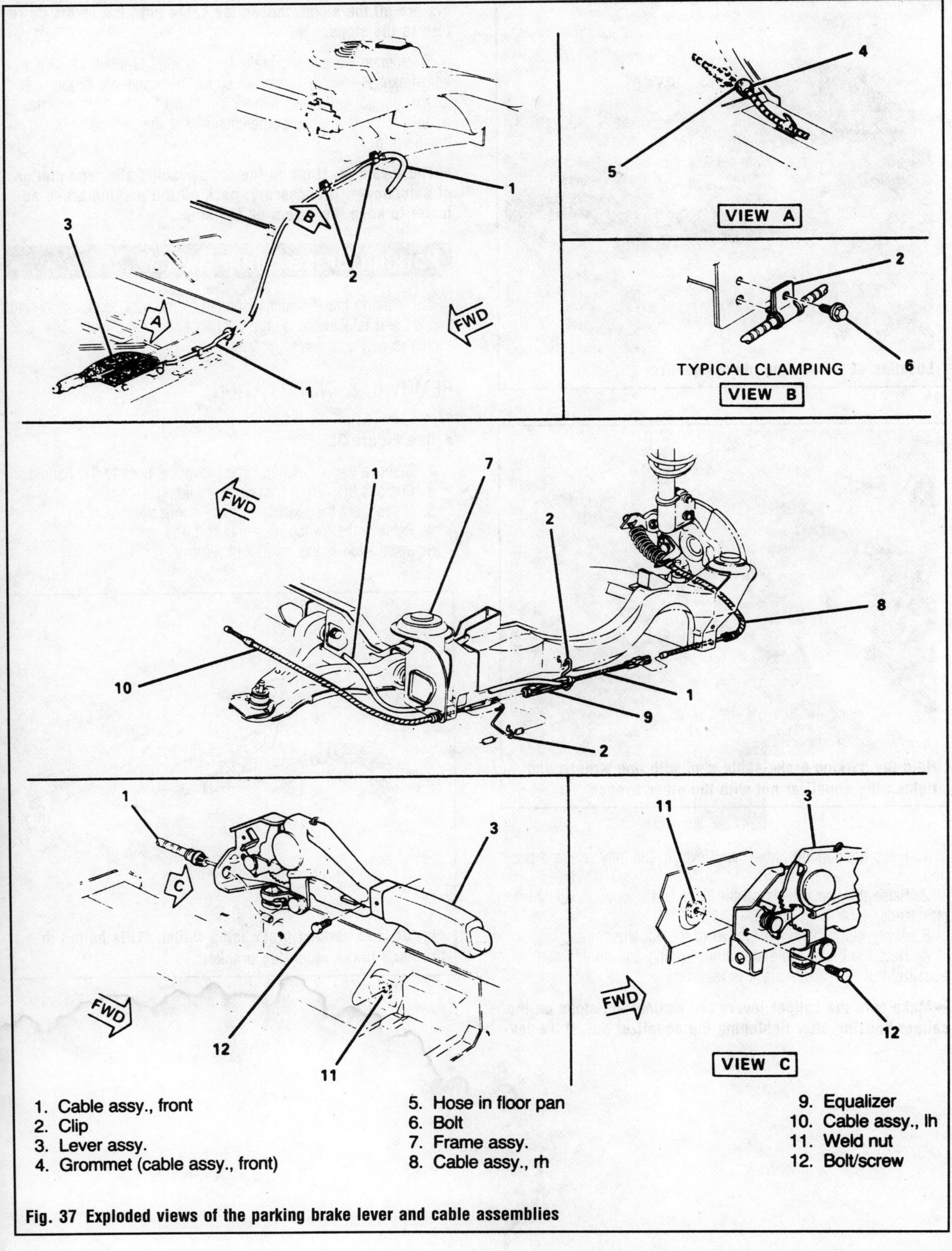

1. Cable assy., front
2. Clip
3. Lever assy.
4. Grommet (cable assy., front)
5. Hose in floor pan
6. Bolt
7. Frame assy.
8. Cable assy., rh
9. Equalizer
10. Cable assy., lh
11. Weld nut
12. Bolt/screw

Fig. 37 Exploded views of the parking brake lever and cable assemblies

Location of the parking brake equalizer

Hold the parking brake cable stud with one wrench and tighten the equalizer nut with the other wrench

1. Place the parking brake hand lever in the fully released position.
2. Raise the rear wheels off the floor and support it safely with jackstands.
3. Apply lubricant to the groove in the equalizer nut.
4. Hold the brake cable stud from turning and tighten the equalizer nut until cable slack is removed.

➡Make sure the caliper levers are against the stops on the caliper housing after tightening the equalizer nut. If the levers are off the stops, loosen the cable until the levers do return to the stops.

5. Operate the parking brake lever several times to check the adjustment. If the parking brake shoes and cable are properly adjusted, the parking brake handle will move five to eight notches when a force is applied perpendicularly at the mid-point of the handle grip.

➡The levers must be on the caliper stops after completion of adjustment. If necessary, back off the parking brake adjuster to keep the levers on the stops.

Parking Brake Lamp Switch

The parking brake switch is bolted to the hand brake mounting bracket and is actuated by the parking brake hand lever. The switch is non-adjustable.

REMOVAL & INSTALLATION

➧ See Figure 38

1. Remove the retainer holding the brake boot to the handle.
2. Remove the carpet trim finish molding.
3. Disconnect the switch electrical connector.
4. Remove the switch retaining bolt and switch.
5. Installation is the reverse of removal.

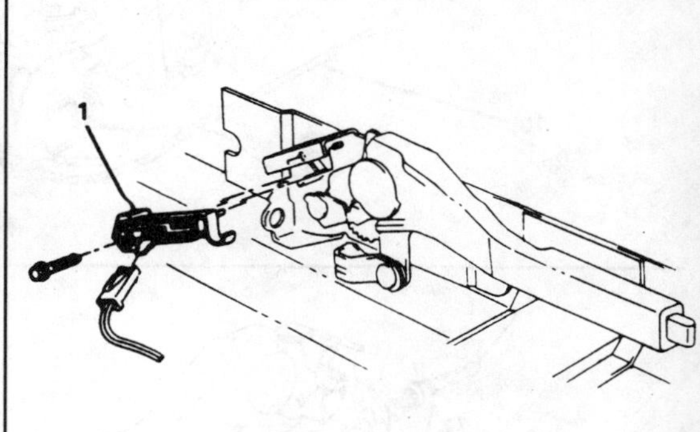

Fig. 38 The parking brake lamp switch (1) is bolted to the hand brake mounting bracket

Troubleshooting the Brake System

Problem	Cause	Solution
Low brake pedal (excessive pedal travel required for braking action.)	• Excessive clearance between rear linings and drums caused by inoperative automatic adjusters	• Make 10 to 15 alternate forward and reverse brake stops to adjust brakes. If brake pedal does not come up, repair or replace adjuster parts as necessary.
	• Worn rear brakelining	• Inspect and replace lining if worn beyond minimum thickness specification
	• Bent, distorted brakeshoes, front or rear	• Replace brakeshoes in axle sets
	• Air in hydraulic system	• Remove air from system. Refer to Brake Bleeding.
Low brake pedal (pedal may go to floor with steady pressure applied.)	• Fluid leak in hydraulic system	• Fill master cylinder to fill line; have helper apply brakes and check calipers, wheel cylinders, differential valve tubes, hoses and fittings for leaks. Repair or replace as necessary.
	• Air in hydraulic system	• Remove air from system. Refer to Brake Bleeding.
	• Incorrect or non-recommended brake fluid (fluid evaporates at below normal temp).	• Flush hydraulic system with clean brake fluid. Refill with correct-type fluid.
	• Master cylinder piston seals worn, or master cylinder bore is scored, worn or corroded	• Repair or replace master cylinder
Low brake pedal (pedal goes to floor on first application—o.k. on subsequent applications.)	• Disc brake pads sticking on abutment surfaces of anchor plate. Caused by a build-up of dirt, rust, or corrosion on abutment surfaces	• Clean abutment surfaces
Fading brake pedal (pedal height decreases with steady pressure applied.)	• Fluid leak in hydraulic system	• Fill master cylinder reservoirs to fill mark, have helper apply brakes, check calipers, wheel cylinders, differential valve, tubes, hoses, and fittings for fluid leaks. Repair or replace parts as necessary.
	• Master cylinder piston seals worn, or master cylinder bore is scored, worn or corroded	• Repair or replace master cylinder
Decreasing brake pedal travel (pedal travel required for braking action decreases and may be accompanied by a hard pedal.)	• Caliper or wheel cylinder pistons sticking or seized	• Repair or replace the calipers, or wheel cylinders
	• Master cylinder compensator ports blocked (preventing fluid return to reservoirs) or pistons sticking or seized in master cylinder bore	• Repair or replace the master cylinder
	• Power brake unit binding internally	• Test unit according to the following procedure: (a) Shift transmission into neutral and start engine (b) Increase engine speed to 1500 rpm, close throttle and fully depress brake pedal (c) Slow release brake pedal and stop engine (d) Have helper remove vacuum check valve and hose from power unit. Observe for backward movement of brake pedal. (e) If the pedal moves backward, the power unit has an internal bind—replace power unit

Troubleshooting the Brake System (cont.)

Problem	Cause	Solution
Spongy brake pedal (pedal has abnormally soft, springy, spongy feel when depressed.)	• Air in hydraulic system	• Remove air from system. Refer to Brake Bleeding.
	• Brakeshoes bent or distorted	• Replace brakeshoes
	• Brakelining not yet seated with drums and rotors	• Burnish brakes
	• Rear drum brakes not properly adjusted	• Adjust brakes
Hard brake pedal (excessive pedal pressure required to stop vehicle. May be accompanied by brake fade.)	• Loose or leaking power brake unit vacuum hose	• Tighten connections or replace leaking hose
	• Incorrect or poor quality brakelining	• Replace with lining in axle sets
	• Bent, broken, distorted brakeshoes	• Replace brakeshoes
	• Calipers binding or dragging on mounting pins. Rear brakeshoes dragging on support plate.	• Replace mounting pins and bushings. Clean rust or burrs from rear brake support plate ledges and lubricate ledges with molydisulfide grease. **NOTE:** If ledges are deeply grooved or scored, do not attempt to sand or grind them smooth—replace support plate.
	• Caliper, wheel cylinder, or master cylinder pistons sticking or seized	• Repair or replace parts as necessary
	• Power brake unit vacuum check valve malfunction	• Test valve according to the following procedure: (a) Start engine, increase engine speed to 1500 rpm, close throttle and immediately stop engine (b) Wait at least 90 seconds then depress brake pedal (c) If brakes are not vacuum assisted for 2 or more applications, check valve is faulty
	• Power brake unit has internal bind	• Test unit according to the following procedure: (a) With engine stopped, apply brakes several times to exhaust all vacuum in system (b) Shift transmission into neutral, depress brake pedal and start engine (c) If pedal height decreases with foot pressure and less pressure is required to hold pedal in applied position, power unit vacuum system is operating normally. Test power unit. If power unit exhibits a bind condition, replace the power unit.
	• Master cylinder compensator ports (at bottom of reservoirs) blocked by dirt, scale, rust, or have small burrs (blocked ports prevent fluid return to reservoirs).	• Repair or replace master cylinder **CAUTION:** Do not attempt to clean blocked ports with wire, pencils, or similar implements. Use compressed air only.
	• Brake hoses, tubes, fittings clogged or restricted	• Use compressed air to check or unclog parts. Replace any damaged parts.
	• Brake fluid contaminated with improper fluids (motor oil, transmission fluid, causing rubber components to swell and stick in bores	• Replace all rubber components, combination valve and hoses. Flush entire brake system with DOT 3 brake fluid or equivalent.
	• Low engine vacuum	• Adjust or repair engine

Troubleshooting the Brake System (cont.)

Problem	Cause	Solution
Grabbing brakes (severe reaction to brake pedal pressure.)	• Brakelining(s) contaminated by grease or brake fluid	• Determine and correct cause of contamination and replace brakeshoes in axle sets
	• Parking brake cables incorrectly adjusted or seized	• Adjust cables. Replace seized cables.
	• Incorrect brakelining or lining loose on brakeshoes	• Replace brakeshoes in axle sets
	• Caliper anchor plate bolts loose	• Tighten bolts
	• Rear brakeshoes binding on support plate ledges	• Clean and lubricate ledges. Replace support plate(s) if ledges are deeply grooved. Do not attempt to smooth ledges by grinding.
	• Incorrect or missing power brake reaction disc	• Install correct disc
	• Rear brake support plates loose	• Tighten mounting bolts
Dragging brakes (slow or incomplete release of brakes)	• Brake pedal binding at pivot	• Loosen and lubricate
	• Power brake unit has internal bind	• Inspect for internal bind. Replace unit if internal bind exists.
	• Parking brake cables incorrrectly adjusted or seized	• Adjust cables. Replace seized cables.
	• Rear brakeshoe return springs weak or broken	• Replace return springs. Replace brakeshoe if necessary in axle sets.
	• Automatic adjusters malfunctioning	• Repair or replace adjuster parts as required
	• Caliper, wheel cylinder or master cylinder pistons sticking or seized	• Repair or replace parts as necessary
	• Master cylinder compensating ports blocked (fluid does not return to reservoirs).	• Use compressed air to clear ports. Do not use wire, pencils, or similar objects to open blocked ports.
Vehicle moves to one side when brakes are applied	• Incorrect front tire pressure	• Inflate to recommended cold (reduced load) inflation pressure
	• Worn or damaged wheel bearings	• Replace worn or damaged bearings
	• Brakelining on one side contaminated	• Determine and correct cause of contamination and replace brakelining in axle sets
	• Brakeshoes on one side bent, distorted, or lining loose on shoe	• Replace brakeshoes in axle sets
	• Support plate bent or loose on one side	• Tighten or replace support plate
	• Brakelining not yet seated with drums or rotors	• Burnish brakelining
	• Caliper anchor plate loose on one side	• Tighten anchor plate bolts
	• Caliper piston sticking or seized	• Repair or replace caliper
	• Brakelinings water soaked	• Drive vehicle with brakes lightly applied to dry linings
	• Loose suspension component attaching or mounting bolts	• Tighten suspension bolts. Replace worn suspension components.
	• Brake combination valve failure	• Replace combination valve
Chatter or shudder when brakes are applied (pedal pulsation and roughness may also occur.)	• Brakeshoes distorted, bent, contaminated, or worn	• Replace brakeshoes in axle sets
	• Caliper anchor plate or support plate loose	• Tighten mounting bolts
	• Excessive thickness variation of rotor(s)	• Refinish or replace rotors in axle sets
Noisy brakes (squealing, clicking, scraping sound when brakes are applied.)	• Bent, broken, distorted brakeshoes	• Replace brakeshoes in axle sets
	• Excessive rust on outer edge of rotor braking surface	• Remove rust

Troubleshooting the Brake System (cont.)

Problem	Cause	Solution
Noisy brakes (squealing, clicking, scraping sound when brakes are applied.) (cont.)	• Brakelining worn out—shoes contacting drum of rotor	• Replace brakeshoes and lining in axle sets. Refinish or replace drums or rotors.
	• Broken or loose holdown or return springs	• Replace parts as necessary
	• Rough or dry drum brake support plate ledges	• Lubricate support plate ledges
	• Cracked, grooved, or scored rotor(s) or drum(s)	• Replace rotor(s) or drum(s). Replace brakeshoes and lining in axle sets if necessary.
	• Incorrect brakelining and/or shoes (front or rear).	• Install specified shoe and lining assemblies
Pulsating brake pedal	• Out of round drums or excessive lateral runout in disc brake rotor(s)	• Refinish or replace drums, re-index rotors or replace

Brake Specifications

All measurements in inches unless noted

Year	Model	Lug Nut Torque (ft. lbs.)	Master Cylinder Bore	Brake Disc Minimum Thickness	Brake Disc Maximum Runout	Standard Brake Drum Diameter	Minimum Lining Thickness Front	Minimum Lining Thickness Rear
1984–87	Front	100	1.00	①	0.005	③	0.062	—
	Rear	100	1.00	②	0.005	③	—	0.062
1988	Front	100	1.00	④	0.005	③	0.062	—
	Rear	100	1.00	④	0.005	③	—	0.062

① Minimum refinish thickness (front) 0.44, minimum discard thickness (front) 0.39.
② Minimum refinish thickness (rear) 0.50, minimum discard thickness (rear) 0.45.
③ Vehicle equipped with four wheel disc brakes.
④ Minimum refinish thickness (front & rear) 0.70, minimum discard thickness (front & rear) 0.68.

10
BODY
EXTERIOR 10-2
INTERIOR 10-15

EXTERIOR

Doors

REMOVAL & INSTALLATION

➧ **See Figure 1**

1. Disconnect the negative (−) battery cable.
2. Remove the door trim panel as outlined in the "Door Trim Panel" procedure in this section.
3. Remove the water reflector and the front run channel.
4. Remove the upper door panel assembly.
5. Support the door on a floor jack. Use a large towel or piece of rubber to pad the bottom of the door.
6. Remove the upper and lower hinge strap bolts at the front of the door.
7. Disconnect the wiring harness conduit at the body and pull the harness through the body, if so equipped. Have an assistant hold the door at this point.

To install:

1. Position the door assembly to the hinges. Install the two bolts at the upper hinge. Coat the door and bolt threads with silicone sealer. Install the two lower hinge bolts coated with sealer.
2. Install the outer door panel assembly as outlined in this section.

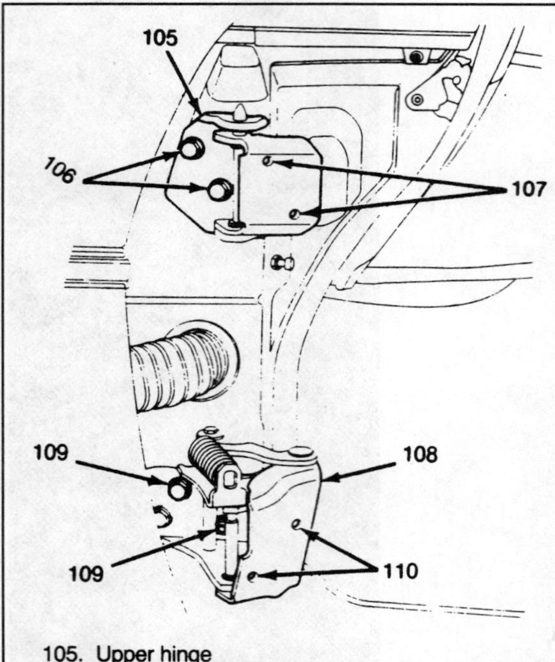

105. Upper hinge
106. Upper hinge to body bolts
107. Upper hinge to door (tapped) attachment points
108. Lower hinge
109. Lower hinge to body bolts
110. Lower hinge to door (tapped) attachment points

Fig. 1 Door hinge components

3. Install the wiring conduit and reconnect the wiring harness to the door.
4. Prior to closing the door completely, inspect for proper door assembly engagement at the striker and correct door clearance with the fender. The clearance between the door and fender should be 5/32 in. (4mm).
5. Torque the hinge bolts to 14–20 ft. lbs. (20–28 Nm). Make sure the door closes properly and all electrical devices work properly.
6. Install the front run channel, water deflector and door trim panel.

ADJUSTMENT

The door is adjusted by the door hinges and striker bolt. The door trim panel and water reflector has to be removed to gain access to the hinge bolts.

Door Lock Striker

1. Remove the striker with a lock striker Torx® tool J-23457 or equivalent.
2. Install a spacer or spacers as required to obtain correct alignment. A 3/32 in. (2mm) spacer can be used to obtain the desired alignment.
3. Replace the striker bolt and torque to 34–46 ft. lbs. (40–60 Nm).
4. Check for up and down, in and out alignment and adjust accordingly.

Hood

REMOVAL & INSTALLATION

➧ **See Figure 2**

➥**Scribe a line around the hinge on the hood inner panel and front panel to indicate the original position.**

1. With as assistant, remove the two upper support attaching bolts.
2. Remove the hinge-to-body nuts and remove the hood.

To install:

3. With an assistant, position the hood into position and install the body nuts and hinge bolts. Torque the hinge nuts and bolts to 15–25 ft. lbs. (20–34 Nm).

ADJUSTMENT

Slotted holes are provided at all hood hinge attaching points. The hood can be adjusted vertically fore and aft.

Hood Too High or Low at the Front Corners

a. Loosen the hinge nuts.
b. Reposition the hood assembly.
c. Torque the nuts to 15–25 ft. lbs. (20–34 Nm).

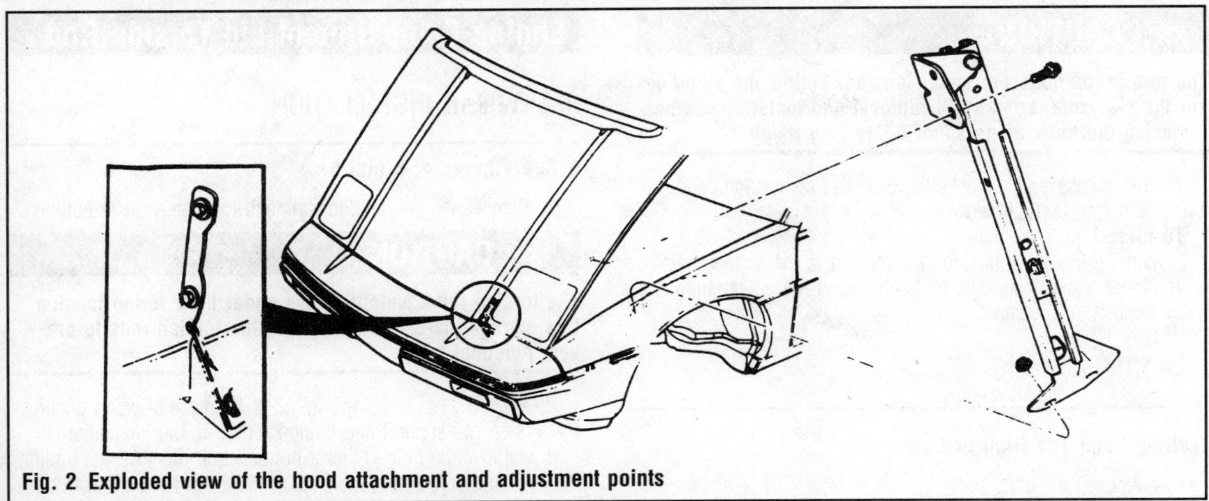

Fig. 2 Exploded view of the hood attachment and adjustment points

Hood Too High or Low at the Rear Corners

a. Determine the amount and direction of adjustment needed.
b. Adjust the hood bumper accordingly.

Hood Too Far Fore or Aft

a. Loosen the hinge bolts.
b. Reposition the hood assembly.
c. Torque the bolts to 15–25 ft. lbs. (20–34 Nm).

Engine Compartment Lid

REMOVAL & INSTALLATION

See Figure 3

Scribe a line around the hinge on the engine compartment lid inner panel and rear panel to indicate the original position.

Matchmark the position of the hinge before removal. This will aid in installation

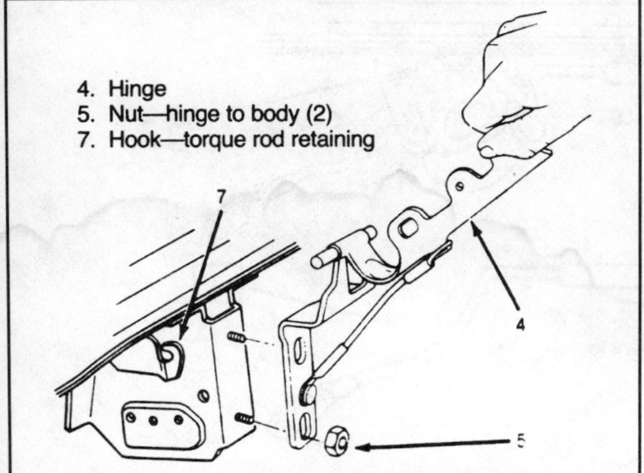

Fig. 3 The engine compartment lid hinge is retained using nuts

Disengage the hinge retaining bolts, then with the help of an assistant remove the lid

✲✲ CAUTION

The torque rod bolts are under tension. Follow the steps under the rear compartment lid removal and installation when removing the bolts as personal injury may result.

1. With an assistant, remove the electrical connections and hinge mounting bolts. Remove the rear lid.

To install:

2. With an assistant, position the rear lid to the scribed areas on the inner panel. Install the bolts and close the lid carefully and check for proper alignment.

ADJUSTMENT

Trailing Edge Too High or Low

a. Loosen the bolts.
b. Raise or lower the striker as required.
c. Tighten the bolts to 15–20 ft. lbs. (20–27 Nm).

Lock Assembly Binding on Side of Striker

a. Loosen the bolts on both hinges.
b. Move the striker right or left as required.
c. Tighten the bolts to 15–20 ft. lbs. (20–27 Nm).

Leading Edge Too High or Low (Either Side)

a. Loosen the nuts on both hinges.
b. Remove both hinges left or right as required.
c. Tighten the nuts to 15–20 ft. lbs. (20–27 Nm).

Lid Too Far Left or Right

a. Loosen the nuts on both hinges.
b. Move the striker right or left as required.
c. Tighten the bolts to 15–20 ft. lbs. (20–27 Nm).

Engine Compartment Lid Torsion Rod

REMOVAL & INSTALLATION

See Figures 4, 5 and 6

1. Remove the engine compartment lid as previously outlined.

✲✲ CAUTION

The torsion rod assemblies are under high spring tension. Use extreme care when servicing the torsion rods to prevent personal injury.

2. Place a 1⅜ in. × 1⅜ in. × 4 in. piece of wood under the torsion rod support and torsion rod as in the illustration.
3. Remove the hinge bracket nut and bolt. Remove the torsion rod retaining screw after the tension has been released from the torsion rod.
4. Remove the hinge assembly.
5. Remove the torsion rod retaining pin with the end of the torsion rod resting against a piece of 12 × 12 × ½ in. plywood as shown in the illustration.
6. Grasp the U end of the rod and pull rearward to release the pin.
7. Remove the rod from the hook and the torsion rod from the vehicle.

To install:

1. Install the torsion rod assembly and position the rod into the hook.
2. Install the pin by resting the rod against the plywood and grasp the U end of the rod and pull rearward to insert the pin. Release the U end of the rod and be sure that the end is hooked over the pin.
3. Install the hinge assembly using a piece of 1 in. × 18 in. pipe.

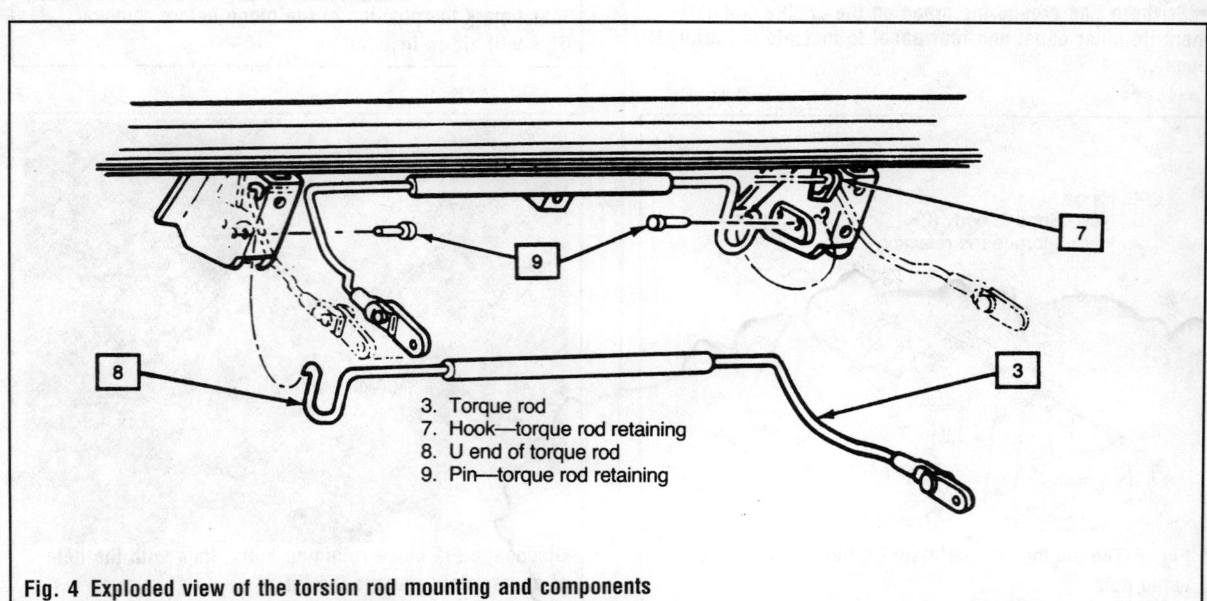

Fig. 4 Exploded view of the torsion rod mounting and components

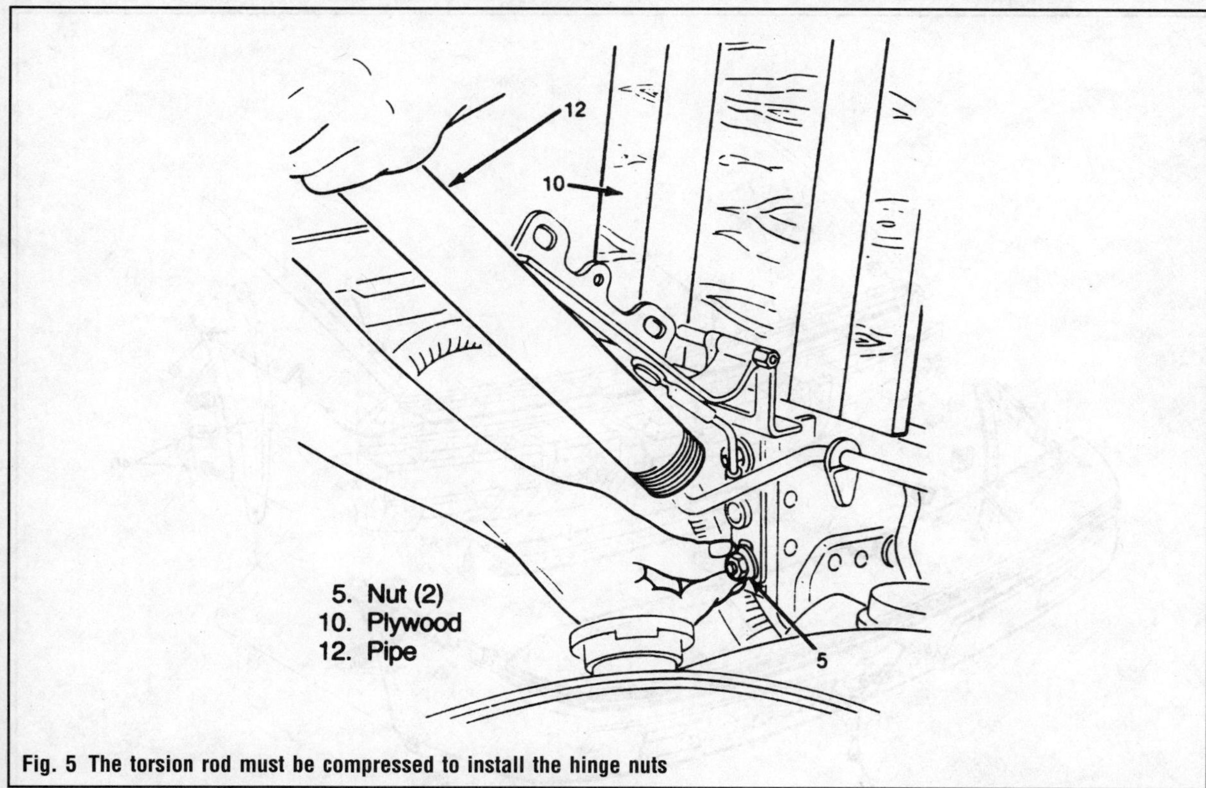

Fig. 5 The torsion rod must be compressed to install the hinge nuts

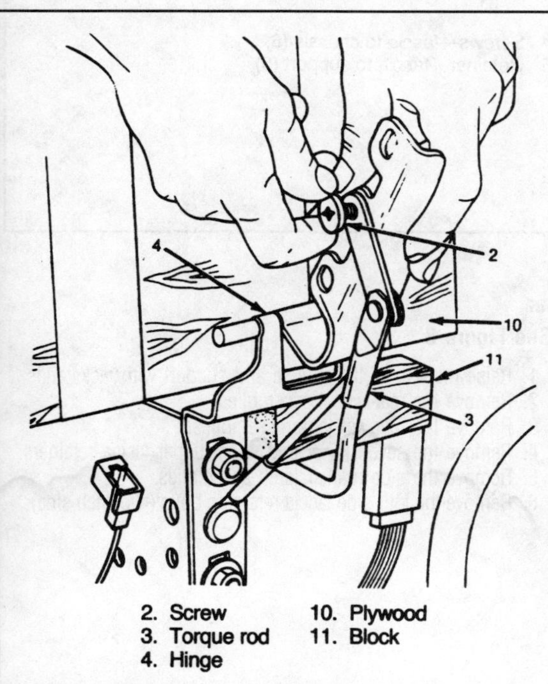

Fig. 6 Install the torque rod pin by resting the rod against the plywood and pulling the U-joint rearward

4. Install the nut and bolt and torque to 15–20 ft. lbs. (20–27 Nm).
5. To increase the tension on the torsion rods, move the pin rearward one hole.
6. With as assistant, install the compartment lid to the hinges and line up the marks on the hinges for proper alignment. Torque the retaining bolts to 15 ft. lbs. (20 Nm).
7. Close very carefully to check proper adjustment. Adjust as necessary.
8. Connect the electrical connectors to the engine compartment lid.

Bumpers

REMOVAL & INSTALLATION

Front

➧ **See Figure 7**

1. Raise the front of the vehicle and support with jackstands.
2. Remove the front wheel assemblies.
3. Remove the six phillips® head screws at the chassis.
4. Remove the two side marker lamp assemblies.
5. Remove the bolts attaching the fascia (cover)-to-fender at side marker lamp, inner wheel well-to-fascia and fascia support. Remove the fascia assembly.

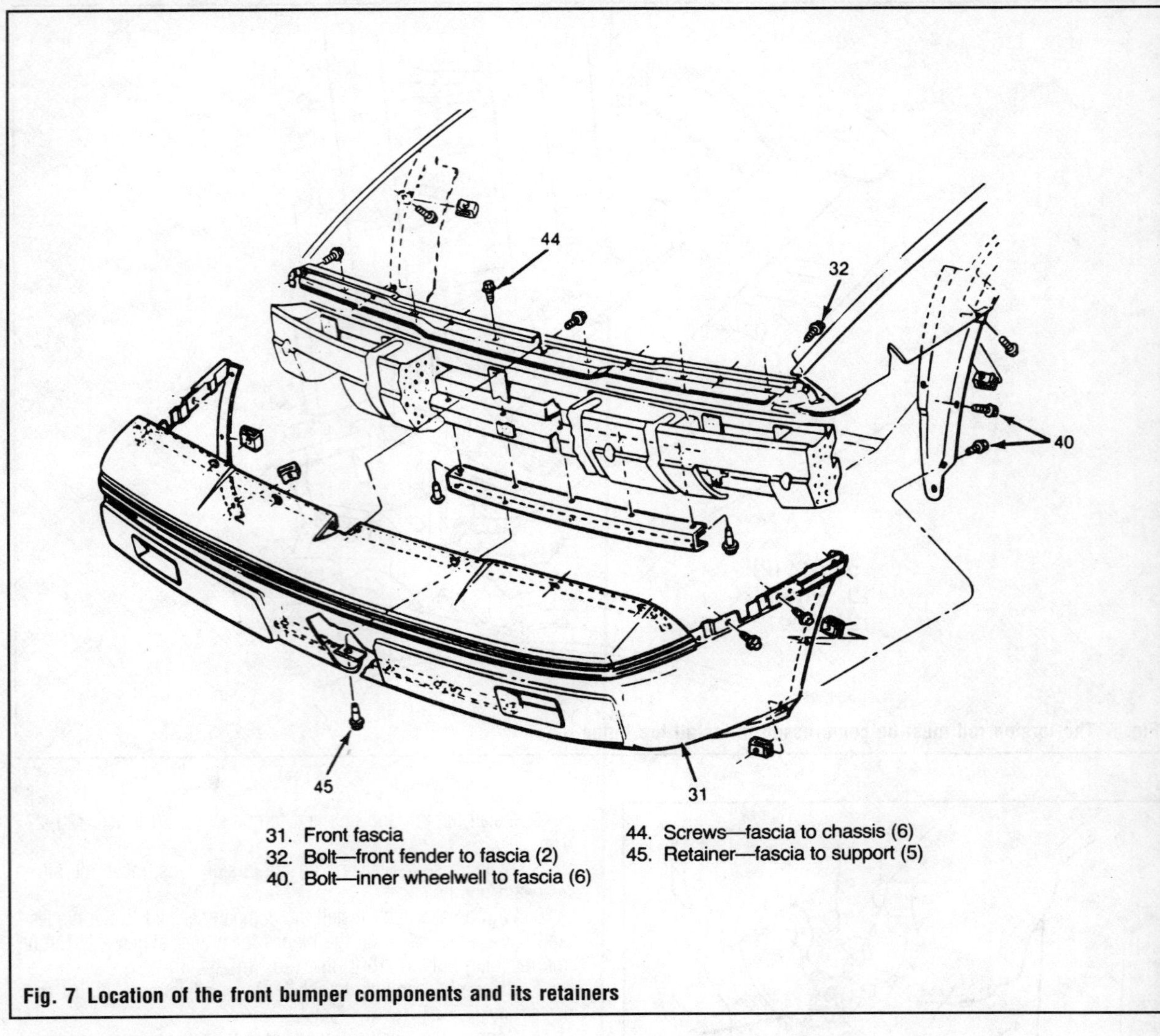

Fig. 7 Location of the front bumper components and its retainers

To install:

6. Position the fascia into place and install attaching bolts for the support, inner wheel well and fascia-to-fender at the marker lamp.
7. Install the 6 phillips® screws at the chassis.
8. Check the fascia-to-hood clearance, should not be no more than 5⁄32 in. (4mm).
9. Install the front wheel assemblies and torque the lug nuts to 100 ft. lbs. (136 Nm). Lower the vehicle.

Rear

➧ **See Figure 8**

1. Raise the rear of the vehicle and support with jackstands.
2. Remove the rear wheel assemblies.
3. Remove the rear tail lamp assemblies.
4. Remove the seven lower and seven upper fascia retainers.
5. Remove the side marker lamp assemblies.
6. Remove the four side fascia retaining bolts (two each side).

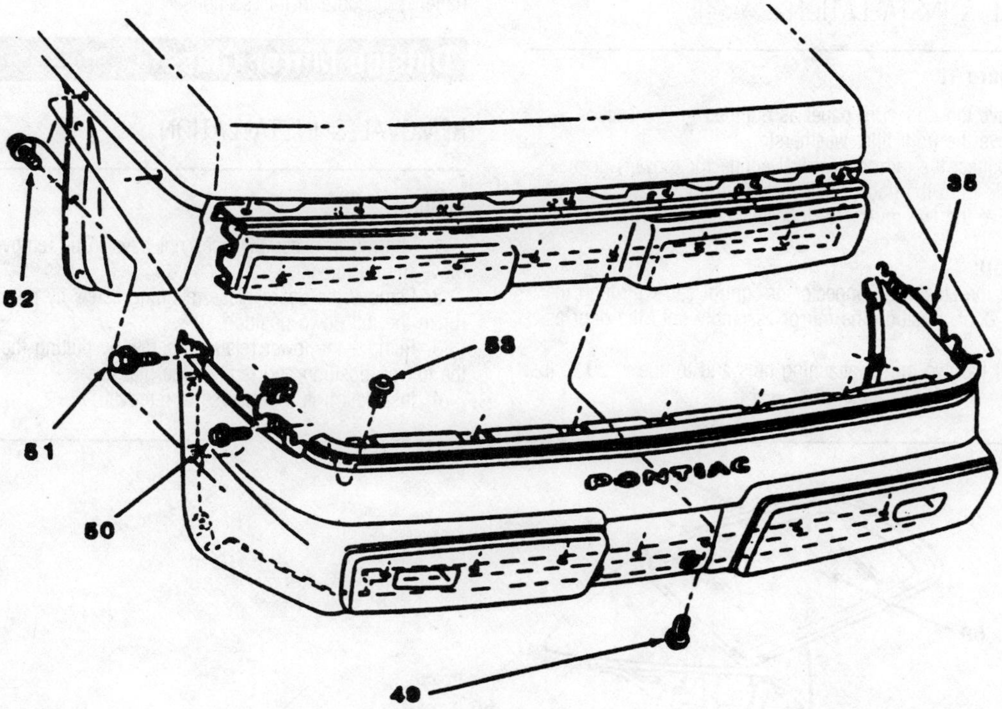

35. Rear fascia
49. Retainers (7)
50. Bolt (2)
51. Bolt (2)
52. Bolt (6)
53. Retainers (7)

Fig. 8 Exploded view of the rear bumper assembly

7. Remove the two wheel well retaining bolts (one each side) and remove the fascia.

To install:

8. Position the fascia onto the bumper reinforcement.
9. Install the seven upper and seven lower retainers.
10. Install the four side fascia retaining bolts. Install the two wheel well retaining bolts.
11. Install the side marker lamp and tail lamp assemblies.
12. Install the front wheel assemblies and torque the lug nuts to 100 ft. lbs. (136 Nm). Lower the vehicle.

Grille

REMOVAL & INSTALLATION

➧ **See Figure 9**

1. Raise the front of the vehicle and support with jackstands.
2. Remove the six grille-to-fascia attaching screws and remove the grille assembly.

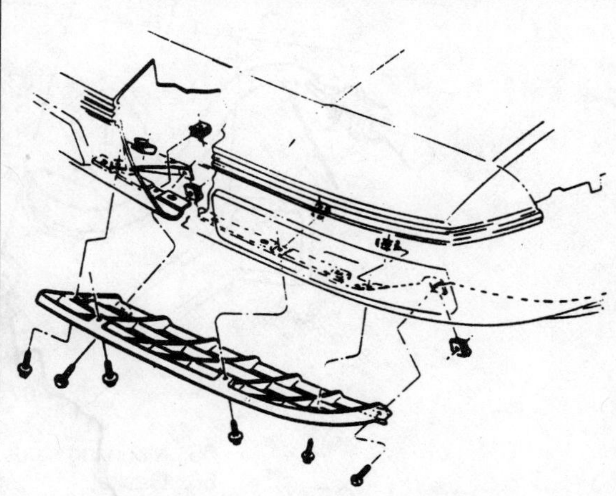

Fig. 9 Unfasten the grille retainers, then remove the grille assembly

Outside Mirrors

REMOVAL & INSTALLATION

➧ **See Figure 10**

1. Remove the door trim panel as outlined in this section.
2. Remove the front filler weatherstrip.
3. Disconnect the mirror electrical connector (power) or the control cable from the door trim panel (remote).
4. Remove the two mirror-to-door attaching nuts and remove the mirror.

To install:

5. Insert the electrical connector or control cable through the hole in the door. Position the mirror assembly onto the door assembly.
6. Install the two mirror attaching nuts and torque to 20 ft. lbs. (27 Nm).
7. Install the control cable to the door trim panel (remote). Check for proper operation before installing the trim panel.
8. Install the door trim panel as outlined in the "Door Trim Panel" procedure in this section.

Outside Mirror Glass

REMOVAL & INSTALLATION

Manual

1. The mirror assembly does not have to be removed to remove the mirror glass.
2. Remove the upper glass retaining screw by putting the mirror in the full down position.
3. Remove the lower retaining screw by putting the mirror in the full up position and remove the glass.
4. Installation is the reverse of removal.

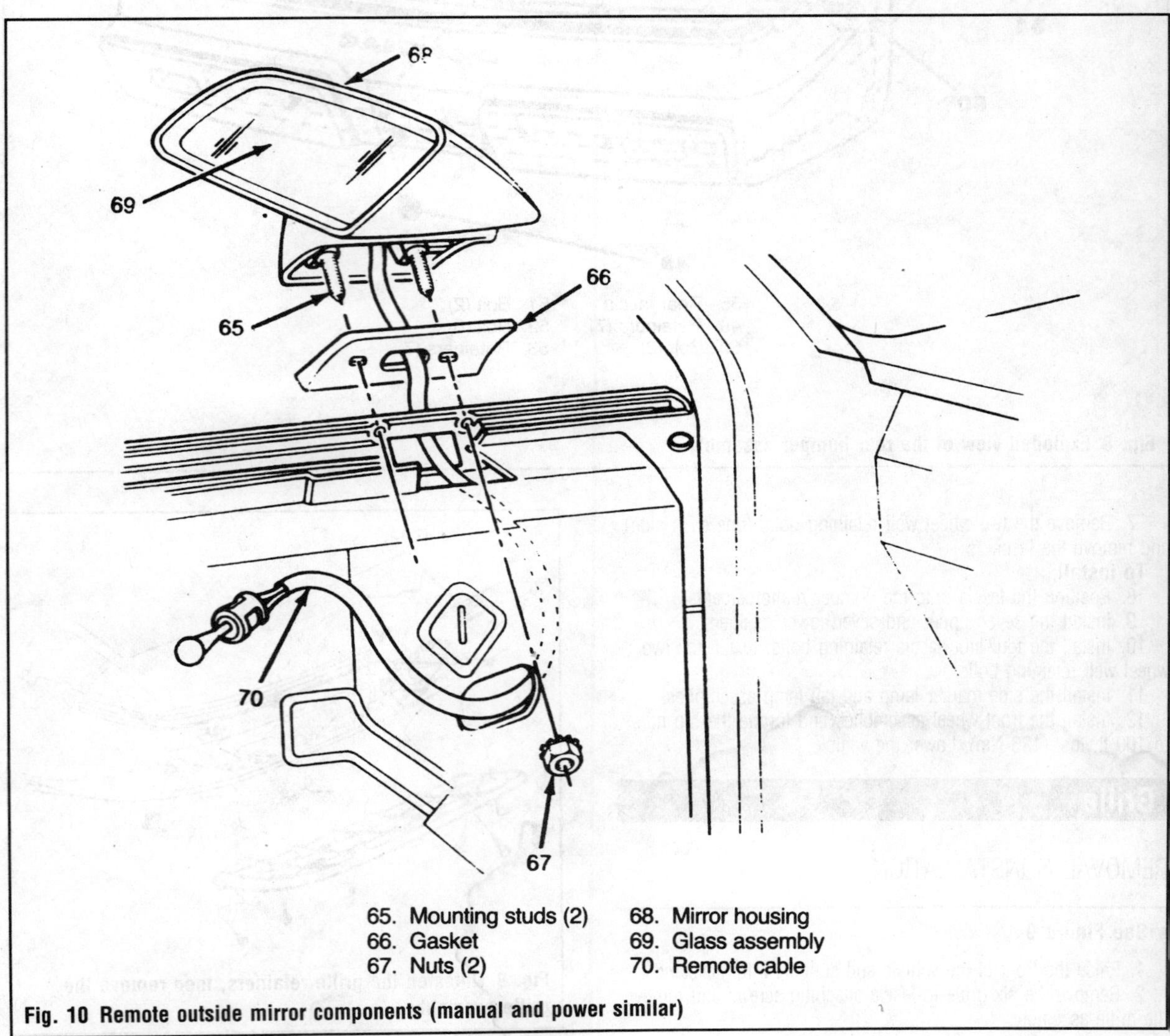

Fig. 10 Remote outside mirror components (manual and power similar)

Power

1. The mirror assembly does not have to be removed to remove the mirror glass.
2. Grasp the inboard and outboard edges on the glass with your fingers. Pull rearward to disengage the glass from the pivot.

To install:

3. Align both worm gears shafts on the glass with the drive gears.
4. Press in on the glass until it snaps into position on the pivot. Check for proper operation.

Antenna

The fixed antenna is mounted on the right front fender and cannot be adjusted up or down. The fixed antenna is made to withstands most car washes without damage. If the mast becomes bent, you can straighten it by hand. The antenna must be kept clean for good performance.

Outer Body Panels

See Figures 11 thru 25

The Fiero is equipped with a completely removable plastic body bolted on a metal sub-assembly. The outer body panels are made of reaction Injection Molded urethane (RIM), glass fiber Reinforced Reaction Molded urethane (RRIM), Sheet Molded Compound (SMC) and Thermoplastic Olefin (TPO). They are rust resistant and can sustain minor impact without damage.

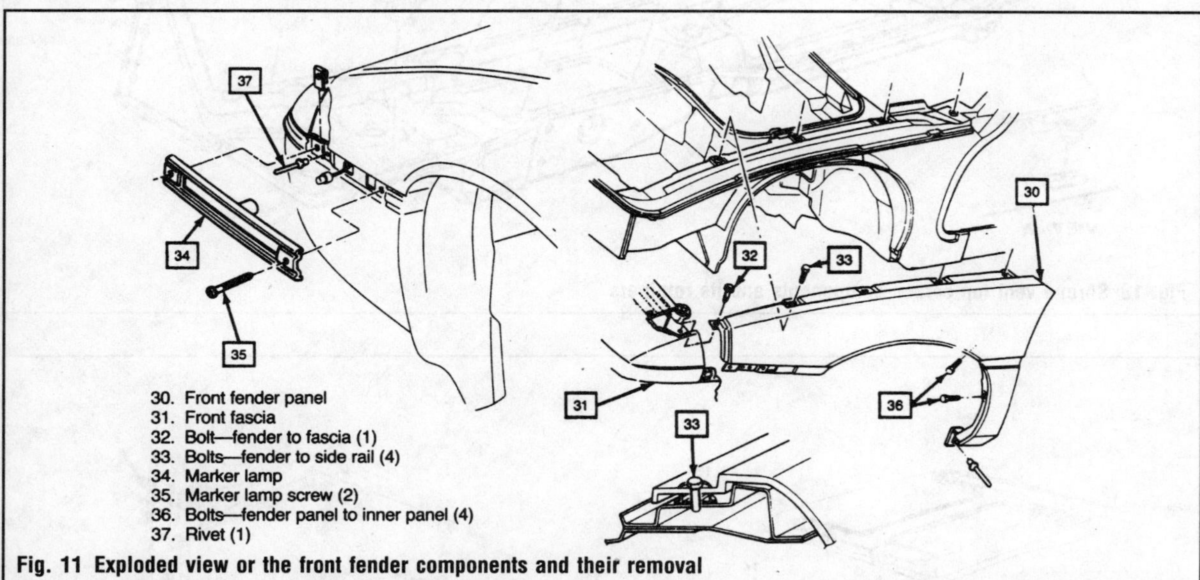

Fig. 11 Exploded view or the front fender components and their removal

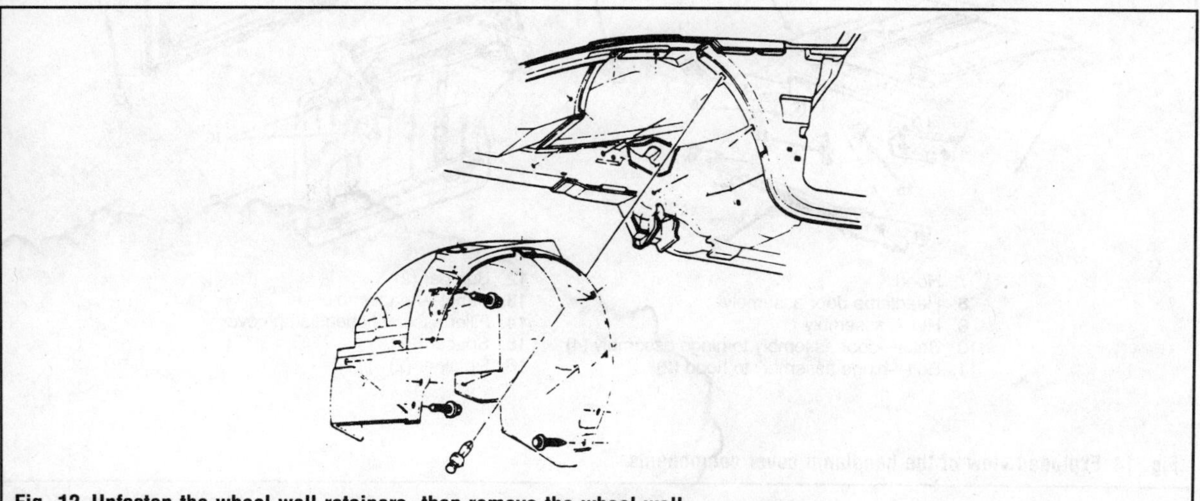

Fig. 12 Unfasten the wheel well retainers, then remove the wheel well

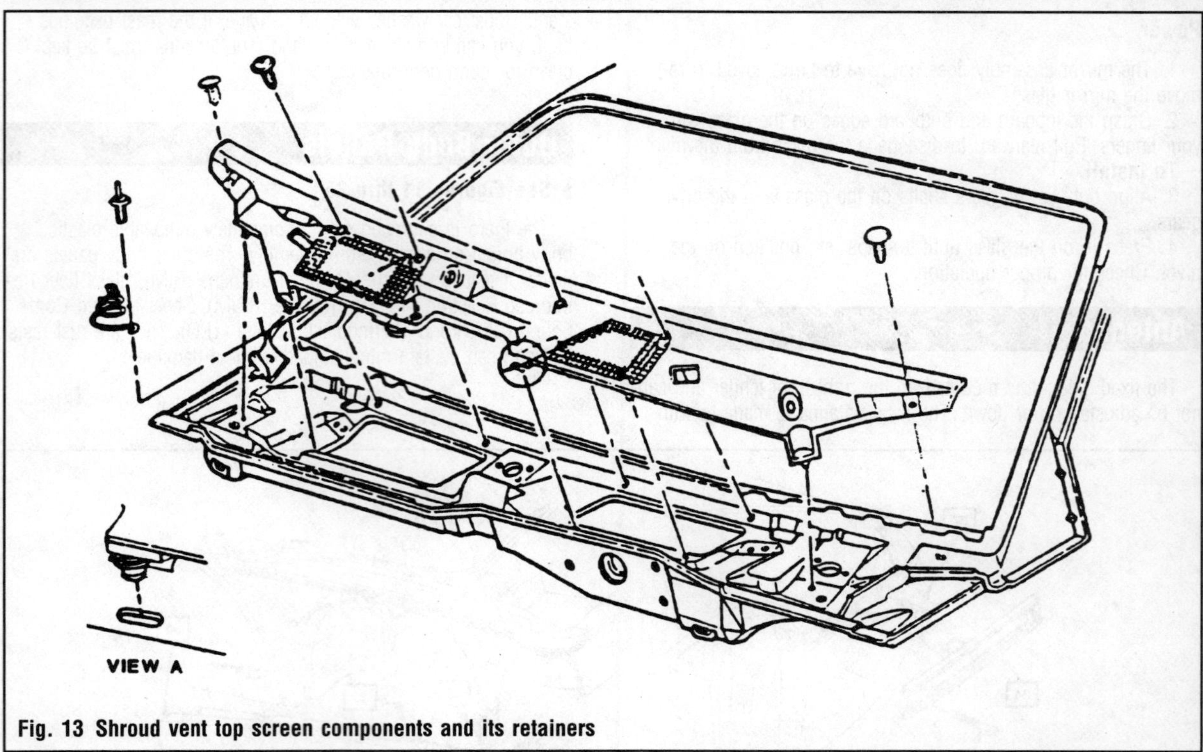

Fig. 13 Shroud vent top screen components and its retainers

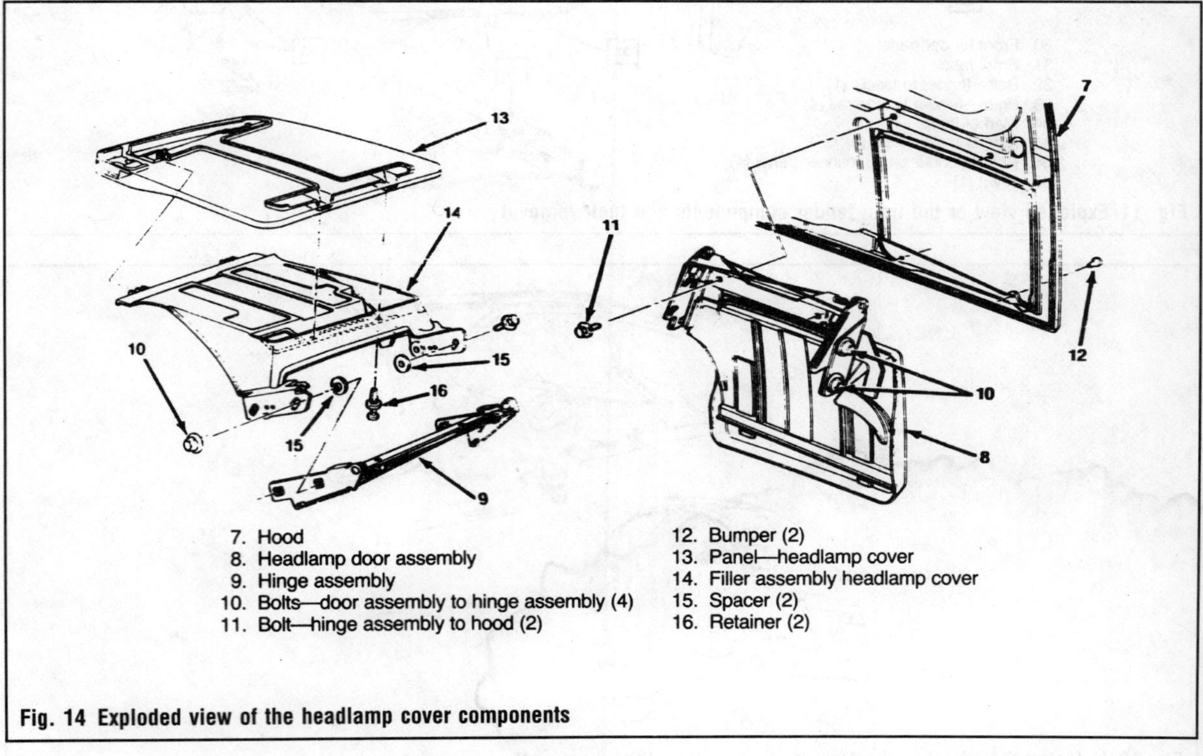

Fig. 14 Exploded view of the headlamp cover components

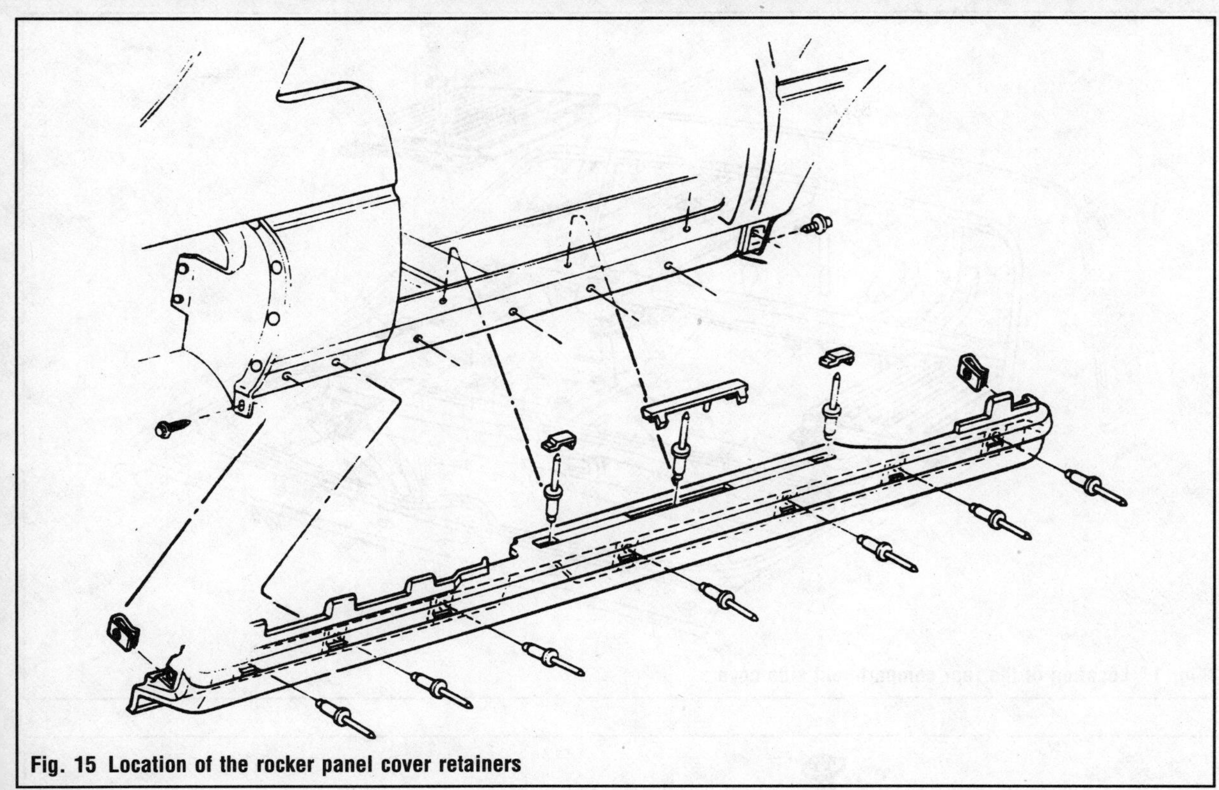

Fig. 15 Location of the rocker panel cover retainers

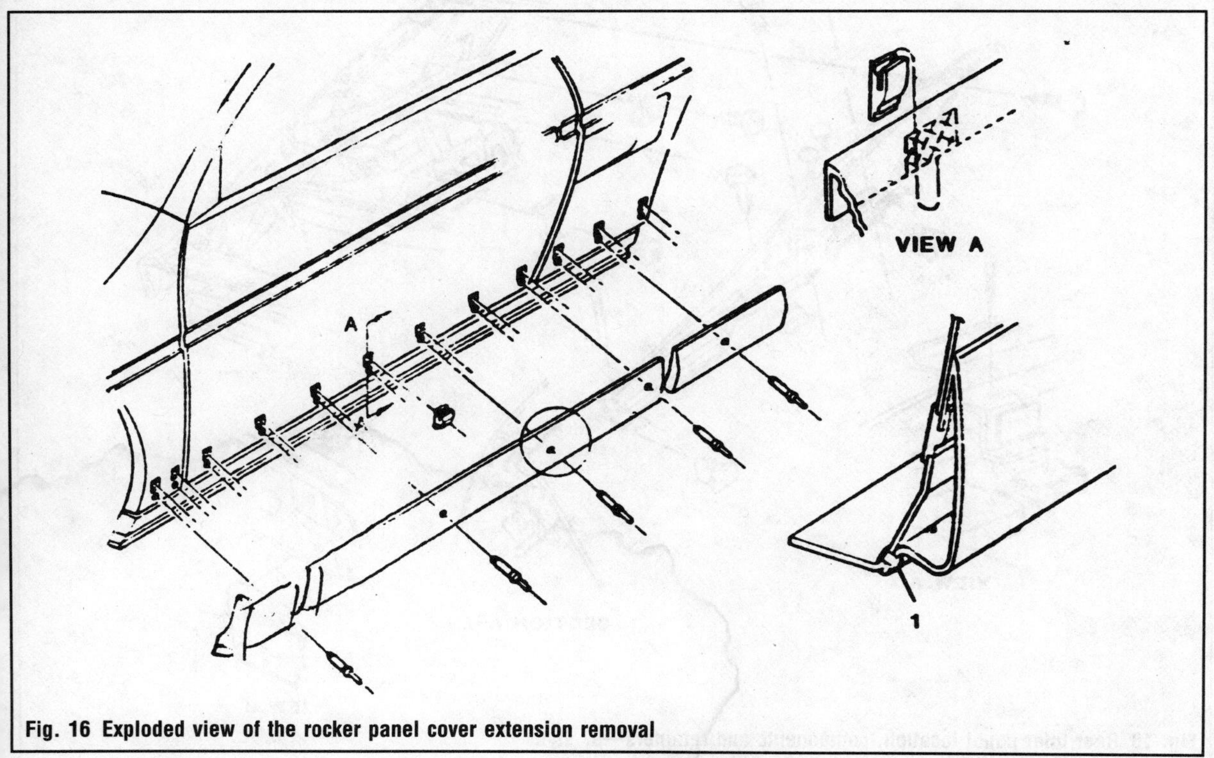

Fig. 16 Exploded view of the rocker panel cover extension removal

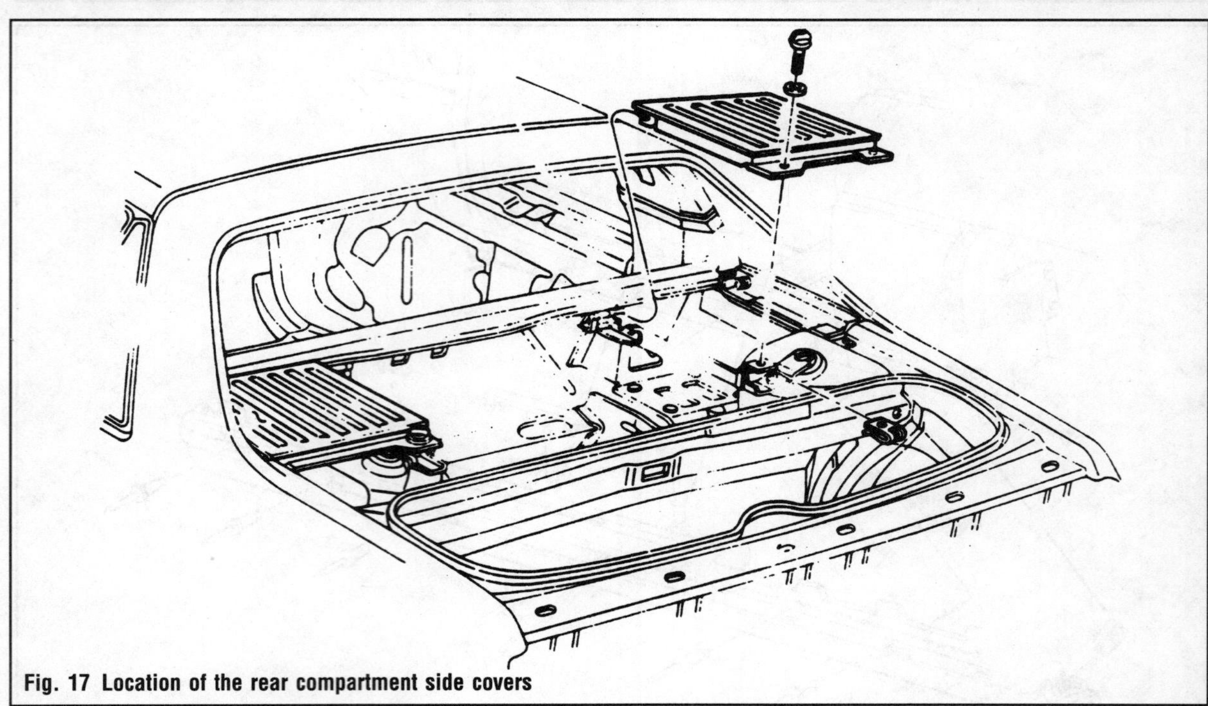
Fig. 17 Location of the rear compartment side covers

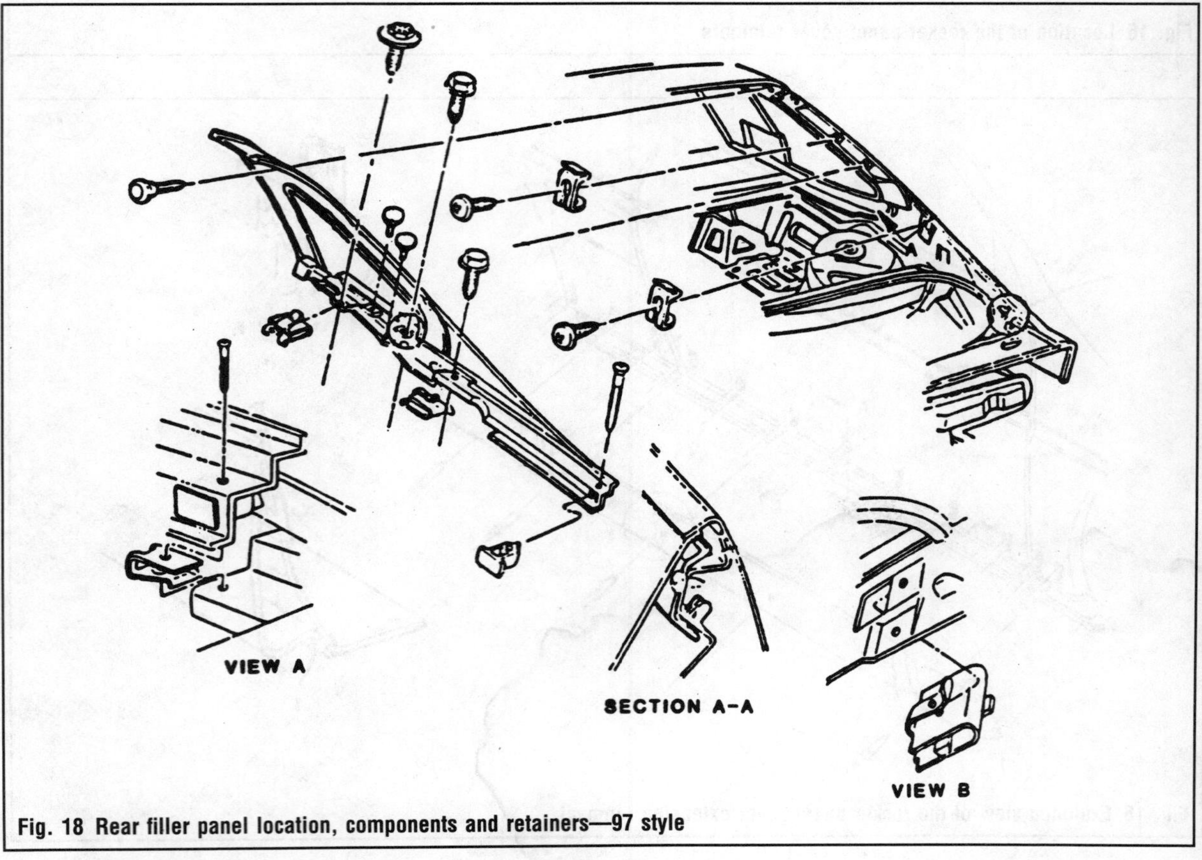

Fig. 18 Rear filler panel location, components and retainers—97 style

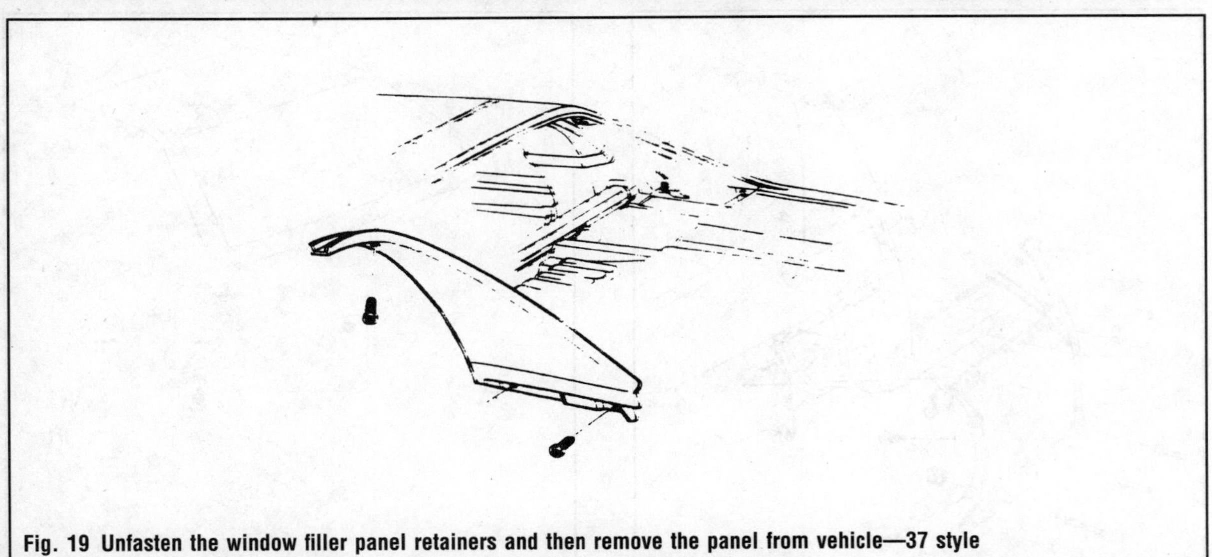

Fig. 19 Unfasten the window filler panel retainers and then remove the panel from vehicle—37 style

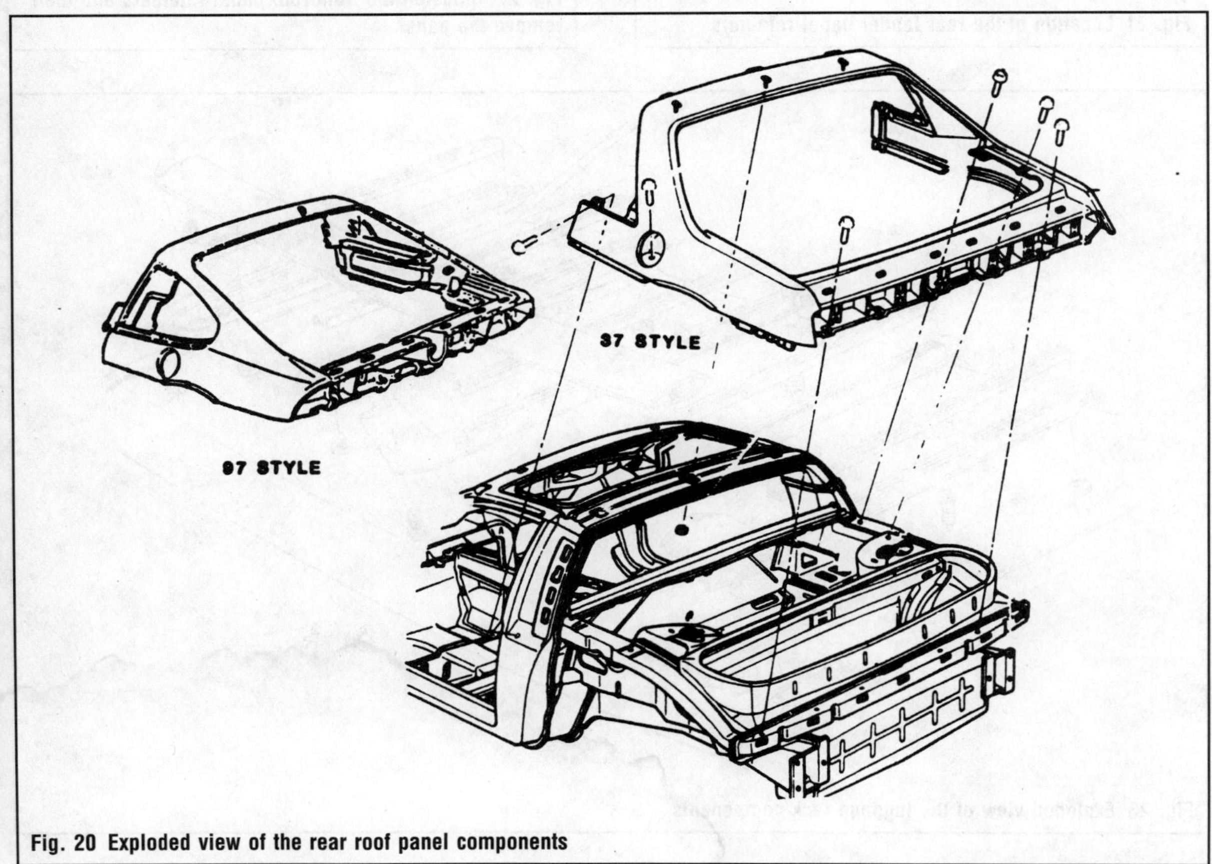

Fig. 20 Exploded view of the rear roof panel components

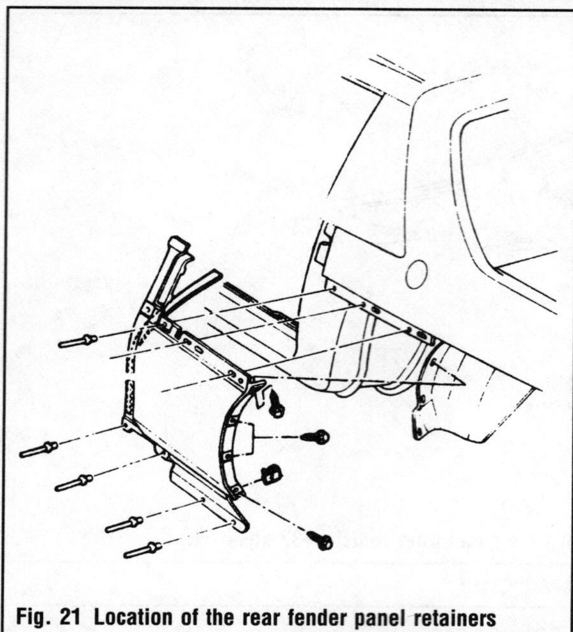
Fig. 21 Location of the rear fender panel retainers

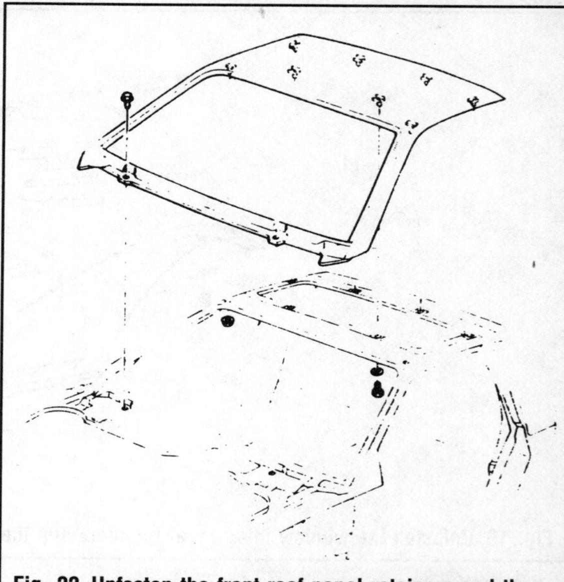
Fig. 22 Unfasten the front roof panel retainers and then remove the panel

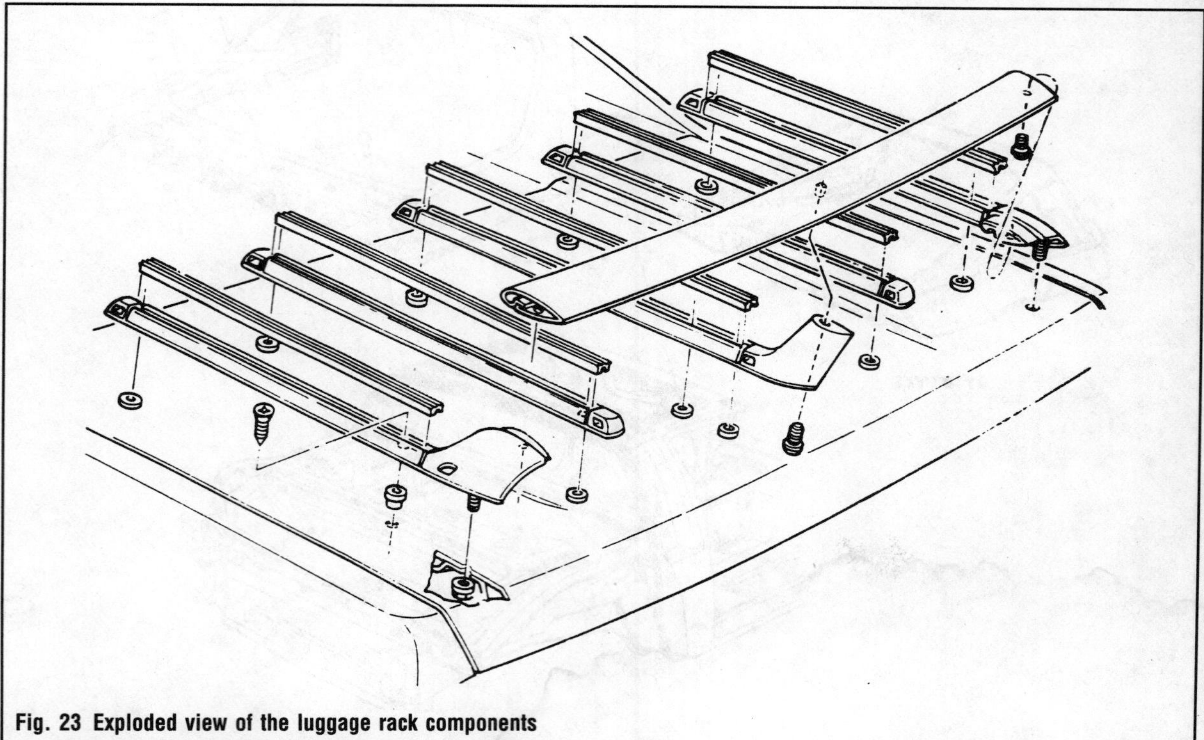
Fig. 23 Exploded view of the luggage rack components

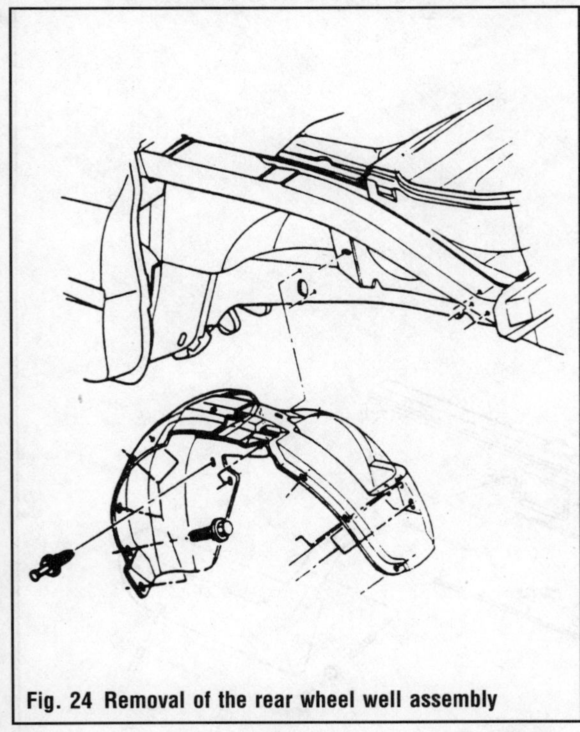

Fig. 24 Removal of the rear wheel well assembly

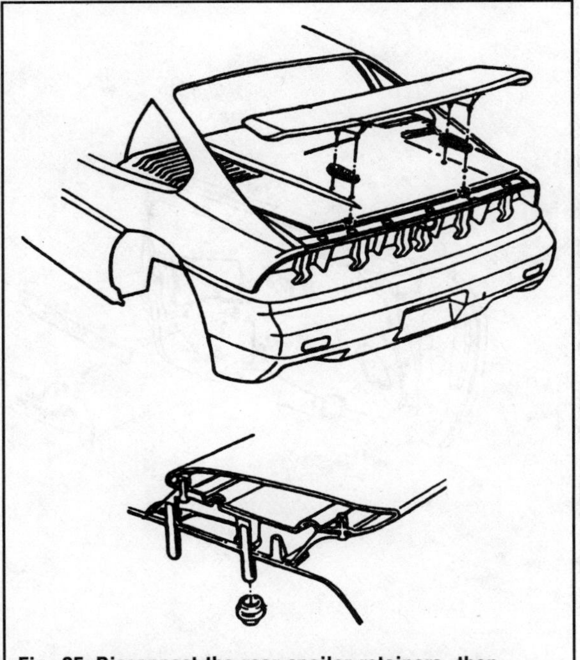

Fig. 25 Disconnect the rear spoiler retainers, then remove the spoiler assembly from the vehicle

INTERIOR

Door Trim Panels

REMOVAL & INSTALLATION

See Figures 26 and 27

1. Remove the armrest by removing the upper armrest plug and three attaching screws.
2. Remove the window regulator handle using a regulator handle removing tool J-9886 or equivalent.
3. Remove the remote door handle bezel.
4. Remove the plastic retainers from the perimeter of the door using a door panel removing tool J-9886 or equivalent. Remove the trim panel by pulling outward to disengage from the retainer at the beltline.

Do not force the trim panel if it will not remove easily. Damage to the panel retainer holes may result, causing an irregular fit after installation.

5. Disconnect the electrical connections and mirror control cable, if so equipped.

To install:

1. Inspect the panel retainers for damage and proper alignment. To correct, insert the flange into the hole and rotate the retainer to engage.
2. Install the remote control mirror cable and wiring harness, if so equipped.
3. Install the trim panel by inserting the top of the panel into

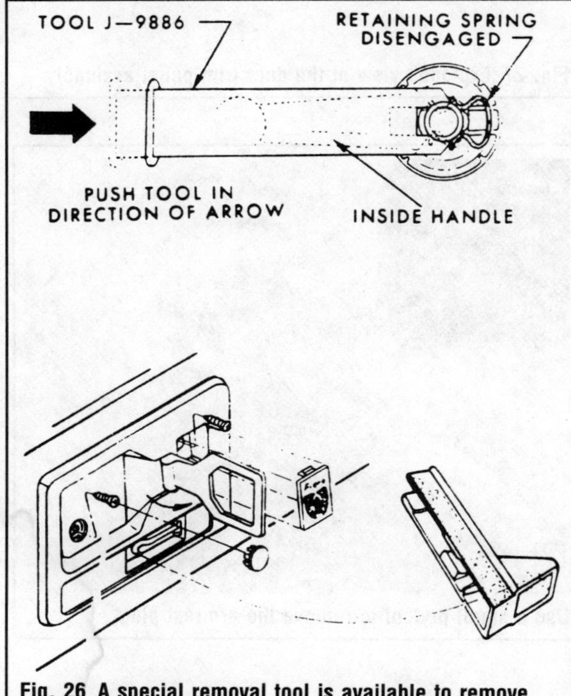

Fig. 26 A special removal tool is available to remove the regulator handle

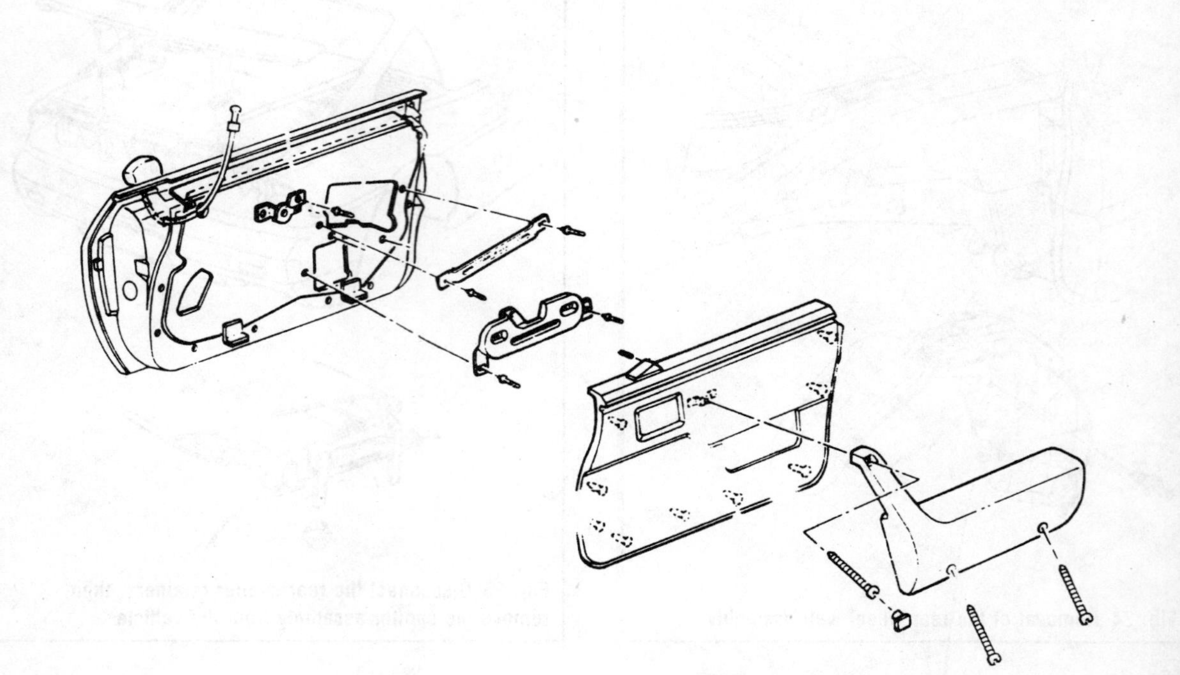

Fig. 27 Exploded view of the door trim panel assembly

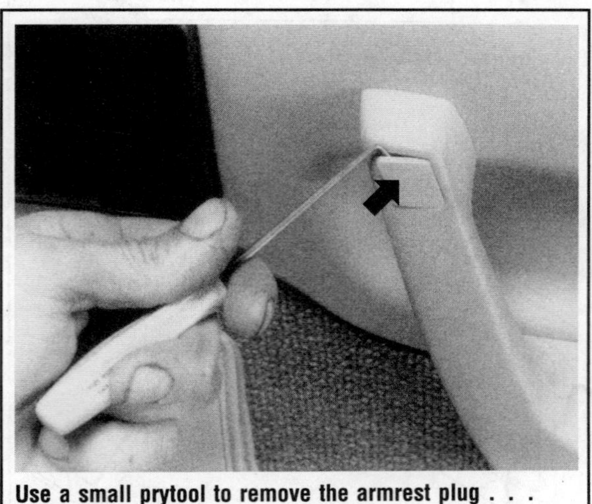

Use a small prytool to remove the armrest plug . . .

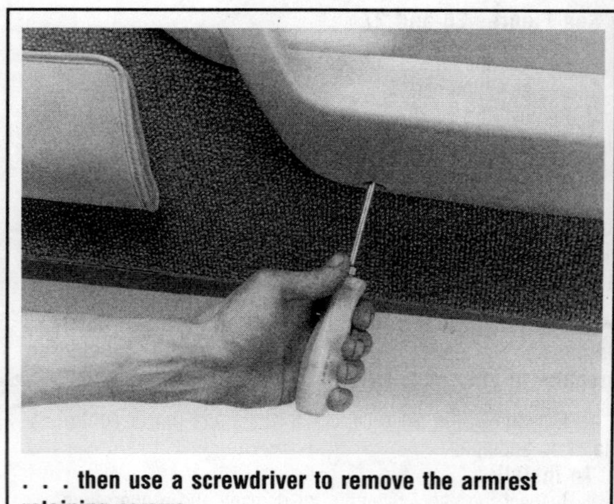

. . . then use a screwdriver to remove the armrest retaining screws

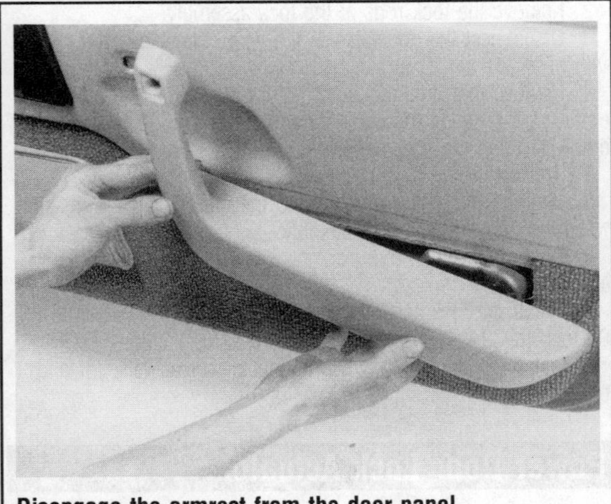
Disengage the armrest from the door panel

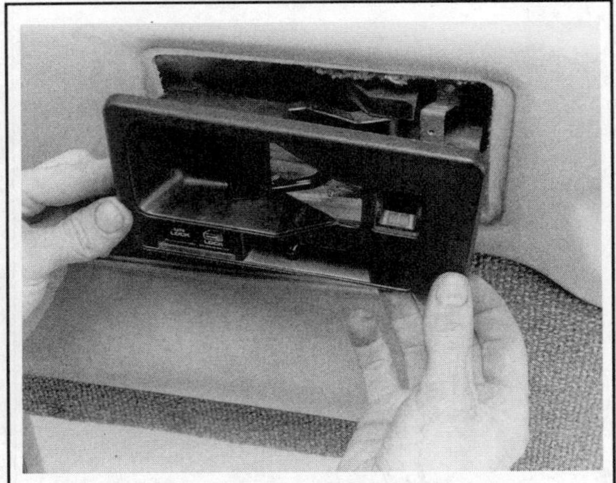
. . . then remove the trim from the door panel

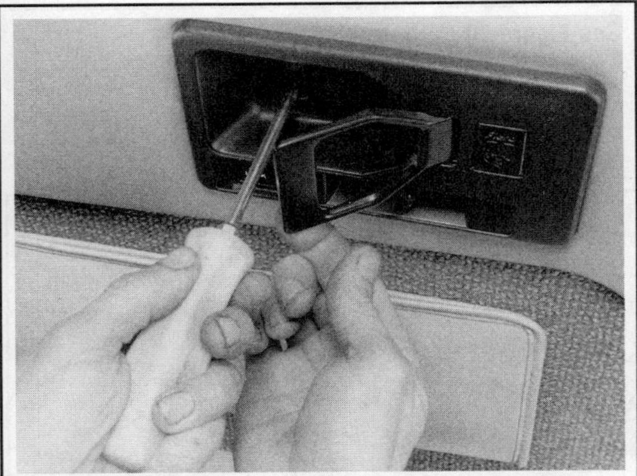
Pull the door handle out to gain access to the bezel retaining screw

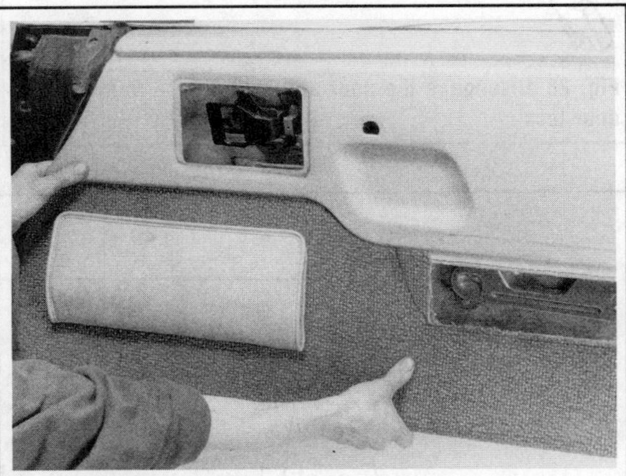
Disengage the retainers from the perimeter of the trim panel and remove the panel from the door

Remove the door handle trim bezel plug and unfasten the screw . . .

the retainer, insert the remote door handle through the panel, align the retainer with the holes in the door and tap into place with the palm of your hand or a clean rubber mallet. DO NOT FORCE.

4. Install the door handle bezel, lock knob, window regulator handle and armrest.

Door Lock Assembly

REMOVAL & INSTALLATION

See Figures 28 and 29

➡Do not attempt to correct any lock discrepancies. Make corrections through the replacement of the lock assembly.

1. Remove the door trim panel and water deflector as previously outlined in this chapter.

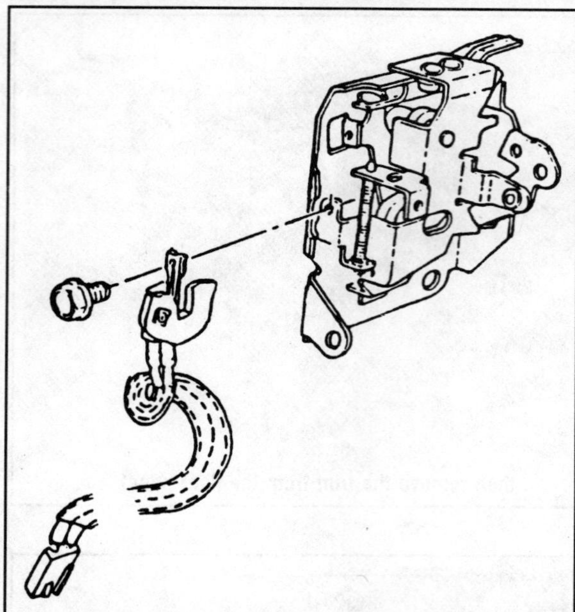

Fig. 28 Disengage the door ajar switch wire from the door lock

2. Remove the lock rods at the lock assembly.

3. Disconnect the door ajar switch wire connector from the main harness.

4. Remove the three lock assembly screws and lower the assembly to disengage the outside handle lock bar. Remove the assembly through the access hole in the inner door panel.

To install:

5. Position the lock assembly into the mounting area. Install the spring clip on the lock assembly.

6. Connect the lock rods to the respective clips on the assembly.

7. Install the lock assembly retaining screws and torque to 80–100 inch lb. (9–11 Nm). Inspect for proper operation.

8. Install the door ajar switch connector, water deflector and door trim panel.

Power Door Lock Actuator

REMOVAL & INSTALLATION

➧ See Figure 30

1. Remove the door trim panel and water deflector as previously outlined in this chapter.

2. Disconnect the actuator electrical connectors.

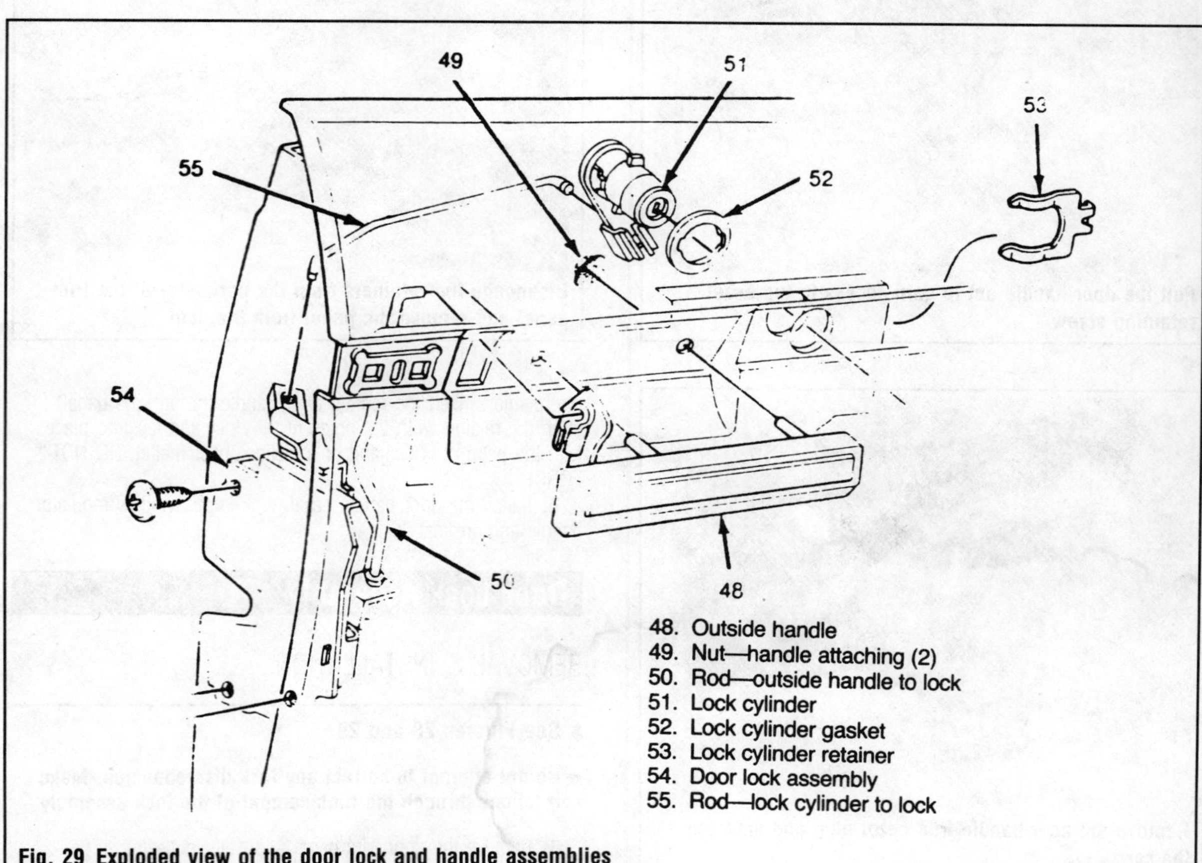

Fig. 29 Exploded view of the door lock and handle assemblies

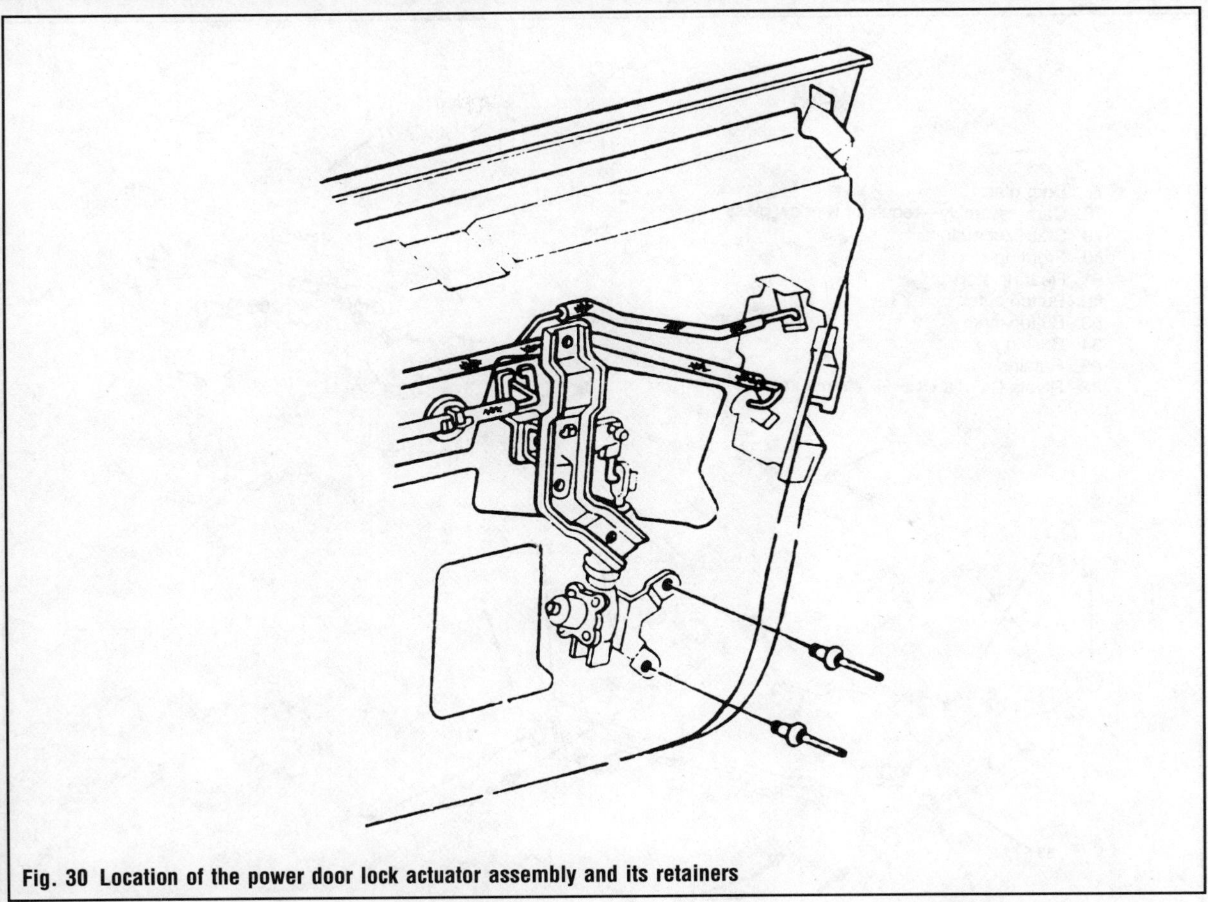

Fig. 30 Location of the power door lock actuator assembly and its retainers

3. Drill out the two actuator rivets with a ¼ inch drill bit.
4. Remove the actuator rod from the bell crank and remove the actuator.

To install:

5. Position the actuator into the door and locate the rivet holes.
6. Install the two attaching rivets (¼ × ½ in.) or two nut and bolt sets. If nut and bolts are used, coat the threads with locking compound before installation.
7. Connect the actuator lock rod and electrical connector. Inspect for proper operation.
8. Install the water deflector and trim panel.

Door Glass

REMOVAL & INSTALLATION

➧ **See Figure 31**

1. Remove the door trim panel and water deflector as previously outlined in this chapter.
2. Remove the front and rear filler sealing strips.
3. Drill out the rivets at the cam assembly, front stop and rear stop with a ¼ inch drill bit.
4. Remove the front and rear glass stops.
5. Loosen and move back the door glass stabilizers.
6. Remove all bushings from the glass before removing the glass. Carefully remove the glass.

To install:

7. Insert all the bushings in the glass before installing the glass in the door.
8. Install the glass to the cam assembly.
9. Install the front and rear stops.
10. Install the rivets (¼ dia. × ½ in.) for the front stop, rear stop and cam assembly. Nut and bolt sets can be used, but have to be coated with thread locking compound before installation.
11. Check the window for proper operation. Adjust as necessary.
12. Install the front and rear filler sealing strip, water deflector and door trim panel.

ADJUSTMENT

Window Rotated

a. The water deflector and door trim panel must be removed to adjust the door window.
b. Loosen the up-stop bolts.

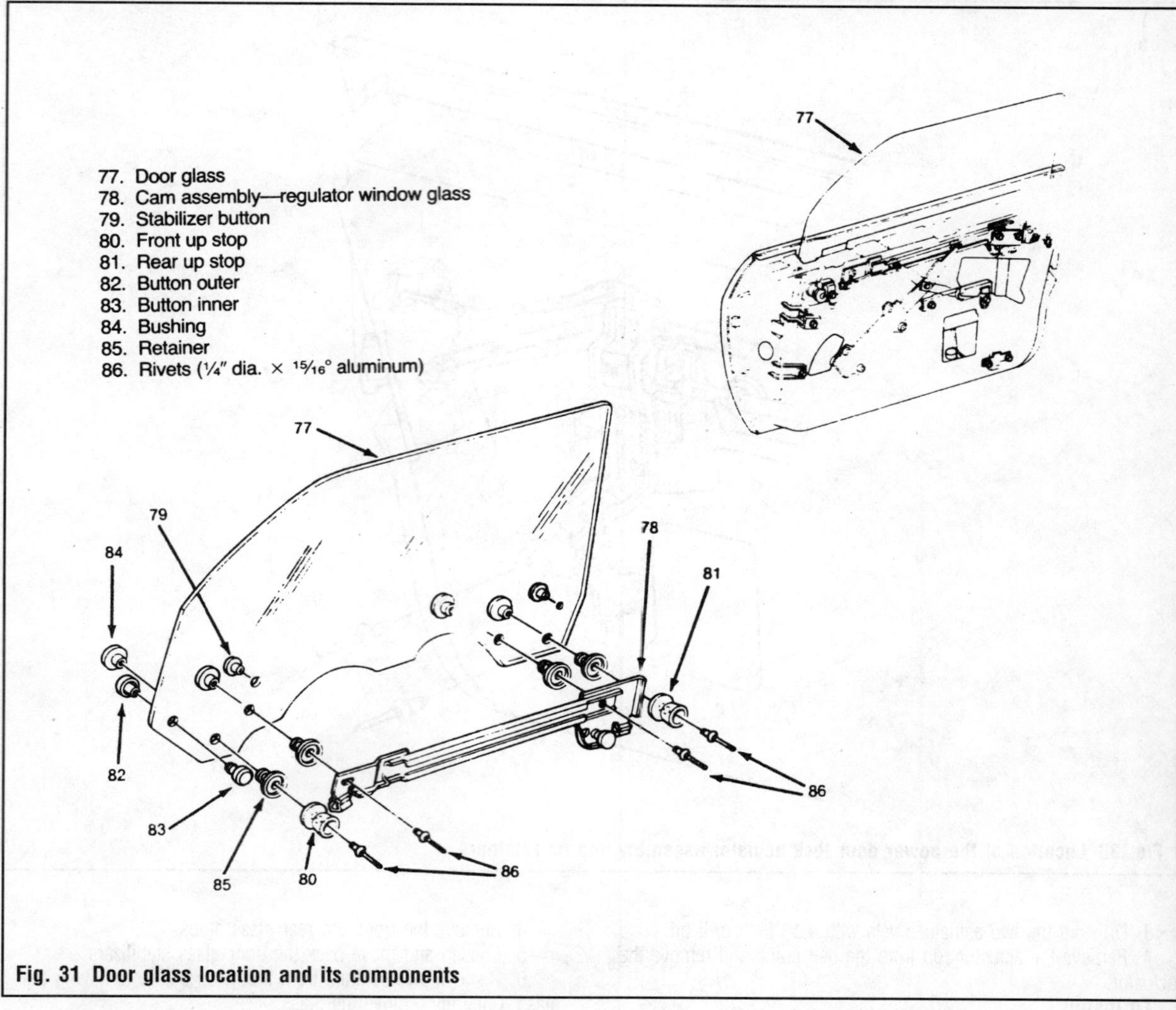

Fig. 31 Door glass location and its components

c. Adjust the inner panel cam bolts

d. Adjust the window so that the upper edge of the glass is parallel with the roof rail weatherstrip.

e. Tighten attaching bolts.

Window Upper Edge Inboard or Outboard

a. Loosen the front retainer bolt.

b. Loosen the rear cam guide to support bolts.

c. Loosen the rear up-stop.

d. Loosen the front and rear glass stabilizer screws.

e. Adjust the vertical guide and rear up-stop support in or out as required and tighten the attaching screws.

Window Too Far Foreward and Rearward

a. Loosen the front run channel bolts.

b. Loosen the rear cam guide assembly.

c. Align the glass in the correct up position.

d. Tighten the upper bolt on the front run channel.

e. Tighten the upper bolts on the rear cam guide.

f. Lower the glass.

g. Tighten the lower bolt on the front run channel.

h. Tighten the lower bolts on the rear cam guide.

Window Too High or Low in the Up Position

Adjust the front and rear up-stop bolts and retighten the bolts.

Window Binds or Has Inboard/Outboard Movement

a. Loosen the glass stabilizers.

b. Place the glass in half-up position.

c. Push the stabilizers against the glass with only enough pressure to eliminate inboard outboard movement.

d. Tighten the glass stabilizers.

e. If the cam channels and rollers lack lubrication, lubricate with part No. 1052196 or Lubriplate Auto-Lube A or another equivalent.

Window Regulator

REMOVAL & INSTALLATION

➧ **See Figure 32**

1. Disconnect the negative (−) battery cable.
2. Put the window in the full-up position and block in place.
3. Remove the door trim panel and water deflector.
4. Remove the window regulator cam assembly from the window.
5. Remove the cam assembly through the inner door panel.
6. Remove the bell crank and bracket assembly.
7. Drill out the rivets from the regulator with a 1/4 inch drill bit. Disconnect wiring harness (if electric).
8. Remove the regulator through the rear access hole.

To install:

9. Position the regulator assembly into the rear access hole and connect wiring harness (if electric).
10. Install the regulator-to-door rivets (1/4 dia. × 1/2 in.). Nuts and bolts can be used, but thread locking compound will have to be used before installation.
11. Install the cam assembly through the front door inner panel.
12. Install the bell crank and bracket assembly.
13. Install the window regulator cam assembly.
14. Remove the block of wood and check for proper operation. Adjust if necessary.
15. Install the water deflector and trim panel as outlined in the "Door Trim Panel" procedure in this section.

Inside Rear View Mirror

REPLACEMENT

➧ **See Figure 33**

The rearview mirror is attached to a support which is secured to the windshield glass. A service replacement windshield glass has the support bonded to the glass assembly. To install a detached mirror support or install a new part, use the following procedures to complete the service.

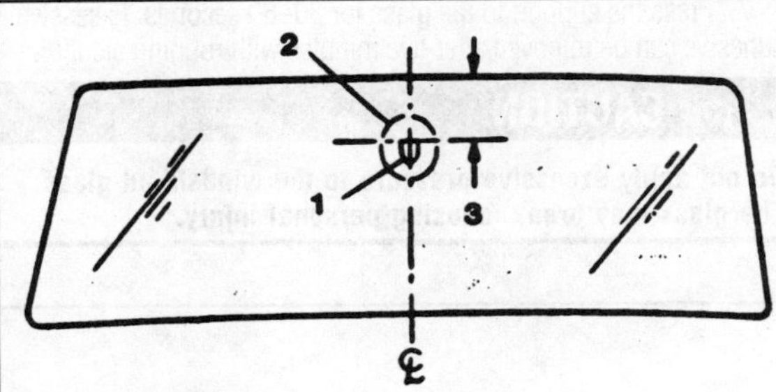

1. Mirror support
2. Circle on outside glass surface indicates area to be cleaned
3. 114 mm (4–1/2") from top of windshield to top of support

Fig. 33 Properly position the mirror mount at the point shown

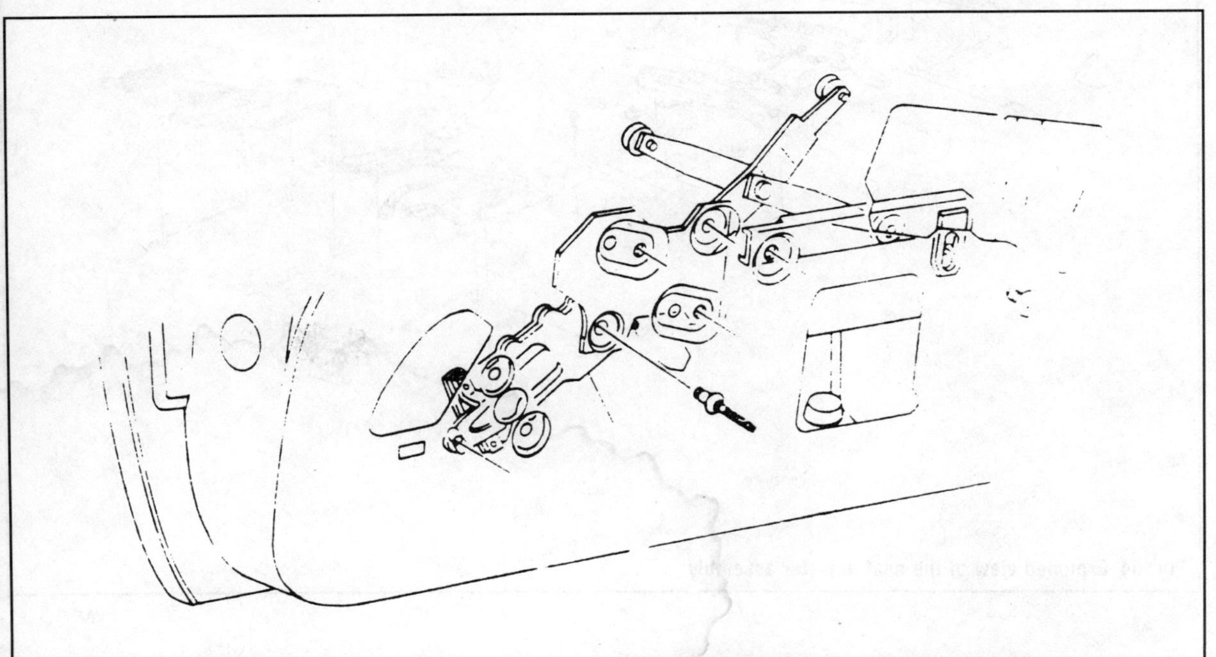

Fig. 32 The door trim panel and water deflector must be removed to gain access to the window regulator

1. Locate the support position at the center of the glass 4½ in. from the top of the glass to the top of the support.
2. Circle the location on the outside of the glass with a wax pencil or crayon. Draw a large circle around the support circle.
3. Clean the area within the circle with household cleaner and dry with a clean towel. Repeat the procedures using rubbing alcohol.
4. Sand the bonding surface of the support with fine grit (320–360) emery cloth or sandpaper. If the original support is being used, remove the old adhesive with rubbing alcohol and a clean towel.
5. Apply the adhesive as outlined in the kit instructions.
6. Position the support to the marked location with the rounded end up.
7. Press the support to the glass for 30–60 seconds. Excessive adhesive can be removed after five minutes with rubbing alcohol.

CAUTION

Do not apply excessive pressure to the windshield glass. The glass may break, causing personal injury.

Seats

REMOVAL & INSTALLATION

See Figure 34

1. The seat assemblies are mounted to the floor pan by nuts installed onto studs welded into the floor pan.
2. Move the seat the most forward position.
3. Remove the adjuster-to-floor pan attaching nuts.
4. Move the seat the most rearward position.
5. Remove the adjuster-to-floor pan attaching nuts and remove the seat assembly.

To install:

6. Position the seat assembly onto the floor pan studs.
7. Move the seat to the rearward position and install the two forward nuts. Torque the nuts to 15–21 ft. lbs. (20–28 Nm). Move the seat to the forward position and torque the rearward nuts to 15–21 ft. lbs. (20–28 Nm).

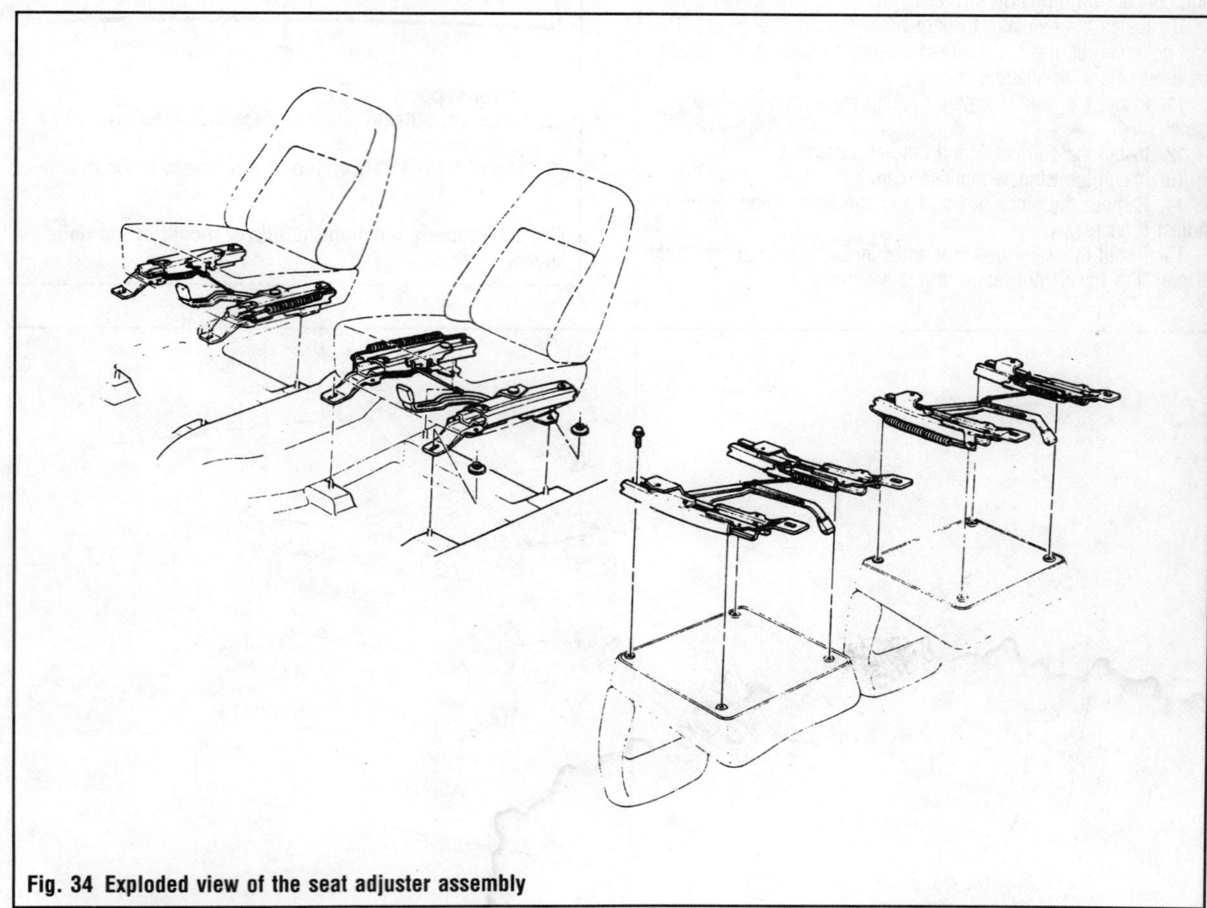

Fig. 34 Exploded view of the seat adjuster assembly

Seat Adjuster Assembly

REMOVAL & INSTALLATION

To remove the seat adjuster assembly from the seat, remove the seat assembly as previously outlined and remove the two bolts per adjuster. To install, position the adjuster and bolts onto seat and torque the bolts to 15–21 ft. lbs. (20–28 Nm).

Pneumatic Seat Bladder Bag

REMOVAL & INSTALLATION

See Figure 35

1. Remove the seat assembly from the vehicle as previously outlined.
2. Remove the recliner cover attaching screws and slide the cover downward and rearward of the seat.
3. Unzip the underside of the seatback trim cover and remove the hog rings from the bottom corners of the seatback cover. The hog rings can be removed using side cutters.
4. Remove the hog rings from the trim curtain on the underside of the seat cushion.
5. Remove the air tube harness connector out from the under inboard edge of the foam underside of cushion.
6. Raise the corner of the seatback trim over the upper portion of the recliner. Remove the recline mechanism to expose the two hinge recliner bolts. Remove the two bolts. Remove the inner hinge arm attaching bolt and remove the seatback. Work the seatback bladder bag tubes out from the under cushion.
7. Remove the hog rings from the side rods and support wires securing the trim cover to seatback frame. Remove the seatback cover.
8. Remove the hog rings securing the upper and lower edges of the bladder bag to the seatback. Carefully peel the cemented area of the bladder bag away from the foam cushion. Do not tear the foam. Remove the bladder bag.

To install:

During installation, apply a nonstaining spray adhesive such as 3M® Super Trim Adhesive 08090 or equivalent to the bladder bag area marked on the foam where the bladder bag is located. Use new hog rings to install the seat trim covers. Be careful not to damage the trim cover while installing.

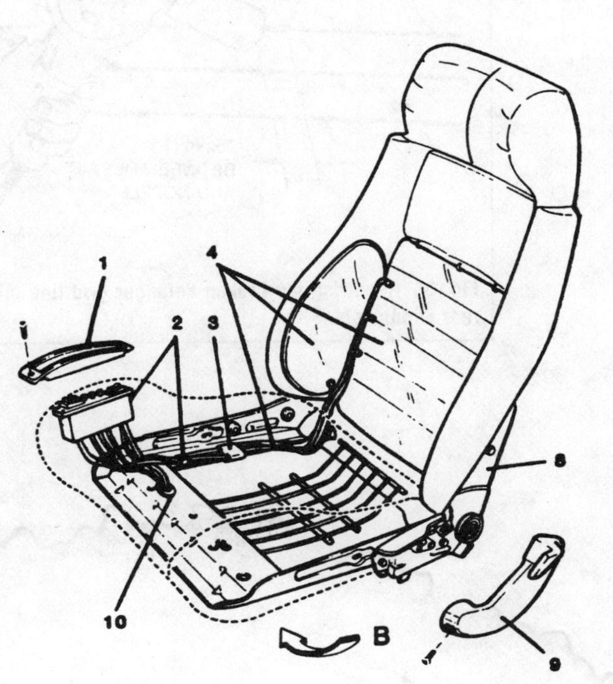

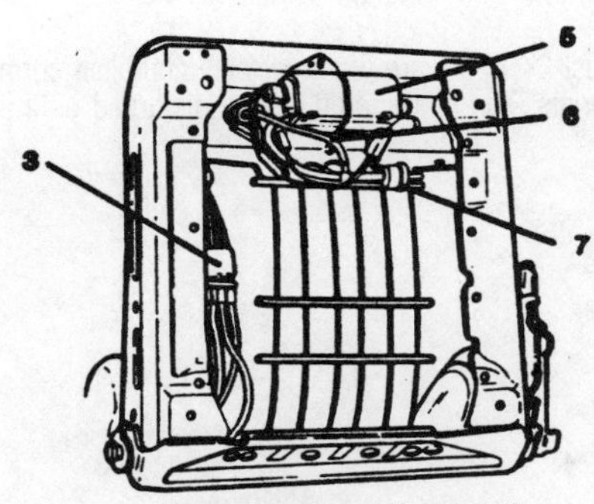

Fig. 35 View of the pneumatic seat assembly and its related components

Rear Window Defogger

GRID LINE REPAIR

➧ **See Figure 36**

1. Remove the battery feed to the rear defogger.
2. Mark the broken grid lines on the outside of the glass with a grease pencil or crayon.
3. Clean the grid line area to be fixed by buffing with fine steel wool and wiping clean using a rubbing alcohol dampened cloth. Buff and clean about 1/4 in. (6mm) beyond each side of the break in the guide line.
4. Install the grid line repair decal or two strips of tape positioned above and below the repair area. The repair decal must be used to control the width of the repair area.
5. Remove the clamp (separator) from the grid repair container. Mix the hardener and silver plastic thoroughly. If the hardener has crystallized, immerse the packet in hot water until liquified.
6. Apply the repair material to the area using a small wood stick or spatula. Carefully remove the decal or tape.

➡The repair material must be cured with heat. Protect the interior trim at the point of repair from heat.

7. Using a heat gun or hair dryer, apply heat to the repair area for one to two minutes. Hold the heat gun nozzle 1 in. (25mm) from the surface. The minimum temperature of 300°F (149°C) is required.
8. At least 24 hours are required for a complete curing of the repair materials. The unit should not be disturbed until after that time.

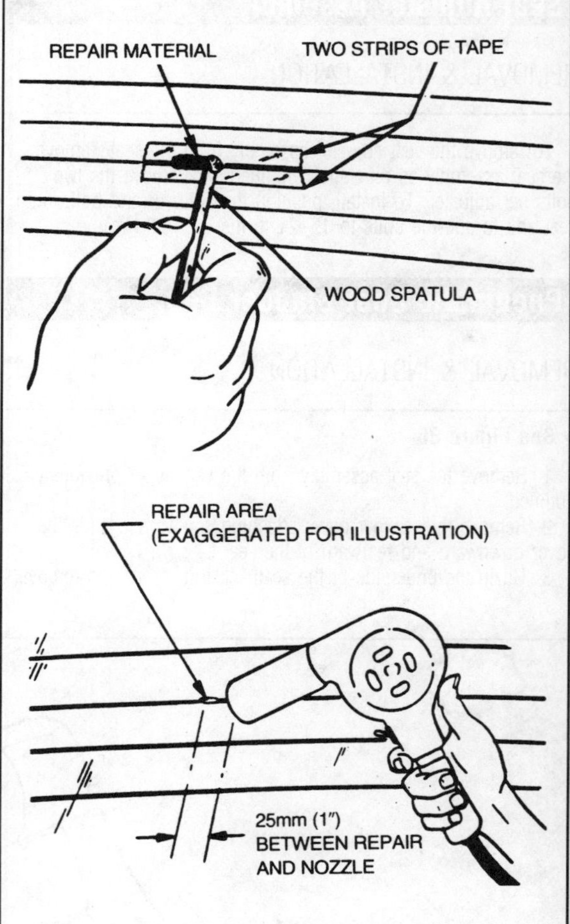

Fig. 36 Repairing the broken defogger grid line on the rear windshield

How to Remove Stains from Fabric Interior

For rest results, spots and stains should be removed as soon as possible. Never use gasoline, lacquer thinner, acetone, nail polish remover or bleach. Use a 3′ x 3″ piece of cheesecloth. Squeeze most of the liquid from the fabric and wipe the stained fabric from the outside of the stain toward the center with a lifting motion. Turn the cheesecloth as soon as one side becomes soiled. When using water to remove a stain, be sure to wash the entire section after the spot has been removed to avoid water stains. Encrusted spots can be broken up with a dull knife and vacuumed before removing the stain.

Type of Stain	How to Remove It
Surface spots	Brush the spots out with a small hand brush or use a commercial preparation such as K2R to lift the stain.
Mildew	Clean around the mildew with warm suds. Rinse in cold water and soak the mildew area in a solution of 1 part table salt and 2 parts water. Wash with upholstery cleaner.
Water stains	Water stains in fabric materials can be removed with a solution made from 1 cup of table salt dissolved in 1 quart of water. Vigorously scrub the solution into the stain and rinse with clear water. Water stains in nylon or other synthetic fabrics should be removed with a commercial type spot remover.
Chewing gum, tar, crayons, shoe polish (greasy stains)	Do not use a cleaner that will soften gum or tar. Harden the deposit with an ice cube and scrape away as much as possible with a dull knife. Moisten the remainder with cleaning fluid and scrub clean.
Ice cream, candy	Most candy has a sugar base and can be removed with a cloth wrung out in warm water. Oily candy, after cleaning with warm water, should be cleaned with upholstery cleaner. Rinse with warm water and clean the remainder with cleaning fluid.
Wine, alcohol, egg, milk, soft drink (non-greasy stains)	Do not use soap. Scrub the stain with a cloth wrung out in warm water. Remove the remainder with cleaning fluid.
Grease, oil, lipstick, butter and related stains	Use a spot remover to avoid leaving a ring. Work from the outisde of the stain to the center and dry with a clean cloth when the spot is gone.
Headliners (cloth)	Mix a solution of warm water and foam upholstery cleaner to give thick suds. Use only foam—liquid may streak or spot. Clean the entire headliner in one operation using a circular motion with a natural sponge.
Headliner (vinyl)	Use a vinyl cleaner with a sponge and wipe clean with a dry cloth.
Seats and door panels	Mix 1 pint upholstery cleaner in 1 gallon of water. Do not soak the fabric around the buttons.
Leather or vinyl fabric	Use a multi-purpose cleaner full strength and a stiff brush. Let stand 2 minutes and scrub thoroughly. Wipe with a clean, soft rag.
Nylon or synthetic fabrics	For normal stains, use the same procedures you would for washing cloth upholstery. If the fabric is extremely dirty, use a multi-purpose cleaner full strength with a stiff scrub brush. Scrub thoroughly in all directions and wipe with a cotton towel or soft rag.

GLOSSARY

AIR/FUEL RATIO: The ratio of air-to-gasoline by weight in the fuel mixture drawn into the engine.

AIR INJECTION: One method of reducing harmful exhaust emissions by injecting air into each of the exhaust ports of an engine. The fresh air entering the hot exhaust manifold causes any remaining fuel to be burned before it can exit the tailpipe.

ALTERNATOR: A device used for converting mechanical energy into electrical energy.

AMMETER: An instrument, calibrated in amperes, used to measure the flow of an electrical current in a circuit. Ammeters are always connected in series with the circuit being tested.

AMPERE: The rate of flow of electrical current present when one volt of electrical pressure is applied against one ohm of electrical resistance.

ANALOG COMPUTER: Any microprocessor that uses similar (analogous) electrical signals to make its calculations.

ARMATURE: A laminated, soft iron core wrapped by a wire that converts electrical energy to mechanical energy as in a motor or relay. When rotated in a magnetic field, it changes mechanical energy into electrical energy as in a generator.

ATMOSPHERIC PRESSURE: The pressure on the Earth's surface caused by the weight of the air in the atmosphere. At sea level, this pressure is 14.7 psi at 32°F (101 kPa at 0°C).

ATOMIZATION: The breaking down of a liquid into a fine mist that can be suspended in air.

AXIAL PLAY: Movement parallel to a shaft or bearing bore.

BACKFIRE: The sudden combustion of gases in the intake or exhaust system that results in a loud explosion.

BACKLASH: The clearance or play between two parts, such as meshed gears.

BACKPRESSURE: Restrictions in the exhaust system that slow the exit of exhaust gases from the combustion chamber.

BAKELITE: A heat resistant, plastic insulator material commonly used in printed circuit boards and transistorized components.

BALL BEARING: A bearing made up of hardened inner and outer races between which hardened steel balls roll.

BALLAST RESISTOR: A resistor in the primary ignition circuit that lowers voltage after the engine is started to reduce wear on ignition components.

BEARING: A friction reducing, supportive device usually located between a stationary part and a moving part.

BIMETAL TEMPERATURE SENSOR: Any sensor or switch made of two dissimilar types of metal that bend when heated or cooled due to the different expansion rates of the alloys. These types of sensors usually function as an on/off switch.

BLOWBY: Combustion gases, composed of water vapor and unburned fuel, that leak past the piston rings into the crankcase during normal engine operation. These gases are removed by the PCV system to prevent the buildup of harmful acids in the crankcase.

BRAKE PAD: A brake shoe and lining assembly used with disc brakes.

BRAKE SHOE: The backing for the brake lining. The term is, however, usually applied to the assembly of the brake backing and lining.

BUSHING: A liner, usually removable, for a bearing; an anti-friction liner used in place of a bearing.

CALIPER: A hydraulically activated device in a disc brake system, which is mounted straddling the brake rotor (disc). The caliper contains at least one piston and two brake pads. Hydraulic pressure on the piston(s) forces the pads against the rotor.

CAMSHAFT: A shaft in the engine on which are the lobes (cams) which operate the valves. The camshaft is driven by the crankshaft, via a belt, chain or gears, at one half the crankshaft speed.

CAPACITOR: A device which stores an electrical charge.

CARBON MONOXIDE (CO): A colorless, odorless gas given off as a normal byproduct of combustion. It is poisonous and extremely dangerous in confined areas, building up slowly to toxic levels without warning if adequate ventilation is not available.

CARBURETOR: A device, usually mounted on the intake manifold of an engine, which mixes the air and fuel in the proper proportion to allow even combustion.

CATALYTIC CONVERTER: A device installed in the exhaust system, like a muffler, that converts harmful byproducts of combustion into carbon dioxide and water vapor by means of a heat-producing chemical reaction.

CENTRIFUGAL ADVANCE: A mechanical method of advancing the spark timing by using flyweights in the distributor that react to centrifugal force generated by the distributor shaft rotation.

CHECK VALVE: Any one-way valve installed to permit the flow of air, fuel or vacuum in one direction only.

CHOKE: A device, usually a moveable valve, placed in the intake path of a carburetor to restrict the flow of air.

CIRCUIT: Any unbroken path through which an electrical current can flow. Also used to describe fuel flow in some instances.

CIRCUIT BREAKER: A switch which protects an electrical circuit from overload by opening the circuit when the current flow exceeds a predetermined level. Some circuit breakers must be reset manually, while most reset automatically.

COIL (IGNITION): A transformer in the ignition circuit which steps up the voltage provided to the spark plugs.

COMBINATION MANIFOLD: An assembly which includes both the intake and exhaust manifolds in one casting.

COMBINATION VALVE: A device used in some fuel systems that routes fuel vapors to a charcoal storage canister instead of venting them into the atmosphere. The valve relieves fuel tank pressure and allows fresh air into the tank as the fuel level drops to prevent a vapor lock situation.

COMPRESSION RATIO: The comparison of the total volume of the cylinder and combustion chamber with the piston at BDC and the piston at TDC.

CONDENSER: 1. An electrical device which acts to store an electrical charge, preventing voltage surges. 2. A radiator-like device in the air conditioning system in which refrigerant gas condenses into a liquid, giving off heat.

CONDUCTOR: Any material through which an electrical current can be transmitted easily.

CONTINUITY: Continuous or complete circuit. Can be checked with an ohmmeter.

COUNTERSHAFT: An intermediate shaft which is rotated by a mainshaft and transmits, in turn, that rotation to a working part.

CRANKCASE: The lower part of an engine in which the crankshaft and related parts operate.

CRANKSHAFT: The main driving shaft of an engine which receives reciprocating motion from the pistons and converts it to rotary motion.

CYLINDER: In an engine, the round hole in the engine block in which the piston(s) ride.

CYLINDER BLOCK: The main structural member of an engine in which is found the cylinders, crankshaft and other principal parts.

CYLINDER HEAD: The detachable portion of the engine, usually fastened to the top of the cylinder block and containing all or most of the combustion chambers. On overhead valve engines, it contains the valves and their operating parts. On overhead cam engines, it contains the camshaft as well.

DEAD CENTER: The extreme top or bottom of the piston stroke.

DETONATION: An unwanted explosion of the air/fuel mixture in the combustion chamber caused by excess heat and compression, advanced timing, or an overly lean mixture. Also referred to as "ping".

DIAPHRAGM: A thin, flexible wall separating two cavities, such as in a vacuum advance unit.

DIESELING: A condition in which hot spots in the combustion chamber cause the engine to run on after the key is turned off.

DIFFERENTIAL: A geared assembly which allows the transmission of motion between drive axles, giving one axle the ability to turn faster than the other.

DIODE: An electrical device that will allow current to flow in one direction only.

DISC BRAKE: A hydraulic braking assembly consisting of a brake disc, or rotor, mounted on an axle, and a caliper assembly containing, usually two brake pads which are activated by hydraulic pressure. The pads are forced against the sides of the disc, creating friction which slows the vehicle.

DISTRIBUTOR: A mechanically driven device on an engine which is responsible for electrically firing the spark plug at a predetermined point of the piston stroke.

DOWEL PIN: A pin, inserted in mating holes in two different parts allowing those parts to maintain a fixed relationship.

DRUM BRAKE: A braking system which consists of two brake shoes and one or two wheel cylinders, mounted on a fixed backing plate, and a brake drum, mounted on an axle, which revolves around the assembly.

DWELL: The rate, measured in degrees of shaft rotation, at which an electrical circuit cycles on and off.

ELECTRONIC CONTROL UNIT (ECU): Ignition module, module, amplifier or igniter. See Module for definition.

ELECTRONIC IGNITION: A system in which the timing and firing of the spark plugs is controlled by an electronic control unit, usually called a module. These systems have no points or condenser.

END-PLAY: The measured amount of axial movement in a shaft.

ENGINE: A device that converts heat into mechanical energy.

EXHAUST MANIFOLD: A set of cast passages or pipes which conduct exhaust gases from the engine.

FEELER GAUGE: A blade, usually metal, of precisely predetermined thickness, used to measure the clearance between two parts.

FIRING ORDER: The order in which combustion occurs in the cylinders of an engine. Also the order in which spark is distributed to the plugs by the distributor.

FLOODING: The presence of too much fuel in the intake manifold and combustion chamber which prevents the air/fuel mixture from firing, thereby causing a no-start situation.

FLYWHEEL: A disc shaped part bolted to the rear end of the crankshaft. Around the outer perimeter is affixed the ring gear. The starter drive engages the ring gear, turning the flywheel, which rotates the crankshaft, imparting the initial starting motion to the engine.

FOOT POUND (ft. lbs. or sometimes, ft.lb.): The amount of energy or work needed to raise an item weighing one pound, a distance of one foot.

FUSE: A protective device in a circuit which prevents circuit overload by breaking the circuit when a specific amperage is present. The device is constructed around a strip or wire of a lower amperage rating than the circuit it is designed to protect. When an amperage higher than that stamped on the fuse is present in the circuit, the strip or wire melts, opening the circuit.

GEAR RATIO: The ratio between the number of teeth on meshing gears.

GENERATOR: A device which converts mechanical energy into electrical energy.

HEAT RANGE: The measure of a spark plug's ability to dissipate heat from its firing end. The higher the heat range, the hotter the plug fires.

HUB: The center part of a wheel or gear.

HYDROCARBON (HC): Any chemical compound made up of hydrogen and carbon. A major pollutant formed by the engine as a byproduct of combustion.

HYDROMETER: An instrument used to measure the specific gravity of a solution.

INCH POUND (inch lbs.; sometimes in.lb. or in. lbs.): One twelfth of a foot pound.

INDUCTION: A means of transferring electrical energy in the form of a magnetic field. Principle used in the ignition coil to increase voltage.

INJECTOR: A device which receives metered fuel under relatively low pressure and is activated to inject the fuel into the engine under relatively high pressure at a predetermined time.

INPUT SHAFT: The shaft to which torque is applied, usually carrying the driving gear or gears.

INTAKE MANIFOLD: A casting of passages or pipes used to conduct air or a fuel/air mixture to the cylinders.

JOURNAL: The bearing surface within which a shaft operates.

KEY: A small block usually fitted in a notch between a shaft and a hub to prevent slippage of the two parts.

MANIFOLD: A casting of passages or set of pipes which connect the cylinders to an inlet or outlet source.

MANIFOLD VACUUM: Low pressure in an engine intake manifold formed just below the throttle plates. Manifold vacuum is highest at idle and drops under acceleration.

MASTER CYLINDER: The primary fluid pressurizing device in a hydraulic system. In automotive use, it is found in brake and hydraulic clutch systems and is pedal activated, either directly or, in a power brake system, through the power booster.

MODULE: Electronic control unit, amplifier or igniter of solid state or integrated design which controls the current flow in the ignition primary circuit based on input from the pick-up coil. When the module opens the primary circuit, high secondary voltage is induced in the coil.

NEEDLE BEARING: A bearing which consists of a number (usually a large number) of long, thin rollers.

OHM: (Ω) The unit used to measure the resistance of conductor-to-electrical flow. One ohm is the amount of resistance that limits current flow to one ampere in a circuit with one volt of pressure.

OHMMETER: An instrument used for measuring the resistance, in ohms, in an electrical circuit.

OUTPUT SHAFT: The shaft which transmits torque from a device, such as a transmission.

OVERDRIVE: A gear assembly which produces more shaft revolutions than that transmitted to it.

OVERHEAD CAMSHAFT (OHC): An engine configuration in which the camshaft is mounted on top of the cylinder head and operates the valve either directly or by means of rocker arms.

OVERHEAD VALVE (OHV): An engine configuration in which all of the valves are located in the cylinder head and the camshaft is located in the cylinder block. The camshaft operates the valves via lifters and pushrods.

OXIDES OF NITROGEN (NOx): Chemical compounds of nitrogen produced as a byproduct of combustion. They combine with hydrocarbons to produce smog.

OXYGEN SENSOR: Used with the feedback system to sense the presence of oxygen in the exhaust gas and signal the computer which can reference the voltage signal to an air/fuel ratio.

PINION: The smaller of two meshing gears.

PISTON RING: An open-ended ring which fits into a groove on the outer diameter of the piston. Its chief function is to form a seal between the piston and cylinder wall. Most automotive pistons have three rings: two for compression sealing; one for oil sealing.

PRELOAD: A predetermined load placed on a bearing during assembly or by adjustment.

PRIMARY CIRCUIT: The low voltage side of the ignition system which consists of the ignition switch, ballast resistor or resistance wire, bypass, coil, electronic control unit and pick-up coil as well as the connecting wires and harnesses.

PRESS FIT: The mating of two parts under pressure, due to the inner diameter of one being smaller than the outer diameter of the other, or vice versa; an interference fit.

RACE: The surface on the inner or outer ring of a bearing on which the balls, needles or rollers move.

REGULATOR: A device which maintains the amperage and/or voltage levels of a circuit at predetermined values.

RELAY: A switch which automatically opens and/or closes a circuit.

RESISTANCE: The opposition to the flow of current through a circuit or electrical device, and is measured in ohms. Resistance is equal to the voltage divided by the amperage.

RESISTOR: A device, usually made of wire, which offers a preset amount of resistance in an electrical circuit.

RING GEAR: The name given to a ring-shaped gear attached to a differential case, or affixed to a flywheel or as part of a planetary gear set.

ROLLER BEARING: A bearing made up of hardened inner and outer races between which hardened steel rollers move.

ROTOR: 1. The disc-shaped part of a disc brake assembly, upon which the brake pads bear; also called, brake disc. 2. The device mounted atop the distributor shaft, which passes current to the distributor cap tower contacts.

SECONDARY CIRCUIT: The high voltage side of the ignition system, usually above 20,000 volts. The secondary includes the ignition coil, coil wire, distributor cap and rotor, spark plug wires and spark plugs.

SENDING UNIT: A mechanical, electrical, hydraulic or electromagnetic device which transmits information to a gauge.

SENSOR: Any device designed to measure engine operating conditions or ambient pressures and temperatures. Usually electronic in nature and designed to send a voltage signal to an on-board computer, some sensors may operate as a simple on/off switch or they may provide a variable voltage signal (like a potentiometer) as conditions or measured parameters change.

SHIM: Spacers of precise, predetermined thickness used between parts to establish a proper working relationship.

SLAVE CYLINDER: In automotive use, a device in the hydraulic clutch system which is activated by hydraulic force, disengaging the clutch.

SOLENOID: A coil used to produce a magnetic field, the effect of which is to produce work.

SPARK PLUG: A device screwed into the combustion chamber of a spark ignition engine. The basic construction is a conductive core inside of a ceramic insulator, mounted in an outer conductive base. An electrical charge from the spark plug wire travels along the conductive core and jumps a preset air gap to a grounding point or points at the end of the conductive base. The resultant spark ignites the fuel/air mixture in the combustion chamber.

SPLINES: Ridges machined or cast onto the outer diameter of a shaft or inner diameter of a bore to enable parts to mate without rotation.

TACHOMETER: A device used to measure the rotary speed of an engine, shaft, gear, etc., usually in rotations per minute.

THERMOSTAT: A valve, located in the cooling system of an engine, which is closed when cold and opens gradually in response to engine heating, controlling the temperature of the coolant and rate of coolant flow.

TOP DEAD CENTER (TDC): The point at which the piston reaches the top of its travel on the compression stroke.

TORQUE: The twisting force applied to an object.

TORQUE CONVERTER: A turbine used to transmit power from a driving member to a driven member via hydraulic action, providing changes in drive ratio and torque. In automotive use, it links the driveplate at the rear of the engine to the automatic transmission.

TRANSDUCER: A device used to change a force into an electrical signal.

TRANSISTOR: A semi-conductor component which can be actuated by a small voltage to perform an electrical switching function.

TUNE-UP: A regular maintenance function, usually associated with the replacement and adjustment of parts and components in the electrical and fuel systems of a vehicle for the purpose of attaining optimum performance.

TURBOCHARGER: An exhaust driven pump which compresses intake air and forces it into the combustion chambers at higher than atmospheric pressures. The increased air pressure allows more fuel to be burned and results in increased horsepower being produced.

VACUUM ADVANCE: A device which advances the ignition timing in response to increased engine vacuum.

VACUUM GAUGE: An instrument used to measure the presence of vacuum in a chamber.

VALVE: A device which control the pressure, direction of flow or rate of flow of a liquid or gas.

VALVE CLEARANCE: The measured gap between the end of the valve stem and the rocker arm, cam lobe or follower that activates the valve.

VISCOSITY: The rating of a liquid's internal resistance to flow.

VOLTMETER: An instrument used for measuring electrical force in units called volts. Voltmeters are always connected parallel with the circuit being tested.

WHEEL CYLINDER: Found in the automotive drum brake assembly, it is a device, actuated by hydraulic pressure, which, through internal pistons, pushes the brake shoes outward against the drums.

MASTER
INDEX

TROUBLESHOOTING THE BRAKE SYSTEM 9-33
TROUBLESHOOTING THE IGNITION SWITCH 8-39
TROUBLESHOOTING THE MANUAL STEERING GEAR 8-42
TROUBLESHOOTING THE MANUAL TRANSMISSION 7-4
TROUBLESHOOTING THE POWER STEERING GEAR 8-43
TROUBLESHOOTING THE POWER STEERING PUMP 8-45
TROUBLESHOOTING THE STEERING COLUMN 8-38
TROUBLESHOOTING THE TURN SIGNAL SWITCH 8-40